The Eloquent Shakespeare

The Eloquent Shakespeare

*A Pronouncing Dictionary for the Complete Dramatic Works
with Notes to Untie the Modern Tongue*

GARY LOGAN

The University of Chicago Press CHICAGO AND LONDON

The University of Chicago Press, Chicago 60637
The University of Chicago Press, Ltd., London
© 2008 by Gary Logan
All rights reserved. Published 2008.
Paperback edition 2012
Printed in the United States of America

21 20 19 18 17 16 15 14 13 12   2 3 4 5 6

ISBN-13: 978-0-226-00631-4 (paper)
ISBN-10: 0-226-00631-X (paper)
ISBN-13: 978-0-226-01679-5 (e-book)
ISBN-10: 0-226-01679-X (e-book)

Library of Congress Cataloging-in-Publication Data

Logan, Gary.
    The eloquent Shakespeare : a pronouncing dictionary for the complete
dramatic works with notes to untie the modern tongue / Gary Logan.
        p. cm.
    ISBN:-13: 978-0-226-49115-8 (alk. paper)
    ISBN-10: 0-226-49115-3 (alk. paper)
    1. Shakespeare, William, 1564–1616—Language—Glossaries, etc.
    2. English language—Early modern, 1500–1700—Pronunciation—
    Dictionaries. I. Title.
    PR3081.L64 2008
    822.3'3—dc22

                                                            2008023296

⊗ This paper meets the requirements of ANSI/NISO Z39.48-1992
(Permanence of Paper).

For Teresa and Andrew

CONTENTS

PREFACE

How many words are in the complete works of Shakespeare? No one can say for sure. Many variables make for vastly different estimates, usually ranging from about 25,000 to 30,000. For instance, how many works actually constitute the 'complete works?' The First Folio of 1623 consists of thirty-six plays, but subsequent editions added another play, *Pericles*, to the canon. For centuries, scholars have vied to introduce other plays into that august group. *The Two Noble Kinsmen* is now generally accepted as a quasi-Shakespearean play, as evidence of his collaborative hand has gained ground. Other works are still waiting in the wings. For some of the plays that were included in the First Folio, quarto versions already existed (eighteen—a full half of them), and they vary greatly in size and vocabulary from their folio counterparts.

Also, does a word count as another word when the spelling changes? Shakespeare uses 'murder' and 'murther.' They mean the same thing, but someone who is in the business of signifying words' distinctions (lexicographers, philologists, orthoepists, etc.) would most certainly count them as two different words. Are 'goes' and 'goeth' two different words, even though they are the same thing but are simply on either side of the fence that delineates the archaic from the modern? And what about nouns that Shakespeare is wont to verbify, such as 'to chapel' or 'to history?' Technically speaking, 'chapel' and 'history' are thus new words. Hyphenated words that join two common words to create a brand new word are eligible, aren't they? 'Key-cold' and 'none-sparing' are examples. And Shakespeare's penchant for taking almost any word and giving it the prefix 'un-' may try some counters' patience at times, but surely words such as 'undreamed,' 'uncuckolded,' and 'unbodied' must qualify as new and different words.

In Alexander Schmidt's *Shakespeare Lexicon and Quotation Dictionary* (1875), E. A. Abbott's *A Shakespearian Grammar* (1870), and C. T. Onions' *A Shakespeare Glossary* (1911), a fine-toothed comb has been dragged through every line of Shakespeare's works, helping to untangle the meaning of his language. Their unrivaled studies, their glossaries, lexicons, and grammars were exhaustive and comprehensive—in their time—when it came to the definitions of Shakespeare's words in their context. Newer, and nearly as thorough, is *Shakespeare's Words; A Glossary & Language Companion* (2002), by David and Ben Crystal, which benefits from fresher, even sounder sources of information and scholarship. Augmented by the myriad modern editors of the plays and poems whose annotations continue to elucidate meanings not just of words, but of terms, phrases, tropes, and so forth, and the advent of countless books about Shakespeare's language intent on aiding both the seasoned and the uninitiated, the modern actor or reader of Shakespeare is more equipped now than ever to glean the most out of his words. *The Eloquent Shakespeare* is intended to be another kind of companion to Shakespeare's works, providing a thorough look at Shakespeare's immense and marvelous vocabulary in terms of how the words sound when actually spoken.

Peppering all of Shakespeare's works are a multitude of words no longer in common usage—words considered to be archaic or obsolete, even mysterious, but which still serve as lively particles of speech via his dramatic literature. For instance, try to pronounce these words used by Shakespeare: *charneco*, *lazar*, *eyrie*, *disme*, *Guysors*, *cacodemon*, *insanie*, *chanson*, *quaestor*, *chough*, *chequins*, *rigol*, *phantasime*, *chimera*, and *escot*. How did you do? Where do you check to see if you're right? *The Oxford English Dictionary* is the likeliest candidate, simply for its sheer number of entries, but it won't always hazard a guess as to how a particular word is to be pronounced—and when it does, the pronunciation is (of course) British. *The Eloquent Shakespeare* gathers together words such as these, alongside thousands of words still in common usage. It is designed especially for actors, directors, stage managers, teachers, and public speakers. It offers American English pronunciations that for the most part travel the path of least overall resistance through America's different regions, dialectal groups, and social strata.

The model for pronunciation used in *The Eloquent Shakespeare* is a modified version of the Standard American Stage Dialect, sometimes known as American Stage Standard—a *modern* model of pronunciation, not to be confused with the 'mid-Atlantic' dialect of old. It offers recommended, or preferred, pronunciations and must therefore be considered more prescriptive than descriptive. It cannot—nor should it—insist on the pronunciation choices ultimately decided by the speaker, but it does furnish standard pronunciations as a basis by which one can knowledgeably make comparisons and judgments. In most (if not all) cases, the transcriptions in this book reflect current phonological proclivities in American English pronunciation, while remaining faithful to traditional characteristics of stage speech.

There is no attempt on my part to include all of the various pronunciations of a word, even though many (usually dialectal) pronunciations for that word may exist in acceptable speech. In instances where a word has more than one *standard* pronunciation, however, all are given in order of preference as common usage, tradition, and consensus of opinion dictate. In other instances where the syllabic stress of a standard pronunciation is altered due to the word's position within a metrical line of Shakespearean verse, the altered pronunciation is also given and its reference point in literature cited. To guide me toward the most suitable pronunciations for proper names and archaic words thought to be questionable (or arguable), I depend on practical experience, tradition, orthoepy, Elizabethan spelling practices, etymological evidence, the conventions governing scansion dynamics in Shakespearean verse, and for some of the entries, the way in which the English language digests foreign words. All of the proper nouns mentioned in Shakespeare are given, and so are the intermittent foreign phrases interspersed throughout his works.

The entries' transcriptions are presented in a narrow form of the International Phonetic Alphabet (IPA), except when they are not. That's the fairest way of putting it, because in some instances I resort to using diacritics and symbols that technically fall outside the International Phonetic Association's sanctioned usage, in order to better serve a particularly rare or elusive phoneme. The list of sounds provided (Introduction §§ 2.1 and 2.2) are limited to the necessary few that are relative to this dictionary's purpose. A knowledge of the IPA is necessary to interpret the pronunciations; therefore, a complete table of sounds common to the English language is provided to instruct or refresh, whichever the case may be. Because many French, Spanish, Italian, and Latin words and phrases are used in Shakespearean texts, some additional IPA symbols are included. The IPA in this dictionary follows the Kiel Convention, revised to 1993 and corrected in 1996 (except for those rare instances when it does not follow).

I acknowledge John S. Kenyon (1874–1959) and Thomas A. Knott (1880–1945), professors of English at Hiram College and the University of Michigan, respectively. In the preface to their book, *A Pronouncing Dictionary of American English* (1944), they rightly point out that the pioneer in the field of pronunciation is Daniel Jones (1881–1967), professor of phonetics at the University of London, who published his first edition of *An English Pronouncing Dictionary* in 1917, and who "has placed all later lexicographers under inescapable obligation to him."

Originally, Jones' *English Pronouncing Dictionary* represented the pronunciation of the speech spoken by a limited though widespread and highly influential segment of English society—a manner of speech or dialect known as Received Pronunciation (RP). A. C. Gimson (1917–1985), also professor of phonetics at the University of London, became the eminent editor of the dictionary after Jones' death, and although he retained the term RP, he attempted to broaden its utility, to widen its application by introducing "certain changes in the phonetic transcription as well as amendments to the pronunciations recorded, with the aim of reflecting more faithfully the current state of the style of speech on which the Dictionary had traditionally been based."

When Kenyon and Knott embarked on their task in the 1930s, they admitted that their aim was much different from that of Daniel Jones. *A Pronouncing Dictionary of American English* broadly transcribes into the IPA common words that are classified into specific regional dialects of the then forty-eight United States. As they state in their book, "Our problem has been to record without prejudice or preference several different types of speech used by large bodies of educated and cultivated Americans in widely separated areas and with markedly different backgrounds of tradition and culture."

With deference to the pursuits of professors Kenyon and Knott, the aim of this book is more in accord with professor Gimson's declaration—intended, however, for the subject who speaks, or wishes to speak, a modern standard English of the American variety. It does not restrict itself solely to the words encountered in the works of William Shakespeare, but it most certainly concentrates on them, seeking to supply the largest repository of his words with regard to their pronunciation. *The Eloquent Shakespeare* strives to reflect forms of pronunciation consistent with current usage—although judging what the current usage actually is for many of the words entered into this dictionary leaves some room for debate. Revisions are inevitable and justifiable; I therefore welcome the suggestions anyone may have toward making this work more useful and accurate.

GL
Washington, DC—2008

ACKNOWLEDGMENTS

There are several people whose contributions to this endeavor were invaluable to me. I would like to extend my special thanks for the generosity and graciousness with which they shared their ideas, professional expertise, and support.

Gabriella Cavallero was my consultant for the Spanish, French, and Italian words and phrases that intermittently appear in Shakespeare; David Pelizzari was my consultant for the sizable amount of Latin words and phrases—I could not have wished for more expert advice from two more gifted linguists; The Stratford Festival of Canada generously granted me a Tyrone Guthrie Award, helping to further my study of Shakespeare's usage of foreign languages; Lib Logan copyedited early editions, greatly improving the manner of my explication; Dr. Peter Ladefoged helped me scrutinize and codify a particularly narrow phoneme; Dr. Brad Story provided scientific data pertaining to that narrow phoneme; Rocco Dal Vera offered valuable advice on writing; Brad Gibson provided technical support and was instrumental in making the manuscript more reader friendly. At the beginning of the process, Rod Menzies shared his opinions on form, content, and clarity, and his contributions greatly added to the directness and purpose of this work; Linda Halvorson, Chris Rhodes, Anita Samen, and Paul Schellinger guided me when I finally sought to publish. Linda's support and expert direction were pivotal.

Others deserving mention of my deepest appreciation: Eric Armstrong, Tony Church, Linda Eller, Dale Genge, Judith Koltai, Teleté Zorayda Lawrence, Dawn McCaugherty, Gayle Murphy, Victor Pappas, Janine Pearson, Ian Raffel, Dr. Ron Scherer, Edith Skinner, Archie Smith, David Smukler, Deborah Sussel, Gerry Trentham, and Catherine Weidner. These individuals represent colleagues, former instructors, and/or mentors perhaps never aware of their impact on this project, or until now, my eternal gratitude.

Finally, my thanks to my former students and colleagues of The National Theatre Conservatory at The Denver Center for the Performing Arts, the annual participants of Canada's National Voice Intensive, Vancouver, British Columbia, and the students and faculty of The Shakespeare Theatre Company's Academy for Classical Acting at The George Washington University, Washington, DC.

INTRODUCTION

1.0 The Pronunciation Paradigm

The Actors' Tradition

1.1 Among broadcasters (e.g., radio commentators, voice-over artists, television newscasters), public speakers (e.g., the clergy, lawyers, politicians, lecturers), and actors rendering works from the classical repertoire of plays, standard pronunciations are usually preferred. The Standard American Stage Dialect is thought to be, with few exceptions, the most correct and acceptable speech because it is deemed to be the least regional. It also reflects qualities of cultivation and education while remaining 'regular' to most Americans, drawing as little attention to itself as possible. Admittedly, *cultivation* and *education* are loaded terms; however, the aim of the Standard American Stage Dialect is far from the presumptive aim of an acrolect—any ostentatious dialect with pretensions of higher status. In actuality, it is remarkably close to the speech most Americans already speak. Adjustments to what is loosely referred to as General American speech are usually made for the sake of clarity of meaning and for the distinction of one's speech. For words in common usage, the transcriptions in this dictionary represent pronunciations that are thought to resonate most broadly through the mainstream of American society.

1.2 Standard American Stage Dialect (sometimes called American Stage Standard) is the name commonly given to the standard pronunciation used by actors in the United States. It is the medley of sounds in our language said to have the least regional influence and can thus be regarded as neutral or universal, the most productive bridge across the boundaries of social class structure and indigenous speech patterns. Today's version of the Standard American Stage Dialect (SASD) is the grandchild of William Tilly's (1860–1935) mid-Atlantic dialect, the dialect actors (especially for the screen) once learned from elocutionists circa 1930–1945; what Kenyon and Knott might have called formal American English of public address. To fully appreciate its system of phonology, it is important to remember that the term 'mid-Atlantic' refers not to the states along the eastern seaboard but to that imaginary place somewhere in the mid-Atlantic between the United States and Great Britain. It sought to marry the most euphonious sounds of British Received Pronunciation with the more frank patterns of speech in the United States. Current SASD pronunciation bears a resemblance to its grandsire, and even more so to its immediate predecessor (what Edith Skinner [1902–1981] called Good Speech for the American Stage), but significant generational changes have occurred in response to modern proclivities in American English pronunciation warranting some subtle (and some not-so-subtle) modifications.

The Idiolect

1.3 Belonging to every region of the United States are the dialects peculiar to that region's native people. The particular sounds causing a speaker from one area of the country to pronounce words in a markedly different manner from that of a speaker in another area are what designate us as indigenous speakers. For every area there are pronunciations considered the most correct and acceptable by its inhabitants. When a word is spoken by someone from a different locality, that word might be thought to sound somewhat foreign, even if foreign means a subtle influence from the next county over. The distinctions can be clear even though the areas are relatively close in proximity to one another,—for example, the Queens and Brooklynese dialects. However, dialects rarely if ever follow state, county, or city boundary lines in the United States, preferring instead major geographical contours, population densities, and various social strata, including ethnicity, education, and even the differences between generations.

1.4 When one moves to another locale or to another (usually higher) social stratum, the individual will, for the most part, defer to the colloquial pronunciations of that specific region or social group, despite the judgments and preferences of pronunciation previously held onto by that individual. This is called *code-shifting*—modifying one's pronunciation so one may be regarded by the new majority as correct, acceptable, or standard. This should not imply that a standard pronunciation at the local level is always classified as correct and acceptable by broader segments of society, but merely by the immediate social group into which one has joined. It would be inadvisable, for instance, to visit the towns of Cairo ['keɪɹoʊ], Illinois, Milan ['maɪlən], Tennessee, or Beatrice [biˈætɹɪs], Nebraska, and inform the local townspeople that their pronunciation is wrong (because they are not wrong), that their towns' names are really ['kaɪɹoʊ], [mɪˈlɑn], and ['bɪətɹɪs], respectively.

An American Model

1.5 Citing a definition supplied by the *Oxford English Dictionary* (OED, new shorter ed.), a *dialect* is a variety of language with nonstandard vocabulary, pronunciations, or idioms. The suggestion here is that if there is a nonstandard form of pronunciation in our language, then there must be a standard form of pronunciation, the corruption of which spawns our various dialects. In England the standard is known as Received Pronunciation (a term coined by professor Henry Cecil Wyld [1870–1945] of Oxford University), or Received Standard. Again citing from the *OED*, RP is "the form of spoken English based on educated speech in southern England and considered to be least regional." In the United States there is no such authoritative model of pronunciation serving as a standard for comparison or judgment. The correct pronunciations of a word can be as numerous as the number of dictionaries referenced. Typically, the (British) *OED* has the last say whenever the pronunciation of a particularly contentious word is sought— not surprising, considering the sheer number of entries in the *OED*. But American traditions of pronunciation are sufficiently dissimilar from British traditions of pronunciation to warrant, whenever possible, a distinctly American authority by which such comparisons and judgments can be made.

1.6 The Standard American Stage Dialect might well be regarded as such an authority. Its custom of promulgating pronunciations that are wholly American make it as likely a candidate as any other school or system of phonology in the United States. It has always attempted to neutralize (not neuter) strong regionalisms for the sake of making the speakers (when they desire) seem as if they are of one kind—similar in nature, and linguistically indistinguishable in terms of geographic origin. However, distinctions must be drawn between that which is called *correct speech* and that which is known as *standard speech*. As previously illustrated (introduction § 1.4), a standard pronunciation may not always be the correct one in all circumstances. In other words, a word given a nonstandard pronunciation does not necessitate the conclusion that the word has been pronounced incorrectly. One must never presume that a dialect in and of itself is either incorrect or *sub*standard speech. A regional or colloquial dialect is simply nonstandard.

1.7 To clarify further what standard speech is and what it is not, another distinction must be drawn between it and that which is called General American speech. General American is one of three broad classifications of dialect in the United States and applies to a vast area embracing all of the Plains, the Rocky Mountains, the Pacific Coast, the Southwest, and even parts of the Alleghenies and New York State. Strictly speaking, this gross misnomer implies that people from Chicago, Oklahoma City, and Los Angeles all speak the same dialect. The other two dialects are Eastern and Southern. Due perhaps to its predominant size over the other two, General American is often confused with being the speech of 'regular, everyday Americans everywhere,' regardless of their origin. This confusion can lead anyone who esteems himself or herself to be the regular, everyday kind of person to falsely suppose that if he or she is speaking General American (substitute 'properly'), everyone else is then speaking a dialect. The term *General American* is vague, potentially confusing, and goes against common logic. It seeks to identify and linguistically represent the dialect of the people who live in the largest, most populated geographical region on the North American continent. General American might have been a suitable name for what we now call *standard*, but as it is, the term should be avoided altogether for want of greater specificity and clarity.

2.0 The Phonetic Transcription of Sounds in American English (SASD)

2.1 The *pure vowels*, *diphthongs*, and *triphthongs* are transcribed as follows:

Pure vowels
s**ea**t [i], c**i**ty [ɨ], s**i**t [ɪ], s**e**t [e], s**a**t [æ], s**a**mple [a]
s**ir** [ɝ], s**a**voy [ə], s**u**p [ʌ], s**u**pper [ɚ]
s**oo**n [u], s**oo**t [ʊ], s**o**journ (*v.*) [o], s**aw** [ɔ], s**o**b [ɒ], sp**a** [ɑ]

Diphthongs (falling)
s**ay** [eɪ̆], s**igh** [aɪ̆], s**oy** [ɔɪ̆], s**o** [oʊ̆], sn**ou**t [aʊ̆]
s**ere** [ɪɚ], sh**are** [ɛɚ], s**ure** [ʊɚ], s**ore** [ɔɚ], sp**ar** [ɑɚ]

Diphthongs (rising)
c**our**teous [ĭə], confl**ue**nce [ŭə]
Note: Though not restricted to poetic usage, rising diphthongs are customarily used when the demands of versification require the elision of two distinct, unstressed syllables into one syllabic phoneme or monophthong; for example,

˘ ´ ˘ ´ ˘ ´ ˘ ´ ˘ ´ ˘ ´
Or such / ambi / **guou**s gi / ving out, / to note
HAM, I.v.186

Triphthongs
s**ire** [aɪ̆ɚ], s**our** [aʊ̆ɚ]

2.2 The *consonants* are transcribed as follows:

Fricatives
s**ee** [s], **z**oo [z], **f**ew [f], **v**iew [v], **sh**ow [ʃ], plea**s**ure [ʒ],
thought [θ], ba**the** [ð], **h**old [h], be**h**ind [ɦ], (Ba**ch**, lo**ch** [x])

Stops
pop [p], **bib** [b], **tote** [t], **dad** [d], **gig** [g], **cake** [k],
church [tʃ], **judge** [dʒ], di**tt**o [t̬] (see introduction § 3.13)

Nasals
mom [m], **noon** [n], si**ng** [ŋ]

Glides
whale [ʍ], **w**in [w], **y**es [j], **r**igid/tomorrow [ɹ]

Voiced Lateral Continuant
linen [l]

3.0 The Properties of Standard American Stage Dialect

3.1 *Vowels*

The vowels are relatively unimpeded as the voiced breathstream passes through the oral passage. If the articulated shape of the mouth remains somewhat still (or static) during phonation then a pure vowel is created. Since the resultant sound is subject to a free, phonated breathstream, the vowel is capable of being short or continuing into a sustained (or long) vowel. If the articulated shape of the mouth is in motion during phonation then a diphthong or triphthong is created. A *diphthong* is one sound consisting of the blending of two elements, one (almost always the initial element) receiving more energy than the other. The result is what is known as a *falling diphthong*. A *triphthong* is one sound consisting of three elements, the initial one always receiving more energy than the other two that follow.

3.2 *Vowel Length and Vowel Reduction*

The vowels [ɪ], [e], [æ], [ʌ], [ʊ], and [ɒ] are generally regarded as *short vowels* in the SASD. There are advantages in keeping them as short as possible; however, it must be acknowledged that their lengths will vary slightly depending on what consonant sound immediately follows. For instance, the [ɪ] in /bid/ is appreciably longer than the [ɪ] in /bit/, and the [æ] in /badge/ is longer than the [æ] in /batch/. Whenever these vowel sounds are immediately followed by the [b], [d], [dʒ], [g], [m], and [n] phonemes, their values, in terms of length, are somewhat fuller (longer).

Vowel length—any vowel's length—is relative to the length of every other sound around it. The five pure vowels (sometimes known as the *long vowels*) given greater latitude in length quality are [iː], [ɝː], [uː], [ɔː], and [ɑː]. Three potential degrees of length —long, half-long, and short—exist in the SASD and are determined by syllabic stress and whatever sounds, if any, immediately follow.

The vowels' lengths, generally speaking, are: *short* in unstressed syllables or in weak forms of words, for example, /curtail/ [kɚˈteɪl] and /he/ [ˈhi]; *half-long* in stressed syllables before one or more voiceless consonants, for example, /boost/ [ˈbuˑst], when the vowel is followed by a voiced consonant that is then followed by a voiceless consonant, for example, /salt/ [ˈsɑˑlt], or when one of these vowels precedes another vowel sound, for example, /idea/ [aɪˈdiˑə]; and *long* in stressed syllables when the vowel is the last sound in the word, for example, /spree/ [ˈspɹiː], or when it occurs before one or more voiced consonants, for example, /fiends/ [ˈfiːnːdz].

The [ɨ] is a high centralized vowel splitting the difference, as it were, between the highest front vowel [i] and the second highest front vowel [ɪ]. In the mid-Atlantic dialect and in Edith Skinner's *Good Speech for the American Stage*, the word /city/ is pronounced with the same vowel sound in both syllables, that is, [ˈsɪtɪ]. In the modernized Standard American Stage Dialect, however, current practice acknowledges the subtle yet significant distinction between the two vowels in the word /city/ and is transcribed [ˈsɪtɨ] (or [ˈsɪɾɨ]) accordingly. It is also the sound commonly heard in the final, unstressed syllable in words such as /ability/, /frankly/, /fancy/, /itchy/, and /Daphne/.

The [ɪ] is a semi-high front unrounded vowel. Characteristic of the SASD, /-less/ and /-ness/ at the ends of words retain the [ɪ] sound to accentuate a higher (brighter) value through forward placement. This is in contrast to the neutral schwa [ə] usually heard in the bald speech habits of most informal speakers in the United States today.

/-ace/ in words such as /preface/, /grimace/, /surface/, and /solace/ retains the [ɪ].

/-age/, /-ege/, and /-ige/ in words such as /message/, /bandage/, /cabbage/, /college/, and /vestige/ also retain the [ɪ].

/-ate/ in both nouns and adjectives such as /temperate/, /desperate/, /choco-late/, and /postulate (in its subject form rather than verb form)/ retains the [ɪ] as well.

/be-/, /de-/, /re-/, and /pre-/ at the beginning of words such as /befall/, /de-ceive/, /reproach/, and /predict/ retain the [ɪ]. This pertains to weak syllables only, so words such as /reinvent/, /deactivate/, and /predetermine/ will not share this trait.

/-est/ at the end of words such as /largest/, /briefest/, and /safest/ retains the [ɪ].

/-es/ and /-ed/ endings in words such as /horses/ and /appointed/ likewise retain the [ɪ].

/e-/, /em-/, /en-/, and /ex-/ at the beginning of words such as /evaluate/, /em-balm/, /engulf/, and /example/ will reliably retain the [ɪ]. This is essentially true for all words beginning with an /e/ and when that /e/ immediately precedes a consonant sound and is part of the weak-stressed syllable.

3.3 *The Intermediate /a/ in the SASD*

Determination of when to use the Intermediate /a/ or [a] in the SASD (short of looking the word up in this dictionary) can be made by following a fairly reliable pattern. There are words such as /can't/, /dance/, and /ask/ for which the British Standard for Received Pronunciation requires an Italian (broad) /a/ or [ɑ] as in /father/. These same words are typically pronounced in the United States with what is called the Short /a/ or [æ] as in /pan/. In the SASD, words of this nature require an Intermediate /a/ or [a]. For example:

	American [æ]	**British RP** [ɑ]	**SASD** [a]
/advantage/	[æd'væntədʒ]	[əd'vɑntɪdʒ]	[əd'vantɪdʒ]
/bath/	['bæθ]	['bɑθ]	['baθ]
/demand/	[də'mænd]	[dɪ'mɑnd]	[dɪ'mand]
/pass/	['pæs]	['pɑs]	['pas]
/telegraph/	['teləgɹæf]	['telɪgɹɑf]	['teləgɹaf]

Hundreds of other words fall into this category. All of them, insofar as I am aware, are represented in this dictionary.

3.4 *The Vowels Given R-Coloration:* [ɝ] *and* [ɚ]
(See introduction § 3.8)

3.5 *The Liquid U*

A very distinct feature of the SASD is the so-called "Liquid U." In some instances, when [u] follows [d], [n], and [t], it is customary to intervene with the consonant [j], as in /duke/ ['djuk], /news/ ['njuz], and /attitude/ ['æɾɪtjud]. Personal aesthetics and one's own discretion influence whether to do the same when [u] follows [l] or [s] as in /lute/ ['ljut], and /pursue/ [pɚ'sju]. Even less frequently, [u] following [z] is 'liquified;' for example, /Zeus/ ['zjus]. Entries in this dictionary usually give both options in accordance with and in order of SASD preferences.

3.6 *Consonants*

Consonants are classified into five different categories: fricatives, stops, nasals, glides, and the voiced lateral continuant. Their names are derived from what each group does with the breathstream.

Fricatives are the result of forcing breath through a constricted passage. All are continuants. Unlike vowels, the articulated constriction is acute, and each voiced fricative has a voiceless cognate, for example, [ʒ/ʃ], with the exception of [h/ɦ].

The *stops* so impede the breathstream as to cause a complete cessation of flow, sometimes resulting in a plosive release, for example, [b/g]. Like the fricatives, each voiced stop has a voiceless cognate, for example, [p/k].

The *nasals* are the result of a redirection of the breathstream through the nasal passage due to a complete closure of the oral aperture, that is, [m/n/ŋ]. Nasals are also continuant sounds.

Other consonants require a stationary placement of the articulators. The *glides*, however, are sounds (both voiced and unvoiced) whose productions rely on the motion of the articulators from beginning to end, for example, [w/ʍ].

The *voiced lateral continuant*, once considered a lateral glide, requires the breathstream to escape through lateral secondary apertures created when the tongue tip is against the alveolar ridge, that is, [l].

3.7 *Aspiration and Nonaspiration of* [t], [p], *and* [k]

There are times when one aspirates (breathes) through the release of the voiceless plosives [t], [p], and [k], and times when one is compelled to articulate these sounds with the articulators but not aspirate through a release. *The six rules for aspiration are as follows:*

1. Aspirate the [t], [p], and [k] sounds whenever they appear alone as mere phonetic symbols, for example, **[t]**, **[p]**, or **[k]**.
2. Aspirate [t], [p], and [k] whenever they are the last sound in a word of text appearing by itself, for example, /no**pe**/.
3. Aspirate [t], [p], and [k] whenever they are followed immediately in a word by a vowel sound, for example, /s**t**one/, /**p**eas/, /eure**k**a/.
4. Aspirate [t], [p], and [k] whenever they are the last sound in a word within a sentence and the next word in the sentence begins with a vowel sound, for example, /I don'**t** abide them/.
5. Aspirate [t], [p], and [k] whenever they are the last sound of a verse line, regardless of whether a consonant sound begins the following line of verse,

   /Or else you are that shrewd and knavish sprite
   Call'd Robin Goodfellow. Are not you he/

6. Aspirate [t], [p], and [k] whenever they are immediately followed by a full-stop punctuation such as a period, a colon, an exclamation mark, and so forth, /. . . unless he pay me tribute; there shall not a maid be married, . . . / Sometimes emphasis will warrant the aspiration of one of these sounds whether followed by a comma (which, under normal circumstances, is a less frequent choice), or even when the next word in the sentence begins with a consonant sound, for example, /I said, 'DON'**T** DO IT!'/

The two rules for nonaspiration are as follows:

1. Do not aspirate [t], [p], or [k] when they are followed immediately in a word by a consonant sound, for example, /tigh**t**back/, /lo**p**sided/, /ha**c**kneyed/

2. Do not aspirate [t], [p], or [k] when they are the last sound in a word within a sentence and the next word in the sentence begins with a consonant sound, for example /Don't be foolish./ There are two exceptions to this rule, both of them covered in the explication of rules numbered five and six for aspiration. In the case of rule number five for aspiration, the integrity of the verse line is retained to a degree by releasing through the [t], [p], and [k], particularly when the next verse line begins with a consonant sound; and as for rule number six, emphatic statements may sometimes warrant an affected over-articulation characterized by aspirating the [t], [p], and [k], even when a consonant sound immediately follows.

3.8 *The Consonant* [ɹ] *and the Vowels Given R-Coloration* [ɝ] *and* [ɚ]
The consonant [ɹ]:

The consonant [ɹ] phoneme is a nonsyllabic retroflex and occurs only in initial and medial positions. In the initial position, the [ɹ] is always immediately followed by a vowel sound. The initial position is when [ɹ] begins a word or syllable (including ones beginning with consonant blends) regardless of what type of sound (consonant or vowel), if any, precedes it, for example /right/, /spring/, /golden rule/, /cartridge/. The medial position simply means whenever /r/ is sandwiched in between two vowel sounds, for example, /porridge/, /ferry/, /parents/.

The vowels given r-coloration; [ɝ] and [ɚ]:
In terminal positions of /r/, represented orthographically by an /r/ followed immediately with either (a) nothing, (b) a silent vowel, or (c) a consonant, the sound becomes a frictionless [ɹ] used as a vowel, for example, /butter/, /there/, /stars/, /paired/, /cartridge/. The only exception in English is the word 'colonel,' in which no /r/ appears in the spelling. Still, the resultant midvowel sounds are rhoticized (given r-coloration) to follow the current proclivities of popular American English pronunciation. In the mid-Atlantic dialect, and even Edith Skinner's Good Speech for classic and elevated texts (also called Theatre Standard and Eastern Standard), these midvowel sounds should be pronounced (in accordance with their conventions and traditions) without r-coloration. The midvowel [ɚ] occurs exclusively in unstressed syllables. The midvowel [ɝ] usually occurs only in stressed syllables, but there are some exceptions, for example, /curtail/, /verbose/, /surmise/.

Note: As one can see in words such as /carpenter/, /parking/, and /person/, a terminal /r/ doesn't have to be at the end of a word to be considered terminal. However, words that *do* have a terminal /r/ at their ends, such as /butter/ and /care/, are frequently followed in a sentence by a word beginning with a vowel sound. In such cases, the /r/ is considered sandwiched in between two vowel sounds, resulting in a consonant [ɹ], as in the sentences /Refer it to the boss./, /Butter again?/, and /There isn't a way out./ This is commonly known as *r-linking*. It keeps the breathstream flowing and is transcribed [ˈbʌtə˞ ɹəˈgen]. It is important to remember that giving the vowel r-coloration can never (in and of itself) suffice for a retroflexed consonant [ɹ].

3.9 *Syllabic Consonants*

Three syllabic consonants appear in this dictionary, reflecting the preferences of SASD pronunciation. They are: [m], [n], and [l]. It is considered overly affected and pedantic to pronounce the word /button/, for instance, with an aspirated [t] followed by the schwa [ə]. The principle feature of a schwa is that it is a reduced vowel. Still, when this reduced vowel is so imperceptible as not to intervene certain sonorant combinations, the result is the [m], [n], and [l] becoming syllabic and transcribed [m̩], [n̩], and [l̩].

The consonant [m] is usually syllabic following [z] in words such as /racism/ and /escapism/. Exceptions occur when (as is customary) one opts for an intervening schwa in words such as /prism/ and /schism/.

The consonant [n] is often syllabic following [d], [s], [t], [z], [ʃ], and [ʒ], as in /garden/, /bosun/, /button/, /cousin/, /invitation/, and /evasion/. Common to Shakespeare's understanding and usage of sound blends, the [n] is often syllabic following [v], as in [ˈhevn̩]. This should not imply that it is *always* so with Shakespeare. In Sonnet 29, /heaven/ is used twice. Scanning the lines, one sees the [n] as a syllabic consonant in the first instance, and with the intervening schwa the second time.

The consonant [l] is often syllabic following [d], [g], [p], [s], [t], and [z], as in /ladle/, /gaggle/, /people/, /hassle/, /acquittal/, and /puzzle/.

3.10 *The* [ʍ]

Characteristic of SASD, the [ʍ] ([hw] in broad transcription) is retained. It is a voiceless rounded labiovelar approximant initiated by a slight puff of breath at the onset. It is distinct from the [w] because it is devoiced. It is heard in words such as /whet/, /which/, and /whether/.

3.11 *The* [x]

This sound, a voiceless velar fricative, is, only in the narrowest sense, a phoneme of English. It is included because of the option one has in SASD when pronouncing some Scottish English words such as /loch/. The same option exists with some German words such as /Bach/ or /achtung/.

3.13 *The* [ɾ̥], *the So-called Logan-Ladefoged*

This is a phonetic symbol specifically designed for this dictionary by taking the IPA phonetic symbol [ɾ] (known as the fish-hook r) and adding to it the subscript circle, or under-ring.

The [ɾ] stands for a voiced alveolar flap—the single apical flap, as spoken in Spanish words such as /toro (bull)/ and /fiero (fierce)/. The [̥] is the IPA symbol used diacritically to denote devoicing, or the diminishment of voice. Together, these symbols ([ɾ̥]) suggest a nearly voiceless apico-alveolar flap.

The need to create and utilize this symbol arises from the desire to more narrowly describe the distinct difference between the [t] as spoken in the initial position of a word such as /take/, and the type of /t/ spoken in the medial position of certain words such as /matter/ and /lottery/ (in American English).

In between a pedantic and affected-sounding ['mætɚ] and ['lɒtɚɹɪ], and the altogether mispronounced versions ['mædɚ] and ['lɒdɚɹɪ], there is a pronunciation considered entirely proper in the Standard American Stage Dialect; the phonetic characteristics of which the [ɾ̥] can sufficiently signify in terms of articulation and vocality.

It is my hope that readers will accept this symbol as the only plausible compromise short of inventing a new symbol using demarcations unrecognized by the IPA.

Anytime that this sound is preferred, [ɾ̥] is used in the phonetic transcription of the entry word. Simply because a /t/ is in a medial position of a word does not justify the use of [ɾ̥]. The word /ability/, for instance, retains the [t]. In the word /attitude/, the first set of /t/s receive the [ɾ̥] and the last /t/ retains the [t].

There is no rule per se of either spelling or pronunciation governing the usage of the [ɾ̥], although when it occurs it is consistently intervocalic and immediately precedes an unstressed syllable. At first glance, one might believe that the [ɾ̥] is reserved only for sets of double /t/s as in each of the preceding examples, but a reminder of words such as /literal/, /totem/, /critical/, /Toto/, and /Saturn/ should dispel any such beliefs.

3.14 *Symbols for Diacritical Marks and "Foreign" Sounds*
Every so often, it is necessary to incorporate into the phonetic transcription of an entry word (or even the word's spelling) certain symbols to designate sounds considered uncommon in the English language. The following constitutes a list of these symbols, along with descriptions and corresponding words:

[ɛ]   denotes the (**ê**) sound, as in the French word /**crêpe**/ or the vowel sound in the German word /**wenn**/. SASD adopts this sound as an acceptable pronunciation for the first vowel heard in words such as /**debut**/, /**prelude**/, /**deluge**/, and the Latin pronunciation of /**credo**/

[ɛ̃]   denotes the nasalized vowel sound (**in**), as in the French name /**Gauguin**/

[ɑ̃]   denotes the nasalized vowel sounds (**an**), as in the French word /**franc**/, and (**en**), as in the French words /**pense**/ and /**enchanté**/

[ɔ̃] denotes the nasalized vowel sound (**on**), as in the French word /**mont**/

[œ̃] denotes the nasalized vowel sound (**un**), as in the French words /**un**/ and /**lundi**/

[ʎ] denotes the (**u**) sound, as in the French words /**sur**/, /**sucre**/, and /**tu**/

[ø] denotes the (**eu**) sound, as in the French words /**Dieu**/, /**bleu**/, and /**oeufs**/

[˜] denotes nasalization

[ħ] denotes the voiceless pharyngeal central fricative (**j**), as in the Spanish word /**mujer**/

[ʀ] denotes the voiced uvular trill, as in the French word /**rouge**/

[ʁ] denotes a voiced uvular frictionless approximant, as in the French word /**maître**/

[ᴚ] denotes an inclination toward the voiced uvular frictionless approximant, for example, /**Port le Blanc**/ (q.v.)

[ɾ] denotes a voiced apico-alveolar flap (**r**), as in the Spanish word /**pero**/

[r] denotes the voiced apico-alveolar trilled or rolled /r/ (**rr**), as in the Spanish word /**perro**/

[ç] denotes the (**ch**) sound, as in the German word /**nicht**/, and distinct from [x] (see introduction § 3.11)

[ʔ] denotes a glottal stop, as in the native pronunciation of /**Hawaii**/

[̯] denotes dentalization; [t], [d], [n], and [l] are dentalized whenever they are followed immediately by either the [θ] or [ð], as in /**eighth**/ (['eɪt̯θ]), /**width**/ (['wɪd̯θ]), /**ninth**/ (['naɪn̯θ]), and /**wealth**/ (['wel̯θ])

[̥] denotes devoicing (see introduction § 3.13)

[ɸ] denotes a bilabial /f/ rather than the standard labio-dental /f/, as in the alternative pronunciation of the interjection /**pah**/

[¨] denotes a dieresis (also diaeresis)—not an umlaut—when employed in the spelling of an entry word. It is sometimes placed over the second of two adjacent vowels to indicate that two distinct syllabic phonemes are to be pronounced rather than a diphthong or monophthong, as in the alternative spelling of words such as /**coöperative**/, /**coördinate**/, /**noël**/, or /**naïve**/ (cf. diaeresis, Fowler's *A Dictionary of Modern English Usage*). Many editors of Shakespeare utilize this customary English device to eke out of words the extra syllable necessary to the metric fulfillment of a verse line; thus, /**statuë**/ and /**Weïrd Sister, -s**/ (q.v.)

[.] denotes syllabication (see interpretation of entries § 9)

[ǀ] denotes an ingressive dental click, the sound of condemnation or rejection usually represented in English by the interjection **tut, tut**, or **tut-tut**, or simply **tut** (q.v.)

[ĭo] denotes the rising diphthong (**io**) sound, as in the Italian words /**seraglio**/, /**finocchio**/, /**intermedio**/, and /**municipio**/

[ʰ] denotes full aspiration. Typically, aspiration and nonaspiration are implied under the rules governing usage (see introduction, § 3.7) and are not therefore explicitly indicated in this dictionary's phonetic transcription. Explicit indication of its use is given, however, when it is used counter to the rules cited, for example, /**Anthony**/ (q.v.)

[¹]   denotes an inclination toward the voiced alveolar fricative (r-sound), for example /**marry**/ (q.v.)

INTERPRETATION OF ENTRIES

1. A Common Entry

apace ə'peɪs

The phonetic transcription is intended to reflect a pronunciation in accordance with the conventions of the Standard American Stage Dialect as outlined in the introduction, and my discretion (based on practice and observation).

2. Subjects, Verbs, and Adjectives

dam, -s, -ming, -med 'dæm, -z, -ɪŋ, -d

A word such as **dam** is pronounced the same whether one means to use it in its substantive form or its verb form, so no declarative notation of form is given.

object (*s.*)**, -s** 'ɒbdʒɪkt, -s

object (*v.*)**, -s, -ing, -ed** əb'dʒekt, -s, -ɪŋ, -ɪd

A word such as **object** is pronounced differently depending on whether one intends to use it as a substantive or as a verb, so the appropriate notation is given in such cases.

confederate (C.) (*s., adj.*)**, -s** kən'fedəˑɹɪt, -s

confederat|e (*v.*)**, -es, -ing, -ed** kən'fedəˑɹeɪt, -s, -ɪŋ, -ɪd

Likewise, when a word such as **confederate** changes pronunciation due to its usage as either a substantive, a verb, or an adjective, an appropriate notation appears in the entry.

3. Capital Letters

jack (J.), -s 'dʒæk, -s

A capital letter in parentheses after an initial entry implies that the word is capable of being either a common word or a proper noun, depending on usage and meaning.

Jefferson 'dʒefəˑsn̩

An entry given with a capital letter implies that it is always considered a proper noun.

4. Parentheses

spake (*archaic p.t. of* **speak**) 'speĭk
gimmer (*corruption of* **gimmal**), **-s** 'dʒɪmɚ, -z

Clarifications following the entry word are contained within parentheses. They are typically, though not always, editorial comments.

Poi(c)tiers pɔĭ'tɪɚ-z [pwɑ'tjeĭ]

Parentheses may also appear within the entry word to indicate that the practice of spelling that word changes and that the letter/s surrounded by the parentheses may or may not be included in the regular spelling of the word.

5. Brackets

Hector 'hektɚ [-tɔɚ]
alarum ə'lɑɹəm [ə'læɹəm]

Variant pronunciations are contained within brackets. In most cases, the initial entry implies a primary preferred pronunciation (according to the conventions of the Standard American Stage Dialect as outlined in the introduction), and the bracketed variants imply secondary and sometimes even tertiary choices. Usage is essentially governed, however, by the discretion of the speaker when many factors (see introduction §§ 1.1 through 1.4) are considered.

6. Italics

hindmost 'haĭn*d*moŭst
mickle 'mɪkəl

Italics within the phonetic transcription itself indicate a phoneme that is virtually, yet not entirely, absent from the pronunciation of the word.

recount (*v.*) (*counting over*), **-s, -ing, -ed** ˌɹi'kaŏnt, -s, -ɪŋ, -ɪd
recount (*v.*) (*to tell*), **-s, -ing, -ed** ɹɪ'kaŏnt, -s, -ɪŋ, -ɪd

Essentially anything within parentheses is in italics; word form, editorial comments, and **Notes** (q.v.).

7. Notes

puissan|ce, -t 'pwisən|s ['pjuɪsən|s], -t
Note.—Poetic meter sometimes requires [pju'ɪs-]
misconstr|ue, -ues, -uing, -ued ˌmɪskən'stɹu, -z, -ɪŋ, -d
Note.—The Folios and Quartos of S. use 'misconster' mostly. Whenever modern editors replace it with 'misconstrue,' the stress falls on the second syllable, that is, [mɪs'kɒnstɹu]. *The only possible exception is* 1HVI, II.iii.72, *depending on how one scans the line*
mispriz|e, -es, -ing, -ed mɪs'pɹaĭz, -ɪz, -ɪŋ, -d
Note.—In MSND, III.ii.74, *the first syllable of 'mispriz'd' is arguably the stressed one*

A note beneath an entry word allows me to expound on the dramatic and literary conditions that can often cause the pronunciation of a word to alter.

8. Syllabic Stress

quite ˈkwaɪ̆t
gaffer, -s ˈgæfɚ, -z
predetermination ˌpɹɪdɪˌtɝˈmɪˈneɪ̆ʃn̩

The entries above represent the three most common notations of syllabic stress in this dictionary.

Primary stress is marked diacritically with [ˈ] immediately preceding the syllable intended to have primary stress—usually treated vocally by heightening one's pitch intonation relative to the other syllables (in polysyllabic words). It should be noted that monosyllabic words in this dictionary also have this diacritical mark preceding them due to the narrowness of the transcription, and to remind the reader that monosyllabic words are not inherently weak.

Secondary stress is marked diacritically with [ˌ] immediately preceding the syllable intended to have secondary stress relative to the syllables considered to have primary stress.

Weak syllables are not marked diacritically.

abstract (*s., adj.*), **-s, -ly, -ness** ˈæbstɹækt, -s, -lɨ [-ˈ--], -nɪs [-ˈ--]
Javanese ˌdʒɑvəˈniz (*when att.,* [ˈ---])

As seen above, words that may have alternative syllabic stress depending on usage and meaning are so indicated by substituting a dash for each syllable.

9. Syllabication (*The Division of Syllables*)

Syllabication is not ordinarily indicated in this dictionary.

Wiltshire ˈwɪlt.ʃɚ [ˈwɪlt.ʃɪɚ]

Sometimes, however, it is necessary to indicate syllabication. The example above illustrates the need to syllabically separate the [t] from the [ʃ] so that the reader is not led to the conclusion that the affricate phoneme [tʃ] exists in the word. Syllabication will be indicated diacritically with [.] in between the syllables in question.

10. The Vertical Stroke

yeo|man, -men ˈjoʊ|mən, -mən
zipp|y, -ier, -iest ˈzɪp|ɨ, -ɨɚ, -ɨɪst
culpab|le, -ly, -leness ˈkʌlpəb|l̩, -lɨ, -l̩nɪs

The vertical stroke in this dictionary is employed for the sole purpose of separating the head-word from the terminating parts that may alter either the spelling of the word or its pronunciation after assimilation.

This vertical stroke is not to be confused with any phonetic symbol, that is, the 'single bar' or the 'pipe' representing a dental (/alveolar) click (cf. Pullum and Ladusaw, *Phonetic Symbol Guide,* The University of Chicago Press, 1986, pp. 192f.).

11. American Spelling

It is important to realize that there are sometimes differences between the way the British spell and the way Americans (U.S.) spell. Shakespeare was, of course, British, and many of the finest editions of his works are edited using the traditional British spellings.

Traditional U.S. spellings are used in this dictionary. Familiarity with the differences between U.S. and British customs of spelling is always useful, but it is not essential in referencing a word in this dictionary.

center, -s, -ing, -ed 'sentɚ, -z, -ɹɪŋ, -d

color, -s, -ing, -ed 'kʌlɚ, -z, -ɹɪŋ, -d

organiz|e, -es, -ing, -ed 'ɔɚ-gənaɪz, -ɪz, -ɪŋ, -d

Words such as the three above are not orthographically far from their British counterparts **centre**, **colour**, and **organise** (a spelling often used). One is able to find them in reasonably the same proximity as their counterpart.

mould (*chiefly Brit. var. of* **mold**, *q.v.*) 'moŭld

Entry words not quite as close in proximity to their counterparts are included (as illustrated above with the word **mould**). The full entry for the word (with its phonetic transcription) will be found under **mold**.

12. Strong and Weak Forms

a (*the indefinite article*), 'eĭ (*strong form*), 'ə (*weak form*)

This distinction is determined by usage in connected speech; that is, how pronunciation is affected by the position of a word relative to the words surrounding it when speaking. The word **from**, for instance, is weak in the sentence /She came in from the garden./; however, in the exchange /Died? What from?/ the word **from** is considered strong, thus changing its pronunciation.

With such words, both the strong and the weak form are given.

13. Foreign Words and Phrases

veni, vidi, vici (*L.*) 'vɛnɪ 'vidɪ 'vitʃɪ

Definitively foreign words found in Shakespeare are listed alphabetically, and foreign phrases are listed in their entirety, alphabetically, using the first word of the phrase as the key entry word. These entries are italicized. When known, the language of origin is given parenthetically.

It must be admitted that customs of English pronunciation rarely allow foreign words to be pronounced with very much of their native integrity. Foreign words are typically acculturated, or anglicized, so that, though still considered foreign, the word has a distinctly English flavor. This is acute in Shakespeare's works (see chapter entitled Shakespeare's Verse § 1.8). There are exceptions, of course; for example, the extensive passages spoken in French in *Henry V*. A reminder, though; to these speakers, the French language is not foreign at all.

14. Homonyms, Homophones, and Parts of Grammar

con, -s, -ning, -ned ˈkɒn, -z, -ɪŋ, -d

Taken into account for each entry are the various meanings the word may have and its part in grammar (e.g., subject, verb, adjective). In the example above, it isn't necessary to distinguish **con** meaning to defraud and **con** meaning to study carefully (or any of its other meanings) because the pronunciation of the word never changes due to meaning. Nor does it ever change due to whether it is a transitive verb (**con** meaning to direct the steering of a vessel) or a noun (such as the short form for **convict**, meaning one who is found guilty of a crime and is serving time in prison).

When pronunciation does change due to its part in grammar, it is so cited with more than one entry:

contract (*s.*), **-s** ˈkɒntɹækt, -s

contract (*v.*), **-s, -ing, -ed** kənˈtɹækt, -s, -ɪŋ, -ɪd

Likewise, when the pronunciation changes due to meaning only, regardless of whether the part of grammar is the same, more than one entry is cited:

depot (*transit station or warehouse*), **-s** ˈdipoŭ, -z

depot (*military usage*), **-s** ˈdepoŭ, -z

15. Shakespeare's Proper Names

The entries of proper names found in Shakespeare will frequently include variant pronunciations (usually dictated by the metrical patterns of verse). In such cases where a name may be pronounced differently due to versification, the alternate pronunciations are provided. They are typically not in brackets because the alternate pronunciation is not considered secondary, but simply different due to the metrical pattern in particular lines of verse. For instance:

Troilus (ADO, *TC*, TN, TS) ˈtɹoɹləs, ˈtɹɔïləs

Depending on the number of beats needed in a line of verse, this name may be either one choice or the other. Note that the play or poem in which a proper noun is mentioned is also given. When dealing with personages, the abbreviation for the play and/or poem is given whether the character is an actual speaking role or simply mentioned. If the character is one of the *dramatis personae*, the name of the play is italicized.

Shakespeare notoriously anglicized foreign names. Attempts to purify or give native integrity to the names in question invariably lead one upstream against the flow of the metrical scheme or Shakespeare's attempts, in some cases, to rhyme or pun. Shakespeare, it may be argued, went to great lengths in his orthography to guide one toward the correct—his correct—pronunciation. For instance, the

French town of Calais [kalɛ] is spelled Callis and Callice in the earliest editions of his plays, indicating a pronunciation of [ˈkælɪs]. Having said that, some latitude ought to be given to the integrity of such names' pronunciations (as well as other French words), depending on whose cause the speaker is allied to: the French or the British.

16. The Reference Source for Shakespeare's Plays in this Dictionary

The Arden Shakespeare editions are the reference source for this dictionary. They were chosen for their practicality, as well as a decades-old tradition of fine scholarship and ample annotations. They are practical in that they are extremely portable for the actor—one small book per play—and because they essentially allow the actor to become his or her own quasi editor by providing a cross-reference of alternative choices from the various Quartos, Folios, and illustrious Shakespearean commentators throughout the centuries.

    undid ˌʌnˈdɪd ([ˈ-ˌ-] *in* AC, II.ii.205)

Line assignations from one *Arden Shakespeare* edition to another are typically reliable. However, because line assignation may vary from one editor's version to another (outside of *The Arden Shakespeare*), other editions referenced using this dictionary's citation may require a shallow search for the entry word. Typically, it will be found in the general area of the line cited. For instance, In G. B. Harrison's edition (*Shakespeare, The Complete Works*, Harcourt Brace Jovanovich) the word cited above ('undid') is found nearby in AC, II.ii.210, and in *The Oxford Shakespeare* (*William Shakespeare, The Complete Works; Compact Edition*. Stanley Wells and Gary Taylor, eds., Oxford University Press), it is found in AC, II.ii.212.

SHAKESPEARE'S VERSE

1.0 Four Hundred Years Later

The Actor's Task

1.1 This dictionary is designed to guide one toward pronunciations that will best serve the versified text, bearing in mind the actor's deepest desire: that of being understood. Every actor, every public speaker, and so on, has the responsibility of being audible and intelligible to the audience, but being understood is more than sheer volume and articulation. Understandability has to do with using the words to convey meaning—meaning of the words themselves in an association with one's authentic responses to the given circumstances of the material. Shakespeare employs two manners of speech—or modes of communication—that convey particular meaning, apart from some of the more conventional forms of understandability. These two manners of speech are verse and prose, which may be a conscious statement the character is making about itself and its perception of the world around it. The manner of speech chosen by the character in any given moment thus takes on special meaning, linguistically reflecting the character's present condition or circumstance.

1.2 When the text is in verse, then prosody (the analysis of poetry) comes into play. Studying the metrical structure of the verse (also known as scansion dynamics) may lead to particular ways of utterance. For example, words of a certain length at first glance may be pronounced with more syllables or fewer syllables, depending on the number of metrical beats required by the verse line. This is not so unusual an idea when one looks at how moderns generally accept different numbers of syllables in commonly used words today, such as /interesting/, /comfortable/ (both with either three or four syllables), and /different/ (with either two or three syllables). Also, scanning the verse can sometimes lead one to give primary stress to a syllable other than the one typically adopted by the speaker, but which better fits the scheme of the iambic pentameter. Modern examples of this practice are found in words such as /detail (s.)/, /applicable/, and /formidable/. Whether it's considered irregular or not, each word may be given primary stress on either the first or second syllable. A brief overview of how Shakespeare's verse works is therefore worthwhile (insofar as it will affect pronunciation choices).

The Principle of Prosody

1.3 View the rules governing scansion dynamics like any other set of rules: there are always exceptions to them, and they were made to be broken. Rules, however, are meant to provide a fairly reliable reference point. That point may also become one of departure if one so chooses. As a friend of mine always says, "The map is never the territory." Only when you are on your feet in the midst of the event of rehearsal and performance will you know for certain how the advice in this chapter—even the pronunciation choices proffered throughout this entire dictionary—will best serve you.

Verse versus Prose

1.4 Shakespeare wrote his plays using two distinctly different linguistic styles: a poetic style of verse called *iambic pentameter*, and a nonpoetic style called *prose*. With only two exceptions, he concurrently employed both styles in his plays. The density of poetry in his plays ranges from 100 percent in *Richard II* and *King John*, to only 13.4 percent in *The Merry Wives of Windsor*. In the main, though, his plays are predominantly in a form of poetic verse, that is, iambic pentameter. In *Romeo and Juliet*, for instance, over 87 percent of the text is in verse—a fairly high percentage.

1.5 But why write in two styles? What does it signify? It might have something to do with who is doing the talking. Everyone in Shakespeare, it seems, is capable of speaking in prose—a colloquial, unstructured, and random way of speaking. Everyone from prince to pauper in what has been called "the Chain of Being" may speak it. One might say that it is everyone's natural birthright to speak in prose, the manner of speech we naturally inherit. Both verse and prose are available to the characters in the verse-speaking category, and such characters may thus adopt either the form of verse or prose—whichever best suits their needs, speaking in the manner that best reflects their present condition or circumstance. Some, with an overdeveloped sense of their own nobility, never deign to speak in prose. In contrast, some high-born characters in Shakespeare avoid speaking in verse outright (e.g., Falstaff), unless they are addressing the sovereignty, in which case, verse-speaking becomes a must. One conspicuous exception—there are always exceptions—is that pe-

riod in *Hamlet* when Hamlet speaks to Claudius in prose. But one must remember, it is within that portion of the play Hamlet assumes an "antic disposition" (serving to express his contempt for Claudius and Claudius' claim to the
throne).

1.6 Verse-speaking may also signify 'Love.' In order for the upper class in Shakespeare to distinguish themselves linguistically from the lower class, as they do in
manner and apparel, a different form of speech is required. The elite don a verbal manner, as it were—an extravagant mantle of words and style—lording the
language of verse over those incapable of study, leisure, and the pursuit of noble
thought. One notable exception to this is in the case of anyone smitten by Love.
Love, the highest of high emotion in Elizabethan cosmology, is evidently capable
of ennobling the simplest of souls, endowing them with the ability to speak in
the heightened ways of verse. Love being blind, the upper class does not have a
singular right to its possession, nor in such instances can it claim sole possession
of Love's by-product, the language of verse.

The Prevailing Rhythm

1.7 Is there a difference in the way in which each style is spoken? In Shakespeare,
there is a structural scheme to the verse. The result has been likened to the human
heartbeat. Its practice does not require a didactic overattention to the rhythm, but
the acknowledgment of it has its rewards. For one thing, its general regularity
provides an assurance of a universe in order. The language thus becomes a kind
of cosmological barometer. Fluctuations in the language—either verse shifting
into prose, prose into verse, or the subtleties of pattern variances within the verse
form itself—indicate shifts of balance in the macrocosmic universe, and shifts of
balance in the hearts of the characters' universe in microcosm.

    Each line of verse usually has five metrical units, known as feet, and each foot
is usually comprised of one short beat followed by a long one. This scheme is
known as iambic pentameter. Thus, there are usually ten syllables—five weak,
five strong—in a verse line.

Take the line: *Before a true and lawful magistrate—*

ˇ ´ ˇ ´   ˇ ´   ˇ ´   ˇ ´
Before / a true / and law / ful ma / gistrate
3HVI, I.ii.23

    No special attention need be given the cadence here because the mere utter-
ance of the words fits naturally into the iambic form of a short beat followed by a
long one. Every so often, though, a word, in order to fulfill the urges of the subtly
rhythmic undercurrent, will distort itself. There are between 80 and 100 instances

of words in Shakespeare's canon that, when necessary to the metrical integrity of a line of verse, adopt a different syllabic stress from the way in which we customarily speak them today; a fairly negligible amount, considering the fact that Shakespeare's works add up to well over 100,000 lines. In *A Midsummer Night's Dream*, for instance, Theseus says:

Long with' / ring out / a young / man's re / venue.
MSND, I.i.9

Here, the first syllable of /revenue/ is stressed just as we pronounce it today. Elsewhere in *A Midsummer Night's Dream* (the very same scene, in fact), Lysander says:

Of great / reve / nue, and / she hath / no child,
MSND, I.i.168

Notice that the word /revenue/ is here stressed on the second syllable rather than the first. Obviously, the dramatists during the Elizabethan period—particularly Shakespeare—felt that words could bear the strain of shifts in their syllabic stress as long as general understandability wasn't compromised; that audiences would benefit more by their responses to the overall effects of the meter and rhythm, as long as the word's meaning was essentially there. This poetic device is known as 'recessive accenting.'

/Complete/, /extreme/, /secure/, /supreme/, and /profound/ are just a few of many disyllabic adjectives and participles able to take the stress on either syllable, and which are often stressed on the first syllable to fit the meter of the verse line (see Appendix I.1, Schmidt's *Shakespeare Lexicon and Quotation Dictionary*), as well as comply with the aesthetic values of recessive accenting. Each of the words above (along with scores of others) is entered into this dictionary, giving both its modern pronunciation and its pronunciation with shifted syllabic stress (when applicable). Each entry of this kind will cite where in Shakespeare's works such aberrant pronunciations are to be found.

Shakespeare: Always the Englishman

1.8 Shakespeare (almost obstinately) requires most foreign words (including, and perhaps especially, names) to be pronounced in an anglicized manner. Under this precept, the name of the incurable melancholic, Jaques (*Fr.* [ʒɑk]), in *As You Like It*, may be pronounced ['dʒeĭks] (just as it still is when referring to the British surname). For Shakespeare there is an advantage in anglicizing because the anglicized form helps to retain a homophonic pun on privies and melancholia—

jakes, in English, means latrine or dung heap, and the humor 'melancholy' is associated with the earth (soil), one of the four principal elements (cf. 'la Pucelle' in the dictionary). It is worth mentioning that in the Second Quarto version of LEAR, II.ii.64, the common noun 'jakes' is spelled 'jaques.' (For a more in-depth discussion, see Agnes Latham's Introduction to her edition of *As You Like It* for *The Arden Shakespeare*, 1975, p. lxviii.)

But it doesn't stop there. Shakespeare always resorts to the privileges of his poetic license—thinking nothing of taking the name, Jaques ['dʒeɪ̆ks], and sometimes (at least four, but no more than six, times) making it two syllables (['dʒeɪ̆kɪs] or perhaps ['dʒeɪ̆kɪz]) to fit it rightly into the verse line. For example:

Of Ja / ques Fal / conbridge, / solem / nized
LLL, II.i.42

Another example using an even more familiar name:

I am / the son / of He / nry / the Fifth,
3HVI, I.i.107

Here, Shakespeare takes the name, Henry (typically disyllabic), and sifts from it an extra syllable, thus securing another (albeit a very weak) beat necessary to the meter. The result is a pronunciation close to ['henəɹɪ]—not far from the trisyllabic variant still spoken by some dialectal groups today. The instances illustrated above are perhaps less obvious than the '-ed' endings where one usually looks to find the elusive beat in a verse line that (at first glance) is seemingly too short. Proper names shifting in length—telescoping into more than the usual number of syllabic phonemes or by syncope shrinking into fewer syllabic phonemes—are so cited in this dictionary.

Rhyme and Reason

1.9 When it comes to the question (or importance) of rhyme nowadays, there is little one can do about a perceived dissonance in what otherwise would have rhymed in Shakespeare's time. Some vowel sounds have shifted in the last four hundred years, the /o/ in particular. Realizing that a couplet's prosperity lies in its ability to rhyme with itself, this shift has caused several couplets of Shakespeare's to fall desperately short of their intended goal. In LLL, IV.i.138–140, 'foul' wants to rhyme with 'bowl,' but then 'bowl' turns right around and attempts to rhyme with 'owl.' The couplets concluding many of Shakespeare's sonnets provide some other examples, for example, 'noon/son,' 'tongue/song,' 'gone/alone,' 'one/alone,' 'moan/gone,' 'forth/worth,' 'belovèd/removèd,' and, 'love(d)/prove(d),' just to name a few. One is forced to forsake the longed-for rhyme in favor of the pronunciation that will reconcile intelligibility, meaning, and regularity.

1.10 On the other hand, there is a stark contradiction to what I have just stated when the element of meter is considered. Intelligibility, meaning, and regularity give over (somewhat) to requirements of metrical patterns when necessary, because Shakespeare's verse is double-pronged. The meaning of words is in a dynamic tension with the overall rhythm underlying the text. This rhythm creates a subtle cadence. Simply put, cadence is syllabic stress—the value of strong next to weak, long next to short, or hard next to soft. This pervasive undercurrent of rhythm beneath the surface of the verse—and the effect of these rhythms—is quasi-subliminal in that the stimuli to which one responds are not just apparent in the word meanings themselves but in the subtleties of cadence as well; and with few exceptions the cadence traditionally prevails over pronunciation.

SHAKESPEARE'S FOREIGN LANGUAGES

1.0 Latin

Decriers of 'Low' Latin

1.1 The bibliography of contemporaneous material related to how Latin was pronounced in Shakespeare's time is extremely thin. There were some in his day who bemoaned misusages and common modes of speech finding their way into what was considered the classical (albeit English) pronunciation of Latin. Most notable of these was Roger Ascham (1515–1568), the Latin and Greek tutor to Princess Elizabeth (later to become Queen Elizabeth I). His lengthy treatise, *The Scholemaster*, published posthumously in 1570, is full of opinions and advice on how best to cope with pervasive influences that he felt were deteriorating the edges of properly spoken Latin, finding great fault with students who were learning, as he puts it, "an evil choice of words (and right words, saith Caesar, is the foundation of eloquence) . . . a wrong placing of words: and lastly, an ill framing of the sentence, with a perverse judgment, both of words and sentences." Long-held traditions of scholarship were evidently giving way to popular—some might say vulgar—educational forms, promulgated by the many (and growing number of) grammar schools and colleges. Ascham unabashedly places most of the blame squarely on the shoulders of exactly the type of school Shakespeare is said to have attended. As for the learning of the Latin tongue, Ascham says, "But now, commonly, in the best schools in England, for words, right choice is smally regarded, true propriety wholly neglected, confusion is brought in, barbariousness is bred up so in young wits, as afterward they be not only marred for speaking, but also corrupted in judgment: as with much ado or never at all, they be brought to right frame again." Needless to say, had Ascham lived to hear any of Shakespeare's plays or read any of his Latin therein, he would have felt mostly vindicated by the vehemence of his pronouncements.

1.2 Exactly how Ascham would have prescribed the proper sounding of English Latin we will never know. He breaks *The Scholemaster* into six parts: Translatio Linguarum, Paraphrasis, Metaphrasis, Epitome, Imitatio, and Declamatio. These are the stages and techniques for the proper study of Latin and its execution that Ascham believes will root out coarse habits, creating the very best speakers and thinkers. More than just a syllabus, all but the final chapter contain ample material—always infused with his rebukes and chastisements—to further the knowledge and perfection of Latin. In his last chapter, Declamatio, one presumes (or hopes) he will speak directly to the utterance of Latin, the shape of sounds as he would have wanted to hear them. Unfortunately, and somewhat mysteriously, the treatise is published with that (and only that) particular chapter wholly omitted. In any case, it's obvious that Ascham was a pedant of the first order, futilely trying to hold back the tide of what he saw as *his* Latin being corrupted by modernists as well as the indolent. And though Ascham does not give commentary on what sounds particularly bothered him in terms of inflection, shape, duration, and placement, nor of his preferences, one thing may easily be deduced from *The Scholemaster*; that in Shakespeare's day, Latin was a *living* dead language, and as with all languages living or otherwise, that it was—is—subject to evolution and adaptation.

A Look into the Past

1.3 Literally, only one small piece of concrete evidence exists related to how Latin was pronounced in England some four centuries ago. The phonetician, Robert Robinson, produced a humble-sized pamphlet, a treatise entitled *The Art of Pronuntiation*, printed in London in 1617. Virtually nothing is known about Robinson, except that he was a Londoner and that at the time of printing he was a relatively young man. H. G. Fiedler, Professor and Fellow of The Queen's College, Oxford University, brought the small pamphlet to light in 1919 after having uncovered the only known copy to exist from the shelves of the Bodleian Library. Included in this inspired (and exceptionally rare) handbook is a phonetic code—an alphabet of sorts, a chart of tongue arch placement in relation to particular vowel sounds, and the phonetic transcription of poems in Latin, presumed to be of Robinson's own composition. Although far ahead of its time, *The Art of Pronuntiation* isn't thoroughly systemic and offers few surprises. It is Robinson's phonetic transcription of Latin, however, that uniquely characterizes the English Latin of his day, the pronunciations promoted by the English Latin schools of the early seventeenth century.

1.4 Professor Fiedler printed a thorough summation of Robinson's work in his own *A Contemporary of Shakespeare on Phonetics and on the Pronunciation of English and Latin* (Oxford University Press, 1936), transposing into modern phonetics (modern for the time) Robinson's phonetic transcription of a poem in Latin. As mentioned above, there is nothing too surprising, except perhaps that it confirms certain notions modern phoneticians and orthoepists have held about how particular vowel sounds were spoken in London four hundred years ago, and that the approach to Latin pronunciation, then as now, is come to by way of the speakers' language or dialect spoken in their particular country or region. In other words, the features of the speakers' mother tongue points the way toward what is thought to be the proper pronunciation of Latin. When *The Classical Review* printed their commentary on Robinson's treatise via Fiedler's study, they concluded that Latin in Shakespeare's day was, "usually pronounced on the same principles as the vernacular."

Latin as the Lingua Franca

1.5 Four hundred years ago, when foreign speakers wanted to communicate, and whose native languages were different from one another, a common language had to be adopted between them. Typically, that language was Latin. If you will imagine a supposed conversation in 1530 between Erasmus, Thomas More, Cardinal Wolsey, Martin Luther, and Pope Clement VII of Rome, their natural instincts would have been to converse in Latin. Latin stood out as the universal language of the learned, especially for liturgical discourse, and it would have been the one language in which all five were entirely conversant. But Erasmus, More, Wolsey, and Luther might have strained a little (or a lot) to thoroughly understand the Latin of Clement VII, an Italian. Clement VII, More, Wolsey, and Luther might have strained to understand Erasmus, who was Dutch. Besides the fact that Erasmus was both famed and defamed in his day for speaking an incorrect Latin "far from classical models," he would also have spoken his Latin in a Dutch accent, just as Clement VII would have spoken his in an Italian, Martin Luther in a German, and so on and so forth. Also, when conversing in Latin, grammatical rules governing formations of sentences, the speakers' knowledge of how declension works in Latin grammar, as well as a retention of the Latin vocabulary, would all be informed and influenced by the precepts and customs of their own mother tongues, contributing to their own particular linguistic idiosyncrasies.

1.6 Much the same is true today. When businesspersons from around the world gather, they commonly choose English as their lingua franca to discuss international matters, such as science, commerce, fashion, and diplomacy. In many parts of the world, English is taught in schools as the first language, even if it is not—or only one of several of—that particular country's 'official' language, very much the way Latin was taught and used throughout Europe in Shakespeare's day. And today, when English is learned and spoken in Singapore, Amsterdam, New Delhi, and the Philippines, it is influenced by the rhythms, inflections, and placement (both tonal and articulatory) of the speakers' various mother tongues, as well as the grammatical rules governing formations of sentences, and other precepts and customs derived thereof; one such custom being whether the English aspired to is that of the British or of the American ilk, or a curious combination of both. Accents and dissimilarities in pronunciation forms are enough to distinguish the various forms, but rarely if ever do they stand in the way of intelligibility or acceptance.

A Bridge for the Actor

1.7 The idea that Latin was pronounced more or less on the same principles as the vernacular sheds some light on how contemporaneous speakers might have spoken some of Shakespeare's English Latin, so that meaning to the characters and the audience in the context of their respective worlds would make sense. But as we don't now attempt to speak the English of Shakespeare's plays based on the principles of the vernacular of his time, but rather the present, a study simply of how English Latin was pronounced then as opposed to now is somewhat beside the point, except where it liberates us from our sense of any obligation to speak it as they did, and where moments of potential humor arise, stemming from confusions with, and corruptions of, Latin to English and vice versa in the ear of an Elizabethan or Jacobean. Sometimes, the so-called corruptions of Latin in Shakespeare's plays are a comment on pronunciation forms, both for Latin and for English of the period; "haud credo" being taken for "old grey doe" (LLL, IV.ii.11–20) is an example. Despite whatever concerns Ascham had over the state of Latin, Shakespeare was not writing classical essays for the court, for academic circles, nor for liturgical purposes; and perhaps it's stating the obvious, but it's worthwhile reminding ourselves that Shakespeare was writing plays for consumption by a general public, about real life sorts of characters who aren't typically preoccupied with whether they're getting it right.

1.8 Contrary to what some might assume when perusing Shakespeare's Latin, other studies have been made that argue in favor of Shakespeare's proficiency and adroitness in his knowledge of Latin. J. W. Binns submitted *Shakespeare's Latin Citations: The Editorial Problem* to the *Shakespeare Survey: An Annual Survey of Shakespearian Study and Production*) (Stanley Wells ed., Cambridge University Press, 1982). In his article, Binns says, "Shakespeare could, and instinctively would, have got his Latin right when he wanted to. Therefore, the errors found in the First Folio and the Quartos are either deliberate—for dramatic effect—or a result of corruptions to the text after it had passed beyond Shakespeare's control . . ." What is also of acute interest is how his characters thus unwittingly characterize themselves by uttering either perfect or imperfect Latin. The evidence suggests (aside from the errors attributed to the compositors and scribes, and others who knew Latin less well than Shakespeare) that the accuracy of the Latin text in his works is more indicative of the characters' acumen, or lack thereof, and less indicative of Shakespeare's ability.

Shakespeare's Latin without a Legend

1.9 There are around 130 instances of Latin used in Shakespeare's plays and poems, some of them quotations, some short phrases, and some miscellaneous words and grammatical tags. The Latin in his works constitutes three times the amount of other foreign matter (the French, Spanish, and Italian) and thus present today's actors and readers, most of whom are illiterate when it comes to Latin, with the sizable task of seeking a legend to explain pronunciation; and for a type of Latin not all of which is, or ever was, considered regular. Finding such a legend or pronunciation guide is all but impossible, and whenever sources are found that attempt to set forth guidelines, the language used to explain them is invariably equivocal and incomplete. The *Oxford Latin Dictionary* (Oxford University Press, 1982) is an eleven-pound tome of well over 2,000 pages, with over 40,000 entries drawn from over a million original quotations, and yet nowhere in it (quite prudently) can one find a guide to pronunciation. Certain assertions for rules of pronunciation proffered by some might be more reliable than others, but in all honesty, there is no way to know exactly how it was meant to be pronounced, and the nineteenth century movement to reform Latin, to find (or propose) what the original Latin of pre-Christian Rome might have sounded like, has only served to confuse the modern reader even further.

1.10 With all this in mind (on top of the belief that Shakespeare was first and foremost a dramatist) I propose speaking the Latin in his plays with the goal of accomplishing two things: making it as understandable to a modern audience as possible, while retaining as much as possible the integrity of the characters' situations in the context of their world within the world of the play. This means that I am *not* recommending a standardized pronunciation of the Latin throughout, old or new, but one that sometimes relies on how Americans already pronounce certain sounds and draw on recognizable analogies. I recommend that in most instances the speakers should in some way 'italicize' their Latin for the sake of setting it apart (being a foreign language) from their colloquial vernacular, and that, depending on a character's status and intention, the pronunciation should reflect meaning to the modern ear; an audience that, for the most part, is as illiterate as the actor/speaker when it comes to the understanding of Latin. Most of the Latin will in fact be exactly what one would expect it to be, with relatively few modifications, and those only for the sake of meaning within context. Syllabic stress is given, but it must be understood that no one knows for sure how Latin is to be stressed. I depend on certain traditions, euphony, and (sometimes) analogies of recessive accenting in the English vernacular. The pronunciations suggested do stay within certain confines, but are unfettered by rigidly consistent regulations or any obligation to get the Latin exactly right, whatever one may assume that is.

Entries

1.11 Latin words in this dictionary, as with the other foreign language matter, are entered alphabetically. With a sentence or a series of words in a phrase, the first word is used as the head word. The entries are italicized to set the entry apart from English, especially when the word or phrase has not wholly been absorbed into the English lexicon, as with common phrases such as *in vino veritas*, *per diem*, *ad infinitum,* or *etcetera*, and also italicized for ease on the eye when searching. The reference line for the word or phrase is always cited. Since context is everything (to include the situation in a particular moment in a play, the status of the character speaking, his or her educational level, mother tongue, etc.) pronunciations proffered here are not necessarily recommendations for the pronunciation of a particular Latin word or phrase in general, only *in situ*.

2.0 French, Spanish, and Italian

2.1 All languages vary in terms of where the resonance and tone are focused in the mouth. For instance, French is focused very much toward the lips, whereas Italian seeks a higher placement somewhere between the alveolar ridge and the palate, yet relies heavily on a muscularity of the lips. In contrast, typical American English is thought to be focused mainly toward the back and middle of the mouth. Phonetic transcription does not accommodate these variances of 'tone-focus,' nor can the International Phonetic Alphabet (IPA) describe the widely varying pitch intonations and inflections characterizing various languages when spoken. Even when one is talking about a merely dialectal variance of speech in English, the IPA simply cannot manifest precisely how one speaker sounds in contrast to another speaker. Take the words 'exact' and 'inhibit,' for example ([ɪɡˈzækt] and [ɪnˈhɪbɪt], respectively). They are both transcribed the same way, whether speaking in a standard American or British dialect, but sound different somehow when coming from an American or British speaker. What the IPA can provide, however, is an approximate idea of vowel placement, consonants (and sometimes vowels) unique to other tongues, and (usually) relative syllabic stress. Users of *The Eloquent Shakespeare* will get a rough idea as to how to pronounce certain foreign words, realizing that a phonetic transcription in and of itself is never a substitute for a knowledge of the foreign sounds of other languages.

2.2 Instances of French, Spanish, and Italian in Shakespeare's works are relatively sparse. With the exception of extensive amounts of French in *Henry V*, there are a little over 40 examples of words and phrases borrowed from French, Spanish, and Italian. When deciding on their pronunciation, there are several things to consider. For one, the foreign words in Shakespeare's works are as old as the plays themselves, just like the English. French, Spanish, and Italian four hundred years ago is not always the French, Spanish, and Italian of today. Certain words continue to challenge, even mystify, modern-day scholars and are often emended. Other things to consider: whether the character speaking the foreign word/s is fluent in the foreign language, or merely taking an illiterate stab at it; whether the foreign term/s retains any of its native integrity, or is thoroughly assimilated into the English vernacular and thus thoroughly anglicized; and finally, whether the foreignness of what's being spoken is being mocked, and by whom— Shakespeare, the character speaking, or both. I suppose one other consideration many editors must ponder is whether or not apparent errors are Shakespeare's, the characters', or early compositors'. Georgio Melchiori, editor of *The Merry Wives of Windsor* (*The Arden Shakespeare*, 2000), expresses in one annotation the frustration most editors must experience (in attempting to discern how best to convey foreign words in Shakespeare) when he says, "French words and expressions are hopelessly confused in [the Folio's] attempt at phonetic rendering."

Entries

2.3 Like the Latin entries, the French, Spanish, and Italian words and phrases are entered into this dictionary alphabetically. With a sentence or a series of words in a phrase, the first word is used as the head word. The entries are italicized to set the entry apart from English, and also italicized for ease on the eye when searching. The reference line for the word or phrase is always cited. Much of the sizable amount of French contained in *Henry V*, including that spoken by the French Soldier and Boy in Act IV, and Katherine, Alice, and the King in Act V, has been omitted due to its scope, a study unto itself.

3.0 Accents: Welsh, Irish, Scottish, and French

3.1 Aside from Shakespeare's usage of country dialects to distinguish a character's identity—such as the rustic dialect Edgar in *King Lear* adopts when disguising himself as Poor Tom: using 'zir' for 'sir,' 'vor' for 'for,' and so on— there are a handful of characters who speak English with the accents natural to their own native tongues. Shakespeare seems to employ semiphonetic spellings in some instances in order to guide the actor toward the Welsh, Irish, Scottish, and French accents signifying places of origin. For example, the Welshmen, Fluellen in *Henry V* and Evans in *The Merry Wives of Windsor*, say, 'ploody' for 'bloody,' 'pless' for 'bless,' and 'Cheshu' for 'Jesu.' The Irishman, Captain Macmorris in *Henry V*, says, 'trompet' for 'trumpet,' 'ish' for 'is,' and 'beseeched' for 'besieged.' Captain Jamy, a Scotsman in *Henry V*, says, 'bath' for 'both,' 'wad' for 'would,' and 'grund' for 'ground.' Finally, Dr. Caius, a Frenchman in *The Merry Wives of Windsor*, says, 'varld' for 'world,' 'Pible' for 'Bible,' and 'trot' for 'troth.' Often, the point is to demonstrate the speakers' inept handling of English, for the sake of wringing the most satire out of plays on words stemming from confusions with, and corruptions of, English pronunciation via a foreign tongue. A strong example of this is Fluellen's usage of "Alexander the Pig" ('Pig' for 'Big') in his exchange with Gower in HV, IV.vii.12–18. There is no way to know exactly how each of these characters sounded in Shakespeare's day, and it's probably fair to say that Shakespeare is only hinting through a few particular words the degree to which a character of foreign origin—and perhaps the listener as well—is suffering through the mangling of English.

3.2 Also, there may be other opportunities in Shakespeare's plays to employ accents, despite the fact that Shakespeare doesn't explicitly write them that way. For example, Don Adriano de Armado in *Love's Labor's Lost* is typically played with a Spanish accent, and Navarre and his Lords (also in *Love's Labor's Lost*) are almost required to assume a Russian accent when masquerading as the Muscovites before the Ladies of France.

REFERENCE GUIDE

The selection of books and articles listed below provide valuable information elaborating on and augmenting the topics touched on in the Introduction to this dictionary, and some of the editorial notes following many of the entry-words.

Abbott, E. A. *A Shakespearian Grammar* (Dover), 1966.

American Heritage Dictionary Second College Edition (Houghton Mifflin), 1985.

Compact Edition of the Oxford English Dictionary (Oxford University Press), 1988.

Fowler, H. W. (rev. and ed. by Sir Ernest Gowers). *A Dictionary of Modern English Usage, Second Edition* (Oxford University Press), 1985.

Freeborn, Dennis. *From Old English to Standard English, Second Edition* (University of Ottawa Press), 1998.

Irvine, Theodora. *A Pronouncing Dictionary of Shakespearean Proper Names* (Barnes & Noble), 1944.

Jones, Daniel, *An Outline of English Phonetics* (Cambridge University Press), 1976.

———— (extensively rev. and ed. by A. C. Gimson). *Everyman's English Pronouncing Dictionary, Fourteenth Edition* (J. M. Dent & Sons), 1984.

Kenyon, John Samuel, and Thomas Albert Knott. *A Pronouncing Dictionary of American English* (G. & C. Merriam), 1953.

Kökeritz, Helge. *Shakespeare's Names: A Pronouncing Dictionary* (Yale University Press), 1972.

————. *Shakespeare's Pronunciation* (Yale University Press), 1966.

Larsen, Thorlief, and Francis C. Walker. *Pronunciation: A Practical Guide to Spoken English in Canada and the United States* (Oxford University Press), 1930.

McArthur, Tom. *The Oxford Companion to the English Language* (Oxford University Press), 1992.

Onions, C. T. *The Oxford Dictionary of English Etymology* (Clarendon Press), 1995.

———— (enlarged and rev. by Robert D. Eagleson). *A Shakespeare Glossary* (Oxford at the Clarendon Press), 1988.

Pullum, Geoffrey K., and William A. Ladusaw. *Phonetic Symbol Guide* (The University of Chicago Press), 1986.

Schmidt, Alexander (rev. and enlarged by Gregor Sarrazin). *Shakespeare Lexicon and Quotation Dictionary, Third Edition in Two Volumes* (Dover), 1971.

Severance, W. Murray. *Pronouncing Bible Names* (Holman Bible Publishers), 1985.

Shipley, Joseph T. *Dictionary of Early English* (Littlefield, Adams), 1963.

Skeat, Walter W. (ed. with additions by A. L. Mayhew). *A Glossary of Tudor and Stuart Words, Especially from the Dramatists* (Oxford at the Clarendon Press), 1914.

Skinner, Edith Warman (rev. with new material added by Timothy Monich and Lilene Mansell; ed. by Lilene Mansell). *Speak with Distinction* (Applause Theatre Book Publishers), 1990.

Stokes, Francis Griffin. *Who's Who in Shakespeare; The Characters, Proper Names, and Plot Sources in the Plays and Poems* (Studio Editions), 1992.

Tiffany, William R., and James Carrell. *Phonetics, Theory and Application* (McGraw-Hill), 1977.

Trask, R. L. *A Dictionary of Phonetics and Phonology* (Routledge), 1996.

Wise, Claude Merton. *Applied Phonetics* (Prentice-Hall), 1957.

Zimmerman, J. E., *Dictionary of Classical Mythology* (Harper & Row), 1964.

ABBREVIATIONS

Shakespeare's Plays and Poems

AC	*Antony and Cleopatra*
ADO	*Much Ado About Nothing*
ALL'S	*All's Well That Ends Well*
AYLI	*As You Like It*
COM	*The Comedy of Errors*
COR	*Coriolanus*
CYM	*Cymbeline*
HAM	*Hamlet*
1HIV	*The First Part of Henry the Fourth*
2HIV	*The Second Part of Henry the Fourth*
HV	*Henry the Fifth*
1HVI	*The First Part of Henry the Sixth*
2HVI	*The Second Part of Henry the Sixth*
3HVI	*The Third Part of Henry the Sixth*
HVIII	*Henry the Eighth*
JUL	*Julius Caesar*
KJ	*King John*
LC	*A Lover's Complaint*
LEAR	*King Lear*
LLL	*Love's Labour's Lost*
LUC	*The Rape of Lucrece*
MAC	*Macbeth*
MEAS	*Measure for Measure*
MSND	*A Midsummer Night's Dream*
MV	*The Merchant of Venice*
MWW	*The Merry Wives of Windsor*
OTH	*Othello*
PER	*Pericles*
PP	*The Passionate Pilgrim*
PT	*The Phoenix and the Turtle*
RII	*King Richard the Second*
RIII	*King Richard the Third*
RJ	*Romeo and Juliet*
TC	*Troilus and Cressida*
TEM	*The Tempest*
TGV	*The Two Gentlemen of Verona*
TIM	*Timon of Athens*
TIT	*Titus Andronicus*
TN	*Twelfth Night, or What You Will*
TNK	*The Two Noble Kinsmen*
TS	*The Taming of the Shrew*
VA	*Venus and Adonis*
WT	*The Winter's Tale*

Dictionary Terms

adj.	adjective
adv.	adverb
alt.	alternative or alternate
att.	attributive
Brit.	British
cf.	confer (compare)
contr.	contraction
e.g.	exempli gratia (for example)
et al.	et alia (and others)
F.	Folio
Fr.	French
i.e.	id est (that is)
Ind.	Induction
interj.	interjection
IPA	International Phonetic Alphabet or International Phonetic Association
It.	Italian
L.	Latin
ln.	line
nom.	nominative
n.	noun
OED	Oxford English Dictionary
OF	Old French
p.	page
pers.	person
pl.	plural
pp.	pages
p.p.	past participle
prep.	preposition
Pro.	Prologue
pron.	pronoun
p.t.	past tense
Q.	Quarto
q.v.	quod vide (which see)
S.	Shakespeare (-'s, -an)
s.	substantive (noun)
sing.	singular
Sonn.	Sonnet (-s)
Sp.	Spanish
U.S.	United States
var.	variant or various/ly
v.	verb
viz.	videlicet (namely)
vs.	versus (in contrast with)
§	section
§§	sections

Aa

A (*the letter*), -'s 'eɪ, -z

a (*the indefinite article*), 'eɪ (*strong form*), 'ə (*weak form*)

a *or* a' (*archaic weak form of the prepositions* at, in, of, *or* on) 'ə
Note.—*These forms are not peculiar to S. Examples follow illustrating what was once a common practice of Elizabethan pronunciation, due in part to grammatical evolution, and to rapidly spoken colloquial speech. Remnants of this practice survive today, e.g., 'aboard' and 'Oh, a-hunting we will go.' Opinion of the citations below will vary depending on the edition referenced, whether Folio, Quarto, or modern (cf. Abbott's A Shakespearian Grammar, § 24, et al.):
". . . , it was not altogether your brother's evil disposition made him seek his death, but a provoking merit, set* a (= at) *work by a reproveable badness in himself." (*LEAR, III.v.4–6*); "Like rats, oft bite the holy cords* a-(= in) *twain" (*LEAR, II.ii.80*); "One good woman in ten, madam, which is a purifying* a'(= of) *th' song." (*ALL'S, I.iii.79, 80*); "God's blessing* a (= on) *your beard!" (*LLL, II.i.202*)

a *or* 'a' (*contr. of* ha *or* ha' = have) 'æ (*strong form*), 'ə (*weak form*)

a *or* 'a *or* a' (*personal pronoun* he) 'i (*strong form*), 'ɪ (*weak form*)
Note.—*This is a common substitution in Elizabethan English for the personal pronoun 'he,' and often used in S., e.g., "I saw him once;* a *was a goodly king." (*HAM, I.ii.186*); ". . . a man may draw his heart out ere* 'a *pluck one." (*ALL'S, I.iii.85, 86*); ". . . but* a' *must fast three days a week." (*LLL, I.ii.121*)

Aaron (*TIT*), -s 'ɛɹɪən, -z

aback ə'bæk

abacus 'æbəkəs

abaft ə'baft

abandon (*s.*), -er/s ə'bændən, -ɚ/z

abandon (*v.*), -s, -ing, -ed, -edly, -ment ə'bændən, -z, -ɪŋ, -d, -dlɪ, -mənt

abas|e, -es, -ing, -ed, -ement ə'beɪs, -ɪz, -ɪŋ, -t, -mənt

abash, -es, -ing, -ed ə'bæʃ, -ɪz, -ɪŋ, -t

abat|e, -es, -ing, -ed, -ement/s ə'beɪt, -s, -ɪd, -mənt/s

a-bat-fowling ə'bæt,faʊlɪŋ

Abba 'abə

abbess, (A.) (*COM*) -es 'æbɪs, -ɪz

abbey (A.), -s 'æbɪ, -z

abbot, (A.) -s 'æbət, -s

abbreviat|e, -es, -ing, -ed, -or/s ə'bɹivɪeɪt, -s, -ɪŋ, -ɪd, -ɚ/z

abbreviation, -s ə,bɹivɪ'eɪʃn̩, -z

ABC *or* abc, -'s ,eɪbi'si, -z

abdicat|e, -es, -ing, -ed 'æbdɪkeɪt, -s, -ɪŋ, -ɪd

abdication, -s ,æbdɪ'keɪʃn̩, -z

abdomen, -s 'æbdəmən, -z

abdomin|al, -ally æb'dɒmɪn|l̩, -əlɪ

abduct, -s, -ing, -ed, -or/s æb'dʌkt, -s, -ɪŋ, -ɪd, -ɚ/z

abduction, -s æb'dʌkʃn̩, -z

a(-)bed ə'bed

a-begging ə'begɪŋ

Abel (1HVI, RII) 'eɪbl̩

Abergavenny, Lord (*HVIII*) 'lɔɚd ,æbɚgə'venɪ
Note.—*In HVIII, I.i.211 and I.ii.137, this name wants to be trisyllabic, i.e.,* [,æbɚ'genɪ] *or* ['æbɚ,genɪ], *which follows the Folio spelling, 'Aburgany'*

aberran|ce, -cy, -t ə'beɹən|s, -sɪ, -t

aberrat|e, -es, -ing, -ed 'æbəɹeɪt, -s, -ɪŋ, -ɪd

aberration, -s ,æbə'ɹeɪʃn̩, -z

---

i we ɪ city ɪ hit e let ɛ debut æ can a pass ɝ bird ʌ hut ə again ɚ supper u you ʊ should o obey ɔ awl ɒ cop ɑ father eɪ paid aɪ high oʊ go ɔɪ voice aʊ found ɪɚ ear ɛɚ air ʊɚ poor ɔɚ fork ɑɚ park aɪɚ fire aʊɚ hour b boy p pit d dog t top g got k kid h how ɸ behave dʒ jot tʃ chew z zany s soft v vat f fat ʒ treasure ʃ ship ð the θ thin m man n no ŋ hang l lip j yes w won ʍ whew ɹ rigger, airy ɾ matter

abe|t, -ts, -tting, -tted, -ttor/s, -tment
ə'be|t, -ts, -ɾɪŋ, -ɪd, -ɾɚ/z, -tmənt

abeyance ə'beïəns

abhominable ə'bɒmɪnəbļ, æb'fiɒmɪnəbļ
[əb'fi-]

*Note.—In LLL, V.i.16–25, the pedant
Holofernes is commenting on "rackers
of orthography," elaborating on the
misapprehended mispronunciation of
words such as 'doubt,' 'debt,' 'calf,'
'half,' 'neighbor,' and 'abhominable.' It
is clear that he insists on pronouncing
what now are (and even then were)
considered silent letters, i.e., 'b,' 'l,' 'g,'
and the curious 'h' appearing in the
spelling of 'abominable,' a common
spelling of that word at the time.
Incidentally, Holofernes is absolutely
correct regarding 'abhominable' (see §
'abominable,' The Oxford Dictionary of
English Etymology, edited by C. T.
Onions). Confusion arises when editors
(or especially speakers) pay no heed to
Holofernes' scheme*

abhor, -s, -ring, -red, -rer/s əb'fiɔɚ, -z,
-ɹɪŋ, -d, -ɹɚ/z

abhorren|ce, -t əb'fiɒɹən|s, -t

Abhorson (*MEAS*) əb'fiɔɚsən

abid|e, -es, -ing ə'baïd, -z, -ɪŋ

abilit|y, -ies ə'bɪlɪt|ɨ, -ɨz

a-billing ə'bɪlɪŋ

a-birding ə'bɝdɪŋ

abject, -ly, -ness 'æbdʒekt, -lɨ, -nɪs

abjection æb'dʒekʃn̩

abjects (*neologism from RIII, I.i.106*)
æb'dʒekts

abjur|e, -s, -ing, -ed, -er/s æb'dʒʊɚ [əb-],
-z, -ɹɪŋ, -d, -ɹɚ/z

ablation æb'leïʃn̩

ablaze ə'bleïz

ab|le, -ler, -lest, -ly 'eïb|əl, -lɚ, -lɪst, -lɨ

able-bodied 'eïbļ,bɒdɨd

a-bleeding ə'blidɪŋ

ablution, -s æb'luʃn̩, -z

Abner 'æbnɚ

abnorm|al, -ally æb'nɔɚm|ļ, -əlɨ

abnormalit|y, -ties ,æbnɔɚ'mælɪt|ɨ, -ɨz

aboard ə'bɔɚd

abod|e, -es, -ing, -ed, -ement/s ə'boŭd,
-z, -ɪŋ, -ɪd, -mənt/s

abolish, -es, -ing, -ed, -er/s, -ment
ə'bɒlɪʃ, -ɪz, -ɪŋ, -t, -ɚ/z, -mənt

abolition, -ist/s ,æbo'lɪʃn̩, -ɪst/s

abominab|le, -ly ə'bɒmɪnəb|ļ, -lɨ

abomination, -s ə,bɒmɪ'neïʃn̩, -z

aboriginal ,æbə'ɹɪdʒɪnļ

aborigines ,æbə'ɹɪdʒɪnɨz

abort, -s, -ing, -ed ə'bɔɚt, -s, -ɪŋ, -ɪd

abortion, -s, -ist/s ə'bɔɚʃn̩, -z, -ɪst/s

abortive, -s; -ly, -ness ə'bɔɚtɪv, -z; -lɨ, -nɪs

abound, -s, -ing, -ed ə'baŭnd, -z, -ɪŋ, -ɪd

about ə'baŭt

above ə'bʌv

above-board ə'bʌvbɔɚd

above-mentioned ə,bʌv'menʃn̩d (*when
att.*, [-'----])

abracadabra ,æbɹəkə'dæbɹə

Abraham (*RII, RJ, MWW*), -'s
'eïbɹə,fiæm, [-fiem] -z

*Note.—In RJ, II.i.13 and RIII, IV.iii.38,
this name is syncopated for the sake of
the meter and is pronounced* ['eïbɹəm]
or ['eïbɹæm]

abram 'ɑbɹəm

*Note.—This is a colloquial corruption or
var. of 'auburn,' which was formerly
also written 'abern,' 'abron,' and
'abrun.' In COR, II.iii.20 it is meant to
stand for the color (associated with the
name, Abram), traditionally a light
yellow, in contrast to the brown already
mentioned in the passage. The OED
does not assert a pronunciation for
'abram.' My assertion to pronounce it*
['ɑbɹəm] *stems mainly from a desire on
my part to hear it sound as close to the
modern 'auburn' as possible*

Abram (*MV, RJ*) 'eïbɹəm

abrasion, -s ə'bɹeïʒn̩, -z

abrasive (*adj., s.*), **-s, -ness** ə'bɹeïsɪv, -z,
-nɪs

abreast ə'bɹest

a-breeding ə'bɹidɪŋ

a-brewing ə'bɹuɪŋ

abridg|e, -es, -ing, -ed, -(e)ment/s
ə'bɹɪdʒ, -ɪz, -ɪŋ, -d, -mənt/s

abroach əˈbɹoŭtʃ
abroad əˈbɹɔd
abrogate (*adj.*) ˈæbɹʊgɪt
abrogat|e (*v.*), **-es, -ing, -ed** ˈæbɹʊgeĭt, -s,
  -ɪŋ, -ɪd
abrogation, -s ˌæbɹʊˈgeĭʃn̩, -z
abrook əˈbɹʊk
abrupt, -est, -ly, -ness əˈbɹʌpt, -ɪst,
  -lɨ, -nɪs
abruption, -s əˈbɹʌpʃn̩, -z
Absalom ˈæbsəlɒm [-ləm]
abscess, -es ˈæbses, -ɪz
abscond, -s, -ing, -ed əbˈskɒnd, -z, -ɪŋ, -ɪd
absence, -s ˈæbsəns, -ɪz
absent (*adj.*), **-ly** ˈæbsənt, -lɨ
absent (*v.*), **-s, -ing, -ed** æbˈsent, -s,
  -ɪŋ, -ɪd
absentee, -s, -ism ˌæbsənˈti, -z, -ɪzm̩
absent-minded, -ly, -ness
  ˌæbsəntˈmaĭndɪd (*when att.,* [ˈ--ˌ--]), -lɨ,
  -nɪs
Absey (KJ) (*for 'A-B-C'*) ˈeĭbsɨ
absinth(e) ˈæbsɪnθ
absolute, -ness ˌæbsəˈlut [-ˈljut], -nɪs
absolutely (*depending on one's meaning,*
  this word may be stressed either of two
  ways:) ˈæbsəlutlɨ [-ˈljutlɨ], æbsəˈlutlɨ
  [-ˈljutlɨ]
absolution, -s ˌæbsəˈluʃn̩ [-ˈljuʃn̩], -z
absolv|e, -es, -ing, -ed, -er/s əbˈzɒlv, -z,
  -ɪŋ, -d, -ə/z
absorb, -s, -ing/ly, -ed, -edly; -able;
  -ent/ly əbˈsɔ˞b [əbˈzɔ˞b], -z, -ɪŋ/lɨ, -d,
  -ɪdlɨ; -əbl̩; -ənt/lɨ
absorption əbˈsɔ˞pʃn̩ [əbˈzɔ˞p-]
absque (obsque) hoc nihil est (*L.*) (2HIV,
  V.v.28) ˈɒbskwɛ (ˈɒbskwɛ) ˈhok ˈnifiil ˈɛst
abstain, -s, -ing, -ed, -er/s əbˈsteĭn [æb-],
  -z, -ɪŋ, -d, -ə/z
abstemious, -ly, -ness æbˈstimɪəs [əb-],
  -lɨ, -nɪs
abstention, -s əbˈstenʃn̩ [æb-], -z
abstinen|ce, -t ˈæbstɪnən|s, -t

abstract (*s., adj.*), **-s, -ly, -ness** ˈæbstɹækt,
  -s, -lɨ (-ˈ---), -nɪs (-ˈ--)
abstract (*v.*), **-s, -ing, -ed/ly, -edness**
  æbˈstɹækt, -s, -ɪŋ, -ɪd/lɨ, -ɪdnɪs
abstraction, -s æbˈstɹækʃn̩, -z
absurd, -est, -ly, -ness; -ity, -ities əbˈsɜ˞d,
  -ɪst, -lɨ, -nɪs; -ɪtɨ, -ɪtɨz
Note.—Sometimes stressed on the first
  syllable in S. [ˈæbsɜ˞d], *e.g.,* HAM,
  III.ii.60
Absyrtus (2HVI) æbˈsɜ˞təs
abundan|ce, -t/ly əˈbʌndən|s, -t/lɨ
abuse (*s.*), **-s** əˈbjus, -ɪz
abus|e (*v.*), **-es, -ing, -ed, -er/s** əˈbjuz, -ɪz,
  -ɪŋ, -d, -ə/z
abusive, -ly, -ness əˈbjusɪv, -lɨ, -nɪs
abut, -s, -ting, -ted, -ment/s əˈbʌt, -s, -ɪŋ,
  -ɪd, -mənt/s
aby əˈbaĭ
abysm, -s əˈbɪzəm, -z
abyss, -es əˈbɪs, -ɪz
Abyssinia, -n/s ˌæbɪˈsɪnɪə, -n/z
acacia, -s əˈkeĭʃə, -z
academe (A.), **-s** ˌækəˈdim, -z
academic, -ally ˌækəˈdemɪk, -əlɨ
academician, -s ˌækədəˈmɪʃn̩ [-dɪ-], -z
a-cap'ring əˈkeĭpɹɪŋ
acced|e, -es, -ing, -ed, -er/s əkˈsid [æk-],
  -z, -ɪŋ, -ɪd, -ə/z
accelerat|e, -es, -ing, -ed əkˈseləɹeĭt, -s,
  -ɪŋ, -ɪd
acceleration, -s əkˌseləˈɹeĭʃn̩, -z
accelerator, -s əkˈseləɹeĭɾə˞, -z
accent (*s.*), **-s** ˈæksənt [-sent], -s
accent (*v.*), **-s, -ing, -ed** ækˈsent, -s, -ɪŋ,
  -ɪd
accept, -s, -ing, -ed əkˈsept [æk-], -s, -ɪŋ,
  -ɪd
acceptability əkˌseptəˈbɪlɪtɨ [æk-]
acceptab|le, -ly, -leness əkˈseptəb|l̩ [æk-],
  -lɨ, -l̩nɪs
acceptan|ce, -ces, -cy, -t/s əkˈseptən|s,
  -sɪz, -sɨ, -t/s [æk-]

---

i wɛ ɨ city ɪ hit e let ɛ debut æ can a pass ɜ˞ bird ʌ hut ə again ə˞ supper u you
ʊ should o obey ɔ awl ɒ cop ɑ father eĭ paid aĭ high oŭ go ɔĭ voice aŭ found ɪ˞ ear
ɛ˞ air ʊ˞ poor ɔ˞ fork ɑ˞ park aĭə˞ fire aŭə˞ hour b boy p pit d dog t top g got
k kid h how fi behave dʒ jot tʃ chew z zany s soft v vat f fat ʒ treasure ʃ ship ð the
θ thin m man n no ŋ hang l lip j yes w won ʍ whew ɹ rigger, airy ɼ matter

access, -es, -ing, -ed 'ækses, -ɪz, -ɪŋ, -t
Note.—Sometimes [æk'ses] *in S., e.g.,*
2HIV, IV.i.78; HVIII, III.ii.17; MEAS,
II.ii.18; RJ, II.Pro.9; OTH, III.i.36; TGV,
III.i.109, III.ii.60, IV.ii.4; WT, II.ii.11,
V.i.87; TN, I.iv.16; TS, I.ii.126, 259,
267, II.i.97

accessor|y *or* **accessar|y, -ies** ək'sesə-ɹ|ɪ,
-ɪz
*Note.—Most editors agree that S. always
gives these words primary syllabic stress
on the first syllable, i.e.,* ['æksəsə-ɹɪ,
'æksesə-ɹɪ], *asserting that it was the
normal pronunciation in his day. This
pronunciation is practically inescapable
in some lines, e.g.,* LUC, 922, 1658;
Sonn. 35.13. *However, by simply eliding
'I am' in* ALL'S, II.i.35 *and 'be
accessary' in* RIII, I.ii.195, *a modern
pronunciation* ([ək'sesə-ɹɪ]) *is reconciled
without sacrificing conventions of
scansion dynamics (cf. Note for*
confessor*)*

accidence 'æksɪdəns

accident, -s 'æksɪdənt, -s

accit|e (*to summon or call; to induce or
excite*)**, -es, -ing, -ed** æk'saɪt, -s, -ɪŋ, -ɪd

acclaim, -s, -ing, -ed ə'kleɪm, -z, -ɪŋ, -d

acclamation, -s ˌæklə'meɪʃn, -z

accolade, -s 'ækəleɪd [-lɑd], -z

accommodat|e, -es, -ing/ly, -ed, -or/s
ə'kɒmədeɪt, -s, -ɪŋ/lɪ, -ɪd, -ə-/z

accommodation, -s əˌkɒmə'deɪʃn, -z

accommodo (*from L. 'accommodare,'
meaning 'to make comfortable'*) (2HIV,
III.ii.70) ɑ'komodo [ɑ'kɒmədoŭ]
*Note.—The modern ear is more likely to
hear 'accommodate' in the second
pronunciation, but in this instance, it's
probably more beneficial that the
modern audience knows they're being
spoken to in a 'tried' Latin*

accompaniment, -s ə'kʌmpənɪmənt, -s

accompan|y, -ies, -ying, -ied ə'kʌmpən|ɪ,
-ɪz, -ɪɪŋ, -ɪd

accomplice, -s ə'kɒmplɪs, -ɪz

accomplish, -es, -ing, -ed, -ment/s
ə'kɒmplɪʃ, -ɪz, -ɪŋ, -t, -mənt/s

accompt, -s, -ing, -ed (*archaic form of
account*) ə'kaŏnt, -s, -ɪŋ, -ɪd

accord, -s, -ing/ly, -ed ə'kɔɔ-d, -z, -ɪŋ/lɪ,
-ɪd

accordan|ce, -t ə'kɔɔ-dən|s [-dn̩-], -t

accost, -s, -ing, -ed ə'kɒst, -s, -ɪŋ, -ɪd

Accost, Mistress Mary (TN) 'mɪstɹɪs
'mɛɹ-ɹɪ ə'kɒst

accouter, -s, -ing, -ed, -ment/s ə'kutə-, -z,
-ɹɪŋ, -d, -mənt/s

accouterment *or* **accoutrement, -s**
ə'kutɹəmənt [-tə-m-], -s

accru|e, -es, -ing, -ed ə'kɹu, -z, -ɪŋ, -d

accumulat|e, -es, -ing, -ed, -or/s
ə'kjumjŭleĭt, -s, -ɪŋ, -ɪd, -ə-/z

accumulation, -s əˌkjumjŭ'leĭʃn, -z

accumulative, -ly, -ness ə'kjumjŭlətɪv,
-lɪ, -nɪs

accuracy 'ækjʊɹəsɪ [-ɹɪsɪ]

accurate, -ly, -ness 'ækjʊɹət [-ɹɪt], -lɪ,
-nɪs

accurs|ed, -t, -edly ə'kɜ-s|ɪd, -t, -ɪdlɪ
Note.—In RIII, I.ii.124, TIM, IV.ii.42
and WT, III.iii.52, *'accurs'd' is
disyllabic and thus pronounced* [ə'kɜ-st]

accusation, -s ˌækjʊ'zeĭʃn, -z

accusative, -s ə'kjuzətɪv, -z

accusativo, hinc (*L.*) (MWW, IV.i.39)
ɑˌkuzə'tivoŏ 'hiŋk

accus|e, -es, -ing, -ed, -er/s ə'kjuz, -ɪz,
-ɪŋ, -d, -ə-/z

ac|e, -es, -ing, -ed 'eĭs, -ɪz, -ɪŋ, -t

acerb, -ic ə'sɜ-b, -ɪk

ach|e (*pain*)**, -es, -ing, -ed** 'eĭk, -s, -ɪŋ, -t
Note.—In TEM, I.ii.372, *the word
'aches' is disyllabic. There is no
apparent pun on the letter 'h' in the*
TEM *passage (as there is in* AC,
IV.vii.7, 8 *and* ADO, III.iv.56) *but the
word in this instance is, according to
most, still to be pronounced* ['eĭtʃɪz].
*There is a tradition based on etymologi-
cal grounds (cf. Kökeritz's* Shakespeare's Pronunciation, *pp. 89 ff.) to
retain the* [tʃ] *when referring to the noun
(in proper context), particularly when
pluralized and versified (as in the* TEM
passage cited above and TIM, I.i.247,

V.i.198). Be that as it may, the meaning in these passages would not suffer were 'aches' to be pronounced ['eĭkɪz]

Acheron (MAC, MSND, TIT) 'ækə-ɹɒn

achiev|e, -es, -ing, -ed, -er/s, -ement/s; -able ə'tʃiv, -z, -ɪŋ, -d, -ə-/z, -mənt/s; -əbl̩

Achilles (2HVI, LLL, *TC*) ə'kɪlɪz

Achitophel (2HIV) ə'kɪtoˌfel [-'kɪtə-]

a'clock ə'klɒk

a-cold ə'koŭld

a-coming ə'kʌmɪŋ

aconitum (*highly poisonous plant*) ˌækə'naĭtəm

acquaint, -s, -ing, -ed ə'kweĭnt, -s, -ɪŋ, -ɪd

acquaintance, -s ə'kweĭntəns [-tn̩s], -ɪz

acquit, -s, -ting, -ted; -tal/s, -tance/s ə'kwɪt, -s, -ɪŋ, -ɪd; -l̩/z, -n̩s/ɪz

acre, -s 'eĭkə-, -z

acreage 'eĭkə-ɹɪdʒ

across ə'kɹɒs

act, -s, -ing, -ed, -or/s 'ækt, -s, -ɪŋ, -ɪd, -ə-/z

Actaeon (TIT) æk'tiən

Actaeon, Sir (MWW) ˌsɜ- (ɪ)æk'tiən

action, -s 'ækʃn̩, -z

actionable 'ækʃn̩əbl̩

action-taking 'ækʃn̩ˌteĭkɪŋ

Actium (AC) 'æktɪəm, 'ækʃɪəm, -tjəm, -ʃjəm

activat|e, -es, -ing, -ed 'æktɪveĭt, -s, -ɪŋ, -ɪd

active, -ly, -ness 'æktɪv, -lɪ, -nɪs

active-valiant 'æktɪv'væljənt

activist, -s 'æktɪvɪst, -s

activit|y, -ies æk'tɪvɪt|ɪ, -ɪz

actor, -s 'æktə-, -z

actress, -es 'æktɹɪs, -ɪz

acture 'æktʃə-

acute, -r, -st, -ly, -ness ə'kjut, -ə-, -ɪst, -lɪ, -nɪs

adage, -s 'ædɪdʒ, -ɪz

Adallas (AC) ə'dæləs

Adam (ADO, *AYLI*, COM, HAM, HV, LLL, TS) 'ædəm

adamant 'ædəmənt

ad Apollinem (*L.*) (TIT, IV.iii.54) ˌad ə'polɪnem

a-days ə'deĭz

adder (**A.**), **-s** 'ædə-, -z

adder's-tongue 'ædə-zˌtʌŋ

adder's-wort 'ædə-zˌwɜ-t [-ˌwɔə-t]

addict, -s, -ing, -ed ə'dɪkt, -s, -ɪŋ, -ɪd

addiction, -s ə'dɪkʃn̩, -z

add|le, -les, -ling, -led 'ædl̩, -l̩z, -lɪŋ [-lɪŋ], -l̩d

address, -es, -ing, -ed ə'dɹes ['æddɹes], -ɪz, -ɪŋ, -t

Note.—In LLL, V.ii.92, the reference is a pun on disguises and is usually spelled 'addrest;' it is stressed on the second syllable and completes a couplet with 'rest'

adieu, -s ə'dju, -z

Note.—Although this word has been firmly part of the English language since the fourteenth century, and has thus been wholly anglicized to the pronunciation given above, there are times in S. when the Fr. pronunciation, i.e., [adjø] *is preferred, e.g., when Dr. Caius uses it in MWW, IV.v.84, et al.*

adjoin, -s, -ing, -ed ə'dʒɔĭn, -z, -ɪŋ, -d

ad Jovem (*L.*) (TIT, IV.iii.54) ˌad 'dʒovɛm

Note.—In S., it's more beneficial that the audience understands that they are hearing 'Jove' than it is that they hear interpretations of Latin pronunciation that perhaps carry it away from direct understanding, e.g., ['jovɛm]

adjudg|e, -es, -ing, -ed, -ment/s ə'dʒʌdʒ, -ɪz, -ɪŋ, -d, -mənt/s

adjunct, -s 'ædʒʌŋkt, -s

adjust, -s, -ing, -ed, -able, -ment/s ə'dʒʌst, -s, -ɪŋ, -ɪd, -əbl̩, -mənt/s

---

i w**e** ɪ c**i**ty ɪ h**i**t e l**e**t ɛ d**e**but æ c**a**n a p**a**ss ɜ- b**i**rd ʌ h**u**t ə **a**gain ə- supp**e**r u y**ou** ʊ sh**ou**ld o **o**bey ɔ **aw**l ɒ c**o**p ɑ f**a**ther eĭ p**ai**d aĭ h**igh** oŭ g**o** ɔĭ v**oi**ce aŭ f**ou**nd ɪə- **ear** ɛə- **air** ʊə- p**oor** ɔə- f**or**k ɑə- p**ar**k aĭə- f**ire** aŭə- h**our** b **b**oy p **p**it d **d**og t **t**op g **g**ot k **k**id h **h**ow fi be**h**ave dʒ **j**ot tʃ **ch**ew z **z**any s **s**oft v **v**at f **f**at ʒ trea**s**ure ʃ **sh**ip ð **th**e θ **th**in m **m**an n **n**o ŋ ha**ng** l **l**ip j **y**es w **w**on ʍ **wh**ew ɹ **r**igger, ai**r**y ꬵ ma**tt**er

ad manes fratrum (*L.*) (TIT, I.i.101) ˌɑd
ˈmɑnɛs ˈfɹɑtɹʊm
ad Martem (*L.*) (TIT, IV.iii.55) ˌɑd
ˈmɑɚ̆tɛm
administ|er, -ers, -ering, -ered
əd'mɪnɪst|ɚ, -ɚz, -əɹɪŋ, -ɚd
administration, -s əd,mɪnɪ'stɹeɪʃn̩, -z
admiral, -s 'ædməɹəl, -z
admiralt|y, -ies 'ædmɚɹəlt|ɪ, -ɪz
admiration ,ædmɪ'ɹeɪʃn̩
admir|e, -es, -ing/ly, -ed, -er/s əd'maɪɚ̆,
-z, -ɹɪŋ/lɪ, -d, -ɹɚ/z
admit, -s, -ting, -ted/ly; -tance/s æd'mɪt
[əd-], -s, -ɪŋ, -ɪd/lɪ; -n̩s/ɪz
admonish, -es, -ing, -ed; -ment əd'mɒnɪʃ,
-ɪz, -ɪŋ, -t; -mənt
ado ə'du
a-doing ə'duɪŋ
Adon (PP, VA), -s 'ædɒn ['ædoʊn], -z
Adonis (1HVI, PP, Sonn. 53, TS, VA)
ə'dɒnɪs [ə'doʊnɪs]
a-doors ə'dɔɚ̆z
adopt, -s, -ing, -ed/ly; -ive ə'dɒpt, -s, -ɪŋ,
-ɪd/lɪ; -ɪv
adoption, -s ə'dɒpʃn̩, -z
adoptious ə'dɒpʃəs
adoration, -s ,ædə'ɹeɪʃn̩, -z
ador|e, -es, -ing/ly, -ed, -er/s ə'dɔɚ̆, -z,
-ɹɪŋ/lɪ, -d, -ɹɚ/z
adorn, -s, -ing/s, -ed, -ment/s ə'dɔɚ̆n, -z,
-ɪŋ/z, -d, -mənt/s
a-doting ə'doʊtɪŋ (*see Note for* nothing)
adown-a ə'daʊnə (*see Note for* down-a)
Adramadio, Dun (LLL) 'dʌn
,ædɹə'mɑdɪoʊ
*Note.—This is Costard's bumbling
attempt to say 'Don Armado' in LLL,
IV.iii.196*
Adrian (COR, TEM) 'eɪdɹɪən
Adriana (*COM*) ,eɪdɹɪ'ɑnə ['-'eɪnə]
Adriatic Sea (TS) ,eɪdɹɪ'ætɪk ['-'æɾɪk] 'si
adsum (*L.*) (2HVI, I.iv.23) ,ad'sʊm
a-ducking ə'dʌkɪŋ
adult, -s ə'dʌlt ['ædʌlt], -s
adulterate (*adj.*) ə'dʌltəɹɪt
adulterat|e (*v.*), -es, -ing, -ed, -or/s
ə'dʌltəɹeɪt, -s, -ɪŋ, -ɪd, -ɚ/z
adulteration, -s ə,dʌltə'ɹeɪʃn̩, -z
adulterer, -s ə'dʌltəɹɚ, -z

adulteress, -es ə'dʌltɹɪs [-təɹɪs], -ɪz
adulterous, -ly ə'dʌltəɹəs, -lɪ
adulter|y, -ies ə'dʌltəɹ|ɪ, -ɪz
adultress, -es ə'dʌltɹɪs, -ɪz
advanc|e, -es, -ing, -ed, -er/s; -ement/s
əd'vans, -ɪz, -ɪŋ, -t, -ɚ/z; -mənt/s
advantag|e, -es, -ing, -ed; -eable
əd'vantɪdʒ, -ɪz, -ɪŋ, -d; -əbl̩
adventur|e, -es, -ing, -ed, -er/s
əd'ventʃɚ, -z, -ɹɪŋ, -d, -ɹɚ/z
adventurous, -ly, -ness əd'ventʃəɹəs, -lɪ,
-nɪs
adverb, -s 'ædvɝb, -z
adversar|y, -ies 'ædvəsəɹ|ɪ, -ɪz
adverse, -ly æd'vɝs ['--], -lɪ
adversit|y (A.) (3HVI), -ies æd'vɝsɪt|ɪ,
-ɪz
advertis|e, -es, -ing, -ed, -er/s 'ædvɚtaɪz,
-ɪz, -ɪŋ, -d, -ɚ/z
*Note.—Sometimes 'advertised' is
[əd'vɝtɪsɪd] in S., e.g.,* 2HVI, IV.ix.23;
3HVI, II.i.116; RIII, IV.iv.449; *also*
[əd'vɝtɪst], *e.g.,* 3HVI, IV.v.9, V.iii.18;
TC, II.ii.212. *In TNK, III.i.58, it may be
either* [əd'vɝtɪsɪd], [əd'vɝtɪst], *or*
['ædvɚtaɪzd], *depending on how one
chooses to scan the line. When it is
simply 'advertise' in S., it is always
given primary syllabic stress on the
second syllable, i.e.,* [əd'vɝtɪs], *as in*
HVIII, II.iv.176 *and* MEAS, I.i.41
advertisement, -s ,ædvɚ'taɪzmənt
[æd'vɝɹɪzmənt, -ɾɪsm-], -s ([-'----] *in*
ADO, V.i.32; 1HIV, III.ii.172, IV.i.36)
advice, -s əd'vaɪs, -ɪz
advis|e, -es, -ing/s, -ed, -edly, -edness
əd'vaɪz, -ɪz, -ɪŋ/z, -d, -ɪdlɪ, -ɪdnɪs
adviser *or* advisor, -s əd'vaɪzɚ, -z
advisor|y, -ies əd'vaɪzəɹ|ɪ, -ɪz
advocate (*s.*), -s 'ædvʊkɪt, -s
advocat|e (*v.*), -es, -ing, -ed, -or/s
'ædvʊkeɪt, -s, -ɪŋ, -ɪd, -ɚ/z
advocation ,ædvʊ'keɪʃn̩
a-dying ə'daɪɪŋ
Æacida (2HVI) i'æsɪdə
Æacides (TS) i'æsɪdɪz
ædile (Æ.) (COR), -s 'idaɪl, -z
Ægeon, Aegeon, *or* Egeon (*COM*) i'dʒɪən
Ægle (MSND) 'iglɪ

Æmilia (*COM*) i'mɪlɪə, -ljə
Note.—See Note for **Emilia**
Æmilius *or* Emillius (*TIT*) i'mɪlɪəs, -ljəs
Æneas *or* Aeneas (AC, CYM, 2HVI, *TC*,
    TEM, TIT, TNK) i'niəs
Æolus (2HVI) 'ioləs ['ɪəl-]
aerial, -s, -ly 'ɛɚ̣.ɪɪəl, -z, -ɨ
aerie *or* aery (*var. of* eyrie), -s 'ɛɚ̣.ɪɪ
    ['ɪɚ̣.ɪ-, 'aɪɚ̣.ɪ-], -z
Æsculapius *or* Aesculapius (MWW,
    PER) ,ɪskjʊ'leɪpɪəs, -pjəs
Æson (MV) 'isɒn [-sən]
Æsop *or* Aesop (3HVI) 'isɒp
Ætna *or* Etna (*the volcano*) (LUC,
    MWW, TIT) 'etnə
afar ə'fɑɚ̣
afeard ə'fɪɚ̣d
a-feasting ə'fistɪŋ
affab|le, -ly, -leness 'æfəb|l̩, -lɨ, -l̩nɪs
affability ,æfə'bɪlɪtɨ
affair, -s ə'fɛɚ̣, -z
affect, -s, -ing/ly, -ed/ly, -edness ə'fekt,
    -s, -ɪŋ/lɨ, -ɪd/lɨ, -ɪd/nɪs
    Note.—In TIM, I.ii.31, *primary syllabic
    stress is given (arguably) on the first
    syllable, i.e.,* ['æfekt]
affectation, -s ,æfek'teɪʃn̩, -z
affection (A.), -s ə'fekʃn̩, -z
affectionate, -ly, -ness ə'fekʃn̩ɪt, -lɨ, -nɪs
affective ə'fektɪv [æ'f-]
affeer, -s, -ing, -ed, -er/s a'fɪɚ̣, -z, -ɪɪŋ,
    -d, -ɪɚ̣/z
affianc|e, -es, -ing, -ed ə'faɪəns, -ɪz,
    -ɪŋ, -t
affidavit, -s ,æfɪ'deɪvɪt, -s
affiliat|e, -es, -ing, -ed ə'fɪlɪeɪt, -s, -ɪŋ, -ɪd
affiliation, -s ə,fɪlɪ'eɪʃn̩, -z
affined ə'faɪnd
affinit|y, -ies ə'fɪnɪt|ɨ, -ɨz
affirm, -s, -ing, -ed ə'fɝm, -z, -ɪŋ, -d
affirmation, -s ,æfɚ'meɪʃn̩, -z
affirmative, -s; -ly ə'fɝmətɪv, -z; -lɨ
afflict, -s, -ing, -ed ə'lɪkt, -s, -ɪŋ, -ɪd
affliction (A.), -s ə'flɪkʃn̩, -z

afford, -s, -ing, -ed ə'fɔɚ̣d, -z, -ɪŋ, -ɪd
affright, -s, -ing, -ed ə'fɪaɪt, -s, -ɪŋ, -ɪd
affront, -s, -ing, -ed ə'fɪʌnt, -s, -ɪŋ, -ɪd
aff|ly, -ies, -ying, -ied ə'f|aɪ, -aɪz, -aɪɪŋ,
    -aɪd
afield ə'fild
afire ə'faɪɚ̣
aflame ə'fleɪm
afloat ə'floʊt
a(-)foot ə'fʊt
afore ə'fɔɚ̣
aforesaid ə'fɔɚ̣sed
afraid ə'fɪeɪd
afresh ə'fɪeʃ
Afric (COR, CYM, TC, TEM) 'æfɪɪk
Africa (2HIV, TEM), -n 'æfɪɪkə, -n
aft 'aft
after 'aftɚ
after-dinner 'aftɚ,dɪnɚ
after-eye 'aftɚ,ɪaɪ
afterglow, -s 'aftɚgloʊ, -z
after-hours 'aftɚ,ɪɑʊɚ̣z
after-inquiry 'aftɚ,ɪɪn'kwaɪɚ̣.ɪɪ [-ɪŋ'k-,
    'aftɚ,ɪɪnkwə.ɪɪ, -,ɪɪŋk-]
after-love 'aftɚ,lʌv
aftermath, -s 'aftɚmæθ [-maθ], -s
after-meeting 'aftɚ,mitɪŋ
afternoon, -s ,aftɚ'nun (*when att.,* ['---]),
    -z
after-nourishment 'aftɚ,nʌɪɪʃmənt
after-supper ,aftɚ'sʌpɚ
afterthought, -s 'aftɚθɔt, -s
after-times 'aftɚ,taɪmz
afterward, -s 'aftɚwɚd, -z
again, -st ə'gen, -st
Agamemnon (2HIV, HV, 3HVI, *TC*), -s
    ,ægə'memnɒn, -z
agate, -s 'ægɪt, -s
agate-ring 'ægɪt,ɪɪŋ
agaze, -d ə'geɪz, -d
ag|e (*s., v.*), -es, -ing, -ed 'eɪdʒ, -ɪz, -ɪŋ, -d
aged (*adj.*), -ly, -ness 'eɪdʒɪd, -lɨ, -nɪs
ageless, -ly, -ness 'eɪdʒlɪs, -lɨ, -nɪs
Agenor (TS) ə'dʒinɔɚ̣

---

i w**e** ɨ c**i**ty ɪ h**i**t e l**e**t ɛ d**e**but æ c**a**n a p**a**ss ɝ b**ir**d ʌ h**u**t ə **a**g**ai**n ɚ supp**er** u y**ou**
ʊ sh**ou**ld o **o**bey ɔ **a**wl ɒ c**o**p ɑ f**a**ther eɪ p**ai**d aɪ h**igh** oʊ g**o** ɔɪ v**oi**ce aʊ f**ou**nd ɪɚ̣ **ear**
ɛɚ̣ **air** ʊɚ̣ **poor** ɔɚ̣ **fork** ɑɚ̣ **park** aɪɚ̣ **fire** aʊɚ̣ **hour** b **b**oy p **p**it d **d**og t **t**op g g**o**t
k **k**id h **h**ow fi be**h**ave dʒ **j**ot tʃ **ch**ew z **z**any s **s**oft v **v**at f **f**at ʒ trea**s**ure ʃ **sh**ip ð **th**e
θ **th**in m **m**an n **n**o ŋ ha**ng** l **l**ip j **y**es w **w**on ʍ **wh**ew ɹ **r**igger, ai**r**y ɡ̊ ma**tt**er

agent, -s 'eɪdʒənt, -s
aggravat|e, -es, -ing/ly, -ed 'ægɹəveɪt, -s, -ɪŋ/lɪ, -ɪd
aggravation, -s ˌægɹə'veɪʃn, -z
aggressive, -ly, -ness ə'gɹesɪv, -lɪ, -nɪs
aghast ə'gast
Agincourt (HV) 'ædʒɪnkɔɚ̯t
agitat|e, -es, -ing, -ed, -or/s 'ædʒɪteɪt, -s, -ɪŋ, -ɪd, -ɚ/z
agitation, -s ˌædʒɪ'teɪʃn, -z
aglet, -s 'æglɪt, -s
aglet-baby 'æglɪtˌbeɪbɪ
agnize (recognize; confess; own with joy) æg'naɪz
ago ə'goʊ
agog ə'gɒg
a-going ə'goʊɪŋ
agone ə'gɒn
agoniz|e, -es, -ing/ly, -ed 'ægənaɪz, -ɪz, -ɪŋ/lɪ, -d
agon|y, -ies 'ægən|ɪ, -ɪz
agree, -s, -ing, -d, -ment/s ə'gɹi, -z, -ɪŋ, -d, -mənt/s
agreeab|le, -ly, -leness ə'gɹiəb|l̩, -lɪ, -l̩nɪs
agriculture 'ægɹɪkʌltʃɚ
Agrippa (AC) ə'gɹɪpə
Agrippa, Menenius (COR) mə'ninɪəs, -njəs, ə'gɹɪpə
aground ə'gɹaʊnd
a-growing ə'gɹoʊɪŋ
ague, -s, -d 'eɪgju, -z, -d
Aguecheek, Sir Andrew (TN) ˌsɝ̯'(ɹ)ændɹu 'eɪgjuˌtʃik
Agueface, Sir Andrew (TN) ˌsɝ̯'(ɹ)ændɹu 'eɪgjuˌfeɪs
ague-proof 'eɪgjuˌpɹuf
ah 'ɑ
aha ɑ'hɑ
a-hanging ə'hæŋɪŋ
ahead ə'hed
a-height ə'haɪt
a-high ə'haɪ
a-hooting ə'hutɪŋ
a-horseback ə'hɔɚ̯sbæk
ahoy ə'hɔɪ
a-hungry ə'hʌŋgɹɪ
a-hunting ə'hʌntɪŋ
aid, -s, -ing, -ed, -er/s 'eɪd, -z, -ɪŋ, -ɪd, -ɚ/z

aidance 'eɪdn̩s
aidant 'eɪdn̩t
aidless 'eɪdlɪs
ail, -s, -ing, -ed, -ment/s 'eɪl, -z, -ɪŋ, -d, -mənt/s
aim, -s, -ing, -ed 'eɪm, -z, -ɪŋ, -d
aimless, -ly, -ness 'eɪmlɪs, -lɪ, -nɪs
Aio (te) Aeacida, Romanos vincere posse (L.) (2HVI, I.iv.60,61) 'aɪo (tɛ) ˌɪə'sidə ɹo'mɑnos 'vinsɛɹɛ 'posɛ
air, -s, -ing, -ed 'ɛɚ̯, -z, -ɹɪŋ, -d
Aire, Joan of (1HVI) 'dʒoʊn əv 'ɛɚ̯
airless 'ɛɚ̯lɪs
air|y, -ier, -iest, -ily, -iness 'ɛɚ̯|ɹɪ, -ɹɪɚ, -ɹɪɪst, -ɹɪlɪ, -ɹɪnɪs
Ajax (AC, CYM, 2HVI, LEAR, LLL, LUC, TC, TIT, TS) 'eɪdʒæks
Note.—In LLL, V.ii.572, a pun is made with the name 'Ajax.' It is meant to be homophonic with 'a jakes,' meaning 'privy.' There is ample evidence to conclude that in S.'s day the pronunciation was indeed more akin to the L. pronunciation of a long 'a' in the second syllable (cf. Kökeritz's Shakespeare's Pronunciation, p. 177). The name would probably have sounded more like [ɛdʒɛks]. In order for this pun to truly prosper, a fairly consistent pronunciation of the name throughout LLL is called for, but then it is likely to compromise understandability (the modern ear being so accustomed to the universally accepted ['eɪdʒæks])
a-killing ə'kɪlɪŋ
akin ə'kɪn
alabaster 'æləbastɚ
alablaster (archaic common form of alabaster) 'æləblastɚ
alack ə'læk
alacrity ə'lækɹɪtɪ
a-land ə'lænd
Alarbus (TIT) ə'lɑɚ̯bəs
alarum, -s, -ed ə'lɑɹəm [ə'læɹəm], -z, -d
alas ə'læs
Alban 'ɔlbən
Albany, Duke of (LEAR) ˌdjuk əv 'ɔlbənɪ
Note.—'Albany' is most likely disyllabic, i.e., ['ɔlbnɪ], in LEAR, I.i.66

albeit ɔl'biːt
Albion (HV, 3HVI, LEAR) 'ælbɪən, -bjən
alchemist, -s 'ælkɪmɪst, -s
alchemy 'ælkɪmɨ
Alcibiades (*TIM*) ˌælsɪ'baɪədɪz, -baĭdɪz
Alcides (AC, 1HVI, KJ, MV, TIT, TNK, TS) æl'saĭdɪz
alderliefest 'ɔldɚ'lifɪst
alder|man, -men 'ɔldɚ|mən, -mən
ale(-)hou|se, -ses 'eĭlfiaŭ|s, -zɪz
Alecto (2HIV, KJ) ə'lektoŭ
Alençon (HV, *1HVI*, 2HVI, HVIII, LLL) ə'lensən
Aleppo (MAC, OTH) ə'lepoŭ
aleven *or* **a leven** (*archaic form of* **eleven**) ə'levən
ale-wi|fe, -ves 'eĭlˌwaĭ|f, -vz
Alexander (AC, COR, HAM, HV, LLL, *TC*, WT), **-s** ˌælɪg'zandɚ, -z
Alexandria (AC), **-n/s** ˌælɪg'zandˌɪɪə, -n/z
Alexas (*AC*) ə'leksəs
alias, -es 'eĭlɪəs, -ɪz
Alice (*HV*, TS) 'ælɪs
   Note.—This name, in the First Folio version of TS, IND.ii.111, is spelled 'Alce,' and might be interpreted as being merely the syncopated form of 'Alice,' in which case the name could very well be pronounced as ['æls]
Aliena (*AYLI*) ˌeĭlɪ'rinə, ˌeĭlɪ'eĭnə (*alias* Celia)
alight, -s, -ing, -ed ə'laĭt, -s, -ɪŋ, -ɪd
Alisander (LLL) ˌælɪ'zandɚ [-'san-]
all-admiring 'ɔləd'maĭɚ̌ˌɹɪŋ
Alla nostra casa ben venuto, molto honorato signor mio Petricio (*It.*) (TS, I.ii.25) allɑ 'nostrɑ 'kɑzɑ bɛn vɛ'nuːto 'molto ono'rɑto 'sinjɔr mio pɛ'truːtʃo
alla stoccata (*It.*) (RJ, III.i.73) allɑ sto'kɑːtɑ
allay, -s, -ing, -ed, -ment/s ə'leĭ, -z, -ɪŋ, -d, -mənt/s
all-binding 'ɔl'baĭndɪŋ
all-changing 'ɔl'tʃeĭndʒɪŋ

all-cheering 'ɔl'tʃɪɚ̌ˌɹɪŋ (*when att.,* [-'---])
all-dreaded 'ɔl'dɹedɪd
all-eating 'ɔlˌiɾɪŋ
allegation, -s ˌælɪ'geĭʃn [-lə-], -z
alleg|e (*v.*), **-es, -ing, -ed** ə'ledʒ, -ɪz, -ɪŋ, -d
alleged (*adj.*) ə'ledʒd [ə'ledʒɪd]
allegedly ə'ledʒɪdlɨ
allegian|ce, -t ə'lidʒən|s, -t
all-ending ˌɔl'endɪŋ [-'---]
all-feared ˌɔl'fɪɚ̌d (*when att.,* ['-,-])
all-hail 'ɔl'heĭl
All-hallond Eve (MEAS) ɔlˌhælənd'iv
Allhallowmas (MWW) ˌɔl'hæloŭməs
All-hallown (1HIV) ˌɔl'hæloŭn
all-hating ˌɔl'heĭtɪŋ
all-honored 'ɔl'ɒnɚd
alliance, -s ə'laĭəns, -ɪz
alligant 'ælɪgænt
   Note.—This word, appearing in MWW, *II.ii.65, is perhaps (in Mistress Quickly's mind) meant to be 'elegant' or 'eloquent,'—so say some editors—but she says 'alligant' instead, coming from the word 'alicant,' which is a kind of wine from Alicante, Spain. Other editors suggest that 'alligant' is a conflation of 'elegant' and 'eloquent,' or that it is merely a malapropism, but the word in this context is far from being a ludicrous misusage. She is saying that courtiers' terms are analogous to wine—she immediately goes on to extol the virtues of wine—much in the way that Berowne (cf.* LLL, V.ii.406, 407) *analogizes phrases, terms, and hyperboles to fabric, i.e., taffeta, silk, and the richest velvet. There are at least four other instances of the word's usage in plays by S.'s contemporaries (cf. Walter Skeat's A Glossary of Tudor and Stuart Words, Especially from the Dramatists, Oxford, 1914, p. 8), so attempts to emend 'alligant' or its meaning to anything else*

i wɛ ɨ city ɪ hit e let ɛ debut æ can a pass ɝ bird ʌ hut ə again ɚ supper u you
ʊ should o obey ɔ awl ɒ cop ɑ father eĭ paid aĭ high oŭ go ɔĭ voice aŭ found ɪɚ̌ ear
ɛɚ̌ air ʊɚ̌ poor ɔɚ̌ fork ɑɚ̌ park aĭɚ̌ fire aŭɚ̌ hour b boy p pit d dog t top g got
k kid h how fi behave dʒ jot tʃ chew z zany s soft v vat f fat ʒ treasure ʃ ship ð the
θ thin m man n no ŋ hang l lip j yes w won ʍ whew ɹ rigger, airy ɾ matter

seems ultimately unprofitable. (Cf.
pulsidge*)*
all-licensed 'ɔl'laɪsə nst
all-noble ˌɔl'noŭbļ
all-obeying ˌɔlo'beɪ̆ɪŋ
allons (Fr.) (LLL, IV.iii.379, V.i.142) alɔ̃
allo|t, -ts, -tting, -tted, -tment/s ə'lɒ|t, -ts, -tɪŋ [-ɾɪŋ], -tɪd [-ɾɪd], -tmənt/s
allottery ə'lɒɾəɹɪ
allow, -s, -ing, -ed ə'laŭ, -z, -ɪŋ, -d
allowanc|e, -es, -ing, -ed ə'laŭəns, -ɪz, -ɪŋ, -t
all-praised ˌɔl'pɹeɪ̆zɪd
all-royal ˌɔl'ɹɔɪ̆əl
all's *(contr. of* **all is)** 'ɔlz
all-seeing 'ɔlˌsiɪŋ [ˌ-'--]
All-seer (RIII) 'ɔlˌsiə˞ [ˌ-'--]
all-shaking 'ɔlˌʃeɪ̆kɪŋ ['-'-]
All-Soul's Day (RIII) 'ɔlˌsoŭlz ˌdeɪ̆
all-thing 'ɔlˌθɪŋ
all-too-precious 'ɔlˌtu'pɹeʃəs *(when att.,* ['-ˌ-'--])
allur|e, -es, -ing/ly, -ed, -ement/s ə'ljʊ˞ [ə'lʊ˞], -z, -ɹɪŋ/lɪ, -d, -mənt/s
all-worthy ˌɔl'wɝ˞ðɪ
all|y *(s.)*, **-ies** æl|aɪ̆ [ə'laɪ̆], -aɪ̆z ([-'-] *in* RJ, III.i.111; AYLI, V.iv.188; 1HIV, I.i.16)
all|y *(v.)*, **-ies, -ying, -ied** ə'l|aɪ̆, -aɪ̆z, -aɪ̆ɪŋ, -aɪ̆d *(may be* ['ælaɪ̆d] *when att.)*
allycholy *or* **allicholy** 'ælɪkəlɪ [-kɒlɪ]
Note.—In TGV, IV.ii.26, *this is the Host's error for 'melancholy.' It is also considered a corruption of 'malecholie,' a var. of 'melancholy,' in* LLL, IV.iii.13 *and in* MWW, I.iv.142
Almain (OTH) 'ælmeɪ̆n
almanac, -s 'ɒlmənæk ['ɔl-]
almighty (A.) ɔl'maɪ̆tɪ
almond, -s 'ɑmənd, -z
almost 'ɔlmoŭst ([-'-] *in* OTH, V.ii.16; WT, V.i.104)
alms 'ɑmz
alms-drink 'ɑmzdɹɪŋk
almshouse, -s 'ɑmzɦaŭ|s, -zɪz [-sɪz]
alms|man, -men 'ɑmz|mən, -mən
aloe, -s 'æloŭ, -z
aloft ə'lɒft
alone, -ness ə'loŭn, -nɪs

along, ə'lɒŋ
alongside əˌlɒŋ'saɪ̆d
Alonso *(TEM)* ə'lɒnzoŭ [-nsoŭ]
aloof, -ness ə'luf, -nɪs
aloud ə'laŭd
alow ə'loŭ
Note.—This word, appearing in a jingle of Edgar's (LEAR, III.iv.76*), can be taken to mean any one of several things, each contributing to the bawdy innuendo of the passage: it can stand for the hunter's cry inciting the hounds to chase; a reference to that which is below; the lower part of a vessel (the cabin or hold as opposed to the deck); or something ablaze, or in flame (a crude allusion to venereal disease so often plied in S.). None of these meanings are mutually exclusive, of course, and the pronunciation remains the same, regardless*
Alow, the George (TNK) ðə 'dʒɔ˞dʒ ə'loŭ *(a ship; see Note for* **alow)**
alp (A.), **-s** 'ælp, -s
alphabet, -s 'ælfəbet [-bɪt], -s
Alphonso, Don (TGV) 'dɒn æl'fɒnzoŭ [-'fɔn-, -nsoŭ]
Alps (AC, HV, KJ, RII) 'ælps
already ɔl'ɹedɪ ([ˈ-ˌ--] *when immediately preceding a stress)*
also 'ɔlsoŭ
altar, -s 'ɔltə˞, -z
alt|er, -ers, -ering, -ered; -erable 'ɔlt|ə˞, -ə˞z, -ə˞ ɹɪŋ, -ə˞d; -ə˞ ɹəbļ
alteration, -s ˌɔltə˞'ɹeɪ̆ʃn, -z
altercation, -s ˌɔltə˞'keɪ̆ʃn, -z
alternate *(s., adj., adv.)*, **-ly, -ness** 'ɔltə˞nɪt, -lɪ, -nɪs
alternat|e *(v.)*, **-es, -ing, -ed** 'ɔltə˞neɪ̆t, -s, -ɪŋ, -ɪd
Althaea *or* **Althæa** (2HIV, 2HVI) æl'θiə
although ɔl'ðoŭ
altogether ˌɔltʊ'geðə˞ *(when att.,* ['--ˌ--])
Alton (1HVI) 'ɔltən
alway 'ɔlweɪ̆
always 'ɔlweɪ̆z
am 'æm
Ama(i)mon (1HIV, MWW) ə'meɪ̆mɒn
amain ə'meɪ̆n

a-making ə'meĭkɪŋ

a-Maying ɔ'meĭɪŋ

amaz|e, -es, -ing/ly, -ed, -edly, -edness, -ement/s ə'meĭz, -ɪz, -ɪŋ/lɪ, -d, -ɪdlɪ, -ɪdnɪs, -mənt/s

Amazon (1HVI, 3HVI, KJ, MSND, TIM), **-s** 'æməzɒn, -z

Amazonian (COR, 3HVI, TNK) ˌæmə'zoŭnɪən, -njən

ambassador, -s æm'bæsɪdɚ [-səd-, -dɔɚ], -z

amber 'æmbɚ

ambiguit|y, -ies ˌæmbɪ'gjuɪt|ɪ, -ɪz

ambition (**A.**), **-s** æm'bɪʃn, -z

ambitious, -ly, -ness æm'bɪʃəs, -lɪ, -nɪs

amb|le, -les, -ling, -led, -ler/s 'æmb|l̩, -l̩z, -lɪŋ [-l̩ɪŋ], -l̩d, -lɚ/z [-l̩ɚ/z]

ambush, -es, -ing, -ed 'æmbʊʃ, -ɪz, -ɪŋ, -t

amen (**A.**), **-s** ˌɑ'men [ˌeĭ'men], -z

amend, -s, -ing, -ed, -ment/s ə'mend, -z, -ɪŋ, -ɪd, -mənt/s

a-mending ə'mendɪŋ

amerc|e, -es, -ing, -ed, -ement/s ə'mɝs, -ɪz, -ɪŋ, -t, -mənt/s

America (COM), **-s, -n/s** ə'meɹɪkə, -z, -n/z

ames-ace 'eĭmzeĭs

amiab|le, -ly, -leness 'eĭmɹəb|l̩, -lɪ, -l̩nɪs

Amiens (*AYLI*) 'eĭmjənz ['ɑmjənz], [*Fr.* amjɛ̃]

amiss ə'mɪs

amit|y, -ies 'æmɪt|ɪ, -ɪz

amorous, -ly, -ness 'æməɹəs, -lɪ, -nɪs

amort ə'mɔɚt

Amphimacus (TC) æm'fɪməkəs

amp|le, -ler, -lest, -ly, -leness 'æmp|l̩, -lɚ, -l̩st [-lɪst], -lɪ, -l̩nɪs

amplif|y, -ies, -ying, -ied, -ier/s 'æmplɪf|aĭ, -aĭz, -aĭɪŋ, -aĭd, -aĭɚ/z

Ampthill (HVIII) 'æmtɪl [-təl]

Amurath (2HVI) 'ɑmʊˌɹɑt, 'æmʊˌɹɑθ

Note.—*This name for a particular Turkish sultan, appearing twice in 2HVI, V.ii.48, is anglicized. Sources admit that*

there might be several different ways of pronouncing it. The two proffered above are only suggestions gleaned from the many ways to read the name. Even primary syllabic stress itself might very well be on the third rather than first syllable. My advice is to let euphony be your guide

Amyntas *or* **Amintas** (AC) ə'mɪntəs

an (*indefinite article*) 'æn (*strong form*), 'ən (*weak form*)

an *or* **an'** (*conjunction; archaic for* **and** *if; if*) 'æn

An (MWW) 'æn

Note.—*Technically speaking, this word (in MWW, I.i.117) is meant to be an alternative spelling of 'Anne,' but is taken to mean the indefinite article*

anatomiz|e, -es, -ing, -ed ə'næɾəmaĭz, -ɪz, -ɪŋ, -d

anatom|y, -ies ə'næɾəm|ɪ, -ɪz

ancestor, -s 'ænsestɚ, -z

ancestral æn'sestɹəl

ancestr|y, -ies 'ænsestɹ|ɪ, -ɪz

Anchises (2HVI, JUL, TC) æŋ'kaĭsɪz [æn'k-]

anchor, -s, -ing, -ed; -age 'æŋkɚ, -z, -ɹɪŋ, -d; -ɹɪdʒ

Ancient (2HIV) 'eĭnʃənt

Note.—*This word is sometimes capitalized in* 2HIV, II.iv.67, *et al. to signify Pistol's rank; 'Ancient' in this instance is thought to be a corruption of 'Ensign'*

ancient, -s, -est, -ly, -ness, -ry 'eĭnʃənt, -s, -ɪst, -lɪ, -nɪs, -ɹɪ

andiron, -s 'ændaĭɚn, -z

Andren (HVIII) 'ændɹən

Andrew (MV, TN) 'ændɹu

Andromache (*TC*) æn'dɹɒməkɪ

Note.—*In* TC, V.iii.84, *this name is meant to be trisyllabic, suggesting a pronunciation of* [æn'dɹɒm'kɪ]

Andronici (TIT) æn'dɹɒnɪsaĭ

---

i w**e** ɪ cit**y** ɪ h**i**t e l**e**t ɛ d**e**but æ c**a**n a p**a**ss ɝ b**i**rd ʌ h**u**t ə **a**gain ɚ supp**er** u y**ou** ʊ sh**ou**ld o **o**bey ɔ **a**wl ɒ c**o**p ɑ f**a**ther eĭ p**ai**d aĭ h**igh** oŭ g**o** ɔĭ v**oi**ce aŭ f**ou**nd ɪɚ **ear** ɛɚ **air** ʊɚ **poor** ɔɚ **fork** ɑɚ **park** aĭɚ **fire** aŭɚ **hour** b **b**oy p **p**it d **d**og t **t**op g **g**ot k **k**id h **h**ow fi be**h**ave dʒ **j**ot tʃ **ch**ew z **z**any s **s**oft v **v**at f **f**at ʒ trea**s**ure ʃ **sh**ip ð **th**e θ **th**in m **m**an n **n**o ŋ ha**ng** l **l**ip j **y**es w **w**on ʍ **wh**ew ɹ **r**igger, ai**r**y ɾ ma**tt**er

Andronicus, Marcus (*TIT*) 'mɑɑ̆ːkəs
æn'dɹɒnɪkəs, -'dɹɒnˈkəs (*e.g.*, TIT, I.i.50)
Andronicus, Titus (*TIT*) 'taɪ̯ɾəs ['taɪ̆təs]
æn'dɹɒnɪkəs
and's (*contr. of* **and his**) 'ændz
anel|e, -es, -ing, -ed ə'nil, -z, -ɪŋ, -d
anew ə'nju
angel (**A.**), **-s** 'eɪ̆ndʒəl, -z
angel-husband ˌeɪ̆ndʒəl'hʌzbənd
angelic, -al, -ally æn'dʒelɪk, -ḷ, -ə lɪ
Angelica (RJ) æn'dʒelɪkə
angel-like 'eɪ̆ndʒəlˌlaɪ̆k
Angelo (*COM, MEAS*) 'ændʒɪloŏ, -dʒḷoŏ
anger, -s, -ing, -ed 'æŋgɚ, -z, -ɹɪŋ, -d
angerly 'æŋgɚlɪ
Angiers (KJ) 'ændʒɪɚz
Note.—*In KJ, II.i.1, this name is
apparently given primary stress on the
second syllable, i.e.,* [æn'dʒɪɚz]*;
otherwise* ['--]
ang|le, -les, -ling, -led, -ler/s 'æŋg|ḷ, -ḷz,
-lɪŋ [-ḷɪŋ], -ḷd, -lɚ/z [-ḷɚ/z]
Anglish (HV) 'æŋglɪʃ (*'English' in Alice's
Fr. accent, HV, V.ii.260*)
angr|y, -ier, -iest, -ily, -iness 'æŋgɹ|ɪ, -ɪɚ,
-ɪɪst, -ɪlɪ, -ɪnɪs
Angus (1HIV, *MAC*) 'æŋgəs
an-hungry (*var. of* **a-hungry**) æn'hʌŋgɹɪ
[ən'h-]
a-night, -s ə'naɪ̆t, -s
Anjou (1HVI, 2HVI, KJ) 'ændʒu [-'-]
[*Fr.* ɑ̃ŋʒu]
ankle, -s 'æŋkḷ, -z
Anna (TS) 'ænə
Anne, Lady (*RIII*) 'leɪ̆dɪ 'æn
annex (*s.*), **-es** 'æneks, -ɪz
annex (*v.*), **-es, -ing, -ed, -ment/s** æ'neks,
-ɪz, -ɪŋ, -t, -mənt/s
annexion, -s æ'nekʃn̩, -z
Note.—*This word's appearance in LC,
208 presents scansionists with rare
choices. The common pronunciation (as
asserted by the OED, et al.) is as above;
however, in order to retain this common
pronunciation, one must either consider
this line (208) as headless or endow the
preceding line with a feminine ending,
thereby supplying line 208 with the extra
beat it wants at its beginning. This then*

*necessitates making a feminine ending
of the three lines, 205, 207, and 208, to
fit the metrical and rhyming scheme of
the stanza*
anniversar|y, -ies ˌænɪ'vɝˈsəɹ|ɪ, -ɪz
annoy, -s, -ing/ly, -ed; -ance/s ə'nɔɪ̆, -z,
-ɪŋ/lɪ, -d; -əns/ɪz
annul, -s, -ling, -led, -ment/s ə'nʌl, -z,
-ɪŋ, -d, -mənt/s
anoint, -s, -ing, -ed, -ment/s ə'nɔɪ̆nt, -s,
-ɪŋ, -ɪd, -mənt/s
anon ə'nɒn
another ə'nʌðɚ
Anselm(e), County (RJ) 'kaŏntɪ 'anselm
Note.—*Though the pronunciation given
is traditional, it poses somewhat of a
problem in its only appearance in S., i.e.,
RJ, I.ii.65. If one subscribes to the
notion that the section in which it
appears is verse (and editors usually
do), then it creates the unusual (though
not unique) occurrence of a fully
trochaic line. If one wishes to avoid this,
the original spelling in the First Folio,
'Anselme,' might be taken as a hint to
pronounce the name with three syllables,
i.e.,* [an'selmɛ]*, thus providing the
semblance of a regular line of verse, as
well as keeping with the particularly
Italian flavor of the passage*
Answer (KJ) 'ansɚ
answer, -s, -ing, -ed, -er/s; -able, -ably
'ansɚ, -z, -ɹɪŋ, -d, -ɹɚ/z; -ɹəbḷ, -ɹəblɪ
ant, -s 'ænt, -s
an't (*archaic and dialectal contr. of* **and
it**; *contr. of* **an it**, *meaning 'if it'; see* **an**
(*conjunction*)) 'ænt
an't (*colloquial weakened form of* **on't**,
q.v.) 'ænt ['ənt]
Antenor (*TC*) æn'tinɚ [-nɔɚ]
Antenorides (TC) ˌæntɪ'nɔɚˌɹɪdɪz
anthem, -s 'æn̯θəm, -z
Anthony (*AC*, HV, RJ) 'æn̯θənɪ, 'æntənɪ
Note.—*The traditional Brit. pronunciation, i.e.,* ['æntənɪ]*, is also the traditional pronunciation of the name
anywhere in S., but particularly when
referring to the Roman, Marcus
Antonius, also set down as* '(Mark)

Anthony' in the Folio version of AC.
*Also, this name is often meant to be
disyllabic due to the metrical require-
ments of verse. In such cases, either*
['æntʰnɨ] *or* ['æntnɨ] *will serve*
Anthropophagi (OTH) ˌænθɹoˈpɒfədʒaɪ̈
Anthropophaginian (MWW)
ˌænθɹoŭˌpɒfəˈdʒɪnɪən, -njən
Antiates (COR) 'ænʃɪeɪ̈ts
Antic (1HIV) 'æntɪk
antic, -s, -ked; -ly 'æntɪk, -s, -t; -lɨ
antidote, -s 'æntɪdoŭt, -s
Antigonus (*WT*) æn'tɪgənəs
Antioch (*PER*) 'æntɪɒk, -tjɒk
Antiochus (*PER*) æn'taɪ̈əkəs, -'taɪ̈(ə)kəs
Antiopa (MSND) æn'taɪ̈əpə
antipath|y, -ies æn'tɪpəθ|ɨ, -ɨz
Antipholus (*COM*) æn'tɪfələs
Antipodes (ADO, 3HVI, MSND, MV,
RII) æn'tɪpədɨz [-pod-]
antiquar|y, -ies 'æntɪkwəɹ|ɨ, -ɨz
antiqu|e, -es, -ing, -ed, -ely, -eness æn'tik,
-s, -ɪŋ, -t, -lɨ, -nɪs
Note.—Stressed on the first syllable
['æntik] *in* AYLI, II.i.31, II.iii.57; COR,
II.iii.118; HAM, V.ii.346; HV, V.
Chorus.26; KJ, IV.ii.21; MSND, V.i.3;
OTH, V.ii.217; Sonn. 17.12, 19.10, 59.7,
68.9, 106.7
antiquit|y, -ies æn'tɪkwɪt|ɨ, -ɨz
Antium (COR) 'ænʃɪəm, -ʃjəm
antler, -s, -ed 'æntlə-, -z, -d
Antoniad (AC) æn'toŭnɪæd
Antonio (*ADO*, ALL'S, *MV, TGV, TEM,
TN*, TS) æn'toŭnɪoŭ, -njoŭ
*Note.—The Folio version also gives
'Anthonio.' In any case, it is pronounced
as indicated above*
Antonius, Marcus (*AC*, HV, MAC, *JUL*)
'mɑɹ̈kəs æn'toŭnɪəs, -njəs
Note.—Sometimes given as **Mark** *(or*
Marc*) Ant(h)ony* ['mɑɹ̈k 'æntənɨ]
Antony (*AC*, ADO, RJ) (*cf.* **Antonius,
Marcus**) 'æntənɨ, -tnɨ

Note.—Regardless of its spelling, i.e.,
Anthony *or* **Antony**, *this name in* S. *is
pronounced as indicated above (see
Note for* **Anthony***)*
antres *or* **antars** (*caves*) 'æntə-z
anus, -es 'eɪ̈nəs, -ɪz
anvil, -s 'ænvɪl [-vl̩], -z
anybody 'enɨˌbɒdɨ [-bədɨ]
anyhow 'enɨhaŭ
anyone 'enɨwʌn
anypody (*from 'anybody'*) 'enɨˌpɒdɨ
[-pədɨ] (*see* **prings**)
anything 'enɨθɪŋ
anyway 'enɨweɪ̈
anywhere 'enɨʍɛɹ̈
ap (*occasional Welsh prefix to surnames
denoting pedigree; 'son of'*) 'æp ['əp]
Note.—The name Rice ap Thomas in
RIII, IV.v.15 *appears with 'ap' in the
First Folio and the Sixth Quarto, and
with 'up' ('vp') in the First through
Fifth Quartos, indicating the pronunciation* ['ʌp], *or perhaps the even weaker*
['əp]
apace ə'peɪ̈s
ap|e, -es, -ing, -ed 'eɪ̈p, -s, -ɪŋ, -t
ape-bearer 'eɪ̈pbɛɹ̈-ɹə-
Apemantus (*TIM*) ˌæpə'mæntəs
Apennines (KJ) 'æpɪnaɪ̈nz
a-piece, -s ə'pis, -ɪz
apish, -ly, -ness 'eɪ̈pɪʃ, -lɨ, -nɪs
Apollo (LEAR, LLL, MSND, PER, TC,
TIT, TS, WT) ə'pɒloŭ
Apollodorus (AC) əˌpɒloˈdɔɹəs
apoplex|ed, -y, -ies 'æpəpleks|t, -ɨ, -ɨz
apostrophus ə'pɒstɹəfəs
apothecar|y, -ies ə'pɒθɪkəɹɨ, -z
appaid ə'peɪ̈d
appal, -s, -ling/ly, -led ə'pɔl, -z, -ɪŋ/lɨ, -d
apparel, -s, -(l)ing, -(l)ed ə'pæɹəl, -z, -ɪŋ,
-d
apparent, -ly, -ness ə'pæɹənt [-pɛɹ̈-ɹ-],
-lɨ, -nɪs
apparition, -s ˌæpə'ɹɪʃn̩, -z

i wɛ ɨ city ɪ hit e let ɛ debut æ can a pass ɝ bird ʌ hut ə again ə- supper u you
ʊ should o obey ɔ awl ɒ cop ɑ father eɪ̈ paid aɪ̈ high oŭ go ɔɪ̈ voice aŭ found ɪɚ̈ ear
ɛɚ̈ air ʊɚ̈ poor ɔɚ̈ fork ɑɚ̈ park aɪ̈ɚ̈ fire aŭɚ̈ hour b boy p pit d dog t top g got
k kid h how fi behave dʒ jot tʃ chew z zany s soft v vat f fat ʒ treasure ʃ ship ð the
θ thin m man n no ŋ hang l lip j yes w won ʍ whew ɹ rigger, airy ɾ matter

appeach, -es, -ing, -ed, -er/s ə'pitʃ, -ɪz,
-ɪŋ, -t, -ə·/z
appeal, -s, -ing, -ed, -er/s ə'pil, -z, -ɪŋ,
-d, -ə·/z
appealing, -ly, -ness ə'pilɪŋ, -lɪ, -nɪs
appear, -s, -ing, -ed, -er/s; -ance/s ə'pɪə·,
-z, -ɹɪŋ, -d, -ɹə·/z; -ɹə ns/ɪz
appeas|e, -es, -ing/ly, -ed, -er/s; -able
ə'piz, -ɪz, -ɪŋ/lɪ, -d, -ə·/z; -əbl̩
appellant, -s ə'pelənt, -s
*Note.—This pronunciation (with the
primary stress on the second syllable) is
difficult in RII, IV.i.104. One may be
tempted to pronounce the word
[*'æpələnts]*, but one must be aware that
the Folio's representation of verse in the
section from which this line assignation
is derived (lines 101 through 106) is at
odds with the conventions of scansion
dynamics. Reconciling a recommended
pronunciation , i.e.,* [ə'pelənts]*, requires
that the caesura occurring in line 104
absorb the value of one metrical beat*
append, -s, -ing, -ed; -age/s ə'pend, -z,
-ɪŋ, -ɪd; -ɪdʒ/ɪz
append|ix, -xes, -ces ə'pend|ɪks, -ɪksɪz,
-ɪsɪz
apperil (*rare alt. form of* **peril**) ə'peɹəl
appertain, -s, -ing/s, -ed ˌæpə·'teɪn, -z,
-ɪŋ/z, -d
appertinent, -s ə'pɝ·tɪnənt [æ'p-, -tn̩ənt],
-s
appetite, -s 'æpɪtaɪt, -s
applaud, -s, -ing/ly, -ed, -er/s ə'plɔd, -z,
-ɪŋ/lɪ, -ɪd, -ə·/z
applause ə'plɔz
apple, -s 'æpl̩, -z
apple-cart 'æpl̩ˌkɑ˞t
apple-john, -s 'æpl̩ˌdʒɒn, -z
apple-tree, -s 'æpl̩ˌtɹi, -z
applicab|le, -ly, -leness 'æplɪkəb|l̩
[ə'plɪkəb|l̩], -lɪ, -l̩nɪs
application, -s ˌæplɪ'keɪʃn̩, -z
appl|y, -ies, -ying, -ied ə'plaɪ, -z, -ɪŋ, -d
appoint, -s, -ing, -ed, -ment/s ə'pɔɪnt, -s,
-ɪŋ, -ɪd, -mənt/s
apportion, -s, -ing, -ed, -ment/s ə'pɔə·ʃn̩,
-z, -ɪŋ, -d, -mənt/s
appreciation, -s əˌpɹiʃɪ'eɪʃn̩, -z

apprehend, -s, -ing, -ed ˌæpɹɪ'hend, -z,
-ɪŋ, -ɪd
apprehension, -s ˌæpɹɪ'henʃn̩, -z
apprentic|e, -es, -ing, -ed; -ehood/s
ə'pɹentɪs, -ɪz, -ɪŋ, -t; -fʊd/z
approach, -es, -ing, -ed, -er/s; -able
ə'pɹoʊtʃ, -ɪz, -ɪŋ, -t, -ə·/z; -əbl̩
approbation, -s ˌæpɹoʊ'beɪʃn̩ [-pɹʊ'b-], -z
approof ə'pɹuf
appropriation, -s əˌpɹoʊpɹɪ'eɪʃn̩, -z
**approv|e, -es, -ing/ly, -ed, -er/s; -able,
-al/s** ə'pɹuv, -z, -ɪŋ/lɪ, -d, -ə·/z;
-əbl̩, -l̩/z
appurtenan|ce, -ces, -t ə'pɝ·tɪnən|s
[-tnə-], -sɪz, -t
a-praying ə'pɹeɪɪŋ
apricock, -s 'eɪpɹɪkɒk ['æp-], -s
apricot, -s 'eɪpɹɪkɒt ['æp-], -s
April (AC, AYLI, KJ, LC, LUC, MV,
MWW, RJ, Sonn. 3, 21, 24, 98, 104,
TC, TEM, TGV, TIT, TIM, WT)**, -s**
'eɪpɹəl, -z
apron, -s, -ing, -ed 'eɪpɹən, -z, -ɪŋ, -d
apron-men 'eɪpɹənˌmen
apt, -er, -est, -ly, -ness 'æpt, -ə·, -ɪst, -lɪ,
-nɪs
Aquilon (TC) 'ækwɪlɒn
Aquitaine (LLL) ˌækwɪ'teɪn ['---]
aqua(-)vitae ˌɑkwə'vaɪti [ˌakw-]
Arabia (AC, COR, MAC, MV, TEM)
ə'ɹeɪbɪə, -bjə
Arabian (AC, CYM, OTH, PT)**, -s**
ə'ɹeɪbɪən, -z, -bjən, -z
Aragon (ADO) 'æɹəgɒn
araise ə'ɹeɪz
arbitrament *or* **arbitrement, -s**
ɑ˞'bɪtɹəmənt, -s
arbitrat|e, -es, -ing, -ed, -or/s 'ɑ˞bɪtɹeɪt,
-s, -ɪŋ, -ɪd, -ə·/z
arbor, -s 'ɑ˞bə·, -z
Arcas (*TNK*) 'ɑ˞kəs
arch, -es, -ing, -ed 'ɑ˞tʃ, -ɪz, -ɪŋ, -t
archangel, -s 'ɑ˞kˌeɪndʒl̩ [ˌ-'--], -z
archbishop, -s ˌɑ˞tʃ'bɪʃəp ['-ˌ--], -s
Archbishop (1HIV, HVIII) 'ɑ˞tʃbɪʃəp
[ˌ-'--]
archbishopric, -s ˌɑ˞'bɪʃəpˌɹɪk, -s
Archdeacon (1HIV) 'ɑ˞tʃdikən [ˌ-'--]
Archelaus (AC) ˌɑ˞kɪ'leɪəs

arch-heretic ˌɑɚ̇-tʃˈheˌɹtɪk
Archibald, Earl of Douglas (*1HIV,*
  2HIV) 'ɑɚ̇-tʃɪbɔld 'ɝ-l əv 'dʌɡləs
Archidamus (*WT*) ˌɑɚ̇-kɪ'deɪ̆məs
architect, -s 'ɑɚ̇-kɪtekt, -s
archive, -s 'ɑɚ̇-kaɪ̆v, -z
arch-mock ˌɑɚ̇-tʃ'mɒk
arch-one 'ɑɚ̇-tʃˌwʌn
arch-villain, -s ˌɑɚ̇-tʃˈvɪlɪn, -z
Arcite (*TNK*) 'ɑɚ̇-sɪt [-saɪ̆t]
Arde (HVIII) 'ɑɚ̇-d
Ardea (LUC) 'ɑɚ̇-dɪə, -djə
Arden, Forest of (AYLI) ˌfɒɹɪst əv 'ɑɚ̇-dn̩
ardency, 'ɑɚ̇-dənsɨ [-dn̩-]
ardent, -ly 'ɑɚ̇-dənt [-dn̩-], -lɨ
are 'ɑɚ̇-
a-repairing əɹɪ'pɛɚ̇-ɹɪŋ
argal (*corruption of* **argo,** *q.v.*) 'ɑɚ̇-ɡɑl
  ['ɑɚ̇-ɡəl, 'ɑɚ̇-ɡɑl]
argentine (*of or resembling silver*)
  'ɑɚ̇-dʒənˌtaɪ̆n [-ˌtin]
Argier (TEM) ɑɚ̇-'dʒɪɚ̇-
argo (*corruption of* **ergo,** *q.v.*) 'ɑɚ̇-ɡoŭ
argos|y, -ies 'ɑɚ̇-ɡəs|ɨ, -ɨz
argot, -s 'ɑɚ̇-ɡoŭ, -z
argument, -s 'ɑɚ̇-ɡjʊmənt, -s
Argus (LLL, MV, TC) 'ɑɚ̇-ɡəs
Ariachne (TC) ˌæɹɪ'æknɨ
Ariadne (MSND, TGV) ˌæɹɪ'ædnɨ
Ariel (*TEM*) 'ɛɚ̇-ɹɪəl ['æɹ-, -ɪel], 'ɛɚ̇-ɹɪ̆əl
  ['æɹ-, -ɪel]
Aries (TIT) 'ɛɚ̇-zɪz ['æɹ-]
aright ə'ɹaɪ̆t
Arion (TN) ə'ɹaɪ̆ən
a-ripening ə'ɹaɪ̆pn̩ɪŋ [-pən-]
aris|e, -es, -ing, arose, arisen ə'ɹaɪ̆z, -ɨz,
  -ɪŋ, ə'ɹoŭz, -ə'ɹɪzn̩
Aristotle (TC, TS) 'æɹɪˌstɒtl̩
arithmetic, -s ə'ɹɪθmətɪk [-mɪt-], -s
arithmetician, -s əˌɹɪθmə'tɪʃn̩ [-mɪ't-], -z
arm, -s, -ing, -ed 'ɑɚ̇-m, -z, -ɪŋ, -d
armada (A.), -s ɑɚ̇-'mɑdə [-'meɪ̆d-], -z
armado (*archaic var. of* **armada**), **-es**
  ɑɚ̇-'mɑdoŭ, -z

Armagnac (1HVI) 'ɑɚ̇-mənˌjæk
armament, -s 'ɑɚ̇-məmənt, -s
Armenia (AC) ɑɚ̇-'minɪə, -njə
armful, -s 'ɑɚ̇-mfʊl, -z
arm-gaunt 'ɑɚ̇-m'ɡɔnt (*when att.,* [ˈ-ˌ-])
Armigero (*L.*) (MWW, I.i.8,9)
  ˌɑɚ̇-mɪ'dʒɛɾo
armipotent ɑɚ̇-'mɪpətənt
armor, -s, -ing, -ed, -er/s 'ɑɚ̇-mə-, -z,
  -ɹɪŋ, -d, -ɹə-/z
armor|y, -ies 'ɑɚ̇-mə-ɹ|ɨ, -ɨz
arm|y, -ies 'ɑɚ̇-m|ɨ, -ɨz
a-rolling ə'ɹoŭlɪŋ
aroma, -s ə'ɹoŭmə, -z
aromatic, -s ˌæɹo'mæɾɪk, -s
a-row ə'ɹoŭ
aroynt *or* **aroint** ə'ɹɔɪ̆nt
Arragon, The Prince of (*MV*) ðə ˌpɹɪns
  əv 'æɹəɡɒn
arraign, -s, -ing, -ed, -er/s, -ment/s
  ə'ɹeɪ̆n, -z, -ɪŋ, -d, -ə-/z, -mənt/s
arrant, -ly 'æɹənt, -lɨ
arras, -es 'æɹəs, -ɪz
array, -s, -ing, -ed ə'ɹeɪ̆, -z, -ɪŋ, -d
arrear, -s, -age/s ə'ɹɪɚ̇-, -z, -ɹɪdʒ/ɪz
arrest, -s, -ing, -ed ə'ɹest, -s, -ɪŋ, -ɪd
arrivance ə'ɹaɪ̆vəns
arriv|e, -es, -ing, -ed; -al/s ə'ɹaɪ̆v, -z, -ɪŋ,
  -d; -l/z
arrogan|ce, -cy, -t/ly 'æɹʊɡən|s [-ɹəɡ-],
  -sɨ, -t/lɨ
arros|e (*obsolete var. of* **arrouse**, *meaning*
  'to sprinkle or moisten; to bedew'), **-es,**
  -ing, -ed ə'ɹɑŭz, -ɪz, -ɪŋ, -d
Note.—This word, appearing in TNK,
V.iv.104, is given as 'arrouse,' 'arowze,'
'arowse,' etc. in different versions of the
play. The OED does not conjecture a
pronunciation for the spelling 'arrose,'
even by implication as a var. of
'arrouse.' One could argue that it should
be pronounced [ə'ɹoŭz]*; however, I offer*
the pronunciation given above due to
certain benefits inherent if it is (coinci-

---

i wˉe ɨ cˉity ɪ hˉit e lˉet ɛ dˉebut æ cˉan a pˉass ɝ bˉird ʌ hˉut ə agˉain ɚ suppˉer u yˉou
ʊ shˉould o obˉey ɔ aˉwl ɒ cˉop ɑ fˉather eɪ̆ paˉid aɪ̆ hˉigh oŭ gˉo ɔɪ̆ vˉoice aŭ foˉund ɪɚ̇- eˉar
ɛɚ̇- aˉir ʊɚ̇- poˉor ɔɚ̇- fˉork ɑɚ̇- pˉark aɪ̆ɚ̇- fˉire aŭɚ̇- hˉour b bˉoy p pˉit d dˉog t tˉop g gˉot
k kˉid h hˉow fi behˉave dʒ jˉot tʃ chˉew z zˉany s sˉoft v vˉat f fˉat ʒ treaˉsure ʃ shˉip ð thˉe
θ thˉin m mˉan n nˉo ŋ haˉng l lˉip j yˉes w wˉon ʍ whˉew ɹ rˉigger, aiɹy ɾ matˉter

dentally) pronounced as a homophone of 'arouse'

arrow, -s 'æɹoʊ̆, -z

art (A.), -s 'ɑꜱ̆t, -s

Artemidorus (*JUL*) ˌɑꜱ̆tɪmɪ'dɔɹəs

Artesius (*TNK*) ɑꜱ̆'tisɪəs, -zjəs

'arth 'ꜱ̆θ

Note.—In TEM, I.ii.390, *The Arden Shakespeare (1994, Frank Kermode, ed.) publishes '. . . the 'arth?' which not only goes against the First Folio's '. . . th' earth?,' but which also goes against the natural rhythm of the line. In the later 1998 version (*The Arden Shakespeare Complete Works*), it is emended to the proper '. . . th' earth?'*

Arthur (2HIV, HV, HVIII, *KJ*) 'ɑꜱ̆θꜱ̆

articulate (*adj.*), **-ly, -ness** ɑꜱ̆'tɪkjʊlɪt, -lɪ, -nɪs

articulat|e (*v.*), **-es, -ing, -ed, -or/s** ɑꜱ̆'tɪkjʊleɪt, -s, -ɪŋ, -ɪd, -ꜱ̆/z

artificer, -s ɑꜱ̆'tɪfɪsꜱ̆ ['----], -z

artifici|al, -ally, -alness ˌɑꜱ̆ɹ'fɪʃl̩ (*when att.,* ['----]), -əlɪ, -əlnɪs

artiller|y, -ies ɑꜱ̆'tɪləɹ|ɪ, -ɪz

artire, -s 'ɑꜱ̆tɪꜱ̆, -z

Artois (1HVI) ɑꜱ̆'twɑ

Note.—Talbot (since he is English) most likely pronounces the name [ɑꜱ̆'tɔɪz] *(cf. 'Shakespeare's Verse' § 1.8 of this dictionary)*

Art to Love, The (TS) ðɪ 'ɑꜱ̆t tʊ 'lʌv

Arundel (RII) 'æɹəndl̩ [-del]

Arviragus (*CYM*) ˌɑꜱ̆vɪ'ɹeɪgəs

Note.—In L., the penultimate is short, i.e., [ɑꜱ̆'vɹɪəgəs], *but in its only two appearances in S., it is stressed as given above*

as 'æz (*strong form*), 'əz (*weak form*)

Ascanius (2HVI) æs'keɪnɪəs, -njəs

ascend, -s, -ing, -ed ə'send, -z, -ɪŋ, -ɪd

ascension, -s ə'senʃn̩, -z

Ascension-day (KJ), **-s** ə'senʃn̩ˌdeɪ, -z

ascent, -s ə'sent, -s

ascrib|e, -es, -ing, -ed; -able ə'skɹaɪb, -z, -ɪŋ, -d; -əbl̩

ash, -es 'æʃ, -ɪz

a-shaking ə'ʃeɪkɪŋ

asham|ed, -edly, -edness ə'ʃeɪm|d, -ɪdlɪ, -ɪdnɪs

ashen 'æʃn̩

Asher-house (HVIII) 'æʃꜱ̆ˌhaʊs

Ashford (2HVI) 'æʃfꜱ̆d

ashore ə'ʃɔꜱ̆

a-shouting ə'ʃaʊ̆tɪŋ

Ash-Wednesday (MV), **-s** ˌæʃ'wenzdɪ [-deɪ], -z

ash|y, -ier, -iest, -iness 'æʃ|ɪ, -ɪꜱ̆, -ɪɪst, -ɪnɪs

Asia (AC, ADO, COM, 2HIV) 'eɪʒə, -ʒɪə, -ʒɪeɪ ['eɪʃə, -ʃɪeɪ]

Note.—This word is pronounced trisyllabically in AC, I.ii.98; COM, I.i.133; and 2HIV, II.iv.162. Kökeritz asserts that in the last example, the final syllable rhymes with 'day,' hence [-ɪeɪ] *(cf. Kökeritz's* Shakespeare's Names: A Pronouncing Dictionary, *p. 18, and his* Shakespeare's Pronunciation, *pp. 174 f.). This applies also to PER, I.chorus.19, 20, where 'Syria' wants to rhyme with 'say'. The rhymes in such cases, however, are typically forsaken*

asinico or assinego (obsolete or dialectal var. of Sp. 'asnico' ['little ass '], a diminutive of 'asno' ['ass ']) (TC, II.i.44) ˌasɪ'niko *or* ˌasɪ'nego

askance ə'skæns [-kans]

askant (*var. of* **askance**) ə'skænt [-kant]

asleep ə'slip

a-sleeping ə'slipɪŋ

Asmath (2HVI) 'æzməθ ['æzmæθ]

Note.—The two pronunciations proffered above are speculative, but traditional. The name is meant to stand for a demonic spirit, possibly the devil himself, conjured by the Duchess, Marjorie Jourdain in 2HVI, I.iv.23. Andrew S. Cairncross (editor of 2HVI, The Arden Shakespeare, *1957) asserts that the name "is simply a minim misprint for* Asnath, *an anagram of* Sathan" *(an archaic var. spelling of 'Satan'). How this would affect the pronunciation isn't entirely clear, due to the fact that the 'th' is the type found in 'Thomas' or 'Theresa.' Literally speaking, the result might be something like* ['eɪsnət], *but I fear this result*

*verges on over-ingeniousness. I
recommend the traditional pronunciations, regardless of one's opinion as to
the name's origin*

aspect, -s 'æspekt, -s
*Note.—Always stressed on the second
syllable in S., i.e.,* [æ'spekt/s], *when in
verse*

aspen, -s 'æspɪn, -z

aspersion, -s ə'spɜ˞ʒn̩ [æ's-, -ɜ˞ʃn̩], -z

aspic, -s 'æspɪk, -s

aspicious (*Dogberry's corruption of*
suspicious *in* ADO, III.v.44) ə'spɪʃəs
*Note.—There is certainly the chance that
Dogberry pronounces this word as*
[æ'spɪʃəs] *or* ['æspɪʃəs], *thus mining (for
the actor) even more of the nonce-word's
comedic value*

aspir|e, -es, -ing, -ed, -er/s ə'spaɪ˞, -z,
-ɹɪŋ, -d, -ɹɚ/z

asquint ə'skwɪnt

ass, -es 'æs, -ɪz

assail, -s, -ing, -ed; -able, -ant/s ə'seɪl,
-z, -ɪŋ, -d; -əbl̩, -ənt/s

assay, -s, -ing, -ed, -er/s æ'seɪ, -z, -ɪŋ,
-d, -ɚ/z

assemblage, -s ə'semblɪdʒ, -ɪz

assemb|le, -les, -ling, -led, -ler/s
ə'sembl̩, -l̩z, -lɪŋ [-lɪŋ], -l̩d, -l̩ɚ/z
[-lɚ/z]

assembl|y, -ies ə'sembl|ɪ, -ɪz
Note.—In ADO, V.iv.34, *'assembly' is
four syllables, i.e.,* [ə'sembəlɪ] *due to the
metrical requirements of the verse line*

ass-head, -s 'æs,hed, -z

assign, -s, -ing, -ed, -er/s, -ment/s; -able
ə'saɪn, -s, -ɪŋ, -d, -ɚ/z, -mənt/s; -əbl̩

assort, -s, -ing, -ed, -ment/s ə'sɔɚt, -s,
-ɪŋ, -ɪd, -mənt/s

assuag|e, -es, -ing, -ed, -ement ə'sweɪdʒ,
-ɪz, -ɪŋ, -d, -mənt

assubjugate ə'sʌbdʒʊgeɪt

assurance, -s ə'ʃʊɚ˞ɹəns, -ɪz

assur|e, -es, -ing, -ed, -er/s; -edly,

-edness ə'ʃʊɚ˞, -z, -ɹɪŋ, -d, -ɹɚ/z; -ɹɪdlɪ,
-ɹɪdnɪs
Note.—In CYM, I.vii.159, *'assured' is
stressed on the first syllable, i.e.,*
['æʃʊɚ˞d]

Assyrian (2HIV, HV) ə'sɪɹɪən, -ɹjən

as't (*contr. of* **as it**) 'æzt

astonish, -es, -ing/ly, -ed/ly, -ment
ə'stɒnɪʃ, -ɪz, -ɪŋ/lɪ, -t/lɪ, -mənt

astound, -s, -ing, -ed ə'staʊnd, -z, -ɪŋ, -ɪd

Astraea (1HVI, TIT) æs'tɹiə

astray ə'stɹeɪ

astride ə'stɹaɪd

astrologer, -s ə'stɹɒlədʒɚ, -z

astrology ə'stɹɒlədʒɪ

astronomer, -s ə'stɹɒnəmɚ, -z

astronomic, -al, -ally ˌæstɹə'nɒmɪk, -l̩,
-əlɪ

astronom|y, -ies ə'stɹɒnəm|ɪ, -ɪz

asunder ə'sʌndɚ

a-swearing ə'swɛɚ˞ɹɪŋ

asylum, -s ə'saɪləm, -z

Atalanta (AYLI) ˌæɾə'læntə

a-talking ə'tɔkɪŋ

at 'æt (*strong form*), 'ət (*weak form*)

ate (*p.t. of* **eat**, *q.v.*) 'eɪt
*Note.—Sometimes in S., it may be best to
pronounce this word in the chiefly Brit.
manner, i.e.,* ['et]

Ate (ADO, JUL, KJ, LLL), **-s** 'eɪtɪ
['ateɪ], -z
*Note.—There is also a popular, pseudo-
Latinized pronunciation, i.e.,* ['ɑteɪ]

Athenian (LEAR, MSND, TC, TIM), **-s**
ə'θiniən, (-njən) -z

Athens (AC, MSND, TC, TIM, TNK)
'æθɪnz

Athol, Earl of (1HIV) 'ɜ˞l əv 'æθəl

a-Thursday ə'θɜ˞zdɪ

athversar|y, -ies (*from 'adversar/y, -ies'*)
'æθfəsəɹ|ɪ, -ɪz
Note.—Fluellen (in HV) *is a Welshman,
and speaks in a Welsh accent, if
somewhat inconsistently. This is an*

---

i w**e** ɪ c**i**ty ɪ h**i**t e l**e**t ɛ d**e**but æ c**a**n a p**a**ss ɜ˞ b**ir**d ʌ h**u**t ə **a**gain ɚ supp**er** u y**ou**
ʊ sh**ou**ld o **o**bey ɔ **aw**l ɒ c**o**p ɑ f**a**ther eɪ p**ai**d aɪ h**igh** oʊ g**o** ɔɪ v**oi**ce aʊ f**ou**nd ɪɚ **ear**
ɛɚ **air** ʊɚ **poor** ɔɚ f**or**k ɑɚ p**ar**k aɪɚ **fire** aʊɚ h**our** b **b**oy p **p**it d **d**og t **t**op g **g**ot
k **k**id h **h**ow fi be**h**ave dʒ **j**ot tʃ **ch**ew z **z**any s **s**oft v **v**at f **f**at ʒ trea**s**ure ʃ **sh**ip ð **th**e
θ **th**in m **m**an n **n**o ŋ ha**ng** l **l**ip j **y**es w **w**on ʍ **wh**ew ɹ **r**igger, ai**r**y ɾ ma**tt**er

example of S.'s direction to the actor (by way of semiphonetic spellings) to adopt such an accent, more or less, for the sake of wringing the most satire out of plays on words stemming from confusions with, and corruptions of, English pronunciation via the Welsh tongue

athwart ə'θwɔʒ·t

a-tiptoe ə'tɪptoŭ

Atlas (3HVI) 'ætləs

atlas, -es 'ætləs, -ɪz

atmosphere, -s 'ætmə,sfɪʒ·, -z

atoll, -s 'æ,tɒl, -z

atom, -s, -ies 'æɾəm, -z, -ɪz

atomi 'æɾəmaĭ

atomic ə'tɒmɪk

atom|y, -ies 'æɾəm|ɪ, -ɪz

Note.—This word can mean an atom or a mote, a very small being such as a mite or pigmy, and even a very emaciated person. It is also the aphæretic form of 'anatomy,' and used thus by Hostess Quickly in the Quarto version of 2HIV, V.iv.29. However, when editors (such as A. R. Humphreys, editor of 2HIV, The Arden Shakespeare, 1966) suggest that 'atomy' in this particular line is a blunder, they are at odds with the OED, which asserts that this aphæretic form was at one time both popular and well established, and they may also be guilty of a pervading bias—negatively—concerning Hostess Quickly's eloquence (see pulsidge)

aton|e, -es, -ing/ly, -ed, -er/s, -ment/s ə'toŭn, -z, -ɪŋ/lɪ, -d, -ʒ·/z, -mənt/s

Atropos (2HIV) 'ætɹəpɒs

attach, -es, -ing, -ed, -ment/s; -able ə'tætʃ, -ɪz, -ɪŋ, -t, -mənt/s; -əbl̩

attack, -s, -ing, -ed, -er/s ə'tæk, -s, -ɪŋ, -t, -ʒ·/z

attainder, -s ə'teĭndʒ·, -z

attaint, -s, -ing, -ed ə'teĭnt, -s, -ɪŋ, -ɪd

attainture, -s ə'teĭntʃʒ·, -z

attasked ə'taskt

attempt, -s, -ing, -ed, -er/s; -able ə'tempt, -s, -ɪŋ, -ɪd, -ʒ·/z; -əbl̩

attend, -s, -ing, -ed, -er/s ə'tend, -z, -ɪŋ, -ɪd, -ʒ·/z

attendan|ce, -ces, -t/s ə'tedən|s, -ɪz, -t/s

attendure (*var. of 'attaindure,' which is obsolete for 'attainder'*) ə'tendʒ·

attent ə'tent

attentive, -ly, -ness ə'tentɪv, -lɪ, -nɪs

attest, -s, -ing, -ed, -er/s, -or/s; -able ə'test, -s, -ɪŋ, -ɪd, -ʒ·/z, -ʒ·/z; -əbl̩

attir|e, -es, -ing, -ed ə'taĭʒ·, -z, -ɹɪŋ, -d

attitude, -s 'æɾɪtjud, -z

attorney, -s, -ed; -ship/s ə'tɜ·nɪ, -z, -d; -ʃɪp/s

attorney-general, attorneys-general ə,tɜ·nɪ'dʒenɹəl, ə,tɜ·nɪz'dʒenɹəl

attribute (*s.*), **-s** 'ætɹɪbjut, -s

attribut|e (*v.*), **-es, -ing, -ed** ə'tɹɪbjut, -s, -ɪŋ [-bjʊtɪŋ], -ɪd [-bjʊtɪd]

attribution, -s ,ætɹɪ'bjuʃn̩, -z

attributive, -ly ə'tɹɪbjʊtɪv, -lɪ

a-turning ə'tɜ·nɪŋ

a(-)twain ə'tweĭn

Aubrey (3HVI) 'ɔbɹɪ (*see* **Vere**)

auburn 'ɔbʒ·n [-bɜ·n]

audacious, -ly, -ness ɔ'deĭʃəs, -lɪ, -nɪs

audacit|y (A.), -ies ɔ'dæsɪt|ɪ, -ɪz

audit, -s, -ing, -ed, -or/s 'ɔdɪt, -s, -ɪŋ, -ɪd, -ʒ·/z

auditor|y, -ies 'ɔdɪtʒ·ɹ|ɪ, -ɪz

Audrey (*AYLI*) 'ɔdɹɪ

Aufidiuses (COR) (*pl. of 'Aufidius'*) ɔ'fɪdjəsɪz

Aufidius, Tullus (*COR*) 'tʌləs ɔ'fɪdɪəs

auger, -s 'ɔgʒ·, -z

aught 'ɔt

augment (*s.*), **-s** 'ɔgmənt [-ment], -s

augment (*v.*), **-s, -ing, -ed; -able** ɔg'ment, -s, -ɪŋ, -ɪd; -əbl̩

augur, -s, -ing, -ed, -er/s 'ɔgʒ·,-z, -ɹɪŋ, -d, -ɹʒ·/z

august (*adj.*), **-est, -ly, -ness** ɔ'gʌst, -ɪst, -lɪ, -nɪs

August (*s.*) (1HVI, TEM), **-s** 'ɔgəst, -s

Augustus (CYM) ɔ'gʌstəs

auger, -s 'ɔgʒ·, -z

auger-hole, -s 'ɔgʒ·,hoŭl, -z

augur|y, -ies 'ɔgjʊɹ|ɪ, -ɪz

Aulis (TNK) 'ɔlɪs

Aumerle, Duke of (*RII*) 'djuk əv ɔ'mɜ·l [o'm-]

aunt, -s 'ant, -s

auricular, -ly ɔ'ɹɪkjʊlɚ, -lɪ
Aurora (MSND, RJ) ɔ'ɹɔɚɹə
auspicious, -ly, -ness ɔ'spɪʃəs, -lɪ, -nɪs
austere, -r, -st, -ly, -ness ɔ'stɪɚ [ɒ's-],
 -ɹɚ, -ɹɪst, -lɪ, -nɪs
austerit|y, -ies ɔ'steɹɪt|ɪ [ɒ'ste-], -ɪz
Austria (ALL'S, KJ), **-n/s** 'ɔstɹɪə [-tɹɪə],
 -n/z
authentic, -ally ɔ'θentɪk, -ə lɪ
author, -s; -ship 'ɔθɚ, -z; -ʃɪp
authorit|y (A.), **-ies** ɔ'θɒɹɪt|ɪ, -ɪz
authorization, -s ˌɔθɚɹɪ'zeɪʃn̩, -z
authoriz|e, -es, -ing, -ed 'ɔθɚɹaɪz, -ɪz,
 -ɪŋ, -d
*Note.—This word is traditionally given
primary syllabic stress on the second
syllable, i.e.,* [ɔ'θɒɹaɪz(-d, -ɪŋ)] *in* MAC,
III.iv.65; LC, 104; Sonn. 35.6 *(cf. Note
for* **canonize***)*
Autolycus (*WT*) ɔ'tɔlɪkəs
Auvergne, Countess of (*1HVI*) 'kaʊntɪs
 əv o'vɛɚn
avaricious, -ly, -ness ˌævə'ɹɪʃəs, -lɪ, -nɪs
avast ə'vast
avaunt ə'vɔnt
ave (A.), **-s** 'aveɪ, -z
Ave-Maries (2HVI, 3HVI) ˌaveɪ'mɛɚɹɪz
avenue, -s 'ævɪnju, -z
aver, -s, -ring, -red, -ment/s ə'vɝ, -z,
 -ɹɪŋ, -d, -mənt/s
averag|e, -es, -ing, -ed 'ævɹɪdʒ [-vəɹ-],
 -ɪz, -ɪŋ, -d
aversion, -s ə'vɝʒn̩ [-'vɝʃn̩], -z
avert, -s, -ing, -ed; -ible ə'vɝt, -s, -ɪŋ,
 -ɪd; -ɪbl̩
avid, -ly 'ævɪd, -lɪ
a(-)vised (*obsolete form of* **advised**)
 ə'vaɪzd
avoid, -s, -ing, -ed; -able ə'vɔɪd, -z, -ɪŋ,
 -ɪd; -əbl̩
avoirdupois (*weight, heaviness*)
 ˌævɚdʊ'pɔɪz
avouch, -es, -ing, -ed, -ment ə'vaʊtʃ, -ɪz,
 -ɪŋ, -t, -mənt

avow, -s, -ing, -ed, -er/s, -edly ə'vaʊ, -z,
 -ɪŋ, -d, -ɚ/z, -ɪdlɪ
avowal, -s ə'vaʊəl, -z
await, -s, -ing, -ed ə'weɪt, -s, -ɪŋ, -ɪd
awak|e, -es, -ing, -ed, awoke ə'weɪk, -s,
 -ɪŋ, -t, ə'woʊk
awaken, -s, -ing/s, -ed ə'weɪkən, -z,
 -ɪŋ/z, -d
award, -s, -ing, -ed ə'wɔɚd, -z, -ɪŋ, -ɪd
aware, -ness ə'wɛɚ, -nɪs
awash ə'wɒʃ
away ə'weɪ
aw|e, -es, -ing, -ed 'ɔ, -z, -ɪŋ, -d
a(-)weary ə'wɪɚɹɪ
aweless, -ness 'ɔlɪs, -nɪs
a-Wednesday ə'wenzdɪ [-deɪ]
a-weeping ə'wipɪŋ
awful, -ness 'ɔfʊl [-fl̩], -nɪs
awfully 'ɔfʊlɪ [-flɪ]
awhile ə'ʍaɪl
awkward, -est, -ly, -ness 'ɔkwəd, -ɪst,
 -lɪ, -nɪs
awoke (*p.t. of* **awake***, q.v.*) ə'woʊk
a-wooing ə'wuɪŋ
a(-)work ə'wɝk
awry ə'ɹaɪ
ax|e, -es, -ing, -ed 'æks, -ɪz, -ɪŋ, -t
axle(-)tree, -s 'æksl̩tɹi, -z
aye (*forever*) 'eɪ
ay(e) (*yes*), **-s** 'aɪ, -z
azure, -d 'æʒɚ, -d

Bb

B (*the letter*), **-'s** 'bi:, -z
baa, -s, -ing, -ed 'ba ['bɑ], -z, -ɪŋ, -d
Baal 'beɪəl
babb|le, -les, -ling, -led, -ler/s 'bæb|l̩, -l̩z,
 -l̩ɪŋ [-lɪŋ], -l̩d, -lɚ/z [-lɚ/z]
babe, -s 'beɪb, -z
babel (B.) 'beɪbl̩ ['bæbl̩]
baboon, -s bæ'bun, -z

i w**e** ɪ cit**y** ɪ h**i**t e l**e**t ɛ d**e**but æ c**a**n a p**a**ss ɝ b**ir**d ʌ h**u**t ə **a**gain ɚ supp**er** u y**ou**
ʊ sh**ou**ld o **o**bey ɔ **aw**l ɒ c**o**p ɑ f**a**ther eɪ p**ai**d aɪ h**igh** oʊ g**o** ɔɪ v**oi**ce aʊ f**ou**nd ɪɚ **ear**
ɛɚ **air** ʊɚ p**oor** ɔɚ f**or**k ɑɚ p**ar**k aɪɚ f**ire** aʊɚ h**our** b **b**oy p **p**it d **d**og t **t**op g **g**ot
k **k**id h **h**ow fi be**h**ave dʒ **j**ot tʃ **ch**ew z **z**any s **s**oft v **v**at f **f**at ʒ trea**s**ure ʃ **sh**ip ð **th**e
θ **th**in m **m**an n **n**o ŋ ha**ng** l **l**ip j **y**es w **w**on ʍ **wh**ew ɹ **r**igger, ai**r**y ɾ ma**tt**er

Note.—In MAC, IV.i.37 *and* PER, IV. vi.177, *this word is stressed on the first syllable, i.e.,* ['bæbun]

bab|y, -ies 'beɪb|ɪ, -ɪz

babyish, -ly, -ness 'beɪbɪɪʃ, -lɪ, -nɪs

Babylon (HV, TN) 'bæbɪlɒn [-lən]

Babylonia|n, -s ˌbæbə'loŭnɪə|n, -z

baby-sitt|er/s, -ing 'beɪbɪsɪtʃ|ə˞/z, -ɪŋ

baccalaureate, -s ˌbækə'lɔɪɪt, -s

baccarat 'bækəɪɑ ['bɑkə-]

baccare, bacare, or backare (L.) (TS, II.i.73) 'bɑkɑɾɛ, bɑ'kɑɾɛ, *or* 'bæk'ɑ˞ɪ

Note.—This is a made-up verb—a crude nonce-word in a mock foreign tongue: perhaps bad Latin, or Italian mixed with English—spoken emphatically so that the person to whom it is addressed (Petruchio) will 'move back!' The final one in the sequence is spelled (and thus pronounced) in such a way as to suggest 'back up!'

Bacchae 'bækɪ

bacchanal (B.) (AC, MSND), -s ˌbækə'nɑl [-'næl, 'bækənəl], -z

bacchanalia, -n/s ˌbækə'neɪlɪə, -n/z

bacchant, -s bə'kænt ['bækənt], -s

bacchic 'bækɪk

Bacchus (AC, LLL) 'bækəs

Bach 'bɑx ['bɑk]

bachelor, -s; -hood, -ship 'bætʃɪlə˞, -z; -hʊd, -ʃɪp

back, -s, -ing, -ed, -er/s 'bæk, -s, -ɪŋ, -t, -ə˞/z

backache, -s 'bækeɪk, -s

backbit|e, -es, -ing, -er/s 'bækˌbaɪt, -s, -ɪŋ, -ə˞/z

backbit, backbitten 'bækbɪt, 'bækˌbɪtn̩

backboard, -s 'bækbɔ˞d, -z

backbone, -s 'bækboŭn, -z

backdat|e, -es, -ing, -ed 'bækˌdeɪt, -s, -ɪŋ, -ɪd

back-door, -s 'bæk'dɔ˞, -z [(v.) ,-'-]

backfir|e, -es, -ing, -ed 'bækˌfaɪ˞, -z, -ɪɪŋ, -d

back-friend, -s 'bækˌfɪɛnd, -z

backgammon 'bækˌgæmən

background, -s 'bækgɪɑŭnd, -z

back-hand, -s, -ing, -ed, -er/s 'bækˌhænd, -z, -ɪŋ, -ɪd, -ə˞/z

backing (s.), -s 'bækɪŋ, -z

backlash, -es, -ing, -ed 'bæklæʃ, -ɪz, -ɪŋ, -t

backlog, -s, -ging, -ged 'bæklɒg, -z, -ɪŋ, -d

back-pedal, -s, -ling, -led 'bækˌpedl̩, -z, -ɪŋ, -d

backside, -s 'bæksaɪd, -z

backslid 'bækslɪd

backslid|e, -es, -ing, -er/s 'bækslaɪd, -z, -ɪŋ, -ə˞/z

backspin 'bækspɪn

backstage 'bæk'steɪdʒ

backstairs 'bæk'stɛ˞z (when att., ['--])

backstitch, -es, -ing, -ed 'bækstɪtʃ, -ɪz, -ɪŋ, -t

back-trick, -s 'bækˌtɪɪk, -s

backward, -s, -ly, -ness 'bækwə˞d, -z, -lɪ, -nɪs

back-wounding 'bækˌwundɪŋ

bacon 'beɪkən

bacon-fed 'beɪkənˌfed

bad, -der, -dest, -ly, -ness 'bæd, -ə˞, -ɪst, -lɪ, -nɪs

bad-causer 'bædˌkɔzə˞

bade (p.t. of **bid**, q.v.) 'bæd ['beɪd]

badg|e, -es, -ing, -ed 'bædʒ, -ɪz, -ɪŋ, -d

bae (Scotch for **baa**, the bleat of a sheep), **-s** 'ba, -z

Bagot (RII) 'bægət

bagpipe, -s, -r/s 'bægpaɪp, -s, -ə˞/z

bail, -s, -ing, -ed 'beɪl, -z, -ɪŋ, -d

bairn, -s 'bɛ˞n, -z

bait, -s, -ing, -ed 'beɪt, -s, -ɪŋ, -ɪd

Bajazet(h) (ALL'S) ˌbædʒə'zet

bald, -ing; -er, -est, -ly, -ness 'bɔld, -ɪŋ; -ə˞, -ɪst, -lɪ, -nɪs

Baldpate (MEAS) 'bɔldpeɪt

bald-pated 'bɔldˌpeɪtɪd

baldric(k), -s 'bɔldɪɪk, -s

bal|e, -es, -ing, -ed 'beɪl, -z, -ɪŋ, -d

bale|ful, -fully, -fulness 'beɪl|fʊl, -fəlɪ, -fʊlnɪs

balk or baulk, -s, -ing, -ed 'bɔk, -s, -ɪŋ, -t

ballad, -s 'bæləd, -z

ballad-maker, -s 'bælədˌmeɪkə˞, -z

ballad-monger, -s 'bælədˌmʌŋgə˞, -z

ballast, -s, -ing 'bæləst, -s, -ɪŋ

ballow (cudgel) 'bæloŭ

balm, -s, -ed 'bɑm, -z, -d
balsam 'bɔlsəm
balsamum 'bɔlsəməm
Balthasar or **Balthazar** (*ADO, COM,*
MV, RJ) ˌbælθə'zɑ˞ ['--ˌ-], bæl'θæzə˞
Note.—*Stressed* [ˌ--'-, '--ˌ-] *in* RJ, V.i.12;
COM, III.i.22, V.i.223. *May be stressed*
[-'--] *in* COM, III.i.19 *but to do so seems*
unprofitable since the same speaker
pronounces it [ˌ--'-, '--ˌ-] *only three lines*
later, and that the entire section of verse
in which it awkwardly appears (lines
11–84) is dubious. Still, Irvine recom-
mends only primary stress on the second
syllable, ever, and proffers [bæl'tɑzɑ˞,
bɑl'tɑzɑ˞, bæl'θæzɑ˞, bɑl'tɑzɑ˞, *and*
bæl'θeɪzə˞]
'Ban (*TEM*) (*from* **Caliban**) 'bæn
ban, -s, -ning, -ned 'bæn, -z, -ɪŋ, -d
Banbury (MWW) 'bænbə˞ɹɪ
banditto bæn'dɪtoʊ
ban-dogs 'bænˌdɒgz
band|y, -ies, -ying, -ied 'bænd|ɪ, -ɪz, -ɪɪŋ,
-ɪd
bane or **bain, -s, -ed** 'beɪn, -z, -d
bane|ful, -fully 'beɪn|fʊl, -fəlɪ
bang, -s, -ing, -ed 'bæŋ, -z, -ɪŋ, -d
bangle, -s, -d 'bæŋgl̩, -z, -d
banish, -es, -ing, -ed, -er/s, -ment/s
'bænɪʃ, -ɪz, -ɪŋ, -t, -ə˞/z, -mənt/s
Banister (HVIII) 'bænɪstə˞
Note.—*This name of a servant in* HVIII,
II.i.109 *is either three syllables (as given*
above) or two syllables (['bænˌstə˞]*),*
depending on whether one scans the line
as having eleven beats or twelve beats
banister, -s 'bænɪstə˞, -z
bank, -s, -ing, -ed, -er/s 'bæŋk, -s, -ɪŋ, -t,
-ə˞/z
bankrout (*var. of* **bankrupt**)**, -s** 'bæŋk-
ɹaʊt [-ɹʊt], -s
Note.—*In older editions of S., this is the*
form often used; still employed by many
modern editors. The OED *lists several*
var. spellings of 'bankrout' but never
asserts a pronunciation, so those
suggested above must be considered
conjectural, due mainly to the many
ways one might interpret the 'ou' in
English
bankrupt, -s 'bæŋkɹʌpt, -s
banner, -s 'bænə˞, -z
banneret, -s 'bænə˞ɹɪt [-ɹet], -s
bannerette (*var. of* **banneret**)**, -s**
ˌbænə˞'ɹet, -s
banns 'bænz
banquet, -s, -ing, -ed 'bæŋkwɪt, -s, -ɪŋ,
-ɪd
Banquo (*MAC*) 'bæŋkwoʊ
Baptista (HAM, *TS*) bæp'tɪstə
baptiz|e, -es, -ing, -ed bæp'taɪz ['--], -ɪz,
-ɪŋ, -d
Bar (HV) 'bɑ˞
bar, -s, -ring, -red 'bɑ˞, -z, -ɹɪŋ, -d
Barabbas (MV) bə'ɹæbəs
Note.—*If and when editors of S. decide*
upon this spelling (in reference to MV,
IV.i.292*), then the pronunciation is*
['bæɹəbəs, -bæs] (*see* **Barrabas**)
barbarism, -s 'bɑ˞bəɹɪzm̩, -z
barbarit|y, -ies bɑ˞'bæɹɪt|ɪ, -ɪz
barbarous, -ly, -ness 'bɑ˞bəɹəs, -lɪ, -nɪs
Barbary (AYLI, HAM, 1HIV, 2HIV, MV,
OTH, RII, *TNK*) 'bɑ˞bə˞ɹɪ, -bɹɪ
Barbary-a (TNK) 'bɑ˞bə˞ɹɪə
Note.—*This word, along with 'three-a,'*
'bound-a,' and 'sound-a,' appears in the
ditty sung by the Gaoler's Daughter in
TNK, III.v; *the extra syllable there*
merely to provide for another musical
beat in the tetrameter line of song
Barbason (HV, MWW) 'bɑ˞bəsən
barber, -s 'bɑ˞bə˞, -z
barber-monger, -s 'bɑ˞bə˞ˌmʌŋgə˞, -z
bard, -s, -ic 'bɑ˞d, -z, -ɪk
Bardolph (*1HIV, 2HIV, HV, MWW*)
'bɑ˞dɔlf
Note.—*In* 2HIV, III.ii.215, *'Master*

---

i wɛ ɪ city ɪ hɪt e lɛt ɛ dɛbut æ can a pass ɝ bird ʌ hut ə again ə˞ suppər u you
ʊ should o obey ɔ awl ɒ cop ɑ father eɪ paid aɪ high oʊ go ɔɪ voice aʊ found ɪɚ ear
ɛɚ air ʊɚ poor ɔɚ fork ɑɚ park aɪɚ fire aʊɚ hour b boy p pit d dog t top g got
k kid h how fi behave dʒ jot tʃ chew z zany s soft v vat f fat ʒ treasure ʃ ship ð the
θ thin m man n no ŋ hang l lip j yes w won ʍ whew ɹ rigger, airy ᶅ matter

Corporate Bardolph' is merely Bullcalf's blunder for 'Master Corporal Bardolph'

bar|e, -es, -ing, -ed; -er, -est, -ly, -ness 'bɛɚ, -z, -ɹɪŋ, -d; -ɹɚ, -ɹɪst, -lɨ, -nɪs
Note.—In Frank Kermode's (editor, The Arden Shakespeare, *1958) annotation for TEM, I.ii.53, there is a brief but valuable discussion about monosyllabic words that sometimes receive the value of two metric beats in S. lines of verse "whether or no [they are] pronounced disyllabically . . ." In TEM, I.ii.206, 'brave' is arguably pronounced disyllabically or given, as Kermode puts it, "a heavy emphasis." Walter Skeat, erstwhile Professor of Anglo-Saxon at University of Cambridge, suggests that 'bare' in TNK, I.ii.15 is disyllabic. Cf. Abbott's* A Shakespearian Grammar, *§§ 475, 479*

bare-armed 'bɛɚ-ɹaɚ-md
bareback, -ed 'bɛɚ-bæk, -t
bare-bone 'bɛɚ-ˌboŏn
bare-fac|ed, -edly, -edness 'bɛɚ-feĭs|t, -tlɨ [-ɪdlɨ], -tnɪs
barefoot 'bɛɚ-fʊt
bare-gnawn 'bɛɚ-ˌnɔn
bare(-)headed 'bɛɚ-ˌhedɪd [ˌ-'--]
bare-picked 'bɛɚ-ˌpɪkt
bare-ribbed 'bɛɚ-ˌɹɪbd
barful (*full of impediments*) 'baɚ-fʊl
bargain, -s, -ing, -ed, -er/s 'baɚ-gɪn, -z, -ɪŋ, -d
barg|e (*s., v.*), **-es, -ing, -ed** 'baɚ-dʒ, -ɪz, -ɪŋ, -d
Bargulus (2HVI) 'baɚ-gələs, -gjʊləs
bark *or* **barque** (*sailing ship*), **-s** 'baɚ-k, -s
bark, -s, -ing, -ed, -er/s 'baɚ-k, -s, -ɪŋ, -t, -ɚ/z
Barkloughly Castle (RII) baɚ-k'loŏlɨ, baɚ-k'lɒklɨ 'kasḷ
barky 'baɚ-kɨ
barley 'baɚ-lɨ
barley-break 'baɚ-lɨˌbɹeĭk
barm, -y, -ier, -iest 'baɚ-m, -ɨ, -ɪɚ, -ɪɪst
barn, -s 'baɚ-n, -z
barnacle, -s 'baɚ-nəkḷ, -z
Barnardine (*MEAS*) 'baɚ-nəˌdin

*Note.—Kökeritz (*Shakespeare's Names: A Pronouncing Dictionary, *p. 34) suggests that this name is possibly stressed [-'--] in MEAS, IV.ii.63. I favor consistency, especially when it comes to the pronunciation of S.'s names (see* **Gonzalo***), and the integrity of the pronunciation given above is easily retained by scanning the line with an epic caesura*

barne (*obsolete form of* **bairn**), **-s** 'bɛɚ-n, -z
Barnes, George (2HIV) 'dʒɔɚ-dʒ 'baɚ-nz
Barnet (3HVI) 'baɚ-nɪt
baron (**B.**), **-s** 'bæɹən, -z
baronet, -s 'bæɹənɪt [-net], -s
baron|y, -ies 'bæɹən|ɨ [-ɹn̩|ɨ], -ɨz
barque *or* **bark** (*sailing ship*), **-s** 'baɚ-k, -s
Barrabas (MV) 'bæɹəbəs [-bæs]
Note.—This is the First Folio's spelling of the name we now commonly spell 'Barabbas,' and pronounce [bə'ɹæbəs]. The spelling 'Barrabas' is usually retained by editors of this passage mainly to impress upon the reader/actor that in its only appearance in S., i.e., MV, IV.i.292, it scans with primary stress on the first rather than the second syllable, in order to fit rightly into the metrical pattern of the verse line. In Marlowe's 'The Jew of Malta,' the name is spelled 'Barabas,' and as in MV, the second syllable is always unstressed
barred-up 'baɚ-dʌp
barr|en, -enest, -enly, -enness 'bæɹ|ən, -ənɪst, -ənlɨ, -ənnɪs
barricad|e, -es, -ing, -ed ˌbæɹɪ'keĭd, -z, -ɪŋ, -ɪd ['---]
barricado, -es ˌbæ ɹɪ'kɑdoŏ [-'keĭdoŏ], -z
barrow, -s 'bæɹoŏ, -z
Barson (2HIV) 'baɚ-sn̩
barter, -s, -ing, -ed 'baɚ-tɚ, -z, -ɹɪŋ, -d
Bartholomew (2HIV, TS) baɚ-'θɒləmju, 'baɚ-tḷmju
Note.—In the First Folio's edition of TS, specifically line TS, IND.i.103, 'Bartholomew' is spelled 'Bartholmew,' indicating one of the pronunciations

common in S.'s day, i.e., ['baɔ̌ˈtl̩mju].
*Some modern editiors emend it to
'Barthol'mew.' However, if one chooses
to retain the customary (modern) way of
pronouncing the name, i.e.,*
[baɔ̌ˈθɒləmju], *one can easily do so
while still remaining within the
conventions of S. scansion dynamics,
despite Kökeritz's assertion (and
somewhat coercive rhetoric) that it is
"clearly stressed"* ['--,-] (*Shakespeare's
Names: A Pronouncing Dictionary, p.
34). By simply making 'Sirrah, go' the
first foot of the line (cf. Note for* **marry**),
*'Bartholomew' falls out nicely in the
modern way*

Bartholomew-tide (HV)
baɔ̌ˈθɒləmjuˌtaɪ̆d
Basan (AC) 'beɪ̆sæn [-sən]
bas|e, -es, -ing, -ed; -er, -est, -ely, -eness
'beɪ̆s, -ɪz, -ɪŋ, -t; -ɚ, -ɪst, -lɪ, -nɪs
baseless, -ly, -ness 'beɪ̆slɪs, -lɪ, -nɪs
basement, -s 'beɪ̆smənt, -s
base-string 'beɪ̆sˌstɹɪŋ
bash, -es, -ing, -ed 'bæʃ, -ɪz, -ɪŋ, -t
Basilisco-like (KJ) ˌbæzɪ'lɪskoŭˌlaɪ̆k
basilisk, -s 'bæzɪlɪsk, -s
Basimecu, Mounsieur (2HVI) mə'sjɚ
ˌbazɪmə'kju
*Note.—As Stokes puts it, this is a "ribald
nonce-name" given by Jack Cade to the
Dauphin of France in* 2HVI, IV.vii.26. *It
is to be pronounced more or less like the
Fr. 'baisez mon cul' which basically
means 'kiss my arse'*
basin, -s 'beɪ̆sn̩, -z
Basingstoke (2HIV) 'beɪ̆zɪŋstoŭk
bask, -s, -ing, -ed 'bask, -s, -ɪŋ, -t
basket, -s 'baskɪt, -s
basket-hilt 'baskɪtˌhɪlt
bass (*musical instrument, singer, pitch,
etc.*) 'beɪ̆s, -ɪz
bass (*fish, plant fiber [var. of 'bast']*), **-es**
'bæs, -ɪz

Bassanio (*MV*) ba'sɑnɪoŭ, -njoŭ
*Note.—In S., this name is always
trisyllabic, i.e.,* [ba'sɑnjoŭ]. *The Folio
also gives 'Bassiano,' in which case the
pronunciation may be* [ba'sjanoŭ]
Bassianus (*TIT*) ˌbasɪ'anəs [ˌbasɪ'eɪ̆nʊs]
Basset (*1HVI*) 'bæsɪt
bass-viol, -s 'beɪ̆s'vaɪ̆əl, -z
basta (*It.*) (TS.I.i.98) 'bɑˈstɑ
bastard (**B.**), **-s, -y** 'bæstɚd ['bas-], -z, -ɪ
bastardiz|e, -es, -ing, -ed 'bæstɚˈdaɪ̆z
['bas-], -ɪz, -ɪŋ, -d
bastardly 'bæstɚˈdlɪ ['bas-]
bast|e, -es, -ing, -ed, -er/s 'beɪ̆st, -s, -ɪŋ,
-ɪd, -ɚ/z
bastinado, -es, -ing, -ed ˌbæstɪ'neɪ̆doŭ
[-'nɑd-], -z, -ɪŋ, -d
batch, -es 'bætʃ, -ɪz
bate (*apheitc form of* **abate**) 'beɪ̆t
bat|e, -es, -ing, -ed 'beɪ̆t, -s, -ɪŋ, -ɪd
bate-breeding 'beɪ̆tˌbɹidɪŋ
bateless 'beɪ̆tlɪs
Bates, John (*HV*) 'dʒɒn 'beɪ̆ts
bat-fowling 'bætfaŭlɪŋ
batler (*wooden instrument for beating
clothes in the wash*) 'bætlɚ
batlet (*wooden instrument for beating
clothes in the wash*) 'bætlɪt
battalia bə'tæljə
batten, -s, -ing, -ed 'bætn̩, -z, -ɪŋ, -d
batter, -s, -ing, -ed 'bæɾɚ, -z, -ɹɪŋ, -d
batter|y, -ies 'bæɾɹɪ|ɪ, -ɪz
batt|le, -les, -ling, -led 'bætl̩, -l̩z, -l̩ɪŋ, -l̩d
battle(-)axe, -s 'bætl̩ˌæks, -ɪz
battlefield, -s 'bætl̩ˌfild, -z
battle(-)ground, -s 'bætl̩ˌgɹaŭnd, -z
battlement, -s, -ed 'bætl̩mənt, -s, -ɪd
bauble, -s 'bɔbl̩, -z
baubling 'bɔblɪŋ
Bavian (*TNK*) 'beɪ̆vɪən, -vjən
bavin (*kindling; brushwood*) 'bævɪn
bawcock, -s 'bɔkɒk, -s
Bawd (*PER*) 'bɔd
bawd, -s; -ry, -y 'bɔd, -z; -ɹɪ, -ɪ

---

i w**e** ɪ c**i**ty ɪ h**i**t e l**e**t ɛ d**e**but æ c**a**n a p**a**ss ɚ b**i**rd ʌ h**u**t ə **a**gain ɚ supp**er** u y**ou**
ʊ sh**ould** o **o**bey ɔ **aw**l ɒ c**o**p ɑ f**a**ther eɪ̆ p**ai**d aɪ̆ h**igh** oŭ g**o** ɔɪ̆ v**oi**ce aŭ f**ou**nd ɪɚ **ear**
ɛɚ **air** ʊɚ **poor** ɔɚ **fork** ɑɚ **park** aɪ̆ɚ **fire** aŭɚ **hour** b **b**oy p **p**it d **d**og t **t**op g **g**ot
k **k**id h **h**ow fi be**h**ave dʒ **j**ot tʃ **ch**ew z **z**any s **s**oft v **v**at f **f**at ʒ trea**s**ure ʃ **sh**ip ð **th**e
θ **th**in m **m**an n **n**o ŋ ha**ng** l **l**ip j **y**es w **w**on ʍ **wh**ew ɹ **r**igger, ai**r**y ɾ ma**tt**er

bawdy-hou|se, -ses 'bɔdɪˌhaʊ|s, -zɪz
bawl, -s, -ing, -ed, -er/s 'bɔl, -z, -ɪŋ, -d,
 -ə·/z
bay, -s, -ing, -ed 'beɪ̆, -z, -ɪŋ, -d
Baynard's Castle (RIII) 'beɪ̆nə·dz 'kasl̩
Bayonne (HVIII) beɪ̆'ɔn [-'on]
bay-tree, -s 'beɪ̆tɹi, -z
be, being, been 'bi, 'biɪŋ, 'bɪn
 Note.—For the sake of the metrical
 requirements of the verse in S., 'being'
 often becomes monosyllabic, i.e., ['bɪŋ]
beach, -es, -ing, -ed; -y 'bitʃ, -ɪz, -ɪŋ, -t; -ɪ
beacon, -s 'bikən, -z
bead, -s, -ing, -ed, -er/s 'bid, -z, -ɪŋ, -ɪd,
 -ə·/z
beadle, -s 'bidl̩, -z
beadsman 'bidzmən
beagle, -s 'bigl̩, -z
beak, -ed 'bik, -s, -t
beam, -s, -ing, -ed 'bim, -z, -ɪŋ, -d
bean, -s 'bin, -z
bear, -s, -ing, bore, born(e), bearer/s
 'bɛə·, -z, -ɹɪŋ, 'bɔə·, 'bɔə·n, 'bɛə·ɹə·/z
 Note.—In TIM, I.i.179, *'bear' is*
 arguably disyllabic, i.e., ['bɛə·] *in order*
 to fulfill the metrical requirements of the
 verse line (cf. Note for **brave***)*
bear(-)bating, -s 'bɛə·beɪ̆tɪŋ, -z
beard, -s, -ed 'bɪə·d, -z, -ɪd
beardless 'bɪə·dlɪs
bear-herd, -s 'bɛə·ˌhɜ·d ['bɛə·ɹə·d], -z
 (*see* **bearward** *and* **berrord**)
bearing (*s.*), **-s** 'bɛə·ɹɪŋ, -z
bearing-cloth 'bɛə·ɹɪŋˌklɒθ
bearward (*bear-keeper*), **-s** 'bɛə·ɹə·d
 [-ɹɔə·d, 'bɛə·wɔə·d], -z
 Note.—This word in ADO, II.i.36
 appears as 'berrord' in the Quarto and
 First and Second Folio versions. It is
 meant to stand for either 'bearward' or
 'bearherd'. The spelling in the Quarto
 and Folios is a pronunciation-spelling
 indicating a colloquial pronunciation,
 analogous to 'bosun' to indicate the
 usual pronunciation for 'boatswain' (cf.
 berrord*)*
bear-whelp, -s 'bɛə·ˌʍelp, -s
beast, -s 'bist, -s

beastl|y, -ier, -iest, -iness 'bistl|ɪ, -ɪə·,
 -ɪɪst, -ɪnɪs
beat, -s, -ing/s, -en, -er/s 'bit, -s, -ɪŋ/z,
 -n̩, -ə·/z
beated (*archaic form of* **beaten**) 'bitɪd
Beatrice (*ADO*) 'biətɹɪs
 Note.—In ADO, III.i.21, 24, 37, 43 *the*
 name is a disyllable, i.e., ['bitɹɪs]; *in all*
 other instances, it is trisyllabic, as
 indicated above
Beaufort (HV, *1HVI, 2HVI,* 3HVI)
 'boʊ̆fə·t
Beaufort, Cardinal (*2HVI*) 'kaə·dn̩l̩
 'boʊ̆fə·t
Beaufort, Henry (*1HVI, 2HVI*) 'henɹɪ
 'boʊ̆fə·t (*see Note for* **Henry**)
Beaufort, John (*1HVI*) 'dʒɒn 'boʊ̆fə·t
Beaufort, Thomas (*1HVI*) 'tɒməs 'boʊ̆fə·t
Beaumont *or* **Beaumond** (HV, RII)
 'boʊ̆mɒnt (*sometimes* [-'-]), [*Fr.* bomɔ̃]
beautiful 'bjuɾɪfʊl [-utɪ-]
beautifully 'bjuɾɪflɪ [-utɪ-]
beauti|fy, -fies, -fying, -fied 'bjuɾɪ|faɪ̆
 [-utɪ-], -faɪ̆z, -faɪ̆ɪŋ, -faɪ̆d
beaut|y (B.), **-ies** 'bjut|ɪ [-uɡ̊|ɪ], -ɪz
beauty-waning 'bjuɾɪ'weɪ̆nɪŋ [-utɪ'w-]
beaver, -s 'bivə·, -z
bechance, -d bɪ'tʃans, -t
beck, -s, -ing 'bek, -s, -ɪŋ
beckon, -s, -ing, -ed 'bekən, -z, -ɪŋ, -d
becom|e, -es, -ing/ly, -ingness, -ings,
 became bɪ'kʌm, -z, -ɪŋ/lɪ, -ɪŋnɪs, -ɪŋz,
 bɪ'keɪ̆m
becomed (*adj.*) bɪ'kʌmɪd
becomed (*archaic form of* **become** [*p.t.*])
 bɪ'kʌmd
bed, -s, -ding, -ded 'bed, -z, -ɪŋ, -ɪd
bedabbled bɪ'dæbl̩d
bedashed bɪ'dæʃt
bedaub, -s, -ing, -ed bɪ'dɔb, -z, -ɪŋ, -d
bedazz|le, -les, -ling, -led bɪ'dæz|l̩, -l̩z,
 -l̩ɪŋ [-lɪŋ], -l̩d
bedeck, -s, -ing, -ed bɪ'dek, -s, -ɪŋ, -t
bedew, -s, -ing, -ed bɪ'dju, -z, -ɪŋ, -d
bedfellow, -s 'bedˌfeloʊ̆, -z
Bedford (*HV, 1HVI,* 2HVI) 'bedfə·d
bed-hanger, -s 'bedˌhæŋə·, -z
bedim, -s, -ming, -med bɪ'dɪm, -z, -ɪŋ, -d

bedlam (B.) (HV, 2HVI, KJ, LEAR)
'bedləm
bed-mate, -s 'bedˌmeɪt, -s
bed-presser 'bedˌpɹesəˑ
bedrench bɪ'dɹentʃ
bed(-)rid, -den 'bedˌɹɪd, -n̩
bed-right (var. of **bed-rite**) 'bedˌɹaɪt
bed-swerver, -s 'bedswɝˑvəˑ, -z
bed-vow 'bedˌvaʊ
bedward 'bedwəˑd
bed-work 'bedˌwɝk
bee, -s 'bi, -z
bee|f, -fs, -ves 'bi|f, -fs, -vz
beef-witted 'bɪfˌwɪtɪd [-ˌwɪɾɪd]
Beelzebub (HV, MAC, TN) bi'elzɪbʌb
Note.—In S., this name for 'the prince of
devils' is spelled 'Belzebub,' and is
pronounced ['belzɪbʌb]
beest-eating 'bistˌitɪŋ
beetle, -s 'bitl̩, -z
beetle-headed 'bitl̩ˌhedɪd
beeves (pl. of **beef**) 'bivz
be|fall, -falls, -falling, -fallen, -fell bɪ'fɔl,
-'fɔlz, -'fɔlɪŋ, -'fɔlən, -'fel
befell (p.t. of **befall**, q.v.) bɪ'fel
befit, -s, -ting/ly, -ted bɪ'fɪt, -s, -ɪŋ/lɪ, -ɪd
before bɪ'fɔɚˑ
beforehand bɪ'fɔɚˑfiænd
beforetime bɪ'fɔɚˑtaɪm
befortune bɪ'fɔɚˑtʃʊn [-tʃən, -tjun]
befriend, -s, -ing, -ed bɪ'fɹɛnd, -z, -ɪŋ, -ɪd
be-gar (from 'by God') bɪ'gaʁ ['gaɚˑ]
Note.—Doctor Caius (in MWW) *is the*
stereotypical foreigner—and French, to
boot—given to foolish arrogance, and
ineptly handling English pronunciation.
This is an example of S.'s direction to the
actor (by way of semiphonetic spellings)
to adopt such an accent, more or less,
for the sake of wringing the most satire
out of plays on words stemming from
confusions with, and corruptions of,

English pronunciation via the French
tongue
be|get, -gets, -getting, -gat, -got, -gotten
bɪ'|get, -'gets, -'getɪŋ, -'gæt, -'gɒt, -'gɒtn̩
beggar (B.), -s 'begəˑ, -z
beggared 'begəˑd
beggar-fear 'begəˑˌfɪɚˑ
beggarl|y, -iness 'begəˑl|ɪ, -ɪnɪs
beggary 'begəˑɹɪ
begnaw, -n bɪ'nɔ, -n
begone bɪ'gɒn
begot (from **beget**), **-ten** bɪ'gɒt, -n̩
begrimed bɪ'gɹaɪmd
beguil|e, -es, -ing/ly, -ed bɪ'gaɪl, -z, -ɪŋ/lɪ,
-d
behalf, -s bɪ'fiaf, -s
behav|e, -es, -ing, -ed bɪ'fieɪ̆v, -z, -ɪŋ, -d
behavior, -s; -al, -ally bɪ'fieɪ̆vjəˑ, -z; -ɹəl,
-ɹəlɪ
behead, -s, -ing, -ed bɪ'fied, -z, -ɪŋ, -ɪd
behest, -s bɪ'fiest, -s
behind bɪ'fiaɪnd
behind-door-work bɪ'fiaɪnd'dɔɚˑˌwɝk
behind-hand bɪ'fiaɪndˌfiænd
be|hold, -holds, -holding, -held,
-holder/s bɪ'|fioʊld, -'fioʊldz, -'fioʊldɪŋ,
-'field, -'fioʊldəˑ/z
beholden bɪ'fioʊldən
behoof bɪ'fiuf
behoov|e, -es, -ing, -ed bɪ'fiuv, -z, -ɪŋ, -d
behov|e, -es, -ing, -ed bɪ'fioʊv, -z, -ɪŋ, -d
behoveful bɪ'fioʊvfʊl
being, -s 'biɪŋ, -z
Note.—Very often monosyllabic in S.,
i.e., ['bɪŋ]
Bel (ADO) 'bel
Belarius (CYM) bə'lɛɚˑɹɪəs, -ɹĭəs
belch, -es, -ing, -ed, -er/s 'beltʃ, -ɪz, -ɪŋ,
-t, -əˑ/z
Belch, Sir Toby (TN) ˌsɝˑ 'toʊbɪ 'beltʃ
beldam, -s 'beldəm, -z
belfr|y, -ies 'belfɹɪ, -ɪz

---

i w<u>e</u> ɪ cit<u>y</u> ɪ h<u>i</u>t e l<u>e</u>t ɛ d<u>e</u>but æ c<u>a</u>n a p<u>a</u>ss ɝ b<u>ir</u>d ʌ h<u>u</u>t ə <u>a</u>gain ɚ supp<u>er</u> u y<u>ou</u>
ʊ sh<u>ou</u>ld o <u>o</u>bey ɔ <u>aw</u>l ɒ c<u>o</u>p ɑ f<u>a</u>ther eɪ p<u>ai</u>d aɪ h<u>igh</u> oʊ g<u>o</u> ɔɪ v<u>oi</u>ce aʊ f<u>ou</u>nd ɪɚ <u>ear</u>
ɛɚ <u>air</u> ʊɚ p<u>oor</u> ɔɚ f<u>ork</u> ɑɚ p<u>ark</u> aɪɚ f<u>ire</u> aʊɚ h<u>our</u> b <u>b</u>oy p <u>p</u>it d <u>d</u>og t <u>t</u>op g g<u>o</u>t
k <u>k</u>id h <u>h</u>ow fi be<u>h</u>ave dʒ <u>j</u>ot tʃ <u>ch</u>ew z <u>z</u>any s <u>s</u>oft v <u>v</u>at f <u>f</u>at ʒ trea<u>s</u>ure ʃ <u>sh</u>ip ð <u>th</u>e
θ <u>th</u>in m <u>m</u>an n <u>n</u>o ŋ ha<u>ng</u> l <u>l</u>ip j <u>y</u>es w <u>w</u>on ʍ <u>wh</u>ew ɹ <u>r</u>igger, ai<u>r</u>y ɾ ma<u>tt</u>er

Belgia (COM, 3HVI) 'bɛldʒɪə
bel|ie, -ies, -ying, -ied bɪ'l|aĭ, -aĭz, -aĭɪŋ, -aĭd
belief, -s bɪ'lif, -s
believability bɪˌlivə'bɪlɪtɨ
believ|e, -es, -ing/ly, -ed, -er/s; -able, -ably bɪ'liv, -z, -ɪŋ/lɨ, -d, -ə˞/z; -əbḷ, -əblɨ
belike bɪ'laĭk
Bellario, Doctor (MV) 'dɒktə˞ be'lɑɹɪoŭ, -ɹjoŭ
bell|man, -men 'bel|mən, -mən
Bellona (MAC, TNK) be'loŭnə
bellow, -s, -ing, -ed, -er/s 'beloŭ, -z, -ɪŋ, -d, -ə˞/z
bellows-mender 'beloŭzˌmendə˞
bell-wether, -s 'belˌweðə˞, -z
bell|y, -ies, -ying, -ied 'bel|ɨ, -ɨz, -ɨɪŋ, -ɨd
bellyful, -s 'belɨfʊl, -z
belly-pinched 'belɨˌpɪntʃt
Belman (TS) 'belmən
Belmont (MV) 'belmɒnt
belocked bɪ'lɒkt
belong, -s, -ing/s, -ed bɪ'lɒŋ, -z, -ɪŋ/z, -d
below bɪ'loŭ
Belzebub (HV, MAC, TN) (*see* **Beelzebub**) 'belzɪbʌb
bemadding bɪ'mædɪŋ
be-met bɪ'met
bemete (*measure*) bɪ'mit
bemoan, -s, -ing, -ed bɪ'moŭn, -z, -ɪŋ, -d
bemock bɪ'mɒk
bemocked-at bɪ'mɒktæt
bemoiled (*made filthy with mire*) bɪ'mɔĭld
be-monster bɪ'mɒnstə˞
bench, -es, -ing, -ed 'bentʃ, -ɪz, -ɪŋ, -t
bencher, -s 'bentʃə˞, -z
bench-hole, -s 'bentʃˌɦoŭl, -z
bend, -s, -ing, -ed, bent 'bend, -z, -ɪŋ, -ɪd, 'bent
bene (*L.*) (LLL, V.i.27) 'bɛnɛ
benedicite (*L.*) (MEAS, II.iii.39; RJ, II.iii.27) ˌbɛnɛ'disitɛ [-'ditʃitɛ]
Benedick (*ADO*) 'benɪdɪk [-ned-]
Note.—*The Folio version also has 'Benedicke' and 'Benedict'*
benediction, -s ˌbenɪ'dɪkʃn, -z
benedictus (*L.*) (ADO, III.iv.72,73) bɛnɛ'diktus (*from* **carduus benedictus**, *q.v.*)

benefaction, -s ˌbenɪ'fækʃn ['----], -z
benefactor, -s 'benɪfæktə˞, -z
benefice, -s, -d 'benɪfɪs, -ɪz, -t
benefit, -s, -(t)ing, -(t)ed 'benɪfɪt, -s, -ɪŋ, -ɪd
benetted bɪ'netɪd
benign, -est, -ly bɪ'naĭn, -ɪst, -lɨ
Note.—*In PER, II.3 (Chorus), this word is given primary stress on the first syllable, i.e.,* ['bɪnaĭn]
benison, -s 'benɪzn̩ [-ɪsn̩], -z
bent, -s 'bent, -s
Bentii (ALL'S) 'benʃɪaĭ
Bentivolii (TS) ˌbentɪ'voŭlɪaĭ
benumb, -s, -ing, -ed bɪ'nʌm, -z, -ɪŋ, -d
ben venuto (*It.*) (TS, I.ii.280) bɛn vɛ'nuˈto
Benvolio (*RJ*) ben'voŭlɪoŭ, -ljoŭ
bepaint, -ed bɪ'peĭnt, -ɪd
bepray bɪ'pɹeĭ
bequea|th, -ths, -thing, -thed bɪ'kwi|ð [-i|θ], -ðz [-i|θs], -ðɪŋ, -ðd [-i|θt]
berattl|e, -es, -ing, -ed bɪ'ɹætḷ, -z, -ɪŋ, -d
beray (*befoul, defile, dirty*), **-ed** bɪ'ɹeĭ, -d
bereav|e, -es, -ing, -ed, bereft bɪ'ɹiv, -z, -ɪŋ, -d, bɪ'ɹeft
bereavement, -s bɪ'ɹivmənt, -s
bereft (*from* **bereave**, *q.v.*) bɪ'ɹeft
Bergamo (TS) 'bɝ˞gəmoŭ
Bergomask (MSND) 'bɝ˞gəmask
berhyme, -d bɪ'ɹaĭm, -d
Berkeley (1HIV, *RII, RIII*) 'bɑ˞klɨ
Note.—*In deference to the fact that this name in S. appears only in the Histories, I recommend the regular and traditional Brit. Pronunciation, viz. that given above*
ber Lady *or* **by-Lady** bə˞'leĭdɨ, bɪ'leĭdɨ
Bermoothes (TEM) bə˞'mudəz [-ð̞ɛz]
Note.—*Both Irvine and Kökeritz give this not-so-troublesome-a-word in TEM, I.ii.229 (standing for the Bermudas) a voiced interdental fricative (*[ð]*) for the 'th' while admitting that it "is clearly a phonetic rendering of the Sp. Bermudez"* (Kökeritz's Shakespeare's Names: A Pronouncing Dictionary, *p. 36*). *I offer the pronunciations above to provide a happy median between the Folio's spelling and what I believe is intended,*

*reconciling the archaic with the modern,
and to elucidate for the sake of meaning
(see* **murther** *and* **quotha***)*
Bernardo (*HAM*) bəˈnɑ˞ˈdoŏ
Berowne, Beroune, *or* **Biron** (*LLL*) bɪˈɹun
*Note.—In LLL, IV.iii.226, 228, the
rhyme-pattern suggests that this name is
to match 'moon.' Despite this, the name
is (just like so many other names in S.)
the subject of much discussion and
debate. Since the vowel sound in the
word 'moon' itself has shifted over the
past 400 years, there is little chance
everyone will ever see eye-to-eye.
However, notwithstanding the vowel
shift, no other pronunciation choice
proffered (and there are at least three
others) can make the same irrefutable
claim of rhyming with a particular word.
(See 'Shakespeare's Verse' § 1.8 of this
dictionary)*
berrord (*see* **bearward**) ˈbɛ˞ɹə˞d
berr|y, -ies ˈbeɹ|ɨ, -ɨz
Berry *or* **Berri, Duke of** (*HV*) ˈdjuk əv
ˈbeɹɨ
Bertram (*ALL'S*) ˈbɝˈtɹəm
*Note.—In ALL'S, I.i.81, pronounced
trisyllabically, i.e.,* [ˈbɝˈɾə˞ɹəmz]
Berwick (*2HVI, 3HVI*) ˈbeɹɪk
*Note.—The First Folio gives the alt.
spelling 'Barwick(e),' which might
indicate a pronunciation closer to*
[ˈbɑɹɪk], *analogous to our pronunciation
of 'sergeant,' and the traditional Brit.
pronunciations of 'clerk' and 'derby'*
bescreened bɪˈskɹind
beseech, -es, -ing/ly, -ed, -er/s bɪˈsitʃ, -ɪz,
-ɪŋ/lɨ, -t, -ə˞/z (*see* **besought**)
beseek bɪˈsik
beseem, -s, -ing, -ed bɪˈsim, -z, -ɪŋ, -d
bese|t, -ts, -tting bɪˈse|t, -ts, -ɾɪŋ
beshrew bɪˈʃɹu
besieg|e, -es, -ing, -ed, -er/s bɪˈsidʒ, -ɪz,
-ɪŋ, -d, -ə˞/z

beslubber bɪˈslʌbə˞
besmear, -s, -ing, -ed bɪˈsmɪ˞, -z, -ɹɪŋ, -d
besmirch, -es, -ing, -ed bɪˈsmɝtʃ, -ɪz, -ɪŋ,
-t
besom, -s ˈbizəm, -z
Besonian *or* **Bezonian** (*2HIV*) bɪˈzoŏnɪən,
-njən
besort bɪˈsɔ˞t
besot, -s, -ting, -ted bɪˈsɒt, -s, -ɪŋ, -ɪd
besought (*alt. p.t. of* **beseech,** *q.v.*) bɪˈsɔt
bespake bɪˈspeɪk
bespectacled bɪˈspektɪkl̩d
bespice bɪˈspaɪs
bespeak bɪˈspik
bespoke bɪˈspoŏk
Bess (*3HVI*) ˈbes
Bessy (*LEAR*) ˈbesɨ
Best (*2HVI, WT*) ˈbest
best (**B.**)**, -s, -ing, -ed** ˈbest, -s, -ɪŋ, -ɪd
bestained bɪˈsteɪnd (-nɪd *in* KJ, IV.iii.24)
best-boding ˈbestˌboŏdɪŋ (*when att.,* [ˌ-ˈ--])
best-governed ˈbestˌɡʌvə˞nd
bestial, -ly, -ism ˈbestjəl [ˈbestʃəl], -ɨ,
-ɪzm̩
bestir, -ring, -red bɪˈstɝ, -z, -ɹɪŋ, -d
bestow, -s, -ing, -ed bɪˈstoŏ, -z, -ɪŋ, -d
bestraught (*distracted; out of one's mind*)
bɪˈstɹɔt
bestrew, -s, -ing, -ed, -n bɪˈstɹu, -z, -ɪŋ,
-d, -n
bestrid (*p.t. and p.p. of* **bestride,** *q.v.*)
bɪˈstɹɪd
**be|stride, -strides, -striding, -strode,
-strid, -stridden** bɪˈstɹaɪd, -ˈstɹaɪdz,
-ˈstɹaɪdɪŋ, -ˈstɹoŏd, -ˈstɹɪd, -ˈstɹɪdn̩
best-tempered ˈbestˌtempə˞d
bet, -s, -ting, -ted, -tor/s ˈbet, -s, -ɪŋ, -ɪd,
-ə˞/z [ˈbeɾə˞/z]
be't (*contr. of* **be it**) ˈbit
be|take, -takes, -taking, -took, -taken
bɪˈteɪk, -ˈteɪks, -ˈteɪkɪŋ, -ˈtŏk, -ˈteɪkən
beteem bɪˈtim
bethink, -ing bɪˈθɪŋk, -ɪŋ
bethought bɪˈθɔt

i we ɨ city ɪ hit e let ɛ debut æ can a pass ɝ bird ʌ hut ə again ə˞ supper u you
ŏ should o obey ɔ awl ɒ cop ɑ father eɪ paid aɪ high oŏ go ɔɪ voice aŏ found ɪ˞ ear
ɛ˞ air ŏ˞ poor ɔ˞ fork ɑ˞ park aɪ˞ fire aŏ˞ hour b boy p pit d dog t top g got
k kid h how fi behave dʒ jot tʃ chew z zany s soft v vat f fat ʒ treasure ʃ ship ð the
θ thin m man n no ŋ hang l lip j yes w won ʍ whew ɹ rigger, airy ɾ matter

bethumped brˈθʌmpt
betid brˈtɪd
betid|e, -es, -ing, -ed brˈtaɪd, -z, -ɪŋ, -ɪd
betime, -s brˈtaɪm, -z
betoken, -s, -ing, -ed brˈtoʊkən, -z, -ɪŋ, -d
betook (p.t. of betake) brˈtʊk
betoss, -ed brˈtɒs, -t
betray, -s, -ing, -ed, -er/s brˈtɹeɪ, -z, -ɪŋ,
    -d, -ɚ/z
betrayal, -s brˈtɹeɪəl, -z
betrim, -s, -ming, -med brˈtɹɪm, -z, -ɪŋ, -d
betroth, -s, -ing, -ed brˈtɹoʊð, -z, -ɪŋ, -d
betrothal, -s brˈtɹoʊðəl, -z
betrothed (adj.) brˈtɹoʊðɪd (as in HV,
    II.iv.108)
better, -s, -ing, -ed ˈbeɾɚ, -z, -ɹɪŋ, -d
better-fashioned ˈbeɾɚˌfæʃnd
betterment ˈbeɾɚmənt
betumbled brˈtʌmbl̩d
between brˈtwin
betwixt brˈtwɪkst
bevel, -s, -ling, -led ˈbevl̩, -z, -ɪŋ, -d
beverage, -s ˈbevɹɪdʒ [ˈbevɚɹɪdʒ], -ɪz
Bevis, George (2HVI) ˈdʒɔɚdʒ ˈbevɪs
    [ˈbivɪs]
Bevis of Hampton (HVIII) ˈbevɪs [ˈbivɪs]
    əv ˈhæmptən
bev|y, -ies ˈbev|ɪ, -ɪz
bewail, -s, -ing, -ed brˈweɪl, -z, -ɪŋ, -d
bewar|e, -es, -ing, -ed brˈwɛɚ, -z, -ɹɪŋ, -d
beweep, -s, -ing, bewept brˈwip, -s, -ɪŋ,
    brˈwept
bewept (p.t. of beweep, q.v.) brˈwept
bewet brˈwet
bewhored brˈhɔɚd
bewitch, -es, -ing/ly, -ed, -ment/s brˈwɪtʃ,
    -ɪz, -ɪŋ/lɪ, -t, -mənt/s
bewray, -s, -ing, -ed bɪ ˈɹeɪ, -z, -ɪŋ, -d
beyond brˈjɒnd [brˈɒnd]
bezel, -z ˈbezl̩, -z
Bezonian or Besonian (2HVI) brˈzoʊnɪən,
    -njən
bezonian, -s brˈzoʊn ɪən, -z
Bianca (OTH, TS) brˈɑŋkə, bjɑŋkə
bias, -(s)es, -(s)ing, -(s)ed ˈbaɪəs, -ɪz, -ɪŋ,
    -t
bias-drawing ˈbaɪəsˌdɹɔɪŋ
bib, -s ˈbɪb, -z
bibble babble (nonsense-talk) ˈbɪbl̩ ˈbæbl̩

bicker, -s, -ing/s, -ed, -er/s ˈbɪkɚ, -z,
    -ɹɪŋ/z, -d, -ɹɚ/z
bid, -s, -ding, bade, bidden ˈbɪd, -z, -ɪŋ,
    ˈbæd [ˈbeɪd], ˈbɪdn̩
bidder, -s ˈbɪdɚ, -z
bidd|y, -ies ˈbɪd|ɪ, -ɪz
bid|e, -es, -ing, -ed ˈbaɪd, -z, -ɪŋ, -ɪd
bier, -s ˈbɪɚ, -z
bifold ˈbaɪfoʊld
big (B.), -ger, -gest, -ness ˈbɪg, -ɚ, -ɪst,
    -nɪs
bigamist, -s ˈbɪgəmɪst, -s
bigam|y, -ies ˈbɪgəm|ɪ, -ɪz
big-bellied ˈbɪgˌbelɪd
big-boned ˈbɪgˌboʊnd
biggen or biggin (nightcap) ˈbɪgən [-gɪn]
    Note.—This word, given as 'biggen' in
    2HIV, IV.v.26, is an obsolete, archaic
    var. of 'biggin,' and means 'nightcap,'
    'hood,' or 'coif of a sergeant-at-law.'
    Even though modern editors typically
    define 'biggen' as a 'nightcap,' perhaps
    there is something in the 'coif of a
    sergeant-at-law,' given that the next line
    refers to "the watch of night;" an
    allusion to he who is asleep at his weary
    post
bigger-looked ˈbɪgɚˌlʊkt
Bigot, Lord (KJ) ˈlɔɚd ˈbɪgət
big-swollen ˈbɪgˌswoʊlən
bilberr|y, -ies ˈbɪlbəˌɹ|ɪ, -ɪz
bilbo, -es ˈbɪlboʊ, -z
bile ˈbaɪl
bill, -s ˈbɪl, -z
billet, -s, -ing, -ed ˈbɪlɪt, -s, -ɪŋ, -ɪd
billiard, -s ˈbɪljəd, -z
billow, -s, -ing, -ed; -y ˈbɪloʊ, -z, -ɪŋ, -d;
    -ɪ
bin, -s ˈbɪn, -z
bind, -s, -ing, bound ˈbaɪnd, -z, -ɪŋ,
    ˈbaʊnd
binder, -s ˈbaɪndɚ, -z
Biondello (TS) ˌbɪənˈdeloʊ
binge, -s ˈbɪndʒ, -ɪz
birch, -es, -ing, -ed ˈbɝtʃ, -ɪz, -ɪŋ, -t
bird, -s ˈbɝd, -z
bird-bolt, -s ˈbɝdˌboʊlt, -s
birding-pieces ˈbɝdɪŋˌpisɪz
Birnam (MAC) ˈbɝnəm

birth, -s, -ing, -ed 'bɝ·θ, -s, -ɪŋ, -t
birth-child 'bɝ·θ,tʃaɪld
birth(-)day, -s 'bɝ·θdeǐ, -z
birthdom 'bɝ·θdəm
birthright, -s 'bɝ·θ,ɹaɪt, -s
birth-strangled 'bɝ·θ,stɹæŋgl̩d
bis coctus (*L.*) (LLL, IV.ii.21) 'bis 'koktus
bishop (**B.**), **-s; -ric/s** 'bɪʃəp, -s; -ɹɪk/s
bisson 'bɪsən
bitch, -es 'bɪtʃ, -ɪz
bitch-wol|f, -ves 'bɪtʃwʊl|f, -vz
bitter, -s; -er, -est, -ly, -ness 'bɪɾɚ, -z;
   -ɹɚ·, -ɹɪst, -lɨ, -nɪs
bittersweet 'bɪɾɚ,swit [,--'-]
bitumed bɪ'tjumd ['--]
blab, -s, -bing, -bed, -ber/s 'blæb, -z, -ɪŋ,
   -d, -ɚ/z
black, -s, -ing, -ed; -er, -est, -ly, -ness
   'blæk, -s, -ɪŋ, -t; -ɚ·, -ɪst, -lɨ, -nɪs
blackamoor, -s 'blækəmʊɝ·, -z
blackball, -s, -ing, -ed 'blækbɔl, -z, -ɪŋ, -d
blackbird, -s 'blækbɝ·d, -z
black-browed 'blæk,bɹɑǔd
black-cornered 'blæk,kɔɝ·nɚd
black-faced 'blækfeǐst
Blackfriars *or* **Black-Friars** (HVIII)
   'blæk'fɹaǐɚz
black-haired 'blæk,heɝ·d
Blackheath (HV, 2HVI) 'blæk,fiiθ
blackish 'blækɪʃ
Blackmere (1HVI) 'blækmɪɚ·
Black-Monday (MV) ,blæk'mʌndɪ [-deǐ]
Black Prince (HV, RII) 'blæk 'pɹɪns
blain, -s 'bleǐn, -z
Blanch (LEAR) 'blantʃ
blanch, -es, -ing, -ed 'blantʃ, -ɪz, -ɪŋ, -t
Blanch(e) (*KJ*) 'blantʃ
blasphem|e, -es, -ing/ly, -ed, -er/s
   blas'fim, -z, -ɪŋ/lɨ, -d, -ɚ/z
blasphem|y, -ies 'blasfɪm|ɨ, -ɨz
blast, -s, -ing, -ed 'blast, -s, -ɪŋ, -ɪd
blastment, -s 'blastmənt, -s
blaz|e, -es, -ing, -ed 'bleǐz, -ɪz, -ɪŋ, -d
blazer, -s 'bleǐzɚ·, -z

blazon, -s, -ing, -ed; -ry, -ries 'bleǐzn̩, -z,
   -ɪŋ, -d; -ɹɨ, -ɹɨz
bleach, -es, -ing, -ed, -er/s 'blitʃ, -ɪz, -ɪŋ,
   -t, -ɚ/z
bleak, -er, -est, -ly, -ness 'blik, -ɚ·, -ɪst,
   -lɨ, -nɪs
blear, -s, -ing, -ed 'blɪɚ·, -z, -ɹɪŋ, -d
bleat, -s, -ing, -ed 'blit, -s, -ɪŋ, -ɪd
bleed, -s, -ing, bled 'blid, -z, -ɪŋ, 'bled
blench, -es, -ing, -ed 'blentʃ, -ɪz, -ɪŋ, -t
blend, -s, -ing, -ed, blent 'blend, -z, -ɪŋ,
   -ɪd, 'blent
blender, -s 'blendɚ·, -z
blent (*p.t. and p.p. of* **blend**, *q.v.*) 'blent
bless, -es, -ing, -ed, blest 'bles, -ɪz, -ɪŋ, -t,
   'blest
blessed (*adj.*), **-ly, -ness** 'blesɪd, -lɨ, -nɪs
blessing (*s.*), **-s** 'blesɪŋ, -z
blew (*p.t. of* **blow**, *q.v.*) 'blu
blind, -s, -ing, -ed; -er -est, -ly, -ness
   'blaǐnd, -z, -ɪŋ, -ɪd; -ɚ·, -ɪst, -lɨ, -nɪs
blind-worm, -s 'blaǐnd,wɝ·m, -z
blink, -s, -ing, -ed 'blɪŋk, -s, -ɪŋ, -t
bliss 'blɪs
bliss|ful, -fully, -fulness 'blɪs|fʊl, -fʊlɨ,
   -fʊlnɪs
blister, -s, -ing, -ed 'blɪstɚ·, -z, -ɹɪŋ, -d
blithe, -r, -st, -ly, -ness 'blaǐð, -ɚ·, -ɪst, -lɨ,
   -nɪs
Blithild (HV) 'blɪðɪld ['blɪθɪld]
blob, -s 'blɒb, -z
block, -s, -ing, -ed, -er/s 'blɒk, -s, -ɪŋ, -t,
   -ɚ/z
blockhead, -s 'blɒkfied, -z
blockish, -ly, -ness 'blɒkɪʃ, -lɨ, -nɪs
Blois (1HVI) 'blwɑ ['blɔǐz]
bloke, -s 'bloǔk, -s
blood, -s 'blʌd, -z
blood-boltered 'blʌd,boǔltɚd
blood-drinking 'blʌd,dɹɪŋkɪŋ
blood-sacrifice, -s 'blʌd,sækɹɪfaǐs, -ɪz
bloodshed 'blʌdʃed
blood-sized 'blʌd,saǐzd
bloodstained 'blʌd,steǐnd

---

i w**e** ɪ c**i**ty ɪ h**i**t e l**e**t ɛ d**e**but æ c**a**n a p**a**ss ɝ· b**i**rd ʌ h**u**t ə **a**gain ɚ supp**er** u y**ou**
ʊ sh**ou**ld o **o**bey ɔ **aw**l ɒ c**o**p ɑ f**a**ther eǐ p**ai**d aǐ h**igh** oǔ g**o** ɔǐ v**oi**ce aǔ f**ou**nd ɪɚ **ear**
ɛɚ **air** ʊɚ **poor** ɔɚ **fork** ɑɚ **park** aǐɚ **fire** aǔɚ **hour** b **b**oy p **p**it d **d**og t **t**op g g**o**t
k **k**id h **h**ow fi be**h**ave dʒ **j**ot tʃ **ch**ew z **z**any s **s**oft v **v**at f **f**at ʒ trea**s**ure ʃ **sh**ip ð **th**e
θ **th**in m **m**an n **n**o ŋ ha**ng** l **l**ip j **y**es w **w**on ʍ **wh**ew ɹ **r**igger, ai**r**y ɡ̊ ma**tt**er

blood(-)sucker, -s 'blʌd,sʌkə, -z
blood|y, -ier, -iest, -ily, -iness 'blʌd|ɪ, -ɪə,
 -ɪɪst, -ɪlɪ, -ɪnɪs
bloody-faced 'blʌdɪ,feɪst
bloody-minded 'blʌdɪ,maɪndɪd
bloody-sceptered 'blʌdɪ,septəd
bloom, -s, -ing, -ed 'blum, -z, -ɪŋ, -d
blossom, -s, -ing, -ed 'blɒsəm, -z, -ɪŋ, -d
blot, -s, -ting, -ted 'blɒt, -s, -ɪŋ, -ɪd
blotter, -s 'blɒɾə, -z
blow, -s, -ing, -er/s, blew, blown 'bloŭ,
 -z, -ɪŋ, -ə/z, 'blu, 'bloŭn
blowed (archaic form of blown) 'bloŭd
blows|y or blowz|y, -ier, -iest, -ily, -iness
 'blaŭz|ɪ, -ɪə, -ɪɪst, -ɪlɪ, -ɪnɪs
blowze, -s 'blaŭz, -ɪz
blubber, -s, -ing, -ed, -er/s 'blʌbə, -z,
 -ɹɪŋ, -d, -ɹə/z
blue, -s, -ing, -d; -r, -st 'blu, -z, -ɪŋ, -d;
 -ə, -ɪst
bluebottle, -s 'blubɒtl̩, -z
blue-cap (Scotsman), -s 'blu,kæp, -s
blue-veined 'blu,veɪnd
bluish 'bluɪʃ
blunder, -s, -ing, -ed, -er/s 'blʌndə, -z,
 -ɹɪŋ, -d, -ɹə/z
blunt, -s, -ing, -ed; -er, -est, -ly, -ness
 'blʌnt, -s, -ɪŋ, -ɪd; -ə, -ɪst, -lɪ, -nɪs
Blunt or Blount, Sir James (RIII) ,sɜ
 'dʒeɪmz 'blʌnt
Blunt or Blount, Sir John (2HIV) ,sɜ
 'dʒɒn 'blʌnt
Blunt or Blount, Sir Thomas (RII) ,sɜ
 'tɒməs 'blʌnt
Blunt or Blount, Sir Walter (1HIV) ,sɜ
 'wɔltə 'blʌnt
blunt-witted 'blʌnt,wɪtɪd
blur, -s, -ring, -red 'blɜ, -z, -ɹɪŋ, -d
blurt, -s, -ing, -ed 'blɜt, -s, -ɪŋ, -ɪd
blush, -es, -ing/ly, -ed, -er/s 'blʌʃ, -ɪz,
 -ɪŋ/lɪ, -t, -ə/z
bluster, -s, -ing/ly, -ed, -er/s 'blʌstə, -z,
 -ɹɪŋ/lɪ, -d, -ɹə/z
boa, -s 'boŭə, -z
boar, -s 'bɔə, -z
board, -s, -ing, -ed, -er/s 'bɔəd, -z, -ɪŋ,
 -ɪd, -ə/z
boar-pig, -s 'bɔə,pɪg, -z
boar-spear, -s 'bɔə,spɪə, -z

boast, -s, -ing, -ed, -er/s 'boŭst, -s, -ɪŋ,
 -ɪd, -ə/z
boat, -s, -ing, -er/s 'boŭt, -s, -ɪŋ, -ə/z
boatswain (B.), -s 'boŭsn̩, -z
bob, -s, -bing, -bed 'bɒb, -z, -ɪŋ, -d
bobbin, -s 'bɒbɪn, -z
bobtail, -s 'bɒbteɪl, -z
Bocchus (AC) 'bɒkəs
bod|e, -es, -ing, -ed, -ment/s 'boŭd, -z,
 -ɪŋ, -ɪd, -mənt/s
bodkin, -s 'bɒdkɪn, -z
bod|y, -ies 'bɒd|ɪ, -ɪz
body-curer 'bɒdɪ,kjŭəɹə
body(-)kins 'bɒdɪkɪnz
bog, -s 'bɒg, -z
bogg|le, -les, -ling, -led, -ler/s 'bɒg|l̩, -l̩z,
 -lɪŋ [-l̩ɪŋ], -l̩d, -l̩ə/z [-lə/z]
Bohemia (WT) bo'himɪə
Bohemian (MEAS) bo'himɪən
Bohemian-Tartar (MWW) bo'himɪən
 'taətə ['taəɾə]
Bohun, Edward (HVIII) 'edwəd 'bun
boil, -s, -ing, -ed, -er/s 'bɔɪl, -z, -ɪŋ, -d,
 -ə/z
boiled-brains 'bɔɪld,bɹeɪnz
boisterous, -ly, -ness 'bɔɪstəɹəs, -lɪ, -nɪs
boisterous-rough 'bɔɪstəɹəs,ɹʌf
bold, -er, -est, -ly, -ness 'boŭld, -ə, -ɪst,
 -lɪ, -nɪs
boldened 'boŭldənd
bolin, -s 'boŭlɪn, -z
Note.—This word in PER, III.i.43 (pl.) is
 an older form of 'bow-lines,' and like
 many nautical words and terms, reflects
 its customary pronunciation, despite the
 fact that 'bow' by itself is pronounced
 ['baŭ] (cf. Note for mainsail)
Bolingbroke (1HIV, 2HIV, 1HVI, 2HVI,
 RII) 'bɒlɪŋbɹʊk [-lɪn-]
Bolingbroke, Henry (2HVI, RII) 'henɹɪ
 'bɒlɪŋbɹʊk [-lɪn-]
Bolingbroke, Roger (2HVI) 'ɹɒdʒə
 'bɒlɪŋbɹʊk [-lɪn-]
bollen (obsolete archaic word meaning
 'swollen') 'boŭlən ['boŭln]
Note.—Some editions of S. retain the
 older form 'boln(e)' in LUC, 1417, to
 reflect its metric value as a monosyllable; others give 'boll'n'

bolster, -s, -ing, -ed 'boŭlstə˞, -z, -ɹɪŋ, -d
bolt, -s, -ing, -ed 'boŭlt, -s, -ɪŋ, -ɪd
bolter, -s 'boŭltə˞, -z
bolting-hutch 'boŭltɪŋˌhʌtʃ
bomb, -s, -ing, -ed 'bɒm, -z, -ɪŋ, -d
bombard (*s.*), **-s** 'bɒmbɑ˞d, -z
bombard (*v.*), **-s, -ing, -ed, -ment/s**
  bɒm'bɑ˞d [bəm-], -z, -ɪŋ, -ɪd, -mənt/s
bombast 'bɒmbæst
bombastic bɒm'bæstɪk
Bona, Lady (*3HVI*, RIII) 'leĭdɨ 'boŭnə
bona-roba (*It.*) (2HIV, III.ii.22) (*hand-some wench, up-market whore*), **-s**
  'bɒnɑ'robɑ, -z
bona terra, mala gens (*L.*) (2HVI, IV.
  vii.54) ˌbɒnɑ 'tɛɾɑ ˌmɑlɑ 'ʤɛnz
bond, -s, -ing, -ed; -age 'bɒnd, -z, -ɪŋ,
  -ɪd; -ɪdʒ
bondmaid, -s 'bɒn*d*meĭd, -z
bond|man, -men 'bɒnd|mən, -mən
bond(-)slave, -s 'bɒn*d*sleĭv, -z
bon|e, -es, -ing, -ed 'boŭn, -z, -ɪŋ, -d
bone-ache 'boŭnˌeĭk
bonfire, -s 'bɒn faĭ˞, -z
bonfire-light 'bɒn faĭ˞ˌlaĭt
bonnet, -s, -ing, -ed 'bɒnɪt, -s, -ɪŋ, -ɪd
bonn|y, -ier, -iest, -ily, -iness 'bɒn|ɨ, -ɪə˞,
  -ɪɪst, -ɪlɨ, -ɪnɪs
bonos dies (*L.*) (TN, IV.ii.13) 'bonos 'diɛs
  Note.—This is merely a bad form of
  Latin, the correct form being 'bonus
  dies'
Bonville, Lord (3HVI) ˌbɔ˞d 'bɒnvɪl
book, -s, -ing, -ed, -er/s 'bʊk, -s, -ɪŋ, -t,
  -ə˞/z
bookish, -ly, -ness 'bʊkɪʃ, -lɨ, -nɪs
book-mate, -s 'bʊkˌmeĭt, -s
Book of Numbers (HV) ˌbʊk əv 'nʌmbə˞z
Book of Riddles (MWW) ˌbʊk əv 'ɹɪdl̩z
  Note.—This is the title of a book,
  mentioned in MWW, I.i.186, 188
boon, -s 'bun, -z
boor, -s 'bʊ˞, -z
boorish, -ly, -ness 'bʊ˞ɹɪʃ, -lɨ, -nɪs

boost, -s, -ing, -ed, -er/s 'bust, -s, -ɪŋ, -ɪd,
  -ə˞/z
boot, -s, -ing, -ed 'but, -s, -ɪŋ, -ɪd
bootee *or* **bootie** (*shoe for a baby*), **-s** 'butɨ
  ['buɾɨ], -z
boo|th, -s 'bu|θ, -ðz [-θs]
boot-hose 'butˌfioŭz
bootless, -ly, -ness 'butlɪs, -lɨ, -nɪs
  Note.—In 1HIV, III.i.63, this word is
  arguably pronounced trisyllabically, to
  fit the metrical requirement of the line,
  and perhaps owing to the speaker's
  (Owen Glendower of Wales) dialect—
  S. often wrote in dialectal form for some
  of his Welshmen (see **prings**). *Perhaps*
  the extra beat at the end of the previous
  line is sufficient to make up the differ-
  ence. If three syllables are desired, then
  the pronunciation ['buətlɪs] *is recom-*
  mended
boot|y (*plunder or gain*), **-ies** 'buɾ̥|ɨ, -ɨz
bo-peep (**B.**) bo'pip [boŭ'p-]
Borachio (*ADO*) bo'ɹɑkɪoŭ [-'ɹɑtʃɪoŭ]
Boreas (TC) 'bɔɹɪəs, -ɹĭəs
Bordeaux (2HIV, 1HVI, HVIII, RII)
  bɔ˞'doŭ ['--]
  Note.—The common spelling of this
  name in S., i.e., 'Burde(a)ux,' and the
  fact that it is always given primary stress
  on the first syllable lends weight to the
  notion that the typical pronunciation in
  S.'s day was probably—and especially
  when spoken by those allied to the
  English cause—akin to a stubbornly
  anglicized ['bɝdəks] (*cf. 'Shakespeare's*
  Verse' § 1.8 of this dictionary; and see
  Calais*)*
boresprit, -s 'bɔ˞spɹɪt, -s
born (*p.p. of* **bear**; *bring to life*) 'bɔ˞n
borne (*from* **bear**; *support or carry*)
  'bɔ˞n
borough, -s 'bʌɹoŭ [bʊɹ-, -ɹə], -z
borrow, -s, -ing, -ed, -er/s 'bɒɹoŭ, -z, -ɪŋ,
  -d, -ə˞/z

i w**e** ɨ c**i**ty ɪ h**i**t e l**e**t ɛ d**e**but æ c**a**n a p**a**ss ɝ b**ir**d ʌ h**u**t ə **a**gain ə˞ s**u**pp**er** u y**ou**
ʊ sh**ou**ld o **o**bey ɔ **aw**l ɒ c**o**p ɑ f**a**ther eĭ p**ai**d aĭ h**igh** oŭ g**o** ɔĭ v**oi**ce aŭ f**ou**nd ɪ˞ **ear**
ɛ˞ **air** ʊ˞ **poor** ɔ˞ **fork** ɑ˞ **park** aĭ˞ **fire** aŭ˞ **hour** b b**oy** p p**i**t d d**o**g t t**o**p g g**o**t
k k**i**d h h**ow** fi be**h**ave dʒ j**o**t tʃ **ch**ew z **z**any s **s**oft v **v**at f f**a**t ʒ trea**s**ure ʃ **sh**ip ð **th**e
θ **th**in m **m**an n **n**o ŋ ha**ng** l l**i**p j **y**es w **w**on ʍ **wh**ew ɹ **r**igger, ai**r** ɾ̥ ma**tt**er

bosky 'bɒskɨ
bosom, -s, -ed 'bʊzəm, -z, -d
boss, -es, -ing, -ed 'bɒs, -ɪz, -ɪŋ, -t
boss|y, -ier, -iest, -ily, -iness 'bɒs|ɨ, -ɪə˞,
  -ɪɪst, -ɪlɨ, -ɪnɪs
bo(')sun (var. of boatswain), -s 'boŭsn̩, -z
botch, -es, -ing, -ed, -er/s; -y 'bɒtʃ, -ɪz,
  -ɪŋ, -t, -ə˞/z; -ɨ
bot(t) (parasitic worms, larvae, mag-
  gots), -s 'bɒt, -s
bottl|e, -es, -ing, -ed, -er/s 'bɒtl̩, -z, -ɪŋ,
  -d, -ə˞/z
bottle-ale 'bɒtl̩ˌeɪl
bottom, -s, -ing, -ed; -less 'bɒɾəm, -z, -ɪŋ,
  -d; -lɪs
Bottom, Nick (MSND) 'nɪk 'bɒtəm
  ['bɒɾəm]
Boucicault (HV) 'busɨkɔl(t) [Fr. busɨko]
bough, -s 'baŭ, -z
bought (p.t. and p.p. of buy, q.v.) 'bɔt
Boult (PER) 'boŭlt
bound, -s, -ing, -ed 'baŭnd, -z, -ɪŋ, -ɪd
bound (p.t. and p.p. of bind, q.v.) 'baŭnd
bound-a 'baŭndə
  Note.—This word, along with 'sound-a,'
  'Barbary-a,' and 'three-a,' appears in
  the ditty sung by the Gaoler's Daughter
  in TNK, III.v; the extra syllable there
  merely to provide for another musical
  beat in the tetrameter line of song
bounden 'baŭndən
boundless, -ly, -ness 'baŭndlɪs, -lɨ, -nɪs
bounteous, -ly, -ness 'baŭntɪəs [-tjəs], -lɨ,
  -nɪs
bount|y (B.), -ies 'baŭnt|ɨ, -ɨz
Bourbon, Duke of (HV) 'djuk əv
  'buˤ˞bən [Fr. buᵏbɔ̃]
Bourbon, High Admiral (3HVI) 'haɪ
  'ædmə˞ɹəl 'buˤ˞bən [Fr. buᵏbɔ̃]
Bourchier, Lord Cardinal (RIII) 'lɔˤ˞d
  'kaˤ˞dn̩l 'baŭtʃə˞
bourn(e), -s 'buˤ˞n ['bɔˤ˞n], -z
bout, -s 'baŭt, -s
'bout (from about) 'baŭt
'bove (from above) 'bʌv
bow-back 'boŭˌbæk
bow-boy, -s 'boŭˌbɔɪ, -z
bow-case 'boŭˌkeɪs

bowel, -s 'baŭəl, -z
bower, -s 'baŭˤ˞, -z
bowline, -s 'boŭlɪn, -z
bowsprit, -s 'baŭspɹɪt, -s
bow(-)string, -s 'boŭstɹɪŋ, -z
box, -es, -ing, -ed, -er/s 'bɒks, -ɪz, -ɪŋ, -t,
  -ə˞/z
box-tree, -s 'bɒksˌtɹi, -z
boy (B.) (ADO, HV, Sonn. 126), -s 'bɔɪ,
  -z
Boyet (LLL) bɔɪ'et
  Note.—In yet another example of how S.
  treats foreign words (especially names),
  this name rhymes with 'debt' in LLL,
  V.ii.333, 334 (see 'Shakespeare's Verse'
  § 1.8 of this dictionary—also cf.
  Berowne and **Longaville**)
boyhood, -s 'bɔɪfiʊd, -z
boyish, -ly, -ness 'bɔɪɪʃ, -lɨ, -nɪs
boy-queller 'bɔɪˌkwelə˞
bra, -s 'bɹɑ, -z
Brabant (HV, LLL) bɹə'bænt ['bɹæbənt]
  Note.—This name is always ['bɹæbənt]
  in S.
Brabantio (OTH) bɹə'bænjoŭ
brabb|le, -les, -ling, -led, -ler/s 'bɹæb|l̩,
  -l̩z, -l̩ɪŋ [-lɪŋ], -l̩d, -lə˞/z [-lə˞/z]
Brabbler (TC) 'bɹæblə˞
brac|e, -es, -ing, -ed 'bɹeɪs, -ɪz, -ɪŋ, -t
bracelet, -s 'bɹeɪslɪt, -s
brach (bitch-hound), -es 'bɹætʃ, -ɪz
brach (used in prosody), -s 'bɹæk, -s
Brach, Lady (LEAR) 'leɪdɨ 'bɹætʃ
  Note.—This may or may not be a proper
  name. There is some debate among
  editors about the term in LEAR,
  I.iv.110. 'Brach' is another word for a
  bitch-hound, so presumably to avoid a
  seeming redundancy (female
  female-dog), 'the Lady Brach' is often
  emended to 'Lady the brach' (the pet
  bitch-hound named Lady). However, 'the
  Lady Brach' plays every bit as well if the
  Fool is making an ironic reference to
  Goneril or Regan
Bracy, Sir John (1HIV) ˌsɚ 'dʒɒn 'bɹeɪsɨ
brag, -s, -ging, -ged, -ger/s 'bɹæg, -z, -ɪŋ,
  -d, -ə˞/z

braggard (*form of* braggart), -ism
'bɹægəˑd, -ızm̩

braggart, -s 'bɹægəˑt, -s

bragless 'bɹæglıs

braid, -s, -ing, -ed 'bɹeĭd, -z, -ıŋ, -ıd

brain, -s, -ing, -ed 'bɹeĭn, -z, -ıŋ, -d

brainless, -ness 'bɹeĭnlıs, -nıs

brain(-)sick, -ly 'bɹeĭnsık, -lɪ

brain|y, -ier, -iest, -ish 'bɹeĭn|ɪ, -ɪəˑ, -ɪıst, -ıʃ

brais|e, -es, -ing, -ed 'bɹeĭz, -ız, -ıŋ, -d

brak|e, -es, -ing, -ed 'bɹeĭk, -s, -ıŋ, -t

Brakenbury, Sir Robert (*RIII*) ˌsɜˑ 'ɹɒbəˑt 'bɹækənbəˑɹɪ

bramble, -s 'bɹæmbl̩, -z

bran 'bɹæn

branch, -es, -ing, -ed; -less 'bɹantʃ, -ız, -ıŋ, -t; -lɪs

Brandon, Charles (*HVIII*) 'tʃɑ˞lz 'bɹændən

Brandon, Sir William (*RIII*) ˌsɜˑ 'wıljəm 'bɹændən

brat (*ill-mannered child*), -s 'bɹæt, -s

brav|e, -es, -ing, -ed; -er, -est, -ely, -eness 'bɹeĭv, -z, -ıŋ, -d; -əˑ, -ıst, -lɪ, -nıs

Note.—In Frank Kermode's (editor, The Arden Shakespeare, 1958) annotation for TEM, I.ii.53, there is a brief but valuable discussion about monosyllabic words that sometimes receive the value of two metric beats in S. lines of verse "whether or no it is [they are] pronounced disyllabically . . ." In TEM, I.ii.206, 'brave' is arguably pronounced disyllabically or given, as Kermode puts it, "a heavy emphasis." Cf. Abbott's A Shakespearian Grammar, §§ 475, 479, 484

brawl, -s, -ing, -ed, -er/s 'bɹɔl, -z, -ıŋ, -d, -əˑ/z

brawn, -s 'bɹɔn, -z

brawn-buttock 'bɹɔnˌbʌɣək

brawn|y, -ier, -iest, -iness 'bɹɔn|ɪ, -ɪəˑ, -ɪıst, -ınıs

bray, -s, -ing, -ed 'bɹeĭ, -z, -ıŋ, -d

braz|e, -es, -ing, -ed 'bɹeĭz, -ız, -ıŋ, -d

brazen, -ly, -ness 'bɹeĭzn̩, -lɪ, -nıs

brazen-face, -d 'bɹeĭzn̩ˌfeĭs, -t

brazier, -s 'bɹeĭʒəˑ, -z

breach, -es, -ing, -ed 'bɹitʃ, -ız, -ıŋ, -t

bread, -s 'bɹed, -z

bread-chipper 'bɹedˌtʃıpəˑ

breadth, -s 'bɹedθ, -s

break, -s, -ing, broke, broken 'bɹeĭk, -s, -ıŋ, 'bɹoŭk, 'bɹoŭkən

breakable, -s 'bɹeĭkəbl̩, -z

breaker, -s 'bɹeĭkəˑ, -z

breakfast, -s, -ing, -ed 'bɹekfəst, -s, -ıŋ, -ıd

break-neck 'bɹeĭknek

break-promise 'bɹeĭkˌpɹɒmıs

break-vow 'bɹeĭkˌvaŭ

breast, -s, -ing, -ed 'bɹest, -s, -ıŋ, -ıd

breast-deep 'bɹestˌdip

breath, -s 'bɹeθ, -s

breath|e, -es, -ing, -ed 'bɹið, -z, -ıŋ, -d

breathed (*adj.*) 'bɹeθt, 'bɹiðd

Note.—The OED cites that, "In early instances it is not easy to separate the verbal from the noun-derivative, nor to fix the pronunciation." In AC, III. xiii.178, the word treble modifies sinew, heart, and breath; therefore, it is most likely pronounced ['bɹeθt] rather than ['bɹiðd]; likewise in AYLI, I.ii.206, meaning 'well-exercised' (cf. **out-breathed**). In TS, Ind.ii.49, it means 'strong-winded' or 'long-winded,' and because it must be disyllabic (due to the metrical requirements of the verse line), it is either ['bɹeθıd] or ['bɹiðıd]

breather, -s 'bɹiðəˑ, -z

breathiness 'bɹeθınıs

breathings 'bɹiðıŋz

breathless, -ly, -ness 'bɹeθlıs, -lɪ, -nıs

---

i we ɪ city ɪ hit e let ɛ debut æ can a pass ɜˑ bird ʌ hut ə again əˑ supper u you
ʊ should o obey ɔ awl ɒ cop ɑ father eĭ paid aĭ high oŭ go ɔĭ voice aŭ found ɪ˞ ear
ɛɜˑ air ʊɜˑ poor ɔɜˑ fork ɑɜˑ park aĭɜˑ fire aŭɜˑ hour b boy p pit d dog t top g got
k kid h how fi behave dʒ jot tʃ chew z zany s soft v vat f fat ʒ treasure ʃ ship ð the
θ thin m man n no ŋ hang l lip j yes w won ʍ whew ɹ rigger, airy ɾ matter

breath|y, -ier, -iest 'bɹeθ|ɪ, -ɪə·, -ɪɪst
Brecknock (RIII) 'bɹeknək [-nɒk]
breech (*of firearms, etc.*), **-es, -ing, -ed** 'bɹɪtʃ, -ɪz, -ɪŋ, -t
breeches (*clothing*) 'bɹɪtʃɪz
breeching, -s 'bɹɪtʃɪŋ ['bɹɪtʃɪŋ], -z
breed, -s, -ing, bred 'bɹid, -z, -ɪŋ, 'bɹed
breed-bate (*trouble-maker*), **-s** 'bɹid,beɪt, -s
breeder, -s 'bɹidə·, -z
breese, -s 'bɹiz, -ɪz
breeze, -s 'bɹiz, -ɪz
breez|y, -ier, -iest, -ily, -iness 'bɹiz|ɪ, -ɪə·, -ɪɪst, -ɪlɪ, -ɪnɪs
breff (*from 'brief '*) 'brɛˑf
Note.—Jamy (in HV) is a Scotsman, and speaks with a Scots accent, if somewhat inconsistently. This is an example of S.'s direction to the actor (by way of semiphonetic spellings) to adopt such an accent, more or less. Note the trilled (or fluttered) [r] characteristic of the Scots tongue (see 'Shakespeare's Foreign Languages' § 3.1 of this dictionary)
Brentford (MWW) 'bɹentfə·d
Note.—In both the Folio and Quarto versions of MWW, this name is always spelled 'Brain(e)ford,' indicating the pronunciation ['bɹeɪnfəd], *which Kökeritz asserts is still the pronunciation locally (cf. Kökeritz's* Shakespeare's Names: A Pronouncing Dictionary, *1972, p. 38)*
Bretagne (HV, 2HVI, RII, RIII) 'bɹɪtən [-tn̩]
brethren 'bɹeðɹɪn
Note.—Often trisyllabic in S., i.e., ['bɹeðə·ɹɪn]. *Early texts sometimes spell the word as 'bretheren' (cf. TIT, I.i.353, First Quarto version, and TIT, I.i.362, Third Quarto version)*
Breton *or* **Briton** (RII, RIII) 'bɹɪtən [-tn̩]
Note.—In the Folio and Quartos, this name is always spelled 'Brit(t)aine'
brevity 'bɹevɪtɪ
brew, -s, -ing, -ed, -er/s; -age 'bɹu, -z, -ɪŋ, -d, -ə·/z; -ɪdʒ
brewer|y, -ies 'bɹuə·ɹ|ɪ ['bɹuə·-], -ɪz

brew-hou|se, -ses 'bɹu,haŏ|s, -zɪz
briar, -s 'bɹaɪə·, -z
Briareus (TC) bɹaɪ'ɛə·ɹɪəs
brib|e, -es, -ing, -ed, -er/s 'bɹaɪb, -z, -ɪŋ, -d, -ə·/z
briber|y, -ies 'bɹaɪbə·ɹ|ɪ, -ɪz
brick, -s, -ing, -ed 'bɹɪk, -s, -ɪŋ, -t
bricklayer, -s 'bɹɪkleɪə·, -z
bricklaying 'bɹɪkleɪɪŋ
bridal 'bɹaɪdl̩
bride, -s, -ed 'bɹaɪd, -z, -ɪd
bride-chamber, -s 'bɹaɪd,tʃeɪmbə·, -z
bridegroom, -s 'bɹaɪdgɹum [-gɹʊm], -z
bride-habited 'bɹaɪd,fiæbɪtɪd
bride-hou|se, -ses 'bɹaɪdfiaŏ|s, -zɪz
bridesmaid, -s 'bɹaɪdzmeɪd, -z
bridg|e (B.), **-es, -ing, -ed** 'bɹɪdʒ, -ɪz, -ɪŋ, -d
Bridg(e)north (1HIV) 'bɹɪdʒnɔə·θ
Bridget (COM, MEAS, MWW) 'bɹɪdʒɪt
brid|le, -les, -ling, -led 'bɹaɪd|l̩, -l̩z, -l̩ɪŋ [-lɪŋ], -l̩d
brief, -s, -ing/s, -ed; -er, -est, -ly, -ness 'bɹif, -s, -ɪŋ/z, -t; -ə·, -ɪst, -lɪ, -nɪs
brier, -s 'bɹaɪə·, -z
brig, -s 'bɹɪg, -z
brigand, -s 'bɹɪgənd, -z
bright, -er, -est, -ly, -ness 'bɹaɪt, -ə·, -ɪst, -lɪ, -nɪs
bright-burning 'bɹaɪt,bə·nɪŋ
bright|en, -ens, -ening, -ened 'bɹaɪt|n̩, -n̩z, -n̩ɪŋ [-nɪŋ], -n̩d
brim, -s, -ming, -med 'bɹɪm, -z, -ɪŋ, -d
brim(-)ful(l) ,bɹɪm'fʊl ['-]
brimstone 'bɹɪmstoŏn
brinded 'bɹɪndɪd
brin|e, -es, -ing, -ed, -ey, -ish 'bɹaɪn, -z, -ɪŋ, -d, -ɪ, -ɪʃ
brine-pit, -s 'bɹaɪnpɪt, -s
bring, -s, -ing, brought, bringer/s 'bɹɪŋ, -z, -ɪŋ, 'bɹɔt, 'bɹɪŋə·/z
bringings-forth ,bɹɪŋɪŋz'fɔə·θ
bringing-up ,bɹɪŋɪŋ'ʌp
brisk, -er, -est, -ly, -ness, -y 'bɹɪsk, -ə·, -ɪst, -lɪ, -n ɪs, -ɪ
brist|le, -les, -ling, -led 'bɹɪs|l̩, -l̩z, -l̩ɪŋ [-lɪŋ], -l̩d
bristly 'bɹɪslɪ [-slɪ]

Bristow (1HIV, 2HVI, RII) 'bɹɪstoŭ
Note.—This is the older form of, and the Folio's way of spelling, 'Bristol,' and most likely represents a more traditional pronunciation
Britain (CYM, HVIII, KJ, LLL) 'bɹɪtn̩ [-tən]
Britain, Duke of (*HV*) 'djuk əv 'bɹɪtn̩ [-tən]
Britany, Brittany, *or* **Britanny** (3HVI, RII, RIII) 'bɹɪtn̩ɨ [-tənɨ]
British (CYM, LEAR) 'bɹɪtɪʃ [-ɪɾɪʃ]
Briton (CYM), **-s** 'bɹɪtn̩ [-tən], -z
Brit(t)aine (RII, RIII) 'bɹɪtən [-tn̩]
Note.—This name is usually emended to 'Breton' or 'Briton'
brittle, -r, -st, -ly, -ness 'bɹɪtl̩, -ɚ, -ɪst, -lɨ, -nɪs
broach, -es, -ing, -ed 'bɹoŭtʃ, -ɪz, -ɪŋ, -t
broad, -er, -est, -ly, -ness 'bɹɔd, -ɚ, -ɪst, -lɨ, -nɪs
broadside, -s 'bɹɔdsaɪd, -z
broadsword, -s 'bɹɔdsɔɚd, -z
Broc(c)as (RII) 'bɹɔkəs
brock, -s 'bɹɒk, -s
brogue, -s 'bɹoŭg, -z
broil, -s, -ing, -ed, -er/s 'bɹɔɪl, -z, -ɪŋ, -d, -ɚ/z
brok|e, -es, -ing, -ed 'bɹoŭk, -s, -ɪŋ, -t
broke (*p.t. of* **break**, *q.v.*), **-n/ly** 'bɹoŭk, -ən/lɨ
broker-lackey 'bɹoŭkɚˌlækɨ
Note.—This word, supplied for TC, V.x.33 *and adopted by some modern editors, is a conjectural creation of Lewis Theobald, a classical scholar and S. editor in the early eighteenth century. The First Folio gives (aptly enough) 'Hence broker, lackie, ignomy, and shame'*
brokers-between 'bɹoŭkɚzbɪˈtwin
bronz|e, -es, -ing, -ed 'bɹɒnz, -ɪz, -ɪŋ, -d
brooch, -es, -ed 'bɹoŭtʃ, -ɪz, -t

brood, -s, -ing, -ed 'bɹud, -z, -ɪŋ, -ɪd
brood|y, -ily, -iness 'bɹud|ɨ, -ɪlɨ, -ɨnɪs
Brook (MWW) 'bɹʊk
Brook, Edmund (3HVI) 'edmənd 'bɹʊk
brook, -s, -ing, -ed 'bɹʊk, -s, -ɪŋ, -t
broom, -s 'bɹum, -z
broom-grove, -s 'bɹum'gɹoŭv, -z
broomstaff 'bɹumstaf
Broom, The (TNK) (*a song*) ðə 'bɹum
broth, -s 'bɹɔθ ['bɹɒθ], -s ['bɹɔðz, 'bɹɒðz]
brothel, -s 'bɹɒθl̩, -z
brothel-hou|se, -ses 'bɹɒθl̩ɦɑŭ|s, -zɪz
brother, -s 'bɹʌðɚ, -z
brother-cardinals ˌbɹʌðɚˈkɑɚdn̩lz
brother-justice ˌbɹʌðɚˈdʒʌstɪs
brought (*p.t. and p.p. of* **bring**, *q.v.*) 'bɹɔt
brow, -s 'bɹɑŭ, -z
brow-bound 'bɹɑŭˌbɑŭnd
brown, -s, -ing, -ed; -er, -est, -ness 'bɹɑŭn, -z, -ɪŋ, -d; -ɚ, -ɪst, -nɪs
brownish 'bɹɑŭnɪʃ
Brownist (TN) 'bɹɑŭnɪst
browny 'bɹɑŭnɨ
brows|e, -es, -ing, -ed, -er/s 'bɹɑŭz, -ɪz, -ɪŋ, -d, -ɚ/z
browzing 'bɹɑŭzɪŋ
bruis|e, -es, -ing, -ed, -er/s 'bɹuz, -ɪz, -ɪŋ, -d, -ɚ/z
bruit, -s, -ing, -ed 'bɹut, -s, -ɪŋ, -ɪd
Brundusium (AC) bɹʌnˈdjuzɪəm
brute, -s 'bɹut, -s
brutish, -ly, -ness 'bɹutɪʃ, -lɨ, -nɪs
Brutus, Decius (*JUL*) 'diʃɪəs, -ʃjəs, 'bɹutəs
Brutus, Junius (*COR*, TIT) 'dʒunjəs 'bɹutəs
Brutus, Marcus (2HVI, LUC, *JUL*) 'mɑɚkəs 'bɹutəs
bubb|le, -les, -ling, -led, -ler/s; -ly 'bʌbl̩, -lz, -l̩ɪŋ [-lɪŋ], -l̩d, -lɚ/z [-lɚ/z]; -lɨ [-lɨ]
bubo, -es 'bjuboŭ, -z
bubonic bju'bɒnɪk
bubuncles (*perhaps a conflation of 'buboes' and 'carbuncles'*) 'bjubʌŋkl̩z

Note.—In the Folio version of HV, *III.vi.101, the word Fluellen speaks is 'bubukles,' which in all likelihood is a compositor error (omitting the 'n')*

buck, -s, -ing, -ed 'bʌk, -s, -ɪŋ, -t

buck-basket 'bʌk‚baskɪt

bucket, -s 'bʌkɪt, -s

bucketful, -s 'bʌkɪtfʊl, -z

Buckingham (*2HVI*, 3HVI, *HVIII, RIII*) 'bʌkɪŋəm ['bʌkɪŋ‚ɦæm]

buck|le, -les, -ling, -led 'bʌk|l̩, -l̩z, -lɪŋ [-l̩ɪŋ], -l̩d

buckler, -s 'bʌklə˞, -z

Bucklersbury (MWW) 'bʌklə˞zbə˞ɹɨ

buckram, -s 'bʌkɹəm, -z

buck-washing 'bʌk‚wɒʃɪŋ

bud, -s, -ding, -ded 'bʌd, -z, -ɪŋ, -ɪd

budg|e, -es, -ing, -ed, -er 'bʌdʒ, -ɪz, -ɪŋ, -d, -ə˞

budget, -s, -ing, -ed, -ary 'bʌdʒɪt, -s, -ɪŋ, -ɪd, -ə˞ɹɨ

buff, -s, -ing, -ed, -er/s 'bʌf, -s, -ɪŋ, -t, -ə˞/z

buffet (*sideboard, meal*), **-s** bʊ'feĭ, -z

buffet (*to hit*), **-s, -ing, -ed** 'bʌfɪt, -s, -ɪŋ, -ɪd

bug, -s, -ging, -ged 'bʌg, -z, -ɪŋ, -d

bugbear, -s 'bʌgbɛə˞, -z

bugle, -s 'bjugl̩, -z

bugle-bracelet 'bjugl̩‚bɹeĭslɪt

build, -s, -ing/s, -ed, built, builder/s 'bɪld, -z, -ɪŋ/z, -ɪd, 'bɪlt, 'bɪldə˞/z

bulg|e, -es, -ing, -ed 'bʌldʒ, -ɪz, -ɪŋ, -d

bulk, -s, -ing, -ed 'bʌlk, -s, -ɪŋ, -t

bulkhead, -s 'bʌlkɦed, -z

bulk|y, -ier, -iest, -ily, -iness 'bʌlk|ɨ, -ɪə˞, -ɪɪst, -ɪlɨ, -ɪnɪs

bull (B.), -s, -ing, -ed 'bʊl, -z, -ɪŋ, -d

bull-bearing 'bʊl‚bɛə˞ɹɪŋ

bull-cal|f, -ves 'bʊl‚ka|f, -vz

Bullcalf, Peter (*2HIV*) 'piɾə˞ 'bʊl‚kaf

Bullen *or* **Boleyn, Anne** (*HVIII*) 'æn 'bʊlɪn

Bullen, Sir Thomas (HVIII) ‚sə˞ 'tɒməs 'bʊlɪn

bullet, -s 'bʊlɪt, -s

bulletin, -s 'bʊlɪtɪn, -z

bullock, -s 'bʊlək, -s

bull's-pizzle 'bʊlz‚pɪzl̩

bull|y, -ies, -ying, -ied 'bʊl|ɨ, -ɪz, -ɪɪŋ, -ɪd

bully-monster 'bʊlɨ'mɒnstə˞

Bulmer, Sir William (HVIII) ‚sə˞ 'wɪljəm 'bʊlmə˞

bulrush, -es 'bʊlɹʌʃ, -ɪz

bulwark, -s 'bʊlwə˞k, -s

bum, -s, -ming, -med 'bʌm, -z, -ɪŋ, -d

bum-bail|y, -ies 'bʌm‚beĭl|ɨ, -ɪz

bump, -s, -ing, -ed 'bʌmp, -s, -ɪŋ, -t

bun, -s 'bʌn, -z

bunch, -es, -ing, -ed 'bʌntʃ, -ɪz, -ɪŋ, -t

bunch-backed 'bʌntʃ‚bækt

Bunch of Grapes, the (MEAS) ðə 'bʌntʃ əv 'gɹeĭps

bung, -s, -ing, -ed 'bʌŋ, -z, -ɪŋ, -d

bung-hole, -s 'bʌŋ‚ɦoŏl, -z

bunker, -s, -ing, -ed 'bʌŋkə˞, -z, -ɹɪŋ, -d

bunn|y, -ies 'bʌn|ɨ, -ɪz

bunt, -s, -ing/s, -ed 'bʌnt, -s, -ɪŋ/z, -ɪd

buoy, -s, -ing, -ed 'buɨ ['bɔĭ], -z, -ɪŋ, -d

bur, -s 'bə˞, -z

Burdeaux, Richard of (RII) 'ɹɪtʃə˞d əv 'bə˞dəks

Note.—The common spelling in S. of the name 'Bo(u)rdeaux,' and the fact that it is always given primary stress on the first syllable lends weight to the notion that the typical pronunciation in S.'s day was probably—and especially when spoken by those allied to the English cause—akin to a stubbornly anglicized ['bə˞dəks] *(cf. 'Shakespeare's Verse'* § *1.8 of this dictionary; and see* **Calais***)*

burden, -s, -ing, -ed 'bə˞dn̩, -z, -ɪŋ, -d

burdensome 'bə˞dn̩səm

burden-wise 'bə˞dn̩‚waĭz

burdock, -s 'bə˞dɒk, -s

burgeon, -s, -ing, -ed 'bə˞dʒən, -z, -ɪŋ, -d

burgess, -es 'bə˞dʒɪs, -ɪz

burgh, -s 'bʌɹə, -z

Burgh 'bə˞g (*sometimes* ['bʌɹə])

burgher, -s 'bə˞gə˞, -z

burglar, -s 'bə˞glə˞, -z

burglar|y, -ies 'bə˞glə˞ɹ|ɨ, -ɪz

burgomaster, -s 'bə˞go‚mastə˞, -z

burgonet 'bə˞gənɪt [‚bə˞gə'net]

Burgundy (HV, *1HVI*, 3HVI, LEAR, RIII) 'bə˞gəndɨ

Burgundy, Duchess of (3HVI) ˌdʌtʃɪs əv
'bɝˑɡəndɨ

Burgundy, Duke of (*HV, 1HVI, LEAR*)
ˌdjuk əv 'bɝˑɡəndɨ

burgund|y, -ies 'bɝˑɡənd|ɨ, -ɨz

burier (*from bury, q.v.*), **-s** 'beɹɪɚ, -z

burlap, -s 'bɝˑlæp, -s

burl|y, -ier, -iest, -iness 'bɝˑl|ɨ, -ɪɚ, -ɪɪst,
-ɪnɪs

burn, -s, -ing, -ed, burnt 'bɝˑn, -z, -ɪŋ, -d,
'bɝˑnt

burner, -s 'bɝˑnɚ, -z

burnet (*plant*) 'bɝˑnɪt [bɝˑ'net]

burnish, -es, -ing, -ed, -er/s 'bɝˑnɪʃ, -ɪz,
-ɪŋ, -t, -ɚ/z

burr, -s 'bɝˑ, -z

burrow, -s, -ing, -ed 'bʊɹoʊ ['bʌɹ-], -z,
-ɪŋ, -d

bursar, -s 'bɝˑsɚ, -z

bursar|y, -ies 'bɝˑsɚɹ|ɨ, -ɨz

burst, -s, -ing 'bɝˑst, -s, -ɪŋ

burthen (*obsolete form of* **burden**; *see
Note for* **murther**), **-s** 'bɝˑðn̩, -z

burthenous 'bɝˑð̩ənəs (*see Note for*
murther)

Burton (1HIV) 'bɝˑtn̩

Burton-heath (TS) 'bɝˑtn̩'hiθ

Bury (2HVI, KJ) 'beɹɪ

bur|y, -ies, -ying, -ied 'beɹ|ɨ, -ɨz, -ɪɪŋ, -ɨd

bush, -es, -ing, -ed 'bʊʃ, -ɪz, -ɪŋ, -t

bushel, -s 'bʊʃl̩ [-ʃəl], -z

bush|y, -ier, -iest, -ily, -iness 'bʊʃ|ɨ, -ɪɚ,
-ɪɪst, -ɪlɨ, -ɪnɪs

Bushy, Sir John (*RII*) ˌsɝˑ 'dʒɒn 'bʊʃɨ

busilest 'bɪzɨlɪst

*Note.—This word, which appears in
TEM, III.i.15, is possibly the result of a
compositor's error and the pronunciation provided here is entirely conjectural.
For an in-depth discussion on the matter,
refer to Kermode's editorial in* The
Arden Shakespeare *(1994) pp. 71–73*

business (*occupation, patronage, etc.*),
-es 'bɪznɪs ['bɪznɪs], -ɪz

buskin, -s, -ed 'bʌskɪn, -z, -d

buss, -es, -ing, -ed 'bʌs, -ɪz, -ɪŋ, -t

bust, -s, -ing, -ed 'bʌst, -s, -ɪŋ, -ɪd

bust|le, -les, -ling, -led 'bʌs|l̩, -l̩z, -lɪŋ
[-lɪŋ], -l̩d

bus|y, -ies, -ying, -ied 'bɪz|ɨ, -ɨz, -ɪɪŋ, -ɨd

bus|y, -ier, -iest, -ily, -yness 'bɪz|ɨ, -ɪɚ,
-ɪɪst, -ɪlɨ, -ɪnɪs

but 'bʌt (*strong form*), 'bət (*weak form*)

butcher, -s, -ing, -ed 'bʊtʃɚ, -z, -ɪɪŋ, -d

Butler (1HIV) 'bʌtlɚ

butler, -s 'bʌtlɚ, -z

butt, -s, -ing, -ed 'bʌt, -s, -ɪŋ ['bʌɾɪŋ],
-ɪd

butt-end, -s 'bʌtend, -z

butter, -s, -ing, -ed 'bʌɾɚ, -z, -ɹɪŋ, -d

butter-|woman, -women 'bʌɾɚ|ˌwʊmən,
-ˌwɪmɪn

butter|y, -ies 'bʌɾɚɹ|ɨ ['bʌtɹ|ɨ], -ɨz

buttock, -s 'bʌɾək, -s

button, -s, -ing, -ed 'bʌtn̩, -z, -ɪŋ, -d

buttress, -es 'bʌtɹɪs, -ɪz

Butts, Sir William (*HVIII*) ˌsɝˑ 'wɪljəm
'bʌts

butt-shaft, -s 'bʌt.ʃaft, -s

buxom, -ness 'bʌksəm, -nɪs

buy, -s, -ing, bought 'baɪ, -z, -ɪŋ, 'bɔt

buyer, -s 'baɪɚ, -z

buz(z), -es, -ing, -ed, -er/s bʌz, -ɪz, -ɪŋ,
-d, -ɚ/z

buzzard, -s 'bʌzɚd, -z

by 'baɪ

by-dependances ˌbaɪdɪ'pendənsɪz

by-drinkings 'baɪˌdɹɪŋkɪŋz

by-gone, -s 'baɪɡɒn, -z

by-Lady *or* **ber Lady** bɪ'leɪdɨ, bɚ'leɪdɨ

by-pa|th, -ths 'baɪpa|θ, -ðz

by-peeping 'baɪˈpipɪŋ

by'r Lady *or* **by'rlady** baɪɚˈleɪdɨ

byrlakin *or* **by'r lakin** baɪɚˈleɪkɪn
[bɝˑl-]

by-room, -s 'baɪˌɹum, -z

by't (*contr. of* **by it**) 'baɪt

Byzantium (TIM) bɪ'zæntɪəm [-nʃɪəm]

---

i wɛ ɨ city ɪ hit e let ɛ debut æ can a pass ɝ bird ʌ hut ə again ɚ supper u you
ʊ should o obey ɔ awl ɒ cop ɑ father eɪ paid aɪ high oʊ go ɔɪ voice aʊ found ɪɚ ear
ɛɚ air ʊɚ poor ɔɚ fork ɑɚ park aɪɚ fire aʊɚ hour b boy p pit d dog t top g got
k kid h how fi behave dʒ jot tʃ chew z zany s soft v vat f fat ʒ treasure ʃ ship ð the
θ thin m man n no ŋ hang l lip j yes w won ʍ whew ɹ rigger, airy ɾ matter

Cc

C (*the letter*), **-'s** 'siː, -z
cab, -s 'kæb, -z
cabbage, -s 'kæbɪdʒ, -ɪz
caber, -s 'keɪbɚ, -z
cabileros ˌkæbə'liɚ.ɹos [-.ɹoʊz]
 Note.—*This word, meaning 'gallant*
 knights' or 'gentlemen,' appears in the
 Quarto version of 2HIV, *V.iii.57, and*
 may either be a corruption of the Sp.
 'caballeros,' or (as the Folio version
 seems to indicate with its 'cavileroes') it
 may be an alt. form of 'cavalieroes' (see
 cavaliero*)*
cabin, -s, -ed 'kæbɪn, -z, -d
cab|le, -les, -ling, -led 'keɪb|l̩, -l̩z, -l̩ɪŋ
 [-lɪŋ], -l̩d
Cacaliban (TEM) (*in song*) kə'kælɪbæn
cache, -s 'kæʃ, -ɪz
cack|le, -les, -ling, -led, -ler/s 'kæk|l̩, -l̩z,
 -l̩ɪŋ [-lɪŋ], -l̩d, -l̩ɚ/z [-lə-/z]
cacodemon, -s kæko'dimən
caddis *or* **caddice, caddisses** *or* **caddices**
 'kædɪs, -ɪz
caddis-garter 'kædɪsˌgɑɚ.tɚ
cade, -s 'keɪd, -z
Cade, John 'Jack' (*2HVI*) 'dʒɒn 'dʒæk
 'keɪd
cadent 'keɪdn̩t
Cadmus (MSND) 'kædməs
caduce|us, -i kə'djusɪ|əs, -aɪ
Cadwal (CYM) 'kædwɔl
Cadwallader (HV) kæd'wɔlədɚ
Cælius (AC) 'siljəs, -lɪəs
Cæsar *or* **Caesar** (*AC*, ALL'S, AYLI,
 CYM, HAM, 2HIV, HV, 1HVI, 2HVI,
 3HVI, *JUL*, LLL, MAC, MEAS, MWW,
 OTH, RII, RIII, TIT), **-s** 'sizɚ, -z
Cæsar *or* **Caesar, Augustus** (CYM)
 ɔ'gʌstəs 'sizɚ
Cæsarion (AC) si'zɛɚ.ɹɪən, -.ɹɪən
Cæsar *or* **Caesar, Julius** (AC, ALL'S,
 AYLI, CYM, HAM, 2HIV, 1HVI, 2HVI,
 2HVI, HV, *JUL*, MEAS, LLL, RII, RIII)
 'dʒuljəs 'sizɚ
Cæsar *or* **Caesar, Octavius** (*AC*, *JUL*)
 ɒk'teɪvɪəs, -vjəs 'sizɚ

Cain (HAM, 2HIV, 1HVI, KJ, LLL, RII)
 'keɪn
Cain-colored (MWW) 'keɪnˌkʌlɚd
Ca(i)thnes(s) (*MAC*) 'keɪθnes
caitiff, -s 'keɪtɪf, -s
caitiv|e (*v.; obsolete form of* **caitiff**), **-es,**
 -ing, -ed 'keɪtɪv, -z, -ɪŋ, -d
Caius (*character in S., Roman name*)
 'kaɪəs ['keɪəs]
Caius (*College of Cambridge, England*)
 'kiz
Caius (*TIT*) 'kaɪəs ['keɪəs]
Caius, Doctor (*MWW*) 'dɒktɚ 'kiz
Calaber (2HVI) 'kæləbɚ
Calais (HV, 1HVI, 3HVI, KJ, RII) 'kæleɪ
 ['kælɪs]
 Note.—*This name is also spelled 'Callis'*
 and 'Callice' in S., indicating the
 anglicized pronunciation ['kælɪs]*, e.g.,*
 1HVI, *IV.i.9 and 170, especially when*
 spoken by those allied to the English
 cause (cf. **Bordeaux, la Pucelle,** *and*
 'Shakespeare's Verse' § *1.8 of this*
 dictionary). It is worthwhile mentioning
 Calais, Vermont and Calais, Maine.
 Both were settled in the eighteenth
 century, and both retain the anglicized
 pronunciation ['kælɪs]*; this despite (or*
 perhaps indeed due to) their relatively
 close proximity to the Canadian border
 and the influence of the French on early
 settlers of the region
calamit|y, -ies kə'læmɪt|ɪ, -ɪz
Calchas (*TC*) 'kælkəs
calculat|e, -es, -ing, -ed, -or/s 'kælkjʊleɪt,
 -s, -ɪŋ, -ɪd, -ɚ/z
calculation, -s ˌkælkjʊ'leɪʃn, -z
calendar, -s, -ing, -ed 'kæləndɚ, -z, -.ɹɪŋ,
 -d
calf, calves 'kaf, 'kavz
 Note.—*In* LLL, *V.i.22, the pedant,*
 Holofernes, insists on the pronunciation
 ['kalf] *for 'calf,' as he does* ['half] *for*
 'half' (see **abhominable***)*
Caliban (*TEM*), **-s** 'kælɪbæn [-lɪb-], -z
Calipolis (2HVI) kə'lɪpəlɪs

caliver (*musket*), **-s** kæˈlivɚ [kəˈl-, ˈkælɪvɚ], -z

calk, -s, -ing, -ed ˈkɔk, -s, -ɪŋ, -t

calkin, -s ˈkɔkɪn [ˈkælkɪn], -z

call, -s, -ing, -ed, -er/s ˈkɔl, -z, -ɪŋ, -d, -ɚ/z

callat, callet, *or* **callot** (*slut, trull, or whore*), **-s** ˈkælət, -s

callet, -s ˈkælət, -s

Callice (HV, KJ, RII) (*for 'Calais,' q.v.*) ˈkælɪs

callot, -s ˈkælət, -s

Calp(h)urnia (*JUL*) kælˈpɜ˞nɪə, -njə

calumniat|e, -es, -ing, -ed, -or/s kəˈlʌmnɪeɪt, -s, -ɪŋ, -ɪd, -ɚ/z

calumniation, -s kəˌlʌmnɪˈeɪʃn, -z

calumnious kəˈlʌmnɪəs

calumn|y, -ies ˈkæləmn|ɪ, -ɪz

calv|e, -es, -ing, -ed ˈkav, -z, -ɪŋ, -d

calves'-guts ˈkavzˌɡʌts

calveskin, -s ˈkavskɪn, -z

calve's-skin ˈkavzˌskɪn

Calydon (2HVI) ˈkælɪdɒn

cam, -s ˈkæm, -z

Cambio (TS) ˈkæmbɪoʊ, -bjoʊ

Cambria (CYM) ˈkæmbɹɪə

cambric ˈkeɪmbɹɪk

Cambridge (*HV*, 1HVI, 2HVI) ˈkeɪmbɹɪdʒ

Cambyses, King (1HIV) ˈkɪŋ kæmˈbaɪsɪz

came (*p.t. of* **come***, q.v.*) ˈkeɪm

camel, -s ˈkæml, -z

Camelot (LEAR) ˈkæmɪlɒt

came't (*contr. of* **came it**) ˈkeɪmt

Camillo (*WT*) kəˈmɪloʊ

camlet *or* **chamblet** ˈkæmlɪt

camomile ˈkæməmaɪl [-mom-]

Campeius, Cardinal (*HVIII*) ˈkaɔ˞dn̩l [-dnəl] kæmˈpiəs [-ˈpeɪəs]

can (*auxiliary v.*) ˈkæn (*strong form*), ˈkən (*weak form*)

can (*s., v.*), **-s, -ning, -ned, -ner/s** ˈkæn, -z, -ɪŋ, -d, -ɚ/z

canal, -s kəˈnæl, -z

canar|y, -ies kəˈnɛɚ.ɹ|ɪ, -ɪz

cancel, -s, -(l)ing, -(l)ed ˈkænsəl, -z, -ɪŋ, -d

Cancer (TC) ˈkænsɚ

candidatus (*L.*) (TIT, I.i.185) ˌkandɪˈdɑtus

Note.—If one ever finds it utterly necessary to wring from this word its meaning ('one electable'), one might opt for [ˌkændɪˈdeɪtəs]; *however, in doing so, any advantage there may be in phrasing it in Latin is virtually lost, aside from metrical value*

candle-case, -s ˈkændl̩ˌkeɪs, -ɪz

candle-holder, -s ˈkændl̩ˌfioʊldɚ, -z

candle-mine ˈkændl̩ˌmaɪn

candle-waster, -s ˈkændl̩ˌweɪstɚ, -z

cand|y (**C.**), **-ies, -ying, -ied** ˈkænd|ɪ, -ɪz, -ɪɪŋ, -ɪd

Canidius (*AC*) kæˈnɪdɪəs [kəˈn-]

canker, -s, -ing, -ed ˈkæŋkɚ, -z, -ɪɪŋ, -d

canker-bit ˈkæŋkɚˌbɪt

canker-blossom, -s ˈkæŋkɚˌblɒsəm, -z

canker-sorrow ˈkæŋkɚˌsɒɹoʊ

cannibal (**C.**), **-s; -ly** ˈkænɪbl̩, -z; -ɪ

cannikin, -s ˈkænɪkɪn, -z

cannon, -s ˈkænən, -z

cannon-bullet, -s ˈkænənˌbʊlɪt, -s

cannoneer, -s ˌkænəˈnɪɚ, -z

cannot ˈkænɒt

canoniz|e, -es, -ing, -ed ˈkænənaɪz, -ɪz, -ɪŋ, -d

Note.—This word is stressed on the second syllable [kæˈnɒnaɪz(d)], *as was normal in S's. time, in* HAM, I.iv.47; 2HVI, I.iii.60; KJ, III.i.103, III.iii.52; TC, II.ii.203

canop|y, -ies, -ying, -ied ˈkænəp|ɪ, -ɪz, -ɪɪŋ, -ɪd

canstick (*candlestick*), **-s** ˈkænstɪk, -s

Canterbury (1HIV, *HV*, HVIII, KJ, RII) ˈkæntɚbə.ɹɪ [-bɹɪ]

cantle, -s ˈkæntl, -z

canto, -s ˈkæntoʊ, -z

canton (*songs; var. form of 'canto'*), **-s**
'kæntən [-tɒn], -z

canus (*L.*) (LLL, V.ii.584) 'kɑnus ['keɪ̆nus]
Note.—*Some important circumstances must be considered before deciding on which pronunciation to use for this word. Holofernes, the blowhard pedant, speaks this word in the amateur play-within-the-play in LLL. He uses this incorrect form of (L.) 'canis' (meaning 'dog'), presumably to rhyme more closely with its rhyme-mate, 'manus.' The reference to 'dog' is usually clear due to what's happening visually in the scene; however, if one also wants to aurally evoke 'dog' to the modern ear, then perhaps* ['keɪ̆nus] *is best because of its closeness to the more familiar 'canine.' Whichever pronunciation one chooses, one should take care to match it with 'manus,' meaning that 'manus' might be either* ['mɑnus] *or* ['meɪ̆nus]. *The comedic value might be raised by using the latter set (i.e.,* ['keɪ̆nus/'meɪ̆nus]*) because, by the time Holofernes reaches 'manus,' the audience to the play-within-the-play might be somewhat apprehensive that Holofernes' "Thus did he strangle serpents in his . . ." could just as likely end with 'anus' instead of 'manus'; base humor a la the amateur (and sometimes bawdy) play-within-the-play in* MSND

canvas, -es 'kænvəs, -ɪz

canvass, -es, -ing, -ed, -er/s 'kænvəs, -ɪz, -ɪŋ, -t, -ɚ/z

canyon, -s 'kænjən, -z

canzonet, -s ˌkænzə'net, -s

cap, -s, -ping, -ped 'kæp, -s, -ɪŋ, -t

capacit|y, -ies kə'pæsɪt|ɪ, -ɪz

Capaneus, King (TNK) 'kɪŋ ˌkæpə'niəs
Note.—*Lois Potter, editor of* TNK *(The Arden Shakespeare, 1997) cites that this name (in other forms) would be given primary stress on the second syllable, i.e.,* [kə'peɪ̆nɪəs, -njəs], *and that in Greek, it is spoken in three syllables, supporting a tradition of primary stress on the second syllable. However, in*

TNK, I.i.59, *it is clear that the meter and rhythm of the line require the pronunciation proffered above; as Lois Potter puts it, "here it is stressed on the first and third."*

cap-à-pie *or* **cap-a-pe** ˌkæpə'pi

caparison, -s, -ing, -ed kə'pæɹɪsən, -z, -ɪŋ, -d

Capels (RJ) 'kæpl̩z

cap|er, -ers, -ering, -ered, -erer/s 'keɪ̆p|ɚ, -ɚz, -ɚɪŋ, -ɚd, -ɚɹɚ/z

Caper, Master (MEAS) ˌmɑstɚ 'keɪ̆pɚ

Capet, Hugh (HV) 'hju 'keɪ̆pɪt ['kæpɪt]

Caphis (*TIM*) 'keɪ̆fɪs

Capilet (TN) 'kæpɪlɪt [-let]

Capilet, Diana (*ALL'S*) daɪ̆'ænə 'kæpɪlɪt [-let]

Capilet, Widow (*ALL'S*) 'wɪdoʊ̆ 'kæpɪlɪt [-let]

capitol (C.), **-s** 'kæpɪtl̩, -z

capitulat|e, -es, -ing, -ed kə'pɪtjʊleɪ̆t, -s, -ɪŋ, -ɪd

capon, -s 'keɪ̆pɒn [-pən], -z

Cappadocia (AC) ˌkæpə'doʊ̆ʃɪə, -ʃjə

capriccio (*It.*) (ALL'S, II.iii.289), **-s** kɑ'pritʃo, -z
Note.—*G. K. Hunter (editor,* The Arden Shakespeare, *1962) calls this word, meaning 'caprice,' "an affected word" and probably carries with it little of its native integrity in terms of pronunciation, in which case it probably sounds more like* [kə'pɹitʃɪoʊ̆, -z]

caprice, -s kə'pɹis, -ɪz

capricious, -ly, -ness kə'pɹɪʃəs [-'pɹiʃ-], -lɪ, -nɪs

captain (C.), **-s, -ing, -ed; -ship/s** 'kæptɪn, -z, -ɪŋ, -d; -ʃɪp/s

captain-general ˌkæptɪn'dʒenəɹəl

captious, -ly, -ness 'kæpʃəs, -lɪ, -nɪs

captivate (*adj.*) 'kæptɪvɪt

captivat|e, -es, -ing, -ed 'kæptɪveɪ̆t, -s, -ɪŋ, -ɪd

captive, -s, -d 'kæptɪv, -z, -d

Capuchius (*HVIII*) kə'pjuʃəs [-'pjutʃəs]

Capulet (*RJ*), **-s** 'kæpjʊlɪt, -s

Capulet, Lady (*RJ*) 'leɪ̆dɪ 'kæpjʊlɪt

car, -s 'kɑɚ, -z

caract, -s 'kæɹækt, -s

carafe, -s kə'ɹaf, -s
carat, -s 'kæɹət, -s
caraway, -s 'kæɹəweĭ, -z
carbonado or carbinado, -(e)s, -ing, -ed ˌkaɚˈbə'nadoŭ [-'neĭd-, -bĭ'n-], -z, -ɪŋ, -d
carbuncle, -s, -ed 'kaɚ-bʌŋkl̩, -z, -d
carcanet, -s 'kaɚ-kəˌnet [-kənɪt]
carcase, -s 'kaɚ-kəs, -ɪz
carcass, -es 'kaɚ-kəs, -ɪz
card, -s, -ing, -ed 'kaɚ-d, -z, -ɪŋ, -ɪd
cardecu(e) (coinage; anglicized spelling of Fr. 'quart d'écu') 'kaɚ-dɪkju
carder (wool-comber), -s 'kaɚ-dɚ, -z
cardinal (C.) (1HVI, RIII), -s, -ly; -ship/s 'kaɚ-dn̩l, -z, -ɪ; -ʃɪp/s
cardmaker, -s 'kaɚ-dmeĭkɚ, -z
carduus benedictus (L.) (ADO, III.iv.68) 'kaɚ-dʊəs bɛnɛ'diktus
car|e, -es, -ing, -ed 'kɛɚ-, -z, -ɹɪŋ, -d
care-crazed 'kɛɚ-ˌkɹeĭzd
careen, -s, -ing, -ed kə'ɹin, -z, -ɪŋ, -d
career, -s, -ing, -ed kə'ɹɪɚ, -z, -ɹɪŋ, -d
caret (L.) (LLL, IV.ii.118; MWW, IV.i.46) 'kaɹɛt

Note.—For the humor to play in MWW, it is necessary for the hearer to confuse this word (enough) with 'carrot,' a euphemism here for 'penis'

care-tuned 'kɛɚ-ˌtjund
carl(e) (peasant, serf, rude person, or churl), -s 'kaɚ-l, -z
Carlisle (RII) kaɚ-'laĭl
Carlot (AYLI) or carlot 'kaɚ-lət

Note.—This rare word appears in AYLI, III.v.108 and essentially means 'peasant,' derived from 'carl' (q.v.). It is probably a coinage of S.'s and its only use in literature may be in this line. Since it is italicized in the First Folio—a custom reserved for proper names (among other things)—some editors surmise this word to be the name of a particular (if insignificant) person

car|man, -men 'kaɚ-|mən, -mən

carn|al, -ally 'kaɚ-n|l̩, -əlɨ
Carnarvonshire (HVIII) kaɚ-'naɚ-vənʃɪɚ- [kə-'n-, -ʃɚ-]
carnation, -s kaɚ-'neĭʃn̩, -z
carous|e, -es, -ing, -ed kə'ɹaŭz, -ɪz, -ɪŋ, -d
carp, -s, -ing, -ed, -er/s 'kaɚ-p, -s, -ɪŋ, -t, -ɚ/z
carpet-monger, -s 'kaɚ-pɪtˌmʌŋgɚ, -z
carrack, -s 'kæɹək, -s
carrat (form of carat and var. of karat), -s 'kæɹət, -s
carrick (var. spelling of carrack), -s 'kæɹɪk, -s
carrion, -s 'kæɹɪən [-ɹ ĭən], -z
carr|y, -ies, -ying, -ied, -ier/s 'kæɹ|ɪ, -ɪz, -ɪŋ, -ɪd, -ɪɚ/z
carry't (contr. of carry it) 'kæɹɪt
carry-tale, -s 'kæɹɪˌteĭl, -z
cart, -s, -ing, -ed 'kaɚ-t, -s, -ɪŋ, -ɪd
carter, -s 'kaɚ-tɚ, -z
Carthage (MSND, MV, TEM, TS) 'kaɚ-θɪdʒ
carv|e, -es, -ing, -ed, -er/s 'kaɚ-v, -z, -ɪŋ, -d, -ɚ/z
Casca (JUL) 'kæskə
cascad|e, -es, -ing, -ed kæ'skeĭd, -z, -ɪŋ, -ɪd
cas|e, -es, -ing, -ed 'keĭs, -ɪz, -ɪŋ, -t
casement, -s 'keĭsmənt, -s
cash, -es, -ing, -ed 'kæʃ, -ɪz, -ɪŋ, -t
cashier, -s, -ing, -ed kæ'ʃɪɚ, -z, -ɹɪŋ, -d
cask, -s, -ing, -ed 'kask, -s, -ɪŋ, -t
casket, -s, -ed 'kaskɪt, -s, -ɪd
casque, -s 'kæsk, -s
Cassandra (TC) kə'sændɹə
Cassibelan (CYM) kæ'sɪbələn [kə's-]
Cassio, Michael (OTH) 'maĭkl̩ 'kæsɪoŭ, -sjoŭ
Cassius, Caius (AC, JUL) 'kaĭəs ['keĭəs] 'kæsɪəs, -sjəs
cassock, -s, -ed 'kæsək, -s, -t
cast, -s, -ing, -ed 'kast, -s, -ɪŋ, -ɪd
Castalion or Castalian (MWW) kə'steĭlɪən

i we ɪ city ɪ hit e let ɛ debut æ can a pass ɝ bird ʌ hut ə again ɚ supper u you ʊ should o obey ɔ awl ɒ cop ɑ father eĭ paid aĭ high oŭ go ɔĭ voice aŭ found ɪɚ- ear ɛɚ- air ʊɚ- poor ɔɚ- fork aɚ- park aĭɚ- fire aŭɚ- hour b boy p pit d dog t top g got k kid h how fi behave dʒ jot tʃ chew z zany s soft v vat f fat ʒ treasure ʃ ship ð the θ thin m man n no ŋ hang l lip j yes w won ʍ whew ɹ rigger, airy ɾ matter

*Note.—This is from a puzzling se-
quence of words and dialogue (*MWW,
II.iii.24–31*) wherein the Host calls the
arrogant Doctor Caius by the satirical
epithet of "Castalion-king-Urinal."
Editors often emend the spelling to
better suit their idea of its origin and
meaning. Some prefer to spell the word
'Castilian' with a reference to Spain and
King Philip II of Castile. What is
uncontested is that doctors and the
subject of urine were inextricably
associated, due to the fact that their
diagnoses were based on the inspection
thereof. 'Stale' is another word for urine
(usually of beasts, such as horses, cattle,
camels, etc.), and the Host has already
(in the section cited above) referred to
the doctor as "bully stale." With these
factors in mind,* [-'steĭl-] *in the second
syllable is recommended*

castaway, -s 'kastəweĭ, -z
caste, -s 'kast, -s
castigat|e, -es, -ing, -ed, -or/s 'kæstɪgeĭt,
-s, -ɪŋ, -ɪd, -ɚ/z
castigation, -s ˌkæstɪ'geĭʃn̩, -z
Castiliano vulgo (*pseudo-Sp.*) (TN,
I.iii.42) ˌkɑstilⁱɑno 'vulgo
casting (*s.*), **-s** 'kastɪŋ, -z
castle (**C.**), **-s** 'kasl̩, -z
Castor (TNK) 'kæstɚ
casual, -ly, -ness 'kæʒʊəl, -ɨ, -nɪs
casualt|y, -ies 'kæʒʊəlt|ɨ [-ʒʊl-], -ɪz
cat, -s; -like 'kæt, -s; -laĭk
Cataian *or* **Catayan** (MWW, TN)
kə'teĭən [kæt-]
catalogu|e, -es, -ing, -ed 'kæɾəlɒg, -z, -ɪŋ,
-d
cat-a-mountain 'cæɾəˌmɑʊntɪn [ˌ--'--]
cataplasm, -s 'kætəplæzm̩ ['kæɾə-], -z
cataract, -s 'kæɾəɹækt, -s
catarrh, -s, -al, -ous kə'tɑɚ, -z, -ɹəl, -ɹəs
catastrophe, -s kə'tæstɹəfɨ, -z
catastrophic ˌkæɾə'stɹɒfɪk
catch, -es, -ing, caught 'kætʃ, -ɪz, -ɪŋ, 'kɔt
catched (*archaic form of* **caught**) 'kætʃt
catcher, -s 'kætʃɚ, -z
cate, -s 'keĭt, -s
catechism, -s 'kæɾəkɪzəm, -z

catechist, -s 'kæɾəkɪst, -s
catechiz|e, -es, -ing, -ed, -er/s 'kæɾəkaĭz,
-ɪz, -ɪŋ, -d, -ɚ/z
cate-log 'kætl̩ɒg ['keĭtəlɒg]
*Note.—This word in TGV, III.i.272 is
probably to suggest a whore, in which
case either 'cat' or the common name
'Kate' works. Though the* OED *admits
'cateloge' to be an archaic variant of
'catalog,' the First Folio's hyphen
implies punning and may thus (depending on one's intention) influence
pronunciation*

cater, -s, -ing, -ed, -er/s 'keĭɾɚ, -z, -ɹɪŋ,
-d, -ɹɚ/z
cater-cousins *or* **catercosins** 'keĭtɚˈkʌzn̩z
caterpillar, -s 'kæɾɚˈpɪlɚ [-ɾəp-], -z
caterwaul, -s, -ing, -ed 'kæɾɚˈwɔl, -z, -ɪŋ,
-d
Catesby, Sir William (*RIII*) ˌsɚ 'wɪljəm
'keĭtsbɨ
*Note.—In RIII, III.i.157, 'Catesby'
appears to be a trisyllable, i.e.,
[*'keĭtɪsbɨ] or ['keĭtɪzbɨ]. A case might be
made that RIII, III.ii.73 includes an epic
caesura, which would precipitate a
trisyllabic pronunciation of Catesby
there as well. Also, there is no harm in
entertaining the idea that this name, in
accord with pronunciation practices
in S.'s time, is meant to be pronounced
[*'kætsbɨ] *throughout; perhaps corresponding in nature to 'Ratcliffe,' also in
RIII*

Cathay kæ'θeĭ
Cathayan (MWW, TN) kæ'θeĭən [kə'θ-]
*Note.—This is a var. of 'Cataian,' and so
might be interpreted as* [kæ'teĭən, kə't-]
catling, -s 'kætlɪŋ, -z
Catling, Simon (RJ) 'saĭmən 'kætlɪŋ
Cato (*JUL*) 'keĭtoŭ
Cato, Marcus (COR, *JUL*, MV) 'mɑɚkəs
'keĭtoŭ
Cats, King of (RJ) ˌkɪŋ əv 'kæts
Cats, Prince of (RJ) ˌpɹɪns əv 'kæts
Caucasus (RII, TIT) 'kɔkəsəs
caudle 'kɔdl̩
cauf (*cf.* **calf**) 'kaf
cauldron, -s 'kɔldɹən, -z

caulk, -s, -ing, -ed ˈkɔk, -s, -ɪŋ, -t

caus|e, -es, -ing, -ed, -er/s ˈkɔz, -ɪz, -ɪŋ, -d, -ɚ/z

'cause (*from* **because**) ˈkɒz (*strong form*), ˈkəz (*weak form*)

causeless, -ly ˈkɔzlɪs, -lɨ

cautel, -s, -ous/ly, -ousness ˈkɔtḷ, -z, -əs/lɨ, -əsnɪs

cauteriz|e, -es, -ing, -ed ˈkɔɾəˌɹaɪz, -ɪz, -ɪŋ, -d

caution, -s, -ing, -ed, -er/s ˈkɔʃn̩, -z, -ɪŋ, -d, -ɚ/z

cautious, -ly, -ness ˈkɔʃəs, -lɨ, -nɪs

cavalery (C.) (*var. of* **cavaleiro** *in MSND*) ˈkævələˌɹɨ

cavalier, -s ˌkævəˈlɪɚ, -z

cavaliero *or* **cavaleiro** (*alt. form of* **cavalier**) ˌkævəˈlɪɚˌɹoʊ

cavalleria (*It.*) (PER, IV.vi.12) ˌkavɑlɛˈriɑ

cavalr|y, -ies ˈkævḷˌɹ|ɨ, -ɪz

cav|e, -es, -ing, -ed ˈkeɪv, -z, -ɪŋ, -d

cave-keeper, -s ˈkeɪvˌkipɚ, -z

cave-keeping ˈkeɪvˌkipɪŋ

cavern, -s ˈkævɚn, -z

cavernous, -ly ˈkævɚnəs, -lɨ

caveto (*L.*) (HV, II.iii.51) kɑˈvito [kəˈv-]

caviar|e, -y, -ie ˌkavɪˈɑɚˌɹ|ə, -ɨ, -ɨ

cavil, -s, -ling, -led, -ler/s ˈkævḷ, -z, -ɪŋ, -d, -ɚ/z

Cawdor (MAC) ˈkɔdɚ [-dɔɚ]

ceas|e, -es, -ing, -ed ˈsis, -ɪz, -ɪŋ, -t

ceaseless, -ly, -ness ˈsislɪs, -lɨ, -nɪs

cedar, -s ˈsidɚ, -z

ced|e, -es, -ing, -ed ˈsid, -z, -ɪŋ, -ɪd

Cedius (TC) ˈsidɪəs, -djəs

ceiling, -s ˈsilɪŋ, -z

ceinture ˈseɪntjʊɚ [-tʃʊɚ, -tʃɚ] [*Fr.* sɛ̃tʌʁ]
Note.—This word (rare in English) is found in many versions of S., but isn't, technically speaking, part of the canon. In KJ, IV.iii.155 and 1HVI, II.ii.6, the words given in the Folio are 'center' and 'centure,' respectively. In both cases, the word means 'girdle,' 'belt,' or

'encircling ring.' Most modern editors, presumably to move the meaning away from the present-day meaning of 'in the middle,' emend the words 'center' and 'centure' (in these instances) to 'ceinture' or the even more familiar 'cincture'

celebrat|e, -es, -ing, -ed, -or/s ˈselɪbɹeɪt, -s, -ɪŋ, -ɪd, -ɚ/z

celebration, -s ˌselɪˈbɹeɪʃn̩, -z

celerity sɪˈleɹɪtɨ

celestial, -ly sɪˈlestjəl [-tɪəl], -ɨ

Celia (*AYLI*) ˈsilɪə, -ljə

cellar, -s; -age, -er/s ˈselɚ, -z; -ɪdʒ, -ɹɚ/z

cement, -s, -ing, -ed sɪˈment, -s, -ɪŋ, -ɪd
Note.—Stressed on the first syllable, i.e., [ˈsiment] *in AC, II.i.48; III.ii.29; PP, XIII.10*

censer, -s ˈsensɚ, -z

Censorinus (COR) ˌsensoˈɹaɪnəs [-səˌɹ-]

censur|e, -es, -ing, -ed, -er/s ˈsenʃɚ, -z, -ɹɪŋ, -d, -ɹɚ/z

centaur (C.) (COM, TIT), **-s** ˈsentɔɚ, -z

centurion, -s senˈtjʊɚˌɹɪən, -z

Cephalus ˈsefələs
Note.—Technically speaking, this name doesn't appear in S. Cephalus was the devoted husband of Procris, and it was he of whom the goddess Aurora was enamored. In MSND, Bottom blunders, calling him 'Shafalus' (q.v.)

Cerberus (2HIV, LLL, TC, TIT) ˈsɝbəˌɹəs, -bɹəs

cer|e, -es, -ing, -ed ˈsɪɚ, -z, -ɹɪŋ, -d

cere(-)cloth, -s ˈsɪɚklɒθ, -s [-klɔðz]

cerements ˈsɪɚmənts

Ceres (2HVI, *TEM*, TNK) ˈsɪɚˌɹiz

Cerimon (*PER*) ˈseɹɪmɒn

'cerns (*from* **concerns**) ˈsɝnz

certain, -ly ˈsɝtn̩ [-tɪn], -lɨ

certainer ˈsɝtn̩ɚ

certaint|y, -ies ˈsɝtn̩t|ɨ [-tɪnt-], -ɪz

certes ˈsɝtɪz [ˈsɝts]

---

i wɛ ɨ cɪty ɪ hɪt e lɛt ɛ debut æ can a pass ɝ bɪrd ʌ hut ə again ɚ suppɚr u you ʊ should o obey ɔ awl ɒ cop ɑ father eɪ paɪd aɪ high oʊ go ɔɪ voɪce aʊ found ɪɚ ear ɛɚ air ʊɚ poor ɔɚ fork ɑɚ park aɪɚ fire aʊɚ hour b boy p pit d dog t top g got k kid h how fi behave dʒ jot tʃ chew z zany s soft v vat f fat ʒ treasure ʃ ship ð the θ thin m man n no ŋ hang l lip j yes w won ʍ whew ɹ rigger, airy ɾ matter

Cesario (*TN*) seˈzɑɹɪoʊ̆, -ɑʲjoʊ̆ (*alias Viola*)

cess(e) ˈses

chaf|e, -es, -ing, -ed ˈtʃeɪ̆f, -s, -ɪŋ, -t

chafer, -s ˈtʃeɪ̆fɚ, -z

chaff, -s, -ing/ly, -ed, -er/s ˈtʃaf, -s, -ɪŋ/lɪ, -t, -ɚ/z

chaffless ˈtʃaflɪs

chaff|y, -iness ˈtʃaf|ɪ, -ɪnɪs

chain, -s, -ing, -ed ˈtʃeɪn, -z, -ɪŋ, -d

chair, -s, -ing, -ed ˈtʃɛɚ, -z, -ɹɪŋ, -d

chair|man, -men ˈtʃɛɚ|mən, -mən

chalice, -s, -d ˈtʃælɪs, -ɪz, -t

chalk, -s, -ing, -ed ˈtʃɔk, -s, -ɪŋ, -t

chalk|y, -ier, -iest, -ily, -iness ˈtʃɔk|ɪ, -ɪɚ, -ɪɪst, -ɪlɪ, -ɪnɪs

challeng|e, -es, -ing, -ed, -er/s ˈtʃælɪndʒ, -ɪz, -ɪŋ, -d, -ɚ/z

Cham (ADO) ˈkæm

chamber, -s, -ed ˈtʃeɪ̆mbɚ, -z, -d

chamber-council, -s ˈtʃeɪ̆mbɚˌkaʊ̆nsl̩, -z

chamberer, -s ˈtʃeɪ̆mbəɹɚ, -z

chamber-hanging ˈtʃeɪ̆mbɚˌfiæŋɪŋ

chamberlain, -s ˈtʃeɪ̆mbɚlɪn, -z

Chamberlain, Lord (*HVIII*, RIII) ˈlɔɚ̆d ˈtʃeɪ̆mbɚlɪn

chamber-lye ˈtʃeɪ̆mbɚˌlaɪ̆

chamber-maid (C.), **-s** ˈtʃeɪ̆mbɚ meɪ̆d, -z

chamber-pot, -s ˈtʃeɪ̆mbɚpɒt, -s

chamber-window ˈtʃeɪ̆mbɚwɪndoʊ̆

chamblet (*obsolete form of* **camlet**) ˈkæmlɪt

chameleon, -s kəˈmiljən [-lɪən], -z

champ, -s, -ing, -ed ˈtʃæmp, -s, -ɪŋ, -t

champaign, -s ˈtʃæmpeɪ̆n, -z

Champa(i)gne (1HVI) ʃæmˈpeɪ̆n

champion, -s, -ing, -ed; -ship/s ˈtʃæmpɪən, -z, -ɪŋ, -d; -ʃɪp/s

chanc|e (C.), **-es, -ing, -ed** ˈtʃans, -ɪz, -ɪŋ, -t

chancel, -s ˈtʃansl̩, -z

chandler, -s ˈtʃandlɚ, -z

chang|e, -es, -ing, -ed, -er/s ˈtʃeɪ̆ndʒ, -ɪz, -ɪŋ, -d, -ɚ/z

changeful ˈtʃeɪ̆ndʒfʊl

changeless ˈtʃeɪ̆ndʒlɪs

changeling, -s ˈtʃeɪ̆ndʒlɪŋ, -z

Note.—*May be trisyllabic in S., i.e.,* [ˈtʃeɪ̆ndʒəlɪŋ], *e.g.,* MSND, I.i.23

channel, -s, -ling, -led ˈtʃænl̩, -z, -ɪŋ, -d

chanson, -s ʃɑnˈsɔn, -z

chant, -s, -ing, -ed, -er/s ˈtʃant, -s, -ɪŋ, -ɪd, -ɚ/z

chanticleer, -s ˈtʃæntɪklɪɚ̆ [ˈʃæn-, ˈtʃan-, ˈʃan-, ˌ-ˈ-], -z

chantr|y, -ies ˈtʃantɹ|ɪ, -ɪz

chaos (C.) (LUC, OTH, VA) ˈkeɪ̆ɒs

chaotic keɪ̆ˈɒɾɪk

chap, -s, -ping, -ped ˈtʃæp, -s, -ɪŋ, -t

chape, -s; -less ˈtʃeɪ̆p, -s; -lɪs

chapel, -s ˈtʃæpl̩, -z

chaplain (C.) (3HVI), **-s** ˈtʃæplɪn, -z

chapless ˈtʃæplɪs

chaplet, -s ˈtʃæplɪt, -s

chap|man, -men ˈtʃæp|mən, -mən

chapter, -s ˈtʃæptɚ, -z

char, -s, -ring, -red ˈtʃɑɚ̆, -z, -ɹɪŋ, -d

character, -s, -ed; -less ˈkæɹɪktɚ, -z, -d; -lɪs

Note.—*Sometimes* [kəˈɹæktɚ(-z, -d; -lɪs)] *in S., e.g.,* 2HVI, III.i.300; HAM, I.iii.59; LUC, 807; RIII, III.i.81; TC, III.ii.186; TGV, II.vii.4

charactery kəˈɹæktɚɹɪ

Charbon (ALL'S) ˈʃɑɚ̆bɒn

char(e) (*s.*) (*chore*), **-s** ˈtʃɑɚ̆ [ˈtʃɛɚ̆], -z

char|e (*v.*) (*to turn (away); to do odd jobs*), **-es, -ing, -ed** ˈtʃɛɚ̆, -z, -ɹɪŋ, -d

charg|e, -es, -ing, -ed; -ful ˈtʃɑɚ̆dʒ, -ɪz, -ɪŋ, -d; -fʊl

charging-staff ˈtʃɑɚ̆dʒɪŋˌstaf

Charing Cross (1HIV) ˌtʃæɹɪŋ ˈkɹɒs [ˌtʃɛɚ̆ˈɹɪŋ-]

chariot, -s ˈtʃæɹɪət, -s

charioteer, -s ˌtʃæɹɪəˈtɪɚ̆, -z

charitab|le, -ly, -leness ˈtʃæɹɪtəb|l̩, -lɪ, -l̩nɪs

charit|y (C.), **-ies** ˈtʃæɹɪt|ɪ, -ɪz

charlatan, -s ˈʃɑɚ̆lətən, -z

Charlemagne (ALL'S, HV) ˈʃɑɚ̆ləmeɪ̆n [ˈ--ˈ-]

Charlemain (HV) ˈʃɑɚ̆ləmeɪ̆n [ˈ--ˈ-]

Charles (*AYLI*, 1HIV, *HV*, *1HVI*, 2HVI, HVIII, LLL) ˈtʃɑɚ̆lz

Charles the Great (HV) ˈtʃɑɚ̆lz ðə ˈgɹeɪ̆t

Charles the Sixth (*HV*) ˈtʃɑɚ̆lz ðə ˈsɪksθ

charm, -s, -ing/ly, -ed, -er/s ˈtʃɑɚ̆m, -z, -ɪŋ/lɪ, -d, -ɚ/z

Charmian (*AC*) ˈkɑə̆-mɪən [ˈtʃɑə̆-], -mjən
charneco ʃɑə̆-ˈneĭku [-koŭ]
charnel ˈtʃɑə̆-nl̩
charnel-hou|se, -ses ˈtʃɑə̆-nl̩ˌhaŭ|s, -zɪz
Charolois *or* **Charolais** (HV) ˈʃaɹolɔĭz, ˌʃaɹoˈleĭ [*Fr.* ʃaʁolɛ]
Charon (TC) ˈkɛə̆-ɹən
chart, -s ˈtʃɑə̆-t, -s
charter, -s, -ing, -ed, -er/s ˈtʃɑə̆-tə-, -z, -ɹɪŋ, -d, -ɹə-/z
Chartham (2HVI) ˈtʃɑə̆-ɾ̥əm
Chartreux (HVIII) ˈʃɑə̆-tɹu [-tɹuz]
char|y, -iest, -iness ˈtʃɛə̆-ɹ|ɨ, -ɨɪst, -ɨnɪs
Charybdis (MV) kəˈɹɪbdɪs
chas|e, -es, -ing, -ed, -er/s ˈtʃeĭs, -ɪz, -ɪŋ, -t, -ə-/z
chaste, -ly, -ness ˈtʃeĭst, -lɨ, -nɪs
chastis|e, -es, -ing, -ed, -er/s tʃæˈstaĭz [*infrequently* ˈtʃæstaĭz], -ɪz, -ɪŋ, -d, -ə-/z
chastisement, -s ˈtʃæstɪzmənt [tʃæˈstaĭzmənt], -s
Note.—Always stressed on the first syllable in S. [ˈtʃæstɪzmənt], *e.g.*, 1HVI, IV.i.69; MEAS, V.i.257; KJ,V.ii.147; RII, I.i.106, IV.i.22, *etc.*
chastity ˈtʃæstɪtɨ
chat, -s, -ting, -ted ˈtʃæt, -s, -ɪŋ, -ɪd
Chatillon (*KJ*) ʃəˈtɪljən, -lɪən [*Fr.* ʃatɪjɔ̃]
Note.—Although this character in KJ *is French, his name is always given primary stress on the second syllable. The Folio gives 'Chatillion' and 'Chattylion' (see 'Shakespeare's Verse' § 1.8 of this dictionary)*
Chatillon, Jaques (HV) ˈdʒeĭkɪz ʃəˈtɪljən [*Fr.* ʒɒk ʃatɪjɔ̃]
Note.—In HV, III.v.43, *'Jaques' may be pronounced as either one or two syllables. Depending on how one chooses to say it, i.e.,* [ˈʒɒk, ˈdʒeĭks, ˈdʒeĭkɪs, *or* ˈdʒeĭkɪz] *(see Note for* **Jacques***), the name 'Chatillon' will shift syllabic stress, and 'Rambures' will shift between being two and three syllables. Spelling in the First Folio favors the first, more anglicized, version given above (*[ˈdʒeĭkɪz ʃəˈtɪljən]*), despite the fact that it is the French King who is speaking (cf.* **Chatillon***)*
chattel, -s ˈtʃætl̩, -z
chatter, -s, -ing, -ed, -er/s ˈtʃæɾ̥ə-, -z, -ɹɪŋ, -d, -ɹə-/z
Chaucer (TNK) ˈtʃɔsə-
chaudron, -s ˈtʃɔdɹən, -z
cheap, -er, -est, -ly, -ness ˈtʃip, -ə-, -ɪst, -lɨ, -nɪs
Cheapside (2HVI) ˈtʃipˌsaĭd
cheat, -s, -ing, -ed, -er/s ˈtʃit, -s, -ɪŋ, -ɪd, -ə-/z
check, -s, -ing, -ed ˈtʃek, -s, -ɪŋ, -t
checker, -s, -ing, -ed ˈtʃekə-, -z, -ɹɪŋ, -d
cheek, -s, -ing, -ed ˈtʃik, -s, -ɪŋ, -t
cheekbone, -s ˈtʃikboŭn, -z
cheek-roses ˈtʃikˌɹoŭzɪz
cheep, -s, -ing, -ed ˈtʃip, -s, -ɪŋ, -t
cheer, -s, -ing, -ed, -er ˈtʃɪə̆-, -z, -ɹɪŋ, -d, -ɹə-
cheer|ful, -fully, -fulness ˈtʃɪə̆-|fʊl, -fʊlɨ, -fʊlnɪs
cheerless, -ly, -ness ˈtʃɪə̆-lɪs, -lɨ, -nɪs
cheerly ˈtʃɪə̆-lɨ
cheer|y, -ier, -iest, -ily, -iness ˈtʃɪə̆-ɹ|ɨ, -ɨɪst, -ɪlɨ, -ɨnɪs
chequer (*chiefly Brit. var. of* **checker**, *q.v.*) ˈtʃekə-
chequin (*var. of 'chequeen', a gold coin*)**, -s** tʃɪˈkin, -z
cherish, -es, -ing, -ed, -er/s ˈtʃeɹɪʃ, -ɪz, -ɪŋ, -t, -ə-/z
cherr|y, -ies ˈtʃeɹ|ɨ, -ɨz
cherry-lips ˈtʃeɹɨlɪps
Chertsey (RIII) ˈtʃɜ-tsɨ
cherub, -s ˈtʃeɹəb, -z
cherubic tʃeˈɹubɪk [tʃɪˈɹ-]
cherubim ˈtʃeɹʊbɪm
cherubin (C.), -s ˈtʃeɹʊbɪn, -z
Cheshu (HV) ˈtʃiʃju [-ʃu]
Note.—This is the dialectal corruption

i w**e** ɨ cit**y** ɪ h**i**t e l**e**t ɛ d**e**but æ c**a**n a p**a**ss ɜ- b**ir**d ʌ h**u**t ə **a**gain ə- supp**er** u y**ou**
ʊ sh**ou**ld o **o**bey ɔ **aw**l ɒ c**o**p ɑ f**a**ther eĭ p**ai**d aĭ h**igh** oŭ g**o** ɔĭ v**oi**ce aŭ f**ou**nd ɪə̆- **ear**
ɛə̆- **air** ʊə̆- p**oor** ɔə̆- f**or**k ɑə̆- p**ar**k aĭə̆- f**ire** aŭə̆- h**our** b **b**oy p **p**it d **d**og t **t**op g **g**ot
k **k**id h **h**ow ɦ be**h**ave dʒ **j**ot tʃ **ch**ew z **z**any s **s**oft v **v**at f **f**at ʒ trea**s**ure ʃ **sh**ip ð **th**e
θ **th**in m **m**an n **n**o ŋ ha**ng** l **l**ip j **y**es w **w**on ʍ **wh**ew ɹ **r**igger, air**y** ɾ̥ ma**tt**er

of 'Jesu,' spoken by Fluellen, a Welshman in HV. *This is an example of S.'s direction to the actor (by way of semiphonetic spellings) to adopt a Welsh accent, more or less. (See 'Shakespeare's Foreign Languages' § 3.2 of this dictionary)*

chess 'tʃes

chest, -s 'tʃest, -s

Chester (2HIV) 'tʃestɚ

Chetas (TC) 'kitəs

chevalier, -s ˌʃevə'lɪɚ, -z

cheveril *or* **chev'ril** 'ʃevəɹɪl [-ɹəl]

chew, -s, -ing, -ed 'tʃu, -z, -ɪŋ, -d

chewet 'tʃuɪt ['ʃuɪt, -uet]

Note.—This word, appearing in 1HIV, *V.i.29, is typically defined as a noisy, quibbling prater; a jackdaw. It is a rare, obsolete word, and since it is adopted from the Fr. 'chouette,' (and as the* OED *does not assert a pronunciation) both an anglicized and a quasi-French pronunciation are proffered here*

chick, -s 'tʃɪk, -s

chicken, -s 'tʃɪkɪn, -z

chid (*p.t. of* **chide**, *q.v.*) 'tʃɪd

chid|e, -es, -ing, -ed, chid, chidden 'tʃaɪd, -z, -ɪŋ, -ɪd, 'tʃɪd, 'tʃɪdn̩

chider, -s 'tʃaɪdɚ, -z

chief (C.), -s; -est, -ly 'tʃif, -s; -ɪst, -lɪ

child, children 'tʃaɪld, 'tʃɪldɹən

Note.—There is some awkwardness about TIT, II.ii.115. *In it, Tamora says, "Or be ye not henceforth called my children." Editors attempt to reconcile this seemingly oddly scanned line by emending 'henceforth' to 'henceforward', or by deleting the word 'ye' entirely. But there is another (and perhaps even more euphonic) way to reconcile the line. By eliding 'be ye,' 'ye' stays in the first foot, and 'children' becomes trisyllabic, i.e.,* ['tʃɪldɚɹən], *lending strength to the force of the line and the word, and thus Tamora's grip on her sons (cf.* **brethren** *and* **empress***)*

child(-)bed 'tʃaɪldbed

child-changed 'tʃaɪldˌtʃeɪndʒɪd

childed 'tʃaɪldɪd

Childeric (HV) 'tʃɪldəɹɪk

childing 'tʃaɪldɪŋ

childish, -ly, -ness 'tʃaɪldɪʃ, -lɪ, -nɪs

childish-foolish ˌtʃaɪldɪʃ'fulɪʃ

children (*p.t. of* **child**, *q.v.; and see Note*)

chimney, -s 'tʃɪmnɪ, -z

chimney-piece, -s 'tʃɪmnɪˌpis, -ɪz

chimney-sweeper, -s 'tʃɪmnɪˌswipɚ, -z

chimney-top, -s 'tʃɪmnɪˌtɒp, -s

China-dishes (MEAS) 'tʃaɪnəˌdɪʃɪz

chine (*fissure; backbone*) 'tʃaɪn (*see Note for* **mose**)

chink, -s 'tʃɪŋk, -s

chip, -s, -ping, -ped, -per/s 'tʃɪp, -s, -ɪŋ, -t, -ɚ/z

Chiron (*TIT*) 'kaɪɹɒn

chirrah (*perhaps a corruption of the Greek 'chaere' in* LLL, V.i.31, 32) 'tʃɪɹə

chirurgeon, -s; -ly kaɪ'ɹɜˑdʒən, -z; -lɪ

chisel, -s, -ling, -led 'tʃɪzl̩, -z, -ɪŋ, -d

Chitopher (ALL'S) 'kɪɹəfɚ ['tʃɪɹ-]

chitterlings 'tʃɪtlɪnz

chivalric 'ʃɪvl̩ɹɪk [ʃɪ'vælɹɪk]

chivalry 'ʃɪvl̩ɹɪ [-vəl-]

choice, -s; -r, -st, -ly, -ness 'tʃɔɪs, -ɪz; -ɚ, -ɪst, -lɪ, -nɪs

choir, -s, -ed 'kwaɪɚ, -z, -d

chok|e, -es, -ing, -ed 'tʃoŭk, -s, -ɪŋ, -t

choler, -s 'kɒlɚ, -z

choleric 'kɒləɹɪk [kə'leɹɪk]

choos|e, -es, -ing, chose, chooser/s 'tʃuz, -ɪz, -ɪŋ, 'tʃoŭz, 'tʃuzɚ/z

choos|y, -ier, -iest, -iness 'tʃuz|ɪ, -ɪɚ, -ɪɪst, -ɪnɪs

chop, -s, -ping, -ped, -per/s 'tʃɒp, -s, -ɪŋ, -t, -ɚ/z

chop-fallen 'tʃɒpˌfɔlən

chopine tʃoŭ'pin

chopless 'tʃɒplɪs

chopp|y, -ier, -iest, -ily, -iness 'tʃɒp|ɪ, -ɪɚ, -ɪɪst, -ɪlɪ, -ɪnɪs

chopt (*var. of the participial adj.* **chopped**, *meaning chapped*) 'tʃɒpt

chord, -s 'kɔˑd, -z

chore, -s 'tʃɔˑ, -z

chorister (C.) (HVIII), **-s** 'kɒɹɪstɚ, -z

Chorus (HV, PT, *RJ*) 'kɔɹəs

chorus, -es, -ing, -ed 'kɔɹəs, -ɪz, -ɪŋ, -t

chorus-like 'kɔɹəsˌlaɪk

chose (*p.t. of* **choose**, *q.v.*) 'tʃoŏz
chosen 'tʃoŏzn̩
chough, -s 'tʃʌf, -s
Chrish (HV) 'kɹaĭʃ
   *Note.—This is the dialectal corruption
of 'Christ,' spoken by Macmorris, an
Irishman in HV. This is an example of
S.'s direction to the actor (by way of
semiphonetic spellings) to adopt an Irish
accent, more or less. (See 'Shakespeare's Foreign Languages' § 3.1 of
this dictionary)*
Christ (1HIV, HV, 1HVI, 2HVI, RII)
   'kɹaĭst
christen, -s, -ing, -ed 'kɹɪsn̩, -z, -ɪŋ, -d
Christendom (1HIV, 1HVI, 2HVI, 3HVI,
   HVIII, KJ, TS) 'kɹɪsn̩dəm
christendom (*baptism*), **-s** 'kɹɪsn̩dəm, -z
christening, -s 'kɹɪsnɪŋ, -z
Christian, -s 'kɹɪstʃən, -z
Christian-like 'kɹɪstʃənlaĭk
Christmas (LLL, TS), **-es** 'kɹɪsməs
   [-stm-], -ɪz
christom 'kɹɪsəm
chronic|le (**C.**), **-les, -ling, -led, -ler/s**
   'kɹɒnɪkl̩, -z, -ɪŋ, -d, -ə˞/z
chrysolite, -s 'kɹɪsəlaĭt, -s
chubb|y, -ier, -iest, -ily, -iness 'tʃʌb|ɪ, -ɪə˞,
   -ɪst, -ɪlɪ, -ɪnɪs
chuck, -s, -ing, -ed 'tʃʌk, -s, -ɪŋ, -t
chuff, -s 'tʃʌf, -s
church (**C.**), **-es, -ing, -ed** 'tʃɜ˞tʃ, -ɪz, -ɪŋ,
   -t
church-bench 'tʃɜ˞tʃbentʃ
church|man, -men 'tʃɜ˞tʃ|mən, -mən
churchyard, -s 'tʃɜ˞tʃjɑ˞d, -z
churl, -s 'tʃɜ˞l, -z
churlish, -ly, -ness tʃɜ˞lɪʃ, -lɪ, -nɪs
Chus (MV) 'kʌʃ ['kʊs, 'kus, 'kuʃ]
   *Note.—It is hard to land on one single
preferred pronunciation of this name.
About the only thing that may be said for
sure about this name is that it is
certainly monosyllabic. It is perhaps*

*etymologically related to 'Cush'
(commonly pronounced* ['kʌʃ]*), son of
Ham in the Old Testament*
cicatrice, -s 'sɪkətɹɪs, -ɪz
Cicely (COM, TNK, TS) 'sɪsəlɪ, -slɪ
Cicero (*JUL*) 'sɪsə˞ɹoŏ
Ciceter (RII) 'sɪsɪtə˞
'cide (*aphaeretic form of* **decide**) 'saĭd
Cilicia (AC) saĭ'lɪʃɪə [sɪ'lɪʃɪə, -'lɪsɪə,
   -'lɪsɪə], -ʃjə, -sjə
Cimber, Metellus (*JUL*) mɪ'teləs 'sɪmbə˞
Cimmerian (TIT) sɪ'mɪə˞ɹɪən
cinch, -es, -ing, -ed 'sɪntʃ, -ɪz, -ɪŋ, -t
cinder, -s 'sɪndə˞, -z
Cinna (*JUL*) 'sɪnə
cinnamon 'sɪnəmən
cinque(-)pace *or* **sink(e)-a-pace**
   'sɪŋkə͵peĭs
Cinque-ports (HVIII) 'sɪŋk'pɔ˞ts
cinque-spotted (*with five spots*)
   'sɪŋk'spɒtɪd
ciph|er, -ers, -ering, -ered 'saĭf|ə˞, -ə˞z,
   -ə˞ɹɪŋ, -ə˞d
Circe (COM, 1HVI) 'sɜ˞sɪ
circ|le, -les, -ling, -led 'sɜ˞k|l̩, -l̩z, -lɪŋ
   [-lɪŋ], -l̩d
circlet, -s 'sɜ˞klɪt, -s
circuit, -s 'sɜ˞kɪt, -s
circumcis|e, -es, -ing, -ed 'sɜ˞kəmsaĭz,
   -ɪz, -ɪŋ, -d
circumcision, -s ͵sɜ˞kəm'sɪʒn̩, -z
circumference, -s sə˞'kʌmfɹəns [-fə˞ɹ-],
   -ɪz
circumflex, -es 'sɜ˞kəmfleks, -ɪz
circummured ͵sɜ˞kəm'mjʊə˞d
circumscrib|e, -es, -ing, -ed
   'sɜ˞kəmskɹaĭb, -z, -ɪŋ, -d
circumscription, -s ͵sɜ˞kəm'skɹɪpʃn̩, -z
circumspect, -ly 'sɜ˞kəmspekt, -lɪ
circumspection, -s ͵sɜ˞kə m'spekʃn̩, -z
circumstance, -s, -d 'sɜ˞kəmstəns
   [-stans], -ɪz, -t
circumstanti|al, -ally ͵sɜ˞kəm'stanʃl̩,
   -əlɪ

---

i w**e** ɪ cit**y** ɪ h**i**t e l**e**t ɛ d**e**but æ c**a**n a p**a**ss ɜ˞ b**i**rd ʌ h**u**t ə **a**gain ə˞ supp**er** u y**ou**
ʊ sh**ould** o **o**bey ɔ **aw**l ɒ c**o**p ɑ f**a**ther eĭ p**ai**d aĭ h**igh** oŏ g**o** ɔĭ v**oi**ce aŏ f**ou**nd ɪə˞ **ear**
ɛə˞ **air** ʊə˞ p**oor** ɔə˞ f**or**k ɑə˞ p**ar**k aĭə˞ f**ire** aŏə˞ h**our** b **b**oy p **p**it d **d**og t **t**op g g**o**t
k **k**id h **h**ow fi be**h**ave dʒ **j**ot tʃ **ch**ew z **z**any s **s**oft v **v**at f **f**at ʒ trea**s**ure ʃ **sh**ip ð **th**e
θ **th**in m **m**an n **n**o ŋ ha**ng** l **l**ip j **y**es w **w**on ʍ **wh**ew ɹ **r**igger, ai**r**y ɾ ma**tt**er

circumvent, -s, -ing, -ed ˌsɝˈkəmˈvent, -s, -ɪŋ, -ɪd

circumvention, -s ˌsɝˈkəmˈvenʃn̩, -z

cistern, -s ˈsɪstɚn, -z

citadel, -s ˈsɪɡədəl [-del], -z

cital (*reproof; impeachment*) ˈsaɪtl̩

cit|e, -es, -ing, -ed ˈsaɪt, -s, -ɪŋ, -ɪd

cittern, -s ˈsɪɡɚn [-ɟɝn], -z

cittern-head, -s ˈsɪɡɚnˈhed [-ɟɝn-], -z

cit|y (C.), -ies ˈsɪɡ|ɪ, -ɪz

city-woman ˈsɪɡɪˌwʊmən

civet, -s ˈsɪvɪt, -s

civic, -s ˈsɪvɪk, -s

civil, -ly ˈsɪvl̩, -ɪ

civilian, -s sɪˈvɪljən, -z

civilit|y, -ies sɪˈvɪlɪt|ɪ, -ɪz

clack, -s, -ing, -ed ˈklæk, -s, -ɪŋ, -t

clack-dish, -es ˈklækˌdɪʃ, -ɪz

clad ˈklæd

clamb|er, -ers, -ering, -ered ˈklæmb|ɚ, -ɚz, -əɹɪŋ, -ɚd

clamor, -s, -ing, -ed, -er/s ˈklæmɚ, -z, -ɹɪŋ, -d, -ɹɚ/z

clamorous, -ly, -ness ˈklæməɹəs, -lɪ, -nɪs

clan, -s ˈklæn, -z

clangor, -s, -ing, -ed ˈklæŋɚ [-æŋɡɚ], -z, -ɹɪŋ, -d

clannish, -ly, -ness ˈklænɪʃ, -lɪ, -nɪs

clap, -s, -ping, -ped ˈklæp, -s, -ɪŋ, -t

clapboard, -s, -ing, -ed ˈklæbɚd [ˈklæpbɔɝd], -z, -ɪŋ, -ɪd

clapper, -s ˈklæpɚ, -z

clapper-claw, -ing ˈklæpɚˌklɔ, -ɪŋ

clapper-de-claw (*from 'clapper-claw'*) ˈklæpɚdəˌklɔ (*see* **dat**)

Clarence (*HV*, 1HVI, 2HVI, *3HVI*, *RIII*) ˈklæɹəns

Clarence, Thomas Duke of (*2HIV, HV*) ˈtɒməs ˈdjuk əv ˈklæɹəns

claret, -s ˈklæɹɪt, -s

Claribel (TEM) ˈklæɹɪbel

clarification ˌklæɹɪfrˈkeɪʃn

clari|fy, -fies, -fying, -fied, -fier/s ˈklæɹɪ|faɪ, -faɪz, -faɪɪŋ, -faɪd, -faɪɚ/z

clarinet, -s ˌklæɹɪˈnet, -s

clarion, -s ˈklæɹɪən, -z

clarity ˈklæɹɪtɪ

clash, -es, -ing, -ed ˈklæʃ, -ɪz, -ɪŋ, -t

clasp, -s, -ing/s, -ed ˈklasp, -s, -ɪŋ/z, -t

class, -es, -ing, -ed ˈklas, -ɪz, -ɪŋ, -t

classic, -s, -al, -ally, -alness ˈklæsɪk, -s, -əl, -lɪ, -əlɪ

classification, -s ˌklæsɪfrˈkeɪʃn, -z

classi|fy, -fies, -fying, -fied, -fier/s ˈklæsɪ|faɪ, -faɪz, -faɪɪŋ, -faɪd, -faɪɚ/z

clatter, -s, -ing, -ed ˈklæɡɚ, -z, -ɹɪŋ, -d

Claudio (*ADO*, HAM, *MEAS*) ˈklɔdɪoʊ, -djoʊ

Claudius (*HAM, JUL*) ˈklɔdɪəs, -djəs

clause, -s ˈklɔz, -ɪz

claw, -s, -ing, -ed ˈklɔ, -z, -ɪŋ, -d

clay, -s ˈkleɪ, -z

clay-brained ˈkleɪˌbɹeɪnd

claymore, -s ˈkleɪmɔɚ, -z

clean, -s, -ing, -ed, -er/s; -er, -est, -ly, -ness ˈklin, -z, -ɪŋ, -d, -ɚ/z; -ɚ, -ɪst, -lɪ, -nɪs

cleanl|y, -ier, -iest, -iness ˈklenl|ɪ, -ɪɚ, -ɪɪst, -ɪnɪs

cleanly-coined ˈklinlɪˌkɔɪnd

clean-timbered ˈklinˌtɪmbɚd

clear, -s, -ing, -ed; -er, -est, -ly, -ness ˈklɪɚ, -z, -ɹɪŋ, -d; -ɹɚ, -ɹɪst, -lɪ, -nɪs
Note.—In PER, IV.vi.105, *'clear' is a disyllable. In Frank Kermode's (editor, The Arden Shakespeare, 1958) annotation for TEM, I.ii.53, there is a brief but valuable discussion about monosyllabic words that sometimes receive the value of two metric beats in S. lines of verse* "whether or no it is [they are] *pronounced disyllabically . . ." In* PER, IV.vi.105, *'clear' is arguably pronounced disyllabically or given, as Kermode puts it,* "a heavy emphasis." *Cf. Abbott's* A Shakespearian Grammar, *§§ 475, 479, 484*

clear-spirited ˌklɪɚˈspɪɹɪtɪd

cleav|e, -es, -ing, -ed, -er/s, cleft, clove, cloven ˈkliv, -z, -ɪŋ, -d, -ɚ/z, ˈkleft, ˈkloʊv, ˈkloʊvn̩

clef, -s ˈklef, -s

cleft (*adj., and a p.t. and p.p. of v.* **cleave**, *q.v.*) ˈkleft

cleft (*s.*)**, -s** ˈkleft, -s

clemen|cy, -t/ly ˈklemən|sɪ, -t/lɪ

Clement's Inn (2HIV) ˈklemənts ˈɪn

Cleomenes (*WT*) kliˈɒmɪnɪz

Cleon (*PER*) 'kliɒn
Cleopatra (*AC*, RJ) ˌklio'patɹə [ˌkliə'p-, -'peɪtɹə]
clep|e, -es, -ing, -ed, clept 'klip, -s, -ɪŋ, -t, 'klept
clept (*from* clepe) 'klept
clerestor|y, -ies 'klɪɝˌstɔɝˌɹ|ɪ [-stəɹ|ɪ], -ɪz
clergy 'klɝˌdʒɪ
clergy|man, -men 'klɝˌdʒɪ|mən, -mən
clerk (C.), -s; -ly 'klɝˌk, -s; -lɪ
Note.—The standard Brit. pronunciation is ['klɑːk], *lending itself to the Americanized version* ['klɑɝk] *in some instances, such as the rhyme of 'dark/clerk' in* MV, V.i.305
clerk-like 'klɝˌkˌlaɪk
clew, -s, -ing, -ed 'klu, -z, -ɪŋ, -d
cliff, -s 'klɪf, -s
cliff-hanger, -s 'klɪfˌhæŋɝ, -z
Clifford (*2HVI*, *3HVI*), -s 'klɪfɝd, -z
Clifton (1HIV) 'klɪftən
climature, -s 'klaɪmətʃɝ, -z
climb, -s, -ing, -ed, -er/s 'klaɪm, -z, -ɪŋ, -d, -ɝ/z
climber-upward ˌklaɪmɝ-'ɹʌpwɝd
clime, -s 'klaɪm, -z
cling, -s, -ing, clung 'klɪŋ, -z, -ɪŋ, 'klʌŋ
clink, -s, -ing, -ed, -er/s 'klɪŋk, -s, -ɪŋ, -t, -ɝ/z
clinquant (*glittering as of gold or silver*) 'klɪŋkənt
clip, -s, -ping/s, -ped 'klɪp, -s, -ɪŋ/z, -t
clipper, -s 'klɪpɝ, -z
clipt (*var. of* clept *from* clepe) 'klɪpt
Clitus (*JUL*) 'klaɪtəs
cloak, -s, -ing, -ed 'kloŏk, -s, -ɪŋ, -t
cloak-bag, -s 'kloŏkˌbæg, -z
clock, -s, -ing, -ed 'klɒk, -s, -ɪŋ, -t
clock-setter 'klɒkˌseɾɝ
clod, -s; -dy 'klɒd, -z; -ɪ
clodpole, -s 'klɒdpoŏl, -z
clog, -s, -ging, -ged 'klɒg, -z, -ɪŋ, -d
cloister, -s, -ing, -ed 'klɔɪstɝ, -z, -ɹɪŋ, -d
cloistress, -es 'klɔɪstɹɪs, -ɪz

clos|e (*v.*), -es, -ing, -ed, -er/s 'kloŏz, -ɪz, -ɪŋ, -d, -ɝ/z
close-stool, -s 'kloŏsˌstul ['kloŏzˌstul], -z
closet, -s, -ing, -ed 'klɒzɪt, -s, -ɪŋ, -ɪd
close-tongued 'kloŏsˌtʌŋd
closet-war 'klɒzɪtˌwɔɝ
closure, -s 'kloŏʒɝ, -z
clot, -s, -ting, -ted 'klɒt, -s, -ɪŋ, -ɪd
Cloten (*CYM*), -s 'klɒtn̩, 'kloŏtn̩, -z
cloth, -s 'klɒθ, -s *or* 'klɒðz ['klɔθ, -s *or* 'klɔðz]
Clothair, King (HV) 'kɪŋ 'kloŏtɛɝ ['kloŏθɛɝ]
Clotharius (HVIII) klo'tɛɝˌɹɪəs [-'θɛɝ-]
cloth|e, -es, -ing, -ed 'kloŏð, -z, -ɪŋ, -d
clothier, -s 'kloŏðɪɝ [-ðjɝ], -z
clotpoll, -s 'klɒtpoŏl, -z
cloud, -s, -ing, -ed 'klaŏd, -z, -ɪŋ, -ɪd
cloud-burst, -s 'klaŏdˌbɝst, -s
cloud-capped 'klaŏdˌkæpt
clout, -s, -ing, -ed 'klaŏt, -s, -ɪŋ, -ɪd
clove (*s.*), -s 'kloŏv, -z
clove (*v.*) (*p.t. and archaic p.p. of* cleave, *q.v.*) 'kloŏv
cloven (*p.p. of* cleave, *q.v.*) 'kloŏvən
clover, -s 'kloŏvɝ, -z
Clowder (TS) 'klaŏdɝ
Clown (AC, ALL'S, HAM, MEAS, OTH, TIT, TN, WT) 'klaŏn
clown (C.), -s, -ing, -ed 'klaŏn, -z, -ɪŋ, -d
clownish, -ly, -ness 'klaŏnɪʃ, -lɪ, -nɪs
cloy, -s, -ing, -ed, -ment; -less 'klɔɪ, -z, -ɪŋ, -d, -mənt; -lɪs
club, -s, -bing, -bed 'klʌb, -z, -ɪŋ, -d
cluck, -s, -ing, -ed 'klʌk, -s, -ɪŋ, -t
clu|e, -es, -ing, -ed 'klu, -z, -ɪŋ, -d
clung (*p.t. and p.p. of* cling, *q.v.*) 'klʌŋ
cluster, -s, -ing, -ed 'klʌstɝ, -z, -ɹɪŋ, -d
clutch, -es, -ing, -ed 'klʌtʃ, -ɪz, -ɪŋ, -t
clyster, -s 'klɪstɝ, -z
clyster-pipe, -s 'klɪstɝˌpaɪp, -s
Clytus, Clitus *or* Cleitus (HV) 'klaɪtəs
Cnidos (*var. of* Cnidus) (JUL) 'naɪdɒs
Cnidus (*var. of* Cnidos) (JUL) 'naɪdəs

coach, -es, -ing, -ed, -er/s ˈkoŏtʃ, -ɪz, -ɪŋ, -t, -ɚ/z

coach-fellow, -s ˈkoŏtʃˌfeloŏ, -z

coachmaker, -s ˈkoŏtʃmeĭkɚ, -z

co-act ˌkoŏˈækt

coac|tion, -tive koŏˈæk|ʃn̩, -tɪv

coagulate (adj.) koŏˈægjʊlɪt

coagulat|e (v.), -es, -ing, -ed koŏˈægjʊleĭt, -s, -ɪŋ, -ɪd

coal-black ˌkoŏlˈblæk (when att., [ˈ-ˌ-])

coarse, -r, -st, -ly, -ness ˈkɔɚs, -ɚ, -ɪst, -lɪ, -nɪs

coarse-frieze ˈkɔɚsˈfɹiz

cob, -s ˈkɒb, -z

cobb|le, -les, -ling, -led, -ler/s ˈkɒb|l̩, -l̩z, -l̩ɪŋ [-lɪŋ], -l̩d, -lɚ/z

Cobham, Eleanor (2HVI) ˈelɪnɚ ˈkɒbəm
Note.—Sometimes 'Eleanor,' in accordance with the occasional Quarto spelling 'Elnor,' wants to be disyllabic, i.e., [ˈelnɚ] in a metrical line of verse, e.g., 2HVI, II.iii.1

Cobham, Lord (3HVI, RII) ˈlɔɚd ˈkɒbəm

cobloaf ˈkɒbloŏf

cobweb, -s ˈkɒbweb, -z

Cobweb, Master (MSND) ˈmastɚ ˈkɒbweb

cock (C.) (a corruption of God in HAM, IV.v.61), -s, -ing, -ed ˈkɒk, -s, -ɪŋ, -t

cock a diddle dow ˈkɒk ə ˌdɪdl̩ ˈdaŏ
Note.—In TEM, I.ii.389, Ariel rhymes this in a song with the dog's bark, 'bow-wow'

cock-a-hoop ˌkɒkəˈhup [ˈ---]

cockatrice, -s ˈkɒkətɹɪs [-tɹaĭs], -ɪz

cocker (pamper, coddle), -ed ˈkɒkɚ, -d

cockerel, -s ˈkɒkəɹəl, -z

cockl|e, -es, -ing, -ed ˈkɒkl̩, -z, -ɪŋ, -d

cocklight ˈkɒklaĭt

cockney (C.), -s ˈkɒknɪ, -z

cock-pigeon, -s ˈkɒkˌpɪdʒən, -z

cock(-)sure, -ly, -ness ˌkɒkˈʃʊɚ, -lɪ, -nɪs

cockshut ˈkɒkʃʌt

Cocytus (TIT) koˈsaĭtəs

cod, -s ˈkɒd, -z

codding (lecherous) ˈkɒdɪŋ

codification, -s ˌkɒdɪfɪˈkeĭʃn̩ [ˌkoŏd-], -z

codif|y, -ies, -ying, -ied ˈkɒdɪf|aĭ [ˈkoŏd-], -aĭz, -aĭɪŋ, -aĭd

codling, -s ˈkɒdlɪŋ, -z

cod(-)piece, -s ˈkɒdpis, -ɪz

coelo (L.) (LLL, IV.ii.5) ˈsilo
Note.—Holofernes, the affected pedant in LLL, is waxing eloquent in Latin to Sir Nathaniel about the ground ('terra') and the sky ('coelo'); and though the Latin pronunciation of 'coelo' may also be [ˈtʃilo], the pronunciation given above might provide for humor (unbeknownst to Holofernes) if he indicates the sky but says, "coelo" to sound like 'see low'

co-equal ˈkoŏikwəl [ˌ-ˈ--]

Coeur-de-lion or Cœur-de-lion (1HVI, KJ) ˌkɚ də ˈliðŋ

coffer, -s ˈkɒfɚ, -z

coffer-lid, -s ˈkɒfɚˌlɪd, -z

coffin, -s, -ing, -ed ˈkɒfɪn, -z, -ɪŋ, -d

cog, -s, -ging, -ged ˈkɒg, -z, -ɪŋ, -d

cogitat|e, -es, -ing, -ed, -or/s ˈkɒdʒɪteĭt, -s, -ɪŋ, -ɪd, -ɚ/z

cogitation, -s ˌkɒdʒɪˈteĭʃn̩, -z

cognition, -s kɒgˈnɪʃn̩, -z

cognitive ˈkɒgnɪtɪv

cognizan|ce, -ces, -t ˈkɒgnɪzən|s, -sɪz, -t

cogscomb (from 'cockscomb') ˈkɒgzkoŏm (see prings)

co-heirs ˌkoŏˈɛɚz

coher|e, -es, -ing, -ed koŏˈhɪɚ [koˈh-], -z, -ɹɪŋ, -d

coif (tight-fitting cap), -s, -ing, -ed ˈkɔĭf, -s, -ɪŋ, -t

coif (short for coiffure; to dress one's hair), -s, -ing, -ed ˈkwɑf, -s, -ɪŋ, -t

coign, -s ˈkɔĭn, -z

coin, -s, -ing, -ed, -er/s ˈkɔĭn, -z, -ɪŋ, -d, -ɚ/z

coinage, -s ˈkɔĭnɪdʒ, -ɪz

coistrel ˈkɔĭstɹəl

co-join koŏˈdʒɔĭn

Colbrand (HVIII, KJ) ˈkoŏlbɹænd

Colchis (MV) ˈkɒlkɪs

Colchos (MV) (var. of Colchis) ˈkɒlkəs [-kɒs]

cold, -s; -er, -est, -ly, -ness ˈkoŏld, -z; -ɚ, -ɪst, -lɪ, -nɪs
Note.—In 1HIV, IV.iii.7; MAC, IV.i.6, this word is arguably disyllabic, i.e., [ˈkoŏəld] (see Note for brave)

cold-blooded, -ly, -ness ˌkoŏld'blʌdɪd
 (*when att.,* [ˈ-,--]), -lɪ, -nɪs
cold-moving ˈkoŏldˌmuvɪŋ
Coldspur (2HIV) ˈkoŏldspɝ
Colebrook *or* **Colnbrook** (MWW)
 ˈkoŏlbɹʊk
Colevil(l)e, Sir John (*2HIV*) ˌsɝ ˈdʒɒn
 ˈkoŏlvɪl
 Note.—Most editors suggest that in
 2HIV, IV.iii.71, *'Colevile' is meant to be*
 trisyllabic—or something near it in
 terms of metric value—in order to
 rightly fit the metrical requirements of
 the verse line. This may be accomplished
 by pronouncing the name [ˈkoŏəlvɪl] *or*
 [ˈkoŏləvɪl]
colic, -ky ˈkɒlɪk, -ɨ
collateral, -ly kə'læɾəɹəl, -ɨ
Collatine (LUC) ˈkɒlətaĭn
Collatinus (LUC) ˌkɒlə'taĭnəs
Collatium (LUC) kə'leĭʃɪəm, -ʃĭəm
 [koˈl-]
colleague, -s ˈkɒlig, -z
collect, -s, -ing, -ed, -er/s kə'lekt, -s, -ɪŋ,
 -ɪd, -ɚ/z
collection, -s kə'lekʃn̩, -z
collective, -ly kə'lektɪv, -lɨ
collector, -s kə'lektɚ, -z
college, -s ˈkɒlɪdʒ, -ɪz
collid|e, -es, -ing, -ed kə'laĭd, -z, -ɪŋ, -ɪd
collied ˈkɒlɨd
collier, -s ˈkɒlɪɚ [ˈkɒljɚ], -z
collision, -s kə'lɪʒn̩, -z
collop, -s ˈkɒləp, -s
Colme-kill (MAC) ˈkoŏmkɪl
coloquintida (*colocynth or bitter apple,*
 from which a purgative is derived)
 ˌkɒlu'kwɪntɪdə
color, -s, -ing, -ed ˈkʌlɚ, -z, -ɹɪŋ, -d
colorab|le, -ly ˈkʌlɚəb|l̩, -lɨ
Coloss|us (1HIV, JUL), -i kə'lɒs|əs, -aĭ
colossus-wise kə'lɒsəsˌwaĭz
colt, -s ˈkoŏlt, -s
colted (*cheated or tricked*) ˈkoŏltɪd

columbine, -s ˈkɒləmbaĭn, -z
column, -s, -ed ˈkɒləm, -z, -d
Comagene (AC) ˌkɒmə'dʒinɨ
 Note.—The First Folio gives 'Comageat'
 in AC, III.vi.74, perhaps a misspelling
 meant to stand for Comagena or
 Comagean, an ancient part of Syria. It is
 either trisyllabic, i.e., [ˈkɒmədʒin] *or*
 tetrasyllabic, i.e., [ˌkɒmə'dʒinɨ]
 depending on how one chooses to scan
 the line. [ˈkɒmədʒin] *is recommended in*
 this instance
co-mate, -s ˈkoŏ'meĭt, -s
comb, -s, -ing, -ed, -er/s ˈkoŏm, -z, -ɪŋ,
 -d, -ɚ/z
combat (*s.*) ˈkɒmbæt
combat (*v.*), -s, -(t)ing, -(t)ed kəm'bæt
 [ˈkɒmbæt], -s, -ɪŋ, -ɪd
combatant, -s kəm'bætn̩t, -s
 Note.—Sometimes [ˈkɒmbətənt] *in S.,*
 e.g., RII, I.iii.117; TC, IV.v.5, IV.v.92;
 1HIV, I.iii.106
combination, -s ˌkɒmbɪ'neĭʃn̩, -z
combine (*s.*), -s ˈkɒmbaĭn, -z
combin|e (*v.*), -es, -ing, -ed kəm'baĭn, -z,
 -ɪŋ, -d
combinate (*adj.*) ˈkɒmbɪnɪt
combless ˈkoŏmlɪs
combustion, -s kəm'bʌs.tʃən, -z
combustious kəm'bʌs.tʃĭəs
com|e, -es, -ing/s, came ˈkʌm, -z, -ɪŋ/z,
 ˈkeĭm
comel|y, -ier, -iest, -iness ˈkʌml|ɪ, -ɪɚ,
 -ɪst, -ɪnɪs
comer, -s ˈkʌmɚ, -z
comes (*aphetic form of* **becomes**) ˈkʌmz
comet, -s ˈkɒmɪt, -s
Comfect, Count (ADO) ˈkoŏnt ˈkʌmfɪt
comfort, -s, -ing, -ed, -er/s ˈkʌmfɚt, -s,
 -ɪŋ, -ɪd, -ɚ/z
comfort-killing ˈkʌmfɚˌt̩kɪlɪŋ
comfortless ˈkʌmfɚtlɪs
comic, -s; -al, -ally, -alness ˈkɒmɪk, -s;
 -əl, -əlɨ, -əlnɪs

coming-in, comings-in ˌkʌmɪŋ'ɪn,
ˌkʌmɪŋz'ɪn
coming-on ˌkʌmɪŋ'ɒn
Cominius (*COR*) ko'mɪnɪəs, -njəs
comma, -s 'kɒmə, -z
command, -s, -ing, -ed, -er/s kə'mand,
-z, -ɪŋ, -ɪd, -ɚ/z
commandement, -s kə'mandəmənt, -s
Note.—This old spelling of 'command-
ment' facilitates the necessary number of
beats required to metrically fulfill the
verse lines in MV, IV.i.447 *and* 1HVI,
I.iii.20; *also* PP, XX.44
commandment, -s kə'mandmənt, -s (*see*
commandement)
commeddl|e, -es, -ing, -ed kə'medl̩
[kɒ'm-, koʊ'm-], -z, -ɪŋ, -d
commenc|e, -es, -ing, -ed, -ement/s
kə'mens, -ɪz, -ɪŋ, -t, -mənt/s
commend, -s, -ing, -ed kə'mend, -z, -ɪŋ,
-ɪd
commendab|le, -ly, -leness kə'mendəb|l̩,
-lɪ, -l̩nɪs
Note.—Stressed on the first syllable
['kɒmɪndəbl̩] *in* 1HVI, IV.vi.57; ADO,
III.i.71, 73; COR, IV.vii.51, *and also,*
depending on how one chooses to scan
the line, HAM, I.ii.87; TS, IV.iii.102
commendation, -s ˌkɒmən'deɪʃn̩, -z
comment, -s, -ing, -ed 'kɒment, -s, -ɪŋ,
-ɪd
commentar|y (C.) (2HVI), **-ies**
'kɒməntə·ɹ|ɪ, -ɪz
commerce 'kɒmɚs (*stressed* [-'-] *in* TC,
I.iii.105, III.iii.204)
commiserat|e, -es, -ing, -ed kə'mɪzəɹeɪt,
-s, -ɪŋ, -ɪd
commiseration kəˌmɪzə'ɹeɪʃn̩
commission, -s, -ing, -ed, -er/s kə'mɪʃn̩,
-z, -ɪŋ, -d, -ɚ/z
commit, -s, -ting, -ted, -ter/s, -ment/s
kə'mɪt, -s, -ɪŋ, -ɪd, -ɚ/z, -mənt/s
committee, -s kə'mɪt̬ɪ, -z
commix, -es, -ing, -ed kɒ'mɪks [kə'm-],
-ɪz, -ɪŋ, -t
commixtion kɒ'mɪkstʃən
commixture kɒ'mɪkstʃɚ [kə'm-]
commodious, -ly, -ness kə'moʊdɪəs, -lɪ,
-nɪs

commodit|y, -ies kə'mɒdɪt|ɪ, -ɪz
commodore, -s 'kɒmədɔ˞, -z
common, -s; -er, -est, -ly, -ness 'kɒmən,
-z; -ɚ, -ɪst, -lɪ, -nɪs
commonalt|y, -ies 'kɒmənəlt|ɪ, -ɪz
commoner, -s 'kɒmənɚ, -z
common-hackneyed 'kɒmənˌhæknɪd
common-kissing 'kɒmənˌkɪsɪŋ
Commons (HV) 'kɒmənz
commonweal 'kɒmənˌwil
commonwealth, -s 'kɒmənwel̩θ, -s
commotion, -s kə'moʊʃn̩, -z
commune (*s.*), **-s** 'kɒmjun, -z
commun|e (*v.*), **-es, -ing, -ed** kə'mjun, -z,
-ɪŋ, -d
Note.—As a var. form of 'common,' this
word may be stressed on the first
syllable ['kɒmjun], *e.g.,* HAM, IV.v.199;
MEAS, IV.iii.103. *As a shortened form*
of 'communicate' in TS, Ind.i.101, *and*
due to where it falls in the verse line, it
is given primary stress on the first
syllable here as well, i.e., ['kɒmjun]
communicat|e, -es, -ing, -ed, -or/s
kə'mjunɪkeɪt, -s, -ɪŋ, -ɪd, -ɚ/z
communication, -s kəˌmjunɪ'keɪʃn̩, -z
communicative, -ly, -ness kə'mjunɪkətɪv
[-keɪt-], -lɪ, -nɪs
communion, -s kə'mjunjən, -z
commutual kə'mjutʃʊəl [kɒ'm-, koʊ'm-]
comonty 'kɒməntɪ
Note.—This highly contested word
appears in TS, Ind.ii.137. *It is consid-*
ered to be an error or a humorous
blunder on the part of the character
(Sly), and is typically emended to either
'comedy' or 'commodity'; two very
different words—the heart of the
controversy. The line itself (as given in
the Folio) is defective, or hypermetrical;
however, if one chooses to retain
'comonty,' then one should probably
regard it as being a hint to Sly's
pronunciation, as may also be indicated
by his 'gambold' instead of 'gambol'
only three words later
compact (*adj.*) kəm'pækt [kɒm'-, 'kɒm-]
compact (*s.*), **-s** 'kɒmpækt, -s
Note.—Sometimes stressed [kɒm'pækt]

in S., e.g., AYLI, V.iv.5; COM, II.ii.161; JUL, III.i.215; RIII, II.ii.133. *It may be stressed on either the first or second syllable in* TN, V.i.158, *depending on how one treats the word 'ceremony' in the line*

compact (*v.*)**, -s, -ing, -ed** kɒmˈpækt, -s, -ɪŋ, -ɪd

companion, -s, -ship kəmˈpænjən, -z, -ʃɪp

compan|y, -ies ˈkʌmpən|ɨ, -ɨz

comparab|le, -ly, -leness ˈkɒmpəˌɹəb|ļ, -lɨ, -ļnɪs

comparative, -s, -ly kəmˈpæɹətɪv, -z, -lɨ

compar|e, -es, -ing, -ed kəmˈpɛɚ, -z, -ɹɪŋ, -d

comparison, -s kəmˈpæɹɪsn̩, -z

compartment, -s kəmˈpɑɚtmənt, -s

compass, -es, -ing, -ed ˈkʌmpəs, -ɪz, -ɪŋ, -t

compassion kəmˈpæʃn̩

compassionate, -ly, -ness kəmˈpæʃn̩ɪt, -lɨ, -nɪs

compatibility kəmˌpæɡɨˈbɪlɪtɨ

compatib|le, -ly, -leness kəmˈpæɡɨb|ļ, -lɨ, -ļnɪs

compeer, -s ˈkɒmpɪɚ [kəmˈp-, kɒmˈp-], -z

compel, -s, -ling, -led; -lable kəmˈpel, -z, -ɪŋ, -d; -əbļ
Note.—Stressed on the first syllable, i.e., [ˈkɒmpeld] *in* HVIII, II.iii.87; MEAS, II.iv.57; TNK, III.i.68

compendium, -s kəmˈpendɪəm, -z

compensat|e, -es, -ing, -ed ˈkɒmpənseɪt, -s, -ɪŋ, -ɪd

compensation, -s ˌkɒmpənˈseɪʃn̩, -z

compet|e, -es, -ing, -ed kəmˈpit, -s, -ɪŋ, -ɪd

competen|ce, -cy, -t/ly ˈkɒmpɪtən|s, -sɨ, -t/lɨ

compil|e, -es, -ing, -ed kəmˈpaɪl, -z, -ɪŋ, -d

complain, -s, -ing, -ed, -er/s kəmˈpleɪn, -z, -ɪŋ, -d, -ɚ/z

complaint, -s kəmˈpleɪnt, -s

complement (*s.*)**, -s** ˈkɒmplɪmənt, -s

complement (*v.*)**, -s, -ing, -ed** ˈkɒmplɪment, -s, -ɪŋ, -ɪd

complet|e (*adj.*)**, -est, -ely, -eness** kəmˈplit, -ɪst, -lɨ, -nɪs
Note.—Stressed on the first syllable, i.e., [ˈkɒmplit] *in* 1HVI, I.ii.83; HAM, I.iv.52; LLL, I.i.135; RIII, IV.iv.190; MEAS, I.iii.3; TC, III.iii.181, IV.i.28

complet|e (*v.*)**, -es, -ing, -ed** kəmˈplit, -s, -ɪŋ, -ɪd

complexion, -s, -ed kəmˈplekʃn̩, -z, -d

complexit|y, -ies kəmˈpleksɪt|ɨ, -ɨz

complian|ce, -ces, -t/ly kəmˈplaɪən|s, -sɪz, -t/lɨ

complicat|e, -es, -ing, -ed ˈkɒmplɪkeɪt, -s, -ɪŋ, -ɪd

complication, -s ˌkɒmplɪˈkeɪʃn̩, -z

complice, -s ˈkɒmplɪs, -ɪz

complicity kəmˈplɪsɪtɨ

compliment (*s.*)**, -s** ˈkɒmplɪmənt, -s

compliment (*v.*)**, -s, -ing, -ed** ˈkɒmplɪment [ˌ--ˈ-], -s, -ɪŋ, -ɪd

complimental ˌkɒmplɪˈmentəl

complot (*s.*)**, -s** ˈkɒmplɒt, -s
Note.—Stressed on the second syllable, i.e., [kɒmˈplɒts] *in* RIII, III.i.192

complotted (*v.*) kɒmˈplɒtɪd

compl|y, -ies, -ying, -ied kəmˈpl|aɪ, -aɪz, -aɪɪŋ, -aɪd

component, -s kəmˈpoʊnənt, -s

comport, -s, -ing, -ed, -ment kəmˈpɔɚt, -s, -ɪŋ, -ɪd, -mənt

compos|e, -es, -ing, -ed, -er/s kəmˈpoʊz, -ɪz, -ɪŋ, -d, -ɚ/z

composition, -s ˌkɒmpəˈzɪʃn̩, -z

composture kəmˈpɒstʃɚ [kɒmˈp-]

composure kəmˈpoʊʒɚ

compound (*adj., s.*)**, -s** ˈkɒmpaʊnd, -z

compound (*v.*)**, -s, -ing, -ed** kɒmˈpaʊnd [kəm-], -z, -ɪŋ, -ɪd

comprehend, -s, -ing, -ed ˌkɒmpɹɪˈhend, -z, -ɪŋ, -ɪd

comprehension ˌkɒmpɹɪˈhenʃn̩

---

i w**e** ɨ c**i**ty ɪ h**i**t e l**e**t ɛ d**e**but æ c**a**n a p**a**ss ɝ b**i**rd ʌ h**u**t ə **a**gain ɚ supp**er** u y**ou** ʊ sh**ou**ld o **o**bey ɔ **a**wl ɒ c**o**p ɑ f**a**ther eɪ p**ai**d aɪ h**igh** oʊ g**o** ɔɪ v**oi**ce aʊ f**ou**nd ɪɚ **ear** ɛɚ **air** ʊɚ **poor** ɔɚ f**or**k ɑɚ p**ar**k aɪɚ f**ire** aʊɚ h**our** b b**oy** p p**i**t d d**o**g t t**o**p g g**o**t k k**i**d h h**ow** fi be**h**ave dʒ j**o**t tʃ **ch**ew z **z**any s **s**oft v **v**at f **f**at ʒ trea**s**ure ʃ **sh**ip ð **th**e θ **th**in m **m**an n **n**o ŋ ha**ng** l **l**ip j **y**es w **w**on ʍ **wh**ew ɹ **r**igger, ai**r**y ɾ ma**tt**er

comprehensive, -ly, -ness ˌkɒmpɹɪˈhensɪv,
-lɪ, -nɪs
compremises ˈkɒmpɹʊmaɪ̆zɪz,
kɒmˈpɹemɪsɪz [kəm-]
*Note.—There is a bit of contention about
this word (appearing in* MWW, I.i.30*).
Most editors agree that 'compremises'
(in the First Folio) is merely an alt.
spelling of 'compromises,' and that both
words are therefore pronounced*
[ˈkɒmpɹʊmaɪ̆zɪz]. *However, Giorgio
Melchiori, editor of* MWW *(The Arden
Shakespeare, 2000), suggests that
"Evans may be thinking in terms of
'premises' for reconciliation." His
meaning of premises here is as in logic,
law, and argument. Under this precept,
the secondary pronunciation is proffered
as a sensible, if unusual, solution.
Melchiori points out that "The preten-
tious use and misuse of legal terminol-
ogy is another aspect of the 'comedy of
language' in this play" (cf.* MWW,
I.i.34–5, *line annotation,* The Arden
Shakespeare, *Giorgio Melchiori, editor,
2000)*
compress (*s.*), **-es** ˈkɒmpɹes, -ɪz
compress (*v.*), **-es, -ing, -ed, -or/s**
kəmˈpɹes, -ɪz, -ɪŋ, -t, -ɚ/z
compression, -s kəmˈpɹeʃn̩, -z
comprimise (*var. of* **compromise**, *q.v.*)
ˈkɒmpɹɪmaɪ̆z
compris|e, -es, -ing, -ed kəmˈpɹaɪ̆z, -ɪz,
-ɪŋ, -d
compromis|e, -es, -ing, -ed, -er/s
ˈkɒmpɹʊmaɪ̆z, -ɪz, -ɪŋ, -d, -ɚ/z
compt (*archaic var. spelling of* **count**),
-less ˈkaʊ̆nt, -lɪs
comptible (*archaic var. spelling of*
countable) ˈkaʊ̆ntɪbl̩
comptroller, -s kənˈtɹoʊ̆lɚ, -z
compulsion kəmˈpʌlʃn̩
compulsive, -ly, -ness kəmˈpʌlsɪv, -lɪ,
-nɪs
compunctious kəmˈpʌŋkʃəs
computation, -s ˌkɒmpjuˈteɪ̆ʃn̩ [-pjʊ-], -z
comrade, -s, -ship ˈkɒmɹæd [-ɹɪd], -z, -ʃɪp
([ˌkɒmˈɹædz] *in* 1HIV, IV.i.96)
con, -s, -ning, -ned ˈkɒn, -z, -ɪŋ, -d

concave ˌkɒnˈkeɪ̆v [ˈ--] [ˌkɒŋˈk-]
concavities ˌkɒnˈkævɪtɪz [ˌkɒŋˈk-]
conceal, -s, -ing, -ed, -ment/s; -able
kənˈsil, -z, -ɪŋ, -d, -mənt/s; -əbl̩
Note.—Stressed on the first syllable, i.e.,
[ˈkɒnsild] *in* RJ, III.iii.97; *and probably
in* AYLI, III.ii.196*—despite its being in
prose—by way of recessive accenting*
conceit, -s, -ing, -ed kənˈsit, -s, -ɪŋ, -ɪd
conceited, -ly, -ness kənˈsitɪd, -lɪ, -nɪs
conceitless kənˈsitlɪs
conceivab|le, -ly, -leness kənˈsivəbl̩, -lɪ,
-l̩nɪs
conceiv|e, -es, -ing, -ed kənˈsiv, -z,
-ɪŋ, -d
concent kənˈsent
concentrat|e, -es, -ing, -ed ˈkɒnsn̩tɹeɪ̆t, -s,
-ɪŋ, -ɪd
concentration, -s ˌkɒnsn̩ˈtɹeɪ̆ʃn̩, -z
concept, -s ˈkɒnsept, -s
conception, -s kənˈsepʃn̩, -z
conceptious kənˈsepʃəs
concern (*s., v.*), **-s, -ing, -ed, -ment/s**
kənˈsɝn, -z, -ɪŋ, -d, -mənt/s
concernanc|y, -ies kənˈsɝnəns|ɪ, -ɪz
concern|ed (*adj.*), **-edly, -edness**
kənˈsɝn|d, -ɪdlɪ, -ɪdnɪs
concert (*s.*), **-s** ˈkɒnsɝt [-sɚt], -s
concert (*v.*), **-s, -ing, -ed** kənˈsɝt, -s, -ɪŋ,
-ɪd
concertina, -s ˌkɒnsəˈtinə, -z
concession, -s kənˈseʃn̩, -z
concis|e, -er, -est, -ely, -eness kənˈsaɪ̆s,
-ɚ, -ɪst, -lɪ, -nɪs
conclave, -s ˈkɒnkleɪ̆v [ˈkɒŋk-], -z
conclud|e, -es, -ing, -ed kənˈklud [kəŋˈk-],
-z, -ɪŋ, -ɪd
conclusion, -s kənˈkluʒn̩ [kəŋˈk-], -z
conclusive, -ly, -ness kənˈklusɪv [kəŋˈk-],
-lɪ, -nɪs
concoct, -s, -ing, -ed, -er/s kənˈkɒkt
[kəŋˈk-], -s, -ɪŋ, -ɪd, -ɚ/z
concoction, -s kənˈkɒkʃn̩ [kəŋˈk-], -z
Concolinel (LLL) kɒnˈkɒlɪnel
*Note.—The pronunciation of this
obscure word, thought to be the title of
Moth's song at the beginning of Act III
in* LLL, *changes depending on one's
interpretation of its origin. Suggestions*

range from Italian to a corruption of the Irish 'Can cailin gheal' which, translated, means 'Sing, maiden fair'

concord (*s.*), **-s** 'kɒnkɔɚd ['kɒŋ-], -z

concord (*v.*), **-s, -ing, -ed** kənˈkɔɚd [kəŋ-], -z, -ɪŋ, -ɪd

concordant kənˈkɔɚdn̩t [kəŋ-]

concubine, -s 'kɒŋkjʊbaɪn ['kɒnk-], -z

concuby (*obsolete, abbreviated form of* **concubine**) 'kɒŋkjʊbɪ ['kɒnk-]

concupiscen|ce, -t kɒnˈkjupɪsən|s, -t

concupiscible kɒnˈkjupɪsɪbl̩

concupy (*obsolete, rare form of* **concuby**, *meaning concubine*) 'kɒnkjʊpɪ

condemn, -s, -ing, -ed; -able kənˈdem, -z, -ɪŋ, -d; -nəbl̩
Note.—Arguably stressed on the first syllable ['kɒndemd] *in AC, I.iii.49. Also, when 'condemned' is to be three syllables to fulfill metrical requirements of S.'s verse, the 'n' is sounded, i.e.,* [kənˈdemnɪd], *in HV, IV.Chorus.22; KJ, V.vii.48; RJ, V.iii.226; TIT, III.i.8; Sonn. 99.6*

condign, -ly, -ness kənˈdaɪn, -lɪ, -nɪs
Note.—Can be ['kɒndaɪn] *in S., e.g., 2HVI, III.i.130; and perhaps LLL, I.ii.25*

condol|e, -es, -ing, -ed, -ement/s kənˈdoʊl, -z, -ɪŋ, -d, -mənt/s

conduc|e, -es, -ing, -ed, -ement/s kənˈdjus, -ɪz, -ɪŋ, -t, -ment/s

conduct (*s.*), **-s** 'kɒndʌkt, -s
Note.—In TIT, IV.iv.64, this words looks like it wants to be given primary syllabic stress on the second syllable, i.e., [kɒnˈdʌkt]; *however, by simply giving 'amain' in the verse line slightly more length or heavier emphasis, 'conduct' falls out normally, creating a feminine ending*

conduct (*v.*), **-s, -ing, -ed, -or/s** kənˈdʌkt, -s, -ɪŋ, -ɪd, -ɚ/z

conduit, -s 'kɒndɪt ['kɒndjʊɪt, 'kʌn-], -s

confection, -s, -ing, -ed, -er/s kənˈfekʃn̩, -z, -ɪŋ, -d, -ɚ/z

confectionary kənˈfekʃnəɹɪ

confederate (*s., adj.*), **-s** kənˈfedəɹɪt, -s

confederat|e (*v.*), **-es, -ing, -ed** kənˈfedəɹeɪt, -s, -ɪŋ, -ɪd

confederation, -s kənˌfedəˈɹeɪʃn̩, -z

confer, -s, -ring, -red kənˈfɝ, -z, -ɹɪŋ, -d

confess, -es, -ing, -ed, -edly kənˈfes, -ɪz, -ɪŋ, -t, -ɪdlɪ
Note.—In TNK, III.i.35, 'confessed' is arguably stressed primarily on the first syllable, i.e., ['kɒnfest], *or it is simply elongated, i.e.,* [kənˈfesɪd]

confession, -s kənˈfeʃn̩, -z

confessor, -s kənˈfesɚ, -z
Note.—Can also be ['kɒnfesɚ, -sɔɚ] *in S., e.g., HVIII, I.i.218; RJ, II.vi.21, III.iii.49; MEAS, IV.iii.128, and arguably in MEAS, II.i.35*

confid|e, -es, -ing/ly, -ed, -er/s kənˈfaɪd, -z, -ɪŋ/lɪ, -ɪd, -ɚ/z

confiden|ce, -ces, -t/ly 'kɒnfɪdən|s, -sɪz, -t/lɪ (*see Note for* **demure**)

confidenti|al, -ally ˌkɒnfɪˈdenʃ|l̩, -əlɪ

confine (*s.*), **-s** 'kɒnfaɪn
Note.—In TEM, IV.i.121, this word is arguably stressed on the second syllable [kɒnˈfaɪn(z)]; *also, AYLI, II.i.24; KJ, IV.ii.246. It is definitely stressed on the second syllable in LEAR, II.ii.337 and Sonn. 84.3. In OTH, I.ii.27, it is stressed on either the first or second syllable, depending on how many syllables one gives 'circumscription'*

confin|e (*v.*), **-es, -ing, -ed, -eless, -ement/s** kənˈfaɪn, -z, -ɪŋ, -d, -lɪs, -mənt/s
Note.—Arguably stressed on the first syllable, i.e., ['kɒnfaɪnd] *in Sonn. 107.4*

confiner (*inhabitant*), **-s** kənˈfaɪnɚ, -z
Note.—In CYM, IV.ii.337, this word is given primary stress on the first syllable, i.e., ['kɒnfaɪnɚz]

---

i wˌe ɪ city ɪ hˌit e lˌet ɛ debut æ cˌan a pˌass ɝ bˌird ʌ hˌut ə again ɚ suppˌer u yˌou ʊ shˌould o ˌobey ɔ ˌawl ɒ cˌop ɑ fˌather eɪ pˌaid aɪ hˌigh oʊ gˌo ɔɪ vˌoice aʊ fˌound ɪɚ ˌear ɛɚ ˌair ʊɚ pˌoor ɔɚ fˌork ɑɚ pˌark aɪɚ fˌire aʊɚ hˌour b bˌoy p pˌit d dˌog t tˌop g gˌot k kˌid h hˌow fi behˌave dʒ jˌot tʃ chˌew z zˌany s sˌoft v vˌat f fˌat ʒ treaˌsure ʃ shˌip ð thˌe θ thˌin m mˌan n nˌo ŋ haˌng l lˌip j yˌes w wˌon ʍ whˌew ɹ rˌigger, aiˌry ɾ matˌter

confirm, -s, -ing, -ed, -er/s kənˈfɝˑm, -z,
-ɪŋ, -d, -ɚ/z
*Note.—In ADO, V.iv.17, this word is
stressed on the first syllable, i.e.,*
[ˈkɒnfɝˑm(d)]
confirmation, -s ˌkɒnfɚˈmeɪʃn̩, -z
confirmities kənˈfɝˑmɪtɪz
confiscate (*adj.*) ˈkɒnfɪskɪt
Note.—Stressed on the second syllable
[kɒnˈfɪskɪt, kən-] *in* CYM, V.v.324
confiscat|e, -es, -ing, -ed, -or/s
ˈkɒnfɪskeɪt, -s, -ɪŋ, -ɪd, -ɚ/z
*Note.—Stressed on the second syllable,
i.e.,* [kɒnˈfɪskeɪt] *in* COM, I.i.20
confix, -es, -ing, -ed kənˈfɪks [kɒn-], -ɪz,
-ɪŋ, -t
conflict (*s.*), **-s** ˈkɒnflɪkt, -s
conflict (*v.*), **-s, -ing, -ed** kənˈflɪkt, -s, -ɪŋ,
-ɪd
confluence, -s ˈkɒnfluəns, -ɪz
confluent, -s, -ly ˈkɒnfluənt, -s, -lɪ
conflux ˈkɒnflʌks
*Note.—Stressed on the second syllable,
i.e.,* [kɒnˈflʌks] *in* TC, I.iii.7
conform, -s, -ing, -ed, -er/s; -able
kənˈfɔˑm, -z, -ɪŋ, -d, -ɚ/z; -əbl̩
conformation, -s ˌkɒnfɚˈmeɪʃn̩, -z
conformist, -s kənˈfɔˑmɪst, -s
confound (*v.*), **-s, -ing, -ed** kənˈfaʊnd, -z,
-ɪŋ, -ɪd
*Note.—When spoken as an oath, e.g.,
'confound it,' the pronunciation is
usually* [ˌkɒnˈfaʊnd, ˈkɒnˌfaʊnd]
confounded (*adj., adv.*), **-ly** ˌkɒnˈfaʊndɪd
[kən-], -lɪ
confus|e, -es, -ing, -ed; -edly, -edness
kənˈfjuz, -ɪz, -ɪŋ, -d; -ɪdlɪ, -ɪdnɪs
confusion, -s kənˈfjuʒn̩, -z
confutation, -s ˌkɒnfjuˈteɪʃn̩, -z
confut|e, -es, -ing, -ed kənˈfjut, -s, -ɪŋ, -ɪd
congeal, -s, -ing, -ed, -ment/s; -able
kənˈdʒil, -z, -ɪŋ, -d, -mənt/s; -əbl̩
*Note.—Arguably stressed on the first
syllable, i.e.,* [ˈkɒndʒild] *in* RIII, I.ii.56
congee, congé, *or* **congie** (*take ceremoni-
ous leave of; courteous bow or curtsy*)
ˈkɒndʒɪ (*Fr.* kɔ̃ʒe)
conger, -s ˈkɒŋgɚ [ˈkʌŋgɚ], -z
congest, -s, -ing, -ed kənˈdʒest, -s, -ɪŋ, -ɪd

congratulat|e, -es, -ing, -ed, -or/s
kənˈgɹætʃuleɪt [kəŋˈgɹ-], -s, -ɪŋ, -ɪd,
-ɚ/z
congratulation, -s kənˌgɹætʃuˈleɪʃn̩
[kəŋˈgɹ-], -z
congree (*cf.* **congrue**), **-ing** kəŋˈgɹi, -ɪŋ
congreeted kəŋˈgɹitɪd
congregat|e, -es, -ing, -ed ˈkɒŋgɹɪgeɪt, -s,
-ɪŋ, -ɪd
congregation, -s ˌkɒŋgɹɪˈgeɪʃn̩, -z
congru|e, -ing kənˈgɹu [ˈkɒŋgɹu], -ɪŋ
*Note.—Alexander Schmidt notes that in
the First Quarto's reading of* HV, I.
ii.182, *'congrueth' is spurious, opting
instead for the First Folio's 'congree-
ing.' In either case, the stress is on the
second syllable. In* HAM, IV.iii.67,
*'congruing,' taken from the Second
Quarto version, is stressed on the first
syllable. The First Folio in this instance
gives the word 'conjuring'*
congruen|ce/s, -cy, -cies, -t/ly
ˈkɒŋgɹuən|s/ɪz [kənˈgɹuən|s/ɪz], -sɪ, -sɪz,
-t/lɪ
cong|y (*obsolete form of* **congee**, *q.v.*),
-ied ˈkɒndʒ|ɪ, -ɪd
conject (*guess; surmise*), **-s, -ing, -ed**
kənˈdʒekt, -s, -ɪŋ, -ɪd
conjecturable kənˈdʒektʃəɹəbl̩
conjectural, -ly kənˈdʒektʃəɹəl, -ɪ
conjectur|e, -es, -ing, -ed kənˈdʒektʃ|ɚ,
-ɚz, -əɹɪŋ, -ɚd
conjoin, -s, -ing, -ed kənˈdʒɔɪn, -z,
-ɪŋ, -d
conjoint, -ly kənˈdʒɔɪnt [kɒn-], -lɪ
conjunct kənˈdʒʌŋkt
conjunction, -s kənˈdʒʌŋkʃn̩, -z
conjunctive, -ly kənˈdʒʌŋktɪv, -lɪ
conjuration, -s ˌkʌndʒuˈɹeɪʃn̩, -z [ˌkɒn-]
conjur|e (*entreating solemnly*), **-es,
-ing/s, -ed** kənˈdʒuɚ, -z, -ɹɪŋ/z, -d
con|jure (*summon spirits or to use
magic*), **-jures, -juring, -jured,
-jurer/s, [-juror/s]** ˈkʌn|dʒɚ [ˈkɒn-],
-ɚz, -dʒə·ɹɪŋ, -dʒə·d, -dʒə·ɹɚz,
[-dʒə·ɹɚ/z]
conjuro te (*L.*) (2HVI, I.iv.sd) kənˈdʒuro
ˈtɛ
Note.—This portion of a Latin conjura-

tion appears in the Stage Direction
between lines 22 and 23 in Act I, scene
iv, of 2HVI and is read aloud by either
Bolingbroke or Southwell

conniv|e, -es, -ing, -ed, -er/s; -ery
kə'naɪv, -z, -ɪŋ, -d, -ɚ/z; -ə·ɹɨ

conquer, -s, -ing, -ed, -or/s 'kɒŋkɚ, -z,
-ɹɪŋ, -d, -ɹɚ/z

Conqueror, Richard (TS) 'ɹɪtʃɚd
'kɒŋkə·ɹɚ

conquest, -s 'kɒŋkwest, -s

Conrade (ADO) 'kɒnɹæd

consanguine kɒn'sæŋgwɪn [kən-]

consanguineous, -ly ˌkɒnsæŋ'gwɪnɪəs, -lɨ

consanguinity ˌkɒnsæŋ'gwɪnɪtɨ

conscience (C.), -s 'kɒnʃəns, -ɪz

conscionab|le, -ly, -leness 'kɒnʃn̩əb|l̩
[-ʃnə-, -ʃənə-], -lɨ, -l̩nɪs

conscious, -ly, -ness 'kɒnʃəs, -lɨ, -nɪs

consecrat|e, -es, -ing, -ed, -or/s
'kɒnsɪkɹeɪt, -s, -ɪŋ, -ɪd, -ɚ/z
Note.—In COM, II.ii.132, S. uses
'consecrate' to represent a past tense, a
custom lasting well into the nineteenth
century, and is pronounced the same
whether a verb or a past participle, i.e.,
['kɒnsɪkɹeɪt]; similarly, in Sonn. 74.6
(cf. Note for **create**)

consecration, -s ˌkɒnsɪ'kɹeɪʃn̩, -z

consent, -s, -ing, -ed kən'sent, -s, -ɪŋ, -ɪd

conservation, -ist/s ˌkɒnsə·'veɪʃn̩, -ɪst/s

conserve (s.), -s kən'sɜ·v ['kɒnsɜ·v], -z

conserv|e (v.), -es, -ing, -ed kən'sɜ·v, -z,
-ɪŋ, -d

consider, -s, -ing/s, -ed kən'sɪdɚ, -z,
-ɹɪŋ/z, -d

considerab|le, -ly, -leness kən'sɪdə·ɹəb|l̩,
-lɨ, -l̩nɪs

considerance kən'sɪdə·ɹəns

considerate, -ly, -ness kən'sɪdə·ɹɪt, -lɨ,
-nɪs

consideration, -s kənˌsɪdə·'ɹeɪʃn̩, -z

consign, -s, -ing, -ed, -er/s, -ment/s
kən'saɪn, -z, -ɪŋ, -d, -ɚ/z, -mənt/s

Note.—Stressed on the first syllable, i.e.,
['kɒnsaɪnd] in TC, IV.iv.44

consist, -s, -ing, -ed kən'sɪst, -s, -ɪŋ, -ɪd

consistor|y, -ies kən'sɪstəɹ|ɨ, -ɨz
Note.—In HVIII, II.iv.90 and RIII, II.
ii.151, 'consistory' is given primary
stress on the first syllable, i.e.,
['kɒnsɪstə·ɹɨ]

consolate (v.) 'kɒnsəleɪt

consolation, -s ˌkɒnsə'leɪʃn̩ [-sʊ'l-], -z

consonanc|e, -es, -y 'kɒnsənəns, -ɪz, -ɨ

consort (s.), -s 'kɒnsɔ·t, -s

consort (v.), -s, -ing, -ed kən'sɔ·t, -s, -ɪŋ,
-ɪd

conspectuit|y, -ies ˌkɒnspek'tjuɪt|ɨ, -ɨz

conspirac|y, -ies kən'spɹɪəs|ɨ, -ɨz

conspirator, -s kən'spɹɪətɚ, -z

conspir|e, -es, -ing, -ed, -er/s kən'spaɪɚ,
-z, -ɹɪŋ, -d, -ɹɚ/z

conspirant (conspirator) kən'spaɪɚɹənt

constable (C.) (ADO, HV), -s 'kʌnstəbl̩
['kɒn-], -z

constabular|y, -ies kən'stæbjʊləɹ|ɨ, -ɨz

Constance (KJ) 'kɒnstəns

constancy 'kɒnstənsɨ

Constantine (1HVI) 'kɒnstəntin

Constantinople (HV) ˌkɒnstæntɹ'noʊpl̩

constellation, -s ˌkɒnstɹ'leɪʃn̩, -z

conster (construe), -s 'kɒnstɚ, -z

constrain, -s, -ing, -ed, -edly; -able
kən'stɹeɪn, -z, -ɪŋ, -d, -ɪdlɨ; -əbl̩

constring|e, -es, -ing, -ed kən'stɹɪndʒ, -ɪz,
-ɪŋ, -d

constru|e, -es, -ing, -ed kən'stɹu, -z, -ɪŋ,
-d
Note.—Some modern dictionaries allow
for the s. form to be pronounced with
primary stress on the first syllable, i.e.,
['kɒnstɹu]. In S.'s day, the v. form of
'construe' was given primary stress on
the first syllable, as was the older form
of the word that typically appears in the
Folio, i.e., 'conster'—modern editors
usually emending to 'construe.'

---

i wɛ ɨ cɨty ɪ hɪt e lɛt ɛ dɛbut æ cæn a pæss ɝ bɝd ʌ hʌt ə again ɚ suppɚ u you
ʊ shoʊld o ObeY ɔ awl ɒ cɒp ɑ fɑther eɪ paɪd aɪ hɪgh oʊ go ɔɪ voɪce aʊ foʊnd ɪɚ ear
ɛɚ air ʊɚ poor ɔɚ fork ɑɚ park aɪɚ fire aʊɚ hour b boy p pit d dog t top g got
k kid h how fi behave dʒ jot tʃ chew z zany s soft v vat f fat ʒ treasure ʃ ship ð the
θ thin m man n no ŋ hang l lip j yes w won ʍ whew ɹ rigger, aiɹy ɟ matter

*Regardless of which word the editor
chooses to use, it is given first-syllable
stress in JUL, I.ii.44, I.iii.34, II.i.307;
TGV, I.ii.56; TS, III.i.30, 40 (see*
misconstrue*)*

consul, -s; -ship/s 'kɒnsəl, -z; -ʃɪp/s
consult, -s, -ing, -ed kən'sʌlt, -s, -ɪŋ, -ɪd
consultant, -s kən'sʌltənt, -s
consultation, -s ˌkɒnsəl'teɪʃn̩, -z
consum|e, -es, -ing, -ed, -er/s kən'sjum,
-z, -ɪŋ, -d, -ɚ/z
consummate (*adj.*), **-ly** kən'sʌmɪt, -lɪ
*Note.—In MEAS, V.i.376, this word is
given primary stress on the first syllable,
i.e.,* ['kɒnsʊmɪt, -meɪt]. *In this instance,
'consummate' is a participle, a word
formed from a verb and used as an
adjective or a noun; in ADO, III.ii.1,
this word might appear at first to be an
adj. when it is actually a p.p. Here, S.
follows a rule whereby the final 'd'
indicating past tense is often omitted. In
this case, it is pronounced* ['kɒnsʊmeɪt]
(cf. Abbott's A Shakespearian Grammar
§ 342; and see Note for **consecrate***)*
consummat|e (*v.*), **-es, -ing, -ed, -or/s**
'kɒnsjʊmeɪt, -s, -ɪŋ, -ɪd, -ɚ/z
consummation, -s ˌkɒnsjʊ'meɪʃn̩ [-sʌm-],
-z
consumption, -s kən'sʌmpʃn̩, -z
consumptive, -s; -ly, -ness kən'sʌmptɪv,
-z; -lɪ, -nɪs
contact (*s.*), **-s** 'kɒntækt, -s
contact (*v.*), **-s, -ing, -ed** 'kɒntækt
[kən'tækt], -s, -ɪŋ, -ɪd
contagion, -s kən'teɪdʒn̩ [-dʒən, -dʒɪən],
-z
contagious, -ly, -ness kən'teɪdʒəs, -lɪ,
-nɪs
contain, -s, -ing, -ed, -er/s; -able
kən'teɪn, -z, -ɪŋ, -d, -ɚ/z; -əbl̩
contaminate (*adj.*) kən'tæmɪnɪt
contaminat|e (*v.*), **-es, -ing, -ed, -er/s**
kən'tæmɪneɪt, -s, -ɪŋ, -ɪd, -ɚ/z
contamination, -s kənˌtæmɪ'neɪʃn̩, -z
contemn, -s, -ing, -ed, -er/s kən'tem, -z,
-ɪŋ, -d, -ɚ/z [-nɚ/z]
*Note.—In TN, I.v.274, the metrical
demands of the line require 'contemned'*

*to be trisyllabic, and thus the 'n' is
pronounced, i.e.,* [kən'temnɪd]
contemplat|e, -es, -ing, -ed, -or/s
'kɒntəmpleɪt, -s, -ɪŋ, -ɪd, -ɚ/z
contemplation, -s ˌkɒntəm'pleɪʃn̩, -z
contemplative, -ly, -ness kən'templətɪv
['kɒntəmpleɪtɪv], -lɪ, -nɪs
contempt, -s kən'tempt, -s
contempt (*confusion with, and perhaps
corruption of,* **content** (*s.*) *in LLL and
MWW*), **-s** 'kɒntempt [kɒn'tempt], -s
contemptibility kənˌtemptɪ'bɪlɪtɪ
contemptib|le, -ly, -leness kən'temptɪbl̩,
-lɪ, -l̩nɪs
contemptuous, -ly, -ness kən'temptjʊəs,
-lɪ, -nɪs
contend, -s, -ing, -ed, -er/s kən'tend, -z,
-ɪŋ, -ɪd, -ɚ/z
content (*s.*), **-s** 'kɒntent, -s
Note.—Can be [kɒn'tent(s)] *in S., e.g.,*
AYLI, IV.iii.8, 21, V.iv.129; LC, 19, 56;
LEAR, II.ii.224; MEAS, IV.ii.93;
MWW, IV.vi.13; MV, III.ii.242; OTH,
II.i.196; RII, V.ii.38; WT, III.i.20; Sonn.
55.3
content (*v., adj.*), **-s, -ing, -ed/ly, -edness,
-ment** kən'tent, -s, -ɪŋ, -ɪd/lɪ, -ɪdnɪs,
-mənt
content-a kən'tentə (*see* **dat**)
contention, -s kən'tenʃn̩, -z
contentious, -ly, -ness kən'tenʃəs, -lɪ, -nɪs
contentless kən'tentlɪs
contestation, -s ˌkɒntes'teɪʃn̩, -z
continen|ce, -cy 'kɒntɪnən|s, -sɪ
continent, -s 'kɒntɪnənt, -s
continental ˌkɒntɪ'nentl̩
continual, -ly kən'tɪnjʊəl, -ɪ
continuance, -s kən'tɪnjʊəns, -ɪz
continuant, -s, -ly kən'tɪnjʊənt, -s, -lɪ
continuate kən'tɪnjʊɪt
continu|e, -es, -ing, -ed, -er/s kən'tɪnju,
-z, -ɪŋ, -d, -ɚ/z
continuous, -ly, -ness kən'tɪnjʊəs, -lɪ, -nɪs
contract (*s.*), **-s** 'kɒntɹækt, -s
Note.—Sometimes [kɒn'tɹækt] *in S.,
e.g.,* 1HVI, V.i.46, V.iv.156, V.v.28;
RJ, II.ii.117; ALL'S, II.iii.178; WT,
IV.iv.418; RIII, III.vii.5, 6; MEAS,
I.ii.134, V.i.208

contract (*v.*), **-s, -ing, -ed** kən'tɹækt, -s, -ɪŋ, -ɪd

contraction, -s kən'tɹækʃn̩, -z

contractor, -s 'kɒntɹæktɚ [kən'tɹ-], -z

contradict, -s, -ing, -ed ‚kɒntɹə'dɪkt, -s, -ɪŋ, -ɪd

contradiction, -s ‚kɒntɹə'dɪkʃn̩, -z

contraption, -s kən'tɹæpʃn̩, -z

contrariet|y, -ies ‚kɒntɹə'ɹaɪ̆t|ɨ, -ɨz

contrarious, -ly kən'tɹɛȝ̆·ɹɪəs, -lɨ

contrar|y, -ies, -ily 'kɒntɹəɹ|ɨ, -ɪz, -ɪlɨ
Note.—This word in KJ, IV.ii.198 *is an adj. and happens to scan with primary stress on the second syllable, i.e.,* [kən'tɹɛȝ̆·ɹɨ]. *In* RJ, I.v.84, *this word is made into a verb meaning 'to oppose,' and likewise should be given primary stress on the second syllable*

contrar|y, -ily (*to be stubborn*) kən'tɹɛȝ̆·ɹ|ɨ, -ɪlɨ

contrite, -ly, -ness kən'tɹaɪ̆t, -lɨ, -nɪs (['kɒntɹaɪ̆t] *in* LUC, 1727*; and arguably so in* HV, IV.i.293)

contriv|e, -es, -ing, -ed, -er/s kən'tɹaɪ̆v, -z, -ɪŋ, -d, -ɚ/z
Note.—Arguably given primary stress on the first syllable, i.e., ['kɒntɹaɪ̆vd] *in* OTH, I.ii.3

control, -s, -ling, -led, -ler/s, -ment; -lable kən'tɹoŭl, -z, -ɪŋ, -d, -ɚ/z, -mənt; -əbl̩

controversia|l, -ly ‚kɒntɹʊ'vȝ·ʃə|l [-'vȝ·sɪə|l], -lɨ

controvers|y, -ies 'kɒntɹəvȝ·s|ɨ [-tɹʊv-], -ɨz

contumelious, -ly, -ness ‚kɒntju'milĭəs [-tjʊ-], -lɨ, -nɪs

contumel|y, -ies 'kɒntjuml|ɨ [-tjʊm-, 'kɒntjʊmɪlɨ, -məlɨ], -ɨz

contusion, -s kən'tju3n̩, -z

con tutto il cuore, ben trovato (*It.*) (TS, I.ii.24) kon 'tuˑtto il kʊ'ɔˑɾɛ bɛn tro'vɑˑto

conundrum, -s kə'nʌndɹəm, -z

conven|e, -es, -ing, -ed, -er/s kən'vin, -z, -ɪŋ, -d, -ɚ/z

convenien|ce, -ces, -t/ly kən'vinjən|s, -sɪz, -t/lɨ

conveniency kən'vinjənsɨ

convent (*s.*) (*religious community*), **-s** 'kɒnvent [-vənt], -s

convent (*v.*) (*to assemble, to summon*), **-s, -ing, -ed** kɒn'vent [kən-], -s, -ɪŋ, -ɪd

conventicle, -s kən'ventɪkl̩, -z
Note.—Sometimes ['kɒnven‚tɪkl̩(z)] *in* S., *e.g.,* 2HVI, III.i.166

conversant, -ly kən'vȝ·sənt ['kɒnvɚ·sənt], -lɨ

convers|e, -es, -ing, -ed kən'vȝ·s, -ɪz, -ɪŋ, -t
Note.—In OTH, III.i.38, *'converse' is a subject noun (to stand for 'conversation'), and although it is still given primary stress on the second syllable, it probably warrants a pronunciation closer to* [kɒn'vȝ·s]

conversion, -s kən'vȝ·3n̩, -z

convert (*s.*), **-s** 'kɒnvȝ·t, -s

convert (*v.*), **-s, -ing, -ed, -er/s** kən'vȝ·t, -s, -ɪŋ, -ɪd, -ɚ/z

convertite, -s 'kɒnvȝ·taɪ̆t, -s

convey, -s, -ing, -ed, -er/s; -able kən'veĭ, -z, -ɪŋ, -d, -ɚ/z; -əbl̩

conveyance, -s kən'veĭəns, -ɪz

convive kɒn'viv [kən-, -'vaɪ̆v]

convocation, -s ‚kɒnvoŏ'keĭʃn̩, -z

convoy, -s, -ing, -ed 'kɒnvɔĭ, -z, -ɪŋ, -d

con|y, -ies 'koŏn|ɨ ['kʌn|ɨ], -ɨz

cony-catch, -ing, -ed 'koŏnɨ‚kætʃ ['kʌnɨ-], -ɪŋ, -t

coo, -es, -ing, -ed 'ku, -z, -ɪŋ, -d

cook, -s, -ing, -ed 'kʊk, -s, -ɪŋ, -t

Cook, William (2HIV) 'wɪljəm 'kʊk
Note.—Some editors prefer not to capitalize 'cook' in 2HIV, V.i.9, *but* S. *supplies many other such instances of characters whose names are extensions of their trade. There is no reason to*

---

suppose that this instance does not follow suit, and so I have included it as a full proper noun

cooker|y, -ies ˈkʊkə˞ɹ|ɪ, -ɪz

cookie, -s ˈkʊkɪ, -z

cool, -s, -ing, -ed; -er, -est, -ly, -ness ˈkul, -z, -ɪŋ, -d; -ə˞, -ɪst, -lɪ, -nɪs

cooler, -s ˈkulə˞, -z

coop, -s, -ing, -ed ˈkup, -s, -ɪŋ, -t

cop, -s, -ping, -ped ˈkɒp, -s, -ɪŋ, -t

co-partners ˌkoʊˈpɑ˞tnə˞z

copatain (*high-crowned hat in the shape of a sugar-loaf*) ˈkɒpəteɪn, ˈkɒpətɪn *Note.—This obsolete and rare word in TS,V.i.59 is presumably the same as 'copintank.' The OED does not assert a pronunciation for either of these words, but I have included both of these (conjectural) pronunciations based on the ideas that* [ˈkɒpəteɪn], *particularly in the last syllable, could be very near to the sound in 'copintank,' and* [ˈkɒpətɪn], *also particular to the last syllable, is possibly analogous to many other words, such as 'mountain,' 'captain,' and 'villain.' It might be worth mentioning that in the First Folio, 'copatain' is spelled 'copataine,' and the word 'villain' is spelled 'villaine,' appearing in the line just preceding 'copataine.' The customary spelling for 'villain' in the First Folio is 'villaine'*

cop|e, -es, -ing, -ed ˈkoʊp, -s, -ɪŋ, -t

copesmate ˈkoʊpsmeɪt

Cophetua, King (2HIV, LLL, RJ) ˈkɪŋ koˈfetjʊə [-tʃʊə], -twə [-tʃwə]

copious, -ly, -ness ˈkoʊpɪəs, -lɪ, -nɪs

copper, -s, -ing, -ed ˈkɒpə˞, -z, -ɹɪŋ, -d

Copperspur, Master (MEAS) ˌmastə˞ ˈkɒpə˞spɚ

coppice, -s ˈkɒpɪs, -ɪz

copse, -s ˈkɒps, -ɪz

copulat|e, -es, -ing, -ed ˈkɒpjʊleɪt, -s, -ɪŋ, -ɪd

copulation, -s ˌkɒpjʊˈleɪʃn, -z

copulative, -s ˈkɒpjʊlətɪv [-leɪt-], -z

cop|y, -ies, -ying, -ied, -ier/s ˈkɒp|ɪ, -ɪz, -ɪɪŋ, -ɪd, -ɪə˞/z

copy-book, -s ˈkɒpɪˌbʊk, -s

copyright, -s, -ing, -ed ˈkɒpɪɹaɪt, -s, -ɪŋ, -ɪd

corag(g)io (*It.*) koˈrɑdʒɪo [-dʒɪo]

coral, -s ˈkɒɹəl, -z

Corambus (ALL'S) koˈɹæmbəs

coranto, -s kəˈɹɑntoʊ [kɒˈɹ-, -ˈɹæn-], -z

cord, -s, -ing, -ed; -age ˈkɔ˞d, -z, -ɪŋ, -ɪd; -ɪdʒ

Cordelia (*LEAR*) kɔ˞ˈdiljə

cordial, -s; -ly ˈkɔ˞dʒl̩, -z; -lɪ

co-responsive ˌkoʊɹɪˈspɒnsɪv [ˈ--,--]

Corin (AYLI, MSND) ˈkɒɹɪn

Corinth (COM, TIM) ˈkɒɹɪnθ

Corinthian (1HIV) kəˈɹɪnθɪən

Coriolanus (*COR*, TIT) ˌkɒɹɪoˈleɪnəs, -ɹɪˈə'l-

Corioles (COR) kɒˈɹaɪələs, -ˈɹaɪləs

Corioli (COR) kɒˈɹaɪəlaɪ

co-rival, -s, -ling, led ˌkoʊˈɹaɪvl̩, -z, -ɪŋ, -d

cork, -s, -ing, -ed, -er/s; -age ˈkɔ˞k, -s, -ɪŋ, -t, -ə˞/z; -ɪdʒ

cork|y, -ier, -iest, -iness ˈkɔ˞k|ɪ, -ɪə˞, -ɪɪst, -ɪnɪs

cormorant, -s ˈkɔ˞məɹənt, -s

corn, -s, -ing, -ed ˈkɔ˞n, -z, -ɪŋ, -d

Cornelia (TIT) kɔ˞ˈnilɪə, -ljə

Cornelius (*CYM*, *HAM*) kɔ˞ˈniljəs

corner, -s, -ing, -ed ˈkɔ˞nə˞, -z, -ɹɪŋ, -d

cornet, -s ˈkɔ˞nɪt, -s

cornice, -s ˈkɔ˞nɪs, -ɪz

Cornish (HV) ˈkɔ˞nɪʃ

cornuto (*cuckold*) kɔ˞ˈnjutoʊ

Cornwall, Duke of (*LEAR*) ˌdjuk əv ˈkɔ˞nwəl, -wɒl

corollar|y, -ies ˈkɒɹələɹ|ɪ [ˈkɒɹ-, -leɹɪ], -ɪz *Note.—In TEM, IV.i.57, the chiefly Brit. pronunciation of* [kəˈɹɒleɹɪ] *is justified, though not necessary, depending on how one chooses to scan the line. If one chooses to scan with an epic caesura and then a trochee in the third foot, an accepted pronunciation is* [kəˈɹɒləɹɪ]

coron|a, -ae, -as kəˈɹoʊn|ə, -i, -əz

coronal (*s.*), **-s** ˈkɒɹənl̩, -z

coronation, -s ˌkɒɹəˈneɪʃn, -z

coroner, -s ˈkɒɹənə˞, -z

coronet, -s ˈkɒɹənet [-nɪt], -s

corpor|al (C.), -als, -ally ˈkɔɚpəɹ|əl, -əlz, -əlɨ

Note.—In CYM, II.iv.119 (The Arden Shakespeare, 1955, J. M. Nosworthy, editor), there appears to be a glaring error that subsequently found itself carried on into numerous reprintings spanning decades, including The Arden Shakespeare Complete Works, 1998. The Arden Shakespeare editions are well known for their meticulous scholarship, and it may simply be (uncharacteristically) a proofing error, but it is an error nonetheless. Because the word 'to' is dropped from the line "Render to me some corporal sign about her" one is left to assume that 'corporal' is arguably given primary stress on the second syllable, i.e., [kɔɚˈpɔɚɹəl], which would, of course, be an erroneous conclusion

corporate, -ly, -ness ˈkɔɚpəɹɪt, -lɨ, -nɪs

corps (sing.) ˈkɔɚ (pl.) ˈkɔɚz

corpse, -s ˈkɔɚps, -ɪz

corpulen|ce, -cy, -t/ly ˈkɔɚpjʊlən|s, -sɨ, -t/lɨ

correct, -s, -ing, -ed, -or/s; -est, -ly, -ness kəˈɹekt, -s, -ɪŋ, -ɪd, -ɚ/z; -ɪst, -lɨ, -nɪs

correction, -s kəˈɹekʃn̩, -z

correctioner, -s kəˈɹekʃnɚ, -z

correspond, -s, -ing/ly, -ed ˌkɔɹɪˈspɒnd, -z, -ɪŋ/lɨ, -ɪd

corresponden|ce/s, -t/s ˌkɔɹɪˈspɒndən|s/ɪz, -t/s

corridor, -s ˈkɔɹɪdɚ [-dɔɚ], -z

corrigible ˈkɔɹɪdʒɪbl̩

corrival, -s koˈɹaɪvl̩, -z

corroborat|e, -es, -ing, -ed, -or/s kəˈɹɒbəɹeɪt, -s, -ɪŋ, -ɪd, -ɚ/z

corrod|e, -es, -ing, -ed kəˈɹoʊd, -z, -ɪŋ, -ɪd

corrosive, -s, -ly, -ness kəˈɹoʊsɪv, -z, -lɨ, -nɪs

Note.—Sometimes [ˈkɔɹəsɪv] *in S., e.g.,*

1HVI, III.iii.3; 2HVI, III.ii.402. *In Jonson's Every Man Out of His Humour, I.i.7, for instance, the iambic pentameter of the line reads, "I send nor Balmes, nor Cor'sives to your wound"*

corrupt, -s, -ing, -ed, -er/s; -er, -est, -ly, -ness kəˈɹʌpt, -s, -ɪŋ, -ɪd, -ɚ/z; -ɚ, -ɪst, -lɨ, -nɪs

corse, -s ˈkɔɚs, -ɪz

cors(e)let, -s ˈkɔɚslɪt, -s

Corydon (PP) ˈkɔɹɪdən [-dɒn]

Cosmo (ALL'S) ˈkɒzmoʊ

cost, -s, -ing ˈkɒst, -s, -ɪŋ

costard, -s ˈkɒstɚd, -z

Costard (LLL) ˈkɒstɚd

costermonger, -s ˈkɒstɚˌmʌŋgɚ, -z

costl|y, -ier, -iest, -iness ˈkɒstl|ɨ, -ɪɚ, -ɪɪst, -ɪnɪs

costume (s.), -s ˈkɒstjum, -z

costum|e (v.), -es, -ing, -ed kɒˈstjum [ˈ--], -z, -ɪŋ, -d

co-supremes ˌkoʊsjuˈpɹimz [-sʊˈp-]

cos|y (var. of cozy), -ies, -ying, -ied; -ier, -iest, -ily, -iness ˈkoʊz|ɨ, -ɪz, -ɪɪŋ, -ɪd; -ɪɚ, -ɪɪst, -ɪlɨ, -ɪnɪs

cot, -s ˈkɒt, -s

cot|e, -es, -ing, -ed ˈkoʊt, -s, -ɪŋ, -ɪd

cot(-)quean, -s ˈkɒtkwin, -z

Cotsall (MWW) ˈkɒtsɔl [-səl]

Note.—This is a dialectal pronunciation spelling of 'Cotswold,' in MWW, I.i.83 (see Note for **Cotsole***)*

Cotshall (RII) ˈkɒtsɔl [-səl]

Cotsole (2HIV) ˈkɒtsoʊl [-səl]

Note.—This is a dialectal pronunciation spelling of 'Cotswold,' in 2HIV, III.ii.20 (see Note for **Cotsall***)*

cotton, -s, -ing, -ed ˈkɒtn̩, -z, -ɪŋ, -d

Cotus (COR) ˈkoʊtəs

couch, -es, -ing/s, -ed ˈkaʊtʃ, -ɪz, -ɪŋ/z, -t

cougar, -s ˈkugɚ, -z

cough, -s, -ing, -ed, -er/s ˈkɒf, -s, -ɪŋ, -t, -ɚ/z

could (from can, q.v.) ˈkʊd

---

i w**e** ɨ c**i**ty ɪ h**i**t e l**e**t ɛ d**e**but æ c**a**n a p**a**ss ɝ b**i**rd ʌ h**u**t ə **a**gain ɚ supp**er** u y**ou**
ʊ sh**ou**ld o **o**bey ɔ **a**wl ɒ c**o**p ɑ f**a**ther eɪ p**ai**d aɪ h**i**gh oʊ g**o** ɔɪ v**oi**ce aʊ f**ou**nd ɪɚ **ear**
ɛɚ **air** ʊɚ p**oor** ɔɚ f**or**k ɑɚ p**ar**k aɪɚ f**ire** aʊɚ h**our** b **b**oy p **p**it d **d**og t **t**op g g**o**t
k **k**id h **h**ow fi be**h**ave dʒ **j**ot tʃ **ch**ew z **z**any s **s**oft v **v**at f **f**at ʒ trea**s**ure ʃ **sh**ip ð **th**e
θ **th**in m **m**an n **n**o ŋ ha**ng** l **l**ip j **y**es w **w**on ʍ **wh**ew ɹ **r**igger, ai**r**y ɟ **m**a**tt**er

couldn't (*contr. of* **could not**) 'kʊdn̩t
coulter, -s 'koŭltɚ, -z
council (C.) (1HIV, HV), **-s** 'kaŏnsl̩, -z
Council-board (1HIV) 'kaŏnsl̩ˌbɔɚ̆d
council-house 'kaŏnsl̩ˌhaŏs
councillor, -s 'kaŏnsɪlɚ, -z
council-table 'kaŏnsl̩ˌteĭbl̩
counsel, -s, -ling, -led, -lor/s 'kaŏnsl̩, -z, -ɪŋ, -d, -ɚ/z
counsel-keeper 'kaŏnsl̩ˌkipɚ
counsel-keeping 'kaŏnsl̩ˌkipɪŋ
count (C.), -s, -ing, -ed, -er/s 'kaŏnt, -s, -ɪŋ, -ɪd, -ɚ/z
countenanc|e, -es, -ing, -ed 'kaŏntɪnəns, -ɪz, -ɪŋ, -t
Counter-gate (MWW) 'kaŏntɚˌgeĭt
*Note.—As Francis Griffin Stokes
(*Who's Who in Shakespeare; The
Characters, Proper Names, and Plot
Sources in the Plays and Poems, *Studio
Editions Ltd, 1992, p. 77) puts it, this is
"not strictly a proper name. Any one of
the prisons for debtors in London and
Southwark was called a 'counter,' later
'compter.'"*
counter, -s, -ing, -ed 'kaŏntɚ, -z, -ɹɪŋ, -d
counter-caster 'kaŏntɚˈkastɚ
counterchange 'kaŏntɚtʃeĭndʒ
countercheck 'kaŏntɚˌtʃek
Countercheck Quarrelsome (AYLI)
ˌkaŏntɚtʃek 'kwɒɹəlsəm
counterfeit, -s, -ing, -ed, -er/s 'kaŏntɚfɪt, -s, -ɪŋ, -ɪd, -ɚ/z
counterfeitly 'kaŏntɚfɪtlɨ
countermand, -s, -ing, -ed ˌkaŏntɚˈmand ['--], -z, -ɪŋ, -ɪd
counter(-)part, -s 'kaŏntɚˌpaɚ̆t
counterpoint, -s 'kaŏntɚpɔĭnt, -s
counter(-)pois|e, -es, -ing, -ed 'kaŏntɚpɔĭz, -ɪz, -ɪŋ, -d
counter-reflect 'kaŏntɚˌɹɪflekt
countersealed ˌkaŏntɚˈsild
countervail, -s, -ing, -ed ˌkaŏntɚˈveĭl ['---], -z, -ɪŋ, -d
countess (C.), -es 'kaŏntɪs, -ɪz
countr|y, -ies 'kʌntɹ|ɨ, -ɨz
Note.—Sometimes trisyllabic ['kʌntɚˌɹɨ] *in S., e.g.,* 2HVI, I.i.207
count|y (C.), -ies 'kaŏnt|ɨ, -ɨz

coup|le, -les, -ling, -led, -lement 'kʌp|l̩, -l̩z, -l̩ɪŋ [-lɪŋ], -l̩d, -l̩mənt
courage (C.), -s 'kʌɹɪdʒ, -ɪz
cours|e, -es, -ing, -ed, -er/s 'kɔɚ̆s, -ɪz, -ɪŋ, -t, -ɚ/z
Court, Alexander (*HV*) ˌælɪgˈzandɚ 'kɔɚ̆t
court, -s, -ing, -ed 'kɔɚ̆t, -s, -ɪŋ, -ɪd
court-cardinal 'kɔɚ̆tˌkaɚ̆dn̩l
court-comtempt ˌkɔɚ̆tkənˈtempt
courtesan [-zan], -s 'kɔɚ̆tɪzən [-ˌzæn], -z
courtes|y, -ies 'kɚtɪs|ɨ, -ɨz
Court-gate (HVIII) 'kɔɚ̆tˌgeĭt
courtier, -s 'kɔɚ̆tjɚ [-tĭɚ], -z
Court(e)ney, Sir Edward (RIII) ˌsɚ '(ɹ)edwɚd 'kɔɚ̆tnɨ
court-odor 'kɔɚ̆tˌoŭdɚ
court-word 'kɔɚ̆tˌwɜ̆d
cousin, -s 'kʌzn̩ [-zɪn], -z
cousin-german ˌkʌzn̩ˈdʒɜ̆mən
cout (*obscure dialectal form of* **colt**) 'kaŏt
cove, -s 'koŭv, -z
coven, -s 'kʌvn̩, -z
covenant, -s, -ing, -ed, -er/s 'kʌvənənt [-vn̩ənt], -s, -ɪŋ, -ɪd, -ɚ/z
covent 'kʌvənt ['kɒv-]
Coventry (1HIV, 2HIV, 3HVI, RII) 'kʌvəntɹɨ ['kɒvənt ɹɨ]
cov|er, -ers, -ering, -ered 'kʌv|ɚ, -ɚz, -ɚɹɪŋ, -ɚd
coverlet, -s 'kʌvɚˌlɪt, -s
covert (*adj.*), **-ly, -ness** 'koŭvɚt ['kʌvɚt, koˈvɜ̆t], -lɨ, -nɪs
covert (*s.*), **-s** 'kʌvɚt, -s ['kʌvɚ, -z]
coverture 'kʌvɚˌtʃʊɚ̆ [-vɚtʃɚ]
covet, -s, -ing/s, -ed 'kʌvɪt, -s, -ɪŋ/z, -ɪd
covetous, -ly, -ness 'kʌvɪtəs, -lɨ, -nɪs
cow, -s, -ing, -ed 'kaŏ, -z, -ɪŋ, -d
coward, -s; -ship 'kaŏɚd, -z; -ʃɪp
cowarded 'kaŏɚˌdɪd
cowardice 'kaŏɚˌdɪs
cowardl|y, -iness 'kaŏɚˌdl̩|ɨ, -ɨnɪs
cow-dung 'kaŏˌdʌŋ
cower, -s, -ing, -ed 'kaŏɚ, -z, -ɹɪŋ, -d
cowish, -ly, -ness 'kaŏɪʃ, -lɨ, -nɪs
cowl, -s 'kaŏl, -z
cowlike 'kaŏlaĭk
cowl-staff 'kaŏl̩ˌstaf
cowshed, -s 'kaŏʃed, -z

cowslip, -s 'kɑʊslɪp, -s

cox (C.) (*a corruption of* **God's** *in* ALL'S, V.ii.42), **-es** 'kɒks, -ɪz

coxcomb, -s 'kɒkskoʊm, -z

coy, -ed; -er, -est, -ly, -ness 'kɔɪ, -d; -ɚ, -ɪst, -lɪ, -nɪs

coyish, -ly, -ness 'kɔɪɪʃ, -lɪ, -nɪs

coz 'kʌz

coz|en, -ens, -ening, -ened, -ener/s; -enage 'kʌz|n̩, -n̩z, -n̩ɪŋ, -n̩d, -n̩ɚ/z; -n̩ɪdʒ

cozier (*s.*) (*cobbler*), **-s** 'koʊzjɚ, -s

coz|y *or* **cos|y, -ies, -ying, -ied; -ier, -iest, -ily, -iness** 'koʊz|ɪ, -ɪz, -ɪɪŋ, -ɪd; -ɪɚ, -ɪɪst, -ɪlɪ, -ɪnɪs

Crab (TGV) 'kɹæb

crab (*v.*), **-s, -bing, -bed** 'kɹæb, -z, -ɪŋ, -d

crabbed (*adj.*), **-ly, -ness** 'kɹæbɪd, -lɪ, -nɪs

crab(-)tree, -s 'kɹæb͵tɹi, -z

crack, -s, -ing, -ed 'kɹæk, -s, -ɪŋ, -t

cracker, -s 'kɹækɚ, -z

crack-hemp 'kɹæk͵ɦemp

cradle-clothes 'kɹeɪdl̩͵kloʊðz

craft, -s, -ing, -ed 'kɹaft, -s, -ɪŋ, -ɪd

crafts|man, -men, -manship 'kɹafts|mən, -mən, -mənʃɪp

craft|y, -ier, -iest, -ily, -iness 'kɹaft|ɪ, -ɪɚ, -ɪɪst, -ɪlɪ, -ɪnɪs

crafty-sick 'kɹaftɪ͵sɪk

crag, -s 'kɹæg, -z

cragg|y, -ier, -iest, -ily, -iness 'kɹæg|ɪ, -ɪɚ, -ɪɪst, -ɪlɪ, -ɪnɪs

crak|e, -es, -ing, -ed 'kɹeɪk, -s, -ɪŋ, -t

cram, -s, -ming, -med 'kɹæm, -z, -ɪŋ, -d

cramp, -s, -ing, -ed 'kɹæmp, -s, -ɪŋ, -t

cran|e, -es, -ing, -ed 'kɹeɪn, -z, -ɪŋ, -d

crank, -s, -ing, -ed 'kɹæŋk, -s, -ɪŋ, -t

Cranmer, Thomas (*HVIII*) 'tɒməs 'kɹænmɚ

crann|y, -ies, -ied 'kɹæn|ɪ, -ɪz, -ɪd

crants *or* **crance** 'kɹants

Crassus (MEAS) 'kɹæsəs

Crassus, Marcus (AC) 'mɑɚkəs 'kɹæsəs

crater, -s 'kɹeɪɽɚ, -z

crav|e, -es, -ing/s, -ed, -er/s 'kɹeɪv, -z, -ɪŋ/z, -d, -ɚ/z

craven, -s 'kɹeɪvən, -z

craz|e, -es, -ing, -ed 'kɹeɪz, -ɪz, -ɪŋ, -d

craz|y, -ier, -iest, -ily, -iness 'kɹeɪz|ɪ, -ɪɚ, -ɪɪst, -ɪlɪ, -ɪnɪs

creak, -s, -ing, -ed 'kɹik, -s, -ɪŋ, -t

creak|y, -ier, -iest, -ily, -iness 'kɹik|ɪ, -ɪɚ, -ɪɪst, -ɪlɪ, -ɪnɪs

cream, -s, -ing, -ed 'kɹim, -z, -ɪŋ, -d

creamer, -s 'kɹimɚ, -z

cream-faced 'kɹim͵feɪst

cream|y, -ier, -iest, -ily, -iness 'kɹim|ɪ, -ɪɚ, -ɪɪst, -ɪlɪ, -ɪnɪs

creas|e, -es, -ing, -ed 'kɹis, -ɪz, -ɪŋ, -t

creat|e, -es, -ing, -ed kɹɪ'eɪt [kɹɪ'eɪt], -s, -ɪŋ, -ɪd

Note.—In KJ, IV.i.106, *S. uses 'create' to represent a past tense, an archaic custom waning by his day; still, it satisfies the metrical requirements of the verse line. This same scheme also applies to 'create' in* MSND, V.i.391 *(cf. Note for* **consecrate***)*

creation (C.), -s kɹɪ'eɪʃn [kɹɪ'eɪʃn̩], -z

creative, -ly, -ness kɹɪ'eɪtɪv, -lɪ, -nɪs

creativity ͵kɹɪeɪ'tɪvɪtɪ [͵kɹɪeɪ-]

Creator (3HVI, TC) kɹɪ'eɪɽɚ

creature, -s 'kɹitʃɚ, -z

credence 'kɹidn̩s [-dəns]

credent, -ly 'kɹidn̩t, -lɪ

credit, -s, -ing, -ed, -or/s 'kɹedɪt, -s, -ɪŋ, -ɪd, -ɚ/z

credo, -s 'kɹidoʊ ([*L.*] 'kɹɛdo; *cf. Note for* **haud credo**), -z

credulity kɹɪ'djulɪtɪ

credulous, -ly, -ness 'kɹedjʊləs, -lɪ, -nɪs

creed, -s 'kɹid, -z

creep, -s, -ing, crept 'kɹip, -s, -ɪŋ, 'kɹept

Creon (TNK) 'kɹɪɒn

crept (*p.t. of* **creep**, *q.v.*) 'kɹept

crescent, -s 'kɹesn̩t, -s

crescive 'kɹesɪv

---

i w**e** ɪ c**i**t**y** ɪ h**i**t e l**e**t ɛ d**e**but æ c**a**n a p**a**ss ɝ b**ir**d ʌ h**u**t ə **a**gain ɚ supp**er** u y**ou** ʊ sh**ou**ld o **o**bey ɔ **aw**l ɒ c**o**p ɑ f**a**ther eɪ p**ai**d aɪ h**igh** oʊ g**o** ɔɪ v**oi**ce aʊ f**ou**nd ɪɚ **ear** ɛɚ **air** ʊɚ p**oor** ɔɚ f**or**k ɑɚ p**ar**k aɪɚ **fire** aʊɚ **hour** b **b**oy p **p**it d **d**og t **t**op g **g**ot k **k**id h **h**ow fi be**h**ave dʒ **j**ot tʃ **ch**ew z **z**any s **s**oft v **v**at f **f**at ʒ trea**s**ure ʃ **sh**ip ð **th**e θ **th**in m **m**an n **n**o ŋ ha**ng** l **l**ip j **y**es w **w**on ʍ **wh**ew ɹ **r**igger, ai**r**y ɽ ma**tt**er

cresset, -s ˈkɹɛsɪt, -s
Cressid (ALL'S, HV, MV, *TC*), -s ˈkɹɛsɪd, -z
Cressida (*TC*, TN) ˈkɹɛsɪdə
Cressy (HV) ˈkɹɛsɪ
crest, -s, -ing, -ed ˈkɹɛst, -s, -ɪŋ, -ɪd
crest(-)fallen ˈkɹɛstˌfɔlən
crest-wounding ˈkɹɛstˌwundɪŋ
Cretan (TS) ˈkɹitn̩
Crete (HV, 1HVI, 3HVI, MSND) ˈkɹit
crevice, -s ˈkɹɛvɪs, -ɪz
crew, -s ˈkɹu
crib, -s, -bing, -bed, -ber/s ˈkɹɪb, -z, -ɪŋ, -d, -ɚ/z
cribbage ˈkɹɪbɪdʒ
cribbage-board, -s ˈkɹɪbɪdʒbɔɚd, -z
crick, -s, -ing, -ed ˈkɹɪk, -s, -ɪŋ, -t
cricket, -s ˈkɹɪkɪt, -s
crimeful ˈkɹaɪmfʊl
crimson, -s, -ing, -ed ˈkɹɪmzn̩, -z, -ɪŋ, -d
cring|e, -es, -ing, -ed, -er/s ˈkɹɪndʒ, -ɪz, -ɪŋ, -d, -ɚ/z
cripp|le, -les, -ling, -led ˈkɹɪp|l̩, -l̩z, -l̩ɪŋ [-lɪŋ], -l̩d
cris|is, -es ˈkɹaɪs|ɪs, -iz
crisp, -er, -est, -ly, -ness ˈkɹɪsp, -ɚ, -ɪst, -lɨ, -nɪs
Crispian, Crispin (HV) ˈkɹɪspɪn ˈkɹɪspɪən, -pjən
Crispianus (HV) ˌkɹɪspɨˈɑnʊs
croak, -s, -ing/s, -ed, -er/s ˈkɹoʊk, -s, -ɪŋ/z, -t, -ɚ/z
crocodile, -s ˈkɹɒkədaɪl, -z
Cromer, Sir James (2HVI) ˌsɚ ˈdʒeɪmz ˈkɹoʊmɚ
Cromwell (1HVI, HVIII) ˈkɹɒmwel [ˈkɹʌmwəl]
Cromwell, Thomas (*HVIII*) ˈtɒməs ˈkɹɒmwel [ˈkɹʌmwəl]
crone, -s ˈkɹoʊn, -z
crook (*s., v.*), -s, -ing, -ed ˈkɹʊk, -s, -ɪŋ, -t (*p.p.*)
crooked (*adj.*) (*curved or bent*), -er, -est, -ly, -ness ˈkɹʊkɪd, -ɚ, -ɪst, -lɨ, -nɪs
crooked-pated ˈkɹʊkɪdˌpeɪtɪd
crop, -s, -ping, -ped ˈkɹɒp, -s, -ɪŋ, -t
crop-ear ˈkɹɒpˌɪɚ
Crosby Place (RIII) ˈkɹɒzbɨ ˈpleɪs
'cross (*from across*) ˈkɹɒs

cross, -es, -ing, -ed; -er, -est, -ly, -ness ˈkɹɒs, -ɪz, -ɪŋ, -t; -ɚ, -ɪst, -lɨ, -nɪs
cross(-)bow (C.), -s ˈkɹɒsboʊ, -z
cross-garter|ing, -ed ˈkɹɒsˌgɑɚtɚ|ɹɪŋ, -d
cross-lightning ˈkɹɒsˌlaɪtnɪŋ [-tn̩ɪŋ]
cross-row, -s ˈkɹɒsˌɹoʊ, -z
crost (*var. of* crossed) ˈkɹɒst
crotchet, -s, -y, -iness ˈkɹɒtʃɪt, -s, -ɨ, -ɪnɪs
crouch, -es, -ing, -ed ˈkɹaʊtʃ, -ɪz, -ɪŋ, -t
crow, -s, -ing, -ed, crew ˈkɹoʊ, -z, -ɪŋ, -d, ˈkɹu
crowd, -s, -ing, -ed ˈkɹaʊd, -z, -ɪŋ, -ɪd
crowkeeper, -s ˈkɹoʊˌkipɚ, -z
crown (C.), -s, -ing, -ed ˈkɹaʊn, -z, -ɪŋ, -d
crownet (*var. of* coronet, *cf.* crowner), -s ˈkɹaʊnɪt, -s
crowner (*var. of* coroner, *cf.* crownet), -s ˈkɹaʊnɚ, -z
crude, -r, -st, -ly, -ness ˈkɹud, -ɚ, -ɪst, -lɨ, -nɪs
crudy (*curdy, thick*) ˈkɹudɨ
cruel, -ler, -lest, -ly, -ness ˈkɹuəl [ˈkɹuəl], -ɚ, -ɪst, -ɨ, -nɪs
cruel-hearted ˈkɹuəlˌhɑɚtɪd [ˈkɹuəl-]
cruis|e, -es, -ing, -ed, -er/s ˈkɹuz, -ɪz, -ɪŋ, -d, -ɚ/z
crumb, -s, -ing, -ed ˈkɹʌm, -z, -ɪŋ, -d
crunch, -es, -ing, -ed ˈkɹʌntʃ, -ɪz, -ɪŋ, -t
crupper, -s ˈkɹʌpɚ, -z
crusad|e, -es, -ing, -ed, -er/s kɹuˈseɪd, -z, -ɪŋ, -ɪd, -ɚ/z
crusado, -es kɹuˈseɪdoʊ [-ˈsɑdoʊ], -z
Note.—*This word, in OTH, III.iv.22, is the name of a Portuguese coin, the pronunciation of which is generally anglicized. If one cares to give it a Spanish flavor, then one should aim for* [kɹuˈsɑdo]; *if Portuguese,* [kɹuˈzɑdu]
crush, -es, -ing, -ed, -er/s ˈkɹʌʃ, -ɪz, -ɪŋ, -t, -ɚ/z
crust, -s, -ing, -ed ˈkɹʌst, -s, -ɪŋ, -ɪd
crutch, -es, -ed ˈkɹʌtʃ, -ɪz, -t
cr|y, -ies, -ying, -ied, -ier/s ˈkɹ|aɪ, -aɪz, -aɪɪŋ, -aɪd, -aɪɚ/z
crypt, -s ˈkɹɪpt, -s
crystal, -s ˈkɹɪstl̩, -z
crystal-button ˈkɹɪstl̩ˌbʌtn̩
crystalline ˈkɹɪstəlɪn [-laɪn]
Note.—[ˈkɹɪstəlaɪn] *is the chiefly Brit.*

way of pronouncing this word—also an accepted way of saying it in the United States—and should be pronounced so in CYM, V.iv.113. *In this instance, it preserves the integrity of the rhyming couplet ('mine/ crystalline')*

cub, -s, -bing, -bed 'kʌb, -z, -ɪŋ, -d

cub-drawn 'kʌb,dɹɔn

cub|e, -es, -ing, -ed 'kjub, -z, -ɪŋ, -d

cubicle, -s 'kjubɪkl̩, -z

cubiculo kju'bɪkjuloŏ [-jʊl-]
Note.—Essentially, this word means 'small bed-chamber.' There is a fair amount of discussion about its origin and how it is used in TN, III.ii.50. *C. T. Onions notes that it is the "ablative of L. 'cubiculum,'"* while the OED *says it is "either a humorous use of Latin, from the phrase 'in cubiculo,' or affected use of Ital. 'cubiculo'"*

cubit, -s, -al 'kjubɪt, -s, -l̩

cuckold, -s, -ing, -ed; -y 'kʌkoŏld, -z, -ɪŋ, -ɪd; -ɨ ['kʌkəldɨ]

cuckoldly 'kʌkəldlɨ

cuckold-maker 'kʌkoŏld,meɪkə
Note.—This word appears twice in S., HVIII, V.iii.24 and TC, V.vii.9. In both instances, it is used explicitly in comparison with 'cuckold' and should thus be pronounced [,kʌkoŏld'meɪkə]

cuckoldry 'kʌkəldɹɨ

cuckoo, -s, -ing, -ed 'kʊku [kʊ'ku], -z, -ɪŋ, -d

cuckoo-bird, -s 'kʊku,bɜd, -z

cuckoo-flowers 'kʊku,flaŏə, -z

cucullus non facit monachum (*L.*) (MEAS, V.i.261; TN, I.v.53) 'kʊkʊlʊs non 'fatʃit 'mɒnakʊm

cudg|el, -els, -elling, -elled 'kʌdʒ|əl, -əlz, -l̩ɪŋ [-əlɪŋ], -əld

cu|e, -es, -ing, -ed 'kju, -z, -ɪŋ, -d

cuff, -s, -ing, -ed 'kʌf, -s, -ɪŋ, -t

cuirass, -es kwɪ'ɹæs, -ɪz

cuisses (*thigh-armor*) 'kwɪsɪz (*see* **cushes**)

cull, -s, -ing, -ed 'kʌl, -z, -ɪŋ, -d

cullion, -s; -ly, -ry 'kʌljən, -z; -lɨ, -ɹɨ

culminat|e, -es, -ing, -ed 'kʌlmɪneɪt, -s, -ɪŋ, -ɪd

culpab|le, -ly, -leness 'kʌlpəb|l̩, -lɨ, -l̩nɪs

culprit, -s 'kʌlpɹɪt, -s

cult, -s 'kʌlt, -s

cultivat|e, -es, -ing, -ed, -or/s 'kʌltɪveɪt, -s, -ɪŋ, -ɪd, -ə/z

culture, -s, -d 'kʌltʃə, -z, -d

culverin, -s 'kʌlvəɹɪn, -z

cumber, -s, -ing, -ed, -er/s 'kʌmbə, -z, -ɹɪŋ, -d, -ɹə/z

Cumberland (MAC) 'kʌmbələnd

cum privilegio (*L.*) (HVIII, I.iii.34) 'kum pɹivi'lɛdʒɪo

cum privilegio ad impremendum solum (*L.*) (TS, IV.iv.89) 'kum pɹivi'lɛdʒɪo ɑd ,impɹi'mɛndʊm 'solʊm

cunning, -ly, -ness 'kʌnɪŋ, -lɨ, -nɪs

cup, -s, -ping, -ped 'kʌp, -s, -ɪŋ, -t

cupboard, -s, -ing 'kʌbəd, -z, -ɪŋ

Cupid (LLL, MV, MWW, Sonn. 153, TIM, VA), -s 'kjupɪd, -z

cur, -s; -rish/ly 'kɜ, -z; -ɹɪʃ/lɨ

Curan (LEAR) 'kʌɹən

curate, -s 'kjʊɜɹɪt, -s

curb, -s, -ing, -ed 'kɜb, -z, -ɪŋ, -d

curd, -s 'kɜd, -z

curdied (*from the v. form of* **curdy**) 'kɜdɪd

cur|e, -es, -ing, -ed, -er/s 'kjʊɜ, -z, -ɹɪŋ, -d, -ɹə/z

cureless 'kjʊɜlɪs

curfew, -s 'kɜfju, -z

Curio (TN) 'kjʊɜɹɪoŏ

curl, -s, -ing, -ed, -er/s 'kɜl, -z, -ɪŋ, -d, -ə/z

curl|y, -ier, -iest 'kɜl|ɨ, -ɪə, -ɪɪst

curmudgeon, -s kɜ'mʌdʒən, -z

currant, -s 'kʌɹənt, -s

currence (*flow*) 'kʌɹəns

current, -s, -ly, -ness 'kʌɹənt, -s, -lɨ, -nɪs

curs|e (*s., v.*), -es, -ing, -ed, curst 'kɝ·s, -ɪz, -ɪŋ, -t, 'kɝ·st
cursed (*adj.*), -ly, -ness 'kɝ·sɪd, -lɪ, -nɪs
cursed-blessed 'kɝ·sɪd'blesɪd
cursitory 'kɝ·sɪtəɹɪ
curst (*p.t. and p.p. of* curse, *q.v.*) 'kɝ·st
curster (*a form used for a comparative degree*) 'kɝ·stə·
curstest (*superlative form of the participial adj.*) 'kɝ·stɪst
curstness 'kɝ·stnɪs
cur's|y (*archaic var. of* curtsy/courtesy), -ies 'kɝ·s|ɪ ['kɝ·ʔs|ɪ], -ɪz
curtail, -s, -ing, -ed, -ment/s kɝ·'teɪl, -z, -ɪŋ, -d, -mənt/s (['--] *in* RIII, I.i.18)
curtain, -s, -ing, -ed 'kɝ·tn̩, -z, -ɪŋ, -d
curtal 'kɝ·tl̩
Curtis (*TS*) 'kɝ·ɾɪs
curtle-axe *or* curtal-ax(e), -s 'kɝ·tl̩ˌæks, -ɪz
curts|y, -ies, -ying, -ied 'kɝ·ts|ɪ, -ɪz, -ɪŋ, -ɪd
curvet, -s, -(t)ing, -(t)ed kɝ·'vet, -s, -ɪŋ, -ɪd
cushes 'kʊʃɪz
Note.—*This word, meaning armor that protects the front of the thighs, appears in* 1HIV, IV.i.105 (*in both the Quarto and Folio editions*), *and is presumed to simply be a pronunciation spelling for 'cuisses' or 'cuishes,' pronounced* ['kwɪsɪz] *and* ['kwɪʃɪz], *respectively. 'Cushes' is only one of several alt. spellings for 'cuisses' cited in the OED, and some modern editors prefer to retain the spelling (and thus pronunciation) 'cushes' in the passage*
cushion, -s, -ing, -ed 'kʊʃn̩, -z, -ɪŋ, -d
cusp, -s 'kʌsp, -s
cuss, -es 'kʌs, -ɪz
custard, -s 'kʌstə·d, -z
custard-coffin, -s 'kʌstə·dˌkɒfɪn, -z
custalorum (*L.*) (*corruption of Latin 'custos rotulorum'*) (MWW, I.i.6) ˌkʌstə'lɔɹum
custody 'kʌstədɪ
custom, -s 'kʌstəm, -z
customed (*aphaeretic form of* accustomed) 'kʌstəmd

Note.—*When this word appears in* KJ, III.iii.155, *an extra syllable eked out of the final '-ed' ending is pronounced, i.e.,* ['kʌstəmɪd]
customer, -s 'kʌstəmə·, -z
custom-shrunk 'kʌstəmʃɹʌŋk
Cut (1HIV) 'kʌt
cu|t, -ts, -tting/s, -tter/s 'kʌ|t, -ts, -ɾɪŋ/z, -ɾə·/z
cute, -r, -st, -ly, -ness 'kjut, -ə·, -ɪst, -lɪ, -nɪs
cutler, -s, -y 'kʌtlə·, -z, -ɹɪ
cutpurs|e, -es 'kʌtˌpɝ·s, -ɪz
cutter-off ˌkʌɾə·'ɹɒf
cut-throat, -s 'kʌtˌθɹoʊt, -s
cuttle, -s 'kʌtl̩, -z
Cyclops (HAM, TIT) 'saɪklɒps
Cydnus (AC, CYM) 'sɪdnəs
cygnet, -s 'sɪgnɪt, -s
Cymbeline (*CYM*) 'sɪmbəlin
cyme, -s 'saɪm, -z
cynic, -s, -al, -ally 'sɪnɪk, -s, -l̩, -lɪ [-lɪ]
Cynthia (PER, RJ, TNK, VA) 'sɪn̪θɪə, -θjə
cypress, -es 'saɪpɹɪs, -ɪz
Cyprus (AC, OTH) 'saɪpɹəs
Cyrus (1HVI) 'saɪɹəs
Cytherea (CYM, PP, TS, WT) ˌsɪθə'ɹɪə

Dd

D (*the letter*), -'s 'diː, -z
d. (*L.*) dɪ'neɝ·ɹɪəs (*sing.*) dɪ'neɝ·ɹɪaɪ (*pl.*)
Note.—*This abbreviation, originally standing for the Roman coin divided or counted by tens, became the common abbreviation in England for the penny; so when in S. 's plays one sees '4d.,' for instance, it is commonly said as 'four pence' (*['fɔɝ· 'pens] *or* ['fɔɝ·pəns])
dab, -s, -bing, -bed, -ber/s 'dæb, -z, -ɪŋ, -d, -ə·/z
dabb|le, -les, -ling, -led, -ler/s 'dæb|l̩, -l̩z, -l̩ɪŋ [-lɪŋ], -l̩d, -l̩ə·/z [-lə·/z]
dabchick, -s 'dæbtʃɪk, -s
da capo dɑ 'kɑpoʊ
dace, -s 'deɪs, -ɪz

dachshund, -s 'dɑksfʊnt, -s [-sənd, -z]
dacha, -s 'dɑtʃə, -z
dacoit, -s, -age də'kɔĭt, -s, -ɪdʒ
dacron (D.) 'dækɹɒn
dactyl, -s 'dæktɪl [-təl], -z
dactylic dæk'tɪlɪk
dactylogram, -s dæk'tɪləgɹæm, -z
dactylography ˌdæktɪ'lɒgɹəfɨ
dad, -s 'dæd, -z
Dada, -ist, -ism 'dɑdɑ, -ɪst, -ɪzm̩
dadd|y, -ies 'dæd|ɨ, -ɪz
daddy longlegs ˌdædɨ'lɒŋlegz
dado, -es, -ing, -ed 'deĭdoŭ, -z, -ɪŋ, -d
daedal 'didl̩
Daedalus (3HVI, TNK) 'didələs, 'didl̩əs
　['dedələs, 'dedl̩əs]
daemon (*var. of* **demon**, *q.v.*)**, -s** 'dimən,
　-z
daff (*archaic var. of* **doff***; to put off or
　aside*)**, -ed** 'daf ['dɒf], -t
daffadill|y, -ies 'dæfədɪl|ɨ, -ɪz
daffodil, -s 'dæfədɪl, -z
daff|y, -ier, -iest, -iness 'dæf|ɨ, -ɪə˞, -ɪɪst,
　-ɪnɪs
daff't *or* **daft** (*a var. contr. of* **doff it**) 'daft
　['dɒft]
daft, -er, -est, -ly, -ness 'daft, -ə˞, -ɪst, -lɨ,
　-nɪs
dag, -s 'dæg, -z
dagger, -s 'dægə˞, -z
dago, -es 'deĭgoŭ, -z
Dagon 'deĭgɒn [-gən]
Dagonet, Sir (2HIV) ˌsɜ˞ 'dægənet [-nɪt]
daguerr(e)otyp|e, -es, -ing, -ed
　də'geɹəˌtaĭp [-'gɛ˞ɹə-], -s, -ɪŋ, -t
dagwood (D.) 'dægwʊd
dah, -s 'dɑ, -z
dahlia, -s 'dɑljə, -z
　Note.—One of only a few words (cf.
　pecan*) still used to retain strong
　regional and cultural identity among its
　speakers in terms of pronunciation
　rather than dialect. 'Dahlia' is variously*
　['deĭljə, 'dɑljə, 'dɑljə, 'dæljə]. *Deference*

*to one's audience or company is
advisable; otherwise,* ['dɑljə] *is the
preferred pronunciation suggested for
SASD. The genus name of flower was
given this New Latin term after Anders
Dahl*

Daintry (3HVI) 'dæntɹɨ ['deĭntɹɨ]
　*Note.—This is an alt. spelling for
　'Daventry' in 3HVI, V.i.6, merely
　indicating a more colloquial or dialectal
　pronunciation for the town in Northamp-
　tonshire*
daint|y, -ies; -ier, -iest, -ily, -iness 'deĭnt|ɨ,
　-ɪz; -ɪə˞, -ɪɪst, -ɪlɨ, -ɪnɪs
dais|y, -ies, -ied 'deĭz|ɨ, -ɪz, -ɪd
dale (D.), -s 'deĭl, -z
dalliance 'dælɪəns [-ljəns]
dall|y, -ies, -ying, -ied, -ier/s 'dæl|ɨ, -ɪz,
　-ɪŋ, -ɪd, -ɪə˞/z
Dalmatian (CYM), **-s** dæl'meĭʃɪən, -ʃn̩, -z
dam, -s, -ming, -med 'dæm, -z, -ɪŋ, -d
damag|e, -es, -ing, -ed 'dæmɪdʒ, -ɪz, -ɪŋ,
　-d
Damascus (1HVI) də'mæskəs
damask, -s, -ed 'dæməsk, -s, -t
dame (D.), -s 'deĭm, -z
damn (*v.*)**, -s, -ing, -ed** 'dæm, -z, -ɪŋ, -d
damnab|le, -ly, -ness 'dæmnəb|l̩, -lɨ, -l̩nɪs
damnation, -s dæm'neĭʃn̩, -z
damned (*adj.*)**, -er, -est** 'dæmd, -ə˞, -ɪst
　*Note.—There is a custom among modern
　editors to set a grave accent over the 'e'
　in 'damnèd' in 2HIV, II.iv.153, indicat-
　ing a pronounced 'e' in what is usually a
　nonsyllabic '-ed' ending. It is a common
　device, but is typically reserved for use
　in poetry when the meter is at stake.
　Here, the word appears in prose, so it is
　presumed that this custom is followed
　for the sake of euphony, and to clarify
　the meaning of the phrase "Pluto's
　damned lake"—emphasizing the
　adjectival quality of 'damned' rather
　than confusing it with the profane*

---

i w**e** ɨ c**i**ty ɪ h**i**t e l**e**t ɛ d**e**but æ c**a**n a p**a**ss ɜ˞ b**ir**d ʌ h**u**t ə **a**gain ə˞ supp**er** u y**ou**
ʊ sh**ou**ld o **o**bey ɔ **aw**l ɒ c**o**p ɑ f**a**ther eĭ p**ai**d aĭ h**igh** oŭ g**o** ɔĭ v**oi**ce aŭ f**ou**nd ɪ˞ **ear**
ɛ˞ **air** ʊ˞ p**oor** ɔ˞ f**or**k ɑ˞ p**ar**k aĭ˞ **fire** aŭ˞ **hour** b **b**oy p **p**it d **d**og t **t**op g **g**ot
k **k**id h **h**ow fi be**h**ave dʒ **j**ot tʃ **ch**ew z **z**any s **s**oft v **v**at f **f**at ʒ trea**s**ure ʃ **sh**ip ð **th**e
θ **th**in m **m**an n **n**o ŋ ha**ng** l **l**ip j **y**es w **w**on ʍ **wh**ew ɹ **r**igger, ai**r**y ɟ **m**a**tt**er

expletive. So, in this instance, it is pronounced ['dæmnɪd]. *In* PER, IV.vi.118 *and* LC, 54, *'damned' is a disyllable for the sake of the metrical requirements of the verse line*

Damon (HAM) 'deĭmɒn [-mən]

damosella 'dæməˌzelə

damsel, -s 'dæmzl̩, -z

damson, -s 'dæmzən, -z

dan (D.) 'dæn

danc|e, -es, -ing, -ed, -er/s 'dans, -ɪz, -ɪŋ, -t, -ɚ/z

dancing-rapier, -s 'dansɪŋˌɹeĭpɪɚ [-pjɚ], -z

dand|le, -les, -ling, -led 'dænd|l̩, -l̩z, -l̩ɪŋ [-əlɪŋ], -l̩d

Dane (ALL'S, HAM), **-s** 'deĭn, -z

danger (D.) (HVIII, JUL), **-s** 'deĭndʒɚ, -z

dangerous, -ly, -ness 'deĭndʒɚˌɹəs, -lɪ, -nɪs

Daniel (MV) 'dænjəl

Note.—This name is mentioned twice in MV, IV.i.329, *and in its first instance is meant to be trisyllabic, i.e.,* ['dænɪəl]

danish (D.) (HAM), **-es** 'deĭnɪʃ, -ɪz

dank (*from 'thank'*) 'dæŋk (*see* **dat**)

dank, -er, -est, -ish, -ly, -ness 'dæŋk, -ɚ, -ɪst, -ɪʃ, -lɪ, -nɪs

Dansker (HAM), **-s** 'dænskɚ, -z

Daphne (MSND, TC, TS) 'dæfnɪ

dapp|le, -les, -ling, -led 'dæp|l̩, -l̩z, -l̩ɪŋ [-lɪŋ], -l̩d

Dardan (LUC, TC) 'daɚ·dn̩ [-dən]

Dardanian (MV) daɚ·'deĭnɪən, -njən

Dardanius (*JUL*) daɚ·'deĭnɪəs, -njəs

dar|e, -es, -ing, -ed, durst 'dɛɚ, -z, -ɹɪŋ, -d, 'dɚst

dareful 'dɛɚ·fʊl

daring-hardy ˌdɛɚ·ɹɪŋ'haɚ·dɪ

Darius (1HVI) də'ɹaĭəs

dark, -s; -er, -est, -ly, -ness 'daɚ·k, -s; -ɚ, -ɪst, -lɪ, -nɪs

dark|en, -ens, -ening, -ened 'daɚ·k|ən, -ənz, -nɪŋ [-ənɪŋ], -ənd

darking 'daɚ·kɪŋ

darkish 'daɚ·kɪʃ

darkling 'daɚ·klɪŋ

darkness (D.) 'daɚ·knɪs

darksome 'daɚ·ksəm

darling, -s 'daɚ·lɪŋ, -z

darnel 'daɚ·nl̩

darraign, -s, -ing, -ed də'ɹeĭn, -z, -ɪŋ, -d

dart, -s, -ing, -ed 'daɚ·t, -s, -ɪŋ, -ɪd

dash, -es, -ing, -ed, -er/s 'dæʃ, -ɪz, -ɪŋ, -t, -ɚ/z

dastard, -s, -ly, -liness 'dæstɚ·d ['das-], -z, -lɪ, -lɪnɪs

dat (*from 'that'*) dat

Note.—Doctor Caius (in MWW*) is the stereotypical foreigner, given to foolish arrogance, and ineptly handling English pronunciation. This is an example of S.'s direction to the actor (by way of semiphonetic spellings) to adopt such an accent, more or less, for the sake of wringing the most satire out of plays on words stemming from confusions with, and corruptions of, English pronunciation via the French tongue*

data (*pl. of* **datum**, *q.v.*) 'deĭɽə ['daɽə]

Datchet Lane (MWW) 'dætʃɪt 'leĭn

Datchet Mead (MWW) 'dætʃɪt 'mid

dat|e, -es, -ing, -ed 'deĭt, -s, -ɪŋ, -ɪd

dateless 'deĭtlɪs

dat|um, -a 'deĭɽ|əm ['daɽ-], -ə

daub, -s, -ing, -ed, -er/s 'dɔb, -z, -ɪŋ, -d, -ɚ/z

daubery 'dɔbɚ·ɹɪ

daughter, -s 'dɔɽɚ, -z

daunt, -s, -ing, -ed 'dɔnt, -s, -ɪŋ, -ɪd

dauntless, -ly, -ness 'dɔntlɪs, -lɪ, -nɪs

Dauphin (*HV*, 1HVI, 3HVI) 'dɔfɪn, [*Fr.* dofɛ̃]

Note.—In the First Folio, this title is always spelled 'Dolphin,' lending itself to the play on words in 1HVI, I.iv.106. *The humor is lost throughout if this French word is not anglicized—at least by those allied to the English cause (see 'Shakespeare's Verse' § 1.8 of this dictionary), and accordingly, primary stress is on the first syllable*

Dauphin, Sir Guichard (HV) ˌsɚ 'gɪtʃɚ·d 'dɔfɪn (*see* **Dauphin**) [*Fr.* gɪʃaʁ dofɛ̃]

Note.—There is no evidence in HV *that either S. or Henry V intends to say the Fr. names in anything but an English 'accent.' In fact, the names (based on*

*their spellings in the Folios and
Quartos, and how they sit metrically in
the verse) seem to be stubbornly
anglicized, especially when spoken by
those allied to the English cause. In
Henry the Fifth's case, the contrast is
made more profound as he moves from
English conqueror to conciliatory wooer
of Katherine, doing so by adopting the
Fr. tongue (cf. 'Shakespeare's Verse'
§ 1.8 of this dictionary; and see* **Calais***)*

Daventry (1HIV) 'dævəntɹɪ, 'dæntɹɪ
['deĭntɹɪ]

*Note.—This name appears as 'Daintry'
in 3HVI, V.i.6, merely indicating the
more colloquial or dialectal pronunciation for the town in Northamptonshire.
In 1HIV, IV.ii.47, the name appears as
'Daventry,' 'Dauintry,' and 'Daintry,'
depending on the version of Quarto or
Folio*

Davy (*2HIV*, HV) 'deĭvɪ

daw, -s 'dɔ, -z

dawn, -s, -ing, -ed 'dɔn, -z, -ɪŋ, -d

day (D.), -s 'deĭ, -z

day-bed, -s 'deĭˌbed, -z

daylight 'deĭlaĭt

day-wearied 'deĭˌwɪɚ˞ɹɪd

day-woman *or* **dey-woman** (*dairy-maid*)
'deĭˌwʊmən

daz|e, -es, -ing, -ed, -edly 'deĭz, -ɪz, -ɪŋ,
-d, -ɪdlɪ

dazz|le, -les, -ling/ly, -led 'dæz|əl, -əlz,
-l̩ɪŋ/lɪ, -əld

de (*from 'the'*) 'də (*see* **dat**)

dead 'ded

dead-cold 'ded'koŭld ['-,-]

dead-killing 'dedˌkɪlɪŋ

deadline, -s 'dedlaĭn, -z

deadlock, -s 'dedlɒk, -s

deadl|y, -ier, -iest, -iness 'dedl|ɪ, ɪɚ˞, -ɪɪst,
-ɪnɪs

deadly-handed 'dedlɪˌhændɪd

deadly-standing 'dedlɪˌstandɪŋ

deaf, -er, -est, -ly, -ness 'def, -ɚ˞, -ɪst, -lɪ,
-nɪs

deafed 'deft

deafen, -s, -ing, -ed 'defn̩, -z, -ɪŋ, -d

deafing 'defɪŋ

deal, -s, -ing/s, dealt 'dil, -z, -ɪŋ/z, 'delt

dealer, -s 'dilɚ˞, -z

dean, -s; -ship/s 'din, -z; -ʃɪp/s

deaner|y, -ies 'dinə˞ɹ|ɪ, -ɪz

dear, -s; -er, -est, -ly, -ness 'dɪɚ˞, -z; -ɹɚ˞,
-ɹɪst, -lɪ, -nɪs

*Note.—In Frank Kermode's (editor, The
Arden Shakespeare, 1958) annotation
for TEM, I.ii.53, there is a brief but
valuable discussion about monosyllabic
words that sometimes receive the value
of two metric beats in S. lines of verse
"whether or no it is* [they are] *pronounced disyllabically . . ." In ADO,
IV.i.45 and PER, IV.vi.178, 'dear' is
arguably pronounced disyllabically or
given, as Kermode puts it, "a heavy
emphasis." Cf. Abbott's A Shakespearian Grammar, §§ 475, 479, 484*

dear-a 'dɪɚ˞ɹə

*Note.—This word, along with its
counterparts, 'wear-a' and 'ware-a,'
appears in a ditty in WT, IV.iv.316–324;
the extra syllable there merely to provide
for another musical beat in the line of
song. An attempt to retain a strict rhyme
with its counterparts—as once they
presumably could rhyme (cf. Kökeritz's
Shakespeare's Pronunciation, p. 208)—
is unprofitable*

dear-bought 'dɪɚ˞ˌbɔt

deared (*aphaeretic form of* **endeared**)
'dɪɚ˞d

dearest-valued 'dɪɚ˞ɹɪst'væljud

dearly 'dɪɚ˞lɪ

*Note.—This word is arguably trisyllabic,
i.e., ['dɪə˞lɪ], in 1HIV, V.i.84, in order to
regularize the meter of the verse line
(see* **reason** *and* **brave***)*

---

i w**e** ɪ c**i**ty ɪ h**i**t e l**e**t ɛ d**e**but æ c**a**n a p**a**ss ɝ b**i**rd ʌ h**u**t ə **a**g**ai**n ɚ supp**er** u y**ou**
ʊ sh**ou**ld o **o**bey ɔ **aw**l ɒ c**o**p ɑ f**a**ther eĭ p**ai**d aĭ h**igh** oŏ g**o** ɔĭ v**oi**ce aŏ f**ou**nd ɪɚ˞ **ear**
ɛɚ˞ **air** ʊɚ˞ p**oor** ɔɚ˞ f**ork** ɑɚ˞ p**ark** aĭɚ˞ **fire** aŏɚ˞ **hour** b **b**oy p **p**it d **d**og t **t**op g **g**ot
k **k**id h **h**ow fi be**h**ave dʒ **j**ot tʃ **ch**ew z **z**any s **s**oft v **v**at f **f**at ʒ trea**s**ure ʃ **sh**ip ð **th**e
θ **th**in m **m**an n **n**o ŋ ha**ng** l **l**ip j **y**es w **w**on ʍ **wh**ew ɹ **r**igger, ai**r**y f̢ **m**a**tt**er

de Armado, Don Adriano (*LLL*) ˌdɒn ˌeɪdɪɪˈɑnoʊ dɛ ɑ˞ˈmɑdoʊ, [*Sp.* ˌdon ˌa̠ð̠ɾiˈano dɛ aɾˈma̠ð̠o]
Note.—Whereas the Fr. characters in LLL are the convention, and thus speak 'normally,' Don Adriano de Armado, the 'fantastical Spaniard,' is typically accented. His uncommon treatment of the vernacular in Navarre ("... and with his royal finger, thus, dally with my excrement, with my mustachio ...") is usually cause to treat his speech in the play as 'foreign.' And since he speaks his own name, I include the second pronunciation, which is more in keeping with the native Sp. integrity of his name. The First Folio also gives his name as 'de Armatho' (cf. Note for **murther***)*

dear-purchased ˈdɪ˞ˌpɝˈtʃɪst
dearth, -s ˈdɝθ, -s
death (D.) (2HIV, 1HVI, KJ, LLL, RII, Sonn. 32), **-s** ˈdeθ, -s
death(-)bed, -s ˈdeθˌbed, -z
death-boding ˈdeθˌboʊdɪŋ
death-darting ˈdeθˌdɑ˞ˈtɪŋ
deathful ˈdeθfʊl
deathlike ˈdeθlaɪk
death-marked ˈdeθˌmɑ˞ˈkt
death-practiced ˈdeθˈpɹæktɪst [ˈ-ˌ--]
death's-bed ˈdeθsˌbed
death's-head ˈdeθsˌhed
deaths|man, -men ˈdeθs|mən, -mən
death-token, -s ˈdeθˌtoʊkən, -z
death-worthy ˈdeθˌwɝˈðɫ
debar, -s, -ring, -red diˈbɑ˞ [dɪˈbɑ˞], -z, -ɹɪŋ, -d
debas|e, -es, -ing, -ed, -ement dɪˈbeɪs, -ɪz, -ɪŋ, -t, -mənt
debat|e, -es, -ing, -ed, -er/s, -ement dɪˈbeɪt, -s, -ɪŋ, -ɪd, -ə˞/z, -mənt
debauch, -es, -ing, -ed, -er/s dɪˈbɔtʃ, -ɪz, -ɪŋ, -t, -ə˞/z
debaucher|y, -ies dɪˈbɔtʃə˞ɹ|ɫ, -ɪz
debile ˈdibaɪl
debility dɪˈbɪlɪtɫ
debit, -s, -ing, -ed ˈdebɪt, -s, -ɪŋ, -ɪd
debitor, -s ˈdebɪtə˞, -z
debonair(e), -ly, -ness ˌdebəˈnɛ˞, -lɫ, -nɪs
Deborah (1HVI) ˈdebə˞ɹə

deboshed dɪˈboʊʃt [-bɒʃt]
Note.—Essentially, this word is 'debauched' [dɪˈbɔtʃt], but there is a good case for pronouncing it with the [oʊ]. *Kermode, editor of The Tempest for The Arden Shakespeare (1954), cites Cotgrave's translation of 'Desbauché' as 'Deboshed' (see his annotation for the word in TEM, III.ii.25)*
de Boys *or* **Bois, Jaques** (AYLI) ˈdʒeɪks dɛ ˈbɔɪs [*Fr.* ʒɑk dɛbwɑ] (*see chapter 'Shakespeare's Verse' § 1.8 of this dictionary*)
de Boys *or* **Bois, Sir Rowland** (AYLI) ˌsɝˈɹoʊlənd dɛ ˈbɔɪs [*Fr.* ʁolɑ dɛbwɑ] (*see chapter 'Shakespeare's Verse,' § 1.8 of this dictionary*)
debt, -s, -ed, -or/s ˈdet, -s, -ɪd, -ə˞/z
Note.—In LLL, V.i.21, the pedant, Holofernes, insists on the pronunciation [ˈdebt] *for* **debt***, as he does* [ˈdaʊbt] *for* **doubt**
de Burgh, Hubert (*KJ*) ˈhjubə˞t dɛ ˈbɝg
debuty (*alt. form of 'deputy'*) ˈdebjʊtɫ
de Cassado, Gregory (HVIII) ˈgɹegə˞ɹɪ, -gɹɫ dɛ kəˈsadoʊ
decay, -s, -ing, -ed, -er dɪˈkeɪ, -z, -ɪŋ, -d, -ə˞
deceas|e, -es, -ing, -ed dɪˈsis, -ɪz, -ɪŋ, -t
deceit (D.) (3HVI), **-s** dɪˈsit, -s
deceit|ful, -fully, -fulness dɪˈsit|fʊl, -fəlɫ, -fʊlnɪs
deceiv|e, -es, -ing, -ed, -er/s; -able dɪˈsiv, -z, -ɪŋ, -d, -ə˞/z; -əbḷ
December (ADO, AYLI, CYM, RII, Sonn. 97, TN, WT), **-s** dɪˈsembə˞, -z
decent, -ly, -ness ˈdisənt, -lɫ, -nɪs
deception, -s dɪˈsepʃn̩, -z
deceptious dɪˈsepʃəs
deceptive, -ly, -ness dɪˈseptɪv, -lɫ, -nɪs
decern, -s (*Dogberry's confusion for 'concerns' in* ADO, III.v.3) dɪˈsɝn, -z
decid|e, -es, -ing, -ed/ly, -er/s dɪˈsaɪd, -z, -ɪŋ, -ɪd/lɫ, -ə˞/z
decimat|e, -es, -ing, -ed, -or/s ˈdesɪmeɪt, -s, -ɪŋ, -ɪd, -ə˞/z
decimation ˌdesɪˈmeɪʃn̩
decipher, -s, -ing, -ed, -er/s; -able dɪˈsaɪfə˞, -z, -ɹɪŋ, -d, -ɹə˞/z; -ɹəbḷ

decision, -s dɪˈsɪʒn̩, -z
decisive, -ly, -ness dɪˈsaɪsɪv, -lɪ, -nɪs
Decius (JUL) ˈdiʃɪəs, -ʃjəs
deck, -s, -ing, -ed ˈdek, -s, -ɪŋ, -t
declaration, -s ˌdekləˈɹeɪʃn̩, -z
declar|e, -es, -ing, -ed, -er/s dɪˈklɛɚ, -z,
 -ɹɪŋ, -d, -ɹɚ/z
declension, -s dɪˈklenʃn̩, -z
declin|e, -es, -ing, -ed, -er/s; -able
 dɪˈklaɪn, -z, -ɪŋ, -d, -ɚ/z; -əbl̩
decoct, -s, -ing, -ed dɪˈkɒkt, -s, -ɪŋ, -ɪd
decorum dɪˈkɔɚ̆ɹəm
decreas|e (v.), -es, -ing/ly, -ed dɪˈkɹiːs, -ɪz,
 -ɪŋ/lɪ, -t
 *Note.—When this word is used as a
 comparative (explicitly or implicitly)
 with 'increase,' the first syllable is given
 primary stress, i.e.,* [ˈdikɹis]
decree, -s, -ing, -d dɪˈkɹi, -z, -ɪŋ, -d
decrepit, -ness; -ude dɪˈkɹepɪt, -nɪs; -jud
Decretas (AC) dɪˈkɹitəs
 Note.—See Kökeritz's Shakespeare's
 Names: A Pronouncing Dictionary,
 p. 21, and M. R. Ridley's note for the
 Stage Direction, *AC, V.i.3, in his edition
 of* The Arden Shakespeare, *1954. If its
 alternate, 'Dercetas,' is opted for, the
 pronunciation is* [dɚˈsitəs]
dedicate (adj.), -s ˈdedɪkɪt, -s
dedicat|e (v.), -es, -ing, -ed ˈdedɪkeɪt, -s,
 -ɪŋ, -ɪd
deed, -s, -ing, -ed; -less ˈdid, -z, -ɪŋ, -ɪd;
 -lɪs
deed-achieving ˈdidəˌtʃivɪŋ
deem, -s, -ing, -ed ˈdim, -z, -ɪŋ, -d
deep, -s, -er, -est, -ly, -ness ˈdip, -s, -ɚ,
 -ɪst, -lɪ, -nɪs
deep-brained ˈdipˌbɹeɪnd
deep-contemplative ˌdipkənˈtemplətɪv
deep-drawing ˈdipˌdɹɔɪŋ
deepen, -s, -ing, -ed ˈdipən, -z, -ɪŋ, -d
deep-fet ˈdipˌfet
deep-mouthed ˈdipˌmaʊ̆ðd [-ˌmaʊ̆θt]
deep-revolving ˈdipɹɪˌvɒlvɪŋ

deep-sunken ˈdipˌsʌŋkən
deep-sworn ˈdipˌswɔɚ̆n
Deep-vow, Master (MEAS) ˌmastɚ
 ˈdipˌvaʊ
deer ˈdɪɚ̆
defac|e, -es, -ing, -ed, -er/s, -ement/s
 dɪˈfeɪs, -ɪz, -ɪŋ, -t, -ɚ/z, -mənt/s
defam|e, -es, -ing, -ed, -er/s dɪˈfeɪm, -z,
 -ɪŋ, -d, -ɚ/z
default, -s, -ing, -ed, -er/s dɪˈfɔlt, -s, -ɪŋ,
 -ɪd, -ɚ/z
defeat, -s, -ing, -ed dɪˈfit, -s, -ɪŋ, -ɪd
defeatur|e, -es, -ing, -ed dɪˈfitʃɚ, -z, -ɹɪŋ,
 -d
defect (s.), -s ˈdifekt [dɪˈfekt], -s
defect (v.), -s, -ing, -ed, -or/s dɪˈfekt, -s,
 -ɪŋ, -ɪd, -ɚ/z
defection, -s dɪˈfekʃn̩, -z
defective, -ly, -ness dɪˈfektɪv, -lɪ, -nɪs
defend, -s, -ing, -ed, -er/s dɪˈfend, -z, -ɪŋ,
 -ɪd, -ɚ/z
defendant, -s dɪˈfendənt, -s
defense, -s dɪˈfens (in sports, often
 [ˈdifens]), -ɪz
defensib|le, -ly dɪˈfensɪb|l̩, -lɪ
defer, -s, -ring, -red, -rer/s dɪˈfɝ, -z, -ɹɪŋ,
 -d, -ɹɚ/z
defil|e, -es, -ing, -ed, -er/s, -ement dɪˈfaɪl,
 -z, -ɪŋ, -d, -ɚ/z, -mənt
defin|e, -es, -ing, -ed, -er/s, -ment dɪˈfaɪn,
 -z, -ɪŋ, -d, -ɚ/z, -mənt
definite, -ly, -ness ˈdefɪnɪt [-fn̩ɪt], -lɪ, -nɪs
definition, -s ˌdefɪˈnɪʃn̩, -z
definitive, -ly, -ness dɪˈfɪnɪtɪv, -lɪ, -nɪs
deflower, -s, -ing, -ed dɪˈflaʊ̆ɚ̆ [ˌdiˈf-], -z,
 -ɹɪŋ, -d
deform, -s, -ing, -ed, -er/s dɪˈfɔɚ̆m, -z,
 -ɪŋ, -d, -ɚ/z
Deformed (ADO) dɪˈfɔɚ̆md
deformit|y (D.) (3HVI), -ies dɪˈfɔɚ̆mɪt|ɪ,
 -ɪz
defrock, -s, -ing, -ed ˌdiˈfɹɒk, -s, -ɪŋ, -t
deft, -er, -est, -ly, -ness ˈdeft, -ɚ, -ɪst, -lɪ,
 -nɪs

i wɛ ɪ city ɪ hit e let ɛ debut æ can a pass ɝ bird ʌ hut ə again ɚ supper u you
ʊ should o obey ɔ awl ɒ cop ɑ father eɪ paid aɪ high oʊ go ɔɪ voice aʊ found ɪɚ ear
ɛɚ air ʊɚ poor ɔɚ fork ɑɚ park aɪɚ fire aʊɚ hour b boy p pit d dog t top g got
k kid h how fi behave dʒ jot tʃ chew z zany s soft v vat f fat ʒ treasure ʃ ship ð the
θ thin m man n no ŋ hang l lip j yes w won ʍ whew ɹ rigger, airy ɾ matter

defunct, -s dɪˈfʌŋkt, -s
defunction dɪˈfʌŋkʃn̩
defunctive dɪˈfʌŋktɪv
defus|e, -es, -ing, -ed ˌdiˈfjuz, -ɪz, -ɪŋ, -d
def|y, -ies, -ying, -ied, -ier/s dɪˈf|aɪ, -aɪz, -aɪɪŋ, -aɪd, -aɪə/z
degenerate (*adj.*), **-ly, -ness** dɪdʒenəˈɹɪt, -lɪ, -nɪs
degenerat|e (*v.*), **-es, -ing, -ed** dɪˈdʒenəˈɹeɪt, -s, -ɪŋ, -ɪd
degrad|e, -es, -ing/ly, -ed dɪˈgɹeɪd, -z, -ɪŋ/lɪ, -ɪd
degree, -s dɪˈgɹi, -z
deif|y, -ies, -ying, -ied ˈdiɪf|aɪ, -aɪz, -aɪɪŋ, -aɪd
deign, -s, -ing, -ed ˈdeɪn, -z, -ɪŋ, -d
Deiphobus (*TC*) diˈɪfəbəs
deit|y (**D.**), **-ies** ˈdiɪt|ɫ [ˈdeɪɪt|ɫ], -ɪz
deject, -s, -ing, -ed/ly, -edness dɪˈdʒekt, -s, -ɪŋ, -ɪd/lɪ,-ɪdnɪs
dejection dɪˈdʒekʃn̩
Delabreth, Charles (*HV*) ˈtʃɑˈlz ˌdɛlaˈbɹeθ [-ˈbɹet]
de la Car, John (HVIII) ˈdʒɒn ˌdɛ lə ˈkɑˈ
de la Pole, William (2HVI) ˈwɪljəm ˌdɛ lə ˈpoʊl [-ˈpul]
delay, -s, -ing, -ed dɪˈleɪ, -z, -ɪŋ, -d
delet|e, -es, -ing, -ed dɪˈlit, -s, -ɪŋ, -ɪd
deletion, -s dɪˈliʃn̩, -z
deliberate (*adj.*), **-ly, -ness** dɪˈlɪbɹɪt, -lɪ, -nɪs
deliberat|e (*v.*), **-es, -ing, -ed, -or/s** dɪˈlɪbəˈɹeɪt, -s, -ɪŋ, -ɪd, -ə/z
delicate, -ly, -ness ˈdelɪkɪt, -lɪ, -nɪs
delicious, -ly, -ness dɪˈlɪʃəs, -lɪ, -nɪs
delight, -s, -ing, -ed/ly dɪˈlaɪt, -s, -ɪŋ, -ɪd/lɪ
delight|ful, -fully, -fulness dɪˈlaɪt|fʊl, -fəlɫ [-fʊlɫ], -fʊlnɪs
deliver, -s, -ing, -ed, -er/s dɪˈlɪvə, -z, -ɪɪŋ, -d, -ɹə/z
deliverance, -s dɪˈlɪvəˈɹəns, -ɪz
deliverly dɪˈlɪvəˈlɪ
deliver't (*contr. of* **deliver it**) dɪˈlɪvəˈt
deliver|y, -ies dɪˈlɪvəˈɹ|ɫ, -ɪz
Delphos (WT) ˈdelfɒs
delta, -s ˈdeltə, -z
delud|e, -es, -ing, -ed, -er/s dɪˈlud [-ˈlju-], -z, -ɪŋ, -ɪd, -ə/z

delug|e, -es, -ing, -ed ˈdɛljudʒ, -ɪz, -ɪŋ, -d
delusion, -s dɪˈluʒn̩ [-ˈlju-], -z
delv|e, -es, -ing, -ed, -er/s ˈdelv, -z, -ɪŋ, -d, -ə/z
Delver, Goodman (HAM) ˈgʊdmən ˈdelvə
demand, -s, -ing, -ed dɪˈmand, -z, -ɪŋ, -ɪd
demean, -s, -ing, -ed dɪˈmin, -z, -ɪŋ, -d
demeanor, -s dɪˈminə, -z
demerit, -s dɪˈmeɹɪt [di'm-], -s
demesne, -s dɪˈmeɪn [-ˈmin], -z
Demetrius (*AC, MSND, TIT*) dɪˈmitɹɪəs
demi-Atlas (AC) ˈdemɪˈætləs
demi-cannon ˈdemɪˌkænən
demi-coronal ˈdemɪˌkɒɹənl̩
demi-devil ˈdemɪˈdevl̩
demi(-)god, -s ˈdemɪgɒd, -z
demi-natured ˈdemɪˌneɪtʃəd
demi-paradise ˌdemɪˈpæɹədaɪs
demi-puppet, -s ˈdemɪˌpʌpɪt, -s
demis|e, -es, -ing, -ed dɪˈmaɪz, -ɪz, -ɪŋ, -d
demi-wol|f, -ves ˈdemɪˌwʊl|f, -vz
democrac|y, -ies dɪˈmɒkɹəs|ɫ, -ɪz
demolish, -es, -ing, -ed, -er/s dɪˈmɒlɪʃ, -ɪz, -ɪŋ, -t, -ə/z
demon *or* **daemon, -s** ˈdimən, -z
demonstrab|le, -ly dɪˈmɒnstɹəb|ɫ, -lɪ
 Note.—In OTH, III.iv.139, *the most advisable pronunciation of 'demon-strable' is* [ˈdemənstɹəbɫ], *which follows the metrical rhythm of the verse line, and which also happens to follow the pronunciation still preferred in standard Brit. English today (cf.* **medicine***)*
demonstrat|e, -es, -ing, -ed, -or/s ˈdemənstɹeɪt, -s, -ɪŋ, -ɪd, -ə/z
 Note.—In OTH, I.i.61, III.iii.437, *this word is arguably given primary stress on the second syllable, i.e.,* [dɪˈmɒnstɹeɪt], *depending on how much one cares to ad-here to the iambic rhythm of the line, and/or echo 'demonstrative.' In* TIM, I.i.93, *it is certainly given primary stress on the second syllable*
demsel, -s ˈdemzl̩, -z
demur, -s, -ring, -red dɪˈmɜ, -z, -ɹɪŋ, -d
demure, -r, -st, -ly, -ness dɪˈmjʊə, -ɹə, -ɹɪst, -lɪ, -nɪs
 Note.—There is an instance of this word

being made a verb in AC, IV.xv.29, *i.e.,*
demuring [dɪ'mjʊɚ̯.ɹɪŋ] *(cf. Furness'*
New Variorum Edition *[1907] p. 318).*
Also, in HVIII, I.ii.167, *this word may*
be given primary stress on the first
syllable, i.e., ['demjʊɚ̯], *depending on*
how one chooses to scan the line. S.
often shifts the stress of adjectives this
way (see Shakespeare's Verse § 1.7 of
this dictionary); and in this case, doing
so requires there to be an epic caesura
in the line. If one chooses not to scan the
line with an epic caesura, then the
unusual option of giving the word
'confidence' primary syllabic stress on
its second syllable results. And if that's
the case, then I recommend pronouncing
it [kən'faɪ̆dn̩s]—*an option, perhaps,*
resounding with the word's root
den (*from 'good even[ing]' '*) 'dɪn
Note.—Don Pedro says, "Good den,
good den" in ADO, V.i.46, *a short form*
of 'God give you good even.' In this
instance, it's best to pronounce 'den'
in a way that reflects its essential
meaning
den, -s 'den, -z
denay, -s, -ing, -ed dɪ'neǐ, -s, -ɪŋ, -d
denial, -s dɪ'naɪ̆əl, -z
denier (*from* **deny**, *q.v.*), **-s** dɪ'naɪ̆ɚ̯, -z
denier (*small coin*), **-s** dɪ'nɪɚ̯, -z
denigrat|e, -es, -ing, -ed 'denɪg.ɹeǐt, -s,
 -ɪŋ, -ɪd
denigration ,denɪ'g.ɹeǐʃn̩
denim, -s 'denɪm, -z
denizen, -s 'denɪzn̩, -z
Denmark (HAM) 'denmaɚ̯k
Dennis (*AYLI*) 'denɪs
Denny, Sir Anthony (*HVIII*) ,sɜ˞
 '(ɹ)æn̩θənɪ ['æntənɪ] 'denɪ
denot|e, -es, -ing, -ed, -ement/s dɪ'noǔt,
 -s, -ɪŋ, -ɪd, -mənt/s
denounc|e, -es, -ing, -ed, -er/s, -ement/s
 dɪ'naǔns, -ɪz, -ɪŋ, -t, -ɚ̯/z, -mənt/s

dense, -r, -st, -ly, -ness 'dens, -ɚ̯, -ɪst, -lɪ,
 -nɪs
dent, -s, -ing, -ed 'dent, -s, -ɪŋ, -ɪd
dentist, -s, -ry 'dentɪst, -s, -ɹɨ
denunciat|e, -es, -ing, -ed, -or/s
 dɪ'nʌnsɪeǐt, -s, -ɪŋ, -ɪd, -ɚ̯/z
denunciation, -s dɪ,nʌnsɪ'eǐʃn̩, -z
den|y, -ies, -ying, -ied, -ier/s dɪ'n|aǐ, -aǐz,
 -aǐɪŋ, -aǐd, -aǐɚ̯/z
depart, -s, -ing, -ed dɪ'paɚ̯t, -s, -ɪŋ, -ɪd
department, -s dɪ'paɚ̯tmənt, -s
departure, -s dɪ'paɚ̯tʃɚ̯, -z
depend, -s, -ing, -ed, -er dɪ'pend, -z, -ɪŋ,
 -ɪd, -ɚ̯
dependable, -ness dɪ'pendəbl̩, -nɪs
dependant, -s dɪ'pendənt, -s
dependen|ce, -cy, -cies, -t/s, -tly
 dɪ'pendən|s, -sɨ, -sɨz, -t/s, -tlɨ
depict, -s, -ing, -ed dɪ'pɪkt, -s, -ɪŋ, -ɪd
depiction, -s dɪ'pɪkʃn̩, -z
deplet|e, -es, -ing, -ed dɪ'plit, -s, -ɪŋ, -ɪd
deplorab|le, -ly, -leness dɪ'plɔɚ̯.ɹəb|l̩, -lɨ,
 -l̩nɪs
deplor|e, -es, -ing, -ed dɪ'plɔɚ̯, -z,
 -.ɹɪŋ, -d
deploy, -s, -ing, -ed, -ment dɪ'plɔǐ, -z, -ɪŋ,
 -d, -mənt
depopulat|e, -es, -ing, -ed, -or/s
 ,di'pɒpjʊleǐt, -s, -ɪŋ, -ɪd, -ɚ̯/z
depos|e, -es, -ing, -ed dɪ'poǔz, -ɪz, -ɪŋ, -d
deposit, -s, -ing, -ed, -or/s dɪ'pɒzɪt, -s,
 -ɪŋ, -ɪd, -ɚ̯/z
depositar|y, -ies dɪ'pɒzɪtə.ɹ|ɨ, -ɨz
deposition, -s ,depʊ'zɪʃn̩
depositor|y, -ies dɪ'pɒzɪtɔɚ̯.ɹ|ɨ, -ɨz
depot (*transit station or warehouse*), **-s**
 'dipoǔ, -z
depot (*military usage*), **-s** 'depoǔ, -z
depravation ,depɹə'veǐʃn̩
deprav|e (*v.*), **-es, -ing, -ed** dɪ'pɹeǐv, -z,
 -ɪŋ, -d
deprav|ed (*adj.*), **-edly, -edness**
 dɪ'pɹeǐv|d, -ɪdlɨ [-dlɨ], -ɪdnɪs [-dnɪs]
depravit|y, -ies dɪ'pɹævɪt|ɨ, -ɨz

depress, -es, -ing/ly, -ed, -or/s dɪˈpɹɛs,
 -ɪz, -ɪŋ/lɪ, -t, -ɚ/z
depression, -s dɪˈpɹɛʃn̩, -z
depriv|e, -es, -ing, -ed dɪˈpɹaɪ̆v, -z, -ɪŋ, -d
depth, -s ˈdepθ, -s
de Pucelle, Joan (*var. of* **la Pucelle**)
 (1HVI) ˈdʒoŭn ˌdɛ pjuˈsel [ˌdɛ ˈpʌzəl]
 *Note.—Var. spellings appear in the
 Folio, e.g., 'Puzel,' 'Pucell,' & 'Pussel.'
 The* OED *also cites 'puzzel' and 'puzzle'
 as obsolete forms of 'Pucelle.' These
 spellings, along with where the name
 falls in the verse line, suggest that the
 pronunciation may be (is probably)
 [ˈpjusel], [ˈpʌsəl], or—perhaps even
 better—[ˈpʌzəl]; thus, a homophonic
 pun about confusion and perplexity is
 retained. I will assert that S. also
 intended (or at least enjoyed) a double
 entendre; 'puzzle' was the colloquial
 slang for a slattern, a whore, or a slut.
 The irony and ambiguity of the name is
 not lost on Talbot, who remarks on it in
 1HVI, I.iv.106. In any case, Pucelle in S.
 is given primary stress on the first
 syllable. See 1HVI, I.ii.110, I.iv.100,
 106, I.vi.3, II.i.20, III.ii.20, 58, 121, III.
 iii.40. In lines I.v.36, III.ii.38, and III.
 iii.88, the name (contained in the first
 foot in each) is presumably trochaic.
 (Cf.* **Bordeaux***)*
deputation, -s ˌdepjʊˈteɪʃn̩, -z
deput|e, -es, -ing, -ed dɪˈpjut, -s, -ɪŋ, -ɪd
deracinat|e, -es, -ing, -ed dɪˈɹæsɪneɪ̆t, -s,
 -ɪŋ, -ɪd
Derby (RII, *RIII*) ˈdɑɚ̆bɪ
 *Note.—In deference to the fact that this
 name in S. only appears in the Histories,
 I recommend the regular and traditional
 Brit. pronunciation, viz. that given
 above*
Dercetas (*AC*) dɚˈsitəs (*see Note for*
 Decretas*)*
der(e) (*from 'there'*) ˈdɛʁ [ˈd̪ɛɚ̆] (*see Note
 for* **varld***)*
derid|e, -es, -ing/ly, -ed, -er/s dɪˈɹaɪ̆d, -z,
 -ɪŋ/lɪ, -ɪd, -ɚ/z
derision dɪˈɹɪʒn̩
derivation, -s ˌdeɹɪˈveɪ̆ʃn̩, -z

derivative, -s, -ly, -ness dɪˈɹɪvətɪv, -z, -lɪ,
 -nɪs
deriv|e, -es, -ing, -ed; -able dɪˈɹaɪ̆v, -z,
 -ɪŋ, -d; -əbl̩
dern *or* **dearn(e)** (*dark, dreadful, wild*)
 ˈdɪɚ̆n
 Note.—The OED *does not assert a
 pronunciation for this obsolete, archaic
 word used in* LEAR *and* PER, *except to
 say that 'darn' is a dialectal var. of
 'dern.' The 11 different spellings cited in
 the* OED *also suggest that the pronunciation widely varied from one region to
 another, of which* [ˈdɪɚ̆n, ˈdɝn, ˈdɑɚ̆n]
 are the most reasonably conjectured
derogate (*adj.*) ˈdeɹəgɪt
derogat|e (*v.*), **-s, -ing, -ed** ˈdeɹəgeɪ̆t, -s,
 -ɪŋ, -ɪd
derogately ˈdeɹəˌgeɪ̆tlɪ [-ɹəgɪtlɪ]
derogation ˌdeɹəˈgeɪ̆ʃn̩
derr|y, -ies ˈdeɹ|ɪ, -ɪz
de Santrailles, Lord Ponton (1HVI)
 ˈlɔɚ̆d ˈpɒntən ˌdə sænˈtɹeɪ̆l
desartless (*obsolete form of* **desertless**)
 dɪˈzɑɚ̆tlɪs
 Note.—In Sonn. 17, *'deserts' is meant to
 rhyme with 'parts,' or at least it once
 was (cf.* **clerk** *and* **termagant***)*
descant (*s.*), **-s** ˈdeskænt, -s
descant (*v.*), **-s, -ing, -ed** dɪˈskænt [deˈs-,
 ˈ--], -s, -ɪŋ, -ɪd
descend, -s, -ing, -ed dɪˈsend, -z, -ɪŋ, -ɪd
descendant, -s dɪˈsendənt, -s
descension dɪˈsenʃn̩
descent, -s dɪˈsent, -s
describ|e, -es, -ing, -ed, -er/s; -able
 dɪˈskɹaɪ̆b, -z, -ɪŋ, -d, -ɚ/z; -əbl̩
description, -s dɪˈskɹɪpʃn̩, -z
descriptive, -ly, -ness dɪˈskɹɪptɪv, -lɪ, -nɪs
descr|y, -ies, -ying, -ied dɪˈskɹ|aɪ̆, -aɪ̆z,
 -aɪ̆ɪŋ, -aɪ̆d
Desdemon (*OTH*) ˌdezdɪˈmoŭn
Desdemona (*OTH*) ˌdezdɪˈmoŭnə
 *Note.—The Quarto(s) and Folio
 versions of Othello are sometimes—
 three times, to be exact—at odds with
 one another when it comes to how and
 when the full 'Desdemona' is used, or
 when its diminutive form, 'Desdemon'*

should be used instead. In OTH, III.i.54; III.iii.56; and IV.ii.42, the First Folio gives the diminutive form, 'Desdemon,' whereas the Quarto versions give 'Desdemona.' Editors who adopt the Quartos' version not only disturb the natural rhythm and meter of the verse, but they also miss a golden opportunity to intensify the plot. Relationships are easily misconstrued (even by an audience) when both Cassio and Othello say 'Desdemon' with the same measure of familiarity, thus heightening the dramatic tension in the play

des(e) (*from 'these'*) ˈd̥is (*see Note for* **varld**)

desert (*s.*) (*due recompense; merit*), **-s** dɪˈzɝt, -s

Note.—In Sonn. 17.2, 'deserts' wants to rhyme with 'parts,' analogous to words such as 'sergeant,' and the chiefly Brit. pronunciations of 'clerk' and 'Derby' (cf. **clerk** *and* **termagant***). Typically, the rhyme in this instance is forsaken in favor of the modern pronunciation, i.e.,* [dɪˈzɝts]; *an irony considering* Sonn. *17's declaration in the final couplet,* "But were some child of yours alive that time, / You should live twice: in it, and in my rhyme." *Similarly, in* Sonn. *49.10 and 72.6, and just like* Sonn. *17, the rhyme is typically forsaken*

desert (*adj., s.*) (*barren region*), **-s** ˈdezɝt, -s

desert (*v.*) (*abandon*), **-s, -ing, -ed, -er/s** dɪˈzɝt, -s, -ɪŋ, -ɪd, -ɚ/z

deserv|e, -es, -ing/ly, -ed, -er/s dɪˈzɝv, -z, -ɪŋ/lɪ, -d, -ɚ/z

Note.—In COR, II.iii.113, 'deserve' is meant to rhyme with 'starve,' or at least it once was (cf. **clerk** *and* **termagant***)*

deserv|ed, -edly, -edness dɪˈzɝv|d, -ɪdlɪ, -ɪdnɪs

deservings dɪˈzɝvɪŋz

design, -s, -ing, -ed, -er/s, -ment/s dɪˈzaɪn, -z, -ɪŋ, -d, -ɚ/z, -mənt/s

desir|e (D.), -es, -ing, -ed, -er/s dɪˈzaɪɚ, -z, -ɹɪŋ, -d, -ɹɚ/z

desirous, -ly dɪˈzaɪɚɹəs, -lɪ

desist, -s, -ing, -ed dɪˈzɪst [dɪˈsɪst], -s, -ɪŋ, -ɪd

desolation ˌdesəˈleɪʃn̩

despair, -s, -ing/ly, -ed dɪˈspɛɚ, -z, -ɹɪŋ/lɪ, -d

despatch, -es, -ing, -ed, -er/s dɪˈspætʃ, -ɪz, -ɪŋ, -t, -ɚ/z

desperate, -ly, -ness ˈdespəɹɪt, -lɪ, -nɪs

desperation, -s ˌdespəˈɹeɪʃn̩, -z

despis|e, -es, -ing, -ed, -er/s dɪˈspaɪz, -ɪz, -ɪŋ, -d, -ɚ/z

despite, -ful, -fully dɪˈspaɪt, -fʊl, -fʊlɪ

despoil, -s, -ing, -ed, -er/s dɪˈspɔɪl, -z, -ɪŋ, -d, -ɚ/z

despos|e (*obsolete form of* **depose** *and* **dispose**), **-es, -ing, -ed** dɪˈspoʊz, -ɪz, -ɪŋ, -d

destin|y (D.), -ies ˈdestɪn|ɪ, -ɪz

destitute, -ly, -ness ˈdestɪtjut, -lɪ, -nɪs

destitution ˌdestɪˈtjuʃn̩

destroy, -s, -ing, -ed, -er/s dɪˈstɹɔɪ, -z, -ɪŋ, -d, -ɚ/z

destruction dɪˈstɹʌkʃn̩

destructive, -ly, -ness dɪˈstɹʌktɪv, -lɪ, -nɪs

detail (*s.*), **-s** ˈditeɪl [dɪˈteɪl], -z

detail (*v.*), **-s, -ing, -ed** dɪˈteɪl, -z, -ɪŋ, -d

detailed (*adj.*) dɪˈteɪld [ˈditeɪld]

detain, -s, -ing, -ed dɪˈteɪn, -z, -ɪŋ, -d

detect, -s, -ing, -ed, -or/s; -able dɪˈtekt, -s, -ɪŋ, -ɪd, -ɚ/z; -əbl̩

detection, -s dɪˈtekʃn̩, -z

detective, -s dɪˈtektɪv, -z

detention, -s dɪˈtenʃn̩, -z

determinate, -ly, -ness dɪˈtɝmɪnɪt, -lɪ, -nɪs

Note.—In RJ, I.iii.150, this word is made into a verb, thus requiring the pronunciation [dɪˈtɝmɪneɪt]

determination, -s dɪˌtɝmɪˈneɪʃn̩, -z

determin|e, -es, -ing, -ed dɪ'tɝˑmɪn, -z,
-ɪŋ, -d

detest, -s, -ing, -ed dɪ'test, -s, -ɪŋ, -ɪd

detestab|le, -ly, -leness dɪ'testəb|l̩, -lɪ,
-l̩nɪs
Note.—Stressed on the first syllable, i.e.,
['ditestəbl̩] *in* KJ, III.iii.29; RJ, IV.v.56,
V.iii.45; TIM, IV.i.33; TIT, V.i.94

detract, -s, -ing/ly, -ed, -or/s dɪ'tɹækt, -s,
-ɪŋ/lɪ, -ɪd, -ɚ/z

detraction, -s dɪ'tɹækʃn̩, -z

detriment, -s 'detɹɪmənt, -s

detrimental ˌdetɹɪ'mentl̩

Deucalion (COR, WT) dju'keɪlɪən, -ljən

deuce, -s 'djus, -ɪz

deuce-ace (*'three' in a throw of dice;*
hence, bad luck or low rate) 'djusˌeɪs ['-'-]

deuced (*adj.*)**, -ly** 'djusɪd, -lɪ

devastat|e, -es, -ing, -ed 'devəsteɪt, -s,
-ɪŋ, -ɪd

devastation, -s ˌdevə'steɪʃn̩, -z

devesting (*undressing*) ˌdi'vestɪŋ

deviant, -s 'divɪənt, -s

deviat|e, -es, -ing, -ed, -or/s 'divɪeɪt, -s,
-ɪŋ, -ɪd, -ɚ/z

deviation, -s ˌdivɪ'eɪʃn̩, -z

device, -s dɪ'vaɪs, -ɪz

devil (D.), -s, -ling, -led 'devl̩ ['devəl], -z,
-ɪŋ, -d

devilish, -ly, -ness 'devl̩ɪʃ [-vlɪʃ], -lɪ, -nɪs

devil-porter 'devl̩ˌpɔɚˑɾɚ

devis|e, -es, -ing, -ed, -er/s; -able dɪ'vaɪz,
-ɪz, -ɪŋ, -d, -ɚ/z; -əbl̩

devision (*from 'devise'*) dɪ'vɪʒn̩

devoid dɪ'vɔɪd

Devonshire (RIII) 'devn̩ʃɪɚ [-ʃɚ]

devot|e, -es, -ing, -ed/ly, -edness dɪ'voʊt,
-s, -ɪŋ, -ɪd/lɪ, -ɪdnɪs

devotion (D.), -s; -al/s, -ally dɪ'voʊʃn̩, -z;
-əl/z, -lɪ

devour, -s, -ing, -ed, -er/s dɪ'vɑʊɚ, -z,
-ɹɪŋ, -d, -ɹɚ/z

devout, -er, -est, -ly, -ness dɪ'vɑʊt, -ɚ,
-ɪst, -lɪ, -nɪs

dew, -s, -ed 'dju, -z, -d

Dew, Signieur (HV) 'sɪnjɚ 'dju
Note.—This term in HV, IV.iv.7 is
Pistol's mocking pronunciation of
'Seigneur Dieu,' Fr. for 'Lord God'

dew-bedabbled 'djubɪ'dæbl̩d

dewberr|y, -ies 'djubeɹ|ɪ [-bəɹ-], -ɪz

dew-claw, -s 'djuˌklɔ, -z

dew-drop, -s, -ping 'djudɹɒp, -s, -ɪŋ

dew(-)lap, -s, -ped 'djulæp, -s, -t

dew|y, -iness 'dju|ɪ, -ɪnɪs

dexter 'dekstɚ

dexteriously (*archaic var. of* **dexter-**
ously) dek'steɹɪəslɪ [-'stɪɚ-ɹ-]
Note.—Both of these pronunciations are
conjectural; the first being parallel to
'dexterity,' and the second being
analogous to 'mysterious' and accepted
pronunciations of 'hysteria' and
'steroid'

dexterity dek'steɹɪtɪ

dexterous, -ly, -ness 'dekstɚəs, -lɪ, -nɪs

dey-woman *or* **day-woman** (*dairy-maid*)
'deɪˌwʊmən

diable (*Fr.*) (MWW, III.i.81) di'ablə

Diablo (*Sp.*) (OTH, II.iii.152) di'ɑˑblo

diadem, -s 'daɪədem [-dəm], -z

dial, -s, -(l)ing, -(l)ed 'daɪəl, -z, -ɪŋ, -d

dialect, -s 'daɪəlekt, -s

dialectic, -s, -al, -ally ˌdaɪə'lektɪk, -s, -l̩,
-əlɪ

dialogue, -s, -d 'daɪəlɒg, -z, -d

Dian (ADO, COR, CYM, 3HVI, MSND,
OTH, PER, RJ, Sonn. 153, TIM, TIT,
TS, VA) 'daɪæn ['daɪən]

Diana (ADO, *ALL'S*, AYLI, 1HIV,
MSND, MV, *PER*, TC, TN) daɪ'ænə

diapason, -s ˌdaɪə'peɪzən [-'peɪsən], -z

diaper, -s 'daɪəpɚ, -z

dibb|le, -les, -ling, -led, -ler/s 'dɪb|l̩, -l̩z,
-lɪŋ [-l̩ɪŋ], -l̩d, -lɚ/z [-l̩ɚ/z]

dice (*pl. of* **die** [*game piece], q.v.*) 'daɪs

dicer, -s 'daɪsɚ, -z

dich 'dɪtʃ
Note.—This word in TIM, I.ii.72 *is*
somewhat of a mystery. H. J. Oliver,
editor of TIM (The Arden Shakespeare,
1959) says, "Not satisfactorily ex-
plained but generally taken as a
corruption of "do it" (do it ye—dit
ye—dich ye)

Dick (COR, 1HIV, *2HVI*, 3HVI, LLL)
'dɪk

dickens 'dɪkɪnz

Dickon (RIII) 'dɪkn̩
Dicky (3HVI) 'dɪkɪ
diction 'dɪkʃn̩
dictionar|y, -ies 'dɪkʃnə˞ɹ|ɪ, -ɪz
Dictynna (LLL) 'dɪktɪnə [-'--]
*Note.—This alt. name for the goddess
Diana is the word most editors assume
is meant in LLL, IV.ii.35, 36, even
though var. versions of the text (two
Quartos and four Folios) give 'Dictis-
sima,' 'Dictinna,' 'Dictima," and
'Dictisima' only*
did (*p.t. of* **do**, *q.v.*) 'dɪd
Dido (AC, HAM, MV, RJ, TEM, TIT,
TNK) 'daɪdŏ
die (*game piece*), **dice** 'daɪ, 'daɪs
di'e (*contr. of* **do ye**) 'dɪɪ ['djɪ]
die (*stamp; cut*), **-s** 'daɪ, -z
d|ie (*expire*), **-ies, -ying, -ied** 'd|aɪ, -aɪz,
-aɪɪŋ, -aɪd
diet, -s, -ing, -ed 'daɪɪt ['daɪət], -s, -ɪŋ,
-ɪd
dieter, -s 'daɪɪtə˞ ['daɪətə˞], -z
Dieu de batailles (*Fr.*) (HV, III.v.15) 'dø
də bɑ'taɪj
*Dieu vous garde, monsieur.—Et vous
aussi, votre serviteur* (*Fr.*) (TN,
III.i.72,73) 'dø vu 'gɑʁd mɪsʎ et vu o'si
votʁ seʁvɪ'tœʁ
Di faciant laudis summa sit ista tuae (*L.*)
(3HVI, I.iii.47) 'di 'fasɪɑnt 'laŏdis 'suma
'sit 'ista 'tuaɪ
differ, -s, -ing, -ed 'dɪfə˞, -z, -ɹɪŋ, -d
differen|ce, -ces, -cy, -t/ly 'dɪfɹən|s
[-fə˞ɹən-], -sɪz, -sɪ, -t/lɪ
diffiden|ce, -ces, -t/ly 'dɪfɪdən|s, -sɪz, -t/lɪ
diffuse (*adj.*), **-ly, -ness** dɪ'fjus, -lɪ, -nɪs
diffus|e (*v.*), **-es, -ing, -ed, -edly, -edness,
-er/s** dɪ'fjuz, -ɪz, -ɪŋ, -d, -ɪdlɪ, -ɪdnɪs,
-ə˞/z
diffusion dɪ'fjuʒn̩
dig, -s, -ging, -ged, dug 'dɪg, -z, -ɪŋ, -d,
'dʌg
digest (*s.*), **-s** 'daɪdʒest, -s

digest (*v.*), **-s, -ing, -ed** daɪ'dʒest [dɪ'dʒ-],
-s, -ɪŋ, -ɪd
digestion, -s daɪ'dʒestʃn̩ [dɪ'dʒ-], -z
Dighton, John (RIII) 'dʒɒn 'daɪtn̩
digni|fy, -fies, -fying, -fied 'dɪgnɪ|faɪ,
-faɪz, -faɪɪŋ, -faɪd
dignit|y, -ies 'dɪgnɪt|ɪ, -ɪz
digress, -es, -ing, -ed daɪ'gɹes [dɪ'g-], -ɪz,
-ɪŋ, -t
digression, -s daɪ'gɹeʃn̩ [dɪ'g-], -z
digs (*s.*) 'dɪgz
digt (*from* '*digged*') 'dɪkt
*Note.—Fluellen (in HV) is a Welshman,
and speaks in a Welsh accent, if
somewhat inconsistently. This is an
example of S.'s direction to the actor (by
way of semiphonetic spellings) to adopt
such an accent, more or less, for the
sake of wringing the most satire out of
plays on words stemming from confusions with, and corruptions of, English
pronunciation via the Welsh tongue. The
fact that he uses 'digged' ('digt') instead
of 'dug' is not inherently a Welsh-ism; S.
uses only 'digged' throughout his works*
dig-you-den, God 'gɒd,dɪgjʊ'den [-ju'd-,
-ʊ'din]
*Note.—This is an obscure dialectal
mutilation of "God give you good even
(-ing)." Cf. OED "good-even"*
dilat|e, -es, -ing, -ed, -er/s; -able daɪ'leɪt
['daɪleɪt], -s, -ɪŋ, -ɪd, -ə˞/z; -əbl̩
dilatorily ,dɪlə'tɔɹɪlɪ
dilator|y, -iness 'dɪlətə˞ɹ|ɪ [-tɔ˞-ɹɪ], -ɪnɪs
dild (*corruption of* **yield**) 'dild
*Note.—This word is a colloquial
corruption of the word 'yield' and is
found in the archaism 'good dild you' to
stand for 'God yield you,' the way
'good-bye' stands for 'God be with you
(ye).' In HAM, IV.v.42, the word
appears as 'dild,' 'dil'd,' or 'yeeld' in
the Second Quarto, First Folio, and
First Quarto versions, respectively.*

---

i w**e** ɪ c**i**t**y** ɪ h**i**t e l**e**t ɛ d**e**but æ c**a**n a p**a**ss ɝ b**ir**d ʌ h**u**t ə **a**gain ə˞ supp**er** u y**ou**
ʊ sh**ould** o **o**bey ɔ **aw**l ɒ c**o**p ɑ f**a**ther eɪ p**ai**d aɪ h**igh** oŏ g**o** ɔɪ v**oi**ce aŏ f**ou**nd ɪɝ **ear**
ɛɝ **air** ʊɝ **poor** ɔɝ **fork** ɑɝ **park** aɪɝ **fire** aŏɝ **hour** b **b**oy p **p**it d **d**og t **t**op g **g**ot
k **k**id h **h**ow fi be**h**ave dʒ **j**ot tʃ **ch**ew z **z**any s **s**oft v **v**at f **f**at ʒ trea**s**ure ʃ **sh**ip ð **th**e
θ **th**in m **m**an n **n**o ŋ ha**ng** l **l**ip j **y**es w **w**on ʍ **wh**ew ɹ **r**igger, ai**r**y ɼ ma**tt**er

'God-eyld' [ˌɡɒˈdild] *is given in the Folio version of* MAC, I.vi.13, *sometimes emended to* 'God 'ild'

dildo(e), -(e)s 'dɪldoʊ̆, -z

dilemma, -s dɪˈlemə, -z

dilículo súrgere (*L.*) (TN, II.iii.2) diˈlikulo 'sɜˈdʒɛɾe

diligen|ce, -t/ly 'dɪlɪdʒən|s, -t/lɪ

dim, -s, -ming, -med; -mer, -mest, -ly, -ness 'dɪm, -z, -ɪŋ, -d; -ə-, -ɪst, -lɪ, -nɪs

dimension, -s, -ing, -ed dɪˈmenʃn̩ [daɪˈm-], -z, -ɪŋ, -d

diminitive (*var. of* **diminutive**), **-ly, -ness** dɪˈmɪnɪtɪv, -lɪ, -nɪs

diminution, -s ˌdɪmɪˈnjuʃn̩, -z

diminutive, -s; -ly, -ness dɪˈmɪnjʊtɪv, -z; -lɪ, -nɪs

dimp|le, -les, -ling, -led 'dɪmp|l̩, -l̩z, -lɪŋ [-l̩ɪŋ], -l̩d

din, -s, -ning, -ned 'dɪn, -z, -ɪŋ, -d

din|e, -es, -ing, -ed, -er/s 'daɪn, -z, -ɪŋ, -d, -ə-/z

ding, -s, -ing, -ed 'dɪŋ, -z, -ɪŋ, -d

dining-chamber, -s 'daɪnɪŋˌtʃeɪmbə-, -z

dinner, -s 'dɪnə-, -z

dinner-time, -s 'dɪnə-ˌtaɪm, -z

dint 'dɪnt

Diomed (AC, 3HVI, TC) 'daɪəmed *Note.—Sometimes this name is syncopated into two syllables (*['daɪ(ə)med]*), e.g.,* AC, IV.xiv.128; TC,V.ii.74

Diomede (*var. of* 'Diomed') (3HVI) 'daɪəmid

Diomedes (AC, TC) ˌdaɪəˈmidɪz

Dion (WT) 'daɪən

Dionyza (PER) ˌdaɪəˈnaɪzə

dire, -r, -st, -ness 'daɪə-, -ɪə-, -ɪɪst, -nɪs

direct, -s, -ing, -ed, -or/s; -ly, -ness dɪˈɹekt, -s, -ɪŋ, -ɪd, -ə-/z; -lɪ, -nɪs *Note.—In* OTH, I.ii.86, *this word is given primary stress on the first syllable, i.e.,* ['daɪɹekt] *and thus takes on a pronunciation more closely related to the modern, chiefly Brit. pronunciation, particularly when (as in this instance) it is attributive. (Cf.* **medicine**)

direction, -s dɪˈɹekʃn̩, -z

directitude dɪˈɹektɪtjud

directive, -s dɪˈɹektɪv, -z

dire|ful, -fully, -fulness 'daɪə-|fʊl, -fəlɪ, -fʊlnɪs

dire-lamenting 'daɪə-ləˌmentɪŋ

dirge, -s 'dɜˈdʒ, -ɪz

dirk, -s 'dɜˈk, -s

dirt 'dɜˈt

dirt-rotten 'dɜˈtˌɹɒtn̩ (*when att.,* ['-,--])

dirt|y, -ies, -ying, -ied; -ier, -iest, -ily, -iness 'dɜˈɾ|ɪ, -ɪz, -ɪɪŋ, -ɪd; -ɪə-, -ɪɪst, -ɪlɪ, -ɪnɪs

Dis (TEM, TNK, WT) 'dɪs

disabilit|y, -ies ˌdɪsəˈbɪlɪt|ɪ, -ɪz

disab|le, -les, -ling, -led dɪˈseɪb|l̩, -l̩z, -lɪŋ [-lɪŋ], -l̩d

disadvantag|e, -es, -ing, -ed ˌdɪsədˈvantɪdʒ, -ɪz, -ɪŋ, -d

disagree, -s, -ing, -d, -ment/s ˌdɪsəˈɡɹi, -z, -ɪŋ, -d, -mənt/s

disagreeab|le, -ly, -leness ˌdɪsəˈɡɹɪəb|l̩, -lɪ, -l̩nɪs

disallow, -s, -ing, -ed ˌdɪsəˈlaʊ̆, -z, -ɪŋ, -d

disanimat|e, -es, -ing, -ed dɪsˈænɪmeɪt, -s, -ɪŋ, -ɪd

disannul, -s, -ling, -led, -ment/s ˌdɪsəˈnʌl, -z, -ɪŋ, -d, -mənt/s

disappoint, -s, -ing, -ed, -ment/s ˌdɪsəˈpɔɪnt, -s, -ɪŋ, -ɪd, -mənt/s

disarm, -s, -ing, -ed dɪˈsɑə-m [dɪsˈɑə-m], -z, -ɪŋ, -d

disaster, -s dɪˈzastə-, -z

disastrous, -ly, -ness dɪˈzastɹəs, -lɪ, -nɪs

disbenched dɪsˈbentʃt

disbranch dɪsˈbɹantʃ

disburdened dɪsˈbɜˈdnd

disburs|e, -es, -ing, -ed, -ement/s dɪsˈbɜˈs, -ɪz, -ɪŋ, -t, -mənt/s

discand|y, -ies, -ying, -ied dɪsˈkænd|ɪ, -ɪz, -ɪŋ, -ɪd

discard (s.), **-s** 'dɪskɑə-d, -z

discard (v.), **-s, -ing, -ed** dɪˈskɑə-d, -z, -ɪŋ, -ɪd

discase dɪsˈkeɪs

discern, -s, -ing/s, -ed, -er/s, -ment dɪˈsɜˈn [dɪˈzɜˈn], -z, -ɪŋ/z, -d, -ə-/z, -mənt

discharge (s.), **-s** 'dɪstʃɑə-dʒ [dɪsˈtʃɑə-dʒ], -ɪz

discharg|e (v.), **-es, -ing, -ed, -er/s** dɪsˈtʃɑə-dʒ, -ɪz, -ɪŋ, -d, -ə-/z

disciple, -s, -d; -ship dɪˈsaɪpl̩, -z, -d; -ʃɪp
disciplin|e, -es, -ing, -ed ˈdɪsɪplɪn, -z, -ɪŋ,
 -d
disclaim, -s, -ing, -ed, -er/s dɪsˈkleɪm, -z,
 -ɪŋ, -d, -ɚ/z
disclos|e, -es, -ing, -ed dɪsˈkloŭz, -ɪz, -ɪŋ,
 -d
disclosure, -s dɪsˈkloŭʒɚ, -z
discolor, -s, -ing, -ed dɪsˈkʌlɚ, -z, -ɹɪŋ,
 -d
discoloration, -s dɪsˌkʌlɚˈɹeɪʃn̩, -z
discomfit, -s, -ing, -ed dɪsˈkʌmfɪt, -s, -ɪŋ,
 -ɪd
discomfiture dɪsˈkʌmfɪtʃɚ
discomfort, -s, -ing, -ed, -able
 dɪsˈkʌmfɚt, -s, -ɪŋ, -ɪd, -əbl̩
discommend ˌdɪskəˈmend
disconsolate, -ly, -ness dɪsˈkɒnsəlɪt, -lɪ,
 -nɪs
discontent (D.), -s, -ing, -ed, -edly,
 -edness ˌdɪskənˈtent, -s, -ɪŋ, -ɪd, -ɪdlɪ,
 -ɪdnɪs
discontinuance ˌdɪskənˈtɪnjʊəns
discontin|ue, -ues, -uing, -ued
 ˌdɪskənˈtɪn|ju, -juz, -juɪŋ, -jud
discontinuit|y, -ies ˌdɪskɒntɪˈnjuɪt|ɪ
 [-ˌ--ˈ---], -ɪz
discord (s.)**, -s** ˈdɪskɔɚd, -z
discord (v.)**, -s, -ing, -ed** dɪˈskɔɚd, -z, -ɪŋ,
 -ɪd
discord-dulcet ˈdɪskɔɚdˈdʌlsɪt
discourse (s.)**, -s** ˈdɪskɔɚs [dɪˈskɔɚs], -ɪz
discours|e (v.)**, -es, -ing, -ed, -er/s**
 dɪˈskɔɚs, -ɪz, -ɪŋ, -t, -ɚ/z
discourtes|y, -ies dɪsˈkɝtɪs|ɪ, -ɪz
discover, -s, -ing, -ed dɪˈskʌvɚ, -z, -ɹɪŋ,
 -d
Note.—When this word is used to mean
‘reveal’ or ‘uncover,’ as it is in 1HVI,
V.iv.60, etc., there may be some
advantage in rendering the more literal
pronunciation [dɪsˈkʌvɚ]
discoverer, -s dɪˈskʌvəɹɚ, -z
discover|y, -ies dɪˈskʌvəɹ|ɪ, -ɪz

discredit, -s, -ing, -ed dɪsˈkɹedɪt [ˌdɪsˈk-],
 -s, -ɪŋ, -ɪd
discreet, -ly, -ness dɪˈskɹit, -lɪ, -nɪs
discretion, -s dɪˈskɹeʃn̩, -z
discuss, -es, -ing, -ed dɪˈskʌs, -ɪz, -ɪŋ, -t
discussion, -s dɪˈskʌʃn̩, -z
disdain, -s, -ing, -ed dɪsˈdeɪn, -z, -ɪŋ, -d
disdain|ful, -fully, -fulness dɪsˈdeɪn|fʊl,
 -fəlɪ, -fʊlnɪs
Disdain, Lady (ADO) ˈleɪdɪ dɪsˈdeɪn
disease, -s, -d dɪˈziz, -ɪz, -d
 Note.—In CYM, I.vii.123, TIM, III.i.53
 and WT, I.ii.386, *‘disease’ wants to scan*
 [ˈ--], *possibly lending itself to a*
 somewhat more pedantic pronunciation,
 i.e., [ˈdɪsˌiz]
disedged ˌdɪsˈedʒd
disembark, -s, -ing, -ed ˌdɪsɪmˈbaɚk, -s,
 -ɪŋ, -t
disfigur|e, -es, -ing, -ed, -ement/s
 dɪsˈfɪgjɚ, -z, -ɹɪŋ, -d, -mənt/s
disfurnish dɪsˈfɝnɪʃ
disgorg|e, -es, -ing, -ed dɪsˈgɔɚdʒ, -ɪz,
 -ɪŋ, -d
disgrac|e, -es, -ing, -ed, -er/s dɪsˈgɹeɪs, -ɪz, -ɪŋ,
 -t
disgraceful, -ly, -ness dɪsˈgɹeɪsfʊl, -ɪ, -nɪs
disgracious dɪsˈgɹeɪʃəs
disguis|e, -es, -ing, -ed, -er/s dɪsˈgaɪz, -ɪz,
 -ɪŋ, -d, -ɚ/z
dish, -es, -ing, -ed ˈdɪʃ, -ɪz, -ɪŋ, -t
dishabit, -s, -ing, -ed dɪsˈfiæbɪt, -s, -ɪŋ,
 -ɪd
dishclout, -s ˈdɪʃklaŭt, -s
dishearten, -s, -ing, -ed dɪsˈfiaɚtn̩, -z, -ɪŋ,
 -d
dishevel, -s, -ling, -led dɪˈʃevl̩, -z, -ɪŋ, -d
dishonest, -ly dɪsˈɒnɪst, -lɪ
dishonest|y, -ies dɪsˈɒnɪst|ɪ, -ɪz
dishonor, -s, -ing, -ed dɪsˈɒnɚ, -z, -ɹɪŋ,
 -d
dishonorab|le, -ly, -leness dɪsˈɒnəɹəb|l̩
 [-nɹəb-], -lɪ, -l̩nɪs
dishorn dɪsˈhɔɚn

---

i wᴇ ɪ city ɪ hit e lᴇt ɛ debut æ can a pass ɝ bird ʌ hut ə again ɚ suppᴇr u you
ʊ should o obey ɔ awl ɒ cop ɑ father eɪ paid aɪ high oŭ go ɔɪ voice aŭ found ɪɚ ear
ɛɚ air ʊɚ poor ɔɚ fork ɑɚ park aɪɚ fire aŭɚ hour b boy p pit d dog t top g got
k kid h how fi behave dʒ jot tʃ chew z zany s soft v vat f fat ʒ treasure ʃ ship ð the
θ thin m man n no ŋ hang l lip j yes w won ᴍ whew ɹ rigger, airy ɼ matter

disinherit, -s, -ing, -ed ˌdɪsɪnˈheɹɪt, -s, -ɪŋ, -ɪd

disinsanity ˌdɪsɪnˈsænɪtɨ

disjoin, -s, -ing, -ed dɪsˈdʒɔɪn, -z, -ɪŋ, -d

disjoint, -s, -ing, -ed/ly, -edness dɪsˈdʒɔɪnt, -s, -ɪŋ, -ɪd/lɨ, -ɪdnɪs

disjunction, -s dɪsˈdʒʌŋkʃn̩, -z

dislik|e, -es, -ing, -ed dɪsˈlaɪk, -s, -ɪŋ, -t

disliken dɪsˈlaɪkən

dislimn, -s, -ing, -ed dɪsˈlɪm, -z, -ɪŋ, -d

dislocat|e, -es, -ing, -ed ˈdɪslokeɪt [dɪsˈloŏkeɪt], -s, -ɪŋ, -ɪd

dislocation, -s ˌdɪsloˈkeɪʃn̩, -z

dislodg|e, -es, -ing, -ed dɪsˈlɒdʒ, -ɪz, -ɪŋ, -d

disloyal, -ly, -ty dɪsˈlɔɪəl, -ɨ, -tɨ

dism|al, -ally, -alness ˈdɪzm|əl, -əlɨ, -əlnɪs

dismall'st ˈdɪzməlst

dismantl|e, -es, -ing, -ed dɪsˈmæntl̩, -z, -ɪŋ, -d

dismask, -s, -ing, -ed dɪsˈmask, -s, -ɪŋ, -t

dismay, -s, -ing, -ed dɪsˈmeɪ, -z, -ɪŋ, -d

disme (var. of **dime**; archaic for tenth, tithe, or decimal), **-s** ˈdaɪm, -z

dismember, -s, -ing, -ed, -ment dɪsˈmembə, -z, -ɹɪŋ, -d, -mənt

dismiss, -es, -ing, -ed dɪsˈmɪs, -ɪz, -ɪŋ, -t

dismissal, -s dɪsˈmɪsl̩, -z

dismission dɪsˈmɪʃn̩

dismount, -s, -ing, -ed dɪsˈmaʊnt, -s, -ɪŋ, -ɪd

disnatured dɪsˈneɪtʃəd

disobedien|ce, -t|ly ˌdɪsəˈbidɪən|s, -t/lɨ

disobey, -s, -ing, -ed ˌdɪsəˈbeɪ, -z, -ɪŋ, -d

disorbed dɪsˈɔːbd

disorder, -s, -ing, -ed dɪsˈɔːdə, -z, -ɹɪŋ, -ɪd

disparag|e, -es, -ing/ly, -ed, -ment/s dɪˈspæɹɪdʒ, -ɪz, -ɪŋ/lɨ, -d, -mənt/s

disparate, -ly, -ness ˈdɪspəɹɪt, -lɨ, -nɪs

disparit|y, -ies dɪˈspæɹɪt|ɨ, -ɨz

disparked dɪˈspaːkt (arguably [ˈdɪspaːkt] in RII, III.i.23)

dispatch, -es, -ing, -ed, -er/s dɪˈspætʃ, -ɪz, -ɪŋ, -t, -ə/z

dispens|e, -es, -ing, -ed, -er/s dɪˈspens, -ɪz, -ɪŋ, -t, -ə/z

dispers|e, -es, -ing, -ed, -er/s dɪˈspɜːs, -ɪz, -ɪŋ, -t, -ə/z ([ˈdɪspɜːst] in LUC, 1805)

dispersedly dɪˈspɜːsɪdlɨ

dispiteous (without pity) dɪsˈpɪtɪəs [-ɪɟɪəs, -ɪtjəs]

displac|e, -es, -ing, -ed, -ement/s dɪsˈpleɪs, -ɪz, -ɪŋ, -t, -mənt/s

displant, -s, -ing, -ed dɪsˈplant, -s, -ɪŋ, -ɪd

display, -s, -ing, -ed, -er/s dɪˈspleɪ, -z, -ɪŋ, -d, -ə/z

displeas|e, -es, -ing/ly, -ingness, -ed dɪsˈpliz, -ɪz, -ɪŋ/lɨ, -ɪŋnɪs, -d

displeasure dɪsˈpleʒə

disponge (var. form of **dispunge**, q.v.) dɪˈspʌndʒ

disport, -s, -ing, -ed dɪˈspɔːt, -s, -ɪŋ, -ɪd

dispos|e, -es, -ing, -ed, -er/s; -able, -al/s dɪˈspoʊz, -ɪz, -ɪŋ, -d, -ə/z; -əbl̩, -əl/z

disposition, -s ˌdɪspʊˈzɪʃn [-pəˈz-], -z

dispossess, -es, -ing, -ed ˌdɪspʊˈzes, -ɪz, -ɪŋ, -t

disprais|e, -es, -ing/ly, -ed dɪsˈpɹeɪz, -ɪz, -ɪŋ/lɨ, -d ([ˈ--] in AC, II.v.108)

dispriz|e, -es, -ing, -ed dɪsˈpɹaɪz, -ɪz, -ɪŋ, -d

dispropertied dɪsˈpɹɒpətɨd

disproportion, -ed ˌdɪspɹʊˈpɔːʃn [ˈ--ˌ--], -d

disprov|e, -es, -ing, -ed dɪsˈpɹuv, -z, -ɪŋ, -d

dispung|e, -es, -ing, -ed dɪˈspʌndʒ, -ɪz, -ɪŋ, -d

disputable dɪˈspjuɟəbl̩ [ˈdɪspjuɟəbl̩]

disputation, -s ˌdɪspjʊˈteɪʃn, -z

disput|e, -es, -ing, -ed, -er/s dɪˈspjut, -s, -ɪŋ, -ɪd, -ə/z

disquantity dɪsˈkwɒntɪtɨ

disquiet, -s, -ing, -ed dɪsˈkwaɪət, -s, -ɪŋ, -ɪd

disquietly dɪsˈkwaɪətlɨ

disrelish dɪsˈɹelɪʃ

disrob|e, -es, -ing, -ed dɪsˈɹoʊb, -z, -ɪŋ, -d

disroot, -s, -ing, -ed dɪsˈɹut, -s, -ɪŋ, -ɪd

disseat, -s, -ing, -ed ˌdɪsˈsit, -s, -ɪŋ, -ɪd

dissemb|le, -les, -ling, -led, -ler/s dɪˈsembl̩, -l̩z, -l̩ɪŋ, -l̩d, -lə/z [-l̩ə/z]

dissembly (Dogberry's perversion [perhaps intentional] of **assembly** in ADO, IV.ii.1) dɪˈsemblɨ

dissension, -s dɪˈsenʃn̩, -z

dissent, -s, -ing, -ed, -er/s dɪ'sent, -s, -ɪŋ, -ɪd, -ɚ/z

dissentious dɪ'senʃəs

dissev|er, -ers, -ering, -ered, -erer/s, -erment; -erance dɪ'sev|ɚ, -ɚz, -ɚɹɪŋ, -ɚd, -ɚɹɚ/z, -ɚmənt; -ɹəns

dissipat|e, -es, -ing, -ed 'dɪsɪpeɪ̆t, -s, -ɪŋ, -ɪd

dissipation, -s ˌdɪsɪ'peɪ̆ʃn̩, -z

dissolute, -s, -ly, -ness 'dɪsəlut [-ljut], -s, -lɪ, -nɪs

dissolution, -s ˌdɪsə'luʃn̩ [-ljuʃ-], -z

dissolv|e, -es, -ing, -ed; -able dɪ'zɒlv, -z, -ɪŋ, -d; -əbl̩

dissuad|e, -es, -ing, -ed dɪ'sweɪ̆d, -z, -ɪŋ, -ɪd

dissuasion dɪ'sweɪ̆ʒn̩

distaff, -s 'dɪstaf, -s

distaff-women 'dɪstafˌwɪmɪn

distain, -s, -ing, -ed dɪ'steɪ̆n, -z, -ɪŋ, -d

distanc|e, -es, -ing, -ed 'dɪstəns, -ɪz, -ɪŋ, -t

distant, -ly 'dɪstənt, -lɪ

distaste, -s, -ed ˌdɪs'teɪ̆st, -s, -ɪd

distaste|ful, -fully, -fulness dɪs'teɪ̆st|fʊl, -fəlɪ, -fʊlnɪs

distemper, -ing, -ed dɪs'tempɚ, -ɹɪŋ, -d

distemperature, -s dɪs'tempɹətʃɚ, -z

distil, -s, -ling, -led, -ler/s dɪ'stɪl, -z, -ɪŋ, -d, -ɚ/z

distillation, -s ˌdɪstɪ'leɪ̆ʃn̩, -z

distinct, -ly, -ness dɪ'stɪŋkt, -lɪ, -nɪs
Note.—Stressed on the first syllable ['dɪstɪŋkt] in MV, II.ix.61; TC, IV.iv.44

distinguish, -es, -ing, -ed, -ment/s; -able, -ably dɪ'stɪŋgwɪʃ, -ɪz, -ɪŋ, -t, -mənt/s; -əbl̩, -əblɪ

distort, -s, -ing, -ed/ly, -edness dɪ'stɔɚt, -s, -ɪŋ, -ɪd/lɪ, -ɪdnɪs

distortion, -s dɪ'stɔɚʃn̩, -z

distract, -s, -ing, -ed/ly, -edness dɪ'stɹækt, -s, -ɪŋ, -ɪd/lɪ, -ɪdnɪs

distraction, -s dɪ'stɹækʃn̩, -z

distrain, -s, -ing, -ed, -er/s; -able dɪ'stɹeɪ̆n, -z, -ɪŋ, -d, -ɚ/z; -əbl̩

distress, -es, -ing/ly, -ed dɪ'stɹes, -ɪz, -ɪŋ/lɪ, -t
Note.—Sometimes stressed on the first syllable in S. ['dɪstɹes], e.g., 1HVI, IV.iii.30

distress|ful, -fully dɪ'stɹes|fʊl, -fʊlɪ [-fəlɪ]

district, -s 'dɪstɹɪkt, -s

distrust, -s, -ing, -ed dɪs'tɹʌst, -s, -ɪŋ, -ɪd

distrust|ful, -fully, -fulness dɪs'tɹʌst|fʊl, -fəlɪ, -fʊlnɪs

disturb, -s, -ing, -ed, -er/s dɪ'stɜɚb, -z, -ɪŋ, -d, -ɚ/z

disturbance, -s dɪ'stɜɚbəns, -ɪz

disunit|e, -es, -ing, -ed ˌdɪsju'naɪ̆t [-jʊ'n-], -s, -ɪŋ, -ɪd

disvalu|e, -es, -ing, -ed dɪs'vælju, -z, -ɪŋ, -d

disvouched dɪs'vɑʊ̆tʃt

ditch, -es, -ing, -ed, -er/s 'dɪtʃ, -ɪz, -ɪŋ, -t, -ɚ/z

ditch-delivered 'dɪtʃdɪˌlɪvɚd

ditch-dog, -s 'dɪtʃˌdɒg, -z

ditto, -s 'dɪɾoʊ, -z

ditt|y, -ies 'dɪɾ|ɪ, -ɪz

diurn|al, -als, -ally daɪ'ɜɚn|l̩, -lz, -lɪ

div|e, -es, -ing, -ed, -er/s 'daɪ̆v, -z, -ɪŋ, -d, -ɚ/z

dive-dapper, -s 'daɪ̆vˌdæpɚ, -z

divel, -s 'dɪvl̩ ['dɪvəl], -z
Note.—S. uses this archaic var. of 'devil' throughout, e.g., KJ, II.i.567; IV.iii.95, 100; V.iv.4. Some modern editors prefer to retain this form rather than emending to the modern 'devil.' There doesn't appear to be a rationale for this retention related to any particular character or dialectal disposition, only the modern editors' tastes. I do admit, however, that the archaic form, when the word wants to be monosyllabic for the sake of the meter, is easier to pronounce monosyllabically

divers (adj.) (several; sundry) 'daɪ̆vɚz

divers-colored 'daɪ̆vɚzˌkʌlɚd

---

i wĕ ɨ cĭtŭy ɪ hĭt e lĕt ɛ dĕbut æ căn a pằss ɜ bĭrd ʌ hŭt ə agằin ɚ suppĕr u yŏu ʊ shŏuld o ŏbey ɔ ăwl ɒ cŏp ɑ făther eɪ̆ pằid aɪ̆ hĭgh oʊ̆ gŏ ɔɪ vŏice aʊ̆ fŏund ɪɚ̆ ĕar ɛɚ̆ ăir ʊɚ̆ pŏor ɔɚ̆ fŏrk ɑɚ̆ părk aɪ̆ɚ̆ fĭre ɑʊ̆ hŏur b bŏy p pĭt d dŏg t tŏp g gŏt k kĭd h hŏw ɦ behằve dʒ jŏt tʃ chĕw z zăny s sŏft v văt f făt ʒ treằsure ʃ shĭp ð thĕe θ thĭn m măn n nŏ ŋ hằng l lĭp j yĕs w wŏn ʍ whĕw ɹ rĭgger, aɪry ɣ mătter

divert, -s, -ing/ly, -ed, -er/s dı'vɜ·t [daĭv-], -s, -ıŋ/lɪ, -ıd, -ə·/z

dividant 'dıvɪdənt

Note.—This word in TIM, IV.iii.5 (its only appearance in S.) means 'separable' or 'divisible' and is an alt. form of 'divident.' Due to where it is situated in the line, there is a rational temptation to scan giving primary syllabic stress to the second syllable, i.e., [dı'vaĭdṇt]

divid|e, -es, -ing, -ed/ly, -er/s; -able dı'vaĭd, -z, -ıŋ, -ıd/lɪ, -ə·/z; -əbḷ

Note.—In TC, I.iii.105, this word is arguably given primary stress on the first syllable, i.e., ['dıvɪdəbḷ]

dividual dı'vɪdjʊəl [-dʒʊəl]

Note.—This word does not technically appear anywhere in S. but is often adopted to emend the Quarto's 'individuall' in TNK, I.iii.82. 'Dividual' is apt enough in this instance and better fits the meter of the line

divination, -s ˌdıvɪ'neĭʃṇ, -z

divin|e, -es, -ing, -ed, -er/s; -est, -ly, -ness dı'vaĭn, -z, -ıŋ, -d, -ə·/z; -ıst, -lɪ, -nıs

Note.—Stressed on the first syllable, i.e., ['dıvaĭn] in COR, IV.v.105; CYM, II.i.56, IV.ii.170; OTH, II.i.73

divinit|y, -ies dı'vɪnɪt|ɪ, -ɪz

division, -s dı'vɪʒṇ, -z

divisive, -ly, -ness dı'vaĭsıv, -lɪ, -nıs

divorc|e, -es, -ing, -ed, -ment/s dı'vɔ·ə·s, -ız, -ıŋ, -t, -mənt/s

divot, -s 'dıvət, -s

divulg|e, -es, -ing, -ed dı'vʌldʒ, -ız, -ıŋ, -d

Dizie or **Dizy** (MEAS) 'daĭsɪ ['dızɪ]

Note.—This name, appearing in MEAS, IV.iii.12, is usually given the pronunciation ['dızɪ]. Pompey's descriptive names of several prisoners, including Dizie, presumably say something about their character. Most sources assert the pronunciation ['dızɪ], but the assertion is as conjectural as any other viable pronunciation posited (cf. J. W. Lever's annotation for the line in the 1965 edition of The Arden Shakespeare). It is perhaps a var. of Dicey

dizz|y, -ies, -ying, -ied; -ier, -iest, -ily, -iness 'dız|ɪ, -ɪz, -ɪıŋ, -ɪd; -ɪə·, -ɪıst, -ɪlɪ, -ɪnıs

dizzy-eyed 'dızɪˌaĭd

do (first note of diatonic scale) 'doʊ

do. (abbreviation for **ditto**, q.v.) 'dıṭoʊ

do (v.), **does, doing, did, done, doer/s** 'du, 'dʌz, 'duıŋ, 'dıd, 'dʌn, 'duə·/z

Dobbin (MV) 'dɒbın

dock, -s, -ing, -ed, -er/s 'dɒk, -s, -ıŋ, -t, -ə·/z

Doctor (TNK) 'dɒktə·

doctor (D.), **-s, -ing, -ed** 'dɒktə·, -z, -ııŋ, -d

doctorate, -s 'dɒktəɹıt, -s

doctor-like 'dɒktə·ˌlaĭk

doctrine, -s 'dɒktɹın, -z

document (s.) **-s** 'dɒkjʊmənt, -s

document (v.) **-s, -ing, -ed** 'dɒkjʊment, -s, -ıŋ, -ıd

do, de, do, de, do, de 'duˌdı'duˌdı'duˌdı

Note.—This phrase of Edgar's (as Poor Tom) from LEAR, III.iv.57 is somewhat mystifying, but not nearly as mystifying as the general note found in various glossaries and line annotations, defining it as 'the inarticulate sound of chattering teeth;' in order, I presume, to attach it in meaning to the "Tom's a-cold" which immediately precedes it. But the Folio's punctuation is clear, and indicates instead an attachment in meaning to the following thought concerning that which one must do, i.e., 'do bless thee from whirlwinds,' and 'do Poor Tom some charity.' The pronunciation given above is entirely conjectural, but is asserted with this in mind. When a form of the phrase is repeated, i.e., "Do, de, de, de": (LEAR, III.vi.71: following the Folio's punctuation), it may again be inferred as concerning that which one must do—in this case "cessez!" ("stop!"). Another thought: because the Poor Tom persona is a lunatic, and is given to lunatic bans, prayers, and roaring voices, he often spouts rhymed incantations and what may be interpreted as bits of song. "Do,

de, do, de, do, de," and "do, de, de, de"
(as interludes of nonsensical sing-song)
would go a long way toward convincing
others that Poor Tom is mentally
deranged

dodg|e, -es, -ing, -ed, -er/s 'dɒdʒ, -ɪz, -ɪŋ, -d, -ɚ/z

doer, -s 'duɚ, -z

doesn't 'dʌzn̩t

doff, -s, -ing, -ed, -er/s 'dɒf, -s, -ɪŋ, -t, -ɚ/z

dog (*s., v.*)**, -s, -ging, -ged** 'dɒg, -z, -ɪŋ, -d

dog-ape, -s 'dɒg͵eɪp, -s

Dogberry (*ADO*) 'dɒgbeɹɪ [-bəɹɪ]

dog-days 'dɒg͵deɪz

doge, -s 'doʊdʒ, -ɪz

dog-fox 'dɒg͵fɒks

dogged (*adj.*)**, -ly, -ness** 'dɒgɪd, -lɪ, -nɪs

dog-hearted 'dɒg͵hɑɚtɪd

dogskin 'dɒgskɪn

dog-weary 'dɒg͵wɪɚɹɪ [͵-'--]

dogwood 'dɒgwʊd

doil|y, -ies 'dɔɪl|ɪ, -ɪz

doing, -s 'duɪŋ, -z

doit, -s 'dɔɪt, -s

Doit, John (2HIV) 'dʒɒn 'dɔɪt

Dolabella (*AC*) ͵dɒlə'belə

doldrum, -s 'doʊldɹəm ['dɔl-, 'dɒl-], -z

dol|e, -es, -ing, -ed 'doʊl, -z, -ɪŋ, -d

dole|ful, -fully, -fulness 'doʊl|fʊl, -fʊlɪ, -fʊlnɪs

doll, -s, -ing, -ed 'dɒl, -z, -ɪŋ, -d

dollar, -s 'dɒlɚ, -z

dollop, s 'dɒləp, -s

doll|y, -ies 'dɒl|ɪ, -ɪz

dolor, -s 'doʊlɚ ['dɒlɚ], -z

dolorous, -ly, -ness 'doʊlɚɹəs ['dɒlɚ-], -lɪ, -nɪs

dolphin, -s 'dɒlfɪn, -z

Dolphin (2HIV, KJ, LEAR) 'dɒlfɪn (*see Note for* **Dauphin**)

dolphin-like 'dɒlfɪn͵laɪk

dolt, -s 'doʊlt, -s

doltish, -ly, -ness 'doʊltɪʃ, -lɪ, -nɪs

domain, -s doʊ'meɪn, -z

dome, -s, -d 'doʊm, -z, -d

Domesday (AC, COM, HAM, JUL, LLL) 'dumzdeɪ

domestic, -s; -ally do'mestɪk [də'm-], -s; -əlɪ

domesticat|e, -es, -ing, -ed do'mestɪkeɪt [də'm-], -s, -ɪŋ, -ɪd

domestication do͵mestɪ'keɪʃn̩ [də͵m-]

domicil|e, -es, -ing, -ed 'dɒmɪsaɪl ['doʊm-, -sɪl], -z, -ɪŋ, -d

dominant, -s; -ly 'dɒmɪnənt, -s; -lɪ

dominat|e, -es, -ing, -ed, -or/s 'dɒmɪneɪt, -s, -ɪŋ, -ɪd, -ɚ/z

domination, -s ͵dɒmɪ'neɪʃn̩, -z

domineer, -s, -ing, -ed ͵dɒmɪ'nɪɚ, -z, -ɹɪŋ, -d

dominical də'mɪnɪkl̩

dominie, -s (*schoolmaster*) 'dɒmɪnɪ ['doʊm-], -z

dominion, -s də'mɪnjən, -z

domino, -es 'dɒmɪnoʊ, -z

Domitius (AC) do'mɪʃɪəs, -ʃəs

Dommelton, Dumbleton, Dumbledon, or Dombledon (2HIV) 'dʌml̩tən, 'dʌmbl̩tən, *or* 'dʌmbl̩dən

don (**D.**) (*s.*)**, -s** 'dɒn, -z

don (*v.*)**, -s, -ning, -ned** 'dɒn, -z, -ɪŋ, -d

Donalbain (*MAC*) 'dɒnl̩beɪn

donat|e, -es, -ing, -ed, -or/s 'doʊneɪt [do'neɪt], -s, -ɪŋ, -ɪd, -ɚ/z

donation, -s doʊ'neɪʃn̩ [do'n-], -z

Doncaster (1HIV) 'dɒŋkəstɚ

done (*p.p. of* **do**, *q.v.*) 'dʌn

done't (*contr. of* **done it**) 'dʌnt

donkey, -s 'dɒŋkɪ, -z

donor, -s 'doʊnɚ, -z

don't (*contr. of* **do not**) 'doʊnt

doom, -s, -ing, -ed 'dum, -z, -ɪŋ, -d

doomsday (**D.**) (AC, COM, HAM, JUL, LLL) 'dumzdeɪ

door, -s 'dɔɚ, -z (*arguably disyllabic, i.e.,* ['dɔɚ] *in* TIT, I.i.292; *see Note for* **brave***)*

door-keeper, -s 'dɔɚ͵kipɚ, -z
dop|e, -es, -ing, -ed 'doŏp, -s, -ɪŋ, -t
Dorcas (*WT*) 'dɔɚkəs
Doreus (TC) 'dɔɹɪəs, -ɹïəs
Doricles (WT) 'dɔɹɪklɨz
dor|mouse, -mice 'dɔɚ|maŏs, -maïs
Dorothy (CYM, 2HIV) 'dɒɹəθɨ
Dorset (HVIII, RIII) 'dɔɚsɪt
Dorset, Lord Marquess (HVIII, *RIII*)
'lɔɚd 'maɚkwɪs 'dɔɚsɪt
do's (*contr. of* do his) 'duz
dos|e, -es, -ing, -ed 'doŏs, -ɪz, -ɪŋ, -t
dost 'dʌst (*strong form*), 'dəst (*weak
form*)
do't (*contr. of* do it) 'dut
dot, -s, -ting, -ted 'dɒt, -s, -ɪŋ, -ɪd
dotage 'doŏtɪdʒ
dotant, -s 'doŏɾ̣ənt ['doŏtn̩t], -s
dotard, -s 'doŏɾ̣ɚd, -z
dot|e, -es, -ing/ly, -ed, -er/s 'doŏt, -s,
-ɪŋ/lɨ, -ɪd, -ɚ/z
doth 'dʌθ (*strong form*), 'dəθ (*weak
form*)
Double (2HIV) 'dʌbl̩
doub|le, -ly, -leness; -les, -ling, -led
'dʌbl̩, -lɨ, -l̩nɪs; -l̩z, -l̩ɪŋ [-l̩ɪŋ], -l̩d
double-charge 'dʌbl̩͵tʃaɚdʒ
double-damned 'dʌbl̩͵dæmd
double-dealer, -s 'dʌbl̩͵dilɚ [͵--'--], -z
double-dealing 'dʌbl̩͵dilɪŋ [͵--'--]
double-fatal 'dʌbl̩͵feïtl̩
double-horned 'dʌbl̩͵fiɔɚnd
double-lock 'dʌbl̩͵lɒk
double-man 'dʌbl̩͵mæn
doubler 'dʌbl̩ɚ
doublet, -s 'dʌblɪt, -s
doubt, -s -ing/ly, -ed, -er/s 'daŏt, -s,
-ɪŋ/lɨ, -ɪd, -ɚ/z
Note.—In LLL, V.i.20, *the pedant,
Holofernes, insists on the pronunciation*
['daŏbt] *for 'doubt,' as he does* ['debt]
for 'debt' (see **abhominable***)*
doubt|ful, -fully, -fulness 'daŏt|fʊl, -fəlɨ,
-fʊlnɪs
doubtless, -ly 'daŏtlɪs, -lɨ
dough 'doŏ
dought|y, -ier, -iest, -ily, -iness 'daŏt|ɨ
['daŏɾ̣|ɨ], -ɪɚ, -ɪɪst, -ɪlɨ, -ɪnɪs
doughty-handed 'daŏɾ̣ɨ͵hændɪd

dough|y, -ier, -iest, -iness 'doŏ|ɨ, -ɪɚ, -ɪɪst,
-ɪnɪs
Douglas, Archibald (1HIV, 2HIV)
'aɚtʃɪ͵bɔld 'dʌgləs
dout, -s, -ing, -ed, -er/s 'daŏt, -s, -ɪŋ, -ɪd,
-ɚ/z
dove (**D.**) (PT), -s 'dʌv, -z
dove-cote, -s 'dʌvkoŏt [-kɒt], -s
dove-drawn 'dʌv'dɹɔn
dove-feathered 'dʌv͵feðɚd
dovehouse 'dʌvfiaŏs
dove-like 'dʌv͵laïk
Dover (1HVI, LEAR) 'doŏvɚ
Dover Castle (KJ) 'doŏvɚ 'kasl̩
dowager (**D.**), -s 'daŏədʒɚ ['daŏɪ-], -z
dowd|y, -ies, -ier, -iest, -ily, -iness 'daŏd|ɨ,
-ɪz, -ɪɚ, -ɪɪst, -ɪlɨ, -ɪnɪs
dower, -s, -ed; -less 'daŏɚ, -z, -d; -lɪs
dowlas 'daŏləs
dowl(e) (*feather down*), -s 'daŏl, -z
down, -s, -ing, -ed, -er/s 'daŏn, -z, -ɪŋ, -d,
-ɚ/z
down-a 'daŏnə
*Note.—This common refrain of song
appears in various forms in* HAM,
IV.v.169,170; MWW, I.iv.39; TNK, IV.
iii.12. *Other ditties in* S. *provide more
examples where '-a-' is attached,
presumably there merely to supply an
additional beat to the music, e.g.,
'wear-a,' 'dear-a,' 'stile-a,' and 'mile-a.'
The pronunciation given above is
traditional; however, when one's
intentions warrant it, the pronunciation
is perhaps* ['daŏni] *(see* **a** = *personal
pronoun 'he')*
down-bed 'daŏn͵bed
down(-)fall, -s; -en 'daŏn͵fɔl, -z; -ən
down-gyved 'daŏn͵dʒaïvd
down-pillow, -s 'daŏn͵pɪloŏ, -z
downright, -ness 'daŏn͵ɹaït, -nɪs
down-roping (*running down in rope-like
strands*) 'daŏn͵ɹoŏpɪŋ
down(-)stairs ͵daŏn'stɛɚz (*when att.,*
['-͵-])
Downs, the (2HVI) 'ðə 'daŏnz
down(-)trod, -den 'daŏn͵tɹɒd, -n̩
downward, -s 'daŏnwɚd, -z
down|y, -ier, -iest 'daŏn|ɨ, -ɪɚ, -ɪɪst

dowr|y, -ies 'daʊɹɪ|ɪ, -ɪz ['daʊ͞ɤ͜ɹ-]

Dowsabel (*from Fr. 'douce et belle'*)
(COM) 'dusəbel ['daʊs-]

dowset (*an alt. form of 'doucet'* ['dusɪt]),
-s 'daʊsɪt, -s

dox|y, -ies 'dɒks|ɪ, -ɪz

doz|e, -es, -ing, -ed, -er/z 'doʊz, -ɪz, -ɪŋ,
-d, -ɚ/z

dozen, -s 'dʌzn̩, -z

doz|y, -ier, -iest, -ily, -iness 'doʊz|ɪ, -ɪə͞,
-ɪɪst, -ɪlɪ, -ɪnɪs

drab, -s, -bing, -bed, -ber, -best, -ly,
-ness 'dɹæb, -z, -ɪŋ, -d, -ə͞, -ɪst, -lɪ, -nɪs

drachm|a, -as, -ae, -aes 'dɹɑkm|ə
['dɹækm|ə], -əz, -ɪ, -ɪz

draff 'dɹaf

draft, -s, -ing, -ed, -er/s 'dɹaft, -s, -ɪŋ,
-ɪd, -ɚ/z

dragon, -s; -ish 'dɹægən, -z; -ɪʃ

dragon-like 'dɹægənlaɪ̆k

drain, -s, -ing, -ed, -er/s; -age 'dɹeɪ̆n, -z,
-ɪŋ, -d, -ɚ/z; -ɪdʒ

drake, -s 'dɹeɪ̆k, -s

dram, -s, -ming, -med 'dɹæm, -z, -ɪŋ, -d

drama, -s 'dɹɑmə, -z

drank (*p.t. of* drink, *q.v.*) 'dɹæŋk

draught (*chiefly Brit. var. of* draft, *q.v.*),
-s 'dɹaft, -s

draught-oxen 'dɹaft͵ɒksn̩

drave (*archaic p.t. of* drive) 'dɹeɪ̆v

draw, -s, -ing/s, drew, drawn 'dɹɔ, -z,
-ɪŋ/z, 'dɹu, 'dɹɔn

drawer (*one who draws pictures, or ale =
tapster*), -s 'dɹɔ͞ɚ, -z

drawer (*sliding boxlike compartment*), -s
'dɹɔ͞ɚ, -z

drawers (*clothing*) 'dɹɔ͞ɚz

draw(-)bridge, -s 'dɹɔbɹɪdʒ, -ɪz

drawl, -s, -ing, -ed, -er/s 'dɹɔl, -z, -ɪŋ, -d,
-ɚ/z

drawling-affecting 'dɹɔlɪŋə͵fektɪŋ

dray|man, -men 'dɹeɪ̆|mən, -mən

dread, -s, -ing, -ed 'dɹed, -z, -ɪŋ, -ɪd

dread-bolted 'dɹed͵boʊ̆ltɪd

dread|ful, -fully, -fulness 'dɹed|fʊl, -fʊlɪ,
-fʊlnɪs

dreadnought, -s 'dɹednɔt, -s

dream, -s, -ing, -ed, dreamt 'dɹim, -z, -ɪŋ,
-d, 'dɹempt ['dɹemt]

dreamer, -s 'dɹimə͞, -z

dream|y, -ier, -iest, -ily, -iness 'dɹim|ɪ,
-ɪə͞, -ɪɪst, -ɪlɪ, -ɪnɪs

drear|y, -ier, -iest, -ily, -iness, -isome
'dɹɪ͞ɚ|ɹɪ, -ɹɪə͞, -ɹɪɪst, -ɹɪlɪ, -ɹɪnɪs, -ɹɪsəm

dredg|e, -es, -ing, -ed, -er/s 'dɹedʒ, -ɪz,
-ɪŋ, -d, -ɚ/z

dreg (*v.*), -s, -ging, -ged 'dɹeg, -z, -ɪŋ, -d

dregs (*s.*) 'dɹegz

drench, -es, -ing, -ed 'dɹentʃ, -ɪz, -ɪŋ, -t

dress, -es, -ing/s, -ed, -er/s 'dɹes, -ɪz,
-ɪŋ/z, -t, -ɚ/z

drest (*var. p.t. and participle of* dressed)
'dɹest

drift, -s, -ing, -ed, -er/s 'dɹɪft, -s, -ɪŋ, -ɪd,
-ɚ/z

drink, -s, -ing, drank, drunk 'dɹɪŋk, -s,
-ɪŋ, 'dɹæŋk, 'dɹʌŋk

drinker, -s 'dɹɪŋkə͞, -z

drinkings 'dɹɪŋkɪŋz

driv|e, -es, -ing, drove, driven 'dɹaɪ̆v, -z,
-ɪŋ, 'dɹoʊ̆v, 'dɹɪvən

driv|el, -els, -elling, -elled, -eller/s 'dɹɪv|l̩,
-l̩z, -l̩ɪŋ [-lɪŋ], -l̩d, -l̩ə͞/z [-lə͞/z]

driver, -s 'dɹaɪ̆və͞, -z

drizz|le, -les, -ling, -led 'dɹɪz|l̩, -l̩z, -l̩ɪŋ
[-lɪŋ], -l̩d

droll, -er, -est, -y 'dɹoʊ̆l, -ə͞, -ɪst, -lɪ

droller|y, -ies 'dɹoʊ̆lə͜ɹ|ɪ, -ɪz

Dromio (*COM*) 'dɹoʊ̆mɪoʊ̆, -mjoʊ̆

dron|e, -es, -ing, -ed 'dɹoʊ̆n, -z, -ɪŋ, -d

drone-like 'dɹoʊ̆n͵laɪ̆k

droop, -s, -ing, -ed 'dɹup, -s, -ɪŋ, -t

drop, -s, -ping/s, -ped 'dɹɒp, -s, -ɪŋ/z, -t

Drop-heir (MEAS) 'dɹɒpfiɛ͞ [-p͵ɛ͞]

droplet, -s 'dɹɒplɪt, -s

drops|y, -ies, -ied 'dɹɒps|ɪ, -ɪz, -ɪd

dross, -y 'dɹɒs, -ɪ

drouth (*aridness, lack of moisture*) 'dɹaʊ̆θ

drove (*p.t. of* **drive**, *q.v.*) 'dɹoŭv
droven (*archaic p.p. of* **drive**) 'dɹoŭvn̩
drover, -s 'dɹoŭvɚ, -z
drovier (*drover*), **-s** 'dɹoŭvɪɚ [-vjɚ], -z
drown, -s, -ing, -ed 'dɹɑŭn, -z, -ɪŋ, -d
drowning-mark, -s 'dɹɑŭnɪŋˌmɑᵊk, -s
drows|e, -es, -ing, -ed 'dɹɑŭz, -ɪz, -ɪŋ, -d
drows|y, -ier, -iest, -ily, -iness 'dɹɑŭz|ɪ, -ɪɚ, -ɪɪst, -ɪlɪ, -ɪnɪs
drudg|e, -es, -ing/ly, -ed 'dɹʌdʒ, -ɪz, -ɪŋ/lɪ, -d
drudger|y, -ies 'dɹʌdʒɚ.ɪ|ɪ, -ɪz
drug, -s, -ging, -ged 'dɹʌg, -z, -ɪŋ, -d
drug-damned 'dɹʌgˌdæmd
druggist, -s 'dɹʌgɪst, -s
Drum, John (ALL'S) 'dʒɒn 'dɹʌm
Drum, Tom (ALL'S) 'tɒm 'dɹʌm
drum, -s, -ming, -med, -mer/s 'dɹʌm, -z, -ɪŋ, -d, -ɚ/z
drumble (*dawdle*) 'dɹʌmbl̩
drumstick, -s 'dɹʌmstɪk, -s
drunk (*p.p. of* **drink**, *q.v.; s.*) 'dɹʌŋk
drunkard, -s 'dɹʌŋkɚd, -z
drunken, -ly, -ness 'dɹʌŋkən, -lɪ, -nɪs
dr|y, -ies, -ying, -ied, -ier/s; -ier, -iest, -yly, -yness 'dɹ|aɪ, -aɪz, -aɪɪŋ, -aɪd, -aɪɚ/z; -aɪᵊ, -aɪɪst, -aɪlɪ, -aɪnɪs
dry-beat, -en 'dɹaɪˌbit [-'-], -n̩
dry(-)foot (*hunt; foot-scent*) 'dɹaɪˌfʊt
dub, -s, -bing, -bed 'dʌb, -z, -ɪŋ, -d
ducat, -s 'dʌkə t, -s
ducdame 'djukdəmi ['djuxdəmɪ, dʊk'dɑmi, -'dæmɪ, -mɛ]
Note.—This word in AYLI, II.v.51 *is one of the most mysterious words to appear in S., and the correct pronunciation (as indicated by the several choices offered above) is entirely conjectural. One's choice will typically depend on the speaker's intention; what language one decides is being spoken (if not gibberish), which then suggests what message is being translated, how the word fits the meter of the verse, and so on. It has been proposed by var. editors that 'ducdame' may derive from Italian, Gaelic, Latin, Romani, or Cymric. It may simply be a nonce-word coined for the song in which it appears, as Walter Skeat and*

*A. L. Mayhew suggest (*A Glossary of Tudor and Stuart Words, Especially from the Dramatists, *Oxford Press, 1914; p. 124). It is not included in the* OED. *I am in favor of Agnes Latham's analysis (see her line annotations 51, 54, and 56 'a Greek invocation,' *The Arden Shakespeare, *1975), which leans toward the Welsh for 'come hither,' viz. 'dewch da mi'*
du Champ, Richard (CYM) 'ɹɪtʃɚd dʊ [djʊ] 'tʃæmp ['ʃæmp]
duchess (**D.**), **-es** 'dʌtʃɪs, -ɪz
duch|y, -ies 'dʌtʃ |ɪ, -ɪz
duck, -s, -ing, -ed 'dʌk, -s, -ɪŋ, -t
dudgeon, -s 'dʌdʒən, -z
due, -s 'dju, -z
duer 'djuɚ
duel, -s, -ling, -led, -ler/s 'djuəl ['djʊəl], -z, -ɪŋ, -d, -ɚ/z
duella (*var. of* **duello**) djʊ'elə
duellist, -s 'djuəlɪst ['djʊəl-], -s
duello (*rules of engagement*) djʊ'eloŭ
Duff (MAC) 'dʌf
dug (*s.*), **-s** 'dʌg, -z
dug (*v.*) (*p.t. and p.p. of* **dig**, *q.v.*) 'dʌg
Duke (*AYLI*) 'djuk
duke (**D.**), **-s** 'djuk, -s
dukedom, -s 'djukdəm, -z
dulcet 'dʌlsɪt
dull, -er, -est, -ness, -y; -s, -ing, -ed 'dʌl, -ɚ, -ɪst, -nɪs, -lɪ; -z, -ɪŋ, -d
dullard, -s 'dʌlɚd, -z
dull-brained 'dʌlˌbɹeɪnd
Dull, Constable Anthony (LLL) 'kʌnstəbl̩ ['kɒn-] 'æn̩θənɪ [-ntə-] 'dʌl
dull-eyed 'dʌl ˌaɪd
dullish 'dʌlɪʃ
dulness (*var. of* **dullness**; *see* **dull**) 'dʌlnɪs
Dumain(e) (LLL) dju'meɪn
Dumb (2HIV) 'dʌm
dumb, -s, -ing, -ed; -ly, -ness 'dʌm, -z, -ɪŋ, -d; -lɪ, -nɪs
dumb-discoursive 'dʌmdɪˌskɚsɪv
dumb-show, -s 'dʌmʃoŭ, -z
dump, -s, -ing, -ed 'dʌmp, -s, -ɪŋ, -t
Dun (RJ) 'dʌn
dun, -s, -ning, -ned; -ner, -nest 'dʌn, -z, -ɪŋ, -d; -ɚ, -ɪst

Duncan (*MAC*) 'dʌŋkən
dunce, -s 'dʌns, -ɪz
dung 'dʌŋ
dunghill, -s 'dʌŋhɪl, -z
dungy 'dʌŋɫ
Dunsinane (MAC) 'dʌnsɪˌneĭn
    [ˌdʌnsɪ'neĭn]
*Note.—This word is a curiosity. The
Scottish place-name in Tayside is now
Dunsinnan and stressed on the penult,
i.e., [dʌn'sɪnən], just as it is apparently
stressed (some say demanded) in* MAC,
IV.i.93. Both pronunciations ([-'--]* and
['--,-]) are (and seem to always have
been) common; however, in every other
instance of the word in* MAC, *the word
is stressed either* ['--,-] *or* [ˌ--'-], *rhyming
with 'bane' in* MAC, *V.iii.59. Although
most sources concede that it is most
likely stressed on the penult in* MAC,
IV.i.93, it is incongruous (cf. **Gonzalo***);
therefore, another look at the line might
be in order. S. frequently relies on
trochees to effect his attack on key-
idea words, so strict adherence to the
iambic here (*MAC, *IV.i.93) seems
unprofitable*
Dunsmore (3HVI) 'dʌnzmɔˑᵊ
Dunstable (HVIII) 'dʌnstəbl̩
dup (*from* **do up***, cf.* **doff** *and* **don***)*, **-s,
-ping, -ped** 'dʌp, -s, -ɪŋ, -t
durance 'djʊᵊɹəns
dure (*archaic and dialectal word meaning
'hard, lasting existence'*) 'djʊᵊ
durst (*archaic p.t. and p.p. of* **dare***, q.v.*)
    'dɝst
dusk, -s, -ing, -ed 'dʌsk, -s, -ɪŋ, -t
dusk|y, -ier, -iest, -ily, -iness 'dʌsk|ɫ, -ɪᵊ,
    -ɪɪst, -ɪlɫ, -ɪnɪs
dust, -s, -ing, -ed, -er/s 'dʌst, -s, -ɪŋ, -ɪd,
    -ᵊ/z
dust|y, -ier, -iest, -ily, -iness 'dʌst|ɫ, -ɪᵊ,
    -ɪɪst, -ɪlɫ, -ɪnɪs
Dutch (MWW) 'dʌtʃ

Dutch, Low (ALL'S) 'loŭ 'dʌtʃ
Dutch|man (ADO, ALL'S, CYM, LLL,
    TN), **-men** 'dʌtʃ|mən, -mən
duteous, -ly, -ness 'djutɪəs, -lɫ, -nɪs
dut|y, -ies 'djuɾ|ɫ, -ɪz
dwar|f, -fs, -ves, -fing, -fed 'dwɔˑᵊ|f, -fs,
    -vz, -fɪŋ, -ft
dwarfish, -ly, -ness 'dwɔˑᵊfɪʃ, -lɫ, -nɪs
dwell, -s, -ing/s, -ed, dwelt, dweller/s
    'dwel, -z, -ɪŋ/z, -d, 'dwelt, 'dwelᵊ/z
dwelling-place, -s 'dwelɪŋˌpleĭs, -ɪz
dwelling-hou|se, -ses 'dwelɪŋˌhaŭ|s, -zɪz
dye, -s, -ing, -d, -r/s 'daĭ, -z, -ɪŋ, -d, -ᵊ/z
dying (*declining*) (*p.t. of* **die***, q.v.*) 'daĭɪŋ
dyk|e, -es, -ing, -ed 'daĭk, -s, -ɪŋ, -t

Ee

E (*the letter*), **-'s** 'iː, -z
eager, -ly, -ness 'igᵊ, -lɫ, -nɪs
ean, -s, -ing, -ed 'in, -z, -ɪŋ, -d
eanling, -s 'inlɪŋ -z
ear (*s.*), **-s** 'ɪᵊ, -z
ear (*v.*) (*plowing; to hear*), **-s, -ing, -ed**
    'ɪᵊ, -z, -ɪɪŋ, -d
ear-bussing 'ɪᵊˌbʌsɪŋ
ear-deafening 'ɪᵊˌdefn̩ɪŋ ([ˌ-'--] *in* WT,
    III.i.9)
ear-kissing 'ɪᵊˌkɪsɪŋ
earl (E.), **-s; -dom, -s** 'ɝl, -z; -dəm, -z
earl|y, -ier, -iest, -iness 'ɝl|ɫ, -ɪᵊ, -ɪɪst,
    -ɪnɪs
earn, -s, -ing, -ed, -er/s 'ɝn, -z, -ɪŋ, -d,
    -ᵊ/z
earnest, -ly, -ness 'ɝnɪst, -lɫ, -nɪs
earnest-gaping 'ɝnɪstˌgeĭpɪŋ
earnings 'ɝnɪŋz
ear-piercing 'ɪᵊˌpɪᵊsɪŋ
earring, -s 'ɪᵊˌɹɪŋ, -z
earshot 'ɪᵊʃɒt
earth, -s, -ing, -ed 'ɝθ, -s, -ɪŋ, -t
earth(-)bound (ɝθbaŭnd

---

i we ɪ city ɪ hit e let ɛ debut æ can a pass ɝ bird ʌ hut ə again ᵊ supper u you
ʊ should o obey ɔ awl ɒ cop ɑ father eĭ paid aĭ high oŭ go ɔĭ voice aŭ found ɪᵊ ear
ɛᵊ air ʊᵊ poor ɔᵊ fork ɑᵊ park aĭᵊ fire aŭᵊ hour b boy p pit d dog t top g got
k kid h how fi behave dʒ jot tʃ chew z zany s soft v vat f fat ʒ treasure ʃ ship ð the
θ thin m man n no ŋ hang l lip j yes w won ʍ whew ɹ rigger, airy ɾ matter

earthl|y, -ier, -iest, -iness 'ɝ·θl|ɪ, -ɪə·, -ɪɪst, -ɪnɪs

earth-treading 'ɝ·θ‚tɹedɪŋ

earth-vexing 'ɝ·θ‚veksɪŋ

earth|y, -ier, -iest, -iness 'ɝ·θ|ɪ, -ɪə·, -ɪɪst, -ɪnɪs

eas|e, -es, -ing, -ed 'iz, -ɪz, -ɪŋ, -d

ease|ful, -fully, -fulness 'iz|fʊl, -fəlɪ, -fʊlnɪs

easilest 'izɪlɪst ['izljɪst, -lĭəst]
Note.—This word in CYM, IV.ii.206 *appears as 'easilest' in the First Folio version, and as 'easil'st' in the Second Folio version. It essentially means 'easiest' and some believe that 'easilest' is simply a misreading of 'easiest.' In S.'s day, however, the word 'easily' was capable of being comparative, i.e., 'easilier' and 'easiliest,' so it is not unreasonable to assume that 'easilest' is just as likely to be a misreading for 'easiliest.' But I will assert that a misreading (if any) stems from either the inversion of the letters 'i' and 'l' ('easilest' vs. 'easiliest') or the accidental omission of the second 'i' from 'easiliest.' In any case, the word in* CYM, IV.ii.206 *is to be disyllabic, so either of the suggested pronunciations proffered above will in this instance suit*

east (E.) (AC, ADO, CYM, 1HIV, KJ, LLL, MAC, MSND, OTH, RII, RIII, RJ, Sonn. 132) 'ist

Eastcheap (1HIV, 2HIV) 'isʧip

Easter (RJ)**, -s** 'istə·, -z

easterl|y, -ies 'istə·l|ɪ, -ɪz

East Indies (MWW) 'ist 'ɪndɪz

eas|y, -ier, -iest, -ily, -iness 'iz|ɪ, -ɪə·, -ɪɪst, -ɪlɪ, -ɪnɪs

easy-held 'izɪ‚held

easy-melting 'izɪ‚meltɪŋ

easy-yielding 'izɪ‚jildɪŋ

eat (*p.t.*) 'et (*as in* ADO, IV.i.194)

eat, -s, -ing, ate, eaten 'it, -s, -ɪŋ, 'eĭt, 'itn̩

eaten 'itn̩
Note.—In MAC, IV.i.64,65, *the words 'eaten' and 'sweaten' (q.v.) are meant to rhyme, and the rhyme here needn't be forsaken. Reconciling this rhyme simply*

requires that the reader/speaker understand a couple of things: first, that 'sweaten' is an irregular participial formation of the v. 'sweat' created specifically for this particular rhyme; and second, that among the Brit., the still typical, primary, or preferred pronunciation of the word 'ate' is ['et]. *Therefore, it isn't so great a stretch to accept that the p.p. of the v. 'eat,' i.e., 'eaten,' adopts a pronunciation of* ['etn̩] *in this case. Obscuring the sense and meaning of the lines by attempting to say 'sweaten' as* ['switn̩] *verges on absurdity. (Cf.* AYLI, II.v.37, 38; *also Kökeritz's* Shakespeare's Pronunciation, *pp. 185–203)*

eater, -s 'i̥ɾə·, -z

eave, -s 'iv, -z

eavesdrop, -s, -ping, -ped, -per/s 'ivzdɹɒp, -s, -ɪŋ, -t, -ə·/z

ebb, -s, -ing, -ed 'eb, -z, -ɪŋ, -d

ebon, -ite 'ebən, -aĭt

ebony 'ebənɪ

Ebrew (*for 'Hebrew'*) (1HIV) 'ibɹu

ecce signum (*L.*) (1HIV, II.iv.167) 'ɛkɛ 'signum ['eʧɛ 'sinjum]

ech|e, -es, -ing, -ed 'ik ['iʧ], -s, -ɪŋ, -t
Note.—The OED *does not assert a pronunciation for this word, though etymology and orthography favor the first pronunciation given for its usage in* MV, III.ii.23. *The Folio and Quartos provide variously 'ich,' 'ech,' 'eck,' and 'eech.' The second pronunciation given above is preferential in* PER, III.Pro.13 *where it is meant to rhyme with 'speech'*

Echo (TS) 'ekoŭ

echo (E.), -es, -ing, -ed 'ekoŭ, -z, -ɪŋ, -d

eclips|e, -es, -ing, -ed ɪ'klɪps, -ɪz, -ɪŋ, -t

ecstas|y, -ies 'ekstəs|ɪ, -ɪz

edd|y, -ies, -ying, -ied 'ed|ɪ, -ɪz, -ɪɪŋ, -ɪd

Eden (RII) 'idn̩

Edgar (*LEAR*) 'edgə·

edg|e, -es, -ing, -ed 'edʒ, -ɪz, -ɪŋ, -d

edgeless 'edʒlɪs

edict, -s 'idɪkt, -s
Note.—Often [i'dɪkt, -s] *in S., e.g.*, 2HVI,

III.ii.257; LLL, I.i.11; MSND, I.i.151;
MEAS, II.ii.93; PER, I.i.112

edifice, -s 'edɪfɪs, -ɪz

edif|y, -ies, -ying, -ied 'edɪf|aɪ, -aɪz, -aɪɪŋ, -aɪd

Edmund (2HVI, *3HVI, LEAR, RII*) 'edmənd

educat|e, -es, -ing, -ed, -or/s 'edjʊkeɪt ['edʒʊ-], -s, -ɪŋ, -ɪd, -ɚ/z

education ˌedjʊ'keɪʃn [ˌedʒʊ-]

Edward (2HIV, HV, 1HVI, *2HVI, 3HVI,* HVIII, MAC, *RIII*) 'edwɚd

Edward Confessor (HVIII) 'edwɚd kən'fesɚ

Edward the Fourth (*3HVI, RIII*) 'edwɚd ðə 'fɔɚθ

Edward the Third (HV) 'edwɚd ðə 'θɚd

eech, -s, -ing, -ed 'ik ['itʃ], -s, -ɪŋ, -t
Note.—The OED does not assert a pronunciation for this word, though etymology and orthography favor the first pronunciation given for its usage in MV, III.ii.23. The Folio and Quartos provide variously 'ich,' 'ech,' 'eck,' and 'eech.' The second pronunciation given above is preferential in PER, III.Pro.13 where it is meant to rhyme with 'speech'

eel, -s 'il, -z

eel-skin, -s 'il,skɪn, -z

e'en (*from even*) 'in

e'er (*from ever*) 'ɛɚ

e'er-remaining ˌɛɚ.ɹɪ'meɪnɪŋ

effect, -s, -ing, -ed ɪ'fekt, -s, -ɪŋ, -ɪd

effective, -ly, -ness ɪ'fektɪv, -lɪ, -nɪs

effectless ɪ'fektlɪs

effectual, -ly ɪ'fektʃʊəl, -ɪ

effeminate (*adj.*), **-ly, -ness** ɪ'femɪnɪt, -lɪ, -nɪs

effeminat|e (*v.*), **-es, -ing, -ed** ɪ'femɪneɪt, -s, -ɪŋ, -ɪd

effigies (*L.*) ɛ'fɪdʒɪɪs [-dʒɪs]
Note.—In AYLI, II.vii.196, this word—the singular form for 'likeness' or 'copy'—retains its L. pronunciation,

with the primary stress on the second syllable, i.e., [ɛ'fɪdʒɪs], thus fitting rightly into the metrical pattern of the verse line

effig|y, -ies 'efɪdʒ|ɪ, -ɪz (*see* **effigies**)

effus|e, -es, -ing, -ed ɪ'fjuz, -ɪz, -ɪŋ, -d

effusion, -s ɪ'fjuʒn, -z

eftest (*Dogberry's nonce-word for 'best; most efficient' in* ADO, IV.ii.33) 'eftɪst

eftsoon (*adv.*), **-s** 'eftsun, -z

egal|l, -ly, -ness 'igl, -ɪ, -nɪs
Note.—Neither the OED nor Onions assert a proper pronunciation for this word; therefore, the pronunciation provided here must be considered conjectural, though probable, considering its close relationship to 'equal,' and the fact that its metrical stress in S. confirms primary stress on the first syllable

Egeon *or* **Aegeon** (COM) i'dʒiən

Egeus (*MSND*) i'dʒiəs

egg, -s, -ing, -ed 'eg, -z, -ɪŋ, -d

egg-shaped 'eg,ʃeɪpt

eggshell, -s 'egʃel, -z

Eglamour, Sir (*TGV*) ˌsɚ '(ɹ)egləmʊɚ [-mɔɚ]

eglantine 'egləntaɪn

egma 'egmə
Note.—This word, appearing only once in literature, i.e., LLL, III.i.69, is Costard's blunderous attempt at the word 'enigma'

ego, -s 'igoʊ ['egoʊ], -z

egregious, -ly, -ness ɪ'gɹidʒəs, -lɪ, -nɪs

egress, -es 'igɹes, -ɪz

Egypt (AC, ALL'S, HVIII, MSND) 'idʒɪpt

Egyptian (AC, OTH, PER, TN), **-s** ɪ'dʒɪpʃn, -z

eh 'eɪ

eider, -s 'aɪdɚ, -z

eiderdown, -s 'aɪdɚdaʊn, -z

eight, -s 'eɪt, -s

eight|pence, -penny 'eɪt|pəns, -pənɪ

i wﻯe ɪ city ɪ hﻯit e lﻯet ɛ debut æ can a pass ɚ bird ʌ hut ə again ɚ supper u you
ʊ should o obey ɔ awl ɒ cop ɑ father eɪ paid aɪ high oʊ go ɔɪ voice aʊ found ɪɚ ear
ɛɚ air ʊɚ poor ɔɚ fork ɑɚ park aɪɚ fire aʊɚ hour b boy p pit d dog t top g got
k kid h how fi behave dʒ jot tʃ chew z zany s soft v vat f fat ʒ treasure ʃ ship ð the
θ thin m man n no ŋ hang l lip j yes w won ʍ whew ɹ rigger, airy ɾ matter

Note.—See Note for **halfpenny**
eisel(l) 'aɪsəl [-sel, 'aɪzəl]
Note.—This obsolete word for vinegar,
appearing in HAM, V.i.271, is cited in
the OED with over twenty var. spellings—it is spelled 'eysell' in the Quarto
version of Sonn. 111.10. The First Folio
and Second Quarto editions of HAM
both give the spelling 'Esile,' perhaps
indicating a pronunciation of ['esaɪl],
['esil], or ['esəl]. Interestingly, the First
Quarto edition of HAM gives the word
'vessels' instead
either 'aɪðə·
ek|e, -es, -ing, -ed 'ik, -s, -ɪŋ, -t
Elbe (HV) 'elb
Elbow (MEAS) 'elboŏ
elbow, -s, -ing, -ed 'elboŏ, -z, -ɪŋ, -d
Elbow, Mistress (MEAS) ˌmɪstɹɪs
'elboŏ
elbow-room 'elboŏˌɹum
eld 'eld
elder, -s 'eldə·, -z
elder-gun 'eldə·ˌgʌn
eldest 'eldɪst
Eleanor or **Elinor** (2HVI, KJ) 'elɪnə·
Note.—Sometimes 'Eleanor,' in
accordance with the occasional Quarto
spelling 'Elnor,' wants to be disyllabic,
i.e., ['elnə·]
elect, -s, -ing, -ed, -or/s ɪ'lekt, -s, -ɪŋ, -ɪd,
-ə·/z
election, -s ɪ'lekʃn̩, -z
elective, -ly ɪ'lektɪv, -lɪ
elegan|ce, -t/ly 'elɪgən|s, -t/lɪ
elegancy 'elɪgənsɪ
eleg|y, -ies 'elɪdʒ|ɪ, -ɪz
element, -s 'eləmənt, -s
elephant, -s 'elɪfənt, -s
Elephant, the (TN) ðɪ 'elɪfənt
ele|ven, -vens, -venth/s ɪ'le|vn̩ [-vən],
-vn̩z [-vənz], -vn̩θ/s
el|f, -ves 'el|f, -vz
elf-lock, -s 'elfˌlɒk, -s
elf-skin 'elfˌskɪn
Elinor or **Eleanor** (2HVI, KJ) 'elɪnə·
Note.—Sometimes 'Eleanor,' in
accordance with the occasional Quarto

spelling 'Elnor,' wants to be a disyllable,
i.e., ['elnə·]
Elizabeth (3HVI, RIII) ɪ'lɪzəbəθ
Elizium (VA) ɪ'lɪzɪəm, -zjəm
'ell 'el
ell, -s 'el, -z
Ellen (2HIV) 'elən
eloquen|ce, -t/ly 'eləkwən|s, -t/lɪ
else 'els
elsewhere 'elsʌɛ̆ə· [ˌels'ʌɛ̆ə·]
Elsinore (HAM) 'elsɪnɔ̆ə·
Eltham Place (1HVI) 'eltəm ['elθəm]
'pleɪs
elves (pl. of **elf**) 'elvz
elvish-marked 'elvɪʃmăə·kt
Ely (HV, HVIII, RII, RIII) 'ilɪ
Ely House (RII) 'ilɪ ˌhaŏs
Elysium (CYM, HV, 2HVI, 3HVI, TGV,
TN, TNK, VA) ɪ'lɪzɪəm [-ʒɪəm]
'em (weak form of **them**) 'əm
embalm, -s, -ing, -ed, -er/s ɪm'bɑm, -z,
-ɪŋ, -d, -ə·/z
embank, -s, -ing, -ed, -ment/s ɪm'bæŋk,
-s, -ɪŋ, -t, -mənt/s
embare (make bare) ɪm'bɛ̆ə·
embark, -s, -ing, -ed, -ment ɪm'băə·k, -s,
-ɪŋ, -t, -mənt
embarquement, -s ɪm'băə·kmənt, -s
Note.—The OED cites 'embarque'
merely as an obsolete var. of 'embark,'
but in his annotation for COR, I.x.22
(The Arden Shakespeare, 1976), Philip
Brockbank makes a sound case for
defining its meaning to be 'impediments,
hindrances'—also C. T. Onions in his
A Shakespeare Glossary—giving cause
to retain this spelling
embarrass, -es, -ing, -ed, -ment/s
ɪm'bæɹəs, -ɪz, -ɪŋ, -t, -mənt/s
embassade ˌembə'sad [-'seɪd]
embassador (var. of **ambassador**, q.v.)
ɪm'bæsɪdə· [em-, -səd-, -dɔ̆ə·]
embassage 'embəsɪdʒ
embass|y, -ies 'embəs|ɪ, -ɪz
embattailed ɪm'bætl̩ɹd
Note.—This archaic var. spelling of
'embattled' is typically retained in KJ,
IV.ii.200 in order to eke from it the four

syllables necessary to the metrical
requirements of the verse line
embattl|e, -es, -ing, -ed ɪm'bæɡl̩, -z, -ɪŋ,
-d
embayed ɪm'beɪd
ember, -s 'embɚ, -z
ember-eve (E.), -s 'embɚ,(ɹ)iv, -z
emblaz|e, -es, -ing, -ed ɪm'bleɪz, -ɪz, -ɪŋ,
-d
emblem, -s 'embləm, -z
embod|y, -ies, -ying, -ied, -iment/s
ɪm'bɒd|ɪ, -ɪz, -ɪɪŋ, -ɪd, -ɪmənt/s
embold|en, -ens, -ening, -ened
ɪm'boʊld|ən, -ənz, -n̩ɪŋ, -ənd
emboss, -es, -ing, -ed, -er/s, -ment/s
ɪm'bɒs, -ɪz, -ɪŋ, -t, -ɚ/z, -mənt/s
embounded ɪm'baʊndɪd
embowel, -s, -(l)ing, -(l)ed ɪm'baʊəl, -z,
-ɪŋ, -d
embrac|e, -es, -ing, -ed, -er/s, -ement/s
ɪm'bɹeɪs, -ɪz, -ɪŋ, -t, -ɚ/z, -mənt/s
embrasure, -s ɪm'bɹeɪʒɚ [-ʃɚ], -z
embroider, -s, -ing, -ed, -er/s ɪm'bɹɔɪdɚ,
-z, -ɹɪŋ, -d, -ɹɚ/z
embroider|y, -ies ɪm'bɹɔɪdɚ,ɹ|ɪ, -ɪz
embroil, -s, -ing, -ed, -ment/s ɪm'bɹɔɪl,
-z, -ɪŋ, -d, -mənt/s
embryo, -s 'embɹɪoʊ, -z
embryonic ,embɹɪ'ɒnɪk
emend, -s, -ing, -ed; -able ɪ'mend, -z, -ɪŋ,
-ɪd; -əbl̩
emendation, -s ɪmen'deɪʃn̩ [,imen-], -z
emerald, -s 'emɚɹəld ['emɹəld], -z
Emilia (*COM, OTH, WT, TNK*) ɪ'milɪə,
-ljə
Note.—In some versions or editions of
COM, *the spelling 'Æmilia' is retained;*
therefore, the pronunciation [ɪ'mɪlɪə,
-ljə] *is optional*
Emillius or Æmilius (*TIT*) ɪ'mɪlɪəs,
-ljəs
eminen|ce, -ces, -cy, -t/ly 'emɪnən|s, -sɪz,
-sɪ, -t/lɪ

Emmanuel (2HVI) ɪ'mænjʊəl
emmew ɪ'mju
emotion, -s; -less ɪ'moʊʃn̩, -z; -lɪs
emotional, -ly ɪ'moʊʃənl̩, -ɪ
empale (*var. of* **impale**, *q.v.*) ɪm'peɪl
empanel, -s, -ling, -led ɪm'pænl̩, -z, -ɪŋ,
-d
empatron ɪm'peɪtɹən
empathy 'empəθɪ
emperal 'empɚɹəl
Note.—This word, though sometimes
indicated as a malapropism spoken by
the Clown in TIT, IV.iii.93, *may not in*
fact be a blunder for 'emperor.' True, the
Clown has already botched Jupiter's
name, but 'emperal's' in the line cited
above (in the First Quarto—
'emperiall's' in the Second and Third
Quartos and First Folio) might be a
compositor error, later emended.
'Emperial' (also appearing in TIT,
IV.iv.40*) is an obsolete form of 'impe-*
rial'. Still, there can be a pathetic humor
in 'emperal' as it sounds unlearned and
unsophisticated, therefore a conjectured
pronunciation is provided
emperial (*obsolete var. of* **imperial**, *q.v.;*
and see Note for **emperal**) ɪm'pɪɚ,ɹɪəl
emperious (*obsolete var. of* **imperious**,
q.v.) ɪm'pɪɚ,ɹɪəs
emperor (E.), -s 'empɚɹɚ, -z
emper|y, -ies 'empɚ,ɹ|ɪ, -ɪz
empha|sis, -ses 'emfə|sɪs, -sɪz
empire, -s 'empaɪɚ, -z
empiric, -s, -al, -ally ɪm'pɪɹɪk, -s, -l̩, -əlɪ
Note.—The First Folio gives 'empericks'
in ALL'S, II.i.121 *(commonly emended*
to 'empirics'), and should be given
primary stress on the first syllable, i.e.,
['empɚ,ɹɪks]
empiricutic ,empɹɪ'kjutɪk [ɪm,pɹɪ'k-]
empleached (*intertwined*) ɪm'plitʃt (*see*
Note for **annexions**)

---

i w**e** ɪ c**i**ty ɪ h**i**t e l**e**t ɛ d**e**but æ c**a**n a p**a**ss ɝ b**i**rd ʌ h**u**t ə **a**gain ɚ supp**er** u y**ou**
ʊ sh**ould** o **o**bey ɔ **aw**l ɒ c**o**p ɑ f**a**ther eɪ p**ai**d aɪ h**igh** oʊ g**o** ɔɪ v**oi**ce aʊ f**ou**nd ɪɚ **ear**
ɛɚ **air** ʊɚ p**oor** ɔɚ f**or**k ɑɚ p**ar**k aɪɚ f**ire** aʊɚ h**our** b **b**oy p **p**it d **d**og t **t**op g **g**ot
k **k**id h **h**ow fi be**h**ave dʒ **j**ot tʃ **ch**ew z **z**any s **s**oft v **v**at f **f**at ʒ trea**s**ure ʃ **sh**ip ð **th**e
θ **th**in m **m**an n **n**o ŋ ha**ng** l **l**ip j **y**es w **w**on ʍ **wh**ew ɹ **r**igger, ai**r**y ɼ ma**tt**er

employ, -s, -ing, -ed, -er/s, -ment/s ɪmˈplɔɪ̆, -z, -ɪŋ, -d, -ɚ/z, -mənt/s

empoison, -s, -ing, -ed ɪmˈpɔɪ̆zn̩, -z, -ɪŋ, -d

empress (E.), -es ˈempɹɪs, -ɪz
Note.—This word is pronounced trisyllabically, i.e., [ˈempə-ɹɪs] *in several instances in* TIT, *fulfilling the metrical requirements of the verse lines, and following the spelling 'emperesse' often given in the First Quarto version*

empt|y, -ies, -ying, -ied; -ier, -iest, -ily, -iness ˈempt|ɨ, -ɨz, -ɨɪŋ, -ɨd; -ɨɚ, -ɨɪst, -ɨlɨ, -ɨnɪs

empty-hearted ˈemptɨˌhɑɚ̆-tɪd

emulat|e, -es, -ing, -ed, -or/s ˈemjʊleɪ̆t, -s, -ɪŋ, -ɪd, -ɚ/z

emulation, -s ˌemjʊˈleɪ̆ʃn̩, -z

emulous, -ly ˈemjʊləs, -lɨ

enact, -s, -ing, -ed, -or/s, -ment/s; -ive ɹˈnækt, -s, -ɪŋ, -ɪd, -ɚ/z, -mənt/s; -ɪv

enacture, -s ɹˈnæktʃɚ, -z

enamel, -s, -(l)ing, -(l)ed ɹˈnæm|l̩, -l̩z, -l̩ɪŋ [-əlɪŋ], -l̩d

enamor, -s, -ing, -ed ɹˈnæmɚ, -z, -ɹɪŋ, -d

encag|e, -es, -ing, -ed ɪnˈkeɪ̆dʒ [ɪŋˈk-], -ɪz, -ɪŋ, -d

encamp, -s, -ing, -ed, -ment/s ɪnˈkæmp [ɪŋˈk-], -s, -ɪŋ, -t, -mənt/s

encave ɪnˈkeɪ̆v

Enceladus (TIT) enˈselədəs

enchafed ɪnˈtʃeɪ̆fɪd

enchant, -s, -ing/ly, -ment/s ɪnˈtʃant, -s, -ɪŋ/lɨ, -ɪd, -mənt/s

enchantress, -es ɪnˈtʃantɹɪs, -ɪz

enchas|e, -es, -ing, -ed ɪnˈtʃeɪ̆s, -ɪz, -ɪŋ, -t

encieled ɪnˈsild
Note.—Arguably stressed on the first syllable, i.e., [ˈenˌsild] *in* MEAS, II.iv.80. *It must be acknowledged that 'encieled,' which appears as 'en-shield' in the First Folio, is the conjectural interpretation of J. W. Lever's, editor of the 1965 edition of* The Arden Shakespeare. *Lever makes a plausible argument in his annotation for the line cited above, q.v.*

encirc|le, -les, -ling, -led, -lement/s ɪnˈsɚk|l̩, -l̩z, -l̩ɪŋ [-lɪŋ], -l̩d, -l̩mənt/s

enclog ɪnˈklɒg

enclos|e, -es, -ing, -ed ɪnˈkloʊ̆z [ɪŋˈk-], -ɪz, -ɪŋ, -d

enclosure, -s ɪnˈkloʊ̆ʒɚ [ɪŋˈk-], -z

encloud, -s, -ing, -ed ɪnˈklɑʊ̆d, -z, -ɪŋ, -ɪd

encompass, -es, -ing, -ed, -ment ɪnˈkʌmpəs [ɪŋˈk-], -ɪz, -ɪŋ, -t, -mənt

encounter, -s, -ing, -ed, -er/s ɪnˈkɑʊ̆ntɚ [ɪŋˈk-], -z, -ɹɪŋ, -d, -ɹɚ/z

encrimsoned ɪnˈkɹɪmzənd [ɪŋˈk-]

encumber, -s, -ing, -ed, -er/s ɪnˈkʌmbɚ [ɪŋˈk-], -z, -ɹɪŋ, -d, -ɹɚ/z

end, -s, -ing, -ed ˈend, -z, -ɪŋ, -ɪd

endamag|e, -es, -ing, -ed, -ement ɪnˈdæmɪdʒ, -ɪz, -ɪŋ, -d, -mənt

endart ɪnˈdɑɚ̆-t

endear, -s, -ing, -ed, -ment ɪnˈdɪɚ̆, -z, -ɹɪŋ, -d, -mənt

endeavor, -s, -ing, -ed ɪnˈdevɚ, -z, -ɹɪŋ, -d

ending, -s ˈendɪŋ, -z

endite *or* **indite, -d** ɪnˈdaɪ̆t, -ɪd
Note.—The OED *cites this word to be an obsolete form of* **indict**. *Brian Gibbons, editor of* The Arden Shakespeare's RJ *(1980), suggests, "Jestingly Benvolio offers a malapropism for 'invite'; . . ." (cf. RJ, II.iv.127, also 2HIV, II.i.26)*

endless, -ly, -ness ˈendlɪs, -lɨ, -nɪs

endow, -s, -ing, -ed, -ment/s ɪnˈdɑʊ̆, -z, -ɪŋ, -d, -mənt/s

endu|e, -es, -ing, -ed ɪnˈdju, -z, -ɪŋ, -d

endur|e, -es, -ing, -ed; -ance ɪnˈdjʊɚ̆, -ɹɪŋ, -d; -ɹəns

Endymion (MV) enˈdɪmɪən

enem|y (E.), -ies ˈenɪm|ɨ, -ɨz
Note.—Often disyllabic in S., *e.g.,* [ˈenˈmɨ]

enew ɹˈnju

enfeeb|le, -les, -ling, -led, -lement ɪnˈfib|l̩, -l̩z, -l̩ɪŋ [-lɪŋ], -l̩d, -l̩mənt

enfeoff, -s, -ing, -ed, -ment ɪnˈfif, -s, -ɪŋ, -t, -mənt

enfetter, -s, -ing, -ed ɪnˈfeɡɚ, -z, -ɹɪŋ, -d

enfold, -s, -ing/s, -ed, -ment ɪnˈfoʊ̆ld, -z, -ɪŋ/z, -ɪd, -mənt

enforc|e, -es, -ing, -ed, -er/s, -ement; -eable ɪnˈfɔɚ̆s, -ɪz, -ɪŋ, -t, -ɚ/z, -mənt; -əbl̩

enforcedly (*adj.*) ɪnˈfɔɚ̆sɪdlɨ

enfranch, -es, -ing, -ed ɪnˈfɹæntʃ, -ɪz, -ɪŋ, -t

Note.—The adj. in AC, III.xiii.149 *must be pronounced trisyllabically, i.e.,* [ɪnˈfɹæntʃɪd]

enfranchis|e, -es, -ing, -ed ɪnˈfɹæntʃaɪz, -ɪz, -ɪŋ, -d

enfranchisement ɪnˈfɹæntʃaɪzmənt [-tʃɪz-]

enfreed ɪnˈfɹid

enfreedoming ɪnˈfɹidəmɪŋ

engag|e, -es, -ing/ly, -ed, -ement/s ɪnˈgeɪdʒ [ɪŋˈg-], -ɪz, -ɪŋ/lɪ, -d, -mənt/s

engaol, -s, -ing, -ed ɪnˈdʒeɪl, -z, -ɪŋ, -d

engender, -s, -ing, -ed ɪnˈdʒendɚ, -z, -ɹɪŋ, -d

engild, -s ɪnˈgɪld [ɪŋˈg-], -z

engin|e, -es, -ing, -ed, -er/s ˈendʒɪn, -z, -ɪŋ, -d, -ɚ/z

engineer, -s, -ing, -ed ˌendʒɪˈnɪɚ, -z, -ɹɪŋ, -d

engirt ɪnˈgɝt [ɪŋˈg-]

England (AYLI, HAM, HV, 3HVI, KJ, MAC, MV, OTH, TEM, TN)**, -er/s** ˈɪŋglənd [-ŋl-], -ɚ/z

English (HV, 3HVI)**, -ed** ˈɪŋglɪʃ, -t

English|man (HV, PP)**, -men** ˈɪŋglɪʃ|mən, -mən

Englishwoman (HV) ˈɪŋglɪʃˌwʊmən

englut, -s, -ted ɪnˈglʌt [ɪŋˈg-], -s, -ɪd

engraffed ɪnˈgɹaft

engraft, -s, -ing, -ed ɪnˈgɹaft [ɪŋˈg-], -s, -ɪŋ, -ɪd

engrav|e, -es, -ing/s, -ed, -er/s ɪnˈgɹeɪv [ɪŋˈg-], -z, -ɪŋ/z, -d, -ɚ/z

engraven ɪnˈgɹeɪvn̩ [ɪŋˈg-]

engross, -es, -ing, -ed, -er/s, -ment/s ɪnˈgɹoʊs [ɪŋˈg-], -ɪz, -ɪŋ, -t, -ɚ/z, -mənt/s

enguard ɪnˈgɑɚd [ɪŋˈg-]

enigma, -s ɪˈnɪgmə, -z

enigmatic, -al, -ally ˌenɪgˈmætɪk, -l̩, -lɪ

enjoin, -s, -ing, -ed, -er/s ɪnˈdʒɔɪn, -z, -ɪŋ, -d, -ɚ/z

Note.—Arguably stressed on the first

syllable, i.e., [ˈendʒɔɪnd] *in* ALL'S, III.v.93

enjoy, -s, -ing, -ed, -er/s, -ment/s ɪnˈdʒɔɪ, -z, -ɪŋ, -d, -ɚ/z, -mənt/s

enkind|le, -les, -ling, -led ɪnˈkɪnd|l̩, -l̩z, -lɪŋ [-lɪŋ], -l̩d

enlard ɪnˈlɑɚd

enlarg|e, -es, -ing, -ed, -ement/s ɪnˈlɑɚdʒ, -ɪz, -ɪŋ, -d, -mənt/s

enlighten, -s, -ing, -ed, -ment ɪnˈlaɪtn̩, -z, -ɪŋ, -d, -mənt

enlinked ɪnˈlɪŋkt

enlist, -s, -ing, -ed, -ment/s ɪnˈlɪst, -s, -ɪŋ, -ɪd, -mənt/s

enmesh, -es, -ing, -ed ɪnˈmeʃ, -ɪz, -ɪŋ, -t

enmit|y, -ies ˈenmɪt|ɪ, -ɪz

ennob|le, -les, -ling, -led, -lement rˈnoʊb|l̩, -l̩z, -lɪŋ, -l̩d, -l̩mənt

Enobarb (AC) ˈinəˌbɑɚb, ˈenə-

Enobarbus, Domitius (AC) doˈmɪʃɪəs, -ʃəs ˌinəˈbɑɚbəs, ˌenə- [-nəˈb-]

Note.—The name from AC *is, in verse, often with only one stress, as if it were but three syllables instead of four, i.e.,* [ɪnˈbɑɚbəs, enˈb- (ɪnəˈb-, enəˈb-)]

enormit|y, -ies rˈnɔɚmɪt|ɪ, -ɪz

enormous, -ly, -ness rˈnɔɚməs, -lɪ, -nɪs

enough rˈnʌf

enow rˈnaʊ

enpierced ɪnˈpɪɚst

enquir|e (var. of **inquire**)**, -es, -ing, -ed, -er/s** ɪnˈkwaɪɚ [ɪŋˈk-], -z, -ɹɪŋ, -d, -ɹɚ/z

enquir|y (var. of **inquiry**)**, -ies** ɪnˈkwaɪɚ|ɹɪ [ɪŋˈk-, ˈɪnkwɹə]ɪ, ˈɪŋk-], -ɪz

enrag|e, -es, -ing, -ed ɪnˈɹeɪdʒ, -ɪz, -ɪŋ, -d

enrank, -s, -ing, -ed ɪnˈɹæŋk, -s, -ɪŋ, -t

enrapt ɪnˈɹæpt

enraptur|e, -es, -ing, -ed ɪnˈɹæptʃɚ, -z, -ɹɪŋ, -d

enrich, -es, -ing, -ed, -ment ɪnˈɹɪtʃ, -ɪz, -ɪŋ, -t, -mənt

enring, -s, -ing, -ed ɪnˈɹɪŋ, -z, -ɪŋ, -d

enrob|e, -es, -ing, -ed ɪnˈɹoʊb, -z, -ɪŋ, -d

i wɛ ɪ city ɪ hɪt e lɛt ɛ dɛbut æ cạn a pạss ɝ bɪrd ʌ hut ə again ɚ supper u you
ʊ should o ọbey ɔ awl ɒ cọp ɑ fạther eɪ pạid aɪ hịgh oʊ gọ ɔɪ vọice aʊ fọund ɪɚ ẹar
ɛɚ ạir ʊɚ pọor ɔɚ fọrk ɑɚ pạrk aɪɚ fịre aʊɚ họur b bọy p pit d dọg t tọp g gọt
k kịd h họw fi behave dʒ jọt tʃ chew z zany s sọft v vạt f fạt ʒ treạsure ʃ shịp ð thẹ
θ thịn m mạn n nọ ŋ hang l lịp j yẹs w wọn ʍ whẹw ɹ rịgger, aiɹy f matter

enrol, -s, -ling, -led, -ment/s ɪnˈɹɔl, -z, -ɪŋ, -d, -mənt/s

enrooted ɪnˈɹutɪd

enround, -s, -ing, -ed ɪnˈɹɑʊnd, -z, -ɪŋ, -ɪd

enscheduled ɪnˈskedʒʊəld

ensconc|e, -es, -ing, -ed ɪnˈskɒns, -ɪz, -ɪŋ, -t

enseam, -s, -ing, -ed ɪnˈsim, -z, -ɪŋ, -d

ensear, -s, -ing, -ed ɪnˈsɪɚ, -z, -ɹɪŋ, -d

ensheltered ɪnˈʃeltəˑd

ensign (the flag or emblem), -s ˈensaɪn [ˈensn̩], -z

ensign (the officer), -s ˈensn̩, -z

ensign (v.), -s, -ing, -ed ɪnˈsaɪn, -z, -ɪŋ, -d

ensinewed ɪnˈsɪnjud

enskied ɪnˈskaɪd

ensnar|e, -es, -ing, -ed ɪnˈsnɛɚ, -z, -ɹɪŋ, -d

ensteeped ɪnˈstipt

ensu|e, -es, -ing, -ed ɪnˈsju, -z, -ɪŋ, -d

enswathed ɪnˈswɒθt [-ˈswɔθt], [-ˈswɒðd, -ˈswɔðd]

entail, -s, -ing, -ed, -ment ɪnˈteɪl, -z, -ɪŋ, -d, -mənt

entame (subdue) ɪnˈteɪm

entang|le, -les, -ling, -led, -lement/s ɪnˈtæŋg|l̩, -l̩z, -l̩ɪŋ [-lɪŋ], -l̩d, -l̩mənt/s

ent|er, -ers, -ering, -ered, -erer/s ˈent|ɚ, -ɚz, -əɹɪŋ, -əˑd, -əɹəˑ/z

enterpris|e, -es, -ing/ly ˈentɚˑpɹaɪz, -ɪz, -ɪŋ/lɨ

entertain, -s, -ing/ly, -ed, -er/s, -ment/s ˌentəˑˈteɪn, -z, -ɪŋ/lɨ, -d, -əˑ/z, -mənt/s

enthral, -s, -ling, -led, -ment ɪnˈθɹɔl, -z, -ɪŋ, -d, -mənt

enthron|e, -es, -ing, -ed, -ement/s ɪnˈθɹoʊn, -z, -ɪŋ, -d, -mənt/s

entic|e, -es, -ing/ly, -ed, -er/s, -ement/s ɪnˈtaɪs, -ɪz, -ɪŋ/lɨ, -t, -əˑ/z, -mənt/s

entire, -ly, -ness ɪnˈtaɪɚ, -lɨ, -nɪs

entiret|y, -ies ɪnˈtaɪɹɪt|ɨ, -ɨz

entit|le, -les, -ling, -led, -lement/s ɪnˈtaɪt|l̩, -l̩z, -l̩ɪŋ [-lɪŋ], -l̩d, -l̩mənt/s

entitul|e (archaic for entitle), -es, -ing, -ed ɪnˈtɪtjul, -z, -ɪŋ, -d

entomb, -s, -ing, -ed, -ment/s ɪnˈtum, -z, -ɪŋ, -d, -mənt/s

entrails ˈentɹeɪlz

entrance (s.) (entryway; act of entering), -s ˈentɹəns, -ɪz
Note.—In MAC, I.v.39, this word (in order for the verse line to scan properly) adopts another, albeit slight, syllable through the process of syncope, i.e., [ˈenˈtəˑɹəns]

entranc|e (v.) (to put into a trance; fill with delight or wonder), -es, -ing/ly, -ed, -ement/s ɪnˈtɹans, -ɪz, -ɪŋ/lɨ, -t, -mənt/s

entrap, -s, -ping, -ped, -per/s, -ment ɪnˈtɹæp, -s, -ɪŋ, -t, -əˑ/z, -mənt

entreasured ɪnˈtɹeʒəˑd

entreat, -s, -ing/ly, -ed, -ment ɪnˈtɹit, -s, -ɪŋ/lɨ, -ɪd, -mənt

entreat|y, -ies ɪnˈtɹit|ɨ, -ɨz

entrench, -es, -ing, -ed, -ment/s ɪnˈtɹentʃ, -ɪz, -ɪŋ, -t, -mənt/s

entwist, -s, -ing, -ed ɪnˈtwɪst, -s, -ɪŋ, -ɪd

envenom, -s, -ing, -ed ɪnˈvenəm, -z, -ɪŋ, -d

enviab|le, -ly, -leness ˈenviəb|l̩, -lɨ, -l̩nɪs

envious, -ly, -ness ˈenviəs, -lɨ, -nɪs

environ, -s, -ing, -ed, -ment/s ɪnˈvaɪɹən, -z, -ɪŋ, -d, -mənt/s

envisag|e, -es, -ing, -ed ɪnˈvɪzɪdʒ, -ɪz, -ɪŋ, -d

envoy or envoi, -s ˈenvɔɪ [ˈɒnvɔɪ], -z

env|y (E.), -ies, -ying, -ied, -ier/s ˈenv|ɨ, -ɨz, -ɨɪŋ, -ɨd, -ɨəˑ/z
Note.—In TS, II.i.18 and Sonn. 128.5, 'envy' is given primary stress on the second syllable, i.e., [enˈvaɪ], a common practice in S.'s day when (as in these instances) it was in the v. form (cf. E. A. Abbott's A Shakespearian Grammar, § 490)

enwheel ɪnˈʍil

enwomb, -s, -ing, -ed ɪnˈwum, -z, -ɪŋ, -d

enwrap, -s, -ping, -ped ɪnˈɹæp, -s, -ɪŋ, -t

enwreath|e, -es, -ing, -ed ɪnˈɹið, -z, -ɪŋ, -d

Ephesian (2HIV, MWW), -s ɪˈfiʒn̩ [-ʒɪən], -z

Ephesus (COM, PER) ˈefisəs

epicure, -s ˈepɪˌkjuɚ, -z

Epicurean (AC, MWW) ˌepɪkjʊˈɹiən

epicurean, -s ˌepɪkjʊˈɹiən, -z

epicurism 'epɪkjʊɝ˞ɪzəm

Note.—Some will assert—including Kökeritz (cf. his Shakespeare's Pronunciation, *p. 398)—that this word is given primary stress on the second syllable, i.e.,* [e'pɪkjʊɝ˞ɪzəm] *in* LEAR, I.iv.235, *in order to scan iambically. However, there is nothing out of the ordinary if one chooses to retain primary stress on the first syllable; S. often accentuates the beginning of a new thought with a trochaic foot (particularly when it lands in the middle of a verse line, and especially when it immediately follows the natural caesura in the line)*

Epicurus (JUL) ˌepɪ'kjʊɝ˞ɹəs

Epidamnum (COM) ˌepɪ'dæmnəm

Epidaurus (COM) ˌepɪ'dɔɹəs

epigram, -s 'epɪgɹæm, -z

epigraph, -s 'epɪgɹaf, -s

epilepsy 'epɪlepsɪ

epileptic, -s ˌepɪ'leptɪk, -s

epilogue (E.), -s 'epɪlɒg, -z

epiphan|y, -ies ɪ'pɪfən|ɪ, -ɪz

episode, -s 'epɪsoʊd, -z

epistle, -s ɪ'pɪsl̩, -z

Epistrophus (TC) ɪ'pɪstɹəfəs

epitaph, -s 'epɪtaf, -s

epithet, -s 'epɪθet, -s

epitheton e'pɪθətɒn

epitome, -s ɪ'pɪɾəmɪ, -z

epoch, -s 'ipɒk, -s

equal, -s, -ling, -led; -ly, -ness 'ikwəl, -z, -ɪŋ, -d; -ɪ, -nɪs

equinoctial, -s ˌikwɪ'nɒkʃl̩ [ˌekwɪ-], -z

equinox, -es 'ikwɪnɒks ['ekwɪ-], -ɪz

equip, -s, -ping, -ped, -ment/s ɪ'kwɪp, -s, -ɪŋ, -t, -mənt/s

equipage, -s 'ekwɪpɪdʒ, -ɪz

equitab|le, -ly, -leness 'ekwɪɾəb|l̩, -lɪ, -l̩nɪs

equit|y (E.), -ies 'ekwɪt|ɪ, -ɪz

equivoc|al, -ally, -alness ɪ'kwɪvʊk|l̩, -əlɪ, -l̩nɪs

equivocat|e, -es, -ing, -ed, -or/s ɪ'kwɪvʊkeɪt, -s, -ɪŋ, -ɪd, -ɚ/z

equivocation, -s ɪˌkwɪvʊ'keɪʃn̩, -z

'er (*from* **her**) 'ɚ (*as it's a weak form*)

Ercles (MSND) 'ɝ˞klɪz

Note.—Said to be a corruption of 'Hercules' *in* MSND, I.ii.25, 36; *however, in* TNK, I.i.66, 'Hercules' *is to be disyllabic in order to fit metrically into the verse line.* 'Ercles' *is thus an option, or* 'Hercles' ['hɝ˞klɪz], *an accepted form of either* 'Hercules' *or* 'Heracles'

ere 'ɛɝ˞

Erebus (2HIV, JUL, MV) 'eɹɪbəs

erect, -s, -ing, -ed; -ly, -ness ɪ'ɹekt, -s, -ɪŋ, -ɪd; -lɪ, -nɪs

erection, -s ɪ'ɹekʃn̩, -z

ere't (*contr. of* **ere it**) 'ɛɝ˞t

erewhile ɛɝ˞'ʍaɪl

ergo (L.) (COM, IV.iii.55; LLL, V.ii.588) 'ɛɝ˞go ['ɝ˞go]

eringo *or* **eryngo** (*aphrodisiac*), **-es** ɪ'ɹɪŋgoʊ, -z

Ermengard, Lady (HV) 'leɪdɪ 'ɝ˞mənˌgɑɝ˞d

ern, -ed 'ɝ˞n, -d

Eros (*AC*) 'ɪɝ˞ɹɒs ['eɹ-, 'ɪɹ-, -ɹɒs]

Note.—This name, whether speaking of the Greek god of love or the character in AC, *is stressed on the first syllable as indicated above; however, there are two lines in* AC *(IV.xiv.35, 41) that, when scanned, suggest that the stress be placed on the second syllable instead. Generally speaking, I favor consistency when it comes to the pronunciation of proper names in* S. *(see* **Gonzalo**). *Most unusual is* AC, IV.xiv.35, *where one is faced with either a rare trochee in the second foot, or a pronunciation of the name incongruous with its other references in this play and other literature*

i we ɪ city ɪ hit e let ɛ debut æ can a pass ɝ bird ʌ hut ə again ɚ supper u you
ʊ should o obey ɔ awl ɒ cop ɑ father eɪ paid aɪ high oʊ go ɔɪ voice aʊ found ɪɝ˞ ear
ɛɝ˞ air ʊɝ˞ poor ɔɝ˞ fork ɑɝ˞ park aɪɝ˞ fire aʊɝ˞ hour b boy p pit d dog t top g got
k kid h how fi behave dʒ jot tʃ chew z zany s soft v vat f fat ʒ treasure ʃ ship ð the
θ thin m man n no ŋ hang l lip j yes w won ʍ whew ɹ rigger, airy ɾ matter

Erpingham, Sir Thomas (*HV*, RII) ˌsɜ˞
ˈtɒməs ˈɜ˞pɪŋəm

err, -s, -ing, -ed ˈɜ˞, -z, -ɹɪŋ, -d

errand, -s ˈeɹənd, -z

errant, -ly, -ry ˈeɹənt, -lɪ, -ɹɪ

erroneous, -ly, -ness ɪˈɹoʊnɪəs, -lɪ, -nɪs

error (E.) (JUL), **-s** ˈeɹɚ, -z

erst ˈɜ˞st

erstwhile ˈɜ˞stʍaɪl

erudite, -ly, -ness ˈɛɹ˞jʊdaɪt [ˈeɹʊ-], -lɪ,
-nɪs

erudition ˌɛɹ˞jʊˈdɪʃn̩ [ˈeɹʊ-]

erupt, -s, -ing, -ed ɪˈɹʌpt, -s, -ɪŋ, -ɪd

eruption, -s ɪˈɹʌpʃn̩, -z

eryngo *or* **eringo** (*aphrodisiac*), **-es**
ɪˈɹɪŋgoʊ, -z

Escalus (ALL'S, *MEAS, RJ*) ˈeskələs

Escanes (*PER*) ˈeskəˌniz

escap|e, -es, -ing, -ed, -ement/s ɪˈskeɪp,
-s, -ɪŋ, -t, -mənt/s

escapend (*escaping*) ɪˈskeɪpənd
Note.—F. D. Hoeniger (editor for PER,
The Arden Shakespeare, 1963) cites that
this is a present participle rather than a
past participle, as numerous editors
have asserted

eschew, -ing, -ed ɪsˈtʃu [esˈtʃu], -z, -ɪŋ,
-d

escot, -s, -ting, -(t)ed, -ter/s ɪˈskɒt, -s, -ɪŋ,
-ɪd, -ɚ/z

Esculapius (MWW, PER) (*var. of*
Aesculapius, *q.v.*) ˌeskjʊˈleɪpɪəs, -pjəs

especi|al, -ally ɪˈspeʃl̩, -əlɪ

esperance (E.) (1HIV) ˈespəˌɹəns

espial, -s ɪˈspaɪəl, -z

espous|e, -es, -ing, -ed, -er/s; -al/s
ɪˈspaʊz, -ɪz, -ɪŋ, -d, -ɚ/z; -l̩/z

esp|y, -ies, -ying, -ied ɪˈspaɪ, -z, -ɪŋ, -d

esquire (E.), -s ˈeskwaɪɚ [ɪˈskwaɪɚ], -z

essay (*s.*), **-s** ˈeseɪ, -z

essay (*v.*), **-s, -ing, -ed, -er/s** eˈseɪ [ˈeseɪ],
-z, -ɪŋ, -d, -ɚ/z

essence, -s ˈesəns, -ɪz

essen|tial, -tially, -tialness ɪˈsenʃl̩, -ʃlɪ
[-ʃəlɪ], -ʃnɪs

Essex (3HVI, *KJ*) ˈesɪks

establish, -es, -ing, -ed, -er/s, -ment/s
ɪˈstæblɪʃ, -ɪz, -ɪŋ, -t, -ɚ/z, -mənt/s

estate (E.), -s ɪˈsteɪt, -s

esteem, -s, -ing, -ed ɪˈstim, -z, -ɪŋ, -d

estimab|le, -ly, -leness ˈestɪməbl̩, -lɪ,
-l̩nɪs

estimate (*s.*), **-s** ˈestɪmɪt, -s

estimat|e (*v.*), **-es, -ing, -ed, -or/s**
ˈestɪmeɪt, -s, -ɪŋ, -ɪd, -ɚ/z

estimation, -s ˌestɪˈmeɪʃn̩, -z̪

estrang|e, -es, -ing, -ed, -edness,
-ement/s ɪˈstɹeɪndʒ, -ɪz, -ɪŋ, -d, -ɪdnɪs,
-mənt/s

estridge, -s ˈestɹɪdʒ, -ɪz

Et bonum quo antiquius eo melius (*L.*)
(PER, I.Gower.10) ɛt ˈbonum kwo
ɑnˈtikwɪus eo ˈmelɪus

etc., etcetera, et cetera, *or* **&c., -s**
ɪtˈseɹ˞ɹə [etˈs-, -ˈsetɹə], -z

etch, -es, -ing/s, -ed, -er/s ˈetʃ, -ɪz, -ɪŋ/z,
-t, -ɚ/z

etern|al (E.), -ally ɪˈtɜ˞n̩l̩, -əlɪ [-l̩ɪ]

eterne ɪˈtɜ˞n

eternit|y, -ies ɪˈtɜ˞nɪt|ɪ, -ɪz

eternized ɪˈtɜ˞naɪzd

-eth (*archaic suffix; forming the third*
person present singular indicative of
verbs) -ɪθ

Ethiop (AYLI, RJ, PER) ˈiθɪɒp [-θɪəp],
-θjɒp [-θjɔp, -θjəp]

Ethiope (ADO, AYLI, LLL, MSND,
PER, PP, RJ, TGV) ˈiθɪoʊp [-θɪəp]

Ethiopian (MWW, WT) ˌiθɪˈoʊpɪən, -pjən

Etna *or* **Ætna** (*the volcano*) (MWW, TIT)
ˈetnə

Eton (MWW) ˈitn̩

Et tu, Brute? (*L.*) (JUL, III.i.77) ˈɛt ˈtu
ˈbrutɛ

eunuch, -s ˈjunək, -s

Euphrates (AC) juˈfɹeɪtɪz
Note.—Irvine, Kökeritz, and Schmidt
each agree that in AC, I.ii.98, the stress
is on the first syllable, i.e., [ˈjufɹətiz,
-ɹat-]; it is the only time in S.'s canon the
name is used, and Irvine asserts that
the stress on the first syllable was the
common Elizabethan pronunciation.
Certainly, pronouncing it this way
(along with trisyllabicizing 'asia' in the
line) adheres to the metric requirements
of iambic pentameter, but there is
another way to scan the line which

reconciles a modern pronunciation of 'Euphrates,' giving primary stress to the second syllable. By allowing the full-stop punctuation to absorb the value of a beat (a not uncommon device identically employed in AC, IV.ii.27, IV.viii.7, IV.xiv.103, and V.ii.66) and finishing with a feminine ending, one retains the modern pronunciation, i.e., [juˈfɹeɪ̆tɪz]

Euphronius (*AC*) juˈfɹoʊ̆nɪəs, -njəs

Euriphile (CYM) jʊˈɹɪfɪlɪ

Europa (ADO, MWW) jʊˈɹoʊ̆pə

Europe (CYM, 1HIV, 2HIV, HV, 1HVI, 3HVI, TEM, WT) ˈjʊ̆ɝ̆ɹəp

evad|e, -es, -ing, -ed, -er/s ɪˈveɪ̆d, -z, -ɪŋ, -ɪd, -ɚ/z

Evans, Sir Hugh (*MWW*) sɝ ˈhju ˈevənz
  Note.—He is also called 'Master Parson' [ˈmɑstɚ ˈpɑɝ̆sn̩]

evasion, -s ɪˈveɪ̆ʒn̩, -z

Eve (LLL, MWW, RII, TGV, TN, Sonn. 93) ˈiv

ev|en (*s., adj., v., adv.*), **-enly, -enness; -ens, -ening, -ened** ˈiv|ən [ˈiv|n̩], -ənlɪ [-n̩lɪ], -ənnɪs [-n̩nɪs]; -ənz, -n̩ɪŋ, -ənd [-n̩d]

even-Christen ˈivənˌkɹɪsn̩ [ˈivn̩-]

evening (*time of day*), **-s** ˈivnɪŋ, -z

even-pleached ˈivənˌplitʃt [-ˌpleɪ̆tʃt]

event, -s ɪˈvent, -s

event|ful, -fully, -fulness ɪˈvent|fʊl, -fəlɪ, -fʊlnɪs

ever ˈevɚ

ever-blinded ˌevɚˈblaɪ̆ndɪd

ever-burning ˌevɚˈbɝ̆nɪŋ (*when att.,* [ˈ--ˌ--])

ever-during (*eternal, everlasting*) ˌevɚˈdjʊ̆ɝ̆ɹɪŋ (*when att.,* [ˈ--ˌ--])

ever-gentle ˌevɚˈdʒentl̩

everlasting (**E.**) (HAM), **-ly, -ness** ˌevɚˈlastɪŋ, -lɪ,-nɪs

evermore ˌevɚˈmɔɝ̆ [ˈ---]

every ˈevɹɪ

everyone ˈevɹɪwʌn

everything ˈevɹɪθɪŋ

everywhere ˈevɹɪʍɛɝ̆

evidenc|e, -es, -ing, -ed ˈevɪdəns, -ɪz

evident, -ly ˈevɪdənt, -lɪ
  Note.— 'Evidently,' depending on its usage, is sometimes pronounced [ˌevɪˈdentlɪ]

ev|il (**E.**), **-ils, -illy** ˈivɪ|l [-ɪl], -l̩z [-ɪlz], -əlɪ [-lɪ]
  Note.—As with so many other words in S. ('warrant,' 'spirit,' 'heaven,' 'even,' 'devil,' etc.), this typically disyllabic word is sometimes pronounced as a monosyllable (absorbing only one metrical beat in the verse), thus the secondary pronunciations proffered above. When 'evilly' wants to reduce into only two syllables (e.g., KJ, III.iii.149), I see no reason why the 'v' might not be fully retained, so that the pronunciation becomes simply [ˈivlɪ]

evil-eyed ˈivl̩ˌaɪ̆d

evitate (*avoid*) ˈevɪteɪ̆t

evolv|e, -es, -ing, -ed ɪˈvɒlv, -z, -ɪŋ, -d

ev'n (*from* **even**) ˈin [ˈivn̩]
  Note.—In combination with a word beginning with 'n,' e.g., 'ev'n now' in TN II.ii.1, the pronunciation may conceivably be [ˈiv]

ewe, -s ˈju, -z

ewer, -s ˈjuɝ̆, -z

exact, -s, -ing, -ed, -er/s; -or/s; -est, -ness ɪɡˈzækt, -s, -ɪŋ, -ɪd, -ɚ/z, -ɚ/z; -ɪst, -nɪs
  Note.—Stressed on the first syllable, i.e., [ˈeɡzækt] *in* 1HIV, IV.i.46; TC, IV.v.231 *(see Note for* **secure**)

exactest ɪɡˈzæktɪst

exaction, -s ɪɡˈzækʃn̩, -z

exactly ɪɡˈzæktlɪ

exalt, -s, -ing, -ed ɪɡˈzɔlt [-ˈzɒlt], -s, -ɪŋ, -ɪd

exaltation, -s ˌeɡzɔlˈteɪ̆ʃn̩ [-ˈzɒlt], -z

---

i wɛ ɪ cit**y** ɪ h**i**t e l**e**t ɛ d**e**but æ c**a**n a p**a**ss ɝ b**ir**d ʌ h**u**t ə **a**gain ɚ supp**er** u y**ou**
ʊ sh**ou**ld o **o**bey ɔ **aw**l ɒ c**o**p ɑ f**a**ther eɪ̆ p**ai**d aɪ̆ h**igh** oʊ̆ g**o** ɔɪ̆ v**oi**ce aʊ̆ f**ou**nd ɪɝ̆ **ear**
ɛɝ̆ **air** ʊɝ̆ **poor** ɔɝ̆ f**or**k ɑɝ̆ p**ar**k aɪɚ̆ f**ire** aʊɚ̆ h**our** b **b**oy p **p**it d **d**og t **t**op g **g**ot
k **k**id h **h**ow fi be**h**ave dʒ **j**ot tʃ **ch**ew z **z**any s **s**oft v **y**at f **f**at ʒ trea**s**ure ʃ **sh**ip ð **th**e
θ **th**in m **m**an n **n**o ŋ ha**ng** l **l**ip j **y**es w **w**on ʍ **wh**ew ɹ **r**igger, ai**r**y ɾ ma**tt**er

exam, -s ɪɡ'zæm, -z

examination, -s ɪɡ,zæmɪ'neɪʃn̩, -z

examin|e, -es, -ing, -ed, -er/s ɪɡ'zæmɪn, -z, -ɪŋ, -d, -ə˞/z

examp|le, -les, -ling, -led ɪɡ'zæmp|l̩, -l̩z, -lɪŋ [-l̩ɪŋ], -l̩d

exasperate (*adj.*) ɪɡ'zæspə˞.ɹɪt

exasperat|e (*v.*)**, -es, -ing, -ed, -or/s** ɪɡ'zæspə˞.ɹeɪt, -s, -ɪŋ, -ɪd, -ə˞/z

exasperation ɪɡ,zæspə˞'ɹeɪʃn̩

excavat|e, -es, -ing, -ed, -or/s 'ekskəveɪt, -s, -ɪŋ, -ɪd, -ə˞/z

excavation, -s ,ekskə'veɪʃn̩, -z

exceed, -s, -ing, -ed ɪk'sid, -z, -ɪŋ, -ɪd

exceedingly ɪk'sidɪŋlɪ

excel, -s, -ling, -led ɪk'sel, -z, -ɪŋ, -d

excellen|ce, -ces, -cy, -cies, -t/ly 'eksələn|s, -sɪz, -sɪ, -sɪz, -t/lɪ

except, -s, -ing, -ed ɪk'sept, -s, -ɪŋ, -ɪd

exception, -s ɪk'sepʃn̩, -z

exceptless ɪk'septlɪs

excess (*s.*)**, -es** ɪk'ses, -ɪz (*when att.,* ['ekses])

excess (*v.*)**, -es, -ing, -ed** ɪk'ses, -ɪz, -ɪŋ, -t

excessive, -ly, -ness ɪk'sesɪv, -lɪ, -nɪs

exchang|e, -es, -ing, -ed, -er/s ɪks'tʃeɪndʒ, -ɪz, -ɪŋ, -d, -ə˞/z

exchequer, -s eks'tʃekə˞, -z

excit|e, -es, -ing, -ed/ly, -edness, -ement/s; -able/ness ɪk'saɪt, -s, -ɪŋ, -ɪd/lɪ, -ɪdnɪs, -mənt/s; -əbl̩/nɪs

exclaim, -s, -ing, -ed, -er/s ɪk'skleɪm, -z, -ɪŋ, -d, -ə˞/z

exclamation, -s ,eksklə'meɪʃn̩, -z

exclamatory ɪk'sklæmətə˞.ɹɪ

exclud|e, -es, -ing, -ed ɪk'sklud, -z, -ɪŋ, -ɪd

exclusion, -s ɪk'skluʒn̩, -z

exclusive, -ly, -ness ɪk'sklusɪv, -lɪ, -nɪs

excommunicate (*s., adj.*)**, -s** ,ekskə'mjunɪkɪt, -s

excommunicat|e (*v.*)**, -es, -ing, -ed** ,ekskə'mjunɪkeɪt, -s, -ɪŋ, -ɪd
Note.—This word, when it appears in KJ, III.i.99 and 149, is a perfect example of S.'s custom of occasionally omitting the final '-d' on the past tense of a verb that ends with '-te' (cf. Abbott's A Shakespearian Grammar, §§ 341, 342)

excommunication, -s ,ekskə,mjunɪ'keɪʃn̩, -z

excrement, -s 'ekskɹɪmənt, -s

excruciat|e, -es, -ing/ly, -ed ɪk'skɹuʃɪeɪt, -s, -ɪŋ/lɪ, -ɪd

excruciation ɪk,skɹuʃɪ'eɪʃn̩

excursion, -s ɪk'skɜ˞.ʒn̩, -z

excuse (*s.*)**, -s** ɪk'skjus, -ɪz

excus|e (*v.*)**, -es, -ing, -ed** ɪk'skjuz, -ɪz, -ɪŋ, -d

execrab|le, -ly, -leness 'eksɪkɹəb|l̩, -lɪ, -l̩nɪs

execrat|e, -es, -ing, -ed 'eksɪkɹeɪt, -s, -ɪŋ, -ɪd

execration, -s ,eksɪ'kɹeɪʃn̩, -z

execut|e, -s, -ing, -ed, -er/s 'eksɪkjut, -s, -ɪŋ, -ɪd, -ə˞/z

execution, -s ,eksɪ'kjuʃn̩, -z

executioner, -s ,eksɪ'kjuʃnə˞, -z

executive, -s ɪɡ'zekjʊtɪv, -z

executor, -s ɪɡ'zekjʊtə˞, -z

exempt, -s, -ing, -ed ɪɡ'zempt, -s, -ɪŋ, -ɪd

exemption, -s ɪɡ'zempʃn̩, -z

exequies 'eksɪkwɪz

exercis|e, -es, -ing, -ed, -er/s 'eksə˞saɪz, -ɪz, -ɪŋ, -d, -ə˞/z

Exeter (*HV, 1HVI, 3HVI,* RII, RIII) 'eksətə˞

exeunt (*L.*) 'eksɪ̩ʊnt [-sɪənt]

exhalation, -s ,eksɸɪə'leɪʃn̩, -z

exhal|e, -es, -ing, -ed eks'ɸeɪl, -z, -ɪŋ, -d (['--] in 1HIV, V.i.19)

exhaust, -s, -ing, -ed ɪɡ'zɔst, -s, -ɪŋ, -ɪd

exhaustion ɪɡ'zɔstʃən

exhibit, -s, -ing, -ed, -or/s ɪɡ'zɪbɪt, -s, -ɪŋ, -ɪd, -ə˞/z

exhibition, -s ,eksɪ'bɪʃn̩, -z

exigen|ce, -ces, -t/ly 'eksɪdʒən|s ['eɡzɪ-], -sɪz, -t/lɪ

exile (*s.*)**, -s** 'eɡzaɪl ['eksaɪl], -z
Note.—Stressed on the second syllable, i.e., [-'-], *in* AYLI, II.i.1; COR, V.iii.96; CYM, IV.iv.26; RJ, V.iii.210; RII, I.iii.217; TGV, III.ii.3

exil|e (*v.*)**, -es, -ing, -ed** 'eɡzaɪl ['eksaɪl], -z, -ɪŋ, -d
Note.—[-'-] *in* AYLI, V.iv.164

exion 'ekʃn̩, 'eksɪən
Note.—The pronunciations proffered for

this word appearing in 2HIV, II.i.29 *are entirely conjectural. The OED and various other sources cite that 'exion' is Mistress Quickly's blunder for 'action,' as she is elsewhere prone to seeming blunders and malapropisms. But orthoepically speaking, 'exion' more than likely represents an obsolete var. spelling (and thus pronunciation) of 'action,' rather than any sort of blunder. (Cf.* **alligant***)*

exorcis|e, -es, -ing, -ed, -er/s 'eksɔɚˌsaɪz [-səˌsaɪz], -ɪz, -ɪŋ, -d, -ɚ/z

exorcism, -s 'eksɔɚˌsɪzm̩ [-səˌsɪzm̩], -z

exorcist, -s 'eksɔɚˌsɪst [-səˌsɪst], -s

expect, -s, -ing, -ed, -er/s ɪk'spekt, -s, -ɪŋ, -ɪd, -ɚ/z

expectan|ce, -cy, -cies, -t/ly ɪk'spektən|s, -sɪ, -sɪz, -t/lɪ

expectation (E.) (HV)**, -s** ˌekspek'teɪʃn̩, -z

expedien|ce, -cy, -t/ly ɪk'spidɪən|s, -sɪ, -t/lɪ

expedit|e, -es, -ing, -ed 'ekspɪdaɪt, -s, -ɪŋ, -ɪd

expedition, -s ˌekspɪ'dɪʃn̩, -z

expeditious, -ly, -ness ˌekspɪ'dɪʃəs, -lɪ, -nɪs

expel, -s, -ling, -led ɪk'spel, -z, -ɪŋ, -d

expend, -s, -ing, -ed; -able/s ɪk'spend, -z, -ɪŋ, -ɪd; -əbl̩/z

expense, -s ɪk'spens, -ɪz

expensive, -ly, -ness ɪk'spensɪv, -lɪ, -nɪs

experienc|e, -es, -ing, -ed ɪk'spɪɚˌɹɪəns, -ɪz, -ɪŋ, -t

experiment (*s.*)**, -s** ɪk'speɹɪmənt, -s

experiment (*v.*)**, -s, -ing, -ed** ɪk'speɹɪment, -s, -ɪŋ, -ɪd

experiment|al, -ally ɪkˌspeɹɪ'ment|l̩ [-əl], -lɪ [-əlɪ]

expert (*adj.*)**, -ly, -ness** 'ekspɝt [ɪk'spɝt], -lɪ, -nɪs

expert (*s.*)**, -s** 'ekspɝt, -s

expertise ˌekspɝ'tiz

expiat|e, -es, -ing, -ed, -or/s 'ekspɪeɪt, -s, -ɪŋ, -ɪd, -ɚ/z

expiation, -s ˌekspɪ'eɪʃn̩, -z

experation, -s ˌekspə'ɹeɪʃn̩ [-spɹɪ-], -z

expir|e, -es, -ing, -ed ɪk'spaɪɚ, -z, -ɹɪŋ, -d (*arguably* ['ekspaɪɚd] *in* LUC, 26)

exploit (*s.*)**, -s** 'eksplɔɪt, -s
Note.—Often [ɪk'splɔɪt(s), ek's-] *in S., e.g.,* HAM, IV.vii.63; HV, I.ii.121; 1HIV, I.iii.197; 1HVI, II.i.43, II.iii.5; 2HVI, I.i.195; JUL, II.i.317, 318; LEAR, II.ii.121; LUC, 429; MAC, IV.i.144; MSND, III.ii.157; MV, III.ii.60; RIII, V.iii.331; TIT, V.i.11

exploit (*v.*)**, -s, -ing, -ed** ɪk'splɔɪt, -s, -ɪŋ, -ɪd

exposition, -s ˌekspə'zɪʃn̩, -z

exposit|or/s, -ory ɪk'spɒzɪt|ɚ/z [ek's-], -əɹɪ

expostulat|e, -es, -ing, -ed, -or/s ɪk'spɒstjʊleɪt [ek's-], -s, -ɪŋ, -ɪd, -ɚ/z

expostulation, -s ɪkˌspɒstjʊ'leɪʃn̩, -z

exposture ɪk'spɒstʃɚ

exposure, -s ɪk'spoʊʒɚ, -z

expound, -s, -ing, -ed, -er/s ɪk'spaʊnd, -z, -ɪŋ, -ɪd, -ɚ/z

express, -es, -ing, -ed; -ly, -ness ɪk'spɹes, -ɪz, -ɪŋ, -t; -lɪ, -nɪs
Note.—In KJ, IV.ii.234, *this word is optionally given primary syllabic stress on the first syllable, i.e.,* ['ekspɹes]

expressure ɪk'spɹeʃɚ

expuls|e, -es, -ing, -ed ɪk'spʌls, -ɪz, -ɪŋ, -t

expulsion, -s ɪk'spʌlʃn̩ [ek's-], -z

exquisite, -ly, -ness 'ekskwɪzɪt [ɪk'skwɪzɪt], -lɪ, -nɪs

exsufflicate ek'sʌflɪkɪt
Note.—This rare word (adj.), of obscure origin and doubtful meaning, appears in OTH, III.iii.185, *and perhaps nowhere else in literature. Most editors agree that it is a contemptable term, probably meaning 'blown-up,' 'puffed-up,' or 'windy'*

---

i w**e** ɪ c**i**t**y** ɪ h**i**t e l**e**t ɛ d**e**but æ c**a**n a p**a**ss ɝ b**i**rd ʌ h**u**t ə **a**gain ɚ supp**er** u y**ou**
ʊ sh**ou**ld o **o**bey ɔ **aw**l ɒ c**o**p ɑ f**a**ther eɪ p**ai**d aɪ h**i**gh oʊ g**o** ɔɪ v**oi**ce aʊ f**ou**nd ɪɚ **ear**
ɛɚ **air** ʊɚ p**oor** ɔɚ f**or**k ɑɚ p**ar**k aɪɚ f**ire** aʊɚ h**our** b b**oy** p p**i**t d d**o**g t t**o**p g g**o**t
k k**i**d h **h**ow fi be**h**ave dʒ j**o**t tʃ **ch**ew z **z**any s **s**oft v **v**at f **f**at ʒ trea**s**ure ʃ **sh**ip ð **th**e
θ **th**in m **m**an n **n**o ŋ ha**ng** l l**i**p j **y**es w **w**on ʍ **wh**ew ɹ **r**igger, ai**r**y ɾ ma**tt**er

extant ɪkˈstænt [ekˈs-, ˈekstənt, ˈekstænt]
   ([ˈ--] *in* Sonn. 83.6)
extas|y (*obscure form of* **ecstasy**), **-ies**
   ˈekstəs|ɪ, -ɪz
extemporal, -ly ɪkˈstempəɹəl [ek-], -ɪ
extempore ɪkˈstempə·ɹɪ
extend, -s, -ing, -ed ɪkˈstend, -z, -ɪŋ, -ɪd
extension, -s ɪkˈstenʃn̩, -z
extensive, -ly, -ness ɪkˈstensɪv, -lɪ, -nɪs
extent, -s ɪkˈstent, -s
extenuat|e, -es, -ing/ly, -ed ɪkˈstenjʊeɪt,
   -s, -ɪŋ/lɪ, -ɪd
extenuation, -s ɪkˌstenjʊˈeɪʃn̩, -z
exterior, -s, -ly ɪkˈstɪɚ·ɹɪɚ, -z, -lɪ
extermined ɪkˈstɚ·mɪnd
extern, -s ekˈstɚ·n, -z
external, -s; -ly ɪkˈstɚ·nl̩, -z; -ɪ
extinct, -ed ɪkˈstɪŋkt, -ɪd
extincture ɪkˈstɪŋktʃɚ
extinguish, -es, -ing, -ed, -er/s; -able
   ɪkˈstɪŋgwɪʃ, -ɪz, -ɪŋ, -t, -ɚ·/z; -əbl̩
extirp, -s, -ing, -ed ɪkˈstɚ·p, -s, -ɪŋ, -t
extirpat|e, -es, -ing, -ed ˈekstə·peɪt
   [-tɚ·p-], -s, -ɪŋ, -ɪd
   Note.—In TEM, I.ii.125, *this verb scans*
   with the stress falling on the second
   syllable, i.e., [ɪkˈstɚ·peɪt, -pɪt]
extol, -s, -ling, -led, -ment ɪkˈstoʊl, -z,
   -ɪŋ, -d, -mənt
Exton, Sir Piers *or* **Pierce of** (*RII*) ˌsɚ·
   ˈpɪɚ·s əv ˈekstən
extort, -s, -ing, -ed, -er/s ɪkˈstɔ·t, -s, -ɪŋ,
   -ɪd, -ɚ·/z
extortion, -s ɪkˈstɔ·ɚ·ʃn̩, -z
extract (*s.*), **-s** ˈekstɹækt, -s
extract (*v.*), **-s, -ing, -ed, -or/s; -able**
   ɪkˈstɹækt, -s, -ɪŋ, -ɪd, -ɚ·/z; -əbl̩
extraordinar|y, -ily, -iness ɪkˈstɹɔ·ɚ·dn̩əɹ|ɪ
   [ˌekstɹə·ˈɔ·ɚ·dn̩əɹ|ɪ], -ɪlɪ
   [ɪkˌstɹɔ·ɚ·dn̩ˈɛɚ·ɹɪlɪ], -ɪnɪs
   Note.—This word is pronounced
   [ˈekstɹə·ɔ·ɚ·dn̩ə·ɹɪ] *in* 1HIV, III.i.38;
   III.ii.78
extraught ɪkˈstɹɔt
extravagan|ce, -ces, -cy, -t/ly
   ɪkˈstɹævɪgən|s, -sɪz, -sɪ, -t/lɪ
extreme, -s, -st, -ly, -ness ɪkˈstɹim, -z, -ɪst,
   -lɪ, -nɪs
   Note.—Sometimes stressed on the first

syllable, i.e., [ˈekstɹim] *in* S., *e.g.,*
ALL'S, III.iii.6; COR, IV.v.70; 1HIV,
I.iii.30; LLL, V.ii.732; LUC, 230; TGV,
II.vii.22; RIII, III.v.43, IV.iv.186; RJ,
II.Pro.14; TS, II.i.135; TIT, V.i.113;
arguably in MWW, IV.iv.12
extremit|y, -ies ɪkˈstɹemɪt|ɪ, -ɪz
exud|e, -es, -ing, -ed ɪgˈzjud, -z, -ɪŋ, -ɪd
exult, -s, -ing/ly, -ed ɪgˈzʌlt, -s, -ɪŋ/lɪ, -ɪd
exultation ˌegzl̩ˈteɪʃn̩ [ˌeksl̩-]
eyas, -es ˈaɪəs, -ɪz
eyas-musket (*young male sparrow-*
   hawk), **-s** ˈaɪəsˌmʌskɪt, -s
eye, -s, -ing, -d ˈaɪ, -z, -ɪŋ, -d
eye(-)ball, -s, -ing, -ed ˈaɪˌbɔl, -z, -ɪŋ, -d
eye-brim ˈaɪˌbɹɪm
eyebrow, -s ˈaɪbɹɑʊ, -z
eye-drop, -s ˈaɪˌdɹɒp, -s
eye-glance ˈaɪˌglans
eye-glass, -es ˈaɪˌglas, -ɪz
eyeless ˈaɪlɪs
eyelid, -s ˈaɪlɪd, -z
eye-offending ˈaɪəˌfendɪŋ
eyesight ˈaɪsaɪt
eye(-)sore, -s ˈaɪsɔɚ·, -z
eye-strings ˈaɪˌstɹɪŋz
eye-wink, -s ˈaɪˌwɪŋk, -s
eye-witness, -es ˌaɪˈwɪtnɪs, -ɪz
eyne (*archaic pl. from* **eye**) ˈaɪn
eyr|ie (*var. of* **aerie**), **-y, -ies** ˈɛɚ·ɹ|ɪ [ˈɪɚ·ɹ-,
   ˈaɪɚ·ɹ-], -ɪ, -ɪz

Ff

F (*the letter*), **-'s** ˈef, -s
fa (*fourth note of diatonic scale*) ˈfɑ
Fabian (*TN*) ˈfeɪbɪən
fable, -s, -d ˈfeɪbl̩, -z, -d
fabric, -s ˈfæbɹɪk, -s
fabricat|e, -es, -ing, -ed, -or/s ˈfæbɹɪkeɪt,
   -s, -ɪŋ, -ɪd, -ɚ·/z
fabrication, -s ˌfæbɹɪˈkeɪʃn̩, -z
fabulous, -ly, -ness ˈfæbjʊləs, -lɪ, -nɪs
façade, -s fəˈsad, -z
fac|e, -es, -ing, -ed ˈfeɪs, -ɪz, -ɪŋ, -t
facere (*L.*) (LLL, IV.ii.14) ˈfasɛɾɛ
face-royal ˌfeɪsˈɹɔɪəl

facet, -s, -(t)ed 'fæsɪt, -s, -ɪd
facetious, -ly, -ness fə'siʃəs, -lɪ, -nɪs
faci|al, -ally 'feɪʃ|l̩, -əlɪ
facile, -ly, -ness 'fæsl̩ [-sɪl, -saɪl], -ɪ, -nɪs
Facile precor gelida quando pecus omne
sub umbra Ruminat (L.) (LLL, IV.ii.90)
'fɑsɪlɛ 'prɛkɔɚ 'dʒɛlɪdɑ 'kwɑndo 'pɛkus
'omnɛ sub 'umbɹɑ 'rumɪnɑt
facilitat|e, -es, -ing, -ed fə'sɪlɪteɪt, -s, -ɪŋ,
-ɪd
facilit|y, -ies fə'sɪlɪt|ɪ, -ɪz
facinerious *or* **facinorious** ˌfæsɪ'nɪɚɹɪəs,
ˌfæsɪ'nɔɚɹɪəs
facsimile, -s fæk'sɪmɪlɪ, -z
fact, -s 'fækt, -s
faction, -s; -ary 'fækʃn̩, -z; -əɹɪ
factious, -ly, -ness 'fækʃəs, -lɪ, -nɪs
factor, -s, -ing, -ed 'fæktəɚ, -z, -ɹɪŋ, -d
factor|y, -ies 'fæktəɹ|ɪ, -ɪz
facult|y, -ies 'fækl̩t|ɪ, -ɪz
fad, -s 'fæd, -z
fad|e (*v.*), **-es, -ing, -ed** 'feɪd, -z, -ɪŋ, -ɪd
fadge 'fædʒ
fading (*s.*), **-s** 'feɪdɪŋ, -z
fad(d)om (*obsolete form of* **fathom**; *see*
murther), **-s** 'fædəm ['fæd̩əm], -z
fag, -s, -ging, -ged 'fæg, -z, -ɪŋ, -d
faggot, -s 'fægət, -s
fail, -s, -ing/s, -ed 'feɪl, -z, -ɪŋ/z, -d
failure, -s 'feɪljəɚ, -z
fain, -ing 'feɪn, -ɪŋ
faint, -s, -ing, -ed; -ly, -ness 'feɪnt, -s, -ɪŋ,
-ɪd; -lɪ, -nɪs
faint-hearted, -ly, -ness 'feɪntˌfiɑɚtɪd, -lɪ,
-nɪs
fair, -s, -er, -est, -ly, -ness 'fɛɚ, -z, -ɹɚ,
-ɹɪst, -lɪ, -nɪs
fairest-boding 'fɛɚɹɪstˌboŭdɪŋ
fair-eyed 'fɛɚˌɹaɪd
fair-faced ˌfɛɚ'feɪst (*when att.,* ['-ˌ-])
fairings 'fɛɚɹɪŋz
fair-play 'fɛɚˌpleɪ
fair|y, -ies 'fɛɚɹ|ɪ, -ɪz
fairy-like 'fɛɚɹ|ɹɪˌlaɪk

fair-spoken 'fɛɚˌspoŭkən
Fairy Queen (MSND, MWW) 'fɛɚɹɪ
'kwin
faith, -s 'feɪθ, -s
faith-breach 'feɪθ'bɹɪtʃ
faithed (*believed*) 'feɪθt
faithless, -ly, -ness 'feɪθlɪs, -lɪ, -nɪs
faitor (*rogue; deceiver*), **-s** 'feɪɾɚ, -z
fak|e, -es, -ing, -ed, -er/s 'feɪk, -s, -ɪŋ, -t,
-ɚ/z
falchion, -s 'fɔltʃən, -z
falcon, -s, -er/s 'fɑlkən ['fɔl-, 'fɔk-], -z,
-ɚ/z ['fɔknɚ/z]
Falconbridge (1HVI, 3HVI, MV)
'fɔkənbɹɪdʒ ['fɔlk-, 'falk-]
Falconbridge, Jacques (LLL) 'dʒeɪkɹs,
[-kɹz] 'fɔkənbɹɪdʒ ['fɔlk-, 'falk-] (*see*
Note for '**Jacques** *or* **Jaques**')
Falconbridge, Robert (*KJ*) 'ɹɒbɚt
'fɔkənbɹɪdʒ ['fɔlk-, 'falk-]
falconry 'falkənɹɪ ['fɔl-, 'fɔk-]
fall, -s, -ing, fell, fallen 'fɔl, -z, -ɪŋ, 'fel,
'fɔlən
falliable 'fælɪəbl̩
fallib|le, -ly, -leness 'fælɪb|l̩, -lɪ, -l̩nɪs
falling-sickness 'fɔlɪŋˌsɪknɪs
fall'n (*contr. of* **fallen** *through syncope*)
'fɔln
fall'n-off 'fɔlnˌɒf
fallow, -s, -ing, -ed; -ness 'fæloŭ, -z, -ɪŋ,
-d; -nɪs
falorous (*from* '*valorous*') 'fæləɹəs (*see*
Note for **digt**)
false, -r, -st, -ly, -ness 'fɔls, -ɚ, -ɪst, -lɪ,
-nɪs
false-boding 'fɔlsˌboŭdɪŋ
false-derived 'fɔlsdɪˌɹaɪvd
false-faced 'fɔlsˌfeɪst
false-hearted 'fɔlsˌfiɑɚtɪd
falsehood, -s 'fɔlsfiʊd, -z
false-played 'fɔls'pleɪd
false-speaking 'fɔlsˌspikɪŋ
falsing 'fɔlsɪŋ
Falstaff, Sir John 'Jack' (*1HIV, 2HIV,*

i wé ɪ city ɪ hit e let ɛ debut æ can a pass ɝ bird ʌ hut ə again ɚ supper u you
ʊ should o obey ɔ awl ɒ cop ɑ father eɪ paid aɪ high oŭ go ɔɪ voice aŭ found ɪɚ ear
ɛɚ air ʊɚ poor ɔɚ fork ɑɚ park aɪɚ fire aŭɚ hour b boy p pit d dog t top g got
k kid h how fi behave dʒ jot tʃ chew z zany s soft v vat f fat ʒ treasure ʃ ship ð the
θ thin m man n no ŋ hang l lip j yes w won ʍ whew ɹ rigger, aiɹy ɾ matter

HV, 1HVI, *MWW*) ˌsɝ ˈdʒɒn ˈdʒæk
ˈfɔlstaf

falt|er, -ers, -ering/ly, -ered, -erer/s
ˈfɔlt|ɚ, -ɚz, -ɚˌɹɪŋ/lɪ, -ɚd, -ɚˌɹɚ/z

fame (F.), -d ˈfeɪm, -d

Fame, Lady (ADO) ˈleɪdɪ ˈfeɪm

familiar, -s, -ly fəˈmɪljɚ, -z, -lɪ

famil|y, -ies ˈfæməl|ɪ, -ɪz

famine (F.) (HV), -s ˈfæmɪn, -z

famish, -es, -ing, -ed ˈfæmɪʃ, -ɪz, -ɪŋ, -t

famous, -ly, -ness ˈfeɪməs, -lɪ, -nɪs

famoused ˈfeɪməst ([ˈfeɪməsɪd] *in* Sonn. 25.9)

fan, -s, -ning, -ned ˈfæn, -z, -ɪŋ, -d

fanatic, -s fəˈnæɡɪk, -s

fanc|y (F.), -ies, -ying, -ied; -ier, -iest, -yness ˈfæns|ɪ, -ɪz, -ɪɪŋ, -ɪd; -ɪɚ, -ɪɪst, -ɪnɪs

fancy-monger ˈfænsɪˌmʌŋɡɚ

fancy-sick ˈfænsɪˌsɪk

fane, -s ˈfeɪn, -z

fanfare, -s ˈfænfɛɚ, -z

Fang (2HIV) ˈfæŋ

fang, -s, -ed; -less ˈfæŋ, -z, -d; -lɪs

fangled (*contemptuous word for 'overly adorned; given to fopperies'*) ˈfæŋɡl̩d

fantastic, -al/s, -ally, -alness fænˈtæstɪk, -l̩/z, -əlɪ, -l̩nɪs

fantas|y, -ies, -ied ˈfæntəs|ɪ, -ɪz, -ɪd

fap (*obsolete for 'drunk'*) ˈfæp

far ˈfɑɚ

farborough, -s ˈfɑɚˌbʌɹə [-bʊɹə, -bʌɹoʊ], -z

farce, -s ˈfɑɚs, -ɪz

farced ˈfɑɚsɪd

fardel, -s ˈfɑɚˌdl̩, -z (*see* **murther**)

far|e, -es, -ing, -ed ˈfɛɚ, -z, -ɹɪŋ, -d

fare-thee-well ˌfɛɚˈðɪˈwel

farewell, -s ˌfɛɚˈwel, -z

far-fet ˈfɑɚ ˈfet

farm, -s, -ing, -ed, -er/s ˈfɑɚm, -z, -ɪŋ, -d, -ɚ/z

farre (*comparative of* **far** *in* WT, IV. iv.432) ˈfɑɚ

farrow, -s, -ing, -ed ˈfæɹoʊ, -z, -ɪŋ, -d

farth|er, -est ˈfɑɚ-ð|ɚ, -ɪst

farthing, -s ˈfɑɚˌðɪŋ, -z

farthingale, -s ˈfɑɚˌðɪŋɡeɪl, -z

fartuous ˈfɑɚˌtjʊəs [-tʃʊəs]

Note.—This is Mistress Quickly's malapropism for 'virtuous' (MWW, II.ii.92). *The comic value is obvious, but there is also the echo of 'fatuous' inherent*

fashion, -s, -ing, -ed, -er/s ˈfæʃn̩, -z, -ɪŋ, -d, -ɚ/z

fashion-monger, -s ˈfæʃn̩ˌmʌŋɡɚ, -z

fashion-monging ˈfæʃn̩ˌmʌŋɪŋ [-ŋɡɪŋ]

fast, -s, -ing, -ed; -er/s, -est, -ness ˈfast, -s, -ɪŋ, -ɪd; -ɚ/z, -ɪst, -nɪs

fast-closed ˈfastˌkloʊzd ([ˌfastˈkloʊzɪd] *in* KJ, II.i.447)

fasten, -s, -ing, -ed ˈfasn̩, -z, -ɪŋ, -d

fastener, -s ˈfasnɚ [-sn̩ɚ], -z

fast-growing ˈfastˌɡɹoʊɪŋ

fasting-days ˈfastɪŋˌdeɪz

fastly ˈfastlɪ

Fastolfe, Sir John (1HVI) ˌsɝ ˈdʒɒn ˈfastɔlf

fat, -s, -ting, -ted; -ter, -test, -ness ˈfæt, -s, -ɪŋ, -ɪd; -ɚ [ˈfæɡɚ], -ɪst, -nɪs

fatal, -ly ˈfeɪtl̩, -ɪ

fatalit|y, -ies feɪˈtælɪt|ɪ [fɛˈt-], -ɪz

fatal-plotted ˈfeɪtl̩ˌplɒtɪd

fat-already ˈfætəˌlɹedɪ [ˈfæɡɔl-]

fat-brained ˈfætˌbɹeɪnd

fat|e (F.), -es, -ed ˈfeɪt, -s, -ɪd

father (F.), -s, -ing, -ed ˈfɑðɚ, -z, -ɹɪŋ, -d

fatherhood ˈfɑðɚˌfʊd

father-in-law, fathers-in-law ˈfɑðɚˌɹɪnˌlɔ, ˈfɑðɚzɪnˌlɔ

fatherless ˈfɑðɚlɪs

fatherl|y, -iness ˈfɑðɚl|ɪ, -ɪnɪs

fathom, -s, -ing, -ed; -able, -less ˈfæðəm, -z, -ɪŋ, -d; -əbl̩, -lɪs

fathom-line, -s ˈfæðəmˌlaɪn, -z

fatigate ˈfæɡɪɡeɪt

Note.—In COR, II.ii.117, *this word might appear at first to be an adj. when it is actually a p.p. here. S. follows a rule whereby the final 'd' indicating past tense is often omitted (cf. Abbott's* A Shakespearian Grammar *§ 342)*

fat-kidneyed ˈfætˌkɪdnɪd

fat-witted ˈfætˌwɪtɪd

Fauconbridge (HV) ˈfɔkənbɹɪdʒ

faucet, -s ˈfɔsɪt, -s

faucet-seller ˈfɔsɪtˌselɚ

faugh or **fough** (*interj.*) (*expression of contempt*) 'fɔ ['ɸɔ]

Faulconbridge, Lady (*KJ*) 'leɪdɪ 'fɔkənbɹɪdʒ ['fɔlk-]

Faulconbridge, Philip (*KJ*) 'fɪlɪp 'fɔkənbɹɪdʒ ['fɔlk-]

Faulconbridge, Robert (*KJ*) 'ɹɒbɚt 'fɔkənbɹɪdʒ ['fɔlk-]

fault, -s, -ing, -ed 'fɔlt, -s, -ɪŋ, -ɪd

faultless, -ly, -ness 'fɔltlɪs, -lɪ, -nɪs

fault|y, -ier, -iest, -ily, -iness 'fɔlt|ɪ, -ɪɚ, -ɪɪst, -ɪlɪ, -ɪnɪs

faul' or **fall** (*from 'fault'; see* **'orld**) 'fɔl

Fauste, precor gelida quando pecus omne sub umbra Ruminat (*L.*) (LLL, IV.ii.90) 'faʊstɛ 'pɾɛkɔɚ 'dʒɛlɪda 'kwando 'pɛkus 'omnɛ sub 'umbɹɑ 'rumɪnɑt

Faustus, Doctor (MWW) 'dɒktɚ 'faʊstəs
*Note.—Bardolph's pl. 'Doctor Faustasses' (*MWW, IV.v.67*) is often emended to a more regular 'Doctor Faustuses,' but there may be something to gain (comedically) in retaining a pronunciation that alludes to 'asses' (cf. Giorgio Melchiori's line annotation,* The Arden Shakespeare*, 2000)*

fav|or, -ors, -oring, -ored, -orer/s 'feɪv|ɚ, -ɚz, -ɚɪŋ, -ɚd, -ɚɹɚ/z

favorab|le, -ly, -leness 'feɪvɚɹəb|l̩, -lɪ, -l̩nɪs

favorit|e, -es; -ism 'feɪvɚɹɪt [-vɹɪt], -s; -ɪzəm

fawn, -s, -ing/ly, -ed, -er/s 'fɔn, -z, -ɪŋ/lɪ, -d, -ɚ/z

fay, -s 'feɪ, -z

faz|e (*v.*) (*obsolete var. of 'feaze,' meaning 'to fray' or 'unravel'*), **-es, -ing, -ed** 'feɪz, -ɪz, -ɪŋ, -d

fealty 'fiəltɪ

fear, -s, -ing, -ed 'fɪɚ, -z, -ɹɪŋ, -d

fear|ful, -fully, -fulness 'fɪɚ|fʊl, -fəlɪ, -fʊlnɪs

fearful-bloody 'fɪɚfʊl̩blʌdɪ

fearless, -ly, -ness 'fɪɚlɪs, -lɪ, -nɪs

fearsome, -ly, -ness 'fɪɚsəm, -lɪ, -nɪs

feast, -s, -ing, -ed 'fist, -s, -ɪŋ, -ɪd

Feast, Mistress o' th' (WT) 'mɪstɹɪs əð 'fist

feat, -s, -ly; -er, -est 'fit, -s, -lɪ; -ɚ, -ɪst

feated 'fitɪd
Note.—This word, appearing in CYM, *I.i.49, has been the subject of much debate and is often emended. Interpretations range from 'constrained to propriety,' to the aphaeretic form of 'defeated'*

feather, -s, -ing, -ed 'feðɚ, -z, -ɹɪŋ, -d

featur|e, -es, -ing, -ed; -eless 'fitʃɚ, -z, -ɹɪŋ, -d; -lɪs

February (ADO) 'febɹʊəɹɪ

feckless, -ly, -ness 'feklɪs, -lɪ, -nɪs

federal, -ly 'fedɚɹəl, -ɪ

federary 'fedəɹɪ
Note.—Spelled 'federarie' in the First Folio, this word in WT, *II.i.90 appears nowhere else in S. It is a form of 'feudary.' Its misassociation with the word 'foedary,' and the fact that the meter of the line requires that it be pronounced trisyllabically, leads to the pronunciation given above. An alternate pronunciation (through syncope) might be* ['fedɹəɹɪ]

fee, -s, -ing, -d 'fi, -z, -ɪŋ, -d

Feeble, Francis (*2HIV*) 'fɹænsɪs 'fibl̩

feeb|le, -ling, -led; -ler, -lest, -ly, -leness 'fib|l̩, -lɪŋ, -l̩d; -lɚ, -lɪst, -lɪ, -l̩nɪs

feed, -s, -ing, fed, feeder/s 'fid, -z, -ɪŋ, 'fed, 'fidɚ/z

fee'd 'fid
Note.—This is an editor's common emendation for the phrase 'feed post' (one who is paid or receives a reward for delivering messages) in TN, *I.v.288*

fee-farm 'fiˌfaɚm

fee-grief 'fiˌgɹif ['-'-]

feel, -s, -ing, felt 'fil, -z, -ɪŋ, 'felt

---

i w**e** ɪ cit**y** ɪ h**i**t e l**e**t ɛ d**e**but æ c**a**n a p**a**ss ɝ b**ir**d ʌ h**u**t ə **a**gain ɚ supp**er** u y**ou** ʊ sh**ou**ld o **o**bey ɔ **aw**l ɒ c**o**p ɑ f**a**ther eɪ p**ai**d aɪ h**igh** oʊ g**o** ɔɪ v**oi**ce aʊ f**ou**nd ɪɚ **ear** ɛɚ **air** ʊɚ p**oor** ɔɚ f**ork** ɑɚ p**ark** aɪɚ f**ire** aʊɚ h**our** b b**oy** p p**it** d d**og** t t**op** g g**ot** k k**id** h **how** ɸ be**h**ave dʒ j**ot** tʃ **ch**ew z **z**any s **s**oft v **v**at f **f**at ʒ trea**s**ure ʃ **sh**ip ð **th**e θ **th**in m **m**an n **n**o ŋ ha**ng** l **l**ip j **y**es w **w**on ʍ **wh**ew ɹ **r**igger, ai**r**y ɾ ma**tt**er

feeler, -s 'filɚ, -z

feeling, -s, -ly 'filɪŋ, -z, -lɪ

fee-simple, -s ˌfiˈsɪmpl̩, -z

feet (*pl. of* **foot** *(s.), q.v.*) 'fit

feez|e, -es, -ing, -ed 'fiz ['feĭz], -ɪz, -ɪŋ, -d

Note.—['feĭz] *is sanctioned by American dictionaries, though the many var. spellings represented in the* OED *strongly suggest the primary pronunciation as given above, i.e.,* ['fiz]

fehemently (*from 'vehemently'*) 'fiɪməntlɪ (*see* **dat**)

feign, -s, -ing, -ed, -edly, -edness 'feĭn, -z, -ɪŋ, -d, -ɪd (*adj.*), -ɪdlɪ, -ɪdnɪs

felicitate (*adj., p.p.*) (*archaic, obsolete for 'made happy'*) fəˈlɪsɪteĭt [frˈl-, -tɪt]

felicitat|e (*v.*), **-es, -ing, -ed** fəˈlɪsɪteĭt [frˈl-], -s, -ɪŋ, -ɪd

felicit|y, -ies fəˈlɪsɪt|ɪ [frˈl-], -ɪz

fell, -s, -ing, -ed, -er/s 'fel, -z, -ɪŋ, -d, -ɚ/z

fellest 'felɪst

fellow (F.), -s; -ly 'feloŭ, -z; -lɪ

Note.—*This word is sometimes spoken colloquially as* ['felə]

fellow-councillor 'feloŭˌkaŭnsɪlɚ

fellow-fault 'feloŭˌfɔlt

fellow-partner 'feloŭˌpaʊ̌·tnɚ

fellow-servant 'feloŭˌsɜ·vənt

fellowship, -s 'feloŭ̌ʃɪp, -s

fell|y, -ies 'fel|ɪ, -ɪz

felon, -s 'felən, -z

felonious, -ly, -ness fəˈloŭnĭəs, -lɪ, -nɪs

felt (*s.*), **-s** 'felt, -s

felt (*p.t. of* **feel***, q.v.*) 'felt

fen, -s 'fen, -z

fenc|e, -es, -ing, -ed, -er/s; -eless 'fens, -ɪz, -ɪŋ, -t, -ɚ/z; -lɪs

fennel 'fenl̩

fenny 'fenɪ

fen-sucked 'fenˌsʌkt

Fenton (*MWW*) 'fentən

feodary *or* **fedarie** 'fedɚˌɪɪ

Ferdinand (HVIII, *LLL, TEM*, TS) 'fɜ·dɪˌnænd, 'fɜ·dn̩ənd, 'fɜ·dn̩ænd

fere (*spouse*), **-s** 'fɪɚ, -z

fern, -s 'fɜ·n, -z

fern-seed 'fɜ·n̩ˌsid

ferocious, -ly, -ness fəˈɪoŭʃəs, -lɪ, -nɪs

ferocity fəˈɪɒsɪtɪ

Ferrara (HVIII) fəˈɪɑɪə

Ferrers, Lord (RIII) 'lɔɚ̌·d 'feɪə·z

ferret, -s, -ing, -ed 'feɪɪt, -s, -ɪŋ, -ɪd

fer(r)y (*from 'very'*) 'feɪɪ

Note.—*Evans (in* MWW) *is a Welshman, and speaks in a Welsh accent, if somewhat inconsistently. This is an example of S.'s direction to the actor (by way of semiphonetic spellings) to adopt such an accent, more or less, for the sake of wringing the most satire out of plays on words stemming from confusions with, and corruptions of, English pronunciation via the Welsh tongue*

ferr|y, -ies, -ying, -ied 'feɪɪ, -ɪz, -ɪɪŋ, -d

ferry|man, -men 'feɪɪ|mən, -mən

fertile, -ly, -ness 'fɜ·tl̩, -ɪ, -nɪs

fertile-fresh 'fɜ·tl̩ˈfɪeʃ

ferula (*L.*) 'feɪʊlə ['fɛ·ˈjulɑ]

ferven|cy, -t/ly, -tness 'fɜ·vən|sɪ, -t/lɪ, -tnɪs

fervor 'fɜ·vɚ

fescue, -s 'feskju, -z

Feste (*TN*) 'festɪ

fester, -s, -ing, -ed 'festɚ, -z, -ɪɪŋ, -d

festinate (*adj.*), **-ly** 'festɪnɪt, -lɪ

festinat|e, -es, -ing, -ed 'festɪneĭt, -s, -ɪŋ, -ɪd

festival, -s 'festɪvl̩, -z

fet (*related to, synonym of, or archaic obsolete form of* **fetch** *(cf.* OED*)*) 'fet

fetch, -es, -ing, -ed, -er/s 'fetʃ, -ɪz, -ɪŋ, -t, -ɚ/z

fetch't (*contr. of* **fetch it**) 'fetʃt

fetlock, -s, -ed 'fetlɒk, -s, -t

fetter, -s, -ing, -ed 'feɾɚ, -z, -ɪɪŋ, -d

fett|le, -les, -ling, -led 'fetl̩, -l̩z, -l̩ɪŋ, -l̩d

fever, -s, -ed 'fivɚ, -z, -d

feverish, -ly, -ness 'fivɚ·ɪʃ, -lɪ, -nɪs

feverous, -ly, -ness 'fivɚ·ɪəs, -lɪ, -nɪs

fever-weakened 'fivɚˌwikənd

few, -er, -est, -ness 'fju, -ɚ, -ɪst, -nɪs

fia (*var. of* **via***, meaning 'hurry away'*) 'faĭə

fick|le, -ler, -lest, -leness 'fɪk|l̩, -l̩ɚ, -l̩ɪst, -l̩nɪs

fico (*It.*) (MWW, I.iii.27) 'fiko

fiction, -s 'fɪkʃn̩, -z

fidd|le, -les, -ling, -led, -ler/s 'fɪd|l̩, -l̩z, -l̩ɪŋ [lɪŋ], -l̩d, -lɚ/z [l̩ɚ/z]

fiddle(-)stick, -s 'fɪdl̩stɪk, -s

Fidele (CYM) fɪ'dilɨ

fidelicet (*L.*) (*corruption of 'videlicet',* *q.v.*) (MWW, I.i.138) vɪ'dɛlɨkɛt

Note.—Evans (in MWW *) is a Welsh-man, and speaks in a Welsh accent, if somewhat inconsistently. This may be an example of S.'s direction to the actor (by way of semiphonetic spellings) to adopt such an accent, more or less, for the sake of wringing the most satire out of plays on words stemming from confu-sions with, and corruptions of, English pronunciation via the Welsh tongue*

fidelity fɪ'dɛlɪtɨ [faɪ'd-]

'fidiussed (*from* **Aufidius** *in COR*) 'fɪdɪəst

fie 'faɪ

fief, -s 'fif, -s

fie, foh and fum 'faɪ 'foʊ ˌænd 'fʌm

Note.—This phrase from LEAR, III.iv.179 *is from the familiar (if some-what altered) passage contained in the old children's story of Jack the Giant-killer (Jack and the Beanstalk). 'Fie,' 'foh,' and 'fum' are each cries, or excla-mations, of disgust and indignation— the sort of reaction one might have at smelling an abhorrent odor—and not to be regarded merely as nonsense words for the sake of the ballad's meter and rhyme (cf.* **foh**)

field, -s, -ing, -ed, -er/s 'fild, -z, -ɪŋ, -ɪd, -ɚ/z

field-bed, -s 'fild,bɛd, -z

field-dew 'fild,dju

fiend, -s; -like 'find, -z; -laɪk

fiendish, -ly, -ness 'findɪʃ, -lɨ, -nɪs

fierce, -r, -st, -ly, -ness 'fɪɚs, -ɚ, -ɪst, -lɨ, -nɪs

fier|y, -ily, -iness 'faɪɚ,ɹ|ɨ, -ɪlɨ, -ɨnɪs

fiery-footed 'faɪɚ,ɹɨˌfʊtɪd

fiery-pointed 'faɪɚ,ɹɨˌpɔɪntɪd

Fife (MAC) 'faɪf

fif|e, -es, -ing, -ed, -er/s 'faɪf, -s, -ɪŋ, -t, -ɚ/z

fift (*obsolete form of 'fifth'*) 'fɪft

fifteen fɪf'tin ['--]

fifteenth fɪf'tin̩θ ['--]

fifth, -s 'fɪfθ, -s

fig, -s, -ging, -ged 'fɪg, -z, -ɪŋ, -d

figment, -s 'fɪgmənt, -s

fight, -s, -ing, fought, fighter/s 'faɪt, -s, -ɪŋ, 'fɔt, 'faɪtɚ/z

fig-lea|f, -ves 'fɪg,li|f, -vz

figment, -s 'fɪgmənt, -s

fig's-end 'fɪgz,ɛnd

figur|e (F.), -es, -ing, -ed 'fɪgjɚ, -z, -ɹɪŋ, -d

filament, -s 'fɪləmənt, -s

filbert, -s 'fɪlbɚt, -s

filch, -es, -ing, -ed, -er/s 'fɪltʃ, -ɪz, -ɪŋ, -t, -ɚ/z

fil|e, -es, -ing, -ed 'faɪl, -z, -ɪŋ, -d

filet (*s.*) (*type of lace*), **-s** fɪ'leɪ ['fɪleɪ], -z

filet (*s., v.*) (*s., boneless strip of meat or fish; v., to bone or make into fillets*) (*var. of* **fillet**), **-s, -ing, -ed** fɪ'leɪ ['fɪleɪ], -z, -ɪŋ, -d

filial, -ly, -ness 'fɪlɪəl, -lɨ, -nɪs

fill, -s, -ing/s, -ed, -er/s 'fɪl, -z, -ɪŋ/z, -d, -ɚ/z

fillet, -s, -ing, -ed 'fɪlɪt, -s, -ɪŋ, -ɪd

fillip, -s, -ing, -ed 'fɪlɪp, -s, -ɪŋ, -t

fill|y, -ies 'fɪl|ɨ, -ɨz

film, -s; -y, -ier, -iest, -ily, -iness 'fɪlm, -z; -ɨ, -ɨɚ, -ɨɪst, -ɨlɨ, -ɨnɪs

filter, -s, -ing, -ed 'fɪltɚ, -z, -ɹɪŋ, -d

filth, -s; -y, -ier, -iest, -ily, -iness 'fɪl̩θ, -s; -ɨ, -ɨɚ, -ɨɪst, -ɨlɨ, -ɨnɪs

fin, -s 'fɪn, -z

final, -ly 'faɪnl̩, -ɨ

finalist, -s 'faɪnl̩ɪst, -s

finaliz|e, -es, -ing, -ed 'faɪnl̩aɪz, -ɪz, -ɪŋ, -d

i wɛ ɨ city ɪ hit e let ɛ debut æ can a pass ɝ bird ʌ hut ə again ɚ supper u you
ʊ should o obey ɔ awl ɒ cop ɑ father eɪ paid aɪ high oʊ go ɔɪ voice aʊ found ɪɚ ear
ɛɚ air ʊɚ poor ɔɚ fork ɑɚ park aɪɚ fire aʊɚ hour b boy p pit d dog t top g got
k kid h how fi behave dʒ jot tʃ chew z zany s soft v vat f fat ʒ treasure ʃ ship ð the
θ thin m man n no ŋ hang l lip j yes w won ʍ whew ɹ rigger, airy ɾ matter

finch, -es 'fɪntʃ, -ɪz
find, -s, -ing/s, found, finder/s 'faɪnd, -z, -ɪŋ/z, 'faŏnd, 'faɪndə/z
fin|e, -es, -ing, -ed; -er, -est, -ly, -ness 'faɪn, -z, -ɪŋ, -d; -ə, -ɪst, -lɨ, -nɪs
fine-baited 'faɪn‚beɪtɪd
fineless 'faɪnlɪs
finery 'faɪnə‚ɹɨ
finess|e, -es, -ing, -ed fɪ'nes, -ɪz, -ɪŋ, -t
finger, -s, -ing, -ed 'fɪŋgə, -z, -ɹɪŋ, -d
finic|al, -ally, -alness 'fɪnɪk|ḷ, -əlɨ, -ḷnɪs
finish, -es, -ing, -ed, -er/s 'fɪnɪʃ, -ɪz, -ɪŋ, -t, -ə/z
finite, -ly, -ness 'faɪnaɪt, -lɨ, -nɪs
Finsbury (1HIV) 'fɪnzbə‚ɹɨ, -bɹɨ
fir, -s 'fɝ, -z
firago (*var. of* **virago**) fɪ‚ɹeɪgoŏ [-'ɹɑgoŏ]
fir|e, -es, -ing, -ed, -er/s 'faɪə, -z, -ɹɪŋ, -d, -ɹə/z
firebrand, -s 'faɪə‚bɹænd, -z
fire-drake 'faɪə‚dɹeɪk
fire-eyed 'faɪə‚ɹaɪd
fire-new 'faɪə‚nju ['-'-]
fire-robed 'faɪə‚ɹoŏbd
firm, -s, -ing, -ed; -er, -est, -ly, -ness 'fɝm, -z, -ɪŋ, -d; -ə, -ɪst, -lɨ, -nɪs
firmament, -s 'fɝməmənt, -s
first, -ly 'fɝst, -lɨ
first(-)born 'fɝst‚bɔə̆n
first-fruit, -s 'fɝstfɹut, -s
firstling, -s 'fɝstlɪŋ, -z
firth, -s 'fɝθ, -s
fish, -es, -ing, -ed, -er/s 'fɪʃ, -ɪz, -ɪŋ, -t, -ə/z
fishified 'fɪʃɪfaɪd
fishmonger, -s 'fɪʃ‚mʌŋgə, -z
Fish Street (2HVI) 'fɪʃ ‚stɹit
fish|y, -ier, -iest, -ily, -iness 'fɪʃ|ɨ, -ɪə, -ɹɪst, -ɪlɨ, -ɨnɪs
fisnomy, fisnomie or **fisnamy** (*archaic and obsolete forms of* **physiognomy**) 'fɪznəmɨ
fist, -s, -ing, -ed 'fɪst, -s, -ɪŋ, -ɪd
fistul|a, -as, -ar, -ous 'fɪstjʊl|ə, -əz, -ə, -əs
fit, -s, -ting/ly, -ted, -ter/s; -test, -ly, -ness 'fɪt, -s, -ɪŋ/lɨ, -ɪd, -ə/z ['fɪɾə/z]; -ɪst, -lɨ, -nɪs
fitchew, -s 'fɪtʃu, -z

fitchook or **fichooke** (*rare dialectal var. of* **fitchew***; polecat*)**, -s** 'fɪtʃʊk, -s
fit|ful, -fully, -fulness 'fɪt|fʊl, -fəlɨ, -fʊlnɪs
fitly 'fɪtlɨ
fitment (*a preparation; device*) 'fɪtmənt
Fitzwater or **Fitzwalter** (*RII*) fɪts'wɔ‚ɾə
Note.—Evidently, in S.'s time, the 'l' was traditionally silent in names such as 'Walter' and 'Fitzwalter.' A play on words in 2HVI, IV.i.31–38 *depends on this precept (cf.* **Whitmore, Walter***)*
five-and-thirty ‚faɪvənd'θɝɾɨ
five-and-twenty ‚faɪvənd'twentɨ
five-finger-tied ‚faɪv‚fɪŋgə'taɪd
five-fold 'faɪv‚foŏld
fix, -es, -ing, -ed 'fɪks, -ɪz, -ɪŋ, -t
fixture, -s 'fɪkstʃə, -z
fixure 'fɪkʃə ['fɪksjə]
flag, -s, -ging, -ged 'flæg, -z, -ɪŋ, -d
flak|e, -es, -ing, -ed 'fleɪk, -s, -ɪŋ, -t
flak|y, -ier, -iest, -ily, -iness 'fleɪk|ɨ, -ɪə, -ɹɪst, -ɪlɨ, -ɨnɪs
flagon, -s 'flægən, -z
flam|e, -es, -ing, -ed 'fleɪm, -z, -ɪŋ, -d
flame-colored 'fleɪm‚kʌlə-d
flamen, -s 'fleɪmən [-men], -z
Flaminius (*TIM*) flə'mɪnɪəs
Flanders (3HVI, HVIII) 'flændə-z ['flandə-z]
flank, -s, -ing, -ed, -er/s 'flæŋk, -s, -ɪŋ, -t, -ə/z
flannel, -s, -led 'flænḷ, -z, -d
flap, -s, -ping, -ped, -per/s 'flæp, -s, -ɪŋ, -t, -ə/z
flap(-)dragon, -s, -ed 'flæpdɹægən, -z, -d
flap-eared 'flæp‚ɪə-d
flap(-)jack, -s 'flæp‚dʒæk, -s
flap-mouthed 'flæp‚maŏθt
flar|e, -es, -ing/ly, -ed 'fleə, -z, -ɹɪŋ/lɨ, -d
flash, -es, -ing, -ed, -er/s 'flæʃ, -ɪz, -ɪŋ, -t, -ə/z
flat, -s; -ter, -test, -ly, -ness 'flæt, -s; -ə, -ɪst, -lɨ, -nɪs
flat-long 'flætlɒŋ
flatten, -s, -ing, -ed 'flætṇ, -z, -ɪŋ, -d
flatter, -s, -ing/ly, -ed, -er/s 'flæɾə, -z, -ɹɪŋ/lɨ, -d, -ɹə/z
flatter|y, -ies 'flæɾə|ɹɨ, -ɹɨz

flaunt, -s, -ing/ly, -ed, -er/s 'flɔnt, -s, -ɪŋ/lɪ, -ɪd, -ɚ/z

Flavina (TNK) flə'vaɪ̆nə [-'vinə]

Flavio (JUL) 'fleɪ̆vɪŏ, -vjŏ

Flavius (*JUL*, MEAS, *TIM*) 'fleɪ̆vɪəs, -vjəs

flaw, -s, -ing, -ed 'flɔ, -z, -ɪŋ, -d

flawless, -ly, -ness 'flɔlɪs, -lɪ, -nɪs

flax, -en 'flæks, -ən

flax-wench, -es 'flæks‚wentʃ, -ɪz

flay, -s, -ing, -ed, -er/s 'fleɪ̆, -z, -ɪŋ, -d, -ɚ/z

flea, -s 'fli, -z

Fleance (*MAC*) 'fliəns

fleck, -s, -ing, -ed 'flek, -s, -ɪŋ, -t

fleckled 'flek‚d

fleckted 'flektɪd

fledg|e, -es, -ing, -ed 'fledʒ, -ɪz, -ɪŋ, -d

fledg(e)ling, -s 'fledʒlɪŋ, -z

flee, -s, -ing, fled 'fli, -z, -ɪŋ, 'fled

fleec|e, -es, -ing, -ed, -er/s 'flis, -ɪz, -ɪŋ, -t, -ɚ/z

fleer (*to smirk*)**, -s, -ing, -ed** 'flɪɚ̆, -z, -ɹɪŋ, -d

fleet (**F.**)**, -s, -ing/ly, -ed; -er, -est, -ly, -ness** 'flit, -s, -ɪŋ/lɪ, -ɪd; -ɚ, -ɪst, -lɪ, -nɪs

fleet-foot 'flit‚fʊt

Fleming (MWW) (*inhabitant of Flanders*) 'flemɪŋ

Flemish (MWW) 'flemɪʃ

flesh, -es, -ing, -ed 'fleʃ, -ɪz, -ɪŋ, -t

flesh-fl|y, -ies 'fleʃfl|aɪ̆, -aɪ̆z

flesh|ly, -liness 'fleʃ|lɪ, -lɪnɪs

fleshment 'fleʃmənt

fleshmonger, -s 'fleʃmʌŋgɚ, -z

flesh|y, -iness 'fleʃ|ɪ, -ɪnɪs

fletcher, -s 'fletʃɚ, -z

fleur-de-luce ‚flɜdə'lus [‚flʊɚ̆-, -'ljus]

flew (*p.t. of* **fly**, *q.v.*) 'flu

flew|s, -ed 'flu|z, -d

flex, -es, -ing, -ed 'fleks, -ɪz, -ɪŋ, -t

flexure, -s 'flekʃɚ, -z

Flibbertigibbet (LEAR) 'flɪbɚ‚tɪ‚dʒɪbɪt [-bɚ‚ɡɪ-]

Note.—This name for a fiend, or devil, is variously spelled 'Stiberdigebit,' 'Fliberdegibek,' 'Sirberdegibit,' and 'Sriberdegibit,' but the Folio's version (given above) is now the universally accepted form

flick, -s, -ing, -ed 'flɪk, -s, -ɪŋ, -t

flicker, -s, -ing, -ed 'flɪkɚ, -z, -ɹɪŋ, -d

flier, -s 'flaɪ̆ɚ̆, -z

flight, -s 'flaɪ̆t, -s

flight|y, -ier, -iest, -ily, -iness 'flaɪ̆t|ɪ, -ɪɚ, -ɪɪst, -ɪlɪ, -ɪnɪs

flims|y, -ier, -iest, -ily, -iness 'flɪmz|ɪ, -ɪɚ, -ɪɪst, -ɪlɪ, -ɪnɪs

flinch, -es, -ing/ly, -ed 'flɪntʃ, -ɪz, -ɪŋ/lɪ, -t

fling, -s, -ing, flung 'flɪŋ, -z, -ɪŋ, 'flʌŋ

flint, -s 'flɪnt, -s

Flint Castle (RII) 'flɪnt 'kas‚

flint-hearted 'flɪnt‚hɑɚ̆tɪd

flint|y, -ier, -iest, -ily, -iness 'flɪnt|ɪ, -ɪɚ, -ɪɪst, -ɪlɪ, -ɪnɪs

flip, -s, -ping, -ped 'flɪp, -s, -ɪŋ, -t

flipper, -s 'flɪpɚ, -z

flirt, -s, -ing/ly, -ed 'flɜt, -s, -ɪŋ/lɪ, -ɪd

flirtation, -s flɜ'teɪ̆ʃn, -z

flirtatious, -ly, -ness flɜ'teɪ̆ʃəs, -lɪ, -nɪs

flirt-gill, -s 'flɜt‚dʒɪl, -z

float, -s, -ing, -ed, -er/s; -able 'floʊt, -s, -ɪŋ, -ɪd, -ɚ/z; -əb‚

floatation flo'teɪ̆ʃn

flock, -s, -ing, -ed 'flɒk, -s, -ɪŋ, -t

flog, -s, -ging/s, -ged 'flɒg, -z, -ɪŋ/z, -d

flood, -s, -ing, -ed 'flʌd, -z, -ɪŋ, -ɪd

flood(-)gate, -s 'flʌdgeɪ̆t, -s

floor, -s, -ing, -ed 'flɔɚ̆, -z, -ɹɪŋ, -d

flop, -s, -ping, -ped 'flɒp, -s, -ɪŋ, -t

flopp|y, -ier, -iest, -ily, -iness 'flɒp|ɪ, -ɪɚ, -ɪɪst, -ɪlɪ, -ɪnɪs

flora (**F.**) (WT) 'flɔɹə

floral 'flɔɹəl

Florence (ADO, TS) 'flɒɹəns

Florence, Duke of (*ALL'S*) ‚djuk əv 'flɒɹəns

---

i w**e** ɪ city ɪ h**i**t e l**e**t ɛ d**e**but æ c**a**n a p**a**ss ɝ b**i**rd ʌ h**u**t ə **a**gain ɚ supp**er** u y**ou** ʊ sh**ou**ld o **o**bey ɔ **aw**l ɒ c**o**p ɑ f**a**ther eɪ̆ p**ai**d aɪ̆ h**igh** oŏ **go** ɔɪ̆ v**oi**ce aʊ̆ f**ou**nd ɪɚ̆ **ear** ɛɚ̆ **air** ʊɚ̆ p**oor** ɔɚ̆ f**or**k ɑɚ̆ p**ar**k aɪ̆ɚ̆ f**ire** aʊ̆ɚ̆ h**our** b **b**oy p **p**it d **d**og t **t**op g **g**ot k **k**id h **h**ow fi be**h**ave dʒ **j**ot tʃ **ch**ew z **z**any s **s**oft v **v**at f **f**at ʒ trea**s**ure ʃ **sh**ip ð **th**e θ **th**in m **m**an n **n**o ŋ ha**ng** l **l**ip j **y**es w **w**on ʍ **wh**ew ɹ **r**igger, ai**r**y ɾ ma**tt**er

Florentine (ADO, OTH), **-s** 'flɒɹəntin
  [-taĭn], -z
Florentius (TS) flɒ'ɹenʃəs
florid, -ly, -ness 'flɒɹɪd, -lɪ, -nɪs
Florizel (*WT*) 'flɔɹɪzel ['--,-]
flote, -s 'floŭt, -s
flotsam 'flɒtsəm
flounc|e, -es, -ing, -ed 'flaŭns, -ɪz, -ɪŋ, -t
flounder, -s, -ing, -ed 'flaŭndə˞, -z, -ɹɪŋ, -d
flour, -s, -ing, -ed 'flaŭə˞, -z, -ɹɪŋ, -d
flourish, -es, -ing/ly, -ed 'flʌɹɪʃ, -ɪz, -ɪŋ/lɪ,
  -t
flout, -s, -ing/ly, -ed 'flaŭt, -s, -ɪŋ/lɪ, -ɪd
flow, -s, -ing/ly, -ingness, -ed 'floŭ, -z,
  -ɪŋ/lɪ, -ɪŋnɪs, -d
flower, -s, -ing, -ed, -er/s; -y 'flaŭə˞, -z,
  -ɹɪŋ, -d, -ɹə˞/z; -ɹɪ
flower-de-luce, -s 'flaŭə˞də'lus [-'ljus],
  -ɪz
floweret, -s 'flaŭə˞ɹɪt, -s
flown (*from* **fly**, *q.v.*) 'floŭn
Fluellen (*HV*) flu'elən
  Note.—This the anglicized spelling of
  'Llewelyn'
fluen|cy, -t/ly, -tness 'fluən|sɪ, -t/lɪ, -tnɪs
flung (*from* **fling**, *q.v.*) 'flʌŋ
flurted (*scorned*) 'flɜ˞tɪd
flush, -es, -ing, -ed 'flʌʃ, -ɪz, -ɪŋ, -t
fluster, -s, -ing, -ed 'flʌstə˞, -z, -ɹɪŋ, -d
**flut|e, -es, -ing, -ed; -y, -ier, -iest, -iness;
  -ist/s** 'flut, -s, -ɪŋ, -ɪd; -ɪ, -ɪə˞, -ɪɪst, -ɪnɪs;
  -ɪst/s
Flute, Francis (*MSND*) 'fɹansɪs 'flut
flutter, -s, -ing, -ed, -er/s 'flʌɾə˞, -z, -ɹɪŋ,
  -d, -ɹə˞/z
flux, -es 'flʌks, -ɪz
fluxive 'flʌksɪv
fl|y, -ies, -ying, flew, flown 'fl|aĭ, -aĭz,
  -aĭŋ, 'flu, 'floŭn
fly-bitten 'flaĭ,bɪtn̩
fly-blowing 'flaĭ,bloŭɪŋ
fo (*var. of* **foh**) 'pfɑ ['pfɸ]
foal, -s, -ing, -ed 'foŭl, -z, -ɪŋ, -d
**foam, -s, -ing, -ed; -y, -ier, -iest, -ily,
  -iness** 'foŭm, -z, -ɪŋ, -d; -ɪ, -ɪə˞, -ɪɪst,
  -ɪlɪ, -ɪnɪs
fob, -s, -bing, -bed 'fɒb, -z, -ɪŋ, -d
focative (*from* '*vocative*') 'fɒkətɪv (*see*
  prings)

fodder 'fɒdə˞
foe, -s 'foŭ, -z
foe|man, -men 'foŭ|mən, -mən
fog, -s, -ging, -ged 'fɒg, -z, -ɪŋ, -d
fogg|y, -ier, -iest, -ily, -iness 'fɒg|ɪ, -ɪə˞,
  -ɪɪst, -ɪlɪ, -ɪnɪs
foh (*interj.*) 'pfɑ ['pfɸ]
foible, -s 'fɔĭbl̩, -z
foil, -s, -ing, -ed 'fɔĭl, -z, -ɪŋ, -d
foin, -s, -ing, -ed 'fɔĭn, -z, -ɪŋ, -d
foison, -s 'fɔĭzn̩, -z
foist, -s, -ing, -ed 'fɔĭst, -s, -ɪŋ, -ɪd
Foix (HV) 'fɔĭz [*Fr.* fwɑ]
fold, -s, -ing, -ed, -er/s 'foŭld, -z, -ɪŋ, -ɪd,
  -ə˞/z
foll|y, -ies 'fɒl|ɪ, -ɪz
folly-fall'n 'fɒlɪ,fɔln
fond, -er, -est, -ly, -ness 'fɒnd, -ə˞, -ɪst,
  -lɪ, -nɪs
fond|le, -les, -ling, -led, -ler/s 'fɒnd|l̩, -l̩z,
  -l̩ɪŋ [-lɪŋ], -l̩d, -l̩ə˞/z [-lə˞/z]
font, -s, -al 'fɒnt, -s, -l̩
Fontibell *or* **Fontybell** (ALL'S)
  'fɒntɪ,bel
Fool (*LEAR, TIM*) 'ful
fool (F.), **-s, -ing, -ed** 'ful, -z, -ɪŋ, -d
fool-born 'ful,bɔ˞n
fooler|y, -ies 'fulə˞ɹ|ɪ, -ɪz
fool(-)hard|y, -ier, -iest, -ily, -iness
  'fulfiɑ˞d|ɪ, -ɪə˞, -ɪɪst, -ɪlɪ, -ɪnɪs
foolish, -ly, -ness 'fulɪʃ, -lɪ, -nɪs
foolish-compounded 'fulɪʃkəm'paŭndɪd
  [-kɒm-]
foot (*s.*), **feet** 'fʊt, 'fit
foot (*v.*), **-s, -ing, -ed** 'fʊt, -s, -ɪŋ, -ɪd
football, -s 'fʊtbɔl, -z
footboy, -s 'fʊtbɔĭ, -z
foot(-)cloth 'fʊt,klɒθ
footfall, -s 'fʊtfɔl, -z
foot-landrakers ,fʊt'lændɹeĭkə˞z
fop, -s, -ped 'fɒp, -s, -t
fopper|y, -ies 'fɒpə˞ɹ|ɪ, -ɪz
foppish, -ly, -ness 'fɒpɪʃ, -lɪ, -nɪs
forag|e, -es, -ing, -ed, -er/s 'fɒɹɪdʒ, -ɪz,
  -ɪŋ, -d, -ə˞/z
forbad(e) (*p.t. of* **forbid**, *q.v.*) fɔ˞'bæd
forbear *or* **forebear** (*s.*) (*ancestor*), **-s**
  'fɔ˞bɛə˞, -z
forbear (*v.*), **-s, -ing/ly, forbore,**

forborne fɔɚˈbɛɚ, -z, -ɹɪŋ/lɪ, fɔɚˈbɔɚ, fɔɚˈbɔɚn

forbearance fɔɚˈbɛɚɹəns

forbid, -s, -ing/ly, forbad(e), forbidden fɔɚˈbɪd [fəˈb-], -z, -ɪŋ/lɪ, fɔɚˈbæd, fɔɚˈbɪdn̩

forbod (*archaic form of* forbade) fɔɚˈbɒd

forc|e, -es, -ing, -ed, -er/s; -edly, -edness ˈfɔɚs, -ɪz, -ɪŋ, -t, -ɚ/z; -ɪdlɪ, -ɪdnɪs

forceless ˈfɔɚslɪs

ford, -s, -ing, -ed; -able ˈfɔɚd, -z, -ɪŋ, -ɪd; -əbl̩

Ford, Alice (*MWW*) ˈælɪs ˈfɔɚd

Ford, Frank (*MWW*) ˈfɹæŋk ˈfɔɚd

fordid (*killed*) fɔɚˈdɪd

fordone (*killed*) fɔɚˈdʌn

fore ˈfɔɚ

'fore (*from* before) ˈfɔɚ

fore-advised ˌfɔɚɹədˈvaɪzd

forearm, -s ˈfɔɚɹɑɚm, -z

fore-bemoaned ˈfɔɚbɪˌmoʊnɪd

fore-betrayed ˈfɔɚbɪˌtɹeɪd

forebod|e, -es, -ing/ly, -ed, -er/s fɔɚˈboʊd, -z, -ɪŋ/lɪ, -ɪd, -ɚ/z

forecast (*s.*), -s ˈfɔɚkast, -s ([fɔɚ ˈkast] *in* 3HVI, V.i.42)

forecast (*v.*), -s, -ing, -ed, -er/s ˈfɔɚkast [fɔɚ ˈkast], -s, -ɪŋ, -ɪd, -ɚ/z

for(e)|do, -does, -doing, -did, -done fɔɚˈdu, -ˈdʌz, -ˈduɪŋ, -ˈdɪd, -ˈdʌn

fore-duteous ˌfɔɚˈdjutɪəs

fore-end ˈfɔɚˌend [ˈfɔɚˌɹend]

forefend (*var. of* forfend, *q.v.*) fɔɚˈfend

forefinger, -s ˈfɔɚfɪŋgɚ, -z ([ˌ-ˈ--] *in* RJ, I.iv.56)

fore-foot ˈfɔɚˌfʊt

fore|go, -goes, -going, -went, -gone, -goer/s fɔɚˈgoʊ, -ˈgoʊz, -ˈgoʊɪŋ, -ˈwent, -ˈgɒn ([--] *when used as an adj.*), -ˈgoʊɚ/z

forehand, -ed ˈfɔɚfiænd, -ɪd

'forehand (*from* aforehand) ˈfɔɚfiænd

forehead, -s ˈfɒɹɪd, -z

fore(-)horse, -s ˈfɔɚfiɔɚs, -ɪz

fore|know, -knows, -knowing, -knew, -known fɔɚˈ|noʊ, -ˈnoʊz, -ˈnoʊɪŋ, -ˈnju, -ˈnoʊn

foreknowledge ˌfɔɚˈnɒlɪdʒ

forename, -d ˈfɔɚneɪm, -d

forenoon, -s ˈfɔɚnun, -z

fore-rank ˈfɔɚˌɹæŋk

fore-recited ˈfɔɚˌɹɪˌsaɪtɪd

fore|run, -runs, -running, -ran fɔɚˈ|ɹʌn, -ˈɹʌnz, -ˈɹʌnɪŋ, -ˈɹæn

forerunner, -s ˈfɔɚˌɹʌnɚ, -z
Note.—This word is arguably pronounced [-ˈ--] *in* KJ, II.i.2

foresaid ˈfɔɚsed

foresay (*predict or determine*) fɔɚˈseɪ

fore|see, -sees, -seeing, -saw, -seen fɔɚˈ|si, -ˈsiz, -ˈsiɪŋ, -ˈsɔ, -ˈsin

foreshadow, -s, -ing, -ed, -er/s fɔɚˈʃædoʊ, -z, -ɪŋ, -d, -ɚ/z

foreshow fɔɚˈʃoʊ

foresight, -s ˈfɔɚsaɪt, -s

foreskirt, -s ˈfɔɚskɚt, -s

forespent ˈfɔɚspent [-ˈ-]

fore-spurrer ˈfɔɚspɚɹɚ

forest, -s ˈfɒɹɪst, -s

forestall, -s, -ing, -ed, -er/s fɔɚˈstɔl, -z, -ɪŋ, -d, -ɚ/z

forest-born ˈfɒɹɪstˌbɔɚn

forester, -s ˈfɒɹɪstɚ, -z

forestry ˈfɒɹɪstɹɪ

fore|tell, -tells, -telling, -told, -teller/s fɔɚˈ|tel, -ˈtelz, -ˈtelɪŋ, -ˈtoʊld, -ˈtelɚ/z

forethink, -ing fɔɚˈθɪŋk, -ɪŋ

forethought ˈfɔɚθɔt

forever fɔɚˈɹevɚ [fəˈɹ-]

fore-vouched ˈfɔɚˈvaʊtʃt

forewarn, -s, -ing, -ed fɔɚˈwɔɚn, -z, -ɪŋ, -d

forfeit, -s, -ing, -ed, -er/s; -able ˈfɔɚfɪt, -s, -ɪŋ, -ɪd, -ɚ/z; -əbl̩

forfeiture, -s ˈfɔɚfɪtʃɚ, -z

forfend, -s, -ing, -ed fɔɚˈfend, -z, -ɪŋ, -ɪd

for|get, -gets, -getting, -got, -gotten fəˈ|get, -ˈgets, -ˈgeɾɪŋ, -ˈgɒt, -ˈgɒtn̩

---

i w**e** ɪ cit**y** ɪ h**i**t e l**e**t ɛ d**e**but æ c**a**n a p**a**ss ɝ b**i**rd ʌ h**u**t ə **a**gain ɚ supp**er** u y**ou** ʊ sh**ou**ld o **o**bey ɔ **aw**l ɒ c**o**p ɑ f**a**ther eɪ p**ai**d aɪ h**igh** oʊ g**o** ɔɪ v**oi**ce aʊ f**ou**nd ɪɚ **ear** ɛɚ **air** ʊɚ p**oor** ɔɚ f**ork** ɑɚ p**ark** aɪɚ f**ire** aʊɚ h**our** b **b**oy p **p**it d **d**og t **t**op g g**o**t k **k**id h **h**ow fi be**h**ave dʒ **j**ot tʃ **ch**ew z **z**any s **s**oft v **v**at f **f**at ʒ trea**s**ure ʃ **sh**ip ð **th**e θ **th**in m **m**an n **n**o ŋ ha**ng** l **l**ip j **y**es w **w**on ʍ **wh**ew ɹ **r**igger, ai**r**y ɾ ma**tt**er

forget|ful, -fully, -fulness fɚ-'gɛt|fʊl, -fəlɪ, -fʊlnɪs

forgetive fɚ-'gɛtɪv [-'gɛʃɪv]

for|go, -goes, -going, -went, -gone fɔɚ-|'goʊ, -'goʊz, -'goʊɪŋ, -'wɛnt, -'gɒn

fork, -s, -ing, -ed 'fɔɚ-k, -s, -ɪŋ, -t

forlorn, -ly, -ness fɔɚ-'lɔɚ-n [fɚ-'l-], -lɪ, -nɪs (['--] in TGV, V.iv.12; Sonn. 33.7)

form, -s, -ing, -ed 'fɔɚ-m, -z, -ɪŋ, -d

former, -ly 'fɔɚ-mɚ-, -lɪ

formless, -ness 'fɔɚ-mlɪs, -nɪs

fornicat|e, -es, -ing, -ed, -or/s 'fɔɚ-nɪkeɪt, -s, -ɪŋ, -ɪd, -ɚ/z

fornication ,fɔɚ-nɪ'keɪʃn̩

fornicatress, -es 'fɔɚ-nɪˌkeɪtɹɪs, -ɪz

For(r)es (MAC) 'fɔɹɪs

Note.—It is generally accepted that the Folio's 'Soris' in MAC, I.iii.39 (and throughout in the settings for several of the scenes) is meant to be 'For(r)es,' a town near Inverness in the north-central part of Scotland; and so it is generally emended

Forrest, Miles (RIII) 'maɪlz 'fɔɹɪst

for's (*contr. of* for his) 'fɔɚ-z

for|sake, -sakes, -saking, -sook, -saken fɔɚ-|'seɪk, -'seɪks, -'seɪkɪŋ, -'sʊk, -'seɪkən

forslow fɔɚ-'sloʊ

forsook (*p.t. of* forsake, *q.v.*) fɔɚ-'sʊk

forsooth fɔɚ-'suθ [fɔ's-]

forspent fɔɚ-'spɛnt

forspoke fɔɚ-'spoʊk

forswear, -s, -ing, forswore, forsworn fɔɚ-'swɛɚ-, -z, -ɹɪŋ, fɔɚ-'swɔɚ-, fɔɚ-'swɔɚ-n

fort, -s 'fɔɚ-t, -s

for't (*contr. of* for it) 'fɔɚ-t

forted (*participial adj. meaning fortified*) 'fɔɚ-tɪd

forth 'fɔɚ-θ

Forthright, Master (MEAS) ,mastɚ- 'fɔɚ-θɹaɪt

forthright, -ly, -ness 'fɔɚ-θɹaɪt, -lɪ, -nɪs ([-'-] in TC, III.iii.158)

forthwith ,fɔɚ-θ'wɪð [-'wɪθ] (['--] in MV, I.iii.168)

fortif|y, -ies, -ying, -ied, -ier/s 'fɔɚ-tɪf|aɪ, -aɪz, -aɪɪŋ, -aɪd, -aɪɚ-/z

Fortinbras (*HAM*) 'fɔɚ-tɪnbɹæs [-bɹɑs, -bɹas]

fortitude (F.) 'fɔɚ-tɪtjud [-ɔɚ-ʃɪ-]

fortuna de la guerra (*Sp.*) (LLL, V.ii.526) fɔɹ'tuna dɛ la 'gɛra

fortune, -s, -d; -less 'fɔɚ-tʃʊn [-tʃən, -tjun], -z, -d; -lɪs

Fortune (AC, ALL'S, AYLI, COR, CYM, HAM, HV, 3HVI, KJ, LEAR, LUC, MAC, MV, PER, PP, Sonn. 111; 124, TIM, WT), (Lady) (*personification or surname*) ('leɪdɪ) 'fɔɚ-tjun

fortune(-)tell, -er/s 'fɔɚ-tʃʊnˌtɛl, [-tʃən-], -ɚ-/z

fortunetelling 'fɔɚ-tʃʊnˌtɛlɪŋ [-tʃən-]

forty-thousandfold ,fɔɚ-tɪ'θaʊzəndfoʊld

for|um, -ums, -a 'fɔɚ-|ɹəm, -ɹəmz, -ɹə

forward, -s, -ing, -ed; -ly, -ness, -er, -est 'fɔɚ-wɚ-d, -z, -ɪŋ, -ɪd; -lɪ, -nɪs, -ɚ-, -ɪst

forwearied fɔɚ-'wɪɚ-ɹɪd

foster, -s, -ing, -ed 'fɒstɚ-, -z, -ɹɪŋ, -d

foster-nurse, -s 'fɒstɚ-ˌnɚ-s, -ɪz

fough *or* faugh (*interj.*) (*expression of contempt*) 'fɔ ['φɔ]

fought (*p.t. of* fight, *q.v.*) 'fɔt

foul, -s, -ing, -ed; -er, -est, -ly, -ness 'faʊl, -z, -ɪŋ, -d; -ɚ-, -ɪst, -lɪ, -nɪs

foul-faced 'faʊlˌfeɪst

foul-mouthed 'faʊlˌmaʊðd [-ˌmaʊθt]

foul-play 'faʊlˌpleɪ ['-']

foul-spoken 'faʊlˌspoʊkən

foul-tainted 'faʊl'teɪntɪd

found (*p.t. of* find, *q.v.*) 'faʊnd

founder, -s, -ing, -ed, -er/s 'faʊndɚ-, -z, -ɹɪŋ, -d, -ɹɚ-/z

fount, -s 'faʊnt, -s

Note.—This word and this pronunciation are for the meanings 'fountain' or 'source.' This spelling, however, also occurs as the chiefly British var. of 'font.' In such cases, its pronunciation can become ['fɒnt]

four, -s 'fɔɚ-, -z

four-and-twenty ,fɔɚ-ɹænd'twentɪ

fourscore ,fɔɚ-'skɔɚ- ['-,-]

fourth, -s, -ly 'fɔɚ-θ, -s, -lɪ

foutre *or* footra (*thing of basest quality*) 'fuɹɚ- ['futɹə, 'futʀ]

fox, -es, -ing, -ed 'fɒks, -ɪz, -ɪŋ, -t
foxship 'fɒksʃɪp
fracted 'fɹæktɪd
fraction, -s 'fɹækʃn̩, -z
fragality fɹʊ'gælɪtɨ
fragment (s.), **-s** 'fɹægmənt, -s
fragment (v.), **-s, -ing, -ed** fɹæg'ment, -s, -ɪŋ, -ɪd
fragran|ce, -cy, -t/ly, -tness 'fɹeɪɡɹən|s, -sɨ, -t/lɨ, -tnɪs
frail, -er, -est, -ly, -ness 'fɹeɪl, -ɚ, -ɪst, -lɨ, -nɪs
frailt|y, -ies 'fɹeɪlt|ɨ, -ɨz
fram|e, -es, -ing, -ed, -er/s 'fɹeɪm, -z, -ɪŋ, -d, -ɚ/z
frampold 'fɹæmpl̩d
frampul (var. of **frampold**) 'fɹæmpl̩
France (ALL'S, HV, 3HVI, KJ, LEAR, LLL) 'fɹans
France, Princess of (LLL) 'pɹɪnses əv 'fɹans
Frances (LLL) 'fɹansɪs
franchise, -s 'fɹæntʃaɪz, -ɪz
Francis (ADO, 1HIV, 2HIV, LLL, MSND, RII) 'fɹansɪs
Francis, Friar (ADO) 'fɹaɪɚ 'fɹansɪs
Francisca (MEAS) fɹan'sɪskə
Francisco (HAM, MWW, TEM) fɹan'sɪskoŭ
François (HV, MWW) fɹan'swɑ
Note.—In HV, V.ii.199, this is an old form of 'français,' meaning the Fr. language. In MWW, II.iii.25, it is a modernized interpretation of the Quarto's 'Francoyes,' which (as a pronunciation-spelling) follows S.'s penchant for anglicizing foreign words, particularly the Fr. ones (see 'Shakespeare's Verse' § 1.8 of this dictionary). There might be some comedic value to holding on to the Quarto's suggested pronunciation, i.e., [fɹæŋ'kɔɪs, -'kɔɪz], since the Host is amusing himself at the Fr. Doctor Caius'

expense—a Frenchman, by the way, who consistently mispronounces English
Frank (MWW) 'fɹæŋk
frank (F.), **-er, -est, -ly, -ness; -s, -ing, -ed** 'fɹæŋk, -ɚ, -ɪst, -lɨ, -nɪs; -s, -ɪŋ, -t
Frankfort (MV) 'fɹæŋkfɚt
franklin, -s 'fɹæŋklɪn, -z
frantic, -ally, -ness, -ly 'fɹæntɪk, -əlɨ, -nɪs, -lɨ
Frateretto (LEAR) ˌfɹatə'ɹetoŭ
fraud, -s 'fɹɔd, -z
fraudful 'fɹɔdfʊl
fraught, -ing, -ed 'fɹɔt, -ɪŋ, -ɪd
fraughtage 'fɹɔtɪdʒ
fray, -s, -ing, -ed 'fɹeɪ, -z, -ɪŋ, -d
freck|le, -les, -ling, -led 'fɹek|l̩, -l̩z, -l̩ɪŋ [-lɪŋ], -l̩d
freckle-faced 'fɹekl̩feɪst
Frederick, Duke (AYLI) 'djuk 'fɹedɚɹɪk
Note.—In AYLI, I.ii.223, this name is trisyllabic; in AYLI, V.iv.153, it is disyllabic, i.e., ['fɹedɹɪk]
free, -r, -st, -ly; -s, -ing, -d 'fɹi, -ɚ, -ɪst, -lɨ; -z, -ɪŋ, -d
free-hearted 'fɹiˌhaɚtɪd
freelier 'fɹilɪɚ
freeness 'fɹinɪs
freestone-colored 'fɹistoŭnˌkʌlɚd
free't (contr. of **free it**) 'fɹit
Freetown (RJ) 'fɹitaŏn
freez|e, -es, -ing/s, froze/n, freezer/s 'fɹiz, -ɪz, -ɪŋ/z, 'fɹoŭz/n̩, 'fɹizɚ/z
freight, -s, -ing, -ed, -er/s 'fɹeɪt, -s, -ɪŋ, -ɪd, -ɚ/z
French (3HVI, PER) 'fɹentʃ
French|man (ALL'S, HV, KJ), **-men** 'fɹentʃ|mən, -mən
Frenchwoman (2HVI, 3HVI) 'fɹentʃwʊmən
frenz|y, -ies, -ying, -ied 'fɹenz|ɨ, -ɨz, -ɨɪŋ, -ɨd
frequent (adv.), **-ly, -ness** 'fɹikwənt, -lɨ, -nɪs

---

i wɛ ɨ citɨ ɪ hɪt e lɛt ɛ dɛbut æ cæn a pæss ɝ bɪrd ʌ hʌt ə agaɪn ɚ suppɚr u yóu
ʊ shoŭld o obey ɔ awl ɒ cop ɑ father eɪ paɪd aɪ hɪgh oŭ go ɔɪ voɪce aŏ foŭnd ɪɚ ear
ɛɚ air ʊɚ poor ɔɚ fork aɚ park aɪɚ fire aŏɚ hour b boy p pit d dog t top g got
k kid h how fi behave dʒ jot tʃ chew z zany s soft v vat f fat ʒ treasure ʃ ship ð the
θ thin m man n no ŋ hang l lip j yes w won ʍ whew ɹ rigger, airy ɾ matter

frequent (*v.*), **-s, -ing, -ed, -er/s** fɪɪ'kwent, -s, -ɪŋ, -ɪd, -ə·/z

fresh, -er, -est, -ly, -ness 'fɹeʃ, -ə·, -ɪst, -lɪ, -nɪs

freshen, -s, -ing, -ed 'fɹeʃn̩, -z, -ɪŋ, -d

fresh-new 'fɹeʃˌnju

fret, -s, -ting, -ted, -ter/s 'fɹet, -s, -ɪŋ, -ɪd, -ə·/z

fret|ful, -fully, -fulness 'fɹet|fʊl, -fʊlɪ, -fʊlnɪs

fretten (*archaic form of* **fretted**) 'fɹetn̩

Friday (AYLI, MEAS, TC), **-s** 'fɹaɪdɪ [-deɪ̆], -z

friend, -s, -ed 'fɹend, -z, -ɪd

friendless, -ness 'fɹendlɪs, -nɪs

friendl|y, -ier, -iest, -iness 'fɹendl|ɪ, -ɪə·, -ɪɪst, -ɪnɪs

friendship, -s 'fɹendʃɪp, -s

frieze, -s 'fɹiz, -ɪz

frigate, -s 'fɹɪgɪt, -s

fright, -s, -ing, -ed 'fɹaɪt, -s, -ɪŋ, -ɪd

frigid, -ly, -ness 'fɹɪdʒɪd, -lɪ, -nɪs

frigidity fɹɪ'dʒɪdɪtɪ

fring|e, -es, -ing, -ed; -eless 'fɹɪndʒ, -ɪz, -ɪŋ, -d; -lɪs

fripper|y, -ies 'fɹɪpə·ɹ|ɪ, -ɪz

frisk, -s, -ing, -ed, -er/s 'fɹɪsk, -s, -ɪŋ, -t, -ə·/z

friskin (*lively, playful action*), **-s** 'fɹɪskɪn, -z

frisk|y, -ier, -iest, -ily, -iness 'fɹɪsk|ɪ, -ɪə·, -ɪɪst, -ɪlɪ, -ɪnɪs

fritter, -s, -ing, -ed 'fɹɪɡ̊ə·, -z, -ɹɪŋ, -d

frivolous, -ly, -ness 'fɹɪvl̩əs, -lɪ, -nɪs

Friz (*TNK*) 'fɹɪz

fro 'fɹoŭ

frock, -s 'fɹɒk, -s

frog, -s 'fɹɒg, -z

Frogmore (MWW) 'fɹɒgmɔ·

Froissart (1HVI) 'fɹɔɪ̆saɾ·t

frolic, -s, -king, -ked 'fɹɒlɪk, -s, -ɪŋ, -t

frolicsome, -ness 'fɹɒlɪksəm, -nɪs

from 'fɹɒm (*strong form*), 'fɹəm (*weak form*)

from's (*contr. of* **from us**) 'fɹɒms (*strong form*), 'fɹəms (*weak form*)

from't (*contr. of* **from it**) 'fɹɒmt (*strong form*), 'fɹəmt (*weak form*)

frond, -s 'fɹɒnd, -z

front, -s, -ing, -ed; -less 'fɹʌnt, -s, -ɪŋ, -ɪd; -lɪs

frontage, -s 'fɹʌntɪdʒ, -ɪz

frontal, -s; -ly 'fɹʌntl̩, -z; -ɪ

frontier, -s fɹʌn'tɪɹ̆ [fɹɒn-, '--], -z

frontispiece, -s 'fɹʌntɪsˌpis, -ɪz

frontlet, -s 'fɹʌntlɪt, -s

frost, -s, -ing, -ed 'fɹɒst, -s, -ɪŋ, -ɪd

frost|y, -ier, -iest, -ily, -iness 'fɹɒst|ɪ, -ɪə·, -ɪɪst, -ɪlɪ, -ɪnɪs

frosty-spirited 'fɹɒstɪˌspɪɹɪtɪd (*cf.* **spirit**)

froth, -s, -ing, -ed 'fɹɔθ ['fɹɒθ], -s, -ɪŋ, -t

Froth, Master (*MEAS*) ˌmastə· 'fɹɔθ

froth|y, -ier, -iest, -ily, -iness 'fɹɔθ|ɪ ['fɹɒθ|ɪ], -ɪə·, -ɪɪst, -ɪlɪ, -ɪnɪs

froward, -ly, -ness 'fɹoŭə·d, -lɪ, -nɪs

frown, -s, -ing/ly, -ed, -er/s 'fɹaŭn, -z, -ɪŋ/lɪ, -d, -ə·/z

froze (*from* **freeze**, *q.v.*), **-n** 'fɹoŭz, -n̩

fructif|y, -ies, -ying, -ied 'fɹʌktɪf|aɪ̆ ['fɹʊk-], -aɪ̆z, -aɪ̆ɪŋ, -aɪ̆d

frug|al, -ally, -alness 'fɹug|l̩, -əlɪ, -l̩nɪs

fruit, -s, -ing, -ed 'fɹut, -s, -ɪŋ, -ɪd

fruit-dish, -es 'fɹutˌdɪʃ, -ɪz

fruiterer, -s 'fɹutə·ɹə· [-uɾə·-], -z

fruit|ful, -fully, -fulness 'fɹut|fʊl, -fʊlɪ, -fʊlnɪs

fruition fɹu'ɪʃn̩

fruitless, -ly, -ness 'fɹutlɪs, -lɪ, -nɪs

fruit-tree 'fɹutˌtɹi

frush, -es, -ing, -ed 'fɹʌʃ, -ɪz, -ɪŋ, -t

frustrate (*adj.*) 'fɹʌstɹɪt

frustrat|e (*v.*), **-es, -ing, -ed** 'fɹʌstɹeɪ̆t, -s, -ɪŋ, -ɪd

frutify (*perhaps a corruption of and/or confusion with* **fructify**) 'fɹʌtɪfaɪ̆

fr|y, -ies, -ying, -ied 'fɹ|aɪ̆, -aɪ̆z, -aɪ̆ɪŋ, -aɪ̆d

fub (*var. of* **fob**) (*with 'off' means 'tricked,' 'cheated,' or 'deceived'*), **-s, -bing, -bed** 'fʌb, -z, -ɪŋ, -d

fudg|e, -es, -ing, -ed 'fʌdʒ, -ɪz, -ɪŋ, -d

fuel, -s, -(l)ing, -(l)ed 'fjʊəl ['fjul], -z, -ɪŋ, -d

fugue, -s 'fjug, -z

fulfill, -s, -ing, -ed fʊl'fɪl, -z, -ɪŋ, -d

full-acorned 'fʊl'eɪ̆kɔ·nd

fullam (*s.*) (*var. form of 'fulham'; loaded die/dice*), **-s** 'fʊləm, -z

full-charged 'fʊlˌtʃɑɝ·dʒd
fuller, -s 'fʊlə·, -z
full-fed 'fʊlˌfed
full-flowing 'fʊlˌfloŭɪŋ
full-fortuned 'fʊlˈfɔɝ·tʃʊnd [-tʃənd,
 -tjund]
full-fraught 'fʊlˈfɹɔt (*when att.,* ['--])
full-gorged 'fʊlˌgɔɝ·dʒd
full-hearted 'fʊlˌhɑɝ·ɾɪd
full-manned ˌfʊl'mænd
full-winged 'fʊlˌwɪŋd
fulsome, -ly, -ness 'fʊlsəm, -lɪ, -nɪs
Fulvia (AC) 'fʌlvjə, -vɪə
fumb|le, -les, -ling, -led, -ler/s 'fʌmb|l̩,
 -l̩z, -l̩ɪŋ [-lɪŋ], -l̩d, -lə·/z [-lə·/z]
fum|e, -es, -ing, -ed 'fjum, -z, -ɪŋ, -d
fumiter 'fjumɪtə·
 *Note.—This word appears in the Folio
 version of* LEAR, IV.iv.3 *as 'fenitar'*
 ['fenɪtə·], *and in the Quarto version as
 'femiter'* ['femɪtə·]. *All three specimens
 ('fumiter,' 'fenitar,' and 'femiter') are
 assumed to be forms of 'fumitory,' a
 weed also known as 'smoke of the earth'*
fumitory 'fjumɪtəɹɪ
fun 'fʌn
function, -s, -ing, -ed 'fʌŋkʃn̩, -z, -ɪŋ, -d
fund, -s, -ing, -ed 'fʌnd, -z, -ɪŋ, -ɪd
funeral, -s 'fjunəɹəl, -z
funereal fju'nɪɝ·ɹɪəl [fjʊ'n-]
funnel, -s, -(l)ing, -(l)ed 'fʌnl̩, -z, -ɪŋ, -d
funn|y, -ier, -iest, -ily, -iness 'fʌn|ɪ, -ɪə·,
 -ɪɪst, -ɪlɪ, -ɪnɪs
fur, -s, -ring, -red 'fɝ·, -z, -ɪɪŋ, -d
furbish, -es, -ing, -ed 'fɝ·bɪʃ, -ɪz, -ɪŋ, -t
furious, -ly, -ness 'fjʊɝ·ɹɪəs, -lɪ, -nɪs
furl, -s, -ing, -ed 'fɝ·l, -z, -ɪŋ, -d
furlong, -s 'fɝ·lɒŋ, -z
furlough, -s 'fɝ·loŭ, -z
furnace, -s 'fɝ·nɪs, -ɪz
furnish, -es, -ing/s, -ed, -er/s 'fɝ·nɪʃ, -ɪz,
 -ɪŋ/z, -t, -ə·/z
furniture 'fɝ·nɪtʃə·
Furnival (1HVI) 'fɝ·nɪvəl

furrow, -s, -ing, -ed; -y 'fʌɹoŭ, -z, -ɪŋ, -d;
 -ɪ
furrow-weeds 'fʌɹoŭˌwidz
furr|y, -ier, -iest, -iness 'fɝ·ɹ|ɪ, -ɪə·, -ɪɪst,
 -ɪnɪs
further, -s, -ing, -ed, -er/s 'fɝ·ðə·, -z, -ɪɪŋ,
 -d, -ɪə·/z
furtherance 'fɝ·ðəɹəns
furthest 'fɝ·ðɪst
furtive, -ly, -ness 'fɝ·tɪv, -lɪ, -nɪs
fur|y (F.) (3HVI, TIT), **-ies** 'fjʊɝ·ɹ|ɪ, -ɪz
fury-innocent 'fjʊɝ·ɹɪ'ɪnəsn̩t
furze, -s 'fɝ·z, -ɪz
furzebush, -es 'fɝ·zbʊʃ, -ɪz
fus|e, -es, -ing, -ed 'fjuz, -ɪz, -ɪŋ, -d
fusion, -s 'fjuʒn̩, -s
fuss, -es, -ing, -ed, -er/s 'fʌs, -ɪz, -ɪŋ, -t,
 -ə·/z
fuss|y, -ier, -iest, -ily, -iness 'fʌs|ɪ, -ɪə·,
 -ɪɪst, -ɪlɪ, -ɪnɪs
fustian 'fʌstɪən
fustigat|e, -es, -ing, -ed 'fʌstɪgeɪ̆t, -s, -ɪŋ,
 -ɪd
fustigation, -s ˌfʌstɪ'geɪ̆ʃn̩, -z
fustilarian ˌfʌstɪ'lɛɝ·ɹɪən
 *Note.—This word, appearing in 2HIV,
 II.i.58, is a mystery. It seems to be a
 nonce-word of a contemptuous nature,
 perhaps of a person who resembles that
 which smells of mildew (fustiness)*
fust|y, -ier, -iest, -ily, -iness 'fʌst|ɪ, -ɪə·,
 -ɪɪst, -ɪlɪ, -ɪnɪs
fut (*interj.*) 'fʊt
 Note.—This word in LEAR, I.ii.131
 *(Quarto only) is taken to be a profane
 oath, short for 'Christ's foot,' not a var.
 spelling of the echoic sound, 'phut'*
 ['fʌt]
futtock, -s 'fʌɾək, -s
future, -s 'fjutʃə·, -z
futurely 'fjutʃə·lɪ
futuristic ˌfjutʃʊ'ɹɪstɪk
futurit|y, -ies fju'tjʊɝ·ɹɪt|ɪ, -ɪz
fuzz, -es, -ing, -ed 'fʌz, -ɪz, -ɪŋ, -d

i w**e** ɪ city ɪ h**i**t e l**e**t ɛ d**e**but æ c**a**n a p**a**ss ɝ b**i**rd ʌ h**u**t ə **a**gain ə· supp**er** u y**ou**
ʊ sh**ou**ld o **o**bey ɔ **a**wl ɒ c**o**p ɑ f**a**ther eɪ̆ p**ai**d aɪ h**i**gh oŭ g**o** ɔɪ v**oi**ce aŭ f**ou**nd ɪɝ̆ **ear**
ɛɝ̆ **air** ʊɝ̆ p**oor** ɔɝ̆ f**or**k ɑɝ̆ p**ar**k aɪɝ̆ f**ire** aʊɝ̆ **hour** b **b**oy p **p**it d **d**og t **t**op g **g**ot
k **k**id h **h**ow fɪ be**h**ave dʒ **j**ot tʃ **ch**ew z **z**any s **s**oft v **v**at f **f**at ʒ trea**s**ure ʃ **sh**ip ð **th**e
θ **th**in m **m**an n **n**o ŋ ha**ng** l **l**ip j **y**es w **w**on ʌ **wh**ew ɹ **r**igger, ai**r**y ɾ ma**tt**er

fuzz|y, -ier, -iest, -ily, -iness 'fʌz|ɨ, -ɪəˑ,
  -ɪɪst, -ɪlɨ, -ɪnɪs

Gg

G (*the letter*), **-'s** 'dʒiː, -z
gab, -s, -bing, -bed, -ber/s 'gæb, -z, -ɪŋ,
  -d, -əˑ/z
gabb|le, -les, -ling, -led, -ler/s 'gæb|ḷ, -ḷz,
  -ḷɪŋ, -ḷd, -ləˑ/z [-ḷəˑ/z]
gaberdine, -s 'gæbəˑdin [ˌ-'-], -z
gable, -s, -d 'geɪbḷ, -z, -d
Gabriel (TS) 'geɪbɹɪəl, -bɹəl
  Note.—In TS, IV.i.120, this name is
  disyllabic, i.e., ['geɪbɹəlz], *in accor-*
  dance with the First Folio's spelling
  'Gabrels,' and the meter of the verse line
gad, -s, -ding, -ded 'gæd, -z, -ɪŋ, -ɪd
gadabout, -s 'gædəbaʊt, -s
gadfl|y, -ies 'gædfl|aɪ, -aɪz
gadget, -s, -ry 'gædʒɪt, -s, -ɹɨ
Gadshill (*1HIV*, 2HIV) 'gædzfɪl
Gad's Hill (1HIV) 'gædz 'hɪl
gadzooks ˌgæd'zuks
Gaelic 'geɪlɪk ['gælɪk]
gaff, -s, -ing, -ed 'gæf, -s, -ɪŋ, -t
gaffer, -s 'gæfəˑ, -z
gag, -s, -ging, -ged 'gæg, -z, -ɪŋ, -d
gag|e (*including aphaeretic form of*
  engage), **-es, -ing, -ed** 'geɪdʒ, -ɪz, -ɪŋ, -d
gaggle, -s 'gægḷ, -z
gaiet|y, -ies 'geɪɪt|ɨ, -ɪz
gaily *or* **gayly** 'geɪlɨ
gain, -s, -ing/s, -ed, -er/s; -able, -less
  'geɪn, -z, -ɪŋ/z, -d, -əˑ/z; -əbḷ, -lɪs
gaingiving 'geɪnˌgɪvɪŋ
gain|say, -says, -saying, -sayed, -said,
  -sayer/s ˌgeɪn|'seɪ, -'seɪz, [-'sez], -'seɪɪŋ,
  -'seɪd, -'seɪd [-'sed], -'seɪəˑ/z (['--] *in*
  WT, III.ii.56)
'gainst (*from* **against**) 'genst
gait, -s 'geɪt, -s
gaiter, -s 'geɪtəˑ ['geɪɣəˑ], -z
gala, -s 'geɪlə ['gɑlə, 'galə], -z
galactic gə'læktɪk
Galathe (TC) 'gæləθɨ
galax|y, -ies 'gæləks|ɨ, -ɪz

gale, -s 'geɪl, -z
Galen (ALL'S, COR, 2HIV, MWW)
  'geɪlɪn [-lən]
Galilee 'gælɪli
gall, -s, -ing, -ed 'gɔl, -z, -ɪŋ, -d
gallant (*s.*), **-s** 'gælənt, -s
gallant (*adj.*), **-ly, -ness** 'gælənt, -lɨ, -nɪs
gallantry 'gæləntɹɨ
gallant-springing 'gælənt'spɹɪŋɪŋ
galleon, -s 'gælɪən [-ljən], -z
galler|y, -ies 'gæləɹ|ɨ, -ɪz
galley, -s 'gælɨ, -z
Gallia (CYM, HV, 1HVI, 3HVI) 'gælɪə,
  -ljə
Gallian (CYM, 1HVI) 'gæljən
galliard, -s 'gæljəˑd [-lɹɑɝˑd], -z
galliass (*sea vessel*), **-es** 'gælɪæs, -ɪz
gallimaufr|y, -ies ˌgælɪ'mɔfɹ|ɨ, -ɪz
gallon, -s 'gælən, -z
gallop, -s, -ing, -ed, -er/s 'gæləp, -s, -ɪŋ,
  -t, -əˑ/z
gallow (*frighten*) 'gæloʊ
Galloway (2HIV) 'gæluweɪ
Gallo(w)glasses (2HVI, MAC)
  'gæloʊˌglasɪz
gallows, -es 'gæloʊz, -ɪz
Gallus (*AC*) 'gæləs
galore gə'lɔɝˑ
Gam, Davy (HV) 'deɪvɨ 'gæm
gambit, -s 'gæmbɪt, -s
gamb|ol, -ols, -olling, -olled 'gæmb|ḷ, -ḷz,
  -ḷɪŋ [-əlɪŋ], -ḷd
gam|e, -es; -er, -est, -ely, -eness; -ing, -ed
  'geɪm, -z; -əˑ, -ɪst, -lɨ, -nɪs; -ɪŋ, -d
gamesome, -ly, -ness 'geɪmsəm, -lɨ, -nɪs
gamester, -s 'geɪmstəˑ, -z
gamma, -s 'gæmə, -z
gammon, -s, -ing, -ed 'gæmən, -z, -ɪŋ, -d
gamut, -s 'gæmət, -s
gam|y, -ier, -iest, -iness 'geɪm|ɨ, -ɪəˑ, -ɪɪst,
  -ɪnɪs
(')gan (*aphaeretic form of* **began**) 'gæn
gander, -s 'gændəˑ, -z
gang, -s, -ing, -ed 'gæŋ, -z, -ɪŋ, -d
gangren|e, -es, -ing, -ed 'gæŋgɹin, -z, -ɪŋ,
  -d
gangrenous 'gæŋgɹɪnəs
Ganymede (*AYLI*, TNK) 'gænɪmid (*alias*
  Rosalind in AYLI)

gaol, -s, -ing, -ed, -er/s 'dʒeĭl, -z, -ɪŋ, -d, -ɚ/z

gap, -s 'gæp, -s

gap|e, -es, -ing, -ed, -er/s 'geĭp, -s, -ɪŋ, -t, -ɚ/z

gar (*from 'God'*) 'gaʀ ['gaɚ] (*see Note for* **varld**)

garb, -s, -ed 'gaɚb, -z, -d

garbage 'gaɚbɪdʒ

garboil, -s 'gaɚbɔĭl, -z

gard|en, -ens, -ening, -ened, -ener/s 'gaɚd|n̩, -n̩z, -nɪŋ [-nɪŋ], -n̩d, -nɚ/z

garden-hou|se, -ses 'gaɚdn̩haŏ|s, -zɪz

Gardiner, Stephen (*HVIII*) 'stivn̩ 'gaɚdnɚ [-dn̩ɚ]

gardon 'gaɚdn̩

Note.—This spelling is an obscure var. form of 'guerdon' (q.v.) rather than the Fr. word for a type of roach; however, LLL, III.i.163–170 might present a clever play on words, regarding bugs, since Berowne's line immediately following Costard's 'gardon' contains the word 'beadle,' very close in sound to 'beetle.' It's worthwhile reminding the reader that LLL takes place in Navarre, a kingdom in the southwestern part of France, and that Berowne and his companions are courting the Princess of France and her ladies. In this context, Elizabethan audiences might have been prepared for plays on words stemming from confusions with, and corruptions of, Fr. pronunciations and accents. If one chooses to play on these words, it's advisable in both 'guerdon' and 'gardon' to accept a pronunciation of [-dən] or, better yet, [-dɒn] in the second syllable

Gargantua (AYLI) gaɚ'gæntjʊə [-tʃʊə]

gargoyle, -s 'gaɚgɔĭl, -z

Gargrave, Sir Thomas (*1HVI*) ‚sɚ 'tɒməs 'gaɚgɹeĭv

garish, -ly, -ness 'gɛɚɹɪʃ, -lɨ, -nɪs

garland, -s 'gaɚlənd, -z

garlic, -ky 'gaɚlɪk, -ɨ

garlic-eater, -s 'gaɚlɪkˌiɾɚ, -z

garment, -s, -ed 'gaɚmənt, -s, -ɪd

Garmombles, Cozen(-) (MWW) 'kʌzn̩ 'dʒɜ·mʌmbl̩z ['dʒaɚm-, ‚-'--]

*Note.—This appellation, spoken by Evans in MWW, IV.v.74, appears only in the First and Second Quartos, later emended in the First Folio to 'Cozen-Iermans' (Jermans). Its meaning has confounded editors for centuries, even to this day. There are some useful suggestions as to its meaning in Giorgio Melchiori's line annotation (*The Arden Shakespeare, 2000*), and in Francis Griffin Stokes' Who's Who in Shakespeare; The Characters, Proper Names, and Plot Sources in the Plays and Poems, Studio Editions Ltd, 1992, p. 122. Until a more definitive light is shed on the matter, however, it must be acknowledged that the pronunciations proffered above are entirely conjectural*

garner, -s, -ing, -ed 'gaɚnɚ, -z, -ɹɪŋ, -d

garnet, -s 'gaɚnɪt, -s

garnish, -es, -ing, -ed, -ment/s 'gaɚnɪʃ, -ɪz, -ɪŋ, -t, -mənt/s

garret, -s 'gæɹɪt [-ɹət], -s

garris|on, -ons, -oning, -oned 'gæɹɪs|ən, -ənz, -nɪŋ, -ənd

Garter (*HVIII*, MWW) 'gaɚɾɚ

garter (G.), -s, -ing, -ed 'gaɚtɚ ['gaɚɾɚ], -z, -ɹɪŋ, -d

gash, -es, -ing, -ed 'gæʃ, -ɪz, -ɪŋ, -t

gaskin, -s 'gæskɪn, -z

gat (*aphaeretic form of* **begat**) 'gæt

gat|e, -es, -ing, -ed 'geĭt, -s, -ɪŋ, -ɪd

gath|er, -ers, -ering, -ered, -erer/s 'gæð|ɚ, -ɚz, -ɚɹɪŋ, -ɚd, -ɚɹɚ/z

gaud, -s, -ed 'gɔd, -z, -ɪd

gaud|y, -ier, -iest, -ily, -iness 'gɔd|ɨ, -ɪɚ, -ɪɪst, -ɪlɨ, -ɪnɪs

gaug|e, -es, -ing, -ed 'geĭdʒ, -ɪz, -ɪŋ, -d

i we ɪ city ɪ hit e let ɛ debut æ can a pass ɜ· bird ʌ hut ə again ɚ supper u you ʊ should o obey ɔ awl ɒ cop ɑ father eĭ paid aĭ high oŏ go ɔĭ voice aŏ found ɪɚ· ear ɛɚ· air ʊɚ· poor ɔɚ· fork aɚ· park aĭɚ· fire aŏɚ· hour b boy p pit d dog t top g got k kid h how ɸ behave dʒ jot tʃ chew z zany s soft v vat f fat ʒ treasure ʃ ship ð the θ thin m man n no ŋ hang l lip j yes w won ʍ whew ɹ rigger, airy ɾ matter

Gaul (MWW), -s; -ish 'gɔl, -z; -ɪʃ
Gaultier *or* Gualtier (2HVI) goŏtjə·
Gaultree Forest (2HIV) 'gɔltɹi [-tɹɨ]
'fɒɹıst
gaunt (G.), -er, -est, -ly, -ness 'gɔnt, -ə·,
-ıst, -lɨ, -nıs
Gaunt, John a (2HIV) 'dʒɒn ə 'gɔnt
Gaunt, John of (1HVI, 2HVI, 3HVI, *RII*)
'dʒɒn əv 'gɔnt
gauntlet, -s, -ed 'gɔntlıt, -s, -ıd
gawd, -s 'gɔd, -z
*Note.—'Gawds,' appearing in TS, II.i.3,
is a var. form of 'gauds,' meaning
'baubles,' but is typically emended to
'goods'*
Gawsey, Sir Nicholas (1HIV) ,sɜ·
'nikələs (-kl-) 'gɔzɨ ['gɔsɨ]
gay, -s; -er, -est, gaily, gayness 'geĭ, -z;
-ə·, -ıst, 'geĭlɨ, 'geĭnıs
gaz|e, -es, -ing, -ed, -er/s 'geĭz, -ız, -ıŋ,
-d, -ə·/z
gear, -s, -ing, -ed 'gɪə·, -z, -ɹıŋ, -d
geck(e) (*fool*), -s 'gek, -s
geese (*pl. of* goose, *q.v.*) 'gis
geld, -s, -ing, -ed, gelt 'geld, -z, -ıŋ, -ıd,
'gelt
gelding, -s 'geldıŋ, -z
gelt (*Yiddish slang for money; p.t. and
p.p. of* geld, *q.v.*) 'gelt
gem, -s 'dʒem, -z
gemini (*L.*) (MWW, II.ii.8) 'dʒemɨnaĭ
*Note.—This pronunciation enables the
modern listener to grasp that the speaker
is referring to 'a pair,' whereas* ['dʒɛmɨni]
(or the more anglicized ['dʒɛmɪnɨ]*) might
not succeed as well. In this instance, it is
doubtful that Falstaff is speaking
(strictly) Latin, any more than he is when
he uses 'gratis' only eight lines later*
gemini (G.) 'dʒemɪnaĭ [-ni]
gender, -s, -ing, -ed 'dʒendə·, -z, -ɹıŋ, -d
gene, -s 'dʒin, -z
gener|al, -als, -ally 'dʒenəɹ|əl ['dʒenɹ|əl],
-əlz, -əlɨ
general (G.) (*rank*), -s 'dʒenɹəl, -z
generat|e, -es, -ing, -ed, -or/s 'dʒenə·ɹeĭt,
-s, -ıŋ, -ıd, -ə·/z
generation, -s ,dʒenə·ɹeĭʃn̩, -z
generative 'dʒenə·ɹətıv

generosity ,dʒenə·'ɹɒsıtɨ
generous, -ly, -ness 'dʒenə·ɹəs, -lɨ, -nıs
gene|sis (G.), -ses 'dʒenı|sıs, -sɨz
genetive, -s 'dʒenıtıv, -z
*genitivo, hujus [. . .] horum, harum,
horum* (*L.*) (MWW, IV.i.38, 53)
,dʒenɨ'tivo 'hujus 'hɔɹʊm 'hɑɹʊm 'hɔɹʊm
ge|nius (G.), -nii, -niuses 'dʒi|njəs [-nıəs],
-nɪaĭ, -njəsɪz [-nɪəsɪz]
gennet (*obsolete form of* jennet) (*small
Sp. saddle horse*), -s 'dʒenıt, -s
Genoa (MV, TS) 'dʒenoə
gentility dʒen'tılıtɨ
gent|le, -ler, -lest, -ly, -leness 'dʒentl̩,
-lə·, -l̩ıst, -lɨ, -l̩nıs
gentlefolk, -s 'dʒentl̩foŏk, -s
gentle-hearted 'dʒentl̩,hɑə·tıd
gentle|man, -men 'dʒentl̩|mən, -mən
gentleman(-)like 'dʒentl̩mənlaĭk
gentle|woman, -women 'dʒentl̩|,wʊmən,
-,wımın
gentility dʒen'tılıtɨ
gentry 'dʒentɹɨ
Geoffrey (KJ) 'dʒefɹɨ
George (*2HVI, 3HVI, RIII*) (*also emblem
of St. George = Order of the Garter*)
'dʒɔɹ·dʒ
Gerald (*TNK*) 'dʒeɹəld
german (G.) (ADO, ALL'S, CYM, 2HIV,
HV, 3HVI, LLL, MV, MWW, OTH), -s
'dʒɜ·mən, -z
germane dʒɜ·'meĭn
Germany (HV, HVIII, KJ, LEAR, MV)
'dʒɜ·mənɨ
germen *or* germain(e) (*cf. var.* germin),
-s 'dʒɜ·mən, -z
germin, -s 'dʒɜ·mın, -z
Gertrude (*HAM*) 'gɜ·tɹud
gest(e), -s 'dʒest, -s
gestur|e, -es, -ing, -ed 'dʒestʃə·, -z, -ɹıŋ,
-d
get, -s, -ting, got 'get, -s, -ıŋ ['geɟıŋ], 'gɒt
getter (*aphaeretic form of* begetter)
'geɟə·
getting (*aphaeretic form of* begetting)
'geɟıŋ
ghasted 'gastıd
ghastl|y, -ier, -iest, -iness 'gastl|ɨ, -ıə·,
-ɨıst, -ɨnıs

ghost (G.) (CYM, HAM, JUL, RIII), **-s; -ed; -like** 'goŏst, -s; -ɪd; -laɪk
ghostl|y, -iness 'goŏstl|ɪ, -ɪnɪs
ghoul, -s 'gul, -z
ghoulish, -ly, -ness 'gulɪʃ, -lɪ, -nɪs
giant, -s; -like 'dʒaɪənt, -s; -laɪk
giantess, -es 'dʒaɪəntes [ˌ--'-], -ɪz
giant-rude 'dʒaɪənt͵rud
gib (*cat, iron hook*), **-s** 'gɪb, -z
gib (*to disembowel*), **-s, -bing, -bed** 'gɪb, -z, -ɪŋ, -d
gib (*a prison*), **-s** 'dʒɪb, -z
gibbe (*archaic var. of* **gib***; a cat*), **-s** 'gɪb, -z
gibber, -s, -ing, -ed 'dʒɪbə, -z, -ɹɪŋ, -d
gibber (*large stone*), **-s** 'gɪbə, -z
gibbet, -s, -ing, -ed 'dʒɪbɪt, -s, -ɪŋ, -ɪd
gibbet-maker 'dʒɪbɪt͵meɪkə
gib|e, -es, -ing/ly, -ed, -er/s 'dʒaɪb, -z, -ɪŋ/lɪ, -d, -ə/z
gidd|y, -ier, -iest, -ily, -iness 'gɪd|ɪ, -ɪə, -ɪɪst, -ɪlɪ, -ɪnɪs
giddy-paced (*adj.*) 'gɪdɪ͵peɪsɪd
gi'en (*from* **given**) 'gɪn
gift, -s 'gɪft, -s
gifted, -ness 'gɪftɪd, -nɪs
gig, -s 'gɪg, -z
giglet, -s 'gɪglɪt, -s
giglot 'gɪglət
gild, -s, -ing, -ed, gilt, gilder/s 'gɪld, -z, -ɪŋ, -ɪd, 'gɪlt, 'gɪldə/z
Gilliams (1HIV) 'gɪljəmz
Gillian (COM, MWW) 'dʒɪlɪən, -ljən
gilly(-)vor, -s 'dʒɪlɪvə, -z
gillyflower, -s 'dʒɪlɪ͵flaŏə, -z
gilt (*s.*) (*p.t. and p.p. of* **gild**, *q.v.*) 'gɪlt
gimmal, -s, -ed 'dʒɪml̩, -z, -d
gimmer (*corruption of* **gimmal**), **-s** 'dʒɪmə, -z
gin (*s.*) (*all meanings*), **-s** 'dʒɪn, -z
(')gin (*from* **begin**), **-s** 'gɪn, -z
ginger, -s 'dʒɪndʒə, -z
Ginn (COM) 'dʒɪn
gins *or* **'gins** (*from* **begins**) 'gɪnz

gipes (*from* '*gibes*') 'dʒaɪps (*see Note for* **pridge**)
gips|y, -ies 'dʒɪps|ɪ, -ɪz
Giraldo (TNK) gɪ'raldo
Note.—The Jailer's Daughter refers to Emilia's schoolmaster, Master Gerald, with this name instead. It is presumably so said to lend it (if sarcastically) airs of the "fantastical"
gird, -s, -ing, -ed 'gɜd, -z, -ɪŋ, -ɪd
girdl|e, -es, -ing, -ed 'gɜdl̩, -z, -ɪŋ, -d
girt, -s, -ing, -ed 'gɜt, -s, -ɪŋ, -ɪd
girt (*p.t. and p.p. of* **gird**) 'gɜt
girth, -s 'gɜθ, -s
Gis *or* **Jis** (*corruption of* **Jesus**) 'dʒɪs
gist, -s 'dʒɪst, -s
'give (*from* '*God give*') 'gɪv
giv|e, -es, -ing, gave, giv|en, -er/s 'gɪv, -z, -ɪŋ, 'geɪv, 'gɪv|n̩, -ə/z
give-a 'gɪvə (*see* **dat**)
'give-ye-good-ev'n ͵gɪvjigŏd'ivn̩
Note.—This was probably colloquialized into something like [ˌgɹŭgŏ'din] (*see* **God gi' good e'en**)
glad (*adj.*), **-der, -dest, -ly, -ness** 'glæd, -ə, -ɪst, -lɪ, -nɪs
glad (*v.*), **-s, -ding, -ded** 'glæd, -z, -ɪŋ, -ɪd
glade, -s 'gleɪd, -z
Glamis (MAC) 'glɑmɪz, 'glɑmz
glanc|e, -es, -ing/ly, -ed 'glans, -ɪz, -ɪŋ/lɪ, -t
gland, -s 'glænd, -z
glander|s, -ed 'glandə|z, -d
Glansdale, Sir William (*1HVI*) ͵sɜ 'wɪljəm 'glænzdeɪl [-dl̩]
glar|e, -es, -ing/ly, -ed 'glɛə, -z, -ɹɪŋ/lɪ, -d
glass, -es, -ed 'glas, -ɪz, -t
glass-faced 'glas͵feɪst
glass-gazing 'glas͵geɪzɪŋ
glass|y, -ier, -iest, -ily, -iness 'glas|ɪ, -ɪə, -ɪɪst, -ɪlɪ, -ɪnɪs
glaz|e, -es, -ing, -ed, -er/s 'gleɪz, -ɪz, -ɪŋ, -d, -ə/z

---

i wɛ ɪ city ɪ hɪt e lɛt ɛ dɛbut æ cæn a pɑss ɜ bɜd ʌ hʌt ə again ə suppə u yŏu
ŏ shŏuld o ŏbey ɔ awl ɒ cɒp ɑ fɑther eɪ paɪd aɪ hɪgh oŏ go ɔɪ voɪce aŏ foŏnd ɪə ear
ɛə air ŏə poor ɔə fork ɑə park aɪə fire aŏə hour b boy p pit d dog t top g got
k kid h how fi behave dʒ jot tʃ chew z zany s soft v vat f fat ʒ treasure ʃ ship ð the
θ thin m man n no ŋ hang l lip j yes w won ʍ whew ɹ rigger, airy ɾ matter

glean, -s, -ing/s, -ed 'glin, -z, -ɪŋ/z, -d
glebe, -s 'glib, -z
glee, -s 'gli, -z
glee|ful, -fully, -fulness 'gli|fʊl, -fəlɪ, -fʊlnɪs
gleek, -s, -ing 'glik, -s, -ɪŋ
Glendor (RII) 'glendɔ˞ (*alt. spelling of 'Glendower' in* RII, III.i.43)
Glendower, Owen (*1HIV*, 2HIV, 2HVI, RII) 'oʊɪn 'glendɑʊ˞ [-dɑʊə˞], glen'dɑʊ˞
Note.—'Glendower,' depending on where it falls in the metrical line of verse, may be either disyllabic or trisyllabic, and given primary stress on either the first or second syllable
glib, -ber, -best, -ly, -ness 'glɪb, -ə˞, -ɪst, -lɪ, -nɪs
glimmer, -s, -ing, -ed 'glɪmə˞, -z, -ɹɪŋ, -d
glimps|e, -es, -ing, -ed 'glɪmps, -ɪz, -ɪŋ, -t
glint, -s, -ing, -ed 'glɪnt, -s, -ɪŋ, -ɪd
glister, -s, -ing, -ed 'glɪstə˞, -z, -ɹɪŋ, -d
global, -ly 'gloʊbl̩, -ɪ
globe, -s 'gloʊb, -z
globy 'gloʊbɪ
gloom, -s, -ing, -ed 'glum, -z, -ɪŋ, -d
gloom|y, -ier, -iest, -ily, -iness 'glum|ɪ, -ɪə˞, -ɪɪst, -ɪlɪ, -ɪnɪs
glori|fy, -fies, -fying, -fied 'glɔɹɪ|faɪ, -faɪz, -faɪɪŋ, -faɪd
glorious, -ly, -ness 'glɔɹɪəs, -lɪ, -nɪs
glor|y, -ies, -ying, -ied 'glɔɹ|ɪ, -ɪz, -ɹɪŋ, -ɪd
glos|e *or* **gloz|e, -es, -ing, -ed** 'gloʊz, -ɪz, -ɪŋ, -d
gloss, -es, -ing, -ed, -er/s 'glɒs, -ɪz, -ɪŋ, -t, -ə˞/z
gloss|y, -ies; -ier, -iest, -ily, -iness 'glɒs|ɪ, -ɪz; -ɪə˞, -ɪɪst, -ɪlɪ, -ɪnɪs
Gloucester (*HV, 1HVI*, 2HVI, 3HVI, *LEAR*, MWW, *RII*, RIII) 'glɔstə˞ ['glɒs-]
Note.—Often trisyllabic ['glɔsɪstə˞] *in S., e.g.*, 1HVI, I.iii.4, 6, 62, III.i.142, III.iv.13
Gloucester, Duchess of (*RII*) 'dʌtʃɪs əv 'glɔstə˞
Gloucester, Humphrey Duke of (*2HIV, 1HVI*) 'hʌmfɹɪ 'djuk əv 'glɔstə˞ (*see Notes for* **Humphrey** *and* **Gloucester**)

Gloucestershire (1HIV, 2HIV, RII, MWW) 'glɔstə˞ʃə˞ ['glɒs-, -ʃɪə˞]
glov|e, -es, -ing, -ed 'glʌv, -z, -ɪŋ, -d
glover, -s 'glʌvə˞, -z
glow, -s, -ing/ly, -ed 'gloʊ, -z, -ɪŋ/lɪ, -d
glower, -s, -ing, -ed 'glɑʊ˞, -z, -ɹɪŋ, -d
glow-worm, -s 'gloʊˌwɝm, -z
gloz|e *or* **glos|e, -es, -ing, -ed** 'gloʊz, -ɪz, -ɪŋ, -d
glu|e, -es, -ing, -ed, -er/s 'glu, -z, -ɪŋ, -d, -ə˞/z
glut, -s, -ting, -ted 'glʌt, -s, -ɪŋ, -ɪd
glutton, -s, -ing; -y 'glʌtn̩, -z, -ɪŋ; -ɪ
glutton-like 'glʌtn̩ˌlaɪk
gluttonous, -ly 'glʌtṇəs, -lɪ
gnarl, -s, -ing, -ed 'nɑ˞l, -z, -ɪŋ, -d
gnash, -es, -ing, -ed 'næʃ, -ɪz, -ɪŋ, -t
gnat, -s 'næt, -s
gnaw, -s, -ing, -ed, -er/s, -n 'nɔ, -z, -ɪŋ, -d, -ə˞/z, -n
go, -es, -ing, went, gone, goer/s 'goʊ, -z, -ɪŋ, 'went, 'gɒn, 'goʊə˞/z
goad, -s, -ing, -ed 'goʊd, -z, -ɪŋ, -ɪd
goat, -s 'goʊt, -s
goatish 'goʊtɪʃ ['goʊɾɪʃ]
gobbet, -s 'gɒbɪt, -s
Gobbo, Launcelot (*MV*) 'lɑnsəlɒt, -slɒt 'gɒboʊ
Gobbo, Old (*MV*) 'oʊld 'gɒboʊ
go-between, -s 'goʊbɪˌtwin, -z
goblet, -s 'gɒblɪt, -s
goblin, -s 'gɒblɪn, -z
god, -s, -ded 'gɒd, -z, -ɪd
God 'gɒd
God Almighty 'gɒd ɔl'maɪɾɪ
God-a-mercy 'gɒdə'mɝsɪ
God bu'y (*colloquial corruption of 'God be with you'*) ˌgɒd'baɪ [gʊd'baɪ]
god-daughter, -s 'gɒdˌdɔɾə˞, -z
God(-)den (*colloquial corruption of God gi' good e'en*) gɒ'den [gʊ'den, -'din]
goddess, -es 'gɒdɪs, -ɪz
goddess-like 'gɒdɪsˌlaɪk
God-eyld (*see* dild) ˌgɒ'dild
godfather, -s 'gɒdˌfɑðə˞, -z
Godgigoden (*colloquial corruption of God gi' good e'en*) ˌgɒdgɪgʊ'den [-ˌ--'-, -gʊ'din]

God gi' good e'en ˌgɒd gɪ gʊˈdin [-ˌ--'-, -gʊˈden]

godhead (G.), -s 'gɒdfied, -z

God 'i' good e'en ˌgɒdɪgʊˈdin

godlike 'gɒdlaɪk

godl|y, -ier, -iest, -iness 'gɒdl|ɨ, -ɪə˞, -ɪɪst, -ɪnɪs

godmother, -s 'gɒdˌmʌðə˞, -z

Godsake 'gɒdseɪk

godsforbot (G.) (3HVI) ˌgɒdzfɔ˞ˈboʊt [-fə˞'b-]

godson, -s 'gɒdsʌn, -z

goer-back ˌgoʊə˞ˈbæk

goers-between 'goʊə˞zbɪˈtwin

Goffe or **Gough, Matthew** (2HVI) 'mæθju 'gɔf

gog's-wouns (from 'by God's wounds') 'gɒgzˈwunz

going-out 'goʊɪŋˈaʊt

gold 'goʊld

golden, -ly 'goʊldən, -lɨ

Golden Age (AYLI, LUC, TEM) 'goʊldən 'eɪdʒ

Golgatha (MAC, RII) 'gɒlgəθə

Goliah (MWW) gəˈlaɪə

Goliases (1HVI) gəˈlaɪəsɪz

Goliath (MWW) gəˈlaɪəθ

Note.—In MWW, V.i.21, the First Folio gives 'Goliah' (q.v.), and 'Goliases' in 1HVI, I.ii.33

gondola, -s 'gɒndələ, -z

gondolier, -s ˌgɒndəˈlɪə˞, -z

Goneril (LEAR) 'gɒnəˌrɪl [-ˌrəl]

Gonzago (HAM) gənˈzɑgoʊ

Gonzalo (TEM) gənˈzɑloʊ

Note.—TEM, V.i.68 is an irregular line, potentially—depending on one's scansion of the line—leading one to the erroneous pronunciation ['gɒnzəˌloʊ] (cf. Kökeritz's Shakespeare's Names: A Pronouncing Dictionary, p. 55). By merely extending the word 'reason,' however, perhaps even into three syllables (not at all an uncommon device

in S.), the line becomes five and a half feet and the name 'Gonzalo' then retains its integrity with proper stress on the second syllable

good, -s, -ness 'gʊd, -z, -nɪs

good-conceited 'gʊdkənˌsitɪd

good(-)den (colloquial abbreviation for 'God give you good even(ing)') gʊˈden [gʊˈdin]

good-faced 'gʊdfeɪst

goodfellow, -s 'gʊdˌfeloʊ, -z

Goodfellow, Robin (MSND) 'rɒbɪn 'gʊdˌfeloʊ (also called **Puck**, q.v.)

goodfellowship gʊdˈfeloʊʃɪp

Good Friday (1HIV, KJ), -s 'gʊd 'frːaɪdɪ [-deɪ], -z

good-limbed 'gʊdˌlɪmd

goodl|y, -ier, -iest, -iness 'gʊdl|ɨ, -ɪə˞, -ɪɪst, -ɪnɪs

good|man, -men 'gʊd|mən, -mən

good-morrow, -s ˌgʊdˈmɒroʊ, -z

good-night, -s ˌgʊdˈnaɪt, -s

Goodrig (1HVI) 'gʊdˌrɪg

goodsooth gʊdˈsuθ

goodwi|fe, -ves 'gʊdwaɪ|f, -vz

Goodwins (MV) 'gʊdwɪnz

Goodwin Sands (KJ, MV) 'gʊdwɪn 'sændz

good(-)year, -s 'gʊdjɪə˞ [-jə˞], -z

goose (s.) (bird), **geese** 'gus, 'gis

goose (s.) (tailor's iron), -s 'gus, -ɪz

goos|e (v.) (to poke or pinch), -es, -ing, -ed 'gus, -ɪz, -ɪŋ, -t

gooseberr|y, -ies 'gʊzbə˞ˌrɨ|ɨ ['gusb-, -beˌrɪ-], -ɪz

goose(-)quill, -s 'gusˌkwɪl, -z

goot (from 'good') 'gʊt

Note.—Evans (in MWW) is a Welsh-man, and speaks in a Welsh accent, if somewhat inconsistently. This is an example of S.'s direction to the actor (by way of semiphonetic spellings) to adopt such an accent, more or less, for the sake of wringing the most satire out of

i w**e** ɪ c**i**ty ɪ h**i**t e l**e**t ɛ d**e**but æ c**a**n a p**a**ss ɝ b**i**rd ʌ h**u**t ə **a**gain ɚ supp**er** u y**ou** ʊ sh**ou**ld o **o**bey ɔ **aw**l ɒ c**o**p ɑ f**a**ther eɪ p**ai**d aɪ h**igh** oʊ g**o** ɔɪ v**oi**ce aʊ f**ou**nd ɪɚ **ear** ɛɚ **air** ʊɚ p**oor** ɔɚ f**or**k ɑɚ p**ar**k aɪɚ **fire** aʊɚ h**our** b b**oy** p p**i**t d d**o**g t t**o**p g g**o**t k k**i**d h h**ow** fi be**h**ave dʒ **j**ot tʃ **ch**ew z **z**any s **s**oft v va**t** f **f**at ʒ trea**s**ure ʃ **sh**ip ð **the** θ **th**in m **m**an n **n**o ŋ ha**ng** l **l**ip j **y**es w **w**on ʍ **wh**ew ɹ **r**igger, ai**r**y ɼ ma**tt**er

plays on words stemming from confu-
sions with, and corruptions of, English
pronunciation via the Welsh tongue

gorbell|y, -ies, -ied 'gɔɚˌbel|ɪ, -ɪz, -ɪd

Gorboduc, King (TN) 'kɪŋ 'gɔɚˌbodʌk

Gordian (CYM, HV) 'gɔɚdjən

gor|e, -es, -ing, -ed 'gɔɚ, -z, -ɹɪŋ, -d

gore-blood 'gɔɚˌblʌd

gorg|e, -es, -ing, -ed 'gɔɚdʒ, -ɪz, -ɪŋ, -d

gorget, -s 'gɔɚdʒɪt, -s

Gorgon (AC, MAC), **-s** 'gɔɚgən, -z

gormandiz|e, -es, -ing, -ed, -er/s
'gɔɚməndaɪz, -ɪz, -ɪŋ, -d, -ɚ/z

gor|y, -ier, -iest, -ily, -iness 'gɔɚɹ|ɪ, -ɪɚ,
-ɪɪst, -ɪlɪ, -ɪnɪs

gosling, -s 'gɒzlɪŋ, -z

gospel (**G.**), **-s, -led** 'gɒspl̩, -z, -d

gossamer, -s 'gɒsəmɚ, -z

goss(e) (*var. of* **gorse**) 'gɒs

gossip, -s, -ing, -ed; -y 'gɒsɪp, -s, -ɪŋ, -t;
-ɪ

gossip-like 'gɒsɪpˌlaɪk

Got (*from 'God'*) 'gɒt
Note.—Evans (in MWW *) is a Welsh-*
man, and speaks in a Welsh accent, if
somewhat inconsistently. This is an
example of S.'s direction to the actor (by
way of semiphonetic spellings) to adopt
such an accent, more or less, for the
sake of wringing the most satire out of
plays on words stemming from confu-
sions with, and corruptions of, English
pronunciation via the Welsh tongue

Goth, -s (AYLI, TIT) 'gɒθ, -s
Note.—This word, when it appears in
AYLI, *III.iii.5–6 (and to a certain*
degree TIT, *II.ii.110), is undoubtedly to*
be pronounced (as it evidently was in
S.'s day) in a similar way to 'goats';
otherwise, the pun is lost and the wit is
pointless. In TIT, *IV.ii.174, 'Goths' is*
interestingly juxtaposed with 'goat' in
TIT, *IV.ii.180. Kökeritz asserts that the*
[θ] pronounced in the word today is a
spelling-pronunciation; that the 'th' in
'Goth' was like the 'th' in 'Thomas,'
'Theresa' and 'thyme' (cf. Kökeritz's
Shakespeare's Pronunciation,
pp. 109–110). If one chooses not to

pronounce it exactly like 'goats,' then
the pronunciation ['goːθs] *is recom-*
mended (see Note for **moth***)*

gots 'gɒts

goug|e, -es, -ing, -ed, -er/s 'gaʊdʒ, -ɪz,
-ɪŋ, -d, -ɚ/z

Gough *or* **Goffe, Matthew** (2HVI)
'mæθju 'gɒf

gourd, -s 'gɔɚd ['gʊɚd], -z

gout, -s; -y, -ily, -iness 'gaʊt, -s; -ɪ, -ɪlɪ,
-ɪnɪs

govern, -s, -ing, -ed; -able 'gʌvɚn, -z,
-ɪŋ, -d; -əbl̩

governess, -es 'gʌvɚnɪs, -ɪz

governor (**G.**), **-s** 'gʌvənɚ [-vnɚ], -z

government, -s 'gʌvɚnmənt, -s

Gower (*2HIV, HV*) 'gaʊɚ

Gower, John (*PER*) 'dʒɒn 'gaʊɚ

gown, -s, -ed 'gaʊn, -z, -d

grac|e (**G.**), **-es, -ing, -ed** 'gɹeɪs, -ɪz, -ɪŋ, -t

grace|ful, -fully, -fulness 'gɹeɪs|fʊl, -fʊlɪ
[-fəlɪ], -fʊlnɪs

graceless, -ly, -ness 'gɹeɪslɪs, -lɪ, -nɪs

gracious, -ly, -ness 'gɹeɪʃəs, -lɪ, -nɪs

gradation, -s gɹeɪ'deɪʃn, -z

grad|e, -es, -ing, -ed 'gɹeɪd, -z, -ɪŋ, -ɪd

graff (*archaic form of* **graft**), **-s, -ing, -ed**
'gɹaf, -s, -ɪŋ, -t

graft, -s, -ing, -ed, -er/s 'gɹaft, -s, -ɪŋ, -ɪd,
-ɚ/z

grail, -s 'gɹeɪl, -z

grain, -s, -ing, -ed, -er/s; -y 'gɹeɪn, -z,
-ɪŋ, -d, -ɚ/z; -ɪ

gramerc|y (*from OF 'grant merci'*), **-ies**
gɹə'mɚs|ɪ, -ɪz

Gramercy Park (*from Dutch 'Krummer-*
see') 'gɹaməˌsɪ 'paɚk

grammar, -s 'gɹæmɚ, -z

gran|d, -der, -dest, -dly, -dness 'gɹæn|d,
-dɚ, -dɪst, -dlɪ, -dnɪs

grandam, -s 'gɹændæm, -z

grandjuror, -s ˌgɹænd'dʒʊɚɹɚ, -z

grand-jurymen ˌgɹænd'dʒʊɚɹɪmən

grandsire, -s 'gɹændsaɪɚ, -z

grandfather, -s 'gɹændˌfaðɚ, -z

Grandpré (*HV*) gɹand'pɹi

grange, -s, -r/s 'gɹeɪndʒ, -ɪz, -ɚ/z

granite, -s 'gɹænɪt, -s

grant, -s, -ing, -ed 'gɹant, -s, -ɪŋ, -ɪd

grape, -s 'ɡɹeɪ̆p, -s

graph, -s 'ɡɹaf, -s

grapp|le, -les, -ling, -led, -ler/s 'ɡɹæp|l̩, -l̩z, -l̩ɪŋ [-lɪŋ], -l̩d, -lə/z [-lə/z]

grasp, -s, -ing/ly, -ed, -er/s 'ɡɹasp, -s, -ɪŋ/lɨ, -t, -ə/z

grass, -es, -ing, -ed 'ɡɹas, -ɪz, -ɪŋ, -t

grass|y, -ier, -iest 'ɡɹas|ɨ, -ɪə, -ɪɪst

grat|e, -es, -ing/ly, -ed, -er/s 'ɡɹeɪ̆t, -s, -ɪŋ/lɨ, -ɪd, -ə/z

grate|ful, -fully, -fulness 'ɡɹeɪ̆t|fʊl, -fʊlɨ [-fəlɨ], -fʊlnɪs

Gratiano (*MV, OTH*) ˌɡɹɑʃɹˈɑnoŭ [ˌɡɹeɪ̆ʃ-, -ʃˈjɑnoŭ]

grati|fy, -fies, -fying, -fied, -fier/s 'ɡɹæɹɪ|faɪ̆, -faɪ̆z, -faɪ̆ɪŋ, -faɪ̆d, -faɪ̆ə/z

Gratii (*ALL'S*) 'ɡɹeɪ̆ʃɹaɪ̆

gratil(l)ity ɡɹəˈtɪlɪtɨ

Note.—The OED *asserts that this word is the Clown's "humorous perversion" of 'gratuity' in TN, II.iii.27; but this "perversion" might also arise from the chance that it may be a portmanteau-word of 'gratuity' and 'civility' as well (cf.* **impeticos**)

gratis 'ɡɹatɪs ['ɡɹeɪ̆tɪs]

gratitude 'ɡɹæɹɪtjud

gratulat|e, -es, -ing, -ed 'ɡɹætjʊleɪ̆t ['ɡɹætʃʊ-], -s, -ɪŋ, -ɪd

grave (*in music, slowly and solemnly*) 'ɡɹɑvɛ

grave (*diacritical mark above a letter denoting accent, as in Fr.*) 'ɡɹɑv

grave (*aphaeretic form of* **engrave**), **-s, -d, -er/s** 'ɡɹeɪ̆v, -s, -d, -ə/z

grave (**G.**) (*all other meanings*), **-s; -r, -st, -ly, -ness** 'ɡɹeɪ̆v, -z; -ə, -ɪst, -lɨ, -nɪs

grave-beseeming 'ɡɹeɪ̆vbɪˌsimɪŋ

gravel, -s, -ling, -led, -ly 'ɡɹævl̩, -z, -ɪŋ, -d, -ɨ

gravel-blind 'ɡɹævl̩ˌblaɪ̆nd

graven (*p.p. of* **grave** (*sculpt or carve*)) 'ɡɹeɪ̆vən [-vn̩]

graver, -s 'ɡɹeɪ̆və, -z

grave-stone, -s 'ɡɹeɪ̆vˌstoŭn, -z

gravity 'ɡɹævɪtɨ

gravure ɡɹəˈvjʊə

grav|y, -ies 'ɡɹeɪ̆v|ɨ, -ɪz

gray *or* **grey, -s; -er, -est, -ness** 'ɡɹeɪ̆, -z; -ə, -ɪst, -nɪs

graybeard, -s 'ɡɹeɪ̆ˌbɪə-d, -z

grayish 'ɡɹeɪ̆ɪʃ

Graymalkin (MAC) ɡɹeɪ̆ˈmɔkɪn [-ˈmɔlkɪn]

Gray's Inn (2HIV) 'ɡɹeɪ̆z 'ɪn

graz|e, -es, -ing, -ed 'ɡɹeɪ̆z, -ɪz, -ɪŋ, -d

grease (*s.*), **-s** 'ɡɹis, -ɪz

greas|e (*v.*), **-es, -ing, -ed, -er/s** 'ɡɹis ['ɡɹiz], -ɪz, -ɪŋ, -t ['ɡɹizd], -ə/z

greas|y, -ier, -iest, -ily, -iness 'ɡɹis|ɨ ['ɡɹiz|ɨ], -ɪə, -ɪɪst, -ɪlɨ, -ɪnɪs

great, -er, -est, -ly, -ness 'ɡɹeɪ̆t, -ə, -ɪst, -lɨ, -nɪs

great-bellied 'ɡɹeɪ̆tˌbelɨd

great-eyed 'ɡɹeɪ̆tˌaɪ̆d

great-grandsire, -s 'ɡɹeɪ̆tˌɡɹandsaɪ̆ə, -z

great-grown 'ɡɹeɪ̆tˌɡɹoŭn

great-sized 'ɡɹeɪ̆tˌsaɪ̆zd

great-uncle, -s 'ɡɹeɪ̆tˈʌŋkl̩, -z

grece (*stairsteps; cf.* **grise** *and* **grize**) 'ɡɹis

Grecian (ALL'S, AYLI, COR, MV, Sonn. 53, TC), **-s** 'ɡɹiʃn̩, -z

(')gree, -ing, -d 'ɡɹi, -ɪŋ, -d

Note.—This is usually considered an aphetic form of 'agree' in S., but some editors quibble, citing that 'gree'—a word in its own right—means 'to be in concord,' 'suiting one's opinion via compromise,' and 'to accommodate' (all of which are blanketed by 'agree')

Greece (COM, COR, 1HVI, 3HVI, LUC, MWW, PER, TC, TS) 'ɡɹis

Greece, Isles of (TC) 'aɪ̆lz əv 'ɡɹis

greed, -y, -ier, -iest, -ily, -iness 'ɡɹid, -ɨ, -ɪə, -ɪɪst, -ɪlɨ, -ɪnɪs

Greek (3HVI, LUC, TC), **-s; -ish** 'ɡɹik, -s; -ɪʃ

---

i wᴇ ɨ city ɪ hɪt e lᴇt ɛ dᴇbut æ cᴀn a pᴀss ɝ bɪrd ʌ hᴜt ə agᴀin ɚ suppᴇr u yᴏu
ʊ shᴏuld o ᴏbey ɔ ᴀwl ɒ cᴏp ɑ fᴀther eɪ̆ pᴀid aɪ̆ hɪgh oŭ gᴏ ɔɪ vᴏice aŭ fᴏund ɪ͡ɚ ᴇar
ɛ͡ɚ ᴀir ʊ͡ɚ pᴏor ɔ͡ɚ fᴏrk ɑ͡ɚ pᴀrk aɪ̆͡ɚ fɪre aʊ͡ɚ hᴏur b bᴏy p pɪt d dᴏg t tᴏp g gᴏt
k kɪd h hᴏw ɦ behᴀve dʒ jᴏt tʃ chᴇw z zᴀny s sᴏft v yᴀt f fᴀt ʒ treᴀsure ʃ shɪp ð thᴇ
θ thɪn m mᴀn n nᴏ ŋ hᴀng l lɪp j yᴇs w wᴏn ʍ whᴇw ɹ rɪgger, airy ɾ mᴀtter

green, -s, -ing, -ed; -er, -est, -ly, -ness
'gɹin, -z, -ɪŋ, -d; -ɚ, -ɪst, -lɨ, -nɪs
green-a-box 'gɹinə'bɒks (*see* des(e))
Green(e), Sir Henry (*RII*) ˌsɚ 'henɹɨ 'gɹin
green-eyed 'gɹinˌaĭd ['gɹinaĭd]
green-sickness 'gɹinˌsɪknɪs
Greensleeves (MWW) (*an ancient tune*)
'gɹinslivz
green(-)sward 'gɹinswɔɚd
Greenwich (HVIII) 'gɹenɪdʒ [-nɪtʃ]
greenwood, -s 'gɹinwʊd, -z
greet, -s, -ing/s, -ed, -er/s 'gɹit, -s, -ɪŋ/z,
-ɪd, -ɚ/z
Gregory (1HIV, HVIII, *RJ*, TS) 'gɹegɚˌɹɨ,
-gɹɨ
Gremio (*TS*) 'gɹemɪoŭ ['gɹim-], -mjoŭ
grenade, -s gɹɪ'neĭd, -z
grew (*from* grow, *q.v.*) 'gɹu
Grey, Lady Elizabeth (*3HVI, RIII*) 'leĭdɨ
ɪ'lɪzəbəθ 'gɹeĭ
Grey, Lord (*RIII*) 'lɔɚd 'gɹeĭ
Grey, Sir John (3HVI, RIII) ˌsɚ 'dʒɒn
'gɹeĭ
Grey, Sir Thomas (*HV*) ˌsɚ 'tɒməs 'gɹeĭ
grey *or* gray, -s; -er, -est, -ness 'gɹeĭ, -z;
-ɚ, -ɪst, -nɪs
greybeard, -s 'gɹeĭˌbɪɚd, -z
grey-eyed 'gɹeĭˌaĭd
greyhound, -s 'gɹeĭˌɦɑŭnd, -z
grid, -s 'gɹɪd, -z
griddle, -s 'gɹɪdl̩, -z
gride *or* gryde (*v.*) (*to pierce through with
a weapon*) 'gɹaĭd
*Note.—In his annotation for TIT,
II.ii.260 (q.v.), Jonathan Bate (editor,
The Arden Shakespeare, 1995) makes
the case for there having been a minim
error made by the first compositor of
TIT. The word 'griude' appears in the
First Quarto version, later emended to
'greeu'd/grieu'd' in subsequent quarto
versions and the First Folio. Most
modern editors give 'grieved' but Bate's
argument is compelling*
grief (G.), -s 'gɹif, -s
grief-shot 'gɹifˌʃɒt
grievance, -s 'gɹivəns, -ɪz
griev|e, -es, -ing/ly, -ed, -er/s 'gɹiv, -z,
-ɪŋ/lɨ, -d, -ɚ/z

grievous, -ly, -ness 'gɹivəs, -lɨ, -nɪs
griffin, -s 'gɹɪfɪn, -z
Griffith (*HVIII*) 'gɹɪfɪθ
grill, -s, -ing, -ed 'gɹɪl, -z, -ɪŋ, -d
grim, -mer, -mest, -ly, -ness 'gɹɪm, -ɚ,
-ɪst, -lɨ, -nɪs
grimac|e, -es, -ing, -ed 'gɹɪməs [gɹɪ'meĭs],
-ɪz, -ɪŋ, -t
grimalkin, -s gɹɪ'mɔkɪn [-'mɔlk-, -'malk-],
-z
grim|e, -es, -ing, -ed 'gɹaĭm, -z, -ɪŋ, -d
grim-grinning 'gɹɪmˌgɹɪnɪŋ
grim-looked 'gɹɪmˌlʊkt
grim-visaged 'gɹɪmˌvɪzɪdʒd
grim|y, -ier, -iest, -ily, -iness 'gɹaĭm|ɨ,
-ɪɚ, -ɪɪst, -ɪlɨ, -ɪnɪs
grin, -s, -ning, -ned, -ner/s 'gɹɪn, -z, -ɪŋ,
-d, -ɚ/z
grind, -s, -ing, ground 'gɹaĭnd, -z, -ɪŋ,
'gɹɑŭnd
grinder, -s 'gɹaĭndɚ, -z
Grindstone, Susan (RJ) 'suzn̩
'gɹaĭndstoŭn
*Note.—Kökeritz asserts that this
surname from RJ was more than likely
pronounced ['gɹɪnstən] in S.'s day, but to
say it thus today might diminish its
descriptiveness*
grip, -s, -ping, -ped 'gɹɪp, -s, -ɪŋ, -t
grip|e, -es, -ing, -ed 'gɹaĭp, -s, -ɪŋ, -t
grise (*rare, obsolete form of* grece; *a
stairsteps*) 'gɹiz ['gɹis]
grisled 'gɹɪzl̩d
grisl|y, -ier, -iest, -iness 'gɹɪzl|ɨ, -ɪɚ, -ɪɪst,
-ɪnɪs
Grissel (TS) 'gɹɪsl̩
grist 'gɹɪst
gristle 'gɹɪsl̩
gristly 'gɹɪslɨ [-slɨ]
grit, -s, -ting, -ted 'gɹɪt, -s, -ɪŋ, -ɪd
gritt|y, -ier, -iest, -ily, -iness 'gɹɪɡ|ɨ, -ɪɚ,
-ɪɪst, -ɪlɨ, -ɪnɪs
grize (*rare, obsolete form of* grece; *a
stairsteps*) 'gɹiz
grizzle, -d 'gɹɪzl̩, -d
groan, -s, -ing/s, -ed 'gɹoŭn, -z, -ɪŋ/z, -d
groat (*money*), -s 'gɹoŭt, -s
groats (*hulled, usually crushed grain*)
'gɹoŭts

groin, -s 'gɹɔĭn, -z
gross, -er, -est, -ly, -ness 'gɹoŭs, -ɚ, -ɪst, -lɪ, -nɪs
ground, -s, -ing, -ed, -er/s 'gɹaŭnd, -z, -ɪŋ, -ɪd, -ɚ/z
groundling, -s 'gɹaŭndlɪŋ, -z
ground-piece 'gɹaŭnd͵pis
grove, -s 'gɹoŭv, -z
grov|el, -els, -elling, -elled, -eller/s 'gɹɒv|l̩, -l̩z, -l̩ɪŋ, -l̩d, -l̩ɚ/z
gr|ow, -ows, -owing, grew, -own, -ower/s 'gɹ|oŭ, -oŭz, -oŭɪŋ, 'gɹu, -oŭn, -oŭɚ/z
growl, -s, -ing, -ed, -er/s 'gɹaŭl, -z, -ɪŋ, -d, -ɚ/z
grub, -s, -bing, -bed, -ber/s 'gɹʌb, -z, -ɪŋ, -d, -ɚ/z
grudg|e, -es, -ing/ly, -ed, -er/s 'gɹʌdʒ, -ɪz, -ɪŋ/lɪ, -d, -ɚ/z
gruel 'gɹuəl ['gɹuəl]
grumb|le, -les, -ling/s, -led, -ler/s 'gɹʌmb|l̩, -l̩z, -lɪŋ/z [-l̩ɪŋ/z], -l̩d, -lɚ/z [-l̩ɚ/z]
Grumio (*TS*) 'gɹumɪoŭ, -mjoŭ
grump|y, -ier, -iest, -ily, -iness 'gɹʌmp|ɪ, -ɪɚ, -ɪɪst, -ɪlɪ, -ɪnɪs
grunt, -s, -ing, -ed 'gɹʌnt, -s, -ɪŋ, -ɪd
Gualtier or **Gaultier** (2HVI) goŭtjɚ
guarantee, -s, -ing, -d ͵gæɹən'ti, -z, -ɪŋ, -d
guarantor, -s ͵gæɹən'tɔɚ, -z
guarant|y, -ies 'gæɹənt|ɪ, -ɪz
guard, -s, -ing, -ed; -age 'gɑɚd, -z, -ɪŋ, -ɪd; -ɪdʒ
guardant 'gɑɚdn̩t
guarded|ly, -ness 'gɑɚdɪd|lɪ, -nɪs
guardian, -s; -ship/s 'gɑɚdɪən, -z; -ʃɪp/s
guards|man, -men 'gɑɚdz|mən, -mən
gudgeon, -s 'gʌdʒən, -z
guerdon, -s, -ing, -ed 'gɝdn̩, -z, -ɪŋ, -d
guess, -es, -ing/ly, -ed, -er/s; -work 'ges, -ɪz, -ɪŋ/lɪ, -t, -ɚ/z; -wɝk
guest, -s 'gest, -s
guest(-)wise 'gest͵waĭz
guffaw, -s, -ing, -ed gə'fɔ, -z, -ɪŋ, -d

Guiana (MWW) gi'ɑnə [gi'ænə, gaĭ'ænə]
guid or **gud** (*from* '*good*') 'gɪd̥
Note.—Jamy (in HV) is a Scotsman, and speaks with a Scots accent, if somewhat inconsistently. This is an example of S.'s direction to the actor (by way of semiphonetic spellings) to adopt such an accent, more or less. The Folio gives 'gud' and modern editors often emend to 'guid' to reflect a common spelling (see 'Shakespeare's Foreign Languages' § 3.1 of this dictionary)
guidance 'gaĭdn̩s
guid|e, -es, -ing, -ed, -er 'gaĭd, -z, -ɪŋ, -ɪd, -ɚ
Guiderius (*CYM*) gwɪ'dɪɚɹɪəs, -ɹĭəs
guidon, -s 'gaĭdɒn [-dn̩], -z
Guienne (1HVI) gi'en
guild, -s 'gɪld, -z
Guildenstern (*HAM*) 'gɪldənstɝn
guilder, -s 'gɪldɚ, -z
Guildhall (RIII) 'gɪld͵hɔl
guil|e, -es, -ing, -ed 'gaĭl, -z, -ɪŋ, -d
guile|ful, -fully, -fulness 'gaĭl|fʊl, -fʊlɪ, -fʊlnɪs
Guilford or **Guildford, Richard** (RIII) 'ɹɪtʃɚd 'gɪlfɚd ['gɪldfɚd]
Guilford or **Guildford, Sir Henry** (*HVIII*) ͵sɝ 'henɹɪ 'gɪlfɚd ['gɪldfɚd]
Guiltian (ALL'S) 'gɪlʃɪən, -ʃjən ['gɪltɪən, -tjən]
guilt, -y, -ier, -iest, -ily, -iness 'gɪlt, -ɪ, -ɪɚ, -ɪɪst, -ɪlɪ, -ɪnɪs
guiltless, -ly, -ness 'gɪltlɪs, -lɪ, -nɪs
guilts 'gɪlt, -s
guilty-like 'gɪltɪ͵laĭk
guinea(-)hen, -s 'gɪnɪ͵hen, -z
Guinover or **Guinever, Queen** (LLL) 'kwin 'gwɪnəvɚ ['gɪn-, -novɚ]
guise, -s 'gaĭz, -ɪz
guitar, -s gɪ'tɑɚ, -z
guitarist, -s gɪ'tɑɚɹɪst, -s
gulch, -es 'gʌltʃ, -ɪz
gules 'gjulz

---

i we ɪ city ɪ hit e let ɛ debut æ can a pass ɝ bird ʌ hut ə again ɚ supper u you
ʊ should o obey ɔ awl ɒ cop ɑ father eĭ paid aĭ high oŭ go ɔĭ voice aŭ found ɪɚ ear
ɛɚ air ʊɚ poor ɔɚ fork ɑɚ park aĭɚ fire aŭɚ hour b boy p pit d dog t top g got
k kid h how ɦ behave dʒ jot tʃ chew z zany s soft v vat f fat ʒ treasure ʃ ship ð the
θ thin m man n no ŋ hang l lip j yes w won ʍ whew ɹ rigger, airy ɾ matter

gulf, -s 'gʌlf, -s
gull, -s, -ing, -ed 'gʌl, -z, -ɪŋ, -d
gull-catcher, -s 'gʌlˌkætʃəˑ, -s
gullet, -s 'gʌlɪt, -s
gullible 'gʌləbl̩
gull‖y, -ies 'gʌl‖ɪ, -ɪz
gulp, -s, -ing, -ed 'gʌlp, -s, -ɪŋ, -t
gum, -s, -ming, -med 'gʌm, -z, -ɪŋ, -d
gun, -s, -ning, -ned, -ner/s 'gʌn, -z, -ɪŋ,
-d, -əˑ/z
gunpowder 'gʌnpaʊdəˑ
gun-stone, -s 'gʌnˌstoʊn, -z
gunwale, -s 'gʌnl̩, -z
gurg‖le, -les, -ling, -led 'gɝˑg‖l̩, -l̩z, -l̩ɪŋ,
-l̩d
gurnet, -s 'gɝˑnɪt, -s
Gurney, James (KJ) 'dʒeɪmz 'gɝˑnɪ
gush, -es, -ing, -ed, -er/s 'gʌʃ, -ɪz, -ɪŋ, -t,
-əˑ/z
gusset, -s 'gʌsɪt, -s
gust, -s, -ing, -ed 'gʌst, -s, -ɪŋ, -ɪd
gusto 'gʌstoʊ
gust‖y, -ier, -iest, -ily, -iness 'gʌst‖ɪ, -ɪəˑ,
-ɪɪst, -ɪlɪ, -ɪnɪs
gu‖t, -ts, -tting, -tted 'gʌ‖t, -ts, -t̩ɪŋ, -t̩ɪd
guts-griping 'gʌtsˌgɹaɪpɪŋ
gutter, -s, -ing, -ed 'gʌɾəˑ, -z, -ɹɪŋ, -d
guy, -s 'gaɪ, -z
Guynes (HVIII) 'gin
Guy, Sir (HVIII) ˌsɝˑ 'gaɪ
Guysors (1HVI) ʒiˈzɔɝˑ [dʒiˈzɔɝˑ(z),
giˈzɔɝˑz]
gym, -s 'dʒɪm, -z
gyps‖y, -ies 'dʒɪps‖ɪ, -ɪz
gyv‖e, -es, -ing, -ed 'dʒaɪv, -z, -ɪŋ, -d

Hh

H (the letter), -'s 'eɪtʃ, -ɪz
ha' (colloquial form of have) 'hæ ['fɪæ]
ha, -'s 'hɑ, -z
haberdasher, -s, -y 'hæbəˑdæʃəˑ, -z, -ɹɪ
habiliment, -s həˈbɪlɪmənt, -s
habit, -s, -ing, -ed 'hæbɪt, -s, -ɪŋ, -ɪd
habitat, -s 'hæbɪtæt, -s
habitation, -s ˌhæbɪˈteɪʃn̩, -z
habitude, -s 'hæbɪtjud, -z

hack, -s, -ing, -ed, -er/s 'hæk, -s, -ɪŋ, -t,
-əˑ/z
Hacket, Cicely (TS) 'sɪsɪlɪ, -slɪ 'hækɪt
Hacket, Marian (TS) 'mɛɝˑɹɪən ['mæɹ-]
'hækɪt
hackney, -s, -ing, -ed 'hæknɪ, -z, -ɪŋ, -d
had‖e, -es, -ing, -ed 'heɪd, -z, -ɪŋ, -ɪd
Hades 'heɪdɪz
hag, -s 'hæg, -z
Hagar (MV) 'heɪgɑɝˑ
hag-born 'hægˌbɔɝˑn
haggard, -s; -est, -ly, -ness 'hægəˑd, -z;
-ɪst, -lɪ, -nɪs
haggish, -ly, -ness 'hægɪʃ, -lɪ, -nɪs
hag-seed, -s 'hægˈsid, -z
hail, -s, -ing, -ed 'heɪl, -z, -ɪŋ, -d
hailstone, -s 'heɪlstoʊn, -z
hailstorm, -s 'heɪlstɔɝˑm, -z
hair, -s 'hɛɝˑ, -z
hair-breadth 'hɛɝˑbɹedθ
hairsbreadth or hair's-breadth
'hɛɝˑzbɹedθ
hairbrush, -es 'hɛɝˑbɹʌʃ, -ɪz
haircut, -s 'hɛɝˑkʌt, -s
hairless 'hɛɝˑlɪs
hair-worth 'hɛɝˑˈwɝˑθ [ˈ-ˌ-]
hair‖y, -ier, -iest, -iness 'hɛɝˑɹ‖ɪ, -ɪəˑ, -ɪɪst,
-ɪnɪs
Hal, Prince (1HIV, 2HIV) 'pɹɪns 'hæl
halberd, -s 'hælbəˑd ['hɔl-], -z
halcyon, -s 'hælsɪən, -z
hal‖e (adj.), -er, -est 'heɪl, -əˑ, -ɪst
hal‖e (v.), -es, -ing, -ed 'heɪl, -z, -ɪŋ, -d
half, halves 'haf, 'havz
Note.—In LLL, V.i.22, the pedant,
Holofernes, insists on the pronunciation
['half] for 'half,' as he does ['kalf] for
'calf' (see Note for abhominable)
half-a-dozen 'hafəˈdʌzn̩
half-blooded 'hafˌblʌdɪd
half-blown 'hafˌbloʊn
Half(-)can (MEAS) 'hafˌkæn
half-cap, -s 'hafˌkæp, -s
half-cheek, -ed 'hafˌtʃik [ˈ-ˈ-], -t
half-conquered 'hafˌkɒŋkəˑd
half-face, -d 'hafˌfeɪs, -t
half-kirtle, -s 'hafˌkɝˑtl̩, -z
Half-moon (1HIV) 'hafˌmun
half-part 'hafˌpɑɝˑt

half(-)pence 'heĭpəns (*see Note for*
  halfpenny)
halfpenn|y, -ies; -yworth/s 'heĭpn̩|ɨ
  [-pənɨ], -ɪz; -ˌɪwɝ·θ/s [-ɪwɚ·θ/s]
  Note.—This is a chiefly Brit. word
  requiring a Brit. pronunciation in
  context. If Americanized, the pronun-
  ciation becomes ['hafˌpenɨ] *or*
  [ˌhaf'penɨ]
half-pint, -s 'hafpaĭnt, -s
half-sight, -s 'hafˌsaĭt, -s
half-supped ˌhaf'sʌpt (*when att.,* ['-ˌ-])
half-through 'hafˌθɪu
half-way 'hafweĭ ['-'-]
half-workers 'hafwɝ·kɚ·z
half-yard 'hafjɑɚ·d
halidom, hallidome, hollidam,
  holydame, holidame, *or* **holy-dam**
  'hɒlɪdəm
hall, -s 'hɔl, -z
halloo, -s, -ing, -ed hæ'lu [hə'l-], -z, -ɪŋ,
  -d
hall|ow, -ows, -owing, -owed 'hæl|oŭ,
  -oŭz, -oŭɪŋ, -oŭd [-oŭɪd]
Hallowmas (MEAS, RII, TGV), **-es**
  'hæloŭməs, -ɪz
halt, -s, -ing/ly, -ed 'hɔlt, -s, -ɪŋ/lɨ, -ɪd
halter, -s, -ing, -ed 'hɔltɚ·, -z, -ɪɪŋ, -d
ham, -s 'hæm, -z
Ham(m)es Castle (3HVI) 'hæmz ['heĭmz]
  'kasl̩
Hamlet (*HAM*) 'hæmlɪt
hamlet, -s 'hæmlɪt, -s
hammer, -s, -ing, -ed 'hæmɚ·, -z, -ɪɪŋ, -d
hammock, -s, -ed 'hæmək, -s, -t
hamper, -s, -ing, -ed 'hæmpɚ·, -z, -ɪɪŋ, -d
Hampton (HV) 'hæmptən
hand, -s, -ing, -ed 'hænd, -z, -ɪŋ, -ɪd
hand-fast 'hændˌfast
handicraft, -s 'hændɪkɪaft, -s
hand-in-hand ˌhændɪn'hænd
handkercher, -s 'hæŋkɚ·tʃɚ·, -z
handker|chief, -s 'hæŋkɚ·|tʃɪf [-tʃif, -s, *or*
  -tʃivz] -s

hand|le, -les, -ling, -led, -ler/s 'hænd|l̩,
  -l̩z, -lɪŋ [-lɪŋ], -l̩d, -lɚ·/z [-l̩ɚ·/z]
handless 'hændlɪs
hand(-)maid, -s, -en/s 'hændmeĭd, -z,
  -n̩/z
handsaw, -s 'hændsɔ, -z
handsome, -r, -st, -ly, -ness 'hænsəm, -ɚ·,
  -ɪst, -lɨ, -nɪs
hand|y, -ier, -iest, -ily, -iness 'hænd|ɨ, -ɪɚ·,
  -ɪɪst, -ɪlɨ, -ɪnɪs
handy-dandy 'hændɪ'dændɨ
hang, -s, -ing/s, -ed, hung, hanger/s
  'hæŋ, -z, -ɪŋ/z, -d, 'hʌŋ, 'hæŋɚ·/z
hang-hog 'hæŋˌfiɒg
hang|man, -men 'hæŋ|mən, -mən
Hannibal (1HVI, LLL, MEAS) 'hænɪbəl
hap, -s, -ping, -ped 'hæp, -s, -ɪŋ, -t
hapless, -ly, -ness 'hæplɪs, -lɨ, -nɪs
haply 'hæplɨ
happ|en -ens, -ening/s, -ened 'hæp|ən,
  -ənz, -ənɪŋ/z [-n̩ɪŋ/z], -ənd
happies 'hæpɪz
happ|y, -ier, -iest, -ily, -iness 'hæp|ɨ, -ɪɚ·,
  -ɪɪst, -ɪlɨ, -ɪnɪs
harbinger, -s 'hɑɚ·bɪndʒɚ·, -z
harbor, -s, -ing, -ed; -age 'hɑɚ·bɚ·, -z,
  -ɪɪŋ, -d; -ɪɪdʒ
Harcourt (*2HIV*) 'hɑɚ·kɔɚ·t [-kɚ·t]
hard, -er, -est, -ly, -ness 'hɑɚ·d, -ɚ·, -ɪst,
  -lɨ, -nɪs
hard-a-keeping 'hɑɚ·dəˌkipɪŋ
hard-favored 'hɑɚ·dˌfeĭvɚ·d
hard-haired 'hɑɚ·dˌfiɛɚ·d
hard-hearted 'hɑɚ·dˌhɑɚ·tɪd [-dˌfiɑɚ·-]
hardiment 'hɑɚ·dɪmənt [-dɪm-]
hard-ruled 'hɑɚ·dˌɪuld
hard|y, -ier, -iest, -ily, -iness 'hɑɚ·d|ɨ, -ɪɚ·,
  -ɪɪst, -ɪlɨ, -ɪnɪs
hare, -s 'hεɚ·, -z
harebell, -s 'hεɚ·bel, -z
hare-brained 'hεɚ·ˌbɪeĭnd
hare-finder, -s 'hεɚ·faĭndɚ·, -z
hare-heart, -s 'hεɚ·ˌhɑɚ·t, -s
hare(-)lip, -s, -ped 'hεɚ·lɪp, -s, -t

Harfleur (HV) ˈhɑɚ̆ˑflɜˑ

Harfleur, Governor of (*HV*) ˈgʌvənəˑ [-vn̩əˑ] əv ˈhɑɚ̆ˑflɜˑ

Ha'rford-west (RIII) ˈhɑɚ̆ˑfəˑdˈwest

hark, -s, -ing, -ed ˈhɑɚ̆ˑk, -s, -ɪŋ, -t

harlot, -s, -ry ˈhɑɚ̆ˑlət, -s, -ɹɨ

harm, -s, -ing, -ed ˈhɑɚ̆ˑm, -z, -ɪŋ, -d

harm-doing ˈhɑɚ̆ˑmˌduɪŋ

harm|ful, -fully, -fulness ˈhɑɚ̆ˑm|fʊl, -fʊlɨ [-fəlɨ], -fʊlnɪs

harmless, -ly, -ness ˈhɑɚ̆ˑmlɪs, -lɨ, -nɪs

harness, -es, -ing, -ed, -er/s ˈhɑɚ̆ˑnɪs, -ɪz, -ɪŋ, -t, -əˑ/z

harp, -s, -ing, -ed, -er/s ˈhɑɚ̆ˑp, -s, -ɪŋ, -t, -əˑ/z

Harpier (MAC) ˈhɑɚ̆ˑpjəˑ

harp|y (H.), -ies ˈhɑɚ̆ˑp|ɨ, -ɨz

harrow, -s, -ing/ly, -ed ˈhæɹoŭ, -z, -ɪŋ/lɨ, -d

harr|y (H.), -ies, -ying, -ied ˈhæɹɨ|ɨ, -ɨz, -ɨɪŋ, -ɨd

Harry the Sixth (RIII) ˈhæɹɨ ðə ˈsɪksθ

harsh, -er, -est, -ly, -ness ˈhɑɚ̆ˑʃ, -əˑ, -ɪst, -lɨ, -nɪs

harsh-resounding ˈhɑɚ̆ˑʃɹɪˌzaŏndɪŋ

harsh-sounding ˈhɑɚ̆ˑʃˌsaŏndɪŋ

hart, -s ˈhɑɚ̆ˑt, -s

harvest, -s, -ing, -ed, -er/s ˈhɑɚ̆ˑvɪst, -s, -ɪŋ, -ɪd, -əˑ/z

harvest-home ˌhɑɚ̆ˑvɪstˈhoŏm

'has *or* **h'as** (*contr. of* he has) ˈhjæz [ˈhæz]

Note.—This contraction, appearing in HVIII, I.iii.59, III.i.119, is a somewhat modern editorial emendation for the First Folio's typical "Ha's," which might induce one to say the just-as-likely pronunciation [ˈhĭəz] *(note the rising rather than falling diphthong), accentuating 'he' more than 'has.' Another common form of the contraction in S.'s day was "h'as." In HVIII, V.iv.75, the Folio gives "'has"*

hash, -es, -ing, -ed ˈhæʃ, -ɪz, -ɪŋ, -t

hasn't ˈhæzn̩t

hasp, -s, -ing, -ed ˈhasp, -s, -ɪŋ, -t

hast ˈhæst (*strong form*), ˈhɨəst (*weak form*)

hast|e, -es, -ing, -ed ˈheĭst, -s, -ɪŋ, -ɪd

hasten, -s, -ing, -ed ˈheĭsn̩, -z, -ɪŋ, -d

haste-post-haste ˈheĭstˌpoŏstˈheĭst

Hastings (*2HIV, 3HVI, RIII*) ˈheĭstɪŋz

hast|y, -ier, -iest, -ily, -iness ˈheĭst|ɨ, -ɨəˑ, -ɨɪst, -ɨlɨ, -ɨnɪs

hasty-witted ˈheĭstɨˌwɪɽɪd

hat, -s ˈhæt, -s

ha't (*contr. of* have it) ˈhæˑt

hatch, -es, -ing, -ed ˈhætʃ, -ɪz, -ɪŋ, -t

hatchet, -s ˈhætʃɪt, -s

hatchment, -s ˈhætʃmənt, -s

hat|e, -es, -ing, -ed, -er/s ˈheĭt, -s, -ɪŋ, -ɪd, -əˑ/z

hate|ful, -fully, -fulness ˈheĭt|fʊl, -fʊlɨ [-fəlɨ], -fʊlnɪs

Hatfield, William of (2HVI) ˈwɪljəm əv ˈhætfild

hath (*from* have) ˈhæθ (*strong form*), ˈhɨəθ (*weak form*)

'hath (*contr. of* he hath) ˈhjæθ [ˈhæθ] *(see Note for* **'has***)*

hatred ˈheĭtɹɪd

hatter, -s ˈhæɡəˑ, -z

hauberk, -s ˈhɔbɚ̆k, -s

haud credo (*L.*) (LLL, IV.ii.11,12,19,20) ˈhaŏd [ˈhɔd] ˈkɹedo

Note.—In LLL, IV.ii.11–20, the L. "haud credo" is taken to mean "old grey doe," therefore, the phrase may require a dialectal pronunciation (somewhat) if the homophonic pun is to work (cf. Kökeritz's Shakespeare's Pronunciation, *pp. 112ff.)*

hauf (*cf.* half) ˈhaf

haught ˈhɔt

haught|y, -ier, -iest, -ily, -iness ˈhɔɡ|ɨ, -ɨəˑ, -ɨɪst, -ɨlɨ, -ɨnɪs

haunch, -es ˈhɔntʃ, -ɪz

haunt, -s, -ing/ly, -ed ˈhɔnt, -s, -ɪŋ/lɨ, -ɪd

haut|boy *or* **haut|bois, -boys** *or* **-bois** ˈhoŏ|bɔĭ [ˈoŏ|bɔĭ], -bɔĭz

have (*v.*); **has; having; had** ˈhæv (*strong form*), ˈhɨəv (*weak form*); ˈhæz (*strong form*), ˈhɨəz (*weak form*); ˈhævɪŋ; ˈhæd (*strong form*), ˈhɨəd (*weak form*)

haves (*s.*) (*those with more than ample means*) ˈhævz

haven, -s ˈheĭvn̩, -z

haver (*one who has*) ˈhævəˑ

havings (*possessions*) 'hævɪŋz
(')havior, -s 'heɪ̆vjɚ, -z
havoc 'hævək
hawk, -s, -ing, -ed, -er/s 'hɔk, -s, -ɪŋ, -t,
　-ɚ/z
hawthorn, -s 'hɔθɔ˞n, -z
hawthorn-bud, -s 'hɔθɔ˞n̩bʌd [-θ˞n-],
　-z
hay 'heɪ̆
haystack, -s 'heɪ̆stæk, -s
hazard, -s, -ing, -ed 'hæzɚd, -z, -ɪŋ, -ɪd
hazel, -s; -nut/s 'heɪ̆zl̩, -z; -nʌt/s
hazel-twig, -s 'heɪ̆zl̩twɪg, -z
he (H.) 'hi (*strong form*), 'ɦi ['i, 'ɪ]
　(*colloquial weak forms; see* a =
　personal pronoun '*he*')
head, -s, -ing, -ed 'hed, -z, -ɪŋ, -ɪd
　Note.—In TS, V.ii.40—*unless one scans*
　the line as a headless one (no pun
　intended)—it is possible that '*head*'
　wants to be disyllabic. In Frank
　Kermode's (editor of TEM, The Arden
　Shakespeare, *1958) annotation for*
　TEM, I.ii.53, *there is a brief but*
　valuable discussion about monosyllabic
　words that sometimes receive the value
　of two metric beats in S. lines of verse
　"*whether or no it is* [they are] *pro-*
　nounced disyllabically . . ." *In* TS,
　V.ii.40 '*head*' *is arguably pronounced*
　disyllabically or given, as Kermode puts
　it, "*a heavy emphasis.*" *Cf. Abbott's*
　A Shakespearian Grammar, *§§ 475, 479,*
　484
headach|e, -es, -y 'hedeɪ̆k, -s, -ɪ
headband, -s 'hedbænd, -z
Headborough (ADO) 'hedbɚɹə
header, -s 'hedɚ, -z
headless 'hedlɪs
headline, -s 'hedlaɪ̆n, -z
headlong 'hedlɒŋ [ˌ-'-]
head-lugged 'hedˌlʌgd
headpiece, -s 'hedpis, -ɪz
heads|man, -men 'hedz|mən, -mən

headstall 'hedstɔl
headstrong 'hedstɹɒŋ
head|y, -ier, -iest, -ily, -iness 'hed|ɪ, -ɪɚ,
　-ɪɪst, -ɪlɪ, -ɪnɪs
heal, -s, -ing, -ed, -er/s 'hil, -z, -ɪŋ, -d,
　-ɚ/z
health, -s 'helθ, -s
health|ful, -fully, -fulness 'helθ|fʊl, -fəlɪ,
　-fʊlnɪs
healthsome 'helθsəm
health|y, -ier, -iest, -ily, -iness 'helθ|ɪ, -ɪɚ,
　-ɪɪst, -ɪlɪ, -ɪnɪs
heap, -s, -ing, -ed 'hip, -s, -ɪŋ, -t
hear, -s, -ing/s, heard, hearer/s 'hɪ˞, -z,
　-ɹɪŋ/z, 'h˞d, 'hɪ˞ɹɚ/z
heard (*p.t. of* hear, *q.v.*) 'h˞d
hearken, -s, -ing, -ed 'hɑ˞kən, -z, -ɪŋ,
　-d
hearsay 'hɪ˞seɪ̆
hear't (*from* hear it) 'hɪ˞t
heart, -s, -ed 'hɑ˞t, -s, -ɪd
heartache 'hɑ˞ɹeɪ̆k
heart-beat, -s 'hɑ˞tˌbit, -s
heart-blood 'hɑ˞tˌblʌd
heart(-)burn, -ing, -ed 'hɑ˞tb˞n, -ɪŋ,
　-d
heartburnt 'hɑ˞tb˞nt
heart-deep 'hɑ˞tˌdip
heart-easing 'hɑ˞tˌizɪŋ
heartfelt 'hɑ˞tfelt
heart-grief 'hɑ˞tˌgɹif
hearth, -s 'hɑ˞θ, -s
heart-hardening 'hɑ˞tˌhɑ˞dnɪŋ
heart-heaviness 'hɑ˞tˌhevɪnɪs
heart-inflaming 'hɑ˞tɪnˌfleɪ̆mɪŋ
heartless, -ly, -ness 'hɑ˞tlɪs, -lɪ, -nɪs
heartling, -s 'hɑ˞tlɪŋ, -z
heart-pierced 'hɑ˞tˌpɪ˞st
heart(-)sick, -ness 'hɑ˞tsɪk, -nɪs
heart-sore 'hɑ˞tˌsɔ˞
heart-sorrowing 'hɑ˞tˌsɒɹoʊ̆ɪŋ
heart-string, -s 'hɑ˞tˌstɹɪŋ, -z
heart-struck 'hɑ˞tˌstɹʌk
heart-whole ˌhɑ˞t'hoʊ̆l

i wᴇ ɪ city ɪ hɪt e lᴇt ɛ dᴇbut æ cᴀn a pᴀss ɝ bɪrd ʌ hut ə again ɚ suppᴇr u yᴏu
ʊ shᴏuld o ᴏbey ɔ ᴀwl ɒ cᴏp ɑ fᴀther eɪ̆ pᴀid aɪ̆ hɪgh oʊ̆ gᴏ ɔɪ vᴏice aʊ̆ fᴏund ɪ˞ ᴇar
ɛ˞ ᴀir ʊ˞ pᴏor ɔ˞ fᴏrk ɑ˞ pᴀrk aɪ̆˞ fɪre aʊ̆˞ hᴏur b bᴏy p pit d dᴏg t tᴏp g gᴏt
k kᴉd h hᴏw fi behᴀve dʒ jᴏt tʃ chᴇw z zᴀny s sᴏft v vᴀt f fᴀt ʒ treᴀsure ʃ shᴉp ð thᴇ
θ thᴉn m mᴀn n nᴏ ŋ hᴀng l lᴉp j yᴇs w wᴏn ʍ whᴇw ɹ rᴉgger, aiɹy ɽ maᴛᴛer

heart-wished 'hɑɚ-t͜wɪʃt

heart|y, -ier, -iest, -ily, -iness 'hɑɚ-ɾ|ɪ, -ɪɚ-,
-ɪɪst, -ɪlɪ, -ɪnɪs

heat, -s, -ing, -ed 'hit, -s, -ɪŋ, -ɪd

heath, -s 'hiθ, -s

heathen, -s, -dom 'hiðn̩, -z, -dəm

heathenish 'hiðn̩ɪʃ

heather, -s, -y 'heðɚ-, -z, -ɹɪ

heav|e, -es, -ing/s, -ed, hove, heaver/s
'hiv, -z, -ɪŋ/z, -d, 'hoŏv, 'hivɚ-/z

heaved-up 'hivdˌʌp

heaven (H.), -s 'hevən ['hevn̩], -z (see
spirit)

heaven-bred 'hevn̩ˌbɹed

heaven-hued 'hevn̩ˌfijud

heaven|ly, -liness 'hevn̩|lɪ, -lɪnɪs

heavenly-harnessed 'hevn̩lɪˌhɑɚ-nɪst

heaven-moving 'hevn̩ˌmuvɪŋ

heavenward, -s 'hevn̩wɚ-d, -z

heav|y, -ier, -iest, -ily, -iness 'hev|ɪ, -ɪɚ-,
-ɪɪst, -ɪlɪ, -ɪnɪs

heavy-gaited 'hevɪˌgeɪ̆tɪd

hebenon 'hebɹnən

Hebrew (MV, TGV), -s 'hibɹu, -z

Hecate (HAM, 1HVI, LEAR, MAC,
MSND) 'hekətɪ, 'hekɪt
Note.—With only one exception, i.e.,
1HVI, III.ii.64, this name is always a
disyllable in S.

Hector (AC, ADO, COR, 2HVI, 1HVI,
3HVI, LLL, LUC, MWW, TC, TIT), -s
'hektɚ- [-tɔɚ-], -z

Hecuba (COR, CYM, HAM, LUC, TC,
TIT) 'hekjubə

he'd (contr. of either he had or he would)
'hid (see he'ld)

hedg|e, -es, -ing, -ed, -er/s 'hedʒ, -ɪz, -ɪŋ,
-d, -ɚ-/z

hedgecorner, -s 'hedʒˌkɔɚ-nɚ-, -z

hedgehog, -s 'hedʒˌfɒg, -z

hedge-pig, -s 'hedʒˌpɪg, -z

hedge-priest 'hedʒˌpɹist

hedge-sparrow, -s 'hedʒˌspæɹoŏ, -z

heed, -s, -ing, -ed 'hid, -z, -ɪŋ, -ɪd

heed|ful, -fully, -fulness 'hid|fʊl, -fəlɪ,
-fʊlnɪs

heedfullest 'hidfʊlɪst

heedless, -ly, -ness 'hidlɪs, -lɪ, -nɪs

heft, -s, -ing, -ed 'heft, -s, -ɪŋ, -ɪd

heft|y, -ier, -iest, -ily, -iness 'heft|ɪ, -ɪɚ-,
-ɪɪst, -ɪlɪ, -ɪnɪs

heifer, -s 'hefɚ-, -z

heigh 'heĭ

heigh-ho 'heĭˌhoŏ

height, -s 'haĭt, -s

heighth 'haĭtθ ['haĭθ]

heinous, -ly, -ness 'heĭnəs, -lɪ, -nɪs

heir, -s; -dom, -less 'ɛɚ-, -z; -dəm, -lɪs

heir-apparent, heirs-apparent
ˌɛɚ-ɹə'pæɹənt, ˌɛɚ-zə'pæɹənt

held (p.t. of hold, q.v.) 'held

he'ld 'hid
Note.—This word (the contr. of 'he
would') appears as 'heel'd' in the Folio
version of CYM, II.i.61. Modern editors
have played fast and loose with the
spelling of the word, and particularly
with the punctuation surrounding it, in
order to underpin their own interpretation of the line (and thus its meaning—
caveat emptor). For an in-depth
discussion of the matter, see the line
annotation in H. H. Furness' New
Variorum Edition of Cymbeline, 1913

Helen (CYM, 2HIV, 1HVI, 3HVI, LUC,
RJ, Sonn. 53, TC) 'helɪn

Helena (ALL'S, MSND, RJ) 'helɪnə
Note.—In MSND, I.i.200, the iambic
pentameter requires this name to be
spoken disyllabically, i.e., ['helnə]. It is
also pronounced [hə'linə] when
referring to St. Helena, the British
island-colony in the South Atlantic
(where Napoleon I was exiled)

Helenus (TC) 'helɪnəs

Helias (TC) 'hilɪəs, -ljəs

Helicane (PER) 'helɪkeĭn

Helicanus (PER) ˌhelɪ'keĭnəs

Helicons (2HVI) 'helɪkɒnz

hell (H.), -s 'hel, -z

hell-black 'helˌblæk

hell-born 'helˌbɔɚ-n

hell-bro|th, -s 'helbɹɔ|θ [-bɹɒ|-], -θs [-ðz]

Hellespont (AYLI, OTH, TGV) 'helɪspɒnt

hell-fire 'helˌfaĭɚ-

Hell Gate 'helˌgeɪt

hell-governed 'helˌgʌvɚ-nd

hell-hated 'helˌheĭtɪd

Hell-hound (MAC), **-s** 'helfiaʊnd, -z
hellhound, -s 'helfiaʊnd, -z
hellish, -ly, -ness 'helɪʃ, -lɪ, -nɪs
Hell-kite (MAC) 'helkaɪt
hello he'loʊ
helm, -s 'helm, -z
helmet, -s, -ing, -ed 'helmɪt, -s, -ɪŋ, -ɪd
help, -s, -ing, -ed, -er/s 'help, -s, -ɪŋ, -t, -ɚ/z
helter-skelter 'heltɚ'skeltɚ
hem, -s, -ming, -med 'hem, -z, -ɪŋ, -d
Note.—When referring to a short cough, or the sound one makes when clearing the throat, it's sometimes difficult to determine whether one is to say the word 'hem,' or rather enact the inarticulate sound suggestive of throat-clearing. In AYLI, I.iii.17, 2HIV, III.ii.212, *and* TC, I.iii.165, *one might opt to make the sound of throat-clearing, but in* OTH, IV.ii.29, *one might opt to simply speak the word. Likewise with a few other words, such as 'pah' and 'tut' (q.v.)*
hemlock, -s 'hemlɒk, -s
hemp 'hemp
hempen 'hempən
hempseed 'hempsid
hen, -s 'hen, -z
hence 'hens
hence|forth, -forward ,hens|'fɔɚθ, -'fɔɚwɚd
hence-going 'hens,goʊɪŋ
henpeck, -s, -ing, -ed 'henpek, -s, -ɪŋ, -t
Henry 'henɹɪ
Note.—Sometimes trisyllabic ['henəɹɪ] *in* S., *e.g.,* 1HVI, II.v.82, III.i.76; 2HVI, III.ii.130, IV.viii.34, V.i.48; 3HVI, I.i.143, I.ii.10, III.i.94; RII, IV.i.112; RIII, II.iii.16
Henry, Earl of Richmond (*3HVI*) 'henɹɪ 'ɝl əv 'ɹɪtʃmənd (*see Note for* **Henry**)
Henry, Prince (*1HIV, 2HIV, KJ*) 'pɹɪns 'henɹɪ (*see Note for* **Henry**)

Henry the Eighth (*HVIII*) 'henɹɪ ðɪ 'eɪ̯t̪θ (*see Note for* **Henry**)
Henry the Fifth (*HV,* 3HVI) 'henɹɪ ðə 'fɪfθ (*see Note for* **Henry**)
Henry the Fourth (*1HIV, 2HIV,* 3HVI, *RII*) 'henɹɪ ðə 'fɔɚθ (*see Note for* **Henry**)
Henry the Seventh (HVIII, *RIII*) 'henɹɪ ðə 'sevən̩θ (*see Note for* **Henry**)
Note.—In HVIII, II.i.112, *'Henry' wants to be disyllabic, and 'Seventh' wants to be monosyllabic, i.e.,* ['sevn̩θ]
Henry the Sixth (HV, *1HVI, 2HVI, 3HVI,* RIII) 'henɹɪ ðə 'sɪksθ (*see Note for* **Henry**)
hent, -s, -ing, -ed 'hent, -s, -ɪŋ, -ɪd
Henton, Nicholas (HVIII) 'nɪkələs, -kləs 'hentən
Herald (*COR, HV, 1HVI, 2HVI, LEAR, OTH*), **-s** 'heɹəld, -z
herald (H.), -s, -ing, -ed; -ry 'heɹəld, -z, -ɪŋ, -ɪd; -ɹɪ
herb, -s 'ɝb ['hɝb], -z
Herbert, Sir Walter (*RIII*) ,sɝ 'wɔltɚ 'hɝbɚt
Herbert, Sir William (3HVI) ,sɝ 'wɪljəm 'hɝbɚt
herblet, -s 'ɝblɪt ['hɝb-], -s
Herculean (AC) ,hɝkjʊ'liən, hɝ'kjuliən, -ljən
Note.—Stressed on the second syllable in AC, I.iii.84
Hercules (AC, ADO, COR, CYM, HAM, 1HIV, 1HVI, 3HVI, LLL, MSND, MV, TNK, TS) 'hɝkju,liz [-kjʊ,liz-]
Note.—In COR, IV.vi.100, CYM, IV.ii.311 *and* TNK, I.i.66, *this name is pronounced as a disyllable. 'Hercles'* ['hɝklɪz] *is an accepted form of either 'Hercules' or 'Heracles' (see* **Ercles***)*
herd, -s, -ing, -ed 'hɝd, -z, -ɪŋ, -ɪd
herd|man, -men 'hɝd|mən, -mən
herds|man, -men 'hɝdz|mən, -mən
here 'hɪɚ

---

i we ɨ city ɪ hit e let ɛ debut æ can a pass ɝ bird ʌ hut ə again ɚ supper u you
ʊ should o obey ɔ awl ɒ cop ɑ father eɪ paid aɪ high oʊ go ɔɪ voice aʊ found ɪɚ ear
ɛɚ air ʊɚ poor ɔɚ fork ɑɚ park aɪɚ fire aʊɚ hour b boy p pit d dog t top g got
k kid h how fi behave dʒ jot tʃ chew z zany s soft v vat f fat ʒ treasure ʃ ship ð the
θ thin m man n no ŋ hang l lip j yes w won ʍ whew ɹ rigger, airy ɾ matter

Note.—R. A. Foakes (editor, HVIII, The Arden Shakespeare, 1964) says in his annotation for HVIII, I.ii.87, ". . . and the disyllabic force of 'here,' compensate for its [the line's] *shortness." But this suggestion can only be half of the solution for a line appearing to have only eight beats instead of the regular ten. The ceasura that immediately follows 'here' in the line might also absorb the value of a metric beat. In Frank Kermode's (editor, The Tempest, The Arden Shakespeare, 1958) annotation for TEM, I.ii.53, there is a brief but valuable discussion about monosyllabic words that sometimes receive the value of two metric beats in S. lines of verse "whether or no it is* [they are] *pronounced disyllabically . . ." In HVIII, I.ii.87, 'here' is arguably pronounced disyllabically or given, as Kermode puts it, "a heavy emphasis." Cf. Abbott's A Shakespearian Grammar, §§ 475, 479, 484*

hereabout, -s 'hɪɚˌɹəbaʊt [,--'-], -s
hereafter hɪɚ-'ɹaftɚ
here-approach 'hɪɚ-ɹəˌpɹoʊtʃ
hereditary hɪ'ɹedɪtɚˌɹɪ
Hereford (2HIV, *HVIII*, RII, RIII) 'heˌɹɪfɚd, 'hɚfɚd
Note.—This name in S. is typically disyllabic and often spelled 'Herford'
Herefordshire (1HIV) 'heˌɹɪfɚdʃɚ [-ˌʃɪɚ]
Note.—When this name appears in 1HIV, I.i.39, it is trisyllabic, i.e., ['hɚfɚdʃɚ] *(see Note for* **Hereford***)*
hereof ˌhɪɚ-'ɹɒv
here-remain 'hɪɚ-ɹɪˌmeɪn
heres|y, -ies 'heˌɹɪs|ɪ, -ɪz
heretic, -s 'heˌɹɪtɪk, -s
Herford, Harry (RII) 'hæˌɹɪ 'hɚfɚd
Hermes (HV) 'hɚˌmiz
Hermia (*MSND*) 'hɚˌmɪə, -mjə
Hermione (*WT*) hɚ-'maɪənɪ
Note.—This name is arguably trisyllabic, i.e., [hɚ-'maɪnɪ] *in* WT, I.ii.173; V.iii.25
hermit, -s 'hɚˌmɪt, -s
hermitage, -s 'hɚˌmɪtɪdʒ, -ɪz

Herne (MWW) 'hɚn ['hɑɚn]
hero (**H.**), **-es** 'hɪɚˌɹoʊ, -z
Hero (*ADO*, AYLI, RJ, TGV) 'hɪɚˌɹoʊ ['hiˌɹoʊ]
Herod (AC, HAM, HV, MWW), **-s** 'heˌɹəd, -z
Note.—The First Folio also gives 'Herode.' Regardless of the var. spellings, it is still pronounced as indicated above
heroic, -s, -al, -ally hɪ'ɹoʊɪk, -s, -ḷ, -lɪ
herring, -s 'heˌɹɪŋ, -z
herringbone, -s 'heˌɹɪŋboʊn, -z
Hesperides (LLL, PER) həs'peˌɹɪdɪz
Hesperus 'hespɚˌɹəs
hest, -s 'hest, -s
hew, -s, -ing, -ed, -n, -er/s 'hju, -z, -ɪŋ, -d, -n, -ɚ/z
hewgh 'hjuːh:
Note.—This word appears in LEAR, IV.vi.92 (Folio version), apparently there to represent the sound an arrow makes as it rips through the air toward the 'clout' (the target in archery), or perhaps to represent the sound of a diving falcon as it rushes towards its prey, "or simply Lear's startled awareness of Edgar, as 'hagh' (Quarto version) might suggest" (The Arden Shakespeare, 1997, R. A. Foakes, Editor; line annotation)
heyday 'heɪdeɪ
Hibla *or* **Hybla** (1HIV, JUL) 'haɪblə
Hibocrates (MWW) (*from 'Hippocrates'; see* **prings**) hɪ'bɒkɹətɪz
hic, hac (*L.*) (MWW, IV.i.66) 'hɪk 'hak
Note.—As Onions puts it, "with quibbles on 'hiccup' and 'hack,' i.e., cough." That being the case, one might find it more advantageous to pronounce these (in this instance) as ['hɪk 'hæk]
hic et ubique (*L.*) (HAM, I.v.164) 'hɪk ɛt 'ubɪkwɛ
hic ibat Simois, hic est Sigeia tellus; hic steterat Priami . . . regia . . . celsa senis (*L.*) (TS, III.i.28) 'hɪk 'ibat 'simoʊɪs 'hɪk ɛst sɪ'dʒeɪa 'tɛlus 'hɪk 'stɛtɛɹat pɹɪ'amɪ . . . 'ɹedʒɪɑ . . . 'tʃɛlsɑ 'sɛnɪs
hic jacet (*L.*) (ALL'S, III.vi.59) 'hɪk 'jɑtʃɛt

hick, -s 'hɪk, -s
hid|e, -es, -ing, hid, hidden 'haɪd, -z, -ɪŋ,
  'hɪd, 'hɪdn̩
hideous, -ly, -ness 'hɪdɪəs, -lɪ, -nɪs
hie, -s, -ing, -d 'haɪ, -z, -ɪŋ, -d
Hiems (*L.*) (LLL, V.ii.883; MSND,
  II.i.109) 'haɪəmz
high, -s; -er, -est 'haɪ, -z; -ɚ, -ɪst
high-battled 'haɪˌbætl̩d
high-blown 'haɪˌbloʊn
high-colored 'haɪˌkʌlɚd
high-day 'haɪdeɪ
high-engendered 'haɪɪnˌdʒendɚd
Higher Italy (ALL'S) 'haɪɚ '(ɹ)ɪʧəlɪ
highest-peering 'haɪɪstˌpɪɚ.ɹɪŋ
high-grown 'haɪˌɡɹoʊn
high-judging 'haɪˌdʒʌdʒɪŋ
high-lone 'haɪˌloʊn [ˌ-'-, '-'-]
highly 'haɪlɪ
high(-)most 'haɪmoʊst
Highness (*title*)**, -es** 'haɪnɪs, -ɪz
high-proof 'haɪ'pɹuf ['-ˌ-]
high-reaching 'haɪˌɹitʃɪŋ
high-reared 'haɪˌɹɪɚd
high-speeded 'haɪˌspidɪd
High Steward (HVIII) 'haɪ 'stjuɚd
high-stomached ˌhaɪ'stʌməkt
high-swoll'n 'haɪˌswoʊln
hight 'haɪt
high-viced 'haɪˌvaɪst
high-witted 'haɪˌwɪtɪd
high-wrought 'haɪˌɹɔt
hilding, -s 'hɪldɪŋ, -z
hill, -s 'hɪl, -z
hillock, -s 'hɪlək, -s
hillo hɪ'loʊ
hilt, -s, -ed 'hɪlt, -s, -ɪd
him (H.) 'hɪm (*strong form*), 'ɦɪm ['ɪm]
  (*colloquial weak forms*)
himself hɪm'self
Hinckley (2HIV) 'hɪŋklɪ
hind, -s 'haɪnd, -z
hind|er, -ers, -ering, -ered, -erer/s
  'hɪnd|ɚ, -ɚz, -ɚɹɪŋ, -ɚd, -ɚɹɚ/z

hinder-legs 'haɪndɚˌlegz
hindmost 'haɪndmoʊst
hing|e, -es, -ing, -ed 'hɪndʒ, -ɪz, -ɪŋ, -d
hint, -s, -ing, -ed 'hɪnt, -s, -ɪŋ, -ɪd
hip, -s, -ping, -ped 'hɪp, -s, -ɪŋ, -t
Hipparchus (AC) hɪ'pɑɚkəs
Hippolyta (*MSND, TNK*) hɪ'pɒlɪtə
Hiren (2HIV) 'haɪɹən
Hirtius (AC) 'hɝ·ʃəs
his (H.) 'hɪz (*strong form*), 'ɦɪz ['ɪz]
  (*colloquial weak forms*)
his-begot 'hɪzbɪˌgɒt
Hisperia (AYLI) hɪ'spɪɚ.ɹɪə
hiss, -es, -ing, -ed, -er/s 'hɪs, -ɪz, -ɪŋ, -t,
  -ɚ/z
hist 's:t ['hɪst]
hither 'hɪðɚ
hitherto 'hɪðɚtu [ˌ-'-]
hitherward, -s 'hɪðɚwɚd, -z
hiv|e, -es, -ing, -ed 'haɪv, -z, -ɪŋ, -d
hizz, -es, -ing, -ed 'hɪz, -ɪz, -ɪŋ, -d
ho 'hoʊ
hoa 'hoʊ
hoar 'hɔɚ
hoard (*s. v.*)**, -s, -ing, -ed, -er/s** 'hɔɚd, -z,
  -ɪŋ, -ɪd, -ɚ/z
hoarding (*s.*)**, -s** 'hɔɚdɪŋ, -z
hoarse, -r, -st, -ly, -ness 'hɔɚs, -ɚ, -ɪst,
  -lɪ, -nɪs
hoar|y, -ier, -iest, -ily, -iness 'hɔɚ.ɹ|ɪ, -ɪɚ,
  -ɪst, -ɪlɪ, -ɪnɪs
Hob (COR) 'hɒb
hob, -s 'hɒb, -z
Hobbididence (LEAR) ˌhɒbɪ'dɪdəns
  Note.—This name of a fiend, or devil, is
  given in LEAR, IV.i.63*, and is no doubt*
  related to the 'Hoppedance/Hopdance'
  in LEAR, III.vi.30
hobby-horse, -s 'hɒbɪˌhɔɚs, -ɪz
hobgoblin (H.) (MSND, MWW)**, -s**
  'hɒbgɒblɪn [ˌ-'--], -z
hob(-)nail, -s, -ed 'hɒbˌneɪl, -z
hobnob, -s, -bing, -bed 'hɒbnɒb, -z, -ɪŋ,
  -d

---

i wǐ ɪ cit**y** ɪ h**ĭ**t e l**ĕ**t ɛ d**e**but æ c**ă**n a p**a**ss ɝ b**ĭr**d ʌ h**ŭ**t ə **a**gain ɚ supp**er** u y**ou**
ʊ sh**ou**ld o **o**bey ɔ **aw**l ɒ c**o**p ɑ f**a**ther eɪ p**ai**d aɪ h**igh** oʊ g**o** ɔɪ v**oi**ce aʊ f**ou**nd ɪɚ **ear**
ɛɚ **air** ʊɚ p**oor** ɔɚ f**or**k ɑɚ p**ar**k aɪɚ f**ire** aʊɚ h**our** b b**oy** p p**it** d d**og** t t**op** g g**ot**
k k**id** h **h**ow ɦ be**h**ave dʒ j**ot** tʃ **ch**ew z **z**any s **s**oft v v**at** f f**at** ʒ trea**s**ure ʃ **sh**ip ð **the**
θ **th**in m **m**an n **n**o ŋ ha**ng** l l**ip** j **y**es w **w**on ʍ **wh**ew ɹ **r**igger, ai**r**y ɾ ma**tt**er

hodge, -s 'hɒdʒ, -ɪz
hodge-podge 'hɒdʒˌpɒdʒ
hodge-pudding 'hɒdʒˌpʊdɪŋ
hogs(-)head, -s 'hɒgzfied, -z
hois'd (form of hoisted) 'hɔɪst
hoise 'hɔɪs
hoist, -s, -ing, -ed 'hɔɪst, -s, -ɪŋ, -ɪd
Holborn (RIII) 'hoŭbə˞n
hold, -s, -ing/s, held, holder/s 'hoŭld, -z, -ɪŋ/z, 'held, 'hoŭldə˞/z
Note.—In the Quarto versions of OTH, II.iii159, 'hold' (in its first instance in the line) is probably disyllabic, or at least given heavy emphasis via extension. In so doing, the line becomes a very regular alexandrine line. (Cf. the Note for year)
hold-door 'hoŭldˌdɔ˞
holden (archaic form of held) 'held
hol|e, -es, -ing, -ed 'hoŭl, -z, -ɪŋ, -d
Holdfast (HV) 'hoŭldˌfast
hold-fast 'hoŭldˌfast
holidame or holy-dam 'hɒlɪdəm
holiday, -s 'hɒlɪdeɪ, -z
holiday-time 'hɒlɪdeɪˌtaɪm [-dɪˌt-]
holily 'hoŭlɪlɨ
holiness (H.) 'hoŭlɨnɪs
holla, -'d 'hɒlə, -d
Holland (3HVI), -er/s 'hɒlənd, -ə˞/z
holland (lawn), -s 'hɒlənd, -z
Holland, John (HV, 2HVI) 'dʒɒn 'hɒlənd
hollidam, hallidome, halidom, holy-dame, holidame, or holy-dam 'hɒlɪdəm
hollow, -s, -ing, -ed; -er/s; -est, -ly, -ness 'hɒloŭ, -z, -ɪŋ, -d; -ə˞/z; -ɪst, -lɨ, -nɪs
hollow-hearted 'hɒloŭˌhɑ˞tɪd
Hollowmas (RII) 'hɒloŭməs
Holmedon (1HIV) 'hoŭmdən
Holofernes (LLL) ˌhɒlo'fɜ˞nɨz
Note.—Although the pronunciation proffered above is coventional, some thought should be given to S.'s penchant for punning proper nouns, such as Jacques and la Pucelle (q.v.). In the case of this character, an affected pronunciation will easily bring to mind a 'hollow furnace' (i.e., 'hot air')
holp (archaic p.t. of help) 'hoŭlp ['hɒlp]

holpen (archaic p.p. of help) 'hoŭlpən ['hɒlpən]
hol|y (H.), -ier, -iest, -ily, -iness 'hoŭl|ɨ, -ɪə˞, -ɪɪst, -ɪlɨ, -ɪnɪs
holy-ale, -s 'hoŭlɨˌeɪl, -z
Note.—Technically, this word appears nowhere in S., but is the generally accepted emendation for the Quarto's 'Holydayes' in PER, I.6, and thus fulfills the rhyme scheme of Gower's introduction as Chorus
Holy-day (HVIII) 'hoŭlɨˌdeɪ
Holy Land (1HIV, 2HIV, RII) 'hoŭlɨ 'lænd
Holy-rood Day (1HIV) 'hoŭlɨˌrud ˌdeɪ
holy-thistle 'hoŭlɨˌθɪsl̩
holy-thoughted 'hoŭlɨˌθɔtɪd [-ˌθɔɾɪd]
holy-water 'hoŭlɨˌwɔɾə˞
Holy Writ (ALL'S, OTH, RIII) 'hoŭlɨ 'rɪt
homage, -r/s 'hɒmɪdʒ ['ɒm-], -ə˞/z
home, -s 'hoŭm, -z
home-bred 'hoŭm'bɹed (when att., ['--])
homeless, -ness 'hoŭmlɪs, -nɪs
homel|y, -ier, -iest, -iness 'hoŭml|ɨ, -ɪə˞, -ɪɪst, -ɪnɪs
homespun, -s 'hoŭmspʌn, -z
homeward, -s 'hoŭmwə˞d, -z
homil|y, -ies 'hɒmɪl|ɨ, -ɪz
honest, -ly, -est 'ɒnɪst, -lɨ, -ɪst
honester 'ɒnɪstə˞
honest-hearted 'ɒnɪstˌhɑ˞tɪd
honest-natured 'ɒnɪstˌneɪtʃə˞d
honesty (H.) 'ɒnɪstɨ
honey, -s, -ing, -ed 'hʌnɨ, -z, -ɪŋ, -d
honey-bag, -s 'hʌnɨˌbæg, -z
honey-bee, -s 'hʌnɨˌbi, -z
honey(-)dew 'hʌnɨdju
honey-mouthed 'hʌnɨˌmaŭðd [-ˌmaŭθt]
honeyseed 'hʌnɨsid
honey-stalk, -s 'hʌnɨˌstɔk, -s
honeysuckle, -s 'hʌnɨˌsʌkl̩, -z
honey-sweet 'hʌnɨˌswit
Honi soit qui mal y pense (Fr.) (MWW, V.v.69) oni swɑ ki mal ɨ pɑs
honor (H.), -s, -ing, -ed 'ɒnə˞, -z, -ɪŋ, -d
honorab|le, -ly, -leness 'ɒnə˞ɹəb|l̩, -lɨ, -l̩nɪs
honor-flawed ˌɒnə˞'flɔd
honor-giving 'ɒnə˞ˌgɪvɪŋ

honorificabilitudinitatibus (*L.*) (LLL, V.i.39) ɒnɒˌɹɪfɪˈkɑbɪlɪˌtudɪnɪˈtɑtɪbus

hoo 'hu

hood, -s, -ing; -ed; -less 'hʊd, -z, -ɪŋ, -ɪd; -lɪs

hoodman-blind 'hʊdmən'blaɪnd

Hood, Robin (AYLI, 2HIV, TGV, TNK) 'ɹɒbɪn 'hʊd

hoodwink, -s, -ing, -ed 'hʊdwɪŋk, -s, -ɪŋ, -t

hoo|f (*s.*), -ves 'hʊ|f ['hu|f], -vz

hoof (*v.*), -s, -ing, -ed 'hʊf ['huf], -ɪŋ, -t

hook, -s, -ing, -ed, -er/s 'hʊk, -s, -ɪŋ, -t, -ɚ/z

hook-nosed 'hʊknoŭzd

hoot, -s, -ing, -ed 'hut, -s, -ɪŋ, -ɪd

hop, -s, -ping, -ped, -per/s 'hɒp, -s, -ɪŋ, -t, -ɚ/z

hop|e (H.), -es, -ing, -ed 'hoŭp, -s, -ɪŋ, -t

hopeless, -ly, -ness 'hoŭplɪs, -lɪ, -nɪs

Hopkins, Nicholas (HVIII) 'nɪkələs, -kləs 'hɒpkɪnz

Hoppedance *or* Hopdance (LEAR) 'hɒpdans

Note.—This name of a fiend, or devil, is given in LEAR, III.vi.30, *and probably derives from 'Hobbididence' or 'Hoberdidance'*

Horace (LLL, TIT) 'hɒɹɪs

Horatio (*HAM*) hoˈɹeɪʃɪoŭ [həˈɹ-], -ʃjoŭ

horizon, -s həˈɹaɪzn̩, -z

Note.—Stressed on the first syllable ['hɒɹɪzən] *in* 3HVI, IV.vii.81

horn, -s, -ing, -ed 'hɔɚn, -z, -ɪŋ, -d

horn-beast, -s 'hɔɚn̩ˌbist, -s

hornbook, -s 'hɔɚnbʊk, -s

Horner, Thomas (*2HVI*) 'tɒməs 'hɔɚnɚ

horn-mad 'hɔɚnˌmæd

horn-maker 'hɔɚnˌmeɪkɚ

hornpipe, -s 'hɔɚnpaɪp, -s

horologe (*time-piece*), -s 'hɒɹələɒdʒ, -ɪz

horoscope, -s 'hɒɹəskoŭp, -s

horrib|le, -ly, -leness 'hɒɹɪb|l̩, -lɪ, -l̩nɪs

horrid, -er, -est, -ly, -ness 'hɒɹɪd, -ɚ, -ɪst, -lɪ, -nɪs

horrific hɒˈɹɪfɪk

horri|fy, -fies, -fying, -fied 'hɒɹɪ|faɪ, -faɪz, -faɪɪŋ, -faɪd

horror (H.), -s 'hɒɹɚ, -z

hors|e, -es, -ing, -ed 'hɔɚ·s, -ɪz, -ɪŋ, -t

horseback 'hɔɚ·sbæk

horse(-)back-breaker 'hɔɚ·sbækˌbɹeɪkɚ

horse-drench 'hɔɚ·sˌdɹentʃ

horse(-)hair, -s 'hɔɚ·sˌheɚ, -z

horse-leech, -es 'hɔɚ·sˌlitʃ, -ɪz

horse|man, -men; -manship 'hɔɚ·s|mən, -mən; -mənʃɪp

horse-piss 'hɔɚ·sˌpɪs

horseshoe, -s, -ing, -ed 'hɔɚ·ʃʃu ['hɔɚ·sʃu], -z, -ɪŋ, -d

horse-tail 'hɔɚ·sˌteɪl

horseway, -s 'hɔɚ·sˌweɪ, -z

Hortensio (*TS*) hɔɚ·ˈtensɪoŭ, -sjoŭ

Hortensius (*TIM*) hɔɚ·ˈtensɪəs, -sjəs

hos|e, -es, -ing, -ed 'hoŭz, -ɪz, -ɪŋ, -d

hospice, -s 'hɒspɪs, -ɪz

hospitab|le, -ly, -leness 'hɒspɪɾəb|l̩ [-ˈ---], -lɪ, -l̩nɪs

hospital, -s 'hɒspɪtl̩, -z

Host (MWW, *TGV*) 'hoŭst

host (H.), -s, -ing, -ed 'hoŭst, -s, -ɪŋ, -ɪd

hostage, -s 'hɒstɪdʒ, -ɪz

Hostess (HV, *TS*) 'hoŭstɪs

hostess, -es 'hoŭstɪs, -ɪz

hostess-ship 'hoŭstɪsʃɪp

Hostilius (COR, *TIM*) hɒsˈtɪlɪəs, -ljəs

hostler, -s 'hɒslɚ ['ɒslɚ], -z

ho|t, -tter, -ttest, -tly, -tness 'hɒ|t, -ɾɚ, -ɾɪst, -tlɪ, -tnɪs

hot-blooded 'hɒtˌblʌdɪd [ˌ-'--]

hot(-)hou|se, -ses 'hɒtˌhaŭ|s, -zɪz

Hotspur (*1HIV, RII*) 'hɒtspɚ ['hɒt-]

hour, -s, -ly 'aŭɚ, -z, -lɪ

hour-glass, -es 'aŭɚˌglas, -ɪz

hou|se (*s.*) (H.), -ses 'haŭ|s, -zɪz [-sɪz]

hous|e (*v.*), -es, -ing, -ed 'haŭz, -ɪz, -ɪŋ, -d

house-affairs 'haŭsəˌfɛɚ·z

i w**e** ɪ c**i**ty ɪ h**i**t e l**e**t ɛ d**e**but æ c**a**n a p**a**ss ɝ b**i**rd ʌ h**u**t ə **a**gain ɚ supp**er** u y**ou** ʊ sh**ou**ld o **o**bey ɔ **a**wl ɒ c**o**p ɑ f**a**ther eɪ p**ai**d aɪ h**igh** oŭ g**o** ɔɪ v**oi**ce aŭ f**ou**nd ɪɚ **ear** ɛɚ **air** ʊɚ **poor** ɔɚ **fork** ɑɚ **park** aɪɚ **fire** aŭɚ **hour** b **b**oy p **p**it d **d**og t **t**op g **g**ot k **k**id h **h**ow fi be**h**ave dʒ **j**ot tʃ **ch**ew z **z**any s **s**oft v **v**at f **f**at ʒ trea**s**ure ʃ **sh**ip ð **th**e θ **th**in m **m**an n **n**o ŋ ha**ng** l **l**ip j **y**es w **w**on ʍ **wh**ew ɹ **r**igger, ai**r**y ɾ ma**tt**er

house-clogs 'haŏs,klɒgz
house-eaves 'haŏs,ivz
household, -s; -er/s 'haŏsfioŏld, -z; -ɚ/z
Housel 'haŏzl̩
houseless 'haŏslɪs
housewi|fe (married woman), -ves 'haŏswaĭ|f, -vz
Note.—There is a play on words in TN, I.iii.99–101. 'Distaff' can mean the staff (usually on a spinning wheel) that holds the unspun flax from which thread is drawn, and it can mean women and their concerns generally; and 'house-wife' can mean the woman of the house, but also the small container for sewing equipment (pronounced ['hʌzɪf]). In the context of this particular line, the clearest sense is derived from this pronunciation, i.e., ['hʌzɪf]. The same case can be made for the reference in AYLI, I.ii.30. The Folio gives 'house-wife,' while some modern editions emend to 'hussif,' in order to remain consistent with its intended meaning. In this instance, whether spelled 'house-wife' or 'hussif,' the preferred pronunci-ation for the sake of meaning is ['hʌzɪf]
housewi|fe (small container for sewing equipment) -fes, -ves 'hʌzɪ|f, -fs, -vz
housewifery 'haŏs,wɪfə·ɹɪ ['hʌzɪf.ɹɪ]
hovel, -s, -ling, -led, -ler/s 'hʌvl̩ ['hɒv-], -z, -ɪŋ, -d, -ɚ/z
hovel-post 'hʌvl̩,poŏst ['hɒv-]
hover, -s, -ing, -ed 'hʌvə· ['hɒvə·], -z, -ɹɪŋ, -d
how 'haŏ
howbe't (from howbeit) ,haŏ'bit
howbeit ,haŏ'biːt
howe'er haŏ'ɛɚ·
Hower or Houre, Humphrey (RIII) 'hʌmf.ɹɪ 'aŏɚ·
however haŏ'evə·
howl, -s, -ing, -ed, -er/s 'haŏl, -z, -ɪŋ, -d, -ɚ/z
howlet, -s 'haŏlɪt, -s
howsoe'er ,haŏsoŏ'ɛɚ·
howsoever ,haŏsoŏ'evə·
howsome'er ,haŏsʌ'mɛɚ·
howsomever ,haŏsʌ'mevə·

hox, -es, -ing 'hɒks, -ɪz, -ɪŋ
hoy, -s 'hɔĭ, -z
hoy(-)day (obsolete form of hey-day) 'hɔĭdeĭ
hubbub, -s 'hʌbʌb, -z
Hubert (KJ) 'hjubə·t
hue, -s 'hju, -z
huff, -s, -ing, -ed 'hʌf, -s, -ɪŋ, -t
hug, -s, -ging, -ged 'hʌg, -z, -ɪŋ, -d
huge, -r, -st, -ly, -ness 'hjudʒ, -ə·, -ɪst, -lɨ, -nɪs
hugger-mugger 'hʌgə·,mʌgə·
huisht (sound of buzzing night-flies) 'hwɪʃt
hulk, -s, -ing 'hʌlk, -s, -ɪŋ
hull, -s, -ing, -ed 'hʌl, -z, -ɪŋ, -d
hum, -s, -ming, -med 'hʌm, -z, -ɪŋ, -d
Note.—Sometimes, 'hum' is used to represent the obscure interj. 'humh,' depending on whether the editor follows the Folio or the Quarto version (cf. OTH, V.ii.36, and see humh)
humane, -r, -st, -ly, -ness hju'meĭn, -ə·, -ɪst, -lɨ, -nɪs
Note.—This was a common spelling of the word 'human' until the early eighteenth century. In S.'s time 'humane' and 'human' meant the same things and were merely variant spellings of each other. In fact, in MAC, III.iv.75; COR, III.i.324; MV, IV.i.25, 'humane' (as given in the Folios yet often emended) is stressed on the first syllable ['hjumeĭn]. Consideration of this may influence one's pronunciation choice when modern editors have opted for the word (and therefore the spelling) 'human' instead of 'humane' in S.
humb|le, -les, -ling, -led; -ler, -lest, -ly, -leness 'hʌmb|l̩, -l̩z, -l̩ɪŋ, -l̩d; -lə·, -lɪst, -lɨ, -l̩nɪs
humble-bee, -s 'hʌmbl̩,bi, -z
humble-mouthed 'hʌmbl̩,maŏðd [-,maŏθt]
Hume, John (2HVI) 'dʒɒn 'hjum
humh (obscure interjection) 'hʌm: ['hm:]
Note.—This essentially inarticulate sound is ascribed some measure of meaning in LEAR, III.iv.46 and elsewhere (cf. editor Kenneth Muir's

note, MAC, III.ii.42, The Arden Shakespeare*). Given its apparent meanings in the context in which it's used here, and its spelling (related to, but quite different from, 'humph'), I've indicated specificity of length. In* TIM, II.ii.199 *and* III.iii.1 *for instance, there is no special significance to this exclamatory sound of dissatisfaction*

humid, -ly, -ness 'hjumɪd, -lɪ, -nɪs

humidity hju'mɪdɪtɪ

humiliat|e, -es, -ing, -ed hju'mɪlɪeɪt [hjʊ'm-], -s, -ɪŋ, -ɪd

humiliation, -s hju,mɪlɪ'eɪʃn [hjʊ,m-], -z

humility hju'mɪlɪtɪ [hjʊ'm-]

humor, -s, -ing, -ed 'hjumə˞, -z, -ɹɪŋ, -d

humorless, -ly, -ness 'hjumə˞lɪs, -lɪ, -nɪs

humor-letter, humored-letter 'hjumə˞ˌleɾə˞, 'humə˞dˌleɾə˞

humorous, -ly, -ness 'hjumə˞ɹəs, -lɪ, -nɪs

Humphrey (*2HIV*, HV, 1HVI, *2HVI*) 'hʌmfɹɪ
Note.—Sometimes trisyllabic ['hʌmfə˞ɹɪ] *in S., e.g.,* 2HVI, I.i.192, II.ii.73

Hundred Merry Tales (ADO) 'hʌndɹɪd 'meɹɪ 'teɪlz

hung (*p.t. and p.p. of* **hang**, *q.v.*) 'hʌŋ

Hungarian, -s hʌŋ'gɛə˞ɹɪən, -z

Hungary, King of (MEAS) ,kɪŋ əv 'hʌŋgəɹɪ

hunger, -s, -ing, -ed, -er/s 'hʌŋgə˞, -z, -ɹɪŋ, -d, -ɹə˞/z

Hungerford (1HVI, 3HVI) 'hʌŋgə˞fə˞d

hungerly (*adj.*) (*famished; left wanting, hence sparse*) 'hʌŋgə˞lɪ

hungr|y, -ier, -iest, -ily, -iness 'hʌŋgɹɪ, -ɪə˞, -ɪɪst, -ɪlɪ, -ɪnɪs

hunk, -s 'hʌŋk, -s

hunt, -s, -ing, -ed, -er/s 'hʌnt, -s, -ɪŋ, -ɪd, -ə˞/z

Huntingdon (*HV*) 'hʌntɪŋdən

huntress, -es 'hʌntɹɪs, -ɪz

hunts|man, -men 'hʌnts|mən, -mən

hunt's-up 'hʌntsʌp

hurl, -s, -ing, -ed, -er/s 'hɜ˞l, -z, -ɪŋ, -d, -ə˞/z

hurly 'hɜ˞lɪ

hurly-burl|y, -ies ,hɜ˞lɪ'bɜ˞l|ɪ ['--,--], -ɪz

hurricane, -s 'hʌɹɪkeɪn, -z

hurricano, -es ,hʌɹɪ'keɪnoʊ, -z

hurr|y, -ies, -ying, -ied, -iedly 'hʌɹɪ, -ɪz, -ɪɪŋ, -ɪd, -ɪdlɪ

hurt, -s, -ing 'hɜ˞t, -s, -ɪŋ

hurt|ful, -fully, -fulness 'hɜ˞t|fʊl, -fʊlɪ, -fʊlnɪs

hurt|le, -les, -ling, -led 'hɜ˞t|l̩, -l̩z, -l̩ɪŋ, -l̩d

hurtless 'hɜ˞tlɪs

husband, -s, -ing, -ed 'hʌzbənd, -z, -ɪŋ, -ɪd

husbandless 'hʌzbəndlɪs

husbandry 'hʌzbəndɹɪ

hush (*interj.*) 'hʌʃ ['hʃ]

hush (*s., v.*), **-es, -ing, -ed** 'hʌʃ, -ɪz, -ɪŋ, -t

husht 'hʌʃt ['hʃt]

husk, -s, -ing, -ed 'hʌsk, -s, -ɪŋ, -t

hussif, -s 'hʌzɪf, -s (*cf.* **housewife**)

huswife 'hʌzɪf ['hʌzwɪf] (*cf.* **housewife**)

Hybla *or* **Hibla** (1HIV, JUL) 'haɪblə

Hydra (COR, 1HIV, 2HIV, OTH) 'haɪdɹə

Hydra-headed (HV) 'haɪdɹəˌhedɪd

hyena *or* **hyaena, -s** haɪ'inə, -z

hyen (*hyena*) 'haɪɪn

hymen, -s 'haɪmən [-men], -z

Hymen (ADO, *AYLI*, HAM, PER, TEM, TIM, *TNK*) 'haɪmən [-men]

Hymenaeus (TIT) ,haɪmə'niəs

hymn, -s, -ing, -ed 'hɪm, -z, -ɪŋ, -d

hyperbole, -s haɪ'pɜ˞bəlɪ, -z

hyperbolic, -al, -ally ,haɪpə˞'bɒlɪk, -l̩ [-əl], -əlɪ

Hyperion (HAM, HV, TC, TIM, TIT) haɪ'pɪə˞ɹɪən, -ɹɪən

hypocris|y, -ies hɪ'pɒkɹɪs|ɪ, -ɪz

hypocrite, -s 'hɪpəkɹɪt, -s

hypocritic|al, -ally ,hɪpə'kɹɪɾɪk|l̩, -əlɪ

Hyrcan (MAC) 'hɜ˞kən

Hyrcania (3HVI) hɜ˞'keɪnɪə, -njə

i we ɪ city ɪ hit e let ɛ debut æ can a pass ɜ˞ bird ʌ hut ə again ə˞ supper u you ʊ should o obey ɔ awl ɒ cop ɑ father eɪ paid aɪ high oʊ go ɔɪ voice aʊ found ɪə˞ ear ɛə˞ air ʊə˞ poor ɔə˞ fork ɑə˞ park aɪə˞ fire aʊə˞ hour b boy p pit d dog t top g got k kid h how fi behave dʒ jot tʃ chew z zany s soft v vat f fat ʒ treasure ʃ ship ð the θ thin m man n no ŋ hang l lip j yes w won ʍ whew ɹ rigger, airy ɾ matter

Hyrcanian (HAM, MV) hɜˑˈkeɪnɪən,
-njən
hyssop, -s ˈhɪsəp, -s
hysterica passio (*L.*) (LEAR, II.ii.247)
hɪˈstɛɾɪkɑ ˈpɑsɪo

Ii

I (*the letter*), **-'s** ˈaɪ, -z
I (*personal pronoun*) ˈaɪ
i' (*from* **in**) ˈɪ
Iachimo (*CYM*) ˈjɑkɪmoʊ
Iago (*OTH*) iˈɑgoʊ (*perhaps* [ˈjɑgoʊ] *in*
OTH, V.ii.155)
iamb, -s ˈaɪæm(*b*), -z
iambic, -s aɪˈæmbɪk, -s
ibis, -es ˈaɪbɪs, -ɪz
Icarus (1HVI, 3HVI) ˈɪkəɹəs [ˈaɪk-]
ic|e, -es, -ing, -ed ˈaɪs, -ɪz, -ɪŋ, -t
iceberg, -s ˈaɪsbɜˑg, -z
ice-brook's ˈaɪsˌbɹʊks
ice-cream, -s ˌaɪsˈkɹim, -z (*when att.,*
[ˈ-ˌ-])
Iceland (HV) ˈaɪslənd
Icelandic aɪsˈlændɪk
icicle, -s ˈaɪsɪkl̩, -z
icing ˈaɪsɪŋ
icon, -s ˈaɪkɒn, -z
iconic aɪˈkɒnɪk
ic|y, -ier, -iest, -ily, -iness ˈaɪs|ɪ, -ɪɚ, -ɪɪst,
-ɪlɪ, -ɪnɪs
id ˈɪd
I'd (*contr. of* **I had**, **I could**, *or* **I would**)
ˈaɪd
idea, -s aɪˈdɪə, -z
ideal, -s aɪˈdɪəl [aɪˈdil], -z
ideal|ism, -ist/s aɪˈdɪəl|ɪzəm, -ɪst/s
idealistic, -ally aɪˌdɪəˈlɪstɪk, -əlɪ
ideally aɪˈdɪəlɪ
Iden, Alexander (*2HVI*) ˌælɪgˈzandɚ
ˈ(ɹ)aɪdn̩
identit|y, -ies aɪˈdentɪt|ɪ, -ɪz
ides (**I.**) ˈaɪdz
idiom, -s ˈɪdɪəm, -z
idiot, -s ˈɪdɪət [ˈɪdjət], -s
idiot-worshippers ˈɪdjətˌwɜˑʃɪpɚz
id|le, -les, -ling, -led, -ler/s; -ly, -leness

ˈaɪdl̩, -lz, -lɪŋ [-lɪŋ], -l̩d, -lɚ/z [-lɚ/z];
-lɪ, -l̩nɪs
idle-headed ˈaɪdl̩ˌhedɪd
idol, -s ˈaɪdl̩, -z
idolater, -s aɪˈdɒlətɚ, -z
idolatr|y, -ies aɪˈdɒlətɪ|ɪ, -ɪz
idoliz|e, -es, -ing, -ed, -er/s ˈaɪdl̩ˌaɪz, -ɪz,
-ɪŋ, -d, -ɚ/z
if (**I.**) ˈɪf
i'faith (*interj.*) ɪˈfeɪθ
i'fecks (*interj.*) ɪˈfeks
if't (*contr. of* **if it**) ˈɪft
igloo, -s ˈɪglu, -z
ignis fatuus (*L.*) (1HIV, III.iii.38) ˈinjis
ˈfɑtuʊs [ˈignis ˈfɑtuʊs]
ignit|e, -es, -ing, -ed; -able ɪgˈnaɪt, -s, -ɪŋ,
-ɪd; -əbl̩
ignition ɪgˈnɪʃn̩
ignob|le, -ly, -leness ɪgˈnoʊbl̩, -lɪ, -l̩nɪs
ignominious, -ly, -ness ˌɪgnoʊˈmɪnɪəs, -lɪ,
-nɪs
ignomin|y, -ies ˈɪgnəˌmɪn|ɪ, -ɪz
ignomy ˈɪgnəmɪ
*Note.—This word appears in the First
Folio version of MEAS, II.iv.111 and
was an accepted contracted form of
'ignominy' up until the beginning of the
nineteenth century; however, unless one
decides that this line is headless, the
contracted form throws off the scansion
of the line. Adherence to the Second
Folio's 'ignominy' more typically and
more rightly fulfills S.'s metrical pattern
of the line. Not so, however, for TC,
V.x.33, where the contracted form (as
given in the First Folio) is best for the
metrical pattern of the line (cf. Note for*
broker-lackey). *'Ignomy' also appears
in the First Quarto version of TIT,
IV.ii.117 where it fits nicely into the
metrical pattern of the line*
ignoran|ce (**I.**), **-t/ly** ˈɪgnəɹən|s, -t/lɪ
ignor|e, -es, -ing, -ed ɪgˈnɔɚ, -z, -ɹɪŋ, -d
'ild (*see* **dild**) ˈild
Ilion (LLL, LUC, TC) ˈɪlɪən, -ljən
Ilium (HAM, TC) ˈɪlɪəm, -ljəm
ill, -s ˈɪl, -z
I'll (*contr. of* **I will**) ˈaɪl
ill-beseeming ˌɪlbɪˈsimɪŋ

ill-composed ˌɪlkəmˈpoŏzd
ill-dealing ˌɪlˈdilɪŋ
ill-dispersing ˌɪldɪˈspɚˌsɪŋ
ill-desposed ˌɪldɪˈspoŏzd
ill-divining ˌɪldɪˈvaĭnɪŋ
ill-doing ˌɪlˈduɪŋ
ill-done ˌɪlˈdʌn
ill-erected ˌɪlɪˈɹektɪd (['--,--] *in* RII, V.i.2)
ill-favored, -ly, -ness ˌɪlˈfeĭvɚd (*when att.*, ['-,--]), -lɪ, -nɪs
ill-headed ˌɪlˈhedɪd
ill-inhabited ˌɪlɪnˈhæbɪtɪd
illiterate, -s, -ly, -ness ɪˈlɪɾəɹɪt, -s, -lɪ, -nɪs
illness, -es ˈɪlnɪs, -ɪz
ill-nurtured ˈɪlˌnɝtʃɚd
ill-resounding ˈɪlɹɪˌzaŏndɪŋ
ill-roasted ˌɪlˈɹoŏstɪd (['-,--] *in* AYLI, III.ii.36)
ill-rooted ˌɪlˈɹutɪd
ill-seeming ˌɪlˈsimɪŋ
ill-sheathed ˌɪlˈʃiðd
ill-spirited ˌɪlˈspɪɹɪtɪd (*when att.*, ['-,---])
Note.—See the Note for **spirit**
ill-starred (*att.*) ˈɪlˌstɑɹd
ill-ta'en ˌɪlˈteĭn
ill-tuned ˌɪlˈtjund
illum|e, -es, -ing, -ed ɪˈljum [ɪˈlum], -z, -ɪŋ, -d
illumin|e, -es, -ing, -ed ɪˈljumɪn [ɪˈlum-], -z, -ɪŋ, -d
ill-urged ˌɪlˈlɝdʒd
ill-used ˌɪlˈjuzd
illustrate (*adj.*) ɪˈlʌstɹɪt [ˈɪlʌstɹeĭt]
illustrat|e (*v.*), **-es, -ing, -ed, -or/s** ˈɪləstɹeĭt, -s, -ɪŋ, -ɪd, -ɚ/z
Note.—*In* TNK, II.v.22, *this word is given primary stress on the second syllable, i.e.,* [ɪˈlʌstɹeĭt]. *In* HVIII, III.ii.181, *this word (here in past tense) is also situated in the verse line so as to be given primary stress on its second syllable (and thus avoiding an unusual trochee in the second foot), i.e.,*

[ɪˈlʌstɹeĭtɪd, -stɹətɪd], *but euphony always allows for one's own discretion; and in this case, how one decides to stress 'therein' immediately preceding 'illustrated' will help in determining the most desirable pronunciation*
illustration, -s ˌɪləˈstɹeĭʃn, -z
illustrious, -ly, -ness ɪˈlʌstɹɪəs, -lɪ, -nɪs
illustrous (*var. of* **illustrious**) ɪˈlʌstɹəs
Note.—*This word never really appears in S.; however, modern editors often emend 'illustrious' in* CYM, I.vii.109 *(Folio) to 'illustrous,' 'unlustrous,' 'inlustrous,' etc. in order to accomplish two things: to better fit the meter of the line—even though 'illustrious' suits just as well when a rising diphthong is employed (see 'Diphthongs' [rising] § 2.1 of this dictionary); and to better convey the meaning of the word in its context. Here, 'illustrious' doesn't mean excellent, glorious, or shining brightly, as it does elsewhere in S.; instead, it means the opposite of shining brightly, i.e., to lack luster, or perhaps to be ill-lustrous (to be even more precise); thus, the peculiar pronunciation offered above. If one chooses to retain the Folio's 'illustrious,' then the recommended pronunciation is* [ɪlˈlʌstɹĭəs]
ill-uttering ˈɪlˈʌɾəˌɹɪŋ
ill-weaved ˈɪlˌwivd
ill-well ˌɪlˈwel
ill-will ˌɪlˈwɪl
ill-wresting ˈɪlˌɹestɪŋ
Illyria (TN) ɪˈlɪɹɪə
Illyrian (2HVI) ɪˈlɪɹĭən
I'm (*contr. of* **I am**) ˈaĭm
imag|e, -es, -ing, -ed ˈɪmɪdʒ, -ɪz, -ɪŋ, -d
imagination, -s ɪˌmædʒɪˈneĭʃn, -z
imagin|e, -es, -ing/s, -ed, -er/s ɪˈmædʒɪn, -z, -ɪŋ/z, -d, -ɚ/z
imbalance ˌɪmˈbæləns
imbecile, -s ˈɪmbɪsɪl [-səl], -z

i w**e** ɪ c**i**ty ɪ h**i**t e l**e**t ɛ d**e**but æ c**a**n a p**a**ss ɝ b**i**rd ʌ h**u**t ə **a**gain ɚ supp**er** u y**ou**
ʊ sh**ou**ld o **o**bey ɔ **a**wl ɒ c**o**p ɑ f**a**ther eĭ p**ai**d aĭ h**igh** oŏ g**o** ɔĭ v**oi**ce aŏ f**ou**nd ɪ˞ **ear**
ɛ˞ **air** ʊ˞ **poor** ɔ˞ f**or**k ɑ˞ p**ar**k aĭ˞ f**ire** aŏ˞ h**our** b **b**oy p **p**it d **d**og t **t**op g **g**ot
k **k**id h **h**ow fi be**h**ave dʒ **j**ot tʃ **ch**ew z **z**any s **s**oft v **v**at f **f**at ʒ trea**s**ure ʃ **sh**ip ð **th**e
θ **th**in m **m**an n **n**o ŋ ha**ng** l **l**ip j **y**es w **w**on ʍ **wh**ew ɹ **r**igger, ai**r**y ɾ ma**tt**er

imbecilit|y, -ies ˌɪmbɪ'sɪlɪt|ɪ, -ɪz
imbrace (*var. of* **embrace**, *q.v.*) ɪm'bɹeɪs
imbru|e, -es, -ing, -ed ɪm'bɹu, -z, -ɪŋ, -d
imbu|e, -es, -ing, -ed ɪm'bju, -z, -ɪŋ
[ɪm'bjʊɪŋ], -d
imitari (*L.*) (LLL, IV.ii.121) ˌɪmɪ'tɑɹɪ
imitat|e, -es, -ing, -ed, -or/s 'ɪmɪteɪt, -s,
-ɪŋ, -ɪd, -ə/z
imitation, -s ˌɪmɪ'teɪʃn, -z
immaculate, -ly, -ness ɪ'mækjʊlɪt, -lɪ,
-nɪs
immanit|y, -ies ɪ'mænɪt|ɪ, -ɪz
immask ˌɪ'mask
immaterial, -ly ˌɪmə'tɪɹˌɹɪəl, -ɪ
imminen|ce, -t/ly 'ɪmɪnən|s, -t/lɪ
immoderate, -ly, -ness ɪ'mɒdəˌɹɪt, -lɪ, -nɪs
immoderation ɪˌmɒdə'ɹeɪʃn
immodest, -ly ɪ'mɒdɪst, -lɪ
immodesty ɪ'mɒdɪstɪ
immoment ɪm'moʊmənt
immortal, -s, -ly ɪ'mɔːtl̩, -z, -ɪ
immortality ˌɪmɔː'tælɪtɪ
immortaliz|e, -es, -ing, -ed ɪ'mɔːtl̩aɪz,
-ɪz, -ɪŋ, -d
immune ɪ'mjun
immunit|y, -ies ɪ'mjunɪt|ɪ, -ɪz
immur|e, -es, -ing, -ed, -ement ɪ'mjʊə,
-z, -ɹɪŋ, -d, -mənt
Imogen (*CYM*) 'ɪmodʒɪn
imp, -s, -ing, -ed 'ɪmp, -s, -ɪŋ, -t
impaint ɪm'peɪnt
impair, -s, -ing, -ed; -ment ɪm'pɛə, -z,
-ɹɪŋ, -d; -mənt
impal|e, -es, -ing, -ed, -ement ɪm'peɪl, -z,
-ɪŋ, -d, -mənt
impare *or* **impaire** 'ɪmpɛə
impart, -s, -ing, -ed, -ment/s ɪm'paət, -s,
-ɪŋ, -ɪd, -mənt/s
imparti|al, -ally, -alness ɪm'paəʃl̩, -əlɪ,
-l̩nɪs
impartiality ɪmˌpaə'ʃɹælɪtɪ
impasted ɪm'peɪstɪd
impatien|ce, -t/ly ɪm'peɪʃn|s, -t/lɪ
impawn, -ed ɪm'pɔn, -d
**impeach, -es, -ing, -ed, -er/s, -ment/s;
-able** ɪm'pitʃ, -ɪz, -ɪŋ, -t, -ə/z, -mənt/s;
-əbl̩
imped|e, -es, -ing, -ed ɪm'pid, -z, -ɪŋ, -ɪd
impediment, -s ɪm'pedɪmənt, -s

impel, -s, -ling, -led, -ler/s ɪm'pel, -z, -ɪŋ,
-d, -ə/z
impend, -s, -ing, -ed ɪm'pend, -z, -ɪŋ, -ɪd
impenetrab|le, -ly, -leness ˌɪm'penɪtɹəb|l̩,
-lɪ, -l̩nɪs
imperator, -s ˌɪmpə'ɹɑtɔ [-'ɹeɪt-, -tə],
-z
imperfect, -ly, -ness ɪm'pɜfɪkt [ˌɪm'p-],
-lɪ, -nɪs
imperfection, -s ˌɪmpə'fekʃn, -z
imperial (I.), -s, -ly ɪm'pɪəˌɹɪəl, -z, -ɪ
imperious, -ly, -ness ɪm'pɪəˌɹɪəs, -lɪ, -nɪs
imperseverant ˌɪmpɜ'sevəˌɹənt
Note.—The OED *cites only one instance*
of this word, and in its context the prefix
is negative (not persevering), but this
prefix is often intensive, and certainly
means to be so in CYM, IV.i.14, *when it*
stands for "exceedingly perseverant, i.e.,
stubborn, obstinate" (cf. The Arden
Shakespeare, line annotation for CYM,
IV.i.14, *J. M. Nosworthy, editor, 1955)*
impertinen|ce, -cy, -cies, -t/ly
ɪm'pɜtnən|s, -sɪ, -sɪz, -t/lɪ
impeticos (*v.*) ɪm'petɪkɒs [-koʊs]
Note.—This v., meaning 'to impocket in
one's petticoat (literally 'small coat'),' is
the Clown's own coinage of foolery in
TN, II.iii.27. *No other instance of the*
word is cited in the OED, *nor is there a*
pronunciation proffered, so the
pronunciations provided above must be
considered entirely conjectural
impetuosity ɪmˌpetjʊ'ɒsɪtɪ
impetuous, -ly, -ness ɪm'petjʊəs, -lɪ, -nɪs
impiet|y, -ies ɪm'paɪɪt|ɪ, -ɪz
impious, -ly, -ness 'ɪmpɪəs, -lɪ, -nɪs
implacability ɪmˌplækə'bɪlɪtɪ [-'pleɪk-]
implacab|le, -ly, -leness ɪm'plækəb|l̩
[-'pleɪk-], -lɪ, -l̩nɪs
implant (*s.*), -s 'ɪmplant, -s
implant (*v.*), -s, -ing, -ed ɪm'plant, -s, -ɪŋ,
-ɪd
implement (*s.*), -s 'ɪmplɪmənt, -s
implement (*v.*), -s, -ing, -ed 'ɪmplɪment,
-s, -ɪŋ, -ɪd
implementation ˌɪmplɪmen'teɪʃn
implicit, -ly, -ness ɪm'plɪsɪt, -lɪ, -nɪs
implorator, -s ɪm'plɔəˌɹətə, -z

implor|e, -es, -ing/ly, -ed, -er/s ɪmˈplɔɚ,
-z, -ɹɪŋ/lɪ, -d, -ɹɚ/z
imployment (*var. of* **employment**)**, -s**
ɪmˈplɔɪmənt, -s
import (*s.*) ˈɪmpɔɚt
Note.—Stressed [-ˊ-] *in* 1HVI, I.i.91;
AC, III.iv.3; *arguably stressed* [-ˊ-] *in*
TS, III.ii.100
import (*v.*)**, -s, -ing, -ed; -less** ɪmˈpɔɚt,
-s, -ɪŋ, -ɪd; -lɪs
importan|ce, -cy, -t/ly ɪmˈpɔɚtn̩|s, -sɪ,
-t/lɪ
importation, -s ˌɪmpɔɚˈteɪʃn̩, -z
importment (*s.*) ɪmˈpɔɚtmənt
importunacy ɪmˈpɔɚtjʊnəsɪ
Note.—In TGV, IV.ii.108 *and* TIM,
II.ii.47, *this word is given primary stress*
on the third syllable, i.e., [ˌɪmpɔɚˈtjunəsɪ]
importunate (*adj.*) ɪmˈpɔɚtjʊnɪt
importun|e, -es, -ing, -ed ɪmˈpɔɚtjun
[ˌɪmpɔɚˈtjun], -z, -ɪŋ, -d
importunit|y, -ies ˌɪmpɔɚˈtjunɪt|ɪ, -ɪz
impos|e, -es, -ing, -ed, -er/s ɪmˈpoʊz, -ɪz,
-ɪŋ, -d, -ɚ/z
imposition, -s ˌɪmpəˈzɪʃn̩, -z
impossib|le, -ly ɪmˈpɒsɪb|l̩, -lɪ
impost(h)um|e, -es, -ed ɪmˈpɒstjum, -z,
-d
impostor, -s ɪmˈpɒstɚ, -z
impregnab|le, -ly ɪmˈpɹɛgnəb|l̩, -lɪ
impress (*s.*)**, -es** ˈɪmpɹes, -ɪz
impress (*v.*)**, -es, -ing, -ed** ɪmˈpɹes, -ɪz,
-ɪŋ, -t ([ˈɪmpɹest] *in* LEAR, V.iii.51)
impression, -s ɪmˈpɹeʃn̩, -z
impressive, -ly, -ness ɪmˈpɹesɪv, -lɪ, -nɪs
impressure, -s ɪmˈpɹeʃɚ, -z
imprimis (*L.*) (TGV, III.i.272; TS, IV.i.59)
ɪmˈpɹaɪmɪs [-ˈpɹaɪ-]
imprint (*s.*)**, -s** ˈɪmpɹɪnt, -s (*arguably* [-ˊ-]
in Sonn. 77.3)
imprint (*v.*)**, -s, -ing, -ed** ɪmˈpɹɪnt, -s, -ɪŋ,
-ɪd
imprison, -s, -ing, -ed, -ment/s ɪmˈpɹɪzn̩,
-z, -ɪŋ, -d, -mənt/s

improper, -ly ɪmˈpɹɒpɚ, -lɪ
improviden|ce, -t/ly ɪmˈpɹɒvɪdən|s, -t/lɪ
impuden|ce, -cy, -t/ly ˈɪmpjʊdən|s, -sɪ,
-t/lɪ
impugn, -s, -ing, -ed, -er/s ɪmˈpjun, -z,
-ɪŋ, -d, -ɚ/z
impure, -ly, -ness ɪmˈpjʊɚ ([-ˊ-] *in* LUC,
1078; RIII, III.vii.233), -lɪ, -nɪs
impurit|y, -ies ɪmˈpjʊɚɹɪt|ɪ, -ɪz
imputation, -s ˌɪmpjuˈteɪʃn̩ [-pjʊt-], -z
imput|e, -es, -ing, -ed; -able ɪmˈpjut, -s,
-ɪŋ, -ɪd; -əbl̩
in ˈɪn
inaccessib|le, -ly, -leness ˌɪnækˈsesɪb|l̩
[ˌɪnək-], -lɪ, -l̩nɪs
in-a-door (*indoors*) ˌɪnəˈdɔɚ
inaidible ɹˈneɪdɪbl̩
inane, -ly, -ness ɹˈneɪn, -lɪ, -nɪs
incage (*obsolete var. of* **encage**, *q.v.*)
ɪnˈkeɪdʒ [ɪŋˈk-]
incapabilit|y, -ies ɪnˌkeɪpəˈbɪlɪt|ɪ [ɪŋˌk-],
-ɪz
incapable, -ness ɪnˈkeɪpəbl̩ [ɪŋˈk-], -nɪs
in capite (*L.*) (2HVI, IV.vii.118) ɪn ˈkapɪtɛ
incardinate ɪnˈkaɚdɪnɪt [ɪŋˈk-]
Note.—An early malapropism—a
ludicrous misuse of a word. In TN,
V.i.179–180, *this word (a verb pro-*
nounced [ɪnˈkaɚdɪneɪt, ɪŋˈk-]) *is*
employed humorously as an adj. by S. to
stand for Sir Andrew Aguecheek's
intended 'incarnate'
incarnadin|e, -es, -ing, -ed ɪnˈkaɚnədaɪn
[ɪŋˈk-], -z, -ɪŋ, -d
incarnate (*adj.*) ɪnˈkaɚnɪt [ɪŋˈk-, -neɪt]
incarnat|e (*v.*)**, -es, -ing, -ed** ɪnˈkaɚneɪt
[ɪŋˈk-], -s, -ɪŋ, -ɪd
incarnation (**I.**)**, -s** ˌɪnkaɚˈneɪʃn̩ [ˌɪŋk-]
incedent, -s ˈɪnsɪdənt, -s
incense (*s.*) ˈɪnsens
incens|e (*v.*) (*anger*)**, -es, -ing, -ed** ɪnˈsens,
-ɪz, -ɪŋ, -t [-ɪd]
incens|e (*v.*) (*to perfume or burn*)**, -es,**
-ing, -ed ˈɪnsens, -ɪz, -ɪŋ, -t

incensement ɪn'sensmənt
incertain, -ly ɪn's3ˑtn̩, -lɪ
incertaint|y, -ies ɪn's3ˑtn̩t|ɪ, -ɪz
incertitude ɪn's3ˑtɪtjud
incest 'ɪnsest
incestuous, -ly, -ness ɪn'sestjʊəs, -lɪ, -nɪs
inch, -es, -ing, -ed 'ɪntʃ, -ɪz, -ɪŋ, -t
incharitab|le, -ly ɪn'tʃæˌɪɪtəb|l̩, -lɪ
inch-meal 'ɪntʃˌmil
inch-thick 'ɪntʃˌθɪk ['-'-]
inciden|ce, -cy, -t/s 'ɪnsɪdən|s, -sɪ, -t/s
incision, -s ɪn'sɪʒn̩, -z
incit|e, -es, -ing/ly, -ed, -er/s, -ement/s
   ɪn'saɪt, -s, -ɪŋ/lɪ, -ɪd, -ə˞/z, -mənt/s
incivil ˌɪn'sɪvl̩
incivilit|y, -ies ˌɪnsɪ'vɪlɪt|ɪ, -ɪz
inclination, -s ˌɪnklɪ'neɪʃn̩ [ˌɪŋk-], -z
incline (s.), -s 'ɪnklaɪn ['ɪŋk-], -z
inclin|e (v.), -es, -ing, -ed; -able ɪn'klaɪn
   [ɪŋ'k-], -z, -ɪŋ, -d; -əbl̩
inclip, -s, -ping, -ped ɪn'klɪp, -s, -ɪŋ, -t
incomparab|le, -ly, -leness
   ɪn'kɒmpəˌɪəb|l̩ [ɪŋ'k-], -lɪ, -l̩nɪs
incongruit|y, -ies ˌɪnkən'gɪuɪt|ɪ [ˌɪŋk-],
   -ɪz
incongruous, -ly, -ness ɪn'kɒŋgɪʊəs
   [ɪŋ'k-], -lɪ, -nɪs
inconsiderate, -ly, -ness ˌɪnkən'sɪdəˌɪɪt
   [ˌɪŋk-], -lɪ, -nɪs
inconstan|cy, -t/ly ɪn'kɒnstən|sɪ [ɪŋ'k-],
   -t/lɪ
incontinen|ce, -t/ly, -cy ɪn'kɒntɪnən|s
   [ɪŋ'k-, -tn̩-], -t/lɪ, -sɪ
inconvenienc|e, -es, -ing, -ed
   ˌɪnkən'vinjəns [ɪŋ'k-, -nɪəns], -ɪz, -ɪŋ, -t
inconvenient, -ly ˌɪnkən'vinjənt [ɪŋ'k-,
   -nɪənt], -lɪ
incony ɪŋ'kʌnɪ [ɪn'k-]
incorporal ɪn'kɔ˞pəɪəl
incorporate (adj.) ɪn'kɔ˞pəˌɪɪt [ɪŋ'k-]
incorporat|e (v.), -es, -ing, -ed
   ɪn'kɔ˞pə ɪeɪt [ɪŋ'k-], -s, -ɪŋ, -ɪd
incorpsed ɪn'kɔ˞pst
increase (s.), -s 'ɪnkɪis ['ɪŋk-], -ɪz
   Note.—Sometimes [ɪn'kɪis (ɪŋ'k-)], e.g.,
   Sonn. 1.1 and VA, 791
increas|e (v.), -es, -ing/ly, -ed ɪn'kɪis
   [ɪŋ'k-], -ɪz, -ɪŋ/lɪ, -t
increaseful ɪn'kɪisfʊl [ɪŋ'k-]

incur, -s, -ring, -red ɪn'k3˞ [ɪŋ'k3˞], -z,
   -ˌɪɪŋ, -d
incurable, -ness ɪn'kjʊə˞ˌɪəbl̩ [ɪŋ'k-], -nɪs
incursion, -s ɪn'k3˞ʒn̩ [ɪŋ'k-, -3˞ʃn̩], -z
Ind(e) 'ɪnd, 'aɪnd
   Note.—The pronunciation of this word is
   sometimes dictated by a rhyme scheme,
   e.g., LLL, IV.iii.218 and AYLI, III.ii.86
   (see Note for Rosalind)
indeed ɪn'did
indent (s.), -s 'ɪndent [-'-], -s
indent (v.), -s, -ing, -ed ɪn'dent, -s, -ɪŋ,
   -ɪd
indentation, -s ˌɪnden'teɪʃn̩, -z
indentur|e, -es, -ing, -ed ɪn'dentʃə˞, -z,
   -ˌɪɪŋ, -d
ind|ex, -exes, -ices, -exing, -exed 'ɪnd|eks,
   -eksɪz, -ˌɪsiz, -eksɪŋ, -ekst
India (1HIV, HVIII, MSND, MV, TC,
   TN) 'ɪndɪə, -djə
Indian (3HVI, HVIII, MSND, MV,
   TEM), -s 'ɪndɪən, -z, -djən, -z
Indian-like (ALL'S) 'ɪndjənˌlaɪk
indicat|e, -es, -ing, -ed, -or/s 'ɪndɪkeɪt, -s,
   -ɪŋ, -ɪd, -ə˞/z
indication, -s ˌɪndɪ'keɪʃn̩, -z
indict, -s, -ing, -ed, -er/s, -ment/s; -able
   ɪn'daɪt, -s, -ɪŋ, -ɪd, -ə˞/z, -mənt/s; -əbl̩
Indies (COM, HVIII, MV, MWW, TN)
   'ɪndɪz
indifferen|ce, -cy, -t/ly ɪn'dɪfɪən|s
   [-'dɪfə˞ɪ-], -sɪ, -t/lɪ
indigest 'ɪndɪˌdʒest
indigestion ˌɪndɪ'dʒestʃən
indign (unworthy; shameful) ɪn'daɪn
indignant, -ly ɪn'dɪgnənt, -lɪ
indignation ˌɪndɪg'neɪʃn̩
indignit|y, -ies ɪn'dɪgnɪt|ɪ, -ɪz
indigo, -s 'ɪndɪgoʊ, -z
indirect, -ly, -ness ˌɪndɪ'ɪekt, -lɪ, -nɪs
indirection ˌɪndɪ'ɪekʃn̩
indiscreet, -ly, -ness ˌɪndɪ'skɪit, -lɪ, -nɪs
indiscretion, -s ˌɪndɪ'skɪeʃn̩, -z
indispos|e, -es, -ing, -ed ˌɪndɪ'spoʊz, -ɪz,
   -ɪŋ, -d
indisposition, -s ɪnˌdɪspə'zɪʃn̩ ['-,--'--], -z
indissolub|le, -ly, -ness ˌɪndɪ'sɒljʊb|l̩, -lɪ,
   -nɪs
   Note.—In MAC, III.i.17, this word is

stressed on the second syllable, i.e., [ɪnˈdɪsəljʊbl̩], *a pronunciation still considered acceptable (chiefly Brit.)*

indistinct, -ly, -ness ˌɪndɪˈstɪŋkt, -lɪ, -nɪs

indistinguishab|le, -ly, -leness ˌɪndɪˈstɪŋgwɪʃəb|l̩, -lɪ, -l̩nɪs

indit|e, -es, -ing, -ed, -er/s ɪnˈdaɪt, -s, -ɪŋ, -ɪd, -ɚ/z

Note.—See **endite**

individable ˌɪndɪˈvaɪdəbl̩

individual, -s, -ly ˌɪndɪˈvɪdʒʊəl, -z, -ɪ

indrenched ɪnˈdɹentʃt

indubitate (*adj.*) ɪnˈdjubɪtɪt

induc|e, -es, -ing, -ed, -er/s, -ement/s ɪnˈdjus, -ɪz, -ɪŋ, -t, -ɚ/z, -mənt/s

induct, -s, -ing, -ed, -or/s ɪnˈdʌkt, -s, -ɪŋ, -ɪd, -ɚ/z

induction, -s ɪnˈdʌkʃn̩, -z

indu|e (*var. of* **endue**)**, -es, -ing, -ed** ɪnˈdju, -z, -ɪŋ, -d

indulgen|ce, -ces, -t/ly ɪnˈdʌldʒən|s, -sɪz, -t/lɪ

Note.—In AC, I.iv.16, a case can be made for giving the word 'indulgent' primary stress on the first syllable and secondary stress on the last syllable, i.e., [ˈɪndʌl̩dʒənt, ˈɪndəl-]. *Between eighty and ninety other words in S. shift syllabic stress due to where they fall in the metrical pattern of a verse line, but this is probably not one of them. Pope, et al., emends 'Let's' to 'Let us' thereby retaining the familiar form of 'indulgent.' Also, one might allow the full-stop in the middle of the line to absorb the value of a beat (not an uncommon occurrence in S.), which accomplishes the same thing but without any emendation necessary*

indurance ɪnˈdjʊɚəns

indure (*obsolete form of* **endure***, q.v.*) ɪnˈdjʊɚ

indurate (*adj.*) ˈɪndjʊɹɪt [-djʊɚ-]
Note.—Stressed [-́--] *in 3HVI, I.iv.142*

indurat|e (*v.*)**, -es, -ing, -ed** ˈɪndjʊɹeɪt [-djʊɚ-], -s, -ɪŋ, -ɪd

industrial, -s ɪnˈdʌstɹɪəl, -z

industrialization ɪnˌdʌstɹɪəlɪˈzeɪʃn̩

industrializ|e, -es, -ing, -ed ɪnˈdʌstɹɪəlaɪz, -ɪz, -ɪŋ, -d

industrious, -ly ɪnˈdʌstɹɪəs, -lɪ

industr|y, -ies ˈɪndəstɹɪ|ɪ, -ɪz

inequalit|y, -ies ˌɪnɪˈkwɒlɪt|ɪ, -ɪz

inestimab|le, -ly ɪnˈestɪməb|l̩, -lɪ

inevitability ɪnˌevɪɹəˈbɪlɪtɪ

inevitab|le, -ly, -leness ɪˈnevɪɹəb|l̩ [ˌɪnˈe-], -lɪ, -l̩nɪs

inexecrable ɪnˈeksɪkɹəbl̩

inexorab|le, -ly, -leness ɪnˈeksəɹəb|l̩, -lɪ, -l̩nɪs

infallib|le, -ly ɪnˈfælɪb|l̩, -lɪ

infamonize (*perversion of* **infamize** *in LLL*) ɪnˈfæmənaɪz

infamy ˈɪnfəmɪ

infant, -s ˈɪnfənt, -s

infant-like ˈɪnfəntˌlaɪk

infect, -s, -ing, -ed ɪnˈfekt, -s, -ɪŋ, -ɪd

infection, -s ɪnˈfekʃn̩, -z

infectious, -ly, -ness ɪnˈfekʃəs, -lɪ, -nɪs

infer, -s, -ring, -red; -able ɪnˈfɝ, -z, -ɹɪŋ, -d; -ɹəbl̩

inference, -s ˈɪnfəɹəns, -ɪz

inferior, -s ɪnˈfɪɚ̯ɹɪɚ, -z

inferiorit|y, -ies ɪnˌfɪɚ̯ɹɪˈɒɹɪt|ɪ, -ɪz

inferno, -s ɪnˈfɝnoʊ, -z

infest, -s, -ing, -ed ɪnˈfest, -s, -ɪŋ, -ɪd

infestation, -s ˌɪnfeˈsteɪʃn̩, -z

infettered (*var. of* **enfettered**) ɪnˈfeɹɚd

infidel, -s ˈɪnfɪdəl [-fɪdel], -z

infidelit|y, -ies ˌɪnfɪˈdelɪt|ɪ, -ɪz

infinite, -ly, -ness ˈɪnfɪnɪt [-fn̩ɪt], -lɪ, -nɪs

infinitive, -s, -ly ɪnˈfɪnɪtɪv, -z, -lɪ

infinit|y, -ies ˌɪnˈfɪnɪt|ɪ, -ɪz

infirm, -ly ˌɪnˈfɝm, -lɪ

infirmit|y, -ies ɪnˈfɝmɪt|ɪ, -ɪz

infix, -es, -ing, -ed ɪnˈfɪks, -ɪz, -ɪŋ, -t

inflam|e, -es, -ing, -ed ɪnˈfleɪm, -z, -ɪŋ, -d

inflammation, -s ˌɪnfləˈmeɪʃn̩, -z

---

i wᴇ ɪ city ɪ hɪt e lᴇt ɛ dᴇbut æ can a pass ɝ bird ʌ hut ə again ɚ suppᴇr u yᴏu ʊ shᴏuld o ᴏbey ɔ awl ɒ cᴏp ɑ fᴀther eɪ paid aɪ high oʊ gᴏ ɔɪ voice aʊ found ɪɚ ear ɛɚ air ʊɚ poor ɔɚ fork ɑɚ park aɪɚ fire aʊɚ hour b bᴏy p pit d dᴏg t tᴏp g gᴏt k kid h hᴏw fi behave dʒ jot tʃ chew z zany s sᴏft v vᴀt f fᴀt ʒ treaᴤure ʃ ship ð the θ thin m man n no ŋ hang l lip j yes w wᴏn ʍ whew ɹ rigger, airʏ ɾ maᴛter

inflat|e, -es, -ing, -ed ɪnˈfleɪt, -s, -ɪŋ, -ɪd
inflect, -s, -ing, -ed ɪnˈflɛkt, -s, -ɪŋ, -ɪd
inflict, -s, -ing, -ed ɪnˈflɪkt, -s, -ɪŋ, -ɪd
influenc|e, -es, -ing, -ed ˈɪnfluəns, -ɪz, -ɪŋ, -t
influenti|al, -ally ˌɪnfluˈenʃ|l, -əlɪ
infold, -s, -ing, -ed ɪnˈfoʊld, -z, -ɪŋ, -ɪd
inforce (*var. of* **enforce**, *q.v.*) ɪnˈfɔɚs
inform, -s, -ing, -ed, -er/s ɪnˈfɔɚm, -z, -ɪŋ, -d, -ɚ/z
informant, -s ɪnˈfɔɚmənt, -s
information, -s ˌɪnfɚˈmeɪʃn̩, -z
infortunate ɪnˈfɔɚtʃnɪt
infrachisement (*obscure form of* **enfranchisement**, *q.v.*) ɪnˈfɹæntʃaɪzmənt [-tʃɪz-]
infring|e, -es, -ing, -ed, -er/s, -ement/s ɪnˈfɹɪndʒ, -ɪz, -ɪŋ, -d, -ɚ/z, -mənt/s
infus|e, -es, -ing, -ed, -er/s ɪnˈfjuz, -ɪz, -ɪŋ, -d, -ɚ/z
Note.—*Arguably stressed on the first syllable, i.e.,* [ˈɪnfjuz] *in* TNK, I.i.73
infusion, -s ɪnˈfjuʒn̩, -z
ingage (*obscure form of* **engage**, *q.v.*) ɪnˈgeɪdʒ [ɪŋˈg-]
ingenious, -ly, -ness ɪnˈdʒinjəs, -lɪ, -nɪs
ingenuity ˌɪndʒɪˈnjʊɪtɪ [-njuɪ-]
inglorious, -ly, -ness ɪnˈglɔɹɪəs [ɪŋˈg-], -lɪ, -nɪs
ingot, -s ˈɪŋgət, -s
ingraft (*var. of* **engraft**, *q.v.*) ɪnˈgɹaft [ɪŋˈg-]
ingrate, -s ˈɪngɹeɪt [ˈɪŋg-], -s ([-ˈ-] *in* KJ, V.ii.151; TN, V.i.111; 1HIV, I.iii.135; TS, I.ii.268)
ingrateful ɪnˈgɹeɪtfʊl [ɪŋˈg-]
ingratitude, -s ɪnˈgɹæɾɪtjud [ɪŋˈg-], -z
ingredience ɪnˈgɹidɪəns [ɪŋˈg-]
ingredient, -s ɪnˈgɹidɪənt [ɪŋˈg-], -s
ingross (*obscure form of* **engross**, q.v.) ɪnˈgɹoʊs [ɪŋˈg-]
in hac spe vivo (*L.*) (PER, II.ii.43) in ˈhɑk spɛ ˈvivo
in(-)hears|e, -es, -ing, -ed ɪnˈfiɜˑs, -ɪz, -ɪŋ, -t
inherit, -s, -ing, -ed, -or/s; -able, -ance/s ɪnˈfieɹɪt, -s, -ɪŋ, -ɪd, -ɚ/z; -əbl̩, -əns/ɪz
inheritrix, -es ɪnˈfieɹɪtɹɪks, -ɪz
inhibit, -s, -ing, -ed ɪnˈhɪbɪt, -s, -ɪŋ, -ɪd

inhibition, -s ˌɪnfɪˈbɪʃn̩, -z
inhooped ɪnˈhupt
inhospitab|le, -ly, -leness ɪnˈhɒspɪɾəb|l̩ [ˌɪnhɒˈsp-], -lɪ, -l̩nɪs
inhuman ɪnˈhjumən
Note.—*In* MV, IV.i.4, *editors often emend the Folio's 'inhumane' to 'inhuman' (cf. Note for* **humane**). *Great care should be taken, however, in pronouncing the word in accordance with one's meaning, and how one chooses to scan the line: an alexandrine line allows for* [ɪnˈhjumən, ɪnˈhjumeɪn], *and a five-and-a-half foot line allows for* [ˌɪnhjuˈmeɪn]
iniquit|y (I.), -ies ɪˈnɪkwɪt|ɪ, -ɪz
initiate (*s.*), **-s** ɪˈnɪʃɪt [-ʃɪt], -s
initiat|e (*v.*), **-es, -ing, -ed, -or/s** ɪˈnɪʃɪeɪt, -s, -ɪŋ, -ɪd, -ɚ/z
injointed ɪnˈdʒɔɪntɪd
injunction, -s ɪnˈdʒʌŋkʃn̩, -z
injur|e, -es, -ing, -ed, -er/s ˈɪndʒɚ, -z, -ɹɪŋ, -d, -ɹɚ/z
injurious, -ly, -ness ɪnˈdʒʊɚɹɪəs, -lɪ, -nɪs
injur|y, -ies, -ied ˈɪndʒəɹ|ɪ, -ɪz, -ɪd
injustice ɪnˈdʒʌstɪs
inkhorn, -s ɪŋkfiɔɚn, -z
inkle, -s ˈɪŋkl̩, -z
inkling, -s ˈɪŋklɪŋ, -z
ink|y, -ier, -iest, -iness ˈɪŋk|ɪ, -ɪɚ, -ɪɪst, -ɪnɪs
inland, -s, -er/s ˈɪnlənd, -z, -ɚ/z
inlay (*s.*) ˈɪnleɪ
inlay (*v.*), **-s, -ing, inlaid** ˌɪnˈleɪ, -z, -ɪŋ, ˌɪnˈleɪd (*when att.,* [ˈɪnleɪd])
Note.—*Arguably given primary stress on the first syllable, i.e.,* [ˈɪnleɪ] *in* CYM, V.v.353
inly ˈɪnlɪ
inmost ˈɪnmoʊst
inn, -s ˈɪn, -z
innocen|ce, -cy ˈɪnəsn̩|s, -sɪ (*see Note for* **innocent**)
innocent, -s, -ly ˈɪnəsn̩t, -s, -lɪ
Note.—*S. very often syncopates this word into a disyllable, i.e.,* [ˈɪnˑsn̩t], *e.g.,* ADO, IV.i.160, V.i.63, 67, 258; KJ, IV.ii.252, 259; MAC, I.v.65, IV.iii.16; *etc.*
Innocent, Pope (KJ) ˈpoʊp ˈɪnəsn̩t

innovat|e, -es, -ing, -ed, -or/s 'ɪnoveɪt, -s, -ɪŋ, -ɪd, -ə/z

innovation, -s ˌɪno'veɪʃn̩, -z

Inns o' Court ˌɪnz ə'kɔɚt

Inns of Court ˌɪnz əv 'kɔɚt

innumerab|le, -ly, -leness ɪ'njumə·ɹəb|l̩, -lɨ, -l̩nɪs

inoculat|e, -es, -ing, -ed, -or/s ɪ'nɒkjʊleɪt, -s, -ɪŋ, -ɪd, -ə/z

inordinate, -ly, -ness ɪ'nɔɚdɪnɪt [-dn̩ɪt], -lɨ, -nɪs

inprimus (*L.*) (TGV, III.i.275; TS, IV.i.66) ɪn'pɹaɪmus [-'praɪ-]

inquir|e, -es, -ing/ly, -ed, -er/s ɪn'kwaɪɚ [ɪŋ'k-], -z, -ɹɪŋ/lɨ, -d, -ɹə/z

inquisition, -s ˌɪnkwɪ'zɪʃn̩ [ˌɪŋk-], -z

inrich(e) (*obsolete form of* enrich, *q.v.*) ɪn'ɹɪtʃ

inroad, -s 'ɪnɹoŭd, -z

in's (*contr. of* in his) 'ɪnz

insane, -ly, -ness ɪn'seɪn, -lɨ, -nɪs
Note.—*In MAC, I.iii.84, there might be some advantage in scanning the line regularly—that is, iambically—thus putting primary stress on the first syllable rather than the second*

insanie ɪn'seɪnɪə [-ni]
Note.—*This extremely rare word appears in prose in LLL,V.i.25 and is surmised by me to stand for the L. 'insania, -ae' indicating primary stress on the second syllable. It must be acknowledged that the word appearing in its place in the Folios and Quartos is 'infamie.' Evidently, sense and meaning are what motivate modern editors to choose the former over the latter. For a more complete discussion on the matter, see R. W. David's note (found in the line's annotation in* The Arden Shakespeare, *1951)*

insatiate, -ly, -ness ɪn'seɪʃɪɪt [-ʃɪt], -lɨ, -nɪs

insconc|e -es, -ing, -ed ɪn'skɒns, -ɪz, -ɪŋ, -t

inscrib|e, -es, -ing, -ed, -er/s ɪn'skɹaɪb, -z, -ɪŋ, -d, -ə/z

inscription, -s ɪn'skɹɪpʃn̩, -z

inscrolled ɪn'skɹoŭld

inscrutability ɪnˌskɹuɾə'bɪlɪtɨ

inscrutab|le, -ly, -leness ɪn'skɹuɾəb|l̩, -lɨ, -l̩nɪs

insculped ɪn'skʌlpt

insculpture ɪn'skʌlptʃə

insensib|le, -ly, -leness ɪn'sensɪb|l̩, -lɨ, -l̩nɪs

inseparab|le, -ly, -leness ɪn'sepə·ɹəb|l̩, -lɨ, -l̩nɪs

inseparate ɪn'sepə·ɹɪt

insert (*s.*), -s 'ɪnsɝt, -s

insert (*v.*), -s, -ing, -ed ɪn'sɝt, -s, -ɪŋ, -ɪd

inshelled ɪn'ʃeld

inship, -s, -ping, -ped ɪn'ʃɪp, -s, -ɪŋ, -t

insinuat|e, -es, -ing/ly, -ed, -or/s ɪn'sɪnjʊeɪt, -s, -ɪŋ/lɨ, -ɪd, -ə/z

insinuation, -s ɪnˌsɪnjʊ'eɪʃn̩, -z

insist, -s, -ing, -ed ɪn'sɪst, -s, -ɪŋ, -ɪd

insisture ɪn'sɪstʃə

insociab|le, -ly, -leness ɪn'soŭʃəb|l̩, -lɨ, -l̩nɪs

insolen|ce, -t/ly 'ɪnsələn|s [-sʊl-], -t/lɨ

insomuch ˌɪnsoŭ'mʌtʃ

inspect, -s, -ing, -ed, -or/s ɪn'spekt, -s, -ɪŋ, -ɪd, -ə/z

inspection, -s ɪn'spekʃn̩, -z

inspiration, -s ˌɪnspɪ'ɹeɪʃn̩, -z

inspir|e, -es, -ing/ly, -ed, -er/s ɪn'spaɪɚ, -z, -ɹɪŋ/lɨ, -d, -ɹə/z

instigation, -s ˌɪnstɪ'geɪʃn̩, -z

install, -s, -ing, -ed ɪn'stɔl, -z, -ɪŋ, -d

installation, -s ˌɪnstə'leɪʃn̩, -z

instalment, -s ɪn'stɔlmənt, -s

instat|e, -es, -ing, -ed ɪn'steɪt, -s, -ɪŋ, -ɪd

instigat|e, -es, -ing, -ed, -or/s 'ɪnstɪgeɪt, -s, -ɪŋ, -ɪd, -ə/z

instinct (*s.*), -s 'ɪnstɪŋkt, -s
Note.—*Sometimes* [ɪn'stɪŋkt] *in S., e.g.,* 2HIV, I.i.86; 2HVI, III.ii.249; RIII,

II.iii.42, Sonn. 50.7, *and arguably in*
COR, V.iii.35; CYM, IV.ii.177
instinct (*adj.*) ɪn'stɪŋkt
instinctive, -ly ɪn'stɪŋktɪv, -lɪ
institut|e, -es, -ing, -ed 'ɪnstɪtjut, -s, -ɪŋ,
-ɪd
institution, -s; -al ˌɪnstɪ'tjuʃn̩, -z; -l̩
instruct, -s, -ing, -ed, -or/s ɪn'stɹʌkt, -s,
-ɪŋ, -ɪd, -ɚ/z
instruction, -s; -al ɪn'stɹʌkʃn̩, -z; -l̩
instructive, -ly, -ness ɪn'stɹʌktɪv, -lɪ, -nɪs
instrument, -s 'ɪnstɹʊmənt, -s
instrumental, -ly; -ist/s ˌɪnstɹʊ'mentl̩, -ɪ;
-ɪst/s
insufficience ˌɪnsə'fɪʃns
insufficien|cy, -cies, -t/ly ˌɪnsə'fɪʃn̩|sɪ, -sɪz,
-t/lɪ
insult (*s.*), **-s** 'ɪnsʌlt, -s
insult (*v.*), **-s, -ing/ly, -ed, -er/s** ɪn'sʌlt, -s,
-ɪŋ/lɪ, -ɪd, -ɚ/z
insultment ɪn'sʌltmənt
insupportab|le, -ly, -leness ˌɪnsə'pɔɚtəb|l̩,
-lɪ, -l̩nɪs
insuppressib|le, -ly ˌɪnsʊ'pɹesɪb|l̩, -lɪ
insuppressive ˌɪnsʊ'pɹesɪv
insurrection, -s ˌɪnsəɚ'ɹekʃn̩, -z
in't (*contr. of* in it) 'ɪnt
inteemable ɪn'timəbl̩
Integer vitae, scelerisque purus, Non
eget Mauri jaculis, nec arcu (*L.*) (TIT,
IV.ii.20,21) 'ɪntɛdʒɛɚ 'vitaɪ ['viti, 'vaɪti]
ˌsɛlɛ'ɹiskwɛ 'pʊrus non 'ɛdʒɛt 'maʊ̆ɹɪ
'dʒɑkʊlɪs [-kjʊlɪs] nɛk 'ɑɚ̆ku
intelligen|ce, -ces, -cing, -cer/s
ɪn'telɪdʒən|s, -sɪz, -sɪŋ, -sɚ/z
intelligent, -ly ɪn'telɪdʒənt, -lɪ
intemperance ɪn'tempəɹəns [-pɹə-]
intemperate, -ly, -ness ɪn'tempəɹɪt
[-pɹɪ-], -lɪ, -nɪs
intend, -s, -ing, -ed, -ment/s ɪn'tend, -z,
-ɪŋ, -ɪd, -mənt/s
intense, -ly, -ness ɪn'tens, -lɪ, -nɪs
intentively ɪn'tentɪvlɪ
inter (*v.*), **-s, -ring, -red** ɪn'tɜ˞, -z, -ɹɪŋ, -d
inter (*L.*) 'ɪntɚ ['ɪntɛɚ̆]
intercept (*s.*), **-s** 'ɪntəɚsept, -s
intercept (*v.*), **-s, -ing, -ed, -er/s**
ˌɪntəɚ'sept, -s, -ɪŋ, -ɪd, -ɚ/z
interception, -s ˌɪntəɚ'sepʃn̩, -z

interceptor, -s ˌɪntəɚ'septɚ, -z
intercession, -s ˌɪntəɚ'seʃn̩, -z
intercessor, -s ˌɪntəɚ'sesɚ ['----], -z
intercessory ˌɪntəɚ'sesəɹɪ
interchange (*s.*), **-s** 'ɪntəɚtʃeɪ̆ndʒ, -ɪz
interchang|e (*v.*), **-es, -ing, -ed**
ˌɪntəɚ'tʃeɪ̆ndʒ, -ɪz, -ɪŋ, -d
interchangeably ˌɪntəɚ'tʃeɪ̆ndʒəblɪ
interchangement ˌɪntəɚ'tʃeɪ̆ndʒmənt
interdiction, -s ˌɪntəɚ'dɪkʃn̩, -z
interessed (*obsolete p.p. meaning 'propri-*
etary concerns and claims') ˌɪntəɚ'ɹest
interest, -s, -ing, -ed 'ɪntɹɪst ['ɪntəɹest],
-s, -ɪŋ, -ɪd
inter(')gator|y (*syncopated form of*
interrogatory, *q.v.*), **-ies** ɪn'tɜ˞gətəɹ|ɪ, -ɪz
Note.—*This is the typical way of*
pronouncing the word in S.
interim (**I.**), **-s** 'ɪntəɹɪm, -z
interior, -s, -ly ɪn'tɪɚ˞ɹɪɚ, -z, -lɪ
interject, -s, -ing, -ed, -or/s ˌɪntəɚ'dʒekt,
-s, -ɪŋ, -ɪd, -ɚ/z
interjection, -s ˌɪntəɚ'dʒekʃn̩, -z
interjoin ˌɪntəɚ'dʒɔɪ̆n
interlac|e, -es, -ing, -ed ˌɪntəɚ'leɪ̆s, -ɪz, -ɪŋ,
-t
intermingle, -les, -ling, -led ˌɪntəɚ'mɪŋg|l̩,
-l̩z, -lɪŋ, -l̩d
intermission, -s ˌɪntəɚ'mɪʃn̩, -z
intermissive ˌɪntəɚ'mɪsɪv
intermit, -s, -ting/ly, -ted ˌɪntəɚ'mɪt, -s,
-ɪŋ/lɪ, -ɪd
intermittent, -ly ˌɪntəɚ'mɪtn̩t, -lɪ
intermix, -es, -ing, -ed ˌɪntəɚ'mɪks, -ɪz,
-ɪŋ, -t
interpos|e, -es, -ing, -ed, -er/s ˌɪntəɚ'poʊ̆z
['---'], -ɪz, -ɪŋ, -d, -ɚ/z
interpret, -s, -ing, -ed, -er/s ɪn'tɜ˞pɹɪt, -s,
-ɪŋ, -ɪd, -ɚ/z
interpretation, -s ɪnˌtɜ˞pɹɪ'teɪ̆ʃn̩, -z
interpretative, -ly ɪn'tɜ˞pɹɪtətɪv [-ˌteɪ̆tɪv],
-lɪ
In terram Salicam mulieres ne succedant
(*L.*) (HV, I.ii.38) ɪn 'tɛɾɑm 'salɪkɑm
mul'jɛɾɛs nɛ sʊk'sɛdɑnt
interrogat|e, -es, -ing, -ed, -or/s
ɪn'tɛɹʊgeɪ̆t, -s, -ɪŋ, -ɪd, -ɚ/z
interrogation, -s ɪnˌtɛɹʊ'geɪ̆ʃn̩, -z
interrogative, -s, -ly ˌɪntəɚ'ɹɒgətɪv, -z, -lɪ

interrogator|y, -ies ˌɪntəˈɹɒgətəɹ|ɪ, -ɪz
interrupt, -s, -ing, -ed, -er/s ˌɪntəˈɹʌpt,
  -s, -ɪŋ, -ɪd, -ɚ/z
interruption, -s ˌɪntəˈɹʌpʃn̩, -z
intertangled ˌɪntəˈtæŋgl̩d
intertissued ˌɪntəˈtɪʃud
interval, -s ˈɪntəvəl, -z
intervall|um (*interval*), **-a, -ums**
  ˌɪntəˈvæl|ə, -ʊmz
interven|e, -es, -ing, -ed, -er/s ˌɪntəˈvin,
  -z, -ɪŋ, -d, -ɚ/z
intervention, -s ˌɪntəˈvenʃn̩, -z
interview, -s, -ing, -ed, -er/s ˈɪntəvju, -z,
  -ɪŋ, -d, -ɚ/z
intestate (*s., adj.*), **-s** ɪnˈtesteɪt [-stɪt], -s
intimate (*s., adj.*), **-s, -ly** ˈɪntɪmɪt, -s, -lɪ
intimat|e (*v.*), **-es, -ing, -ed** ˈɪntɪmeɪt, -s,
  -ɪŋ, -ɪd
intitle (*var. of* **entitle**, *q.v.*) ɪnˈtaɪtl̩
intitul|e (*archaic for* **entitle**), **-es, -ing,**
  -ed ɪnˈtɪtjul, -z, -ɪŋ, -d
into ˈɪntu [-ˈ-, ˈɪntʊ]
intolerab|le, -ly, -leness ɪnˈtɒləɹəb|l̩, -lɪ,
  -l̩nɪs
intreasured ɪnˈtɹezɚd
intreat (*obscure, archaic form of* **entreat**,
  q.v.) ɪnˈtɹit
intrench, -es, -ing, -ed, -ment/s ɪnˈtɹentʃ,
  -ɪz, -ɪŋ, -t, -mənt/s
intrenchant ɪnˈtɹentʃənt
intrepid, -ly, -ness ɪnˈtɹepɪd, -lɪ, -nɪs
intricate, -ly, -ness ˈɪntɹɪkɪt, -lɪ, -nɪs
intrigue (*s.*), **-s** ˈɪntɹiɡ, -z
intrigu|e (*v.*), **-es, -ing, -ed** ɪnˈtɹiɡ, -z, -ɪŋ,
  -d
intrince ɪnˈtɹɪns
  Note.—This obsolete word is surmised
  to be an abbreviated form of 'intrinsi-
  cate,' meaning intricate, entangled, or
  involved
intrinsicate ɪnˈtɹɪnzɪkɪt [-nsɪkɪt]
intrud|e, -es, -ing, -ed, -er/s ɪnˈtɹud, -z,
  -ɪŋ, -ɪd, -ɚ/z
intrusion, -s ɪnˈtɹuʒn̩, -z

intrusive, -ly, -ness ɪnˈtɹusɪv, -lɪ, -nɪs
inundat|e, -es, -ing, -ed ˈɪnʌndeɪt, -s, -ɪŋ,
  -ɪd
inundation, -s ˌɪnʌnˈdeɪʃn̩, -z
inur|e, -es, -ing, -ed, -ement ɪˈnjʊɚ, -z,
  -ɹɪŋ, -d, -mənt
inurn, -s, -ing, -ed ɪˈnɝn, -z, -ɪŋ, -d
invad|e, -es, -ing, -ed, -er/s ɪnˈveɪd, -z,
  -ɪŋ, -ɪd, -ɚ/z
invaluab|le, -ly, -leness ɪnˈvæljʊəb|l̩, -lɪ,
  -l̩nɪs
invasion, -s ɪnˈveɪʒn̩, -z
invasive ɪnˈveɪsɪv
invective, -s; -ly ɪnˈvektɪv, -z; -lɪ
inveigh, -s, -ing, -ed ɪnˈveɪ, -z, -ɪŋ, -d
inveig|le, -les, -ling, -led, -ler/s,
  -lement/s ɪnˈveɪɡ|l̩ [-ˈviɡ-], -l̩z, -l̩ɪŋ
  [-lɪŋ], -l̩d, -l̩ɚ/z [-lə/z], -l̩mənt/s
invent, -s, -ing, -ed, -or/s ɪnˈvent, -s, -ɪŋ,
  -ɪd, -ɚ/z
invention, -s ɪnˈvenʃn̩, -z
inventorially ˌɪnvənˈtɔɹɪəlɪ
inventor|y, -ies, -ied ˈɪnvəntəɹ|ɪ [-ˌtɔɹɪ],
  -ɪz, -ɪd
inverness (*coat*), **-es** ˌɪnvɚˈnes (*when att.*,
  [ˈ---]), -ɪz
Inverness (*city—once a county—in*
  Scotland) ˌɪnvɚˈnes
invert (*adj., s.*), **-s** ˈɪnvɝt, -s
invert (*v.*), **-s, -ing, -ed** ɪnˈvɝt, -s, -ɪŋ, -ɪd
invest, -s, -ing, -ed, -or/s; -ment/s
  ɪnˈvest, -s, -ɪŋ, -ɪd, -ɚ/z; -mənt/s
inveterate, -ly, -ness ɪnˈveɾəɹɪt, -lɪ, -nɪs
in via (*L.*) (LLL, IV.ii.14) ɪn ˈviɑ
inviolab|le, -ly, -leness ɪnˈvaɪələb|l̩, -lɪ,
  -l̩nɪs

invised ɪnˈvaɪzd
  Note.—This obsolete, rare word
  meaning 'hidden' or 'unseen' appears in
  LC, 212. At first glance, it would seem
  that there is only one way to scan this
  word, giving primary syllabic stress to
  the first syllable, i.e., [ˈɪnvaɪzd]; but a
  more euphonic solution—as well as

---

i wǝ ɪ cɪty ɪ hɪt e lɛt ɛ dɛbut æ can a pass ɝ bɪrd ʌ hut ǝ again ɚ suppǝr u you
ʊ should o obey ɔ awl ɒ cop ɑ father eɪ paɪd aɪ hɪgh oʊ go ɔɪ voɪce aʊ found ɪɚ ear
ɛɚ air ʊɚ poor ɔɚ fork ɑɚ park aɪɚ fɪre aʊɚ hour b boy p pɪt d dog t top g got
k kɪd h how fɪ behave dʒ jot tʃ chew z zany s soft v vat f fat ʒ treasure ʃ ship ð the
θ thin m man n no ŋ hang l lɪp j yes w won ʍ whew ɹ rɪgger, aɪɾy ɾ matter

*being a regular custom in S.—lies in
eliding 'Whereto his,' thereby making
'invised' a trisyllable, i.e.,* [ɪn'vaɪzɪd].
Since the OED *does not hazard a guess
as to pronunciation, the one proffered
above must be considered conjectural,
and might just as likely be* [ɪn'vizɪd]

invisible ˌɪn'vɪzɪbl̩

invitation, -s ˌɪnvɪ'teɪʃn̩, -z

invit|e, -es, -ing/ly, -ed ɪn'vaɪt, -s, -ɪŋ/lɪ, -ɪd

Invitis nubibus (L.) (2HVI, IV.i.98)
in'vitis 'nubɪbus

invocat|e, -es, -ing, -ed 'ɪnvəˌkeɪt, -s, -ɪŋ, -ɪd

invocation, -s ˌɪnvʊ'keɪʃn̩, -z

invok|e, -es, -ing, -ed ɪn'voŏk, -s, -ɪŋ, -t

involv|e, -es, -ing, -ed, -ement ɪn'vɒlv, -z, -ɪŋ, -d, -mənt

invulnerab|le, -ly, -leness ɪn'vʌlnə-ɹəb|l̩, -lɪ, -l̩nɪs

inward, -s, -ly, -ness 'ɪnwə-d, -z, -lɪ, -nɪs
Note.—In OTH, II.i.292, *this word is
used as an informal reference to the
viscera— 'innards' being the common alteration. As such (in this instance),
'inwards' is pronounced* ['ɪnə-dz]

Io (TS) 'aɪoŏ

Io|nia (AC), **-nian/s** aɪ'oŏnɪə, -nɪən/z
[-njən/z]

Ipswich (*HVIII*) 'ɪpswɪtʃ ['ɪpsɪdʒ]

Ira furor brevis est (L.) (TIM, I.ii.28) 'ɪrɑ
['ɪɚ-ɹɑ] 'fjʊɹɔ- ['fʊrɔ-] 'bɹɛvɪs 'ɛst

Iras (*AC*) 'aɪɹəs

ire 'aɪ-

ire|ful, -fully, -fulness 'aɪɚ-|fʊl, -fʊlɪ, -fʊlnɪs

Ireland (HV, 2HVI, 3HVI, KJ) 'aɪɚ-lənd
Note.—In 2HVI, I.i.193, *this name is
technically a trisyllable, i.e.,* ['aɪɚ-lənd],
*in order to better fit the metrical
requirements of the verse line*

Iris (ALL'S, 2HVI, *TEM*, TC) 'aɪɹɪs

iris, -es *or* **irides** 'aɪɹɪs, -ɪz *or* 'aɪɹɪdɪz
['ɪɹɪ-]

Irish (AYLI, 1HIV, RII) 'aɪɹɪʃ

Irish|man (HV, 2HVI, MWW), **-men**
'aɪɹɪʃ|mən, -mən

irk, -s, -ing, -ed '-k, -s, -ɪŋ, -t

irksome, -ly, -ness '-ksəm, -lɪ, -nɪs

iron, -s, -ing, -ed 'aɪə-n, -z, -ɪŋ, -d

ironclad 'aɪə-nklæd

iron-witted 'aɪə-nˌwɪɾɪd

irreconciled ɪˌɹekənsaɪld

irrecoverab|le, -ly, -leness ˌɪɹ'kʌvə-ɹəb|l̩, -lɪ, -l̩nɪs

irregular, -ly ɪ'ɹegjʊlə-, -lɪ

irregulous (*unruly, lawless*) ɪ'ɹegjʊləs

irreligious, -ly, -ness ˌɪɹ'lɪdʒəs, -lɪ, -nɪs

irremoveable ˌɪɹ'muvəbl̩

irreparable, -ness ɪ'ɹepəɹəbl̩, -nɪs

irreparably ɪ'ɹepəɹəblɪ

irresolute, -ly, -ness ɪ'ɹezl̩ut [-l̩jut], -lɪ, -nɪs

irrevocab|le, -ly ɪ'ɹevʊkəb|l̩, -lɪ

is 'ɪz

Isabel (*HV*, *MEAS*, RII) 'ɪzəbel, 'ɪzbel

Isabella (*MEAS*) ˌɪzə'belə

Isadore (TIM) 'ɪzɪdɔ-

Isbel(l) (ALL'S, *HV*, *MEAS*), **-s** 'ɪzbel, -z

Iscariot, Judas (AYLI, 3HVI, LLL, RII, WT) 'dʒudəs ɪ'skæɹɪət

Isis (AC) 'aɪsɪs

island, -s 'aɪlənd, -z

islander, -s 'aɪləndə-, -z

isle, -s 'aɪl, -z

Isle of Man (2HVI) 'aɪl əv 'mæn

isn't 'ɪzn̩t

isolat|e, -es, -ing, -ed 'aɪsəleɪt, -s, -ɪŋ, -ɪd

isolation ˌaɪsə'leɪʃn

Israel (HAM) 'ɪzɹeɪəl ['ɪzɹɪəl]

**iss|ue, -ues, -uing, -ued, -uer/s, -less;
-uable, -uance** 'ɪʃu, -uz, -ʊɪŋ, -ud, -ʊə-/z, -ulɪs; -ʊəbl̩, -ʊəns

is't (*contr. of* is it) 'ɪzt

Italian (ALL'S, CYM, HAM, KJ, MV, TS), **-s** ɪ'tæljən, -z

Italy (AC, ADO, ALL'S, COR, CYM, JUL, LUC, MV, RII, RJ, TEM, TS) 'ɪtlɪ ['ɪɾəlɪ]

itch, -es, -ing, -ed 'ɪtʃ, -ɪz, -ɪŋ, -t

itch|y, -iness 'ɪtʃ|ɪ, -ɪnɪs

item, -s 'aɪɾəm ['aɪtəm], -z

iterat|e, -es, -ing, -ed 'ɪɾə-ɹeɪt, -s, -ɪŋ, -ɪd

iteration ˌɪɾə-'ɹeɪʃn

i'th' (*contr. of* in the) 'ɪð

Ithaca (COR, TC) 'ɪθəkə

its 'ɪts

it's (*contr. of* it is) 'ɪts
itself ɪt'self
I've (*contr. of* I have) 'aĭv
ivor|y, -ies 'aĭvəˑɹ|ɪ, -ɪz
iv|y, -ies, -ied 'aĭv|ɪ, -ɪz, -ɪd
iwis *or* ywis ɪ'wɪs
> Note.—*This archaic word for 'certainly'*
> *or 'assuredly' is often capitalized, i.e.,*
> *'Iwis', and often separated into two*
> *elements, i.e., 'I wis' (cf.* MV, II.ix.68;
> PER, II.2 (Chorus); *and* TS, I.i.62*)*

Jj

J (*the letter*), -'s 'dʒeĭ, -z
jab, -s, -bing, -bed 'dʒæb, -z, -ɪŋ, -d
jabber, -s, -ing, -ed, -er/s 'dʒæbəˑ, -z,
  -ɹɪŋ, -d, -ɹəˑ/z
Jabberwock, -y 'dʒæbəˑwɒk, -ɪ
jabot, -s ʒæ'boŭ, -z
Jack (AC, ADO, COR, 1HIV, LLL,
  MSND, MV, MWW, RIII, RJ, TEM,
  TS), -s 'dʒæk, -s
jack, -s 'dʒæk, -s
jackal, -s 'dʒækəl [-kɔl], -z
Jack-a-Lent (MWW) 'dʒækə'lent
jackanape, -s 'dʒækəˌneĭp, -s
jackanapes, -es 'dʒækəˌneĭps, -ɪz
jackass, -es 'dʒækæs, -ɪz
jack(-)boot, -s 'dʒækbut, -s
jackdaw, -s 'dʒækdɔ, -z
Jack-dog 'dʒækˌdɒg
jacket, -s, -ed 'dʒækɪt, -s, -ɪd
jackhammer, -s, -ing, -ed 'dʒækˌhæməˑ,
  -z, -ɹɪŋ, -d
jack-in-the-box, -es 'dʒækɪnðəbɒks, -ɪz
jackkni|fe (*s.*), -ves 'dʒæknaĭ|f, -vz
jackknif|e (*v.*), -s, -ing, -fed 'dʒæknaĭf,
  -s, -ɪŋ, -ft
Jack'nape (MWW) (*from 'jackanapes'*)
  'dʒækṇeĭp
jack-of-all-trades ˌdʒækəv'ɔlˌtɹeĭdz

jack-o'-lantern, -s 'dʒækoˌlæntəˑn, -z
jackpot, -s 'dʒækpɒt, -s
Jack-priest (MWW) 'dʒækˌpɹist
Jack(-)sauce (HV) 'dʒækˌsɔs
Jack-slave (CYM) 'dʒækˌsleĭv
jack-tar (J.), -s 'dʒæk'tɑˑ, -z
Jacob (MEAS, MV) 'dʒeĭkəb
Jacobean ˌdʒækə'biən [-kʊ-]
Jacobi|te, -tes, -tism 'dʒækəbaĭ|t [-kʊ-],
  -ts,-ˌtɪzṃ
Jacques *or* Jaques (ALL'S, *AYLI*, HV,
  LLL) 'dʒeĭks [*Fr.* ʒɑk]
> Note.—*This name is the source of much*
> *debate and consternation among both*
> *scholars and theater professionals. In*
> *the anglicized pronunciation* ['dʒeĭks], *a*
> *pun on privies, and thus melancholia, is*
> *retained. Sometimes in* S. (*four instances*
> *only*), *a disyllabic* ['dʒeĭkɪs] *or perhaps*
> ['dʒeĭkɪz] *is called for by the meter, i.e.,*
> AYLI, II.i.26; LLL, II.i.42; ALL'S,
> III.iv.4, III.v.98. *In all other instances,*
> *it is monosyllabic. That said, there is a*
> *well-beloved, time-honored tradition of*
> *pronouncing the name as* ['dʒeĭkwɪz] *in*
> *all instances; but in so doing, one must*
> *be aware that—besides missing the play*
> *on words—in most cases this will throw*
> *the rhythm and the meter off somewhat*
> (cf. la Pucelle, *and see 'Shakespeare's*
> *Verse'* § *1.8 of this dictionary*)
jactitation ˌdʒæktɪ'teĭʃṇ
jad|e, -es, -ing, -ed 'dʒeĭd, -z, -ɪŋ, -ɪd
jad'ry 'dʒeĭdɹɪ
jaeger, -s 'jeĭgəˑ, -z
jag (*s.,v.*), -s, -ging, -ged 'dʒæg, -z, -ɪŋ, -d
jagged (*adj.*), -ly, -ness 'dʒægɪd, -lɪ, -nɪs
jaggery 'dʒægəɹɪ
jagg|y, -ier, -iest, -iness 'dʒæg|ɪ, -ɪəˑ, -ɪɪst,
  -ɪnɪs
jaguar (J.), -s 'dʒægwɑˑ ['dʒægjuˌɑˑ], -z
Jahveh (*var. of* Yahweh, *q.v.*) 'jɑveĭ
jail, -s, -ing, -ed 'dʒeĭl, -z, -ɪŋ, -d
jailbird, -s 'dʒeĭlbɝˑd, -z

i wĕ ɪ cĭty ɪ hĭt e lĕt ɛ dĕbut æ căn a păss ɝ bĭrd ʌ hŭt ə again əˑ suppĕr u yŏu
ʊ shŏuld o ŏbey ɔ ăwl ɒ cŏp ɑ făther eĭ păid aĭ hĭgh oŭ gŏ ɔĭ vŏice aŭ fŏund ɪɚ ĕar
ɛɚ ăir ʊɚ pŏor ɔɚ fŏrk ɑɚ părk aĭɚ fĭre aŭɚ hŏur b bŏy p pĭt d dŏg t tŏp g gŏt
k kĭd h hŏw fi behăve dʒ jŏt tʃ chĕw z zany s sŏft v văt f făt ʒ treăsure ʃ shĭp ð thĕ
θ thĭn m măn n nŏ ŋ hăng l lĭp j yĕs w wŏn ʍ whĕw ɹ rĭgger, airɣ ɣ mătter

Jailer *or* **Gaoler** (*TNK*) 'dʒeɪlə˞
Jailer's *or* **Gaoler's Daughter** (*TNK*) 'dʒeɪlə˞z 'dɔɾə˞
jailer (J.), -s 'dʒeɪlə˞, -z
jakes 'dʒeɪks
jalap 'dʒæləp ['dʒɑləp]
jalop|y, -ies dʒə'lɒpɨ, -ɨz
jalousie, -s 'dʒæləsɨ, -z
jam, -s, -ming, -med 'dʒæm, -z, -ɪŋ, -d
Jamaica, -n/s dʒə'meɪkə, -n/z
jamb, -s 'dʒæm, -z
jambalaya ˌdʒʌmbə'laɪə
jambeau, -x 'dʒæmboŭ, -z
jamboree, -s ˌdʒæmbə'ɹi, -z
James (HV, 2HVI, *KJ*, RIII, RJ) 'dʒeɪmz
Jamy (*HV*) 'dʒeɪmɨ
jang|le, -les, -ling, -led, -ler/s 'dʒæŋg|l̩, -l̩z, -l̩ɪŋ, -əld, -l̩ə˞/z
janissar|y, -ies 'dʒænɪsəɹɨ, -z
janitor, -s 'dʒænɪtə˞, -z
janitorial ˌdʒænɪ'tɔɹɪəl
Januar|y (ADO, WT), **-ies** 'dʒænjʊəɹɨ, -z
Janus (MV, OTH) 'dʒeɪnəs
japan (*s., v.*) **(J.), -s, -ning, -ned, -ner/s** dʒə'pæn, -z, -ɪŋ, -d, -ə˞/z
jap|e, -es, -ing, -ed, -er/s; -ery 'dʒeɪp, -s, -ɪŋ, -t, -ə˞/z; -əɹɨ
Japhet (2HIV) 'dʒeɪfet
japonica, -s dʒə'pɒnɪkə, -z
Jaquenetta (*LLL*) ˌdʒækə'netə [-'neɾə]
Jaques *or* **Jacques** (ALL'S, *AYLI*, HV, LLL) 'dʒeɪks [*Fr.* 'ʒɑk] (*see Note for* 'Jacques *or* Jaques')
jar, -s, -ring/ly, -red 'dʒɑ˞, -z, -ɹɪŋ/lɨ, -d
jardinière, -s ˌʒɑ˞-dn̩'jeə˞, -z
jargon (*talk*), **-s, -ing, -ed** 'dʒɑ˞-gən, -z, -ɪŋ, -d
jargon (*variety of zircon*) (*var. of* **jargoon**) dʒɑ˞-'gɒn
jargoon dʒɑ˞-'gun
jarl, -s 'jɑ˞-l, -z
Jarmany (MWW) (*for* 'Germany') 'ʒɑ˞-mənɨ (*see* **Jarteer**)
jarring-concord 'dʒɑ˞-ɹɪŋ'kɒŋkɔ˞-d [-'kɒnk-]
Jarteer *or* **Jarterre** (MWW) ˌʒɑ˞-'tɪə˞, ˌdʒɑ˞-'teə˞
Note.—This word (*in* MWW, I.i.110; III.i.81; IV.v.79) *is a semi-anglicized*

pronunciation-spelling of the Fr. 'jarretière,' *meaning* 'Garter,' *the name of the inn. Doctor Caius* (*in* MWW) *is the stereotypical foreigner, given to foolish arrogance, and ineptly handling English pronunciation. This is an example of S.'s direction to the actor* (*by way of semiphonetic spellings*) *to adopt such an accent, more or less, for the sake of wringing the most satire out of plays on words stemming from confusions with, and corruptions of, English pronunciation via the French tongue*
jasmine 'dʒæzmɪn
Jason (MV), **-s** 'dʒeɪsn̩, -z
jasper, -s 'dʒæspə˞, -z
jaunc|e, -ing 'dʒɔns, -ɪŋ
jaundice, -d 'dʒɔndɪs, -t
jaundies 'dʒɔndɨz
jaunt, -s, -ing, -ed 'dʒɔnt, -s, -ɪŋ, -ɪd
jaunt|y, -ier, -iest, -ily, -iness 'dʒɔnt|ɪ, -ɪə˞, -ɪɪst, -ɪlɨ, -ɪnɪs
Java 'dʒɑvə
Javanese ˌdʒɑvə'niz (*when att.,* ['---])
jave = jane 'dʒeɪn
Note.— 'Jave' is most likely a misprint of 'jane' in the Quarto version of TNK, III.v.8. *'Jane' in this case means common or coarse, but may also be considered an alt. spelling of 'jean,' a type of coarse twilled cotton. The* OED *does not cite the word 'jave' at all*
javelin, -s 'dʒævlɪn ['dʒævəlɪn]
jaw, -s, -ing, -ed 'dʒɔ, -z, -ɪŋ, -d
jawbon|e, -es, -ing, -ed 'dʒɔboŭn, -z, -ɪŋ, -d
jawbreak|er/s, -ing 'dʒɔbɹeɪk|ə˞/z, -ɪŋ
jay, -s 'dʒeɪ, -z
jaybird, -s 'dʒeɪbɜ˞-d, -z
jazz, -es, -ing, -ed 'dʒæz, -ɪz, -ɪŋ, -d
jazzy 'dʒæzɨ
jealous, -ly, -ness 'dʒeləs, -lɨ, -nɪs
Note.—In the Folio version of RII, I.i.92 *this word is spelled 'iealious' (a var. spelling and pronunciation at one time), which is congruent to the meter of the line in that it requires the word (in this instance) to be trisyllabic, i.e.,* ['dʒelɹəs]
jealous-hood, -s 'dʒeləsˌhʊd, -z

jealous|y (J.) (VA), **-ies** 'dʒeləsɪ, -z

jean (*twilled cotton*) 'dʒin ['dʒeĭn]

Jean 'dʒin

jeans (*pants*) 'dʒinz

jeep, -s 'dʒip, -s

jeer, -s, -ing/ly, -ed, -er/s 'dʒɪɚ, -z, -ɹɪŋ/lɪ, -d, -ɹɚ/z

Jehovah dʒɪˈɦoŭvə

jejune, -ly, -ness dʒɪˈdʒun, -lɪ, -nɪs

jejun|um/s, -a dʒɪˈdʒun|əm/z, -ə

jell (*var. of* **gel**), **-s, -ing, -ed** 'dʒel, -z, -ɪŋ, -d

jell|y, -ies, -ying, -ied 'dʒel|ɪ, -ɪz, -ɪɪŋ, -ɪd

jellybean, -s 'dʒelɪbin

jellyfish, -es 'dʒelɪfɪʃ, -ɪz

Jen (COM) 'dʒen

jennet *or* **gennet** (*small Sp. saddle horse*), **-s** 'dʒenɪt, -s

Jenny (MWW) 'dʒenɪ

jeopardiz|e, -es, -ing, -ed 'dʒepɚˌdaĭz, -ɪz, -ɪŋ, -d

jeopardy 'dʒepɚdɪ

Jephthah (HAM, 3HVI) 'dʒefθə

jerk, -s, -ing, -ed 'dʒɝk, -s, -ɪŋ, -t

jerkin, -s 'dʒɝkɪn, -z

jerk|y, -ier, -iest, -ily, -iness 'dʒɝk|ɪ, -ɪɚ, -ɪɪst, -ɪlɪ, -ɪnɪs

Jerusalem (1HIV, 2HIV, 1HVI, 2HVI, 3HVI, KJ) dʒəˈɹusələm

Jeshu (HV, MWW) (*from 'Jesu'; see* **prings**) 'dʒiʃju [-iʃu]

jess, -es, -ing, -ed 'dʒes, -ɪz, -ɪŋ, -t

Jessica (*MV*) 'dʒesɪkə

jest, -s, -ing/ly, -ed, -er/s 'dʒest, -s, -ɪŋ/lɪ, -ɪd, -ɚ/z

jestings 'dʒestɪŋz

Jesu (1HIV, 2HVI, 3HVI, RII, RJ) 'dʒizju [-isu]

Jesus (1HIV, 2HVI, 2HVI, 3HVI, RII) 'dʒizəs

jetsam 'dʒetsəm

jet, -s, -ting, -ted 'dʒet, -s, -ɪŋ, -ɪd

jett|y, -ies 'dʒeʧ|ɪ, -ɪz

Jew (1HIV, MV), **-s** 'dʒu, -z

jewel, -s, -(l)ing, -(l)ed 'dʒʊəl ['dʒuəl], -z, -ɪŋ, -d

jewel-house 'dʒʊəlˌhaŭs ['dʒuəl-]

Jeweller (TIM) 'dʒʊələ˞

jewel(l)er, -s 'dʒʊələ˞, -z

jewel-like 'dʒʊəlˌlaĭk

jewelry 'dʒʊəlɹɪ

Jewes (MV) 'dʒuɪz

Note.—This curious word in MV, II.v.42 (First Quarto and First Folio versions), is often, in an attempt to reconcile the meter, emended to 'Jewess',' even though the Third Folio's 'Jew's' indicates that its quality as a possessive is more germane to its meaning than any specificity of sex. 'Jewes' most likely indicates a disyllabic pronunciation-spelling of 'Jew's' to guide one toward the pronunciation best suited to the verse, while staying in complete accord with the convention (at least in S.'s verse-writing) of being able to pronounce a possessive as an additional syllable (cf. **whales***), as it is derived from 'Jew his'*

Jewish, -ly, -ness 'dʒuɪʃ ['dʒuɪʃ], -lɪ, -nɪs

Jewry (AC, RII, MWW) 'dʒuɹɪ ['dʒuəɹɪ]

Jezebel (TN) 'dʒezəbel [-bl̩]

jib, -s, -bing, -bed 'dʒɪb, -z, -ɪŋ, -d

jib|e, -es, -ing, -ed 'dʒaĭb, -z, -ɪŋ, -d

jig, -s, -ging, -ged 'dʒɪg, -z, -ɪŋ, -d

jigger, -s 'dʒɪgɚ, -z

jig-maker, -s 'dʒɪgˌmeĭkɚ, -z

jigsaw, -s 'dʒɪgsɔ, -z

Jill (LLL, MSND, TS), **-s** 'dʒɪl, -z

jilt, -s, -ing, -ed 'dʒɪlt, -s, -ɪŋ, -ɪd

jing|le, -les, -ling, -led 'dʒɪŋg|l̩ [-g|əl], -əlz, -l̩ɪŋ [-əlɪŋ], -l̩d [-əld]

Jis *or* **Gis** (*corruption of* **Jesus**) 'dʒɪs

Joan (1HVI, 2HVI, KJ, LLL, TS) 'dʒoŏn

Job (2HIV, MWW) 'dʒoŏb

job, -s, -bing, -bed, -ber/s 'dʒɒb, -z, -ɪŋ, -d, -ɚ/z

jockey, -s, -ing, -ed 'dʒɒkɪ, -z, -ɪŋ, -d

---

i wᴇ ɪ city ɪ hɪt e lᴇt ɛ dᴇbut æ cᴀn a pᴀss ɝ bɪrd ʌ hᴜt ə agaɪn ɚ suppᴇr u yᴏu ʊ shᴏuld o ᴏbey ɔ ᴀwl ɒ cᴏp ɑ fᴀther eĭ paɪd aĭ hɪgh oŏ gᴏ ɔĭ vᴏice aŏ foᴜnd ɪɚ **ear** ɛɚ **air** ʊɚ **poor** ɔɚ **fork** ɑɚ **park** aĭɚ **fire** aŏɚ **hour** b bᴏy p pit d dᴏg t tᴏp g gᴏt k kɪd h hᴏw fi behᴀve dʒ jᴏt tʃ **chew** z zany s sᴏft v vᴀt f fᴀt ʒ treasᴜre ʃ **ship** ð **the** θ **thin** m **man** n **no** ŋ hang l lip j yes w wᴏn ʍ **whew** ɹ rigger, airy ɾ mᴀtter

Jockey of Norfolk (RIII) 'dʒɒkɪ əv 'nɔ˞fək

jocund, -ly, -ness 'dʒɒkənd ['dʒoŭkənd], -lɪ, -nɪs

jocundity dʒoŭ'kʌndɪtɪ

jog, -s, -ging, -ged, -ger/s 'dʒɒg, -z, -ɪŋ, -d, -ə˞/z

john (J.) (2HIV, HV, MWW), **-s** 'dʒɒn, -z

John, Don (*ADO*) 'dɒn 'dʒɒn

John, Friar (*RJ*) 'fɹaɪ˞ 'dʒɒn

John, King (*KJ*) 'kɪŋ 'dʒɒn

John, Prester (ADO) 'pɹestə˞ 'dʒɒn

John, Sir (RIII) ˌsɜ˞ 'dʒɒn

John-a-dreams (HAM) ˌdʒɒnə'dɹimz

join, -s, -ing, -ed, -er/s 'dʒɔĭn, -z, -ɪŋ, -d, -ə˞/z

joinder, -s 'dʒɔĭndə˞, -z

joint, -s, -ing, -ed; -ly 'dʒɔĭnt, -s, -ɪŋ, -ɪd; -lɪ

joint-laborer 'dʒɔĭntˌleĭbə˞ɹə˞

jointress, -es 'dʒɔĭntɹɪs, -ɪz

joint-ring, -s 'dʒɔĭntˌɹɪŋ, -z

joint-servant 'dʒɔĭntsɜ˞vənt

joint-stool, -s 'dʒɔĭntˌstul, -z

jointure, -s 'dʒɔĭntʃə˞, -z

jollit|y, -ies 'dʒɒlɪt|ɪ, -ɪz

joll|y, -ier, -iest, -ily, -iness 'dʒɒl|ɪ, -ɪə˞, -ɪɪst, -ɪlɪ, -ɪnɪs

jolt, -s, -ing/ly, -ed 'dʒoŭlt, -s, -ɪŋ/lɪ, -ɪd

jolt(-)head, -s 'dʒoŭltˌhed, -z

jordan (J.), -s 'dʒɔ˞dn̩, -z

Joseph (TS) 'dʒoŭzɪf

Joshua (LLL) 'dʒɒʃʊə

jost|le, -les, -ling, -led 'dʒɒs|l̩, -l̩z, -l̩ɪŋ [-lɪŋ], -l̩d

jot, -s, -ting/s, -ted 'dʒɒt, -s, -ɪŋ/z, -ɪd

jounc|e, -es, -ing, -ed 'dʒaŏns, -ɪz, -ɪŋ, -t

Jourdain, Margery (*2HVI*) 'mɑ˞dʒəɹɪ dʒɜ˞'deĭn [ʒʊ˞'deĭn]

journal, -s 'dʒɜ˞nl̩, -z

journey, -s, -ing, -ed 'dʒɜ˞nɪ, -z, -ɪŋ, -d

journey-bated 'dʒɜ˞nɪˌbeĭtɪd

journey|man, -men 'dʒɜ˞nɪ|mən, -mən

joust, -s, -ing, -ed 'dʒaŏst ['dʒust, 'dʒʌst], -s, -ɪŋ, -ɪd

Jove (AC, ADO, ALL'S, AYLI, COR, CYM, HAM, HV, 2HIV, 2HVI, 3HVI, LEAR, LLL, LUC, MEAS, MSND,

MWW, OTH, PER, PP, RIII, RJ, TC, TEM, TIM, TIT, TN, TS, WT) 'dʒoŭv

Jovial (CYM) 'dʒoŭvjəl

jovial, -ly, -ness 'dʒoŭvɪəl [-vjəl], -ɪ, -nɪs

jovialit|y, -ies ˌdʒoŭvɪ'ælɪt|ɪ, -ɪz

jowl, -s 'dʒaŏl, -z

joy, -s, -ing, -ed 'dʒɔĭ, -z, -ɪŋ, -d

joy|ful, -fullest, -fully, -fulness 'dʒɔĭ|fʊl, -fʊlɪst, -fəlɪ, -fʊlnɪs

joyless, -ly, -ness 'dʒɔĭlɪs, -lɪ, -nɪs

joyous, -ly, -ness 'dʒɔĭəs, -lɪ, -nɪs

Jubiter (TIT) 'dʒubɪtə˞

Note.—This may be the Clown's blunder or dialectal corruption of 'Jupiter' in TIT, IV.iii.84, rather than a compositor's error. Many editors emend this to 'Jupiter' but I agree with Jonathan Bate (editor of TIT, The Arden Shakespeare, 1995) who considers this pronunciation not only necessary for the play on 'gibbet-maker' in line 80, but also to remain consistent with the character of the Clown, who is wont to mispronounce

Judas (AYLI, 3HVI, LLL, RII), **-es** 'dʒudəs, -ɪz

Jude (LLL) 'dʒud

Judean (OTH) dʒu'diən

Note.—This word, from OTH, V.ii.348, is usually emended to 'Indian.' 'Judean' is given in the First Folio, a transposition of the Quartos' 'Indian.' 'Indian' scans more evenly in the line unless one makes an anapest of the first foot (and in OTH, this would be in common with so many other 'seeming' irregularities)

judg|e, -es, -ing, -ed 'dʒʌdʒ, -ɪz, -ɪŋ, -d

judg(e)ment (COM, MEAS), **-s** 'dʒʌdʒmənt, -s

Judgement Day (1HVI) 'dʒʌdʒməntˌdeĭ

judgement-place 'dʒʌdʒməntˌpleĭs

judicious, -ly, -ness dʒu'dɪʃəs [dʒʊ'd-], -lɪ, -nɪs

Jug (LEAR) 'dʒʌg

jug, -s, -ging, -ged 'dʒʌg, -z, -ɪŋ, -d

jugg|le, -les, -ling, -led, -ler/s 'dʒʌg|l̩, -l̩z, -lɪŋ [-l̩ɪŋ], -l̩d, -lə˞/z [-l̩ə˞/z]

juice, -es 'dʒus, -ɪz

juic|y, -ier, -iest, -ily, -iness 'dʒus|ɪ, -ɪə˞, -ɪɪst, -ɪlɪ, -ɪnɪs

Jule (RJ) 'dʒul
Julia (*TGV*) 'dʒulɪə, -ljə
Juliet (*MEAS, RJ*) 'dʒuljət, -lɪət
Julietta (*MEAS*) dʒul'jetə, -lɪ'etə
Julius (AC, CYM, HAM, 1HVI, 2HVI, JUL, RII, RIII) 'dʒuljəs
July (ADO, HVIII, WT) dʒʊ'laĭ [dʒu'laĭ]
Note.—Up until the end of the eighteenth century (to include the English author and lexicographer, Samuel Johnson, and the English poet, William Cowper), this word was commonly pronounced with primary stress on the initial syllable, i.e., ['dʒulaĭ] *or its alternative pronunciation,* ['dʒulɪ]. *Thus, S. gives it first-syllable stress in HVIII, I.i.154 and WT, I.ii.169 (where its pronunciation also complies with the metrical and rythmical requirements of iambic pentameter). It is presumably intended to be spoken the same way in ADO, I.i.264 (Kökeritz and Schmidt both assert that it is), but as this occurrence is in prose, the pronunciation typically gives way to the modern* [dʒʊ'laĭ] *or* [dʒu'laĭ]
jump, -s, -ing, -ed, -er/s 'dʒʌmp, -s, -ɪŋ, -t, -ɚ/z
June (AC, 1HIV, Sonn. 104)**, -s** 'dʒun, -z
junk, -s, -ing, -ed 'dʒʌŋk, -s, -ɪŋ, -t
junket, -s, -ing, -ed 'dʒʌŋkɪt, -s, -ɪŋ, -ɪd
Juno (AYLI, COR, CYM, LLL, PER, PP, *TEM*, TNK, WT) 'dʒunoŭ
Juno-like (COR) 'dʒunoŭˌlaĭk
Jupiter (AC, AYLI, COR, CYM, LEAR, MWW, TC, TEM, TIT, TNK, WT) 'dʒupɪtɚ
jure (*nonce-word (v.) meaning 'to make a juror of'*) 'dʒʊɚ
jurisdiction, -s ˌdʒʊɚˌɹɪs'dɪkʃn̩, -z
juror, -s 'dʒʊɚˌɹɚ, -z
jur|y, -ies 'dʒʊɚˌɹ|ɪ, -ɪz
just, -er, -est, -ly, -ness 'dʒʌst, -ɚ, -ɪst, -lɪ, -nɪs
Note.—The weak form ['dʒəst] *is*

sometimes countenanced when, as an adverb, this word is in an entirely unstressed position
just-borne 'dʒʌstˌbɔɚn
Justice (LUC, *MEAS*, OTH, PER, RII, TIT, TNK) 'dʒʌstɪs
Justice, Cavaliero (MWW) kævɑ'lɪɚˌɹoŭ 'dʒʌstɪs
*Note.— 'Cavaliero' is the Host's coinage, and probably an innocent confusion with the It. 'cavaliere' (*MWW, II.i.176; II.iii.67). *It is somewhat less than the Host's sheer blunder, as it appears elsewhere in S. in several other forms, e.g., 'cavaleiro,' 'cavalera,' 'cavalery,' and 'cavaliery'*
justice, -es 'dʒʌstɪs, -ɪz
justice-like 'dʒʌstɪsˌlaĭk
justicer, -s 'dʒʌstɪsɚ, -z
justification, -s ˌdʒʌstɪfɪ'keĭʃn̩, -z
justif|y, -ies, -ying, -ied, -ier/s 'dʒʌstɪf|aĭ, -aĭz, -aĭɪŋ, -aĭd, -aĭɚ/z
justify't (*contr. of* **justify it**) 'dʒʌstɪfaĭt
justl|e (*form of* **jostle**), **-es, -ing, -ed** 'dʒʌsl̩, -z, -ɪŋ, -d
justs 'dʒʌsts
jut, -s, -ting, -ted 'dʒʌt, -s, -ɪŋ, -ɪd
jutting-out 'dʒʌʧɪŋˌaŭt
jutt|y, -ies 'dʒʌʧ|ɪ, -ɪz
juvenal 'dʒuvɪnl̩

Kk

K (*the letter*)**, -'s** 'keĭ, -z
Kaaba 'kɑbə
kabuki kə'bukɪ
kachina kə'ʧinə
Kaddish 'kɑdɪʃ
Kaf(f)ir, -s 'kæfɚ, -z
kailyard 'keĭlˌjɑɚd
Kaiser *or* **Kaisar** (MWW)**, -s** 'kaĭzɚ, -z
kakemono, -s ˌkɑkə'moŭnoŭ, -z

i wе ɪ city ɪ hit e let ɛ debut æ can a pass ɝ bird ʌ hut ə again ɚ supper u you
ʊ should o obey ɔ awl ɒ cop ɑ father eĭ paid aĭ high oŭ go ɔĭ voice aŭ found ɪɚ ear
ɛɚ air ʊɚ poor ɔɚ fork ɑɚ park aĭɚ fire aŭɚ hour b boy p pit d dog t top g got
k kid h how fɪ behave dʒ jot ʧ chew z zany s soft v vat f fat ʒ treasure ʃ ship ð the
θ thin m man n no ŋ hang l lip j yes w won ʍ whew ɹ rigger, airy ɾ matter

kakistocrac|y, -ies ˌkækɪˈstɒkɹəs|ɪ, -ɪz
kale ˈkeɪl
kaleidoscope, -s kəˈlaɪdəskoʊp, -s
kaleidoscopic kəˌlaɪdəˈskɒpɪk
kalends (*var. of* **calends**) ˈkæləndz
kam (*var. of Welsh* **cam**, *meaning 'crooked, awry'*) ˈkæm
kangaroo, -s ˌkæŋɡəˈɹu, -z
kaolin(e) ˈkeɪəlɪn
kaph ˈkɑf [ˈkɔf]
kapok ˈkeɪpɒk
kappa ˈkæpə
kaput kɑˈpʊt [kə-]
karate kəˈɹɑtɪ
karm|a, -ic ˈkɑɚm|ə [ˈkɝm-], -ɪk
kar(r)oo, -s kəˈɹu, -z
Kate (1HIV, *HV*, *HVIII*, LLL, MEAS, TEM, *TS*), **-s, -d** ˈkeɪt, -s, -ɪd
Kate Hall (TS) ˈkeɪt ˈhɔl
Katherina (*TS*) ˌkætəˈɹinə, kæˈtɹinə
Katherine *or* **Katharine** (2HIV, *HV*, *HVIII*, LLL) ˈkæθəˌɹɪn, -θɹɪn
Note.—Spellings of this name in the First Folio lead one to the conclusion that it was most likely pronounced [ˈkætəˌɹɪn, -tɹɪn] *in S.'s day, with the 'th' as in 'Thomas,' 'Theresa,' or 'thyme'; however, in plays such as HVIII it is advisable to speak it as in modern English, especially by those in the English court*
katydid, -s ˈkeɪɾɪdɪd [-eɪtɪ-], -z
kayak, -s ˈkaɪæk, -s
kazoo, -s kəˈzu, -z
kecksies (*plant*) ˈkeksɪz
keech (*lump of congealed fat*) ˈkitʃ
Keech (2HIV) ˈkitʃ
keel, -s, -ing, -ed ˈkil, -z, -ɪŋ, -d
keen (*adj.*), **-er, -est, -ly, -ness** ˈkin, -ɚ, -ɪst, -lɪ, -nɪs
keen (*v.*), **-s, -ing, -ed** ˈkin, -z, -ɪŋ, -d
keen-edged ˈkinˌedʒd
Keep-down, Mistress Kate (MEAS) ˈmɪstɹɪs ˈkeɪt ˈkipdɑʊn
keeper (**K.**), **-s** ˈkipɚ, -z
keeper-back ˈkipɚˌbæk
keep't (*contr. of* **keep it**) ˈkipt
Keighley, Sir Richard (HV) ˌsɝ ˈɹɪtʃɚd ˈkiθlɪ

Note.—Technically, this name does not appear in S. In HV, IV.viii.105, the Folios and Quartos give 'Ketly,' some modern editors emending to 'Keighley' and pronouncing it as the present-day town in Yorkshire, i.e., [ˈkiθlɪ]
keisar (**K.**) (*obsolete var. of* **kaiser** [*from 'caesar'*] *in* MWW) ˈkaɪzɚ
ken, -s, -ning, -ned ˈken, -z, -ɪŋ, -d
Kendal(-)green (1HIV) ˈkendlˈɡɹin
kennel, -s, -ling, -led ˈkenl̩, -z, -ɪŋ, -d
Kent (1HIV, 2HVI, 3HVI, KJ, RII, RIII) ˈkent
Kent, Earl of (*LEAR*) ˌɝl əv ˈkent
Kentish (2HVI, 3HVI), **-man, -men** ˈkentɪʃ, -mən, -mən
kerchief, -s ˈkɝtʃɪf, -s
kern, -s, -ing, -ed ˈkɝn, -z, -ɪŋ, -d
kerne (**K.**) (2HVI, MAC), **-s** ˈkɝn, -z
kernel, -s ˈkɝnl̩, -z
kersey, -s ˈkɝzɪ, -z
Ketly (HV) ˈketlɪ, ˈkitlɪ (*see* **Keighley**)
kettle, -s ˈketl̩, -z
kettledrum, -s ˈketl̩ˌdɹʌm, -z
key, -s, -ing, -ed ˈki, -z, -ɪŋ, -d
key-cold ˈkiˌkoʊld
key-hole, -s ˈkiˌhoʊl, -z
kibe, -s ˈkaɪb, -z
kick, -s, -ing, -ed, -er/s ˈkɪk, -s, -ɪŋ, -t, -ɚ/z
kicksie-wicksie ˈkɪksɪˈwɪksɪ
kickshaw, -s, -ses ˈkɪkʃɔ, -z, -zɪz
kicky-wicky ˈkɪkɪˈwɪkɪ
kid-fox ˈkɪdˌfɒks
kidnap, -s, -ping, -ped, -per/s ˈkɪdnæp, -s, -ɪŋ, -t, -ɚ/z
kidney, -s ˈkɪdnɪ, -z
Kildare (HVIII) kɪlˈdɛɚ
kill, -s, -ing, -ed, -er/s ˈkɪl, -z, -ɪŋ, -d, -ɚ/z
kill-courtesy ˈkɪlˌkɝtɪsɪ
killen (*archaic p.t. and p.p. of* **kill**) ˈkɪlɪn
Killingworth (2HVI) ˈkɪlɪŋwɝθ
killjoy, -s ˈkɪldʒɔɪ, -z
kiln, -s, -ing, -ed ˈkɪln [ˈkɪl], -z, -ɪŋ, -d
Note.—[ˈkɪl], *when used at all, is usually spoken only by those in the ceramics-firing trade*
kiln-hole ˈkɪlnˌhoʊl [ˈkɪlˌhoʊl]

Note.—See Note for **kiln***; the First Folio gives this word in WT, IV.iv.247 and MWW, IV.ii.54 (the only two appearances of the word in S.) as 'kill-hole'*

kilt, -s, -ing, -ed 'kɪlt, -s, -ɪŋ, -ɪd

Kimmalton *or* **Kymmalton** 'kɪməltən

Note.—This castle, referred to in HVIII, IV.i.34, is modernly known as 'Kimbolton' and pronounced with primary stress on the second syllable, i.e., [kɪm'boŭltən]. *Despite this and the fact that the Third Folio gives 'Kimbolton,' its pronunciation in S. still follows the archaic spellings, spellings that once reflected a now obsolete pronunciation, and that supported the natural rhythm of the line*

kin 'kɪn

kin|d, -ds, -der, -dest, -dly, -dness/es 'kaɪnd, -dz, -dɚ, -dɪst, -dlɪ, -dnɪs/ɪz

kind-hearted 'kaɪndˌfiɑɚtɪd

kind|le, -les, -ling, -led, -ler/s 'kɪndl̩, -l̩z, -lɪŋ [-l̩ɪŋ], -l̩d, -lɚ/z [-l̩ɚ/z]

kindless 'kaɪndlɪs

kindl|y, -ier, -iest, -iness 'kaɪndl|ɪ, -ɪɚ, -ɪɪst, -ɪnɪs

kindred, -s 'kɪndɹɪd, -z

kine *(archaic pl. of 'cow')* 'kaɪn

king (K.), -s, -ed 'kɪŋ, -z, -d

Note.—In CYM, I.i.14, 'king's' is arguably meant to be pronounced disyllabically, i.e., ['kɪŋɪz], *otherwise the line is fully trochaic pentameter instead of the conventional iambic pentameter. Although examples of fully trochaic lines of verse exist in S., such as "Then, the whining schoolboy with his satchel" (AYLI, II.vii.145) and "Never, never, never, never, never" (LEAR, V.iii.307), there are even more examples where the possessive case exerts an influence over the meter and rhythm of a line, e.g., 'moon's' in MSND, II.i.7, 'night's' in MSND, IV.i.95, 'whale's' in LLL,*

V.ii.332, *'month's' in TGV, I.ii.137, etc. (see Abbott's A Shakespearian Grammar, § 217, and The Oxford Companion to the English Language, § 'Apostrophe— Possession,' and see Note for* **whale***)*

king-becoming 'kɪŋbɪˌkʌmɪŋ

king-cardinal 'kɪŋˌkɑɚdn̩l

kingdom (K.), -s, -ed 'kɪŋdəm, -z, -d

king-killer, -s 'kɪŋˌkɪlɚ, -z

kingl|y, -ier, -iest, -iness 'kɪŋl|ɪ, -ɪɚ, -ɪɪst, -ɪnɪs

kingly-poor 'kɪŋlɪˌpʊɚ

kins|man, -men 'kɪnz|mən, -mən

kins|woman, -women 'kɪnz|wʊmən, -wɪmɪn

kirk, -s, -ing 'kɚk, -s, -ɪŋ

kirtle, -s 'kɚtl̩, -z

kiss, -es, -ing, -ed, -er/s 'kɪs, -ɪz, -ɪŋ, -t, -ɚ/z

kissing-comfit, -s 'kɪsɪŋˌkʌmfɪt [-ˌkɒm-], -s

kit, -s 'kɪt, -s

kitchen, -s 'kɪtʃɪn [-tʃən], -z

kitchen-maid, -s 'kɪtʃɪnˌmeɪd [-tʃən], -z

kitchen-trull, -s 'kɪtʃɪnˌtɹʌl [-tʃən-], -z

kitchen-vestal, -s 'kɪtʃɪnˌvestəl [-tʃən-], -z

kitchen-wench, -es 'kɪtʃɪnˌwentʃ [-tʃən-], -ɪz

kite, -s; -flying 'kaɪt, -s; -ˌflaɪɪŋ

kith 'kɪθ

kitten, -s, -ing, -ed 'kɪtn̩, -z, -ɪŋ, -d

kiwi, -s 'kiˌwi ['kiwɪ], -z

Klondike 'klɒndaɪk

knack, -s 'næk, -s

knap, -s, -ping, -ped, -per/s 'næp, -s, -ɪŋ, -t, -ɚ/z

knave, -s 'neɪv, -z

Note.—In TS, IV.i.107, one could argue that 'knaves' is somehow given more value (metrically speaking) than a monosyllable. In Frank Kermode's (editor, The Arden Shakespeare, 1958) annotation for TEM, I.ii.53, there is a brief but valuable discussion about

---

i w**e** ɨ c**i**ty ɪ h**i**t e l**e**t ɛ d**e**but æ c**a**n a p**a**ss ɝ b**ir**d ʌ h**u**t ə **a**gain ɚ supp**er** u y**ou**
ʊ sh**ou**ld o **o**bey ɔ **aw**l ɒ c**o**p ɑ f**a**ther eɪ p**ai**d aɪ h**igh** oŭ g**o** ɔɪ v**oi**ce aŭ f**ou**nd ɪɚ **ear**
ɛɚ **air** ʊɚ **poor** ɔɚ **fork** ɑɚ **park** aɪɚ **fire** aŭɚ **hour** b **b**oy p **p**it d **d**og t **t**op g g**o**t
k **k**id h **h**ow fi be**h**ave dʒ **j**ot tʃ **ch**ew z **z**any s **s**oft v **v**at f **f**at ʒ trea**s**ure ʃ **sh**ip ð **th**e
θ **th**in m **m**an n **n**o ŋ ha**ng** l **l**ip j **y**es w **w**on ʍ **wh**ew ɹ **r**igger, ai**r**y ɟ **m**a**tt**er

monosyllabic words that sometimes receive the value of two metric beats in S. lines of verse "whether or no it is [they are] pronounced disyllabically . . ." In TEM, I.ii.206, 'brave' is arguably pronounced disyllabically or given, as Kermode puts it, "a heavy emphasis." Cf. Abbott's A Shakespearian Grammar, §§ 475, 479, 484

knaver|y, -ies 'neɪvəɹ|ɪ, -ɪz
knavish, -ly, -ness 'neɪvɪʃ, -lɪ, -nɪs
knead, -s, -ing, -ed, -er/s 'nid, -z, -ɪŋ, -ɪd, -ə˞/z
knee, -s, -ing, -d 'ni, -z, -ɪŋ, -d
knee(-)cap, -s 'nikæp, -s
knee-crooking 'ni,kɹʊkɪŋ
knee-deep 'ni'dip *(when att.,* ['--])
kneel, -s, -ing, -ed, knelt 'nil, -z, -ɪŋ, -d, 'nelt

Note.—The line KJ, I.i.161 seems to be lacking a necessary beat that would fulfill the metrical requirements of the verse. Various editors have emended the line by adding words, etc., but the solution may be more simple. In Frank Kermode's (editor, The Arden Shakespeare, 1958) annotation for TEM, I.ii.53 (for the word 'brave'), there is a brief but valuable discussion about monosyllabic words that sometimes receive the value of two metric beats in S. lines of verse "whether or no it is [they are] pronounced disyllabically . . ." In KJ, I.i.161, 'kneel' is arguably pronounced disyllabically or given, as Kermode puts it, "a heavy emphasis." Cf. Abbott's A Shakespearian Grammar, §§ 475, 479, 484

knell, -s, -ing, -ed 'nel, -z, -ɪŋ, -d
knew (*p.t. of* **know**, *q.v.*) 'nju
kni|fe (*s.*), **-ves** 'naɪ|f, -vz
knif|e (*v.*), **-es, -ing, -ed** 'naɪf, -s, -ɪŋ, -t
knight, -s, -ing, -ed 'naɪt, -s, -ɪŋ, -ɪd
knight-errant, knights-errant ,naɪt'eɹənt, ,naɪts'eɹənt
knighthood, -s 'naɪtʰʊd, -z
knightl|y, -ier, -iest, -iness 'naɪtl|ɪ, -ɪə˞, -ɪɪst, -ɪnɪs
Knight of the Burning Lamp (1HIV) ,naɪt əv ðə 'bɝˑnɪŋ 'læmp

knit, -s, -ting, -ted, -ter/s 'nɪt, -s, -ɪŋ, -ɪd, -ə˞/z
knob, -s 'nɒb, -z
Knob, Sir (KJ) ,sɝˑ 'nɒb
knock, -s, -ing, -ed, -er/s 'nɒk, -s, -ɪŋ, -t, -ə˞/z
knog (*from* '*knock*') 'nɒg (*see* **prings**)
knoll, -s, -ed 'noʊl, -z, -d
knot, -s, -ting, -ted 'nɒt, -s, -ɪŋ, -ɪd
knot-grass 'nɒt,gɹas
knott|y, -ier, -iest, -ily, -iness 'nɒt̥|ɪ, -ɪə˞, -ɪɪst, -ɪlɪ, -ɪnɪs
knotty-pated 'nɒt̥ɪ,peɪtɪd
know, -s, -ing, knew, know|n; -able 'noʊ, -z, -ɪŋ, 'nju, 'noʊ|n; -əbl̩
knower 'noʊə˞
know(-)how 'noʊfiɑʊ
knowing, -ly, -ness, -s 'noʊɪŋ, -lɪ, -nɪs, -z
knowist (*var. of* '*knowest*') 'noʊɪst
knowledge 'nɒlɪdʒ
know't (*contr. of* **know it**) 'noʊt
Knox 'nɒks
knuck|le, -les, -ling, -led 'nʌk|l̩, -l̩z, -l̩ɪŋ [-lɪŋ], -l̩d
kosher 'koʊʃə˞
kowtow, -s, -ing, -ed ,kaʊ'taʊ ['--], -z, -ɪŋ, -d

Ll

L (*the letter*)**, -'s** 'el, -z
la (*sixth note of diatonic scale*) 'lɑ
la (*interj.*) 'lɑ (*strong form*) 'lə (*weak form*)
Laban (MV) 'leɪbən
label, -s, -ling, -led 'leɪbl̩, -z, -ɪŋ, -d
Labeo (JUL; *var. of* **Labio**) 'leɪbɪoʊ, -bjoʊ
Labienus (AC) ,leɪbɪ'inəs [,læb-]
labor, -s, -ing, -ed, -er/s 'leɪbə˞, -z, -ɹɪŋ, -d, -ɹə˞/z
laborsome 'leɪbə˞səm
labras (*blunder for* '*labra*') (*L.*) (MWW, I.i.151) 'lɑbrɑs
labyrinth, -s 'læbɪɹɪnθ, -s
lac|e, -es, -ing, -ed 'leɪs, -ɪz, -ɪŋ, -t
Lacedæmon (TIM) ,læsɪ'dimən

lacerat|e, -es, -ing, -ed 'læsəreĭt, -s, -ɪŋ, -ɪd

laceration, -s ˌlæsəˈɹeĭʃn̩, -z

Lacies (2HVI) 'leĭsɪz

lack, -s, -ing, -ed 'læk, -s, -ɪŋ, -t

'lack (*aphetic form of* **alack**) 'læk

Lackbeard, Lord (ADO) 'lɔɚ̃-d 'lækbɪɚ̃-d

lack-brain 'lækˌbɹeĭn

lackey, -s, -ing, -ed 'lækɪ, -z, -ɪŋ, -d

lack-linen 'lækˌlɪnɪn

lack-love 'lækˌlʌv

lack-luster 'lækˌlʌstɚ
Note.—Arguably stressed [ˌ-ˈ--] in AYLI,
II.vii.21

laconic, -al, -ally ləˈkɒnɪk, -l̩, -əlɪ

lactat|e, -es, -ing, -ed 'lækteĭt, -s, -ɪŋ, -ɪd

lactation lækˈteĭʃn̩

lactic 'læktɪk

lad, -s 'læd, -z

ladder, -s 'lædɚ, -z

laddie, -s 'lædɪ, -z

lad|e, -es, -ing, -ed, -en 'leĭd, -z, -ɪŋ, -ɪd, -n̩

lad|y (L.), -ies 'leĭd|ɪ, -ɪz

ladybird, -s 'leĭdɪbɝ-d, -z

ladyship (L.), -s 'leĭdɪʃɪp, -s

Laertes (*HAM*, TIT) leĭˈɛɚ̃-tɪz, leĭˈɝ-tɪz
Note.—The Quarto spelling in HAM *is
'Leartes,' indicating the possible, if
uncommon, pronunciation* [lɪˈɑɚ̃-tɪz]

la Far, Monsieur (LEAR) məˈsjɝ- lə 'fɑɚ̃-

Lafew *or* **Lafeu** (*ALL'S*) ləˈfju

la fin couronne les oeuvres (*Fr.*) (2HVI,
V.ii.28) lə [la] 'fɛ̃ kuˈʀɔ̃ lə 'zøvʀ

lag, -s, -ging, -ged 'læg, -z, -ɪŋ, -d

lager, -s 'lagɚ, -z

lagoon, -s ləˈgun, -z

lain (*p.p. of* **lie**) 'leĭn

lair, -s 'lɛɚ̃-, -z

lake, -s; -side 'leĭk, -s; -saĭd

lam, -s, -ming, -med 'læm, -z, -ɪŋ, -d

lamb, -s, -ing, -ed 'læm, -z, -ɪŋ, -d

lambast|e, -es, -ing, -ed læmˈbeĭst, -s, -ɪŋ, -ɪd

lambkin, -s 'læmkɪn [-mpk-], -z

lambskin, -s 'læmskɪn, -z

lamb's(-)wool 'læmzˌwʊl

lam|e, -es, -ing, -ed; -er, -est, -ely, -eness
'leĭm, -z, -ɪŋ, -d; -ɚ, -ɪst, -lɪ, -nɪs

lament, -s, -ing/s, -ed ləˈment, -s, -ɪŋ, -ɪd

lamentab|le, -ly 'læmɪntəb|l̩ [ləˈmen-], -lɪ

lamentation (L.), -s ˌlæmɪnˈteĭʃn̩, -z

Lammas (RJ), **-tide** 'læməs, -taĭd

Lammas Eve 'læməs 'iv

Lamo(u)nd (HAM) lɑˈmɒnd

Lamord (HAM) lɑˈmɔɚ̃-d

lamp, -s 'læmp, -s

lampas(s) (*horse disease*) 'læmpəs

lampoon, -s, -ing, -ed, -er/s læmˈpun, -z,
-ɪŋ, -d, -ɚ/z

Lamprius (AC) 'læmpɹɪəs

Lancaster (2HIV, 2HVI, 3HVI, RII, RIII)
'læŋkəstɚ
Note.—Though ['læŋˌkæstɚ] *is the
preferred pronunciation for many places
and of many families in the United
States, the only pronunciation used in S.
is* ['læŋkəstɚ]

Lancaster, Henry of (RII) 'henɹɪ əv
'læŋkəstɚ (*see Note for* **Henry** *and*
Lancaster)

Lancaster, House of 'haŭs əv 'læŋkəstɚ

Lancaster, Prince John of (*1HIV, 2HIV*)
'pɹɪns 'dʒɒn əv 'læŋkəstɚ (*see Note for*
Lancaster)

lanc|e (L.), -es, -ing, -ed, -er/s 'lans, -ɪz,
-ɪŋ, -t, -ɚ/z

land, -s, -ing/s, -ed 'lænd, -z, -ɪŋ/z, -ɪd

land-damn ˌlændˈdæm

land-fish 'lændˌfɪʃ

landlocked 'lændlɒkt

landlord, -s 'lændlɔɚ̃-d, -z

land|man, -men 'lænd|mən, -mən

landmark, -s 'lændmɑɚ̃-k, -s

landscap|e, -es, -ing, -ed, -er/s
'lændskeĭp, -s, -ɪŋ, -t, -ɚ/z

land-service 'lændˌsɝ-vɪs

lane, -s 'leĭn, -z

---

i w**e** ɪ c**i**ty ɪ h**i**t e l**e**t ɛ d**e**but æ c**a**n a p**a**ss ɝ b**i**rd ʌ h**u**t ə **a**gain ɚ supp**er** u y**ou**
ʊ sh**ould** o **o**bey ɔ **aw**l ɒ c**o**p ɑ f**a**ther eĭ p**ai**d aĭ h**igh** oŭ g**o** ɔĭ v**oi**ce aŭ f**ou**nd ɪɚ̃- **ear**
ɛɚ̃- **air** ʊɚ̃- **poor** ɔɚ̃- **fork** ɑɚ̃- p**ar**k aĭɚ̃- f**ire** aŭɚ̃- h**our** b **b**oy p **p**it d **d**og t **t**op g g**o**t
k **k**id h **h**ow fi be**h**ave dʒ **j**ot tʃ **ch**ew z **z**any s **s**oft v **v**at f **f**at ʒ trea**s**ure ʃ **sh**ip ð **th**e
θ **th**in m **m**an n **n**o ŋ ha**ng** l **l**ip j **y**es w **w**on ʍ **wh**ew ɹ **r**igger, ai**r**y ɾ ma**tt**er

Langley, Edmund of (1HVI, 2HVI, *RII*) 'edmənd əv 'læŋlɨ

Langton, Stephen (KJ) 'stivn̩ 'læŋtən

language, -s; -less 'læŋgwɪdʒ, -ɪz; -lɨs

languid, -ly, -ness 'læŋgwɪd, -lɨ, -nɪs

languish, -es, -ing/ly, -ed, -ment 'læŋgwɪʃ, -ɪz, -ɪŋ/lɨ, -t, -mənt

languor, -ous/ly 'læŋgə·, -ɹəs/lɨ

lank, -ed; -er, -est, -ly, -ness 'læŋk, -t; -ə·, -ɪst, -nɪs

lank-lean 'læŋk͜lin

lantern, -s 'læntə·n, -z

lanthorn, -s 'læntə·n ['læntfɪɔ͡ə·n], -z
Note.—This is one of many—at least 18, according to the OED—obsolete, archaic, var. spellings of the word 'lantern' and is possibly, if not probably, pronounced the same way, with the 'th' analogous to words such as 'thyme,' 'Thomas,' and 'Theresa.' However, in 2HIV, I.ii.48, there is an advantage to retaining the more pedantic pronunciation of ['læntfɪɔ͡ə·n] *or even* ['læŋθfɪɔ͡ə·n], *since there is a pun being played with "horn of abundance" in the passage*

lap, -s, -ping, -ped, -per/s 'læp, -s, -ɪŋ, -t, -ə·/z

lapel, -s lə'pel, -z

lapis (L.) (MWW, IV.i.27) (*stone*) 'lapɪs ['lapɨs]
Note.—The first pronunciation given above probably carries with it more meaning to the modern ear, as it is still used commonly in 'lapis lazuli'

Lapland (COM), **-er/s** 'læp͜lænd, -ə·/z

laps|e, -es, -ing, -ed 'læps, -ɪz, -ɪŋ, -t

la Pucelle, Joan (*var. of* **de Pucelle**) (*1HVI*) 'dʒoʊn ͜la pju'sel [͜la 'pʌzəl]
Note.—Var. spellings appear in the Folio, e.g., 'Puzel,' 'Pucell,' & 'Pussel.' The OED also cites 'puzzel' and 'puzzle' as obsolete forms of 'Pucelle.' These spellings, along with where the name falls in the verse line, suggest that the pronunciation may be (is probably) ['pjusel], ['pʌsəl], *or—perhaps even better—*['pʌzəl]*; thus, a homophonic pun about confusion and perplexity is retained. I will assert that S. also*

intended (or at least enjoyed) a double entendre; 'puzzle' was the colloquial slang for a slattern, a whore, or a slut. The irony and ambiguity of the name is not lost on Talbot, who remarks on it in 1HVI, I.iv.106. *In any case, Pucelle in S. is given primary stress on the first syllable. See* 1HVI, I.ii.110, I.iv.100, 106, I.vi.3, II.i.20, III.ii.20, 58, 121, III.iii.40. *In lines* I.v.36, III.ii.38, *and* III.iii.88, *the name (contained in the first foot in each) is presumably trochaic. Cf.* **Bordeaux** *and the Note for* **Puzzel**

lapwing, -s 'læpwɪŋ, -z

larcen|y, -ies 'laɚ·sən|ɨ, -ɨz

larch, -es 'laɚ·tʃ, -ɪz

lard, -s, -ing, -ed 'laɚ·d, -z, -ɪŋ, -ɪd

larder, -s 'laɚ·də·, -z

large, -r, -st, -ly, -ness 'laɚ·dʒ, -ə·, -ɪst, -lɨ, -nɪs

large-handed 'laɚ·dʒͺhændɪd

largess|(e), -(e)s laɚ·'ʒes [-'dʒes], -ɪz (['laɚ·dʒes] *in* HV, IV.Chorus.43)

lark, -s, -ing, -ed 'laɚ·k, -s, -ɪŋ, -t

lark's-heel, -s 'laɚ·ksfiil, -z

Lartius, Titus (*COR*) 'taɪtəs 'laɚ·ʃəs

'larum (*from* **alarum**), **-s** 'laɹəm ['læɹəm], -z

'larum-bell, -s 'laɹəmͺbel ['læɹəm], -z

'las (*from* **alas**) 'læs

lascivious, -ly, -ness lə'sɪvɪəs, -lɨ, -nɪs

lass, -es 'læs, -ɪz

lass-lorn 'læs'lɔ͡ə·n (*when att.,* ['-ͺ-])

last, -s, -ing/ly, -ed; -ly 'last, -s, -ɪŋ/lɨ, -ɪd; -lɨ

latch, -es, -ing, -ed 'lætʃ, -ɪz, -ɪŋ, -t

late, -st, -ly, -ness 'leɪt, -ɪst, -lɨ, -nɪs

lated (*perhaps the aphaeretic form of* **belated**) 'leɪtɪd

later 'leɪɾə·

late-walking 'leɪtͺwɔkɪŋ

lath, -s 'laθ, -s [-aðz]

Latin (AYLI, HV, 2HVI, HVIII, LLL, MV, MWW, TS) 'lætn̩ [-tɪn]

latten (*thin sheet of tin*) 'lætn̩ [-tɪn]

latter, -ly 'læɾə·, -lɨ

lattic|e, -es, -ing, -ed 'læɾɪs, -ɪz, -ɪŋ, -t

laud, -s, -ing, -ed 'lɔd, -z, -ɪŋ, -ɪd

laudab|le, -ly, -leness 'lɔdəb|l̩, -lɪ, -l̩nɪs
Launce (*TGV*), **-s** 'lɑns ['lans], -ɪz
Launcelot (*MV*) 'lɑnsəlɒt, -slɒt
launch, -es, -ing, -ed 'lɔntʃ, -ɪz, -ɪŋ, -t
laund, -s 'lɔnd, -z
launder, -s, -ing, -ed, -er/s 'lɔndɚ, -z, -ɹɪŋ, -d, -ɹɚ/z
laundress, -es 'lɔndɹɪs, -ɪz
laundr|y, -ies 'lɔndɹ|ɪ, -ɪz
Laura (*RJ*) 'lɔɹə
laurel, -s, -(l)ing, -(l)ed 'lɒɹəl, -z, -ɪŋ, -d
Laurence, Friar (*RJ*, TGV) 'fɹaɪɚ 'lɔɹəns ['lɒɹ-]
Laus, Deo, bone, intelligo (*L.*) (LLL, V.i.26) 'laŭs 'dεo 'bonε in'tεlɪgo
Lavatch *or* **Lavache** (*ALL'S*) lə'vætʃ [*Fr.* ləvɑʃ]
lav|e, -es, -ing, -ed 'leɪv, -z, -ɪŋ, -d
lavender 'lævɪndɚ
Lavinia (*TIT*) lə'vɪnɪə, -njə
lavolt (*var. of* **lavolta**) lə'vɒlt
lavolta, -s lə'vɒltə [lɑ'v-], -z
law, -s 'lɔ, -z
law-breaker, -s 'lɔˌbɹeɪkɚ, -z
law-day, -s 'lɔˌdeɪ, -z
lawless, -ly, -ness 'lɔlɪs, -lɪ, -nɪs
lawn, -s 'lɔn, -z
Lawrence, Friar 'fɹaɪɚ 'lɔɹəns ['lɒɹ-]
lay, -s, -ing, laid 'leɪ, -z, -ɪŋ, 'leɪd
lay-thoughts 'leɪˌθɔts
lazar, -s 'læzɚ, -z
Lazarus (1HIV) 'læzəɹəs
lazy-puffing 'leɪzɪˌpʌfɪŋ
lea, -s 'li, -z
lead (*to guide*), **-s, -ing, led** 'lid, -z, -ɪŋ, 'led
lead (*soft metal*), **-s, -ing, -ed** 'led, -z, -ɪŋ, -ɪd
leaden 'lednn
leaden-footed 'lednnˌfʊtɪd
lea|f (*s.*), **-ves** 'li|f, -vz
leaf (*v.*), **-s, -ing, -ed** 'lif, -s, -ɪŋ, -t
leafless 'liflɪs
leaflet, -s 'liflɪt, -s

leaf|y, -ier, -iest, -iness 'lif|ɪ, -ɪɚ, -ɪɪst, -ɪnɪs
leagu|e, -es, -ing, -ed 'lig, -z, -ɪŋ, -d
leaguer, -s 'ligɚ, -z
Leah (MV) 'liə
leak, -s, -ing, -ed 'lik, -s, -ɪŋ, -t
lean, -er, -est, -ly, -ness; -s, -ing, -ed, leant 'lin, -ɚ, -ɪst, -lɪ, -nɪs; -z, -ɪŋ, -d, 'lint
Leander (ADO, AYLI, TGV) li'ændɚ [lɪ'æ-]
lean-faced 'linˌfeɪst
lean-looked 'linlʊkt
lean-witted 'linwɪɾɪd [ˌ-'--]
leap, -s, -ing, -ed, leapt 'lip, -s, -ɪŋ, -t, 'lept
leaper, -s 'lipɚ, -z
leapfrog 'lipfɹɒg
leaping-houses 'lipɪŋˌhaŭzɪz
Lear, King (*LEAR*) 'kɪŋ 'lɪɚ
learn, -s, -ing/s, -ed, -t, -er/s 'lɝn, -z, -ɪŋ/z, -d, -t, -ɚ/z
learned (*adj.*), **-ly, -ness** 'lɝnɪd, -lɪ, -nɪs
leas|e, -es, -ing, -ed 'lis, -ɪz, -ɪŋ, -t
leasing (*lie-telling*) 'lisɪŋ ['lizɪŋ]
leather, -s, -ing, -ed 'leðɚ, -z, -ɹɪŋ, -d
leather-coat, -s 'leðɚˌkoŭt, -s
leather-jerkin 'leðɚˌdʒɝkɪn
leathern 'leðɚn
leath|ery, -iness 'leð|ɚɹɪ, -ɚɹɪnɪs
leav|e, -es, -ing/s, left 'liv, -z, -ɪŋ/z, 'left
leaven, -s, -ing, -ed 'levən, -z, -ɪŋ, -d
leave-taking 'livˌteɪkɪŋ
leavy (*earlier form of* **leafy**) 'livɪ
Note.—This word is meant to rhyme with 'heavy' in ADO, II.iii.73, but the rhyme is usually forsaken to preserve a sense of meaning for the modern ear. If one insists on retaining the rhyme, it makes better sense to shift the pronunciation of 'heavy' (in accordance with its root word 'heave'), although dialectally the vowel sound in the first syllable of both words was probably closer to an

i w**e** ɪ cit**y** ɪ h**i**t e l**e**t ε d**e**but æ c**a**n a p**a**ss ɝ b**ir**d ʌ h**u**t ə **a**gain ɚ supp**er** u y**ou** ʊ sh**oul**d o **o**bey ɔ **aw**l ɒ c**o**p ɑ f**a**ther eɪ p**ai**d aɪ h**igh** oŭ g**o** ɔɪ v**oi**ce aŭ f**ou**nd ɪɚ **ear** εɚ **air** ʊɚ **poor** ɔɚ **for**k ɑɚ **par**k aɪɚ f**ire** aŭɚ **hour** b **b**oy p **p**it d **d**og t **t**op g **g**ot k **k**id h **h**ow fi be**h**ave dʒ **j**ot tʃ **ch**ew z **z**any s **s**oft v **v**at f **f**at ʒ trea**s**ure ʃ **sh**ip ð **th**e θ **th**in m **m**an n **n**o ŋ ha**ng** l **l**ip j **y**es w **w**on ʍ **wh**ew ɹ **r**igger, ai**r**y ɾ ma**tt**er

elongated [ɛ] *in S.'s time (cf. Introduction § 3.14 of this dictionary)*

Le Beau (*AYLI*) lə'boŏ

Le Bon, Monsieur (*MV*) mə'sjɔ̃ lə'bɔn

le chavel volant chez les narines de feu
(*Fr.*) (HV, III.vii.14) lʊ ʃə'val vo'lã ʃɛ lə nɑ'ʀin də fø

lecher, -s 'letʃɚ, -z

lecherous, -ly, -ness 'letʃəɹəs, -lɪ, -nɪs

lechery 'letʃəɹɪ

le chien est retourné à son propre
vomissement, et la truie lavée au
bourbier (*Fr.*) (HV, III.vii.65) lʊʃẽ ɛ ʀʊtuʀ'nɛ a sɔ̃ 'pʀopʀ ,vomis'mã ɛ la 'tʀʊi la'vɛ o bu'bjɛ

lectur|e, -es, -ing, -ed, -er/s 'lektʃɚ, -z, -ɹɪŋ, -d, -ɹɚ/z

Leda (MWW, TS) 'lidə

ledge, -s 'ledʒ, -ɪz

ledger, -s 'ledʒɚ, -z

lee, -s 'li, -z

leech, -es 'litʃ, -ɪz

lee'd 'lid

leek, -s 'lik, -s

leer, -s, -ing/ly, -ed 'lɪɚ, -z, -ɹɪŋ/lɪ, -d

leese (*archaic form of 'lose'*) 'lis

leet (*special court of record lords were*
empowered to periodically hold), **-s** 'lit, -s

Le Fer, Monsieur (*HV*) mə'sjɔ̃ lə 'fɛɚ

left (*direction; p.t. of* **leave**, *q.v.*), **-s** 'left, -s

Leg, The (2HIV) ,ðə 'leg

leg, -s, -ging/s, -ged 'leg, -z, -ɪŋ/z, -d

legac|y, -ies 'legəs|ɪ, -ɪz

Legate (1HVI) 'legɪt

legate, -s 'legɪt, -s

legative 'legɪtɪv

lege, domine (*L.*) (LLL, IV.ii.100) 'ledʒɛ 'domɪnɛ

legerity lɪ'dʒeɹɪtɪ

(')leges (*aphetic form of* **alleges**) 'ledʒɪz

legion (**L.**), **-s** 'lidʒən, -z

legitimacy lɪ'dʒɪɾɪməsɪ

legitimate (*adj.*), **-ly, -ness** lɪ'dʒɪɾɪmɪt, -lɪ, -nɪs

legitimat|e (*v.*), **-es, -ing, -ed** lɪ'dʒɪɾɪmeɪt, -s, -ɪŋ, -ɪd

legitimation lɪ,dʒɪɾɪ'meɪʃn̩

legitimiz|e, -es, -ing, -ed lɪ,dʒɪɾɪmaɪz, -ɪz, -ɪŋ, -d

Leicester (HVIII, RIII) 'lestɚ

Leicestershire (3HVI) 'lestɚˌʃɪɚ [-ʃɚ]

leiger 'lidʒɚ

Note.—This word in MEAS, III.i.58 *is*
meant to stand for 'liegeman' or
'ambassador,' and though the OED *cites*
that 'leiger' is an obsolete form of
'leaguer,' which might lead one to the
pronunciation ['ligɚ], *it also cites 'leige'*
as an obsolete form of 'liege'

leisure, -s, -d, -ly, -liness 'leʒɚ, -z, -d, -lɪ, -lɪnɪs

leman, -s 'lemən ['lim-], -z

Lena, Popilius (*JUL*) po'pɪlɪəs, -ljəs 'linə

lend, -s, -ing/s, lent 'lend, -z, -ɪŋ/z, 'lent

length, -s 'leŋkθ, -s

lengthen, -s, -ing, -ed 'leŋkθən, -z, -ɪŋ, -d

lenity 'lenɪtɪ

Len(n)ox (*MAC*) 'lenəks

lent (*p.t. and p.p. of* **lend**, *q.v.*) 'lent

Lent, -en 'lent, -ən

l'envoy 'lɒnvɔɪ

Leonardo (*MV*) ,liə'nɑɚ-doŏ [,lio'n-]
Note.—In MV, II.ii.161, *this name is*
meant to be three syllables to satisfy the
metrical pattern of the line. In this
instance, the name is pronounced as
either [ljə'nɑɚ-doŏ] *or* [lɪ'nɑɚ-doŏ]

Leonati (CYM) lɪə'neɪtaɪ, -'natɪ

Leonato (*ADO*) lɪə'nɑtoŏ
Note.—In ADO, IV.i.244, V.iv.21, *this*
name must be trisyllabic, i.e., [ljə'nɑtoŏ]
to meet the requirements of versification

Leonatus, Posthumus (*CYM*) 'pɒstjuməs, pɒs'hjuməs [pɒs'tj-] lɪə'neɪtəs [lɪə'nɑtəs]
Note.—The words 'posthumous' and
'posthumus' were extremely new to
English in S.'s day (cf. OED). *The*
modern pronunciation of the words
places primary stress on the first
syllable, i.e., ['pɒstjuməs], *following the*
traditional pronunciation dating from at
least A.D. 1757 (James Buchanan's
'Linguae Britannicae vera Pronunciatio
or, A New English Dictionary,' and even
earlier lexicographers). If primary
syllabic stress was ever normally placed

on the second syllable, there is no
evidence for it. Therefore, by applying
primary syllabic stress to the second
syllable, one is practically forced to
suppose that S. is merely dressing his
character in a very thin 'disguise,' as he
does with names such as Abhorson,
Aliena, Holofernes (MEAS, AYLI, and
LLL, respectively), and many, many
others. Perhaps giving this name
traditional stress on the first syllable
would have seemed to S. too obvious
and overly portentous. At first glance,
CYM, I.i.41; III.v.36; and particularly
IV.ii.320 pose a problem by appearing
to appropriate primary stress on the
first syllable, but a clever scansionist
can reconcile these seeming incongrui-
ties using common prosodic devices S.
often employs. I favor consistency when
it comes to a proper name's syllabic
stress in S.'s plays, and it seems
unprofitable to pronounce the name two
different ways in the very same passage
(CYM, IV.ii.308–320). Also see Note for
Balthasar

Leonine (PER) 'lɪənaɪn

Leontes (WT) li'ɒntɨz [lɪ'ɒ-]

leopard, -s 'lepə˞d, -z
Note.—There is a tenable case to
support this word being pronounced as a
trisyllable ['lɪəpaᵊd, -pə˞d] in 1HVI,
I.v.31

Lepidus, Marcus Æmilius (AC, JUL)
'maᵊ˞kəs i'mɪlɪəs 'lepɪdəs
Note.—To retain this accentuation for
'Lepidus' in AC, II.i.14, one must allow
the full-stop punctuation to absorb the
value of a beat, and thus the vowel
sound in the second syllable of 'Lepidus'
is virtually, though not entirely, absent
from pronunciation, i.e., ['lepɪdəs]. In
JUL, III.ii.266, where it appears to scan
[-ˊ--], the line is possibly prose

le Port Blanc (RII) (see **Port le Blan[c]**)
lə 'pɔᵊ˞t 'blaŋk

leprosy 'lepɹəsɨ

leprous, -ly, -ness 'lepɹəs, -lɨ, -nɪs

le Roy, Harry (HV) (alias Henry V) 'hæɹɨ
lə 'ɹɔɪ

less, -er 'les, -ə˞

less|en, -ens, -ening, -ened 'les|n̩ [-s|n̩],
-n̩z, -n̩ɪŋ, -n̩d

lest 'lest

Lestrelles (HV) lɛ'stɹal (may be ['lestɹal]
in HV, III.v.45)

let, -s, -ting 'let, -s, -ɪŋ ['leɡɪŋ]

let-a 'letə (see **dat**)

let-alone 'leɡə'loʊn

letharg|y, -ies, -ied 'leθə˞dʒ|ɨ, -ɨz, -ɨd

lethe (L.) (AC, HAM, 2HIV, RIII, TN)
'liθɨ

let't (contr. of **let it**) 'lett

letter, -s, -ing, -ed 'leɡə˞, -z, -ɹɪŋ, -d

lettuce, -s 'leɡɪs, -ɪz

level, -s, -ling, -led, -ler/s; -ness 'levl̩, -z,
-ɪŋ, -d, -ə˞/z; -nɪs

'leven (from **eleven**) 'levn̩

leven-pence 'levn̩pəns

lev|er, -ers, -ering, -ered 'lev|ə˞ ['liv|ə˞],
-ə˞z, -ə˞ɹɪŋ, -ə˞d

leverag|e, -es, -ing, -ed 'levə˞ɹɪdʒ, -ɪz, -ɪŋ,
-d

leviathan, -s lɪ'vaɪə θn̩, -z

levit|y, -ies 'levɪt|ɨ, -ɨz

lev|y, -ies, -ying, -ied, -ier/s 'lev|ɨ, -ɨz,
-ɨɪŋ, -ɨd, -ɨə˞/z

lewd, -er, -est, -ly, -ness 'ljud ['lud], -ə˞,
-ɪst, -lɨ, -nɪs

lewdster, -s 'ljudstə˞ ['lud-], -z

lewd-tongued 'ljud,tʌnd ['lud-]

Lewis or **Louis** (HV, 3HVI, KJ) 'luɪs
['ljuɪs]
Note.—In 3HVI, this name is spoken
monosyllabically ['lu(ə)s], with the
exception of 3HVI, III.iii.169. Lines
III.iii.23 and IV.i.28 may be treated as
monosyllables, or disyllables if one opts

i we ɪ city ɪ hit e let ɛ debut æ can a pass ɝ bird ʌ hut ə again ə˞ supper u you
ʊ should o obey ɔ awl ɒ cop ɑ father eɪ paid aɪ high oʊ go ɔɪ voice aʊ found ɪᵊ˞ ear
ɛᵊ˞ air ʊᵊ˞ poor ɔᵊ˞ fork ɑᵊ˞ park aɪᵊ˞ fire aʊᵊ˞ hour b boy p pit d dog t top g got
k kid h how fi behave dʒ jot tʃ chew z zany s soft v vat f fat ʒ treasure ʃ ship ð the
θ thin m man n no ŋ hang l lip j yes w won ʍ whew ɹ rigger, airy ɾ matter

to scan these lines with feminine endings. In KJ, *the name is mono-syllabic throughout*

liable 'laɪəbl̩

liand (*see* **ligned**) 'laɪənd

liar, -s 'laɪɚ, -z

libbard (*archaic var. of* **leopard**), **-s** 'lɪbɑɚ̆d ['lɪbəˑd], -z

libel, -s, -ling, -led, -ler/s 'laɪbl̩, -z, -ɪŋ, -d, -ɚ/z

liberal, -s, -ly 'lɪbəˑɹəl [-bɹəl], -z, -ɪ

liberality ˌlɪbəˑ'ɹælɪtɪ

liberat|e, -es, -ing, -ed, -or/s 'lɪbəˑɹeɪ̆t, -s, -ɪŋ, -ɪd, -ɚ/z

liberation ˌlɪbəˑ'ɹeɪ̆ʃn̩

libertine, -s 'lɪbəˑtin, -z

libert|y (L.), -ies 'lɪbəˑt|ɪ [-əˑɾ|ɪ], -ɪz

librar|y, -ies 'laɪbɹəɹ|ɪ, -ɪz

Libya (AC, TC, WT) 'lɪbɪə, -bjə

lice (*p.t. of* **louse** (*s.*)*, q.v.*) 'laɪs

licens|e, -es, -ing, -ed 'laɪsəns, -ɪz, -ɪŋ, -t

licentious, -ly, -ness laɪ'senʃəs, -lɪ, -nɪs

Lichas (AC, MV) 'laɪ̆kəs

lick, -s, -ing, -ed 'lɪk, -s, -ɪŋ, -t

lictor, -s 'lɪktɚ, -z

lie (*s., v.*) (*falsehood, untruth*) **lies, lying, lied** 'laɪ, 'laɪz, 'laɪɪŋ, 'laɪd

lie (*v.*) (*recline; be placed; be situated; consist, etc.*) **lies, lying, lay, lain** 'laɪ, 'laɪz, 'laɪɪŋ, 'leɪ, 'leɪ̆n

Lie Circumstantial ˌlaɪ ˌsɚkəm'stænʃl̩

Lie Direct ˌlaɪ dɪ'ɹekt

lief, -er, -est 'lif, -ɚ, -ɪst

liege (L.), -s, -er/s 'lidʒ, -ɪz, -ɚ/z

liege|man, -men 'lidʒ|mən, -mən

lie-giver 'laɪˌgɪvɚ [ˌ-'--]

lien, -s 'lin ['liən], -z

li'es 'lɪvz ['lɪz]

Note.—This poetic contraction of 'lives' appears in KJ, III.i.264 *(The Arden Shakespeare, 1954, E. A. J. Honigmann, editor), is the brainchild of F. G. Fleay, a nineteenth century S. scholar, and is an equivocation. The couplet in which it appears is,* 'Lewis: *Lady, with me, with me thy fortune lies. /* Blanche: *There where my fortune li'es, there my life dies.' Editors intent on retaining this contrivance never truly commit*

themselves either to 'lives' (the antithesis to 'dies') or to 'lies' (repeating the image of the previous line). It's difficult to see (or rather hear) the advantage in pronouncing the word as indicated by the contraction. The First Folio gives simply 'lives'

lieu 'lju ['lu]

lieutenant (L.), -s; -ry lju'tenənt [lu't-], -s; -ɹɪ

Note.—Certain S. plays are more apt than others to be spoken with a Brit. dialect, e.g., the Histories. 'Lieutenant,' along with a handful of other words ('clerk,' 'corollary,' 'schedule,' etc.), takes on an entirely different (viz. Brit.) pronunciation, in addition to the merely dialectal variances that naturally distinguish Brit. and U.S. English from one another. Thus, when traditional Brit. English is preferred, the pronunciation becomes [lefˈtenənt, ləf-]

li|fe, -ves 'laɪ̆|f, -vz

life-blood 'laɪ̆fˌblʌd

life-harming 'laɪ̆fˌhɑɚ̆mɪŋ

lifeling, -s 'laɪ̆flɪŋ, -z

lifelong 'laɪ̆flɒŋ [ˌ-'-]

life-poisoning 'laɪ̆fˌpɔɪ̆znɪŋ

lifetime, -s 'laɪ̆ftaɪ̆m, -z

life-weary 'laɪ̆fˌwɪɚ̆ɹɪ (*when att.,* [ˌ-'--])

lift, -s, -ing, -ed, -er/s 'lɪft, -s, -ɪŋ, -ɪd, -ɚ/z

ligament, -s 'lɪgəmənt, -s

Ligarius, Caius (*JUL*) 'kaɪ̆əs, 'keɪ̆əs lɪ'gɛɚ̆ɹɪəs, -ɹɪ̆əs

liggens 'lɪggənz

Note.—The pronunciation of this rare word in 2HIV, V.iii.63 *presents less of a challenge than does its meaning. Most modern editors surmise that the oath in which it appears, i.e., "By God's liggens," is saying 'by God's little eyelids.' It's a clever solution and fits with other oaths of this nature found in* S., *e.g., 'sfoot and 'slid. In this case, they conjecture that 'liggens' is derived from 'lidkins' (a word the* OED *never happens to mention). G. B. Harrison (*Shakespeare: The Complete Works, *Harcourt,*

*Brace, Jovanovich, publishers) suggests
that 'liggens' is "probably 'little
legs'—but Shallow has passed beyond
coherence." As both of these etymolo-
gies suggest that the latter part of
'liggens' comes from the diminutive
'-kins,' please note the use of the
same-consonant blend [-ɡɡ-] in the
pronunciation proffered above*

light, -er, -est, -ly, -ness; -s, -ing, -ed, lit
'laɪt, -ɚ, -ɪst, -lɨ, -nɪs; -s, -ɪŋ, -ɪd, 'lɪt
lighter, -s 'laɪɾɚ, -z
lightless 'laɪtlɪs
lightning, -s 'laɪtnɪŋ, -z
lightning-flash, -es 'laɪtnɪŋˌflæʃ, -ɪz
Light o' Love (ADO, TGV, TNK)
(*popular contemporary tune*) ˌlaɪt ə 'lʌv
light-winged 'laɪtˌwɪŋd
ligned 'laɪnd
*Note.—This word, appearing in RJ,
III.v.180 in The Arden Shakespeare
(1980), is the conjectural conclusion of
Harold Jenkins (see his note for the
line). The various Quartos and Folios
give 'liand,' 'allied,' and 'trainde'*
likable 'laɪkəbl̩
lik|e, -es, -ing, -ed 'laɪk, -s, -ɪŋ, -t
likel|y, -ier, -iest, -iness, -ihood/s 'laɪkl|ɨ,
-ɪɚ, -ɪɪst, -ɪnɪs, -ɨhʊd/z
likeness, -es 'laɪknɪs, -ɪz
liker (*one who likes; more alike*), **-s**
'laɪkɚ, -z
*Note.—Given the content of what's being
said in LLL, V.ii.827, 828, the word
'liker' in this instance must be a
contraction or slurring of the words 'like
are'*
likewise 'laɪkwaɪz ([ˌ-'-] *in* TGV, I.i.60)
liking, -s 'laɪkɪŋ, -z
lil|y, -ies 'lɪl|ɨ, -ɨz
lily-livered ˌlɪlɨ'lɪvɚd
lily-tincture ˌlɪlɨ'tɪŋktʃɚ
Limander (*corruption of* **Leander** *in*
MSND) lɪ'mændɚ

limb, -s, -ed 'lɪm, -z, -d
limbeck (*archaic corruption or aphetic
form of* **alembic**), **-s** 'lɪmbek, -s
limber, -s, -ing, -ed 'lɪmbɚ, -z, -ɹɪŋ, -d
limb-meal (*limb from limb*) 'lɪmˌmil
limbo (L.) 'lɪmboʊ
lim|e, -es, -ing, -ed 'laɪm, -z, -ɪŋ, -d
Limehouse (HVIII) 'laɪmfiaʊs ['lɪməs]
lime-kiln, -s 'laɪmˌkɪln [-ˌkɪl], -z (*see* **kiln**)
limit, -s, -ing, -ed/ness, -er/s; -able
'lɪmɪt, -s, -ɪŋ, -ɪd/nɪs, -ɚ/z; -əbl̩
limitation, -s ˌlɪmɪ'teɪʃn, -z
limitless, -ly, -ness 'lɪmɪtlɪs, -lɨ, -nɪs
li|mn, -mns, -mning, -mned, -mner/s
'lɪ|m, -mz, -mnɪŋ [-mɪŋ], -d, -mnɚ/z
Limoges *or* **Lymoges** (*KJ*) lɪ'moʊʒ
*Note.—The pronunciation of this name
(as given above) presents a problem
when it appears in KJ, III.i.40. It seems
that in this line 'Limoges' wants to be
trisyllabic (['lɪmodʒɪs]?), as well as
anglicized, in order to fit rightly into the
verse. If the line is considered headless,
the pronunciation proffered above will
stand (cf. Kökeritz's Shakespeare's
Names: A Pronouncing Dictionary,
p. 24)*
limp, -s, -ing, -ed; -er, -est, -ly, -ness
'lɪmp, -s, -ɪŋ, -t; -ɚ, -ɪst, -lɨ, -nɪs
Lincoln (HVIII) 'lɪŋkən
Lincolnshire (1HIV) 'lɪŋkənʃɚ [-ʃɪɚ]
Lincoln Washes (KJ) 'lɪŋkən 'wɒʃɪz
lineage, -s 'lɪnɪɪdʒ, -ɪz
lineal, -ly 'lɪnɪəl, -ɨ
lineament, -s 'lɪnɪəmənt [-njə-], -s
line-grove, -s 'laɪn'ɡɹoʊv, -z
linen, -s 'lɪnɪn, -z
ling, -s 'lɪŋ, -z
Lingard, Lady (HV) 'leɪdɨ 'lɪŋɡɑɚd
linger, -s, -ing, -ed, -er/s 'lɪŋɡɚ, -z, -ɹɪŋ,
-d, -ɪɚ/z
lingo, -s 'lɪŋɡoʊ, -z
linguist, -s 'lɪŋɡwɪst, -s
linsey-woolsey, -s 'lɪnzɨ'wʊlzɨ, -z

---

i wе ɨ citу ɪ hɪt e lеt ɛ dеbut æ cаn a pаss ɝ bɪrd ʌ hut ə agаin ɚ suppеr u yоu
ʊ shоuld o obеy ɔ аwl ɒ cоp ɑ fаther eɪ pаid aɪ hɪgh oʊ gо ɔɪ vоice aʊ fоund ɪɚ **ear**
ɛɚ **air** ʊɚ **poor** ɔɚ **fork** ɑɚ **park** aɪɚ **fire** aʊɚ **hour** b bоy p pit d dog t top g got
k kid h hоw fi behаve dʒ jot tʃ chew z zаny s soft v vаt f fаt ʒ treаsure ʃ ship ð the
θ thin m mаn n nо ŋ hang l lip j yes w wоn ʍ whew ɹ rigger, airy ɾ matter

linstock 'lınstɒk
lion (L.), -s 'laɪən, -z
Lionel (1HVI, 2HVI) 'laɪənl̩ ['laɪnl̩]
lioness, -es 'laɪənɪs [-nes], -ɪz
lion-gait 'laɪənˌgeɪt
lion-mettled 'laɪənˌmetl̩d
lion-sick 'laɪənˌsɪk
lip, -s, -ping, -ped 'lɪp, -s, -ɪŋ, -t
Lipsbury (LEAR) 'lɪpsbə˞ɪ
liquid, -s; -ly, -ness 'lɪkwɪd, -z; -lɪ, -nɪs
liquidat|e, -es, -ing, -ed, -or/s 'lɪkwɪdeɪt,
  -s, -ɪŋ, -ɪd, -ə˞/z
liquidation, -s ˌlɪkwɪ'deɪʃn̩, -z
liquor, -s, -ing, -ed; -ish 'lɪkə˞, -z, -ɹɪŋ,
  -d; -ɹɪʃ
Lisbon (MV) 'lɪzbən
lisp, -s, -ing, -ed, -er/s 'lɪsp, -s, -ɪŋ, -t,
  -ə˞/z
list, -s, -ing, -ed 'lɪst, -s, -ɪŋ, -ɪd
listless, -ly, -ness 'lɪstlɪs, -lɪ, -nɪs
lit (p.t. and p.p. of v., light, q.v.) 'lɪt
lither 'lɪðə˞
litigant, -s 'lɪʧɪgənt, -s
litigat|e, -es, -ing, -ed 'lɪʧɪgeɪt, -s, -ɪŋ,
  -ɪd
litigation, -s ˌlɪʧɪ'geɪʃn̩, -z
litigious, -ly, -ness lɪ'tɪdʒəs, -lɪ, -nɪs
Litio, Licio, or Lisio (TS) 'lɪʧɪoŭ, -ʃjoŭ
litter, -s, -ing, -ed, -er/s 'lɪʧə˞, -z, -ɹɪŋ, -d,
  -ɹə˞/z
little-a-while 'lɪtələ'waɪl (see dat)
little-seeming 'lɪtl̩ˌsimɪŋ
live (adj.) 'laɪv
liv|e (v.), -es, -ing, -ed, -er/s 'lɪv, -z, -ɪŋ,
  -d, -ə˞/z
livelong 'lɪvlɒŋ
liver, -s 'lɪvə˞, -z
liver|y, -ies, -ied 'lɪvə˞ɪ|ɪ, -ɪz, -ɪd
lives (pl. of life, q.v.) 'laɪvz
Livia (AC, RJ) 'lɪvɪə, -vjə
lo(e) 'loŭ
loach 'loŭʧ
load, -s, -ing, -ed 'loŭd, -z, -ɪŋ, -ɪd
loaden (archaic form of laden) 'loŭdn̩
loa|f (s.), -ves 'loŭ|f, -vz
loaf (v.), -s, -ing, -ed, -er/s 'loŭf, -s, -ɪŋ,
  -t, -ə˞/z
loam 'loŭm
loan, -s, -ing, -ed 'loŭn, -z, -ɪŋ, -d

loath (adj.), -er, -ly, -ness 'loŭθ, -ə˞, -lɪ,
  -nɪs
loath|e (v.), -es, -ing/ly, -ed 'loŭð, -z,
  -ɪŋ/lɪ, -d
loathsome, -st, -ly, -ness 'loŭðsəm
  ['loŭθs-], -ɪst, -lɪ, -nɪs
lob, -s, -bing, -bed, -ber/s 'lɒb, -z, -ɪŋ, -d,
  -ə˞/z
lobb|y, -ies, -ying, -ied 'lɒb|ɪ, -ɪz, -ɪɪŋ, -ɪd
lock, -s, -ing, -ed 'lɒk, -s, -ɪŋ, -t
locker, -s 'lɒkə˞, -z
locket, -s 'lɒkɪt, -s
lockram 'lɒkɹəm
lode(-)star, -s 'loŭdstɑ˞, -z
lodg|e, -es, -ing/s, -ed, -er/s 'lɒdʒ, -ɪz,
  -ɪŋ/z, -d, -ə˞/z
Lodovico (OTH) ˌlɒdo'vikoŭ [loŭdo-]
Lodowick (ALL'S) 'loŭdowɪk ['lɒd-]
Lodowick, Friar (MEAS) ˌfɹaɪə˞
  'loŭdowɪk ['lɒd-]
loffe 'lɔf (to laugh)
  Note.—Its only appearance in S. is in
  MSND, II.i.55, in couplet form meant to
  rhyme with 'cough.' For anyone
  speaking American English, the rhyme is
  typically forsaken in favor of 'laugh'
  (['laf])
loggerhead, -s 'lɒgə˞ˌfied, -z
logger-headed 'lɒgə˞ˌhedɪd
logget or loggat, -s, -ing 'lɒgət, -s, -ɪŋ
log-man 'lɒgmən [-gmæn]
loin, -s 'lɔɪn, -z
loiter, -s, -ing, -ed, -er/s 'lɔɪʧə˞, -z, -ɹɪŋ,
  -d, -ɹə˞/z
loll, -s, -ing, -ed, -er/s 'lɒl, -z, -ɪŋ, -d,
  -ə˞/z
Lombardy (TS) 'lɒmbə˞dɪ
London (HV, 3HVI), -er/s 'lʌndən, -ə˞/z
London Bridge (1HVI, 2HVI) ˌlʌndən
  'bɹɪdʒ
London Stone (2HVI) ˌlʌndən 'stoŭn
lonel|y, -ier, -iest, -iness 'loŭnl|ɪ, -ɪə˞, -ɪɪst,
  -ɪnɪs
long (s., adj.), -s, -er, -est 'lɒŋ, -z, -gə˞,
  -gɪst
long (v.), -s, -ing/ly, -ed, -er/s 'lɒŋ, -z,
  -ɪŋ/lɪ, -d, -ə˞/z
long-a 'lɒŋə
  Note.—This word appears in a ditty in

2HIV, V.iii.46; *the extra syllable at the end merely to provide for another musical beat in the line of song*
Longaville (*LLL*) ˈlɔŋəvɪl
Note.—Perhaps [ˈlɔŋəvaɪ̆l] *is closer to what S. intended, as the name is meant to rhyme with 'mile' and 'compile' in LLL, IV.iii.130, 131 and LLL, V.ii.53, 54, respectively; yet, in both instances, the name is spoken tauntingly (if only teasingly), so that accentuating the end of his name to sound like 'vile' may simply be a device for the occasion. Adding weight to the theory that he is being heckled when he is called 'Longa-vile' is the fact that the name also rhymes with 'ill' in LLL, IV.iii.120 and 121, which better suits the more conventional pronunciation of the name. (Cf.* **Berowne***)*
long-continued ˈlɒŋkənˌtɪnjud
longed-for ˈlɒŋdˌfɔɚ
long-engrafted ˈlɒŋɪnˌɡɹaftɪd [-ɪŋˌɡ-]
'longeth (*see* **'longs**) ˈlɒŋɡɪθ
long-experienced ˌlɒŋɪkˈspɪɚˌɹɪənst
long-grown ˈlɒŋˌɡɹoŏn
Long Lane ˈlɒŋ ˈleɪ̆n
long-lived ˈlɒŋˌlɪvd
long-living ˈlɒŋˌlɪvɪŋ
longly ˈlɒŋlɨ
'longs (*from* **belongs**) ˈlɒŋz
long-staff ˈlɒŋˌstaf
long-tail ˈlɒŋˌteɪ̆l
long-tongued ˈlɒŋˌtʌŋd
long-winded, -ness ˌlɒŋˈwɪndɪd (*when att.,* [ˈ-ˌ--]), -nɪs
(')loo (*hunting cry*) ˈlu:
loofed *or* **looft** (*as in the First Folio*) ˈluft
Note.—The reference in AC, III.x.18 is obscure. It may be a treatment (in an aphetic form) of the adv. 'aloof,' or refer instead to the blade of an oar or rudder (cf. OED, 'loof' and 'aloof'). The word

is often emended to the nautical term 'luffed' [ˈlʌft]
look, -s, -ing, -ed, -er/s ˈlŏk, -s, -ɪŋ, -t, -ɚ/z
looker-on, lookers-on ˌlŏkɚˈɹɒn, ˌlŏkɚˈzɒn
looking-glass, -es ˈlŏkɪŋɡlas, -ɪz
loon, -s ˈlun, -z
loop, -s, -ing, -ed ˈlup, -s, -ɪŋ, -t
loop(-)hole, -s ˈlupˌɦoŏl, -z
loos|e, -es, -ing, -ed; -er, -est, -ely, -eness ˈlus, -ɪz, -ɪŋ, -t; -ɚ, -ɪst, -lɨ, -nɪs
loose-bodied ˈlusˌbɒdɪd
lop, -s, -ping, -ped, -per/s ˈlɒp, -s, -ɪŋ, -t, -ɚ/z
lord (**L.**)**, -s, -ing/s, -ed** ˈlɔɚd, -z, -ɪŋ/z, -ɪd
Lord High Constable (HVIII) ˈlɔɚd ˈhaɪ̆ ˈkʌnstəbl̩ [ˈkɒn-]
lordl|y, -ier, -iest, -iness ˈlɔɚdl|ɨ, -ɪɚ, -ɪɪst, -ɪnɪs
lordship (**L.**)**, -s** ˈlɔɚdʃɪp, -s
Lorenzo (*MV*) loˈɹenzoŏ [lɔˈɹ-]
Lorraine, Duke of (HV) ˈdjuk əv ˈlɔɹeɪ̆n
Note.—Although reliable sources give primary stress to the second syllable of 'Lorraine,' i.e., [lɔˈɹeɪ̆n], *the scansion of the verse favors first syllable stress as proffered above; also, the First Folio's spelling 'Loraine' is like that of 'Millaine' (Milan) and 'villaine,' both of which are given first-syllable stress (see Note for* **Milan***)*
losel, -s ˈloŏzəl, -z
loth (*var. of* **loath**) ˈloŏθ
Louis the Ninth (HV) ˈlu(ə)s ðə ˈnaɪ̆nθ (*see Note for* **Lewis***)*
lour *or* **lower** (*ominous or threatening*), **-s, -ing, -ed** ˈlaŏɚ, -z, -ɹɪŋ, -d
louse (*s.*), **lice** ˈlaŏs, ˈlaɪ̆s
Note.—In MWW, I.i.16, Evans says 'louses' for the pl. form of the s. 'louse' rather than the regular 'lice'
lous|e (*v.*), **-es, -ing, -ed** ˈlaŏs, -ɪz, -ɪŋ, -t

lous|y, -ier, -iest, -ily, -iness 'laŭz|ɪ, -ɪə̆-, -ɪst, -ɪlɪ, -ɪnɪs

lout, -s, -ing, -ed 'laŭt, -s, -ɪŋ, -ɪd

Louvre (HV, HVIII) 'luvɹə (*Fr.* luvʁ) *Note.—It's clear that in HV, II.iv.132 and HVIII, I.iii.23, 'Louvre' wants to be disyllabic. Kökeritz asserts that S. might have anglicized it entirely to* ['luvə̆-(ɹ)] *(cf. Kökeritz's* Shakespeare's Names: A Pronouncing Dictionary, *p. 67). In the Second Folio version of HV, 'Louvre' is spelled 'Loover,' supporting this notion*

lov|e (L.), **-es, -ing/ly, -ed, -er/s** 'lʌv, -z, -ɪŋ/lɪ, -d, -ə̆-/z

love-a 'lʌvə (*see* **dat**)

love-bed, -s 'lʌvˌbed, -z

love-broker, -s 'lʌvˌbɹoŭkə̆-, -z

love-cause 'lʌvˌkɔz

love-day 'lʌvˌdeĭ

love-devouring 'lʌvdɪˌvaŭə̆-ɹɪŋ [ˌ--'--]

love-discourse 'lʌvdɪˌskɔə̆-s

love-juice 'lʌvˌdʒus

love-god, -s 'lʌvˌgɒd, -z

love-in-idleness ˌlʌvɪn'aĭdl̩nɪs

love-kindling 'lʌvˌkɪndlɪŋ

love-lacking 'lʌvˌlækɪŋ

love-letter, -s 'lʌvˌleɾə̆-, -z

Lovell, Sir Thomas (*HVIII, RIII*) ˌsɜ̆- 'tɒməs 'lʌvəl

Love, Monsieur (ADO) məˌsjɜ̆- 'lʌv [--'-]

love-news 'lʌvnjuz

love-performing 'lʌvpə̆-ˌfɔə̆-mɪŋ

love-prate 'lʌvˌpɹeĭt

love-shaft 'lʌvˌʃaft

love-shaked 'lʌvˌʃeĭkt

love-sick, -ness 'lʌvˌsɪk, -nɪs

Love, Signior (AYLI) ˌsinjɔə̆- 'lʌv

love-suit 'lʌvˌsut [-ˌsjut, '-'-]

love-thoughts 'lʌvˌθɔts

loving-jealous ˌlʌvɪŋ'dʒeləs

low, -er, -est, -ness 'loŭ, -ə̆-, -ɪst, -nɪs

low (*sound an ox or cow makes*), **-s, -ing, -ed** 'loŭ, -z, -ɪŋ, -d *Note.—In ADO, V.iv.48, this word wants to rhyme with 'cow' (cf. Kökeritz's* Shakespeare's Pronunciation, *pp. 245f.), but today this rhyme is traditionally forsaken*

low-down 'loŭdaŏn ['-'-]

lower *or* **lour** (*ominous or threatening*), **-s, -ing, -ed** 'laŏə̆-, -z, -ɹ ɪŋ, -d

low-laid 'loŭˌleĭd

lowl|y, -ier, -iest, (L.) -iness 'loŭl|ɪ, -ɪə̆-, -ɪst, -ɪnɪs

lown (*var. of* **loon**) 'laŏn

low-voiced 'loŭˌvɔĭst

loyal, -ly 'lɔĭəl, -ɪ

loyalist, -s 'lɔĭəlɪst, -s

loyalt|y (L.), **-ies** 'lɔĭəlt|ɪ, -ɪz

lozel(l) (*obsolete form of* **losel**), **-s** 'loŭzəl, -z

lozenge, -s 'lɒzɪndʒ, -ɪz

lubber, -s; -ly 'lʌbə̆-, -z; -lɪ

Lubber's *or* **Lubbar's Head** (2HIV) 'lʌbə̆-z 'hed

Luccicos, Marcus (OTH) 'maə̆-kəs lu'tʃikəs [lju'tʃ-]

Luce (*COM, TNK*) 'ljus ['lus]

luce (*the pike, a freshwater fish*), **-s** 'lus ['ljus], -ɪz

Lucentio (RJ, *TS*) lu'senʃĭo [lju's-], -ʃɪoŭ

Lucetta (*TGV*) lu'tʃetə, lu'setə [lju-, -eɾə]

Luciana (*COM*) ˌlusɪ'anə [ˌluʃɪ'ænə, ˌlju-]

Lucianus (HAM) ˌljuʃɪ'anəs [ˌljusɪ'eĭnəs, ˌlu-]

lucid, -ly, -ness 'ljusɪd ['lus-], -lɪ, -nɪs

lucidity lju'sɪdɪtɪ [lu's-]

Lucifer (1HIV, 2HIV, HV, HVIII, KJ, MWW) 'lusɪfə̆- ['lju-]

Lucil(l)ius (AC, *JUL, TIM*) lu'sɪlɪəs, -ljəs [lju's-]

Lucina (PER) lu'saĭnə ['lju-]

Lucio (*MEAS*, RJ) 'luʃĭo ['lju-, -usĭo], -ʃɪoŭ

Lucius (AC, *CYM, JUL, TIM, TIT*) 'luʃɪəs, -ʃjəs, 'lusɪəs, -sjəs ['lju-]

Lucius, Caius (*CYM*) 'kaĭəs ['keĭəs] 'luʃɪəs, -ʃjəs, 'lusɪəs, -sjəs ['lju-]

Lucius, Young (*TIT*) 'jʌŋ 'luʃɪəs, -ʃjəs, 'lusɪəs, -sjəs ['lju-]

lucre 'lukə̆- ['lju-]

Lucrece (LUC, TIT, TN, TS) 'lukɹis ['lju-]

Lucretia (AYLI, LUC) lu'kɹiʃə [lju-]

Lucretius (LUC) lu'kɹiʃɪəs, -ʃəs [lju-]

Lucullus (*TIM*) lu'kʌləs [lju-]

Lucy, Lady Elizabeth (RIII) 'leĭdɨ
r'lɪzəbəθ 'lusɨ [lju-]
Lucy, Sir William (*1HVI*) ˌsɜˑ 'wɪljəm
'lusɨ [lju-]
Lud (CYM) 'lʌd
Ludlow (RIII) 'lʌdloŏ
lug, -s, -ging, -ged 'lʌg, -z, -ɪŋ, -d
luggage 'lʌgɪdʒ
lukewarm, -ly, -ness 'lukwɔɔ̌ˑm ['ljuk-],
-lɨ, -nɪs
lull, -s, -ing, -ed 'lʌl, -z, -ɪŋ, -d
lulla 'lʌlə
Note.—The Fairies in MSND *sing this
in a ditty. It is simply extracted from
'lullaby,' also part of the song*
lullab|y, -ies 'lʌləb|aĭ, -aĭz
lumber, -s, -ing, -ed 'lʌmbəˑ, -z, -ɹɪŋ, -d
Lumbert Street (2HIV) 'lʌmbəˑt 'stɹit
lump, -s, -ing, -ed 'lʌmp, -s, -ɪŋ, -t
lumpish, -ly, -ness 'lʌmpɪʃ, -lɨ, -nɪs
lump|y, -ier, -iest, -iness 'lʌmp|ɨ, -ɨəˑ,
-ɨɪst, -ɨnɪs
Luna (LLL) 'lunə ['ljunə]
lunacy 'lunəsɨ ['ljun-]
lunar 'lunəˑ ['ljunəˑ]
lunatic, -s 'lunətɪk ['ljun-], -s
Note.—In LLL, V.i.16–25, *Holofernes
is lamenting the "rackers of orthography," particularly concerning how one
should pronounce certain words. It
therefore suits the conceit of the
passage, and is—even more to the
matter—just plain funnier in this
instance to pronounce 'lunatic' with
primary stress on the second syllable
rather than the first, i.e.,* [lju'nætɪk]
*(*LLL, V.i.25*)*
lunch, -es, -ing, -ed 'lʌntʃ, -ɪz, -ɪŋ, -t
luncheon, -s 'lʌntʃən, -z
lune, -s 'lun ['ljun], -z
lung, -s 'lʌŋ, -z
lung|e, -es, -ing, -ed 'lʌndʒ, -ɪz, -ɪŋ, -d
Lupercal 'lupəˑkæl ['ljup-]
lurch, -es, -ing, -ed 'lɜˑtʃ, -ɪz, -ɪŋ, -t

lur|e, -es, -ing, -ed 'lŏɔ̌ˑ ['ljŏɔ̌ˑ], -z, -ɹɪŋ, -d
lurid, -ly, -ness 'lŏɔ̌ˑɹɪd ['ljŏɔ̌ˑ-], -lɨ, -nɪs
lurk, -s, -ing, -ed, -er/s 'lɜˑk, -s, -ɪŋ, -t,
-əˑ/z
luscious, -ly, -ness 'lʌʃəs, -lɨ, -nɪs
lush 'lʌʃ
lust, -s, -ing, -ed 'lʌst, -s, -ɪŋ, -ɪd
lust-breathed 'lʌstˌbɹeθɪd
Note.—In LUC, 3, *the metrical
requirements of the verse line prescribes
that this word be spoken as a trisyllable,
as above. See Note for* **breathed** *(*adj.*)*
lust-dieted 'lʌstˌdaĭətɪd
luster, -s, -ing, -ed; -less 'lʌstəˑ, -z, -ɹɪŋ,
-d; -lɪs
lust|ful, -fully, -fulness 'lʌst|fŏl, -fəlɨ,
-fŏlnɪs
lustique *or* **lustick** 'lʌstɪk
lustrous, -ly, -ness 'lʌstɹəs, -lɨ, -nɪs
lust-stained 'lʌstˌsteĭnd
lust|y, -ier, -iest, -ily, -iness, -ihood 'lʌst|ɨ,
-ɨəˑ, -ɨɪst, -ɪlɨ, -ɨnɪs, -ɨfŏd
lute, -s 'lut ['ljut], -s
lute-string, -s 'lutstɹɪŋ ['ljut-], -z
Lutheran (HVIII), -s 'luθəˑɹən, -θɹən, -z
lux tua vita mihi (*L.*) (PER, II.ii.21) 'luks
'tuɑ 'vitɑ 'mihi
luxurious, -ly, -ness lʌg'ʒɜˑɹɪəs ['lʌkʃɜˑ-],
-lɨ, -nɪs
luxur|y (**L.**) (TC), **-ies** 'lʌgʒɜˑɹ|ɨ ['lʌkʃəˑ-],
-ɨz
Lycaonia (AC) ˌlaĭkə'oŏnɪə
Lychorida (*PER*) laĭ'kɔɹɪdə
Lycurgus (COR), **-es** laĭ'kɜˑgəs, -ɪz
Lydia (AC) 'lɪdɪə
lye 'laĭ
lyingest 'laĭɪŋɪst
Lymoges *or* **Limoges** (*KJ*) lɪ'moŏʒ (*see
Note for* **Limoges**)
lynch, -es, -ing, -ed 'lɪntʃ, -ɪz, -ɪŋ, -t
Lynn (3HVI) 'lɪn
lynx, -es 'lɪŋks, -ɪz
Lysander (*MSND*) laĭ'sændəˑ
Lysimachus (*PER*) laĭ'sɪməkəs

i wĕ ɨ cit**y** ɪ hĭt e lĕt ɛ dĕbut æ c**a**n a p**a**ss ɜˑ bĭr**d** ʌ hŭt ə **a**gain əˑ supp**er** u y**ou**
ŏ shŏuld o ŏbey ɔ **aw**l ɒ cŏp ɑ f**a**ther eĭ p**ai**d aĭ h**i**gh oŏ g**o** ɔĭ v**oi**ce aŏ f**ou**nd ɪɔ̌ˑ **ear**
ɛɔ̌ˑ **air** ŏɔ̌ˑ p**oor** ɔɔ̌ˑ f**or**k ɑɔ̌ˑ p**ar**k aĭɔ̌ˑ f**ire** aŏɔ̌ˑ h**our** b b**o**y p p**i**t d d**o**g t t**o**p g g**o**t
k k**i**d h **h**ow fi be**h**ave dʒ **j**ot tʃ **ch**ew z **z**any s **s**oft v **v**at f **f**at ʒ trea**s**ure ʃ **sh**ip ð **th**e
θ **th**in m **m**an n **n**o ŋ han**g** l **l**ip j **y**es w **w**on ʍ **wh**ew ɹ **r**igger, ai**r**y ɼ ma**tt**er

Mm

M (*the letter*), **-s** 'em, -z
'm (*weakest form of* **them**, *q.v.*) 'm
Mab, Queen (RJ) 'kwin 'mæb
Macbeth (*MAC*) mæk'beθ [mək-]
Macbeth, Lady (*MAC*) 'leĭdɪ mæk'beθ
[mək-]
Maccabæus, Judas (LLL) 'dʒudəs
ˌmækə'biəs
Macdonwald (MAC) mæk'dɒnəld [mək-]
Macduff (*MAC*) mæk'dʌf [mək-]
Macduff, Lady (*MAC*) 'leĭdɪ mæk'dʌf
[mək-]
Macedon (HV, PER) 'mæsɪdɒn
Macedon, Philip of (HV) 'fɪlɪp əv
'mæsɪdɒn
Machiavel (1HVI, 3HVI, MWW)
ˌmækɪə'vel ['--,-, -kjə-]
machinat|e, -es, -ing, -ed, -or/s
'mækɪneĭt ['mæʃɪ-], -s, -ɪŋ, -ɪd, -ɚ/z
machination, -s ˌmækɪ'neĭʃn [ˌmæʃɪ-], -z
machin|e, -es, -ing, -ed mə'ʃin, -z, -ɪŋ, -d
Note.—*Probably stressed on the first*
syllable, i.e., ['mæʃin] *in* TNK, III.v.112
machinery mə'ʃinəɹɪ
mackerel, -s 'mækəɹəl ['mækɹəl], -z
Macmorris (*HV*) mæk'mɒɹɪs [mək-]
maculate (*adj.*) 'mækjʊlɪt
maculat|e, -es, -ing, -ed 'mækjʊleĭt, -s,
-ɪŋ, -ɪd
maculation, -s ˌmækjʊ'leĭʃn, -z
mad, -der, -dest, -ly, -ness 'mæd, -ɚ, -ɪst,
-lɪ, -nɪs
madam(e) 'mædəm
mad-brain, -ed 'mæd,bɹeĭn, -d
mad(-)cap, -s 'mædkæp, -s
madded 'mædɪd
madding 'mædɪŋ
made (*p.t. of* **make**, *q.v.*) 'meĭd
Madeira (1HIV) mə'dɪɚ,ɹə
mad-headed 'mæd,hedɪd
madly-used 'mædlɪ,juzd
mad|man, -men 'mæd|mən, -mən
madonna (M.), -s mə'dɒnə, -z
madrigal, -s 'mædɹɪgḷ, -z
Note.—*In* MWW, III.i.17, *this word*
wants to rhyme (more or less) with 'falls'

occurring in the line of song immedi-
ately preceding
mad|woman, -women 'mæd|wʊmən,
-wɪmɪn
Mæcenas, Maecenas, Mecænas, *or*
Mecenas (*AC*) mi'sinəs
ma foi, il fait fort chaud. O, je m'en vois
à la cour—la grande affaire (*Fr.*)
(MWW, I.iv.46.47) ma 'fwa ɪl fɛ fɔʁ 'ʃo
o ʒʊ mɑ̃ 'vwa a lɑ cuʁ la 'gʁɑ̃ dɑ'fɛʁ
maggot, -s, -y 'mægət, -s, -ɪ
magi (M.) (*pl. of* **magus**) 'meĭdʒaĭ
['mædʒaĭ]
magic, -al, -ally 'mædʒɪk, -ḷ, -əlɪ
magician, -s mə'dʒɪʃn̩, -z
magnanimity ˌmægnə'nɪmɪtɪ
magnanimious ˌmægnə'nɪmɪəs
magnanimous, -ly mæg'nænɪməs, -lɪ
Magni dominator poli. Tam lentus audis
scelera? tam lentus vides? (*L.*) (TIT,
IV.i.81,82) 'magni 'domɪnɛtɔ̌ 'polɪ 'tam
'lentus 'aŭdɪs 'sɛlɛɾa 'tam 'lentus 'vidɛs
magnifico, -(e)s mæg'nɪfɪkoŭ, -z
mag(g)ot-pie, -s 'mægət,paĭ, -z
magpie, -s 'mægpaĭ, -z
magus (M.), magi (M.) 'meĭgəs,
'meĭdʒaĭ ['mædʒaĭ]
Mahomet mə'fiɒmɪt ['meĭə,met, 'mɑfiə-,
-əmɪt]
Note.—*In* 1HVI, I.ii.140, *the stress is on*
the first syllable
Mahu (LEAR) 'mɑhu
maid-child 'meĭd,tʃaĭld
maiden, -s 'meĭdn̩, -z
maidenhead (M.), -s 'meĭdn̩,hed, -z
maiden-hearted 'meĭdn̩,fiɑ̌-tɪd
maidenhood, -s 'meĭdn̩,fiʊd, -z
maiden|ly, -liest 'meĭdn̩|lɪ, -lɪɪst
maiden-widowed 'meĭdn̩ ,wɪdoŭd
Note.—*In* RJ, III.ii.135, *this word is*
meant to rhyme with 'bed' in line 134
(cf. **punished***); thus an elongated, if*
somewhat over-conscious, ['meĭdn̩
,wɪdoŭed] *is created*
maidhood 'meĭdfiʊd
maid-pale 'meĭd,peĭl

maim, -s, -ing, -ed 'meɪ̆m, -z, -ɪŋ, -d
main, -s, -ly 'meɪ̆n, -z, -lɪ̵
Maine (1HVI, 2HVI, KJ) 'meɪ̆n
main(-)mast, -s 'meɪ̆nməst [-mast], -s
mainport (*offering*) 'meɪ̆npɔɔ̌·t
mainsail, -s 'meɪ̆nsḷ [-seɪ̆l], -z
*Note.—Like so many other words used
in nautical parlance (e.g., 'forecastle'—*
['fŏŭksḷ] *instead of* ['fɔɔ̌·kasḷ], *'bowline'—*['bŏŭlɪn] *instead of* ['bŏŭlaɪ̆n],
'tompion'—['tɒmpkɪn] *instead of*
['tɒmpɪən], *'boatswain'—*['bŏŭsṇ]
instead of ['bŏŭtsweɪ̆n], *etc.), the
pronunciation is typically governed by
the text; who is speaking, to whom one is
speaking, and all other circumstances
germane*
maintain, -s, -ing, -ed, -er/s; -able
meɪ̆n'teɪ̆n, -z, -ɪŋ, -d, -ə˞/z; -əbḷ
*Note.—In TIT, I.i.546; V.ii.72 and TNK,
III.i.53, 'maintain' is arguably given
primary stress on the first syllable, i.e.,*
['meɪ̆nteɪ̆n]
main-top 'meɪ̆n'tɒp
majestic, -al, -ally mə'dʒestɪk, -ḷ, -əlɪ̵
majest|y (M.), -ies 'mædʒɪst|ɪ̵, -ɪ̵z
major, -s, -ing, -ed 'meɪ̆dʒɝ, -z, -ɹɪŋ, -d
majorit|y, -ies mə'dʒɒɹɪt|ɪ̵, -ɪ̵z
mak|e, -es, -ing/s, made 'meɪ̆k, -s, -ɪŋ/z,
'meɪ̆d
make-a 'meɪ̆kə (*see* dat)
make-believe 'meɪ̆kbɪ,liv
makeless 'meɪ̆klɪs
make-peace 'meɪ̆kpis
maker, -s 'meɪ̆kə˞, -z
makeshift 'meɪ̆kʃɪft
malad|y, -ies 'mæləd|ɪ̵, -ɪ̵z
malapert, -ly, -ness 'mæləˌpɝt, -lɪ̵, -nɪs
Malchus, King (AC) ˌkɪŋ 'mælkəs
['mɔkəs]
Malcolm (*MAC*) 'mælkəm
malcontent, -s 'mælkənˌtent, -s
male, -s 'meɪ̆l, -z
male-child 'meɪ̆lˌtʃaɪ̆ld

malediction, -s ˌmælɪ'dɪkʃn̩, -z
malefaction, -s ˌmælɪ'fækʃn̩, -z
malefactor, -s 'mælɪfæktə˞, -z
malevolen|ce, -t/ly mə'levələn|s [-vḷə-],
-t/lɪ̵
malfunction, -s, -ing, -ed mæl'fʌŋkʃn̩, -z,
-ɪŋ, -d
malice 'mælɪs
malicho *or* **mallico** 'mælɪkŏŭ [-lɪtʃŏŭ]
*Note.—This rare word may derive from
Sp. 'malhecho' and thus may be
pronounced* [mɑ'lɛtʃo]. *Since it is used in
the term 'miching malicho,' there may
be some guidance from the potentially
euphonic combination of the* [tʃ] *sound*
malicious, -ly, -ness mə'lɪʃəs, -lɪ̵, -nɪs
malign, -s, -ing, -ed, -er/s mə'laɪ̆n, -z,
-ɪŋ, -d, -ə˞/z
malignan|cy, -t/ly mə'lɪgnən|sɪ̵, -t/lɪ̵
malkin (M.) (COR) 'mɔkɪn
mall, -s 'mɔl, -z
Mall (TEM, TN) 'mæl
mallard, -s 'mælə˞d, -z
malleable, -ness 'mælɪəbḷ [-ljə-], -nɪs
mallet, -s 'mælɪt, -s
mallow, -s 'mæloŭ, -z
malmsey 'mɑmzɪ̵
malmsey-butt 'mɑmzɪ̵ˌbʌt
malmsey-nose 'mɑmzɪ̵ˌnŏŭz
malt, -s, -ing, -ed 'mɔlt ['mɒlt], -s, -ɪŋ, -ɪd
malthorse, -s 'mɔltfiɔɝ·s ['mɒlt-], -ɪz
maltworm, -s 'mɔltwɝm, -z
Malvolio (*TN*) mæl'voŭlɪŏŭ, -ljoŭ
Mamil(l)ius (*WT*) mə'mɪlɪəs, -ljəs
mammer, -s, -ing, -ed 'mæmə˞, -z, -ɹɪŋ,
-d
mammet (*var. of* **maumet**), -s 'mæmɪt
[-met], -s
mammock, -s, -ing, -ed 'mæmək, -s, -ɪŋ,
-t
man (*s.*) **(M.), men** 'mæn, 'men
man (*v.*), -s, -ning, -ned 'mæn, -z, -ɪŋ, -d
manacl|e, -es, -ing, -ed 'mænəkḷ, -z, -ɪŋ,
-d

---

i wɛ ɪ citɪ ɪ hɪt e lɛt ɛ dɛbut æ cæn a pæss ɝ bɪrd ʌ hʌt ə again ə˞ suppɚ u yọu
ʊ shọuld o ọbey ɔ awl ɒ cɒp ɑ fạther eɪ̆ paɪ̆d aɪ̆ hɪgh oŭ gọ ɔɪ vọice aŭ fọund ɪɝ̆· ẹar
ɛɝ̆· ạir ʊɝ̆· pọor ɔɝ̆· fọrk ɑɝ̆· pạrk aɪ̆ɝ̆· fịre aŭɝ̆· họur b bọy p pit d dọg t tọp g gọt
k kid h họw fi behạve dʒ jot tʃ chew z zany s sọft v vat f fat ʒ treạsure ʃ ship ð thẹ
θ thin m man n nọ ŋ hang l lip j yẹs w wọn ʍ whew ɹ rigger, aiɹy ɼ mạtter

manag|e, -es, -ing, -ed, -er/s, -ment/s 'mænɪdʒ, -ɪz, -ɪŋ, -d, -ɚ/z, -mənt/s

man-at-arms, men-at-arms ˌmænə'ɾɑ˞mz, ˌmenə'ɾɑ˞mz

man-child 'mænˌtʃaɪld

Manchus, King (AC; *var. of* Malchus *and* Mauchus) ˌkɪŋ 'mæŋkəs

mandat|e, -es, -ing, -ed 'mændeɪt, -s, -ɪŋ, -ɪd

mandragora mæn'dɹægəɹə

mandrake, -s 'mændɹeɪk, -s

mane, -s, -d 'meɪn, -z, -d

man-entered 'mænˌentɚd

man|ful, -fully, -fulness 'mæn|fʊl, -fʊlɪ, -fʊlnɪs

manger, -s 'meɪndʒɚ, -z

mang|le, -les, -ling, -led 'mæŋg|l̩, -l̩z, -lɪŋ [-l̩ɪŋ], -l̩d

mango, -es 'mæŋgoʊ, -z

mang|y, -ier, -iest, -ily, -iness 'meɪndʒ|ɪ, -ɪɚ, -ɪɪst, -ɪlɪ, -ɪnɪs

manhood, -s 'mænfʊd, -z

manifest, -s, -ing, -ed; -ly 'mænɪfest, -s, -ɪŋ, -ɪd; -lɪ

manifold, -ly, -ness 'mænɪfoʊld, -lɪ, -nɪs

manikin, -s 'mænɪkɪn, -z

Man i'th' Moon (MSND) ˌmæn ɪð 'mun

mankind 'mænkaɪnd ['-'-]

manlike 'mænlaɪk

man|ly, -ier, -iest, -liness 'mæn|lɪ, -lɪɚ, -lɪɪst, -lɪnɪs

manna 'mænə

manner, -s, -ed 'mænɚ, -z, -d

mannerism, -s 'mænəˌɹɪzəm, -z

manner|ly, -liness 'mænɚ|lɪ, -lɪnɪs

mannerly-modest 'mænɚlɪ'mɒdɪst

Manningtree (1HIV) 'mænɪŋtɹi [-nɪntɹi]

mannish, -ly, -ness 'mænɪʃ, -lɪ, -nɪs

man-of-war, men-of-war ˌmænəv'wɑ˞, ˌmenəv'wɑ˞

manor, -s 'mænɚ, -z

manse, -s 'mæns, -ɪz

mansion, -s 'mænʃn̩, -z

mansionry 'mænʃn̩ɹɪ

mant|le, -les, -ling, -led 'mænt|l̩, -l̩z, -lɪŋ, -l̩d

Mantua (RJ, TS) 'mæntʃʊə [-tʊə, -tjʊə]
Note.—The name is disyllabic in RJ,

III.iii.168, IV.i.124; *suggesting the pronunciation* ['mæntʃwə, -twə]

Mantuan (LLL) 'mæntʃʊən [-tʊən, -tjʊən]

manu cita (L.) (LLL, V.i.62) 'mɑnu 'sitɑ

manur|e, -es, -ing, -ed mə'njʊ˞, -z, -ɹɪŋ, -d

manus (L.) (LLL, V.ii.586) 'mɑnus (*see Note for* canus)

many 'menɪ

many-headed 'menɪˌhedɪd

map, -s, -ping, -ped, -per/s 'mæp, -s, -ɪŋ, -t, -ɚ/z

mappery 'mæpəɹɪ

mar, -s, -ring, -red 'mɑ˞, -z, -ɹɪŋ, -d

marb|le, -les, -ling, -led; -ly 'mɑ˞b|l̩, -l̩z, -lɪŋ [-lɪŋ], -l̩d; -lɪ [-lɪ]

marble-breasted 'mɑ˞bl̩ˌbɹestɪd

marble-constant 'mɑ˞bl̩'kɒnstənt

marble-hearted 'mɑ˞bl̩ˌhɑ˞tɪd

Marcade *or* Mercade (*LLL*) 'mɑ˞kədɪ, 'mɚkədɪ
Note.—Surprising to some, both spellings (according to conventions of English) may indicate the same pronunciation in the first syllable, analogous to words such as 'sergeant,' and the chiefly Brit. pronunciations of 'clerk' and 'Derby.' In the only instance of the name being spoken in S. (LLL, V.ii.708*), the metrical requirements of the verse imply a trisyllable, regardless of whether it is spoken with a Fr. flavor or accent. In R. W. David's edition of* LLL *(*The Arden Shakespeare*, 1951), he cites in the line's annotation, ". . . the Princess should probably give him his 'e' acute and so preserve the blank verse line." I include another pronunciation choice, viz.* ['mɚkədɪ]*, to signify a possible allusion to Mercury, the messenger of the gods, as well as the conductor of the dead to Hades (the abode of the dead). If by saying the name 'Mercade' in a way that somehow echoes 'Mercury,' the nature and impact of Mercade's mission is that much more enhanced, acting as a prodigious precursor to the very last line*

of the play, i.e., 'The words of Mercury
are harsh after the songs of Apollo.
*You that way: we this way' (*LLL,
V.ii.922–923*)*

Marcellus (*HAM*) maɚ'seləs

Marcellus, Caius (AC) 'kaĭəs ['keĭəs]
maɚ'seləs

March (1HIV, JUL, WT) 'maɚtʃ

march, -es, -ing, -ed, -er/s 'maɚtʃ, -ɪz,
-ɪŋ, -t, -ɚ/z

March-chick (ADO) 'maɚtʃ,tʃɪk

March, Earl of (*1HVI*, 2HVI, 3HVI) ,ɚl
əv 'maɚtʃ

Marches, the (3HVI) ,ðə 'maɚtʃɪz

marchioness (**M.**) 'maɚʃənɪs
[,maɚʃə'nes]

Marcus 'maɚkəs

Marcus Æmilius Lepidus (*AC, JUL*)
'maɚkəs i'mɪlɪəs, -ljəs 'lepɪdəs (*see*
Lepidus)

Marcus Justeius (AC) 'maɚkəs dʒʌs'tiəs

Marcus Octavius (AC) 'maɚkəs
ɒk'teĭvɪəs, -vjəs

Mardian (*AC*) 'maɚdɪən, -djən

mare, -s 'mɛɚ, -z

Margarelon (*TC*) maɚ'gænɪlɒn

Margaret (*ADO, 1HVI, 2HVI, 3HVI,
RIII*) 'maɚgəɹɪt, -gɹɪt

margent, -s 'maɚdʒənt, -s

Margery (2HVI, MV, TEM, WT)
'maɚdʒəɹɪ

Maria (*LLL, TN*) mə'ɹiə [mə'ɹaĭə]
*Note.—When the name is meant in
context to be Latinate (as in the phrase
'Jesu Maria'),* [mə'ɹiə] *is the preferred
pronunciation. In some versions of
TN—in one instance only,* II.iii.14—*this
character is addressed as Marian, q.v.*

Marian (COM, LLL, TEM, *TN*)
'mɛɚɹɪən ['mæɹ-]

Mariana (*ALL'S, MEAS*) ,mɛɚɹɪ'ænə
[-ɹɪ'anə]

Marian, Maid (1HIV) 'meĭd 'mɛɚɹɪən

marigold, -s 'mæɹɪgoŭld, -z

Marina (*PER*) mə'ɹinə

marine mə'ɹin

Mariner (*WT*) 'mæɹɪnə

maritime (**M.**), **-s** 'mæɹɪtaĭm, -z

marjoram 'maɚdʒəɹəm

mark, -s, -ing/s, -ed, -edly, -er/s 'maɚk,
-s, -ɪŋ/z, -t, -ɪdlɪ, -ɚ/z

market, -s, -ing, -ed; -able 'maɚkɪt, -s,
-ɪŋ, -ɪd; -əbl̩

market-maid, -s 'maɚkɪt,meĭd, -z

market-men 'maɚkɪt,men

market-place, -s 'maɚkɪtpleĭs, -ɪz

markman 'maɚkmən

marl, -s, -ing, -ed 'maɚl, -z, -ɪŋ, -d

Marle (HV) 'maɚl

marmoset, -s 'maɚməset [-əzet], -s

marquess, -es 'maɚkwɪs, -ɪz

Marquess, Master (RIII) 'mastə
'maɚkwɪs

marriage, -es; -able 'mæɹɪdʒ, -ɪz; -əbl̩
Note.—This word may be trisyllabic
['mæɹɹɪdʒ] *in MV,* II.ix.13 *and TS,*
III.ii.142

marriage-bed 'mæɹɪdʒ,bed

marriage-pleasures 'mæɹɪdʒ,pleʒɚz

marrow, -s, -y 'mæɹoŭ, -z, -ɨ

marrow-eating 'mæɹoŭ,itɪŋ [-,i̥ɹɪŋ]

marrowless 'mæɹoŭlɪs

marr|y, -ies, -ying, -ied 'mæɹ|ɨ, -ɪz, -ɨŋ,
-ɨd
*Note.—The archaic interjection 'marry'
is often collapsed into a monosyllable in
S. For instance, in ADO,* IV.i.81,
"Marry, that . . ." is slurred into
[mɛⁿðæt], *in ADO,* IV.i.210, *"Marry,
this . . ." becomes* [mɛⁿðɪs], *and in
ADO,* V.i.53, *"Marry, thou . . ." is*
[mɛⁿðaŭ]

Mars (AC, ALL'S, COR, CYM, HAM,
1HIV, HV, 1HVI, LLL, MV, MWW, RII,
TC, TEM, TIM, TNK, Sonn. 55) 'maɚz

Marseilles (TS) maɚ'seləs [*Fr.* maʁsɛj]

---

i w**e** ɨ cit**y** ɪ h**i**t e l**e**t ɛ d**e**but æ c**a**n a p**a**ss ɚ b**i**rd ʌ h**u**t ə **a**gain ɚ supp**er** u y**ou**
ʊ sh**ou**ld o **o**bey ɔ **aw**l ɒ c**o**p ɑ f**a**ther eĭ p**ai**d aĭ h**igh** oŭ g**o** ɔĭ v**oi**ce aŭ f**ou**nd ɪɚ **ear**
ɛɚ **air** ʊɚ p**oor** ɔɚ f**or**k ɑɚ p**ar**k aĭɚ f**ire** aŭɚ h**our** b **b**oy p **p**it d **d**og t **t**op g **g**ot
k **k**id h **h**ow fi be**h**ave dʒ **j**ot tʃ **ch**ew z **z**any s **s**oft v **v**at f **f**at ʒ trea**s**ure ʃ **sh**ip ð **th**e
θ **th**in m **m**an n **n**o ŋ ha**ng** l **l**ip j **y**es w **w**on ʍ **wh**ew ɹ **r**igger, ai**r**y ɾ ma**tt**er

Note.—This name (when appearing in the Folio and Quarto versions of TS, *and the First Folio version of* ALL'S*) is given the various spellings 'Marcellus,' 'Marcellæ' (thought by some to be a misreading of 'Marcellus'), and 'Marsellis.' The point is that when it is in verse (*TS, II.i.368 *and* ALL'S, IV.iv.9*), and despite editors' emendation to 'Marseilles,' it is meant to be a trisyllable, as indicated above (see 'Shakespeare's Verse' § 1.8 of this dictionary)*

marsh|al (M.), -als, -al(l)ing, -al(l)ed; -ship 'mɑɚ-ʃl̩, -l̩z, -l̩ɪŋ [-əlɪŋ], -l̩d; -ʃɪp
Note.—In 1HIV, IV.iv.2, *this word is trisyllabic, i.e.,* ['mɑɚ-ɹɪʃl̩] *or* ['mɑ-ɹɪʃl̩], *reflecting its Fr. root-word 'maréchal'; and arguably the same in* LEAR, IV.iii.8. *This trisyllabic pronunciation (with the var. spelling 'marischal') is still used today when referring to Scotland's high officer of state, the Earl Marischal (now defunct). The* OED *gives eleven variant trisyllabic spellings for 'marshal'*

Marshalsea (HVIII) 'mɑɚ-ʃlsi
mart, -s, -ed 'mɑɚ-t, -s, -ɪd
Martext, Sir Oliver (*AYLI***)** ,sɚ '(ɹ)ɒlɪvɚ 'mɑɚ-tɛkst
Martial (CYM) 'mɑɚ-ʃl̩
marti|al, -ally 'mɑɚ-ʃl̩, -əlɪ
martialist, -s 'mɑɚ-ʃəlɪst, -s
Martians (COR) 'mɑɚ-ʃnz
Martino, Signor (RJ) 'sinjɔɚ mɑɚ-'tinoʊ
Martius (*COR, TIT***)** 'mɑɚ-ʃɪəs, -ʃəs
Martius, Ancus (COR) 'æŋkəs 'mɑɚ-ʃɪəs
Martius, Caius (*COR***)** 'kaɪəs 'mɑɚ-ʃɪəs, -ʃəs
Note.—This character is later called **Coriolanus**, *q.v.*
Martius, Young (*COR***)** 'jʌŋ 'mɑɚ-ʃɪəs, -ʃəs
martlet, -s 'mɑɚ-tlɪt, -s
martyr (M.), -s, -ing, -ed; -dom/s 'mɑɚ-tɚ ['mɑɚ-ɾɚ], -z, -ɹɪŋ, -d; -dəm/z
Marullus (*JUL***)** mə'ɹʌləs
marvailous (*marvelous***)** mɑɚ-'veɪləs
Note.—In HV, II.i.48, *this word is meant to have primary stress on the second syllable in order to fit the metrical requirements of the verse line*

marvel, -s, -ling, -led 'mɑɚ-vl̩, -z, -ɪŋ [-vəlɪŋ], -d
marvel(l)ous, -ly, -ness 'mɑɚ-vələs, -lɪ, -nɪs
marvel(l)'s 'mɑɚ-vels [-vəls]
Note.—This word in TC, I.ii.138 *and* HAM, II.i.3, *is conjectured to be an old-fashioned pronunciation-spelling of the adv. 'marvelous'*
Mary (HVIII, RII, TN) 'mɛɚ-ɹɪ
Mary-bud (CYM), -s 'mɛɚ-ɹɪˌbʌd, -z
masculine 'mæskjʊlɪn
masculinity ˌmæskjʊ'lɪnɪtɪ
mash, -es, -ing, -ed, -er/s 'mæʃ, -ɪz, -ɪŋ, -t, -ɚ/z
Masham (HV) 'mæsəm ['mæʃəm]
mask, -s, -ing, -ed, -er/s 'mask, -s, -ɪŋ, -t, -ɚ/z
mason, -s, -ed; -ry 'meɪsn̩, -z, -d; -ɹɪ
masqu|e, -es, -ing 'mask, -s, -ɪŋ
mass (*s.***) (***quantity***), -es** 'mæs, -ɪz
mass (M.) (*s.***) (***celebration of the Eucharist***), -es** 'mæs ['mas], -ɪz
mass (*v.***), -es, -ing, -ed** 'mæs, -ɪz, -ɪŋ, -t
massac|re, -res, -ring, -red 'mæsək|ɚ [-sɪk-], -ɚz, -ɚɹɪŋ, -ɚd
massive, -ly, -ness 'mæsɪv, -lɪ, -nɪs
mass|y, -iness 'mæs|ɪ, -ɪnɪs
mast, -s 'mast, -s
master (M.), -s, -ing, -ed 'mastɚ, -z, -ɹɪŋ, -d
master-cord 'mastɚˌkɔɚd
masterdom 'mastɚdəm
Master Gunner of Orleans (1HVI) 'mastɚ 'gʌnɚ (ɹ)əv 'ɔɚliənz (*see Note for* **Orleans**)
master-leaver 'mastɚˌlivɚ
masterless 'mastɚlɪs
masterl|y, -iness 'mastɚ-l|ɪ, -ɪnɪs
master-reasons 'mastɚˌɹiznz
mastership, -s 'mastɚʃɪp, -s
Master's Mate (2HVI) 'mastɚz 'meɪt
mastic 'mæstɪk
mastiff, -s 'mæstɪf, -s
match, -es, -ing, -ed 'mætʃ, -ɪz, -ɪŋ, -t
matchless, -ly, -ness 'mætʃlɪs, -lɪ, -nɪs
mat|e, -es, -ing, -ed 'meɪt, -s, -ɪŋ, -ɪd
material, -s, -ly mə'tɪɚ-ɹɪəl, -z, -ɪ
math, -s 'mæθ, -s

mathematic, -s ˌmæθɪˈmæɾɪk, -s
mathematic|al, -ally ˌmæθɪˈmæɾɪk|l̩, -l̩ɨ [-lɨ]
matin, -s; -al ˈmætn̩ [-tɪn], -z; -əl
matron, -s; -ly ˈmeɪtɹən, -z; -lɨ
matter, -s, -ing, -ed ˈmæɾɚ, -z, -ɹɪŋ, -d
matter-a ˈmætə-ɹə (*see* **dat**)
mattock, -s ˈmæɾək, -s
matur|e, -es, -ing, -ed; -er, -est, -ely, -eness məˈtjʊɚ [-ˈtʃʊɚ], -z, -ɹɪŋ, -d; -ɹɚ, -ɹɪst, -lɨ, -nɪs
maturity məˈtjʊɚɹɪtɨ [-ˈtʃʊɚɹɪtɨ]
Mauchus, King (AC) ˌkɪŋ ˈmɔkəs
Maud (COM) ˈmɔd
Maudlin (ALL'S, *TNK*) ˈmɔdlɪn
maugre ˈmɔgɚ
maul *or* **mall, -s, -ing, -ed** ˈmɔl, -z, -ɪŋ, -d
maumet, -s ˈmɔmet, -s
maund (*wicker basket with handles*), **-s** ˈmɔnd, -z
Mauritania (OTH) ˌmɔɹɪˈteɪnɪə
maw, -s ˈmɔ, -z
maxim, -s ˈmæksɪm, -z
may ˈmeɪ
May (ADO, AYLI, HAM, 1HIV, LC, LEAR, LLL, MSND, MWW, PP, Sonn. 108, TC, TN, TNK), **-s, -ing** ˈmeɪ, -z, -ɪŋ
maybe ˈmeɪbɨ
mayday (*distress call*), **-s** ˈmeɪˌdeɪ, -z
May(-)day (**D.**) (ALL'S, HVIII) (*celebration*), **-s** ˈmeɪˈdeɪ, -z
Maying (TNK) ˈmeɪɪŋ
May-morn (HV) ˈmeɪˌmɔɚn
Mayor, Lord (HV, 1HVI, HVIII, RIII) ˈlɔɚd ˈmeɪɚ
Note.—Often monosyllabic in S., i.e., [ˈmɛɚ]
maypole (**M.**), **-s** ˈmeɪpoʊl, -z
maze, -s, -d ˈmeɪz, -ɪz, -d
maz(z)ard, -s ˈmæzɑɚd [-zɚd], -z
me (*pron.*) ˈmi (*strong form*) ˈmɪ (*weak form*)
meacock (*milksop*), **-s** ˈmikɒk, -s

mead, -s ˈmid, -z
meadow, -s, -y ˈmedoʊ, -z, -ɨ
meadow-fairies ˈmedoʊˌfɛɚɹɪz
meager *or* **meagre, -er, -est, -ly, -ness** ˈmigɚ, -ɹɚ, -ɹɪst, -lɨ, -nɪs
meal, -s, -ed; -y ˈmil, -z, -d; -ɨ
mean, -s, -ing/s, meant ˈmin, -z, -ɪŋ/z, ˈment
mean-apparelled ˈminəˌpæɹəld
meander (**M.**), **-s, -ing, -ed, -er/s** mɪˈændɚ, -z, -ɹɪŋ, -d, -ɹɚ/z
mean|er, -est, -ly, -ness ˈmɪn|ɚ, -ɪst, -lɨ, -nɪs
meas|les, -ly ˈmiz|l̩z, -lɨ
measur|e (**M.**), **-es, -ing, -ed, -er/s; -ement/s; -eless** ˈmeʒɚ, -z, -ɹɪŋ, -d, -ɹɚ/z; -mənt/s; -lɪs
meat, -s; -less ˈmit, -s; -lɪs
meat|y, -ier, -iest, -iness ˈmiɾ|ɨ, -ɪɚ, -ɹɪst, -ɨnɪs
Mecenas, Mecænas, Mæcenas, *or* **Maecenas** (AC) mɪˈsinəs [mɪˈs-]
mechanic, -s, -al/s, -ally mɪˈkænɪk, -s, -l̩/z, -əlɨ
medal, -s ˈmedl̩, -z
medallion, -s mɪˈdæljən, -z
medallist, -s ˈmedl̩ɪst, -s
medd|le, -les, -ling, -led, -ler/s ˈmedl̩, -lz, -lɪŋ [-lɪŋ], -ld, -l̩ɚ/z [-lɚ/z]
meddlesome, -ly, -ness ˈmedl̩səm, -lɨ, -nɪs
Mede (AC) ˈmid
Medea (2HVI, MV) mɪˈdiə
Media, Great (AC) ˈgɹeɪt ˈmidɪə, -djə
median, -s ˈmedɪən, -z
mediat|e (*v.*), **-es, -ing, -ed** ˈmidɪeɪt, -s, -ɪŋ, -ɪd
mediation, -s ˌmidɪˈeɪʃn̩, -z
mediator, -s ˈmidɪeɪɾɚ, -z
Medice, teipsum (*L.*) (2HVI, II.i.54) ˈmɛdɪsɛ tɛˈɪpsʊm
medicinal, -ly məˈdɪsɪnl̩ [meˈd-, -sn̩l̩], -ɨ
Note.—In OTH, V.ii.352, the Quartos give 'medicinal' and the Folio gives

---

i wᴇ ɨcity ɪ hɪt e lᴇt ɛ dᴇbut æ cᴀn a pᴀss ɚ bɪrd ʌ hᴜt ə again ɚ suppᴇr u yᴏu ʊ shᴏuld o ᴏbey ɔ ᴀwl ɒ cᴏp ɑ fᴀther eɪ pᴀid aɪ hɪgh oʊ gᴏ ɔɪ vᴏice aʊ fᴏund ɪɚ eᴀr ɛɚ ᴀir ʊɚ pᴏor ɔɚ fᴏrk ɑɚ pᴀrk aɪɚ fɪre aʊɚ hᴏur b ʙoy p pɪt d dᴏg t tᴏp g gᴏt k kɪd h hᴏw fi behᴀve dʒ jᴏt tʃ chᴇw z zany s sᴏft v yat f fᴀt ʒ treᴀsure ʃ shɪp ð the θ thin m ᴍan n ɴo ŋ hang l lɪp j yes w wᴏn ʍ whᴇw ɹ rɪgger, airy ɾ matter

'medicinable.' Although some editors will sometimes favor the Quartos' version, it makes for awkward scansion, and also flies in the face of S.'s traditional (Brit.) pronunciation pattern (cf. the Note for **medicine***). Retaining 'medicinal' (as it is customarily pronounced) saddles the line with an undesirable trochee in the second foot, or forces one to (unnecessarily) shift primary syllabic stress to the head of the word. However, if one chooses to go with the Quartos' version, i.e., 'medicinal,' then* ['medɪsɪnl̩] *is the recommended pronunciation; if one chooses the Folio's version, i.e., 'medicinable,' then* ['medsɪnəbl̩] *is preferable*

medicin|e, -es; -able 'medɪsɪn, -z; -əbl̩ ['medsɪnəbl̩]
Note.—In S., this word appears in verse twenty-four times. With the exception of ADO, V.i.24; 2HIV, III.i.43; *and* Sonn. 118.11 *the pronunciation is invariably two syllables* ['medsɪn], *the traditional Brit. pronunciation. Americanizing the word into three syllables may at times be (or seem) necessary; however, in doing so, the integrity of the verse line's pattern may suffer (both rhythmically and metrically). In* ALL'S, II.i.71, *the pronunciation is dependent on the editor's line assignation; cf. G. K. Hunter (*Arden Shakespeare*) versus G. B. Harrison (*The Complete Works, Harcourt Brace Jovanovich*)*

meditance 'medɪtəns

meditat|e, -es, -ing, -ed 'medɪteɪt, -s, -ɪŋ, -ɪd

meditation, -s ˌmedɪ'teɪʃn̩, -z

Mediterranean (TEM) ˌmedɪtə-'ɹeɪnɪən, -njən

Mediterraneum (LLL) ˌmedɪtə-'ɹeɪnɪʊm

medlar, -s 'medlə-, -z

medley, -s 'medlɪ, -z

meed, -s 'mid, -z

meek, -er, -est, -ly, -ness 'mik, -ə-, -ɪst, -lɪ, -nɪs

meet (*adj.*), **-er, -est, -ly, -ness** 'mit, -ə-, -ɪst, -lɪ, -nɪs

meet (*s., v.*), **-s, -ing/s, met** 'mit, -s, -ɪŋ/z, 'met

meet-a 'mitə (*see* **dat**)

meeting-place, -s 'mitɪŋˌpleɪs, -ɪz

Meg (ADO, 2HVI, MWW, TEM) 'meg

Mehercle (*L.*) (LLL, IV.ii.75) mɛ'hɛɹ̆-klɛ

meinie *or* **meiny** (*household retinue*) 'meɪnɪ

Meis(s)en (HV) 'maɪsən

melanchol|y (M.) (MSND) 'melənkəl|ɪ [-ˌkɒl|ɪ], -ɪz

Melancholy, Monsieur (AYLI) mə'sjɜ- 'melənkəlɪ [-ˌkɒlɪ]
Note.—Arguably stressed ['mɪsjɜ- 'melənkəlɪ, -ˌkɒlɪ] *in* AYLI, III.ii.288–289 *due to conventions of recessive accenting*

Meleager (TNK) ˌmelɪ'eɪdʒə-

mell, -s, -ing, -ed 'mel, -z, -ɪŋ, -d

mellifluous, -ly, -ness mə'lɪfluəs, -lɪ, -nɪs

mellow, -s, -ing, -ed; -er, -est, -ness 'meloŭ, -z, -ɪŋ, -d; -ə-, -ɪst, -nɪs

melodious, -ly, -ness mɪ'loŭdɪəs [mə'l-], -lɪ, -nɪs

melt, -s, -ing, -ed 'melt, -s, -ɪŋ, -ɪd

Melun, Count (*KJ*) 'kaŏnt me'lun

member, -s; -ship/s 'membə-, -z; -ʃɪp/s

memento mori (*L.*) (1HIV, III.iii.29) mɛ'mɛnto 'mɔɹɪ

memorand|um, -a, -ums ˌmemə'ɹænd|əm [-muʼr-], -ə, -əmz

Memphis (1HVI) 'memfɪs

men (*pl. of* **man**, *q.v.*) 'men

menac|e, -es, -ing/ly, -ed 'menɪs, -ɪz, -ɪŋ/lɪ, -t

ménage, -s mɛ'nɑʒ [-'naʒ], -ɪz

Menaphon, Duke (COM) 'djuk 'menəfən [-fɒn]

Menas (*AC*) 'minəs

Menecrates (*AC*) mə'nekɹətɪz

Menelaus (3HVI, *TC*) ˌmenɪ'leɪəs

Menon (TC) 'minɒn ['menɒn]

Mente(i)th (1HIV, *MAC*) men'tiθ

Mephostophilus (MWW) ˌmefə'stɒfɪləs

Me pompae provexit apex (*L.*) (PER, II.ii.30) mɛ 'pɒmpɪ pɹo'vɛksɪt 'apɛks

Mercade *or* **Marcade** (*LLL*) 'mɑɹ̆-kəˌdɪ, 'mɜ-kədɪ (*see Note for* **Marcade**)

mercatante (*It.*) (TS, IV.ii.63)
ˌmɛrkɑˈtɑˑnˈtɛ
Note.—*This word does not technically
appear in S. In the First Folio version of*
TS, IV.ii.63, *the word 'marcantant' is
used, which doesn't happen to fit the
meter of the line. Most editors deem it to
be a corruption of the It. 'mercatante,'
and so accordingly emend it to better fit
the metrical requirements of the verse
line*
Mercatio (TGV) mɝˑˈkeɪʃɪoʊ
mercenar|y, -ies 'mɝˑsɪnəɹ|ɪ, -z
mercer, -s 'mɝˑsəˑ, -z
merchandis|e, -es, -ing, -ed, -er/s
'mɝˑtʃəndaɪz [-daɪs], -ɪz, -ɪŋ, -d, -əˑ/z
merchant, -s 'mɝˑtʃənt, -s
Note.—*There is some argument about
the syllabic stress of this word in* COM,
I.i.150 *where the line begins, "Therefore, merchant . . ." Nowhere else does
S. ever attempt to stress the second
syllable of this word, so it's safe to
assume that he plants the unusual
trochee in the second foot for effect*
merchant-marring 'mɝˑtʃəntˌmɑˑˑɹɪŋ
merciless, -ly, -ness 'mɝˑsɪlɪs, -lɪ, -nɪs
Mercurial (CYM) məˈkjʊɹɪəl
Mercur|y (AC, 1HIV, KJ, LLL, RIII, TC,
TIT, TN, WT)**, -ies** 'mɝˑkjʊɹ|ɪ, -ɪz
Mercutio (*RJ*) mɝˑˈkjuʃɪoʊ, -ʃjoʊ
merc|y (M.), -ies 'mɝˑs|ɪ, -ɪz
mere, -s, -st, -ly 'mɪɝˑ, -z, -ɹɪst, -lɪ
mered 'mɪɝˑɹɪd
Note.—*This obscure word, appearing in*
AC, III.xiii.10, *is pronounced disyllabically, as indicated, though it may simply
be the p.t. or p.p. of 'mere.' The* OED
*cites the word as being rare and
obsolete, and as to its origin, the* OED
(*q.v.*) *states, "Formation and sense
doubtful; possibly a corrupt reading"*
merg|e, -es, -ing, -ed, -er/s 'mɝˑdʒ, -ɪz,
-ɪŋ, -d, -əˑ/z

meridian, -s məˈɹɪdɪən, -z
merit, -s, -ing, -ed 'meɹɪt, -s, -ɪŋ, -ɪd
meritorious, -ly ˌmeɹɪˈtɔɹɪəs, -lɪ
Merlin (1HIV, LEAR) 'mɝˑlɪn
mermaid (M.) (3HVI)**, -s** 'mɝˑmeɪd, -z
Merops (TGV) 'mɪɹɒps ['meɹ-]
Merriman (TS) 'meɹɪmən
merriment 'meɹɪmənt
merr|y, -ier, -iest, -ily, -iness 'meɹ|ɪ, -ɪəˑ,
-ɪst, -ɪlɪ, -ɪnɪs
merry-hearted 'meɹɪˌhɑˑˑtɪd
meseems mɪˈsimz
mesh, -es, -ing, -ed 'meʃ, -ɪz, -ɪŋ, -t
Mesopotamia (AC) ˌmesəpəˈteɪmɪə, -mjə
Messala (*JUL*) meˈsɑlə [meˈseɪlə]
Messaline (TN) 'mesəlin
Messina (ADO) meˈsinə
Note.—*In* ADO, V.iv.124, *the verse line
has a feminine ending by virtue of
'armed' being two syllables instead of
one; thus 'Messina' is pronounced as
indicated above*
me't (*contr. of* **me it**) 'mit
metamorphos|e, -es, -ing, -ed
ˌmeʃəˈmɔˑˑfoʊz [-foʊs/t], -ɪz, -ɪŋ, -d
Metamorphosis (TIT) ˌmeʃəˈmɔˑˑfəsɪs
[-fosɪs]
Note.—*Some editors retain this Folio
spelling for Ovid's 'Metamorphoses,'
found in* TIT, IV.i.42
metaphor, -s 'meʃəfɔˑˑ [-fəˑ], -z
metaphysic|s, -al, -ally ˌmeʃəˈfɪzɪk|s, -l̩,
-əlɪ
met|e, -es, -ing, -ed 'mit, -s, -ɪŋ, -ɪd
Metellus (JUL) mɪˈteləs
meteor, -s 'miʃɪə [-ɪɔˑˑ], -z
meteoric ˌmiʃɪˈɒɹɪk
mete-yard, -s 'mitjɑˑˑd, -z
metheglin, -s meˈθeglɪn [mɪˈθ-], -z
methinks mɪˈθɪŋks
methought, -s mɪˈθɔt, -s
metropolis, -es məˈtɹɒpəlɪs [-pl̩ɪs], -ɪz
mettle 'metl̩
mew, -s, -ing, -ed 'mju, -z, -ɪŋ, -d

---

i wᴇ ɪ cit**y** ɪ h**i**t e l**e**t ɛ d**e**but æ c**a**n a p**a**ss ɝ b**ir**d ʌ h**u**t ə **a**gain ɚ supp**er** u y**ou**
ʊ sh**ou**ld o **o**bey ɔ **a**wl ɒ c**o**p ɑ f**a**ther eɪ p**ai**d aɪ h**igh** oʊ g**o** ɔɪ v**oi**ce aʊ f**ou**nd ɪɚ **ear**
ɛɚ **air** ʊɚ **poor** ɔɚ f**or**k ɑɚ p**ar**k aɪɚ f**ire** aʊɚ h**our** b **b**oy p **p**it d **d**og t **t**op g **g**ot
k **k**id h **h**ow fi be**h**ave dʒ **j**ot tʃ **ch**ew z **z**any s **s**oft v **v**at f **f**at ʒ trea**s**ure ʃ **sh**ip ð **th**e
θ **th**in m **m**an n **n**o ŋ ha**ng** l **l**ip j **y**es w **w**on ʍ **wh**ew ɹ **r**igger, ai**r**y ɾ ma**tt**er

mewl, -s, -ing, -ed 'mjul, -z, -ɪŋ, -d
mews (s.) 'mjuz
Mexican, -s 'meksɪkən, -z
Mexico (MV) 'meksɪkoŭ
mi (third note of diatonic scale) 'mi
mice (pl. of mouse) 'maĭs
Michael (2HVI, HVIII, OTH) 'maĭkl̩
Michaelmas (1HIV, MWW) 'mɪkl̩məs
Michael, Sir (1HIV) ˌsɝ 'maĭkl̩
mich|e or mych|e, -es, -ing, -ed, -er/s
  'mɪtʃ, -ɪz, -ɪŋ, -t, -ɚ/z
mickle 'mɪkəl
microcosm, -s 'maĭkɹoŭkɒzəm [-kɹʊk-],
  -z
mid-age 'mɪdeĭdʒ
Midas (MV) 'maĭdəs
mid(-)day 'mɪddeĭ
midnight (M.) 'mɪdnaĭt ([ˌ-'-] in MSND,
  I.i.223)
midriff, -s 'mɪdɹɪf, -s
'midst (aphetic form of amidst) ə'mɪdst
midsummer 'mɪdsʌmɚ
mid(-)way 'mɪdweĭ [ˌ-'-]
midwi|fe, -ves 'mɪdwaĭ|f, -vz
might 'maĭt
mightful 'maĭtfʊl
might|y, -ier, -iest, -ily, -iness 'maĭt|ɪ, -ɪɚ,
  -ɪɪst, -ɪlɪ, -ɪnɪs
Milan (ADO, KJ, TEM, TGV) mɪ'lɑn
  [-'læn], 'mɪlən
  Note.—In TEM and KJ, this word
  appears in verse and is stressed on the
  first syllable, i.e., ['mɪlən] (an older
  accepted pronunciation of the word).
  Elsewhere in S. it is in prose. Its spelling
  in the Folio ('Millaine,' like 'villaine')
  may indicate a preference of first-
  syllable stress throughout
Milan, Duchess of (ADO) 'dʌtʃɪs əv
  'mɪlən (see Note for Milan)
Milan, Duke of (TEM, TGV) 'djuk əv
  'mɪlən (see Note for Milan)
milch 'mɪltʃ
milch-kine (dairy cows) 'mɪltʃˌkaĭn
mild, -er, -est, -ly, -ness 'maĭld, -ɚ, -ɪst,
  -lɪ, -nɪs
mile-a 'maĭələ
  Note.—This word, along with its
  counterpart, 'stile-a,' appears in the

ditty at the end of WT, IV.iii; the extra
  syllable there merely to provide for
  another musical beat in the tetrameter
  line of song
Mile-end Green (ALL'S, 2HIV)
  ˌmaĭələend 'gɹin
Milford (CYM, RIII) 'mɪlfɚd
Milford-Haven (CYM) 'mɪlfɚd 'heĭvn̩
militarist, -s 'mɪlɪtɚɹɪst, -s
military 'mɪlɪtəɹɪ
milk, -s, -ing, -ed, -er/s 'mɪlk, -s, -ɪŋ, -t,
  -ɚ/z
milking-time 'mɪlkɪŋˌtaĭm
milk-livered 'mɪlkˌlɪvɚd
milk-paps 'mɪlkˌpæps
milksop, -s 'mɪlksɒp, -s
milk-white 'mɪlkˌʍaĭt
milk|y, -ier, -iest, -ily, -iness 'mɪlk|ɪ, -ɪɚ,
  -ɪɪst, -ɪlɪ, -ɪnɪs
mill, -s, -ing, -ed, -er/s 'mɪl, -z, -ɪŋ, -d,
  -ɚ/z
milliner, -s 'mɪlɪnɚ, -z
million, -s, -ed 'mɪljən, -z, -d
mill-sixpences 'mɪlˌsɪkspənsɪz
mill(-)stone, -s 'mɪlstoŭn, -z
Milo (TC) 'maĭloŭ
mimic, -s, -king, -ked 'mɪmɪk, -s, -ɪŋ, -t
mimicry 'mɪmɪkɹɪ
minc|e, -es, -ing/ly, -ed, -er/s 'mɪns, -ɪz,
  -ɪŋ/lɪ, -t, -ɚ/z
Minerva (CYM, TS) mɪ'nɝvə
mind, -s, -ing, -ed 'maĭnd, -z, -ɪŋ, -ɪd
mindless, -ly, -ness 'maĭndlɪs, -lɪ, -nɪs
mine (pron.) 'maĭn
min|e (s., v.), -es, -ing, -ed, -er/s 'maĭn,
  -z, -ɪŋ, -d, -ɚ/z
mineral, -s 'mɪnɚɹəl, -z
miniature, -s 'mɪnɪɹətʃɚ, -z
minikin, -s 'mɪnɪkɪn, -z
minimal, -ly 'mɪnɪməl, -ɪ
minime (L.) (LLL, III.i.57) 'mɪnɪmɛ
minim rest, -s 'mɪnɪm ˌɹest, -s
minimus 'mɪnɪməs
minion, -s 'mɪnjən [-nĭən], -z
minist|er, -ers, -ering, -ered 'mɪnɪst|ɚ,
  -ɚz, -ɚɹɪŋ, -ɚd
  Note.—Often disyllabic in S., i.e.,
  ['mɪnstɚ]
ministration, -s ˌmɪnɪ'stɹeĭʃn̩, -z

minnow, -s 'mɪnoŭ, -z
Minola, Baptista (*TS*) bæp'tɪstə 'mɪnolə
  [bæp'tɪstə 'mɪnələ]
Minola, Katherina (*TS*) ˌkætə'ɹinə
  'mɪnolə ['mɪnələ] (*see* **Katherina**)
minor, -s 'maĭnɚ, -z
minorit|y, -ies maĭ'nɒɹɪt|ɪ, -ɪz
Minos (3HVI) 'maĭnɒs
Minotaur (1HVI), **-s** 'mɪnətɔɚ ['maĭn-],
  -z
minstrel, -s; -sy 'mɪnstɹəl, -z; -sɪ
minute (*adj.*) (*exceptionally small*), **-st,
  -ly, -ness** maĭ'njut, -ɪst, -lɪ, -nɪs
minute (*s., v.*) (*increment of time and
  angle*), **-s; -ly** 'mɪnɪt, -s; -lɪ
  Note.—The rare adj. form appears in
  MAC, V.ii.18
minute (*record of proceedings;
  memorandum*), **-s, -ing, -ed** 'mɪnɪt, -s,
  -ɪŋ, -ɪd
minute-jacks *or* **minute-Jacks** (*the bell-
  striking figures in a clock*) 'mɪnɪtˌdʒæks
minx, -es 'mɪŋks, -ɪz
mi perdonato (*It.*) (TS, I.i.25) mi
  ˌpɛɾdo'nɑ'to
mirable 'mɪɹəbl̩
  *Note.—This obsolete word in TC,
  IV.v.141, meaning wonderful and
  marvelous, comes from the L. mīrābilis,
  from mīrāri. Although it shares roots
  with 'admirable,' it is sometimes
  mistaken to be the aphaeretic form of
  'admirable' (with irregular stress given
  to the second syllable, i.e.,*
  [æd'maĭɚɹəbl̩]*), which leads to the
  erroneous pronunciation* ['maĭɚɹəbl̩].
  *For correct pronunciation, it's better to
  think of 'mirable's' other (and closer)
  cousin, 'miracle'*
miracle, -s 'mɪɹɪkl̩, -z
miraculous, -ly, -ness mɪ'ɹækjʊləs, -lɪ,
  -nɪs
mirage, -s mɪ'ɹɑʒ, -ɪz
Miranda (*TEM*) mɪ'ɹændə

mir|e, -es, -ing, -ed 'maĭɚ, -z, -ɹɪŋ, -d
mirth, -ful 'mɜɚθ, -fʊl
mir|y, -ier, -iest, -iness 'maĭɚɹ|ɪ, -ɪɚ,
  -ɪɪst, -ɪnɪs
misadventure, -s ˌmɪsədˌventʃɚ, -z
Misanthropos (TIM) mɪ'sænθɹopɒs
  [-pos]
misbecom|e, -es, -ing/ly, misbecame
  ˌmɪsbɪ'kʌm, -z, -ɪŋ/lɪ, ˌmɪsbɪ'keĭm
misbegot ˌmɪsbɪ'gɒt
misbegotten ˌmɪsbɪ'gɒtn̩ ['-ˌ-]
misbeliev|e, -es, -ing, -ed, -er/s ˌmɪsbɪ'liv,
  -z, -ɪŋ, -d, -ɚ/z (*when att.,* ['mɪsbɪˌlivɪŋ],
  as in TIT, V.iii.142)
miscall, -s, -ing, -ed ˌmɪs'kɔl, -z, -ɪŋ, -d
miscarriage, -s 'mɪskæɹɪdʒ [ˌ-'--], -ɪz
miscarr|y, -ies, -ying, -ied ˌmɪs'kæɹ|ɪ, -ɪz,
  -ɪɪŋ, -ɪd
mischance (**M.**), **-s** mɪs'tʃans, -ɪz
mischief (**M.**), **-s** 'mɪstʃɪf, -s
mischievous, -ly, -ness 'mɪstʃɪvəs, -lɪ, -nɪs
misconception, -s ˌmɪskən'sepʃn̩, -z
misconster (*cf.* **misconstrue**), **-s, -ing,
  -ed** mɪs'kɒnstɚ, -z, -ɹɪŋ, -d
misconstruction, -s ˌmɪskən'stɹʌksn̩, -z
misconstru|e, -es, -ing, -ed ˌmɪskən'stɹu,
  -z, -ɪŋ, -d
  *Note.—The Folios and Quartos of S. use
  'misconster' mostly. Whenever modern
  editors replace it with 'misconstrue,' the
  stress falls on the second syllable, i.e.,*
  [mɪs'kɒnstɹu]. *The only possible
  exception is* 1HVI, II.iii.72, *depending
  on how one scans the line*
miscreant, -s 'mɪskɹɪənt, -s
miscreate ˌmɪskɹɪ'eĭt
misdeed, -s mɪs'did, -z
misdemean|ant/s, -or/s ˌmɪsdɪ'min|ənt/s,
  -ɚ/z
misdemeaned ˌmɪsdɪ'mind
misdoubt, -s, -ing, -ed mɪs'daŭt, -s, -ɪŋ,
  -ɪd
mis-dread ˌmɪs'dɹed
Misena, Mount (AC) ˌmaŭnt maĭ'sinə

---

i we ɪ city ɪ hit e let ɛ debut æ can a pass ɜ bird ʌ hut ə again ɚ supper u you
ʊ should o obey ɔ awl ɒ cop ɑ father eĭ paid aĭ high oŭ go ɔĭ voice aŭ found ɪɚ ear
ɛɚ air ʊɚ poor ɔɚ fork ɑɚ park aĭɚ fire aŭɚ hour b boy p pit d dog t top g got
k kid h how fi behave dʒ jot tʃ chew z zany s soft v vat f fat ʒ treasure ʃ ship ð the
θ thin m man n no ŋ hang l lip j yes w won ʍ whew ɹ rigger, airy ɾ matter

miser, -s 'maĭzɚ, -z

miserab|le, -ly, -leness 'mɪzɹəb|l̩
['mɪzəɹəb|l̩], -lɪ, -l̩nɪs

miser|ly, -liness 'maĭzɚ|lɪ, -lɪnɪs

miser|y (M.) (KJ), -ies 'mɪzɚɹ|ɪ [-zɹ̩-], -ɪz

misfit, -s 'mɪsfɪt, -s

mis|give, -gives, -gave, -given mɪs|'gɪv,
-'gɪvz, -'geĭv, -'gɪvən

misgiving, -s mɪs'gɪvɪŋ, -z

misgovern, -s, -ing, -ed, -ment
ˌmɪs'gʌvɚn, -z, -ɪŋ, -d, -mənt

misguid|e, -ed/ly mɪs'gaĭd, -ɪd/lɪ

mishap, -s 'mɪsfiæp [mɪs'hæp], -s

mishaved mɪs'fieĭvd

misheard mɪs'fiɜd

mis|lead, -leads, -leading, -led ˌmɪs|'lid,
-'lidz, -'lidɪŋ, -'led

misleaders ˌmɪs'lidɚz

mislik|e, -es, -ing, -ed mɪs'laĭk, -s, -ɪŋ, -t

misnomer, -s ˌmɪs'noŭmɚ, -z

misordered mɪs'ɔɚdɚd

misplac|e, -es, -ing, -ed, -ement
ˌmɪs'pleĭs, -ɪz, -ɪŋ, -t, -mənt (*when att.*,
['mɪspleĭst])

misprision mɪs'pɹɪʒn̩

mispriz|e, -es, -ing, -ed mɪs'pɹaĭz, -ɪz, -ɪŋ,
-d
Note.—In MSND, III.ii.74, *the first
syllable of 'mispriz'd' is arguably the
stressed one, i.e.,* ['mɪspɹaĭzd]

misproud (*att.*) 'mɪsˌpɹaŭd

misquotation, -s ˌmɪskwoŭ'teĭʃn̩, -z

misquot|e, -es, -ing, -ed ˌmɪs'kwoŭt, -s,
-ɪŋ, -ɪd

misreport, -s, -ing, -ed ˌmɪsɹɪ'pɔɚt, -s,
-ɪŋ, -ɪd

miss (*s., v.*), **-es, -ing, -ed** 'mɪs, -ɪz, -ɪŋ, -t

mis(-)shapen ˌmɪs'ʃeĭpən [ˌmɪʃʃ-]

misshaped (*archaic form of* **misshapen**)
ˌmɪs'ʃeĭpt [ˌmɪʃʃ-] (['-,-] *in* 3HVI, III.
ii.170)

mis-sheathed mɪs'ʃiðd

missing (*adj., adv.*), **-ly** 'mɪsɪŋ, -lɪ

missive, -s 'mɪsɪv, -z

misspeak mɪs'spik

misspoke mɪs'spoŭk

mist, -s 'mɪst, -s

mista'en mɪs'teĭn

mis|take, -takes, -taking/s, -took,

-taken/ly mɪ's|teĭk, -teĭks, -teĭkɪŋ/z,
-tʊk, -teĭkən/lɪ

mis-take ˌmɪs'teĭk

mistempered mɪs'tempɚd

mister (M.), -s 'mɪstɚ, -z

mistermed mɪs'tɜmd

mistful 'mɪstfʊl

misthink mɪs'θɪŋk

misthought mɪs'θɔt

mistletoe 'mɪsl̩toŭ

mist-like 'mɪstˌlaĭk

mistook (*p.t. of* **mistake**) mɪ'stʊk

mistreadings mɪs'tɹedɪŋz

mistreat, -s, -ing, -ed, -ment mɪs'tɹit, -s,
-ɪŋ, -ɪd, -mənt

mistress, -es 'mɪstɹɪs, -ɪz
Note.—In TS, IV.v.52, *this word is
trisyllabic, i.e.,* ['mɪstəɹɪs]; *and is
arguably trisyllabic in* TS, V.ii.96

mistress-ship 'mɪstɹɪsˌʃɪp

mistrust, -s, -ing, -ed ˌmɪs'tɹʌst, -s, -ɪŋ,
-ɪd

mistrustful mɪs'tɹʌstfʊl

mist|y, -ier, -iest, -ily, -iness 'mɪst|ɪ, -ɪɚ,
-ɪst, -ɪlɪ, -ɪnɪs

misuse (*s.*) ˌmɪs'jus

misus|e (*v.*) ˌmɪs'juz, -ɪz, -ɪŋ, -d

mite, -s 'maĭt, -s

Mithridates (AC) ˌmɪθɹɪ'deĭtɪz

mitigat|e, -es, -ing, -ed 'mɪtɪgeĭt ['mɪɾɪ-],
-s, -ɪŋ, -ɪd

mitigation ˌmɪtɪ'geĭʃn̩ [ˌmɪɾɪ-]

Mitigation, Madam (MEAS) ˌmædəm
ˌmɪɾɪ'geĭʃn̩

mo (*archaic form of* **more***; number*) 'moŭ
(*see Note for* **mo[e]**)

moan, -s, -ing, -ed 'moŭn, -z, -ɪŋ, -d

moat, -s, -ing, -ed 'moŭt, -s, -ɪŋ, -ɪd

mob, -s, -bing, -bed 'mɒb, -z, -ɪŋ, -d

mob(b)led 'mɒbl̩d ['moŭbl̩d]
*Note.—This famous though obscure
word from* HAM, II.ii.498, 499 *may take
either pronunciation depending on
whether one interprets the word to be
the p.p. of the v. 'to mob(b)le' (muffle)
or as an adj. from the n. 'moble'
(movable—capable of being moved)*

mock, -s, -ing/ly, -ed, -er/s; -able 'mɒk,
-s, -ɪŋ/lɪ, -t, -ɚ/z; -əbl̩

mocker|y, -ies 'mɒkəˑɹ|ɨ, -ɨz
mocking-bird, -s 'mɒkɪŋˌbɝˑd, -z
mockvater (*from 'Mockwater'*) 'mɒk-vɑtɚ [-tʁ] (*see* **Mockwater**)
Note.—Doctor Caius (in MWW*) is the stereotypical foreigner, given to foolish arrogance, and ineptly handling English pronunciation. This is an example of S.'s direction to the actor (by way of semiphonetic spellings) to adopt such an accent, more or less, for the sake of wringing the most satire out of plays on words stemming from confusions with, and corruptions of, English pronunciation via the French tongue*
Mock(-)water, Mounseur (MWW)
maŭn'suɝˑ 'mɒkwɔɾɚ [-wɔtɚ]
Note.—The Host, in The Merry Wives of Windsor *(II.iii.53), is amusing himself at the expense of the French foreigner, Dr. Caius, by giving him this appellation. Despite Giorgio Melchiori's (editor,* The Arden Shakespeare*, 2000) dry, if perhaps accurate, annotation for the name, allusions to 'muck-water' (moist animal dung and urine used to fertilize) and 'making water' (urinating) are obvious and unavoidable. Even the Host's corruption of 'monsieur' with 'monsire' (Quarto) or 'mounseur' (First Folio) provides raw material for a jest. 'Sire' (var. of 'syre') is an archaic word for sewer, gutter, or drain, and certainly any clever actor can eke 'sewer' out of 'mounseur.' Editors who over-correct, and emend 'monsire/ mounseur' to 'monsieur' endanger the inherent fun and humor of the exchange*
mode, -s 'moŭd, -z
model, -s, -ling, -led, -ler/s 'mɒdl̩, -z, -ɪŋ, -d, -ɚ/z
Modena (AC) 'mɔdeɪnɑ ['moŭdn̩ə, 'mɔdɛnɑ]
Note.—In S. this name is stressed on the

second syllable, i.e., [moŭ'dinə, mə-, -'deɪnə]
moderate (*s., adj.*), **-s, -ly, -ness** 'mɒdəˑɹɪt, -s, -lɨ, -nɪs
moderat|e (*v.*), **-es, -ing, -ed, -or/s** 'mɒdəˑɹeɪt, -s, -ɪŋ, -ɪd, -ɚ/z
moderation, -s ˌmɒdəˑ'ɹeɪʃn̩, -z
modern, -s, -ly, -ness 'mɒdəˑn, -z, -lɨ, -nɪs
modernity mɒ'dɝˑnɪtɨ
modest, -ly 'mɒdɪst, -lɨ
modest|y (M.), -ies 'mɒdɪst|ɨ, -ɨz
modicum, -s 'mɒdɪkəm, -z
Modo (LEAR) 'moŭdoŭ
module, -s 'mɒdjul, -z
mo(e) (*archaic form of* **more***; greater*) 'moŭ (*see Note for* **mo**)
moiet|y, -ies 'mɔɪɪt|ɨ, -ɨz
moist, -er, -est, -ness 'mɔɪst, -ɚ, -ɪst, -nɪs
moisten, -s, -ing, -ed 'mɔɪsn̩, -z, -ɪŋ, -d
moisture 'mɔɪstʃɚ
mold, -s, -ing, -ed, -er/s 'moŭld, -z, -ɪŋ, -ɪd, -ɚ/z
mold|er, -ers, -ering, -ered 'moŭld|ɚ, -ɚz, -ɚˑɹɪŋ, -ɚd
moldwarp (*mole*), **-s** 'moŭldwɔɝˑp, -s
mole, -s 'moŭl, -z
mole(-)hill, -s 'moŭlhɪl, -z
molest, -s, -ing, -ed, -er/s mə'lest, -s, -ɪŋ, -ɪd, -ɚ/z
molestation, -s ˌmoŭle'steɪʃn̩, -z
mollification ˌmɒlɪfɪ'keɪʃn̩
mollif|y, -ies, -ying, -ied 'mɒlɪf|aɪ, -aɪz, -aɪɪŋ, -aɪd
mollis aer (L.) (CYM, V.v.448) 'mɒlɨs 'ɛɝˑ
molt, -s, -ing, -ed 'moŭlt, -s, -ɪŋ, -ɪd
molten 'moŭltən
mome, -s 'moŭm, -z
moment, -s 'moŭmənt, -s
momentany 'moŭmənteɪnɨ [-tənɨ]
momentarily ˌmoŭmən'tɛɝˑɹɪlɨ
momentary 'moŭməntɚˑɹɨ
monarch, -s 'mɒnɚˑk [-nɑɝ̆k], -s
monarchiz|e, -es, -ing, -ed 'mɒnɚˑkaɪz, -ɪz, -ɪŋ, -d

i w**e** ɨ cit**y** ɪ h**i**t e l**e**t ɛ d**e**but æ c**a**n a p**a**ss ɝ b**i**rd ʌ h**u**t ə **a**gain ɚ supp**er** u y**ou**
ʊ sh**ou**ld o **o**bey ɔ **a**wl ɒ c**o**p ɑ f**a**ther eɪ p**ai**d aɪ h**igh** oŭ g**o** ɔɪ v**oi**ce aŭ f**ou**nd ɪɝ̆ **ear**
ɛɝ̆ **air** ʊɝ̆ **poor** ɔɝ̆ **fork** ɑɝ̆ **park** aɪɝ̆ **fire** aŭɝ̆ **hour** b **b**oy p **p**it d **d**og t **t**op g **g**ot
k **k**id h **h**ow ɦ be**h**ave dʒ **j**ot tʃ **ch**ew z **z**any s **s**oft v **v**at f **f**at ʒ trea**s**ure ʃ **sh**ip ð **th**e
θ **th**in m **m**an n **n**o ŋ ha**ng** l **l**ip j **y**es w **w**on ʍ **wh**ew ɹ **r**igger, ai**r**y ɼ ma**tt**er

Monarcho (LLL) moˈnɑɚˌkoʊ

monarch|y, -ies ˈmɒnəˌk|ɨ [-nɑɚˌk-], -ɨz

monaster|y, -ies ˈmɒnəstəˌɹ|ɨ, -ɨz

Monastery, Chertsey (RIII) ˈtʃɚˌtsɨ ˈmɒnəstəˌɹɨ

Note.—In RIII, I.ii.218, *'Monastery' wants to be trisyllabic, i.e.,* [ˈmɒnəstɹɨ], *to better suit the metrical requirements of the verse line, and still happens to be in keeping with modern Brit. English*

monastic, -al, -ally məˈnæstɪk, -l̩, -əlɨ

Monday (1HIV), **-s** ˈmʌndɪ [-deɪ̌], -z

money, -s, -ed ˈmʌnɨ, -z, -d

'mong (*aphetic form of* **among**) ˈmʌŋ

mongrel, -s ˈmʌŋɡɹəl [ˈmɒŋ-], -z

'mongst (*aphetic form of* **amongst**) ˈmʌŋst [ˈmʌŋkst]

monk, -s ˈmʌŋk, -s

monkey, -s ˈmʌŋkɨ, -z

monkish, -ly, -ness ˈmʌŋkɪʃ, -lɨ, -nɪs

Monmouth (HV, 1HVI) ˈmɒnməθ

Monmouth, Harry (1HIV, 2HVI) ˈhæˌɹɨ ˈmɒnməθ

Monmouth, Henry (1HVI) ˈhenˌɹɨ ˈmɒnməθ

monopoliz|e, -es, -ing, -ed, -er/s məˈnɒpl̩aɪ̌z, -ɪz, -ɪŋ, -d, -ɚ/z

monopol|y, -ies məˈnɒpəl|ɨ, -ɨz

mons (*L.*) (LLL, V.i.76) ˈmɒnz [ˈmonz]

monsieur məˈsjɚ

Note.—Arguably stressed on the first syllable, i.e., [ˈmɪˌsjɚ] *in* AYLI, II.vii.9. *In* MWW, II.iii.53, *some editors will insist on emending 'monsire' (Quarto) or 'mounseur' (First Folio) to 'monsieur,' but in doing so endanger the inherent fun and humor of the exchange (see Note for* **Mock(-)water, Mounseur***)*

monster, -s, -ed ˈmɒnstɚ, -z, -d

Monster, Monsieur (TEM) məˈsjɚ ˈmɒnstɚ

monstrosit|y, -ies mɒnˈstɹɒsɪt|ɨ, -ɨz

monstrous, -ly, -ness ˈmɒnstɹəs, -lɨ, -nɪs

Note.—Depending on how one chooses to scan OTH, II.iii.208—*as either four feet or five— 'monstrous' is justifiably trisyllabic, i.e.,* [ˈmɒnstəˌɹəs]. *In so doing, the line becomes a regular iambic*

pentameter. 'Monstrous' is certainly trisyllabic in MAC, III.vi.8

monstruosity ˌmɒnstɹʊˈɒsɪtɨ

Montacute *or* **Montague, Lord** (HVIII) ˈlɔɚ̌d ˈmɒntəkjut *or* ˈmɒntəɡju

Montague (*RJ*), **-s** ˈmɒntəɡju, -z

Montague, Lady (*RJ*) ˈleɪ̌dɨ ˈmɒntəɡju

Montague, Marquess of (*3HVI*) ˈmɑɚ̌kwɪs əv ˈmɒntəɡju

Montano (*OTH*) mɒnˈtænoʊ [-ˈtɑnoʊ]

montant (*fencing; upright or upward thrust*) ˈmɒntənt

Montferrat, Marquis of (MV) ˈmɑɚ̌kwɪs əv ˌmɒntfəˈɹæt

Montgomery, Sir John (*3HVI*) ˌsɚ ˈdʒɒn mənt ˈɡʌməˌɹɨ

month, -s, -ly ˈmʌnθ, -s, -lɨ

Note.—Possibly disyllabic in TGV, I.ii.137 *to fulfill the metrical requirements of the verse. Editors have endorsed 'monthes' and 'moneths.' As it is a possessive in the line, perhaps there is a more sensible emendation, such as 'month his' (see Note for* **whale***)*

Montjoy (*HV*) ˈmɒntdʒɔɪ̌

monument, -s ˈmɒnjʊmənt, -s

monument|al, -ally ˌmɒnjʊˈment|l̩, -lɨ [-əlɨ]

moo, -s, -ing, -ed ˈmu, -z, -ɪŋ, -d

mooch, -es, -ing, -ed, -er/s ˈmutʃ, -ɪz, -ɪŋ, -t, -ɚ/z

mood, -s ˈmud, -z

mood|y, -ier, -iest, -ily, -iness ˈmud|ɨ, -ɨɚ, -ɨɪst, -ɪlɨ, -ɨnɪs

moody-mad ˈmudɨˌmæd

moon (**M.**), **-s, -ing, -ed** ˈmun, -z, -ɪŋ, -d

moonbeam, -s ˈmunbim, -z

moon-cal|f, -ves ˈmunka|f, -vz

moonish ˈmunɪʃ

moon|light, -lit ˈmun|laɪ̌t, -lɪt

moonshine (**M.**), **-s** ˈmunʃaɪ̌n, -z

moonstruck ˈmunstɹʌk

Moor (MV, OTH, TIT, TNK) ˈmʊɚ̌

Moor(-)ditch (1HIV) ˈmʊɚ̌ˌdɪtʃ

Moorfields (HVIII) ˈmʊɚ̌ˌfildz

moor, -s, -ing/s, -ed ˈmʊɚ̌, -z, -ɹɪŋ/z, -d

moose ˈmus

mop, -s, -ping, -ped ˈmɒp, -s, -ɪŋ, -t

mop|e, -es, -ing/ly, -ed ˈmoʊ̌p, -s, -ɪŋ/lɨ, -t

Mopsa (*WT*) 'mɒpsə
moral, -s; -ly 'mɒɹəl, -z; -ɨ
morale mə'ɹal
moral(l)er, -s 'mɒɹələ˞, -z
moralit|y, -ies mə'ɹælɪt|ɨ, -ɨz
moraliz|e, -es, -ing, -ed, -er/s 'mɒɹəlaɪz, -ɪz, -ɪŋ, -d, -ə˞/z
morbid, -ly, -ness 'mɔ˞bɪd, -lɨ, -nɪs
morbidity mɔ˞'bɪdɪtɨ
Mordake, Earl of Fife (1HIV) 'mɜ˞dɒk ['mɔ˞deɪ̆k, -dək] 'ɜ˞l əv 'faɪ̆f
Note.—Holinshed was S.'s source for this character, and he gives this name (standing for Murdoch) as 'Mordacke.' S. borrows this spelling, and so it might be surmised that S. intended it to be pronounced ['mɔ˞deɪ̆k]. If so, there is certainly the echo of 'death's ache' or 'ache of death' in it's sounding
more, -s 'mɔ˞, -z
Note.—It is important to point out that in TN, V.i.134, (if the scansion of the line weren't clue enough) 'mores' is an unusual usage of the comparative (by making it an object and then pluralizing it), rather than the word that means 'accepted social customs' (cf. **mores***)*
more-having 'mɔ˞ˌfiævɪŋ
more-o'er 'mɔ˞ˌ(ɹ)ɔ˞
moreover mɔ˞'ɹoŭvə˞
mores (*accepted social customs*) 'mɔ˞ɹeɪ̆z [-ɹiz] (*see* **more, -s**)
Morgan (ALL'S, CYM) 'mɔ˞gən
morgue, -s 'mɔ˞g, -z
Morisco (2HVI) mɒ'ɹɪskoŭ
morn, -s 'mɔ˞n, -z
morn-dew 'mɔ˞nˌdju
morning, -s 'mɔ˞nɪŋ, -z
Morocco, The Prince of (*MV*) ðə ˌpɹɪns əv mə'ɹɒkoŭ
morris, -es 'mɒɹɪs, -ɪz
morris-pike, -s 'mɒɹɪsˌpaɪ̆k
morrow, -s 'mɒɹoŭ, -z
morsel, -s 'mɔ˞sḷ, -z

mort, -s 'mɔ˞t, -s
mort|al, -als, -ally 'mɔ˞t|ḷ, -ḷz, -əlɨ
mortalit|y, -ies mɔ˞'tælɪt|ɨ, -ɨz
mortal-staring 'mɔ˞tḷˌstɛ˞ɹɪŋ
mortar, -s 'mɔ˞ɾə˞, -z
mortar-piece, -s 'mɔ˞ɾə˞ˌpis, -ɪz
mort de ma vie (*Fr.*) (HV, III.v.11) mɔʁ dʊ ma 'vi
mort Dieu (*Fr.*) (2HVI, I.i.122) mɔʁ dø
mort du vinaigre (*Fr.*) (ALL'S, II.iii.44) mɔʁ du vɪ'negʁ
mortgag|e, -es, -ing, -ed 'mɔ˞gɪdʒ, -ɪz, -ɪŋ, -d
mortgager *or* **mortgagor, -s** 'mɔ˞gɪdʒə˞, -z
mortification ˌmɔ˞fɪfɪ'keɪ̆ʃn
morti|fy, -fies, -fying, -fied 'mɔ˞tɪ|faɪ̆, -faɪ̆z, -faɪ̆ɪŋ, -faɪ̆d
Mortimer, Edmund (*1HIV, 1HVI, 2HVI*) 'edmənd 'mɔ˞tɪmə˞
Mortimer, Hugh (*3HVI*) 'hju 'mɔ˞tɪmə˞
Mortimer, John (2HVI, *3HVI*) 'dʒɒn 'mɔ˞tɪmə˞
Mortimer, Lady (*1HIV*) 'leɪ̆dɨ 'mɔ˞tɪmə˞
Mortimer, Lord (*1HIV*) 'lɔ˞d 'mɔ˞tɪmə˞
Note.—In 1HIV, I.iii.275, 'Mortimer' becomes disyllabic, i.e., ['mɔ˞tmə˞] *to fit more rightly the metrical requirements of the verse line*
Mortimer, Roger (3HVI) 'ɹɒdʒə˞ 'mɔ˞tɪmə˞
Note.—In 3HVI, I.i.106, 'Mortimer' becomes disyllabic, i.e., ['mɔ˞tmə˞] *to fit more rightly the metrical requirements of the verse line*
morti|se *or* **morti|ce, -ses (-ces), -sing (-cing), -sed (-ced)** 'mɔ˞tɪs, -ɪz, -ɪŋ, -t
Morton (*2HIV*) 'mɔ˞tn̩
Morton, John (*RIII*) 'dʒɒn 'mɔ˞tn̩
mose 'moŭz
Note.—The meaning of this word, and the phrase in which it appears, i.e., 'to mose in the chine' (TS, III.ii.48–49) is a mystery; therefore, the pronunciation

---

i w**e** ɨ cit**y** ɪ h**i**t e l**e**t ɛ d**e**but æ c**a**n a p**a**ss ɜ˞ b**ir**d ʌ h**u**t ə **a**gain ə˞ supp**er** u y**ou**
ʊ sh**ou**ld o **o**bey ɔ **aw**l ɒ c**o**p ɑ f**a**ther eɪ̆ p**ai**d aɪ̆ h**igh** oŭ g**o** ɔɪ̆ v**oi**ce aŭ f**ou**nd ɪ˞ **ear**
ɛ˞ **air** ʊ˞ **poor** ɔ˞ **fork** ɑ˞ p**ar**k aɪ̆ə˞ **fire** aŭə˞ **hour** b **b**oy p **p**it d **d**og t **t**op g **g**ot
k **k**id h **h**ow fi be**h**ave dʒ **j**ot tʃ **ch**ew z **z**any s **s**oft v **v**at f **f**at ʒ trea**s**ure ʃ **sh**ip ð **th**e
θ **th**in m **m**an n **n**o ŋ ha**ng** l **l**ip j **y**es w **w**on ʍ **wh**ew ɹ **r**igge**r**, ai**r**y ɾ ma**tt**er

proffered above is entirely conjectural. 'Mose' doesn't seem to show up anywhere else in literature, though the OED *suggests that it might be a corruption of 'mourn.' Practically all that can be said about it is that it's obviously a verb; but so are 'dose,' 'pose,' and 'lose,' any one of which 'mose' might be analogous to. (See* Brian Morris' *annotation for the line,* The Arden Shakespeare, *1981, for a more in-depth discussion of the matter)*

moss, -es, -ed 'mɒs, -ɪz, -t

moss-grown 'mɒsˌgɹoŭn

moss|y, -ier, -iest, -iness 'mɒs|ɪ, -ɪə˞, -ɪɪst, -ɪnɪs

most, -ly 'moŭst, -lɪ

mot, -s 'moŭ, -z

mote, -s 'moŭt, -s

moth (M.) (*LLL, MSND*), **-s** 'mɒθ, -s ['mɒðz]

Note.—This name in S. (especially LLL*) is traditionally pronounced* ['moŭt]*, as there is little doubt that it was so pronounced in S.'s day (cf. Kökeritz's* Shakespeare's Pronunciation, *p. 320). There is, of course, a pun on the word 'mote,' meaning 'a very small speck' (an allusion to the parable in the Book of Matthew, vii.3). In* MV, *II.ix.79, the word is optionally* ['moŭt, 'moŭθ] *for the sake of assonance if not rhyme, or* ['mɒθ] *for the (seeming) sake of the modern ear. It is also worthwhile mentioning that in* KJ, *IV.i.91 (First Folio version), 'mote'—meaning a small speck—again, from Matthew—is spelled 'moth'*

mother (M.), -s, -ing, -ed; -hood, -less 'mʌðə˞, -z, -ɹɪŋ, -d; -ɦʊd, -lɪs

mother-in-law, -s 'mʌðə˞ɹɪnlɔ, -z

mother-queen 'mʌðə˞ˌkwin [ˌ--'-]

mothers-in-law 'mʌðə˞zɪnlɔ

mother-wit 'mʌðə˞ˌwɪt

motif, -s moŭ'tif, -s

motion, -s, -ing, -ed 'moŭʃn̩, -z, -ɪŋ, -d

motionless 'moŭʃn̩lɪs

motivat|e, -es, -ing, -ed 'moŭtɪveĭt, -s, -ɪŋ, -ɪd

motivation ˌmoŭtɪ'veĭʃn̩

motive, -s 'moŭtɪv, -z

Motley (AYLI) 'mɒtlɪ

motley 'mɒtlɪ

motley-minded 'mɒtlɪˌmaĭndɪd

motor, -s, -ing, -ed 'moŭɾə˞, -z, -ɹɪŋ, -d

motto, -s 'mɒɾoŭ, -z

mought 'moŭt

mould (*chiefly Brit. var. of* **mold***, q.v.*) 'moŭld

Mouldy, Ralph *or* **Rafe** (*2HIV*) 'ɹeĭf ['ɹælf] 'moŭldɪ

mounch, -es, -ing, -ed 'mʌnʃ [-ntʃ], -ɪz, -ɪŋ, -t

mount (M.), -s, -ing, -ed 'maŭnt, -s, -ɪŋ, -ɪd

mountain (M.), -s 'maŭntɪn [-tn̩], -z

mountaineer, -s, -ing ˌmaŭntɪ'nɪə˞ [-t'n̩-], -z, -ɹɪŋ

mountain-foot 'maŭntɪnˌfʊt

mountain-foreigner 'maŭntɪnˌfɔɹɪnə˞ [-tn̩-]

mountain-squire 'maŭntɪnˌskwaĭə˞

mountain-top, -s 'maŭntɪnˌtɒp [-tn̩], -s

mountant 'maŭntənt

Mountanto, Signior (ADO) 'sinjɔ˞ mɒn'tantoŭ

Note.—In ADO, *I.i.28, Beatrice refers to Benedick as Signior Mountanto. He is a soldier, and the term stands for 'fencer' or 'duellist' (deriving from a fencing term for an upright hit or thrust). Depending on how suggestive and/or mocking she's being, it may also be a play on the words 'mount onto' and pronounced as such*

mountebank, -s 'maŭntɪbæŋk, -s

Mount Misena (AC) 'maŭnt mɪ'sinə

mourn, -s, -ing/ly, -ed, -er/s 'mɔ˞n, -z, -ɪŋ/lɪ, -d, -ə˞/z

mourn|ful, -fully, -fulness 'mɔ˞n|fʊl, -fəlɪ, -fʊlnɪs

mouse, mice 'maŭs, 'maĭs

mous|e (*v.*)**, -es, -ing, -ed** 'maŭz ['maŭs, -ɪz, -ɪŋ, -t], -ɪz, -ɪŋ, -d

mouse-hunt 'maŭsˌhʌnt

mouser, -s 'maŭzə˞ [-sə˞], -z

Mouse-trap, The (HAM) ðə 'maŭsˌtɹæp

mou|th (*s.*)**, -ths** 'maŭ|θ, -ðz

mouth (*v.*), **-s, -ing, -ed** 'maʊð, -z, -ɪŋ, -d
mouth-friend, -s 'maʊθ͵fɹend, -z
mouth-honor ͵maʊ'θɒnɚ [-'θɒnɚ]
moveable *or* **movable, -s** 'muvəbl̩, -z
mov|e, -es, -ing/ly, -ed, -er/s -ement/s
'muv, -z, -ɪŋ/lɪ, -d, -ɚ/z, -mənt/s
moving-delicate ͵muvɪŋ'delɪkɪt
mow (*grimace*), **-s, -ing, -ed** 'maʊ, -z, -ɪŋ, -ed
mow (*raze*), **-s, -ing, -ed** 'moʊ, -z, -ɪŋ, -d
Mowbray, John (3HVI) 'dʒɒn 'moʊbɹeɪ
Mowbray, Thomas (*2HIV, RII*) 'tɒməs 'moʊbɹeɪ
moyle (*archaic var. of* **mule**), **-s** 'mɔɪl, -z
much, -ly, -ness 'mʌtʃ, -lɪ, -nɪs
mud, -s, -ding, -ded 'mʌd, -z, -ɪŋ, -ɪd
mudd|y, -ies, -ying, -ied; -ier, -iest, -ily, -iness 'mʌd|ɪ, -ɪz, -ɪɪŋ, -ɪd; -ɪɪst, -ɪlɪ, -ɪnɪs
muddy-mettled 'mʌdɪ͵metl̩d
muff|le, -les, -ling, -led 'mʌf|l̩, -l̩z, -lɪŋ [-lɪŋ], l̩d
muffler, -s 'mʌflɚ, -z
Mugs (1HIV) 'mʌgz
mug, -s, -ging/s, -ged, -ger/s 'mʌg, -z, -ɪŋ/z, -d, -ɚ/z
mugg|y, -ier, -iest, -iness 'mʌg|ɪ, -ɪɚ, -ɪɪst, -ɪnɪs
mulberr|y, -ies 'mʌlbeɹɪ [-bəɹ-], -ɪz
mulch, -es, -ing, -ed 'mʌltʃ, -ɪz, -ɪŋ, -t
mule, -s 'mjul, -z
muleteer, -s ͵mjulɪ'tɪɚ, -z
muleter, -s 'multɚ, -z
mulier (*L.*) (CYM, V.v.449) mul'jɛɚ
mulish, -ly, -ness 'mjulɪʃ, -lɪ, -nɪs
mull, -s, -ing, -ed 'mʌl, -z, -ɪŋ, -d
Mulmutius (CYM) mʌl'mjuʃəs
multiple, -s 'mʌltɪpl̩, -z
multipl|y, -ies, -ying, -ied, -ier/s 'mʌltɪpl|aɪ, -aɪz, -aɪɪŋ, -aɪd, -aɪɚ/z
multipotent mʌl'tɪpətənt
multitude, -s 'mʌltɪtjud, -z
multitudinous, -ly, -ness ͵mʌltɪt'judn̩əs [-dɪnəs], -lɪ, -nɪs

Muly *or* **Muli** (TIT) 'mjulɪ ['mulɪ]
Note.—*The Quartos and the Folio give 'Muliteus' in* TIT, IV.ii.154, *and editors typically emend this to 'Muli lives'*
mum, -s, -ming, -med, -mer/s 'mʌm, -z, -ɪŋ, -d, -ɚ/z
mumble-news 'mʌmbl̩͵njuz
mummi|fy, -fies, -fying, -fied 'mʌmɪ|faɪ, -faɪz, -faɪɪŋ, -faɪd
mumm|y, -ies 'mʌm|ɪ, -ɪz
mundane, -ly ͵mʌn'deɪn, -lɪ (['mʌn deɪn] *in* PER, III.ii.73)
muniment, -s 'mjunɪmənt, -s
munition, -s mju'nɪʃn̩ [mjʊ'n-], -z
mural, -s 'mjʊɚɹəl, -z
Murder (TIT) 'mɝdɚ
murder, -s, -ing, -ed 'mɝdɚ, -z, -ɹɪŋ, -d
murderer, -s 'mɝdɚɹɚ, -z
murderous, -ly 'mɝdəɹəs, -lɪ
mur|e, -es, -ing, -ed 'mjʊɚ, -z, -ɹɪŋ, -d
Murellus (*JUL*) mə'ɹeləs
Note.—*This is a var. of* **Marullus** (*q.v.*) *found in the Folio version of* JUL
murk *or* **mirk** 'mɝk
murk|y, -ier, -iest, -ily, -iness 'mɝk|ɪ, -ɪɚ, -ɪɪst, -ɪlɪ, -ɪnɪs
murm|ur, -urs, -uring, -ured, -urer/s 'mɝm|ɚ, -ɚz, -əɹɪŋ, -ɚd, -əɹɚ/z
murrain, -ed 'mʌɹɪn [-ɹeɪn], -d
Murray (1HIV) 'mʌɹɪ
murrion 'mʌɹɪən (*cf.* **murrain**)
murther (**M.**), **-s, -ing, -ed, -er/s** 'mɝð̩ɚ, -z, -ɹɪŋ, -d, -ɹɚ/z
Note.—*This word is an obsolete archaic var. of 'murder,' and perhaps merely an alternate spelling. The sources I've come across that hazard a guess at its pronunciation suggest the one given above (or something close to it), but it must be acknowledged that in S.'s time the pronunciation of the* [ð] *and the* [d] *in such words as 'fathom/fad(d)om,' 'murther/murder,' 'burthen/burden,' and 'farthell/fardel,' etc., must have been*

---

i wĕ ɪ city ɪ hĭt e lĕt ɛ dĕbut æ căn a păss ɝ bĭrd ʌ hŭt ə again ɚ suppĕr u yŏu ʊ shŏuld o ŏbey ɔ awl ɒ cŏp ɑ făther eɪ păid aɪ hĭgh oʊ gŏ ɔɪ vŏice aʊ fŏund ɪɚ eăr ɛɚ aĭr ʊɚ pŏor ɔɚ fŏrk ɑɚ părk aɪɚ fĭre aʊɚ hŏur b bŏy p pĭt d dŏg t tŏp g gŏt k kĭd h hŏw fi behăve dʒ jŏt tʃ chĕw z zany s sŏft v văt f făt ʒ treăsure ʃ shĭp ð thĕ θ thĭn m măn n nŏ ŋ hăng l lĭp j yĕs w wŏn ʍ whĕw ɹ rĭgger, aiɹy ɾ matter

extremely close to—if not indistinguishable from—one another. In Kökeritz's Shakespeare's Pronunciation *(p. 320), he cites in a footnote Simon Daines' reminder from his* Orthoepia Anglicana *(A.D. 1640) that in some instances "many pronounce 'Th' like 'd';" therefore, it would not be unreasonable to see 'murther,' but say 'murder.' Another similar example of this phenomenon: the word 'Bedlam,' a corruption of the word 'Bethlehem' (see § 'Bedlam,'* The Oxford Dictionary of English Etymology, *edited by C. T. Onions; and see* **quotha***)*

murtherous, -ly 'mɜˑðəˑɹəs, -lɪ (*see* **murther**)

muscadel (*var. of 'muscatel'*) ˌmʌskəˈdel

Muscovite (LLL), **-s** 'mʌskəvaĭt [-kov-], -s
Note.—In LLL, V.ii.265, *this word is meant to rhyme with 'wits,' i.e.,* ['mʌskəvɪts]*, and some editions retain the First Folio spelling 'Muscovits'*

Muscovy (LLL) 'mʌskəvɪ [-kov-]

mus|e (**M.**) (MSND, Sonn. 21, 78, 79, 82, 85, 100, 101, 103), **-es, -ing/s, -ingly, -ed** 'mjuz, -ɪz, -ɪŋ/z, -ɪŋlɪ, -d

mush (*from 'much'*) 'mʌʃ (*see* **nursh-a**)

mush, -es, -ing, -ed 'mʌʃ, -ɪz, -ɪŋ, -t

mushroom, -s 'mʌʃɹum, -z

mushrump, -s 'mʌʃɹəmp, -s

mush|y, -ier, -iest, -iness 'mʌʃ|ɪ, -ɪəˑ, -ɪɪst, -ɪnɪs

music, -s 'mjuzɪk, -s

music|al (*adj.*), **-ally, -alness** 'mjuzɪk|l̩, -əlɪ, -l̩nɪs

musical (*s.*), **-s** 'mjuzɪkl̩, -z

musit *or* **muset** (*hole for hiding*), **-s** 'mjuzɪt, -s

musk, -y, -iness 'mʌsk, -ɪ, -ɪnɪs

musk-cat, -s 'mʌskˌkæt, -s

musket, -s; -ry 'mʌskɪt, -s; -ɹɪ

Muskos 'mʌskɒs [-kos]

musk-rose, -s 'mʌskˌɹoŏz, -ɪz

muss, -es, -ing, -ed 'mʌs, -ɪz, -ɪŋ, -t

mussel, -s 'mʌsl̩, -z

mussel-shell 'mʌsl̩ˌʃel

mustachio mʊˈstaʃjo

mustang, -s 'mʌstæŋ, -z

mustard 'mʌstəˑd

Mustardseed, Master (*MSND*) 'mastəˑ'mʌstəˑdsid

muster, -s, -ing, -ed 'mʌstəˑ, -z, -ɹɪŋ, -d

muster-book, -s 'mʌstəˑˌbʊk, -s

muster-file, -s 'mʌstəˑfaĭl, -z

must|y, -ier, -iest, -ily, -iness 'mʌst|ɪ, -ɪəˑ, -ɪɪst, -ɪlɪ, -ɪnɪs

mutability ˌmjuɾəbɪlɪtɪ

mutable 'mjuɾəbl̩

mutation, -s mjuˈteĭʃn̩ [mjʊˈt-], -z

mut|e, -es, -ing, -ed; -er, -est, -ely, -eness 'mjut, -s, -ɪŋ, -ɪd; -əˑ, -ɪst, -lɪ, -nɪs

mutine, -s 'mjuˌtin, -z

mutineer, -s ˌmjutɪˈnɪɜˑ [-tn̩-], -z

mutiner, -s 'mjutn̩əˑ [-tɪnəˑ], -z

mutinous, -ly, -ness 'mjutɪnəs [-tn̩-], -lɪ, -nɪs

mutin|y, -ies, -ying, -ied 'mjutɪn|ɪ [-tn̩-], -ɪz, -ɪɪŋ, -ɪd

Mutius (*TIT*) 'mjuʃəs, -ʃɪəs

mutter, -s, -ing/ly, -ed, -er/s 'mʌɾəˑ, -z, -ɪŋ/lɪ, -d, -ɹəˑ/z

mutton, -s 'mʌtn̩, -z

mutual, -ly 'mjutʃʊəl, -ɪ

mutualit|y, -ies ˌmjutʃʊˈælɪt|ɪ, -ɪz

muzz|le, -es, -ing, -ed 'mʌzl̩|, -l̩z, -l̩ɪŋ [-lɪŋ], -l̩d

mych|e *or* **mich|e, -es, -ing, -ed, -er/s** 'mɪtʃ, -ɪz, -ɪŋ, -t, -əˑ/z

myn(-)heer (**M.**), **-s** maĭn'heɜˑ [-'hɪɜˑ], -z
Note.—This is a Dutch word ('mijnheer'), meaning 'gentleman' or the title of respect and courtesy equivalent to 'sir.' Many modern editors emend 'An-heires' in MWW, II.i.197 *to 'myn-heers' because 'An-heires' is a mystery that has yet to be sufficiently explained*

myriad 'mɪɹɪəd

Myrmidon (TC, TN), **-s** 'mɜˑmɪdɒn [-dən], -z

myrrh 'mɜˑ

myrtle, -s 'mɜˑtl̩, -z

myrtle-lea|f, -ves 'mɜˑtl̩ˌli|f, -vz

myself maĭ'self

mysterious, -ly, -ness mɪ'stɪɜˑɹɪəs, -lɪ, -nɪs

myster|y, -ies 'mɪstə‧ɹ|ɪ, -ɪz
mystic, -s 'mɪstɪk, -s
myth, -s 'mɪθ, -s
Mytilene (PER) ˌmɪṭɪˈlinɨ [ˌmɪtɪ-]
Note.—In PER, V.i.175, it seems clear that 'Mytilene' wants to be tetrasyllabic, as given above, but in other lines it is equivocal. In PER, V.ii.8, it is usually spelled 'Mytilin' and wants to rhyme with its couplet counterpart, 'din'. It might be either three or four syllables in PER, IV.ii.3; IV.iv.51; V.i.186, 218, and might be pronounced [ˌmɪṭɪˈlɪn] or ['mɪṭɪlɪn]. The Quarto version of PER gives several different spellings, including 'Mittelin,' 'Metiline,' 'Mittelyne,' etc.

Nn

N (*the letter*), **-'s** 'en, -z
nab, -s, -bing, -bed 'næb, -z, -ɪŋ, -d
nabob, -s 'neĭbɒb, -z
nag, -s, -ging, -ged 'næg, -z, -ɪŋ, -d
naiad (N.), -s 'naĭæd, -z
nail, -s, -ing, -ed 'neĭl, -z, -ɪŋ, -d
naked, -ly, -ness 'neĭkɪd, -lɨ, -nɪs
nam|e, -es, -ing, -ed; -eless 'neĭm, -z, -ɪŋ, -d; -lɪs
namely 'neĭmlɨ
namesake, -s 'neĭmseĭk, -s
Nan (MWW, TGV) 'næn
nann|y, -ies 'næn|ɨ, -ɪz
nap, -s, -ping, -ped; -less 'næp, -s, -ɪŋ, -t; -lɪs
nape, -s 'neĭp, -s
napkin, -s 'næpkɪn, -z
Naples 'neĭpl̩z
Naples, King of (1HVI, 2HVI, 3HVI, TEM) ˌkɪŋ əv 'neĭpl̩z
Naples, Queen of ˌkwin əv 'neĭpl̩z
Naps, John (TS) 'dʒɒn 'næps

Narbon, Gerard de (ALL'S) dʒeˈɹɑɝ-d də 'nɑɝ-bən
narciss|us, -es, -i nɑɝ-ˈsɪs|əs, -əsɪz, -aĭ
Narcissus (AC, LUC, TNK, VA) nɑɝ-ˈsɪsəs
narrative, -s 'næɹətɪv, -z
narrow, -s, -ing, -ed; -er, -est, -ly, -ness 'næɹoŭ, -z, -ɪŋ, -d; -ɝ-, -ɪst, -lɨ, -nɪs
narrow-mouthed 'næɹoŭˌmaŭðd [-ˌmaŭθt]
narrow-prying 'næɹoŭˌpɹaĭɪŋ
Narrow Seas (HV, 3HVI, MV) 'næɹoŭ 'siz
Naso, Ovidius (LLL) oˈvɪdɪəs 'neĭzoŭ ['nɑzoŭ]
Note.—There is an alternative which might even more fully satisfy the humor in the mention of this name in LLL, having to do with smell and the nose. By saying ['nɑzoŭ] and connecting the first and last names, there is an echo of the modern 'schnoz' (short for 'schnozzola')—an entirely random coincidence, since the term 'schnoz' didn't originate until the 1940s. At any rate, [oˈvɪdɪəˈsnɑzoŭ] might pay dividends
Nathaniel (TS) nəˈθænjəl
Note.—This name is arguably [nəˈθænɪəl] in TS, IV.i.109
Nathaniel, Sir (LLL) ˌsɝ- nəˈθænjəl
nation, -s 'neĭʃn̩, -z
native, -s, -ly 'neĭtɪv, -z, -lɨ
nativit|y, -ies nəˈtɪvɪt|ɨ, -ɪz
nature (N.), -s, -d 'neĭtʃɝ-, -z, -d
naught *or* **nought, -s** 'nɔt, -s
naught|y, -ier, -iest, -ily, -iness 'nɔt|ɨ, -ɪ‧ɝ-, -ɪɪst, -ɪlɨ, -ɪnɪs
Navarre (LLL) nəˈvɑɝ-
nave, -s 'neĭv, -z
navel, -s 'neĭvəl, -z
navigat|e, -es, -ing, -ed, -or/s 'nævɪgeĭt, -s, -ɪŋ, -ɪd, -ɝ-/z
navigation, -al ˌnævɪˈgeĭʃn̩, -l̩
nav|y, -ies 'neĭv|ɨ, -ɪz

nay, -s 'neɪ, -z

Note.—In A. R. Humphreys' (editor, The Arden Shakespeare, 1960) annotation for 'Nay' in 1HIV, III.i.205, he vaguely acquiesces to other editors' notions that this word (in this instance) is likely protracted "so to be dwelt on in speaking, as to be equivalent to a dissyllable," presumably for the purpose of supplying a beat that the line seems to lack. True, the line as it stands seems to have only nine beats rather than the conventional ten, but protracting 'nay' into a disyllable doesn't reconcile how the line would then be thrown rhythmically out of kilter. If one, however, scans the line so that the caesura in the middle of the line absorbs the value of a beat (a not uncommon device in S.), the line is made regular

nay-ward 'neɪwəˑd

nay(-)word (*byword; password*) 'neɪwəˑd [-wɝˑd]

Nazarite (MV), **-s** 'næzəˌɹaɪt, -s

ne (*conj. meaning 'and not, nor'*) 'ni ['nɛ]

neaf 'nif

Neapolitan (2HVI, MV, TEM, TC, TS), **-s** ˌniəˈpɒlɪtən, -z

Note.—In TS, I.i.205, the meter of the line requires 'Neapolitan' to be (by process of syncope) [ˌniəˈpɒltən]

near, -s, -ing, -ed; -er, -est, -ly, -ness 'nɪɚ, -z, -ɹɪŋ, -d; -ɹɚ, -ɹɪst, -lɪ, -nɪs

neat-herd, -s 'nitˌhɝˑd, -z

neat's-leather 'nitsˌlɛðɚ

near-legged 'nɪɚˌlɛgd

neat's-tongue 'nitsˌtʌŋ

neb, -s 'neb, -z

Nebuchadnezzar *or* **Nabuchadnezzar** (ALL'S) ˌnebjʊkædˈnezɚ [-bʊk-, -kəd-]

necessar|y, -ies, -iness 'nesɪsəɹ|ɪ [-sɪseɹ-], -ɪz, -ɪnɪs

necessit|y (N.) (3HVI), **-ies, -ied** nɪˈsesɪt|ɪ, -ɪz, -ɪd

neck, -s, -ing, -ed, -er/s 'nek, -s, -ɪŋ, -t, -ɚ/z

necklace, -s 'neklɪs, -ɪz

nectar 'nektɚ

Ned (1HIV, 2HIV, 3HVI, RIII) 'ned

Nedar (MSND) 'nidɚ

need, -s, -ing, -ed, -ly 'nid, -z, -ɪŋ, -ɪd, -lɪ

needer, -s 'nidɚ, -z

need|ful, -fully, -fulness 'nid|fʊl, -flɪ [-fʊlɪ], -fʊlnɪs

needle, -s 'nidl̩, -z

Note.—Some regard this disyllabic pronunciation as difficult in RII, V.v.17; MSND, III.ii.204; PER, IV.23 (Chorus) and KJ, V.ii.157, where only one syllable is needed to fulfill the requirements of a (regular) metrical line of verse. Although the First Folio, Quarto, etc., retain the spelling 'needle,' some editors rightly point out that the word has several variant spellings, many of which indicate a monosyllabic pronunciation, e.g., 'neeld,' 'neele,' etc. For the KJ example, the First Folio gives 'Needl's'

needless, -ly, -ness 'nidlɪs, -lɪ, -nɪs

needlework 'nidl̩ˌwɝˑk

needn't 'nidn̩t

need|y, -ier, -iest, -ily, -iness 'nid|ɪ, -ɪɚ, -ɪɪst, -ɪlɪ, -ɪnɪs

neele 'nil (*see Note for* **needle**)

ne'er (*from* **never**) 'nɛɚ

ne'er-changing ˌnɛɚˈtʃeɪndʒɪŋ

ne'er-cloying ˌnɛɚˈklɔɪɪŋ

ne'er-do-well, -s 'nɛɚduˌwel [-dʊˌw-], -z

ne'er-offence ˌnɛɚɹoˈfens [-ɹʊˈf-]

ne'ertheless ˌnɛɚðəˈles

ne'er-touched 'nɛɚˈtʌtʃt (*when att.,* ['-ˌ-])

ne'er-yet-beaten ˌnɛɚjetˈbitn̩

neeze (*from* **sneeze**) 'niz

negat|e, -es, -ing, -ed nɪˈgeɪt, -s, -ɪŋ, -ɪd

negation, -s nɪˈgeɪʃn̩, -z

negative, -s; -ly, -ness 'negətɪv, -z; -lɪ, -nɪs

neglect, -s, -ing, -ed nɪˈglekt, -s, -ɪŋ, -ɪd

neglectingly nɪˈglektɪŋlɪ

neglection nɪˈglekʃn̩

negligen|ce, -es, -t/ly 'neglɪdʒən|s, -ɪz, -t/lɪ

negligib|le, -ly, -leness 'neglɪdʒɪb|l̩, -lɪ, -l̩nɪs

negotiat|e, -es, -ing, -ed, -or/s nɪˈgoʊʃɪeɪt, -s, -ɪŋ, -ɪd, -ɚ/z

negotiation, -s nɪˌgoʊʃɪˈeɪʃn̩, -z

negress, -es 'nigɹɪs, -ɪz

negro (N.), -es 'niɡɹoŭ, -z
neigh, -s, -ing, -ed 'neĭ, -z, -ɪŋ, -d
Note.—Cf. note for **neighbor** regarding
LLL, V.i.23
neighbor (N.), -s, -ing, -ed; -ly, -liness
'neĭbɚ, -z, -ɹɪŋ, -d; -lɪ, -lɪnɪs
Note.—There is enough evidence to
conclude that in LLL, V.i.22, the pedant,
Holofernes, gives a misapprehended
mispronunciation of the word 'neighbor'
by pronouncing the otherwise silent 'g'
(cf. **abhominable**). How it is sounded in
this case (immediately followed by an
'h') is open for debate, but it would
follow that he says ['neĭɡɪbʊɚ] since
the word is from nēah NIGH + ġebūr
BOOR
neighbor-stained 'neĭbɚˌsteĭnd
ne intelligis, domine? (L.) (LLL, V.i.25)
nɛ in'tɛlɪdʒɪs 'domɪnɛ
neither 'naĭðɚ
Nell (COM, *HV*, 2HVI, RJ, TC, *TNK*) 'nel
Nemean (HAM, LLL, TNK) ni'miən,
'nimɪən
Note.—Always ['nimjən] *in S.*
Nemesis (1HVI) 'nemɪsɪs [-məs-]
Neoptolemus (TC) ˌnɪəp'tɒlɪməs [ˌnɪɒp-]
Neptune (AC, COR, CYM, HAM, 2HIV,
KJ, MAC, MSND, PER, RII, TC, TEM,
TIM, WT) 'neptjun
Nereides (AC) nɪ'ɹiɪdɪz
Note.—This name appears in AC,
II.ii.206 and is pronounced as given
above if one scans the line to contain an
epic caesura in the second foot. If one
scans the line without an epic caesura,
then the name is emended to 'Nereids'
(the plural) and is pronounced ['niɹɪdz]
Nereid (AC), **-s** 'niɹɪd, -z
Nerissa (*MV*) ne'ɹɪsə [nə'ɹ-]
Nero (3HVI, KJ, LEAR), **-es** 'niɹoŭ
['nɪɹoŭ], -z
Nero-like (1HVI) 'niɹoŭlaĭk ['nɪɹoŭ-]
Nervii (JUL) 'nɜ·vɪaĭ

nerv|y, -ier, -iest, -ily, -iness 'nɜ·v|ɪ, -ɪɚ,
-ɪɪst, -ɪlɪ, -ɪnɪs
Nessus (AC, ALL'S) 'nesəs
Nestor (LLL, 3HVI, LUC, MV, *TC*)
'nestɚ [-tɔɚ]
Nestor-like (1HVI) 'nestɚˌlaĭk
nether, -most 'neðɚ, -ˌmoŭst
Netherlands (COM) 'neðɚləndz
nether-stocks 'neðɚˌstɒks
nett|le, -les, -ling, -led 'net|l̩, -l̩z, -l̩ɪŋ
[-lɪŋ], -l̩d
nettle-seed, -s 'netl̩ˌsid, -z
neuter, -s, -ing, -ed 'njutɚ, -z, -ɹɪŋ, -d
neutral, -s, -ly 'njutɹəl, -z, -ɪ
neutrality nju'tɹælɪtɪ
never 'nevɚ
never-daunted 'nevɚˌdɒntɪd
never-dying 'nevɚˌdaĭɪŋ
never-erring 'nevɚˌɜ·ɹɪŋ
never-heard-of ˌnevɚ'hɜ·dɒv
never-needed 'nevɚˌnidɪd
never-quenching 'nevɚˌkwentʃɪŋ
never-resting 'nevɚˌɹestɪŋ
nevertheless ˌnevɚðə'les
never-withering 'nevɚˌwɪðɚɹɪŋ
Nevil or **Neville** (1HIV, 2HIV, HV, 2HVI,
3HVI, HVIII, RIII), **-s** 'nevɪl ['nevl̩], -z
new, -er, -est, -ly, -ness 'nju, -ɚ, -ɪst, -lɪ,
-nɪs
new-appearing 'njuəˌpɪɚɹɪŋ
new-bleeding 'njuˌblidɪŋ
new(-)born 'njubɔɚn
new-built 'njuˌbɪlt
new-burned 'njuˌbɜ·nd
new-christened 'njuˈkɹɪsn̩d
new-come 'njuˌkʌm
new-conceived 'njukən'sivd
new-dated 'njuˌdeĭtɪd
new-delivered 'njudɪˌlɪvɚd
new-devised 'njudɪ'vaĭzd
new-enkindled 'njuɪnˌkɪndəld
new-fall'n 'njuˌfɔln
new-fangled 'njuˈfæŋɡl̩d
new-found 'njuˌfaʊnd

i wе ɪ city ɪ hit e let ɛ dеbut æ cаn a pаss ɜ· bird ʌ hut ə again ɚ supper u you
ʊ shоuld o оbey ɔ awl ɒ cоp ɑ fаther eĭ paid aĭ high oŏ go ɔĭ vоice aŏ found ɪɚ ear
ɛɚ air ʊɚ poor ɔɚ fork ɑɚ park aĭɚ fire aʊɚ hour b bоy p pit d dоg t tоp g got
k kid h how fı behave dʒ jоt tʃ chew z zany s sоft v vаt f fat ʒ treаsure ʃ ship ð the
θ thin m mаn n nо ŋ hаng l lip j yes w wоn ʍ whew ɹ rigger, airу f matter

Newgate (1HIV) 'njuɡɪt [-ɡeɪ̆t]
new-healed 'nju‚hild
new-killed 'nju‚kɪld
new-lodged 'nju‚lɒdʒd ([‚-ʹ-] *in* LC, 84)
new-made 'nju‚meɪ̆d
new-married 'nju‚mæ.ɹd
new-repaired 'njuɹɪ‚pɛ˞ʹd
news 'njuz
news-crammed 'njuz'kɹæmd [‚-ʹ-]
new-shed 'nju‚ʃed
newsmonger, -s 'njuzmʌŋɡ˞, -z
new-sprung 'nju‚spɹʌŋ
newt, -s 'njut, -s
new-ta'en 'nju‚teɪ̆n
new-transformed 'njutɹæns‚fɔ˞md
  [-ɹan-] ([-‚fɔ˞‚mɹd] *in* TIT, II.ii.64)
new-trothed ‚nju'tɹoʊ̆ðɪd
next 'nekst
nibb|le, -les, -ling, -led, -ler/s 'nɪb|ḷ, -ḷz,
  -lɪŋ [-ḷɪŋ], -ḷd, -lə˞/z [-ḷə˞/z]
Nicander (PER) naɪ̆'kænd˞
Nicanor (COR) naɪ̆'keɪ̆n˞ [nɪ'k-]
nice, -r, -st, -ly, -ness 'naɪ̆s, -ə˞, -ɪst, -lɪ,
  -nɪs
nicet|y, -ies 'naɪ̆sɹt|ɪ, -ɪz
Nicholas (HVIII, TS) 'nɪkələs, -kləs
nick (N.), -s, -ing, -ed 'nɪk, -s, -ɪŋ, -t
nicknam|e, -es, -ing, -ed 'nɪkneɪ̆m, -z, -ɪŋ,
  -d
niece, -s 'nis, -ɪz
niggard, -s, -ing 'nɪɡə˞d, -z, -ɪŋ
niggardl|y, -iness 'nɪɡə˞dl|ɪ, -ɪnɪs
nigh 'naɪ̆
night (N.), -s 'naɪ̆t, -s
  Note.—In MSND, IV.i.95*—when*
  following the First Quarto version—
  'night's' must be disyllabic in order to
  meet the metrical demands of the verse
  line. It stands for the loosely contracted
  possessive form of 'night his' and is
  pronounced ['naɪ̆tɪz] *or even* ['naɪ̆tɦɪz]
  (cf. TC, IV.v.254, TN, III.iii.26, 3HVI,
  V.vi.89, *and see Abbott's* A Shakespearian Grammar, *§ 217, and* The Oxford
  Companion to the English Language,
  § 'Apostrophe—Possession'). The same
  case could be made for 'moon's' in
  MSND, II.i.7 *(see Note for* **month** *and*
  whale*)*

night-bird, -s 'naɪ̆t‚bɜ˞d, -z
night-brawler, -s 'naɪ̆t‚bɹɔlə˞, -z
night-cap, -s 'naɪ̆t‚kæp, -s
night-crow, -s 'naɪ̆t‚kɹoʊ̆, -z
night-dog, -s 'naɪ̆t‚dɒɡ, -z
nighted 'naɪ̆tɪd
night-fl|y, -ies 'naɪ̆t‚fl|aɪ̆, -aɪ̆z
night(-)gown, -s 'naɪ̆tɡɑʊ̆n, -z
nightingale, -s 'naɪ̆tn̩ɡeɪ̆l ['naɪ̆ɾɪ̩ŋɡeɪ̆l], -z
nightly 'naɪ̆tlɪ
nightmar|e, -es, -ish 'naɪ̆tmɛ˞, -z, -ɹɪʃ
night-oblations 'naɪ̆t o‚bleɪ̆ʃn̩z
night-owl, -s 'naɪ̆tɑʊ̆l, -z
night-raven, -s 'naɪ̆t‚ɹeɪ̆vn̩ [-vən], -z
night-rest 'naɪ̆t‚ɹest
night-shriek, -s 'naɪ̆t‚ʃɹik, -s
night-tripping 'naɪ̆t‚tɹɪpɪŋ
night-walk|ing, -er/s 'naɪ̆t‚wɔk|ɪŋ, -ə˞/z
night-wanderers 'naɪ̆t‚wɑndə‚ɹə˞z
night-wandering 'naɪ̆t‚wɑndə‚ɹɪŋ
Nightwork, Jane (2HIV) 'dʒeɪ̆n
  'naɪ̆twə˞k
Nightwork, Robin (2HIV) 'ɹɒbɪn
  'naɪ̆twə˞k
nil 'nɪl
Nile (AC, CYM) 'naɪ̆l
nill (*archaic for 'will not'*) 'nɪl
Nilus (AC, TIT) 'naɪ̆ləs
Nim *or* **Nym** (HV, MWW) 'nɪm
nimb|le, -ler, -lest, -ly, -leness 'nɪmb|ḷ,
  -ḷə˞ [-lə˞], -ḷɪst [-lɪst], -ḷɪ [-lɪ], -ḷnɪs
nimble-footed 'nɪmbḷ‚fʊtɪd
nimble-pinioned 'nɪmbḷ‚pɪnjənd
nine-men's-morris 'naɪ̆n'menz'mɒɹɪs
Nine Worthies, The (2HIV, LLL) ‚ðə
  'naɪ̆n 'wɜ˞ðɪz
Ninny (*corruption of* **Ninus** *in* MSND)
  'nɪnɪ
ninn|y, -ies 'nɪn|ɪ, -ɪz
Ninus (MSND) 'naɪ̆nəs
Niobe (HAM, TC), -s 'naɪ̆obɪ, -z
nip, -s, -ping, -ped, -per/s 'nɪp, -s, -ɪŋ, -t,
  -ə˞/z
nit, -s 'nɪt, -s
nitty 'nɪɾɪ
no, -es 'noʊ̆, -z
Noah (COM, TN) 'noʊ̆ə
nob, -s 'nɒb, -z
nobilit|y, -ies noʊ̆'bɪlɪt|ɪ, -ɪz

nob|le, -les, -ler, -lest, -ly, -leness 'noŭb|l̩,
-l̩z, -lə-, -lɪst, -lɪ, -l̩nɪs
noble|man, -men 'noŭbl̩|mən, -mən
noble-minded, -ness 'noŭbl̩ˌmaɪndɪd
[ˌ--'--], -nɪs
noblesse no'bles
nobod|y (N.), -ies 'noŭbəd|ɪ ['noŭˌbɒd|ɪ],
-ɪz
no-come ˌnoŭ'kʌm ['-ˌ-]
nod, -s, -ding, -ded 'nɒd, -z, -ɪŋ, -ɪd
noddle, -s 'nɒdl̩, -z
nodd|y, -ies 'nɒd|ɪ, -ɪz
Note.—*In TGV, I.i.109, the humor
depends (or once depended) on this
word being a homophone of the words
'Nod—ay,' as indeed they were
homophonic in S.'s day. Because the
exchange (lines 108–119) hardly makes
sense to us now, the rhyme throughout is
typically forsaken and the pronunciation
given above, i.e.,* ['nɒdɪ] *is probably best*
'nointed (*from* **anointed**) 'nɔɪntɪd
nois|e, -es, -ing, -ed 'nɔɪz, -ɪz, -ɪŋ, -d
noiseless, -ly, -ness 'nɔɪzlɪs, -lɪ, -nɪs
noisemaker, -s 'nɔɪzmeɪkə-, -z
noisome, -ly, -ness 'nɔɪsəm, -lɪ, -nɪs
nole 'noŭl
nominat|e, -es, -ing, -ed, -or/s 'nɒmɪneɪt,
-s, -ɪŋ, -ɪd, -ə-/z
nonage 'nɒnɪdʒ ['noŭnɪdʒ]
nonce 'nɒns
non-come 'nɒn'kʌm [-'kɒm]
Note.—*This is Dogberry's illiterate coinage in ADO, III.v.58, apparently to
stand for (L.) 'non compos'—short for
'of an unsound mind.'*
nonino, nonneno, *or* **nonny-no** (*meaningless refrain in some songs*) ˌnɒnɪ'noŭ
non nobis (*L.*) (HV, IV.viii.124) non
'nobɪs
nonny *or* **nony** 'nɒnɪ
nonpareil ˌnɒnpə'ɹel ['---]
non-payment ˌnɒn'peɪmənt
non-performance ˌnɒnpə-'fɔ˞-məns

non-regardance ˌnɒnɹɪ'gɑ˞-dn̩s ['--'--]
nonsuit, -s, -ing, -ed ˌnɒn'sjut, -s, -ɪŋ, -ɪd
nook, -s 'nʊk, -s
nook-shotten 'nʊkˌʃɒtn̩
noon, -s 'nun, -z
noon(-)day 'nundeɪ
no(-)one 'noŭwʌn (*strong form*), 'noŭən
(*weak form*)
noon(-)tide 'nuntaɪd
Norbery *or* **Norbury, Sir John** (RII) ˌs˞-
'dʒɒn 'nɔ˞-bə-ɹɪ
Norfolk (3HVI) 'nɔ˞-fək
Norfolk, Duke of (2HIV, *3HVI, HVIII,*
RII, *RIII*) 'djuk əv 'nɔ˞-fək
Norman (HAM, HV, 2HVI)**, -s** 'nɔ˞-mən,
-z
Normandy (HAM, 2HVI, LLL)
'nɔ˞-məndɪ
nor's (*contr. of* **nor his**) 'nɔ˞-z
Northampton (3HVI, *HVIII*, RIII)
nɔ˞-'θæmptən [nɔ˞-'θfiæmptən]
Northamptonshire (KJ) nɔ˞-'θæmptənʃə-
[-ʃɪ˞-]
north-east ˌnɔ˞-'θist (*when att. or
comparative,* ['--])
North Gate (1HVI, TGV) 'nɔ˞-θ 'geɪt
['-ˌ-]
North Star 'nɔ˞-θ 'stɑ˞-
Northumberland (1HIV, *2HIV, 3HVI,
HVIII, RII,* RIII)**, -s** nɔ˞-'θʌmbə-lənd, -z
Northumberland, Lady (*2HIV,* HV)
'leɪdɪ nɔ˞-'θʌmbə-lənd
northward, -s, -ly 'nɔ˞-θwə-d, -z, -lɪ
Norway (HAM, MAC)**, -s** 'nɔ˞-weɪ, -z
Norweyan (MAC) nɔ˞-'weɪən
nos|e, -es, -ing, -ed 'noŭz, -ɪz, -ɪŋ, -d
nosegay, -s 'noŭzgeɪ, -z
noseless 'noŭzlɪs
nose-painting 'noŭzpeɪntɪŋ
not 'nɒt
not-appearance ˌnɒtə'pɪ˞-ɹəns
notar|y, -ies 'noŭʃəɹ|ɪ, -ɪz
notation, -s noŭ'teɪʃn̩, -z
notch, -es, -ing, -ed 'nɒtʃ, -ɪz, -ɪŋ, -t

i wǝ ɪ city ɪ hit e let ɛ debut æ can a pass ɝ bird ʌ hut ə again ɚ supper u you
ʊ should o obey ɔ awl ɒ cop ɑ father eɪ paid aɪ high oŭ go ɔɪ voice aŭ found ɪ˞ ear
ɛ˞ air ʊ˞ poor ɔ˞ fork ɑ˞ park aɪ˞ fire aŭ˞ hour b boy p pit d dog t top g got
k kid h how fi behave dʒ jot tʃ chew z zany s soft v vat f fat ʒ treasure ʃ ship ð the
θ thin m man n no ŋ hang l lip j yes w won ʍ whew ɹ rigger, aiɾy ɾ matter

not|e, -es, -ing, -ed/ly 'noŏt, -s, -ɪŋ, -ɪd/lɨ
note(-)book, -s 'noŏtbʊk, -s
noteworth|y, -iness 'noŏt͵wɜˑð|ɨ, -ɨnɪs
not-fearing ͵nɒt'fɪɚˑɹɪŋ
nothing, -s, -ness 'nʌθɪŋ, -z, -nɪs

Note.—There can be little doubt that in S.'s day the word 'nothing' did, or could, rhyme with 'a-doting' (as it does in Sonn. 20.10,12), and was, or could be for the sake of punning, homophonic with 'noting' (as is the case in WT, IV.iv.613–615; ADO, II.iii.54–57; and arguably in 1HIV, III.i.123–128; TEM, III.ii.143; TIM, III.i.21). Without this understanding, the modern reader or actor—and thus, the modern audience—loses both the meaning and the wit of these passages. There is little to do nowadays to reconcile this conundrum except to perhaps offer up dialectal corruptions of 'nothing' e.g., ['noːθɪŋ, 'noːtn̩], etc. (cf. Kökeritz's Shakespeare's Pronunciation, pp. 132, 233, 320). In other instances, the pronunciation may be more literal, explicitly akin to 'no thing,' a sexual reference to that which a female possesses (lack of a penis), in contrast to that which a male possesses. In HAM, III.ii.110–120, Hamlet makes bawdy allusions to sexual organs ('lie in your lap,' 'head upon lap,' 'country matters'), and when Ophelia says "I think nothing, my lord," Hamlet turns her meaning, saying, "That's a fair thought to lie between maids' legs." She asks, "What is, my lord?" and Hamlet's response of, "Nothing" might reasonably precipitate the literal pronunciation of the words 'no thing.' (Cf. Frankie Rubenstein's A Dictionary of Shakespeare's Sexual Puns and their Significance, § "Nothing" p. 172; and The Arden Shakespeare, line annotation for HAM, III.ii.119, Harold Jenkins, editor, 1982)

nothing-gift 'nʌθɪŋ͵gɪft
notic|e, -es, -ing, -ed 'noŏɾɪs, -ɪz, -ɪŋ, -t
noticeab|le, -ly 'noŏɾɪsəb|l̩, -lɨ
notion, -s 'noŏʃn̩, -z

notorious, -ly, -ness no'tɔɹɪəs, -lɨ, -nɪs
not-pated 'nɒt͵peĭtɪd [͵-ˈ--]
Notre très cher fils Henri, Roi d'Angleterre, Heritiér de France (Fr.) (HV, V.ii.333) notʁ 'tʁɛ ʃɛʁ fis ɑ̃'ʁi ʁwɑ dɑ̃glɪ'tɛʁ eʁitɪ'ɛʁ dʊ 'fʁɑ̃s
notwithstanding ͵nɒtwɪð'stændɪŋ
nought or naught, -s 'nɔt, -s
noun, -s 'naŏn, -z
nourish, -es, -ing, -ed, -er/s, -ment 'nʌɹɪʃ, -ɪz, -ɪŋ, -t, -ɚ/z, -mənt
novel, -s 'nɒvl̩, -z
novelist, -s 'nɒvəlɪst, -s
novelt|y, -ies 'nɒvl̩t|ɨ, -ɨz
no-verbs 'noŏ͵vɜˑbz
novice, -s 'nɒvɪs, -ɪz
novi hominem tanquam te (L.) (LLL, V.i.9) 'novɨ '(h)omɪnɛm 'tɑnkwɑm 'tɛ
novum or novem (L.) (LLL, V.ii.544) 'novum or 'novɛm
now 'naŏ
now(-)a(-)days 'naŏə͵deĭz
nowhere 'noŏ͵ʍɛɚˑ
noyance, -s 'nɔĭəns, -ɪz
null 'nʌl
nullit|y, -ies 'nʌlɪt|ɨ, -ɨz
Numa (COR) 'njumə
numb, -s, -ing, -ed, -ly, -ness 'nʌm, -z, -ɪŋ, -d, -lɨ, -nɪs
numb-cold 'nʌm͵koŭld
number, -s, -ing, -ed; -less 'nʌmbɚ, -z, -ɹɪŋ, -d; -lɪs
Numbers (HV) 'nʌmbɚz
nuncio, -s 'nʌnsɪoŭ ['nʊn-, -sjoŭ], -z
nuncle, -s 'nʌŋkl̩, -z
nunner|y, -ies 'nʌnəɹ|ɨ, -ɨz
nuntio or nuncio (L.) (TN, I.iv.28) 'nʊntɪo or 'nʊnsɪo
nuptial, -s 'nʌpʃl̩, -z
nurs|e (N.) (RJ, TIT), -es, -ing, -ed 'nɜˑs, -ɪz, -ɪŋ, -t
nurse-like 'nɜˑs͵laĭk
nursh-a (from 'nurse') 'nɜˑʃə (see Note for varld)
nut, -s 'nʌt, -s
nutcracker, -s 'nʌt͵kɹækɚ, -z
nut(-)hook, -s 'nʌtfʊk, -s
nutmeg, -s 'nʌtmeg, -z
nutrient 'njutɹɪənt

nutriment 'njutɹɪmənt
nutshell, -s 'nʌt.ʃel, -z
nutty 'nʌɾɨ
nuzzl|e, -es, -ing, -ed, -er/s 'nʌzl̩, -z, -ɪŋ, -d, -ə·/z
nyas (*emendation of First Folio's* **neece**), **niess, niësse,** *or* **niaise** 'naɪəs
Nym *or* **Nim** (*HV, MWW*) 'nɪm
nymph (N.) (TEM), **-s, -al** 'nɪmf, -s, -əl
nymph-like 'nɪmf.laɪk

Oo

O (*the letter*), **-'s** 'oŭ, -z
o (O) (*the form, or shape*), **-es** 'oŭ, -z
O (*exclamation*) 'oŭ
Note.—*Appearing throughout S., this word is perhaps best thought of as a vocal expulsion which the letter 'O' attempts to represent. In instances of grief, anguish, temper, etc., any nondescript vocal utterance absorbing the value of one beat is likely to serve. In some cases, however, the exclamation is a double entendre, insinuating the 'nought,' or the vagina, e.g.,* LEAR, IV.vi.266; CYM, II.iv.169. *In such cases, the pronunciation* ['oŭ] *is beneficial and thus should be (more or less) retained*
o' (*from* **of**) 'ə
o' (*from* **on**) 'ɒ
oaf, -s; -ish/ly 'oŭf, -s; -ɪʃ/lɨ
oak, -s 'oŭk, -s
oak-cleaving 'oŭk.klivɪŋ
oaken 'oŭkən
oakum 'oŭkəm
oar, -s, -ing, -ed 'ɔə·, -z, -ɹɪŋ, -d
oarlock, -s 'ɔə·lɒk, -s
oar, -s, -ing, -ed 'ɔə·, -z, -ɹɪŋ, -d
oars|man, -men 'ɔə·z|mən, -mən
oas|is, -es o'eĭs|ɪs, -iz

oast, -s 'oŭst, -s
oat, -s 'oŭt, -s
oatcake, -s 'oŭtkeĭk, -s
Oatcake *or* **Otecake, Hugh** (ADO) 'hju 'oŭtkeĭk
oaten 'oŭtn̩
oa|th, -ths 'oŭ|θ, -ðz [-θs]
oathable 'oŭθəbl̩
oatmeal 'oŭtmil
ob. (*L.*) (*abbreviation for 'obolus'*) 'ɒbolʊs (*sing.*) 'ɒbolaĭ (*pl.*)
Note.—*This abbreviation for an ancient coin worth about one-half of a denarius (cf.* **d.***) became the common abbreviation in England for one halfpenny (cf.* **half-penny***), and is so said, i.e.,* ['heĭpn̩ɨ, 'hafpenɨ] *when encountered in S.'s plays, e.g.,* 1HIV, II.iv.532
Obadiah ˌoŭbə'daĭə
obbliga|to, -tos *or* **-ti** ˌɒblɪ'gɑ|toŭ, -toŭz, -ti
obduracy 'ɒbdjuɹəsɨ
obdurate, -ly, -ness 'ɒbdjuɹɪt [ɒb'djoŭ·ɹɪt], -lɨ, -nɪs
Note.—[ɒb'djoŭ·ɹɪt] *in* 2HVI, IV.vii.110; LUC, 429; MV, IV.i.8; RIII, I.iii.347; TIT, II.ii.160; VA, 199; (*and arguably in* RIII, III.i.39)
obduration ˌɒbdjʊ'ɹeĭʃn̩
obeah 'oŭbɪə
obedien|ce, -t/ly o'bidɪən|s [ə'b-, -djə-], -t/lɨ
o'Bedlam, Tom (LEAR) 'tɒm ə'bedləm
obeisance, -s o'beĭsəns [o'bis-], -ɪz
Note.—*This word appears in* TS, Ind.i.106, *which is perhaps a defective line of verse (only four-and-a-half feet). If the line is interpreted as being regular (five feet), then either one of two unusual things happen to 'obeisance': shifting the primary stress away from the second syllable, i.e.,* ['--,-, ,--'-], *or—which is more likely—the line adopts an epic caesura, and 'obeisance' then becomes*

---

i wᴇ ɪ city ɪ hit e lᴇt ɛ dᴇbut æ can a pass ɝ bird ʌ hut ə again ə· suppᴇr u you
ʊ should ɔ awl ɒ cop ɑ fathᴇr eĭ paid aĭ high oŭ go ɔĭ voice aŭ found ɪɚ· ear
ɛɚ· air ʊɚ· poor ɔɚ· fork ɑɚ· park aĭɚ· fire aŭɚ· hour b boy p pit d dog t top g got
k kid h how fi behave dʒ jot tʃ chew z zany s soft v vat f fat ʒ treasure ʃ ship ð the
θ thin m man n no ŋ hang l lip j yes w won ʍ whew ɹ rigger, airy ɟ matter

somewhat elongated, i.e., [o'beĭəsəns]
(cf. E. A. Abbott's A Shakespearian Grammar, *§§ 475, 479, 484; and see* **brave***)*

obelisk, -s 'ɒbəlɪsk, -s

Oberon (*MSND*) 'oŏbə-ɹɒn

obey, -s, -ing, -ed, -er/s o'beĭ, -z, -ɪŋ, -d, -ə-/z

object (*s.*), **-s** 'ɒbdʒɪkt [-dʒekt], -s

object (*v.*), **-s, -ing, -ed, -or/s** əb'dʒekt, -s, -ɪŋ, -ɪd, -ə-/z

objection, -s əb'dʒekʃn, -z

objectionab|le, -ly əb'dʒekʃnəb|ḷ, -łɪ

objective, -s; -ly, -ness əb'dʒektɪv, -z; -łɪ, -nɪs

objectivity ,ɒbdʒek'tɪvɪtɪ

Obidicut (LEAR) o'bɪdɪkət

oblate (*s.*), **-s** 'ɒbleĭt, -s

oblate (*adj.*) 'ɒbleĭt [ɒ'bleĭt, o'b-]

oblation, -s o'bleĭʃn, -z

obligat|e, -es, -ing, -ed 'ɒblɪgeĭt, -s, -ɪŋ, -ɪd

obligation, -s ,ɒblɪ'geĭʃn, -z

oblig|e, -es, -ing, -ed ə'blaĭdʒ, -ɪz, -ɪŋ, -d

oblique, -ly, -ness o'blik, -łɪ, -nɪs

obliquy 'ɒblɪkwɪ
Note.—This word in TIM, IV.iii.18 *is often emended to 'oblique.' The* OED *cites this word merely as an alt. form of 'obloquy,' which would cause the meaning in this particular instance to stray in the wrong direction. H. J. Oliver (editor,* The Arden Shakespeare, *1959) is in favor of retaining 'obliquy' because, "Obliquity" seems to be the word required here; perhaps 'obliquy' is Shakespeare's own version of it."*

oblivion ə'blɪvɪən

oblivious, -ly, -ness ə'blɪvɪəs, -łɪ, -nɪs

oblong, -s 'ɒblɒŋ, -z

obloquy 'ɒblɪkwɪ

obscene, -ly, -ness ɒb'sin [əb-], -łɪ, -nɪs

obscur|e (*adj.*), **-er, -est, -ely, -eness** əb'skjŏə- [ɒb'skjŏə-], -ɹə-, -ɹɪst, -łɪ, -nɪs
Note.—Stressed on the first syllable ['ɒbskjŏə-] *in* HAM, IV.v.210; MAC, II.iii.58; MV, II.vii.51; RII, III.iii.154; TIT, II.ii.77. *Cf.* **secure** *(adj.)*

obscur|e (*v.*), **-es, -ing, -ed** əb'skjŏə- [ɒb'skjŏə-], -z, -ɹɪŋ, -d

obsequ|y, -ies 'ɒbsɪkw|ɪ,-ɪz

obsequious, -ly, -ness əb'sikwɪəs [ɒb-], -łɪ, -nɪs

observan|ce, -ces, -cy əb'zɜ-vn̩s, -sɪz, -sɪ

observant, -s; -ly əb'zɜ-vn̩t, -s; -łɪ

observation, -s ,ɒbzə-'veĭʃn, -z

observ|e, -es, -ing/ly, -ed, -er/s əb'zɜ-v, -z, -ɪŋ/łɪ, -d, -ə-/z

obsess, -es, -ing, -ed əb'ses [ɒb's-], -ɪz, -ɪŋ, -t

obsession, -s əb'seʃn [ɒb's-], -z

obsessive, -ly, -ness əb'sesɪv [ɒb's-], -łɪ, -nɪs

obsolete, -ly, -ness ,ɒbsə'lit ['---], -łɪ, -nɪs

obsque (absque) hoc nihil est (*L.*) (2HIV, V.v.28) 'ɒbskwɛ ('ɑbskwɛ) 'hok 'nifiil 'ɛst

obstacle, -s 'ɒbstəkḷ, -z

obstinac|y, -ies 'ɒbstɪnəs|ɪ, -ɪz

obstinate, -ly, -ness 'ɒbstɪnɪt, -łɪ, -nɪs

obstruct, -s, -ing, -ed əb'stɹʌkt [-b'z̩t-], -s, -ɪŋ, -ɪd

obstruction, -s əb'stɹʌkʃn [-b'z̩t-], -z

obstructive, -ly, -ness əb'stɹʌktɪv, -łɪ, -nɪs

obtain, -s, -ing, -ed; -able əb'teĭn, -z, -ɪŋ, -d; -əbḷ

occasion, -s, -ing, -ed ə'keĭʒn̩, -z, -ɪŋ, -d

occasional, -ly ə'keĭʒnḷ, -ɪ

occident (O.) 'ɒksɪdənt [-dent]

occidental ,ɒksɪ'dentəl [-tḷ]

occult, -ly, -ness ə'kʌlt [ɒ'k-], -łɪ, -nɪs

occult, -s, -ing, -ed ə'kʌlt [ɒ'k-], -s, -ɪŋ, -ɪd

occupation, -s ,ɒkjŏ'peĭʃn, -z

occup|y, -ies, -ying, -ied, -ier/s 'ɒkjŏp|aĭ, -aĭz, -aĭɪŋ, -aĭd, -aĭə-/z

occur, -s, -ring, -red ə'kɜ-, -z, -ɹɪŋ, -d

occurrence, -s ə'kʌɹəns, -ɪz

occurrent, -s ə'kʌɹənt, -s

ocean, -s 'oŏʃn̩, -z

oceanic ,oŏʃɪ'ænɪk

octagon, -s 'ɒktəgɒn, -z

Octavia (AC) ɒk'teĭvɪə, -vjə

Octavius (AC, JUL) ɒk'teĭvɪəs, -vjəs

October, -s ɒk'toŏbə-, -z

ocular, -ly 'ɒkjŏlə-, -łɪ

odd, -er, -est, -ly, -ness 'ɒd, -ə-, -ɪst, -łɪ, -nɪs

odd-conceited 'ɒdkən,sitɪd

odd-even 'ɒd'ivn̩

oddit|y, -ies 'ɒdɪt|ɨ, -ɨz
odds 'ɒdz
ode, -s 'oŭd, -z
O Dieu vivant (Fr.) (HV, III.v.5) o dφ vivã
odious, -ly, -ness 'oŭdɪəs, -lɨ, -nɪs
o'door (*from* of door) ə'dɔɚ
odor, -s, -ed, -less 'oŭdəˑ, -z, -d, -lɪs
odoriferous, -ly, -ness ˌoŭdə'ɹɪfəˑɹəs, -lɨ, -nɪs
odorous, -ly, -ness 'oŭdəɹəs, -lɨ, -nɪs
'od's *or* 'Od's (*for* 'God's' *in oaths*) 'ɒdz
'od's lifelings (*diminutive plural of the contr.* by God's life) 'ɒdz 'laɪflɪŋz
oeillades *or* œillades 'iljədz, 'ɛlɪədz
Note.—S. never actually uses this word (meaning 'amorous glances'). However, the forms 'aliads,' 'eliads,' and 'illiads' appear in King Lear and The Merry Wives of Windsor—editors typically emending them to reflect the more regular Fr. form. S.'s spellings more than likely suggest a more anglicized (or 'naturalized' as the OED *puts it) pronunciation; thus the alternative pronunciations proffered above*
o'er (*from* over) 'ɔɚ
o'erbear, -ing ɔɚ'bɛɚ, -ɹɪŋ
o'erblows ɔɚ'bloŭz
o'erborne ɔɚ'bɔɚn
o'ercast ɔɚ'kast
o'er-changes ɔɚ'tʃeɪndʒɪz
o'er-charged ɔɚ'tʃɑɚdʒd
o'er-cloyed ɔɚ'klɔɪd
o'ercome ɔɚ'kʌm
o'er-count ɔɚ'kaŭnt
o'er-covered ɔɚ'kʌvəˑd
o'er(-)crows ɔɚ'kɹoŭz
o'erdoing ɔɚ'duɪŋ
o'er-dusted ɔɚ'dʌstɪd
o'er-dyed ɔɚ'daɪd (*when att.,* ['--])
o'er-eaten ɔɚ'itn̩ (*when att.,* ['---'])
o'er-fed ɔɚ'fed (*when att.,* ['--'])
o'er-flourished ɔɚ'flʌɹɪʃt
o'erflow, -s, -ing -ed ɔɚ'floŭ, -z, -ɪŋ, -d

o'er-fraught ɔɚ'fɹɔt
o'er-galled ɔɚ'gɔld
o'er-glanced ɔɚ'glanst
o'er-great ɔɚ'gɹeɪt (*arguably* ['-,-] *in* HVIII, I.i.222)
o'er-green ɔɚ'gɹin
o'er-grown ɔɚ'gɹoŭn (['-,-] *in* MEAS, I.iii.22)
o'erheard ɔɚ'hɝd
o'er-joyed ɔɚ'dʒɔɪd
o'er-labored ɔɚ'leɪbəˑd
o'er|leap, -leaps, -leaping, -leaped, -leapt ɔɚ'lip, -lips, -lipɪŋ, -lept [-'lipt], -lept
o'er-leavens ɔɚ'levn̩z
o'erlook, -ed ɔɚ'lŭk, -t
o'er-looking ɔɚ'lŭkɪŋ
o'er-master, -s, -ing, -ed ɔɚ'mastəˑ, -z, -ɹɪŋ, -d
o'er-matched ɔɚ'mætʃt
o'ermount ɔɚ'maŭnt
o'er-night ɔɚ'naɪt ['--]
o'erpaid ɔɚ'peɪd
o'erparted ɔɚ'pɑɚtɪd
o'erpast ɔɚ'past
o'erpeer ɔɚ'pɪɚ
o'erperch ɔɚ'pɝtʃ
o'er-picturing ɔɚ'pɪktʃəˑɹɪŋ
o'erposting ɔɚ'poŭstɪŋ
o'erpower, -s, -ing/ly, -ed ɔɚ'paŭəˑ, -z, -ɹɪŋ/lɨ, -d
o'er(-)pressed ɔɚ'pɹest (*arguably* ['-,-] *in* COR, II.ii.93 *and* PER, III.ii.86)
o'er-prized ɔɚ'pɹaɪzd
o'er-rank ɔɚ'ɹæŋk (*when att.,* ['-,-])
o'er-rate ɔɚ'ɹeɪt
o'er-raught ɔɚ'ɹɔt
o'erreach, -es, -ing ɔɚ'ɹitʃ, -ɪz, -ɪŋ
o'er-read (*p.t.*) ɔɚ'ɹed
o'er-rule, -d ɔɚ'ɹul, -d
o'er(-)run ɔɚ'ɹʌn
o'erset ɔɚ'set
o'ershade, -s ɔɚ'ʃeɪd, -z
o'ershine ɔɚ'ʃaɪn

---

i we ɨ city ɪ hit e let ɛ debut æ can a pass ɝ bird ʌ hut ə again ɚ supper u you
ʊ should o obey ɔ awl ɒ cop ɑ father eɪ paid aɪ high oŭ go ɔɪ voice aŭ found ɪɚ ear
ɛɚ air ʊɚ poor ɔɚ fork ɑɚ park aɪɚ fire aŭɚ hour b boy p pit d dog t top g got
k kid h how fi behave dʒ jot tʃ chew z zany s soft v vat f fat ʒ treasure ʃ ship ð the
θ thin m man n no ŋ hang l lip j yes w won ʍ whew ɹ rigger, airy ɾ matter

o'ershowered ɔɚ-'ʃɑŏɚ-d
o'er-sized ɔɚ-'saĭzd
o'erskip ɔɚ-'skɪp
o'erslip, -s ɔɚ-'slɪp, -s
o'er-snowed ɔɚ-'snoŏd
o'erspent ɔɚ-'spent
o'er-spreads ɔɚ-'spɹedz
o'erstare ɔɚ-'stɛɚ-
o'erstrawed ɔɚ-'stɹɔd
o'erstunk ɔɚ-'stʌŋk
o'ersway, -s ɔɚ-'sweĭ, -z
o'erswell ɔɚ-'swel
o'erta'en ɔɚ-'teĭn
o'ertake ɔɚ-'teĭk
o'er-teemed ɔɚ-'timd
o'erthrow ɔɚ-'θɹoŏ (['-,-] *in* CYM,
   III.vi.20; WT, IV.i.8)
o'ertook ɔɚ-'tʊk
o'er-top, -ping ɔɚ-'tɒp, -ɪŋ
o'ertrip ɔɚ-'tɹɪp
o'erturn ɔɚ-'tɝ-n
o'ervalues ɔɚ-'væljuz
o'er-walk ɔɚ-'wɔk
o'er-watched ɔɚ-'wɒtʃt
o'erween, -s ɔɚ-'win, -z
o'erweigh, -s ɔɚ-'weĭ, -z
o'erwhelm, -ing ɔɚ-'ʍelm (['-,-] *in* WT,
   IV.i.9), -ɪŋ
o'er-worn ɔɚ-'wɔɚ-n (['-,-] *in* RII, I.i.81)
o'er-wrested ɔɚ-'ɹestɪd
o'er-wrestling ɔɚ-'ɹeslɪŋ [-slɪŋ]
of 'ɒv (*strong form*), 'əv (*weak form*)
off 'ɒf
offal 'ɒfl̩ ['ɔfl̩]
off-cap, -s, -ping, -ped 'ɒf,kæp, -s, -ɪŋ, -t
offend, -s, -ing, -ed, -er/s o'fend, -z, -ɪŋ,
   -ɪd, -ɚ/z
offendress, -es o'fendɹɪs [ə'f-], -ɪz
offense, -s, -less; -ful o'fens [ə'f-], -ɪz,
   -lɪs; -fʊl
off|er, -ers, -ering/s, -ered, -erer/s 'ɒf|ɚ,
   -ɚz, -əɹɪŋ/z, -ɚd, -əɹɚ/z
office, -s 'ɒfɪs, -ɪz
office-badge 'ɒfɪs,bædʒ
officer (O.), -s 'ɒfɪsɚ, -z
officers-at-arms 'ɒfɪsɚzæɹɑɚ-mz [-zəɹ-]
officious, -ly, -ness o'fɪʃəs [ə'f-], -lɪ, -nɪs
offing, -s 'ɒfɪŋ, -z
offspring, -s 'ɒfspɹɪŋ, -z

of's (*contr. of* of his) 'əvz (*weak form*)
oft 'ɒft
often, -er, -times 'ɒfn̩ [-fən], -ɚ, -taĭmz
oft-times 'ɒft,taĭmz
oh 'oŏ
   Note.—Technically speaking, this is a
   var. spelling of 'O' and the pronuncia-
   tion given above is a conservative one.
   If the moment in which it is uttered is
   emotionally charged (in instances of
   grief, anguish, temper, etc.), then any
   nondescript vocal utterance absorbing
   the value of one beat is likely to serve.
   Cf. Note for O *(exclamation)*
oil, -s, -ing, -ed, -er/s 'ɔĭl, -z, -ɪŋ, -d,
   -ɚ/z
oil-dried 'ɔĭl,dɹaĭd
oil|y, -ier, -iest, -iness 'ɔĭl|ɪ, -ɪɚ, -ɪɪst,
   -ɪnɪs
old, -er, -est, -ness 'oŏld, -ɚ, -ɪst, -nɪs
'old (*obsolete form or dialectal var. of*
   wold; *meaning 'upland plain'*) 'oŏld
Old(-)castle (2HIV) 'oŏld,kasl̩
olden 'oŏldən
old-faced 'oŏld,feĭst
Old Man (*LEAR*) 'oŏld 'mæn
olive, -s 'ɒlɪv, -z
olivebranch, -es 'ɒlɪvbɹantʃ, -ɪz
Oliver (*AYLI*, 1HVI), -s 'ɒlɪvɚ, -z
Olivia (*TN*) o'lɪvɪə, -vjə
Olympian (3HVI, TC) o'lɪmpɪən, -pjən
Olympus (COR, HAM, JUL, OTH, TC,
   TIT) o'lɪmpəs
Olympus-high o'lɪmpəs,haĭ
'oman (*from 'woman'*) 'ʊmən (*see* 'orld)
   Note.— 'omans' in MWW, III.iii.205 *is*
   Evans' way of saying 'woman' (follow-
   ing his dialectal penchant—despite this
   erroneous formation—for overpluraliz-
   ing), and is simply pronounced ['ʊmənz]
omen, -s, -ing, -ed 'oŏmən, -z, -ɪŋ, -d
ominous, -ly, -ness 'ɒmɪnəs, -lɪ, -nɪs
omission, -s o'mɪʃn̩, -z
omit, -s, -ting, -ted o'mɪt, -s, -ɪŋ, -ɪd
omittance o'mɪtn̩s [-təns]
omne bene (*L.*) (LLL, IV.ii.31) 'omnɛ
   'bɛnɛ
omnipoten|ce, -t/ly ɒm'nɪpətən|s, -t/lɪ
on 'ɒn

once 'wʌns

one, -s 'wʌn, -z

one-and-twenty ˌwʌnənd'twentɪ

onion, -s, -y 'ʌnjən, -z, -ɪ

onion-eyed 'ʌnjən'aɪd

only 'oŭnlɪ

on's (*contr. of* **on his**) 'ɒnz

onset 'ɒnset

on't (*contr. of* **on it**) 'ɒnt

onward, -s 'ɒnwəˑd, -z

onyers *or* **oneyers** 'wʌnjəˑz, 'oŭnɪəˑz,
ˌoŭen'aĭəˑz, o'enjəˑz

Note.—This word, appearing in 1HIV,
*II.i.75, is somewhat of a mystery. The
pronunciations proffered above are
therefore entirely conjectural, and are in
no particular order of preference.
Editors have surmised several different
meanings and origins for the word, and
have often emended it to entirely
different words to better suit their
arguments. A fairly comprehensive
discussion of this troublesome word can
be found in A. R. Humphreys' line
annotation in his edition of* 1HIV
(*The Arden Shakespeare, 1960*)

ooz|e, -es, -ing, -ed 'uz, -ɪz, -ɪŋ, -d

ooz|y, -ier, -iest, -ily, -iness 'uz|ɪ, -ɪəˑ,
-ɪɪst, -ɪlɪ, -ɪnɪs

opal, -s 'oŭpl̩, -z

opaque, -ly, -ness o'peĭk, -lɪ, -nɪs

op|e, -es, -ing, -ed 'oŭp, -s, -ɪŋ, -t

open, -s, -ing, -ed, -er/s; -ly, -ness
'oŭpən, -z, -ɪŋ, -d, -əˑ/z; -lɪ, -nɪs

open-arse, -s 'oŭpənˌɑ̃ˑs, -ɪz

open't (*contr. of* **open it**) 'oŭpənt

operance 'ɒpəˑɹəns

operant, -s 'ɒpəˑɹənt, -s

operat|e, -es, -ing, -ed, -or/s 'ɒpəˑɹeĭt, -s,
-ɪŋ, -ɪd, -əˑ/z

operation, -s ˌɒpəˑɹeĭʃn̩, -z

operational ˌɒpəˑɹeĭʃn̩l̩

operative, -s; -ly, -ness 'ɒpəˑɹətɪv ['ɒpɹə-],
-z; -lɪ, -nɪs

Ophelia (*HAM*) o'filɪə, -ljə

opin|e, -es, -ing, -ed o'paĭn, -z, -ɪŋ, -d

opinion, -s, -ed; -ated ə'pɪnjən, -z, -d;
-eĭtɪd [-eĭɟɪd]

opportune, -ly, -ness 'ɒpəˑtjun [ˌ--'-], -lɪ,
-nɪs

Note.—Stressed on the second syllable
[ɒ'pɔɝ̃ˑtjun] *in* TEM, IV.i.26; WT,
IV.iv.501

oppos|e, -es, -ing, -ed, -er/s; -able ə'poŭz,
-ɪz, -ɪŋ, -d, -əˑ/z; -əbl̩

opposeless ə'poŭzlɪs

opposite, -ly, -ness 'ɒpəzɪt, -lɪ, -nɪs

opposition, -s ˌɒpə'zɪʃn̩, -z

oppress, -es, -ing, -ed, -or/s o'pɹes, -ɪz,
-ɪŋ, -t, -əˑ/z

opprest o'pɹest

*Note.—This is simply an alt. spelling of
'oppressed,' sometimes retained by
modern editors to more fervidly express
an intended rhyme of 'rest/opprest' in*
CYM, V.iv.97, 99

opprobrious, -ly, -ness ə'pɹoŭbɹɪəs
[ɒ'pɹoŭ-], -lɪ, -nɪs

oppugn, -s, -ing, -ed, -er/s ə'pjun [ɒ'p-],
-z, -ɪŋ, -d, -əˑ/z

oppugnan|cy, -t ɒ'pʌgnən|sɪ, -t

opt, -s, -ing, -ed 'ɒpt, -s, -ɪŋ, -ɪd

option, -s 'ɒpʃn̩, -z

opulen|ce, -cy, -t 'ɒpjʊlən|s, -sɪ, -t

or 'ɔɝ̃ (*strong form*), 'əˑ (*occasional weak
form*)

oracle (**O.**), **-s** 'ɒɹəkl̩, -z

Oracle, Sir (*MV*) ˌsɔɝ̃ '(ɹ)ɒɹəkl̩

Orades (*AC*) (*Folio form of* **Orodes**, *q.v.*)
o'ɹeĭdɪz

orange, -s 'ɒɹɪndʒ, -ɪz

orange-tawny ˌɒɹɪndʒ'tɔnɪ

orange-wife 'ɒɹɪndʒˌwaĭf

orat|e, -es, -ing, -ed ɒ'ɹeĭt ['ɒɹeĭt], -s, -ɪŋ,
-ɪd

oration, -s ɒ'ɹeĭʃn̩, -z

orator (**O.**) (*TIT*) **-s** 'ɒɹɪtəˑ, -z

Note.—In TIT, IV.i.14, *the 'Orator' is*

i wȩ ɨ city ɪ hɪt e lȩt ɛ dȩbut æ cạn a pạss ɝ bird ʌ hut ə again əˑ suppȩr u yoụ
ʊ shoụld o obȩy ɔ awl ɒ cọp ɑ fạther eĭ paịd aĭ hịgh oŭ gọ ɔĭ voịce aŭ foụnd ɪɝ̃ eạr
ɛɝ̃ aịr ʊɝ̃ poọr ɔɝ̃ fọrk ɑɝ̃ pạrk aĭɝ̃ fịre aŭɝ̃ hoụr b boy p pit d dog t top g got
k kịd h họw fi behạve dʒ jot tʃ chew z zany s soft v vạt f fạt ʒ treạsure ʃ shịp ð thȩ
θ thịn m mạn n nọ ŋ hang l lịp j yȩs w wọn ʍ whȩw ɹ rịgger, aịrɣ ɣ mạtter

mentioned. This is the title of one of Cicero's treatises on rhetoric

orator|y, -ies 'ɔɹətə˞.ɹ|ɪ, -ɪz

orb, -s, -ing, -ed 'ɔ˞.b, -z, -ɪŋ, -d

orbit, -s, -ing, -ed 'ɔ˞.bɪt, -s, -ɪŋ, -ɪd

orchard, -s 'ɔ˞.tʃə˞.d, -z

'ord (*from 'word'; see* **'orld**) 'ɜ˞.d

ordain, -s, -ing, -ed, -er/s ɔ˞.'deɪn, -z, -ɪŋ, -d, -ə˞/z

ordeal, -s ɔ˞.'dil, -z

order (O.), -s, -ing, -ed; -less 'ɔ˞.də˞, -z, -ɹɪŋ, -d; -lɪs

orderl|y, -iness 'ɔ˞.də˞.l|ɪ, -ɪnɪs

ordinant 'ɔ˞.dn̩ənt

ordinarily ˌɔ˞.dn̩'ɛ˞.ɹɪlɪ ['ɔ˞.dnə˞.ɹɪlɪ]

ordinar|y, -ies 'ɔ˞.dnə˞.ɹ|ɪ, -ɪz

ordnance 'ɔ˞.dnəns

ordure 'ɔ˞.djə˞

ore, -s 'ɔ˞, -z

organ, -s 'ɔ˞.gən, -z

organ-pipe, -s 'ɔ˞.gən.paɪp, -s

orgulous, -ly, -ness 'ɔ˞.gjʊləs, -lɪ, -nɪs

orient (O.) (*adj., s.*) 'ɔɹɪənt, -ɹĭənt

orient (v.), -s, -ing, -ed 'ɔɹɪent ['ɔɹ-], -s, -ɪŋ, -ɪd

oriental, -s ˌɔɹɪ'entl̩ [ˌɔɹ-], -z

orifex 'ɔɹɪfəks [-feks]

Note.—Though not unique to S. (used by him only once, i.e., TC, V.i.150), the OED calls this word both an obsolete and erroneous form of 'orifice'

origin, -s 'ɔɹɪdʒɪn, -z

original, -s; -ly, -ness ə'ɹɪdʒɪnl̩, -z; -ɪ, -nɪs

orison, -s 'ɔɹɪzən, -z

'ork (*from 'work'*) 'ɜ˞.k

Note.—Evans (in MWW) is a Welshman, and speaks in a Welsh accent, if somewhat inconsistently. This is an example of S.'s direction to the actor (by way of semiphonetic spellings) to adopt such an accent, more or less, for the sake of wringing the most satire out of plays on words stemming from confusions with, and corruptions of, English pronunciation via the Welsh tongue

Orlando (*AYLI*) ɔ˞.'lændoʊ

'orld (*from 'world'*) 'ɜ˞.ld

Note.—Evans (in MWW) is a Welsh-

man, and speaks in a Welsh accent, if somewhat inconsistently. This is an example of S.'s direction to the actor (by way of semiphonetic spellings) to adopt such an accent, more or less, for the sake of wringing the most satire out of plays on words stemming from confusions with, and corruptions of, English pronunciation via the Welsh tongue

Orleans (CYM, *HV, 1HVI*, 2HVI, HVIII) 'ɔ˞.li̩ænz ['ɔ˞.liənz, 'ɔ˞.leɪˌɑ̃ŋ, ɔ˞.'lɪənz, 'ɔ˞.linz]

Note.—Stressed ['--ˌ-] *1HVI, I.i.60, 111, 157; I.ii.6, 125; I.iv.59; I.v.14. Stressed* ['--] *1HVI, I.ii.148; I.iv.1; IV.vi.14, 42 and HVIII, II.iv.172. In all other instances, allow the meter to be your guide*

ornament (*s.*)**, -s** 'ɔ˞.nəmənt, -s

ornament (*v.*)**, -s, -ing, -ed** 'ɔ˞.nəment, -s, -ɪŋ, -ɪd

ornament|al, -ally ˌɔ˞.nə'ment|l̩, -əlɪ

ornamentation, -s ˌɔ˞.nəmen'teɪʃn̩, -z

Orodes (AC) o'ɹoʊdɪz

orphan, -s, -ing, -ed; -hood 'ɔ˞.fən, -z, -ɪŋ, -d; -hʊd

Orpheus (HVIII, LUC, MV, TGV) 'ɔ˞.fjus, 'ɔ˞.fɪəs, -fjəs

Orsino (*TN*) ɔ˞.'sinoʊ

'ort (*from 'word'; see* **'orld**) 'ɜ˞.t

ort, -s 'ɔ˞.t, -s

orthograph|y, -ies ɔ˞.'θɒgɹəf|ɪ, -ɪz

osier, -s 'oʊʒə˞ ['oʊzjə˞], -z

osprey, -s 'ɒspɹɪ ['ɒspɹeɪ], -z

Osric(k) (*HAM*) 'ɒzɹɪk ['ɒsɹɪk]

Ossa (HAM) 'ɒsə

ostensib|le, -ly ɒ'stensɪb|l̩, -lɪ

ostent, -s ɒ'stent, -s

Note.—Editors are convinced that this word, in its appearance in PER, I.ii.26, should replace the alleged compositor misreading of the Quarto's 'the stint'

ostentare (*L.*) (LLL, IV.ii.15) ˌɒsten'tɑɾɛ

Note.—If it seems more important for an audience to detect the word 'ostentation' than the acumen of the speaker's Latin, then a pronunciation of [ˌɒsten'tɑɹɛ] *could be more beneficial*

ostentation ˌɒsten'teɪʃn̩ [-tən-]

ostentatious, -ly, -ness ˌɒstenˈteɪʃəs
  [-tən-], -lɪ, -nɪs
ostler, -s ˈɒslɚ, -z
Ostler, Robin (1HIV) ˈɹɒbɪn ˈɒslɚ
Oswald (*LEAR*) ˈɒzwəld
Othello (*OTH*) oˈθeloŭ
other, -s; -wise ˈʌðɚ, -z; -waĭz
othergates ˈʌðɚgeĭts
otherwhere ˈʌðɚˌʍɛɚ
otherwhiles ˈʌðɚˌʍaĭlz
otter, -s ˈɒɾɚ, -z
Ottoman (OTH) ˈɒtəmən
Ottomites (OTH) ˈɒtəmaĭts
ouch, -es ˈaŭtʃ, -ɪz
ought ˈɔt
oui (*Fr.*) wi
  *Note.—Although S. uses this French
  word meaning 'yes' in HV and MWW,
  its usage in HVIII, I.iii.34 is a modern
  editorial emendation for 'wee' appearing in the First Folio and 'wear(e)'
  appearing in the Second Folio (see
  R. A. Foakes' annotation for the line in
  HVIII, The Arden Shakespeare, 1964)*
Oui, mettez-le au mon pocket; dépêchez
  (*Fr.*) (MWW, I.iv.49) wi meteĭˈlʊ o mɔ̃
  poˈkɛ ˌdeĭpɛˈʃɛ
ounce, -s ˈaŭns, -ɪz
ouph (*elfen child*)**, -es** ˈaŭf, -s
our, -s ˈaŭɚ, -z
ousel *or* **ouzel** (*blackbird*)**, -s** ˈuzl̩, -z
out, -s ˈaŭt, -s
out-bragged ˌaŭtˈbɹægd
outbrave, -s ˌaŭtˈbɹeĭv, -z
out-breasted ˌaŭtˈbɹestɪd
out-breathed (*winded*) ˌaŭtˈbɹeθt *(cf.*
  breathed*)*
outburn ˌaŭtˈbɝn
out-craftied ˌaŭtˈkɹaftɪd
outdare ˌaŭtˈdɛɚ
out-dared ˌaŭtˈdɛɚd (*when att.,* [ˈ--])
outdure ˌaŭtˈdjʊɚ [ˈ--]
outdwell, -s, -ing, -ed ˌaŭtˈdwel, -z, -ɪŋ,
  -d

out(-)fac|e, -es, -ing, -ed ˌaŭtˈfeĭs, -ɪz, -ɪŋ,
  -t
outfrown ˌaŭtˈfɹaŭn (*arguably* [ˈ-ˌ-] *in*
  LEAR, V.iii.6)
outgo (*s.*)**, -es** ˈaŭtgoŭ, -z
out(-)|go (*v.*)**, -goes, -going, -went, -gone**
  ˌaŭtˈ|goŭ, -ˈgoŭz, -ˈgoŭɪŋ, -ˈwent, -ˈgɒn
out-jest ˌaŭtˈdʒest
outlaw (**O.**) (TGV), **-s, -ing, -ed; -ry**
  ˈaŭtlɔ, -z, -ɪŋ, -d; -ɹɪ
outliv|e, -es, -ing, -ed ˌaŭtˈlɪv, -z, -ɪŋ, -d
  *Note.—In OTH, V.ii.246, 'outlive' is
  most likely given primary stress on the
  first syllable, i.e.,* [ˈaŭtˌlɪv]
outlook, -s ˈaŭtlʊk, -s
outlusters ˌaŭtˈlʌstɚz
outlying ˈaŭtˌlaĭɪŋ
out-night ˌaŭtˈnaĭt
out-paramoured ˌaŭtˈpæɹəmʊɚd
out-peer ˌaŭtˈpɪɚ
outpray ˌaŭtˈpɹeĭ (*arguably* [ˈ-ˌ-] *in* RII,
  V.iii.107)
outprized ˌaŭtˈpɹaĭzd
outrag|e, -es, -ing, -ed ˈaŭtɹeĭdʒ, -ɪz, -ɪŋ,
  -d
outrageous, -ly, -ness ˌaŭtˈɹeĭdʒəs, -lɪ,
  -nɪs
outright (*adj.*) ˈaŭtɹaĭt
outright (*adv.*) aŭtˈɹaĭt
outroar, -s, -ing, -ed ˌaŭtˈɹɔɚ, -z, -ɹɪŋ, -d
out-rode ˌaŭtˈɹoŭd
out|run, -runs, -running, -ran ˌaŭtˈ|ɹʌn,
  -ˈɹʌnz, -ˈɹʌnɪŋ, -ˈɹæn
outscold ˌaŭtˈskoŭld
outscorn ˌaŭtˈskɔɚn
out|sell, -sells, -selling, -sold ˌaŭtˈ|sel,
  -ˈselz, -ˈselɪŋ, -ˈsoŭld
out-shining ˈaŭtˈʃaĭnɪŋ
outside, -s ˌaŭtˈsaĭd [ˈ--], -z
outsleep ˌaŭtˈslip
out(-)speaks ˌaŭtˈspiks
outsport ˌaŭtˈspɔɚt
out(-)star|e, -es, -ing, -ed ˌaŭtˈstɛɚ, -z,
  -ɹɪŋ, -d

---

i wĕ ɪ cĭty ɪ hĭt e lĕt ɛ dĕbut æ căn a pass ɝ bĭrd ʌ hŭt ə again ɚ suppĕr u yŏu
ʊ shŏuld o ŏbey ɔ awl ɒ cŏp ɑ fäther eĭ paĭd aĭ hĭgh oŭ go ɔĭ voĭce aŭ fŏund ɪɚ eär
ɛɚ air ʊɚ pŏor ɔɚ fŏrk ɑɚ pärk aĭɚ fĭre aŭɚ hŏur b bŏy p pĭt d dŏg t tŏp g gŏt
k kĭd h hŏw fi behäve dʒ jŏt tʃ chew z zäny s sŏft v vät f fät ʒ treäsure ʃ shĭp ð the
θ thĭn m män n nŏ ŋ hang l lĭp j yes w wŏn ʍ whew ɹ rĭgger, aĭɽy ɟ mätter

outstay, -s, -ing, -ed ˌɑʊ̆t'steĭ, -z, -ɪŋ, -d
outstood ˌɑʊ̆t'stʊd
out-storm ˌɑʊ̆t'stɔɚ-m
outstretch, -es, -ing, -ed ˌɑʊ̆t'stɹetʃ, -ɪz, -ɪŋ, -t (*when att.,* [ˈɑʊ̆tstɹetʃt])
outstrike ˌɑʊ̆t'stɹaĭk (*arguably* [ˈ-ˌ-] *in* AC, IV.vi.36)
outstrip, -s, -ping, -ped ˌɑʊ̆t'stɹɪp, -s, -ɪŋ, -t (*arguably* [ˈ--] *in* RIII, IV.i.41)
outswear, -s, -ing, outswore, outsworn ˌɑʊ̆t'swɛɚ-, -z, -ɹɪŋ, ˌɑʊ̆t'swɔɚ-, ˌɑʊ̆t'swɔɚ-n
out-sweetened ˌɑʊ̆t'switn̩d
out-swell ˌɑʊ̆t'swel
out-talk ˌɑʊ̆t'tɔk
out-tongue ˌɑʊ̆t'tʌŋ [ˈ-ˌ-]
outvenoms ˌɑʊ̆t'venəmz
out(-)vied ˌɑʊ̆t'vaĭd
out-wall (*outward appearance; clothing*) 'ɑʊ̆tˌwɔl
outward, -s, -ly, -ness 'ɑʊ̆twɚ-d, -z, -lɪ, -nɪs
out|wear, -wears, -wearing, -wore, -worn ˌɑʊ̆t|'wɛɚ-, -'wɛɚ-z, -'wɛɚ-ɹɪŋ, -'wɔɚ-, -wɔɚ-n
out(-)went (*p.t. of* **outgo** (*v.*)*, q.v.*) ˌɑʊ̆t'went
outwork (*adj., s.*)**, -s** 'ɑʊ̆twɝ-k, -s
outwork (*v.*)**, -s, -ing, -ed** ˌɑʊ̆t'wɝ-k, -s, -ɪŋ, -t
outworths ˌɑʊ̆t'wɝ-θs
ovator 'oŭvətɚ-
Note.—This word does not technically appear in S., unless one accepts Philip Brockbank's assertion for COR, I.ix.46 *(The Arden Shakespeare, 1976). In his notes he contends that the First Folio's 'overture' might be considered a variant spelling for 'ovator,' which he argues makes as much if not better sense*
over 'oŭvɚ-
overbear, -s, -ing, overbore, overborne ˌoŭvɚ-'bɛɚ-, -z, -ɹɪŋ, ˌoŭvɚ-'bɔɚ-, ˌoŭvɚ-'bɔɚ-n
over(-)|blow, -blows, -blowing, -blew, -blown ˌoŭvɚ-|'bloŭ, -'bloŭz, -'bloŭɪŋ, -'blu, -'bloŭn
overboard 'oŭvɚ-bɔɚ-d
over-boldly ˌoŭvɚ-'boŭldlɪ

over-boots (*adj.*) (*knee-high*) 'oŭvɚ-ˌbuts
overbulk ˌoŭvɚ-'bʌlk
overbuys ˌoŭvɚ-'baĭz
over-careful ˌoŭvɚ-'kɛɚ-fʊl [ˈ--ˌ--]
overcharge (*s.*)**, -s** 'oŭvɚ-tʃɑɚ-dʒ, -ɪz
overcharg|e (*v.*)**, -es, -ing, -ed** ˌoŭvɚ-'tʃɑɚ-dʒ, -ɪz, -ɪŋ, -d
overcharged (*adj.*) 'oŭvɚ-tʃɑɚ-dʒd, [-dʒɪd]
over|come, -comes, -coming, -came ˌoŭvɚ-|'kʌm, -'kʌmz, -'kʌmɪŋ, -'keĭm
over-cool ˌoŭvɚ-'kul
Overdone, Mistress (*MEAS*) ˌmɪstɹɪs 'oŭvɚ-dʌn
over-earnest ˌoŭvɚ-'ɹɝ-nɪst
over-eyeing ˌoŭvɚ-'ɹaĭɪŋ
over(-)far ˌoŭvɚ-'fɑɚ-
over(-)fly ˌoŭvɚ-'flaĭ
over(-)fond ˌoŭvɚ-'fɒnd
over-full 'oŭvɚ-fʊl [ˌ--'-]
overglanc|e, -es, -ing, -ed ˌoŭvɚ-'glans, -ɪz, -ɪŋ, -t
over|go, -goes, -going, -went, -gone ˌoŭvɚ-|'goŭ, -'goŭz, -'goŭɪŋ, -'went, -'gɒn
overgorged ˌoŭvɚ-'gɔɚ-dʒd
over-greedy ˌoŭvɚ-'gɹidɪ
over-handled ˌoŭvɚ-'hændl̩d (*when att.,* [ˈ----])
over|hear, -hears, -hearing, -heard ˌoŭvɚ-|'hɪɚ-, -'hɪɚ-z, -'hɪɚ-ɹɪŋ, -'hɝ-d
overhold ˌoŭvɚ-'hoŭld
overjoy, -s, -ing, -ed ˌoŭvɚ-'dʒɔĭ, -z, -ɪŋ, -d
over-kind, -ness ˌoŭvɚ-'kaĭnd, -nɪs
overleather 'oŭvɚ-leðɚ-
overlive ˌoŭvɚ-'lɪv
over-long ˌoŭvɚ-'lɒŋ
overlook (*s.*)**, -s, -ing** 'oŭvɚ-lʊk, -s, -ɪŋ
overlook (*v.*)**, -s, -ing, -ed** ˌoŭvɚ-'lʊk, -s, -ɪŋ, -t
overlord, -s 'oŭvɚ-lɔɚ-d, -z
over-lusty ˌoŭvɚ-'lʌstɪ
overmaster, -s, -ing, -ed ˌoŭvɚ-'mastɚ-, -z, -ɹɪŋ, -d
overmatching ˌoŭvɚ-'mætʃɪŋ [ˈ--ˌ--]
over-measure 'oŭvɚ-ˌmeʒɚ-
over-merry ˌoŭvɚ-'meɹɪ [ˈ--ˌ--]
over-mounting 'oŭvɚ-ˌmɑʊ̆ntɪŋ
over-much ˌoŭvɚ-'mʌtʃ [ˈ---]
over-name ˌoŭvɚ-'neĭm [ˈ--ˌ-]

overnight (*adv.*) (*course of a night*) ˌoŭvəˈnaĭt

overnight (*s.*) (*yesternight*) ˈoŭvəˌnaĭt

over-partial ˈoŭvəˌpɑ˞ʃḷ

overpass (*s.*) (*passage above another*), **-es** ˈoŭvəˌpas, -ɪz

overpass (*v.*) (*spend; traverse*), **-es, -ing, -ed** ˌoŭvəˈpas [ˈ--ˌ-], -ɪz, -ɪŋ, -t

overpeer, -s, -ing, -ed ˌoŭvəˈpɪ˞, -z, -ɹɪŋ, -d

overplus, -es ˈoŭvə˞plʌs, -ɪz

over(-)proud ˌoŭvəˈpɹɑŭd

overraught ˌoŭvəˈɹɔt

overreach ˌoŭvəˈɹitʃ

over-read (*present tense*) ˌoŭvəˈɹid

over-read (*p.t.*) ˌoŭvəˈɹed

over-red ˌoŭvəˈɹed

overridden ˌoŭvəˈɹidn̩

over-roasted ˌoŭvəˈɹoŭstɪd (*when att.,* [ˈ--ˌ--])

over-rode ˌoŭvəˈɹoŭd

overrul|e, -es, -ing, -ed ˌoŭvəˈɹul, -z, -ɪŋ, -d

overrun, -s, -ning, overran ˌoŭvəˈɹʌn, -z, -ɪŋ, ˌoŭvəˈɹæn
Note.—In HVIII, I.i.143, *'over-running'* is used contrastively with *'outrun'* and is given primary syllabic stress on the first syllable, i.e., [ˈoŭvəˌɹʌnɪŋ]

overscutched (*over-beaten, over-thrashed*) ˌoŭvəˈskʌtʃt [-tʃɪd]
Note.—Editors disagree over the meaning of *'overscutched housewives'* in 2HIV, III.ii.311. Some suggest a literal interpretation , i.e., *'housewives who are often whipped,'* while others take it figuratively to mean *'deadbeat whores,' 'hussies,'* or *'worn out.'* It is in prose, but as it is used as an adj., it may be pronounced [ˌoŭvəˈskʌtʃɪd], analogous to the adj. form of *'learned'* (ˈlɝnɪd])

over|see, -sees, -seeing, -saw, -seen ˌoŭvəˈsi, -ˈsiz, -ˈsiɪŋ, ˈsɔ, -ˈsin

overset (*s.*) ˈoŭvə˞set

overset (*v.*), **-s, -ting** ˌoŭvəˈset, -s, -ɪŋ

overshades ˌoŭvəˈʃeĭdz

over(-)shine, -s ˌoŭvəˈʃaĭn, -z

over(-)shoe, -s ˈoŭvə˞ʃu, -z

over(-)|shoot, -shoots, -shooting, -shot ˌoŭvəˈ|ʃut, -ˈʃuts, -ˈʃutɪŋ, -ˈʃɒt

overslipped ˌoŭvəˈslɪpt

overspread ˌoŭvəˈspɹed

overstained ˌoŭvəˈsteĭnd

overswayed ˌoŭvəˈsweĭd

over-swear ˌoŭvəˈswɛ˞

overt, -ly oˈvɝt [ˈoŭvɝt], -lɪ

overta'en ˌoŭvəˈteĭn

over|take, -takes, -taking, -took, -taken ˌoŭvəˈ|teĭk, -ˈteĭks, -ˈteĭkɪŋ, -ˈtʊk, -ˈteĭkən

overthrow (*s.*), **-s** ˈoŭvə˞θɹoŭ, -z

over|throw (*v., adj.*), **-throws, -throwing, -threw, -thrown** ˌoŭvəˈ|θɹoŭ, -ˈθɹoŭz, -ˈθɹoŭɪŋ, -ˈθɹu, -ˈθɹoŭn

over-topping ˌoŭvəˈtɒpɪŋ

overture, -s ˈoŭvə˞tʃə˞ [-tʃʊ˞], -z

overturn (*s.*), **-s** ˈoŭvə˞tɝn, -z

overturn (*v.*), **-s, -ing, -ed** ˌoŭvəˈtɝn, -z, -ɪŋ, -d

overwatched ˌoŭvəˈwɒtʃt

overweathered ˌoŭvəˈweðə˞d [ˈ--ˌ--]

overween, -s, -ing, -ed ˌoŭvəˈwin (*when att.,* [ˈ--ˌ--]), -z, -ɪŋ, -d

overweigh, -s, -ing, -ed ˌoŭvəˈweĭ, -z, -ɪŋ, -d

overwhelm, -s, -ing/ly, -ed ˌoŭvəˈʍelm, -z, -ɪŋ/lɪ, -d

Ovid (AYLI, TIT, TS) ˈɒvɪd (*see* **Naso, Ovidius**)

owd (*obsolete and dialectal form of 'old'*) ˈʌŭd [ˈoŭd]
Note.—This word appears in the First Quarto version of OTH, II.iii.90, in a song purportedly of northern English or Scottish origin. The First Folio and Second Quarto versions give *'awl'd'* and *'auld,'* respectively. The diphthongs proffered above (which happen to fall

i wĕ ɪ cĭty ɪ hĭt e lĕt ɛ dĕbut æ căn a păss ɝ bĭrd ʌ hŭt ə agaĭn ə˞ suppĕr u yŏu
ʊ shŏuld o ŏbey ɔ awl ɒ cŏp ɑ făther eĭ paĭd aĭ hĭgh oŭ gŏ ɔĭ voĭce aŭ foŭnd ɪ˞ ĕar
ɛ˞ aĭr ʊ˞ pŏor ɔ˞ fŏrk ɑ˞ părk aĭ˞ fĭre aŭ˞ hŏur b bŏy p pĭt d dŏg t tŏp g gŏt
k kĭd h hŏw ɦ behăve dʒ jŏt tʃ chĕw z zăny s sŏft v văt f făt ʒ treăsure ʃ shĭp ð the
θ thĭn m măn n nŏ ŋ hăng l lĭp j yĕs w wŏn ʍ whĕw ɹ rĭgger, aĭry ɾ mătter

outside standard American) are meant to suggest the word's northern English origin

ow|e, -es, -ing, -ed 'oŭ, -z, -ɪŋ, -d

owl, -s 'aŭl, -z

owlet, -s 'aŭlɪt, -s

own, -s, -ing, -ed, -er/s 'oŭn, -z, -ɪŋ, -d, -ɚ/z

ownership 'oŭnɚʃɪp

ox, -en 'ɒks, -ən

ox-beef 'ɒks͵bif

oxbow, -s 'ɒksboŭ, -z

Oxford (2HIV, *3HVI*, HVIII, RII, *RIII*) 'ɒksfɚd

Oxfordshire (3HVI) 'ɒksfɚdʃɚ

ox-head, -s 'ɒks͵hed, -z

oxlip, -s 'ɒkslɪp, -s

oxygen 'ɒksɪdʒən

oyes *or* **oyez** 'oŭjes ['oŭjez, 'oŭjeĭ]
Note.—*It seems that in TC, IV.v.142, this typically disyllabic word is meant to be stressed on the second syllable, depending on whether one decides to retain the line's 'loud'st' (as in the First Folio) or emend it to 'loudest.' In MWW, V.v.41, 'oyez' is in a couplet with 'toys,' and is either monosyllabic, i.e.,* ['ɔĭz], *or (as is more likely) 'toys' is meant in this particular couplet scheme to also be pronounced as a disyllable, as perhaps indicated by the First Folio's spelling, 'toyes'*

oyster, -s; -bed/s 'ɔĭstɚ, -z; -bed/z

oyster-wench 'ɔĭstɚ͵wentʃ

oz., ozs. 'aŭns, 'aŭnsɪz

Pp

P (*the letter*)**, -'s** 'piː, -z

Pabylon (MWW) (*from 'Babylon'; see Note for* **prings**) 'pæbɪlən [-lɒn]

Pace, Doctor (HVIII) 'dɒktɚ 'peĭs

pac|e, -es, -ing, -ed, -er/s 'peĭs, -ɪz, -ɪŋ, -t, -ɚ/z

pacifist, -s 'pæsɪfɪst, -s

pack, -s, -ing/s, -ed, -er/s 'pæk, -s, -ɪŋ/z, -t, -ɚ/z

packag|e, -es, -ing, -ed 'pækɪdʒ, -ɪz, -ɪŋ, -d

packet, -s 'pækɪt, -s

pack(-)horse, -s 'pækfiɔ˞s, -ɪz

pack-saddle, -s 'pæk͵sædl̩, -z

packthread, -s 'pækθɹed, -z

Pacorus (AC) 'pækəɹəs

paction (*compact, agreement*) 'pækʃn̩
Note.—*This word does not actually appear in S. It is a modern conjectural emendation for 'pation/passion' in HV, V.ii.359*

pad (*from 'bad'*) 'pæd (*see* **prings**)

pad, -s, -ding, -ded 'pæd, -z, -ɪŋ, -ɪd

padd|le, -les, -ling, -led, -ler/s 'pædl̩, -l̩z, -lɪŋ [-l̩ɪŋ], -l̩d, -lɚ/z [-lɚ/z]

paddock (P.) (MAC)**, -s** 'pædək, -s

padlock, -s, -ing, -ed 'pædlɒk, -s, -ɪŋ, -t

Padua (ADO, MV, TGV, TS) 'pædjʊə

pagan (P.), -s 'peĭgən, -z

pag|e (P.), -es, -ing, -ed, -er/s 'peĭdʒ, -ɪz, -ɪŋ, -d, -ɚ/z

Page, Anne (*MWW*) 'æn 'peĭdʒ
Note.—*Also called 'Nan'* ['næn]

pageant, -s 'pædʒənt, -s
Note.—*Trisyllabic* ['pædʒɹənt] *in 2HVI, I.ii.67*

Page, George (*MWW*) 'dʒɔ˞dʒ 'peĭdʒ

Page, Margaret (*MWW*) 'mɑ˞gɹɪt 'peĭdʒ
Note.—*Also called 'Meg'* ['meg]

Page, William (*MWW*) 'wɪljəm 'peĭdʒ

pah (*interj.*) 'pɑ ['pɸ]

paid (*p.t. and p.p. of* **pay**, *q.v.*) 'peĭd

pain, -s, -ing, -ed 'peĭn, -z, -ɪŋ, -d

pain|ful, -fully, -fulness 'peĭnfʊl, -fəlɪ, -fʊlnɪs

painless, -ly, -ness 'peĭnlɪs, -lɪ, -nɪs

painstaking, -ly 'peĭnz͵teĭkɪŋ, -lɪ

paint, -s, -ing/s, -ed, -er/s 'peĭnt, -s, -ɪŋ/z, -ɪd, -ɚ/z

Painter (TIM) 'peĭntɚ

pair, -s, -ing, -ed 'peˑ˞, -z, -ɹɪŋ, -d

Pair-Taunt 'peˑ˞͵tɔnt (*see Note for* **pertaunt-like**)

pajock, -s 'pædʒɒk [-dʒək], -s

palabras (*Sp.*) (ADO, III.v.15) pɑ'lɑ'brɑs

Palamedes (TC) ͵pæləˈmidɪz

Palamon (*TNK*) 'pæləmɒn

palate (*s.*)**, -s** 'pælɪt, -s

Palatine, County (MV) 'kaʊntɪ 'pælətaɪn
Note.—The First Quarto and First
Folio versions of MV *give 'Palentine.'*
The Second Quarto gives 'Palatine,'
and is what most editors emend 'Palen-
tine' to
pal|e, -es, -ing, -ed; -er, -est, -ely, -eness
'peɪl, -z, -ɪŋ, -d; -ə‑, -ɪst, -lɪ, -nɪs
Palestine (KJ, OTH) 'pælɪstaɪn
pale-visaged 'peɪl͵vɪzɪdʒd
palfrey, -s 'pɔlfɹɪ, -z
palindrome, -s 'pælɪndɹoʊm, -z
palisado, -es ͵pælɪ'seɪdoʊ [-'sɑd-], -z
pall, -s, -ing, -ed 'pɔl, -z, -ɪŋ, -d
Pallas (TIT, TNK) 'pæləs
pal(l)at|e (*v.*)**, -es, -ing, -ed** 'pælɪt, -s, -ɪŋ,
-ɪd
pallet, -s 'pælɪt, -s
palliament (*robe, gown*)**, -s** 'pælɪəmənt
[-ljə-], -s
palm, -s, -ing, -ed 'pɑm, -z, -ɪŋ, -d
palmer (P.)**, -s** 'pɑmə‑, -z
palm-tree, -s 'pɑm͵tɹi, -z
palm|y, -ier, -iest 'pɑm|ɪ, -ɪə‑, -ɪɪst
palpab|le, -ly, -leness 'pælpəb|l̩, -lɪ, -l̩nɪs
palpable-gross 'pælpəbl̩͵gɹoʊs
pals|y, -ies, -ied 'pɔlz|ɪ, -ɪz, -ɪd
palter, -s, -ing, -ed, -er/s 'pɔltə‑, -z, -ɹɪŋ,
-d, -ɹə‑/z
paltr|y, -ier, -iest, -ily, -iness 'pɔltɹ|ɪ, -ɪə‑,
-ɪɪst, -ɪlɪ, -ɪnɪs
paly 'peɪlɪ
pamper, -s, -ing, -ed, -er/s 'pæmpə‑, -z,
-ɹɪŋ, -d, -ɹə‑/z
pamphlet, -s 'pæmflɪt, -s
pan, -s, -ning, -ned 'pæn, -z, -ɪŋ, -d
pancak|e, -es, -ing, -ed 'pænkeɪk
['pæŋk-], -s, -ɪŋ, -t
panda, -s 'pændə, -z
Pandar (PER, TC)**, -s** 'pændə‑, -z
Pandarus (MWW, *TC*, TN) 'pændəɹəs
pander, -s, -ing, -ed 'pændə‑, -z, -ɹɪŋ, -d
panderly 'pændə‑lɪ
Pandion, King (PP) 'kɪŋ pæn'daɪən

Pandulph, Cardinal (*KJ*) 'kɑə‑dn̩l̩
'pændʌlf
pang, -s, -ing, -ed 'pæŋ, -z, -ɪŋ, -d
pannier, -s 'pænjə‑ [-nɪə‑], -z
Pannonian (CYM)**, -s** pæ'noʊnjən, -z
Pansa (AC) 'pænsə [-nzə]
pans|y, -ies, -ying, -ied 'pænz|ɪ, -ɪz, -ɪɪŋ,
-ɪd
pant (*v.*)**, -s, -ing, -ed** 'pænt, -s, -ɪŋ, -ɪd
pantaloon (P.)**, -s** ͵pæntə'lun, -z
Pantheon (TIT) 'pænθɪən, -θjən [-θɪɒn,
pæn'θɪən]
panther, -s 'pænθə‑, -z
Panthino (*TGV*) pæn̩'θinoʊ
pantingly 'pæntɪŋlɪ
pantler, -s 'pæntlə‑, -z
pants (*s.*) 'pænts
pap, -s 'pæp, -s
paper, -s, -ing, -ed, -er/s 'peɪpə‑, -z, -ɹɪŋ,
-d, -ɹə‑/z
paper-faced 'peɪpə‑͵feɪst
Paphlagonia (AC) ͵pæflə'goʊnɪə, -njə
Paphos (PER, TEM, VA) 'peɪfɒs
papist, -s 'peɪpɪst, -s
par 'pɑə‑
Paracelsus (ALL'S) ͵pæɹə'selsəs
paradise (P.) (ALL'S, COM, TEM)**, -s**
'pæɹədaɪs, -ɪz
paradox, -es 'pæɹədɒks, -ɪz
paragon, -s, -ed 'pæɹəgɒn [-gən], -z, -d
parallel, -s, -ing, -ed; -ism 'pæɹəlel, -z,
-ɪŋ, -d; -ɪzm̩
paramour, -s 'pæɹə ͵mʊə‑ [-͵mɔə‑], -z
parapet, -s, -ed 'pæɹəpɪt [-pet], -s, -ɪd
paraquito ͵pæɹə'kitoʊ
parasite, -s 'pæɹəsaɪt, -s
Parca (HV) 'pɑə‑kə
parcel, -s, -(l)ing, -(l)ed 'pɑə‑sl̩, -z, -ɪŋ, -d
parcel-gilt (*partially gilded*) 'pɑə‑sl̩͵gɪlt
parch, -es, -ing, -ed 'pɑə‑tʃ, -ɪz, -ɪŋ, -t
parchment, -s 'pɑə‑tʃmənt, -s
pard, -s 'pɑə‑d, -z
pardon, -s, -ing, -ed, -er/s 'pɑə‑dn̩, -z,
-ɪŋ, -d, -ə‑/z

pardonami (*It.*) (RJ, II.iv.33) paɾˈdoˈnami
pardonnez(-)moi (*Fr.*) (HV, IV.iv.21; RII,
   V.iii.117) paʁdonɛ ˈmwa
   Note.—In RII, V.iii.117, *York literally*
   says 'pardonne moy,' anglicizing the
   pronunciation to [paɚˈdɒnɛ ˈmɔɪ̆],
   rhyming it with 'destroy' in the couplet
par|e, -es, -ing/s, -ed ˈpɛɚ, -z, -ɹɪŋ/z, -d
parent, -s; -age ˈpɛɚɹənt, -s; -ɪdʒ
parfect (*v.*) (*corruption of v.* **perfect** *in*
   LLL) paɚˈfekt
paring-kni|fe, -ves ˈpɛɚɹɪŋˌnaɪ̆|f, -vz
Paris (HV, 1HVI, 2HVI, LUC, *RJ, TC,*
   TS) ˈpæɹɪs
Paris-ball (HV), **-s** ˈpæɹɪsˌbɔl, -z
parish, -es ˈpæɹɪʃ, -ɪz
Parish-garden (HVIII) ˈpæɹɪʃˌɡaɚˈdn̩
   Note.—This is usually given as 'Paris
   Garden,' in which case the pronuncia-
   tion is [ˈpæɹɪsˌɡaɚˈdn̩]
parishioner, -s pəˈɹɪʃnɚ, -z
Parisian (1HVI), **-s** pəˈɹɪʒn [-ˈɹɪzɪən], -z
paritor, -s ˈpæɹɪtɚ, -z
park, -s, -ing, -ed ˈpaɚk, -s, -ɪŋ, -t
Park-ward (MWW) ˈpaɚkˌwɔɚd
parlance ˈpaɚləns
parle ˈpaɚl
parley, -s, -ing, -ed ˈpaɚlɪ, -z, -ɪŋ, -d
parliament (**P.**), **-s** ˈpaɚlɪmənt [-ljə-], -s
parling (*speaking*) ˈpaɚlɪŋ
parlor, -s ˈpaɚlɚ, -z
   Note.—This word in ADO, III.i.1 *is*
   probably something like a trisyllable,
   i.e., [ˈpaɚɹələ], *or* [ˈpaɚlɪ̆ə], *or*
   perhaps [ˈpaɚlʊə]. *I agree with both*
   the rationale and the recommendation
   of J. C. Smith in the 1902 Warwick
   edition of ADO, *subsequently cited by*
   A. R. Humphreys in his annotation of
   *the line (q.v.) (*The Arden Shakespeare,
   1981; reprinted 1998)
parlous, -ly ˈpaɚləs, -lɪ
parmacity (*archaic distortion of*
   'spermaceti' in 1HIV, I.iii.57; *ointment*
   obtained from the fatty acids of sperm
   whales) ˌpaɚməˈsɪtɪ
Par(r)olles (*ALL'S*) pəˈɹɒlɪs [paˈɹɔles,
   -lɪz]
parricide, -s ˈpæɹɪsaɪ̆d, -z

parrot, -s, -ing, -ed ˈpæɹət, -s, -ɪŋ, -ɪd
parrot-teacher ˈpæɹətˌtitʃɚ, -z
parsley ˈpaɚslɪ
parson, -s ˈpaɚsn̩, -z
Parson, Master (TN) ˈmastɚ ˈpaɚsn̩
part, -s, -ing, -ed ˈpaɚt, -s, -ɪŋ, -ɪd
partak|e, -es, -ing, partook, partak|en,
   -er/s paɚˈteɪ̆k, -s, -ɪŋ, paɚˈtʊk,
   paɚˈteɪ̆k|ən, -ɚ/z
part-created ˈpaɚtkɹɪˌeɪ̆tɪd
Parthia (AC) ˈpaɚθɪə, -θjə
Parthian (AC, CYM, TNK), **-s** ˈpaɚθɪən,
   -z, -θjən, -z
parti|al, -ally, -alness ˈpaɚʃ|l̩, -əlɪ, -l̩nɪs
partialize ˈpaɚʃəlaɪ̆z
participat|e, -es, -ing, -ed, -or/s
   paɚˈtɪsɪpeɪ̆t, -s, -ɪŋ, -ɪd, -ɚ/z
participation, -s paɚˌtɪsɪˈpeɪ̆ʃn̩, -z
parti-coated ˈpaɚtɪˌkoʊtɪd
parti-colored ˈpaɚtɪˌkʌlɚd
particular, -s, -ly paɚˈtɪkjʊlɚ, -z, -lɪ
particularit|y, -ies paɚˌtɪkjʊˈlæɹɪt|ɪ, -ɪz
particulariz|e, -es, -ing, -ed
   paɚˈtɪkjʊləˌɹaɪ̆z, -ɪz, -ɪŋ, -d
partisan (*militant supporter*), **-s; -ship/s**
   ˈpaɚtɪzæn, -z; -ʃɪp/s
partisan (*weapon*), **-s** ˈpaɚtɪzən, -z
partition, -s, -ing, -ed paɚˈtɪʃn̩ [pəˈt-], -z,
   -ɪŋ, -d
Partlet, Dame (1HIV, WT) ˈdeɪ̆m ˈpaɚtlɪt
partly ˈpaɚtlɪ
partner, -s, -ing, -ed; -ship/s ˈpaɚtnɚ,
   -z, -ɹɪŋ, -d; -ʃɪp/s
partridge, -s ˈpaɚtɹɪdʒ, -ɪz
part|y, -ies, -ying, -ied, -ier/s ˈpaɚɟ̥|ɪ, -ɪz,
   -ɪŋ, -ɪd, -ɪɚ/z
party-verdict ˈpaɚɟ̥ɪˌvɝˈdɪkt
pash, -es, -ed ˈpæʃ, -ɪz, -t
pass, -es, -ing, -ed, -er/s ˈpas, -ɪz, -ɪŋ, -t,
   -ɚ/z
passab|le, -ly, -leness ˈpasəb|l̩, -lɪ, -l̩nɪs
passado (LLL, I.ii.168; RJ, II.iv.26,
   III.i.84) pæˈsado
   Note.—This fencing term stems from Fr.
   'passade,' Sp. 'pasada,' or It. 'passata.'
   The OED *cites its usage in* LLL *as the*
   first
passag|e, -es, -ing, -ed ˈpasɪdʒ, -ɪz, -ɪŋ, -d
passant (*of heraldry*) ˈpæsənt

passenger, -s 'pæsɪndʒəˑ, -z
passion, -s 'pæʃn̩, -z
passionate, -ly, -ness 'pæʃnɪt, -lɪ, -nɪs
   Note.—In TIT, III.ii.6 *(First Folio, as*
   this scene does not appear in the
   Quartos), this adjective is used as a verb
   and is thus pronounced ['pæʃəneɪ̆t]
passive, -ly, -ness 'pæsɪv, -lɪ, -nɪs
passport, -s 'paspɔ̌ˑt, -s
passy(-)measures (*var. of 'passe-*
   measures') 'pasɪˌmeʒəˑz
past 'past
past|e, -es, -ing, -ed 'peɪ̆st, -s, -ɪŋ, -ɪd
pastern, -s 'pæstɜˑn, -z
pastime, -s 'pastaɪ̆m, -z
pastor, -s 'pastəˑ, -z
pastoral, -s, -ly 'pastəˑɹəl, -z, -ɪ
pastoralism 'pastəˑɹəlɪzm̩
pastur|e, -es, -ing, -ed 'pastʃəˑ, -z, -ɹɪŋ, -d
past-proportion ˌpastpɹəˈpɔ̌ˑʃn̩ [-pɹʊˈp-]
pastr|y, -ies 'peɪ̆stɹɪ, -ɪz
pastur|e, -es, -ing, -ed 'pastʃəˑ, -z, -ɹɪŋ, -d
past|y (*meat or fish pie*), **-ies** 'pæstɪ, -ɪz
pat, -s, -ting, -ted; -ly, -ness 'pæt, -s, -ɪŋ,
   -ɪd; -lɪ, -nɪs
Patay (1HVI) pæˈteɪ̆
patch, -es, -ing, -ed; -able, -ery 'pætʃ, -ɪz,
   -ɪŋ, -t; -əbl̩, -əˑɹɪ
Patch(-)breech (*PER*) 'pætʃbɹɪtʃ
patch|y, -ier, -iest, -ily, -iness 'pætʃɪ, -ɪəˑ,
   -ɪɪst, -ɪlɪ, -ɪnɪs
pate, -s 'peɪ̆t, -s
paten *or* **patin, -s** 'pætn̩, -z
patent, -s, -ing, -ed 'pætn̩t, -s, -ɪŋ, -ɪd
patently 'peɪ̆tn̩tlɪ
paternal, -ly pəˈtɜˑnl̩, -ɪ
paternity pəˈtɜˑnɪtɪ
pa|th, -ths 'paθ, -ðz
pathetic, -al, -ally pəˈθetɪk [-eɹɪ-], -l̩, -əlɪ
patience (P.) (AYLI, PER, TC, TN), **-s**
   'peɪ̆ʃns [-ʃəns], -ɪz
Patience (*HVIII*) 'peɪ̆ʃns [-ʃəns]
patient, -s, -ly 'peɪ̆ʃənt, -s, -lɪ
patrician, -s pəˈtɹɪʃn̩, -z

Patrick, Friar (TGV) 'fɹaɪ̆əˑ 'pætɹɪk
patrimon|y, -ies 'pætɹɪmən|ɪ, -ɪz
Patroclus (*TC*) pəˈtɹɒŭkləs [-'tɹɒk-]
patron, -s 'peɪ̆tɹən, -z
patronage 'peɪ̆tɹənɪdʒ ['pæt-]
patroness, -es 'peɪ̆tɹənɪs [-nes], -ɪz
pattern, -s, -ed 'pæɾəˑn, -z, -d
pauca verba (*L.*) (LLL, IV.ii.158; MWW,
   I.i.113) 'paŭka 'vɛ̌ˑba
paucas pallabris (TS, Ind.i.5) 'paŭkas
   paˈlabɹis
   Note.—This is deemed to be a corrup-
   tion of the Sp. 'pocas palabris.' If one
   gives it a Spanish pronunciation, it will
   become ['poˑkas paˈlaˑbras]
Paul, Apostle (RIII) əˈpɒsl̩ 'pɔl
Paulina (*WT*) pɔˈlaɪ̆nə
Paul's (1HIV, 2HIV, HVIII, RIII) 'pɔlz
paunch, -es 'pɔntʃ, -ɪz
Paunch, Sir John (1HIV) ˌsɜˑ 'dʒɒn 'pɔntʃ
   Note.—As Stokes puts it, "Nonce-name
   applied to Falstaff by Prince Hal"
paus|e, -es, -ing, -ed, -er/s 'pɔz, -ɪz, -ɪŋ,
   -d, -əˑz
pausingly 'pɔzɪŋlɪ
pavan(e), -z 'pævən [pəˈvan, pəˈvan], -z
pav|e, -es, -ing, -ed, -er/s 'peɪ̆v, -z, -ɪŋ,
   -d, -əˑz
pavement, -s 'peɪ̆vmənt, -s
pavilion, -s, -ing, -ed pəˈvɪljən, -z, -ɪŋ, -d
pavin, -s (*var. of* **pavan[e]**, *q.v.*) 'pævɪn, -z
paw, -s, -ing, -ed 'pɔ, -z, -ɪŋ, -d
pawn, -s, -ing, -ed 'pɔn, -z, -ɪŋ, -d
pax 'pæks
pay, -s, -ing, paid, payer/s, payment/s
   'peɪ̆, -z, -ɪŋ, 'peɪ̆d, 'peɪ̆əˑ/z, 'peɪ̆mənt/s
pea, -s 'pi, -z
peace (P.), **-s** 'pis, -ɪz
peace-a 'pisə (*see* **vere**)
peaceab|le, -ly, -leness 'pisəb|l̩, -lɪ, -l̩nɪs
peace|ful, -fully, -fulness 'pis|fʊl, -fəlɪ,
   -fʊlnɪs
peace-maker, -s 'pisˌmeɪ̆kəˑ, -z
peace-parted 'pis'paǒˑtɪd

---

i wĕ ɪ cit**y** ɪ h**ĭt** e l**ĕt** ɛ d**ĕ**but æ c**ă**n a p**a**ss ɜˑ b**ĭr**d ʌ h**ŭt** ə **a**gain əˑ supp**er** u y**ou**
ʊ sh**ould** o **o**bey ɔ **aw**l ɒ c**o**p ɑ f**a**ther eɪ̆ p**aid** aɪ h**igh** oŭ g**o** ɔɪ v**oi**ce aŏ f**ound** ɪǒˑ **ear**
ɛǒˑ **air** ʊǒˑ **poor** ɔǒˑ **fork** aǒˑ **park** aɪ̆ǒˑ **fire** aŏǒˑ **hour** b b**oy** p p**it** d d**og** t t**op** g g**ot**
k k**id** h h**ow** ɦ be**h**ave dʒ j**ot** tʃ **ch**ew z **z**any s **s**oft v v**a**t f f**a**t ʒ trea**s**ure ʃ **sh**ip ð **th**e
θ **th**in m **m**an n **n**o ŋ ha**ng** l l**ip** j **y**es w **w**on ʍ **wh**ew ɹ **r**igger, ai**r**y ɽ ma**tt**er

peach, -es, -ing, -ed 'pitʃ, -ɪz, -ɪŋ, -t

peach|y, -ier, -iest, -iness 'pitʃ|ɪ, -ɪə˞, -ɪɪst, -ɪnɪs

Pead (MWW) (*from 'Bead' or 'Bede'; see* **prings**) 'pid

peak, -s, -ing, -ed 'pik, -s, -ɪŋ, -t

peal, -s, -ing, -ed 'pil, -z, -ɪŋ, -d

peanut, -s 'pinʌt, -s

pear, -s 'pɛə˞, -z

'pear (*from* **appear**) 'pɪə˞

peard (*from 'beard'*) 'pɪə˞d (*see* **prings**)

pearl, -s, -ing, -ed; -y 'pɜ˞l, -z, -ɪŋ, -d; -ɪ

peasant, -s 'pezn̩t, -s

peasantry 'pezn̩tɪɪ

peascod, -s 'pizkɒd, -z

Peascod, Master (MSND) 'mastə˞ 'pizkɒd

peascod-time 'pizkɒdˌtaɪm

pease 'piz

Peaseblossom, Master (*MSND*) 'mastə˞ 'pizblɒsəm

peas(e)cod, -s 'pizkɒd, -z

peat (*from 'beat'*) 'pit

  Note.—Evans (in MWW*) is a Welsh-man, and speaks in a Welsh accent, if somewhat inconsistently. This is an example of S.'s direction to the actor (by way of semiphonetic spellings) to adopt such an accent, more or less, for the sake of wringing the most satire out of plays on words stemming from confusions with, and corruptions of, English pronunciation via the Welsh tongue*

peat, -bog/s 'pit, -bɒg/z

peaten (*from 'beaten'*) 'pitn̩ (*see* **prings**)

pebble, -s, -d 'pebl̩, -z, -d

pecan, -s pɪ'kɑn, -z

  Note.—One of only a few words (cf. **dahlia***) still used to retain strong regional and cultural identity amongst its speakers in terms of pronunciation rather than dialect. 'Pecan' is variously* ['pikæn, pɪ'kæn, 'pikən]. *Deference to one's audience or company is advisable*

peck, -s, -ing, -ed, -er/s 'pek, -s, -ɪŋ, -t, -ə˞/z

Peck, Gilbert (HVIII) 'gɪlbə˞t 'pek (*see Note for* **Perk, Gilbert**)

peckish, -ly, -ness 'pekɪʃ, -lɪ, -nɪs

peculiar, -s, -ly pɪ'kjuljə˞, -z, -lɪ

Pedant (TS) 'pedn̩t [-dənt]

pedant, -s 'pedn̩t [-dənt], -s

pedantic, -al, -ally pɪ'dæntɪk, -l̩, -əlɪ

pedascule (*little pedant, schoolmaster*) pe'dæskjʊlɪ, [*L.* pe'dɑskʊlɛ]

pedd|le, -les, -ling, -led 'pedl̩|l̩, -l̩z, -l̩ɪŋ, -l̩d

pedigree, -s, -d 'pedɪgɹɪ, -z, -d

pedlar, -s 'pedlə˞, -z

Pedro, Don (*ADO*) 'dɒn 'peɪdɹoʊ ['ped-]

  Note.—There is another pronunciation proffered by very reputable sources, i.e., ['pidɹoʊ], *though its usage in the United States is rare*

peds (*from 'beds'*) 'pedz (*see* **prings**)

peel, -s, -ing/s, -ed, -er/s 'pil, -z, -ɪŋ/z, -d, -ə˞/z

peep, -s, -ing, -ed, -er/s 'pip, -s, -ɪŋ, -t, -ə˞/z

peer (**P.**), **-s, -ing, -ed** 'pɪə˞, -z, -ɹɪŋ, -d

peerless, -ly, -ness 'pɪə˞lɪs, -lɪ, -nɪs

Peesel (2HIV) 'pizl̩ ['pisl̩]

peev|e, -es, -ing, -ed 'piv, -z, -ɪŋ, -d

peevish, -ly, -ness 'pivɪʃ, -lɪ, -nɪs

peevish-fond 'pivɪʃ'fɒnd ['--,-]

peg, -s, -ging, -ged 'peg, -z, -ɪŋ, -d

Peg-a-Ramsey (TN) 'pegə'ɹæmzɪ

Pegasus (1HIV, HV, TS) 'pegəsəs

peis|e *or* **peiz|e, -es, -ing, -ed** 'peɪz ['piz], -ɪz, -ɪŋ, -d

pelf 'pelf

pelican, -s 'pelɪkən, -z

Pelion, Mount (HAM, MWW) 'maʊnt 'pilɪən, -ljən

Pella, Lucius (JUL) 'luʃɪəs, -ʃjəs, 'lusɪəs, -sjəs ['lju-] 'pelə

pellet, -s, -ing, -ed 'pelɪt, -s, -ɪŋ, -ɪd

pell(-)mell 'pel'mel [ˌ-'-]

Peloponnesus (AC) ˌpeləpo'nisəs

Pelops (TNK) 'pilɒps

pelt, -s, -ing, -ed 'pelt, -s, -ɪŋ, -ɪd

Pembroke (*3HVI*, HVIII, *KJ*, RIII) 'pembɹʊk

pen, -s, -ning, -ned 'pen, -z, -ɪŋ, -d

penaliz|e, -es, -ing, -ed 'pinl̩aɪz, -ɪz, -ɪŋ, -d

penalt|y, -ies 'penl̩t|ɪ, -ɪz

penance, -s 'penəns, -ɪz

pencil, -s, -ling, -led 'pensl̩, -z, -ɪŋ, -d

pendant, -s ˈpendənt, -s
pendent, -ly ˈpendənt, -lɪ
pending ˈpendɪŋ
Pendragon (1HVI) penˈdɹægən
pendulous, -ly, -ness ˈpendjʊləs, -lɪ, -nɪs
pendulum, -s ˈpendjʊləm, -z
Pene (Pine) gelidus timor occupat artus
(*L.*) (2HVI, IV.i.116) ˈpɛnɛ (ˈpinɛ) ˈdʒelɪdus ˈtimɔˈ ˈɒkjʊpɑt ˈaˈtus
Note.—The word 'occupat' would normally sound more like [ˈoʊkupɑt], *but the pronunciation given above evokes (to the modern ear mostly unlearned in Latin) more of the sense of the word, i.e., 'occupy' (see 'Shakespeare's Foreign Languages' § 1.10 of this dictionary)*
Penelope (COR) pɪˈneləpɪ
penetrab|le, -ly, -leness ˈpenɪtɹəb|l̩, -lɪ, -l̩nɪs
penetrat|e, -es, -ing/ly, -ed ˈpenɪtɹeɪt, -s, -ɪŋ/lɪ, -ɪd
penetrative, -ly, -ness ˈpenɪtɹətɪv [-tɹeɪt-], -lɪ, -nɪs
penguin, -s ˈpeŋgwɪn, -z
penitence ˈpenɪtəns
penitent, -s, -ly ˈpenɪtənt, -s, -lɪ
Penker, Friar (RIII) ˈfɹaɪˈ ˈpeŋkə
penner, -s ˈpenə
pennon, -s ˈpenən, -z
penn'orth (*from* **pennyworth**) ˈpenəˈθ
penn|y, -ies ˈpen|ɪ, -ɪz
pennyworth, -'s ˈpenɪˌwɜˈθ, -s
Note.—[ˈpenəˈθs] *in* 2HVI, I.i.223; RJ, IV.v.4: [ˈpenɪˌwɜˈθ] *in* ADO, II.iii.42
pension (*s., v.*) (*monetary allowance, usually for retirement*), **-s, -ing, -ed, -er/s** ˈpenʃn̩, -z, -ɪŋ, -d, -əˈ/z
pensive, -ly, -ness ˈpensɪv, -lɪ, -nɪs
pensived (*made melancholic, thoughtful*) ˈpensɪvd
pent ˈpent
Pentapolis (PER) penˈtæpəlɪs
Pentecost (COM, RJ, TGV), **-s** ˈpentɪkɒst, -s

pentecostal ˌpentɪˈkɒstəl
Penthesilea (TN) ˌpenθesɪˈliə
penthou|se, -ses ˈpentfiaʊ|s, -zɪz
pent-up (*att. adj.*) ˈpentˌʌp
penurious, -ly, -ness pɪˈnjʊˈɹəs, -lɪ, -nɪs
penury ˈpenjʊɹɪ
peop|le, -les, -ling, -led ˈpip|l̩, -l̩ɪŋ [-lɪŋ], -l̩d
Pepin, King (ALL'S, HV, HVIII, LLL) ˈkɪŋ ˈpepɪn
Note.—The First Folio also gives the spelling 'Pippin,' so an accepted alt. pronunciation is [ˈpɪpɪn]
pepper, -s, -ing, -ed, -er/s ˈpepəˈ, -z, -ɹɪŋ, -d, -ɹəˈ/z
pepperbox, -es ˈpepəˈbɒks, -ɪz
pepper(-)corn, -s ˈpepəˈkɔˈn, -z
pepper-gingerbread ˈpepəˈˌdʒɪndʒəˈbɹed
peradventure, -s ˌpɜˈɹədˈventʃəˈ [pəɹəd-], -z
perceiv|e, -es, -ing, -ed, -er/s pəˈsiv, -z, -ɪŋ, -d, -əˈ/z
per cent pəˈsent
percentage, -s pəˈsentɪdʒ, -ɪz
perception, -s pəˈsepʃn̩, -z
perceptive, -ly, -ness pəˈseptɪv, -lɪ, -nɪs
perch, -es, -ing, -ed, -er/s ˈpɜˈtʃ, -ɪz, -ɪŋ, -t, -əˈ/z
perchance pəˈtʃans
Perc|y (*1HIV, 2HIV*, 1HVI, 3HVI, *RII*), **-ies** ˈpɜˈs|ɪ, -ɪz
Percy, Harry (*1HIV, RII*) ˈhæɹɪ ˈpɜˈsɪ
Percy, Henry (*1HIV*, 2HIV, *RII*) ˈhenɹɪ ˈpɜˈsɪ (*see Note for* **Henry**)
Percy, Lady (*1HIV, 2HIV*) ˈleɪdɪ ˈpɜˈsɪ
Percy, Thomas (*1HIV*) ˈtɒməs ˈpɜˈsɪ
Perdita (*WT*) ˈpɜˈdɪtə
perdition pəˈdɪʃn̩
perdu(e) pɜˈdju
perdurab|le, -ly pəˈdjʊˈɹəb|l̩, -lɪ
perdy *or* **perdie** pəˈdi
peregrinate (*adj.*) ˈpeɹɪgɹɪˌnɪt
peregrinat|e (*v.*)**, -es, -ing, -ed** ˈpeɹɪgɹɪˌneɪt, -s, -ɪŋ, -ɪd

i w**e** ɪ c**i**ty ɪ h**i**t e l**e**t ɛ d**e**but æ c**a**n a p**a**ss ɜˈ b**i**rd ʌ h**u**t ə **a**gain əˈ supp**er** u y**ou** ʊ sh**oul**d o **o**bey ɔ **aw**l ɒ c**o**p ɑ f**a**ther eɪ p**ai**d aɪ h**igh** oʊ g**o** ɔɪ v**oi**ce aʊ f**ou**nd ɪɚ **ear** ɛɚ **air** ʊɚ **poor** ɔɚ f**or**k ɑɚ p**ar**k aɪɚ f**ire** aʊɚ **hour** b **b**oy p **p**it d **d**og t **t**op g **g**ot k **k**id h **h**ow fi be**h**ave dʒ **j**ot tʃ **ch**ew z **z**any s **s**oft v **v**at f **f**at ʒ trea**s**ure ʃ **sh**ip ð **th**e θ **th**in m **m**an n **n**o ŋ ha**ng** l **l**ip j **y**es w **w**on ʍ **wh**ew ɹ **r**igger, ai**r**y ɾ ma**tt**er

peremptor|y, -ily, -iness pə'ɹemptəɹ|ɪ, -ɪlɪ, -ɪnɪs

Note.— 'Peremptory' is used at least a dozen times in S., where in most cases it is given primary syllabic stress on the first syllable, i.e., ['peɹəmptəɹɪ]. Brian Morris (editor, TS, The Arden Shakespeare, 1981) asserts that 'peremptory' is "always accented on the first syllable, in S." However, it may be given primary syllabic stress on either the first or second syllable in 2HVI, II.i.23; PER, II.v.72; TGV, I.iii.71; TS, II.i.131, depending on how one scans the lines

perfect (*adj., s.*), **-er, -est, -ly, -ness** 'pɜˑfɪkt, -ə˞, -ɪst, -lɪ, -nɪs

perfect (*v.*), **-s, -ing, -ed** pɜˑ'fekt [pə˞'f-], -s, -ɪŋ, -ɪd

Note.—Stressed on the first syllable, i.e., ['pɜˑfekt, -fɪkt] in ALL'S, IV.iv.4; MEAS, IV.iii.141; TGV, I.iii.23

perfidious, -ly, -ness pə˞'fɪdɪəs [pɜˑ'f-], -lɪ, -nɪs

perforce pɜˑ'fɔ˞s

perform, -s, -ing, -ed, -er/s pə˞'fɔ˞m, -z, -ɪŋ, -d, -ə˞/z

performance, -s pə˞'fɔ˞məns, -ɪz

perfume (*s.*), **-s** 'pɜˑfjum, -z ([ˌ-'-] *in* CYM, I.vi.13)

perfum|e (*v.*), **-es, -ing, -ed, -er/s** pɜˑ'fjum, -z, -ɪŋ, -d, -ə˞/z

perge (*L.*) (LLL, IV.ii.51) 'pɛ˞dʒɛ

Note.—This word meaning 'go on' or 'pursue' (when it appears in LLL) might benefit from another pronunciation, potentially heightening its comedic value. Sir Nathaniel could be interpreted as saying 'purge' to Holofernes, which prompts the pronunciation ['pɜˑdʒɛ], or something close to it

periapt, -s 'peɹɪæpt, -s

Pericles (*PER*) 'peɹɪklɪz

Perigenia *or* **Peregenia** (MSND) ˌpeɹɪ'dʒinjə

Perigort, Lord (LLL) ˌlɔ˞d 'peɹɪgɔ˞t [ˌpeɹɪ'gɔ˞(t)]

Perigouna (MSND) ˌpeɹɪ'gunə [-'gaʊnə]

peril, -s 'peɹəl, -z

perilous, -ly, -ness 'peɹɪləs, -lɪ, -nɪs

period, -s 'pɪ˞ɹɪəd, -z

periodic ˌpɪ˞ɹɪ'ɒdɪk

perish, -es, -ing, -ed 'peɹɪʃ, -ɪz, -ɪŋ, -t

perishen 'peɹɪʃɪn [-ʃn̩]

Note.—F. D. Hoeniger (editor for PER, The Arden Shakespeare, 1963) cites that this is the Midland form of the third person plural in early English

periwig, -s 'peɹɪwɪg, -z

periwig-pated 'peɹɪwɪg'peɪtɪd

perjur|e, -es, -ing, -ed, -er/s 'pɜˑdʒə˞, -z, -ɹɪŋ, -d, -ɹə˞/z

perk, -s, -ing, -ed 'pɜˑk, -s, -ɪŋ, -t

Perkes, Clement (2HIV) 'klemənt 'pɑ˞ks

Perk, Gilbert (HVIII) 'gɪlbə˞t 'pɑ˞k

Note.—The Folio gives 'Pecke,' which Stokes says is a var. of 'Sir Gilbert Perke, priest'

perk|y, -ier, -iest, -ily, -iness 'pɜˑk|ɪ, -ɪə˞, -ɪst, -ɪlɪ, -ɪnɪs

per-lady (*from 'by'r lady'*) pə˞'leɪdɪ, [pɜˑ'l-]

Note.—Evans (in MWW) is a Welshman, and speaks in a Welsh accent, if somewhat inconsistently. This is an example of S.'s direction to the actor (by way of semiphonetic spellings) to adopt such an accent, more or less, for the sake of wringing the most satire out of plays on words stemming from confusions with, and corruptions of, English pronunciation via the Welsh tongue

pernicious, -ly, -ness pɜˑ'nɪʃəs [pə˞'n-], -lɪ, -nɪs

peroration, -s ˌpeɹə'ɹeɪʃn, -z

perpend, -s, -ing, -ed pə˞'pend, -z, -ɪŋ, -ɪd

perpendicular, -s, -ly ˌpɜˑpɪn'dɪkjʊlə˞, -z, -lɪ

perpetual, -ly pə˞'petʃʊəl, -ɪ

perpetuit|y, -ies ˌpɜˑpɪ'tjuɪt|ɪ, -ɪz

perplex, -es, -ing/ly, -ed pɜˑ'pleks [pə˞'p-], -ɪz, -ɪŋ/lɪ, -t

perplexed|ly, -ness pɜˑ'pleksɪd|lɪ [pə˞'p-], -nɪs

perplexit|y, -ies pɜˑ'pleksɪt|ɪ, -ɪz

per se (*L.*) (TC, I.ii.15) ˌpɛ˞ 'sɛ

Note.—This is a common term in modern speech and commonly given a

psuedo-anglicized pronunciation of
[ˌpɝˈseɪ̆]

Perseus (HV, TC) ˈpɝˌsjus, -sjəs [-sɪəs]

persever pəˈsevə̆

persever|e, -es, -ing/ly, -ed; -ance
ˌpɝˈsɪˈvɪɝ̆, -z, -ɪɪ̆ŋ/lɪ̆, -d; -ɪəns
*Note.— 'Perseverance' in MAC, IV.iii.93
and TC, III.iii.150 is pronounced*
[pəˈsevɹəns]*, the former regular
pronunciation of the word*

Persia (COM, LEAR, MV), **-n/s** ˈpɝˈʒə,
ˈpɝˈʒn/z

persist, -s, -ing, -ed pəˈsɪst, -s, -ɪɪ̆ŋ, -ɪd

persisten|ce, -cy, -t/ly pəˈsɪstən|s, -sɪ̆,
-t/lɪ̆

persistive pəˈsɪstɪv

person (**P.**), **-s; -able** ˈpɝˈsn̩, -z; -əbl̩

personage, -s ˈpɝˈsn̩ɪdʒ, -ɪz

personal, -ly ˈpɝˈsn̩l̩, -ɪ̆

personaliz|e, -es, -ing, -ed ˈpɝˈsn̩l̩aɪ̆z, -ɪz,
-ɪɪ̆ŋ, -d

personat|e, -es, -ing, -ed, -or/s ˈpɝˈsn̩eɪ̆t,
-s, -ɪɪ̆ŋ, -ɪd, -ə̆/z

Person, Master (LLL) ˈmastə̆ ˈpaɝ̆ˈsn̩
*Note.—The spelling of this word in LLL,
IV.ii.79 meaning 'parson' (a clergyman),
is analogous to how one says 'sergeant,'
and the chiefly Brit. pronunciations of
'clerk,' and 'Derby,' i.e.,* [ˈklɑːk] *and*
[ˈdɑːbɪ]*, which become* [ˈklaɝ̆k] *and*
[ˈdaɝ̆bɪ] *in the United States. For its
relevance in the arcane wit of LLL, IV.ii,
see R. W. David's annotations for lines
80–84 (*The Arden Shakespeare, 1951)

perspective, -s, -ly pɝˈspektɪv, -z, -lɪ̆
*Note.—Stress is on the first syllable
(and, some might add, the third) in RII,
II.ii.18; Sonn. 24.4; ALL'S, V.iii.48,
creating the pronunciation of either*
[ˈpɝˈspektɪv] *or* [ˌpɝˈspekˈtiv]*. It is
arguably stressed likewise in TN,
V.i.215, depending on how one decides
to scan the line, i.e., with or without an
epic caesura. In* The Arden Shakespeare

*edition of TN (edited by J. M. Lothian
and T. W. Craik, 1975), first-syllable
stress is asserted as the only choice*

perspicuous, -ly, -ness pəˈspɪkjʊəs, -lɪ̆,
-nɪs

Per Styga, per manes vehor (*L.*) (TIT,
II.i.136) pɛɝ̆ ˈstidʒɪɑ pɛɝ̆ ˈmanɛs
vɛˈhɔɝ̆ [ˈvihɔɝ̆]
*Note.—Many editors emend 'Styga' to
'Stygia'; and since that is also my
preference, I have transcribed it
accordingly*

persuad|e, -es, -ing, -ed, -er/s pəˈsweɪ̆d,
-z, -ɪɪ̆ŋ, -ɪd, -ə̆/z

persuasion, -s pəˈsweɪ̆ʒn̩, -z

persuasive, -ly, -ness pəˈsweɪ̆sɪv, -lɪ̆,
-nɪs

pert, -est, -ly, -ness ˈpɝˈt, -ɪst, -lɪ̆, -nɪs

pertain, -s, -ing, -ed pɝˈteɪ̆n, -z, -ɪɪ̆ŋ, -d

pertaunt-like, perttaunt-like, *or* **Pair-
Taunt like** [ˈpɛɝ̆ˌtɔntlaɪ̆k [ˈpɝˌt-]
*Note.—Literally, 'pertaunt' or 'pair-
taunt' means possessing four of a kind in
an old game of cards called Post and
Pair, and essentially means (in LLL,
V.ii.67) having the winning or outrank-
ing hand*

perturb, -s, -ing, -ed pɝˈtɝ̆b, -z, -ɪɪ̆ŋ, -d
(*arguably* [ˈ--] *in* CYM, III.iv.107)

perturbation, -s ˌpɝˈtə̆ˈbeɪ̆ʃn̩, -z

perusal, -s pəˈɹuzl̩ [pɹˈɹ-], -z

perus|e, -es, -ing, -ed, -er/s pəˈɹuz, -ɪz,
-ɪɪ̆ŋ, -d, -ə̆/z

perverse, -ly, -ness pɝˈvɝ̆s, -lɪ̆, -nɪs

pervert (*s.*), **-s** ˈpɝˈvɝ̆t, -s

pervert (*v.*), **-s, -ing, -ed, -er/s** pɝˈvɝ̆t,
-s, -ɪɪ̆ŋ, -ɪd, -ə̆/z

pester, -s, -ing, -ed ˈpestə̆, -z, -ɪɪ̆ŋ, -d

pestiferous, -ly peˈstɪfə̆ɹəs, -lɪ̆

pestilence, -s ˈpestɪləns, -ɪz

pestilent, -ly ˈpestɪlənt, -lɪ̆

petard, -s pɹˈtaɝ̆d [peˈtaɝ̆d], -z

Peter (*2HVI, KJ, RJ, TS*) ˈpiɟə̆ [ˈpitə̆]

Peter, Friar (*MEAS*) ˌfɹaɪ̆ɝ̆ ˈpiɟə̆ [ˈpitə̆]

i w**e** ɪ cit**y** ɪ h**i**t e l**e**t ɛ d**e**but æ c**a**n a p**a**ss ɝ b**ir**d ʌ h**u**t ə **a**gain ə supp**er** u y**ou**
ʊ sh**ou**ld o **o**bey ɔ **aw**l ɒ c**o**p ɑ f**a**ther eɪ p**ai**d aɪ h**igh** oʊ g**o** ɔɪ v**oi**ce aʊ f**ou**nd ɪɝ̆ **ear**
ɛɝ̆ **air** ʊɝ̆ **poor** ɔɝ̆ **fork** ɑɝ̆ **park** aɪ̆ɝ̆ **fire** aʊ̆ɝ̆ **hour** b **b**oy p **p**it d **d**og t **t**op g **g**ot
k **k**id h **h**ow fi be**h**ave dʒ **j**ot tʃ **ch**ew z **z**any s **s**oft v **v**at f **f**at ʒ trea**s**ure ʃ **sh**ip ð **th**e
θ **th**in m **m**an n **n**o ŋ ha**ng** l **l**ip j **y**es w **w**on ʍ **wh**ew ɹ **r**igger, ai**r**y ɾ ma**tt**er

petition, -s, -ing, -ed, -er/s pɪˈtɪʃn̩, -z, -ɪŋ, -d, -ɚ/z

petitionary pɪˈtɪʃṇəˌɹɪ

Peto (*1HIV, 2HIV*) ˈpitoŭ [ˈpiɾoŭ]

Petrarch (RJ) ˈpetɹɑɚ̆k

Petruchio (RJ, *TS*) pɪˈtɹukjoŭ, -kɪoŭ
Note.—Kökeritz argues in favor of [pɪˈtɹutʃĭo, -tʃɪoŭ] *(see Kökeritz's* Shakespeare's Names: A Pronouncing Dictionary, *pp. 22, 79), but his scholarship and quest for accuracy in this case is perhaps a mite over-ingenious, since popular acceptance of* [pɪˈtɹukjoŭ, -kɪoŭ] *is nearly universal*

petter (*from 'better'*) ˈpeɾɚ
Note.—Evans (in MWW*) is a Welshman, and speaks in a Welsh accent, if somewhat inconsistently. This is an example of S.'s direction to the actor (by way of semiphonetic spellings) to adopt such an accent, more or less, for the sake of wringing the most satire out of plays on words stemming from confusions with, and corruptions of, English pronunciation via the Welsh tongue*

petticoat, -s, -ed ˈpeɾɪkoŭt, -s, -ɪd

pettish, -ly, -ness ˈpeɾɪʃ, -lɪ, -nɪs

pettitoes ˈpeɾɪtoŭz

pett|y, -ier, -iest, -ily, -iness/es ˈpeɾ|ɪ, -ɪɚ, -ɪɪst, -ɪlɪ, -ɪnɪs/ɪz

Petty-ward (MWW) ˈpeɾɪˌwɔɚ̆d

pew, -s ˈpju, -z

pew-fellow, -s ˈpjuˌfeloŭ, -z

pewter, -s, -er/s ˈpjuɾɚ, -z, -ɹɚ/z

Phaët(h)on (3HVI, RII, RJ, TGV) ˈfeĭəθən [-θɒn, -ətən]

Phaeton (3HVI, RII, RJ, TGV) ˈfeĭətən

phantasime, -s ˈfæntəˌzim [ˈfæntæzɪm, fænˈtæsimɛ], -z
Note.—The pronunciations offered are entirely conjectural. The word appears only once in S., i.e., LLL, IV.i.100 *(or twice if one presumes that 'phantasims' in* LLL, V.i.18 *is meant to be the same word), and perhaps only once in all of English literature (cf.* OED*). In either instance the word is not contained within a verse line of iambic pentameter, so no hint is given as to its correct*

syllabic stress. Two clues of pronunciation are: the It. 'fantasima' or 'fantasma'; and the fact that the English word 'phantasm' has a var. spelling of 'phantasme.' However, Richard W. David, editor of LLL *(*The Arden Shakespeare, *1951) points out that "The sense required is something distinct from 'phantasm'; not a creature of the fancy, but one full of fancies." It is prudent to remember that Boyet, who speaks the word in* LLL, IV.i.100, *is a Frenchman, and that he is speaking to the French Princess about Armado, a Spanish fantastical. In its second instance (*LLL, V.i.18*), Holofernes is also referring to the Spaniard. In any case, the word's pronunciation must ultimately be dictated by its sense, the rhythm of the speech, and euphony. Brian Gibbons, editor of* RJ *(*The Arden Shakespeare, *1980) emends the words 'phantacies' and 'fantasticoes,' found in* RJ, II.iv.28 *in the Folio and Quarto versions respectively, to 'phantasimes'*

phantasm, -s ˈfæntæzəm, -z

phantasma, -s fænˈtæzmə, -z

Pharamond, King (HV) ˈkɪŋ ˈfæɹəmɒnd [-mənd]

Pharaoh (ADO, 1HIV), **-s** ˈfɛɚ̆ɹoŭ, -z

Pharsalia (AC) fɑɚ̆ˈseĭlɪə, -ljə

Pheazar or **Pheezar** (MWW) ˈfizɚ

Phebe or **Phoebe** (*AYLI*, LLL), **-s** ˈfibɪ, -z

Phibbus (*corruption of* **Phoebus** *in* MSND) ˈfɪbəs

Philadelphos (AC) ˌfɪləˈdelfɒs

Philario (*CYM*) fɪˈlɑɚ̆ɹɪoŭ

Philarmonus (CYM) ˌfɪlɑɚ̆ˈmoŭnəs

Philemon (ADO, *PER*) faˈlimən [fɪˈl-, -mɒn]

Philip (HV, *KJ*, MEAS, TS) ˈfɪlɪp

Philip of Macedon (HV) ˈfɪlɪp əv ˈmæsɪdɒn

Philippan (AC) fɪˈlɪpən

Philippe (2HVI) fɪˈlip

Philippi (AC, JUL) fɪˈlɪpaĭ

Phillida (MSND) ˈfɪlɪdə

Philo (*AC*) ˈfaĭloŭ

Philomel (CYM, LUC, MSND, Sonn. 102, TIT, TNK), **-s** 'fɪlomel [-ləm-], -z
Philomela (PP, TIT) 'fɪloɱelə [-ləm-]
Note.—Although TIT, II.iii.38 *(First Quarto) gives 'Philomela,' it is usually emended to 'Philomel,' which scans well and is consistent with the name elsewhere in the text. Jonathan Bate (editor,* The Arden Shakespeare, *1995) is particular about retaining 'Philomela.' In* TIT, IV.i.52, *'Philomela' is appropriate*
philosopher (**P.**), **-s** fɪ'lɒsəfɚ, -z
philosoph|y, -ies fɪ'lɒsəf|ɪ, -ɪz
Philostrate (*MSND*) 'fɪləstɹeɪt
Philoten (PER) 'fɪlətən ['faɪl-]
Philotus (*TIM*) 'fɪlətəs ['faɪl-]
phlegm, -z 'flem, -z
phlegmatic, -s; -al, -ally fleg'mæɾɪk, -s; -ḷ, -əlɪ
Phoebe *or* **Phebe** (*AYLI*, LLL, TIT), **-s** 'fibɪ, -z
Phoebus *or* **Phœbus** (AC, ADO, CYM, HAM, 1HIV, HV, 3HVI, MV, RJ, TC, TEM, WT) 'fibəs
Phoenicia *or* **Phœnicia** (AC) fɪ'niʃɪə, -ʃə
Phoenician *or* **Phœnician** (AC), **-s** fɪ'niʃn̩, -z
phoenix (**P.**) (COM, PT, TN, Sonn. 19), **-es** 'finɪks, -ɪz
phoenix-like 'finɪks,laɪk
Photinus (AC) 'fɒtn̩əs ['foʊt-, -tɪnəs]
phras|e, -es, -ing, -ed 'fɹeɪz, -ɪz, -ɪŋ, -d
phraseless 'fɹeɪzlɪs
Phrygia (TC, TN) 'fɹɪdʒɪə, -dʒjə
Phrygian (LUC, TC, MWW) 'fɹɪdʒɪən, -dʒən
Note.—This word is always disyllabic, i.e., ['fɹɪdʒən] *in* S.
Phrynia (*TIM*) 'fɹɪnɪə
phthisic *or* **tisick** 'tɪzɪk
physic (**P.**), **-s, -king, -ked** 'fɪzɪk, -s, -ɪŋ, -t
physic|al, -ally 'fɪzɪk|ḷ, -əlɪ

physician (**P.**) (LEAR), **-s** fɪ'zɪʃn̩, -z
physiognom|y, -ies ,fɪzɪ'ɒgnəm|ɪ [-'ɒnəm-], -ɪz
pia mater (*L.*) (LLL, IV.ii.68; TC, II.i.73) ,pia 'mɑtɚ ['meɪtɚ]
Note.—This phrase is a common one, still used in modern medicine. When speaking in the modern vernacular, accepted pronunciations are [,piə 'mɑɾɚ] *or* [,paɪə 'meɪɾɚ]
pibble-pabble (*from 'bibble-babble'*) 'pɪbḷ,pæbḷ
Note.—Fluellen (in HV*) is a Welshman, and speaks in a Welsh accent, if somewhat inconsistently. This is an example of S.'s direction to the actor (by way of semiphonetic spellings) to adopt such an accent, more or less. (See 'Shakespeare's Foreign Languages' § 3.1 of this dictionary)*
Pible (*from 'Bible'*) 'paɪbḷ
*Note.—This is a curious blunder by Dr. Caius (*MWW, II.iii.7*), in that it sounds more like the kind one would expect from Evans. Be that as it may, Doctor Caius is the stereotypical foreigner, given to foolish arrogance, and ineptly handling English pronunciation. This is an example of S.'s direction to the actor (by way of semiphonetic spellings) to adopt such an accent, more or less, for the sake of wringing the most satire out of plays on words stemming from confusions with, and corruptions of, English pronunciation via the French tongue*
Picardy (1HVI, 2HVI) 'pɪkɚdɪ
pick, -s, -ing, -ed, -er/s 'pɪk, -s, -ɪŋ, -t, -ɚ/z
pickaxe, -s 'pɪkæks, -ɪz
Pickbone, Francis (2HIV) 'fɹansɪs 'pɪkboʊn
Picked-hatch *or* **Pickt-hatch** (MWW) 'pɪkt,hætʃ

---

i w**e** ɪ cit**y** ɪ h**i**t e l**e**t ɛ d**e**but æ c**a**n ɑ p**a**ss ɝ b**ir**d ʌ h**u**t ə **a**gain ɚ supp**er** u y**ou** ʊ sh**oul**d o **o**bey ɔ **aw**l ɒ c**o**p ɑ f**a**ther eɪ p**ai**d aɪ h**igh** oʊ g**o** ɔɪ v**oi**ce aʊ f**ou**nd ɪɚ **ear** ɛɚ **air** ʊɚ **poor** ɔɚ f**or**k ɑɚ p**ar**k aɪɚ f**ire** aʊɚ h**our** b **b**oy p **p**it d **d**og t **t**op g g**o**t k **k**id h **h**ow fi be**h**ave dʒ **j**ot tʃ **ch**ew z **z**any s **s**oft v **v**at f **f**at ʒ trea**s**ure ʃ **sh**ip ð **th**e θ **th**in m **m**an n **n**o ŋ ha**ng** l **l**ip j **y**es w **w**on ʌ **wh**ew ɹ **r**igger, air**y** ɾ ma**tt**er

picket, -s, -ing, -ed 'pɪkɪt, -s, -ɪŋ, -ɪd

pickl|e, -es, -ing, -ed 'pɪkl̩, -z, -ɪŋ, -d

pickle-herring 'pɪkl̩ˌheɹɪŋ

pick(-)lock, -s 'pɪklɒk, -s

pick-purse, -s 'pɪkˌpɝ·s, -ɪz

pickthanks 'pɪkθæŋks

pictur|e, -es, -ing, -ed 'pɪktʃɚ, -z, -ɹɪŋ, -d

picture-like 'pɪktʃɚˌlaɪk

pid (*from 'bid'*) 'pɪd (*see* **prings**)

pie, -s 'paɪ, -z

'pie (*from* **magpie**) 'paɪ

piebald 'paɪbɔld

piec|e, -es, -ing, -ed, -er/s 'pis, -ɪz, -ɪŋ, -t, -ɚ/z

Pie Corner (2HIV) 'paɪ 'kɔɚ·nɚ

pied, -ness 'paɪd, -nɪs

pier, -s 'pɪɚ·, -z

pierc|e, -es, -ing, -ed, -er/s 'pɪɚ·s, -ɪz, -ɪŋ, -t, -ɚ/z

Note.—In RII, V.iii.125, *'pierce' is meant to rhyme with 'rehearse' in the couplet (as is 'there' to 'ear' in the two preceding lines), but these sorts of rhymes are nowadays typically forsaken, giving over for the sake of meaning to the modern ear*

piety 'paɪɪtɪ

pig, -s, -ging, -ged 'pɪg, -z, -ɪŋ, -d

Note.—This word is used for 'big' in HV, *IV.vii.13–15, and is the source of some humor (though not intentional on the part of the character). Fluellen (in* HV*) is a Welshman, and speaks in a Welsh accent, if somewhat inconsistently. This is an example of S.'s direction to the actor (by way of semiphonetic spellings) to adopt such an accent, more or less, for the sake of wringing the most satire out of plays on words stemming from confusions with, and corruptions of, English pronunciation via the Welsh tongue*

pigeon, -s 'pɪdʒɪn, -z

pight (*archaic p.t. and p.p. of* **pitch**, *as in* tents) 'paɪt

pig-like 'pɪgˌlaɪk

pigment, -s 'pɪgmənt, -s

Pigmies *or* **Pygmies** (ADO) 'pɪgmɪz

pigm|y, -ies 'pɪgm|ɪ, -ɪz

pig(-)nut, -s 'pɪgnʌt, -s

Pigrogromitus (TN) ˌpɪgɹoˈgɹɒmɪtəs

pik|e (P.), -es, -ing, -ed, -er/s 'paɪk, -s, -ɪŋ, -t, -ɚ/z

Pilate (RII, RIII) 'paɪlət

Pilch (*PER*) 'pɪltʃ

pilchard, -s 'pɪltʃɚd, -z

pilcher, -s 'pɪltʃɚ, -z

pil|e, -es, -ing, -ed 'paɪl, -z, -ɪŋ, -d

pilfer, -s, -ing/s, -ed, -er/s 'pɪlfɚ, -z, -ɹɪŋ/z, -d, -ɹɚ/z

pilgrim, -s; -age/s 'pɪlgɹɪm, -z; -ɪdʒ/ɪz

pill, -s, -ing, -ed 'pɪl, -z, -ɪŋ, -d

pillag|e, -es, -ing, -ed, -er/s 'pɪlɪdʒ, -ɪz, -ɪŋ, -d, -ɚ/z

pillar, -s, -ed 'pɪlɚ, -z, -d

Pillicock *or* **Pillycock** (LEAR) 'pɪlɪkɒk

pillor|y, -ies, -ying, -ied 'pɪlə·ɹ|ɪ, -ɪz, -ɪŋ, -ɪd

Pimpernell, Henry (TS) 'henɹɪ 'pɪmpɚnel

pin, -s, -ning, -ned 'pɪn, -z, -ɪŋ, -d

pin-buttock 'pɪnˌbʌɾək

pinch, -es, -ing, -ed, -er/s 'pɪntʃ, -ɪz, -ɪŋ, -t, -ɚ/z

Pinch, Doctor (*COM*) 'dɒktɚ 'pɪntʃ

pinch-spotted 'pɪntʃˌspɒtɪd

Pindarus (*JUL*) 'pɪndəɹəs

pin|e, -es, -ing, -ed 'paɪn, -z, -ɪŋ, -d

Pine (Pene) gelidus timor occupat artus (*L.*) (2HVI, IV.i.116) 'pine ('pɛnɛ) 'dʒɛlɪdus 'timɔɚ· 'ɒkjupɑt 'aɚ·tus *Note.—The word 'occupat' would normally sound more like* ['oŭkupɑt]*, but the pronunciation given above evokes (to the modern ear mostly unlearned in Latin) more of the sense of the word, i.e., 'occupy' (see 'Shakespeare's Foreign Languages' § 1.10 of this dictionary)*

pinfold, -s, -ing, -ed 'pɪnfoŭld, -z, -ɪŋ, -ɪd

pinion, -s, -ing, -ed 'pɪnjən, -z, -ɪŋ, -d

pink, -s, -ing, -ed; -ish 'pɪŋk, -s, -ɪŋ, -t; -ɪʃ

pinnace, -s 'pɪnɪs, -ɪz

pin(-)prick, -s 'pɪnpɹɪk, -s

pinse 'pɪns

pint, -s 'paɪnt, -s

pint-pot, -s 'paɪntˌpɒt, -s

pion, -s, -ing, -ed 'paɪən, -z, -ɪŋ, -d

pioneer, -s, -ing, -ed ˌpaɪəˈnɪɚ, -z, -ɹɪŋ, -d

pioner, -s 'paɪənɚ, -z

pious, -ly, -ness 'paɪ̆əs, -lɪ, -nɪs
pip, -s, -ping, -ped 'pɪp, -s, -ɪŋ, -t
pip|e, -es, -ing, -ed, -er/s 'paɪ̆p, -s, -ɪŋ, -t, -ɚ/z
pipe-wine 'paɪ̆p͵waɪ̆n
pippin, -s 'pɪpɪn, -z
Pippin, King 'kɪŋ 'pɪpɪn
pirat|e, -es, -ing, -ed 'paɪɻ̆ɪt, -s, -ɪŋ, -ɪd
pir|e, -es, -ing, -ed 'paɪ̆ɚ, -z, -ɹɪŋ, -d
Pirithous (*TNK*) paɪ̆'ɹɪθoəs

*Note.—Lois Potter (editor, The Arden
Shakespeare, 1997), in her annotations
for the list of roles, cites that in Act One
of TNK, the name Pirithous "evidently
has three syllables, stressed on the first,"
but that in Act Two, "scansion requires
it to be a four-syllable word, stressed on
the second syllable." I favor consistency,
especially when it comes to those names
pronounced multiple times in a play. By
recognizing that the lines to which Lois
Potter is referring, i.e., TNK, I.i.207,
219, contain epic caesuras, the
pronunciation of the name remains
consistent with that which is proffered
above*

Pisa (TS) 'pizə
Pisanio (*CYM*) pɪ̆'zɑnɪoŏ, -njoŭ
pish (*interj.*) (*expression of disdain*) 'pɪʃ, 'pʃ
pismire, -s 'pɪsmaɪ̆ɚ ['pɪzm-], -z
piss, -es, -ing, -ed 'pɪs, -ɪz, -ɪŋ, -t
pissing-conduit 'pɪsɪŋ 'kɒndɪt [-'kʌndɪt, -djuɪt]
pistol, -s 'pɪstəl, -z
Pistol, Ancient (*2HIV, HV, MWW*)
'eĭnʃənt 'pɪstəl

*Note.—'Ancient' in this instance is
thought to be a corruption of 'Ensign,'
Pistol's rank*

pistol-proof 'pɪstəl͵pɹuf
pit, -s, -ting, -ted 'pɪt, -s, -ɪŋ, -ɪd
pitch, -es, -ing, -ed 'pɪtʃ, -ɪz, -ɪŋ, -t
pitch-balls 'pɪtʃ͵bɔlz

pitchy 'pɪtʃɪ
piteous, -ly, -ness 'pɪɻ̆ɪəs, -lɪ, -nɪs
pitfall, -s 'pɪtfɔl, -z
pith, -s, -less 'pɪθ, -s, -lɪs
pith|y, -ier, -iest, -ily, -iness 'pɪθ|ɪ, -ɪɚ, -ɪɪst, -ɪlɪ, -ɪnɪs
piti|ful, -fully, -fulness 'pɪɻ̆ɪ|fʊl, -flɪ, -fʊlnɪs
pitiful-hearted 'pɪɻ̆ɪfʊl͵hɑɚ̆tɪd
pittance, -s 'pɪtn̩s, -ɪz
pittikins 'pɪɻ̆ɪkɪnz

*Note.—This is a diminutive form of 'pity'
in the mild oath 'od's pittikins' ('God's
pity'—cf. CYM, IV.ii.293)*

pit|y (P.), -ies, -ying/ly, -ied 'pɪɻ̆|ɪ, -ɪz, -ɪŋ/lɪ, -ɪd
Piùe per dolcezza che per forza (*macaronic*) (PER, II.ii.27) 'pĭu pɛɾ dol'tʃɛˈtsɑ kɛ pɛɾ 'fɔɾtsɑ

*Note.—The Quarto gives, "The motto
thus, in Spanish, Pue Per doleera kee per
forsa" but isn't (pure) Spanish at all. It
seems to be a mixture of Spanish,
Italian, and possibly even Portuguese—
with textual errors and corruptions.
Another possible emendation for this
motto is, 'Piu per dolcera que per forca,'
which is more Italian, but not entirely. If
one chooses to say it this way, the
pronunciation is* ['pju pɛɾ dol'tʃɛˈɾɑ kɛ pɛɾ 'fɔɾkɑ]

Pius (TIT) 'paɪ̆əs
plac|e, -es, -ing, -ed, -er/s 'pleĭs, -ɪz, -ɪŋ, -t, -ɚ/z
Placentio, Signor (RJ) 'sinjɔɚ pla'senʃĭo
placket, -s; -hole/s 'plækɪt, -s; -fioŭl/z
plagu|e, -es, -ing, -ed, -er/s 'pleĭg, -z, -ɪŋ, -d, -ɚ/z
plagu|y, -ily, -iness 'pleĭg|ɪ, -ɪlɪ, -ɪnɪs
plain, -s, -er, -est, -ly, -ness 'pleĭn, -z, -ɚ, -ɪst, -lɪ, -nɪs
plain-dealing 'pleĭn͵dilɪŋ
plaining (*aphaeretic form of* **complaining**)**, -s** 'pleĭnɪŋ, -z

i we ɪ city ɪ hit e let ɛ debut æ can a pass ɚ bird ʌ hut ə again ɚ supper u you
ʊ should o obey ɔ awl ɒ cop ɑ father eĭ paid aĭ high oŭ go ɔĭ voice aŭ found ɪɚ̆ ear
ɛɚ̆ air ʊɚ̆ poor ɔɚ̆ fork ɑɚ̆ park aĭɚ̆ fire aŭɚ̆ hour b boy p pit d dog t top g got
k kid h how fi behave dʒ jot tʃ chew z zany s soft v vat f fat ʒ treasure ʃ ship ð the
θ thin m man n no ŋ hang l lip j yes w won ʍ whew ɹ rigger, airy ɾ matter

plain(-)song, -s ˈpleɪ̆nsɒŋ, -z
plaint, -s ˈpleɪ̆nt, -s
plaintful ˈpleɪ̆ntfʊl
plaintiff, -s ˈpleɪ̆ntɪf, -s
plait, -s, -ing, -ed ˈplæt [ˈpleɪ̆t], -s, -ɪŋ,
-ɪd
planched ˈplanʃɪd [-ntʃɪd]
Note.—Although the word 'planch' may
be either a s. (a wooden board or plank)
or a v. (to floor a floor with wooden
boards or planks), in its only instance in
S., i.e., MEAS, IV.i.30, it is used as a
participial adj. (made of wooden boards
or planks) and is thus properly spoken
disyllabically, regardless of the fact that
the line requires a disyllable there
anyhow to fulfill the meter
planet, -s ˈplænɪt, -s
planetary ˈplænɪtə˞ɹɪ
plank, -s, -ing, -ed ˈplæŋk, -s, -ɪŋ, -t
plant, -s, -ing/s, -ed, -er/s ˈplant, -s,
-ɪŋ/z, -ɪd, -ə˞/z
plantage ˈplantɪdʒ
Plantagenet (1HIV, HV, 1HVI, 2HVI,
3HVI, KJ, RII, RIII), -s plænˈtædʒɪnɪt, -s
Note.—At times, this name is trisyllabic,
i.e., [plænˈtædʒnɪt] in order to fit more
rightly the metrical requirements of the
verse line, e.g., 3HVI, I.i.40, 48
Plantagenet, Arthur (KJ) ˈɑ˞θə˞
plænˈtædʒɪnɪt (see Note for Plantagenet)
Plantagenet, Edward (2HVI) ˈedwə˞d
plænˈtædʒɪnɪt (see Note for Plantagenet)
Plantagenet, Henry (HV) ˈhenɹɪ
plænˈtædʒɪnɪt (see Note for Plantagenet)
Plantagenet, Margaret (RIII) ˈmɑ˞gə˞ɹɪt,
[-gɹɪt] plænˈtædʒɪnɪt (see Note for
Plantagenet)
Plantagenet, Richard (1HVI, 2HVI,
3HVI) ˈɹɪtʃə˞d plænˈtædʒɪnɪt (see Note
for Plantagenet)
plantain, -s ˈplæntɪn [ˈplantɪn], -z
plantation, -s planˈteɪ̆ʃn̩, -z
plash, -es, -ing, -ed; -y ˈplæʃ, -ɪz, -ɪŋ, -t;
-ɪ
Plashy (RII) ˈplæʃɪ
plat|e, -es, -ing, -ed ˈpleɪ̆t, -s, -ɪŋ, -ɪd

platform, -s, -ing, -ed ˈplætfɔ˞m, -z, -ɪŋ,
-d
plausib|le, -ly, -leness ˈplɔzɪb|l̩, -lɪ, -l̩nɪs
plausive ˈplɔzɪv [-ɔsɪv]
Plautus (HAM) ˈplɔtəs [ˈplɔɾəs]
play, -s, -ing, -ed, -er/s ˈpleɪ̆, -z, -ɪŋ, -d,
-ə˞/z
Player (HAM), -s ˈpleɪ̆ə˞, -z
playfellow, -s ˈpleɪ̆ˌfeloʊ̆, -z
play(-)fere (playmate), -s ˈpleɪ̆fɪ˞, -z
plea, -s ˈpli, -z
pleach, -es, -ing, -ed ˈplitʃ [ˈpleɪ̆tʃ], -ɪz,
-ɪŋ, -t
plead, -s, -ing/ly, -ed, -er/s ˈplid, -z,
-ɪŋ/lɪ, -ɪd, -ə˞/z
pleasance ˈplezəns
pleasant, -er, -est, -ly, -ness ˈpleznt̩, -ə˞,
-ɪst, -lɪ, -nɪs
pleas|e, -es, -ing/ly, -ed ˈpliz, -ɪz, -ɪŋ/lɪ, -d
please-man ˈplizˌmæn
pleasurab|le, -ly, -leness ˈpleʒə˞ɹəb|l̩, -lɪ,
-l̩nɪs
pleasur|e (P.), -es, -ing, -ed ˈpleʒə˞, -z,
-ɹɪŋ, -d
pleat, -s, -ing, -ed ˈplit, -s, -ɪŋ, -ɪd
pleb, -s ˈpleb, -z
plebeian, -s plɪˈbiən, -z
Note.—Stressed on the first syllable
[ˈplibɪən] in AC, IV.xii.34; COR, I.ix.7,
V.iv.40
plebeii (L.) (COR, II.iii.182) ˈplɛbɪaɪ̆
pled (p.t. and p.p. of plead, q.v.) ˈpled
pledg|e, -es, -ing, -ed, -er/s ˈpledʒ, -ɪz,
-ɪŋ, -d, -ə˞/z
plenitude ˈplenɪtjud
plenteous, -ly, -ness ˈplentɪ̆əs, -lɪ, -nɪs
plenti|ful, -fully, -fulness ˈplentɪ|fʊl, -fəlɪ,
-fʊlnɪs
plent|y, -ies ˈplent|ɪ, -ɪz
pless (from 'bless'), -ing, -ed ˈples, -ɪŋ,
-t, -ɪd (adj.)
Note.—Evans (in MWW) is a Welshman, and speaks in a Welsh accent, if
somewhat inconsistently. This is an
example of S.'s direction to the actor (by
way of semiphonetic spellings) to adopt
such an accent, more or less, for the
sake of wringing the most satire out of
plays on words stemming from confu-

sions with, and corruptions of, English pronunciation via the Welsh tongue

pleurisy 'pluɔ˞ˌɹɪsɫ

pliant, -ly, -ness 'plaɪ̆ənt, -lɪ, -nɪs

pliers 'plaɪ̆ɔ˞z

plight, -s, -ing, -ed 'plaɪ̆t, -s, -ɪŋ, -ɪd

plighter, -s 'plaɪ̆tɔ˞, -z

plod, -s, -ding, -ded, -der/s 'plɒd, -z, -ɪŋ, -ɪd, -ɔ˞/z

plop, -s, -ping, -ped 'plɒp, -s, -ɪŋ, -t

plot, -s, -ting, -ted, -ter/s 'plɒt, -s, -ɪŋ, -ɪd, -ɔ˞/z

plot-proof 'plɒtpɹuf [ˈ-ˈ-]

plough (*chiefly Brit. var. of* **plow**, *q.v.*) 'plaʊ̆

plough-iron (*chiefly Brit. var. of* **plow-iron**, *q.v.*), **-s** 'plaʊ̆ˌaɪ̆ɔ˞n, -z

plow, -s, -ing, -ed, -er/s; -able 'plaʊ̆, -z, -ɪŋ, -d, -ɔ˞/z; -əbl̩
Note.—In HV, IV.viii.15, *this is the Welshman, Fluellen's, substitution for 'blows' and is pronounced* ['ploʊ̆z]. *See 'Shakespeare's Foreign Languages' § 3.1 of this dictionary*

plowboy, -s 'plaʊ̆bɔĭ, -z

plow-iron, -s 'plaʊ̆ˌaɪ̆ɔ˞n, -z

plowman 'plaʊ̆mən

plowmen 'plaʊ̆mən [-men]

ploy, -s 'plɔĭ, -z

pluck, -s, -ing, -ed 'plʌk, -s, -ɪŋ, -t

plug, -s, -ging, -ged 'plʌg, -z, -ɪŋ, -d

plum, -s 'plʌm, -z

plum-broth 'plʌmˌbɹɒθ

plumage, -s 'plumɪdʒ, -ɪz

plumb, -s, -ing, -ed, -er/s 'plʌm, -z, -ɪŋ, -d, -ɔ˞/z

plum-broth 'plʌmˌbɹɒθ

plum|e, -es, -ing, -ed 'plum, -z, -ɪŋ, -d

plume-plucked 'plumˌplʌkt

plummet, -s 'plʌmɪt, -s

plump, -s, -ing, -ed; -er, -est, -ly, -ness 'plʌmp, -s, -ɪŋ, -t; -ɔ˞, -ɪst, -lɪ, -nɪs

plum-pudding, -s ˌplʌm'pʊdɪŋ, -z

plumpy 'plʌmpɫ

plumy 'plumɫ

plunder, -s, -ing, -ed, -er/s; -ous 'plʌndɔ˞, -z, -ɹɪŋ, -d, -ɹɔ˞/z; -ɹəs

plung|e, -es, -ing, -ed, -er/s 'plʌndʒ, -ɪz, -ɪŋ, -d, -ɔ˞/z

plural, -s, -ly 'pluɔ˞ɹəl, -z, -ɫ

Pluto (COR, 2HIV, LUC, TC, TIT) 'plutoʊ̆

Plutus (ALL'S, JUL, TC, TIM) 'plutəs

pl|y, -ies, -ying, -ied 'plaɪ̆, -z, -ɪŋ, -d

Po (KJ, TNK) 'poʊ̆

pocas palabras (*Sp.*) (TS, Ind.i.5) 'pokɑs pɑ'labɹɑs

pock, -s, -ed, -y 'pɒk, -s, -t, -ɫ

pocket, -s, -ing, -ed; -ful/s 'pɒkɪt, -s, -ɪŋ, -ɪd; -fʊl/z

poes|y, -ies 'poʊ̆ɪz|ɫ [-ɪs|ɫ], -ɫz

poem, -s 'poʊ̆ɪm ['poʊ̆əm], -z

Poet (JUL, *TIM*) 'poʊ̆ɪt

poet, -s 'poʊ̆ɪt, -s

poetic, -al, -ally po'eɹɪk, -l̩, -lɫ [əlɫ]

poetry 'poʊ̆tɹɫ

Poi(c)tiers (1HVI, KJ) pɔɪ̆'tɪɔ˞z [pwɑ'tjeɪ̆]

Poins (*1HIV, 2HIV*, MWW) 'pɔɪnz
Note.—The Folio version also spells the name 'Pointz' and 'Points' (among others), indicating a possible alt. pronunciation of ['pɔĭnts]

poinst (*from* **appointest**) 'pɔĭnst

point, -s, -ing, -ed, -er/s 'pɔĭnt, -s, -ɪŋ, -ɪd, -ɔ˞/z

point-blank 'pɔĭnt'blæŋk [ˈ-,-]

point-device ˌpɔĭntdɪ'vaɪ̆s

'point (*from* **appoint**), **-ed** 'pɔĭnt, -ɪd

pointed (*adj.*), **-ly, -ness** 'pɔĭntɪd, -lɪ, -nɪs

pointing-stock, -s 'pɔĭntɪŋˌstɒk, -s

pointless, -ly, -ness 'pɔĭntlɪs, -lɪ, -nɪs

pois|e, -es, -ing, -ed 'pɔĭz, -ɪz, -ɪŋ, -d

poison, -s, -ing, -ed, -er/s 'pɔĭzn̩, -z, -ɪŋ, -d, -ɔ˞/z

poisonous, -ly, -ness 'pɔĭznəs [-znəs], -lɪ, -nɪs

pok|e, -es, -ing, -ed 'poʊ̆k, -s, -ɪŋ, -t

poker, -s 'poʊ̆kɔ˞, -z

---

i wɛ ɪ city ɪ hit e let ɛ debut æ can a pass ɜ˞ bird ʌ hut ə again ɔ˞ supper u you
ʊ should o obey ɔ awl ɒ cop ɑ father eɪ̆ paid aɪ̆ high oʊ̆ go ɔɪ̆ voice aʊ̆ found ɪɔ˞ ear
ɛɔ˞ air ʊɔ˞ poor ɔɔ˞ fork ɑɔ˞ park aɪ̆ɔ˞ fire aʊ̆ɔ˞ hour b boy p pit d dog t top g got
k kid h how ɦ behave dʒ jot tʃ chew z zany s soft v vat f fat ʒ treasure ʃ ship ð the
θ thin m man n no ŋ hang l lip j yes w won ʍ whew ɹ rigger, airy ɟ matter

poking-stick, -s 'pŏŭkɪŋˌstɪk, -s
Polack (HAM), **-s** 'pŏŭlæk, -s
Poland (COM, HAM, MEAS) 'pŏŭlənd
pold (*from 'bold'*) 'pŏŭld (*see* **prings**)
pole (**P.**) (HAM), **-s** 'pŏŭl, -z
pole(-)ax|e, poleax, *or* **pollax|e, -es, -ing, -ed** 'pŏŭlˌæks, -ɪz, -ɪŋ, -t
Pole, William (1HVI) 'wɪljəm 'pŏŭl
polecat, -s 'pŏŭlkæt, -s
pole-clipt (*hedged in with poles*) 'pŏŭlˌklɪpt
Polemon (AC) poˈlimən [-mɔn], 'pɒləmɔn
Note.—This name in AC, III.vi.74 may change syllabic stress depending on how one chooses to scan the line (see **Comagene***); however,* [poˈlimən] *is recommended in this instance*
polic|e, -es, -ing, -ed pʊˈlis [pəˈl-], -ɪz, -ɪŋ, -t
police|man, -men pʊˈlis|mən [pəˈl-], -mən
polic|y, -ies 'pɒlɪs|ɨ, -ɨz
polish, -es, -ing, -ed, -er/s 'pɒlɪʃ, -ɪz, -ɪŋ, -t, -ɚ/z
polite, -st, -ly, -ness pʊˈlaɪt, -ɪst, -lɨ, -nɪs
politic, -s; -ly 'pɒlɪtɪk, -s; -lɨ
politic|al, -ally pəˈlɪɾɪk|ḻ, -əlɨ
politician, -s ˌpɒlɪˈtɪʃn̩, -z
politicly 'pɒlɨˌtɪklɨ
Polixenes (TC, *WT*) pəˈlɪksənɨz [poˈl-], -ˈlɪksnɨz
poll, -s, -ing, -ed 'pŏŭl, -z, -ɪŋ, -d
pollax|e, poleax, *or* **pole(-)ax|e, -es, -ing, -ed** 'pŏŭlæks, -ɪz, -ɪŋ, -t
poll-clipt 'pŏŭlˈklɪpt (*when att.,* ['-,-])
pollen, -s 'pɒlɪn, -z
pollenat|e, -es, -ing, -ed 'pɒlɪneɪt, -s, -ɪŋ, -ɪd
pollenation ˌpɒlɪˈneɪʃn̩
pollut|e, -es, -ing, -ed, -er/s pəˈlut [pəˈljut], -s, -ɪŋ, -ɪd, -ɚ/z
pollution, -s pəˈluʃn̩ [pəˈljuʃn̩], -z
Polonius (*HAM*) pəˈlŏŭnɪəs, -njəs
poltergeist, -s 'pŏŭltɚˌgaɪst, -s
poltroon, -s; -ery pɒlˈtɹun, -z; -əɹɨ
Polydamas (TC) poˈlɪdəməs [ˌpɒlɪˈdæməs, -deɪməs]
Note.—This name in TC, V.v.6 (its only appearance in S.) may be stressed either way, depending on how one chooses to

scan the verse line. If 'fierce' in the line is meant to be monosyllabic, then the former choice is appropriate, and follows the traditional pronunciation. If 'fierce' is meant to be disyllabic, then the latter choice is best. It should be pointed out that the accentuation in the original Greek supports the pronunciation [ˌpɒlɪˈdæməs, -deɪməs]
Polydore (CYM) 'pɒlɪdɔ˞
Polyxena (TC) poˈlɪksɪnə
pomander poˈmændɚ ['pŏŭmændɚ, 'pɒm-]
pomegranate, -s 'pɒmgɹænɪt [-mɪˌg-], -s
Note.—In RJ, III.v.4, the stress is on the second syllable, i.e., [pɒmˈgɹænɪt]
pomewater, -s 'pŏŭmwɔɾɚ [-wɔtɚ-], -z
Pomfret (2HIV, 2HVI, KJ, RII, RIII) 'pʌmfɹɪt ['pɒm-]
Pomgarnet (1HIV) 'pɒmgɑ˞nɪt ['pʌm-, -'--]
pommel (*of a sword*), **-s** 'pɒməl ['pʌm-], -z
pommel (*to beat*), **-s, -ling, -led** 'pʌməl ['pɒm-], -z, -ɪŋ, -d
pomp, -s 'pɒmp, -s
Pompeius, Sextus (*AC*) 'sekstəs pɒmˈpiəs
Pompey (*MEAS*) (*alias for* **Thomas Tapster**, *q.v.*) 'pɒmpɨ
Pompey, Gnaeus *or* **Cneius** (AC) 'niəs 'pɒmpɨ
Pompey the Great (*AC*, HV, LLL) 'pɒmpɨ ðə 'gɹeɪt
Pompey the Huge (LLL) (*satirically mentioned*) 'pɒmpɨ ðə 'hjudʒ
Pompion the Great (2HVI, LLL) ˌpʌmpkɪn ðə 'gɹeɪt (*see Note for* **pompion**)
pompion (**P.**) 'pʌmpkɪn, 'pʌmpɪən
Note.—This word (meaning 'pumpkin') appears in S. technically only once, in LLL, V.ii.500. It is Costard's blunder for, or corruption of, 'Pompey' in 'Pompey the Great,' similar to the kinds of distortions and confusions of names and words made by other S. characters, e.g., Bottom in MSND and Dogberry in ADO, et al. Editors often (rightly) emend 'Pompey' in LLL, V.ii.502 to

read 'Pompion' as well, to reconcile a
seeming inconsistency. Dictionaries that
cite this rare word usually proffer the
conservative pronunciation ['pʌmpɪən],
but there is sufficient evidence to suggest
that it is simply an alt. spelling of
'pumpkin,' and thus pronounced
['pʌmpkɪn], or even ['pʌŋkɪn]. If Costard
happens to wear pumpkin breeches (as
he most likely had done in the original
LLL) then his inference is clear in LLL,
V.i.119, 120, and the sexual innuendo
unmistakable in LLL, V.ii.502–504. To
illustrate this point a little further;
Pompion Hill Chapel in Berkeley
County, South Carolina was established
in A.D. 1703 and still carries over the
pronunciation ['pʌŋkɪn] (cf. Claude and
Irene Neuffer's Correct Mispronuncia-
tions of Some South Carolina Names,
University of South Carolina Press,
1991, p. 141). 'Tompion,' (a disc-shaped
block of wood plugging the bore of a
muzzle-loading gun) is similarly given
the conservative pronunciation
['tɒmpɪən] by most dictionaries, but has
been commonly pronounced ['tɒmpkɪn]
in the navy (see 'pumpkin,' 'pompion,'
'tomkin,' and 'tompion' in the OED). In
any event, there are possible (comedic)
advantages for allowing Costard to read
['pʌmpkɪn] rather than ['pʌmpɪən].
Another version of the word, i.e.,
'pumpion' appears in MWW, III.iii.36
and is likewise pronounced ['pʌmpkɪn]

pomposity pɒm'pɒsɪtɪ
pompous, -ly, -ness 'pɒmpəs, -lɪ, -nɪs
ponce, -s 'pɒns, -ɪz
pond, -s 'pɒnd, -z
ponder, -s, -ing, -ed, -er/s; -able 'pɒndə-,
  -z, -ɹɪŋ, -d, -ɪə-/z; -ɹəbl̩
ponderous, -ly, -ness 'pɒndə-ɹəs, -lɪ, -nɪs
poniard, -s, -ing, -ed 'pɒnjə-d [-jɑ͞ə-d], -z,
  -ɪŋ, -ɪd

Pont, King of (AC) ˌkɪŋ əv 'pɒnt
Pontic (OTH) 'pɒntɪk
pontiff, -s 'pɒntɪf, -s
pontific|al, -s, -ally pɒn'tɪfɪk|l̩, -lz, -əlɪ
pontificate (n.), **-s** pɒn'tɪfɪkɪt [-keɪt], -s
pontificat|e (v.), **-es, -ing, -ed** pɒn'tɪfɪkeɪt,
  -s, -ɪŋ, -ɪd
pool, -s, -ing, -ed 'pul, -z, -ɪŋ, -d
Poole (2HVI) 'pul (see de la Pole)
poop, -s, -ing, -ed 'pup, -s, -ɪŋ, -t
poor, -er, -est, -ly, -ness 'pʊə-, -ɹə-, -ɹɪst,
  -lɪ, -nɪs
Poor-John (TEM) 'pʊə-ˌdʒɒn
Poor Tom (LEAR) 'pʊə- 'tɒm (alias Edgar)
pop, -s, -ping, -ped, -per/s 'pɒp, -s, -ɪŋ,
  -t, -ə-/z
pope (P.), **-s; -dom/s** 'poʊp, -s; -dəm/z
poperin or **poprin** 'pɒpə-ɹɪn
Popilius (JUL) po'pɪlɪəs, -ljəs
popinjay, -s 'pɒpɪndʒeɪ, -z
popish, -ly, -ness 'poʊpɪʃ, -lɪ, -nɪs
popp|y, -ies 'pɒp|ɪ, -ɪz
popular, -ly 'pɒpjʊlə-, -lɪ
popularity ˌpɒpjʊ'læɹɪtɪ
populous, -ly, -ness 'pɒpjʊləs, -lɪ, -nɪs
por|e, -es, -ing, -ed 'pɔə-, -z, -ɹɪŋ, -d
pork, -er/s 'pɔə-k, -ə-/z
porn (from 'born') 'pɔə-n (see Note for
  pridge)
porpentine (P.) (COM), **-s** 'pɔə-pɪntaɪn
  [-pən-], -z
porpoise, -s 'pɔə-pəs, -ɪz
porridge 'pɒɹɪdʒ
porringer, -s 'pɒɹɪndʒə-, -z
port, -s, -ing, -ed 'pɔə-t, -s, -ɪŋ, -ɪd
portability ˌpɔə-ɾə'bɪlɪtɪ
portab|le, -ly, -leness 'pɔə-ɾəb|l̩, -lɪ, -l̩nɪs
portage 'pɔə-ɹɪdʒ
portal, -s 'pɔə-tl̩, -z
portance 'pɔə-təns [-tn̩s]
portcullis, -es, -ed ˌpɔə-t'kʌlɪs, -ɪz, -t
portend, -s, -ing, -ed pɔə-'tend, -z, -ɪŋ,
  -ɪd
portent, -s 'pɔə-tent, -s (arguably [-'-] in

i we ɪ city ɪ hit e let ɛ debut æ can a pass ɝ bird ʌ hut ə again ɚ supper u you
ʊ should o obey ɔ awl ɒ cop ɑ father eɪ paid aɪ high oʊ go ɔɪ voice aʊ found ɪɚ ear
ɛɚ air ʊɚ poor ɔɚ fork ɑɚ park aɪɚ fire aʊɚ hour b boy p pit d dog t top g got
k kid h how fi behave dʒ jot tʃ chew z zany s soft v vat f fat ʒ treasure ʃ ship ð the
θ thin m man n no ŋ hang l lip j yes w won ʍ whew ɹ rigger, airy ɾ matter

JUL, II.ii.80; 1HIV, II.iii.63; TC, I.iii.96;
and certainly in OTH, V.ii.45)
portentous, -ly pɔɹ'tentəs, -lɪ
porter (P.), -s 'pɔɹtɚ, -z
Porter (*MAC*) 'pɔɹtɚ
Portia (*JUL, MV*) 'pɔɹʃɪə, -ʃə
portion, -s, -ing, -ed 'pɔɹʃn̩, -z, -ɪŋ, -d
Port le Blan(c) (RII) 'pɔɹt lə 'blɑŋk, [*Fr.*
pɔʁləblɑ̃]
portl|y, -ier, -iest, -iness 'pɔɹtl|ɪ, -ɪɚ,
-ɪst, -ɪnɪs
portraiture 'pɔɹtɹɪtʃɚ
Portugal, Bay of (AYLI) ˌbeɪ əv
'pɔɹtʃʊgəl [-gl̩]
pos|e, -es, -ing, -ed, -er/s 'poʊz, -ɪz, -ɪŋ,
-d, -ɚ/z
posh 'pɒʃ
posit, -s, -ing, -ed 'pɒzɪt, -s, -ɪŋ, -ɪd
position, -s, -ing, -ed pə'zɪʃn̩ [pʊ'z-], -z,
-ɪŋ, -d
positive, -s, -ly, -ness 'pɒzɪtɪv, -z, -lɪ,
-nɪs
*Note.—Depending on one's intention
and meaning, 'positively' may be given
primary stress on both the first and third
syllables, i.e.,* ['pɒzɪ'tɪvlɪ]
possess, -es, -ing, -ed, -or/s pʊ'zes, -ɪz,
-ɪŋ, -t, -ɚ/z
possession, -s pʊ'zeʃn̩, -z
possessive, -s, -ly, -ness pʊ'zesɪv, -z, -lɪ,
-nɪs
posset 'pɒsɪt
possibilit|y, -ies ˌpɒsɪ'bɪlɪt|ɪ, -ɪz
possib|le, -ly 'pɒsɪb|l̩, -lɪ
possitable 'pɒsɪtəbl̩
*Note.—This is either Evans' blunder or
high-blown parlance, for 'positively' in*
MWW, I.i.220
possum, -s 'pɒsəm, -z
post, -s, -ing, -ed 'poʊst, -s, -ɪŋ, -ɪd
postage, -s 'poʊstɪdʒ, -ɪz
postal 'poʊstəl
postcard, -s 'poʊstkɑɹd, -z
poster, -s 'poʊstɚ, -z
posterior, -s, -ly pɒ'stɪɹɪɚ, -z, -lɪ
posterit|y, -ies pɒ'steɹɪt|ɪ, -ɪz
postern, -s 'poʊstɜn ['pɒs-, -tɚn], -z
post(-)haste ˌpoʊst'heɪst
post(-)horse, -s 'poʊsthɔɹs, -ɪz

posthumous, -ly 'pɒstjʊməs, -lɪ (*see Note
for* **Leonatus, Posthumus**)
post|man, -men 'poʊst|mən, -mən
postmark, -s, -ing, -ed 'poʊstmɑɹk, -s,
-ɪŋ, -t
postmaster, -s 'poʊstˌmastɚ, -z
postpon|e, -es, -ing, -ed, -ement/s
poʊst'poʊn, -z, -ɪŋ, -d, -mənt/s
postscript, -s 'poʊstskɹɪpt, -s
postur|e, -es, -ing, -ed 'pɒstʃɚ, -z, -ɹɪŋ, -d
pos|y, -ies, -ied 'poʊz|ɪ, -ɪz, -ɪd
pot, -s, -ting, -ted 'pɒt, -s, -ɪŋ, -ɪd
potable, -s; -ness 'poʊɾəbl̩, -z; -nɪs
potation, -s po'teɪʃn̩, -z
potato, -es po'teɪɾoʊ, -z
potch (*gouge or poke*) 'pɒtʃ
poten|cy, -t/ly 'poʊtn̩|sɪ, -t/lɪ
potentate, -s 'poʊtn̩teɪt, -s
potential, -s, -ly po'tenʃl̩, -z, -ɪ
potent (*potentate*), **-s** 'poʊtn̩t [-tənt], -s
(')pothecar|y, -ies 'pɒθəkɚɹ|ɪ, -ɪz
pother, -s, -ing, -ed 'pɒðɚ, -z, -ɹɪŋ, -d
potion, -s 'poʊʃn̩, -z
Potpan (RJ) 'pɒtpæn
Pots (MEAS) 'pɒts
*Note.—This 'character,' listed among
several other denizens of the prison by
Pompey in* MEAS, IV.iii.18, *is perhaps
no character at all. The line's meaning is
obscure, open to interpretation, and
some editors will not concede that it
means anything other than metal
containers. They cite that all names in
the First Folio are printed in italics and
that 'pots' in this instance is printed in
roman rather than italics*
potter, -s, -ing, -ed, -er/s 'pɒɾɚ, -z, -ɹɪŋ,
-d, -ɹɚ/z
potter|y, -ies 'pɒɾɚɹ|ɪ, -ɪz
pottle, -s 'pɒtl̩, -z
pottle-deep 'pɒtl̩ˌdip
pottle-pot, -s 'pɒtl̩ˌpɒt, -s
pouch, -es, -ing, -ed 'paʊtʃ, -ɪz, -ɪŋ, -t
poulter, -s 'poʊltɚ, -z
poulterer, -s 'poʊltəɹɚ, -z
poultic|e, -es, -ing, -ed 'poʊltɪs, -ɪz, -ɪŋ, -t
poultry 'poʊltɹɪ
pounc|e, -es, -ing, -ed ˌpaʊns, -ɪz, -ɪŋ, -t
pouncet-box, -es 'paʊnsɪtˌbɒks, -ɪz

pound, -s, -ing, -ed, -er/s 'paʊnd, -z, -ɪŋ, -ɪd, -ɚ/z

pout, -s, -ing/s, -ed, -er/s 'paʊt, -s, -ɪŋ/z, -ɪd, -ɚ/z

poverty 'pɒvɚtɨ

powder, -s, -ing, -ed 'paʊdɚ, -z, -ɹɪŋ, -d

power (P.), -s 'paʊɚ, -z

power|ful, -fully, -fulness 'paʊɚ|fʊl, -fəlɨ, -fʊlnɪs

powdering-tub 'paʊdɚˌɹɪŋˌtʌb

powerless, -ly, -ness 'paʊɚlɪs, -lɨ, -nɪs

pow, waw (*interj. of contempt in* COR, II.i.140) 'paʊ 'wɔ

Poysam (ALL'S) 'pɔɪsəm

pox 'pɒks

'pparel (*from* **apparel**) 'pæɹəl

prabbles (*from* '*brabbles*'?) 'pɹæbl̩z
Note.—Evans (in MWW*) is a Welsh-man, and speaks in a Welsh accent, if somewhat inconsistently. This may be an example of S.'s direction to the actor (by way of semiphonetic spellings) to adopt such an accent, more or less, for the sake of wringing the most satire out of plays on words stemming from confu-sions with, and corruptions of, English pronunciation via the Welsh tongue. It is just as likely to be from an often-used phrase ('pribble and prabble,' or 'pribble-prabble') meaning "petty disputation, paltry discussion, vain chatter" (cf.* OED*, 'pribble')*

practic (*practical*) 'pɹæktɪk

practic|e, -es, -ing, -ed, -er/s 'pɹæktɪs, -ɪz, -ɪŋ, -t, -ɚ/z

practisant, -s 'pɹæktɪsənt, -s

Praeclarissimus filius noster Henricus, Rex Angliae, et Heres Franciae (*L.*) (HV, V.ii.335) ˌpɹaɪklɑˈɹɪsɨmus 'filɨus 'nostɛɚ 'hɛnɹɨkus 'ɹɛks 'ɑŋglɨaɪ ɛt 'hɛɹɛs 'fɹɑnsɨaɪ
Note.—Under normal circumstances, I usually assert a proclivity for pronounc-ing the so-called 'ash' (the digraph

ligature 'æ') as [i]*, but in this instance, I want to avoid hearing the prefix 'pre-' in the first word. In doing so, and by using a completely acceptable phoneme for the 'ash' (*[eɪ] *would also be accept-able), the character's consistency is retained throughout the passage*

praemunire (*writ charging one with paying homage to or recognizing the ascendant power of a foreign authority [e.g., a pope over a monarch], thus challenging the supremacy of one's sovereign*) ˌpɹimjuˈnaɪɹɨ

praetor *or* **prætor, -s; -ship/s** 'pɹitɚ [-tɔɚ], -z; -ʃɪp

Prague, Hermit of (TN) 'hɚmɪt əv 'pɹɑg

prain (*from* '*brain*'), **-s** 'pɹeɪn, -z
Note.—Evans and Fluellen (in MWW *and* HV*, respectively) are Welshmen, and speak in a Welsh accent, if some-what inconsistently. This is an example of S.'s direction to the actor (by way of semiphonetic spellings) to adopt such an accent, more or less, for the sake of wringing the most satire out of plays on words stemming from confusions with, and corruptions of, English pronuncia-tion via the Welsh tongue*

prais|e, -es, -ing, -ed, -er/s 'pɹeɪz, -ɪz, -ɪŋ, -d, -ɚ/z

praiseworth|y, -iness 'pɹeɪzˌwɚ·ð|ɨ, -ɪnɪs

pranc|e, -es, -ing, -ed, -er/s 'pɹans, -ɪz, -ɪŋ, -t, -ɚ/z

prank, -s, -ing, -ed 'pɹæŋk, -s, -ɪŋ, -t

prat 'pɹæt

Prat, Mother (MWW) 'mʌðɚ 'pɹæt

prat|e, -es, -ing, -ed, -er/s 'pɹeɪt, -s, -ɪŋ, -ɪd, -ɚ/z

pratt|le, -les, -ling, -led, -ler/s 'pɹæt|l̩, -l̩z, -l̩ɪŋ, -l̩d, -lɚ/z [-lɚ/z]

prawn, -s 'pɹɔn, -z

pray, -s, -ing, -ed 'pɹeɪ, -z, -ɪŋ, -d

prayer (*the petitioner*), **-s** 'pɹeɪɚ, -z

prayer (*the petition*), **-s** 'pɹɛɚ, -z

---

i w**e** ɨ cit**y** ɪ h**i**t e l**e**t ɛ d**e**but æ c**a**n a p**a**ss ɚ b**i**rd ʌ h**u**t ə **a**gain ɚ supp**e**r u y**ou**
ʊ sh**ou**ld o **o**bey ɔ **aw**l ɒ c**o**p ɑ f**a**ther eɪ p**ai**d aɪ h**igh** oʊ g**o** ɔɪ v**oi**ce aʊ f**ou**nd ɪɚ **ear**
ɛɚ **air** ʊɚ **poor** ɔɚ **fork** ɑɚ **park** aɪɚ **fire** aʊɚ **hour** b **b**oy p **p**it d **d**og t **t**op g **g**ot
k **k**id h **h**ow fi be**h**ave dʒ **j**ot tʃ **ch**ew z **z**any s **s**oft v **v**at f **f**at ʒ trea**s**ure ʃ **sh**ip ð **th**e
θ **th**in m **m**an n **n**o ŋ ha**ng** l **l**ip j **y**es w **w**on ʍ **wh**ew ɹ **r**igger, ai**r**y ɾ ma**tt**er

Note.—Two syllables, i.e., [ˈpɹeɪ̌ə˞z] *in* TNK, II.ii.94

prayer-book, -s ˈpɹɛ̌˞bʊk, -s

preach, -es, -ing, -ed, -er/s, -ment/s ˈpɹitʃ, -ɪz, -ɪŋ, -t, -ə˞/z, -mənt/s

preamble, -s pɹiˈæmbl̩ [pɹɪˈæ-], -z

preambulat(e) pɹiˈæmbjʊlɑt, -jʊlɪt

preceden|ce, -cy ˌpɹiˈsidən|s [pɹɪˈs-], -sɪ

precedent (*adj.*), **-ly** pɹɪˈsidn̩t [-dənt], -lɪ

precedent (*s.*), **-s, -ed** ˈpɹesɪdənt, -s, -ɪd

precept, -s ˈpɹisept, -s ([pɹiˈsepts] *in* HV, III.iii.26)

preceptial ˌpɹiˈsepʃl̩

precinct, -s ˈpɹisɪŋkt, -s

Note.—Stressed on the second syllable [pɹɪˈsɪŋkt] *in* 1HVI, II.i.68

precious, -ly, -ness ˈpɹeʃəs, -lɪ, -nɪs

precious-dear ˈpɹeʃəsˈdɪ˞

precious-princely ˈpɹeʃəsˈpɹɪnslɪ

precipice, -s ˈpɹesɪpɪs, -ɪz

precipitan|ce, -cy pɹɪˈsɪpɪtən|s, -sɪ

precipitate (*adj.*), **-ly** pɹɪˈsɪpɪtɪt, -lɪ

precipitat|e (*v.*), **-es, -ing, -ed** pɹɪˈsɪpɪteɪ̆t, -s, -ɪŋ, -ɪd

precipitation pɹɪˌsɪpɪˈteɪ̆ʃn̩

precipitous, -ly, -ness pɹɪˈsɪpɪtəs, -lɪ, -nɪs

precise, -ly, -ness pɹɪˈsaɪs, -lɪ, -nɪs

Note.—See note for **prenzie**

precisian, -s pɹɪˈsɪʒn̩, -z

precision pɹɪˈsɪʒn̩

pre-contract ˈpɹiˌkɒntɹækt ([ˈ--ˌ-] *in* MEAS, IV.i.72)

precurrer (*precursor*) pɹɪˈkɜ˞ɹə˞

precurse ˌpɹiˈkɜ˞s

precursor, -s pɹɪˈkɜ˞sə˞ [ˈpɹikɜ˞sə˞], -z

predeceas|e, -es, -ing, -ed ˌpɹidɪˈsis, -ɪz, -ɪŋ, -t

predecessor, -s ˈpɹedɪˌsesə˞ [ˈpɹid-], -z

predestinat|e, -es, -ing, -ed ˌpɹiˈdestɪneɪ̆t [pɹɪˈd-], -s, -ɪŋ, -ɪd ([-nɪt] *in* ADO, I.i.124)

predicament, -s pɹɪˈdɪkəmənt, -s

predict, -s, -ing, -ed, -or/s pɹɪˈdɪkt, -s, -ɪŋ, -ɪd, -ə˞/z

predictab|le, -ly pɹɪˈdɪktəb|l̩, -lɪ

prediction, -s pɹɪˈdɪkʃn̩, -z

predominan|ce, -t/ly pɹɪˈdɒmɪnən|s, -t/lɪ

predominat|e, -es, -ing, -ed pɹɪˈdɒmɪneɪ̆t, -s, -ɪŋ, -ɪd

predomination pɹɪˌdɒmɪˈneɪ̆ʃn̩

preeches (*from 'breeches,' Evans' version of 'breeched' in* MWW, *meaning 'whipped'*) ˈpɹitʃɪz (*see* **prings**)

pre-eminen|ce, -t/ly ˌpɹiˈemɪnən|s, -t/lɪ

pre-employed ˌpɹiɪmˈplɔɪ̆d

Note.—It is stressed [ˈ---] *in* WT, II.i.49 *because of the comparative in the line*

prefer, -s, -ring, -red pɹɪˈfɜ˞, -z, -ɹɪŋ, -d

preference, -s ˈpɹefə˞ɹəns [ˈpɹefɹəns], -ɪz

preferment, -s pɹɪˈfɜ˞mənt, -s

prefiguring ˌpɹiˈfɪgjʊɹɪŋ

prefix (*s.*), **-es** ˈpɹifɪks, -ɪz

prefix (*v.*), **-es, -ing, -ed** ˌpɹiˈfɪks [ˈpɹifɪks], -ɪz, -ɪŋ, -t

pre-formed ˌpɹiˈfɔ˞md

pregnan|cy, -t/ly ˈpɹegnən|sɪ, -t/lɪ

prejudicat|e, -es, -ing, -ed pɹiˈdʒudɪkeɪ̆t [pɹɪˈdʒ-], -s, -ɪŋ, -ɪd

prejudic|e, -es, -ing, -ed ˈpɹedʒʊdɪs, -ɪz, -ɪŋ, -t

prejudicial, -ly ˌpɹedʒʊˈdɪʃl̩, -ɪ

prelate, -s ˈpɹelɪt, -s

premeditat|e, -es, -ing, -ed/ly ˌpɹiˈmedɪteɪ̆t [pɹɪˈm-], -s, -ɪŋ, -ɪd/lɪ

premeditation pɹɪˌmedɪˈteɪ̆ʃn̩ [pɹɪˌm-]

premise (*s.*), **-s** ˈpɹemɪs, -ɪz

Note.—R. A. Foakes, editor of HVIII (*The Arden Shakespeare, 1964), spells this word 'premisses' (an alt. spelling) when it appears in* HVIII, II.i.63, *despite the fact that the First Folio gives 'premises.' In this instance—according to the* OED, *Onions, etc.—the word means 'previous circumstances or events.' Schmidt says it means 'conditions, suppositions,' and Foakes asserts 'evidence, proceedings.' Still, Foakes is the only one of all these sources choosing to use its alt. spelling. Regardless, the prununciation remains the same, i.e.,* [ˈpɹemɪsɪz]

premis|e (*v.*), **-es, -ing, -ed** ˈpɹemɪs [pɹɪˈmaɪ̆z], -ɪz, -ɪŋ, ˈpɹemɪst [pɹɪˈmaɪ̆zd]

prenominate (*adj.*) ˌpɹiˈnɒmɪnɪt [pɹɪˈn-]

prenominate (*v.*) ˌpɹiˈnɒmɪneɪ̆t

preordain, -s, -ing, -ed ˌpɹiɔ˞ˈdeɪ̆n, -z, -ɪŋ, -d

pre-ordinance ˌpɹiˈɔ˞dɪnəns

prentice, -s 'pɹentɪs, -ɪz
prenzie 'pɹenzɪ
*Note.—This word in the First Folio
version of* MEAS, III.i.93, 96 *is the
subject of much debate. In the Second
Folio it appears as 'Princely,' and has
been variously emended by moderns to
'priestly,' 'prence' (It.), 'proxy,'
'phrenzied,' etc. It is given as 'precise' in
J. W. Lever's edition of* The Arden
Shakespeare *(1965),* The Oxford
Shakespeare *(1988), etc. If, however, one
settles on 'precise,' one must take care
that syllabic stress is on the first and not
the second syllable. Lever asserts in the
annotation for the lines that 'precise'
"was sometimes accented on the first
syllable (with 'i' normally pronounced
as in French)"*
pre(-)occup|y, -ies, -ying, -ied
ˌpɹiˈɒkjʊp|aɪ, -aɪz, -aɪɪŋ, -aɪd
preordain, -s, -ing, -ed ˌpɹiɔɚˈdeɪn, -z,
-ɪŋ, -d
pre-ordinance ˌpɹiˈɔɚdɪnəns [-dn̩əns]
preparation, -s ˌpɹepəˈɹeɪʃn, -z
**prepar|e, -es, -ing, -ed, -er/s; -edly,
-edness** pɹɪˈpɛɚ, -z, -ɹɪŋ, -d, -ɹɚ/z;
-ɹɪdlɪ, -ɹɪdnɪs
preposterous, -ly, -ness pɹɪˈpɒstəɹəs, -lɪ,
-nɪs
prerogatifs pɹɪˈɹɒɡəˌtɪfs [-ˌtifs]
*Note.—Fluellen's speech is riddled with
dialectal variations. This is from* HV,
IV.i.68. *See Notes for* **digt, prief,** *and
'Shakespeare's Foreign Languages'
§ 3.1 of this dictionary*
prerogative, -s, -d pɹɪˈɹɒɡətɪv, -z, -d
presage (s.), -s 'pɹesɪdʒ, -ɪz
*Note.—Although used in its s. form,
'presage' receives second syllable stress,
i.e.,* [pɹɪˈseɪdʒ] *in Sonn.* 107.6 *and* VA,
457
presag|e (v.), -es, -ing, -ed, -er/s pɹɪˈseɪdʒ
['pɹesɪdʒ], -ɪz, -ɪŋ, -d, -ɚ/z

prescien|ce, -t/ly 'pɹiʃən|s [-ʃɪən-,
'pɹeʃən|s, -ʃɪən-], -t/lɪ
prescrib|e, -es, -ing, -ed, -er/s pɹɪˈskɹaɪb,
-z, -ɪŋ, -d, -ɚ/z
prescript, -s 'pɹiskɹɪpt, -s
prescription, -s pɹɪˈskɹɪpʃn, -z
presence, -s 'pɹezn̩s [-zəns], -ɪz
present (adj.), -ly 'pɹeznt [-zənt], -lɪ
present (s.), -s 'pɹeznt [-zənt], -s
present (v.), -s, -ing, -ed, -ment pɹɪˈzent,
-s, -ɪŋ, -ɪd, -mənt
presentab|le, -ly, -leness pɹɪˈzentəb|l̩, -lɪ,
-l̩nɪs
presentation, -s ˌpɹezənˈteɪʃn, -z
preservation, -s ˌpɹezɚˈveɪʃn, -z
preserv|e, -es, -ing, -ed, -er/s; -able
pɹɪˈzɝv, -z, -ɪŋ, -d, -ɚ/z; -əbl̩
press, -es, -ing/ly, -ed, -er/s 'pɹes, -ɪz,
-ɪŋ/lɪ, -t, -ɚ/z
press-money 'pɹesˌmʌnɪ
pressur|e, -es, -ing, -ed 'pɹeʃɚ, -z, -ɹɪŋ, -d
prest 'pɹest
prestige pɹeˈstiʒ
presumab|le, -ly pɹɪˈzjuməb|l̩, -lɪ
presum|e, -es, -ing/ly, -ed pɹɪˈzjum, -z,
-ɪŋ/lɪ, -d
presumption, -s pɹɪˈzʌmpʃn, -z
presuppos|e, -es, -ing, -ed ˌpɹisəˈpoʊz, -ɪz,
-ɪŋ, -d
presurmise ˌpɹisɚˈmaɪz ['--ˌ-]
**pretence (chiefly Brit. var. of pretense,
q.v.), -s** 'pɹitens [pɹɪˈtens], -ɪz
pretend, -s, -ing, -ed, -er/s pɹɪˈtend, -z,
-ɪŋ, -ɪd, -ɚ/z
pretense, -s 'pɹitens [pɹɪˈtens], -ɪz
prett|y, -ier, -iest, -ily, -iness 'pɹɪt|ɪ
['pɹɪɡ|ɪ], -ɪɚ, -ɪɪst, -ɪlɪ, -ɪnɪs
prevail, -s, -ing, -ed, -ment pɹɪˈveɪl, -z,
-ɪŋ, -d, -mənt
prevent, -s, -ing, -ed; -able pɹɪˈvent, -s,
-ɪŋ, -ɪd; -əbl̩
prevention pɹɪˈvenʃn
prewarn ˌpɹiˈwɔɚn
prey, -s, -ing, -ed 'pɹeɪ, -z, -ɪŋ, -d

Priam (ALL'S, HAM, 2HIV, 3HVI, LUC, *TC*, TIT) 'pɹaĭəm
Priamus (TC) 'pɹaĭəməs
Priapus (PER) pɹaĭ'eĭpəs
pribbles 'pɹɪbl̩z
Note.—*A weakened echo of 'prabble,' from an often-used phrase ('pribble and prabble,' or 'pribble-prabble') meaning "petty disputation, paltry discussion, vain chatter" (cf. OED, 'pribble,' and see* **prabbles***)*
pric|e, -es, -ing, -ed 'pɹaĭs, -ɪz, -ɪŋ, -t
prick, -s, -ing, -ed 'pɹɪk, -s, -ɪŋ, -t
prick-eared 'pɹɪkˌɪ˞d
pricket, -s 'pɹɪkɪt, -s
pricksong 'pɹɪksɒŋ
prid|e, -es, -ing, -ed 'pɹaĭd, -z, -ɪŋ, -ɪd
pridge (*from 'bridge'*) 'pɹɪdʒ
Note.—*Fluellen's speech is riddled with dialectal variations. This is from HV, III.vi.13. See Notes for* **digt, prief** (*just below*), *and 'Shakespeare's Foreign Languages' § 3.1 of this dictionary*
prief (*from 'brief'*) 'pɹif
Note.—*Evans (in MWW) is a Welshman, and speaks in a Welsh accent, if somewhat inconsistently. This is an example of S.'s direction to the actor (by way of semiphonetic spellings) to adopt such an accent, more or less, for the sake of wringing the most satire out of plays on words stemming from confusions with, and corruptions of, English pronunciation via the Welsh tongue*
priest, -s; -hood, -like 'pɹist, -s; -fʊd, -laĭk
prig, -s, -ging, -ged 'pɹɪg, -z, -ɪŋ, -d
priggish, -ly, -ness 'pɹɪgɪʃ, -lɪ, -nɪs
primal 'pɹaĭməl
prim|e, -es, -ing, -ed 'pɹaĭm, -z, -ɪŋ, -d
primer (*one who or that which primes*)**, -s** 'pɹaĭmə˞, -z
primer (*textbook covering the basics*)**, -s** 'pɹɪmə˞, -z
primero pɹɪ'mɛ˞ɹoʊ [-'mɪ˞ɹoʊ]
primest 'pɹaĭmɪst
primitive, -ly, -ness 'pɹɪmɪtɪv, -lɪ, -nɪs
primogenitive ˌpɹaĭmo'dʒɛnɪtɪv
primogenitor, -s ˌpɹaĭmo'dʒɛnɪtə˞, -z

primogeniture ˌpɹaĭmo'dʒɛnɪtʃə˞ [-tʃʊ˞]
primogenity ˌpɹaĭmo'dʒɛnɪtɪ
primo, secundo, tertio (*L.*) (TN, V.i.34) 'pɹimo sɛ'kundo 'tɛ˞ʃɪo
primrose, -s 'pɹɪmɹoʊz, -ɪz
primy 'pɹaĭmɪ
prince (**P.**)**, -s** 'pɹɪns, -ɪz
prince-like 'pɹɪnsˌlaĭk
princel|y, -ier, -iest, -iness 'pɹɪnsl̩ɪ, -ɪə˞, -ɪɪst, -ɪnɪs
princess (**P.**)**, -es** 'pɹɪnses [-'-], -ɪz
principal, -s, -ly 'pɹɪnsɪpəl, -z, -ɪ
principalit|y, -ies ˌpɹɪnsɪ'pælɪt|ɪ, -ɪz
principle, -s, -d 'pɹɪnsɪpl̩ [-pəl], -z, -d
princox 'pɹɪŋkɒks
prings (*from 'brings'*) 'pɹɪŋz
Note.—*Evans (in MWW) is a Welshman, and speaks in a Welsh accent, if somewhat inconsistently. This is an example of S.'s direction to the actor (by way of semiphonetic spellings) to adopt such an accent, more or less, for the sake of wringing the most satire out of plays on words stemming from confusions with, and corruptions of, English pronunciation via the Welsh tongue*
print, -s, -ing/s, -ed, -er/s, -less 'pɹɪnt, -s, -ɪŋ/z, -ɪd, -ə˞/z, -lɪs
prior|y, -ies 'pɹaĭ˞ɹ|ɪ, -ɪz
Priscian (LLL) 'pɹɪʃɪən, -ʃjən
prison, -s, -ed; -ment 'pɹɪzn̩, -z, -d; -mənt
pristine 'pɹɪstɪn [-'-]
Note.—*Stressed on the first syllable in MAC, V.iii.52*
prithee *or* **pr'ythee** 'pɹɪðɪ
privacy 'pɹaĭvəsɪ
private, -s; -ly, -ness 'pɹaĭvɪt, -s; -lɪ, -nɪs
privateer, -s ˌpɹaĭvɪ'tɪ˞, -z
privilege, -s, -d 'pɹɪvɹlɪdʒ [-vl-], -ɪz, -d
privity 'pɹɪvɪtɪ
priv|y, -ies, -ily 'pɹɪv|ɪ, -ɪz, -ɪlɪ
privy-kitchen 'pɹɪvɪˌkɪtʃɪn [-tʃən]
priz|e, -es, -ing, -ed, -er/s 'pɹaĭz, -ɪz, -ɪŋ, -d, -ə˞/z
probab|le, -ly 'pɹɒbəb|l̩, -lɪ
probal 'pɹoʊbl̩
Note.—*The pronunciation proffered above is entirely conjectural. The OED does not assert a pronunciation for this*

*rare word, but wonders if it is possibly
an alteration of 'probable,' in which
case the pronunciation might just as
likely reflect the same vowel sound, i.e.,
['pɹɒbl] (as it might sound if it stood for
a syncopated form of 'probable').
However, 'probal' could also derive
from 'probe.' In* OTH, II.iii.329, *this
nonce-word—in its context—could
certainly mean that Iago is rationalizing
that the advice he has given is capable
of withstanding the probing of curious,
even suspicious, wit or reason ("thinking," to use his own term). The word
'probe' was rather new in S.'s day (the*
OED *citing its earliest use in print as*
A.D. *1580, and then only as a noun), and
it must be acknowledged that S. doesn't
include any other form of the word
anywhere else in his works. Nonetheless,
'probe' comes from the L. 'proba,'
meaning 'a proof,' and later, the
mediæval L. 'probāre,' meaning
'examination.' Incidentally, the Catalan
word 'proba' (from the same L. root) is
the nautical term for 'sounding line,'
which tests the depth of the water. As
any one of these interpretations well
suits Iago's argument—namely, that his
advice is free, honest, and ironclad
against any critical examination (or that
it's test-proof), I will assert (and
assume) that 'probal' is more closely
related to 'probe' (as 'tone' is to 'tonal')
than it is to 'probable.' If 'probal' does
have to do with testing the water's depth
or using a sounding line, it certainly
wouldn't be S.'s only use of the conceit.
In* MEAS *(believed to have been written
within a year of* OTH*), Isabella speaks
of Angelo's wickedness and immorality
when she says, "His filth within being
cast, he would appear / A pond as deep
as hell." In this instance, 'cast' carries*

*the same meaning as 'proba' mentioned
above (cf.* OED, *'CAST' sb.* 1 5 a. *and b.)*

probation, -s pɹoˈbeɪʃn [pɹʊˈb-], -z
prob|e, -es, -ing, -ed ˈpɹoŭb, -z, -ɪŋ, -d
problem, -s ˈpɹɒbləm, -z
proceed (*s.*)**, -s** ˈpɹoŭsid, -z
proceed (*v.*)**, -s, -ing/s, -ed, -er/s** pɹʊˈsid
   [pɹoˈs-], -z, -ɪŋ/z, -ɪd, -ɚ/z
process-server ˈpɹɒsesˌsɝˈvɚ
proclaim, -s, -ing, -ed, -er/s pɹʊˈkleɪm
   [pɹoˈk-], -z, -ɪŋ, -d, -ɚ/z
proclamation, -s ˌpɹɒkləˈmeɪʃn, -z
proconsul, -s ˌpɹoŭˈkɒnsəl, -z
procrastinat|e, -es, -ing, -ing, -or/s
   pɹʊˈkɹæstɪneɪt [pɹoˈk-], -s, -ɪŋ, -ɪd, -ɚ/z
procrastination, -s pɹʊˌkɹæstɪˈneɪʃn
   [pɹoˌk-], -z
procreant, -s ˈpɹoŭkɹɪənt, -s
procreat|e, -es, -ing, -ed ˈpɹoŭkɹɪeɪt, -s,
   -ɪŋ, -ɪd
procreation ˌpɹoŭkɹɪˈeɪʃn
Procris ˈpɹoŭkɹɪs [ˈpɹɒk-]
Procrus (*corruption of* **Procris** *in* MSND)
   ˈpɹoŭkɹəs [ˈpɹɒk-]
Proculeius (*AC*) ˌpɹoŭkjuˈliəs
procurator, -s ˈpɹɒkjʊˌɹeɪʃɚ, -z
procur|e, -es, -ing, -ed, -er/s; -able
   pɹʊˈkjʊɚ [pɹə-], -z, -ɪŋ, -d, -ɹɚ/z; -ɹəbl
procure-a pɹʊˈkjʊɚɹə (*see* **varld**)
procurement pɹʊˈkjʊɚmənt [pɹə-]
Prodigal (2HIV) ˈpɹɒdɪgl
prodig|al (P.), -als, -ally, -alness ˈpɹɒdɪg||l,
   -l̩z, -əlɪ, -l̩nɪs
prodigality ˌpɹɒdɪˈgælɪtɪ
Prodigal Son (WT) ˈpɹɒdɪgl ˈsʌn
prodigious, -ly, -ness pɹəˈdɪdʒəs, -lɪ, -nɪs
prodig|y, -ies ˈpɹɒdɪdʒ|ɪ, -ɪz
proditor, -s ˈpɹɒdɪtɔɚ [-tɚ], -z
produce (*s.*) ˈpɹoŭdjus
produc|e (*v.*)**, -es, -ing, -ed, -er/s** pɹəˈdjus,
   -ɪz, -ɪŋ, -t, -ɚ/z
proface (*Fr.*) (2HVI, V.iii.27) pʀɒfɑs
   [ˈpɹoŭfɑs]
   Note.—This is an English deformation of

i w**e** ɪ cit**y** ɪ h**i**t e l**e**t ɛ d**e**but æ c**a**n a p**a**ss ɝ b**ir**d ʌ h**u**t ə **a**gain ɚ supp**e**r u y**ou**
ʊ sh**ou**ld o **o**bey ɔ **aw**l ɒ c**o**p ɑ f**a**ther eɪ p**ai**d aɪ h**igh** oŭ g**o** ɔɪ v**oi**ce aŭ f**ou**nd ɪɚ **ear**
ɛɚ **air** ʊɚ **poor** ɔɚ **fork** ɑɚ **park** aɪɚ **fire** aŭɚ **hour** b **b**oy p **p**it d **d**og t **t**op g g**o**t
k **k**id h **h**ow fɪ be**h**ave dʒ **j**ot tʃ **ch**ew z **z**any s **s**oft v **v**at f **f**at ʒ trea**s**ure ʃ **sh**ip ð **th**e
θ **th**in m **m**an n **n**o ŋ ha**ng** l **l**ip j **y**es w **w**on ʍ **wh**ew ɹ **r**igger, ai**r**y ɾ ma**tt**er

an old Fr. expression; a salutation, much like saying 'cheers' before drinking or 'here's to your health' before a meal. Technically, the word does not exist in French

profanation, -s ˌpɹɒfəˈneɪʃn̩, -z

profan|e, -es, -ing, -ed, -er/s; -er, -est, -ely, -eness pɹoˈfeɪn, -z, -ɪŋ, -d, -ɚ/z; -ɚ, -ɪst, -lɨ, -nɪs

Note.—In its adj. form in CYM, II.iii.123 and RII, V.i.25, it is arguably stressed on the first syllable, i.e., [ˈpɹoʊfeɪn]

profess, -es, -ing, -ed, -or/s pɹoˈfes [pɹəˈf-], -ɪz, -ɪŋ, -t, -ɚ/z

profession, -s pɹəˈfeʃn̩, -z

professional, -s; -ly pɹəˈfeʃnl̩, -z, -ɨ

proffer, -s, -ing, -ed, -er/s ˈpɹɒfɚ, -z, -ɹɪŋ, -d, -ɹɚ/z

profit, -s, -ing, -ed ˈpɹɒfɪt, -s, -ɪŋ, -ɪd

profitab|le, -ly, -leness ˈpɹɒfɪtəb|l̩, -lɨ, -l̩nɪs

profiteer, -s, -ing, -ed ˌpɹɒfɪˈtɪɚ, -z, -ɹɪŋ, -d

profitless ˈpɹɒfɪtlɪs

profoun|d, -der, -dest, -dly, -dness pɹəˈfaʊn|d [pɹʊˈ-], -dɚ, -dɪst, -dlɨ, -dnɪs

Note.—Stressed on the first syllable [ˈpɹoʊfaʊnd] *in HAM, IV.i.1, and arguably stressed on the first syllable in LLL, IV.iii.165 (cf.* **secure***)*

progenitor, -s pɹoˈdʒenɪtɚ [pɹəˈdʒ-], -z

progen|y, -ies ˈpɹɒdʒɪn|ɨ, -ɨz

Progne (TIT) ˈpɹɒɡnɨ

prognostic pɹɒɡˈnɒstɪk

prognosticat|e, -es, -ing, -ed, -or/s pɹɒɡˈnɒstɪkeɪt, -s, -ɪŋ, -ɪd, -ɚ/z

prognostication, -s ˌpɹɒɡnɒstɪˈkeɪʃn̩, -z

progress (s.), **-es** ˈpɹɒɡɹes, -ɪz *(see Note for* **progress***, the verb)*

progress (v.), **-es, -ing, -ed** pɹəˈɡɹes, -ɪz, -ɪŋ, -t

Note.—In KJ, V.ii.46, this word wants to scan as [ˈpɹɒɡɹes]*, indicating that in this instance it should most likely be considered a noun (a royal procession) instead of a verb*

progression, -s pɹəˈɡɹeʃn̩, -z

project (s.), **-s** ˈpɹɒdʒɪkt [-dʒekt], -s

project (v.), **-s, -ing, -ed** pɹʊˈdʒekt [pɹəˈdʒekt], -s, -ɪŋ, -ɪd

Note.—Stressed on the first syllable [ˈpɹoʊdʒekt] *in AC, V.ii.120*

projection, -s pɹəˈdʒeksn̩, -z

prolixious pɹoˈlɪkʃəs

prolixity pɹoˈlɪksɪtɨ

prologu|e (P.), **-es, -ing, -ed** ˈpɹoʊlɒɡ, -z, -ɪŋ, -d

prologue-like ˈpɹoʊlɒɡˌlaɪk

prolong, -s, -ing, -ed pɹoˈlɒŋ [pɹʊˈl-], -z, -ɪŋ, -d

Promethean (LLL, OTH) pɹoˈmiθɪən, -θjən

Prometheus (TIT) pɹoˈmiθɪəs, -θjəs

promis|e, -es, -ing/ly, -ed, -er/s ˈpɹɒmɪs, -ɪz, -ɪŋ/lɨ, -t, -ɚ/z

promise-breach ˈpɹɒmɪsˌbɹitʃ

promise-breaker ˈpɹɒmɪsˌbɹeɪkɚ

promontor|y, -ies ˈpɹɒməntɚɹ|ɨ, -ɨz

promot|e, -es, -ing, -ed, -er/s pɹəˈmoʊt [pɹʊˈm-], -s, -ɪŋ, -ɪd, -ɚ/z

promotion, -s pɹəˈmoʊʃn̩ [pɹʊˈm-], -z

prompt, -s, -ing/s, -ed, -er/s; -er, -est, -ly, -ness ˈpɹɒmpt, -s, -ɪŋ/z, -ɪd, -ɚ/z; -ɚ, -ɪst, -lɨ, -nɪs

promptitude ˈpɹɒmptɪtjud

prompture ˈpɹɒmptʃɚ

prone, -r, -st, -ly, -ness ˈpɹoʊn, -ɚ, -ɪst, -lɨ, -nɪs

prong, -s, -ing, -ed ˈpɹɒŋ, -z, -ɪŋ, -d

pronoun, -s ˈpɹoʊnaʊn, -z

pronounc|e, -es, -ing, -ed, -edly, -er/s, -ement/s; -eable pɹʊˈnaʊns, -ɪz, -ɪŋ, -t, -ɪdlɨ, -ɚ/z, -mənt/s; -əbl̩

proof, -s, -ing, -ed, -er/s; -less ˈpɹuf, -s, -ɪŋ, -t, -ɚ/z; -lɪs

propagat|e, -es, -ing, -ed, -or/s ˈpɹɒpəɡeɪt, -s, -ɪŋ, -ɪd, -ɚ/z

propagation ˌpɹɒpəˈɡeɪʃn̩

propend, -s, -ing, -ed pɹoˈpend, -z, -ɪŋ, -ɪd

propension pɹʊˈpenʃn̩

proper, -ly, -ness ˈpɹɒpɚ, -lɨ, -nɪs

properer ˈpɹɒpəɹɚ

propert|y, -ies, -ied ˈpɹɒpɚt|ɨ, -ɨz, -ɨd

prophec|y (s.), **-ies** ˈpɹɒfɪs|ɨ, -ɨz

prophes|y (v.), **-ies, -ying, -ied, -ier/s** ˈpɹɒfɪˌs|aɪ, -aɪz, -aɪɪŋ, -aɪd, -aɪɚ/z

prophet, -s ˈpɹɒfɪt, -s
prophetess, -es ˈpɹɒfɪtɪs, -ɪz
prophetic, -al, -ally pɹoˈfeɾɪk [pɹʊˈf-], -ḷ,
-əlɪ
propinquity pɹoˈpɪŋkwɪtɪ
Propontic (OTH) pɹoˈpɒntɪk
proportion, -s, -ing, -ed pɹʊˈpɔɚˌʃn̩, -z,
-ɪŋ, -d
proportionab|le, -ly pɹʊˈpɔɚˌʃn̩ab|ḷ
[-ʃənə-], -lɪ
proposal, -s pɹʊˈpoʊzḷ, -z
propos|e, -es, -ing, -ed, -er/s pɹʊˈpoʊz,
-ɪz, -ɪŋ, -d, -ɚ/z
proposition, -s ˌpɹɒpəˈzɪʃn̩, -z
propound, -s, -ing, -ed, -er/s pɹoˈpaʊnd,
-z, -ɪŋ, -ɪd, -ɚ/z
propriet|y, -ies pɹʊˈpɹaɪət|ɪ, -ɪz
propugnation ˌpɹɒpjʊˈneɪʃn̩
prorogu|e, -es, -ing, -ed pɹʊˈɹoʊg, -z, -ɪŋ,
-d
proscription, -s pɹoˈskɹɪpʃn̩, -z
prosecut|e, -es, -ing, -ed, -or/s ˈpɹɒsɪkjut,
-s, -ɪŋ, -ɪd, -ɚ/z
prosecution, -s ˌpɹɒsɪˈkjuʃn̩, -z
proselyte, -s ˈpɹɒsɪlaɪt, -s
proselytiz|e, -es, -ing, -ed, -er/s
ˈpɹɒsɪlɪtaɪz, -ɪz, -ɪŋ, -d, -ɚ/z
Proserpina (TC, WT) pɹoˈsɝˌpɪnə
Proserpine (TNK) pɹoˈsɝˌpɪnɪ
prospect, -s, -ing, -ed, -or/s ˈpɹɒspekt, -s,
-ɪŋ, -ɪd, -ɚ/z
prospective, -s; -ly, -ness pɹʊˈspektɪv, -z;
-lɪ, -nɪs
Prosper (*TEM*) ˈpɹɒspɚ
prosper, -s, -ing, -ed ˈpɹɒspɚ, -z, -ɹɪŋ, -d
prosperit|y, -ies pɹɒˈspeɹɪt|ɪ, -ɪz
Prospero (*TEM*) ˈpɹɒspəˌɹoʊ
Note.—Possibly disyllabic [ˈpɹɒspɹoʊ] *in*
TEM, II.i.266, *and definitely disyllabic*
in TEM, V.i.211
prosperous, -ly, -ness ˈpɹɒspəˌɹəs, -lɪ,
-nɪs
prostitut|e, -es, -ing, -ed ˈpɹɒstɪtjut, -s,
-ɪŋ, -ɪd

prostrate (*adj.*) ˈpɹɒstɹeɪt
prostrat|e (*v.*), -es, -ing, -ed pɹɒˈstɹeɪt, -s,
-ɪŋ, -ɪd
protect, -s, -ing/ly, -ed pɹəˈtekt [pɹʊ-], -s,
-ɪŋ/lɪ, -ɪd
protector (**P.**) (3HVI), -s; -ship/s
pɹəˈtektɚ [pɹʊ-], -z; -ʃɪp/s
protectress, -es pɹəˈtektɹɪs [pɹʊ-], -ɪz
protest (*s.*), -s ˈpɹoʊtest, -s
Note.—In 1HIV, III.i.249; TC, III.ii.173,
this word is stressed on the second
syllable, i.e., [pɹoˈtest]
protest (*v.*), -s, -ing/s, -ed, -er/s pɹoˈtest
[ˈpɹoʊtest], -s, -ɪŋ/z, -ɪd, -ɚ/z
protestation, -s ˌpɹɒteˈsteɪʃn̩ [ˌpɹoʊt-,
-tɪˈs-], -z
Proteus *or* Protheus (3HVI, *TGV*)
ˈpɹoʊtɪəs, -tjəs [-tjus]
protract, -s, -ing, -ed/ly pɹoˈtɹækt [pɹʊ-,
pɹə-], -s, -ɪŋ, -ɪd/lɪ
protracted|ly, -ness pɹoˈtɹæktɪd|lɪ [pɹʊ-,
pɹə-], -nɪs
protractive pɹoˈtɹæktɪv [pɹʊ-, pɹə-]
proud, -er, -est, -ly, -ness ˈpɹaʊd, -ɚ, -ɪst,
-lɪ, -nɪs
proudlier ˈpɹaʊdlɪɚ
proud-minded ˈpɹaʊdˌmaɪndɪd
prouds ˈpɹaʊdz
provand ˈpɹɒvənd
prov|e, -es, -ing, -en ˈpɹuv, -z, -ɪŋ, -d,
-ən
provender ˈpɹɒvɪndɚ
proverb (**P.**), -s, -ed ˈpɹɒvɝb, -z, -d
proverbial, -ly pɹʊˈvɝbɪəl, -ɪ
provid|e, -es, -ing, -ed, -er/s pɹoˈvaɪd
[pɹʊˈv-], -z, -ɪŋ, -ɪd, -ɚ/z
providen|ce (**P.**), -t/ly ˈpɹɒvɪdən|s, -t/lɪ
provin|cial (**P.**), -cials, -cially pɹʊˈvɪn|ʃl̩,
-ʃlz, -ʃəlɪ
provision, -s, -ing, -ed pɹʊˈvɪʒn̩, -z, -ɪŋ, -d
provisional, -ly pɹʊˈvɪʒnl̩, -ɪ
proviso, -(e)s pɹoˈvaɪzoʊ, -z [pɹʊˈv-]
provocative, -ly, -ness pɹəˈvɒkətɪv, -lɪ,
-nɪs

---

i wᴇ ɪ city ɪ hɪt e lᴇt ɛ dᴇbut æ cᴀn a pᴀss ɝ bird ʌ hᴜt ə again ɚ suppᴇr u yᴏu
ʊ shoᴜld o obᴇy ɔ awl ɒ cop ɑ fᴀther eɪ paᴉd aɪ high oʊ go ɔɪ voᴉce aʊ found ɪɚ ear
ɛɚ air ʊɚ poor ɔɚ fork ɑɚ park aɪɚ fire aʊɚ hour b boy p pit d dog t top g got
k kid h how fi behᴀve dʒ jot tʃ chew z zany s soft v vat f fat ʒ treasure ʃ ship ð the
θ thin m mᴀn n no ŋ hang l lip j yes w won ʍ whew ɹ rigger, aiɹy ɾ matter

provocation, -s ˌpɹɒvəˈkeɪʃn̩, -z

provok|e, -es, -ing/ly, -ed, -er/s pɹʊˈvoŭk, -s, -ɪŋ/lɪ, -t, -ɚ/z

Provost (*MEAS*) ˈpɹoŭvoŭst [ˈpɹɒvəst]

provulgate (*v.*) (*to make public; publish*) ˈpɹɒvl̩geɪt

Note.—This word appears in the First Quarto version of OTH, I.ii.21, emended to 'promulgate' for the Second Quarto and First Folio versions. Some editors prefer to retain the obsolete and rare 'provulgate' rather than concede that it is likely to be a minimal misreading on the part of an early compositor. These editors rightly enjoy an inherent antithesis between the 'vulgus' (common people) barely concealed in 'provulgate' and the 'men of royal siege' in the very next line

Prudence, Good (RJ) ˈgʊd ˈpɹudn̩s

Prudence, Sir (TEM) ˌsɝ ˈpɹudn̩s

pruden|ce, -t/ly ˈpɹudn̩|s, -t/lɪ

prudish, -ly, -ness ˈpɹudɪs, -lɪ, -nɪs

prun|e, -es, -ing, -ed, -er/s ˈpɹun, -z, -ɪŋ, -d, -ɚ/z

pr|y, -ies, -ying, -ied, -ier/s (-yer/s) ˈpɹ|aɪ, -aɪz, -aɪɪŋ, -aɪd, -aɪɚ/z

pr'ythee *or* **prithee** ˈpɹɪðɪ

psalm (**P.**), **-s; -ist/s** ˈsɑm, -z; -ɪst/s

psalter (**P.**), **-s** ˈsɔltɚ, -z

psalter|y, -ies ˈsɔltɚɹ|ɪ, -ɪz

Ptolom|y (AC), **-ies** ˈtɒlɪm|ɪ, -ɪz, ˈtɒlm|ɪ, -ɪz

public, -ly ˈpʌblɪk, -lɪ

publican, -s ˈpʌblɪkən, -z

publication, -s ˌpʌblɪˈkeɪʃn̩, -z

Publicola (AC, COR) pʌˈblɪkələ

publish, -es, -ing, -ed, -er/s ˈpʌblɪʃ, -ɪz, -ɪŋ, -t, -ɚ/z

Publius (COR, *JUL*, *TIT*) ˈpʌblɪəs, -ljəs

Pucelle (*see* **la Pucelle**)

Puck (*MSND*) ˈpʌk

puck, -s ˈpʌk, -s

pucker, -s, -ing, -ed ˈpʌkɚ, -z, -ɹɪŋ, -d

pudder (*obsolete form, or dialectal var. of 'pother'; to stir up into a fuss: see* **murther**) ˈpʌdɚ

Pudding (MEAS) ˈpʊdɪŋ

pudding, -s ˈpʊdɪŋ, -z

pudd|le, -les, -ling, -led ˈpʌd|l̩, -l̩z, -l̩ɪŋ [-lɪŋ], -l̩d

pudency (*modesty*) ˈpjudn̩sɪ

pueritia (*L.*) (LLL, V.i.46) puɛɚˈɹitɪɑ [-ʃɪɑ]

Puff (2HIV) ˈpʌf

puff, -s, -ing, -ed, -er/s ˈpʌf, -s, -ɪŋ, -t, -ɚ/z

puffin, -s ˈpʌfɪn, -z

puff|y, -ier, -iest, -ily, -iness ˈpʌf|ɪ, -ɪɚ, -ɪɪst, -ɪlɪ, -ɪnɪs

pug, -s, -ging, -ged ˈpʌg, -z, -ɪŋ, -d

pugilist, -s ˈpjudʒɪlɪst, -s

puisny *or* **puisne** (*inferior*) ˈpjunɪ

Note.— 'Puny' (q.v.) is the modern phonetic spelling of this word

puissan|ce, -t ˈpwɪsən|s [ˈpjuɪsən|s], -t

Note.—Poetic meter sometimes requires [pjuˈɪs-]

puk|e, -es, -ing, -ed ˈpjuk, -s, -ɪŋ, -t

puke-stocking ˈpjukˌstɒkɪŋ

pulcher (*L.*) (MWW, IV.i.23) (*beautiful*) ˈpulkɛɚ

pul|e, -es, -ing, -ed ˈpjul, -z, -ɪŋ, -d

pull, -s, -ing, -ed, -er/s ˈpʊl, -z, -ɪŋ, -d, -ɚ/z

pullet, -s ˈpʊlɪt, -s

pullet-sperm ˈpʊlɪtˌspɝm

pulpit, -s ˈpʊlpɪt, -s

pulsidge ˈpʌlsɪdʒ

Note.—This nonce-word, spoken by Mistress Quickly in 2HIV, II.iv.23, is often considered a malapropism for 'pulses,' and the OED says it is a "humorous blunder for PULSE," but it is consistent with many other examples of her speech not altogether interpretable as ludicrous misusage (cf. **alligant**). Her speech is florid and somewhat liberal in its freedom to coin words, but there is a certain charm in its rustic fluency

pumpion ˈpʌmpkɪn (*see* **pompion**)

pun, -s, -ning, -ned, -ner/s ˈpʌn, -z, -ɪŋ, -d, -ɚ/z

punch, -es, -ing, -ed, -er/s ˈpʌntʃ, -ɪz, -ɪŋ, -t, -ɚ/z

puncto (*fencing; direct thrust*) 'pʌŋktoŭ

punctur|e, -es, -ing, -ed 'pʌŋktʃɚ, -z, -ɹɪŋ, -d

**punish, -es, -ing, -ed, -er/s, -ment/s;
-able** 'pʌnɪʃ, -ɪz, -ɪŋ, -t, -ɚ/z, -mənt/s;
-əbļ
*Note.—In RJ, V.iii.307, the word
'punished' is meant to rhyme with 'head'
in line 305 (cf.* **maiden-widowed***); thus,
an elongated—if somewhat over-
conscious—*['pʌnɪʃed] *is created*

punk, -s 'pʌŋk, -s

punt, -s, -ing, -ed, -er/s 'pʌnt, -s, -ɪŋ, -ɪd,
-ɚ/z

punto (*fencing; direct thrust*) 'pʌntoŭ

punto reverso (*fencing; back-handed
thrust*) 'pʌntoŭ ɹɪ'vɝsoŭ

pun|y, -ier, -iest, -iness 'pjun|ɫ, -ɪɚ, -ɪɪst,
-ɪnɪs

pup, -s, -ping, -ped 'pʌp, -s, -ɪŋ, -t

pupil, -s 'pjupļ, -z

puppet, -s 'pʌpɪt, -s

puppetr|y, -ies 'pʌpɪtɹ|ɫ, -ɪz

pupp|y, -ies 'pʌp|ɫ, -ɪz

puppy-dog, -s 'pʌpɫ,dɒg, -z

puppy-headed 'pʌpɫ,hedɪd

pur *or* **purr** (*of a card game*)**, -s** 'pɝ, -z

purblin|d, -dness, -dly 'pɝblaɪn|d, -dnɪs,
-dlɫ

purchas|e, -es, -ing, -ed, -er/s 'pɝtʃɪs, -ɪz,
-ɪŋ, -t, -ɚ/z

pure, -r, -st, -ly, -ness 'pjuɚ, -ɹɚ, -ɹlɪst,
-lɫ, -nɪs

purgation, -s pɝ'geĭʃn, -z

purgative, -s 'pɝgətɪv, -s
*Note.—In MAC, V.iii.55, this word is
arguably stressed on the second syllable,
i.e.,* [pɝ'geĭtɪv]

purgatorial ˌpɝgə'tɔɹɪəl

purgator|y, -ies 'pɝgətəɹ|ɫ, -ɪz

purg|e, -es, -ing, -ed 'pɝdʒ, -ɪz, -ɪŋ, -d

purger 'pɝdʒɚ

purification, -s ˌpjuɚɹɪfɪ'keĭʃn, -z

puri|fy, -fies, -fying, -fied, -fier/s
'pjuɚɹɪ|faĭ, -faĭz, -faĭɪŋ, -faĭd, -faĭɚ/z

puritan (P.), -s, -ism 'pjuɚɹɪtən [-tn̩], -z,
-ɪzəm

purity 'puɚɹɪtɫ

purl, -s, -ing, -ed 'pɝl, -z, -ɪŋ, -d

purlieu, -s 'pɝlju, -z

purloin, -s, -ing, -ed pɝ'lɔĭn, -z, -ɪŋ, -d

purp|le, -les, -ling, -led; -ler, -lest 'pɝp|ļ,
-ļz, -ļɪŋ, -ļd; -ļɚ, -ļɪst

purple-colored 'pɝpļ,kʌlɚd

purple-hued 'pɝpļ,hjud

purple-in-grain 'pɝpļɪn,gɹeĭn

purplish 'pɝplɪʃ [-pļɪʃ]

purport, -s, -ing, -ed/ly pɝ'pɔɚt, -s, -ɪŋ,
-ɪd/lɫ

purpos|e, -es, -ing, -ed 'pɝpəs, -ɪz, -ɪŋ, -t

purpose-changer 'pɝpəs,tʃeĭndʒɚ

purposely 'pɝpəslɫ

purr, -s, -ing, -ed 'pɝ, -z, -ɹɪŋ, -d

purs|e, -es, -ing, -ed 'pɝs, -ɪz, -ɪŋ, -t

purse-bearer 'pɝs,bɛɚɹɚ

pursents (*corruption of* **presents** (*v.*) *in
LLL*) pɝ'zents

pursu|e, -es, -ing, -ed, -er/s pə'sju [-'su],
-z, -ɪŋ, -d, -ɚ/z
*Note.—Arguably stressed on the first
syllable, i.e.,* ['pɝsju, -su] *in MV,
IV.i.294*

pursuit, -s pə'sjut [-'sut], -s
Note.—Stressed on the first syllable, i.e.,
['pɝsjut, -sut] *in Sonn. 143.4*

pursuivant (P.), -s 'pɝswɪvənt ['pɝsɪ-], -s

pursuivant-at-arms 'pɝswɪvənɺəɹɑɚmz
['pɝsɪ-, -ntæt-]

purs|y, -iness 'pɝs|ɫ, -ɪnɪs

purvey, -s, -ing, -ed, -or/s pɝ'veĭ, -z, -ɪŋ,
-d, -ɚ/z

push, -es, -ing, -ed, -er/s 'puʃ, -ɪz, -ɪŋ, -t,
-ɚ/z

push-pin 'puʃ,pɪn

pusillanimity ˌpjusɪlə'nɪmɪtɫ

pussel 'pʌsļ, 'pʌzļ

---

i wᴇ ɪ city ɪ hit e let ɛ debut æ can a pass ɝ bird ʌ hut ə again ɚ supper u you
ʊ should o obey ɔ awl ɒ cop ɑ father eĭ paid aĭ high oŭ go ɔĭ voice aŭ found ɪɚ ear
ɛɚ air ʊɚ poor ɔɚ fork ɑɚ park aĭɚ fire aŭɚ hour b boy p pit d dog t top g got
k kid h how fi behave dʒ jot tʃ chew z zany s soft v vat f fat ʒ treasure ʃ ship ð the
θ thin m man n no ŋ hang l lip j yes w won ʍ whew ɹ rigger, airy ɼ matter

Note.—This is an obsolete form of 'puzzle,' which is in turn one of the obsolete forms of 'Pucelle.' S. intended (or at least enjoyed) a double entendre in the name 'la Pucelle' (q.v.); 'puzzle' being the colloquial slang for a slattern, a whore, or a slut. The irony and ambiguity of the name is not lost on Talbot, who remarks on it in 1HVI, I.iv.106. In this line, I recommend [ˈpʌsl̩] for 'Pucelle,' and [ˈpʌzl̩] for 'pussel'

pu|t, -ts, -tting ˈpʊ|t, -ts, -ţɪŋ

putre|fy, -fies, -fying, -fied ˈpjutɹɪ|faɪ, -faɪz, -faɪɪŋ, -faɪd

putrid, -ly, -ness ˈpjutɹɪd, -lɪ, -nɪs

putter (from 'butter') ˈpʌɾɚ (see prings)

putter, -s -ing, -ed, -er/s ˈpʌɾɚ, -z, -ɹɪŋ, -d, -ɹɚ/z

putter-on ˈpʊɾɚˈɹɒn

putter-out ˈpʊɾɚˈɹaʊt

putting-by ˌpʊţɪŋˈbaɪ

putting-on ˌpʊţɪŋˈɒn

puttock, -s ˈpʌɾək, -s

Puzzel (1HVI) ˈpʌzl̩

Note.—S. intended (or at least enjoyed) a double entendre in the name 'la Pucelle' (q.v.); 'puzzle' was the colloquial slang for a slattern, a whore, or a slut. S.'s name for Joan of Arc (la Pucelle) is an old Fr. term for '(virginal) maiden.' The irony and ambiguity of the name is not lost on Talbot, who remarks on it in 1HVI, I.iv.106. In any case, Pucelle in S. is given primary stress on the first syllable (cf. la Pucelle)

puzz|le, -les, -ling/ly, -led, -ler/s ˈpʌz|l̩, -lz, -lɪŋ/lɪ, [-lɪŋ/lɪ], -l̩d, -lɚ/z [-l̩ɚ/z]

Pygmalion (MEAS) pɪɡˈmeɪlɪən

Pygmies or Pigmies (ADO) ˈpɪɡmɪz

pyramid (P.), -s ˈpɪɹəmɪd, -z

pyramides (P.) (archaic, classical plural form of pyramid) pɪˈɹæmɪdɪz

pyramis, -es ˈpɪɹəmɪs, -ɪz [pɪˈɹæmɪsɪz]

Pyramus or Piramus (MSND, TIT) ˈpɪɹəməs

Pyrenean (KJ) ˌpɪɹɪˈniən

py'r lady (from 'by'r lady') ˈpaɪɚˈleɪdɪ [pɚˈleɪdɪ, pɜˈl-]

Note.—Evans (in MWW) is a Welsh-

man, and speaks in a Welsh accent, if somewhat inconsistently. This is an example of S.'s direction to the actor (by way of semiphonetic spellings) to adopt such an accent, more or less, for the sake of wringing the most satire out of plays on words stemming from confusions with, and corruptions of, English pronunciation via the Welsh tongue

Pyrrhus (HAM, LUC, TC) ˈpɪɹəs

Pythagoras (AYLI, MV, TN) pɪˈθæɡəɹəs [paɪˈθ-]

Qq

Q (the letter), -'s ˈkjuː, -z

qua ˈkweɪ [ˈkwɑ]

quack, -s, -ing, -ed; -ery ˈkwæk, -s, -ɪŋ, -t; -əɹɪ

quad, -s ˈkwɒd, -z

quadrangle, -s ˈkwɒdɹæŋ gl̩, -z

quadrangular kwɒˈdɹæŋɡjʊlɚ

quadrant, -s ˈkwɒdɹənt, -s

quadraphonic ˌkwɒdɹəˈfɒnɪk

quadrate (s., adj.), -s ˈkwɒdɹeɪt [-ɹɪt], -s

quadrat|e (v.), -es, -ing, -ed kwɒˈdɹeɪt [ˈkwɒdɹeɪt], -s, -ɪŋ, -ɪd

quadratic kwɒˈdɹætɪk

quadrature ˈkwɒdɹətʃɚ [-ɹɪtʃ-, -tʃʊɚ]

quadrilateral ˌkwɒdɹɪˈlætəɹəl

quadroon, -s kwɒˈdɹun, -z

quadrupl|e, -es, -ing, -ed kwɒˈdɹupl̩, -z, -ɪŋ, -d

quadruplet, -s kwɒˈdɹuplɪt [ˈkwɒdɹʊplɪt], -s

quadruplicate (s., adj.), -s kwɒˈdɹuplɪkɪt, -s

quadruplicat|e (v.), -es, -ing, -ed kwɒˈdɹuplɪkeɪt, -s, -ɪŋ, -ɪd

quaere ˈkwiɹɹɪ

quaestor, -s ˈkwistɚ [ˈkwestɚ], -z

quaff, -s, -ing, -ed, -er/s ˈkwɒf [ˈkwaf], -s, -ɪŋ, -t, -ɚ/z

quag, -s ˈkwæɡ [ˈkwɒɡ], -z

quagga, -s ˈkwæɡə [ˈkwɒɡə], -z

quagmire, -s ˈkwæɡmaɪɚ, -z

quaich or quaigh, -s ˈkweɪx, -s

Qu'ai-je oublié (*Fr.*) (MWW, I.iv.57)
kɛˌʒʊ ublɪ'ɛ

quail, -s, -ing, -ed 'kweĭl, -z, -ɪŋ, -d

quaint, -er, -est, -ly, -ness 'kweĭnt, -ɚ,
-ɪst, -lɨ, -nɪs

quak|e, -es, -ing, -ed 'kweĭk, -s, -ɪŋ, -t

Quaker, -s 'kweĭkɚ, -z

qualification, -s ˌkwɒlɪfɹ'keĭʃn, -z

quali|fy, -fies, -fying, -fied, -fier/s
'kwɒlɪ|faĭ, -faĭz, -faĭɪŋ, -faĭd, -faĭɚ/z

qualitative, -ly 'kwɒlɪˌteĭtɪv, -lɨ

qualit|y, -ies 'kwɒlɪt|ɨ, -ɪz

qualm, -s "kwɑm ['kwɔm], -z

qualmish, -ly, -ness 'kwɑmɪʃ, -lɨ, -nɪs

quandar|y, -ies 'kwɒndɹ|ɨ [-dəɹ-], -ɪz

quanta (*pl. of* **quantum**) 'kwɒntə

quantit|y, -ies 'kwɒntɪt|ɨ, -ɪz

quantum 'kwɒntəm

quare or quari (*L.*) (LLL, V.i.32) 'kwɑɾɛ
or 'kwɑɾɨ

quarrel, -s, -ling, -led, -ler/s 'kwɒɹəl, -z,
-ɪŋ, -d, -ɚ/z

quarrelous 'kwɒɹələs

quarrelsome, -ly, -ness 'kwɒɹəlsəm, -lɨ,
-nɪs

quarr|y, -ies, -ying, -ied 'kwɒɹ|ɨ, -ɪz, -ɪɪŋ,
-ɪd

quarry|man, -men 'kwɒɹɨ|mən, -mən

quart (*measurement*), **-s** 'kwɔɚt, -s

quart (*in fencing*), **-s, -ing, -ed** 'kɑɚt, -s,
-ɪŋ, -ɪd

quarter, -s, -ing, -ed 'kwɔɚˌɾɚ, -z, -ɹɪŋ,
-d

quarter-carrier 'kwɔɚˌɾɚˌkæɹɪɚ

quasi 'kweĭzaĭ ['kwɑzɨ]

quasi (*L.*) (LLL, IV.ii.80) 'kwɑzɨ

quat (*pimple; small boil*) 'kwɒt

quatch-buttock 'kwɒtʃˌbʌɡək

quean, -s 'kwin, -z

queas|y, -iness 'kwiz|ɨ, -ɪnɪs

queen (*s.*) (**Q.**), **-s** 'kwin, -z

queen (*v.*), **-s, -ing, -ed** 'kwin, -z, -ɪŋ, -d

quell, -s, -ing, -ed, -er/s 'kwel, -z, -ɪŋ, -d,
-ɚ/z

quench, -es, -ing, -ed, -er/s; -able
'kwentʃ, -ɪz, -ɪŋ, -t, -ɚ/z; -əbl̩

quenchless 'kwentʃlɪs

quern, -s 'kwɝn, -z

quest, -s, -ing, -ed, -er/s 'kwest, -s, -ɪŋ,
-ɪd, -ɚ/z

questant, -s 'kwestənt, -s

Question (KJ) 'kwestʃən

question, -s, -ing/ly, -ed, -er/s; -able
'kwestʃən, -z, -ɪŋ/lɨ, -d, -ɚ/z; -əbl̩

questionless 'kwestʃənlɪs

questrist, -s (*searcher*) 'kwestɹɪst, -s

Queubus (TN) 'kjubəs

qui, quae, quod (*L.*) (MWW, IV.i.69,70)
'kwi 'kwɛ 'kwod

quick, -s, -er, -est, -ly, -ness 'kwɪk, -s, -ɚ,
-ɪst, -lɨ, -nɪs

quick-answered 'kwɪkˌansɚd

quick-conceiving 'kwɪkkənˌsivɪŋ

quicken, -s, -ing, -ed 'kwɪkən, -z, -ɪŋ, -d

quick-eyed 'kwɪkˌaĭd

quicklier 'kwɪklɪɚ

Quickly, Mistress (*1HIV, 2HIV, HV,
MWW*) 'mɪstɹɪs 'kwɪklɨ
Note.—In HV, *Mistress Quickly is
known simply as 'Hostess' and 'Nell'*

quick-raised 'kwɪkˌɹeĭzd (['-ˌ--] *in* 1HIV,
IV.iv.12)

quick(-)sand, -s 'kwɪksænd, -z

quick-shifting 'kwɪkʃɪftɪŋ

quicksilver, -s, -ing, -ed 'kwɪkˌsɪlvɚ, -z,
-ɹɪŋ, -d

quick-witted 'kwɪkˌwɪɾɪd

quid 'kwɪd

quid for *quo* (*L.*) (1HVI, V.iii.109) 'kwɪd
'fɔɚ 'kwoŭ

quiddet, -s 'kwɪdɪt, -s

quiddit|y, -ies 'kwɪdɪt|ɨ, -ɪz

quier(e) (*obsolete form of* **choir**), **-s**
'kwaĭɚ, -z

quiet, -s, -ing, -ed; -er, -est, -ly, -ness
'kwaĭət [-aĭɪt], -s, -ɪŋ, -ɪd; -ɚ, -ɪst, -lɨ,
-nɪs

quietus kwaĭ'itəs [kwaĭ'eĭtəs]

---

quill, -s, -ing, -ed 'kwɪl, -z, -ɪŋ, -d
quillet, -s 'kwɪlɪt, -s
quillet|y, -ies 'kwɪlɪt|ɨ, -ɨz
quilt, -s, -ing, -ed 'kwɪlt, -s, -ɪŋ, -ɪd
Quinapalus (TN) kwɪ'næpələs
quince, -s 'kwɪns, -ɪz
Quince, Peter (*MSND*) 'pitɚ ['piɾɚ]
    'kwɪns
quintain, -s 'kwɪntn̩ [-tɪn], -z
quintessence kwɪn'tesn̩s
Quintus (COR, *TIT*) 'kwɪntəs
quip, -s, -ping, -ped 'kwɪp, -s, -ɪŋ, -t
Quip Modest (AYLI) ˌkwɪp 'mɒdɪst
quire, -s, -d 'kwaɪɚ, -z, -d ['kwaɪɚd]
quiring (*archaic var. of* **choiring**)
    'kwaɪɚ.ɹɪŋ
quirk, -s 'kwɝk, -s
quis (*L.*) (LLL, V.i.49; MWW, IV.i.69)
    'kwis ['kwɪs]
quit, -s, -ting, -ted 'kwɪt, -s, -ɪŋ, -ɪd
quite 'kwaɪt
'quite (*contr. from* **requite**) 'kwaɪt
quittal 'kwɪtl̩
quittance, -s 'kwɪtn̩s [-təns], -ɪz
quitter, -s 'kwɪɾɚ, -z
quiv|er, -ers, -ering/ly, -ered 'kwɪv|ɚ,
    -ɚz, -ɚ.ɹɪŋ/lɨ, -ɚd
quo 'kwoʊ
Quod me alit, me extinguit (*L.*) (PER,
    II.ii.33) 'kwod ['kwɒd] mɛ 'ɑlit mɛ
    ɛk'stɪŋgwɨt
quoif (*var. of* **coif**; *tight-fitting cap*), **-s**
    'kɔɪf, -s
Quoint *or* **Coint, Francis** (RII) 'fɹansɪs
    'kɔɪnt
quoit, -s 'kɔɪt ['kwɔɪt], -s
quondam 'kwɒndəm [-dæm]
quoniam (*L.*) (LLL, V.ii.587) 'kwoʊnɪəm
    ['kwonɨɑm]
quot|e, -es, -ing, -ed 'kwoʊt, -s, -ɪŋ, -ɪd
quoth 'kwoʊθ
quotha, quoth(')a, *or* **quoth-a** (*from*
    quoth he, *i.e., 'said he'*) 'kwoʊθɨ, [-θə,
    -oʊð̩]
Note.—The OED *asserts only* ['kwoʊðə]
*for the pronunciation of this interjection
meaning 'said he' (quoth he). But it also
lists var. spellings, to include 'quod a'
and 'quodha.' I offer* ['kwoʊθɨ] *and*

['kwoʊð̩] *for two reasons: first, because
the pronunciation of* [ð] *and* [d] *must
have, at times, been extremely close
to—if not indistinguishable from—one
another (see Note for* **murther***), and
because 'a,' "a,' and 'a" can stand for
the personal pronoun 'he,' (see* **a***,* **'a***, or*
a' *= personal pronoun* **he***), as it does in
'quotha.' In rapid colloquial speech, this
blending is more than likely either*
['kwoʊθɨ] *or* ['kwoʊð̩]

quotidian kwoʊ'tɪdɪən
quotient, -s 'kwoʊʃn̩t, -s

Rr

R (*the letter*), **-'s** 'ɑɚ, -z
rabbet, -s 'ɹæbɪt, -s
rabbi, -s 'ɹæbaɪ, -z
rabbinic, -al, -ally ɹə'bɪnɪk, -əl, -əlɨ
rabbit, -s 'ɹæbɪt, -s
rabbit-sucker 'ɹæbɪtˌsʌkɚ
rabble, -s, -ment 'ɹæbl̩, -z, -mənt
rabid, -ly, -ness 'ɹæbɪd, -lɨ, -nɪs
rabies 'ɹeɪbiz [-bɨz]
rable 'ɹæbl̩, 'ɹeɪbl̩
Note.—This word, appearing in TNK,
*III.v.105, is the Quarto version's spelling
of 'rabble,' retained in some editions of
the play to signify the Schoolmaster's pedantic (if erroneous) rhyme for 'fable.' If
one goes so far as to say* ['ɹeɪbl̩], *then it
follows that the same attention should be
given to the implicit rhymes of 'ladies/
made is' and 'here/villager' featured in
the same passage, not to mention the
once authentic rhyme (now typically
forsaken) of 'Host/cost'*
raccoon, (*var. of* **racoon**) **-s** 'ɹæ'kun, -z
rac|e, -es, -ing, -ed, -er/s 'ɹeɪs, -ɪz, -ɪŋ, -t,
    -ɚ/z
rack, -s, -ing, -ed, -er/s 'ɹæk, -s, -ɪŋ, -t,
    -ɚ/z
racket, -s, -ing, -ed 'ɹækɪt, -s, -ɪŋ, -ɪd
racketeer, -s ˌɹækɪ'tɪɚ, -z
racoon, (*var. of* **raccoon**) **-s** ˌɹæ'kun, -z
racquetball, -s 'ɹækɪtbɔl, -z

radar 'ɹeɪ̆dɑɚ̆
radian|ce, -cy, -t/ly 'ɹeɪ̆dɪən|s, -sɪ, -t/lɪ
radish, -es 'ɹædɪʃ, -ɪz
Rafe, Raphe, Ralph, *or* **Ralfe** (1HIV, 2HIV, TS) 'ɹeɪ̆f
raft, -s, -ing, -ed 'ɹaft, -s, -ɪŋ, -ɪd
rafter, -s, -ed 'ɹaftɚ, -z, -d
rag, -s, -ging, -ged 'ɹæg, -z, -ɪŋ, -d
ragamuffin, -s 'ɹægəˌmʌfɪn, -z
rag|e, -es, -ing, -ed 'ɹeɪ̆dʒ, -ɪz, -ɪŋ, -d
ragged (*adj.*)**, -ly, -ness** 'ɹægɪd, -lɪ, -nɪs
Ragozine (MEAS) 'ɹægʊzin
rah, tah, tah (*interj.*) ˌɹɑ tɑ 'tɑ (*note the trilled or rolled 'r'*)
raid, -s, -ing, -ed, -er/s 'ɹeɪ̆d, -z, -ɪŋ, -ɪd, -ɚ/z
rail, -s, -ing, -ed, -er/s 'ɹeɪ̆l, -z, -ɪŋ, -d, -ɚ/z
raiment, -s 'ɹeɪ̆mənt, -s
rain, -s, -ing, -ed; -less 'ɹeɪ̆n, -z, -ɪŋ, -d; -lɪs
rainbow, -s 'ɹeɪ̆nboŭ, -z
raindrop, -s 'ɹeɪ̆ndɹɒp, -s
rainfall, -s 'ɹeɪ̆nfɔl, -z
Rainold, Raynold, *or* **Rainald** (RII) 'ɹenḷd ['ɹeɪ̆nḷd]
rainstorm, -s 'ɹeɪ̆nstɔɚ̆m, -z
rain(-)water 'ɹeɪ̆nˌwɔɾɚ
rain|y, -ier, -iest, -iness 'ɹeɪ̆n|ɪ, -ɪɚ, -ɪɪst, -ɪnɪs
rais|e, -es, -ing, -ed 'ɹeɪ̆z, -ɪz, -ɪŋ, -d
raisin, -s 'ɹeɪ̆zn̩, -z
rak|e, -es, -ing, -ed 'ɹeɪ̆k, -s, -ɪŋ, -t
rakish, -ly, -ness 'ɹeɪ̆kɪʃ, -lɪ, -nɪs
rall|y, -ies, -ying, -ied 'ɹæl|ɪ, -ɪz, -ɪŋ, -ɪd
Ralph (1HIV, 2HIV, TS) 'ɹælf, 'ɹeɪ̆f
Ram (TIT) 'ɹæm
ram, -s, -ming, -med, -mer/s 'ɹæm, -z, -ɪŋ, -d, -ɚ/z
Rambures (*HV*) ɹæm'bʊɚ̆z
Note.—If one opts to go with [ʒɒk ʃatɹjɔ̃] *in HV, III.v.43, 'Rambures' takes on another syllable, i.e.,* [ɹæm'bʊɚ̆ɹɪz]. *(see Note for* **Chatillon, Jaques***)*

ramp, -s, -ing, -ed 'ɹæmp, -s, -ɪŋ, -t
rampage (*s.*)**, -s** 'ɹæmpeɪ̆dʒ, -ɪz
rampag|e (*v.*)**, -es, -ing, -ed** ɹæm'peɪ̆dʒ, -ɪz, -ɪŋ, -d
rampallian (*scoundrel, ruffian*)**, -s** ɹæm'pæljən [-lɪən], -z
rampart, -s 'ɹæmpɑɚ̆t, -s
rampired (*fortified*) 'ɹæmpɪɚ̆d
ramrod, -s 'ɹæmɹɒd, -z
Ramston, Sir John (RII) ˌsɚ 'dʒɒn 'ɹæmstən
Note.—Mentioned in RII, II.ii.283 as 'John,' it was actually 'Thomas' who sailed with Bolingbroke; and anyhow, the name 'John' throws off the rhythm of the line, whereas 'Thomas' rightly fits the meter of the verse line. My recommendation is to say 'Thomas' instead
ram-tender, -s 'ɹæmtendɚ, -z
ranch, -es, -ing, -ed, -er/s ɹantʃ, -ɪz, -ɪŋ, -t, -ɚ/z
rancor (**R.**)**, -s** 'ɹæŋkɚ, -z
rancorous, -ly 'ɹæŋkəɹəs, -lɪ
random, -ly 'ɹændəm, -lɪ
rang (*p.t. of* **ring***, q.v.*) 'ɹæŋ
rang|e, -es, -ing, -ed 'ɹeɪ̆ndʒ, -ɪz, -ɪŋ, -d
ranger, -s 'ɹeɪ̆ndʒɚ, -z
rank, -s, -ing, -ed; -er, -est, -ly, -ness 'ɹæŋk, -s, -ɪŋ, -t; -ɚ, -ɪst, -lɪ, -nɪs
rank|le, -les, -ling, -led 'ɹæŋk|ḷ, -ḷz, -lɪŋ [-l̩ɪŋ], -l̩d
rank-scented 'ɹæŋkˌsentɪd
Rannius (AC) 'ɹænɪəs
ransack, -s, -ing, -ed, -er/s 'ɹænsæk, -s, -ɪŋ, -t, -ɚ/z
ransom, -s, -ing, -ed, -er/s 'ɹænsəm, -z, -ɪŋ, -d, -ɚ/z
ransomless 'ɹænsəmlɪs
rant, -s, -ing, -ed, -er/s 'ɹænt, -s, -ɪŋ, -ɪd, -ɚ/z
rap, -s, -ping, -ped, -per/s 'ɹæp, -s, -ɪŋ, -t, -ɚ/z
Rape (TIT) 'ɹeɪ̆p
rap|e, -es, -ing, -ed 'ɹeɪ̆p, -s, -ɪŋ, -t

---

rapier, -s 'ɹeɪ́pɪə- [-pjə-], -z

Rapine (TIT) 'ɹæpɪn [-paɪ̆n]

rapport ɹə'pɔə- [ɹa'p-]

rapt 'ɹæpt

raptur|e, -es, -ing, -ed 'ɹæptʃə-, -z, -ɹɪŋ, -d

rapturous, -ly 'ɹæptʃə-ɹəs, -lɪ

rare, -r, -st, -ly, -ness 'ɹɛə-, -ɹə-, -ɹɪst, -lɪ, -nɪs

rarit|y, -ies 'ɹɛə-ɹɪt|ɪ, -ɪz

rascal, -s, -ly 'ɹaskəl, -z, -lɪ

rascalliest 'ɹaskəlɪɪst

ras|e (var. of raze), -es, -ing, -ed 'ɹeɪz, -ɪz, -ɪŋ, -d

Note.—In Sonn. 64.3, 'rased' is usually emended to its variant spelling, 'razed.' It is meant to rhyme with 'defaced,' and there is no harm in pronouncing it ['ɹeɪst] as it may be an apheitc form of 'erased.' In any case, the meaning is essentially the same, i.e., 'that which is effaced, scraped away, obliterated'

rash, -es; -er, -est, -ly, -ness 'ɹæʃ, -ɪz; -ə-, -ɪst, -lɪ, -nɪs

rasher (s.), -s 'ɹæʃə-, -z

rash-embraced 'ɹæʃɪm,bɹeɪst

rash-levied 'ɹæʃˌlevɪd

Rash, Master (MEAS) ˌmastə- 'ɹæʃ

rasure 'ɹeɪʒə-

rat-catcher, -s 'ɹætˌkætʃə-, -z

Ratcliffe, Sir Richard (RIII) ˌsɜ- 'ɹɪtʃə-d 'ɹætklɪf

rat|e, -es, -ing, -ed 'ɹeɪt, -s, -ɪŋ, -ɪd

rather, -est 'ɹaðə-, -ɹɪst

ratif|y, -ies, -ying, -ied, -ier/s 'ɹæɡɹɪf|aɪ̆, -aɪ̆z, -aɪ̆ɪŋ, -aɪ̆d, -aɪ̆ə-/z

rational, -ly 'ɹæʃnl̩ [-ʃənl̩], -ɪ

rationaliz|e, -es, -ing, -ed 'ɹæʃnəlaɪ̆z, -ɪz, -ɪŋ, -d

ratsbane 'ɹætsbeɪn

ratt|le, -les, -ling, -led, -ler/s 'ɹæt|l̩, -ˌlz, -ˌlɪŋ [-lɪŋ], -ˌld, -ˌlə-/z [-lə-/z]

raucous, -ly 'ɹɔkəs, -lɪ

raught 'ɹɔt

ravag|e, -es, -ing, -ed, -er/s 'ɹævɪdʒ, -ɪz, -ɪŋ, -d, -ə-/z

rav|e, -es, -ing, -ed 'ɹeɪv, -z, -ɪŋ, -d

raven (bird), -s 'ɹeɪ̆vən, -z

raven-colored 'ɹeɪ̆vənˌkʌlə-d

ravenous, -ly, -ness 'ɹævɪnəs [-vən-], -lɪ, -nɪs

Ravenspurgh (1HIV, 3HVI, RII) 'ɹeɪ̆vnspɜ-(g), 'ɹeɪ̆vnspə-ɹə

Note.—This was the harbor town at the mouth of the Humber in northeast England where Bolingbroke landed returning from exile. The sea has since claimed it, and its name is given variously as 'Ravenspurgh,' 'Raven-spurn,' and even 'Ravenser.' It is disyllabic in 3HVI, IV.vii.8, RII, II.iii.35, and arguably so in 1HIV, I.iii.244; elsewhere, it is trisyllabic. Following traditions of English pronunciation, the disyllabic var. might sound close to ['ɹeɪ̆nspɜ-(g)] or ['ɹeɪ̆vn̩spɜ-(g)]. The weak, or even silent 'v', is analogous to the traditional pronunciation for 'Haverford-west,' or S.'s sometime usage of 'ever = e'er,' 'even = e'en,' 'seven = sev'n,' and 'heaven = heav'n.' The 'g' at the end is entirely optional, although one should be consistent (regarding the pronunciation of the 'g') when the name appears more than once in the play

ravin or raven (devour), -s, -ing, -ed 'ɹævɪn, -z, -ɪŋ, -d

ravish, -es, -ing/ly, -ed, -er/s, -ment 'ɹævɪʃ, -ɪz, -ɪŋ/lɪ, -t, -ə-/z, -mənt

raw, -er, -est, -ly, -ness 'ɹɔ, -ə-, -ɪst, -lɪ, -nɪs

raw-rheumatic 'ɹɔɹuˌmæɡɪk

ray, -s; -less 'ɹeɪ̆, -z; -lɪs

rayed (var., or aphaeretic form, of berayed, meaning 'befouled,' 'defiled,' 'dirtied') 'ɹeɪ̆d

raz|e, -es, -ing, -ed 'ɹeɪz, -ɪz, -ɪŋ, -d (see Note for rase)

razor, -s; -able 'ɹeɪzə-, -z; -ɹəbl̩

razure (var. of rasure) 'ɹeɪʒə-

re (second note of diatonic scale) 'ɹeɪ̆

reach, -es, -ing, -ed 'ɹitʃ, -ɪz, -ɪŋ, -t

read (present tense), -s, -ing 'ɹid, -z, -ɪŋ

read (p.t.) 'ɹed

reader, -s; -ship/s 'ɹidə-, -z; -ʃɪp/s

Reading (MWW) 'ɹedɪŋ

Note.—When the Welshman, Evans says

this name in MWW, IV.v.75, *he pronounces it 'Readins' or 'Readings,' in keeping with his dialectal affectation of pluralizing many of his words that would otherwise be in singular form. Still, he is actually speaking an earlier form of the name, pronounced* [ˈɹednz̩]

readjust, -s, -ing, -ed, -ment/s ˌɹiəˈdʒʌst, -s, -ɪŋ, -ɪd, -mənt/s

read|y, -ier, -iest, -ily, -iness ˈɹed|ɪ, -ɪɚ, -ɪɪst, -ɪlɪ, -ɪnɪs

real (*adj.*) ˈɹɪəl [ˈɹil]

realistic, -ally ˌɹɪəˈlɪstɪk [ˌɹiə-], -əlɪ

realization, -s ˌɹɪəlɪˈzeɪʃn̩, -z

realiz|e, -es, -ing, -ed ˈɹɪəlaɪz, -ɪz, -ɪŋ, -d

realm, -s ˈɹelm, -z

ream, -s, -ing, -ed ˈɹim, -z, -ɪŋ, -d

reap, -s, -ing, -ed, -er/s ˈɹip, -s, -ɪŋ, -t, -ɚ/z

Reapers (TEM) ˈɹipɚz

reappear, -s, -ing, -ed; -ance/s ˌɹiəˈpɪɚ, -z, -ɹɪŋ, -d; -ɹəns/ɪz

rearward, -s ˈɹɪɚˈwɚd, -z

reason (R.) (MWW), **-s, -ing, -ed, -er/s** ˈɹizn̩ [-zən], -z, -ɪŋ, -d, -ɚ/z
Note.—In S.'s verse, this word is susceptible to becoming three syllables, i.e., [ˈɹiəzn̩], *for the sake of the meter, e.g.,* AC, III.xiii.4; TEM, V.i.68 (*cf.* **Gonzalo**). *In* 1HIV, II.iv.230–235, *a play on words suggests that 'reason(s)' is to be pronounced something like 'raisin(s)' (presumeably akin to* [ˈɹeːzn̩(z)]*), in order for an intended pun to pay off*

reasonless ˈɹiznlɪs

reav|e, -es, -ing, -ed, reft ˈɹiv, -z, -ɪŋ, -d, ˈɹeft

rebate (*s.*) (*reduction of payment*), **-s** ˈɹibeɪt

rebat|e (*v.*) (*to make dull*), **-es, -ing, -ed** ɹɪˈbeɪt, -s, -ɪŋ, -ɪd

rebato ɹɪˈbɑtoʊ

Rebeck, Hugh (RJ) ˈhju ˈɹibek

Note.—Kökeritz asserts that in S.'s day, this name was pronounced [ˈɹebɪk] *in accordance with the Folio's spelling, i.e., 'Rebicke,' in* RJ, IV.v.129. *Editors emend the spelling from 'Rebicke' to 'Rebeck' to underpin their argument that the name represents the early musical instrument. The* OED *does not list 'rebicke' as an alt. form of the word 'rebeck,' and does not cite 'rebicke' at all*

rebel (*s.*), **-s** ˈɹebl̩, -z

rebel (*v.*), **-s, -ling, -led** ɹɪˈbel, -z, -ɪŋ, -d

rebel-like ˈɹebl̩ˌlaɪk

rebellion, -s ɹɪˈbeljən, -z

rebellious, -ly, -ness ɹɪˈbeljəs, -lɪ, -nɪs

rebound (*adj.*) ˌɹiˈbaʊnd

rebound (*s.*), **-s** ˈribaʊnd, -z

rebound (*v.*), **-s, -ing, -ed** ɹɪˈbaʊnd, -z, -ɪŋ, -ɪd

rebuk|e, -es, -ing/ly, -ed; -eable ɹɪˈbjuk, -s, -ɪŋ/lɪ, -t; -əbl̩

rebused (*Grumio's blunder for 'abused'* TS, I.ii.7) ɹɪˈbjuzd

recall (*s.*), **-s** ˈɹikɔl, -z

recall (*v.*), **-s, -ing, -ed** ɹɪˈkɔl, -z, -ɪŋ, -d

recant, -s, -ing, -ed, -er/s ɹɪˈkænt, -s, -ɪŋ, -ɪd, -ɚ/z

recantation, -s ˌɹikænˈteɪʃn̩, -z

recaptur|e, -es, -ing, -ed ɹɪˈkæptʃɚ, -z, -ɹɪŋ, -d

reced|e, -es, -ing, -ed ɹɪˈsid, -z, -ɪŋ, -ɪd

receipt, -s, -ing, -ed ɹɪˈsit, -s, -ɪŋ, -ɪd

receiv|e, -es, -ing, -ed, -er/s; -able/s ɹɪˈsiv, -z, -ɪŋ, -d, -ɚ/z; -əbl̩/z

recency ˈɹisn̩sɪ

recent, -ly, -ness ˈɹisn̩t, -lɪ, -nɪs

receptacle, -s ɹɪˈseptɪkl̩, -z
Note.—In TIT, I.i.95; II.ii.235 *and* RJ, IV.iii.39, *this word is typically given primary stress on the initial syllable, i.e.,* [ˈɹisepˌtɪkl̩] (*cf. 'conventicle'*)

reception, -s ɹɪˈsepʃn̩, -z

receptive, -ly, -ness ɹɪˈseptɪv, -lɪ, -nɪs

---

i w**e** ɪ city ɪ h**i**t e l**e**t ɛ d**e**but æ c**a**n a p**a**ss ɝ b**i**rd ʌ h**u**t ə **a**gain ɚ supp**e**r u y**ou** ʊ sh**ou**ld o **o**bey ɔ **a**wl ɒ c**o**p ɑ f**a**ther eɪ p**ai**d aɪ h**i**gh oʊ g**o** ɔɪ v**oi**ce aʊ f**ou**nd ɪɚ **ear** ɛɚ **air** ʊɚ **poor** ɔɚ f**or**k ɑɚ p**ar**k aɪɚ f**ire** aʊɚ **hour** b b**oy** p p**i**t d d**o**g t t**o**p g g**o**t k k**i**d h **h**ow fi be**h**ave dʒ j**o**t tʃ **ch**ew z **z**any s **s**oft v **v**at f **f**at ʒ trea**s**ure ʃ **sh**ip ð **th**e θ **th**in m **m**an n **n**o ŋ ha**ng** l **l**ip j **y**es w **w**on ʍ **wh**ew ɹ **r**igger, ai**r**y ɾ ma**tt**er

recess, -es, -ing, -ed 'ɹises [ɹɪ'ses], -ɪz, -ɪŋ, -t

recession, -s ɹɪ'seʃn̩, -z

recheat, -s ɹɪ'tʃit, -s

recipe, -s 'ɹesɪpi, -z

recipient, -s ɹɪ'sɪpɪənt, -s

reciproc|al, -als, -ally, -alness ɹɪ'sɪpɹək|l̩, -l̩z, -əlɪ, -l̩nɪs

reciprocat|e, -es, -ing, -ed ɹɪ'sɪpɹəkeɪt, -s, -ɪŋ, -ɪd

reciprocation ɹɪˌsɪpɹə'keɪʃn̩

reciprocity ˌɹesɪ'pɹɒsɪtɪ

recital, -s ɹɪ'saɪtl̩, -z

recitation, -s ˌɹesɪ'teɪʃn̩, -z

recit|e, -es, -ing, -ed, -er/s ɹɪ'saɪt, -s, -ɪŋ, -ɪd, -ə/z

reck, -s, -ing, -ed 'ɹek, -s, -ɪŋ, -t

reckless, -ly, -ness 'ɹeklɪs, -lɪ, -nɪs

reck|on, -ons, -oning/s, -oned, -oner/s 'ɹek|ən, -ənz, -n̩ɪŋ/z, -ənd, -n̩ə/z

reclaim, -s, -ing, -ed ɹɪ'kleɪm [ˌɹiˈk-], -z, -ɪŋ, -d

reclamation, -s ˌɹeklə'meɪʃn̩, -z

reclin|e, -es, -ing, -ed, -er/s ɹɪ'klaɪn, -z, -ɪŋ, -d, -ə/z

recluse, -s 'ɹeklus [ɹɪ'klus], -ɪz

reclusive ɹɪ'klusɪv

recognizance, -s ɹɪ'kɒgnɪzəns [-'kɒnɪ-], -ɪz

recoil (*s.*)**, -s** ɹɪ'kɔɪl ['ɹikɔɪl], -z

recoil (*v.*)**, -s, -ing, -ed** ɹɪ'kɔɪl, -z, -ɪŋ, -d

recollect (*remember, recall*)**, -s, -ing, -ed** ˌɹekə'lekt, -s, -ɪŋ, -ɪd

re(-)collect (*gather up; collect again*)**, -s, -ing, -ed** ˌɹikə'lekt, -s, -ɪŋ, -ɪd

recollection, -s ˌɹekə'lekʃn̩, -z

recomforted ɹɪ'kʌmfə·tɪd

recomforture ɹɪ'kʌmfə·tʃə·

recommend, -s, -ing, -ed; -able ˌɹekə'mend, -z, -ɪŋ, -ɪd; -əbl̩

recommendation, -s ˌɹekəmen'deɪʃn̩ [-km̩, -mən-], -z

recompens|e, -es, -ing, -ed 'ɹekəmˌpens, -ɪz, -ɪŋ, -t

reconcil|e, -es, -ing, -ed, -er/s, -ement/s 'ɹekənsaɪl, -z, -ɪŋ, -d, -ə/z, -mənt/s

record (*s.*)**, -s** 'ɹekə·d, -z
Note.—Stressed on the second syllable, i.e., [ɹe'kɔə·d] *in AC, IV.ix.8; RII,*

IV.i.230; RIII, III.i.72, 74, IV.iv.28, V.iii.336; HAM, I.v.99; MEAS, II.ii.40; TC, I.iii.14; TIM, I.i.5; TN, V.i.244; TNK, II.ii.112; Sonn. 59.5, 123.11

record (*v.*)**, -s, -ing, -ed, -er/s; -able** ɹɪ'kɔə·d, -z, -ɪŋ, -ɪd, -ə/z; -əbl̩

recordation, -s ˌɹekɔə·'deɪʃn̩, -z

Recorder (RIII) ɹɪ'kɔə·də·

recorder (*instrument and device*)**, -s** ɹɪ'kɔə·də·, -z

recount (*s.*)**, -s** 'ɹikaʊnt, -s

recount (*v.*) (*counting over*)**, -s, -ing, -ed** ˌɹi'kaʊnt, -s, -ɪŋ, -ɪd

recount (*v.*) (*to tell*)**, -s, -ing, -ed** ɹɪ'kaʊnt, -s, -ɪŋ, -ɪd

recountment, -s ɹɪ'kaʊntmənt, -s

recourse 'ɹikɔə·s [ɹɪ'kɔə·s]

recreant, -s, -ly 'ɹekɹɪənt, -s, -lɪ

recreat|e (*restore or refresh*)**, -es, -ing, -ed** 'ɹekɹɪeɪt, -s, -ɪŋ, -ɪd

re(-)creat|e (*create anew*)**, -es, -ing, -ed** ˌɹikɹɪ'eɪt, -s, -ɪŋ, -ɪd

recti|fy, -fies, -fying, -fied, -fier/s; -fiable 'ɹektɪ|faɪ, -faɪz, -faɪɪŋ, -faɪd, -faɪə·/z; -faɪəbl̩

rector, -s; -ship/s 'ɹektə·, -z; -ʃɪp/s

recure, -d ɹɪ'kjʊə·, -d

red, -s; -der, -dest, -ness 'ɹed, -z; -ə·, -ɪst, -nɪs

redbreast, -s 'ɹedbɹest, -s

redcoat, -s 'ɹedkoʊt, -s

redden, -s, -ing, -ed 'ɹedn̩, -z, -ɪŋ, -d

reddish, -ness 'ɹedɪʃ, -nɪs

rede, -s 'ɹid, -z

redeem, -s, -ing, -ed; -able ɹɪ'dim, -z, -ɪŋ, -d; -əbl̩

redeemer (R.) (RIII)**, -s** ɹɪ'dimə·, -z

redemption, -s ɹɪ'dempʃn̩, -z

redemptive ɹɪ'demptɪv

red-eyed 'ɹedaɪd

red-hot 'ɹed'hɒt (*when att.,* ['-ˌ-])

Redime te captum quam queas minimo
(*L.*) (TS, I.i.162) ɹɛ'dimɛ tɛ 'kɑptum kwɑm 'kwɛəs 'minɪmo

red-lattice 'ɹedˌlæɡɪs

red-looked 'ɹedˌlʊkt

redoub|le, -les, -ling, -led ˌɹi'dʌb|l̩ [ɹɪ'd-], -l̩z, -l̩ɪŋ [-lɪŋ], -l̩d

redoubt, -s, -ed; -able ɹɪ'daʊt, -s, -ɪd; -əbl̩

redound, -s, -ing, -ed ɹɪ'daʊnd, -z, -ɪŋ, -ɪd
redress (*s., v.*) (*rectify*), **-es, -ing, -ed** ɹɪ'dɹes, -ɪz, -ɪŋ, -t
redress (*v.*) (*dress again*), **-es, -ing, -ed** ˌɹi'dɹes, -ɪz, -ɪŋ, -t
reech|y, -ily 'ɹitʃ|ɪ, -ɪlɪ
reed, -s, -ing, -ed 'ɹid, -z, -ɪŋ, -ɪd
re-edified ˌɹi'edɪfaɪd
reef, -s, -ing, -ed 'ɹif, -s, -ɪŋ, -t
reek, -s, -ing, -ed; -y 'ɹik, -s, -ɪŋ, -t; -ɨ
reel, -s, -ing, -ed 'ɹil, -z, -ɪŋ, -d
reeve, -s 'ɹiv, -z
refel, -s, -ling, -led ɹɪ'fel, -z, -ɪŋ, -d
refer, -s, -ing, -ed ɹɪ'fɝ, -z, -ɪŋ, -d
referee, -s ˌɹefə'ɹi, -z
reference, -s 'ɹefəɹəns ['ɹefɹəns], -ɪz
referend|um, -a, -ums ˌɹefə'ɹend|əm, -ə, -əmz
refigured ɹi'fɪgjəd
reflex (*v.*), **-ed** ˌɹi'fleks ['ɹifleks], -t
reflex (*s., adj.*), **-es** 'ɹifleks, -ɪz ([ˌ-'-] *in* RJ, III.v.20)
refract, -s, -ing, -ed, -or/s; -ive ɹɪ'fɹækt, -s, -ɪŋ, -ɪd, -ə/z; -ɪv
refraction, -s ɹɪ'fɹækʃn, -z
refractor|y, -ily, -iness ɹɪ'fɹæktəɹ|ɪ, -ɪlɪ, -ɪnɪs
reft (*p.t. and p.p. of archaic v.* **reave**, *q.v.*), **-s** 'ɹeft, -s
refuge (*s.*), **-s** 'ɹefjudʒ, -ɪz
refuge (*v.*) 'ɹefjudʒ
Note.—The v. form of this word is now rare, and used only once in S., i.e., RII, V.v.26. Its place in this particular line of verse might indicate to some (the strictest of scansionists) that a pronunciation of [ɹɪ'fjudʒ] *is required; however, a reminder that trochees commonly initiate the second part of a line following a caesura should dispel this notion*
refund (*s.*), **-s** 'ɹifʌnd, -z
refund (*v.*), **-s, -ing, -ed** ɹɪ'fʌnd, -z, -ɪŋ, -ɪd
refusal, -s ɹɪ'fjuzl̩, -z

refuse (*adj., s.*) 'ɹefjus
refus|e (*v.*), **-es, -ing, -ed** ɹɪ'fjuz, -ɪz, -ɪŋ, -d
refutable ɹɪ'fjuɾəbl̩ ['ɹefjʊɾəbl̩]
refutation, -s ˌɹefjʊ'teɪʃn, -z
refut|e, -es, -ing, -ed ɹɪ'fjut, -s, -ɪŋ, -ɪd
regain, -s, -ing, -ed ɹɪ'geɪn [ˌɹi'g-], -z, -ɪŋ, -d
reg|al, -ally 'ɹig|l̩, -əlɨ
Regan (*LEAR*) 'ɹigən
regard, -s, -ing, -ed ɹɪ'gɑɹd, -z, -ɪŋ, -ɪd
regardfully ɹɪ'gɑɹdfʊlɨ
regardless, -ly, -ness ɹɪ'gɑɹdlɪs, -lɨ, -nɪs
regenc|y, -ies 'ɹidʒəns|ɨ, -ɨz
regent (**R.**) (1HVI), **-s** 'ɹidʒənt, -s
regentship, -s 'ɹidʒənt.ʃɪp, -s
regiment (*s.*), **-s** 'ɹedʒɪmənt, -s
region, -s 'ɹidʒən, -z
regional, -ly 'ɹidʒənl̩, -ɨ
register, -s, -ing, -ed 'ɹedʒɪstə, -z, -ɪɹɪŋ, -d
regreet, -s, -ing, -ed ɹɪ'gɹit [ɹi'g-], -s, -ɪŋ, -ɪd
regress (*s.*) 'ɹigɹes
regress (*v.*), **-es, -ing, -ed** ɹɪ'gɹes [ˌɹi'g-], -ɪz, -ɪŋ, -t
reguerdon, -s, -ing, -ed ɹɪ'gɝdn̩, -z, -ɪŋ, -d
regulat|e, -es, -ing, -ed, -or/s 'ɹegjʊleɪt, -s, -ɪŋ, -ɪd, -ə/z
regulation, -s ˌɹegjʊ'leɪʃn, -z
rehears|e, -es, -ing, -ed; -al/s ɹɪ'hɝs, -ɪz, -ɪŋ, -t; -l̩/z
reign, -s, -ing, -ed 'ɹeɪn, -z, -ɪŋ, -d
Reignier (*1HVI, 2HVI, 3HVI*) 'ɹeɪnjeɪ ['ɹeɪnɪɝ]
Note.—In Shakespeare's Names: A Pronouncing Dictionary *(Yale University Press, 1972, p. 84), Kökeritz asserts that this name is sometimes given primary stress on the second syllable, i.e.,* [ɹeɪn'jeɪ]*, citing 1HVI, I.ii.61, 65, etc., as examples; however, only the strictest of iambicists would insist that instances such as these (where the name falls in*

---

i wɛ ɨcity ɪ hit e let ɛ debut æ can a pass ɝ bird ʌ hut ə again ɚ supper u you
ʊ should o obey ɔ awl ɒ cop ɑ father eɪ paid aɪ high oʊ go ɔɪ voice aʊ found ɪɚ ear
ɛɚ air ʊɚ poor ɔɚ fork ɑɚ park aɪɚ fire aʊɚ hour b boy p pit d dog t top g got
k kid h how fi behave dʒ jot tʃ chew z zany s soft v vat f fat ʒ treasure ʃ ship ð the
θ thin m man n no ŋ hang l lip j yes w won ʍ whew ɹ rigger, airy ɾ matter

the first foot of the verse line) necessitate
an iamb rather than the typically
trochaic form

rein, -s, -ing, -ed 'ɹeɪn, -z, -ɪŋ, -d

re(-)inforc|e, -es, -ing, -ed, -ement/s ˌɹiɪn'fɔɚs, -ɪz, -ɪŋ, -t, -mənt/s

rejoic|e, -es, -ing/ly, -ed, -er/s ɹɪ'dʒɔɪs, -ɪz, -ɪŋ/lɪ, -t, -ɚ/z

rejoicing-fires ɹɪ'dʒɔɪsɪŋˌfaɪɚz

rejoindure ɹɪ'dʒɔɪndjɚ

rejourn ɹɪ'dʒɜn

relapse (*s.*), **-s** 'ɹilæps, -ɪz

relaps|e (*v.*), **-es, -ing, -ed** ɹɪ'læps ['ɹilæps], -ɪz, -ɪŋ, -t

relat|e, -es, -ing, -ed ɹɪ'leɪt, -s, -ɪŋ, -ɪd

relation, -s; -ship/s ɹɪ'leɪʃn, -z; -ʃɪp/s

relative, -s, -ly 'ɹelətɪv, -z, -lɪ

relax, -es, -ing, -ed ɹɪ'læks, -ɪz, -ɪŋ, -t

relaxation, -s ˌɹilæk'seɪʃn, -z

releas|e, -es, -ing, -ed ɹɪ'lis, -ɪz, -ɪŋ, -t

relent, -s, -ing, -ed ɹɪ'lent, -s, -ɪŋ, -ɪd

relentless, -ly, -ness ɹɪ'lentlɪs, -lɪ, -nɪs

reliability ɹɪˌlaɪə'bɪlɪtɪ

reliab|le, -ly, -leness ɹɪ'laɪəb|l̩, -lɪ, -l̩nɪs

reliance, -s ɹɪ'laɪəns, -ɪz

reliant ɹɪ'laɪənt

relic, -s 'ɹelɪk, -s

relief, -s ɹɪ'lif, -s

reliev|e, -es, -ing, -ed ɹɪ'liv, -z, -ɪŋ, -d

religion, -s ɹɪ'lɪdʒən, -z

religious, -ly, -ness ɹɪ'lɪdʒəs, -lɪ, -nɪs

relish, -es, -ing, -ed 'ɹelɪʃ, -ɪz, -ɪŋ, -t

re-lives ˌɹi'lɪvz

relum|e, -es, -ing, -ed ɹɪ'lum [ˌɹi'l-, -'ljum], -z, -ɪŋ, -d

rel|y, -ies, -ying, -ied, -ier/s ɹɪ'l|aɪ, -aɪz, -aɪɪŋ, -aɪd, -aɪɚ/z

remainder, -s ɹɪ'meɪndɚ, -z

remediate (*adj.*) ɹɪ'midɪɪt

remediat|e (*v.*), **-es, -ing, -ed** ɹɪ'midɪeɪt, -s, -ɪŋ, -ɪd

remember, -s, -ing, -ed ɹɪ'membɚ, -z, -ɹɪŋ, -d

remembrance, -s; -er/s ɹɪ'membɹəns, -ɪz; -ɚ/z

remiss, -ly, -ness ɹɪ'mɪs, -lɪ, -nɪs

remission, -s ɹɪ'mɪʃn, -z

remit, -s, -ting, -ted, -ter/s ɹɪ'mɪt, -s, -ɪŋ, -ɪd, -ɚ/z

remittance, -s ɹɪ'mɪtn̩s, -ɪz

remnant, -s 'ɹemnənt, -s

remonstran|ce, -ces, -t/ly ɹɪ'mɒnstɹən|s, -sɪz, -t/lɪ

remonstrat|e, -es, -ing, -ed ɹɪ'mɒnstɹeɪt, -s, -ɪŋ, -ɪd

Remorse, Monsieur (1HIV) mə'sjɚ ɹɪ'mɔɚs

remorse, -ful, -fully ɹɪ'mɔɚs, -fʊl, -fʊlɪ

remorseless, -ly, -ness ɹɪ'mɔɚslɪs, -lɪ, -nɪs

remote, -ly, -ness ɹɪ'moʊt, -lɪ, -nɪs

remotion (*departure; remoteness*) ɹɪ'moʊʃn

remov|e, -es, -ing, -ed, -er/s; -able ɹɪ'muv, -z, -ɪŋ, -d, -ɚ/z; -əbl̩

removedness ɹɪ'muvɪdnɪs

remunerat|e, -es, -ing, -ed ɹɪ'mjunəɹeɪt, -s, -ɪŋ, -ɪd

remuneration ɹɪˌmjunə'ɹeɪʃn [-ˌmjunə]

rend, -s, -ing, rent 'ɹend, -z, -ɪŋ, 'ɹent

render, -s, -ing, -ed 'ɹendɚ, -z, -ɹɪŋ, -d

rendezvous (*sing.*) 'ɹɒndɛˌvu (*pl.*) 'ɹɒndɛˌvuz

renegado ɹenɪ'geɪdoʊ [-'gɑdoʊ]

reneg|e, -es, -ing, -ed ɹɪ'nɪg [-'neg, -'nig], -z, -ɪŋ, -d

renew, -s, -ing, -ed; -able ɹɪ'nju, -z, -ɪŋ, -d; -əbl̩

Note.—Arguably stressed ['ɹiˌnjud] *in* OTH, II.i.81

renounc|e, -es, -ing, -ed, -ement ɹɪ'naʊns, -ɪz, -ɪŋ, -t, -mənt

renown, -ed ɹɪ'naʊn, -d

rent, -s, -ing, -ed, -er/s 'ɹent, -s, -ɪŋ, -ɪd, -ɚ/z

repaid (*p.t. of* **repay***, q.v.*) ɹɪ'peɪd [ɹi'p-]

repast, -s, -ing, -ed ɹɪ'past, -s, -ɪŋ, -ɪd

repasture ɹɪ'pastʃɚ

re|pay, -pays, -paying, -paid ɹɪ|'peɪ [ɹi'p-], -'peɪz, -'peɪɪŋ, -'peɪd

repeal, -s, -ing, -ed ɹɪ'pil, -z, -ɪŋ, -d

repeat, -s, -ing, -ed/ly, -er/s ɹɪ'pit, -s, -ɪŋ, -ɪd/lɪ, -ɚ/z

repent, -s, -ing, -ed ɹɪ'pent, -s, -ɪŋ, -ɪd

repentan|ce, -ces, -t/ly ɹɪ'pentən|s [-tn̩|s], -sɪz, -t/lɪ

repercussion, -s ˌɹipɚ'kʌʃn, -z

repetition, -s ˌɹepɪ'tɪʃn, -z

repetitive, -ly, -ness ɹɪ'pɛɾɪtɪv, -lɨ, -nɪs
repin|e, -es, -ing, -ed ɹɪ'paĭn, -z, -ɪŋ, -d
replenish, -es, -ing, -ed, -ment ɹɪ'plenɪʃ,
  -ɪz, -ɪŋ, -t, -mənt
replete, -ness ɹɪ'plit, -nɪs
repletion ɹɪ'pliʃn̩
replicat|e, -es, -ing, -ed 'ɹeplɪkeĭt, -s, -ɪŋ,
  -ɪd
replication, -s ˌɹeplɪ'keĭʃn̩, -z
repl|y, -ies, -ying, -ied ɹɪ'pl|aĭ, -aĭz, -aĭɪŋ,
  -aĭd
Reply Churlish (AYLI) ɹɪˌplaĭ 'tʃɝlɪʃ
report (R.) (MV), **-s, -ing/ly, -ed, -er/s**
  ɹɪ'pɔɝt, -s, -ɪŋ/lɨ, -ɪd, -ɚ/z
reposal ɹɪ'poŏzl̩
repos|e, -es, -ing, -ed ɹɪ'poŏz, -ɪz, -ɪŋ, -d
repossess, -es, -ing, -ed ˌɹipə'zes, -ɪz, -ɪŋ,
  -t
reprehend, -s, -ing, -ed ˌɹepɹɪ'fiend, -z,
  -ɪŋ, -ɪd
repress, -es, -ing, -ed ɹɪ'pɹes, -ɪz, -ɪŋ, -t
repriev|e, -es, -ing, -ed ɹɪ'pɹiv, -z, -ɪŋ, -d
reprimand (s.), **-s** 'ɹepɹɪmand, -z
reprimand (v.), **-s, -ing, -ed** 'ɹepɹɪmand
  [ˌɹepɹɪ'm-], -z, -ɪŋ, -ɪd
reprint (s.), **-s** 'ɹipɹɪnt, -s
reprint (v.), **-s, -ing, -ed** ˌɹi'pɹɪnt, -s, -ɪŋ,
  -ɪd
reprisal, -s ɹɪ'pɹaĭzl̩, -z
reproach, -es, -ing, -ed; -able ɹɪ'pɹoŏtʃ,
  -ɪz, -ɪŋ, -t; -əbl̩
reproach|ful, -fully, -fulness ɹɪ'pɹoŏtʃ|fʊl,
  -fəlɨ, -fʊlnɪs
reprobate (adj.) 'ɹepɹʊbeĭt [-bɪt]
reprobate (s.), **-s** 'ɹepɹʊbeĭt, -s
reprobat|e (v.), **-es, -ing, -ed** 'ɹepɹʊbeĭt,
  -s, -ɪŋ, -ɪd
reprobation ˌɹepɹʊ'beĭʃn̩
reproof (s.) ɹɪ'pɹuf
re-proof (v.), **-s, -ing, -ed** ˌɹi'pɹuf, -s, -ɪŋ, -t
Reproof Valiant (AYLI) ɹɪˌpɹuf 'væljənt
reprovable ɹɪ'pɹuvəbl̩
reprov|e, -es, -ing/ly, -ed, -er/s ɹɪ'pɹuv,
  -z, -ɪŋ/lɨ, -d, -ɚ/z

repugn, -s, -ing, -ed ɹɪ'pjun, -z, -ɪŋ, -d
repugnan|ce, -t/ly ɹɪ'pʌgnən|s, -t/lɨ
repuls|e, -es, -ing, -ed ɹɪ'pʌls, -ɪz, -ɪŋ, -t
reputation, -s ˌɹepjʊ'teĭʃn̩, -z
reput|e, -es, -ing, -ed/ly ɹɪ'pjut, -s, -ɪŋ,
  -ɪd/lɨ
reputeless ɹɪ'pjutlɪs
request, -s, -ing, -ed ɹɪ'kwest, -s, -ɪŋ, -ɪd
requickened ˌɹi'kwɪkənd
requir|e, -es, -ed, -ement/s
  ɹɪ'kwaĭɚ, -z, -ɹɪŋ, -d, -mənt/s
requisite, -s, -ly, -ness 'ɹekwɪzɪt, -s, -lɨ,
  -nɪs
requit, -s, -ting, -ted ɹɪ'kwɪt, -s, -ɪŋ, -ɪd
requit|e, -es, -ing, -ed; -al ɹɪ'kwaĭt, -s,
  -ɪŋ, -ɪd; -l̩
rere|mouse, -mice 'ɹɪɚ|maŏs, -maĭs
resalute 'ɹisəˌlut [-ˌljut]
resc|ue, -ues, -uing, -ued, -uer/s 'ɹesk|ju,
  -juz, -jʊɪŋ, -jud, -jʊɚ/z
resemblance, -s ɹɪ'zembləns, -ɪz
resemb|le, -les, -ling, -led ɹɪ'zembl̩, -l̩z,
  -lɪŋ [-l̩ɪŋ], -l̩d
reservation, -s ˌɹezɚ'veĭʃn̩, -z
reserv|e, -es, -ing, -ed ɹɪ'zɝv, -z, -ɪŋ, -d
residence, -s 'ɹezɪdəns, -ɪz
residue, -s 'ɹezɪdju, -z
resist, -s, -ing, -ed ɹɪ'zɪst, -s, -ɪŋ, -ɪd
resistan|ce, -ces, -t ɹɪ'zɪstən|s, -ɪz, -t
resolute, -ly, -ness 'ɹezəˌlut [-ˌljut], -lɨ,
  -nɪs
resolution, -s ˌɹezə'luʃn̩ [-lju-], -z
resolv|e, -es, -ing, -ed; -able ɹɪ'zɒlv, -z,
  -ɪŋ, -d; -əbl̩
resolvedly ɹɪ'zɒlvɪdlɨ
resort, -s, -ing, -ed ɹɪ'zɔɝt, -s, -ɪŋ, -ɪd
resorter, -s ɹɪ'zɔɝtɚ, -z
resound, -s, -ing/ly, -ed ɹɪ'zaŏnd, -z,
  -ɪŋ/lɨ, -ɪd
respect, -s, -ing, -ed ɹɪ'spekt, -s, -ɪŋ, -ɪd
respective, -ly ɹɪ'spektɪv, -lɨ
respice finem (L.) (COM, IV.iv.39)
  ɾɛ'spitʃɛ 'finɛm
respit|e, -es, -ing, -ed 'ɹespɪt, -s, -ɪŋ, -ɪd

---

i w**e** ɨ c**i**ty ɪ h**i**t e l**e**t ɛ d**e**but æ c**a**n a p**a**ss ɝ b**i**rd ʌ h**u**t ə **a**gain ɚ supp**er** u y**ou**
ʊ sh**ou**ld o **o**bey ɔ **aw**l ɒ c**o**p ɑ f**a**ther eɪ p**ai**d aɪ h**igh** oŏ g**o** ɔɪ v**oi**ce aŏ f**ou**nd ɪɚ **ear**
ɛɚ **air** ʊɚ **poor** ɔɚ **fork** ɑɚ **park** aĭɚ **fire** aŏɚ **hour** b **b**oy p **p**it d **d**og t **t**op g **g**ot
k **k**id h **h**ow fi be**h**ave dʒ **j**ot tʃ **ch**ew z **z**any s **s**oft v **v**at f **f**at ʒ trea**s**ure ʃ **sh**ip ð **th**e
θ **th**in m **m**an n **n**o ŋ ha**ng** l **l**ip j **y**es w **w**on ʍ **wh**ew ɹ **r**igger, ai**r**y ɼ ma**tt**er

respond, -s, -ing, -ed ɹɪ'spɒnd, -z, -ɪŋ,
-ɪd

response, -s ɹɪ'spɒns, -ɪz

responsive, -ly, -ness ɹɪ'spɒnsɪv, -lɪ, -nɪs

rest, -s, -ing, -ed; -y 'ɹest, -s, -ɪŋ, -ɪd; -ɪ

restem ˌɹi'stem

rest|ful, -fully, -fulness 'ɹest|fʊl, -fəlɪ,
-fʊlnɪs

restitution ˌɹestɪ'tjuʃn̩

restoration, -s ˌɹestʊ'ɹeɪʃn̩, -z

restorative, -s ɹɪ'stɒɹətɪv [-tɒɹ-], -z
Note.— 'Restoratives' in PER, I.8
*(Gower's introduction as Chorus) is
meant to rhyme with 'lives' (pl. of 'life'),
but the rhyme is best forsaken for the
sake of meaning to the modern ear*

restor|e, -es, -ing, -ed, -er/s; -able
ɹɪ'stɔɚ, -z, -ɹɪŋ, -d, -ɹɚ/z; -ɹəbl̩

restrain, -s, -ing, -ed, -er/s ɹɪ'stɹeɪn, -z,
-ɪŋ, -d, -ɚ/z

restraint, -s ɹɪ'stɹeɪnt, -s

restrict, -s, -ing, -ed; -ive ɹɪ'stɹɪkt, -s, -ɪŋ,
-ɪd; -ɪv

restriction, -s ɹɪ'stɹɪkʃn̩, -z

result, -s, -ing, -ed ɹɪ'zʌlt, -s, -ɪŋ, -ɪd

resum|e, -es, -ing, -ed ɹɪ'zjum, -z, -ɪŋ, -d

re-survey ˌɹisɚ'veɪ

retail *(adj., s.)* 'ɹiteɪl

retail *(v.)*, -s, -ing, -ed, -er/s 'ɹiteɪl [-'-],
-z, -ɪŋ, -d, -ɚ/z
Note.—In 2HIV, I.i.32, *this word scans
with primary stress on the second
syllable*

retain, -s, -ing, -ed, -er/s ɹɪ'teɪn, -z, -ɪŋ,
-d, -ɚ/z

retaliat|e, -es, -ing, -ed ɹɪ'tælɪeɪt, -s, -ɪŋ,
-ɪd

retaliation, -s ɹɪˌtælɪ'eɪʃn̩, -z

retard, -s, -ing, -ed ɹɪ'tɑɚd, -z, -ɪŋ, -ɪd

retardation ˌɹitɑɚ'deɪʃn̩

retell, -s, -ing, retold ˌɹi'tel, -z, -ɪŋ,
ˌɹi'toʊld

retention ɹɪ'tenʃn̩

retentive, -ly, -ness ɹɪ'tentɪv, -lɪ, -nɪs

retinue, -s 'ɹetn̩ju, -z

retir|e, -es, -ing, -ed, -ment/s ɹɪ'taɪɚ, -z,
-ɹɪŋ, -d, -mənt/s

retold *(from* retell, *q.v.)* ˌɹi'toʊld

retort, -s, -ing, -ed ɹɪ'tɔɚt, -s, -ɪŋ, -ɪd

Retort Courteous (AYLI) ɹɪˌtɔɚt 'kɜˑtɪəs,
-tjəs

retract, -s, -ing, -ed; -able ɹɪ'tɹækt, -s,
-ɪŋ, -ɪd; -əbl̩

retraction, -s ɹɪ'tɹækʃn̩, -z

retrograde 'ɹetɹoʊɡɹeɪd [-tɹʊɡ-, -tɹɒɡ-]

return, -s, -ing, -ed ɹɪ'tɜˑn, -z, -ɪŋ, -d

reunion, -s ˌɹi'junjən [ɹɪ'j-], -z

reveal, -s, -ing, -ed, -er/s; -able ɹɪ'vil, -z,
-ɪŋ, -d, -ɚ/z; -əbl̩

revel, -s, -(l)ing, -(l)ed, -(l)er/s 'ɹevəl, -z,
-ɪŋ, -d, -ɚ/z

Revenge (TIT) ɹɪ'vendʒ

reveng|e, -es, -ing/ly, -ed, -ment ɹɪ'vendʒ,
-ɪz, -ɪŋ/lɪ, -d, -mənt

revenge|ful, -fully, -fulness ɹɪ'vendʒ|fʊl,
-fəlɪ, -fʊlnɪs

revenue, -s 'ɹevɪnju, -z
Note.—Often [ɹɪ'venju(z)] *in S., e.g.,* AC,
III.vi.30; HAM, III.ii.58; 2HVI, I.iii.80;
KJ, III.i.95; LEAR, II.i.100; MSND,
I.i.158; RII, IV.i.212; TC, II.ii.207;
TEM, I.ii.98; Sonn. 142.8. *Arguably*
[ɹɪ'venju] *in* LEAR, I.i.138

reverb *(s.)* 'ɹivɜˑb

reverb *(v.)* ɹɪ'vɜˑb

reverberate *(participial adj.)* ɹɪ'vɜˑbəɹɪt

reverberat|e *(v.)*, -es, -ing, -ed
ɹɪ'vɜˑbəɹeɪt, -s, -ɪŋ, -ɪd

reverend, -s 'ɹevəɹənd, -z

revers|e, -es, -ing, -ed ɹɪ'vɜˑs, -ɪz, -ɪŋ, -t

reversion, -s ɹɪ'vɜˑʒn̩, -z

revert, -s, -ing, -ed ɹɪ'vɜˑt, -s, -ɪŋ, -ɪd

review, -s, -ing, -ed, -er/s ɹɪ'vju, -z, -ɪŋ,
-d, -ɚ/z

re-view ˌɹi'vju

revil|e, -es, -ing, -ed, -er/s ɹɪ'vaɪl, -z, -ɪŋ,
-d, -ɚ/z

revis|e, -es, -ing, -ed ɹɪ'vaɪz, -ɪz, -ɪŋ, -d

revision, -s; -ist/s ɹɪ'vɪʒn̩, -z; -ɪst/s

revival, -s ɹɪ'vaɪvl̩, -z

reviv|e, -es, -ing, -ed ɹɪ'vaɪv, -z, -ɪŋ, -d

revok|e, -es, -ing, -ed, -ment/s ɹɪ'voʊk,
-s, -ɪŋ, -t, -mənt/s

revolt, -s, -ing, -ed ɹɪ'voʊlt, -s, -ɪŋ, -ɪd

revolution, -s ˌɹevə'luʃn̩ [-'ljuʃ-], -z

revolutionar|y, -ies ˌɹevə'luʃnəɹ|ɪ [-'ljuʃ-],
-ɪz

revolv|e, -es, -ing, -ed ɹɪ'vɒlv, -z, -ɪŋ, -d

revolver, -s ɹɪ'vɒlvɚ, -z
revulsion, -s ɹɪ'vʌlʃn̩, -z
reward, -s, -ing, -ed, -er/s ɹɪ'wɔɚd, -z, -ɪŋ, -ɪd, -ɚ/z
reword, -s, -ing, -ed ˌɹi'wɜd, -z, -ɪŋ, -ɪd
Reynaldo (*HAM*) ɹeɪ'nɑldoŭ [ɹɪ'n-]
Rheims (1HVI, TS) 'ɹimz
Rhenish (HAM) 'ɹenɪʃ
Rhesus (3HVI) 'ɹisəs
rhetoric 'ɹeɾəɹɪk
rhetoric|al, -ally ɹɪ'tɒɹɪk‖l̩, -əlɨ
rheum, -y 'ɹum, -ɨ
rheumatic, -s ɹu'mætɪk [ɹʊ'm-], -s
  Note.—Sometimes ['ɹuməˌtɪk] *in S., e.g.,*
  MSND, II.i.105; VA, 135
Rhodes (OTH) 'ɹoŭdz
Rhodope (1HVI) 'ɹoŭdoˌpɨ
  Note.—This name, mentioned in 1HVI,
  I.vi.22, *is from 'Rhodopis'* ([ɹo'doŭpɪs]*),
  but altered for the sake of the meter, and
  perhaps euphony*
rhubarb 'ɹubɑɚb
rhym|e, -es, -ing, -ed, -er/s 'ɹaɪm, -z, -ɪŋ, -d, -ɚ/z
rhythm, -s 'ɹɪðəm, -z
rhythmic, -al, -ally 'ɹɪðmɪk, -əl, -əlɨ [-lɨ]
Rialto (MV) ɹi'æltoŭ
rib, -s, -bing, -bed 'ɹɪb, -z, -ɪŋ, -d
ribald, -s; -ry 'ɹɪbəld ['ɹaɪbɒld], -z; -ɹɨ
  *Note.—Although customarily pro-
  nounced* ['ɹɪbəld], *it is known in poetry
  to also rhyme with 'piebald' (not,
  however, in S.)*
riband, -s 'ɹɪbənd, -z
ribaudred (*corruption of* **ribald** *in* AC)
  'ɹɪbəld
  Note.—The OED *cites, "a corrupt
  reading in* Ant. & Cl. III.x.10 *which has
  not yet been satisfactorily emended." It
  seems that no one has been able to
  reconcile this word to the scansion of the
  verse line. Rowe, et al. traditionally
  emend 'ribaudred' to 'ribauld' based on
  the fact that the Fourth Folio did include*

*an 'l' in its edition ('ribauldred'), and
that a two-syllable word best suits the
metricality of the line*
ribbon, -s, -ing, -ed 'ɹɪbən, -z, -ɪŋ, -d
rib-breaking 'ɹɪbˌbɹeɪkɪŋ
Ribs (1HIV) 'ɹɪbz
  *Note.—Some editors assert that this is a
  proper noun in* 1HIV, II.iv.109
Rice *or* **Rhys ap Thomas** (RIII) 'raɪs ˌæp 'tɒməs
  *Note.— 'ap' is the occasional Welsh
  prefix to surnames denoting pedigree;
  'son of,' pronounced* 'æp [ə'p]. *The name
  Rice ap Thomas in* RIII, IV.v.15 *appears
  with 'ap' in the First Folio and the Sixth
  Quarto, and with 'up' ('vp') in the First
  through Fifth Quartos, indicating the
  pronunciation* ['ʌp], *or perhaps the even
  weaker* ['əp]
rich, -es, -er, -est, -ly, -ness 'ɹɪtʃ, -ɪz, -ɚ, -ɪst, -lɨ, -nɪs
Richard (2HIV, HV, *1HVI, 2HVI, 3HVI,*
  KJ, *RII, RIII*) 'ɹɪtʃɚd
Richard the Second (*RII*, RIII) 'ɹɪtʃɚd ðə 'sekənd
Richard the Third (*RIII*) 'ɹɪtʃɚd ðə 'θɜd
rich-built 'ɹɪtʃˌbɪlt
riched 'ɹɪtʃt
rich-left 'ɹɪtʃˌleft
Richmond (3HVI, KJ, RIII) 'ɹɪtʃmənd
rid, -s, -ding 'ɹɪd, -z, -ɪŋ
riddance 'ɹɪdn̩s
rid|e, -es, -ing, rode, ridden 'ɹaɪd, -z, -ɪŋ, 'ɹoŭd, 'ɹɪdn̩
rider, -s; -less 'ɹaɪdɚ, -z; -lɪs
ridg|e, -es, -ing, -ed 'ɹɪdʒ, -ɪz, -ɪŋ, -d
ridicul|e, -es, -ing, -ed 'ɹɪdɪkjul, -z, -ɪŋ, -d
ridiculous, -ly, -ness ɹɪ'dɪkjʊləs, -lɨ, -nɪs
riding-robe, -s 'ɹaɪdɪŋˌɹoŭb, -z
riding-rod, -s 'ɹaɪdɪŋˌɹɒd, -z
riding-suit, -s 'ɹaɪdɪŋˌsjut, -s
rife 'ɹaɪf
rif|le, -les, -ling, -led 'ɹaɪf‖l̩, -lz, -l̩ɪŋ [-lɪŋ], -l̩d

---

i wẹ ɨ cit**y** ɪ h**ịt** e l**ẹt** ɛ d**ẹbut** æ c**ạn** a p**ạss** ɝ b**ịrd** ʌ h**ụt** ə **again** ɚ supp**er** u y**ọu**
ʊ sh**ould** o **ọbey** ɔ **ạwl** ɒ c**ọp** ɑ f**ạther** eɪ p**ạid** aɪ h**ịgh** oŭ g**ọ** ɔɪ v**ọice** aŭ f**ound** ɪɚ **ẹar**
ɛɚ **ạir** ʊɚ p**ọor** ɔɚ f**ọrk** ɑɚ p**ạrk** aɪɚ f**ịre** aŭɚ h**ọur** b **bọy** p p**ịt** d d**ọg** t t**ọp** g g**ọt**
k k**ịd** h **họw** fɪ be**hạve** dʒ j**ọt** tʃ **chẹw** z z**ạny** s s**ọft** v v**ạt** f f**ạt** ʒ tre**ạsure** ʃ **shịp** ð **thẹ**
θ **thịn** m **mạn** n **nọ** ŋ ha**ng** l l**ịp** j y**ẹs** w w**ọn** ʍ **whẹw** ɹ **rịgger**, ai**ɹ**y ɾ ma**ttẹr**

rift, -s, -ing, -ed 'ɹɪft, -s, -ɪŋ, -ɪd
rig, -s, -ging/s, -ged, -ger/s 'ɹɪg, -z, -ɪŋ/z, -d, -ɚ/z
riggish, -ly, -ness 'ɹɪgɪʃ, -lɪ, -nɪs
right, -s, -ing, -ed; -ly, -ness 'ɹaɪt, -s, -ɪŋ, -ɪd; -lɪ, -nɪs
righteous, -ly, -ness 'ɹaɪtʃəs, -lɪ, -nɪs
rigid, -ly, -ness 'ɹɪdʒɪd, -lɪ, -nɪs
rigidity ɹɪ'dʒɪdɪtɨ
rigol (ring, circle; groove, rut), -s 'ɹigoŭl ['ɹig̩l], -z
Note.—The OED asserts neither a pronunciation nor a clear etymology for this unusual word. Walter Skeat, however (in his A Concise Etymological Dictionary of the English Language, Capricorn Books, 1963), provides clues that speak to its pronunciation. In it, he cites its roots in Italian derived from Old High German (O.H.G.), and its meaning is given as 'a circlet,' a 'little wheel,' and the 'line or circumference of a circle.' With influences from O.H.G. and from Italian, one can deduce with some certainty that the 'i' is pronounced [i], and that the 'g' is hard
rigor 'ɹɪgɚ
rigorous, -ly, -ness 'ɹɪgɚɹəs, -lɪ, -nɪs
ril|e, -es, -ing, -ed 'ɹaɪl, -z, -ɪŋ, -d
rim, -s, -ming, -med 'ɹɪm, -z, -ɪŋ, -d
rime, -s 'ɹaɪm, -z
Rinaldo (ALL'S) ɹɪ'nɒldoŭ
rind, -s 'ɹaɪnd, -z
ring, -s, -ing, rang, rung, ringer/s 'ɹɪŋ, -z, -ɪŋ, 'ɹæŋ, 'ɹʌŋ, 'ɹɪŋɚ/z
ringlet, -s 'ɹɪŋlɪt, -s
ring-time 'ɹɪŋtaɪm
Ringwood (MWW) 'ɹɪŋwʊd
rins|e, -es, -ing, -ed 'ɹɪns, -ɪz, -ɪŋ, -t
riot, -s, -ing, -ed, -er/s "ɹaɪət, -s, -ɪŋ, -ɪd, -ɚ/z
riotous, -ly, -ness 'ɹaɪətəs, -lɪ, -nɪs
rip, -s, -ping, -ped, -per/s 'ɹɪp, -s, -ɪŋ, -t, -ɚ/z
ripe, -r, -st, -ly, -ness 'ɹaɪp, -ɚ, -ɪst, -lɪ, -nɪs
rip|en, -ens, -ening, -ened 'ɹaɪp|ən, -ənz, -n̩ɪŋ [-nɪŋ], -ənd
riping 'ɹaɪpɪŋ

ript (from rip) 'ɹɪpt
ris|e, -es, -ing, rose, risen 'ɹaɪz, -ɪz, -ɪŋ, 'ɹoŭz, 'ɹɪzn̩
rite, -s 'ɹaɪt, -s
rivage (shore) 'ɹaɪvɪdʒ
rival, -s, -(l)ing, -(l)ed 'ɹaɪvl̩, -z, -ɪŋ, -l̩d
rival-hating 'ɹaɪvl̩ˌheɪtɪŋ
rivality ɹaɪ'vælɪtɨ
riv|e, -es, -ing, -ed, riven 'ɹaɪv, -z, -ɪŋ, -d, 'ɹɪvən
Rivers (1HVI, 3HVI, RIII) 'ɹɪvɚz
Rivers, Earl (3HVI, RIII) 'ɝl 'ɹɪvɚz
rivet, -s, -ing, -ed, -er/s 'ɹɪvɪt, -s, -ɪŋ, -ɪd, -ɚ/z
road, -s 'ɹoŭd, -z
roam, -s, -ing, -ed 'ɹoŭm, -z, -ɪŋ, -d
roan, -s 'ɹoŭn, -z
roar, -s, -ing, -ed, -er/s 'ɹɔ˞, -z, -ɹɪŋ, -d, -ɹɚ/z
roast, -s, -ing, -ed, -er/s 'ɹoŭst, -s, -ɪŋ, -ɪd, -ɚ/z
rob, -s, -bing, -bed, -ber/s 'ɹɒb, -z, -ɪŋ, -d, -ɚ/z
robber|y, -ies 'ɹɒbɚɹ|ɨ, -ɨz
rob|e, -es, -ing, -ed 'ɹoŭb, -z, -ɪŋ, -d
Robert (KJ, MWW) 'ɹɒbɚt
Robin (HAM, 1HIV, 2HVI, MWW, TN) 'ɹɒbɪn
Note.—Also the given name or forename of Robin Goodfellow (MSND), Robin Nightwork (2HIV), and Robin Hood (mentioned in AYLI, 2HIV, and TGV)
Robin, Bonny (TNK) (a song) 'bɒnɨ 'ɹɒbɪn
robin, -s 'ɹɒbɪn, -z
robin-redbreast, -s ˌɹɒbɪn'ɹedbɹest, -s
robust, -ious, -ly, -ness ɹoŭ'bʌst, -jəs, -lɪ, -nɪs
Rochester (1HIV, HVIII) 'ɹɒtʃɪstɚ
Rochford, Viscount (HVIII) 'vaɪkaŭnt 'ɹɒtʃfɚd ['ɹɒʃfɚd]
rock, -s, -ing, -ed, -er/s 'ɹɒk, -s, -ɪŋ, -t, -ɚ/z
rode (p.t. of ride, q.v.) 'ɹoŭd
Roderigo or Rodorigo (OTH, TN) ˌɹɒdə'ɹigoŭ, -d'ɹigoŭ
roe, -s 'ɹoŭ, -z
Roger (2HVI) 'ɹɒdʒɚ
Rogero (WT) ɹo'dʒɛɹoŭ

rogu|e, -es, -ing 'ɹoʊg, -z, -ɪŋ
roguer|y, -ies 'ɹoʊgəˌɹ|ɪ, -ɪz
roguish, -ly, -ness 'ɹoʊgɪʃ, -lɪ, -nɪs
roil, -s, -ing, -ed 'ɹɔɪl, -z, -ɪŋ, -d
roisting (*archaic, obsolete form of*
  roistering) 'ɹɔɪstɪŋ
  Note.—This word in TC, II.ii.209 is an
  accepted form, and also the word used
  in the First Folio; however, emending it
  to 'roistering,' and then syncopating it
  into 'roist'ring,' i.e., ['ɹɔɪstɹɪŋ] *would*
  harm neither the meter nor the meaning
Roland *or* **Rowland** (1HVI), **-s** 'ɹoʊlənd,
  -z
role, -s 'ɹoʊl, -z
roll, -s, -ing, -ed, -er/s 'ɹoʊl, -z, -ɪŋ, -d,
  -ɚ/z
rollick, -s, -ing, -ed 'ɹɒlɪk, -s, -ɪŋ, -t
Roman (COR, HV, JUL, LUC, TIT), **-s**
  'ɹoʊmən, -z
Roman Brutus (HV) 'ɹoʊmən 'bɹutəs
Roman Empire (AC) 'ɹoʊmən 'empaɪɚ
Romano, Julio (WT) 'dʒuljoʊ ɹo'mɑnoʊ
Rome (AC, HVIII, JUL, KJ, LUC, TIT)
  'ɹoʊm
Romeo (*RJ*) 'ɹoʊmɪoʊ, -mjoʊ
Romish (CYM) 'ɹoʊmɪʃ
romp, -s, -ing, -ed 'ɹɒmp, -s, -ɪŋ, -t
rondure 'ɹɒndjɚ
ronyon *or* **runnion, -s** 'ɹʌnjən, -z
rood (R.), **-s** 'ɹud, -z
rook, -s, -ing, -ed 'ɹʊk, -s, -ɪŋ, -t
rookie (*inexperienced*), **-s** 'ɹʊkɪ, -z
rooky (*adj.*) (*crowlike bird*) 'ɹʊkɪ
root, -s, -ing, -ed/ly 'ɹut, -s, -ɪŋ, -ɪd/lɪ
rop|e, -es, -ing, -ed, -er/s 'ɹoʊp, -s, -ɪŋ, -t,
  -ɚ/z
ropery 'ɹoʊpəˌɹɪ
rope-trick, -s 'ɹoʊpˌtɹɪk, -s
Rosalind (*AYLI*) 'ɹɒzəlɪnd ['ɹoʊz-]
  Note.—The pronunciation of this name
  in AYLI is the subject of considerable
  debate, centering on the character
  Orlando's rhyme scheme in his

*poem dedicated to Rosalind (*AYLI,
III.ii.86–110*). In it, it appears that he*
rhymes every line with 'find' (including
her name). At least three factors should
be considered before ultimately landing
on the desired choice of how to
pronounce Rosalind: (1) Orlando is a
notoriously rotten versifier—note that
Touchstone's immediate reaction to the
poem is, "This is the very false gallop of
verses; why do you infect yourself with
them?" Agnes Latham (editor of AYLI,
The Arden Shakespeare, *1975) says,*
"The modern stage tends to treat
Orlando's rhymes as a joke, an ungifted
amateur's distortion of normal pronun-
ciation," but goes on to say, "It is
unlikely that they sounded so to an
Elizabethan," which brings me to: (2) In
S.'s day, it is possible (if not likely) that
all such words as those found at the end
of each of the poem's verse lines did
indeed rhyme, more or less (Kökeritz's
Shakespeare's Pronunciation, *p. 218),*
rendering a diphthong [əɪ]*, uncommon*
in modern standard parlance, so that
any argument as to whether S. intended
one or another pronunciation is a
modern (and perhaps moot) conundrum.
Finally: (3) The poem's rhyme scheme
may be rationalized if one accepts it as
being in an 'a b a b' pattern rather than
in couplets, in which case her name
would justifiably remain consistent with
the pronunciation given above. It also
happens to cause better euphony for
'Rosalinda' in AYLI, III.ii.134
Rosalinda (*AYLI*) ˌɹɒzə'lɪndə [ˌɹoʊz-] (*see*
  Note for **Rosalind**)
Rosaline (LLL, RJ) 'ɹɒzəlaɪn
Roscius (HAM, 3HVI) 'ɹɔʃɪəs, -ʃəs
rose, -s 'ɹoʊz, -ɪz
rose (*p.t. of* **rise**, *q.v.*) 'ɹoʊz
Rose (AYLI, HVIII) 'ɹoʊz

---

i wᴇ ɪ city ɪ hit e let ɛ debut æ can a pass ɝ bird ʌ hut ə again ɚ supper u you
ʊ should o obey ɔ awl ɒ cop ɑ father eɪ paid aɪ high oʊ go ɔɪ voice aʊ found ɪɚ ear
ɛɚ air ʊɚ poor ɔɚ fork ɑɚ park aɪɚ fire aʊɚ hour b boy p pit d dog t top g got
k kid h how fi behave dʒ jot tʃ chew z zany s soft v vat f fat ʒ treasure ʃ ship ð the
θ thin m man n no ŋ hang l lip j yes w won ʍ whew ɹ rigger, airy ɾ matter

rose-cheeked ˈɹoŭzˌtʃikt
rosed (*made red*) ˈɹoŭzd ([ˈɹoŭzɪd] *in* TIT,
 II.iii.24)
rose-lipped ˈɹoŭzˌlɪpt
Rosencrantz (*HAM*) ˈɹoŭzənkɹænts
rose-water ˈɹoŭzˌwɔɾɚ
Ross(e) (*MAC, RII*) ˈɹɒs
Rossillion *or* Roussillon, Count/ess
 (*ALL 'S*) ˈkɑŭnt/ɪs [-es] ɹɔˈsɪljən [ɹoˈs-,
 ɹuˈs-]
rot, -s, -ting, -ted ˈɹɒt, -s, -ɪŋ [ˈɹɒɾɪŋ], -ɪd
rote, -d ˈɹoŭt, -ɪd
Rotherham, Thomas (*RIII*) ˈtɒməs
 ˈɹɒðɚɹəm
rotten, -est, -ly, -ness ˈɹɒtn̩, -ɪst, -lɨ, -nɪs
rotund, -ity, -ness ɹoˈtʌnd, -ɪtɨ, -nɪs
rotunda, -s ɹoˈtʌndə, -z
Rouen (HV, 1HVI) ˈɹoŭən [ˈɹoŭn, ˈɹuɑ̃]
 *Note.—The pronunciation in S. is
 dictated by the word's place within the
 metrical pattern of the verse line.* 1HVI,
 I.i.60 and I.i.65 *require a disyllabic
 pronunciation; it is usually monosyllabic
 elsewhere. It may be either one or two
 syllables in* 1HVI, III.ii.1
roug|e, -es, -ing, -ed ˈɹuʒ, -ɪz, -ɪŋ, -d
Rougemont (RIII) ˈɹuʒmɔnt
rough, -s, -ing, -ed; -er, -est, -ly, -ness
 ˈɹʌf, -s, -ɪŋ, -t; -ɚ, -ɪst, -lɨ, -nɪs
rough-grown ˈɹʌfˌɡɹoŭn
rough-hew, -s, -ing, -ed, -n ˌɹʌfˈhju, -z,
 -ɪŋ, -d, -n
round, -s, -ing, -ed; -er, -est, -ly, -ness
 ˈɹɑŭnd, -z, -ɪŋ, -ɪd; -ɚ, -ɪst, -lɨ, -nɪs
roundel, -s ˈɹoŭndl̩, -z
rounders ˈɹɑŭndɚz
round-faced ˈɹɑŭndfeĭst
round-hoofed ˈɹɑŭndˌhŭft [-ˌhuft]
roundish, -ness ˈɹɑŭndɪʃ, -nɪs
roundure (*roundness*) ˈɹɑŭndjɚ
round-wombed ˈɹɑŭndˌwumd
rous|e, -es, -ing/ly, -ed ˈɹɑŭz, -ɪz, -ɪŋ/lɨ,
 -d
Roussi (HV) ˈɹuˌsi
rout, -s, -ing, -ed ˈɹɑŭt, -s, -ɪŋ, -ɪd
rov|e, -es, -ing, -ed, -er/s ˈɹoŭv, -z, -ɪŋ,
 -d, -ɚ/z
row, -s, -ing, -ed, -er/s ˈɹoŭ, -z, -ɪŋ, -d,
 -ɚ/z

row (*boisterous argument*), -s, -ing, -ed
 ˈɹɑŭ, -z, -ɪŋ, -d
rowel(l), -s, -ing, -ed ˈɹɑŭəl, -z, -ɪŋ, -d
rowel-head ˈɹɑŭəlˌhed
Rowland(s) (1HVI, MEAS) ˈɹoŭlənd(z)
Rowland, Child(e) (LEAR) ˌtʃaĭld
 ˈɹoŭlənd
Rowland, Sir (AYLI) ˌsɚ ˈɹoŭlənd (*see
 Note for* de Boys, Sir Rowland)
royal, -ly; -ize ˈɹɔĭəl, -ɨ; -aĭz
roynish *or* roinish (*coarse, base*) ˈɹɔĭnɪʃ
rub, -s, -bing, -bed ˈɹʌb, -z, -ɪŋ, -d
rubber, -s ˈɹʌbɚ, -z
rubbish ˈɹʌbɪʃ
rubious ˈɹubɪəs
rubric, -s ˈɹubɹɪk, -s
rub|y, -ies ˈɹub|ɨ, -ɨz
ruby-colored ˈɹubɨˌkʌlɚd
ruddock, -s ˈɹʌdək, -s
rudd|y, -ier, -iest, -ily, -iness ˈɹʌd|ɨ, -ɨɚ,
 -ɨst, -ɪlɨ, -ɨnɪs
rude, -r, -st, -ly, -ness ˈɹud, -ɚ, -ɪst, -lɨ,
 -nɪs
rude-growing ˈɹudˌɡɹoŭɪŋ
rudeliest ˈɹudlɨɪst
rudesby ˈɹudzbɨ
rudiment, -s ˈɹudɪmənt, -s
rue, -s, -ing, -d ˈɹu, -z, -ɪŋ, -d
ruff, -s, -ing, -ed ˈɹʌf, -s, -ɪŋ, -t
ruffian, -s, -ed, -ly; -ism ˈɹʌfɪən, -z, -d,
 -lɨ; -ɪzm̩
ruff|le, -les, -ling, -led ˈɹʌf|l̩, -l̩z, -l̩ɪŋ
 [-lɪŋ], -l̩d
rug, -s ˈɹʌg, -z
Rugby, John (*MWW*) ˈdʒɒn ˈɹʌgbɨ
rug-headed ˈɹʌgˌhedɪd
ruinate ˈɹuɪneĭt
ruinous, -ly, -ness ˈɹuɪnəs, -lɨ, -nɪs
rul|e, -es, -ing/s, -ed, -er/s ˈɹul, -z, -ɪŋ/z,
 -d, -ɚ/z
rumb|le, -les, -ling, -led ˈɹʌmb|l̩, -l̩z, -lɪŋ
 [-l̩ɪŋ], -l̩d
ruminat|e, -es, -ing, -ed ˈɹumɪneĭt, -s, -ɪŋ,
 -ɪd
rumination, -s ˌɹumɪˈneĭʃn̩, -z
rummag|e, -es, -ing, -ed ˈɹʌmɪdʒ, -ɪz, -ɪŋ,
 -d
rumor, -s, -ing, -ed, -er/s ˈɹumɚ, -z, -ɹɪŋ,
 -d, -ɹɚ/z

rumor-monger, -ers, -ing 'ɹuməˌmʌŋgə-,
-ɪə-z, -ɹɪŋ
Rumour (*2HIV*) 'ɹumə-
rump, -s 'ɹʌmp, -s
rump-fed 'ɹʌmpˌfed
rump|le, -les, -ling, -led 'ɹʌmp|l̩, -l̩z, -lɪŋ
[-l̩ɪŋ], -l̩d
run, -s, -ning, ran 'ɹʌn, -z, -ɪŋ, 'ɹæn
runagate, -s 'ɹʌnəgeɪt, -s
runaway, -s 'ɹʌnəweĭ, -z
rune, -s 'ɹun, -z
rung (*p.p. of* **ring**, *q.v.*) 'ɹʌŋ
rung (*s.*), **-s** 'ɹʌŋ, -z
runner, -s 'ɹʌnə-, -z
runneth 'ɹʌnɪθ
*Note.—'-eth' is the suffix used to form
the archaic third person present singular
indicative of verbs, and although it is
employed throughout S., the form is not
typically cited in this dictionary. I
include this particular instance because
it has survived in the saying, 'My cup
runneth over'*
runnion *or* **ronyon, -s** 'ɹʌnjən, -z
runt, -s 'ɹʌnt, -s
runway, -s 'ɹʌnweĭ, -z
ruptur|e, -es, -ing, -ed 'ɹʌptʃə-, -z, -ɹɪŋ,
-d
rural, -ly 'ɹʊə-ɹəl, -ɪ
ruse, -s 'ɹuz, -ɪz
rush, -es, -ing, -ed, -er/s 'ɹʌʃ, -ɪz, -ɪŋ, -t,
-ə-/z
rush-candle, -s 'ɹʌʃˌkændl̩, -z
rushling (*obsolete var. of* '*rustling*')
'ɹʌʃlɪŋ [-ʃlɪŋ]
rushy 'ɹʌʃɪ
russet, -s, -y 'ɹʌsɪt, -s, -ɪ
Russia (MEAS, WT) 'ɹʌʃə
*Note.—In MEAS, II.i.133, this word is
meant to be trisyllabic, i.e.,* ['ɹʌʃɪə]
Russia, Emperor of (MEAS, WT)
'empə-ɹə- (ɹ)əv 'ɹʌʃə
Russian (HV, LLL), **-s** 'ɹʌʃn̩, -z
rust, -s, -ing, -ed 'ɹʌst, -s, -ɪŋ, -ɪd

rustic, -s, -ally 'ɹʌstɪk, -s, -əlɪ
rusticity ɹʌ'stɪsɪtɪ
rust|le, -les, -ling, -led, -ler/s 'ɹʌs|l̩, -l̩z,
-l̩ɪŋ [-lɪŋ], -l̩d, -lə-/z [-lə-/z]
rust|y, -ier, -iest, -iness 'ɹʌst|ɪ, -ɪə-, -ɪɪst,
-ɪnɪs
ru|t, -ts, -tting, -tted 'ɹʌ|t, -ts, -ɾɪŋ, -ɾɪd
Rutland, Edmund (3HVI, RII, RIII)
'edmənd 'ɹʌtlənd
ruth (**R.**) 'ɹuθ
ruth|ful, -fully, -fulness 'ɹuθ|fʊl, -fʊlɪ,
-fʊlnɪs
ruthless, -ly, -ness 'ɹuθlɪs, -lɪ, -nɪs
rut-time 'ɹʌtˌtaɪm
ruttish, -ly, -ness 'ɹʌɾɪʃ, -lɪ, -nɪs
Rycas (*TNK*) 'ɹaĭkəs
rye 'ɹaĭ
Rynaldo *or* **Rinaldo** (ALL'S) ɹɪ'nɒldoŭ

Ss

S (*the letter*), **-'s** 'es, -ɪz
s. (*abbreviation for* '*shilling(s)*') 'ʃɪlɪŋ
(*sing.*) 'ʃɪlɪŋz (*pl.*)
sa 'sɑ (*see* **sa, sa, sa, sa**)
Saba (HVIII) 'seĭbə ['sɑbə]
sabbath (**S.**), **-s** 'sæbəθ, -s
sable, -s 'seĭbl̩, -z
Sack, Sir John (1HIV) ˌsə- 'dʒɒn 'sæk
*Note.—This is a nonce-name that Poins
gives Falstaff in* 1HIV, I.ii.110. *There is
some confusion at to whether Poins calls
him 'Sir John Sack-and-Sugar' or 'Sir
John Sack, and Sugar Jack'*
sack, -s, -ing, -ed, -er/s 'sæk, -s, -ɪŋ, -t,
-ə-/z
sackbut, -s 'sækbʌt, -s
sackcloth 'sækklɒθ
Sackerson (MWW) 'sækə-sn̩
sacral 'seĭkɹəl
sacrament, -s 'sækɹəmənt, -s
sacred, -ly, -ness 'seĭkɹɪd, -lɪ, -nɪs

---

i w**e** ɪ c**i**ty ɪ h**i**t e l**e**t ɛ d**e**but æ c**a**n a p**a**ss ɚ b**i**rd ʌ h**u**t ə **a**gain ɚ supp**e**r u y**ou**
ʊ sh**ou**ld o **o**bey ɔ **aw**l ɒ c**o**p ɑ f**a**ther eĭ p**ai**d aĭ h**igh** oŭ g**o** ɔĭ v**oi**ce aŭ f**ou**nd ɪɚ **ear**
ɛɚ **air** ʊɚ p**oor** ɔɚ f**or**k ɑɚ p**ar**k aĭɚ f**ire** aŭɚ h**our** b b**oy** p p**i**t d d**o**g t t**o**p g g**o**t
k k**i**d h h**ow** fi be**h**ave dʒ j**o**t tʃ **ch**ew z **z**any s **s**oft v **v**at f **f**at ʒ trea**s**ure ʃ **sh**ip ð **th**e
θ **th**in m **m**an n **n**o ŋ ha**ng** l l**i**p j **y**es w **w**on ʍ **wh**ew ɹ **r**igger, ai**ry** ɾ ma**tt**er

sacrific|e, -es, -ing, -ed, -er/s 'sækɹɪfaɪs,
-ɪz, -ɪŋ, -t, -ɚ/z

sacrilege 'sækɹɪlɪdʒ

sacrilegious, -ly, -ness ˌsækɹɪ'lɪdʒəs
[-'lidʒəs], -lɪ, -nɪs

sacring(-)bell 'seɪkɹɪŋˌbel

sad, -der, -dest, -ly, -ness 'sæd, -ɚ, -ɪst,
-lɪ, -nɪs

sad-attending 'sædəˌtendɪŋ

saddlebag, -s 'sædl̩ˌbæg, -z

saddle-bow, -s 'sædl̩ˌboŏ, -z

saddle-horse, -s 'sædl̩ˌhɔ̌ɚs, -ɪz

sad-eyed 'sædˌaɪd

sad-faced 'sædˌfeɪst

sadistic sə'dɪstɪk

safari, -s sə'fɑɹɪ, -z

safe, -s; -r, -st, -ly, -ness 'seɪf, -s; -ɚ, -ɪst,
-lɪ, -nɪs

safed (*v. from* **safe**) 'seɪft

safeguard, -s, -ing, -ed 'seɪfgɑ̌ɚd, -z, -ɪŋ,
-ɪd

safety 'seɪftɪ

saffron 'sæfɹən

sag, -s, -ging, -ged 'sæg, -z, -ɪŋ, -d

sage, -s, -ly, -ness 'seɪdʒ, -ɪz, -lɪ, -nɪs

Sagittar (OTH) 'sædʒɪtɚ [-tɛɚ]

Sagit(t)ary (OTH, TC) 'sædʒɪtɛɚ̌ɹɪ

said (*from* **say**) 'sed

sail, -s, -ing, -ed, -or/s 'seɪl, -z, -ɪŋ, -d,
-ɚ/z

sail-maker, -s 'seɪl̩ˌmeɪkɚ, -z

sain, -s, -ing, -ed 'seɪn, -z, -ɪŋ, -d

saint, -s, -ed 'seɪnt, -s, -ɪd

Saint Alban *or* **Albon(e)** (2HVI) 'seɪnt
'ɔlbən

Saint Alban's *or* **Albon(e)s** (1HIV, 2HIV,
2HVI, 3HVI, RIII) 'seɪnt 'ɔlbənz

Saint Anne (TN, TS) 'seɪnt 'æn

Saint Asaph (HVIII) 'seɪnt 'eɪsəf ['eɪzəf,
'æsəf]

Saint Bennet (TN) 'seɪnt 'benɪt

Saint Charity (HAM) 'seɪnt 'tʃæɹɪtɪ

Saint Clare (MEAS) 'seɪnt 'klɛɚ̌

Saint Colme's Inch (MAC) ˌseɪnt
'kɔlmɪz 'ɪntʃ

*Note.—The name (i.e., 'Colme's') is that
of a small island in the Firth of Forth,
Scotland, and cited in MAC, I.ii.63. It is
meant to be disyllabic for the sake of the*

*meter, and is consistent with a handful of
other possessive words in S. (see Note
for* **whale**). *'Inch' is Scottish for 'island,'
derived from the Gaelic 'innis'*

Saint Cupid (LLL) 'seɪnt 'kjupɪd

Saint Davy (HV) 'seɪnt 'deɪvɪ

Saint Den(n)is (HV, 1HVI, LLL) 'seɪnt
'denɪs

Saint Edmundsbury (KJ) 'seɪnt
'edmən dzbɚ̌ɹɪ, -bɹɪ

Saint Francis (RJ) 'seɪnt 'fɹansɪs

Saint George (HV, 1HVI, 3HVI, KJ,
LLL, TS) 'seɪnt 'dʒɔɚ̌dʒ

Saint George's Field (2HIV, 2HVI) ˌseɪnt
[ˌsn̩t] 'dʒɔɚ̌dʒɪz 'fild

Saint Jamy (TS) 'seɪnt 'dʒeɪmɪ

*Note.—This name in TS, III.ii.79, is
generally accepted to be contained
within the fragment of an old ballad
(despite the fact that the First Folio
prints it as prose); yet, the rhyme is
questionable. If it wants to rhyme with
'penny,' then perhaps a pronunciation
more akin to* ['dʒemɪ] *is more appropriate. If it wants to remain closer to
the pronunciation proffered above—
my recommendation—then perhaps
'penny' and 'many' (or 'meiny'?) shift
a little. Cf. Kökeritz's* Shakespeare's
Pronunciation, *p. 186, and the line
annotations for TS, III.ii.79–83 and
'many' (ln. 83) in TS,* The Arden
Shakespeare, *Brian Morris, editor,
1981*

Saint Jaques le Grand (ALL'S) 'seɪnt
'dʒeɪks lə 'gɹænd

Note.—Sometimes in S. a disyllabic
['dʒeɪkɪs] *is required by the meter, i.e.,
AYLI, II.i.26; LLL, II.i.42; ALL'S,
III.iv.4, III.v.98; see chapter 'Shakespeare's Verse' § 1.8 of this dictionary*

Saint Jeronimy (TS) 'seɪnt dʒɚ'ɹɒnɪmɪ

Saint John (RIII) 'seɪnt 'dʒɒn

Saint Katherine's Church (1HVI) 'seɪnt
'kæθɹɪnz 'tʃɚ̌tʃ

Saint Lambert (RII) 'seɪnt 'læmbɚt

Saint Lawrence Poultney (HVIII) 'seɪnt
'lɔɹəns 'poŏltnɪ

saint(-)like 'seɪntˌlaɪk

Saint Luke's (MEAS, TS) 'seɪnt 'luks ['ljuks]

Saint Magnus (2HVI) 'seɪnt 'mægnəs

Saint Martin (1HVI) 'seɪnt 'mɑɚ̆·tn̩

Saint Mary's Chapel (KJ) 'seɪnt 'mɛɚ̆·ɹɪz 'tʃæpl̩

Saint Michael (1HVI) 'seɪnt 'maɪ̆kl̩

Saint Nic(h)olas (1HIV, TGV) 'seɪnt 'nɪkələs [-kl̩əs]

Saint Patrick (HAM) 'seɪnt 'pætɹɪk

Saint Paul (RIII) 'seɪnt 'pɔl

Saint Peter (OTH) 'seɪnt 'piɾə̆

Saint Peter's Church (RJ) 'seɪnt 'piɾə̆·z 'tʃɚ̆·tʃ

Saint Philip (1HVI) 'seɪnt 'fɪlɪp

saint-seducing 'seɪntsɪˌdjusɪŋ

Saint Stephen (TIT) 'seɪnt 'stivən

Saint Tavy (HV) 'seɪnt 'teɪ̆vɨ
Note.—This is the dialectal corruption of 'Saint Davy,' spoken by Fluellen, a Welshman in HV. This is an example of S.'s direction to the actor (by way of semiphonetic spellings) to adopt a Welsh accent, more or less

Saint Valentine (HAM, MSND) 'seɪnt 'væləntaɪn

saith (*archaic third person singular present of* **say**) 'seθ ['seɪ̆ɪθ]
Note.—Typically, I don't list pronuncia- tions of words employing this archaic suffix (usually ending in '-eth'); forming the third person present singular indicative for verbs. In this case, however, there is a traditional pronunciation not at first apparent to the eye, but commonly heard in the phrase, "saith the Lord." The word is preferably pronounced as a monosyllable, as in Sonn. 114.3

sake, -s 'seɪ̆k, -s

Sala (HV) 'seɪ̆lə

salacious, -ly, -ness sə'leɪ̆ʃəs, -lɨ, -nɪs

salad, -s 'sæləd, -z

salamander, -s 'sæləˌmandə̆·, -z

Salanio (MV) sə'lɑnɪoŭ, -njoŭ

Salarino (MV) sɑlə'ɹinoŭ

salar|y, -ies, -ied 'sæləɹ|ɨ, -ɨz, -ɨd

sale, -s 'seɪl, -z

Salerio (MV) sə'leɹɪoŭ [-'lɪɚ̆·ɹɪoŭ], -'lɪɚ̆·ʲjoŭ
Note.—In S., this name is always trisyllabic, i.e., [sə'leʲjoŭ] *(*[-'lɪɚ̆·ʲjoŭ]*)*

sale-work 'seɪl̩ˌwɜ·k

Salic (HV) 'sælɪk ['seɪlɪk]

Salisbury (HV, 1HVI, 2HVI, HVIII, KJ, RII, RIII) 'sɔlzbə·ɹɨ ['sɒlz-]
Note.—At times, this names is disyllabic, i.e., ['sɔlzbɹɨ ('sɒlz-)], *in order to meet the metrical requirements of the verse line*

sallet, -s 'sælɪt, -s

sall|y, -ies, -ying, -ied 'sæl|ɨ, -ɨz, -ɨŋ, -ɨd

salt, -s, -ing, -ed, -er/s; -er, -est, -ly, -ness, -ish 'sɔlt, -s, -ɪŋ, -ɨd, -ə·/z; -ə·, -ɪst, -lɨ, -nɪs, -ɪʃ

salt-butter 'sɔltˌbʌɾə̆·

salt-fish 'sɔltˌfɪʃ

Saltiers (WT) 'sɔltɪɚ̆·z
Note.—I tend to agree with the editors who suggest that this unusual word is derived from 'leapers' or 'jumpers'

saltpeter 'sɔltˌpitə̆· [-ˌpiɾə̆·]

salt-sea 'sɔltˌsi

salt-water 'sɔltˌwɔɾə̆·

salt|y, -ier, -iest, -iness 'sɔlt|ɨ, -ɪə·, -ɪɪst, -ɪnɪs

salutation, -s ˌsæljʊ'teɪ̆ʃn̩, -z

salut|e, -es, -ing, -ed sə'lut [-'ljut], -s, -ɪŋ, -ɨd

salvag|e, -es, -ing, -ed, -er/s; -eable 'sælvɪdʒ, -ɪz, -ɪŋ, -d, -ə·/z; -əbl̩

salv|e, -es, -ing, -ed (*ointment*) 'sav ['sæv], -z, -ɪŋ, -d

salv|e, -es, -ing, -ed (*rescue*) 'sælv, -z, -ɪŋ, -d

Samingo (2HIV) sæ'mɪŋgoŭ

samphire 'sæmfaɪ̆ə̆·

samp|le, -les, -ling, -led, -ler/s 'samp|l̩, -l̩z, -lɪŋ [-l̩ŋ], -l̩d, -lə·/z [-lə·/z]

i w**e** ɨ cit**y** ɪ h**i**t e l**e**t ɛ d**e**but æ c**a**n a p**a**ss ɜ· b**ir**d ʌ h**u**t ə **a**gain ə· supp**er** u y**ou** ʊ sh**ou**ld o **o**bey ɔ **aw**l ɒ c**o**p ɑ f**a**ther eɪ p**ai**d aɪ h**igh** oŭ g**o** ɔɪ v**oi**ce aŭ f**ou**nd ɪɚ̆· **ear** ɛɚ̆· **air** ʊɚ̆· p**oor** ɔɚ̆· f**or**k ɑɚ̆· p**ar**k aɪɚ̆· f**ire** aŭɚ̆· h**our** b **b**oy p **p**it d **d**og t **t**op g **g**ot k **k**id h **h**ow fi be**h**ave dʒ **j**ot tʃ **ch**ew z **z**any s **s**oft v **v**at f **f**at ʒ trea**s**ure ʃ **sh**ip ð **th**e θ **th**in m **m**an n **n**o ŋ ha**ng** l **l**ip j **y**es w **w**on ʍ **wh**ew ɹ **r**igger, ai**r**y ɾ ma**tt**er

Sampson (*RJ*) 'sæmpsn̩
Samson (1HVI, HVIII, LLL), **-s** 'sæmsn̩
[-mpsn̩], -z
sancta majestas (*L.*) (2HVI, V.i.5) 'saŋktɑ
'madʒɛstɑs
sancti|fy, **-fies, -fying, -fied** 'sæŋktɪ|faɪ̆,
-faɪ̆z, -faɪ̆ɪŋ, -faɪ̆d
sanctimonious, **-ly, -ness**
ˌsæŋktɪ'moŭnɪəs, -lɪ, -nɪs
sanctimony 'sæŋktɪmənɨ
sancti|on, **-ons, -oning, -oned** 'sæŋkʃ|n̩,
-n̩z, -n̩ɪŋ [-ənɪŋ], -n̩d
sanctity 'sæŋktɪtɨ
sanctuarize 'sæŋktʃʊəɹaɪ̆z
sand, **-s, -ing, -ed** 'sænd, -z, -ɪŋ, -ɪd
Sandal Castle (3HVI) 'sændl̩ 'kasl̩
sand-blind 'sændblaɪ̆nd
Sands *or* Sandys, Lord (*HVIII*) 'lɔɔ̆-d
'sændz
sand|y, **-ier, -iest, -iness** 'sænd|ɪ, -ɪə̆-, -ɪɪst,
-ɪnɪs
sandy-bottomed 'sændɪˌbɒɾəmd
sanguine, **-ly, -ness** 'sæŋgwɪn, -lɪ, -nɪs
sanguineous sæŋ'gwɪnɪəs
sanguis (*L.*) (LLL, IV.ii.3) 'saŋgwis
[-wɪs]
sanity 'sænɪtɨ
sans 'sænz [*Fr.* sɑ̃ŋ]
sap, **-s, -ping, -ped, -per/s** 'sæp, -s, -ɪŋ,
-t, -ə̆-/z
sapego (*var. of* serpigo) sə'pigoŭ
Note.—*This word in MEAS, III.i.31, in
the First Folio, is typically emended to
'serpigo,' q.v.*
sapien|ce, **-t/ly** 'seɪ̆pɪən|s, -t/lɨ
sapling, **-s** 'sæplɪŋ, -z
sapphire, **-s** 'sæfaɪ̆ə̆-, -z
sapp|y, **-iness** 'sæp|ɪ, -ɪnɪs
Saracen (RII), **-s** 'sæɹəsn̩ [-sən], -z
Sardian (JUL), **-s** 'sɑɔ̆-dɪən, -z, -djən, -z
Sardinia (AC) sɑɔ̆-'dɪnɪə, -njə
Sardis (JUL) 'sɑɔ̆-dɪs
sarpego sə̆-'pigoŭ
Note.—*This word in MEAS, III.i.31, in
the Second Folio, is typically emended
to 'serpigo,' q.v.*
sarsenet 'sɑɔ̆-snɪt [-net]
Sarum (LEAR) 'sɛɔ̆-ɹəm
sa, sa, sa, sa 'sɑ 'sɑ 'sɑ 'sɑ

Note.—*This phrase in LEAR, IV.vi.199
is arguably derived from the Fr. 'ça, ça,
ça, ça,' meaning, 'there, there, there,
there'*
sash, **-es, -ing, -ed** 'sæʃ, -ɪz, -ɪŋ, -t
Satan (ALL'S, COM, 1HIV, MWW, TN)
'seɪ̆tn̩
satchel, **-s** 'sætʃl̩, -z
sat|e, **-es, -ing, -ed** 'seɪ̆t, -s, -ɪŋ, -ɪd
satiate (*adj.*) 'seɪ̆ʃɪt [-ʃɪt]
satiat|e (*v.*), **-es, -ing, -ed** 'seɪ̆ʃɪeɪ̆t, -s, -ɪŋ,
-ɪd
satiety sə'taɪ̆ɪtɨ ['seɪ̆ʃjətɨ]
Note.—*In the early Quarto and Folio
editions of S., this word is spelled
'society' and 'societie.' For instance, in
the First through Third Folio editions,
TIM, I.i.169 has 'society' in contrast to
the Fourth Folio edition, which gives
'satiety.' Likewise, Quartos One through
Five of VA give 'societie' (VA, 19), and
the Sixth Quarto gives 'satietie' (modern
editors emending to 'satiety'). In both of
these cases, the metricality of the verse
wants them to have primary stress on the
second syllable, i.e.,* [sə'taɪ̆ɪtɨ], *the
pronunciation preferred today. In OTH,
II.i.227, this word in the First Folio is
'Satiety' and although in prose,* [sə'taɪ̆ɪtɨ]
*is recommended. Most dictionaries cite
or sanction this pronunciation as the
only pronunciation of 'satiety'*
satin, **-s, -y** 'sætn̩, -z, -ɨ
satire, **-s** 'sætaɪ̆ə̆-, -z
satiric|al, **-ally, -alness** sə'tɪɹɪk|l̩, -əlɨ,
-l̩nɪs
satirist, **-s** 'sæɾə̆-ɹɪst [-ɾɪ-], -s
Satis quod (quid) sufficit (*L.*) (LLL, V.i.1)
'satɪs kwɒd (kwɪd) sʌ'fiʃɪt [su'fisit]
Note.—[sʌ'fiʃɪt] *is given here to resemble
'sufficient' in some way and to evoke
'sufficient' to the modern ear, an
audience mostly unlearned in Latin*
Saturday (AYLI, LLL), **-s** 'sæɾə̆-dɪ [-deɪ̆],
-z
Saturn (ADO, 2HIV, Sonn. 98, TIT)
'sæɾɔ̆-n
Saturnine (*TIT*) 'sæɾə̆-naɪ̆n ['sætə̆-]
Saturninus (*TIT*) ˌsæɾə̆-'naɪ̆nəs [ˌsætə̆-]

satyr (S.), -s 'seĭtə˞ ['sætə˞], -z
sauc|e, -es, -ing, -ed 'sɔs, -ɪz, -ɪŋ, -t
sauc|y, -ier, -iest, -ily, -iness 'sɔs|ɪ, -ɪə˞,
  -ɪɪst, -ɪlɪ, -ɪnɪs
sausage, -s 'sɒsɪdʒ, -ɪz
savage, -s, -ly, -ness; -ry 'sævɪdʒ, -ɪz, -lɪ,
  -nɪs; -ɹɪ
savage-wild 'sævɪdʒˌwaĭld
'save (*contr. of* God save) 'seĭv [ḑs-]
savior (S.) (HAM), -s 'seĭvjə˞, -z
savor, -s, -ing, -ed, -er/s 'seĭvə˞, -z, -ɹɪŋ,
  -d, -ɹə˞/z
savor|y, -ies; -ily, -iness 'seĭvə˞ɹ|ɪ, -ɪz; -ɪlɪ,
  -ɪnɪs
Savoy (2HVI) sə'vɔĭ
saw (*p.t. of* see, *q.v.*) 'sɔ
saw (*s., v.*) (*familiar saying; tool for and
  act of cutting*), -s, -ing, -ed, -n 'sɔ, -z,
  -ɪŋ, -d, -n
sawpit, -s 'sɔpɪt, -s
saw't (*contr. of* saw it) 'sɔt
Saxon (HV), -s 'sæksn̩, -z
Saxony (HV, MV) 'sæksnɪ [-sənɪ]
Say, Lord (*2HVI*) 'lɔɹ̩-d 'seĭ
s|ay, -ays, -aying/s, -aid 's|eĭ, -ez, -eĭɪŋ/z,
  -ed
'say'd (*aphetic form of* assayed *in* PER,
  I.i.60, 61) 'seĭd
'sblood (*contr. of* God's blood) 'zblʌd
scab, -s, -by, -biness 'skæb, -z, -ɪ, -ɪnɪs
scabbard, -s 'skæbə˞d, -z
scaffold, -s, -ing/s, -ed; -age 'skæfəld
  [-foŭld], -z, -ɪŋ/z, -ɪd; -ɪdʒ
scald, -s, -ing, -ed 'skɔld, -z, -ɪŋ, -ɪd
scal|e, -es, -ing, -ed 'skeĭl, -z, -ɪŋ, -d
Scales (1HVI, 2HVI, 3HVI, RIII) 'skeĭlz
scall 'skɔl
scalp, -s, -ing, -ed, -er/s 'skælp, -s, -ɪŋ, -t,
  -ə˞/z
scal|y, -ier, -iest, -iness 'skeĭl|ɪ, -ɪə˞, -ɪɪst,
  -ɪnɪs
scamb|le, -les, -ling, -led, -ler/s 'skæmb|l̩,
  -lz, -lɪŋ [-l̩ɪŋ], -l̩d, -lə˞/z [-l̩ə˞/z]
Note.—This word, meaning 'rough,

*contentious, or chaotic struggle,'
appears in* ADO, V.i.94 *and* HV, I.i.4,
*etc. Although the pronunciations given
above are in accord with the* OED, *the
var. spellings of the word strongly
suggest that the 'b' can very well be
silent, i.e.,* ['skæm|l̩] *(cf. the alt.
pronunciation of 'clamber'). In* KJ,
IV.iii.146, *its close kinship with
'scramble' (as well as euphony) almost
demands that the 'b' be pronounced*
scamel, -s 'skæməl ['skeĭməl], -z
*Note.—The pronunciations proposed for
this word are entirely conjectural. It
appears in* TEM, II.ii.172, *and is at
times emended to 'sea-mels,' 'sea-mells,'
'seamews,' and even 'shamois'*
scamp, -s, -ing, -ed 'skæmp, -s, -ɪŋ, -t
scamp|er, -ers, -ering, -ered 'skæmp|ə˞,
  -ə˞z, -ə˞ɹɪŋ, -ə˞d
scan, -s, -ning, -ned 'skæn, -z, -ɪŋ, -d
scandal, -s 'skændl̩, -z
scandaliz|e, -es, -ing, -ed 'skændəlaĭz,
  -ɪz, -ɪŋ, -d
scandalous, -ly, -ness 'skændələs, -lɪ, -nɪs
scansion, -s 'skænʃn̩, -z
scant, -s, -ing, -ed; -er, -ly, -ness 'skænt,
  -s, -ɪŋ, -ɪd; -ə˞, -lɪ, -nɪs
scantle (*small amount*) 'skæntl̩
scantling, -s 'skæntlɪŋ [-lɪn], -z
scant|y, -ier, -iest, -ily, -iness 'skænt|ɪ,
  -ɪə˞, -ɪɪst, -ɪlɪ, -ɪnɪs
scap|e (*archaic var. of* escape), -s, -ing,
  -ed 'skeĭp, -s, -ɪŋ, -t
'scap|e (*from* escape), -es, -ing, -ed
  'skeĭp, -s, -ɪŋ, -t
scape (*stalk or column*), -s 'skeĭp, -s
scar, -s, -ring, -red 'skɑɹ̩, -z, -ɹɪŋ, -d
scarc|e, -er, -est, -ely, -eness 'skɛɹ̩-s, -ə˞,
  -ɪst, -lɪ, -nɪs
scarce-cold 'skɛɹ̩-sˌkoŭld
scarcit|y, -ies 'skɛɹ̩-sɪt|ɪ, -ɪz
scar|e, -es, -ing, -ed 'skɛɹ̩-, -z, -ɹɪŋ, -d
scarecrow, -s 'skɛɹ̩-kɹoŭ, -z

i wᴇ ɪcitʏ ɪ hɪt e lᴇt ɛ dᴇbut æ cᴀn a pᴀss ɝ bɪrd ʌ hᴜt ə agᴀin ᵊ suppᴇr u yᴏu
ᴜ shᴏuld o ᴏbey ɔ ᴀwl ɒ cᴏp ɑ fᴀther eĭ pᴀid aĭ hɪgh oŭ gᴏ ɔĭ vᴏice aŭ fᴏund ɪɝ eᴀr
ɛɝ aᴵr ᴜɝ pᴏor ɔɝ fᴏrk ɑɝ pᴀrk aĭɝ fᴵre aŭɝ hᴏur b bᴏy p pit d dᴏg t tᴏp g gᴏt
k kᴵd h hᴏw ɦ behᴀve dʒ jᴏt tʃ chᴇw z zᴀny s sᴏft v ᴠat f fᴀt ʒ treaᴤure ʃ shᴵp ð the
θ thᴵn m ᴍan n nᴏ ŋ haᴎg l lᴵp j yes w wᴏn ʍ whᴇw ɹ ᴙigger, airʏ ɟ matter

scar|f (*s.*), **-ves, -fs** 'skɑɚ·|f, -vz, -fs
scarf (*v.*), **-s, -ing, -ed** 'skɑɚ·f, -s, -ɪŋ, -t
scarlet 'skɑɚ·lɪt
Scarlet (2HIV, MWW) 'skɑɚ·lɪt
scarre 'skɑɚ·, 'skɛɚ·

> *Note.—This obscure word appears in an even more obscure phrase in ALL'S, IV.ii.38. Many have conjectured as to the meaning, usually seeing fit to emend 'scarre' to something else. The pronunciations given here are also entirely conjectural, and yet suitable if one finds the word to be, as the OED cites, an obsolete form for either 'scar' or 'scare'*

Scarus (*AC*) 'skeɪɹəs

> *Note.—The First Folio gives the spelling 'Scarrus,' which suggests also* ['skæɹəs] *or* ['skɑɚ·ɹəs]

scar|y, -ier, -iest 'skɛɚ·ɹ|ɪ, -ɪɚ·, -ɪɪst
scath (*archaic alt. spelling of* **scathe**, *suggesting a different pronunciation*) 'skæθ
scath|e, -es, -ing/ly, -ed; -eless 'skeɪð, -z, -ɪŋ/lɪ, -d; -lɪs
scathful(l) 'skeɪðfʊl

> *Note.—This word, meaning 'harmful' or 'destructive,' appears in TN, V.i.54, and is simply considered a var. spelling of 'scatheful' by the OED. The only benefit of giving the word a spelling pronunciation, i.e.,* ['skæθfʊl], *rests on how far one might intend to go—and it would seem to me highly inadvisable in the context of the scene—for the double entendre with 'noble bottom' ('scathful' taking on a pronunciation similar to 'scatful')*

scatter, -s, -ing, -ed, -er/s 'skæɾɚ·, -z, -ɹɪŋ, -d, -ɹɚ·/z
scaveng|e, -es, -ing, -ed, -er/s 'skævəndʒ [-vɪndʒ], -ɪz, -ɪŋ, -d, -ɚ·/z
scene, -s 'sin, -z
scenery 'sinɚ·ɹɪ
scenic 'sinɪk
scent, -s, -ing, -ed 'sent, -s, -ɪŋ, -ɪd
scent-snuffing 'sent,snʌfɪŋ
sceptre, -s, -d 'septɚ·, -z, -d
schedul|e, -es, -ing, -ed, -er/s 'skedʒʊəl, -z, -ɪŋ, -d, -ɚ·/z

schem|e, -es, -ing, -ed, -er/s 'skim, -z, -ɪŋ, -d, -ɚ·/z
scholar, -s, -ly 'skɒlɚ·, -z, -lɪ
scholarship, -s 'skɒlɚ·ʃɪp, -s
scholastic, -ally skə'læstɪk, -əlɪ [-klɪ]
school, -s, -ing, -ed 'skul, -z, -ɪŋ, -d
school(-)boy, -s 'skulbɔɪ, -z
school-doing 'skul'duɪŋ
schoolfellow, -s 'skul,feloʊ, -z
sciatic, -a/s saɪ'æɹɪk, -ə/z
scimitar, -s 'sɪmɪtɚ· [-tɑɚ·], -z
scion, -s 'saɪən, -z
scissor, -s, -ing, -ed 'sɪzɚ·, -z, -ɹɪŋ, -d
scoff, -s, -ing/ly, -ed, -er/s 'skɒf, -s, -ɪŋ/lɪ, -t, -ɚ·/z
Scoggin, Scoggan, *or* **Skoggin** (2HIV) 'skɒgən
scold, -s, -ing/s, -ed 'skoʊld, -z, -ɪŋ/z, -ɪd
sconc|e, -es, -ing, -ed 'skɒns, -ɪz, -ɪŋ, -t
Scone (MAC) 'skun, 'skoʊn, 'skɒn

> *Note.—Reliable sources sanction all three pronunciations given above. I have listed them in order of personal preference; however, Kökeritz offers yet another—and probably useful—pronunciation of* ['sko:n] *(see Kökeritz's* Shakespeare's Names: A Pronouncing Dictionary, *p. 88). Modern-day Scots pronounce Scone Palace (where generations of kings of Scotland were crowned) closest to the first option proffered above, i.e.,* ['skun]. *Regardless of one's choice, the longed-for rhyme of 'one' with 'Scone,' capping the end of MAC (MAC, V.ix.41, 42) is now typically forsaken (cf. 'Shakespeare's Verse' § 1.9 of this dictionary)*

scoop, -s, -ing, -ed, -er/s 'skup, -s, -ɪŋ, -t, -ɚ·/z
scope, -s 'skoʊp, -s
scorch, -es, -ing/ly, -ed, -er/s 'skɔɚ·tʃ, -ɪz, -ɪŋ/lɪ, -t, -ɚ·/z
scor|e, -es, -ing, -ed, -er/s 'skɔɚ·, -z, -ɹɪŋ, -d, -ɹɚ·/z
scorn (S.), **-s, -ing, -ed** 'skɔɚ·n, -z, -ɪŋ, -d
scorn|ful, -fully, -fulness 'skɔɚ·n|fʊl, -fʊlɪ, -fʊlnɪs
Scotland (COM, 1HIV, 2HIV, HV, 3HVI, MAC, RIII) 'skɒtlənd

Scot (1HIV, 2HIV, HV, 1HVI), **-s** 'skɒt, -s

scotch (**S.**), **-es, -ing, -ed** 'skɒtʃ, -ɪz, -ɪŋ, -t

Scottish (1HIV, MV) 'skɒṭɪʃ

scoundrel, -s 'skɑʊ̆ndɹəl, -z

scour, -s, -ing, -ed 'skɑʊ̆ɚ, -z, -ɹɪŋ, -d

scourg|e (**S.**), **-es, -ing, -ed** 'skɝdʒ, -ɪz, -ɪŋ, -d

scout, -s, -ing, -ed 'skɑʊ̆t, -s, -ɪŋ, -ɪd

scowl, -s, -ing/ly, -ed 'skɑʊ̆l, -z, -ɪŋ/lɪ, -d

scratch, -es, -ing, -ed; -y, -ier, -iest, -ily, -iness 'skɹætʃ, -ɪz, -ɪŋ, -t; -ɪ, -ɪɪst, -ɪlɪ, -ɪnɪs

scrawl, -s, -ing, -ed 'skɹɔl, -z, -ɪŋ, -d

scream, -s, -ing, -ed, -er/s 'skɹim, -z, -ɪŋ, -d, -ɚ/z

screech-owl, -s 'skɹitʃˌɑʊ̆l, -z

screen, -s, -ing/s, -ed, -er/s 'skɹin, -z, -ɪŋ/z, -d, -ɚ/z

screw, -s, -ing, -ed 'skɹu, -z, -ɪŋ, -d

scribb|le, -les, -ling, -led, -ler/s 'skɹɪb|l̩, -l̩z, -l̩ɪŋ [-lɪŋ], -l̩d, -l̩ɚ/z [-lɚ/z]

scribe, -s 'skɹaɪ̆b, -z

scrimer (*aphetic form of* **escrimer**), **-s** 'skɹaɪ̆mɚ, -z

scrimp, -s, -ing, -ed 'skɹɪmp, -s, -ɪŋ, -t

scrip, -s (*from* **script**) 'skɹɪp, -s

scrippage 'skɹɪpɪdʒ

script, -s, -ing, -ed 'skɹɪpt, -s, -ɪŋ, -ɪd

scripture (**S.**) (HAM, MV, RIII), **-s** 'skɹɪptʃɚ, -z

scrivener (*RIII*), **-s** 'skɹɪvnɚ, -z

scroll, -s, -ing, -ed 'skɹoʊ̆l, -z, -ɪŋ, -d

Scroop(e), Henry (*HV*) 'henɹɪ 'skɹup

Scroop(e), Richard (*1HIV, 2HIV*) 'ɹɪtʃɚd 'skɹup

Scroop(e), Sir Stephen (*RII*) ˌsɝ 'stivən 'skɹup

scroyle (*scoundrel, wretch*), **-s** 'skɹɔɪ̆l, -z

scrup|le, -les, -ling, -led 'skɹup|l̩, -l̩z, -l̩ɪŋ [-lɪŋ], -l̩d

scrupulous, -ly, -ness 'skɹupjʊləs, -lɪ, -nɪs

scud, -s, -ding, -ded 'skʌd, -z, -ɪŋ, -ɪd

scul(l) (*s.*) (*grouping* = '*school*'), **-s** 'skul, -z

Note.—In TC, V.v.22, *this word is meant to stand for 'schools.' The First Folio gives the word 'sculs,' an archaic var. of 'schools,' pronounced* ['skulz]. *Kenneth Palmer, editor of 'Troilus and Cressida' for* The Arden Shakespeare, *1982 (et al.) includes the sanctionable extra 'l,' which might lead one to either the pronunciation proffered above or to* ['skʌlz] *if the editors are suggesting a poetic allusion to fish looking like turning paddles on oars*

scull (*s., v.*) (*oar, boat, racing*), **-s, -ing, -ed, -er/s** 'skʌl, -z, -ɪŋ, -d, -ɚ/z

scullion, -s 'skʌljən [-lɪən], -z

sculpt, -s, -ing, -ed 'skʌlpt, -s, -ɪŋ, -ɪd

sculptor, -s 'skʌlptɚ, -z

sculptur|e, -es, -ing, -ed 'skʌlptʃɚ, -z, -ɹɪŋ, -d

scum, -s, -ming, -med 'skʌm, -z, -ɪŋ, -d

scupper, -s 'skʌpɚ, -z

scurril(e) 'skʌɹəl

scurrility skəˈɹɪlɪtɪ [skʌˈɹ-]

scurrilous, -ly, -ness 'skʌɹɪləs, -lɪ, -nɪs

scurv|y, -ier, -iest, -ily, -iness 'skɝv|ɪ, -ɪɚ, -ɪɪst, -ɪlɪ, -ɪnɪs

scurvy-valiant 'skɝvɪˌvæljənt

(')scuse (*from* **excuse** *[s.]*) 'skjus

scut, -s 'skʌt, -s

scutcheon, -s 'skʌtʃən, -z

Scylla (MV) 'sɪlə

scyth|e, -es, -ing, -ed 'saɪ̆ð, -z, -ɪŋ, -d

scythe-tusked 'saɪ̆ðˌtʌskt

Scythia (TIT) 'sɪθɪə ['sɪðɪə, -ðjə], -θjə

Scythian (1HVI, LEAR) 'sɪθɪən ['sɪð-, -ðjən], -θjən

'sdeath (*contr. of* **God's death**) 'zdeθ

sea, -s 'si, -z

sea-bank, -s 'siˌbæŋk, -s

sea-boy, -s 'siˌbɔɪ̆, -z

sea-cap, -s 'siˌkæp, -s

Sea-captain (*TN*) 'siˌkæptɪn

---

i w**e** ɪ c**i**ty ɪ h**i**t e l**e**t ɛ d**e**but æ c**a**n a p**a**ss ɝ b**i**rd ʌ h**u**t ə **a**gain ɚ supp**er** u y**ou** ʊ sh**oul**d o **o**bey ɔ **aw**l ɒ c**o**p ɑ f**a**ther eɪ̆ p**ai**d aɪ̆ h**igh** oʊ̆ g**o** ɔɪ̆ v**oi**ce ɑʊ̆ f**ou**nd ɪɚ̆ **ear** ɛɚ̆ **air** ʊɚ̆ p**oor** ɔɚ̆ f**or**k ɑɚ̆ p**ar**k aɪ̆ɚ̆ f**ire** ɑʊ̆ɚ̆ h**our** b b**oy** p p**i**t d d**o**g t t**o**p g g**o**t k k**i**d h h**ow** fɪ be**h**ave dʒ j**o**t tʃ **ch**ew z **z**any s **s**oft v **v**at f **f**at ʒ trea**s**ure ʃ **sh**ip ð **th**e θ **th**in m **m**an n **n**o ŋ ha**ng** l **l**ip j **y**es w **w**on ʍ **wh**ew ɹ **r**igger, ai**r**y ɾ ma**tt**er

sea-coal 'sikoŏl

Sea-coal *or* **Seacole, Francis** (ADO) 'fɹansɪs 'sikoŏl

Sea-coal *or* **Seacole, George** (ADO) 'dʒɔ˞dʒ 'sikoŏl

seafar|er/s, -ing 'si̩fɛ˞|ɹə˞/z, -ɹɪŋ

sea-fight, -s 'si̩faĭt, -s

sea-going 'si̩goŏɪŋ

seal, -s, -ing, -ed, -er/s 'sil, -z, -ɪŋ, -d, -ə˞/z

sealed-up (*adj.*) 'sildʌp

sea-like 'si̩laĭk

sealing-day 'silɪŋ̩deĭ

seal-ring, -s 'sil̩ɹɪŋ, -z

seam, -s, -ing, -ed; -less 'sim, -z, -ɪŋ, -d; -lɪs

sea-maid, -s 'si̩meĭd, -z

sea|man, -men 'si|mən, -mən

sea-marge, -s 'si̩maʒ˞dʒ, -ɪz

sea-margent 'si̩maʒ˞dʒənt

sea-mark, -s 'si̩maʒ˞k, -s

seamstress, -es 'simstɹɪs, -ɪz

seam|y, -ier, -iest, -iness 'sim|ɪ, -ɪə˞, -ɪɪst, -ɪnɪs

seaport, -s 'sipɔ˞t, -s

sear, -s, -ing, -ed 'sɪə˞, -z, -ɹɪŋ, -d

search, -es, -ing/ly, -ed, -er/s 'sɜ˞tʃ, -ɪz, -ɪŋ/lɪ, -t, -ə˞/z

sea-salt 'si̩sɔlt

seascape, -s 'siskeĭp, -s

seashore, -s 'siʃɔ˞, -z

sea(-)side 'si̩saĭd

season, -s, -ing, -ed 'sizn̩, -z, -ɪŋ, -d

seasoner, -s 'siznə˞ [-znə˞], -z

seat, -s, -ing, -ed 'sit, -s, -ɪŋ, -ɪd

sea-tost 'si̩tɒst

sea-wall, -s, -ed ,si'wɔl ['--], -z, -d

seaweed 'siwid

sea-wing, -s 'si̩wɪŋ, -z

Sebastian (*TEM, TN*) sɪ'bæstɪən, -stjən

second (*military usage*), **-s, -ing, -ed** sɪ'kɒnd, -z, -ɪŋ, -ɪd

second (*all other meanings*), **-s, -ing, -ed** 'sekənd, -z, -ɪŋ, -ɪd

secondarily ,sekən'dɛ˞ɹɪlɪ

secondar|y, -ies 'sekəndəɹ|ɪ, -ɪz

secrecy 'sikɹɪsɪ

secret, -s; -ly 'sikɹɪt, -s; -lɪ

secretar|y, -ies 'sekɹɪtə˞ɹ|ɪ, -ɪz

secret|e, -es, -ing, -ed sɪ'kɹit, -s, -ɪŋ, -ɪd

secretion, -s sɪ'kɹiʃn̩, -z

secretive, -ly, -ness 'sikɹɪtɪv, -lɪ, -nɪs

sect, -s 'sekt, -s

sectar|y, -ies 'sektəɹ|ɪ, -ɪz

section, -s 'sekʃn̩, -z

secur|e, -es, -ing, -ed; -er, -est, -ely; -able sɪ'kjʊə˞, -z, -ɹɪŋ, -d; -ɹə˞, -ɹɪst, -lɪ; -ɹəbl̩
Note.—In its adj. form, it can be, and sometimes is in S., pronounced with the stress on the first syllable, i.e., ['sekjʊə˞], *as in HAM, I.v.61 and OTH, IV.i.71. The scansion of the verse line dictates which pronunciation will prevail*

sedge, -s, -d 'sedʒ, -ɪz, -d

sedgy 'sedʒɪ

sedition, -s sɪ'dɪʃn̩, -z

seditious, -ly, -ness sɪ'dɪʃəs, -lɪ, -nɪs

seduc|e, -es, -ing, -ed, -er/s, -ement/s sɪ'djus, -ɪz, -ɪŋ, -t, -ə˞/z, -mənt/s

see (S.), **-s, -ing, saw, seen, seer/s** 'si, -z, -ɪŋ, 'sɔ, 'sin, 'siə˞/z

seeds|man, -men 'sidz|mən, -mən

seek, -s, -ing, sought 'sik, -s, -ɪŋ, 'sɔt

seeker, -s 'sikə˞, -z

seel, -s, -ing, -ed 'sil, -z, -ɪŋ, -d

Seely, Sir Bennet (RII) ,sɜ˞ 'benɪt 'silɪ

seem, -s, -ing/ly, -ed, -er/s 'sim, -z, -ɪŋ/lɪ, -d, -ə˞/z

seemings 'simɪŋz

seeml|y, -ier, -iest, -iness 'siml|ɪ, -ɪə˞, -ɪɪst, -ɪnɪs

seep, -s, -ing, -ed 'sip, -s, -ɪŋ, -t

seesaw, -s, -ing, -ed 'sisɔ, -z, -ɪŋ, -d

seese (*from 'cheese'*) 'sis, 'siz (*see* **prings**)

see't (*contr. of* **see it**) 'si˙t

seeth|e, -es, -ing, -ed 'sið, -z, -ɪŋ, -d

segment (*s.*), **-s** 'segmənt, -s

segment (*v.*), **-s, -ing, -ed** seg'ment, -s, -ɪŋ, -ɪd

segregat|e, -es, -ing, -ed 'segɹɪgeĭt, -s, -ɪŋ, -ɪd

segregation ,segɹɪ'geĭʃn̩

seignior|y, -ies 'seĭnjə˞ɹ|ɪ, -ɪz

seiz|e, -es, -ing, -ed 'siz, -ɪz, -ɪŋ, -d

seizure, -s 'siʒə˞, -z

seld (*seldom*) 'seld

seldom 'seldəm

seld-shown 'seldʃoŭn
select, -s, -ing, -ed; -ive/ly sɪ'lekt [sə'l-],
  -s, -ɪŋ, -ɪd; -ɪv/lɪ
selection, -s sɪ'lekʃn̩ [sə'lek-], -z
Seleucus (*AC*) se'ljukəs
sel|f, -ves 'sel|f, -vz
self-admission ˌselfəd'mɪʃn̩
self-affairs 'selfə'fɛɔ̈·z
self-affected ˌselfə'fektɪd
self-affrighted ˌselfə'fɹaĭtɪd
self-assumption ˌselfə'sʌmpʃn̩
self-born(e) 'self̩bɔɔ̈·n
self-bounty 'self̩baŭntɪ
self-breath 'self̩bɹeθ
self-charity 'self̩tʃæɹɪtɪ
self-covered 'self̩kʌvə·d ['-ˌ--]
self-danger 'self̩deĭndʒɚ
self-doing 'self̩duɪŋ
self-drawing ˌself̩dɹɔɪŋ ['-ˌ--]
self-endeared ˌselfɪn'dɪɔ̈·d
self-example ˌselfɪg'zampl̩
self-explication ˌself̩eksplɪ'keĭʃn̩
self-figured ˌself̩fɪgjə·d
self-glorious ˌself̩glɔɹĭəs
self-love 'self̩lʌv
self-loving 'self̩lʌvɪŋ ([ˌ-'--] *in* Sonn.
  62.12)
self-mettle ˌself̩metl̩
self-misused ˌselfmɪs'juzd
self-neglecting ˌselfnɪ'glektɪŋ
self-offence, -s ˌselfə'fens [-lfo'f-], -ɪz
self-reproving ˌselfɹɪ'pɹuvɪŋ
self(-)same 'selfseĭm
self-slaughter 'self̩slɔɹ̩ɚ
self-subdued 'self̩səbˌdjud
self-substantial 'self̩səbˌstænʃl̩
self-willed 'self̩wɪld
semblab|le, -ly 'semblab|l̩, -lɪ
semblance, -s 'sembləns, -ɪz
semblative 'semblətɪv
semi(-)circle, -s, -d 'semɪˌsɜ·kl̩, -z, -d
Semiramis (TIT, TS) sə'mɪɹəmɪs
semper idem (*L.*) (2HIV, V.v.28) 'sɛmpɛɔ̈·
  'idɛm

Sempronius (*TIM, TIT*) sem'pɹoŭnɪəs,
  -njəs
sempster, -s 'sempstɚ, -z
senate (S.), **-s** 'senɪt, -s
Senate(-)House 'senɪt 'haŭs
senator (S.), **-s** 'senɪtɚ, -z
send, -s, -ing, sent 'send, -z, -ɪŋ, 'sent
send-a 'sendə (*see* **vere**)
sender, -s 'sendɚ, -z
Seneca (HAM) 'senɪkə
senior, -s 'sinjɚ, -z
Senior, Duke (*AYLI*) 'djuk 'sinjɚ
seniorit|y, -ies ˌsin'jɒɹɪt|ɪ [-nɪ'ɒɹ-], -ɪz
sennight *or* **se'nnight, -s** 'senaĭt, -s
Sennois (*TNK*) se'nɔĭs ['--]
Senoys (ALL'S) 'sinɔĭz ['sen-]
sens|e, -es, -ing, -ed 'sens, -ɪz, -ɪŋ, -t
senseless, -ly, -ness 'senslɪs, -lɪ, -nɪs
senseless-obstinate 'senslɪs'ɒbstɪnɪt
sensual, -ly, -ness 'senʃʊəl, -ɪ, -nɪs
sensuality ˌsenʃʊ'ælɪtɪ
sensuous, -ly, -ness 'senʃʊəs, -lɪ, -nɪs
sent (*p.t. of* **send**, *q.v.*) 'sent
sentenc|e, -es, -ing, -ed 'sentəns, -ɪz, -ɪŋ,
  -t
sententious, -ly, -ness sen'tenʃəs [sən-],
  -lɪ, -nɪs
sentinel (S.) (*1HVI*), **-s, -(l)ing, -(l)ed**
  'sentɪnəl, -z, -ɪŋ, -d
sentr|y, -ies 'sentɹɪ|ɪ, -ɪz
se offendendo (*L.*) (HAM, V.i.9) sɛ
  ˌofɛn'dendo
separab|le, -ly, -leness 'sepəɹəb|l̩, -lɪ,
  -l̩nɪs
separate (*adj.*), **-ly, -ness** 'sepɹɪt
  ['sepəɹɪt], -lɪ, -nɪs
separat|e (*v.*), **-es, -ing, -ed, -or/s**
  'sepəˌɹeĭt, -s, -ɪŋ, -ɪd, -ɚ/z
separation, -s ˌsepəˈɹeĭʃn̩, -z
September, -s sep'tembɚ, -z
Septentrion (3HVI) sep'tentɹɪɒn [-tɹɪən]
sepul|chre, -chres, -chring 'sepəl|kɚ,
  -kɚz, -kɹɪŋ
  Note.—In LUC, 805; RII, I.iii.196; TGV,

i wᴇ ɪ city ɪ hịt e lẹt ɛ dẹbut æ cạn a pạss ɜ· bịrd ʌ hụt ə again ɚ suppẹr u yọu
ʊ shọuld o ọbey ɔ awl ɒ cọp ɑ fạther eĭ pạid aĭ hịgh oŭ gọ ɔĭ vọice aŭ fọund ɪɔ̈· eạr
ɛɔ̈· aịr ʊɔ̈· pọor ɔɔ̈· fọrk ɑɔ̈· pạrk aĭɔ̈· fịre aŭɔ̈· họur b bọy p pịt d dọg t tọp g gọt
k kịd h họw fi behạve dʒ jọt tʃ chẹw z zạny s sọft v vạt f fạt ʒ treạsure ʃ shịp ð thẹ
θ thịn m mạn n nọ ŋ hạng l lịp j yẹs w wọn ʍ whẹw ɹ rịgger, aịry ɡ mạtter

IV.ii.114, *stress is on the second
syllable, i.e.,* [sə'pʊlkə˞, -'pʌl-]

sequel, -s 'sikwəl, -z

sequence, -s 'sikwəns [-kwens], -ɪz

sequent 'sikwənt

sequest|er, -ers, -ering, -ered sɪ'kwest|ə˞,
-ə˞z, -ə˞ɹɪŋ [-ə˞ɹɪŋ], -ə˞d
*Note.—In OTH, III.iv.36, the construc-
tion of the line seems to indicate that
primary stress should be placed on the
first syllable, i.e.,* ['si'kwestə˞]; *it is
almost certainly pronounced with
primary stress on the first syllable in
TIT, II.ii.75*

sequestration, -s ˌsikwe'stɹeɪʃn̩, -z

sere, -s 'sɪə˞, -z

serge, -s 's3˞dʒ, -ɪz

sergeant (S.) (*1HVI, MAC*)**, -s** 'sɑ˞dʒənt,
-s

Sergeant-at-Arms (*HVIII*) 'sɑ˞dʒənt
əɹ'ɑ˞mz

serious, -ly, -ness 'sɪə˞ɹɪəs, -lɪ, -nɪs

serpent, -s; -like 's3˞pənt, -s; -ˌlaɪk

serpentine 's3˞pəntaɪn [-tin]

serpigo sə˞'paɪgoʊ [-'pig-]

servant, -s, -ed 's3˞vənt, -s, -ɪd

servant-monster 's3˞vəntˌmɒnstə˞

serv|e, -es, -ing/s, -ed, -er/s 's3˞v, -z,
-ɪŋ/z, -d, -ə˞/z

servic|e, -es, -ing, -ed 's3˞vɪs, -ɪz, -ɪŋ, -t

serviceability ˌs3˞vɪsə'bɪlɪtɪ

serviceab|le, -ly, -leness 's3˞vɪsəb|l̩, -lɪ,
-l̩nɪs

servile, -ly, -ness 's3˞vaɪl, -lɪ, -nɪs

Servilius (*TIM*) sə˞'vɪlɪəs, -ljəs

serving-creature 's3˞vɪŋˌkɹitʃə˞

serving|man (S.), -men 's3˞vɪŋ|ˌmæn, -ˌmen

servitor, -s 's3˞vɪtə˞, -z

servitude 's3˞vɪtjud

sessa, sese, *or* **sesey** (*halt?; haste away?*)
'sesə, se'sɑ, 'sesɪ, se'seɪ
*Note.—The pronunciations proffered
above are entirely conjectural, as are the
many opinions as to the origin and
meaning of this obscure word. A brief
but insightful discussion of 'sessa' can
be found in Brian Morris' line annotation for TS, Ind.i.5 (The Arden
Shakespeare, 1981)*

session, -s 'seʃn̩, -z

Sestos (*AYLI*) 'sestɒs

Setebos (*TEM*) 'setɪbɒs [-bɔs, -bos]

seven, -s, -th/s; -fold 'sevn̩ [-vən], -z,
-θ/s; -foʊld
*Note.—This word, as with 'warrant,'
'devil,' 'evil,' 'even,' 'heaven,' etc., is
often (though not always) monosyllabic
in S. (absorbing only one metrical beat
in the verse). For instance, in TS,
IV.iii.184, 'seven' is a monosyllable in
order to make a regular line of iambic
pentameter, whereas 'seven' in TS,
IV.iii.188 (just four lines later) is
disyllabic for exactly the same reason.
(Cf.* **spirit***)*

seven-night, -s 'sevnaɪt ['senaɪt], -s

sever, -s, -ing, -ed; -able 'sevə˞, -z, -ɹɪŋ,
-d; -ɹəbl̩

sever|al, -ally 'sevɹ|əl, -əlɪ

severals 'sevɹəlz

severance 'sevɹəns

Severn (*CYM, 1HIV*) 'sevə˞n

sev'n-night *or* **seve'night, -s** 'sevnaɪt
['senaɪt], -s

sew, -s, -ing, -ed, -n 'soʊ, -z, -ɪŋ, -d, -n

sewer (*one who sews*)**, -s** 'soʊə˞, -z

sewer (*underground conduit for drainage;
mediæval server*)**, -s** 'suə˞, -z

sex, -es; -less 'seks, -ɪz; -lɪs

sexton, -s 'sekstən, -z

Seyton (*MAC*) 'sitn̩

'sfoot (*contr. of* **God's foot**) 'sfʊt

Shaa *or* **Shaw, Doctor John** (*RIII*) 'dɒktə˞
'dʒɒn 'ʃɔ

shabb|y, -ier, -iest, -ily, -iness 'ʃæb|ɪ, -ɪə˞,
-ɪɪst, -ɪlɪ, -ɪnɪs

shack|le, -les, -ling, -led 'ʃæk|l̩, -l̩z, -l̩ɪŋ,
-l̩d

Shadow, Simon (*2HIV*) 'saɪmən 'ʃædoʊ

shadow, -s, -ing, -ed; -less 'ʃædoʊ, -z, -ɪŋ,
-d; -lɪs

shadow|y, -iness 'ʃædoʊ |ɪ, -ɪnɪs

shad|y, -ier, -iest, -ily, -iness 'ʃeɪd|ɪ, -ɪə˞,
-ɪɪst, -ɪlɪ, -ɪnɪs

Shafalus (*corruption of* **Cephalus** *in
MSND*) 'ʃæfələs

shaft, -s, -ing, -ed 'ʃaft, -s, -ɪŋ, -ɪd

shag, -s 'ʃæg, -z

shagg|y, -ier, -iest, -ily, -iness ˈʃæg|ɪ, -ɪɚ,
 -ɪɪst, -ɪlɪ, -ɪnɪs
shak|e, -es, -ing, shook, shaken,
 shaker/s ˈʃeɪk, -s, -ɪŋ, ˈʃʊk, ˈʃeɪkn̩,
 ˈʃeɪkɚ/z
shaked (*archaic form of* **shook** *or*
 shaken) ˈʃeɪkt
shak|y, -ier, -iest, -ily, -iness ˈʃeɪk|ɪ, -ɪɚ,
 -ɪɪst, -ɪlɪ, -ɪnɪs
shallenge (*from 'challenge'*) ʃalɛŋʒ
 [ˈʃælɪndʒ] (*see Note for* **varld**)
shall|ow, -ows, -ower, -owest, -owness,
 -owly ˈʃæl|oʊ, -oʊz, -ʊɚ, -ʊɪst, -oʊnɪs,
 -oʊlɪ
shallow-hearted ˈʃæloʊˌfiɑɚtɪd
Shallow, Robert (*2HIV, MWW*) ˈɹɒbɚt
 ˈʃæloʊ
sham, -s, -ming, -med ˈʃæm, -z, -ɪŋ, -d
shamb|le, -les, -ling, -led ˈʃæmb|l̩, -l̩z,
 -l̩ɪŋ [-lɪŋ], -l̩d
sham|e, -es, -ing, -ed ˈʃeɪm, -z, -ɪŋ, -d
shamefac|ed, -edly, -edness ˈʃeɪmfeɪs|t,
 -ɪdlɪ, -ɪdnɪs
shame|ful, -fully, -fulness ˈʃeɪm|fʊl, -fəlɪ,
 -fʊlnɪs
shameless, -ly, -ness ˈʃeɪmlɪs, -lɪ, -nɪs
shameless-desperate ʃeɪmlɪsˈdespɚɹɪt
 [ˈ--ˌ---]
shank, -s ˈʃæŋk, -s
shard, -s, -ed ˈʃɑɚd, -z, -ɪd
shard-born ˈʃɑɚdbɔɚn
sharp, -s; -er, -est, -ly, -ness ˈʃɑɚp, -s;
 -ɚ, -ɪst, -lɪ, -nɪs
sharpen, -s, -ing, -ed, -er/s ˈʃɑɚpən, -z,
 -ɪŋ, -d, -ɚ/z
sharp-pointed ˈʃɑɚpˌpɔɪntɪd
sharp-provided ˈʃɑɚpˌpɹʊˌvaɪdɪd
sharp-toothed ˈʃɑɚpˌtuθt
sh'ath *or* **s'hath** (*contr. of* **she hath**) ˈʃæθ
Shaw *or* **Shaa, Doctor John** (RIII)
 ˈdɒktɚ ˈdʒɒn ˈʃɔ
Shaw, Sir Edmund (RIII) ˌsɚ ˈ(ɹ)edmənd
 ˈʃɔ
she, -s ˈʃi, -z

She, Doctor (ALL'S) ˈdɒktɚ ˈʃi
shea|f, -ves ˈʃi|f, -vz
she-angel ˈʃiˌeɪndʒəl
shear, -s, -ing, -ed, shorn ˈʃɪɚ, -z, -ɹɪŋ,
 -d, ˈʃɔɚn
shea|th, -ths ˈʃi|θ, -ðz [-θs]
sheath|e, -es, -ing, -ed ˈʃið, -z, -ɪŋ, -d
sheaved ˈʃivd
sheaves (*pl. of* **sheaf**, *q.v.*) ˈʃivz
she-beggar ˈʃiˌbegɚ
shed, -s, -ing, -der/s ˈʃed, -z, -ɪŋ, -ɚ/z
sheen ˈʃin
sheep, -s ˈʃip, -s
sheep-biter, -s ˈʃipˌbaɪtɚ, -z
sheep-biting ˈʃipˌbaɪtɪŋ
sheepcote, -s ˈʃipˌkoʊt [-ˌkɒt], -s
sheep-hook, -s ˈʃipˌfiʊk, -s
sheep-shearing ˈʃipˌʃɪɚɹɪŋ
sheepskin, -s ˈʃipskɪn, -z
sheep-whistling ˈʃipʍɪslɪŋ [-slɪŋ]
sheer, -s, -ing, -ed ˈʃɪɚ, -z, -ɹɪŋ, -d
sheet, -s, -ing, -ed ˈʃit, -s, -ɪŋ, -ɪd
Sheffield (1HVI) ˈʃefild
she-lamb, -s ˈʃiˌlæm, -z
shel|f, -ves ˈʃel|f, -vz
shell, -s, -ing, -ed; -y ˈʃel, -z, -ɪŋ, -d; -ɪ
shelter, -s, -ing, -ed; -less ˈʃeltɚ, -z, -ɹɪŋ,
 -d; -lɪs
shelv|e, -es, -ing, -ed ˈʃelv, -z, -ɪŋ, -d
shelvy ˈʃelvɪ
she-Mercury (MWW) ˈʃiˌmɚˈkjʊɹɪ
shent (*p.p. of archaic v.* **shend**) (*disgraced or ruined*) ˈʃent
shepherd, -s, -ing, -ed ˈʃepɚd, -z, -ɪŋ, -ɪd
shepherdess, -es ˈʃepɚdɪs, -ɪz
sheriff, -s ˈʃeɹɪf, -s
sherris (*sherry*) ˈʃeɹɪs
sherris-sack (*sherry*) ˈʃeɹɪsˌsæk
sherr|y, -ies ˈʃeɹ|ɪ, -ɪz
shew, -s, -ing, -ed, -n ˈʃoʊ, -z, -ɪŋ, -d, -n
 Note.—This is an old-fashioned alt.
 spelling for 'show'. However, its
 appearance in PER, I.i.137 *presents a*
 bit of a problem. Several meanings for

---

i w<u>e</u> ɪ cit<u>y</u> ɪ h<u>i</u>t e l<u>e</u>t ɛ d<u>e</u>but æ c<u>a</u>n a p<u>a</u>ss ɚ b<u>ir</u>d ʌ h<u>u</u>t ə <u>a</u>gain ɚ supp<u>er</u> u y<u>ou</u>
ʊ sh<u>ou</u>ld o <u>o</u>bey ɔ <u>aw</u>l ɒ c<u>o</u>p ɑ f<u>a</u>ther eɪ p<u>ai</u>d aɪ h<u>igh</u> oʊ g<u>o</u> ɔɪ v<u>oi</u>ce aʊ f<u>ou</u>nd ɪɚ <u>ear</u>
ɛɚ <u>air</u> ʊɚ p<u>oor</u> ɔɚ f<u>or</u>k ɑɚ p<u>ar</u>k aɪɚ f<u>ire</u> aʊɚ h<u>our</u> b <u>b</u>oy p <u>p</u>it d <u>d</u>og t <u>t</u>op g g<u>o</u>t
k <u>k</u>id h <u>h</u>ow fi be<u>h</u>ave dʒ <u>j</u>ot tʃ <u>ch</u>ew z <u>z</u>any s <u>s</u>oft v <u>v</u>at f <u>f</u>at ʒ trea<u>s</u>ure ʃ <u>sh</u>ip ð <u>th</u>e
θ <u>th</u>in m <u>m</u>an n <u>n</u>o ŋ ha<u>ng</u> l <u>l</u>ip j <u>y</u>es w <u>w</u>on ʍ <u>wh</u>ew ɹ <u>r</u>igger, ai<u>r</u>y ɾ ma<u>tt</u>er

the word in this instance have been put forward, as well as suggested emendations, including 'shun,' 'shy,' and 'schew' (the aphetic form of 'eschew'). If the latter is chosen, the pronunciation is [ˈstʃu]

shield, -s, -ing, -ed ˈʃild, -z, -ɪŋ, -ɪd
shift, -s, -ing, -ed ˈʃɪft, -s, -ɪŋ, -ɪd
shilling, -s ˈʃɪlɪŋ, -z
shimmer, -s, -ing, -ed ˈʃɪmɚ, -z, -ɹɪŋ, -d
shin, -s, -ning, -ned ˈʃɪn, -z, -ɪŋ, -d
shin|e, -es, -ing, -ed, shone ˈʃaɪn, -z, -ɪŋ, -d, ˈʃoŏn [ˈʃɒn]
ship, -s, -ping, -ped, -per/s ˈʃɪp, -s, -ɪŋ, -t, -ɚ/z
ship-boy, -s ˈʃɪpˌbɔĭ, -z
shipmate, -s ˈʃɪpmeĭt, -s
shipment, -s ˈʃɪpmənt, -s
ship-tire, -s ˈʃɪpˌtaĭɚ, -z
shipwrack, -s, -ing, -ed ˈʃɪpɹæk, -s, -ɪŋ, -t
shipwreck, -s, -ing, -ed ˈʃɪpɹek, -s, -ɪŋ, -t
shire, -s ˈʃaĭɚ, -z
shirk, -s, -ing, -ed, -er/s ˈʃɝk, -s, -ɪŋ, -t, -ɚ/z
Shirley (1HIV) ˈʃɝlɨ
shive (*slice of bread*), **-s** ˈʃaĭv, -z
shiv|er, -ers, -ering, -ered ˈʃɪv|ɚ, -ɚz, -ɚɹɪŋ, -ɚd
shoal, -s ˈʃoŏl, -z
shock, -s, -ing/ly, -ed ˈʃɒk, -s, -ɪŋ/lɨ, -t
shodd|y, -ier, -iest, -ily, -iness ˈʃɒd|ɨ, -ɪɚ, -ɪɪst, -ɪlɨ, -ɪnɪs
shoe, -s, -ing, shod ˈʃu, -z, -ɪŋ, ˈʃɒd
shoeing-horn, -s ˈʃuɪŋˌfiɔɚn, -z
Shoe-tie, Master (MEAS) ˌmastɚ ˈʃutaĭ
shoe-tie, -s ˈʃutaĭ, -z
shog (*'go away'*) ˈʃɒg
shone (*p.t. and p.p. of* **shine**, *q.v.*) ˈʃoŏn [ˈʃɒn]
shook (*p.t. of* **shake**, *q.v.*) ˈʃʊk
shoon (*archaic pl. from* **shoe**) ˈʃun
shoot, -s, -ing, shot ˈʃut, -s, -ɪŋ, ˈʃɒt
shooter, -s ˈʃuʈɚ, -z
shop, -s, -ping, -ped, -per/s ˈʃɒp, -s, -ɪŋ, -t, -ɚ/z
shor|e, -es, -ing, -ed ˈʃɔɚ, -z, -ɹɪŋ, -d
Shore, Mistress Jane (RIII) ˈmɪstɹɪs ˈdʒeĭn ˈʃɔɚ

short, -s, -ing, -ed; -er, -est, -ly, -ness ˈʃɔɚt, -s, -ɪŋ, -ɪd; -ɚ, -ɪst, -lɨ, -nɪs
shortage, -s ˈʃɔɚtɪdʒ, -ɪz
short-armed ˈʃɔɚˌɹɑɚmd
Shortcake, Alice (MWW) ˈælɪs ˈʃɔɚtkeĭk
short-legged ˈʃɔɚtˌlegɪd [-ˌlegd]
short-lived ˈʃɔɚtˈlɪvd (*when att.,* [ˈ--])
short-winded ˈʃɔɚtˌwɪndɪd [ˌ-ˈ--]
shot, -s ˈʃɒt, -s
shot-free ˈʃɒtˈfɹi
shotten ˈʃɒtn̩
shough, -s ˈʃʌf [ˈʃɒk], -s
Note.—I list [ˈʃɒk] *as an alternate pronunciation because the OED states that 'shough' is perhaps the same word as 'shock.' Although the relation between the two forms is obscure, both words mean the same thing: a long-haired lapdog. I support the inclusion of the alternate pronunciation by citing that the word 'hough' (the tarsal joint in the hind leg of a quadruped, such as a horse) is pronounced* [ˈhɒk] *(cf. the OED and Fowler's* Modern English Usage, *under "pronunciation,"* § *9. -ough)*
shoulder, -s, -ing, -ed ˈʃoŏldɚ, -z, -ɹɪŋ, -d
shoulder-bone, -s ˈʃoŏldɚboŏn, -z
shoulder-shotten (*dislocated shoulder*) ˈʃoŏldɚʃɒtn̩
shout, -s, -ing, -ed, -er/s ˈʃaŏt, -s, -ɪŋ, -ɪd, -ɚ/z
shov|e, -es, -ing, -ed ˈʃʌv, -z, -ɪŋ, -d
shove-groat ˈʃʌvˌgɹoŏt
shovel, -s, -ling, -led, -ler/s ˈʃʌvl̩, -z, -ɪŋ, -d, -ɚ/z
shovel-board, -s ˈʃʌvl̩ˌbɔɚd, -z
show, -s, -ing, -ed, -n ˈʃoŏ, -z, -ɪŋ, -d, -n
shrank (*p.t. of* **shrink**, *q.v.*) ˈʃɹæŋk
shrape, -s, -d ˈʃɹeĭp, -s, -t
Note.—In TC, IV.v.192, *the First Folio gives the word 'hem'd.' Editors often follow the Quarto's word 'shrupd' (which does not have any representation in the* OED), *emending it to the word 'shrap'd'*
shrew, -s ˈʃɹu, -z
Note.—In TS, IV.i.197; V.ii.28, *and in* TS, V.ii.189 *(in the very last two lines of the play), 'shrew' is in couplet form*

*meant to rhyme with 'show,' 'woe,' and
'so,' respectively*—['ʃɹoŭ] *being an older
Brit. pronunciation. For anyone
speaking American English, the rhyme is
typically (but not necessarily) forsaken
in favor of* ['ʃɹu] *(cf. Kökeritz's* Shakespeare's Pronunciation, *p. 211)*

'shrew (*aphetic form of* **beshrew**) 'ʃɹu

shrewd, -er, -est, -ly, -ness 'ʃɹud, -ɚ, -ɪst,
-lɨ, -nɪs

shrewish, -ly, -ness 'ʃɹuɪʃ, -lɨ, -nɪs

Shrewsbury (1HIV, 2HIV, *1HVI*)
'ʃɹoŭzbɚɹɨ ['ʃɹuz-]

shriek, -s, -ing, -ed 'ʃɹik, -s, -ɪŋ, -t

shrieval 'ʃɹivl̩

shrievalt|y, -ies 'ʃɹivl̩t|ɨ, -ɨz

shrieve, -s 'ʃɹiv, -z

shrift 'ʃɹɪft

shrill, -er, -est, -y, -ness 'ʃɹɪl, -ɚ, -ɪst, -ɨ,
-nɪs

shrill-gorged 'ʃɹɪl̩gɔɹɚd3d

shrill-tongued 'ʃɹɪl'tʌŋd ['-,-]

shrill-voiced 'ʃɹɪl'vɔĭst ['-,-]

**shrink, -s, -ing, shrank, shrunk,
shrunken** 'ʃɹɪŋk, -s, -ɪŋ, 'ʃɹæŋk, 'ʃɹʌŋk,
'ʃɹʌŋkən

shrinkage, -s 'ʃɹɪŋkɪdʒ, -ɪz

**shriv|e, -es, -ing, -ed, shrove, shriven,
shriver/s** 'ʃɹaĭv, -z, -ɪŋ, -d, 'ʃɹoŭv, 'ʃɹɪvn̩,
'ʃɹaĭvɚ/z

shrivel, -s, -ling, -led 'ʃɹɪvl̩, -z, -ɪŋ, -d

shriving-time 'ʃɹaĭvɪŋˌtaĭm

shroud, -s, -ing, -ed 'ʃɹɑŭd, -z, -ɪŋ, -ɪd

shrove (*p.t. of* **shrive**) 'ʃɹoŭv

Shrove-tide (2HIV) 'ʃɹoŭvˌtaĭd

Shrove Tuesday (ALL'S) 'ʃɹoŭv 'tjuzdɪ
[-deĭ]

shrow, -s 'ʃɹoŭ, -z

shrunk (*p.t. and p.p. of* **shrink**, *q.v.*)
'ʃɹʌŋk

shudder, -s, -ing, -ed 'ʃʌdɚ, -z, -ɹɪŋ, -d

shun, -s, -ning, -ned 'ʃʌn, -z, -ɪŋ, -d

shunless 'ʃʌnlɪs

Shylock (*MV*) 'ʃaĭlɒk

sib (*sibling or kinsman*), **-s** 'sɪb, -z

sibyl (S.) (1HVI, OTH, TIT, TS), **-s** 'sɪbɪl
[-bəl], -z

Sibylla (MV) sɪ'bɪlə

sic (*adv.*) (*thus; read as so*) 'sɪk

sic (*v.*) (*to set upon; attack or chase*), **-s,
-cing, -ced** 'sɪk, -s, -ɪŋ, -t

Sicil (2HVI, 3HVI), **-s** 'sɪsɪl, -z

Sicilia (2HVI, WT) sɪ'sɪlɪə, -ljə

Sicilian (WT) sɪ'sɪlɪən, -ljən

Sicilius (CYM) sɪ'sɪlɪəs, -ljəs

Sicily (AC, TIT) 'sɪsɪlɨ, 'sɪslɨ

sick, -er, -est, -ness 'sɪk, -ɚ, -ɪst, -nɪs

sicked (*archaic form of* **sickened**) 'sɪkt

sick-fall'n 'sɪkˌfɔln

sicken, -s, -ing, -ed 'sɪkən, -z, -ɪŋ, -d

sickle, -s 'sɪkl̩, -z

sickle|man, -men 'sɪkl̩|mən, -mən

sickl|y, -ied, -ier, -iest, -iness 'sɪkl|ɨ, -ɪd,
-ɪɚ, -ɪɪst, -ɪnɪs

sick-service 'sɪkˌsɚvɪs

sick-thoughted 'sɪkˌθɔtɪd

Sic spectanda fides (*L.*) (PER, II.ii.38) 'sɪk
spɛk'tɑndɑ 'fidɛs

Sicyon (AC) 'sɪʃɪən [-ʃjən], 'sɪsɪən [-sjən]

sid|e, -es, -ing, -ed 'saĭd, -z, -ɪŋ, -ɪd

sideboard, -s 'saĭdbɔɚd, -z

side-piercing 'saĭdˌpɪɚsɪŋ

siege, -s 'sidʒ, -ɪz

Sien(n)a *or* **Syenna** (CYM) sɪ'enə

siev|e, -es, -ing, -ed 'sɪv, -z, -ɪŋ, -d

*Si fortuna me tormenta, spero me
contenta* (*It.*) (2HIV, V.v.96) si fɔɾ'tuɾnɑ
mɛ tɔɾ'mɛntɑ 'spɛˑɾo mɛ kon'tɛˑn'tɑ

*Si fortune me tormente, sperato me
contento* (*It.*) (2HIV, II.iv.177) si
fɔɾ'tuˑnɛ mɛ tɔɾ'mɛntɛ spɛ'ɾaˑto mɛ
kon'tɛˑn'to

sift, -s, -ing, -ed, -er/s 'sɪft, -s, -ɪŋ, -ɪd,
-ɚ/z

sigh, -s, -ing, -ed 'saĭ, -z, -ɪŋ, -d

sight, -s, -ing, -ed; -less/ness 'saĭt, -s, -ɪŋ,
-ɪd; -lɪs/nɪs

sight-hole, -s 'saĭtˌhoŭl, -z

---

i w**e** ɪ c**i**ty ɪ h**i**t e l**e**t ɛ d**e**but æ c**a**n a p**a**ss ɚ b**i**rd ʌ h**u**t ə **a**gain ɚ supp**er** u y**ou**
ʊ sh**ou**ld o **o**bey ɔ **aw**l ɒ c**o**p ɑ f**a**ther eĭ p**ai**d aĭ h**igh** oŭ g**o** ɔĭ v**oi**ce aŭ f**ou**nd ɪɚ **ear**
ɛɚ **air** ʊɚ **poor** ɔɚ f**or**k ɑɚ p**ar**k aĭɚ f**ire** aŭɚ h**our** b **b**oy p **p**it d **d**og t **t**op g **g**ot
k **k**id h **h**ow fi be**h**ave dʒ **j**ot tʃ **ch**ew z **z**any s **s**oft v **v**at f **f**at ʒ trea**s**ure ʃ **sh**ip ð **th**e
θ **th**in m **m**an n **n**o ŋ ha**ng** l **l**ip j **y**es w **w**on ʍ **wh**ew ɹ **r**igger, ai**r**y ɾ ma**tt**er

sightl|y, -iness 'saĭtl|ɪ, -ɪnɪs

sign, -s, -ing, -ed, -er/s 'saĭn, -z, -ɪŋ, -d, -ɚ/z

signet, -s 'sɪgnɪt, -s

signior (S.) 'sɪnjɔ˞ [-'-]

signor (S.), -s 'sɪnjɔ˞ [-'-], -z

signor|y *or* **signior|y, -ies** 'sɪnjɔɪ|ɪ, -ɪz

Silence (*2HIV*) 'saĭləns

silenc|e, -es, -ing, -ed, -er/s 'saĭləns, -ɪz, -ɪŋ, -t, -ɚ/z

silent, -ly 'saĭlənt, -lɪ

Silius (*AC*) (*the Folio gives Sillius*) 'sɪlɪəs, -ljəs

silk, -s, -en 'sɪlk, -s, -ən

silk|man, -men 'sɪlk|mən, -mən

silkworm, -s 'sɪlkwɝm, -z

silk|y, -ier, -iest, -ily, -iness 'sɪlk|ɪ, -ɪɚ, -ɪɪst, -ɪlɪ, -ɪnɪs

sill, -s 'sɪl, -z

sill|y, -ier, -iest, -ily, -iness 'sɪl|ɪ, -ɪɚ, -ɪɪst, -ɪlɪ, -ɪnɪs

silly-ducking 'sɪlɪˌdʌkɪŋ

Silver (*TS*) 'sɪlvɚ

silver (S.), -s, -ing, -ed; -y, -iness 'sɪlvɚ, -z, -ɹɪŋ, -d; -ɹɪ, -ɹɪnɪs

silver-bright 'sɪlvɚ'bɹaĭt ['--,-]

silverly 'sɪlvɚlɪ

silver-shedding 'sɪlvɚˌʃedɪŋ

silver-voiced 'sɪlvɚˌvɔɪst

Silvia (*TGV*) 'sɪlvɪə, -vjə

Silvius (*AC, AYLI*) 'sɪlvɪəs, -vjəs

simile, -s 'sɪmɪlɪ, -z

Simois (*LUC, TS*) 'sɪmʊɪs, -mwɪs

Simon (*2HVI*) 'saĭmən

Simonides (*PER*) saĭ'mɒnɪdɪz

simony 'saĭmənɪ

Simpcox, Saunder (*2HVI*) 'sɔndɚ 'sɪmpkɒks

simper, -s, -ing, -ed 'sɪmpɚ, -z, -ɹɪŋ, -d

simp|le, -les, -ler, -lest, -ly, -leness 'sɪmp|ḷ, -ḷz, -lɚ [-ḷɚ], -lɪst [-ḷɪst], -lɪ, -ḷnɪs

Simple, Peter (*MWW*) 'piʦɚ 'sɪmpḷ

simpleton, -s 'sɪmpḷtən, -z

simular (*archaic for [adj.] 'sham' [possibly 'specious']; or [s.] one who simulates*) 'sɪmjʊlɚ [-lɑ˞]

sin (*21st letter of Hebrew alphabet*) 'sin ['sɪn]

sin (S.), -s, -ning, -ned, -ner/s 'sɪn, -z, -ɪŋ, -d, -ɚ/z

sin-absolver, -s ˌsɪnəb'zɒlvɚ, -z

sin-concealing 'sɪnkənˌsilɪŋ

sin-conceiving 'sɪnkənˌsivɪŋ

Sinel (*MAC*) 'saĭnəl ['sinəl]

sinew, -s, -ed 'sɪnju, -z, -d

sinewy 'sɪnjuɪ [-njʊɪ]

sing, -s, -ing, sang, sung, singer/s 'sɪŋ, -z, -ɪŋ, 'sæŋ, 'sʌŋ, 'sɪŋɚ/z

singe, -s, -ing, -d 'sɪndʒ, -ɪz, -ɪŋ, -d

singing-man 'sɪŋɪŋˌmæn

sing|le, -ly, -leness 'sɪŋg|ḷ, -lɪ, -ḷnɪs

Singulariter, nominativo, hic, haec, hoc (*L.*) (*MWW, IV.i.36*) ˌsɪŋgju'lɑritɛ˞ ˌnomɪnɑ'tivo 'hik 'heĭk 'hok

singularit|y, -ies ˌsɪŋgjʊ'læɹɪt|ɪ, -ɪz

sinister 'sɪnɪstɚ

sink(e)-a-pace *or* **cinque(-)pace** 'sɪŋkəˌpeĭs

Sinon (*CYM, 3HVI, LUC, TIT*) 'saĭnən

sir (S.), -s 'sɝ, -z (*strong form*), 'sɚ (*weak form*)

sir|e (S.), -es, -ing, -ed 'saĭɚ, -z, -ɹɪŋ, -d

siren, -s 'saĭɹən [-ɹɪn], -z

sirrah 'sɪɹə

sister (S.), -s; -ly 'sɪstɚ, -z; -lɪ

sisterhood, -s 'sɪstɚhʊd, -z

sistering 'sɪstɚɹɪŋ

Sisters Three (*2HIV, MSND, MV*) ˌsɪstɚz 'θɹi

sit, -s, -ting/s, sat, -sitter/s 'sɪt, -s, -ɪŋ/z ['sɪʧɪŋ/z], 'sæt, -'sɪʧɚ/z

sit fas aut nefas (*L.*) (*TIT, II.i.134*) 'sit fas aŏt 'nɛfas

sith 'sɪθ ['sɪð]

sithence 'sɪðns

situate (*adj.*) 'sɪtjʊeĭt [-ʧʊeĭt, -tjʊɪt, -ʧʊɪt]

situat|e (*v.*), **-es, -ing, -ed** 'sɪtjʊeĭt [-ʧʊ-], -s, -ɪŋ, -ɪd

Siward (*MAC*) 'siɚd ['siwɚd]

Siward, Old (*MAC*) 'oŭld 'siɚd ['siwɚd]

six-and-thirty ˌsɪksənd'θɝʧɪ

sixpence 'sɪkspəns

sixpenny 'sɪkspənɪ (*see Note for* **half-penny**)

sixteen, -s, -th/s ˌsiks'tin ['--], -z, -θ/s

sixth, -s 'sɪksθ, -s

sixt|y, -ies, -ieth/s 'sɪkst|ɪ, -ɪz, -ɪɪθ/s

siz|e, -es, -ing, -ed 'saĭz, -ɪz, -ɪŋ, -d
siz(e)able 'saĭzəbl̩
skains-mates 'skeĭnz͵meĭts
skeans-mates 'skinz͵meĭts
skein, -s 'skeĭn, -z
skiff, -s, -ed 'skɪf, -s, -t
skil|ful, -fully, -fulness 'skɪl|fʊl, -fʊlɪ,
    -fʊlnɪs
skill, -s, -ed 'skɪl, -z, -d
skilless 'skɪllɪs
skillet, -s 'skɪlɪt, -s
skim, -s, -ming, -med 'skɪm, -z, -ɪŋ, -d
skin, -s, -ning, -ned, -ner/s 'skɪn, -z, -ɪŋ,
    -d, -ɚ/z
skin-coat 'skɪn͵koŏt
skinless 'skɪnlɪs
skinn|y, -ier, -iest, -iness 'skɪn|ɪ, -ɪɚ, -ɪɪst,
    -ɪnɪs
skip, -s, -ping, -ped 'skɪp, -s, -ɪŋ, -t
skipper, -s 'skɪpɚ, -z
skirmish, -es, -ing, -ed, -er/s 'skɝ·mɪʃ,
    -ɪz, -ɪŋ, -t, -ɚ/z
skirr, -s, -ing, -ed 'skɝ, -z, -ɹɪŋ, -d
skirt, -s, -ing, -ed 'skɝt, -s, -ɪŋ, -ɪd
skit, -s 'skɪt, -s
skittish, -ly, -ness 'skɪʧɪʃ, -lɪ, -nɪs
Skoggin, Scoggin, *or* **Scoggan** (2HIV)
    'skɒgən
skulduggery skʌl'dʌgɚɹɪ
skulk, -s, -ing, -ed 'skʌlk, -s, -ɪŋ, -t
skull, -s 'skʌl, -z
skunk, -s 'skʌŋk, -s
sk|y, -ies, -ying, -ied, -ier/s; -yish 'sk|aĭ,
    -aĭz, -aĭɪŋ, -aĭd, -aĭɚ/z; -aĭʃ
sky-aspiring 'skaĭə͵spaĭɚɹɪŋ
skyey 'skaĭɪ
sky-planted 'skaĭ͵plantɪd
slab, -s, -bing, -bed 'slæb, -z, -ɪŋ, -d
slacks (*s.*) (*trousers*) 'slæks
slack, (*v., adj.*) **-s, -ing, -ed, -er/s; -er,
    -est, -ly, -ness** 'slæk, -s, -ɪŋ, -t, -ɚ/z;
    -ɚ, -ɪst, -lɪ, -nɪs
slain (*p.p. of* **slay***, q.v.*) 'sleĭn
slak|e, -es, -ing, -ed 'sleĭk, -s, -ɪŋ, -t

slam, -s, -ming, -med 'slæm, -z, -ɪŋ, -d
slander, -s, -ing, -ed, -er/s 'slandɚ, -z,
    -ɹɪŋ, -d, -ɹɚ/z
slanderous, -ly, -ness 'slandɚɹəs, -lɪ, -nɪs
slang, -s, -ing, -ed 'slæŋ, -z, -ɪŋ, -d
slant, -s, -ing, -ed 'slant, -s, -ɪŋ, -ɪd
slap, -s, -ping, -ped 'slæp, -s, -ɪŋ, -t
slash, -es, -ing, -ed, -er/s 'slæʃ, -ɪz, -ɪŋ, -t,
    -ɚ/z
slat, -s 'slæt, -s
slattern, -s; -ly, -liness 'slæʧɚn, -z; -lɪ,
    -lɪnɪs
slaughter, -s, -ing, -ed, -er/s; -ous/ly
    'slɔʃɚ, -z, -ɹɪŋ, -d, -ɹɚ/z; -ɹəs/lɪ
slaughter(-)hou|se, -ses 'slɔʃəˌhaŏ|s, -zɪz
slaughter(-)man, -men 'slɔʃɚ͵mən
    [-͵mæn], -mən
slav|e, -es, -ing, -ed, -er/s 'sleĭv, -z, -ɪŋ,
    -d, -ɚ/z
slave-like 'sleĭv͵laĭk
slaver (*slobber*)**, -s, -ing, -ed** 'slævɚ, -z,
    -ɹɪŋ, -d
slavery 'sleĭvɚɹɪ
slavish, -ly, -ness 'sleĭvɪʃ, -lɪ, -nɪs
slay, -s, -ing/s, slew, slain, slayer/s 'sleĭ,
    -z, -ɪŋ/z, 'slu, 'sleĭn, 'sleĭɚ/z
sleav|e, -es, -ing, -ed 'sliv, -z, -ɪŋ, -d
sleek, -s, -ing, -ed; -er, -est, -ly, -ness
    'slik, -s, -ɪŋ, -t; -ɚ, -ɪst, -lɪ, -nɪs
sleek-headed 'slik͵hedɪd
sleep (S.), -s, -ing, slept 'slip, -s, -ɪŋ,
    'slept
sleeper, -s 'slipɚ, -z
sleeping-hours 'slipɪŋ͵aŏɚz
sleep|y, -ier, -iest, -ily, -iness 'slip|ɪ, -ɪɚ,
    -ɪɪst, -ɪlɪ, -ɪnɪs
sleeve, -s, -ed; -less 'sliv, -z, -d; -lɪs
sleeve-hand 'sliv͵hænd
sleided 'sleĭdɪd
    Note.—This word appears in PER, IV.21
    (Chorus) *and* LC, 48, *and is an irregular
    var. of 'sleaved' (p.p.). As the* OED *puts
    it, 'sleave' is "a slender filament of silk
    obtained by separating a thicker*

i w**e** ɪ cit**y** ɪ h**i**t e l**e**t ɛ d**e**but æ c**a**n a p**a**ss ɝ b**i**rd ʌ h**u**t ə **a**gain ɚ supp**er** u y**ou**
ʊ sh**ou**ld o **o**bey ɔ **aw**l ɒ c**o**p ɑ f**a**ther eĭ p**ai**d aĭ h**igh** oŏ g**o** ɔĭ v**oi**ce aŏ f**ou**nd ɪɚ **ear**
ɛɚ **air** ʊɚ **poor** ɔɚ **fork** ɑɚ **park** aĭɚ **fire** aŏɚ **hour** b **b**oy p **p**it d **d**og t **t**op g **g**ot
k **k**id h **h**ow fi be**h**ave dʒ **j**ot ʧ **ch**ew z **z**any s **s**oft v **v**at f **f**at ʒ trea**s**ure ʃ **sh**ip ð **th**e
θ **th**in m **m**an n **n**o ŋ ha**ng** l **l**ip j **y**es w **w**on ʍ **wh**ew ɹ **r**igger, ai**r**y ͼ ma**tt**er

*thread", and is the root of the term
'sleeve(d)-silk.' The pronunciation given
above comes from a form derived from
'slay' (alt. 'sley') which in one particular entry in the* OED *seems to slightly
puzzle the editors, citing only that in one
rare, obsolete usage it is "some kind of
fabric." One definition for 'slay' in the*
OED *(the first given, and with ten var.
spellings, including 'sleie') is, "an
instrument used in weaving to beat up
the weft." The* OED *does not hazard a
guess as to the pronunciation of
'sleided,' but the orthographic evidence
strongly suggests the one proffered
above*

sleight, -s 'slaɪt, -s
slender, -er, -est, -ly, -ness 'slendɚ, -ɪɚ,
   -ɹɪst, -lɪ, -nɪs
Slender, Abraham (*MWW*) 'eɪbɹəfiæm
   'slendɚ
slew (*p.t. of* **slay**, *q.v.*) 'slu
slick, -s, -ing, -ed; -er, -est, -ly, -ness
   'slɪk, -s, -ɪŋ, -t; -ɚ, -ɪst, -lɪ, -nɪs
'slid (*contr. of* **God's eyelid**) 'zlɪd
slid|e, -es, -ing, slid 'slaɪd, -z, -ɪŋ, 'slɪd
slier (*var. of* **slyer** *from* **sly**, *q.v.*) 'slaɪɚ
sliest (*var. of* **slyest** *from* **sly**, *q.v.*) '
   slaɪɪst
slight, -s; -er, -est, -ly, -ness; -ing/ly, -ed
   'slaɪt, -s; -ɚ, -ɪst, -lɪ, -nɪs; -ɪŋ/lɪ, -ɪd
'slight (*contr. of* **God's light**) 'zlaɪt
slily (*var. of* **slyly** *from* **sly**, *q.v.*) 'slaɪlɪ
slim|e, -es, -ing, -ed 'slaɪm, -z, -ɪŋ, -d
slim|y, -ier, -iest, -ily, -iness 'slaɪm|ɪ, -ɪɚ,
   -ɹɪst, -ɪlɪ, -ɪnɪs
slink, -s, -ing, slunk 'slɪŋk, -s, -ɪŋ, 'slʌŋk
slip, -s, -ping, -ped 'slɪp, -s, -ɪŋ, -t
slipper, -s, -ed 'slɪpɚ, -z, -d
slipper|y, -ier, -iest, -ily, -iness 'slɪpɚɹ|ɪ,
   -ɪɚ, -ɹɪst, -ɪlɪ, -ɪnɪs
slipshod 'slɪpʃɒd
slipstream, -s 'slɪpstɹim, -z
slish (*from* '*slish and slash*') 'slɪʃ
slit, -s 'slɪt, -s
sliver, -s, -ing, -ed 'slɪvɚ, -z, -ɹɪŋ, -d
slobber, -s, -ing, -ed; -y 'slɒbɚ, -z, -ɹɪŋ,
   -d; -ɹɪ
slop, -s, -ping, -ped 'slɒp, -s, -ɪŋ, -t

slopp|y, -ier, -iest, -ily, -iness 'slɒp|ɪ, -ɪɚ,
   -ɹɪst, -ɪlɪ, -ɪnɪs
slot, -s, -ting, -ted 'slɒt, -s, -ɪŋ, -ɪd
sloth, -s 'slɔθ ['sloʊθ, 'slɒθ], -s
sloth|ful, -fully, -fulness 'slɔθ| ['sloʊθ-,
   'slɒθ-] fʊl, -fʊlɪ, -fʊlnɪs
slouch, -es, -ing, -ed, -er/s 'slaʊtʃ, -ɪz, -ɪŋ,
   -t, -ɚ/z
slough (*s.*) (*a depression*) 'slu
slough (*v.*) (*snake's skin*)**, -s, -ing, -ed**
   'slʌf, -s, -ɪŋ, -t
slovenl|y, -iness 'slʌvənl|ɪ, -ɪnɪs
slovenry 'slʌvənɹɪ
slow-gaited 'sloʊˌgeɪtɪd
slow-winged 'sloʊˌwɪŋd
slub, -s, -bing, -bed 'slʌb, -z, -ɪŋ, -d
slubber, -s, -ing, -ed 'slʌbɚ, -z, -ɹɪŋ, -d
slug, -s 'slʌg, -z
slug-abed 'slʌgəbed
sluggard, -s; -ised 'slʌgɚd, -z; -aɪzd
sluggish, -ly, -ness 'slʌgɪʃ, -lɪ, -nɪs
sluic|e, -es, -ing, -ed 'slus, -ɪz, -ɪŋ, -t
slumber, -s, -ing, -ed, -er/s; -less, -y
   'slʌmbɚ, -z, -ɹɪŋ, -d, -ɹɚ/z; -lɪs, -ɹɪ
slunk (*p.t. and p.p. of* **slink**, *q.v.*) 'slʌŋk
slut, -s 'slʌt, -s
sluttery 'slʌɾɚɹɪ
sluttish, -ly, -ness 'slʌɾɪʃ, -lɪ, -nɪs
Sly, Christopher (*TS*) 'kɹɪstəfɚ 'slaɪ
Sly, Christophero (*TS*) kɹɪ'stɒfəɹoʊ
   [-fɹoʊ] 'slaɪ
Sly, Stephen (TS) 'stivn̩ 'slaɪ
sly, -er, -est, -ly, -ness 'slaɪ, -ɚ, -ɪst, -lɪ,
   -nɪs
smack, -s, -ing, -ed 'smæk, -s, -ɪŋ, -t
small, -er, -est, -ness; -ish 'smɔl, -ɚ, -ɪst,
   -nɪs; -ɪʃ
Smalus (WT) 'smeɪləs
smart, -s, -ing, -ed; -er, -est, -ly, -ness
   'smaɚt, -s, -ɪŋ, -ɪd; -ɚ, -ɪst, -lɪ, -nɪs
smash, -es, -ing, -ed, -er/s 'smæʃ, -ɪz, -ɪŋ,
   -t, -ɚ/z
smatch 'smætʃ
smatter, -s, -ing/s, -ed, -er/s 'smæɾɚ, -z,
   -ɹɪŋ/z, -d, -ɹɚ/z
smel|l, -ls, -ling, -led, -t 'smel, -z, -ɪŋ, -d,
   -t
smell-less 'smelˌlɪs
smelt, -s, -ing, -ed 'smelt, -s, -ɪŋ, -ɪd

smil|e, -es, -ing/ly, -ed, -er/s 'smaɪl, -z, -ɪŋ/lɨ, -d, -ɚ/z

Smile, Jane (AYLI) 'dʒeɪn 'smaɪl

Smile, Sir (WT) ˌsɝ 'smaɪl

smirch, -es, -ing, -ed 'smɝtʃ, -ɪz, -ɪŋ, -t

smit (*archaic form of* **smitten**) 'smɪt

smit|e, -es, -ing, smote, smit, smitten, smiter/s 'smaɪt, -s, -ɪŋ, 'smoŭt, 'smɪt, 'smɪtn̩, 'smaɪtɚ/z

Smith (*2HVI*) 'smɪθ

Smithfield (2HIV, 2HVI) 'smɪθfild

smock, -s, -ing, -ed 'smɒk, -s, -ɪŋ, -t

smooth, -es, -ing, -ed; -er, -est, -ly, -ness 'smuð, -z, -ɪŋ, -d; -ɚ, -ɪst, -lɨ, -nɪs

Smooth, Master (2HIV) 'mastɚ 'smuð

smooth-faced 'smuð͜feɪst

smooth-pate, -s 'smuð͜peɪt, -s

smooth-tongue, -d 'smuð͜tʌŋ, -d

smote (*p.t. of* **smite**, *q.v.*) 'smoŭt

smother, -s, -ing, -ed 'smʌðɚ, -z, -ɹɪŋ, -d

smug, -ly, -ness 'smʌg, -lɨ, -nɪs

smugg|le, -les, -ling, -led 'smʌg|l̩, -l̩z, -l̩ɪŋ [-lɪŋ], -l̩d

smuggler, -s 'smʌglɚ, -z

Smulkin (LEAR) 'smʌlkɪn

smutched 'smʌtʃt

snaff|le, -les, -ling, -led 'snæf|l̩, -l̩z, -lɪŋ [-l̩ɪŋ], -l̩d

snail-paced 'sneɪl͜peɪst

snake, -s 'sneɪk, -s

snak|y, -iness 'sneɪk|ɨ, -ɨnɪs

snap, -s, -ping, -ped, -per/s 'snæp, -s, -ɪŋ, -t, -ɚ/z

snapper-up 'snæpɚˌɹʌp

Snare (*2HIV*) 'snɛɚ

snar|e, -es, -ing, -ed 'snɛɚ, -z, -ɹɪŋ, -d

snarl, -s, -ing, -ed 'snɑɚl, -z, -ɪŋ, -d

snatch, -es, -ing, -ed, -er/s 'snætʃ, -ɪz, -ɪŋ, -t, -ɚ/z

Sneak (2HIV) 'snik

sneak, -s, -ing, -ed; -y, -ier, -iest, -ily, -iness 'snik, -s, -ɪŋ, -t; -ɨ, -ɨɚ, -ɨɪst, -ɨlɨ, -ɨnɪs

sneaker, -s 'snikɚ, -z

sneak-up (*s.*) 'snikˌʌp

sneap, -s, -ing, -ed 'snip, -s, -ɪŋ, -t

sneck 'snek

sneer, -s, -ing/ly, -ed 'snɪɚ, -z, -ɹɪŋ/lɨ, -d

sneez|e, -es, -ing, -ed 'sniz, -ɪz, -ɪŋ, -d

snide 'snaɪd

sniff, -s, -ing, -ed 'snɪf, -s, -ɪŋ, -t

snigger, -s, -ing, -ed 'snɪgɚ, -z, -ɹɪŋ, -d

snip, -s, -ping, -ped, -per/s 'snɪp, -s, -ɪŋ, -t, -ɚ/z

snip|e, -es, -ing, -ed, -er/s 'snaɪp, -s, -ɪŋ, -t, -ɚ/z

snob, -s; -bery 'snɒb, -z; -ɚˌɹɨ

snobbish, -ly, -ness 'snɒbɪʃ, -lɨ, -nɪs

snooz|e, -es, -ing, -ed 'snuz, -ɪz, -ɪŋ, -d

snor|e, -es, -ing, -ed, -er/s 'snɔɚ, -z, -ɹɪŋ, -d, -ɹɚ/z

snort, -s, -ing, -ed, -er/s 'snɔɚt, -s, -ɪŋ, -ɪd, -ɚ/z

snout, -s 'snaŭt, -s

Snout, Tom (*MSND*) 'tɒm 'snaŭt

snow, -s, -ing, -ed 'snoŭ, -z, -ɪŋ, -d

snowball, -s, -ing, -ed 'snoŭbɔl, -z, -ɪŋ, -d

snow-broth 'snoŭˌbɹɒθ

snow-white 'snoŭˌʍaɪt

snow|y, -ier, -iest, -ily, -iness 'snoŭ|ɨ, -ɨɚ, -ɨɪst, -ɨlɨ, -ɨnɪs

snuff, -s, -ing, -ed 'snʌf, -s, -ɪŋ, -t

snug, -ger, -gest, -ly, -ness 'snʌg, -ɚ, -ɪst, -lɨ, -nɪs

Snug (*MSND*) 'snʌg

sob, -s, -bing, -bed 'sɒb, -z, -bɪŋ, -d

sober, -s, -ing, -ed; -er, -est, -ly, -ness 'soŭbɚ, -z, -ɹɪŋ, -d; -ɹɚ, -ɹɪst, -lɨ, -nɪs

sober-blooded 'soŭbɚˌblʌdɪd

sober-suited 'soŭbɚˌsjutɪd

sobriety so'bɹaɪətɨ

sociab|le, -ly, -leness 'soŭʃəb|l̩, -lɨ, -l̩nɪs

soci|al, -als, -ally 'soŭʃ|l̩, -l̩z, -əlɨ

socializ|e, -es, -ing, -ed 'soŭʃl̩aɪz, -ɪz, -ɪŋ, -d

societ|y, -ies sə'saɪɪt|ɨ, -ɨz

sock, -s, -ing, -ed 'sɒk, -s, -ɪŋ, -t

socket, -s, -ing, -ed 'sɒkɪt, -s, -ɪŋ, -ɪd

---

i wɨ ɨ city ɪ hit e let ɛ dᴇbut æ can a pass ɝ bird ʌ hut ə again ɚ suppᴇr u you
ʊ should o obey ɔ awl ɒ cop ɑ father eɪ paid aɪ high oŏ go ɔɪ voice aŏ found ɪɚ ear
ɛɚ air ʊɚ poor ɔɚ fork ɑɚ park aɪɚ fire aŏɚ hour b boy p pit d dog t top g got
k kid h how fi behave dʒ jot tʃ chew z zany s soft v vat f fat ʒ treasure ʃ ship ð the
θ thin m man n no ŋ hang l lip j yes w won ʍ whew ɹ rigger, airy ꞔ matter

Socrates (TS) 'sɒkɹətiz

sod, -s 'sɒd, -z

sodden, -s, -ing, -ed; -ness 'sɒdn̩, -z, -ɪŋ, -d; -nɪs

sodden-witted 'sɒd n̩wɪtɪd

so-differing 'soʊ'dɪfəɹɪŋ

soe'er soʊ'ɛɚ

soever soʊ'evɚ

so-forth (s.), **-s** 'soʊfɔɚθ, -s

soft, -er, -est, -ly, -ness 'sɒft, -ɚ, -ɪst, -lɨ, -nɪs

soft-conscienced 'sɒftˌkɒnʃənst

soften, -s, -ing, -ed 'sɒfn̩, -z, -ɪŋ, -d

softener, -s 'sɒfnɚ, -z

soft-hearted 'sɒftˌhɑɚtɪd

softly-sprighted 'sɒftlɨˌspɹaɪtɪd

sogg|y, -ier, -iest, -iness 'sɒg|ɨ, -ɪɚ, -ɪɪst, -ɪnɪs

so(-)ho (hunting cry) soʊ'hoʊ

soil, -s, -ing, -ed 'sɔɪl, -z, -ɪŋ, -d

soilure 'sɔɪljɚ

sojourn, -s, -ing, -ed, -er/s 'soʊdʒɝn [so'dʒɝn], -z, -ɪŋ, -d, -ɚ/z

Sol (the sun) (TC) 'sɒl ['soʊl]

sol (var. of **so**) (fifth note of diatonic scale) 'soʊl

sola (adj.) (feminine of **solus**) 'soʊlə

sola (s.) (pl. of **solum**) 'soʊlə

sola (interj.) (a call; a hunter's cry) 'soʊlə

solac|e, -es, -ing, -ed, -ement 'sɒlɪs, -ɪz, -ɪŋ, -t, -mənt

Solanio (MV) so'lɑnɪoʊ, -njoʊ

solder, -s, -ing, -ed, -er/s 'sɒdɚ, -z, -ɹɪŋ, -d, -ɹɚ/z

soldier (S.), **-s, -ing; -ship, -y** 'soʊldʒɚ ['soʊldjɚ], -z, -ɹɪŋ; -ʃɪp, -ɹɨ

soldieress 'soʊldʒəɹɪs ['soʊldjəɹɪs]

soldier-like 'soʊldʒɚˌlaɪk [-ldjɚ-]

sole, -ly 'soʊl, -ɨ

solemn, -ly, -ness 'sɒləm, -lɨ, -nɪs

solemnit|y, -ies sə'lemnɪt|ɨ, -ɪz

solemniz|e, -es, -ing, -ed 'sɒləmnaɪz, -ɪz, -ɪŋ, -d

Note.—Stressed on the second syllable, i.e., [so'lemnɪzɹd], in LLL, II.i.42

sol(-)fa 'soʊlˌfɑ

Note.—This word, appearing in TS,

I.ii.17, is derived from combining two of the syllables from the respective notes of the diatonic scale in music

solicit, -s, -ing/s, -ed sə'lɪsɪt, -s, -ɪŋ/z, -ɪd

solid, -s; -est, -ly, -ness 'sɒlɪd, -z; -ɪst, -lɨ, -nɪs

solidares 'sɒlɪdɛɚz [ˌsolɨ'dɑɹɛz]

Note.—This word found in TIM, III.i.43 is perhaps an error, and the OED does not hazard a guess as to how to say it; therefore, the pronunciations given above are entirely conjectural. Its usage indicates the plural form of a coin now unknown, unless it is meant to be derived from the Roman coin known as the 'solidus' (pl. 'solidi'). The alternative pronunciation proffered above is suggestive of an Italian flavor, and thus apt in the context of TIM's Greco-Roman world from the Elizabethan and Jacobean aesthetic

solidi|fy, -fies, -fying, -fied sə'lɪdɪ|faɪ, -faɪz, -faɪɪŋ, -faɪd

soliloqu|y, -ies sə'lɪləkw|ɨ, -ɪz

Solinus (COM) so'laɪnəs

solitarily ˌsɒlɪ'tɛɚɹɪlɨ

solitariness 'sɒlɪtəɹɪnɪs

solitar|y, -ies 'sɒlɪtəɹ|ɨ, -ɪz

solitude 'sɒlɪtjud

solo, -s 'soʊloʊ, -z

soloist, -s 'soʊloʊɪst, -s

Solomon (LLL) 'sɒləmən

Solon (TIT) 'soʊlɒn

solus (L.) (HV, II.i.46, et al.) 'solus

solv|e, -es, -ing, -ed; -able 'sɒlv, -z, -ɪŋ, -d; -əbl̩

Solyman, Sultan (MV) 'sʌltən 'sɒlɨmən [-mɑn]

some 'sʌm (strong form), 'səm (weak form)

somehow 'sʌmhɑʊ

Somerset (1HVI, 2HVI, 3HVI) 'sʌmɚsɪt [-set, -ˌset]

Somerville, Sir John (3HVI) ˌsɚ 'dʒɒn 'sʌmɚvɪl

something 'sʌmθɪŋ [-mpθ-]

sometime, -s 'sʌmtaɪm, -z (arguably [-'-] in Sonn. 18.7)

somever sʌm evɚ
somewhere 'sʌmʍɛɚ
somewhither 'sʌm͵ʍɪðɚ [͵-'--]
Somme (HV) 'sɒm ['sɔm]
son (3HVI), **-s** 'sʌn, -z
sonance (*sound; resounding ring*)
  'soŏnəns
song, -s 'sɒŋ, -z
song-men 'sɒŋ mən [-͵men]
Songs and Sonnets (MWW) 'sɒŋz ənd
  'sɒnɪts
  Note.—This is the title of a popular
  book, mentioned in MWW, I.i.184
son-in-law, -s, sons-in-law 'sʌnɪn͵lɔ, -z,
  'sʌnzɪn͵lɔ
sonnet, -s, -ing 'sɒnɪt, -s, -ɪŋ
sonneteer, -s, -ing, -ed ͵sɒnɪ'tɪɚ, -z, -ɹɪŋ,
  -d
sont|y, -ies 'sɒnt|ɪ, -ɪz
soon, -er, -est 'sun, -ɚ, -ɪst
soon-believing ͵sunbɪ'livɪŋ
soon-speeding 'sun'spidɪŋ [͵-'--]
soo|t, -ty, -tier, -tiest, -tiness 'sʊ|t, -ɾ,
  -ɾɪɚ, -ɾɪst, -ɾɪnɪs
sooth 'suθ
Sooth, Signior (PER) 'sinjɔɚ 'suθ
sooth|e, -es, -ing/ly, -ed, -er/s 'suð, -z,
  -ɪŋ/lɪ, -d, -ɚ/z
sooth|say, -says, -saying, -said 'suθ͵seĭ,
  -͵sez, -͵seĭɪŋ, -͵sed
Soothsayer (AC, CYM, JUL), **-s**
  'suθ͵seĭɚ, -z
sop, -s, -ping, -ped 'sɒp, -s, -ɪŋ, -t
sophister, -s 'sɒfɪstɚ, -z
sophisticat|e, -es, -ing, -ed sə'fɪstɪkeĭt, -s,
  -ɪŋ, -ɪd
sophistication sə͵fɪstɪ'keĭʃn̩
Sophy (MV, TN) 'soŏfɪ
sorcer|y, -ies; -er/s; -ess/es 'sɔɚ-səɹ|ɪ, -ɪz;
  -ɚ/z; -ɪs/ɪz
sore, -s; -r, -st, -ly, -ness 'sɔɚ, -z; -ɹɚ,
  -ɹɪst, -lɪ, -nɪs
Soris (*see* **For[r]es**) (MAC) 'sɔɹɪs

sor(r)el(l), -s 'sɒɹel, -z
sorrow (S.), **-s, -ing/ly, -ed, -er/s** 'sɒɹoŏ,
  -z, -ɪŋ/lɪ, -d, -ɚ/z
sorrow|ful, -fully, -fulness 'sɒɹoŏ|fʊl,
  -fəlɪ, -fʊlnɪs
sorrow-wreathen 'sɒɹoŏ͵ɹiðən
sorr|y, -ier, -iest, -ily, -iness 'sɒɹ|ɪ, -ɪɚ,
  -ɪɪst, -ɪlɪ, -ɪnɪs
sort, -s, -ing, -ed, -er/s 'sɔɚt, -s, -ɪŋ, -ɪd,
  -ɚ/z
sortance (*agreement, accord*) 'sɔɚtn̩s
  ['sɔɚ͵ɾəns]
so-seeming 'soŏ͵simɪŋ
Sossius (AC) 'sɒʃəs ['sɔʃ-], -ʃjəs
sot, -s, -ted 'sɒt, -s, -ɪd
Soto (TS) 'soŏtoŏ ['soŏɾoŏ]
sottish, -ly, -ness 'sɒɾɪʃ, -lɪ, -nɪs
sought (*p.t. of* **seek**, *q.v.*) 'sɔt
soul, -s 'soŏl, -z
soul-confirming 'soŏlkən͵fɚ-mɪŋ
soul-curer 'soŏl͵kjʊɚ-ɹɚ
soul-fearing 'soŏl'fɪɚ-ɹɪŋ
soulless, -ly, -ness 'soŏllɪs, -lɪ, -nɪs
soul-vexed 'soŏl'vekst
sound, -s, -ing/s, -ed; -er, -est, -ly, -ness
  'saŏnd, -z, -ɪŋ/z, -ɪd; -ɚ, -ɪst, -lɪ, -nɪs
sound-a 'saŏndə
  Note.—This word, along with 'bound-a,'
  'Barbary-a,' and 'three-a,' appears in
  the ditty sung by the Gaoler's Daughter
  in TNK, III.v; *the extra syllable there*
  merely to provide for another musical
  beat in the tetrameter line of song
soundless, -ly, -ness 'saŏndlɪs, -lɪ, -nɪs
Sound(-)post, James (RJ) 'dʒeĭmz
  'saŏndpoŏst
soupçon, -s 'supsɔ̃ŋ, -z
sour, -er, -est, -ly, -ness; -s, -ing, -ed
  'saŏɚ, -ɹɚ, -ɹɪst, -lɪ, -nɪs; -z, -ɹɪŋ, -d
sourest-natured 'saŏɚ-ɹɪst͵neĭtʃɚ-d
sour-eyed 'saŏɚ͵ɹaĭd
sous|e, -es, -ing, -ed 'saŏs, -ɪz, -ɪŋ, -t
south (*s., adj., adv.*) (S.) 'saŏθ

---

i wᴇ ɪ city ɪ hɪt e lᴇt ɛ dᴇbut æ cᴀn a pᴀss ɚ bird ʌ hut ə again ɚ suppᴇr u yọu
ʊ shọuld o ọbey ɔ ạwl ɒ cọp ɑ fạther eĭ pạid aĭ hịgh oŏ gọ ɔĭ vọice aŏ fọund ɪɚ ẹar
ɛɚ ạir ʊɚ pọor ɔɚ fọrk ɑɚ pạrk aĭɚ fịre aŏɚ họur b bọy p pit d dog t top g got
k kid h hơw fi behạve dʒ jot tʃ chew z zany s soft v vat f fat ʒ treạsure ʃ ship ð thẹ
θ thin m mạn n nọ ŋ hang l lip j yẹs w wọn ʍ whew ɹ ɹigger, airy ɾ mạtter

sou|th (*v.*), **-ths, -thing, -thed** 'saŭ|θ [-ð],
-θs [-ðz], -θıŋ [-ðıŋ], -θt [-ðd]
Southam (3HVI) 'sʌðəm
Southampton (HV) saŭˈθæmptən
[saŭθˈfjæmptən]
southerly 'sʌðəᴧlɨ
south-fog 'saŭθˌfɒg
south-north 'saŭθˈnɔɚθ
South Sea (AYLI) 'saŭθ 'si
Southwark (2HVI) 'sʌðəᴧk ['saŭθwəᴧk]
Southwell, John (*2HVI*) 'dʒɒn 'saŭθwəl
['sʌðḷ, -ðəl]
south-wind 'saŭθwınd
sovereign, -s; -est 'sɒvɹın [-vəᴧɹ-], -z; -ıst
sovereignty 'sɒvɹıntɨ
sow (*s.*) (*adult female pig, molded metal
[iron], etc.*), **-s** 'saŭ, -z
sow (*v.*) (*scattering seed*), **-s, -ing, -ed, -n,
-er/s** 'soŭ, -z, -ıŋ, -d, -n, -ɚ/z
sowl (*seize roughly*) 'soŭl ['sul]
Note.—The OED *does not assert a
pronunciation for this dialectal word in*
COR, IV.v.206, *which appears in many
modern editions as a substitution for the
First Folio's 'sole.' The pronunciations
given above are conjectural but
consistent with the var. spellings of the
word as cited in the* OED, *i.e., 'sole,'
'sol(l),' 'sowl(e),' 'soul,' 'soal,' 's'ool,'
'sool(e),' etc.*
sow-skin 'saŭˌskın
sowter (**S.**) (*obsolete var. of 'souter'*), **-s**
'sutəᴧ ['su̱ɚ], -z
*Note.—This word, meaning 'cobbler' or
'maker of shoes,' is the proper name of a
dog in* TN, II.v.124
spa, -s 'spɑ, -z
spac|e, -es, -ing, -ed 'speĭs, -ız, -ıŋ, -t
spacious, -ly, -ness 'speĭʃəs, -lɨ, -nıs
spade, -s 'speĭd, -z
Spain (COM, HV, 3HVI, HVIII, JUL, KJ,
LLL, OTH) 'speĭn
spake (*archaic p.t. of* **speak**, *q.v.*) 'speĭk
span, -s, -ning, -ned 'spæn, -z, -ıŋ, -d
spang|le, -les, -ling, -led 'spæŋg|ḷ, -ḷz, -ḷıŋ
[-lıŋ], -ḷd
Spaniard (ADO, CYM, 2HIV, HVIII,
LLL, PER), **-s** 'spænjəᴧd, -z
spaniel, -s 'spænjəl, -z

spaniel-like 'spænjəlˌlaĭk
Spanish (ALL'S, 1HIV, PER, RJ)
'spænıʃ
spank, -s, -ing/s, -ed, -er/s 'spæŋk, -s,
-ıŋ/z, -t, -ɚ/z
spar, -s, -ring, -red 'spɑɚ, -z, -ɹıŋ, -d
spar|e, -es, -ing/ly, -ed; -eness 'spɛɚ, -z,
-ɹıŋ/lɨ, -d; -nıs
spark, -s, -ing, -ed 'spɑɚk, -s, -ıŋ, -t
spark|le, -les, -ling, -led, -ler/s 'spɑɚk|ḷ,
-ḷz, -ḷıŋ [-lıŋ], -ḷd, -ḷɚ/z [-lɚ/z]
sparrow, -s 'spæɹoŭ, -z
sparse, -ly, -ness 'spɑɚs, -lɨ, -nıs
Sparta (MSND, PER, TC) 'spɑɚtə
Spartan (MSND, OTH), **-s** 'spɑɚtṇ, -z
spavin, -s 'spævın, -z
speak, -s, -ing, spoke, spoken, speaker/s
'spik, -s, -ıŋ, 'spoŭk, 'spoŭkən, 'spikɚ/z
Note.—In Frank Kermode's (editor, The
Arden Shakespeare, *1958) annotation
for* TEM, I.ii.53, *there is a brief but
valuable discussion about monosyllabic
words that sometimes receive the value
of two metric beats in S. lines of verse
"whether or no it is [they are] pronounced disyllabically . . ." In* TIT,
III.i.67, *'speak' is arguably pronounced
disyllabically or given, as Kermode puts
it, "a heavy emphasis." Cf. Abbott's* A
Shakespearian Grammar, *§§ 475, 479,
484*
speak-a 'spikə (*see* **vere**)
spear, -s, -ing, -ed 'spıɚ, -z, -ɹıŋ, -d
spear-grass 'spıɚˌgɹɑs
specialt|y, -ies 'speʃlt|ɨ, -ɨz
specious, -ly, -ness 'spiʃəs, -lɨ, -nıs
spectacle, -s, -d 'spektıkḷ, -z, -d
spectator, -s 'spekteĭɾɚ, -z
spectatorship 'spekteĭɾɚˌʃıp [-ˈ---]
speculative, -ly, -ness 'spekjʊlətıv
[-ˌleĭt-], -lɨ, -nıs
speech, -es 'spitʃ, -ız
speechless, -ly, -ness 'spitʃlıs, -lɨ, -nıs
Speed (*TGV*) 'spid
**speed, -s, -ing, -ed, sped; -y, -ier, -iest,
-ily, -iness** 'spid, -z, -ıŋ, -ıd, 'sped; -ɨ,
-ɨɚ, -ɨıst, -ɨlɨ, -ɨnıs
speed's (*contr. of* **speed us** *in* ADO,
V.iii.32) 'spids

spel|l, -ls, -ling/s, -led, -t, -ler/s 'spel, -z,
-ɪŋ/z, -d, -t, -ɚ/z
spellbound 'spelbɑŭnd
spell-stopped 'spel͵stɒpt
Spencer (RII) 'spensɚ
spen|d, -ds, -ding, -t, -der/s 'spen|d, -dz,
-dɪŋ, -t, -dɚ/z
spendthrift, -s 'spend̦θɹɪft, -s
sperm, -s 'spɝm, -z
spe|t, -ts, -tter/s, -tting/s 'spe|t, -ts,
-͵ɟɚ/z, -͵ɟɪŋ/z
spew, -s, -ing, -ed 'spju, -z, -ɪŋ, -d
sphere, -s, -d 'sfɪɚ, -z, -d
spheric, -s, -al, -ally 'sfɪɚɹɪk ['sfeɹɪk], -s,
-l̩, -əlɨ
sphery 'sfɪɚɹɨ
Sphinx (LLL) 'sfɪŋks
sphinx, -es; -like 'sfɪŋks, -ɪz; -laɪ̆k
spic|e, -es, -ing, -ed; -y, -ier, -iest, -ily,
-iness 'spaɪ̆s, -ɪz, -ɪŋ, -t; -ɨ, -ɪɚ, -ɪɪst,
-ɪlɨ, -ɪnɪs
spicery 'spaɪ̆sɚɹɨ
spider (S.) (CYM), -s 'spaɪ̆dɚ, -z
spider-like 'spaɪ̆dɚ͵laɪ̆k
spigot, -s 'spɪɡət, -s
spik|e, -es, -ing, -ed, -er/s 'spaɪ̆k, -s, -ɪŋ,
-t, -ɚ/z
spik|y, -ier, -iest, -iness 'spaɪ̆k|ɨ, -ɪɚ, -ɪɪst,
-ɪnɪs
spill, -s, -ing, -ed, spilt 'spɪl, -z, -ɪŋ, -d,
'spɪlt
spilth 'spɪl̩θ
spin, -s, -ning, spun, spinner/s 'spɪn, -z,
-ɪŋ, 'spʌn, 'spɪnɚ/z
spinach 'spɪnɪtʃ
spin|e, -es; -eless, -y 'spaɪ̆n, -z; -lɪs, -ɨ
Spinii (ALL'S) 'spaɪ̆nɪaɪ̆ ['spɪn-]
spinster, -s; -hood 'spɪnstɚ, -z; -ɦʊd
spire, -s, -d 'spaɪ̆ɚ, -z, -d
spirit (S.), -s, -ing, -ed, -edly, -edness;
-less 'spɪɹɪt, -s, -ɪŋ, -ɪd, -ɪdlɨ, -ɪdnɪs; -lɪs
Note.—This word, as with 'warrant,'
'devil,' 'evil,' 'even,' 'heaven,' etc., is
often (though not always) monosyllabic

in S. (absorbing only one metrical beat
in the verse). When compelled to use
them in such a way, their pronunciation
can only be accomplished by pronouncing the second syllable in each word
with a vowel that is virtually, though not
entirely, absent, e.g., ['spɪɹɪt] or perhaps
['spɪɚ̆t]
spirit-stirring 'spɪɹɪt͵stɝɹɪŋ
spirt, -s, -ing, -ed 'spɝt, -s, -ɪŋ, -ɪd
sp|it (s., v.) (expectorate, e.g., saliva), -its,
-itting, spat 'sp|ɪt, -ɪts, -ɪɟ̥ɪŋ, 'spæt
sp|it (s., v.) (impale for roasting), -its,
-itting, -itted 'sp|ɪt, -ɪts, -ɪɟ̥ɪŋ, -ɪɟ̥ɪd
spital-house (aphetic form of 'hospital-
house') 'spɪtl͵hɑŭs
spit|e, -es, -ing, -ed; -eful, -efully,
-efulness 'spaɪ̆t, -s, -ɪŋ, -ɪd; -fʊl, -fʊlɨ
[-fəlɨ], -fʊlnɪs
'spite 'spaɪ̆t
Note.—This word appears as 'spight' in
the original quarto version of Sonn.
107.11, and is typically emended to the
aphaeretic form of 'despite'; thus the
apostrophe
spittle 'spɪtl̩
splash, -es, -ing, -ed, -er/s 'splæʃ, -ɪz, -ɪŋ,
-t, -ɚ/z
splay, -s, -ing, -ed 'spleɪ̆, -z, -ɪŋ, -d
spleen, -s; -ful, -fully, -ish/ly; -y 'splin,
-z; -fʊl, -fʊlɨ, -ɪʃ/lɨ; -ɨ
splenative 'splenətɪv [-lin-]
splendid, -ly, -ness 'splendɪd, -lɨ, -nɪs
splint, -s, -ing, -ed 'splɪnt, -s, -ɪŋ, -ɪd
splinter, -s, -ing, -ed 'splɪntɚ, -z, -ɹɪŋ, -d
split, -s, -ting, -ted 'splɪt, -s, -ɪŋ, -ɪd
spoil, -s, -ing, -ed, -t, -er/s 'spɔɪ̆l, -z, -ɪŋ,
-d, -t, -ɚ/z
spoke (s.), -s 'spoŭk, -s
spoken 'spoŭkən
spong|e, -es, -ing, -ed, -er/s 'spʌndʒ, -ɪz,
-ɪŋ, -d, -ɚ/z
spong|y, -ier, -iest, -iness 'spʌndʒ|ɨ, -ɪɚ,
-ɪɪst, -ɪnɪs

sport, -s, -ing, -ed 'spɔɔ̌t, -s, -ɪŋ, -ɪd
sportful 'spɔɔ̌tfʊl
sporting-place 'spɔɔ̌tɪŋˌpleɪ̌s ['spɔɔ̌ˌʄɪŋ-]
sportive, -ly, -ness 'spɔɔ̌tɪv, -lɪ, -nɪs
spot, -s, -ting, -ted, -ter/s 'spɒt, -s, -ɪŋ,
    -ɪd, -ɚ/z
spousal 'spaʊ̌zəl
spouse (S.), -s 'spaʊ̌s, -ɪz
spout, -s, -ing, -ed, -er/s 'spaʊ̌t, -s, -ɪŋ,
    -ɪd, -ɚ/z
sprag (from 'sprack,' meaning 'smart')
    'spɹæg (see prings)
sprang (p.t. of spring [v.], q.v.) 'spɹæŋ
sprat, -s 'spɹæt, -s
sprawl, -s, -ing, -ed, -er/s 'spɹɔl, -z, -ɪŋ,
    -d, -ɚ/z
spray, -s, -ing, -ed, -er/s 'spɹeɪ̌, -z, -ɪŋ,
    -d, -ɚ/z
spread, -s, -ing, -er/s 'spɹed, -z, -ɪŋ,
    -ɚ/z
spree, -s 'spɹi, -z
sprig, -s 'spɹɪg, -z
spright|ful, -fully 'spɹaɪ̌t|fʊl, -fəlɪ
sprightl|y, -ier, -iest, -iness 'spɹaɪ̌tl|ɪ, -ɪɚ,
    -ɪɪst, -ɪnɪs
spring (s.) (S.) (LLL), -s 'spɹɪŋ, -z
spring (v.), -s, -ing, sprang, sprung,
    springer/s 'spɹɪŋ, -z, -ɪŋ, 'spɹæŋ, 'spɹʌŋ,
    'spɹɪŋɚ/z
springe, -s 'spɹɪndʒ, -ɪz
springhalt (condition resulting in horses'
    lameness) 'spɹɪŋɦɔlt
spring(-)time 'spɹɪŋtaɪ̌m
sprink|le, -les, -ling, -led, -ler/s 'spɹɪŋk|l̩,
    ḷz, -lɪŋ [-lɪŋ], -lɚ/z [-ḷɚ/z]
sprint, -s, -ing, -ed, -er/s 'spɹɪnt, -s, -ɪŋ,
    -ɪd, -ɚ/z
sprit|e, -es, -ing, -ly 'spɹɪ aɪ̌t, -s, -ɪŋ, -lɪ
sprout, -s, -ing, -ed 'spɹaʊ̌t, -s, -ɪŋ, -ɪd
spruc|e, -es, -ing, -ed; -er, -est, -ely,
    -eness 'spɹus, -ɪz, -ɪŋ, -t; -ɚ, -ɪst, -lɪ,
    -nɪs
sprung (p.t. and p.p. of spring [v.], q.v.)
    'spɹʌŋ
spun (p.t. and p.p. of spin, q.v.) 'spʌn
spur, -s, -ring, -red 'spɝ, -z, -ɹɪŋ, -d
Spurio, Captain (ALL'S) 'kæptɪn
    'spjuɹɪoʊ̌ ['spjuɹ-]
spurn, -s, -ing, -ed 'spɝn, -z, -ɪŋ, -d

sp|y, -ies, -ying, -ied 'sp|aɪ̌, -aɪ̌z, -aɪ̌ɪŋ,
    -aɪ̌d
squabb|le, -les, -ling, -led, -ler/s 'skwɒb|l̩,
    -ḷz, -lɪŋ [-lɪŋ], -ḷd, -ḷɚ/z [-lɚ/z]
squad, -s 'skwɒd, -z
squadron, -s 'skwɒdɹən, -z
squander, -s, -ing, -ed, -er/s 'skwɒndɚ,
    -z, -ɹɪŋ, -d, -ɹɚ/z
squar|e, -es, -ing, -ed; -er, -est, -ly, -ness
    'skwɛɚ, -z, -ɹɪŋ, -d; -ɹɚ, -ɹɪst, -lɪ, -nɪs
squarer (brawler), -s 'skwɛɚɹɚ, -z
Squash, Mistress (MSND) 'mɪstɹɪs 'skwɒʃ
squash, -es, -ing, -ed 'skwɒʃ, -ɪz, -ɪŋ, -t
Squele, Will (2HIV) 'wɪl 'skwil
squier (obsolete form of square;
    measuring instrument), -s 'skwaɪ̌ɚ, -z
squinies (squints) 'skwɪnɪz
squire (S.) (PER), -s 'skwaɪ̌ɚ, -z
squire-like 'skwaɪ̌ɚˌlaɪ̌k
stab|le, -les, -ling, -led; -ly, (S.) -leness
    'steɪ̌b|l̩, -ḷz, -ḷd; -lɪ [-ḷ], -ḷnɪs
stablish (archaic aphetic var. of
    establish), -ment 'stæblɪʃ, -mənt
Stafford, Edmund (1HIV) 'edmənd
    'stæfɚd
Stafford, Edward (HVIII) 'edwɚd
    'stæfɚd
Stafford, Humphrey (see Note for
    Humphrey) (2HVI, 3HVI) 'hʌmfɹɪ
    'stæfɚd
Stafford, William (2HVI) 'wɪljəm
    'stæfɚd
Staffordshire (2HIV) 'stæfɚdʃɪɚ [-ʃɚ]
stag, -s 'stæg, -z
stag|e, -es, -ing, -ed 'steɪ̌dʒ, -ɪz, -ɪŋ, -d
stagger, -s, -ing, -ed, -er/s 'stægɚ, -z,
    -ɹɪŋ, -d, -ɹɚ/z
stagnat|e, -es, -ing, -ed 'stægneɪ̌t, -s, -ɪŋ,
    -ɪd
stagnation stæg'neɪ̌ʃn̩
staid, -er, -ly, -ness 'steɪ̌d, -ɚ, -lɪ, -nɪs
stain, -s, -ing, -ed, -er/s 'steɪ̌n, -z, -ɪŋ, -d,
    -ɚ/z
Staines (HV) 'steɪ̌nz
stair, -s 'stɛɚ, -z
stair-work 'stɛɚˌwɝk
stak|e, -es, -ing, -ed 'steɪ̌k, -s, -ɪŋ, -t
stale, -d; -r, -st, -ly, -ness 'steɪ̌l, -d; -ɚ,
    -ɪst, -lɪ, -nɪs

stalk, -s, -ing, -ed, -er/s 'stɔk, -s, -ɪŋ, -t,
-ɚ/z

stalking-horse, -s 'stɔkɪŋˌhɔɚ̆s, -ɪz

stall, -s, -ing, -ed 'stɔl, -z, -ɪŋ, -d

stallion, -s 'stæljən, -z

Stamford (2HIV) 'stæmfɚd

stammer, -s, -ing, -ed, -er/s 'stæmɚ, -z,
-ɹɪŋ, -d, -ɹɚ/z

stamp, -s, -ing, -ed, -er/s 'stæmp, -s, -ɪŋ,
-t, -ɚ/z

stamped|e, -es, -ing, -ed stæm'pid, -z, -ɪŋ,
-ɪd

stampt 'stæmpt
*Note.—R. A. Foakes (editor for HVIII,
The Arden Shakespeare, 1964) curiously
retains the Folio's spelling (i.e.,
'stampt') when it appears in his edition
of HVIII, III.ii.325, rather than making
the customary emandation to 'stamp'd.'
Regardless, the pronunciation is the
same, and no special significance need
be inferred by this spelling*

stance, -s 'stans, -ɪz

stanch, -es, -ing, -ed 'stɑntʃ, -ɪz, -ɪŋ, -t

stand, -s, -ing, stood 'stænd, -z, -ɪŋ, 'stʊd

standard, -s 'stændɚd, -z

standardization ˌstændɚdɪ'zeɪʃn̩

standardiz|e, -es, -ing, -ed 'stændɚdaɪz,
-ɪz, -ɪŋ, -d

stander-by 'stændɚˌbaɪ

stander, -s 'stændɚ, -z

standers-by 'stændɚzˌbaɪ

standing (*s.*), **-s** 'stændɪŋ, -z

standing-bed, -s 'stændɪŋˌbed, -z

standing-bowl, -s 'stændɪŋˌboʊl, -z

standpoint, -s 'stændpɔɪnt, -s

standstill, -s 'stændstɪl, -z

staniel, -s 'stænjəl, -z

stank (*p.t. of* **stink**, *q.v.*) 'stæŋk

Stanley, George (RIII) 'dʒɔɚ̆dʒ 'stænlɪ

Stanley, John (2HVI) 'dʒɒn 'stænlɪ

Stanley, Thomas (RIII) 'tɒməs 'stænlɪ

Stanley, William (3HVI, RIII) 'wɪljəm
'stænlɪ

stanza, -s 'stænzə, -z

stanze 'stænzə

stanzo (*var. form of* **stanza**), **-s** 'stænzoʊ̆,
-z

stapl|e, -es, -ing, -ed, -er/s 'steɪpl̩, -z, -ɪŋ,
-d, -ɚ/z

star, -s, -ring, -red 'stɑɚ̆, -z, -ɹɪŋ, -d

star-blasting 'stɑɚ̆ˌblastɪŋ

Star Chamber (MWW) 'stɑɚ̆ 'tʃeɪmbɚ

star|e, -es, -ing/ly, -ed, -er/s 'stɛɚ̆, -z,
-ɹɪŋ/lɪ, -d, -ɹɚ/z

star-gaz|e, -er/s, -ing 'stɑɚ̆ˌgeɪz, -ɚ/z, -ɪŋ

starings 'stɛɚ̆ˌɹɪŋz

stark, -ly, -ness 'stɑɚ̆k, -lɪ, -nɪs

stark-naked 'stɑɚ̆k'neɪkɪd
*Note.—The Folio gives 'starke-nak'd'
['stɑɚ̆k'neɪkt] in AC, V.ii.59; however,
neither scansion nor meaning would
suffer by the creation of an epic caesura
in the line, thereby allowing the
pronunciation* ['stɑɚ̆k'neɪkɪd]

starlight 'stɑɚ̆laɪt

star-like 'stɑɚ̆ˌlaɪk

starling, -s 'stɑɚ̆lɪŋ, -z

starr|y, -iness 'stɑɚ̆ɹ|ɪ, -ɪnɪs

start, -s, -ing, -ed, -er/s 'stɑɚ̆t, -s, -ɪŋ,
-ɪd, -ɚ/z

startingly 'stɑɚ̆tɪŋlɪ

start|le, -les, -ling, -led, -ler/s 'stɑɚ̆t|l̩,
-l̩z, -l̩ɪŋ [-lɪŋ], -l̩d, -l̩ɚ/z

start-up (*upstart*), **-s** 'stɑɚ̆tʌp [-ɑɚ̆ˌɾʌp],
-s

starvation stɑɚ̆'veɪʃn̩

starv|e, -es, -ing, -ed 'stɑɚ̆v, -z, -ɪŋ, -d

Starve-Lackey, Master (MEAS) ˌmastɚ
'stɑɚ̆vˌlækɪ

starveling, -s 'stɑɚ̆vlɪŋ, -z

Starveling, Robin (MSND) 'ɹɒbɪn
'stɑɚ̆vlɪŋ

stat|e (S.), **-es, -ing, -ed, -ement/s** 'steɪt,
-s, -ɪŋ, -ɪd, -mənt/s

state-affairs 'steɪtəˌfɛɚ̆z [ˌ--'-]

state-matters 'steɪtˌmæfɚz

state-statues 'steɪtˌstætjuz [-tʃuz]

i wᴇ ɪ city ɪ hɪt e lᴇt ɛ dᴇbut æ cᴀn a pᴀss ɚ bɪrd ʌ hᴜt ə again ɚ suppᴇr u yᴏu
ʊ shᴏuld o ᴏbey ɔ ᴀwl ɒ cᴏp ɑ fᴀther eɪ pᴀid aɪ hɪgh oʊ̆ gᴏ ɔɪ vᴏice aʊ̆ fᴏund ɪɚ̆ ᴇar
ɛɚ̆ ᴀir ʊɚ̆ pᴏor ɔɚ̆ fᴏrk ɑɚ̆ pᴀrk aɪɚ̆ fɪre aʊ̆ɚ hᴏur b bᴏy p pɪt d dᴏg t tᴏp g gᴏt
k kɪd h hᴏw fi behᴀve dʒ jᴏt tʃ chᴇw z zany s sᴏft v vᴀt f fᴀt ʒ treasure ʃ shɪp ð the
θ thin m mᴀn n nᴏ ŋ hang l lɪp j yes w wᴏn ʍ whᴇw ɹ rɪgger, aiɹy ɾ matter

Statilius (JUL) stə'tɪlɪəs [stæ't-], -ljəs
station, -s, -ing, -ed 'steɪ̆ʃn̩, -z, -ɪŋ, -d
statist, -s 'steɪ̆tɪst, -s
statue, -s 'stætju [-tʃu], -z
  Note.— 'statuë' ['stætjʊə] *in S.'s* 2HVI,
  III.ii.79; JUL, II.ii.76, III.ii.190; RIII,
  III.vii.25 *is trisyllabic, fulfilling the*
  necessary number of beats required by
  the pentameter (cf. 'dieresis,' Introduc-
  tion § 3.14 of this dictionary). 'Statua,' a
  spelling common in S.'s time, is often
  substituted
stature, -s 'stætʃɚ, -z
staunch *or* **stanch, -er, -est, -ly, -ness**
  'stɔntʃ ['stɑntʃ], -ɚ, -ɪst, -lɨ, -nɪs
stav|e, -es, -ing, -ed, stove 'steɪ̆v, -z, -ɪŋ,
  -d, 'stoŏv
stay, -s, -ing, -ed 'steɪ̆, -z, -ɪŋ, -d
stead, -s, -ed 'sted, -z, -ɪd
steadfast, -ly, -ness 'stedfast [-fəst], -lɨ,
  -nɪs
stead|y, -ies, -ying, -ied; -ier, -iest, -ily,
  -iness 'sted|ɨ, -ɨz, -ɨɪŋ, -ɨd; -ɨɚ, -ɨɪst, -ɨlɨ,
  -ɨnɪs
steak, -s 'steɪ̆k, -s
steal, -s, -ing, stole, stolen 'stil, -z, -ɪŋ,
  'stoŏl, 'stoŏlən
stealth, -y, -ier, -iest, -ily, -iness 'ste̢lθ, -ɨ,
  -ɨə, -ɨɪst, -ɨlɨ, -ɨnɪs
steam, -s, -ing, -ed; -y, -ier, -iest, -iness
  'stim, -z, -ɪŋ, -d; -ɨ, -ɨə, -ɨɪst, -ɨnɪs
steed, -s 'stid, -z
steel, -s, -ing, -ed; -y, -ier, -iest, -iness
  'stil, -z, -ɪŋ, -d; -ɨ, -ɨə, -ɨɪst, -ɨnɪs
steep, -s, -ing, -ed; -er, -est, -ly, -ness
  'stip, -s, -ɪŋ, -t; -ɚ, -ɪst, -lɨ, -nɪs
steep-down 'stip͵daŏn
steeple, -s, -d 'stipl̩, -z, -d
steep-up 'stip͵ʌp
steepy 'stipɨ
steer, -s, -ing, -ed, -er/s 'stɪɚ, -z, -ɪɪŋ, -d,
  -ɹə/z
steerage 'stɪɚ͵ɹɪdʒ
stelled (*starry; affixed*) 'stelɹd (['steld] *in*
  LUC, 1444)
stench, -es 'stentʃ, -ɪz
step(-)dame, -s 'stepdeɪ̆m, -z
Stephano (*MV, TEM*) 'stefənoŏ

  Note.—In MV, V.i.51, *the line appears to*
  scan in such a way as to suggest that in
  this instance alone, 'Stephano' is given
  primary stress on the second syllable,
  i.e., [ste'fɑnoŏ]. *I favor consistency,*
  especially when it comes to the
  pronunciation of S.'s names (cf.
  Gonzalo). *With a little imagination—*
  extending 'friend,' and syncopating
  'Stephano' into two syllables, i.e.,
  ['stef͵noŏ]—*one can retain the regular*
  pronunciation of the name without
  sacrificing the conventions of iambic
  pentameter (cf. Kökeritz's Shakespeare's
  Names: A Pronouncing Dictionary,
  p. 23)

Stephen, King (OTH) 'kɪŋ 'stivən
stepmother, -s 'stepmʌðɚ, -z
sterile 'steɹəl
sterility stə'ɹɪlɪtɨ
sterilization, -s ͵steɹɪlɪ'zeɪ̆ʃn̩, -z
sterling 'stɝlɪŋ
stern (*s.*), **-s** 'stɝn, -z
stern (*adj.*), **-er, -est, -ly, -ness** 'stɝn, -ɚ,
  -ɪst, -lɨ, -nɪs
sternage 'stɝnɪdʒ
stew, -s, -ing, -ed 'stju, -z, -ɪŋ, -d
steward (S.), **-s** 'stjuəd, -z
stick (*v.*), **-s, -ing, stuck, sticker/s** 'stɪk,
  -s, -ɪŋ, 'stʌk, 'stɪkɚ/z
sticker (*s.*), **-s** 'stɪkɚ, -z
stickler-like 'stɪklə͵laɪ̆k
stick|y, -ier, -iest, -ily, -iness 'stɪk|ɨ, -ɨə,
  -ɨɪst, -ɨlɨ, -ɨnɪs
stiff, -s, -ing, -ed; -er, -est, -ly, -ness 'stɪf,
  -s, -ɪŋ, -t; -ɚ, -ɪst, -lɨ, -nɪs
stiff-borne 'stɪf͵bɔɚn
stif|le, -les, -ling/ly, -led 'staɪ̆f|l̩, -lz, -l̩ɪŋ/lɨ
  [-lɪŋ/lɨ], -l̩d
stigmatic, -al stɪg 'mætɪk, -əl
  (['stɪgmə͵tɪk] *in* 3HVI, II.ii.136)
stile, -s 'staɪ̆l, -z
stile-a 'staɪ̆lə
  Note.—This word, along with its counter-
  part, 'mile-a,' appears in the ditty at the
  end of WT, IV.iii; *the extra syllable there*
  merely to provide for another musical
  beat in the tetrameter line of song

still, -s, -ing, -ed; -er, -est, -ness 'stɪl, -z, -ɪŋ, -d; -ə·, -ɪst, -nɪs
still-born 'stɪlˌbɔə·n
still-breeding 'stɪlˌbɹidɪŋ
still-discordant 'stɪldɪs'kɔə·dn̩t
stillitory (*obsolete form of* **stillatory**) 'stɪlɹtə·ɹɪ
Note.—This word, meaning 'a still,' is meant to be a disyllable when it appears in VA, 443, *i.e.,* ['stɪltɹɪ]
still-waking 'stɪlˌweɪkɪŋ
still-lasting 'stɪl'lastɪŋ
still-stand 'stɪlˌstænd
sting, -s, -ing, stung 'stɪŋ, -z, -ɪŋ, 'stʌŋ
stinger, -s 'stɪŋə·, -z
stink, -s, -ing/ly, stank, stunk 'stɪŋk, -s, -ɪŋ/lɪ, 'stæŋk, 'stʌŋk
stinker, -s 'stɪŋkə·, -z
stinking-elder 'stɪŋkɪŋ'eldə·
stint, -s, -ing, -ed 'stɪnt, -s, -ɪŋ, -ɪd
stirrup, -s 'stɜ·ɹəp ['stɪɹ-], -s
stitch, -es, -ing, -ed 'stɪtʃ, -ɪz, -ɪŋ, -t
stitchery 'stɪtʃə·ɹɪ
stith|y, -ies, -ied 'stɪð|ɪ ['stɪθ|ɪ], -ɪz, -ɪd
stoccado (*fencing term; thrust or stab*), **-es** sto'kɑdoŭ, -z
stock, -s, -ing, -ed 'stɒk, -s, -ɪŋ, -t
stock(-)fish, -es 'stɒkfɪʃ, -ɪz
Stockfish, Sam(p)son (2HIV) 'sæmsn̩ 'stɒkfɪʃ
stocking, -s, -ed 'stɒkɪŋ, -z, -d
stockish, -ly, -ness 'stɒkɪʃ, -lɪ, -nɪs
stoic, -s, -al, -ally 'stoŭɪk, -s, -l̩, -əlɪ
stoicism 'stoŭɪsɪzəm
Stokesley (HVIII) 'stoŭkslɪ
stole (*p.t. of* **steal**, *q.v.*) 'stoŭl
stolen (*p.p. of* **steal**, *q.v.*) 'stoŭlən
stol'n 'stoŭln
stomach, -s, -ing, -ed 'stʌmək, -s, -ɪŋ, -t
stomacher, -s 'stʌməkə·, -z
stomach-qualmed 'stʌmək'kwɑmd
ston|e, -es, -ing, -ed 'stoŭn, -z, -ɪŋ, -d
stone-bow 'stoŭnˌboŭ

stone-hard 'stoŭnˌhɑə·d
stone-still 'stoŭnˌstɪl
(')stonish (*aphetic form of* **astonish**, *q.v.*), **-ed** 'stɒnɪʃ, -t
ston|y, -ier, -iest, -ily, -iness 'stoŭn|ɪ, -ɪə·, -ɪɪst, -ɪlɪ, -ɪnɪs
stony-hearted 'stoŭnɪˌhɑə·tɪd
Stony(-)Stratford (RIII) 'stoŭnɪ 'stɹætfə·d
stool, -s 'stul, -z
stool-ball 'stulˌbɔl
stoop, -s, -ing, -ed, -er/s 'stup, -s, -ɪŋ, -t, -ə·/z
stop, -s, -ping, -ped, -per/s 'stɒp, -s, -ɪŋ, -t, -ə·/z
stopp|le (*to plug*), **-les, -ling, -led** 'stɒp|l̩, -l̩z, -l̩ɪŋ, -l̩d
Note.—LEAR, V.iii.153 (Quarto version) has 'stople'
storage 'stɔɹɪdʒ
stor|e, -es, -ing, -ed 'stɔə·, -z, -ɹɪŋ, -d
store(-)hou|se, -ses 'stɔə·ˌhaŭ|s, -zɪz
storm, -s, -ing, -ed 'stɔə·m, -z, -ɪŋ, -d
storm-beaten 'stɔə·mˌbitn̩
storm|y, -ier, -iest, -ily, -iness 'stɔə·m|ɪ, -ɪə·, -ɪɪst, -ɪlɪ, -ɪnɪs
stor|y, -ies 'stɔɹ|ɪ, -ɪz
stoup, -s 'stup, -s
stout, -s; -er, -est, -ly, -ness 'staŭt, -s; -ə·, -ɪst, -lɪ, -nɪs
stout-hearted 'staŭtˌhɑə·tɪd
stover (*fodder*) 'stoŭvə·
stow, -s, -ing, -ed; -age 'stoŭ, -z, -ɪŋ, -d; -ɪdʒ
Strachy, Lady of the (TN) 'leɪdɪ əv ðə 'stɹeɪtʃɪ
stragg|le, -les, -ling, -led, -ler/s 'stɹæg|l̩, -l̩z, -l̩ɪŋ [-lɪŋ], -l̩d, -l̩ə·/z [-lə·/z]
straight, -er, -est, -ness 'stɹeɪt, -ə·, -ɪst, -nɪs
straighten, -s, -ing, -ed 'stɹeɪtn̩, -z, -ɪŋ, -d
straight-pight (*tall, erect figure*) 'stɹeɪtˌpaɪt
straightway 'stɹeɪtweɪ

---

strain, -s, -ing, -ed, -er/s 'stɹeĭn, -z, -ɪŋ, -d, -ɚ/z

strait, -s, -ed; -ly, -ness; -er 'stɹeĭt, -s, -ɪd; -lɪ, -nɪs; -ɚ

straiten, -s, -ing, -ed 'stɹeĭtn̩, -z, -ɪŋ, -d

Strange, Lord (1HVI) 'lɔɹ̃d 'stɹeĭndʒ

strange (adj.), -r, -st, -ly, -ness 'stɹeĭndʒ, -ɚ, -ɪst, -lɪ, -nɪs

strange-achieved 'stɹeĭndʒəˌtʃivd

strangely-visited 'stɹeĭndʒlɪ'vɪzɪtɪd

stranger (s.), -s 'stɹeĭndʒɚ, -z

strangered 'stɹeĭndʒɚd

stranger-soul 'stɹeĭndʒɚ'soŭl

strap, -s, -ping, -ped 'stɹæp, -s, -ɪŋ, -t

strapless 'stɹæplɪs

strappado, -es stɹæ'peĭdoŭ [-'pɑd-], -z

stratagem, -s 'stɹætədʒəm [-tɪdʒ-, -dʒɪm], -z

Strato (JUL) 'stɹeĭtoŭ

straw, -s, -y 'stɹɔ, -z, -ɨ

stray, -s, -ing, -ed 'stɹeĭ, -z, -ɪŋ, -d

stream, -s, -ing, -ed, -er/s 'stɹim, -z, -ɪŋ, -d, -ɚ/z

strength, -s; -less 'stɹeŋθ [-ŋkθ], -s; -lɪs

stretch, -es, -ing, -ed, -er/s 'stɹetʃ, -ɪz, -ɪŋ, -t, -ɚ/z

stretch-mouthed 'stɹetʃˌmaŭðd [-ˌmaŭθt]

strew, -s, -ing/s, -ed, -n 'stɹu, -z, -ɪŋ/z, -d, -n

strewment, -s 'stɹumənt, -s

strict, -er, -est, -ly, -ness 'stɹɪkt, -ɚ, -ɪst, -lɪ, -nɪs

stricture, -s 'stɹɪktʃɚ, -z

strid|e, -es, -ing, -er/s, strode, stridden 'stɹaĭd, -z, -ɪŋ, -ɚ/z, 'stɹoŭd, 'stɹɪdn̩

strik|e, -es, -ing/ly, struck, stricken 'stɹaĭk, -s, -ɪŋ/lɪ, 'stɹʌk, 'stɹɪkən

striker, -s 'stɹaĭkɚ, -z

string, -s, -ing, -ed, strung 'stɹɪŋ, -z, -ɪŋ, -d, 'stɹʌŋ

stringless 'stɹɪŋlɪs

strip|e, -es, -ing, -ed 'stɹaĭp, -s, -ɪŋ, -t

stripling, -s 'stɹɪplɪŋ, -z

striv|e, -es, -ing, -ed, strove, striven 'stɹaĭv, -z, -ɪŋ, -d, 'stɹoŭv, 'stɹɪvən

stroken (obscure var. of strucken, q.v.) 'stɹoŭkən

strond, -s 'stɹɒnd, -z

strong-barred 'stɹɒŋˌbɑɹ̃d

strong-bonded 'stɹɒŋˌbɒndɪd

strong-framed 'stɹɒŋˌfɹeĭmd

strong-hearted 'stɹɒŋˌfiɑɹ̃tɪd

strong-necked 'stɹɒŋˌnekt

strong-tempered 'stɹɒŋˌtempɚd

strong-winged 'stɹɒŋˌwɪŋd

strook (archaic form of struck) 'stɹʊk

strooken (archaic form of p.p. from strike) 'stɹʊkən

strosser (trouser), -s 'stɹɒsɚ, -z

strove (p.t. of strive, q.v.) 'stɹoŭv

(')stroyed (obsolete, archaic form, or aphaeretic form of destroyed) 'stɹɔĭd

strucken (archaic form of p.p. from strike) 'stɹʌkən

strumpet, -s, -ed 'stɹʌmpɪt, -s, -ɪd

strung (p.t. and p.p. of string, q.v.) 'stɹʌŋ

stubb|le, -ly 'stʌb|l̩, -lɨ [-lɪ]

stubble-land 'stʌblˌlænd

stubborn, -er, -est, -ly, -ness 'stʌbɚn, -ɚ, -ɪst, -lɪ, -nɪs

stubborn-chaste 'stʌbɚn'tʃeĭst ['--ˌ-]

stubborn-hard 'stʌbɚn'hɑɹ̃d ['--ˌ-]

stuck (p.t. of stick [v.], q.v.) 'stʌk

stud, -s, -ding, -ded 'stʌd, -z, -ɪŋ, -ɪd

studio, -s 'stjudɪoŭ, -z

stuff, -s, -ing, -ed; -y, -ier, -iest, -ily, -iness 'stʌf, -s, -ɪŋ, -t; -ɨ, -ɪɚ, -ɪɪst, -ɪlɨ, -ɪnɪs

stumb|le, -les, -ling, led, -ler/s 'stʌmb|l̩, -l̩z, -lɪŋ [-l̩ɪŋ], -l̩d, -lɚ/z [-l̩ɚ/z]

stump, -s, -ing, -ed; -y, -ier, -iest, -iness 'stʌmp, -s, -ɪŋ, -t; -ɨ, -ɪɚ, -ɪɪst, -ɪnɪs

stun, -s, -ning/ly, -ned 'stʌn, -z, -ɪŋ/lɨ, -d

stung (p.t. and p.p. of sting, q.v.) 'stʌŋ

stunk (p.t. and p.p. of stink, q.v.) 'stʌŋk

stupe|fy, -fies, -fying, -fied 'stjupɪ|faĭ, -faĭz, -faĭɪŋ, -faĭd

stupid, -s, -er, -est, -ly, -ness 'stjupɪd, -z, -ɚ, -ɪst, -lɪ, -nɪs

stupidit|y, -ies stju'pɪdɪt|ɨ, -ɨz

stuprum (L.) (TIT, IV.i.78) 'stupɹʊm

sturd|y, -ier, -iest, -ily, -iness 'stɝd|ɨ, -ɪɚ, -ɪɪst, -ɪlɨ, -ɪnɪs

st|y, -ies 'st|aĭ, -aĭz

Stygian (TC) 'stɪdʒɪən, -dʒjən

styl|e, -es, -ing, -ed 'staĭl, -z, -ɪŋ, -d

Styx (TC, TIT) 'stɪks

subcontract (s.), -s ˌsʌb'kɒntɹækt, -s

sub(-)contract (*v.*), **-s, -ing, -ed**
ˌsʌbkən'tɹækt, -s, -ɪŋ, -ɪd

subdu|e, -es, -ing, -ed, -er/s, -ement/s
səb'dju, -z, -ɪŋ, -d, -ɚ/z, -mənt/s
*Note.—Some might opt to give 'subdued'
primary stress on the first syllable, i.e.,*
['sʌbdjud], *in* OTH, V.ii.349 *(cf.* **secure***)*

subject (*s., adj.*), **-s** 'sʌbdʒɪkt [-dʒekt], -s
Note.—In KJ, II.ii.14, *one could argue
that 'subject' is meant to have primary
stress on the second syllable, i.e.,*
[səb'dʒekt], *because there is cause to
believe that in this instance 'subject' is
not working as an adjective—one who is
under the power or authority of
another—but as the past tense of the
verb. S. employs this method of '-ed'
omission elsewhere for euphony, and not
infrequently (cf. Abbott's* A Shakespearian Grammar, *§§ 341, 342). Although
the line's meaning varies only slightly
depending on which form of 'subject'
one chooses, it's the difference of having
either a verse line in complete iambic
pentameter or one containing a trochee
in the fourth foot following a caesura,
which is also often the case in S.*

subject (*v.*), **-s, -ing, -ed** səb'dʒekt, -s, -ɪŋ,
-ed

subjection səb'dʒekʃn̩

subjective, -ly, -ness səb'dʒektɪv, -lɪ,
-nɪs

subjectivity ˌsʌbdʒek'tɪvɪtɪ

submission, -s səb'mɪʃn̩, -z

submissive, -ly, -ness səb'mɪsɪv, -lɪ, -nɪs

submit, -s, -ting, -ted səb'mɪt, -s, -ɪŋ, -ɪd

subordinate (*s., adj.*), **-s; -ly** sə'bɔɚ-dn̩ɪt,
-s; -lɪ

subordinat|e (*v.*), **-es, -ing, -ed**
sə'bɔɚ-dn̩eɪt, -s, -ɪŋ, -ɪd

subordination, -s sə,bɔɚ-dn̩'eɪʃn̩, -z

suborn, -s, -ing, -ed, -er/s sʌ'bɔɚ-n, -z,
-ɪŋ, -d, -ɚ/z

subornation (S.) ˌsʌbɔɚ-'neɪʃn̩

subpoena, -s, -ing, -ed səb'pinə, -z, -ɪŋ,
-d

subscrib|e, -es, -ing, -ed, -er/s səb'skɹaɪb,
-z, -ɪŋ, -d, -ɚ/z

subscription, -s səb'skɹɪpʃn̩, -z

subsequent, -ly, -ness 'sʌbsɪkwənt, -lɪ,
-nɪs
*Note.—Given primary stress on the
second syllable, i.e.,* [sʌb'sikwənt] *in*
TC, I.iii.344

subsist, -s, -ing, -ed; -ence sʌb'sɪst [səb-],
-s, -ɪŋ, -ɪd; -əns

substance, -s 'sʌbstəns [-bzt-], -ɪz

substractors səb'stɹæktɚz
Note.—C. T. Onions calls this word in
TN, I.iii.34 *a perversion of 'detractors,'
yet it might be purposeful since
'substract' is simply an obsolete, archaic
form of 'subtract,' and which still suits
the meaning of the line*

subt|le, -ler, -lest, -ly, -leness 'sʌt|l̩, -l̩ɚ
[-lə-], -l̩ɪst [-lɪst], -lɪ, -l̩nɪs

subtle-potent 'sʌtl̩ˌpoŭtn̩t

subtlet|y, -ies 'sʌtl̩t|ɪ, -ɪz

subtract, -s, -ing, -ed səb'tɹækt, -s, -ɪŋ,
-ɪd

subtraction, -s səb'tɹækʃn̩, -z

suburb, -s 'sʌbɜ-b, -z

subversion, -s sʌb'vɜ-ʒn̩ [səb-], -z

succeed, -s, -ing, -ed, -er/s sək'sid, -z,
-ɪŋ, -ɪd, -ɚ/z

success, -es; -ful, -fully sək'ses, -ɪz; -fʊl,
-fʊlɪ
Note.—Stressed on the first syllable in
TNK, I.i.209, *i.e.,* ['sʌkses] *(cf.*
successor *in* WT, V.i.48 *and* **successive**
in MEAS, II.ii.99*)*

succession, -s sək'seʃn̩, -z

successive, -ly sək'sesɪv, -lɪ
*Note.—Stressed primarily on the first
syllable in* MEAS, II.ii.99, *i.e.,*
['sʌksesɪv] *(cf.* **successor** *in* HVIII, I.i.60
and WT, V.i.48*)*

successor, -s sək'sesɚ, -z

Note.—In HVIII, I.i.60 *and* WT, V.i.48, *this word is given primary stress on the first syllable, i.e.,* ['sʌksesəˈ] *(cf.* successive *in* MEAS, II.ii.99*)*

succinct, -ly, -ness sək'sɪŋkt [sʌk-], -lɪ, -nɪs

succor, -s, -ing, -ed 'sʌkəˈ, -z, -ɹɪŋ, -d

succumb, -s, -ing, -ed sə'kʌm, -z, -ɪŋ, -d

such 'sʌtʃ

Such-a-one, Lord (HAM) 'lɔɚ̃d 'sʌtʃəˌwʌn

suck, -s, -ing, -ed, -er/s 'sʌk, -s, -ɪŋ, -t, -əˈ/z

suction 'sʌkʃn̩

sudden, -est, -ly, -ness 'sʌdn̩, -ɪst, -lɪ, -nɪs

su|e, -es, -ing, -ed 'sju, -z, -ɪŋ, -d

sued-for 'sjudˌfɔɚ̃

suff|er, -ers, -ering, -ered, -erer/s; -erable 'sʌf|əˈ, -əˈz, -əɹɪŋ, -əˈd, -əɹəˈ/z; -əɹəbl̩

sufferance, -s 'sʌfəɹəns ['sʌfɹəns], -ɪz

suffic|e, -es, -ing, -ed sə'faɪs, -ɪz, -ɪŋ, -t

sufficien|cy, -t/ly sə'fɪʃn̩|sɪ, -t/lɪ

suffigance 'sʌfɪdʒəns, -fɪgəns

Note.—This is Dogberry's illiterate corruption of 'suffisance' (obsolete word meaning 'sufficient') in ADO, III.v.48. *Some editors erroneously suggest that 'suffigance' is merely a corruption of 'sufficient,' leading them to mistakenly assert that the syllabic stress is in the second rather than first syllable*

suffocat|e, -es, -ing/ly, -ed 'sʌfəkeɪt, -s, -ɪŋ/lɪ, -ɪd

Note.—['sʌfəkɪt] *(p.p.) in* 2HVI, I.i.123; TC, I.iii.125

suffocation ˌsʌfə'keɪʃn̩

Suffolk (HV, *1HVI, 2HVI,* 3HVI, *HVIII*) 'sʌfək

suffrage, -s 'sʌfɹɪdʒ, -ɪz

sugar, -s, -ing, -ed 'ʃʊgəˈ, -z, -ɹɪŋ, -d

sugar-candy 'ʃʊgəˈˌkændɪ

Sugarsop (TS) 'ʃʊgəˈsɒp

suggest, -s, -ing, -ed səg'dʒest, -s, -ɪŋ, -ɪd

suggestion, -s səg'dʒestʃən, -z

suggestive, -ly, -ness səg'dʒestɪv, -lɪ, -nɪs

suit, -s, -ing, -ed, -or/s 'sut ['sjut], -s, -ɪŋ, -ɪd, -əˈ/z

suitab|le, -ly, -leness 'suɾəb|l̩ ['sju-], -lɪ, -l̩nɪs

sullen, -ly, -ness 'sʌlən, -lɪ, -nɪs

sull|y, -ies, -ying, -ied 'sʌl|ɪ, -ɪz, -ɪɪŋ, -ɪd

sulphur 'sʌlfəˈ

sulphurous [-lfur-] 'sʌlfəɹəs ['sʌlfjʊɚ̃ɹəs, sʌl'fjʊɚ̃ɹəs]

sultr|y, -ier, -iest, -ily, -iness 'sʌltɹ|ɪ, -ɪəˈ, -ɪɪst, -ɪlɪ, -ɪnɪs

sum, -s, -ming, -med 'sʌm, -z, -ɪŋ, -d

sumless 'sʌmlɪs

summer (S.), **-s, -ed; -time** 'sʌməˈ, -z, -d; -taɪm

summer-seeming 'sʌməˈsimɪŋ

summer-swelling 'sʌməˈswelɪŋ

sumpter, -s 'sʌmptəˈ, -z

sumptuous, -ly, -ness 'sʌmptʃʊəs, -lɪ, -nɪs

sun, -s, -ning, -ned 'sʌn, -z, -ɪŋ, -d

sunbeam, -s 'sʌnbim

sun-bright 'sʌnˌbɹaɪt

sunburn, -s, -ing, -ed, -t 'sʌnbɝ̃n, -z, -ɪŋ, -d, -t

Sunday (ADO, HAM, 1HIV, TC), **-s** 'sʌndɪ [-deɪ], -z

sunder, -s, -ing, -ed 'sʌndəˈ, -z, -ɹɪŋ, -d

sundry 'sʌndɹɪ

sun-expelling 'sʌnɪkˌspelɪŋ

sunn|y, -ier, -iest, -ily, -iness 'sʌn|ɪ, -ɪəˈ, -ɪɪst, -ɪlɪ, -ɪnɪs

sunrise, -s 'sʌnɹaɪz, -ɪz

sun-rising 'sʌn'ɹaɪzɪŋ

sunset, -s 'sʌnset, -s ([ˌ-ˈ-] *in* KJ, III.i.36)

sunshine 'sʌnʃaɪn

sup, -s, -ping, -ped 'sʌp, -s, -ɪŋ, -t

super-dainty ˌsupəˈ'deɪntɪ [ˌsjup-]

superfluit|y, -ies ˌsupəˈ'fluɪt|ɪ [ˌsjup-], -ɪz

superfluous, -ly, -ness su'pɝ̃fluəs [sju'p-, sʊ'p-, sjʊ'p-], -lɪ, -nɪs

superflux 'supəˈflʌks ['sjup-]

supernal (*celestial, divine*) su'pɝ̃nl̩ [sju'p-]

superprais|e, -es, -ing, -ed 'supəˈˌpɹeɪz ['sjup-], -ɪz, -ɪŋ, -d

superscript, -s 'supəˈskɹɪpt ['sjup-], -s

superscription 'supəˈskɹɪpʃn̩ ['sjup-]

super-serviceable 'supəˈsɝ̃vɪsəbl̩ ['sjup-]

superstition, -s ˌsupəˈ'stɪʃn̩ ['sjup-]

superstitious, -ly, -ness ˌsupəˈ'stɪʃəs, ['sjup-], -lɪ, -nɪs

supervis|e, -es, -ing, -ed, -or/s 'supəˑvaĭz
['sjup-], -ɪz, -ɪŋ, -d, - əˑ/z
supervision, -s ˌsupəˑ'vɪʒn̩ [ˌsjup-], -z
supper, -s 'sʌpəˑ, -z
supper-time, -s 'sʌpəˑˌtaĭm, -z
supplant, -s, -ing, -ed, -er/s səˈplant, -s,
-ɪŋ, -ɪd, -əˑ/z
supp|le, -ler, -lest; -leness, -ly 'sʌp|l̩, -ləˑ,
-l̩ɪst [-lɪst]; -l̩nɪs, -lɨ
suppliance səˈplaĭəns
suppliant, -s, -ly 'sʌplɪənt, -s, -lɨ
supplicant, -s 'sʌplɪkənt, -s
supplication, -s ˌsʌplɪˈkeĭʃn, -z
suppl|y, -ies, -ying, -ied, -ier/s səˈpl|aĭ,
-aĭz, -aĭɪŋ, -aĭd, -aĭəˑ/z
supplyant səˈplaĭənt
supplyment səˈplaĭmənt
support, -s, -ing, -ed, -er/s; -able
səˈpɔˑ̆t, -s, -ɪŋ, -ɪd, -əˑ/z; -əbl̩
supportance səˈpɔˑ̆tn̩s [-təns]
supposal, -s səˈpoŭsl̩, -z
supposedly səˈpoŭzɪdlɨ
supposition, -s ˌsʌpʊˈzɪʃn, -z
suppress, -es, -ing, -ed, -or/s səˈpɹes, -ɪz,
-ɪŋ, -t, -əˑ/z
supression, -s səˈpɹeʃn, -z
supremac|y, -ies sjuˈpɹeməs|ɨ [sʊˈp-], -ɨz
supreme, -ly, -ness sjuˈpɹim [sʊˈp-], -lɨ,
-nɪs
Note.—Stressed on the first syllable
['sjupɹim] *in* COR, V.iii.71; 1HVI,
I.iii.57; RIII, II.i.13, III.vii.117; CYM,
I.vii.4; KJ, III.i.81; LUC, 780; VA, 996
sur-addition 'sɜˑɹəˌdɪʃn̩
surance (*pledge, guarantee*) 'ʃʊəˑɹəns
surceas|e, -es, -ing, -ed sɜˑ'sis, -ɪz, -ɪŋ, -t
sure, -r, -st, -ly, -ness 'ʃʊəˑ, -ɹəˑ, -ɹɪst, -lɨ,
-nɪs
Surecard (2HIV) 'ʃʊəˑˌkɑˑ̆d
suret|y, -ies 'ʃʊəˑɹɪtɨ ['ʃʊəˑtɨ], -z
surety-like 'ʃʊəˑɹɪtɨˌlaĭk ['ʃʊəˑtɨ-]
surfeit, -s, -ing, -ed, -er/s 'sɜˑfɪt, -s, -ɪŋ,
-ɪd, -əˑ/z
surfeit-swelled 'sɜˑfɪtˌsweld

surg|e, -es, -ing, -ed 'sɜˑdʒ, -ɪz, -ɪŋ, -d
Surgeon, Dick (TN) 'dɪk 'sɜˑdʒən
surgeon, -s 'sɜˑdʒən, -z
surger|y, -ies 'sɜˑdʒəˑɹ|ɨ, -ɨz
surl|y, -ier, -iest, -iness 'sɜˑl|ɨ, -ɪəˑ, -ɹɪst,
-ɪnɪs
sur mes genoux (*Fr.*) (HV, IV.iv.55) sʌ́
mɛ ʒʊnju
surmise (*s.*), **-s** sɜˑ'maĭz ['sɜˑm-], -ɪz
surmis|e (*v.*), **-es, -ing, -ed** sɜˑ'maĭz
[səˑ'm-], -ɪz, -ɪŋ, -d
surmount, -s, -ing, -ed; -able sɜˑ'maʊnt,
-s, -ɪŋ, -ɪd; -əbl̩
surnam|e (*s., v.*), **-es, -ing, -ed** 'sɜˑneĭm,
-z, -ɪŋ, -d
Note.—Given primary stress on the
second syllable in COR, II.iii.241, *i.e.,*
[sɜˑ'neĭmd], *and arguably also in* TIT,
I.i.23, *i.e.,* [sɜˑ'neĭmɪd]
surpass, -es, -ing/ly, -ed; -able sɜˑ'pas,
-ɪz, -ɪŋ/lɨ, -t; -əbl̩
surplice, -s, -d 'sɜˑplɪs, -ɪz, -t
surplus, -es 'sɜˑpləs [-plʌs], -ɪz
sur-reined (*overridden*) 'sɜˑˌɹeĭnd
Surrey (*2HIV, HVIII, RII, RIII*) 'sʌɹɨ
survey (*s.*), **-s** 'sɜˑveĭ, -z ([--] *in* ALL'S,
V.iii.16; 1HIV, V.iv.81; TIT, I.i.451)
survey (*v.*), **-s, -ing, -ed** sɜˑ'veĭ ['--], -z,
-ɪŋ, -d
surviv|e, -es, -ing, -ed, -or/s; -al/s
səˑ'vaĭv, -z, -ɪŋ, -d, -əˑ/z; -l̩/z
Susan (RJ) 'suzn̩
suspect (*s.*), **-s** 'sʌspekt, -s
Note.—The word 'suspect' in S. can
sometimes stand for the word 'suspi-
cion' and be stressed [-'-], *e.g.,* COM,
III.i.87; RIII, I.iii.89, III.v.32; Sonn.
70.3,13; TIM, IV.iii.516
suspect (*v.*), **-s, -ing, -ed** səˈspekt, -s, -ɪŋ,
-ɪd
suspend, -s, -ing, -ed, -er/s səˈspend, -z,
-ɪŋ, -ɪd, -əˑ/z
suspense səˈspens
suspiration, -s ˌsʌspɪˈɹeĭʃn̩, -z

---

i w**e** ɨ c**i**ty ɪ h**i**t e l**e**t ɛ d**e**but æ c**a**n a p**a**ss ɜˑ b**ir**d ʌ h**u**t ə **a**gain əˑ supp**er** u y**ou**
ʊ sh**ou**ld o **o**bey ɔ **aw**l ɒ c**o**p ɑ f**a**ther eĭ p**ai**d aĭ h**igh** oŭ g**o** ɔĭ v**oi**ce aŭ f**ou**nd ɪɔˑ **ear**
ɛɔˑ **air** ʊɔˑ p**oor** ɔɔˑ f**or**k ɑɔˑ p**ar**k aĭɔˑ f**ire** aŭɔˑ h**our** b **b**oy p **p**it d **d**og t **t**op g g**o**t
k **k**id h **h**ow fi be**h**ave dʒ **j**ot tʃ **ch**ew z **z**any s **s**oft v **v**at f **f**at ʒ trea**s**ure ʃ **sh**ip ð **th**e
θ **th**in m **m**an n **n**o ŋ ha**ng** l **l**ip j **y**es w **w**on ʍ **wh**ew ɹ **r**igger, ai**r**y ɾ ma**tt**er

suspir|e, -es, -ing, -ed səˈspaɪɚ, -z, -ɹɪŋ, -d

sustain, -s, -ing, -ed; -able səˈsteɪn, -z, -ɪŋ, -d; -əbl̩

sustenance ˈsʌstɪnəns

sutler, -s ˈsʌtlɚ, -z

Sutton Co'fil' (1HIV) ˈsʌtn̩ ˈkoŏfɪl

suum cuique (*L.*) (TIT, I.i.284) ˈsuʊm kuˈikwɛ

suum, mun, nonny ˈsuʊm ˈmun [ˈmʊn] ˈnɒnɨ

Note.—This phrase in LEAR, III.iv.97 (Folio)—one of the most mysterious in S.—is unexplained, and is generally defined as 'a sound imitating the rushing wind,' a somewhat insufficient explication considering the fact that each word in the phrase is comprehensible language. Whether or not it is intended, the word 'Suum' is L. for 'one's own,' or 'free,' and S. uses the word elsewhere (TIT, I.i.284) in the L. phrase 'suum cuique' ('to each man his due'). The word 'mun' is used nowhere else in S., but is, nevertheless, a very old word in English, with several possible interpretations. Some of the more helpful ones are: a var. form of 'mone' meaning 'to remember, to bear in mind'; a word standing for any one of many pronouns, including 'them,' 'him,' 'it,' etc.; or a dialectal var. of 'man' (cf. OED, 'MAN' sb. 1 4 e.), used here as a vocative to indicate not only the one being addressed, but with an implication of annoyance or impatience, perhaps used even as a meaningless expletive. The word 'nonny' is the familiar catch-all refrain (or burden) to jingles and ditties of the time, and some editors italicize 'Still through . . . trot by' (LEAR, III.iv.96–98) to indicate that 'suum, mun, nonny' is contained within a song. If the phrase is indeed to stand for the sound of rushing wind, then there is certainly a message borne on the wind. It is also worthwhile bearing in mind that Poor Tom (Edgar's persona in this part of the play) is given

to 'lunatic bans, prayers, and roaring voices'

swab, -s, -bing, -bed, -ber/s ˈswɒb, -z, -ɪŋ, -d, -ɚ/z

swadd|le, -les, -ling, -led ˈswɒd|l̩, -l̩z, -lɪŋ [-l̩ɪŋ], -l̩d

swag ˈswæg

swag-bellied ˈswæg͵belɪd

swagger, -s, -ing/ly, -ed, -er/s ˈswægɚ, -z, -ɹɪŋ/lɨ, -d, -ɹɚ/z

swain, -s ˈsweɪn, -z

swallow, -s, -ing, -ed ˈswɒloŏ, -z, -ɪŋ, -d

swamp, -s, -ing, -ed; -y, -ier, -iest, -iness ˈswɒmp, -s, -ɪŋ, -t; -ɨ, -ɪɚ, -ɪɪst, -ɪnɪs

swan, -s ˈswɒn, -z

swap, -s, -ping, -ped ˈswɒp, -s, -ɪŋ, -t

sware (*archaic p.t. of* **swear**) ˈswɛɚ

swarm, -s, -ing, -ed ˈswɔɚm, -z, -ɪŋ, -d

swart ˈswɔɚt

swart-complexioned ˈswɔɚtkəm͵plekʃn̩d

swarth (*var. of* **swath[e]***; width of the lane of scythed grass or grain*)**, -s** ˈswɔɚθ, -s [ˈswɔɚð, -z]

swarth|y, -ier, -iest, -ily, -iness ˈswɔɚð|ɨ, -ɪɚ, -ɪɪst, -ɪlɨ, -ɪnɪs

swash, -es, -ing, -ed, -er/s ˈswɒʃ, -ɪz, -ɪŋ, -t, -ɚ/z

swath, -s ˈswɒθ [ˈswɔθ], -s [ˈswɒðz, ˈswɔðz]

swathing-clothes ˈsweɪðɪŋ͵kloŏðz

Note.—The OED prefers [ˈsweɪðɪŋ] *from 'swathe'* [ˈsweɪð]*, but the term's kinship to 'swathling/swaddling' (cf.* **swathling***) is so close that a pronunciation of* [ˈswɒðɪŋ͵kloŏðz] *would not be considered unreasonable*

swathling ˈswɒðl̩ɪŋ

Note.—The term 'swathling clothes' is found in 1HIV, III.ii.112, and is an alt. form of 'swaddling clothes.' Its pronunciation is analogous to 'murther/murder,' 'fathom/fadom,' etc. (see Note for **murther***). In other words, by dentalizing the 'th' (*[ð̪]*), it is remarkably close to a 'd' (*[d]*), and thus very close to the more familiar 'swaddling'*

sway, -s, -ing, -ed ˈsweɪ, -z, -ɪŋ, -d

swear, -s, -ing/s, swore, sworn,

swearer/s 'swɛɚ, -z, -ɹɪŋ/z, 'swɔɚ,
'swɔɚn, 'swɛɚɹɚ/z
sweat, -s, -ing, -ed; -y 'swet, -s, -ɪŋ, -ɪd;
-ɨ
sweaten (*irregular p.p. of v.* sweat; *see*
eaten) 'swetn̩
sweater, -s 'sweɾɚ, -z
sweep, -s, -ing/s, swept, sweeper/s 'swip,
-s, -ɪŋ/z, 'swept, 'swipɚ/z
sweet, -s; -er, -est, -ly, -ness 'swit, -s; -ɚ,
-ɪst, -lɨ, -nɪs
sweet-faced 'swit͜feɪst
sweet-favored 'swit͜feɪvɚd
Sweetheart (LEAR) 'switfiɑɚt
sweet(-)heart, -s 'swit͜hɑɚt, -s
sweeting, -s 'switɪŋ, -z
sweetmeat, -s 'switmit, -s
sweet-suggesting 'switsəɡˌdʒestɪŋ
swell, -s, -ing/s, -ed, swollen 'swel, -z,
-ɪŋ/z, -d, 'swoŭlən
swelter, -s, -ing/ly, -ed 'sweltɚ, -z,
-ɹɪŋ/lɨ, -d
Sweno (MAC) 'swinoŭ ['svɛːnoŭ]
swept (*p.t. of* sweep, *q.v.*) 'swept
swerv|e, -es, -ing, -ed 'swɜˑv, -z, -ɪŋ, -d
swift, -er, -est, -ly, -ness 'swɪft, -ɚ, -ɪst,
-lɨ, -nɪs
swill, -s, -ing, -ed 'swɪl, -z, -ɪŋ, -d
swim, -s, -ming/ly, swam, swum 'swɪm,
-z, -ɪŋ/lɨ, 'swæm, 'swʌm
swimmer, -s 'swɪmɚ, -z
swindged (*p.t. var. of* swinge, *q.v.,*
meaning 'thrashed' or 'beaten')
'swɪndʒd
swine 'swaɪn
swine(-)herd, -s 'swaɪnfiɚd, -z
swing|e, -es, -ing, -ed, -er/s 'swɪndʒ, -ɪz,
-ɪŋ, -d, -ɚ/z
swinge-buckler, -s 'swɪndʒˌbʌklɚ, -z
swinish, -ness 'swaɪnɪʃ, -nɪs
Swinstead (KJ) 'swɪnsted
Swithold (LEAR) 'swɪðəld
Note.—This name in LEAR, III.iv.117 *is*
taken to be a contr. of 'St. Withold'

Switzer (HAM), -s 'swɪtsɚ, -z
Switzerland 'swɪtsɚlənd
swoln (*var. spelling of p.p. and participial*
adj. from swell, *q.v.*) 'swoŭln
swoon, -s, -ing, -ed 'swun, -z, -ɪŋ, -d
swoonded (*cf.* swound) 'swundɪd
swoopstake, -s 'swupsteɪk, -s
sword, -s 'sɔɚd, -z
sword-and-buckler ˌsɔɚdənd'bʌklɚ
[-dn̩'b-]
sworder, -s 'sɔɚdɚ, -z
swound (*to swoon*), -s, -ed 'swund, -z,
-ɪd
'swounds (*contr. of God's wounds*)
'zwundz
sycamore, -s 'sɪkəmɔɚ, -z
Sycorax (TEM) 'sɪkəɹæks
Syenna *or* Sien(n)a (CYM) sɪ'enə
Sylla (2HVI) 'sɪlə
syllable, -s 'sɪləbl̩, -z
syllogism, -s 'sɪləŭdʒɪzəm [-ədʒ-], -z
sylvan 'sɪlvən
symbol, -s 'sɪmbl̩, -z
symbolism 'sɪmbl̩ɪzm̩ [-bʊlɪ-]
sympathetic, -al, -ally ˌsɪmpə'θeɾɪk, -l̩,
-əlɨ
sympathiz|e, -es, -ing, -ed 'sɪmpəθaɪz,
-ɪz, -ɪŋ, -d
sympath|y, -ies 'sɪmpəθ|ɨ, -ɨz
synod, -s 'sɪnəd, -z
syntax, -es 'sɪntæks, -ɪz
Syracusa (COM) ˌsɪɹɑ'kuzɑ
Syracuse (COM) 'sɪɹəkjuz ['saɪɚɹ-]
Syracusian (COM), -s ˌsɪɹə'kjuzjən, -z
Syria (AC, PER), -n/s 'sɪɹɪə, -n/z, 'sɪɹɪ̆ə,
-ɹɪ̆ən/z
Note.—In PER, I.chorus.19, 20,
'Syria' wants to rhyme with its counter-
part, 'say,' but this rhyme is nowa-
days typically forsaken (cf. Note for
Asia*)*
Syria, Lower (AC) 'loŭɚ 'sɪɹə
syrup, -s; -y 'sɪɹəp ['sɜˑɹəp], -s; -ɨ
system, -s 'sɪstəm, -z

i wɛ ɨ cityy ɪ hɪt e lɛt ɛ dɛbut æ can a pass ɜˑ bird ʌ hut ə again ɚ supper u you
ʊ should o obey ɔ awl ɒ cop ɑ father eɪ paid aɪ high oŭ go ɔɪ voice aŭ found ɪɚ ear
ɛɚ air ʊɚ poor ɔɚ fork ɑɚ park aɪɚ fire aŭɚ hour b boy p pit d dog t top g got
k kid h how fi behave dʒ jot tʃ chew z zany s soft v vat f fat ʒ treasure ʃ ship ð the
θ thin m man n no ŋ hang l lip j yes w won ʍ whew ɹ rigger, airy ɾ matter

Tt

T (*the letter*), **-'s** 'tiː, -z
ta (*obsolete, dialectal form of 'thou'*) 'tɑ
  Note.—This word in 2HIV, II.i.56 *is in
  the phrase 'wot ta,' meaning 'wilt not
  thou'*
tab, -s 'tæb, -z
taber (*from 'taper'*) 'teĭbɚ (*see* **prings**)
tabernacle, -s 'tæbɚnækl̩, -z
tab|le, -es, -ling, -led 'teĭb|l̩, -l̩z, -l̩ɪŋ
  [-lɪŋ], -l̩d
table-book, -s 'teĭbl̩ˌbʊk, -s
tablespoon, -s 'teĭbl̩spun, -z
table-sport 'teĭbl̩ˌspɔɚt
tablet, -s 'tæblɪt, -s
taboo, -s tə'bu [tæ'bu], -z
tabor, -s, -er/s 'teĭbɚ [-bɔɚ], -z, -ɹɚ/z
taborine *or* **tabourine, -s** ˌteĭbɚ'ɹin, -z
taborins 'teĭbɚɹɪnz
tabulat|e, -es, -ing, -ed, -or/s 'tæbjʊleĭt,
  -s, -ɪŋ, -ɪd, -ɚ/z
tabulation, -s ˌtæbjʊ'leĭʃn̩, -z
tacit, -ly, -ness 'tæsɪt, -lɪ, -nɪs
taciturn, -ly 'tæsɪtɝn, -lɪ
taciturnity ˌtæsɪ'tɝnɪtɪ
tack, -s, -ing, -ed 'tæk, -s, -ɪŋ, -t
tack|le, -les, -ling/s, -led, -ler/s 'tæk|l̩,
  -l̩z, -l̩ɪŋ/z [-lɪŋ/z], -l̩d, -l̩ɚ/z [-lɚ/z]
tact 'tækt
tactless, -ly, -ness 'tæktlɪs, -lɪ, -nɪs
tadpole, -s 'tædpoŭl, -z
ta'en (*from* **taken**) 'teĭn
taffeta 'tæfɪtə [-fɪɾ̬ə]
taffety 'tæfɪtɪ
tag, -s, -ging, -ged 'tæg, -z, -ɪŋ, -d
tag(-)rag 'tægˌɹæg
tail, -s, -ing, -ed; -less 'teĭl, -z, -ɪŋ, -d; -lɪs
tailor, -s, -ing, -ed 'teĭlɚ, -z, -ɹɪŋ, -d
tailor's-yard 'teĭlɚzˌjɑɚd
taint, -s, -ing, -ed; -less 'teĭnt, -s, -ɪŋ, -ɪd;
  -lɪs
taintingly 'teĭntɪŋlɪ
  *Note.—This is probably an error for
  'tauntingly' in* COR, I.i.108
tainture 'teĭntʃɚ
tak|e, -es, -ing, took, taken 'teĭk, -s, -ɪŋ,
  'tʊk, 'teĭkən

take-a 'teĭkə (*see* **dat**)
taker, -s 'teĭkɚ, -z
taking-off ˌteĭkɪŋ'ɒf
Talbonites (1HVI) 'tɒlbənaĭts ['tæl-]
Talbot (HV, *1HVI*, RIII) 'tɒlbət ['tæl-]
Talbot, John (*1HVI*) 'dʒɒn 'tɒlbət ['tæl-]
Talbot, Sir Gilbert (RIII) ˌsɝ 'gɪlbɚt
  'tɒlbət ['tæl-]
talc 'tælk
tale, -s 'teĭl, -z
talent, -s, -ed, -less 'tælənt, -s, -ɪd, -lɪs
Tale(-)porter, Mistress (WT) 'mɪstɹɪs
  'teĭlˌpɔɚtɚ
talk, -s, -ing, -ed, -er/s 'tɔk, -s, -ɪŋ, -t,
  -ɚ/z
tall, -er, -est, -ness 'tɔl, -ɚ, -ɪst, -nɪs
Tallow (1HIV) 'tæloŭ
  *Note.—Some editors assert that this is a
  proper noun in* 1HIV, II.iv.109
tallow, -y 'tæloŭ, -ɪ
tallow-catch 'tæloŭˌkætʃ
tallow-face 'tæloŭˌfeĭs
tall|y, -ies, -ying, -ied 'tæl|ɪ, -ɪz, -ɪɪŋ, -ɪd
talon, -s 'tælən, -z
tam (*from 'tam-o'-shanter'*), **-z** 'tæm, -z
tam (*from 'dam' = 'mother'*) 'tæm
  Note.—Evans (in MWW*) is a Welshman, and speaks in a Welsh accent, if
  somewhat inconsistently. This is an
  example of S.'s direction to the actor (by
  way of semiphonetic spellings) to adopt
  such an accent, more or less, for the
  sake of wringing the most satire out of
  plays on words stemming from confusions with, and corruptions of, English
  pronunciation via the Welsh tongue*
'tame (*aphetic form of* **attame**) (*infiltrate*)
  'teĭm
**tam|e, -es, -ing, -ed, -er/s; -er, -est, -ely,
  -eness** 'teĭm, -z, -ɪŋ, -d, -ɚ/z; -ɚ, -ɪst,
  -lɪ, -nɪs
taming-school, -s 'teĭmɪŋˌskul, -z
Tamora (*TIT*) 'tæməɹə, -mɹə
Tamworth (RIII) 'tæmwɚθ
tan, -s, -ning, -ned, -ner/s 'tæn, -z, -ɪŋ,
  -d, -ɚ/z

tanling, -s 'tænlɪŋ, -z
tang, -s, -ing, -ed 'tæŋ, -z, -ɪŋ, -d
tang|le, -les, -ling, -led 'tæŋg|ḷ, -ḷz, ḷɪŋ
[-lɪŋ], -ḷd
tanling, -s 'tænlɪŋ, -z
Tantaene animis coelistibus irae (*L.*)
(2HVI, II.i.24) tɑn'tɛnɪ 'ɑnɪmus
sɛ'lɛstɪbus 'irɛ
*Note.—The pronunciation for 'coelisti-
bus' recommended above is a departure
from the normal Latin pronunciation for
this spelling, but the pronunciation given
more closely resembles 'celestial'
(something the modern ear—not
altogether familiar with Latin—stands a
chance of apprehending), which is
derived from L. 'caelestis'*
*Tanta est erga te mentis integritas Regina
serenissima* (*L.*) (HVIII, III.i.40,41)
'tɑntɑ ɛst 'ɛɚgɑ tɛ 'mɛntis in'tɛgɹitɑs
ɹɛ'dʒinɑ ˌsɛɹɛ'nisimɑ
Tantalus (LUC, VA) 'tæntələs
tap, -s, -ping, -ped 'tæp, -s, -ɪŋ, -t
tap|e, -es, -ing, -ed 'teɪp, -s, -ɪŋ, -t
taper, -s, -ing, -ed 'teɪpɚ, -z, -ɹɪŋ, -d
taper-light 'teɪpɚˌlaɪt
tapestr|y, -ies 'tæpɪstɹɪ|ɪ, -ɪz
tap(-)hou|se, -ses 'tæpfiɑʊ|s, -zɪz
tapster, -s 'tæpstɚ, -z
Tapster, Thomas (*MEAS*) ˌtɒməs 'tæpstɚ
(*also known as* **Pompey**, *q.v.*)
tar, -s, -ring, -red 'tɑɚ, -z, -ɹɪŋ, -d (*see
Note for* **tarre**)
tardied 'tɑɚdɪd
tard|y, -ier, -iest, -ily, -iness 'tɑɚd|ɪ, -ɪɚ,
-ɪɪst, -ɪlɪ, -ɪnɪs
tardy-apish ˌtɑɚdɪ'(ʔ)eɪpɪʃ
tardy-gaited 'tɑɚdɪˌgeɪtɪd
Tarentum (AC) tə'ɹentəm
targe, -s 'tɑɚdʒ, -ɪz
*Note.—The supposition of some scholars
is that the plural form may have been, at
one time, pronounced monosyllabically,
i.e.,* ['tɑɚgz], *thus reconciling the*

otherwise irregular AC, II.vi.39 *and*
CYM, V.v.5
target, -s, -ing, -ed 'tɑɚgɪt, -s, -ɪŋ, -ɪd
tarnish, -es, -ing, -ed 'tɑɚnɪʃ, -ɪz, -ɪŋ, -t
Tarpeian (COR) tɑɚ'piən
Tarquin (COR, CYM, JUL, LUC, MAC,
TIT), **-s** 'tɑɚkwɪn, -z
tarr|e, -es, -ing, -ed 'tɑɚ, -z, -ɹɪŋ, -d
*Note.—This obsolete archaic word,
meaning 'provoke' or 'incite,' appears in
KJ, IV.i.116, TC, I.iii.392, and HAM,
II.ii.351. Editors sometimes emend it
to 'tar'*
tarriance 'tæɹɪəns
tarr|y, -ies, -ying, -ied 'tæɹ|ɪ, -ɪz, -ɪŋ, -ɪd
tart, -s, -ly, -ness 'tɑɚt, -s, -lɪ, -nɪs
Tartar (ALL'S, COM, HV, MAC,
MSND, MV, MWW, RJ, TN), **-s** 'tɑɚtɚ
['tɑɚɾɚ], -z
Tarus (*AC*) 'tɔɹəs
*Note.—Though this name appears in the
list of dramatis personæ in M. R. Ridley's edition of 'Antony and Cleopatra'
for the 1993 version of* The Arden
Shakespeare *(Routledge), it is obviously
a misprint. In Ridley's earlier versions
(as well as other editors' editions) and in
the subsequent printing of* The Arden
Shakespeare Complete Works *(Thomas
Nelson and Sons Ltd. 1998), the name is
properly listed as* **Taurus**
't'as (*contr. of* **it has**) 'tæz
task, -s, -ing, -ed, -er/s 'task, -s, -ɪŋ, -t,
-ɚ/z
taskmaster, -s 'taskˌmastɚ, -z
tassel, -s, -led 'tæsḷ, -z, -d
tassel-gentle ˌtæsḷ'dʒentəl [-ntḷ]
tast|e, -es, -ing, -ed, -er/s 'teɪst, -s, -ɪŋ,
-ɪd, -ɚ/z
taste-full 'teɪstˌfʊl
tatter, -s, -ed 'tæɾɚ, -z, -d
tatt|le, -les, -ling/s, -led, -ler/s 'tæt|ḷ, -ḷz,
-ḷɪŋ/z [-lɪŋ/z], -ḷd, -ḷɚ/z [-ləɚ/z]
taught (*p.t. and p.p. of* **teach**, *q.v.*) 'tɔt

taunt, -s, -ing/ly, -ed, -er/s 'tɔnt, -s, -ɪŋ/lɪ, -ɪd, -ɚ/z

Taurus (AC, MSND, TIT, TN) 'tɔɹəs

tavern, -s 'tævɚn, -z

tavern-bill, -s 'tævɚnˌbɪl, -z

tawdr|y, -ier, -iest, -ily, -iness 'tɔdɹ|ɪ, -ɪɚ, -ɪɪst, -ɪlɪ, -ɪnɪs

tawdry-lace 'tɔdɹɪˌleɪs

tawn|y, -ier, -iest, -iness 'tɔn|ɪ, -ɪɚ, -ɪɪst, -ɪnɪs

tawny-finned 'tɔnɪˌfɪnd

tax, -es, -ing, -ed 'tæks, -ɪz, -ɪŋ, -t

taxation, -s tæk'seɪʃn, -z

teach, -es, -ing/s, taught, teacher/s 'titʃ, -ɪz, -ɪŋ/z, 'tɔt, 'titʃɚ/z

tear (*lachrymal fluid*), **-s, -ing, -ed** 'tɪɚ, -z, -ɹɪŋ, -d

Note.—*In Frank Kermode's (editor, The Arden Shakespeare, 1958) annotation for TEM, I.ii.53, there is a brief but valuable discussion about monosyllabic words that sometimes receive the value of two metric beats in S. lines of verse "whether or no it is [they are] pronounced disyllabically . . ." In TIT, V.iii.155, 'tear' is arguably pronounced disyllabically or given, as Kermode puts it, "a heavy emphasis." Cf. Abbott's* A Shakespearian Grammar, *§§ 475, 479, 484*

tear (*rip or rend into pieces*), **-s, -ing, tore, torn** 'tɛɚ, -z, -ɹɪŋ, 'tɔɚ, 'tɔɚn

tear-distained 'tɪɚdɪ'steɪnɪd

tear-falling 'tɪɚˌfɔlɪŋ

Tearsheet, Doll (*2HIV, HV*) 'dɔl 'tɛɚʃit

teat, -s 'tit, -s

Te Deum (*L.*) (HV, IV.viii.124) tɛ 'dɛʊm

tediosity ˌtidɪ'ɒsɪtɪ

tedious, -ly, -ness 'tidɪəs, -lɪ, -nɪs

tedium 'tidɪəm

teem, -s, -ing, -ed 'tim, -z, -ɪŋ, -d

teeming-date (*child-bearing years*) 'timɪŋˌdeɪt

teen, -s 'tin, -z

teeter, -s, -ing, -ed 'titɚ, -z, -ɹɪŋ, -d

teeth (*pl. of* **tooth**) 'tiθ

Note.—*In JUL, V.i.41 (First Folio), the pl. form of 'tooth' is given as 'teethes,' which (if not emended to 'teeth') is often*

emended to 'teeths,' thus implying the pronunciation ['tiθs]

teeth|e, -es, -ing, -ed 'tið, -z, -ɪŋ, -d

Telamon (AC) 'teləmɒn

Telamonius, Ajax (2HVI) 'eɪdʒæks ˌtelə'moʊnɪəs

tell, -s, -ing/ly, told 'tel, -z, -ɪŋ/lɪ, 'toʊld

tell-a 'telə (*see* vere)

tell-a-me 'teləmi (*see* vere)

teller, -s 'telɚ, -z

tell(-)tale, -s 'telteɪl, -z

Tellus (HAM, PER) 'teləs

temper, -s, -ing, -ed, -er/s 'tempɚ, -z, -ɹɪŋ, -d, -ɹɚ/z

temperality ˌtempɚ'ɹælɪtɪ

temperance (T.) 'tempəɹəns [-pɹəns]

temperate, -ly, -ness 'tempɚɪt, -lɪ, -nɪs

temperature, -s 'tempɚɹɪtʃɚ, -z [-ɹətʃ-]

tempest, -s 'tempɪst, -s

tempest-tossed 'tempɪstˌtɒst

tempest-tost 'tempɪstˌtɒst

tempestuous, -ly, -ness tem'pestjʊəs, -lɪ, -nɪs

temple (T.) (1HIV), **-s** 'templ, -z

Temple Garden (1HVI) 'templ 'gɑɚdn̩

tempor|al, -ally 'tempɚɹ|əl, -əlɪ

temporiz|e, -es, -ing/ly, -ed, -er/s 'tempɚɹaɪz, -ɪz, -ɪŋ/lɪ, -d, -ɚ/z

tempt, -s, -ing, -ed, -er/s 'tempt, -s, -ɪŋ, -ɪd, -ɚ/z

temptation, -s temp'teɪʃn, -z

tempting, -s; -ly, -ness 'temptɪŋ, -z; -lɪ, -nɪs

ten, -s 'ten, -z

tenab|le, -leness, -ly 'tenəb|l̩, -l̩nɪs, -lɪ

tenant, -s; -less 'tenənt, -s; -lɪs

Tenantius (CYM) tə'nænʃəs

tench, -es 'tentʃ, -ɪz

Ten Commandments (2HVI) ˌten kə'mandmənts

Note.—*In 2HVI, I.iii.141,142 ("Could I come near your beauty with my nails/I'd set my ten commandments in your face."), an allusion is made to the Ten Commandments and sometimes given without capitalization*

tend, -s, -ing, -ed 'tend, -z, -ɪŋ, -ɪd

tendance 'tendəns

Note.—*This word, appearing four times*

*in S. (*CYM, V.v.53; HVIII, III.ii.149;
TIM, I.i.58, 82*), carries with it a
handful of meanings (sometimes
simultaneously), and they are: loving
care of, or attention to; attendants
collectively, or retinue; and it can act as
the aphetic form of 'attendance'*
tender, -s, -ing, -ed; -er, -est, -ly, -ness
'tendɚ, -z, -ɹɪŋ, -d; -ɹɚ, -ɹɪst, -lɪ, -nɪs
tender-bodied 'tendɚˌbɒdɪd
tender-dying 'tendɚˌdaɪ̆ɪŋ
tender-hafted 'tendɚˌhaftɪd
tender-minded 'tendɚˌmaɪ̆ndɪd
tender-smelling 'tendɚˌsmelɪŋ
Tenedos (TC) 'tenədəs [-dɒs]
tenement, -s 'tenɪmənt, -s
ten(-)fold 'tenfoŭld
tenor, -s 'tenɚ, -z
tennis 'tenɪs
tennis-ball, -s 'tenɪsˌbɔl, -z
tennis-court, -s 'tenɪsˌkɔɚt, -s
tent, -s, -ing, -ed 'tent, -s, -ɪŋ, -ɪd
tenth, -s 'ten̪θ, -s
ten-times 'tenˌtaɪ̆mz
tent-royal ˌtent'ɹɔɪ̆əl
tenure, -s, -d 'tenjɚ [-jŭɚ], -z, -d
tercel, -s 'tɝsl̩, -z
Tereu (PP) 'tiɹu
Tereus (CYM, LUC, TIT) 'tiɹus [-ɹĭəs]
term, -s, -ed; -less 'tɝm, -z, -d; -lɪs
termagant (T.) (HAM, 1HIV) 'tɝməgənt
*Note.—In the Quarto version of HAM,
this name is spelled 'Tarmagant,' adding
weight to another pronunciation
sometimes proffered, i.e.,* ['tɑɚ̆məgənt].
*This is generally accepted (as a
secondary choice) even when spelled
'Termagant,' as it may be considered
analogous to words such as 'sergeant'
and 'Derby' (Brit.)*
terminal, -s 'tɝmɪnl̩, -z
terminat|e, -es, -ing, -ed, -or/s 'tɝmɪneɪ̆t,
-s, -ɪŋ, -ɪd, -ɚ/z
termination, -s ˌtɝmɪ'neɪ̆ʃn̩, -z

terra (*L.*) (LLL, IV.ii.6) 'tɛɹɑ ['tɛɹə]
Terras Astraea reliquit (*L.*) (TIT, IV.iii.4)
'tɛɹɑs ɑ'stɹiɑ ɾɛ'likwɪt
terrene 'tɛɹin [tɛ'ɹin]
terrestrial, -ly, -ness tɪ'ɹestɹɪəl [təˈɹ-], -ɪ,
-nɪs
terrib|le, -ly, -leness 'tɛɹɪb|l̩, -lɪ, -l̩nɪs
territorial, -s, -ly ˌtɛɹɪ'tɔɹɪəl, -z, -ɪ
territor|y, -ies 'tɛɹɪtɚ-ɹ|ɪ, -ɪz
terror (T.), -s 'tɛɹɚ, -z
tertian 'tɝʃn̩
test, -s, -ing, -ed 'test, -s, -ɪŋ, -ɪd
testament (T.), -s 'testəmənt, -s
tester, -s 'testɚ, -z
testern (*v.*) (*obsolete form of 'tester'
meaning to give sixpence*), **-ed** 'testɚn,
-d
testicle, -s 'testɪkl̩, -z
testicular te'stɪkjʊlɚ
testimon|y, -ies, -ied 'testɪmən|ɪ, -ɪz, -ɪd
testril (*s.*) (*diminutive of 'tester';
meaning 'sixpence'*) 'testɹəl [-tɹɪl]
test|y, -ier, -iest, -ily, -iness 'test|ɪ, -ɪɚ,
-ɪɪst, -ɪlɪ, -ɪnɪs
tetch|y *or* **tech|y, -ier, -iest, -ily, -iness**
'tetʃ|ɪ, -ɪɚ, -ɪɪst, -ɪlɪ, -ɪnɪs
tether, -s, -ing, -ed 'teðɚ, -z, -ɹɪŋ, -d
tetter 'tetɚ
tevil (*from 'devil'*) 'tevl̩ ['tevəl]
Note.—Evans (in MWW*) is a Welshman, and speaks in a Welsh accent, if
somewhat inconsistently. This is an
example of S.'s direction to the actor (by
way of semiphonetic spellings) to adopt
such an accent, more or less, for the
sake of wringing the most satire out of
plays on words stemming from confusions with, and corruptions of, English
pronunciation via the Welsh tongue*
Tewk(e)sbury (2HIV, 3HVI, RIII)
'tjuksbəɹɪ, -bɹɪ
text, -s 'tekst, -s
Thaisa (*PER*) θɑ'isə, tɑ'i-
Note.—Reputable sources (e.g., Irvine

---

i wɛ ɪ city ɪ hɪt e lɛt ɛ debut æ can a pass ɝ bird ʌ hut ə again ɚ supper u you
ʊ should o obey ɔ awl ɒ cop ɑ father eɪ̆ paid aɪ̆ high oŭ go ɔɪ̆ voice aŭ found ɪɚ̆ ear
ɛɚ̆ air ʊɚ̆ poor ɔɚ̆ fork ɑɚ̆ park aɪ̆ɚ̆ fire aŭɚ̆ hour b boy p pit d dog t top g got
k kid h how ɦ behave dʒ jot tʃ chew z zany s soft v vat f fat ʒ treasure ʃ ship ð the
θ thin m man n no ŋ hang l lip j yes w won ʍ whew ɹ rigger, airy ɾ matter

and Kökeritz) recommend [θeĭˈɪsə], *but euphony, as well as experience of modern tradition, lead me to prefer the choices proffered above. Regardless of which of the above one chooses,* PER, V.i.209 *appears to require that the name be stressed* [ˈ---], *as Kökeritz asserts (p. 93,* Shakespeare's Names: A Pronouncing Dictionary, *1972). But I disagree. Using an often-employed device, 'name' in the line becomes disyllabic (cf. Note for* **brave**), *creating a feminine ending and thereby retaining a consistent pronunciation of Thaisa (*[-ˈ---]*) throughout*

Thaliard (*PER*) ˈθæljə˞d, ˈtæl-

Thames (HV, 2HVI, MWW) ˈtemz

thane (T.), -s ˈθeĭn, -z

thank, -s, -ing/s, -ed, -er/s ˈθæŋk, -s, -ɪŋ/z, -t, -ə˞/z

thankless, -ly, -ness ˈθæŋklɪs, -lɪ, -nɪs

tharborough, -s ˈθɑ˞bʌɹə [-bʊɹə, -bʌɹoŭ], -z

th'are (*contr. of* **they are**) ˈðɛ˞

Tharsus (*var. of* **Tarsus**) (PER) ˈtɑ˞səs

th'art (*contr. of* **thou art**) ˈðɑ˞t

Thasos (JUL) ˈθeĭsɒs

that ˈðæt (*strong form*), ˈðət, ˈðt (*weak forms*)

thatch, -es, -ing, -ed, -er/s ˈθætʃ, -ɪz, -ɪŋ, -t, -ə˞/z

thaw, -s, -ing, -ed ˈθɔ, -z, -ɪŋ, -d

Theban (LEAR, TNK) ˈθibən

Thebes (MSND, TNK) ˈθibz

thee ˈði

theft, -s ˈθeft, -s

them ˈðem (*strong form*), ˈðəm, ˈəm, ˈm (*weak forms*)

theme, -s ˈθim, -z

then ˈðen

thence ˈðens

theor|y, -ies; -ic ˈθɪ˞ɹ|ɪ, -ɪz; -ɪk

there ˈðɛ˞ (*strong form*), ˈðə˞ (*weak form*)

thereabouts ˈðɛ˞ɹəˌbaŭts

thereafter ˌðɛ˞ˈɹaftə˞

thereat ˌðɛ˞ˈɹæt ([ˈ-ˌ-] *in* WT, IV.iv.490)

thereby ˌðɛ˞ˈbaĭ ([ˈ--] *in* MEAS, III.i.6; OTH, III.i.8)

therefor ˌðɛ˞ˈfɔ˞

therefore ˈðɛ˞ˌfɔ˞ (*arguably* [ˌ-ˈ-] *in* Sonn. 41.6)

therein ˌðɛ˞ˈɹɪn [ˈ-ˌ-]

thereon ˌðɛ˞ˈɹɒn

thereto ˌðɛ˞ˈtu [ˈ-ˌ-]

thereunto ˌðɛ˞ˈɹʌntu [-tʊ, ˌðɛ˞ɹʌnˈtu]

therewith ˌðɛ˞ˈwɪð ([ˈ-ˌ-] *in* OTH, I.ii.88, *and arguably in* 1HIV, I.iii.39)

therewithal ˌðɛ˞wɪˈðɔl

Thersites (CYM, *TC*) θɜ˞ˈsaĭtɪz

Theseus (*MSND*, TGV, *TNK*) ˈθisɪəs, -sjəs

Thessalian (MSND) θeˈseĭljən

Thessaly (AC, MSND) ˈθesəlɪ

Thetis (AC, TC) ˈθitɪs

thew, -s, -y ˈθju, -z, -ɪ

they ˈðeĭ

thick, -er, -est, -ly, -ness/es ˈθɪk, -ə˞, -ɪst, -lɪ, -nɪs/ɪz

thick-coming ˈθɪkˌkʌmɪŋ

thicken, -s, -ing, -ed, -er/s ˈθɪkən, -z, -ɪŋ, -d, -ə˞/z

thicket, -s ˈθɪkɪt, -s

thick-eyed ˈθɪkˌaĭd

thick-lipped ˈθɪkˌlɪpt

thicklips ˈθɪklɪps

thick-pleached ˈθɪkˌplitʃt

thick-ribbed ˈθɪkˌɹɪbd
  Note.—In MEAS, III.i.122, *editors often suggest a trisyllabic pronunciation, i.e.,* [ˈθɪkˌɹɪbɪd] *to fulfill the metrical requirements of the line. Perhaps a better, more euphonious, choice is to employ the common S. practice of eking the extra syllable out of the word 'region,' i.e.,* [ˈɹɪdʒɹən], *and thus retaining the disyllabic pronunciation given above*

thick-sighted ˈθɪkˌsaĭtɪd

thick-skin, -ned ˈθɪkˈskɪn, -d (*when att.,* [ˈ-ˌ-])

thick-twined ˈθɪkˌtwaĭnd

Thidias (AC) ˈθɪdɪəs, -djəs

thie|f, -ves ˈθi|f, -vz

thief-stolen ˈθifˌstoŭlən

thiev|e, -es, -ing, -ed; -ery ˈθiv, -z, -ɪŋ, -d; -ə˞ɪ

thievish, -ly, -ness ˈθivɪʃ, -lɪ, -nɪs

thigh, -s ˈθaĭ, -z

thill, -s 'θɪl, -z
thimble, -s; -ful/s 'θɪmbl̩, -z; -fʊl/z
thin, -s, -ning, -ned; -ner, -nest, -ly, -ness
'θɪn, -z, -ɪŋ, -d; -ɚ, -ɪst, -lɪ, -nɪs
thin-belly 'θɪnˌbelɪ
thine 'ðaɪn
thin-faced 'θɪnˌfeɪst
thing, -s 'θɪŋ, -z
think, -s, -ing/s, thought/s 'θɪŋk, -s,
-ɪŋ/z, 'θɔt/s
thinker, -s 'θɪŋkɚ, -z
third, -s, -ly 'θɝd, -z, -lɪ
thirdborough (*constable*)**, -s** 'θɝdbʌɹə,
-z
*Note.—This word does not technically
appear in S.'s works. In* TS, *Ind.i.10, it is
the editorial emendation of Lewis
Theobald's, an eminent early eighteenth
century S. scholar. He emends the First
Folio's 'headborough' to 'thirdborough'
(adopted by most modern editors) to
better suit Sly's response*
thirst, -s, -ing, -ed 'θɝst, -s, -ɪŋ, -ɪd
thirst|y, -ier, -iest, -ily, -iness 'θɝst|ɪ, -ɪɚ,
-ɪɪst, -ɪlɪ, -ɪnɪs
this, these 'ðɪs, 'ðiz
Thisbe (MSND, MV, RJ) 'θɪzbɪ
Thisne (*corruption of* **Thisbe** *in MSND*)
'θɪznɪ
thistle, -s 'θɪsl̩, -z
thither, -ward 'ðɪðɚ ['θɪ-], -wɚd
Thoas (TC) 'θoʊəs
Thomas (*2HVI*) 'tɒməs
Thomas, Friar (*MEAS*) ˌfɹaɪɚ 'tɒməs
thong, -s 'θɒŋ, -z
thorn, -s; -less 'θɔɚn, -z; -lɪs
thorn|y, -ier, -iest, -ily, -iness 'θɔɚn|ɪ,
-ɪɚ, -ɪɪst, -ɪlɪ, -ɪnɪs
tho|rough, -roughly, -roughness 'θʌ|ɹoʊ
[-ɹə], -ɹəlɪ, -ɹənɪs
*Note.—When this word in S. stands for
the archaic form of 'through' (as in* JUL,
*III.i.136; MSND, II.i.3, 5, 106; and RII,
V.vi.43), license may be taken with its*

pronunciation. Acceptable forms are
['θʌɹə, 'θʌɹu]
those (*pl. of* **that**) 'ðoʊz
thou (**T.**) (*archaic familiar—or informal—form of the sing. pron.* **you**) 'ðaʊ
though 'ðoʊ
thought, -s 'θɔt, -s
thoughten (*adj.*) 'θɔtn̩
thought-executing 'θɔtˌeksɪkjutɪŋ
thought|ful, -fully, -fulness 'θɔt|fʊl, -fʊlɪ,
-fʊlnɪs
thoughtless, -ly, -ness 'θɔtlɪs, -lɪ, -nɪs
thought-sick 'θɔtˌsɪk
thou'lt (*contr. of* **thou wilt**) 'ðaʊlt
thou'rt (*contr. of* **thou art**) 'ðaʊɚt
thousan|d, -ds, -dth/s, -d(-)fold
'θaʊzən|d, -dz, -dθʔs, -dfoʊld
Thracian (AC, 3HVI, MSND, TIT)
'θɹeɪʃn̩
thraldom 'θɹɔldəm
thrall, -s, -ing, -ed 'θɹɔl, -z, -ɪŋ, -d
thrash, -es, -ing, -ed, -er/s 'θɹæʃ, -ɪz, -ɪŋ,
-t, -ɚ/z
thrasonical θɹeɪ'sɒnɪkl̩
thread, -s, -ing, -ed 'θɹed, -z, -ɪŋ, -ɪd
threadbare 'θɹedbeɚ
threaden (*adj.*) 'θɹedn̩
threat, -s 'θɹet, -s
threat|en, -ens, -ening/ly, -ened 'θɹet|n̩,
-n̩z, -nɪŋ/lɪ [-nɪŋ/lɪ], -n̩d
threatener 'θɹetn̩ɚ
three, -s 'θɹi, -z
three-a 'θɹiə
*Note.—This word, along with
'Barbary-a,' 'bound-a,' and 'sound-a,'
appears in the ditty sung by the Gaoler's
Daughter in* TNK, *III.v; the extra
syllable there merely to provide for
another musical beat in the tetrameter
line of song*
three-and-twenty ˌθɹiənd'twentɪ
three-farthings 'θɹɪ'faɚðɪŋz
threefold 'θɹifoʊld
three-inch 'θɹiˌɪntʃ

three-legged 'θɹiˌlegd [ˌ-'-] (when att., [ˌ-'-], 'θɹiˌlegɪd)

three-man 'θɹiˌmæn

three-nooked 'θɹiˌnʊkt

threepence, -s 'θɹepəns ['θɹɪp-, 'θɹʌp-], -ɪz

three-pile, -d 'θɹiˌpaɪl, -d

Three-pile, Master (MEAS) ˌmastə 'θɹiˌpaɪl

three-quarter, -s ˌθɹi'kwɔ˞ɾə˞, -z

threescore ˌθɹi'skɔ˞ ['--]

threesome, -s 'θɹisəm, -z

three-suited 'θɹiˌsutɪd [-ˌsjutɪd]

Threne (PT) 'θɹin

Threnos (PT) 'θɹinɒs

thresh, -es, -ing, -ed, -er/s 'θɹeʃ, -ɪz, -ɪŋ, -t, -ə˞/z

threshold, -s 'θɹeʃhoŭld, -z

threw (p.t. of throw, q.v.) 'θɹu

thrice 'θɹaɪs

thrice-crowned ˌθɹaɪs'kɹaŭnd (['θɹaɪs'kɹaŭnɪd] in AYLI, III.ii.2)

thrice-driven 'θɹaɪsˌdɹɪvn̩

thrice-gentle ˌθɹaɪs'dʒentl̩ [-təl]

thrice-gorgeous ˌθɹaɪs'gɔ˞dʒəs

thrice-gracious ˌθɹaɪs'gɹeɪʃəs

thrice-noble 'θɹaɪsˌnoŭbl̩

thrice-nobler ˌθɹaɪs'noŭblə˞

thrice-puissant ˌθɹaɪs'pwɪsənt (['-ˌ--] in HV, I.ii.119)

thrice-repured ˌθɹaɪsˌɹɪ'pjʊ˞d [-ɹi'p-] (['θɹaɪsˌɹɪ'pjʊ˞ɹɪd] in TC, III.ii.20)

thrice-valiant ˌθɹaɪs'væljənt

thrice-worthy ˌθɹaɪs'wɝ˞ðɪ ['-ˌ--]

thrift, -s 'θɹɪft, -s

thriftless, -ly, -ness 'θɹɪftlɪs, -lɪ, -nɪs

thrift|y, -ier, -iest, -ily, -iness 'θɹɪft|ɪ, -ɪə˞, -ɪɪst, -ɪlɪ, -ɪnɪs

thrill, -s, -ing/ly, -ed, -er/s 'θɹɪl, -z, -ɪŋ/lɪ, -d, -ə˞/z

thriv|e, -es, -ing/ly, -ed, -er/s, throve, thriven 'θɹaɪv, -z, -ɪŋ/lɪ, -d, -ə˞/z, 'θɹoŭv, 'θɹɪvn̩

throat, -s, -ed 'θɹoŭt, -s, -ɪd

throat|y, -ier, -iest, -ily, -iness 'θɹoŭt|ɪ, -ɪə˞, -ɪɪst, -ɪlɪ, -ɪnɪs

throb, -s, -bing/ly, -bed 'θɹɒb, -z, -ɪŋ/lɪ, -d

throe, -s 'θɹoŭ, -z

thron|e, -es, -ing, -ed 'θɹoŭn, -z, -ɪŋ, -d

throng, -s, -ing, -ed 'θɹɒŋ, -z, -ɪŋ, -d

throughfare, -s 'θɹufɛ˞, -z

throughly (archaic var. of thoroughly) 'θɹulɪ ['θɹʊlɪ]

throstle, -s 'θɹɒsl̩, -z

throw, -s, -ing, threw, throw|n, -er/s 'θɹoŭ, -z, -ɪŋ, 'θɹu, 'θɹoŭ|n, -ə˞/z

thrower-out ˌθɹoŭə˞'ɹaŭt

throw't (contr. of throw it) 'θɹoŭt

thrum, -s, -ming, -med 'θɹʌm, -z, -ɪŋ, -d

thrush, -es 'θɹʌʃ, -ɪz

thrust, -s, -ing 'θɹʌst, -s, -ɪŋ

thud, -s, -ding, -ded 'θʌd, -z, -ɪŋ, -ɪd

thug, -s 'θʌg, -z

thumb, -s, -ing, -ed 'θʌm, -z, -ɪŋ, -d

thumb-ring 'θʌmˌɹɪŋ

thump (s., v.), -s, -ing, -ed, -er/s 'θʌmp, -s, -ɪŋ, -t, -ə˞/z

thumping (adj., adv.), -ly 'θʌmpɪŋ, -lɪ

Thump, Peter (2HVI) 'piɾə˞ ['pitə˞] 'θʌmp

thunder, -s, -ing/ly, -ed, -er/s 'θʌndə˞, -z, -ɪŋ/lɪ, -d, -ɹə˞/z

thunder-bearer 'θʌndə˞ˌbɛ˞ɹə˞

thunderbolt, -s 'θʌndə˞boŭlt, -s

thunder-clap, -s 'θʌndə˞klæp, -s

thunder-darter 'θʌndə˞ˌdɑ˞tə˞

thunder-like 'θʌndə˞ˌlaɪk

thunder-master 'θʌndə˞ˌmastə˞

thunderous, -ly 'θʌndə˞ɹəs, -lɪ

thunder-stone, -s 'θʌndə˞ˌstoŭn, -z

thunder-storm, -s 'θʌndə˞stɔ˞m, -z

thunder-stroke, -s 'θʌndə˞ˌstɹoŭk, -s

Thurio (TGV) 'tjʊ˞ˌɹoŭ ['tʊ˞-, 'θʊ˞-]

Thursday (1HIV, 2HIV, RJ), -s 'θɝ˞zdɪ [-deĭ], -z

thus, -ly 'ðʌs, -lɪ

thwack, -s, -ing, -ed 'θwæk, -s, -ɪŋ, -t

thwart, -s, -ing/s, -ed 'θwɔ˞t, -s, -ɪŋ/z, -ɪd

thy 'ðaĭ

thyme, -s 'taĭm, -z

Thyreus (AC; usually supplanting Thidias) 'θaĭɹɪəs, -ɹĭəs

thyself ðaĭ'self

Tib (ALL'S, PER) 'tɪb

Tiber (AC, COR, JUL) 'taĭbə˞

Tiberio (RJ) taĭ'bɪ˞ˌɹoŭ

'ticed (aphaeretic form of enticed) 'taĭst

tick|le, -les, -ling, -led, -ler/s 'tɪk|l̩, -l̩z,
  -l̩ŋ [-lɪŋ], -l̩d, -l̩ɚ/z [-lə/z]
tickle-brain 'tɪkl̩ˌbɹeɪn
ticklish, -ly, -ness 'tɪklɪʃ, -lɪ, -nɪs
tick-tack, -s 'tɪkˌtæk, -s
tiddle-taddle 'tɪdl̩ˌtædl̩
tid|e, -es, -ing, -ed 'taɪd, -z, -ɪŋ, -ɪd
'tide (*contr. from* **betide**) 'taɪd
tidings 'taɪdɪŋz
tid|y, ies, -ying, -ied; -ier, -iest, -ily,
  -iness 'taɪd|ɪ, -ɪz, -ɪŋ, -ɪd; -ɪɚ, -ɪɪst, -ɪlɪ,
  -ɪnɪs
tie, -s, tying, tied 'taɪ, -z, 'taɪɪŋ, 'taɪd
tiger (T.) (COM, MAC, TN), **-s** 'taɪgɚ, -z
tiger-footed 'taɪgɚˌfʊtɪd
tight, -s; -er, -est, -ly, -ness 'taɪt, -s; -ɚ,
  -ɪst, -lɪ, -nɪs
tike *or* **tyke (T.), -s** 'taɪk, -s
til|e, -es, -ing, -ed 'taɪl, -z, -(l)ɪŋ, -d
till, -s, -ing, -ed, -er/s; -able, -age 'tɪl, -z,
  -ɪŋ, -d, -ɚ/z; -əbl̩, -ɪdʒ
till't (*contr. of* **till it**) 'tɪlt
tilly-fally (*exclamation of contempt or*
  mild irritation; 'hogwash') 'tɪlɪˌfælɪ
tilly-vally (*exclamation of contempt or*
  mild irritation; 'hogwash') 'tɪlɪˌvælɪ
tilt, -s, -ing, -ed, -er/s 'tɪlt, -s, -ɪŋ, -ɪd,
  -ɚ/z
tilth 'tɪl̩θ
tilt-yard, -s 'tɪltˌjɑɚd, -z
Timandra (*TIM*) tɪˈmændɹə
timber, -s, -ing, -ed 'tɪmbɚ, -z, -ɹɪŋ, -d
Timbria *or* **Tymbria** (TC) 'tɪmbɹɪə
Time (ADO, COM, KJ, LUC, MSND,
  PER, TNK, Sonn. 12; 16; 19; 60; 63; 64;
  65; 115; 116; 123, *WT*) 'taɪm
tim|e (T.), -es, -ing, -ed, -er/s 'taɪm, -z,
  -ɪŋ, -d, -ɚ/z
time-beguiling 'taɪmbɪˌgaɪlɪŋ
time-bettering 'taɪmˌbeɾɚˌɹɪŋ
time-bewasted ˌtaɪmbɪˈweɪstɪd
time-honored 'taɪmˌɒnɚd (*when att.,*
  [ˌ-ˈ--])
timeless, -ly, -ness 'taɪmlɪs, -lɪ, -nɪs

timel|y, -ier, -iest, -iness 'taɪml|ɪ, -ɪɚ,
  -ɪɪst, -ɪnɪs
timely-parted 'taɪmlɪˌpɑɚtɪd
time-pleaser, -s 'taɪmˌplizɚ, -z
timid, -ly, -ness 'tɪmɪd, -lɪ, -nɪs
timidity tɪˈmɪdɪtɪ
Timon (LLL, *TIM*) 'taɪmən
timorous, -ly, -ness 'tɪmə.ɹəs, -lɪ, -nɪs
Timothy (*TNK*) 'tɪməθɪ
tinct, -s 'tɪŋkt, -s
tinctur|e, -es, -ing, -ed 'tɪŋktʃɚ, -z, -ɹɪŋ,
  -d
tinder 'tɪndɚ
tinderbox, -es 'tɪndɚˌbɒks, -ɪz
tinder-like 'tɪndɚˌlaɪk
tinker, -s, -ing, -ed 'tɪŋkɚ, -z, -ɹɪŋ, -d
tinsel 'tɪnsl̩
tip, -s, -ping, -ped 'tɪp, -s, -ɪŋ, -t
tipp|le, -les, -ling, -led, -ler/s 'tɪp|l̩, -l̩z,
  -l̩ŋ, -l̩d, -lə/z
tips|y, -ier, -iest, -ily, -iness 'tɪps|ɪ, -ɪɚ,
  -ɪɪst, -ɪlɪ, -ɪnɪs
tiptoe, -s, -ing, -d 'tɪptoʊ, -z, -ɪŋ, -d
tip-top 'tɪpˌtɒp [ˌ-ˈ-]
tird *or* **turd** (*from 'third'*) 'tɜ·d (*see* **dat**)
tir|e, -es, -ing, -ed/ly, -edness 'taɪɚ, -z,
  -ɹɪŋ, -d/lɪ, -dnɪs
tireless, -ly, -ness 'taɪɚlɪs, -lɪ, -nɪs
tiresome, -ly, -ness 'taɪɚsəm, -lɪ, -nɪs
tire-valiant ˌtaɪɚˈvæljənt
tiring-hou|se, -ses 'taɪɚ.ɹɪŋˌhaʊ|s, -zɪz
tirra-lirra *or* **tirra-Lyra** ˌtɪɹəˈlɪɹə
tirrits (*fit of fear or temper*) 'tɪɹɪts
'tis (*contr. of* **it is**) 'tɪz
Tisick (2HIV) 'tɪzɪk
tisick (*var. of* **phthisic**) 'tɪzɪk
tissue, -s 'tɪʃu, -s
Titan (1HIV, RJ, TC, TIT, VA), **-s** 'taɪtən
  [-tn̩], -z
Titania (*MSND*) tɪˈtɑnɪə, -njə
titely (*with haste*) 'taɪtlɪ
tith|e, -es, -ing, -ed 'taɪð, -z, -ɪŋ, -d
tithe-pig, -s 'taɪðˌpɪg, -z
tithe-woman 'taɪðˌwʊmən

i wᴇ ɪ city ɪ hɪt e lᴇt ɛ dᴇbut æ cᴀn a pᴀss ɝ bɪrd ʌ hᴜt ə again ɚ suppᴇr u yᴏu
ʊ shᴏuld o ᴏbey ɔ ᴀwl ɒ cᴏp ɑ fᴀther eɪ pᴀid aɪ hɪgh oʊ gᴏ ɔɪ vᴏice aʊ fᴏund ɪɚ ᴇar
ɛɚ ᴀir ʊɚ pᴏor ɔɚ fᴏrk ɑɚ pᴀrk aɪɚ fɪre aʊɚ hᴏur b bᴏy p pit d dᴏg t tᴏp g gᴏt
k ᴋid h hᴏw fi behᴀve dʒ jᴏt tʃ chew z zany s sᴏft v yat f fᴀt ʒ treasure ʃ shᴉp ð the
θ thin m ᴍan n ᴎo ŋ haᴎg l lip j yes w wᴏn ʍ whew ɹ rɪgger, aiɾy ɾ matter

Titinius (*JUL*) tɪˈtɪnɪəs, -njəs
titl|e, -es, -ing, -ed; -eless ˈtaɪtḷ, -z, -ɪŋ, -d; -lɪs
title-lea|f, -ves ˈtaɪtḷˌli|f, -vz
title-page, -s ˈtaɪtḷˌpeɪdʒ, -ɪz
titler, -s ˈtaɪtlɚ [-tlɚ-], -z
tittle, -s ˈtɪtḷ, -z
tittle-tattling ˈtɪtḷˌtætlɪŋ [-tlɪŋ]
Titus (*TIM*, TN) ˈtaɪtəs [ˈtaɪɾəs]
toad (**T.**), **-s** ˈtoʊd, -z
toad-spotted ˈtoʊdˌspɒtɪd
toadstool, -s ˈtoʊdstul, -z
toast, -s, -ing, -ed, -er/s ˈtoʊst, -s, -ɪŋ, -ɪd, -ɚ/z
toasting-iron, -s ˈtoʊstɪŋˌaɪɚn, -z
toasts-and-butter ˌtoʊstsənd'bʌɾɚ
to(a)z|e (*to separate or unravel*), **-es, -ing, -ed, -er/s** ˈtoʊz, -ɪz, -ɪŋ, -d, -ɚ/z
to-be-pitied ˌtubiˈpɪtɪd [-bɪˈp-, -pɪɾɪd]
tod, -s ˈtɒd, -z
today *or* **to-day, -s** təˈdeɪ, -z
todpole (*tadpole*), **-s** ˈtɒdpoʊl, -z
toe, -s, -ing, -d ˈtoʊ, -z, -ɪŋ, -d
tofore (*beforehand*) tuˈfɔɚ [tʊˈfɔɚ]
toga, -s, -ed ˈtoʊɡə, -z, -d
toge *and* **toged** ˈtoʊɡ,-ɪd, ˈtʌŋ, -ɪd
Note.—There was a custom in Early Modern English to abbreviate certain kinds of words. Sometimes, a tilde or macron was used above letters in a handwritten word to imply the intended onset of a nasal consonant, and these abbreviations frequently made their way onto the printed page. For instance, the word 'long' (or 'longe' in its alternative form) was often abbreviated 'lõge,' and 'tongue' abbreviated as 'tõge.' But, coincidentally, the word 'toge' (as well as 'togue') is the alternative—now archaic—spelling for 'toga,' the gownlike garment worn by the patricians and senators of ancient Rome. The words 'toge' and 'toged' both appear in certain versions and editions of S., viz. COR, II.iii.114 and OTH, I.i.25, respectively; although it is worthwhile mentioning that in both cases, the First Folio version gives 'tongue' and 'tongued.' Errors arise when editors (not to mention compositors) have failed to recognize this arcane custom of abbreviation. Thus, there is much debate about whether S.'s intention was to mean the garment or the organ of the mouth, which of course becomes an issue of how one is to pronounce them. Both passages allude to Roman consuls, which is why (I presume) many editors have emended 'tongue' and 'tongued' to the irregular 'toge' and 'toged,' yet both passages explicitly refer to begging and proposing, voices and words; all being tasks associated with and especial to the tongue. Therefore, one could read 'toged' in Othello (First Quarto version only), or 'toge' in modern editions of Coriolanus, and reasonably pronounce them as [ˈtʌŋɪd] and [ˈtʌŋ]. Cf. Freeborn's From Old English to Standard English, Second Edition, p. 285, § 15.2.1.1

together, -ness tʊˈɡeðɚ, -nɪs
toil, -s, -ing, -ed, -er/s ˈtɔɪl, -z, -ɪŋ, -d, -ɚ/z
toilet, -s ˈtɔɪlɪt, -s
toiletr|y, -ies ˈtɔɪlɪtɪ|ɪ, -ɪz
token, -s, -ed ˈtoʊkən, -z, -d
told (*p.t. of* **tell**, *q.v.*) ˈtoʊld
Toledo (HVIII) toˈlidoʊ
toll, -s, -ing, -ed, -er/s ˈtoʊl, -z, -ɪŋ, -d, -ɚ/z
tom, -s ˈtɒm, -z
Tom (1HIV, 2HVI, LEAR, LLL) ˈtɒm
tomb, -s; -less ˈtum, -z; -lɪs
tomboy, -s ˈtɒmbɔɪ, -z
Tom o'Bedlam (LEAR) ˈtɒm əˈbedləm (*alias Edgar*)
tomorrow *or* **to-morrow, -s** tʊˈmɒɹoʊ, -z
Note.—This word is sometimes spoken colloquially as [tʊˈmɒɹə] or [tʊˈmɒɹʊ], particularly when preceding words such as 'morning,' 'afternoon,' 'evening,' and 'night'
Tomyris (1HVI) ˈtɒmɹɪs [toˈmaɪɹɪs]
tongs ˈtɒŋ z
tongu|e, -es, -ing, -ed; -eless ˈtʌŋ, -z, -ɪŋ, -d; -lɪs
Note.—In CYM, V.iv.147, this word is

potentially disyllabic, i.e., ['tʌŋə]. *In Frank Kermode's (editor, The Arden Shakespeare, 1958) annotation for* TEM, I.ii.53, *there is a brief but valuable discussion about monosyllabic words that sometimes receive the value of two metric beats in S. lines of verse "whether or no it is* [they are] *pronounced disyllabically . . ." In* CYM, V.iv.147, *'tongue' is arguably pronounced disyllabically or given, as Kermode puts it, "a heavy emphasis." Cf. Abbott's* A Shakespearian Grammar, §§ *475, 479, 484*

Tongue, Lady (ADO) 'leĭdɨ 'tʌŋ

tongue-tied 'tʌŋtaĭd

tonight *or* **to-night, -s** tʉ'naĭt, -s

too 'tu

took (*p.t. of* **take**, *q.v.*) 'tʊk

took't (*contr. of* **took it**) 'tʊkt

tool, -s, -ing, -ed 'tul, -z, -ɪŋ, -d

tooth (*s.*), **teeth** 'tuθ, 'tiθ

tooth (*v.*), **-s, -ing, -ed** 'tuθ, -s, -ɪŋ, -t

toothache 'tuθeĭk

toothdrawer (*one who pulls teeth*), **-s** 'tuθdɹɔə-, -z

tooth(-)pick, -s, -er/s 'tuθpɪk, -s, -ə-/z

too-timely 'tu'taĭmlɨ

too-too 'tu,tu

top, -s, -ping, -ped 'tɒp, -s, -ɪŋ, -t

topaz, -es 'toŭpæz, -ɪz

top(-)ful(l) 'tɒp,fʊl

top(-)gallant ,tɒp'gælənt

topless 'tɒplɪs

topmast, -s 'tɒpməst [-mast], -s

top-proud 'tɒp,pɹaŭd

topsail, -s 'tɒpsl̩ [-seĭl], -z

topsy(-)turv|y, -ily, -iness ,tɒpsɨ'tɜ·v|ɨ, -ɪlɨ, -ɪnɪs

torch, -es, -ing, -ed, -er/s 'tɔə-tʃ, -ɪz, -ɪŋ, -t, -ə-/z

torch-staves 'tɔə-tʃ,steĭvz

tore (*p.t. of* **tear** *[to rend], q.v.*) 'tɔə-

torment (*s.*), **-s** 'tɔə-ment, -s

torment (*v.*), **-s, -ing/ly, -ed, -or/s** tɔə-'ment, -s, -ɪŋ/lɨ, -ɪd, -ə-/z

torn (*p.p. of* **tear** *[to rend], q.v.*) 'tɔə-n

tortive 'tɔə-ɾɪv

tortur|e, -es, -ing, -ed, -er/s 'tɔə-tʃə-, -z, -ɪŋ, -d, -ɹə-/z

Toryne (AC) tɔ'ɹaĭnɨ

Note.—Despite Kökeritz's opinion on the matter (cf. Kökeritz's Shakespeare's Names: A Pronouncing Dictionary, *p. 21), this word (particilarly in* AC, III.vii.23*) is able to retain the pronunciation given above by simply contracting 'You have' into 'You've,' a device S. often employs, e.g.,* AC, III.xi.7

to's (*contr. of* **to us**) 'tus

to's (*contr. of* **to his**) 'tuz

toss, -es, -ing, -ed, -er/s 'tɒs, -ɪz, -ɪŋ, -t, -ə-/z

toss-pot, -s 'tɒs,pɒt, -s

to't (*contr. of* **to it**) 'tut

total, -s, -ling, -led; -ly 'toŭtl̩, -z, -ɪŋ, -d; -ɨ

t'other (*from* **to other**) 'tʌðə-

totter, -s, -ing/ly, -ed, -er/s 'tɒɾə-, -z, -ɹɪŋ/lɨ, -d, -ɹə-/z

touch, -es, -ing, -ed 'tʌtʃ, -ɪz, -ɪŋ, -t

touching, -ly, -ness 'tʌtʃɪŋ, -lɨ, -nɪs

touchstone, -s 'tʌtʃstoŭn, -z

Touchstone (AYLI) 'tʌtʃstoŭn

Touraine (1HVI, KJ) tu'ɹeĭn [-'ɹen]

Note.—In S., 'Touraine' is given primary stress on the first syllable, i.e., ['tuɹeĭn, -ɹen]

tourney, -s 'tŭə-nɨ ['tɜ·nɨ], -z

Tours (1HVI, 2HVI) 'tŭə- ['tŭə-z]

tous|e *or* **towz|e, -es, -ing, -ed** 'taŭz, -ɪz, -ɪŋ, -d

tow, -s, -ing, -ed 'toŭ, -z, -ɪŋ, -d

toward (*adj.*), **-ly, -ness** 'toə-d, -lɨ, -nɪs

toward (*prep.*), **-s; -ly** 'tɔə-d [tʉ'wɔə-d, 'twɔə-d], -z; -lɨ

Note.—In 3HVI, II.ii.66, this word is disyllabic and is stressed on the first

---

i wᴇ ɨ city ɪ hɪt e lᴇt ɛ debut æ can a pass ɝ bird ʌ hut ə again ɚ supper u you ʊ should o obey ɔ awl ɒ cop ɑ father eĭ paid aĭ high oŭ go ɔĭ voice aŭ found ɪɝ ear ɛɝ air ʊɝ poor ɔɝ fork ɑɝ park aĭɝ fire aŭɝ hour b boy p pit d dog t top g got k kid h how fi behave dʒ jot tʃ chew z zany s soft v vat f fat ʒ treasure ʃ ship ð the θ thin m man n no ŋ hang l lip j yes w won ʍ whew ɹ rigger, airy ɾ matter

syllable, i.e., ['tuwəᵈd]. *In order to fufill the couplet rhyme in TS, I.i.68, 69; and* V.ii.183, 184 *of 'toward/froward,' 'toward' is likely to be pronounced* ['toŭwəᵈd] *(cf.* **untoward***)*

Tower (3HVI, HVIII) 'taŏɚ

tower (*that which, or one who, tows*), **-s** 'toŏə, -z

tower (*tall structure; to rise*), **-s, -ing, -ed** 'taŏɚ, -z, -ɹɪŋ, -d

Tower-hill *or* **Tower Hill** (HVIII) 'taŏɚ ˌhɪl

town, -s; -ship/s 'taŏn, -z; -ʃɪp/s

townsfolk 'taŏnzfoŏk

townspeople 'taŏnzˌpipl̩

toy, -s, -ing, -ed 'tɔĭ, -z, -ɪŋ, -d

trac|e, -es, -ing, -ed, -er/s 'tɹeĭs, -ɪz, -ɪŋ, -t, -ɚ/z

tract, -s 'tɹækt, -s

tractab|le, -ly, -leness 'tɹæktəb|l̩, -lɪ, -l̩nɪs

trad|e, -es, -ing, -ed, -er/s 'tɹeĭd, -z, -ɪŋ, -ɪd, -ɚ/z

trade-fallen 'tɹeĭdˌfɔlən

trades|man, -men 'tɹeĭdz|mən, -mən

tradition, -s tɹə'dɪʃn̩, -z

traduc|e, -es, -ing, -ed, -er/s, -ement tɹə'djus, -ɪz, -ɪŋ, -t, -ɚ/z, -mənt

traffic, -s, -king, -ked, -ker/s 'tɹæfɪk, -s, -ɪŋ, -t, -ɚ/z

tragedian, -s tɹə'dʒidɪən, -z

traged|y, -ies 'tɹædʒɪd|ɪ, -ɪz

trail, -s, -ing, -ed, -er/s 'tɹeĭl, -z, -ɪŋ, -d, -ɚ/z

train, -s, -ing, -ed, -er/s 'tɹeĭn, -z, -ɪŋ, -d, -ɚ/z

traitor, -s, -ly 'tɹeĭɽɚ, -z, -lɪ

traitorous, -ly, -ness 'tɹeĭɽəɹəs, -lɪ, -nɪs

traitress, -es 'tɹeĭtɹɪs, -ɪz

traject (*s.*), **-s** 'tɹædʒekt, -s

traject (*v.*), **-s, -ing, -ed** tɹə'dʒekt, -s, -ɪŋ, -ɪd

trajector|y, -ies tɹə'dʒektəɹ|ɪ, -ɪz

trammel, -s, -ling, -led 'tɹæməl, -z, -ɪŋ, -d

tramp, -s, -ing, -ed 'tɹæmp, -s, -ɪŋ, -t

tramp|le, -les, -ling, -led, -ler/s 'tɹæmp|l̩, -l̩z, -lɪŋ [-l̩ɪŋ], -l̩d, -lɚ/z [-l̩ɚ/z]

trance, -s, -d 'tɹans, -ɪz, -t

Tranio (*TS*) 'tɹɑnɪoŏ, -njoŏ

tranquil, -ly, -ness 'tɹæŋkwəl, -ɪ, -nɪs

tranquillity tɹæŋ'kwɪlɪtɪ

transcenden|ce, -cy, -t/ly tɹæn'sendən|s [-ɹan-], -sɪ, -t/lɪ

transfer (*s.*), **-s** 'tɹænsfɚ [-ɹan-], -z

transfer (*v.*), **-s, -ring, -red, -rer/s** tɹæns'fɚ [-ɹan-, '--], -z, -ɹɪŋ, -d, -ɹɚ/z

transfix, -es, -ing, -ed tɹæns'fɪks [-ɹan-], -ɪz, -ɪŋ, -t

transform, -s, -ing, -ed, -er/s; -able tɹæns'fɔɚm [-ɹan-], -z, -ɪŋ, -d, -ɚ/z; -əbl̩

transgress, -es, -ing, -ed, -or/s tɹæns'gɹes [-ɹan-, -nz'g-], -ɪz, -ɪŋ, -t, -ɚ/z

transgression, -s tɹæns'gɹeʃn̩ [-ɹan-, -nz'g-], -z

translat|e (*often stressed on the first syllable*), **-es, -ing, -ed, -or/s; -able** tɹæns'leĭt [-ɹan-, -nz'l-], -s, -ɪŋ, -ɪd, -ɚ/z; -əbl̩

translation, -s tɹæns'leĭʃn̩ [-ɹan-, -nz'l-], -z

transmigrat|e, -es, -ing, -ed, -or/s tɹæns'maĭgɹeĭt [-ɹan-, -nz'm-], -s, -ɪŋ, -ɪd, -ɚ/z

transmutation, -s ˌtɹænzmju'teĭʃn̩ [-ɹan-, -nsm-], -z

transparenc|y, -ies tɹæns'pɛɚɹəns|ɪ [-ɹan-, -nz'p-, -'pæɹ-], -ɪz

transparent, -ly, -ness tɹæns'pɛɚɹənt [-ɹan-, -nz'p-, -'pæɹ-], -lɪ, -nɪs

transport (*s.*), **-s** 'tɹænspɔɚt [-ɹan-, -nzp-], -s

transport (*v.*), **-s, -ing, -ed; -able** tɹæn'spɔɚt [-ɹan-, -nz'p-], -s, -ɪŋ, -ɪd; -əbl̩

transportance tɹæn'spɔɚtns [-ɹan-]

transportation ˌtɹænspɔɚ'teĭʃn̩ [-ɹan-, -nzp-, -pɚ-]

transpos|e, -es, -ing, -ed tɹæns'poŏz [-ɹan-, -nz'p-], -ɪz, -ɪŋ, -d

transshape ˌtɹæns'ʃeĭp [-ɹan-, -nz'ʃ-]

Transylvanian (PER) ˌtɹænsɪl'veĭnjən

trap, -s, -ping/s, -ped, -per/s 'tɹæp, -s, -ɪŋ/z, -t, -ɚ/z

trash, -es, -ing, -ed 'tɹæʃ, -ɪz, -ɪŋ, -t

trash|y, -ier, -iest, -iness 'tɹæʃ|ɪ, -ɪɚ, -ɪɪst, -ɪnɪs

travail, -s, -ing, -ed 'tɹæveĭl [tɹə'veĭl], -z, -ɪŋ, -d

Note.—This word has several meanings in S., including the usual ones one might expect, i.e., 'toil,' 'exertion,' 'tormenting distress,' and 'labor of childbirth.' Interestingly, as was common in his day, it also stands at times for 'difficult journeying,' or just 'journeying' in general. The Folios and Quartos use the spellings 'travail,' 'travaile,' 'travell,' and 'travel,' overlapping meanings with spellings (cf. Sonn. 27.2). Some modern editors differentiate meaning by differentiating spelling, and some do not. Scanning the verse will typically dictate stress, the primary stress usually falling on the first syllable, regardless of spelling

travel, -(1)s, -(1)ing, -(1)ed, -(1)er/s 'tɹævl̩, -z, -ɪŋ, -d, -ɚ/z (*see Note for* **travail**)

Traveller, Monsieur (AYLI) mə'sjɚ 'tɹævlə

Note.—Arguably stressed ['mɪsjɚ 'tɹævlɚ] *in AYLI, IV.i.31 due to customs of recessive accenting*

Travellers (*1HIV*) 'tɹævlɚz

travel-tainted 'tɹævl̩ˌteɪntɪd

Travers (*2HIV*) 'tɹævɚz

traverse (*adj., s.*), **-s** 'tɹævɚs [tɹə'vɝs], -ɪz

travers|e (*v.*), **-es, -ing, -ed** tɹə'vɝs ['tɹævɚs], -ɪz, -ɪŋ, -t

Tray *or* **Trey** (LEAR) 'tɹeɪ̆

tray, -s 'tɹeɪ̆, -z

tray-trip (*card game*) 'tɹeɪ̆ˌtɹɪp

treacher, -s 'tɹetʃɚ, -z

treacherous, -ly, -ness 'tɹetʃəɹəs, -lɪ, -nɪs

treacher|y, -ies 'tɹetʃɚɹ|ɪ, -ɪz

treacle, -s 'tɹikl̩, -z

tread, -s, -ing, trod, trodden, treader/s 'tɹed, -z, -ɪŋ, 'tɹɒd, 'tɹɒdn̩, 'tɹedɚ/z

treason, -s 'tɹizn̩, -z

treasonous, -ly 'tɹizṇəs, -lɪ

treasur|e, -es, -ing, -ed 'tɹeʒɚ, -z, -ɹɪŋ, -d

treasur|y, -ies 'tɹeʒɚɹ|ɪ, -ɪz

treat, -s, -ing, -ed, -ment/s 'tɹit, -s, -ɪŋ, -ɪd, -mənt/s

treatise, -s 'tɹitɪs, -ɪz

treat|y, -ies 'tɹit|ɪ, -ɪz

treb|le, -les, -ling, -led; -ly 'tɹebl̩, -l̩z, -l̩ɪŋ [-lɪŋ], -l̩d; -lɪ

treble-dated 'tɹebl̩ˌdeɪtɪd

treble-sinewed 'tɹebl̩ˌsɪnjud

Trebonius (*JUL*) tɹɪ'boʊnɪəs, -njəs

tree (*from 'three'*) 'tɹi (*see* **varld**)

tree, -s, -ing, -d 'tɹi, -z, -ɪŋ, -d

tremb|le, -les, -ling/ly, -led, -ler/s 'tɹembl̩, -l̩z, -lɪŋ/lɪ, -l̩d, -lɚ/z

tremor cordis (*L.*) (WT, I.ii.110) 'tɹemɚ 'kɔɚdɪs

trempling (*from 'trembling'*) 'tɹempl̩ɪŋ [-plɪŋ]

Note.—Evans (in MWW) is a Welsh- man, and speaks in a Welsh accent, if somewhat inconsistently. This is an example of S.'s direction to the actor (by way of semiphonetic spellings) to adopt such an accent, more or less, for the sake of wringing the most satire out of plays on words stemming from confu- sions with, and corruptions of, English pronunciation via the Welsh tongue

trench, -es, -ing, -ed, -er/s 'tɹentʃ, -ɪz, -ɪŋ, -t, -ɚ/z

trenchan|ce, -t/ly 'tɹentʃən|s, -t/lɪ

trencher, -s, -ed 'tɹentʃɚ, -z, -ɹɪŋ, -d

trencher-friend, -s 'tɹentʃɚˌfɹend, -z

trencher-knight 'tɹentʃɚˌnaɪ̆t

trencher|-man, -men 'tɹentʃɚ|mən [-mæn], -mən

Trent (1HIV, TNK) 'tɹent

trespass, -es, -ing, -ed, -er/s 'tɹespas [-pəs], -ɪz, -ɪŋ, -t, -ɚ/z

tress, -es, -ed 'tɹes, -ɪz, -t

Tressel (*RIII*) 'tɹesl̩

Trey *or* **Tray** (LEAR) 'tɹeɪ̆

trey, -s 'tɹeɪ̆, -z

trial, -s 'tɹaɪ̆əl, -z

---

i w**e** ɨ c**i**ty ɪ h**i**t e l**e**t ɛ d**e**but æ c**a**n a p**a**ss ɝ b**ir**d ʌ h**u**t ə **a**gain ɚ supp**er** u y**ou**
ʊ sh**ou**ld o **o**bey ɔ **aw**l ɒ c**o**p ɑ f**a**ther eɪ p**ai**d aɪ h**igh** oʊ g**o** ɔɪ v**oi**ce aʊ f**ou**nd ɪɚ **ear**
ɛɚ **air** ʊɚ **poor** ɔɚ f**or**k ɑɚ p**ar**k aɪɚ f**ire** aʊɚ h**our** b **b**oy p **p**it d **d**og t **t**op g **g**ot
k **k**id h **h**ow fi be**h**ave dʒ **j**ot tʃ **ch**ew z **z**any s **s**oft v **v**at f **f**at ʒ trea**s**ure ʃ **sh**ip ð **th**e
θ **th**in m **m**an n **n**o ŋ ha**ng** l **l**ip j **y**es w **w**on ʌ **wh**ew ɹ **r**igger, ai**r**y ɾ ma**tt**er

trial-fire 'tɹaɪəlˌfaɪɚ

trib (*from 'trip'*) 'tɹɪb (*see* **prings**)

tribe, -s 'tɹaɪb, -z

tribulation, -s ˌtɹɪbjʊ'leɪʃn̩, -z

tribunal, -s tɹaɪ'bjunl̩ [tɪ'b-], -z

tribune, -s 'tɹɪbjun, -z

Tribunes (*CYM*) 'tɹɪbjunz

tributar|y, -ies 'tɹɪbjʊtɚˌɹ|ɪ, -ɪz

tribute, -s 'tɹɪbjut, -s

trice 'tɹaɪs

trick, -s, -ing, -ed 'tɹɪk, -s, -ɪŋ, -t

trick|le, -les, -ling, -led 'tɹɪk|l̩, -l̩z, -l̩ɪŋ [-lɪŋ], -l̩d

tricksy 'tɹɪksɪ

trident, -s 'tɹaɪdn̩t [-dənt], -s

trifl|e, -es, -ing, -ed, -er/s 'tɹaɪfl̩, -z, -ɪŋ, -d, -ɚ/z

Trigon (2HIV) 'tɹaɪgɒn

trill, -s, -ing, -ed 'tɹɪl, -z, -ɪŋ, -d

trim, -s, -ming/s, -med, -mer/s; -mer, -mest, -ly, -ness 'tɹɪm, -z, -ɪŋ/z, -d, -ɚ/z; -ɚ, -ɪst, -lɪ, -nɪs

Trinculo (*TEM*), **-s** 'tɹɪŋkjʊloʊ, -z

trinit|y (T.), -ies 'tɹɪnɪt|ɪ, -ɪz

trinket, -s 'tɹɪŋkɪt, -s

trio, -s 'tɹioʊ, -z

trip, -s, -ping/ly, -ped 'tɹɪp, -s, -ɪŋ/lɪ, -t

tripartite, -ly ˌtɹaɪ'pɑɚtaɪt ['-ˌ--], -lɪ

tripe, -s 'tɹaɪp, -s

tripe-visaged 'tɹaɪpˌvɪzɪdʒd

trip|le, -les, -ling, -led; -ly 'tɹɪp|l̩, -l̩z, -l̩ɪŋ [-lɪŋ], -l̩d; -lɪ

triplet, -s 'tɹɪplɪt, -s

triple-turned 'tɹɪpl̩ˌtɝnd

triplex 'tɹɪpleks ['tɹaɪp-]

Tripoli (TS) 'tɹɪpəlɪ, -plɪ

Tripolis (MV) 'tɹɪpəlɪs

trist, -ful, -fully 'tɹɪst, -fʊl, -fəlɪ

trite, -r, -st, -ly, -ness 'tɹaɪt, -ɚ, -ɪst, -lɪ, -nɪs

Triton (COR) 'tɹaɪtn̩

triumph, -s, -ing, -ed, -er/s 'tɹaɪəmf ['tɹaɪʌmf], -s, -ɪŋ, -t
Note.—This word is sometimes given primary stress on the second syllable in S., e.g., [tɹaɪ'ʌmfɪŋ] *in* LLL, IV.iii.33; [tɹaɪ'ʌmft] *in* 1HIV, V.iii.15; [tɹaɪ'ʌmfs] *in* 1HIV, V.iv.13; *and* [tɹaɪ'ʌmfɚz] *in* TIM, V.i.195

triumphal tɹaɪ'ʌmfl̩

triumphant, -ly tɹaɪ'ʌmfənt, -lɪ

triumvirate, -s tɹaɪ'ʌmvlɪɪt, -s

triumvir|y, -ies tɹaɪ'ʌmvɚ|ɹɪ [tɹaɪ'ʊm-], -ɹɪz

troat (*from 'throat'*) 'tɹoʊt (*see* **vere**)

trod (*from* **tread**), **-den** 'tɹɒd, -n̩

Troien (TC) 'tɹɔɪən

Troilus (ADO, *TC*, TN, TS), **-es** 'tɹoɪləs, 'tɹɔɪləs, -ɪz
Note.—In S. this name is always disyllabic, with one exception, i.e., TC, V.ii.160, where it is trisyllabic

Trojan (HV, 1HIV, 2HIV, 1HVI, LLL, LUC, MSND, MV, PER, TC), **-s** 'tɹoʊdʒən, -z

troll, -s, -ing, -ed, -er/s 'tɹoʊl, -z, -ɪŋ, -d, -ɚ/z

troll-my-dame, -s 'tɹoʊlmɪˌdeɪm [-mɪˌdæm], -z

troop, -s, -ing, -ed, -er/s 'tɹup, -s, -ɪŋ, -t, -ɚ/z

trope, -s 'tɹoʊp, -s

troph|y, -ies 'tɹoʊf|ɪ, -ɪz

tropic, -s, -al, -ally 'tɹɒpɪk, -s, -l̩, -əlɪ
Note.—In the First Quarto edition of HAM (III.ii.232), the spelling 'trapically' is presumably given to suggest a pun on "The Mousetrap" and would thus assume a pronunciation of ['tɹæpɪkəlɪ]

trot (*from 'troth'*) 'tɹoʊt (*see* **vere**)
Note.—In MWW, IV.v.83, Dr. Caius makes a mild oath, viz. 'by my troth.' 'Trot' in this case is presumably meant to stand for 'troth,' but it is worthwhile noting that from his Fr., 'throat' would sound exactly the same way

trot, -s, -ting, -ted, -ter/s 'tɹɒt, -s, -ɪŋ, -ɪd, -ɚ/z

tro|th, -ths 'tɹoʊ|θ ['tɹɒ|θ, 'tɹɔ|θ], -ðz [-θs]

troth-plight 'tɹoʊθˌplaɪt ['tɹɒθ-, 'tɹɔθ-]

troubadour, -s 'tɹubəˌdɔɚ, -z

troub|le, -les, -ling, -led, -ler/s 'tɹʌb|l̩, -l̩z, -l̩ɪŋ [-lɪŋ], -l̩d, -lɚ/z

troublesome, -ly, -ness 'tɹʌbl̩səm, -lɪ, -nɪs

troublous 'tɹʌbləs

trough, -s 'tɹɒf, -s

trove, -s 'tɪoŭv, -z
trow 'tɪoŭ
trowel, -s, -ling, -led 'tɪɑŭəl, -z, -ɪŋ, -d
Troy (ALL'S, 2HIV, 2HVI, 3HVI, JUL, LLL, LUC, MV, MWW, RII, TC, TIT) 'tɪɔĭ
Troyan (1HIV), **-s** 'tɪɔĭən, -z
Troyant (2HIV) 'tɪɔĭənt
truancy 'tɪuənsɪ
truant, -s 'tɪuənt, -s
truce, -s 'tɪus, -ɪz
truck, -s, -ing, -ed, -er/s 'tɪʌk, -s, -ɪŋ, -t, -ə/z
truckle-bed, -s 'tɪʌkl̩ˌbed, -z
trudg|e, -es, -ing, -ed 'tɪʌdʒ, -ɪz, -ɪŋ, -d
tr|ue, -uer, -uest, -uly, -ueness 'tɪ|u, -uə-, -uɪst, -ulɪ, -unɪs
true-anointed 'tɪuəˌnɔĭntɪd
true-born 'tɪuˌbɔ˞n
true-bred 'tɪuˌbɪed
true-derived 'tɪudɪˌɪaĭvd
true-devoted 'tɪudɪˌvoŭtɪd
true-disposing 'tɪudɪˌspoŭzɪŋ
true-divining 'tɪudɪˌvaĭnɪŋ
true-fixed 'tɪuˌfɪkst
true-hearted 'tɪuˌhɑ˞tɪd (*arguably* [ˌ-ˈ--] *in* HVIII, V.i.154)
true-man 'tɪuˌmæn [-ˌmən]
true-meant 'tɪuˌment
true-owed 'tɪuˌoŭd
truepenny (T.) 'tɪuˌpenɪ ['tɪupənɪ]
truer-hearted 'tɪuə-ˌhɑ˞tɪd
true-telling 'tɪuˌtelɪŋ
trull, -s 'tɪʌl, -z
truly 'tɪulɪ
truly-falsely ˌtɪulɪˈfɔlslɪ
trump, -s, -ing, -ed 'tɪʌmp, -s, -ɪŋ, -t
trumpery 'tɪʌmpə-ɹɪ
trumpet, -s, -ing, -ed, -er/s 'tɪʌmpɪt, -s, -ɪŋ, -ɪd, -ə/z
trumpet-clangor 'tɪʌmpɪtˌklæŋə-
trumpet-tongued 'tɪʌmpɪtˌtʌŋd
truncheon, -s, -ed, -er/s 'tɪʌntʃən, -z, -d, -ə/z

trund|le, -les, -ling, -led 'tɪʌnd|l̩, -l̩z, -l̩ɪŋ, -l̩d
trundle-tail 'tɪʌndl̩ˌteĭl
trunk, -s 'tɪʌŋk, -s
trunk-inheriting 'tɪʌŋkɪnˌheɹɪtɪŋ
trunk-work 'tɪʌŋkˌwɜ˞k
truss, -es, -ing, -ed 'tɪʌs, -ɪz, -ɪŋ, -t
trust (T.), **-s, -ing/ly, -ed, -er/s** 'tɪʌst, -s, -ɪŋ/lɪ, -ɪd, -ə/z
trustless 'tɪʌstlɪs
trust|y, -ier, -iest, -ily, -iness 'tɪʌst|ɪ, -ɪə-, -ɪɪst, -ɪlɪ, -ɪnɪs
tru|th (T.), **-ths** 'tɪu|θ, -ðz [-θs]
tr|y, -ies, -ying, -ied, -ier/s 'tɪ|aĭ, -aĭz, -aĭɪŋ, -aĭd, -aĭə/z
tub, -s, -bing, -bed 'tʌb, -z, -ɪŋ, -d
Tubal(l) (*MV*) 'tjubəl [-bɔl]
tub-fast 'tʌbˌfast
tuck, -s, -ing, -ed 'tʌk, -s, -ɪŋ, -t
tucker, -s, -ing, -ed 'tʌkə-, -z, -ɹɪŋ, -d
tucket, -s 'tʌkɪt, -s
Tudor, -s 'tjudə-, -z
Tuesday (ADO, ALL'S, 1HIV, 2HIV, MAC, MEAS, OTH), **-s** 'tjuzdɪ [-deĭ], -z
tuft, -s, -ing, -ed 'tʌft, -s, -ɪŋ, -ɪd
tug, -s, -ging, -ged, -ger/s 'tʌg, -z, -ɪŋ, -d, -ə/z
tuition, -s tju'ɪʃn̩, -z
tulip, -s 'tjulɪp, -s
Tully (2HVI, TIT) 'tʌlɪ
tumb|le, -les, -ling, -led 'tʌmb|l̩, -l̩z, -lɪŋ [-l̩ɪŋ], -l̩d
tumbler, -s 'tʌmblə-, -z
tumbling-trick 'tʌmblɪŋˌtɪɪk
tumult, -s 'tjumʌlt, -s
tumultuous, -ly, -ness tju'mʌltjŭəs, -lɪ, -nɪs
tun, -s, -ning, -ned 'tʌn, -z, -ɪŋ, -d
tun-dish, -es 'tʌnˌdɪʃ, -ɪz
tundra, -s 'tʌndɹə, -z
tun|e, -es, -ing, -ed, -er/s; -eable 'tjun, -z, -ɪŋ, -d, -ə/z; -əbl̩
tunic, -s 'tjunɪk, -s
Tunis (TEM) 'tjunɪs

---

i wĕ ɨ citỵ ɪ hĭt e lĕt ɛ dĕbut æ căn a păss ɜ˞ bĭrd ʌ hŭt ə agaĭn ə˞ suppĕr u yŏu
ŭ shŏuld o ŏbey ɔ ăwl ɒ cŏp ɑ făther eĭ paĭd aĭ hĭgh oŭ gŏ ɔĭ vŏice aŭ fŏund ɪə˞ ĕar
ɛə˞ ăir ŭə˞ pŏor ɔə˞ fŏrk ɑə˞ părk aĭə˞ fĭre aŭə˞ hŏur b bŏy p pĭt d dŏg t tŏp g gŏt
k kĭd h hŏw ɦ beháve dʒ jŏt tʃ chĕw z zăny s sŏft v vặt f făt ʒ treăsure ʃ shĭp ð thĕ
θ thĭn m măn n nŏ ŋ hăng l lĭp j yĕs w wŏn ʍ whĕw ɹ rĭgger, aiɾỵ ɾ mătter

tup, -s, -ping, -ped 'tʌp, -s, -ɪŋ, -t
turban, -s, -ed 'tɝbən, -z, -d
turbulen|ce, -cy, -t/ly 'tɝbjʊlən|s, -sɪ, -t/lɪ
turd or **tird** (from 'third') 'tɝd (see dat)
turd, -s 'tɝd, -z
tur|f (s.), **-fs, -ves** 'tɝ|f, -fs, -vz
turf (v.), **-s, -ing, -ed** 'tɝf, -s, -ɪŋ, -t
turf|y, -ier, -iest, -iness 'tɝf|ɪ, -ɪɚ, -ɪɪst, -ɪnɪs
Turk (ADO, ALL'S, AYLI, HAM, 1HIV, 2HIV, HV, 1HVI, LEAR, MAC, MV, MWW, OTH, RII, RIII), **-s** 'tɝk, -s
Turkey 'tɝkɪ
turkey, -s 'tɝkɪ, -z
turkey-cock, -s 'tɝkɪkɒk, -s
Turkish (COM, 2HIV, HV, OTH) 'tɝkɪʃ
Turlygod, Poor (LEAR) 'pʊɚ 'tɝlɪgɒd (alias Edgar in LEAR)
turmoil, -s 'tɝmɔɪl, -z
Note.—**turmoiled** in 2HVI, IV.x.16 is pronounced [tɝ'mɔɪlɪd]
turn, -s, -ing, -ed 'tɝn, -z, -ɪŋ, -d
Turnbull Street (2HIV) 'tɝnbʊl 'stɹit
turncoat, -s 'tɝnkoŏt ['tɝŋk-], -s
turnip, -s 'tɝnɪp, -s
Turph, Peter (TS) 'piɾɚ 'tɝf
turpitude 'tɝpɪtjud
turret, -s, -ed 'tʌɹɪt, -s, -ɪd
turtle (**T.**) (PT), **-s** 'tɝtl̩, -z
Tuscan, -s, -y 'tʌskən, -z, -ɪ
tush (buttocks), **-es** 'tʊʃ, -ɪz
tush, -es (interj.) 'tʌʃ, -ɪz
tush (tusk), **-es, -ing, -ed** 'tʌʃ, -ɪz, -ɪŋ, -t
tut (interj.) 'tʌt ['ɪ]
tu|t (s., v.), **-ts, -tting, -tted** 'tʌ|t, -ts, -ɾɪŋ, -ɾɪd
Tuthill Fields (3HVI) 'tʌtfɪɹl 'fildz
tu-whit tʊ'ʍɪt
tu-who(o) tʊ'ʍu [tʊ'wu]
twain 'tweɪn
twang|le, -les, -ling, -led 'twæŋg|l̩, -l̩z, -l̩ɪŋ [-lɪŋ], -l̩d
'twas (contr. of **it was**) 'twɒz (strong form) 'twəz (weak form)
'tween (from **between**) 'twin
twelv(e)month 'twelvmʌnθ [-mənθ]
twent|y, -ies, -ieth/s 'twent|ɪ, -ɪz, -ɪɪθ/s

twenty-six ˌtwentɪ'sɪks (when att., ['--ˌ-])
'twere (contr. of **it were**) 'twɝ
twice 'twaɪs
twice-told 'twaɪsˌtoŏld
twig, -s, -ging, -ged 'twɪg, -z, -ɪŋ, -d
twilight, -s 'twaɪlaɪt, -s
twill, -s, -ing, -ed; -y 'twɪl, -z, -ɪŋ, -d; -ɪ
'twill (contr. of **it will**) 'twɪl
twin, -s, -ning, -ned 'twɪn, -z, -ɪŋ, -d
twin-born 'twɪnˌbɔɝn
twin|e, -es, -ing/ly, -ed 'twaɪn, -z, -ɪŋ/lɪ, -d
twing|e, -es, -ing, -ed 'twɪndʒ, -ɪz, -ɪŋ, -d
twink 'twɪŋk
twink|le, -les, -ling, -led, -ler/s 'twɪŋk|l̩, -l̩z, -lɪŋ [-l̩ɪŋ], -l̩d, -lɚ/z [-l̩ɚ/z]
twire 'twaɪɚ
twirl, -z, -ing, -ed 'twɝl, -z, -ɪŋ, -d
twist, -s, -ing, -ed, -er/s 'twɪst, -s, -ɪŋ, -ɪd, -ɚ/z
twit, -s, -ting/ly, -ted 'twɪt, -s, -ɪŋ/lɪ, -ɪd
twitch, -es, -ing, -ed 'twɪtʃ, -ɪz, -ɪŋ, -t
'twixt (from **betwixt**) 'twɪkst
two, -s 'tu, -z
two-and-twenty ˌtuənd'twentɪ
twofold 'tufoŏld
two-headed 'tuˌhedɪd
two-legged 'tuˌlegd [ˌ-'-] (when att., [ˌ-'-], ˌtu'legɪd)
twopence, -s 'tʌpəns, -ɪz
'twould (contr. of **it would**) 'twʊd
Tybalt (RJ) 'tɪbəlt
Tyburn (LLL) 'taɪbɝn
tying (from **tie**, q.v.) 'taɪɪŋ
tyke or **tike, -s** 'taɪk, -s
Tymbria or **Timbria** (TC) 'tɪmbɹɪə
typ|e, -es, -ing, -ed 'taɪp, -s, -ɪŋ, -t
typhoid 'taɪfɔɪd
Typhon (TC, TIT) 'taɪfɒn
typhoon, -s taɪ'fun, -z
tyrannic|al, -ally, -alness tɪ'ɹænɪk|l̩, -lɪ [-əlɪ], -l̩nɪs
tyranniz|e, -es, -ing, -ed 'tɪɹənaɪz, -ɪz, -ɪŋ, -d
tyrannous, -ly 'tɪɹənəs, -lɪ
tyrann|y, -ies 'tɪɹən|ɪ, -ɪz
tyrant (**T.**), **-s** 'taɪɹənt ['taɪɚˌɹənt], -s
Tyre (PER) 'taɪɚ
Tyrian (PER, TS) 'tɪɹɪən, -ɹĭən

Tyrrel(l), Sir James (*RIII*) ˌsɝ ˈdʒeɪ̆mz
  ˈtɪɹəl
Tyrus (PER) ˈtaɪ̆ɝ-ɹəs
tzar (*var. of* **czar**), **-s** ˈtsɑɝ-, -z

Uu

U (*the letter*), **-'s** juː, -z
ubiquitous, -ly, -ness juˈbɪkwɪtəs, -lɪ, -nɪs
ubiquity juˈbɪkwɪtɪ
udder, -s ˈʌdɝ-, -z
'udge (*from 'judge'; see* **'orld**) ˈʌdʒ, ˈʊdʒ
ud's pity (*corrupt contr. of* **God's pity**)
  ədzˈpɪ̆ɾɪ
ugh ˈʌg, ˈʌx
uglification ˌʌglɪfɪˈkeɪ̆ʃn̩
ugli|fy, -fies, -fying, -fied ˈʌglɪ|faɪ̆, -faɪ̆z,
  -faɪ̆ɪŋ, -faɪ̆d
ugl|y, -ier, -iest, -iness ˈʌgl|ɪ, -ɪɝ-, -ɪɪst,
  -ɪnɪs
uh ˈə
u(h)lan, -s ˈulɑn [ˈjulən, ʊˈlɑn], -z
ulcer, -s ˈʌlsɝ-, -z
ulcerous ˈʌlsə-ɹəs
Ulysses (COR, 3HVI, LUC, *TC*) juˈlɪsɪz
  [jʊˈl-]
umbel, -s ˈʌmbəl, -z
umber, -s, -ing, -ed ˈʌmbɝ-, -z, -ɹɪŋ, -d
umbilical ʌmˈbɪlɪkl̩
umbrage ˈʌmbɹɪdʒ
umbrella, -s ʌmˈbɹelə, -z
Umfrevile, Sir John (2HIV) ˌsɝ- ˈdʒɒn
  ˈʌmfɹɪvɪl
umlaut, -s ˈʊmlaʊ̆t, -s
umpir|e, -es, -ing, -ed ˈʌmpaɪ̆ɝ-, -z, -ɹɪŋ,
  -d
unabashed ˌʌnəˈbæʃt
unabated ˌʌnəˈbeɪ̆tɪd
unable ʌnˈeɪ̆bl̩
unabridged ˌʌnəˈbɹɪdʒd
unacceptable ˌʌnəkˈseptəbl̩
unaccommodated ˌʌnəˈkɒmədeɪ̆tɪd

unaccompanied ˌʌnəˈkʌmpənɪd
unaccountab|le, -ly, -leness
  ˌʌnəˈkaʊntəbl̩|, -lɪ, -l̩nɪs
unaccustomed ˌʌnəˈkʌstəmd
unaching ˌʌnˈeɪ̆kɪŋ
unacknowledged ˌʌnəkˈnɒlɪdʒd
unacquainted ˌʌnəˈkweɪ̆ntɪd
unacted ˌʌnˈæktɪd
unactive ˌʌnˈæktɪv
unadaptable ˌʌnəˈdæptəbl̩
unaddressed ˌʌnəˈdɹest
unadorned ˌʌnəˈdɔɝ-nd
unadvisable ˌʌnədˈvaɪ̆zəbl̩
unadvised ˌʌnədˈvaɪ̆zd
unadvisedly ˌʌnədˈvaɪ̆zɪdlɪ
unagreeable ˌʌnəˈgɹiəbl̩
unaneled ˌʌnəˈnild
unannounced ˌʌnəˈnaʊ̆nst
unanswerable ˌʌnˈansɝ-ɹəbl̩
unanswered ˌʌnˈansɝ-d
unappeased ˌʌnəˈpizd
unapproved ˌʌnəˈpɹuvd ([-vɪd] *in* LC, 53)
unapt, -ness ˌʌnˈæpt, -nɪs
unarm, -s, -ing, -ed ˌʌnˈɑɝ-m, -z, -ɪŋ, -d
unashamed ˌʌnəˈʃeɪ̆md
unasked ˌʌnˈaskt
unaspirated ˌʌnˈæspɹɪeɪ̆tɪd
unassailable ˌʌnəˈseɪ̆ləbl̩
unassisted ˌʌnəˈsɪstɪd
unassuming ˌʌnəˈsjumɪŋ
unattached ˌʌnəˈtætʃt
unattainted ˌʌnəˈteɪ̆ntɪd
unattempted ˌʌnəˈtemptɪd
unattended ˌʌnəˈtendɪd
unauspicious ˌʌnɔˈspɪʃəs
unauthorized ˌʌnˈɔθə-ɹaɪ̆zd
unavoided ˌʌnəˈvɔɪ̆dɪd
unaware, -s ˌʌnəˈwɛɝ-, -z
unback, -s, -ing, -ed ˌʌnˈbæk, -s, -ɪŋ, -t
  ([ˈʌnˌbækt] *in* TEM, IV.i.176; VA, 320)
unbanded ˌʌnˈbændɪd
unbar ˌʌnˈbɑɝ-
unbarbed ˌʌnˈbɑɝ-bd
unbashful ˌʌnˈbæʃfʊl

---

i w**e** ɪ cit**y** ɪ h**i**t e l**e**t ɛ d**e**but æ c**a**n a p**a**ss ɝ b**i**rd ʌ h**u**t ə **a**gain ɝ supp**er** u y**ou**
ʊ sh**ou**ld o **o**bey ɔ **a**wl ɒ c**o**p ɑ f**a**ther eɪ̆ p**ai**d aɪ̆ h**igh** oŭ g**o** ɔɪ̆ v**oi**ce aʊ̆ f**ou**nd ɪ̆ɝ **ear**
ɛɝ **air** ʊɝ p**oor** ɔɝ f**ork** ɑɝ p**ark** aɪ̆ɝ f**ire** aʊ̆ɝ h**our** b **b**oy p **p**it d **d**og t **t**op g **g**ot
k **k**id h **h**ow fi be**h**ave dʒ **j**ot tʃ **ch**ew z **z**any s **s**oft v **v**at f **f**at ʒ trea**s**ure ʃ **sh**ip ð **th**e
θ **th**in m **m**an n **n**o ŋ ha**ng** l **l**ip j **y**es w **w**on ʍ **wh**ew ɹ **r**igger, ai**r**y ɾ ma**tt**er

unbated ˌʌnˈbeɪ̆tɪd
unbattered ˌʌnˈbæɾɚd
unbearab|le, -ly, -leness ˌʌnˈbɛɚ̆ˌɹəb|l̩, -lɪ, -l̩nɪs
unbeatable ˌʌnˈbitəbl̩
unbeaten ˌʌnˈbitn̩
unbecoming, -ly, -ness ˌʌnbɪˈkʌmɪŋ, -lɪ, -nɪs
unbefitting ˌʌnbɪˈfɪɾɪŋ
unbegot, -ten ˌʌnbɪˈgɒt, -n̩
unbeknown, -st ˌʌnbɪˈnoʊ̆n, -st
unbelieved (adj. in MEAS, V.i.122) ˌʌnbɪˈlivɪd
unbelieving ˌʌnbɪˈlivɪŋ
unbend, -s, -ing, unbent ˌʌnˈbend, -z, -ɪŋ, ˌʌnˈbent
unbewailed ˌʌnbɪˈweɪ̆ld
unbidden ˌʌnˈbɪdn̩
unbind, -s, -ing, unbound ˌʌnˈbaɪ̆nd, -z, -ɪŋ, ˌʌnˈbaʊ̆nd
unbitted ˌʌnˈbɪtɪd
unblemished ˌʌnˈblemɪʃt
unbless, -ed (v.) ˌʌnˈbles, -t
unblest (adj.) ˌʌnˈblest
unblowed ˌʌnˈbloʊ̆d ([ˈ-,-] in RIII, IV.iv.10; Q., F.)
unblown ˌʌnˈbloʊ̆n ([ˈ-,-] in RIII, IV.iv.10)
unbodied ˌʌnˈbɒdɪd
unbolt, -s, -ing, -ed ˌʌnˈboʊ̆lt, -s, -ɪŋ, -ɪd
unbonneted ˌʌnˈbɒnɪtɪd
unbookish ˌʌnˈbʊkɪʃ
unborn ˌʌnˈbɔɚ̆n ([ˈ-,-] in 1HIV, V.i.21; RII, II.ii.10)
unbosom ˌʌnˈbʊzəm
unbound, -ed ˌʌnˈbaʊ̆nd ([ˈ-,-] in RJ, I.iii.87), -ɪd
unbowed ˌʌnˈboʊ̆d
unbraced ˌʌnˈbɹeɪ̆st
unbraided ˌʌnˈbɹeɪ̆dɪd
unbred ˌʌnˈbɹed
unbreeched ˌʌnˈbɹitʃt
unbridled ˌʌnˈbɹaɪ̆dl̩d
unbroke ˌʌnˈbɹoʊ̆k ([ˈ-,-] in RII, IV.i.215)
unbroken ˌʌnˈbɹoʊ̆kən
unbruised ˌʌnˈbɹuzd
unbuck|le, -les, -ling, -led ˌʌnˈbʌk|l̩, -l̩z, -l̩ɪŋ [-lɪŋ], -l̩d
unbuild ˌʌnˈbɪld
unburdened ˌʌnˈbɝ̆dn̩d

unburied ˌʌnˈbeˌɹɪd
unburnt ˌʌnˈbɝ̆nt
unburden, -s, -ing, -ed ˌʌnˈbɝ̆dn̩, -z, -ɪŋ, -d
unburthen ˌʌnˈbɝ̆ðən [-ðn̩] (see Note for murther)
unbutton, -s, -ing, -ed ˌʌnˈbʌtn̩, -z, -ɪŋ, -d
uncandied ˌʌnˈkændɪd
uncapable ˌʌnˈkeɪ̆pəbl̩
uncas|e,—ing ˌʌnˈkeɪ̆s, -ɪŋ
uncaught ˌʌnˈkɔt
unceremonious, -ly, -ness ˌʌnˌseˌɹɪˈmoʊ̆nɪəs [ˌ---ˈ---], -lɪ, -nɪs
uncertain, -ly ˌʌnˈsɝ̆tn̩, -lɪ
uncertaint|y, -ies ˌʌnˈsɝ̆tn̩t|ɪ [-tɪnt|ɪ], -ɪz
unchain, -s, -ing, -ed ˌʌnˈtʃeɪ̆n, -z, -ɪŋ, -d
uncharge, -d ˌʌnˈtʃɑɚ̆dʒ, -d (arguably [ˈʌnˌtʃɑɚ̆ˌdʒd] in TIM, V.iv.55)
uncharitab|le, -ly, -leness ˌʌnˈtʃæˌɹɪtəb|l̩, -lɪ, -l̩nɪs
uncharmed ˌʌnˈtʃɑɚ̆md
unchary ˌʌnˈtʃɛɚ̆ˌɹɪ
unchaste ˌʌnˈtʃeɪ̆st (arguably [ˈ-,-] in CYM, V.v.284; LEAR, I.i.230)
unchecked ˌʌnˈtʃekt ([ˈ-,-] in TIM, IV.iii.447)
uncheerful ˌʌnˈtʃɪɚ̆ˌfʊl
unchilded ˌʌnˈtʃaɪ̆ldɪd
unciv|il, -illy ˌʌnˈsɪv|l̩, -əlɪ
uncivilized ˌʌnˈsɪvl̩aɪ̆zd [-vɪlaɪ̆zd]
unclaimed ˌʌnˈkleɪ̆md
unclasp, -s, -ing, -ed ˌʌnˈklasp, -s, -ɪŋ, -t
unclassified ˌʌnˈklæsɪfaɪ̆d
uncle, -s ˈʌŋkl̩, -z
unclean ˌʌnˈklin (when att., [ˈ-,-])
uncleanliness ˌʌnˈklenlɪnɪs
uncleanly ˌʌnˈklenlɪ
uncleanness ˌʌnˈklinnɪs
unclear ˌʌnˈklɪɚ̆
unclew ˌʌnˈklu
unclog ˌʌnˈklɒg
uncoined ˌʌnˈkɔɪ̆nd (probably [ˈʌnˌkɔɪ̆nd] in HV, V.ii.154 as an att.)
uncolted (not tricked or cheated) ˌʌnˈkoʊ̆ltɪd ([ˈ-,--] in 1HIV, II.ii.38)
uncomeliness ˌʌnˈkʌmlɪnɪs
uncomely ˌʌnˈkʌmlɪ
uncomfortab|le, -ly, -leness ˌʌnˈkʌmfɚ̆ˌɾəb|l̩ [-ftɚ̆b-], -lɪ, -l̩nɪs

uncompassionate ˌʌnkəm'pæʃnɪt
uncomprehensive ʌnˌkɒmpɹɪ'fiensɪv
unconfinable ˌʌnkən'faɪnəbl̩
unconfirmed ˌʌnkən'fɜ·md
unconsidered ˌʌnkən'sɪdə·d (*when att.*, ['--ˌ--'])
unconstant ˌʌn'kɒnstənt
unconstrain|ed, -edly ˌʌnkən'stɹeɪn|d, -ɪdlɪ
uncontemned ˌʌnkən'temd
uncontrolled ˌʌnkən'tɹoŭld
uncorrected ˌʌnkə·'ɹektɪd
uncounted ˌʌn'kɑŭntɪd
uncoupl|e, -es, -ing, -es ˌʌn'kʌpl̩ , -z, -ɪŋ, -d
uncourteous ˌʌn'kɜ·tɪəs
uncouth, -ly, -ness ˌʌn'kuθ, -lɪ, -nɪs (*arguably* ['-ˌ-] *in* LUC, 1598; TIT, II. ii.211)
uncover, -s, -ing, -ed ˌʌn'kʌvə·, -z, -ɹɪŋ, -d
uncropped ˌʌn'kɹɒpt ([-pɹd] *in* ALL'S, V.iii.324)
uncross, -es, -ing, -ed ˌʌn'kɹɒs, -ɪz, -ɪŋ, -t (*when att., or in contrast*, ['ʌnˌkɹ-])
unction, -s 'ʌŋkʃn̩, -z
unctuous, -ly, -ness 'ʌŋktʃʊəs, -lɪ, -nɪs
uncuckolded ˌʌn'kʌkoŭldɪd [-'kʌkəld-]
uncurable ˌʌn'kjʊɜ·ɹəbl̩
uncurbable ˌʌn'kɜ·bəbl̩
uncurbed ˌʌn'kɜ·bɹd
uncurrent ˌʌn'kʌɹənt
uncurse ˌʌn'kɜ·s
uncut ˌʌn'kʌt ['-ˌ-]
undaunted, -ly, -ness ˌʌn'dɔntɪd, -lɪ, -nɪs
undeaf ˌʌn'def
undeck ˌʌn'dek
undeeded ˌʌn'didɪd
under 'ʌndə·
underbear (*v.*) ˌʌndə·'bɛɜ·
underbearing (*s.*) 'ʌndə·ˌbɛɜ·ɹɪŋ
underborne 'ʌndə·bɔɜ·n [ˌ--'-]
undercrest 'ʌndə·kɹest
undergarnished ˌʌndə·'gɑɜ·nɪʃt ['--ˌ--]

under-globe 'ʌndə·ˌgloŭb
under|go, -goes, -going, -went, -gone ˌʌndə·|'goŭ, -'goŭz, -'goŭɪŋ, -'went, -'gɒn
underhand 'ʌndə·fiænd [ˌ--'-]
underhanded, -ly, -ness ˌʌndə·'hændɪd, -lɪ, -nɪs
under-hangman 'ʌndə·ˌhæŋmən
under(-)honest ˌʌndə·'ɹɒnɪst
underling, -s 'ʌndə·lɪŋ, -z
undermin|e, -es, -ing, -ed, -er/s ˌʌndə·'maɪn ['--ˌ-], -z, -ɪŋ, -d, -ə·/z
under-peep 'ʌndə·ˌpip
underprizing ˌʌndə·'pɹaɪzɪŋ
underprop, -s, -ping, -ped ˌʌndə·'pɹɒp, -s, -ɪŋ, -t
undershrinker 'ʌndə·ˌʃɹɪŋkə·
understand, -s, -ing/s, understood ˌʌndə·'stænd, -z, -ɪŋ/z, ˌʌndə·'stʊd
underta'en ˌʌndə·'teɪn
under|take, -takes, -taking/s, -took, -taken ˌʌndə·|'teɪk, -'teɪks, -'teɪkɪŋ/z, -'tʊk, -'teɪkən
undertaker (*endeavoring a task*), **-s** ˌʌndə·'teɪkə·, -z
undertaker (*mortician*), **-s** 'ʌndə·teɪkə·, -z
underval|ue, -ues, -uing, -ued ˌʌndə·'væl|ju, -juz, -juɪŋ, -jud
under(-)world 'ʌndə·ˌwɜ·ld
underwrit 'ʌndə·ˌɹɪt
underwrit|e, -es, -ing, underwrote, underwritten 'ʌndə·ɹaɪt [ˌ--'-], -s, -ɪŋ, 'ʌndə·ɹoŭt [ˌ--'-], 'ʌndə·ɹɪtn̩ [ˌ--'--]
underwrought ˌʌndə·'ɹɔt ['--ˌ-]
undescried ˌʌndɪ'skɹaɪd
undeserv|ed, -edly, -edness ˌʌndɪ'zɜ·v|d, -ɪdlɪ, -ɪdnɪs
undeserver, -s ˌʌndɪ'zɜ·və·, -z
undeserving, -ly ˌʌndɪ'zɜ·vɪŋ, -lɪ
undetermined ˌʌndɪ'tɜ·mɪnd
undid ˌʌn'dɪd (['-ˌ-] *in* AC, II.ii.205)
undinted ˌʌn'dɪntɪd
undiscernible ˌʌndɪ'sɜ·nɪbl̩
undiscerning ˌʌndɪ'sɜ·nɪŋ

---

i wĕ ɪ cĭty ɪ hĭt e lĕt ɛ dĕbut æ căn a păss ɜ· bĭrd ʌ hŭt ə agaĭn ə· suppĕr u yŏu
ʊ shŏuld o ŏbey ɔ ăwl ɒ cŏp ɑ făther eɪ paĭd aɪ hĭgh oŭ gŏ ɔɪ vŏice aŭ fŏund ɪɜ· eăr
ɛɜ· aĭr ʊɜ· pŏor ɔɜ· fŏrk ɑɜ· părk aɪɜ· fĭre aŭɜ· hŏur b bŏy p pĭt d dŏg t tŏp g gŏt
k kĭd h hŏw fi behăve dʒ jŏt tʃ chĕw z zăny s sŏft v văt f făt ʒ treăsure ʃ shĭp ð thĕ
θ thĭn m măn n nŏ ŋ hăng l lĭp j yĕs w wŏn ʌ whĕw ɹ rĭgger, airy ɟ matter

undiscovered ˌʌndɪˈskʌvəd (*when att.*, [ˈ--ˌ--])

undistinguished ˌʌndɪˈstɪŋgwɪʃt

undistinguishable ˌʌndɪˈstɪŋgwɪʃəbl̩

undivid|ed, -edly, -edness; -able ˌʌndɪˈvaɪd|ɪd, -ɪdlɪ, -ɪdnɪs; -əbl̩

undivulged ˌʌndɪˈvʌldʒd [-daɪˈv-]

un|do, -does, -doing, -did, -done, -doer/s ˌʌnˈdu, -ˈdʌz, -ˈduɪŋ, -ˈdɪd, -ˈdʌn, -ˈduə-/z

undo't (*contr. of* **undo it**) ˌʌnˈduˈt (*perhaps* [ˈ-ˌ-] *in* OTH, IV.iii.70)

undoubted, -ly ˌʌnˈdaʊtɪd, -lɪ

undoubtful ˌʌnˈdaʊtfʊl

undreamed ˌʌnˈdɹimd ([ˈ-ˌ-] *in* WT, IV. iv.568)

undress, -es, -ing, -ed ˌʌnˈdɹes, -ɪz, -ɪŋ, -t

undrowned ˌʌnˈdɹaʊnd

unduteous ˌʌnˈdjutɪəs [-tjəs]

uneath ˌʌnˈiθ

uneared ˌʌnˈɪə-d (*when att.*, [ˈ-ˌ-])

unearth, -s, -ing, -ed ˌʌnˈɜ-θ, -s, -ɪŋ, -t

unearthl|y, -iness ˌʌnˈɜ-θl|ɪ, -ɪnɪs

uneas|y, -ier, -iest, -ily, -iness ˌʌnˈiz|ɪ, -ɪə-, -ɪɪst, -ɪlɪ, -ɪnɪs

unelected ˌʌnɪˈlektɪd

unequal, -s, -led ˌʌnˈikwəl, -z, -d

uneven, -ly, -ness ˌʌnˈivn̩, -lɪ, -nɪs

unexamined ˌʌnɪgˈzæmɪnd

unexecuted ˌʌnˈeksɪkjutɪd

unexpected ˌʌnɪkˈspektɪd

unexperienced ˌʌnɪkˈspɪə-ɹɪənst

unexperient ˌʌnɪkˈspɪə-ɹɪənt

unexpressive ˌʌnɪkˈspɹesɪv

unfair, -ly, -ness ˌʌnˈfɛə-, -lɪ, -nɪs

unfallible (*var. of* **infallible**) ˌʌnˈfælɪbl̩

unfamed ˌʌnˈfeɪmd

unfasten, -s, -ing, -ed ˌʌnˈfasn̩, -z, -ɪŋ, -d

unfathered ˌʌnˈfɑðə-d

unfeared ˌʌnˈfɪə-d

unfed ˌʌnˈfed ([ˈ-ˌ-] *in* LEAR, III.iv.30)

unfee(')d ˌʌnˈfid (*when att.*, [ˈ-ˌ-])

unfeeling, -ly ˌʌnˈfilɪŋ, -lɪ

unfeigned ˌʌnˈfeɪnd

unfeigned|ly, -ness ˌʌnˈfeɪnɪd|lɪ, -nɪs

unfellowed ˌʌnˈfeloʊd

unfelt ˌʌnˈfelt ([ˈ-ˌ-] *in* LUC, 828)

unfenced ˌʌnˈfenst ([-sɪd] *in* KJ, II.i.386)

unfilial, -ly ˌʌnˈfɪlɪəl, -ɪ

unfilled ˌʌnˈfɪld

unfinished ˌʌnˈfɪnɪʃt (*when att.*, [ˈ-ˌ--])

unfirm ˌʌnˈfɜ-m ([ˈ--] *in* 2HIV, I.iii.73)

unfit (*adj.*), **-ly, -ness** ˌʌnˈfɪt, -lɪ, -nɪs

unfit (*v.*), **-s, -ting, -ted** ˌʌnˈfɪt [ˌʌnˈf-], -s, -ɪŋ, -ɪd

unfix ˌʌnˈfɪks

unfledged ˌʌnˈfledʒd

unfold, -s, -ing, -ed ˌʌnˈfoʊld, -z, -ɪŋ, -ɪd (*arguably* [ˈ-ˌ-] *in* WT, IV.i.2)

unfool ˌʌnˈful

unforfeited ˌʌnˈfɔ-fɪtɪd

unfought ˌʌnˈfɔt

unfrequented ˌʌnfɹɪˈkwentɪd

unfriended ˌʌnˈfɹendɪd

unfriendly ˌʌnˈfɹendlɪ

unfruit|ful, -fully, -fulness ˌʌnˈfɹut|fʊl, -fʊlɪ, -fʊlnɪs

unfurnish, -ed ˌʌnˈfɜ-nɪʃ, -t

ungained ˌʌnˈgeɪnd

ungall, -s, -ing, -ed ˌʌnˈgɔl, -z, -ɪŋ, -d

un garçon, un paysan (*Fr.*) (MWW, V.v.202) œ̃ gaʁˈsɔ̃ œ̃ peɪˈzɑ̃

ungartered ˌʌnˈgɑə-tə-d

ungenerative ˌʌnˈdʒenə-ɹətɪv

ungenitured ˌʌnˈdʒenɪtʃə-d

ungent|le, -ly, -leness ˌʌnˈdʒent|l̩, -lɪ, -l̩nɪs

ungird, -s, -ing, -ed ˌʌnˈgɜ-d, -z, -ɪŋ, -ɪd

unglu|e, -es, -ing, -ed ˌʌnˈglu, -z, -ɪŋ, -d

ungodl|y, -ier, -iest, -iness ˌʌnˈgɒdl|ɪ, -ɪə-, -ɪɪst, -ɪnɪs

ungored ˌʌnˈgɔə-d

ungorged ˌʌnˈgɔə-dʒd

ungot ˌʌnˈgɒt

ungotten ˌʌnˈgɒtn̩

ungovernab|le, -ly, -leness ˌʌnˈgʌvə-nəb|l̩, -lɪ, -l̩nɪs

ungoverned ˌʌnˈgʌvə-nd

ungracious ˌʌnˈgɹeɪʃəs

ungrateful, -ly, -ness ˌʌnˈgɹeɪtfʊl, -ɪ, -nɪs

ungravely ˌʌnˈgɹeɪvlɪ

ungrown ˌʌnˈgɹoʊn ([ˈ-ˌ-] *in* 1HIV, V.iv.22; VA, 526)

unguarded ˌʌnˈgɑə-dɪd

unguem (*ad . . . unguem*) (*L.*) (LLL, V.i.72) ad . . . ˈʌŋgwəm
Note.—Normally, I would recommend [ɑd . . . ˈʊŋgwəm], *but there is some thinly disguised humor in echoing*

'dung.' Costard has just blundered in the line before, with "ad dunghill"
unguided ˌʌnˈɡaɪ̆dɪd
unhacked ˌʌnˈhækt ([ˈ-,-] *in* AC, II.vi.38; KJ, II.i.254)
unhair ˌʌnˈhɛɚ̆
unhaired ˌʌnˈhɛɚ̆d ([ˈ-,-] *in* KJ, V.ii.133)
unhallowed ˌʌnˈhæloŏd
unhandled ˌʌnˈhændl̩d
unhandsome ˌʌnˈhænsəm
unhappied ˌʌnˈhæpɪd
unhapp|y, -ier, -iest, -ily, -iness ˌʌnˈhæp|ɪ, -ɪɚ̆, -ɪɪst, -ɪlɪ, -ɪnɪs
unhardened ˌʌnˈhɑɚ̆dn̩d
unhatched ˌʌnˈhætʃt ([ˈ-,-] *in* OTH, III.iv.138)
unheard ˌʌnˈhɜ̆d
unhearts ˌʌnˈhɑɚ̆ts
unheed|ed, -ing ˌʌnˈhid|ɪd, -ɪŋ
unheed|ful ˌʌnˈhid|fʊl, -fəlɪ
unheedy ˌʌnˈhidɪ
unhidden ˌʌnˈhɪdn̩
unhing|e, -es, -ing, -ed ˌʌnˈhɪndʒ, -ɪz, -ɪŋ, -d
unhopefullest ˌʌnˈhoŏpfʊlɪst
unhors|e, -es, -ing, -ed ˌʌnˈhɔɚ̆s, -ɪz, -ɪŋ, -t
unhospitable ˌʌnˈhɒspɪtəbl̩ [-spɪɾə-, ˌ--ˈ---]
unhous|e, -es, -ing, -ed ˌʌnˈhaŏz, -ɪz, -ɪŋ, -d
unhouseled ˌʌnˈhaŏzl̩d
unhurt, -ful ˌʌnˈhɜ̆t, -fʊl
unicorn, -s ˈjunɪkɔɚ̆n, -z
uninhabitable, -ness ˌʌnɪnˈhæbɪtəbl̩, -nɪs
unintelligent, -ly ˌʌnɪnˈtelɪdʒənt, -lɪ
union, -s ˈjunjən, -z
unit|e, -es, -ing, -ed/ly, -er/s juˈnaɪ̆t [jʊˈn-], -s, -ɪŋ, -ɪd/lɪ, -ɚ̆/z
unit|y, -ies ˈjunɪt|ɪ, -ɪz
universe, -s ˈjunɪvɜ̆s, -ɪz
universit|y, -ies ˌjunɪˈvɜ̆sɪt|ɪ, -ɪz [ˌjʊnɪ-]
unjointed ˌʌnˈdʒɔɪ̆ntɪd
unjust, -ly, -ness ˌʌnˈdʒʌst (*when att.,* [ˈ--]), -lɪ, -nɪs

unkennel ˌʌnˈkenl̩
unkept ˌʌnˈkept
unkin|d, -der, -dest, -dly, -dness ˌʌnˈkaɪ̆n|d, -dɚ̆, -dɪst, -dlɪ, -dnɪs
Note.—[ˈ-,-] *in* 1HIV, V.i.69; RJ, V.iii.145; LEAR, III.iv.70; TS, V.ii.137; *and probably so in* OTH, IV.i.221
unkindl|y, -ier, -iest, -iness ˌʌnˈkaɪ̆ndl|ɪ, -ɪɚ̆, -ɪɪst, -ɪnɪs
unkinged ˌʌnˈkɪŋd ([ˈ-,-] *in* RII, IV.i.220)
unkinglike ˌʌnˈkɪŋlaɪ̆k
unkiss, -ed ˌʌnˈkɪs, -t
unknit ˌʌnˈnɪt
unknown ˌʌnˈnoŏn ([ˈ-,-] *in* ADO, IV.i.135; LUC, 103; OTH, II.i.193; PER, I.iii.34; RIII, I.ii.221; WT, IV.iv.65, IV.iv.492)
unlac|e, -es, -ing, -ed ˌʌnˈleɪ̆s, -ɪz, -ɪŋ, -t
unlaid ˌʌnˈleɪ̆d ([ˈ-,-] *in* PER, I.ii.89)
unlaw|ful, -fully, -fulness ˌʌnˈlɔ|fʊl, -fəlɪ, -fʊlnɪs
unlearn (*v.*)**, -s, -ing, -ed, -t** ˌʌnˈlɜ̆n, -z, -ɪŋ, -d, -t
unlearned (*adj.*)**, -ly, -ness** ˌʌnˈlɜ̆nɪd, -lɪ, -nɪs
unlessoned ˌʌnˈlesn̩d
unlettered ˌʌnˈleɾɚ̆d
unlicensed ˌʌnˈlaɪ̆sənst
unlike ˌʌnˈlaɪ̆k [ˈ--]
unlimited ˌʌnˈlɪmɪtɪd
unlineal ˌʌnˈlɪnɪəl [-njəl]
unlinked ˌʌnˈlɪŋkt
unlived (*deprived of life*) ˌʌnˈlaɪ̆vd
unlooked ˌʌnˈlʊkt ([ˈ-,-] *in* RIII, I.iii.214)
unlooked-for ˌʌnˈlʊktfɔɚ̆
unloos|e, -es, -ing, -ed ˌʌnˈlus, -ɪz, -ɪŋ, -t
unloved ˌʌnˈlʌvd
unloving ˌʌnˈlʌvɪŋ
unluck|y, -ier, -iest, -ily, -iness ˌʌnˈlʌk|ɪ, -ɪɚ̆, -ɪɪst, -ɪlɪ, -ɪnɪs
unmade ˌʌnˈmeɪ̆d ([ˈ-,-] *in* RJ, III.iii.70)
unmake ˌʌnˈmeɪ̆k
unmanl|y, -iness, -ier, -iest ˌʌnˈmænl|ɪ, -ɪnɪs, -ɪɚ̆, -ɪɪst

---

i w**e** ɪ cit**y** ɪ h**i**t e l**e**t ɛ d**e**but æ c**a**n a p**a**ss ɜˑ b**ir**d ʌ h**u**t ə **a**gain ɚ supp**er** u y**ou**
ʊ sh**ou**ld o **o**bey ɔ **aw**l ɒ c**o**p ɑ f**a**ther eɪ p**ai**d aɪ h**igh** oŏ g**o** ɔɪ v**oi**ce aŏ f**ou**nd ɪɚˑ **ear**
ɛɚˑ **air** ʊɚˑ **poor** ɔɚˑ **fork** aɚˑ **park** aɪɚˑ **fire** aŏɚˑ **hour** b **b**oy p **p**it d **d**og t **t**op g **g**ot
k **k**id h **h**ow fi be**h**ave dʒ **j**ot tʃ **ch**ew z **z**any s **s**oft v **v**at f **f**at ʒ trea**s**ure ʃ **sh**ip ð **th**e
θ **th**in m **m**an n **n**o ŋ ha**ng** l **l**ip j **y**es w **w**on ʍ **wh**ew ɹ **r**igger, ai**r**y ɾ ma**tt**er

unmanned ˌʌn'mænd
unmannered ˌʌn'mænəˑd
unmannerl|y, -iness ʌn'mænəˑl|ɪ, -ɪnɪs
unmarried ˌʌn'mæɹɪd
unmask, -s, -ing, -ed ˌʌn'mask, -s, -ɪŋ, -t
    (*arguably* ['-ˌ-] *in* LUC, 940)
unmatchable ˌʌn'mætʃəbl̩
unmatched ˌʌn'mætʃt
unmeasurable ˌʌn'meʒəˑɹəbl̩
unmeet ˌʌn'mit
unmellowed ˌʌn'meloŭd
unmerci|ful, -fully, -fulness ˌʌn'mɜˑsɪ|fʊl,
    -fʊlɪ, -fʊlnɪs
unmeritable ˌʌn'meɹɪtəbl̩
unmeriting ˌʌn'meɹɪtɪŋ
unminded ˌʌn'maĭndɪd
unmind|ful, -fully, -fulness ˌʌn'maĭnd|fʊl,
    -fʊlɪ, -fʊlnɪs
unmingled ˌʌn'mɪŋgl̩d
unmitigable ˌʌn'mɪtɪgəbl̩
unmoaned ˌʌn'moŏnd
unmov(e)able ˌʌn'muvəbl̩
unmoved ˌʌn'muvd
unmoving ˌʌn'muvɪŋ
unmusical ˌʌn'mjuzɪkl̩
unmuzz|le, -les, -ling, -led ˌʌn'mʌz|l̩, -l̩z,
    -l̩ɪŋ [-lɪŋ], -l̩d
unnatural, -ly, -ness ˌʌn'nætʃəˑɹəl, -ɪ, -nɪs
unnecessarily ʌnˌnesɪ'seɹɪlɪ ['ʌnˌnesɪ'seɹɪlɪ]
unnecessary ˌʌn'nesɪsəˑɹɪ
unneighborly ˌʌn'neĭbəˑlɪ
unnoble ˌʌn'noŏbl̩d
unnoted ˌʌn'noŏtɪd
unnumbered ˌʌn'nʌmbəˑd
unordinate ˌʌn'ɔˑˑdn̩ɪt [-dɪn-]
unowed ˌʌn'oŏd (*when att.*, ['--])
unpaid ˌʌn'peĭd
unpaid-for ˌʌn'peĭdfɔˑˑ
unpanged ˌʌn'pæŋd (['-ˌ-] *in* TNK, I.i.169)
unparagoned ˌʌn'pæɹəgɒnd [-gənd]
unparalleled ˌʌn'pæɹələleld [-ləld]
unpartial ˌʌn'pɑˑˑʃl̩
unpathed ˌʌn'paθt (['-ˌ-] *in* WT, IV.iv.568)
unpaved ˌʌn'peĭvd (*when att.*, ['--])
unpay ˌʌn'peĭ
unpeaceable ˌʌn'pisəbl̩
unpeg, -s, -ging, -ged ˌʌn'peg, -z, -ɪŋ, -d
unpeople, -d ˌʌn'pipl̩, -d
unperceived ˌʌnpəˑ'sivd

unperfectness ˌʌn'pɜˑfɪktnɪs
unpicked ˌʌn'pɪkt
unpin, -s, -ning, -ned ˌʌn'pɪn, -z, -ɪŋ, -d
unpinked (*unadorned*) ˌʌn'pɪŋkt
unpitied ˌʌn'pɪtɪd [-'pɪɾɪd]
unpitifully ˌʌn'pɪɾɪfəlɪ
unplagued ˌʌn'pleĭgd
unplausive ˌʌn'plɔzɪv [-ɔsɪv]
unpleased (*adj.*) ˌʌn'plizɪd
unpleasing ˌʌn'plizɪŋ
unplucked ˌʌn'plʌkt
unpolicied ˌʌn'pɒlɪsɪd
unpolished ˌʌn'pɒlɪʃt
unpossessed ˌʌnpə'zest [-po'z-]
unpossessing ˌʌnpə'zesɪŋ [-po'z-]
unpossible ˌʌn'pɒsɪbl̩
unpracticed ˌʌn'pɹæktɪst
unpregnant ˌʌn'pɹegnənt
unprepar|ed, -edly, -edness ˌʌnpɹɪ'pɛˑˑ|d,
    -ɹɪdlɪ, -ɹɪdnɪs
unpressed ˌʌn'pɹest
unprevented ˌʌnpɹɪ'ventɪd
unprizable ˌʌn'pɹaĭzəbl̩
unprized ˌʌn'pɹaĭzd (['-ˌ-] *in* LEAR,
    I.i.261)
unprofitab|le, -ly, -leness ˌʌn'pɹɒfɪtəb|l̩,
    -lɪ, -l̩nɪs
unprofited ˌʌn'pɹɒfɪtɪd
unproper, -ly ˌʌn'pɹɒpəˑ, -lɪ
unprovid|e, -ed ˌʌnpɹo'vaĭd [-pɹʊ'v-], -ɪd
unprovident ˌʌn'pɹɒvɪdənt
unpruned ˌʌn'pɹund
unpurged ˌʌn'pɜˑdʒd (['-ˌ-] *in* JUL,
    II.i.266)
unqualitied ˌʌn'kwɒlɪtɪd
unqueened ˌʌn'kwind
unquiet, -ly, -ness ʌn'kwaĭət, -lɪ, -nɪs
unraked ˌʌn'ɹeĭkt
unread ˌʌn'ɹed
unreal ˌʌn'ɹil [-'ɹiəl]
unreasonab|le, -ly, -leness ˌʌn'ɹiznəb|l̩, -lɪ
    [-'ɹiznəblɪ], -l̩nɪs
unreasoned ˌʌn'ɹiznd
unrecalling ˌʌnɹɪ'kɔlɪŋ
unreconcilable ʌnˌɹekən'saĭləbl̩
unreconciled ˌʌn'ɹekənsaĭld
unreconciliable ʌnˌɹekən'sɪlɪəbl̩
unrecounted ˌʌnɹɪ'kaŏntɪd
unrecuring (*incurable*) ˌʌnɹɪ'kjʊˑˑɹɪŋ

unregarded ˌʌnɹɪˈgɑɚ̆ˈdɪd
unrelenting, -ly, -ness ˌʌnɹɪˈlentɪŋ, -lɪ, -nɪs
unremovab|le, -ly ˌʌnɹɪˈmuvəb|ḷ, -lɪ
unreprievable ˌʌnɹɪˈpɹivəbḷ
unrespected ˌʌnɹɪˈspektɪd
unrespective ˌʌnɹɪˈspektɪv
unrest ˌʌnˈɹest
unrestored ˌʌnɹɪˈstɔɚ̆ˈd
unrestrain|ed, -edly ˌʌnɹɪˈstɹeɪ̆n|d, -ɪdlɪ
unrevenged ˌʌnɹɪˈvendʒd
unreverend ˌʌnˈɹevəˈɹend [-vɹə-]
unreverent ˌʌnˈɹevəɹənt [-vɹə-]
unreversed ˌʌnɹɪˈvɝ̆st
unripe ˌʌnˈɹaɪ̆p (*when att.,* [ˈ-,-])
unrip(ʼst) ʌnˈɹɪp(st) (RIII, I.iv.196)
unrivalled ˌʌnˈɹaɪ̆vḷd
unroll, -s, -ing, -ed ˌʌnˈɹoŭl, -z, -ɪŋ, -d
unroofed ˌʌnˈɹuft
unroosted ˌʌnˈɹustɪd
unrough ˌʌnˈɹʌf ([ˈ-,-] *in* MAC, V.ii.10)
unrul|y, -ier, -iest, -iness ˌʌnˈɹul|ɪ, -ɪɚ̆, -ɪɪst, -ɪnɪs
unsafe ˌʌnˈseɪ̆f ([ˈ-,-] *in* WT, II.ii.30)
unsaluted ˌʌnsəˈlutɪd [-ˈljutɪd]
unsanctified ˌʌnˈsæŋktɪfaɪ̆d
unsatiate ˌʌnˈseɪ̆ʃɪɪt [-ʃɪt]
unsatisf|ied, -ying ˌʌnˈsæɟɪsf|aɪ̆d, -aɪ̆ɪŋ
unsavor|y, -ily, -iness ˌʌnˈseɪ̆vɚ̆ɹ|ɪ, -ɪlɪ, -ɪnɪs
uns|ay, -ays, -aying, -aid ˌʌnˈs|eɪ̆, -ez, -eɪ̆ɪŋ, -ed
unsayʼt (*contr. of* unsay it) ˌʌnˈseɪ̆t
unscal(e)able ˌʌnˈskeɪ̆ləbḷ
unscanned ˌʌnˈskænd
unscarred ˌʌnˈskɑɚ̆ˈd
unscathed ˌʌnˈskeɪ̆ðd
unschooled ˌʌnˈskuld
unscissored ˌʌnˈsɪzɚ̆d
unscoured ˌʌnˈskɑŭɚ̆ˈd ([ˈ-,-] *in* MEAS, I.ii.156)
unscratched ˌʌnˈskɹætʃt
unseal, -s, -ing, -ed ˌʌnˈsil, -z, -ɪŋ, -d
unseamed ˌʌnˈsimd

unseasonab|le, -ly, -leness ˌʌnˈsiznəb|ḷ [-znə-], -lɪ, -ḷnɪs
unseasoned ˌʌnˈsizənd
unseconded ˌʌnˈsekəndɪd (*perhaps* [ˈ-,---] *in* 2HIV, II.iii.34)
unsecret ˌʌnˈsikɹɪt
unseduced ˌʌnsɪˈdjust
unseeing ˌʌnˈsiɪŋ
unseeming ˌʌnˈsimɪŋ
unseeml|y, -iness ˌʌnˈsiml|ɪ, -ɪnɪs
unseen ˌʌnˈsin ([ˈ-,-] *in* LUC, 763, 827; RII, IV.i.297)
unseminared ˌʌnˈsemɪnɑɚ̆d
unsentenced ˌʌnˈsentənst [-tn̩st]
unseparable ˌʌnˈsepəˈɹəbḷ
unset ˌʌnˈset
unsettl|e, -es, -ing, -ed ˌʌnˈsetḷ, -z, -ɪŋ, -d
unsevered ˌʌnˈsevɚ̆d
unsex ˌʌnˈseks
unshaked ˌʌnˈʃeɪ̆kt
unshaken ˌʌnˈʃeɪ̆kən
unshapes ˌʌnˈʃeɪ̆ps
unsheath|e, -es, -ing, -ed ˌʌnˈʃið, -z, -ɪŋ, -d
unshorn ˌʌnˈʃɔɚ̆ˈn ([ˈ-,-] *in* LC, 94)
unshout ˌʌnˈʃɑŭt
unshrinking, -ly ˌʌnˈʃɹɪŋkɪŋ, -lɪ
unshrubbed ˈʌnˌʃɹʌbd
unshunnable ˌʌnˈʃʌnəbḷ
unshunned ˌʌnˈʃʌnd
unsift, -s, -ing, -ed ˌʌnˈsɪft, -s, -ɪŋ, -ɪd
unsinewed ˌʌnˈsɪnjud
unsisting ˌʌnˈsɪstɪŋ
Note.—This word in MEAS, IV.ii.87 (*perhaps used nowhere else in literature*) *is of doubtful meaning according to the* OED, *and is probably an error; cf. J. W. Lever's note in the 1965 edition of* The Arden Shakespeare
unskil|ful, -fully, -fulness ˌʌnˈskɪl|fʊl, -fʊlɪ, -fʊlnɪs
unskilled ˌʌnˈskɪld (*when att.,* [ˈ-,-])
unslipping ˌʌnˈslɪpɪŋ
unsmirched ˌʌnˈsmɝ̆tʃt [-tʃɪd]

---

i wᴇ ɪ city ɪ hit e let ɛ debut æ can a pass ɝ bird ʌ hut ə again ɚ supper u you
ʊ should o obey ɔ awl ɒ cop ɑ father eɪ̆ paid aɪ̆ high oŏ go ɔɪ voice aŏ found ɪɚ̆ ear
ɛɚ̆ air ʊɚ̆ poor ɔɚ̆ fork ɑɚ̆ park aɪ̆ɚ̆ fire aŏɚ̆ hour b boy p pit d dog t top g got
k kid h how fi behave dʒ jot tʃ chew z zany s soft v vat f fat ʒ treasure ʃ ship ð the
θ thin m man n no ŋ hang l lip j yes w won ʍ whew ɹ rigger, aɪɾʏ ɟ matter

unsoiled ˌʌnˈsɔɪld (*arguably* [ˈ-,-] *in* MEAS, II.iv.154)

unsolicited ˌʌnsəˈlɪsɪtɪd

unsorted ˌʌnˈsɔɚ·tɪd

unsought ˌʌnˈsɔt

unsoun|d, -ded; -dly, -dness ˌʌnˈsaʊn|d, -dɪd; -dlɨ, -dnɪs

unspeak, -ing; -able ˌʌnˈspik, -ɪŋ; -əbl̩

unsphere ˌʌnˈsfɪɚ

unspoke ˌʌnˈspoʊk

unspoken ˌʌnˈspoʊkən

unspotted ˌʌnˈspɒtɪd [-ɒɾɪd]

unsquared ˌʌnˈskwɛɚ·d

unstable, -ness ˌʌnˈsteɪbl̩

unstaid ˌʌnˈsteɪd ([ˈ-,-] *in* RII, II.i.2)

unstained ˌʌnˈsteɪnd ([ˈ-,-] *in* RJ, IV.i.88; WT, IV.iv.149)

unstate ˌʌnˈsteɪt

unsta(u)nched ˌʌnˈstɔntʃt [-stɑn-]

unsteadfast, -ly, -ness ˌʌnˈstedfast [-fəst], -lɨ, -nɪs

unstooping ˌʌnˈstupɪŋ

unstringed ˌʌnˈstɹɪŋd

unstuffed ˌʌnˈstʌft ([ˈ-,-] *in* RJ, II.iii.33)

unsubstantial ˌʌnsəbˈstænʃl̩

unsuiting ˌʌnˈsjutɪŋ [-uɾɪŋ]

unsullied ˌʌnˈsʌlɨd

unsunned ˌʌnˈsʌnd

unsure ˌʌnˈʃʊɚ ([ˈ-,-] *in* MAC, V.iv.19)

unsured ˌʌnˈʃʊɚ·d

unsuspected, -ly, -ness ˌʌnsəˈspektɪd, -lɨ, -nɪs

unsuspecting, -ly, -ness ˌʌnsəˈspektɪŋ, -lɨ, -nɪs

unswayed ˌʌnˈsweɪd

unswayable ˌʌnˈsweɪəbl̩

unswear ˌʌnˈswɛɚ

unswept ˌʌnˈswept (*when att.,* [ˈ-,-])

unsworn ˌʌnˈswɔɚ·n

untainted ˌʌnˈteɪntɪd

untalked-of ˌʌnˈtɔktəv [-tɒv]

untang|le, -les, -ling, -led ˌʌnˈtæŋgl̩, -l̩z, -lɪŋ [-l̩ɪŋ], -l̩d

untasted ˌʌnˈteɪstɪd

untaught ˌʌnˈtɔt ([ˈ-,-] *in* MEAS, II.iv.29; 1HIV, I.iii.42)

untempering ˌʌnˈtempɚ·ɹɪŋ

untender, -ed ˌʌnˈtendɚ, -d

untent, -ed ˌʌnˈtent, -ɪd

unthank|ful, -fully, -fulness ˌʌnˈθæŋk|fʊl, -fʊlɨ, -fʊlnɪs

unthink ˌʌnˈθɪŋk

unthought ˌʌnˈθɔt

unthought-of ˌʌnˈθɔtɒv [-ɔɾɒv, -ɔɾəv]

unthought-on ˌʌnˈθɔtɒn [-ɔɾɒn]

unthread, -s, -ing, -ed ˌʌnˈθɹed, -z, -ɪŋ, -ɪd

unthrift ˌʌnˈθɹɪft ([ˈ-,-] *in* MV, V.I.16; Sonn. 9.9)

unthrifts ˈʌnˌθɹɪfts

unthrift|y, -ily, -iness ˌʌnˈθɹɪft|ɨ, -ɪlɨ, -ɪnɪs

unt|ie, -ies, -ying, -ied ˌʌnˈt|aɪ, -aɪz, -aɪɪŋ, -aɪd

untimbered ˌʌnˈtɪmbɚ·d

untimel|y, -iness ˌʌnˈtaɪml|ɨ, -ɪnɪs

untirable ˌʌnˈtaɪɚ·ɹəbl̩

untired ˌʌnˈtaɪɚ·d ([ˈ--] *in* JUL, II.i.227)

untitled ˌʌnˈtaɪtl̩d

unto ˈʌntʊ [-tu]

untouchable, -s ˌʌnˈtʌtʃəbl̩, -z

untouched ˌʌnˈtʌtʃt

untoward, -ly, -ness ˌʌntʊˈwɔɚ·d [ˌʌnˈtɔɚ·d], -lɨ, -nɪs
Note.—In order to fulfill the couplet rhyme in TS, IV.v.77, 78 *of 'froward/ untoward,' 'untoward' is likely to be pronounced* [ˌʌnˈtoʊwɚ·d] *(cf.* **toward***). It is similarly pronounced* [ˌʌnˈtoʊwɚ·d] *in* KJ, I.i.243, *but in this case simply to fulfill the metrical requirements of the verse line*

untraded ˌʌnˈtɹeɪdɪd

untread ˌʌnˈtɹed

untreasured ˌʌnˈtɹeʒɚ·d

untried ˌʌnˈtɹaɪd

untrimmed ˌʌnˈtɹɪmd (*when att.,* [ˈ-,-])

untrod, -den ˌʌnˈtɹɒd ([ˈ-,-] *in* JUL, III.i.136), -n̩

untroubled ˌʌnˈtɹʌbl̩d

untrue ˌʌnˈtɹu

untrussing ˌʌnˈtɹʌsɪŋ

untru|th, -ths ˌʌnˈtɹu|θ, -ðz [-θs]

untuck, -s, -ing, -ed ˌʌnˈtʌk, -s, -ɪŋ, -t

untun|e, -ed; -able ˌʌnˈtjun, -d ([ˈ-,-] *in* LUC, 1214; RII, I.iii.134); -əbl̩

untutored ˌʌnˈtjuɾɚ·d

untwind (*obsolete form of* **untwine**) ˌʌnˈtwaɪnd

untwin|e, -es, -ing, -ed ˌʌn'twaɪn, -z, -ɪŋ, -d

untwist, -s, -ing, -ed ˌʌn'twɪst, -s, -ɪŋ, -ɪd

unurged ʌn'ɝ·dʒd (*when att.,* ['-,-])

unused (*not used*) ˌʌn'juzd (*when att.,* ['-,-])

unused (*not familiar with or accustomed to*) ˌʌn'just

unvalued ˌʌn'væljud

unvarnished ˌʌn'vɑɚ·nɪʃt

unveil, -s, -ing, -ed, -er/s ˌʌn'veɪl, -z, -ɪŋ, -d, -ɚ/z

unvenerable ˌʌn'venəɹəbl̩

unvexed ˌʌn'vekst

unvirtuous ˌʌn'vɝ·tʃʊəs [-tjʊəs]

unvisited ˌʌn'vɪzɪtɪd

unvulnerable ˌʌn'vʌlnɚ·ɹəbl̩

unwappered ˌʌn'wɒpɚ·d

unwares (*from* **unawares**) ˌʌn'wɛɚ·z

unwary ˌʌn'wɛɚ·ɹɪ

unwarily ˌʌn'wɛɚ·ɹɪlɪ

unwashed ˌʌn'wɒʃt (*when att.,* ['-,-])

unwearied ˌʌn'wɪɚ·ɹɪd

unweaves ˌʌn'wivz

unwed ˌʌn'wed (*when att.,* ['-,-])

unwedgeable ˌʌn'wedʒəbl̩

unweigh, -ing, -ed ˌʌn'weɪ, -ɪŋ, -d

unwelcome ˌʌn'welkəm

unwept ˌʌn'wept

unwhipped ˌʌn'ʍɪpt

unwholesome ˌʌn'hoʊlsəm

unwilling, -ly, -ness ˌʌn'wɪlɪŋ, -lɪ, -nɪs

un|wind, -winds, -winding, -wound ˌʌn|'waɪnd, -'waɪndz, -'waɪndɪŋ, -'waʊnd

unwise -ly ˌʌn'waɪz, -lɪ

unwished ˌʌn'wɪʃt

unwitnessed ˌʌn'wɪtnɪst

Note.—In VA, 1023, *this word needs to be four syllables instead of three in order to fulfill the metrical requirements of the verse line; thus, the pronunciation shifts to* [ˌʌn'wɪtnɪsɪd]. *Normally, I do not record how words' pronunciations change due to elision or syncope;*

however, in this instance the additional syllable causes the [t] *to shift to a* [d]

unwitted ˌʌn'wɪɾɪd

unwitting, -ly ˌʌn'wɪɾɪ̥ŋ, -lɪ

unwonted ˌʌn'woʊntɪd

unwooed ˌʌn'wud

unworth|y, -ier, -iest, -ily, -iness ˌʌn'wɝ·ð|ɪ, -ɪɚ·, -ɪɪst, -ɪlɪ, -ɪnɪs

unwrung ˌʌn'ɹʌŋ

unyielding, -ly, -ness ˌʌn'jildɪŋ, -lɪ, -nɪs

unyok|e, -es, -ing, -ed ˌʌn'joʊk, -s, -ɪŋ, -t (['-,-] *in* 1HIV, I.ii.191)

up 'ʌp

upbraid, -s, -ing/s, -ed ʌp'bɹeɪd, -z, -ɪŋ/z, -ɪd

upbringing 'ʌpˌbɹɪŋɪŋ

upcast, -s 'ʌpkast, -s

upfill ʌp'fɪl

uphoard, -s, -ing, -ed ʌp'fiɔɚ·d, -z, -ɪŋ, -ɪd

uplift (*adj., s.*) 'ʌplɪft

uplift (*v.*), **-s, -ing, -ed** ʌp'lɪft, -s, -ɪŋ, -ɪd

up-locked 'ʌpˌlɒkt (['ʌpˌlɒkɪd] *in* Sonn. 52.2)

upmost 'ʌpmoʊst

upon ə'pɒn

Note.—Often ['ʌpɒn] *in* S.

upon't (*contr. of* **upon it**) ə'pɒnt

upreared ʌp'ɹɪɚ·d ([ʌp'ɹɪɚ·ɹɪd] *in* HV, Pro.21)

upright, -ly, -ness 'ʌpˌɹaɪt ([ˌ-'-] *in* RIII, III.ii.38; [ˌ-'--] TIT, I.i.51), -lɪ, -nɪs

uprighteously ʌp'ɹaɪ̆tʃəslɪ

up|rise, -rose, -risen ʌp|'ɹaɪz, -'ɹoʊz, -'ɹɪzn̩

uproar, -s 'ʌpɹɔɚ·, -z

uproot, -s, -ing, -ed ʌp'ɹut, -s, -ɪŋ, -ɪd

uproused ʌp'ɹaʊzd

upset (*adj.*) ʌp'set (*when att.,* ['-,-])

upset (*s.*), **-s** 'ʌpset, -s

upset (*v.*), **-s, -ting** ʌp'set, -s, -ɪŋ

upshoot 'ʌpʃut

upshot 'ʌpʃɒt

up(-)stairs ʌp'stɛɚ·z (*when att.,* ['-,-])

---

i wᴇ ɪ city ɪ hit e let ɛ debut æ can a pass ɝ bird ʌ hut ə again ɚ supper u you
ʊ should o obey ɔ awl ɒ cop ɑ father eɪ paid aɪ high oʊ go ɔɪ voice aʊ found ɪɚ ear
ɛɚ air ʊɚ poor ɔɚ fork ɑɚ park aɪɚ fire aʊɚ hour b boy p pit d dog t top g got
k kid h how fi behave dʒ jot tʃ chew z zany s soft v vat f fat ʒ treasure ʃ ship ð the
θ thin m man n no ŋ hang l lip j yes w won ʍ whew ɹ rigger, airy ɾ matter

up-staring ˌʌp'stɛɚˈɹɪŋ
up-swarmed ˌʌp'swɔɚˈmd
up-till (*up against*) ˌʌp'tɪl
upward, -s, -ly 'ʌpwəˈd, -z, -lɪ
urchin, -s 'ɝˈtʃɪn, -z
Urchinfield (1HVI) 'ɝˈtʃɪnfild
urchin-snouted 'ɝˈtʃɪnˌsnaʊ̆tɪd
urg|e, -es, -ing, -ed, -er/s 'ɝˈdʒ, -ɪz, -ɪŋ,
   -d, -əˈ/z
urgen|cy, -t/ly 'ɝˈdʒən|sɪ, -t/lɪ
urinal, -s 'jʊɚˈɹɪnl̩, -z
urinat|e, -es, -ing, -ed 'jʊɚˈɹɪneɪ̆t, -s, -ɪŋ,
   -ɪd
urination jʊɚˈɹɪ'neɪ̆ʃn̩
urine 'jʊɚˈɹɪn
Ursa Major (*L.*) (LEAR, I.ii.130)
   (*constellation; 'Great Bear'*) 'ɝˈsə
   'meɪ̆dʒəˈ
   Note.—Even though this is Latin,
   there is nothing to be gained here by
   giving it an overly Latinate pronun-
   ciation, and like so many other Latin
   words and phrases in English (e.g.,
   'etcetera,' 'ergo,' 'non compos mentis'),
   'Ursa Major' has been entirely
   anglicized
Ursley (*ADO*) 'ɝˈslɪ (*var. of* Ursula, *q.v.*)
Ursula (*ADO*, 2HIV, TGV) 'ɝˈsələ
   ['ɝˈsjʊlə], 'ɝˈslə
Urswick, Sir Christopher (*RIII*) ˌsɝˈ
   'kɹɪstəfəˈ 'ɝˈzɪk ['ɝˈswɪk]
usable 'juzəbl̩
usage, -s 'jusɪdʒ ['juzɪdʒ], -ɪz
usance, -s 'juzn̩s, -ɪz
usher, -s, -ing, -ed 'ʌʃəˈ, -z, -ɹɪŋ, -d
usurer, -s 'juʒəˈɹəˈ, -z
usuring 'juʒəˈɹɪŋ
usurp, -s, -ing/ly, -ed, -er/s ju'zɝˈp, -s,
   -ɪŋ/lɪ, -t, -əˈ/z
usurpation, -s juzɝˈ'peɪ̆ʃn̩, -z
usur|y, -ies 'juʒəˈɹ|ɪ, -ɪz
utensil, -s ju'tensl̩ [jʊ't-, -sɪl], -z
   Note.—In TEM, III.ii.94, this word is
   given primary stress on the first syllable,
   i.e., ['jutɪnsɪlz], *the standard pronuncia-*
   tion in S.'s time
utis (*festive noise; jollification*) 'jutɪs
utmost 'ʌtmoʊ̆st
Utruvio (RJ) ʊ'tɹuvɪoʊ̆

utter, -s, -ing, -ed, -er/s; -able, -ly, -ness
   'ʌɾəˈ, -z, -ɹɪŋ, -d, -ɹəˈ/z; -ɹəbl̩, -lɪ, -nɪs
utterance, -s 'ʌɾəˈɹəns, -ɪz
utterly 'ʌɾəˈlɪ
uttermost 'ʌɾəˈmoʊ̆st
uvula, -s 'juvjʊlə, -z
uvular 'juvjʊləˈ

Vv

V (*the letter*), -'s 'viː, -z
vacanc|y, -ies 'veɪ̆kəns|ɪ, -ɪz
vacant, -ly 'veɪ̆kənt, -lɪ
vacat|e, -es, -ing, -ed 'veɪ̆keɪ̆t [-'-], -s, -ɪŋ,
   -ɪd
vacation, -s veɪ̆'keɪ̆ʃn̩, -z
vaccinat|e, -es, -ing, -ed, -or/s 'væksɪneɪ̆t
   [-sn̩eɪ̆t], -s, -ɪŋ, -ɪd, -əˈ/z
vaccination, -s ˌvæksɪ'neɪ̆ʃn̩, -z
vaccine, -s væk'sin ['--], -z
vade (*go away; obsolete var. of 'fade'*), -d
   'veɪ̆d, -ɪd
vagabond, -s 'vægəbɒnd, -z
vagar|y, -ies 'veɪ̆gəɹ|ɪ [və'gɛɚˈɹ|ɪ], -ɪz
vagram 'veɪ̆gɹəm
   Note.—Whereas 'vagrom' is Dogberry's
   illiterate alteration or corruption of
   *'vagrant' in ADO, 'vagram' (*MWW,
   III.i.24) is most likely Evans' dialectal
   corruption of 'fragrant' (as already
   established in MWW, III.i.19) *rather*
   than a var. form of 'vagrom' (see prings)
vagrancy 'veɪ̆gɹənsɪ
vagrant, -s 'veɪ̆gɹənt, -s
vagrom (*Dogberry's corruption of*
   vagrant *in* ADO, III.iii.25) 'veɪ̆gɹəm
vague, -r, -st, -ly, -ness 'veɪ̆g, -əˈ, -ɪst, -lɪ,
   -nɪs
vail, -s, -ing, -ed 'veɪ̆l, -z, -ɪŋ, -d
vain, -er, -est, -ly, -ness 'veɪ̆n, -əˈ, -ɪst, -lɪ,
   -nɪs
vainglorious, -ly, -ness ˌveɪ̆n'glɔɹɪəs, -lɪ,
   -nɪs
vain(-)glor|y, -ies 'veɪ̆nˌglɔɹ|ɪ [ˌ-'--], -ɪz
valanc|e, -es, -ing, -ed 'væləns, -ɪz, -ɪŋ, -t
Valdes (PER) 'vældɪz
vale, -s 'veɪ̆l, -z

Valence (1HVI) 'væləns
valenc|e, -es, -y, -ies 'veɪ̈ləns, -ɪz, -ɪ, -ɪz
Valencius (MEAS) vəˈlenʃɪəs, -ʃjəs
Note.—In MEAS, *IV.v.8 (its only appearance in S.) this name presents a problem to the scansion of the line. Editors sometimes emend the name to* **Valentinus**, *or make the first word of the line 'Unto' rather than 'To'*
Valentine (RJ, *TGV, TIT, TN*) 'væləntaɪ̈n
Valentinus (MEAS, *TGV*) ˌvælənˈtaɪ̈nəs (*see Note for* **Valencius**)
Note.—The usage of 'Valentinus' in TGV, *I.iii.67 (First Folio) notwithstanding, in* TGV, *II.iv.192, it may not be the correct choice, as some editors have opted for. In this line, the First Folio gives 'Valentines,' probably to be spoken as a tetrasyllable, i.e.,* [ˌvælənˈtaɪ̈nɪz] *in order to better fit the metrical requirements of the verse line. If one accepts that a possessive case is intended, then S. simply employs a device here that he uses several other times throughout his plays. For a more in-depth discussion on how this works, see the Note for* **whale**. *And see Clifford Leech's (editor of* TGV, The Arden Shakespeare, *1969) line annotation for* TGV, *II.iv.192, as elements of the entire line have been the subject of considerable conjecture and debate. Editors presumably emend the First Folio's 'Valentines' to 'Valentinus' by analogy with S. 's Saturnine to Saturninus in* TIT *and Collatine to Collatinus in* LUC, *etc.*
Valentio, Signor (RJ) 'sinjɚ vəˈlenʃïo [væ'l-]
Valeria (*COR*) vəˈliɚˌɪɪə, -ˌɪĭə
Valerius (*TNK*) vəˈliɚˌɪɪəs, -ˌɪĭəs
valiant, -ly, -ness 'væljənt, -lɪ, -nɪs
valiant-young 'væljəntˈjʌŋ
valid, -ly, -ness 'vælɪd, -lɪ, -nɪs

validat|e, -es, -ing, -ed 'vælɪdeɪ̈t, -s, -ɪŋ, -ɪd
validation ˌvælɪˈdeɪ̈ʃn̩
validity vəˈlɪdɪtɪ
valley, -s 'vælɪ, -z
valley-fountain 'vælɪˌfaʊntɪn
Valour, Sir (TC) ˌsɝ 'vælɚ
valor (V.), -s 'vælɚ, -z
valorous, -ly 'vælɚˌɪəs, -lɪ
valuation, -s ˌvæljʊˈeɪ̈ʃn̩, -z
val|ue, -ues, -uing, -ued 'væl|ju [-jʊ], -juz [-jʊz], -juɪŋ, -jud [-jʊd]
valueless 'væljʊlɪs
valve, -s 'vælv, -z
vambrace, -s 'væmbɹeɪ̈s, -ɪz
vamp, -s, -ing, -ed, -er/s 'væmp, -s, -ɪŋ, -t, -ɚ/z
vampire, -s 'væmpaɪ̈ɚ, -z
van, -s 'væn, -z
vandal (V.), -s 'vændl̩, -z
vandalism 'vændl̩ɪzəm
vane, -s 'veɪ̈n, -z
vanguard, -s 'væŋgɑɚˌd ['væŋg-], -z
vanilla vəˈnɪlə
vanish, -es, -ing, -ed 'vænɪʃ, -ɪz, -ɪŋ, -t
vanit|y (V.), -ies 'vænɪt|ɪ, -ɪz
vanquish, -es, -ing, -ed, -er/s 'væŋkwɪʃ, -ɪz, -ɪŋ, -t, -ɚ/z
vant (*forefront*) 'vɑnt ['vɑnt]
vantage, -s 'vɑntɪdʒ, -ɪz
vantbrace (*var. of* **vambrace**, *q.v.*) 'væntbɹeɪ̈s
Vapians (TN) 'veɪ̈pɪənz
vapid, -ly, -ness 'væpɪd, -lɪ, -nɪs
vapor, -s, -ing, -ed, -er/s 'veɪ̈pɚ, -z, -ɹɪŋ, -d, -ɹɚ/z
vaporiz|e, -es, -ing, -ed, -er/s 'veɪ̈pəˌɹaɪz, -ɪz, -ɪŋ, -d, -ɚ/z
vaporous, -ly, -ness 'veɪ̈pəˌɹəs, -lɪ, -nɪs
vapor-vow 'veɪ̈pɚˌvaʊ
vara (*dialectal var. of* **very**) 'vɛɚˌɹə
variab|le, -ly, -leness 'vɛɚˌɹɪəb|l̩, -lɪ, -l̩nɪs
varian|ce, -t/s 'vɛɚˌɹɪən|s, -t/s
variation, -s ˌvɛɚˌɹɪ'eɪ̈ʃn̩, -z

i w**e** ɪ city ɪ h**i**t e l**e**t ɛ d**e**but æ c**a**n a p**a**ss ɝ b**ir**d ʌ h**u**t ə **a**gain ɚ supp**er** u y**ou** ʊ sh**ou**ld o **o**bey ɔ **aw**l ɒ c**o**p ɑ f**a**ther eɪ̈ p**ai**d aɪ̈ h**igh** oʊ̈ g**o** ɔɪ̈ v**oi**ce aʊ̈ f**ou**nd ɪɚ̈ **ear** ɛɚ̈ **air** ʊɚ̈ p**oor** ɔɚ̈ f**or**k ɑɚ̈ p**ar**k aɪ̈ɚ̈ f**ire** aʊ̈ɚ̈ h**our** b **b**oy p **p**it d **d**og t **t**op g g**o**t k **k**id h **h**ow fi be**h**ave dʒ **j**ot tʃ **ch**ew z **z**any s **s**oft v **v**at f **f**at ʒ trea**s**ure ʃ **sh**ip ð **th**e θ **th**in m **m**an n **n**o ŋ ha**ng** l **l**ip j **y**es w **w**on ʍ **wh**ew ɹ **r**igger, ai**r**y ɾ ma**tt**er

various, -ly, -ness 'vɛɚˌɹəs, -lɪ, -nɪs
varld (*from 'world'*) 'vɑɚld
Note.—Doctor Caius (in MWW*) is the stereotypical foreigner—and French, to boot—given to foolish arrogance, and ineptly handling English pronunciation. This is an example of S.'s direction to the actor (by way of semiphonetic spellings) to adopt such an accent, more or less, for the sake of wringing the most satire out of plays on words stemming from confusions with, and corruptions of, English pronunciation via the French tongue*
varlet, -s, -ry 'vɑɚlɪt, -s, -ɹɪ
varletto vɑɚˈletoʊ
Note.—This is a malapropism of the Host's in MWW, IV.v.63*. He means to say 'valletto,' a steward or attendant, but has instead come fairly close to a term of abuse*
varmint, -s 'vɑɚmɪnt, -s
varnish, -es, -ing, -ed, -er/s 'vɑɚnɪʃ, -ɪz, -ɪŋ, -t, -ɚ/z
Varrius (*AC, MEAS*) 'væɹəs, -ɹĭəs
Varro (*JUL,* TIM) 'væɹoʊ
Varrus (JUL) 'væɹəs
var|y, -ies, -ying, -ied 'vɛɚˌɹ|ɪ, -ɪz, -ɪŋ, -ɪd
vase, -s 'veĭs ['vɑz, 'veĭz], -ɪz
vassal, -s; -age 'væsl̩, -z; -ɪdʒ
vast, -er, -est, -ly, -ness; -y 'vast, -ɚ, -ɪst, -lɪ, -nɪs; -ɪ
vastidity vaˈstɪdɪtɪ
vat, -s, -ting, -ted 'væt, -s, -ɪŋ, -ɪd
vat (*from 'what'*) 'vɒt ['vat] (*see Note for* **varld**)
Vaudemont (HV) 'voʊdəmɒnt [*Fr.* vodɛmɔ̃]
Vaughan, Sir Thomas (*RIII*) ˌsɚ 'tɒməs 'vɔən
Note.—In S., 'Vaughan' is always pronounced as a disyllable
vault, -s, -ing/s, -ed, -er/s; -y 'vɔlt, -s, -ɪŋ/z, -ɪd, -ɚ/z; -ɪ
vaultage, -s 'vɔltɪdʒ, -ɪz
Vaumond (ALL'S) 'voʊmɒnd ['vɔmənd]
vaunt, -s, -ing/ly, -ed, -er/s 'vɔnt, -s, -ɪŋ/lɪ, -ɪd, -ɚ/z
vaunt-couriers 'vɔntˌkʊɹɪɚz [-ˌkʌɹ-]

Vaux, Sir Nicholas (*HVIII*) ˌsɚ 'nɪkələs, -kləs 'vɔks ['vɔz]
Vaux, Sir William (*2HVI*) ˌsɚ 'wɪljəm 'vɒks ['vɔz]
vaward (*forefront*) 'vɔwɚd ['vaw-]
veal 'vil
veer, -s, -ing, -ed 'vɪɚ, -z, -ɹɪŋ, -d
vegetable, -s 'vedʒtəbl̩ [-dʒɪt-], -z
vegetarian, -s, -ism ˌvedʒɪˈtɛɚˌɹɪən, -z, -ɪzəm
vegetat|e, -es, -ing, -ed 'vedʒɪteĭt, -s, -ɪŋ, -ɪd
vegetation, -s ˌvedʒɪˈteĭʃn, -z
vegetive, -s 'vedʒɪtɪv, -z
vehemen|ce, -cy, -t/ly 'viːmən|s, -sɪ, -t/lɪ
veil, -s, -ing/s, -ed 'veĭl, -z, -ɪŋ/z, -d
vein, -s, -ing/s, -ed; -less, -like 'veĭn, -z, -ɪŋ/z, -d; -lɪs, -laĭk
vein|y, -ier, -iest 'veĭn|ɪ, -ɪɚ, -ɪɪst
vell (*from 'well'*) 'vel (*see Note for* **varld**)
vellum, -s 'veləm, -z
velocit|y, -ies vɪˈlɒsɪt|ɪ, -ɪz
velum, -s 'viləm, -z
velure, -s veˈlʊɚ ['veljɚ], -z
Velutus, Sicinius (*COR*) sɪˈsɪnɪəs, -njəs, vəˈlutəs [-ljut-]
velvet, -s, -ed; -y 'velvɪt, -s, -ɪd; -ɪ
velveteen, -s ˌvelvɪˈtin ['---], -z
velvet-guard, -s 'velvɪtˌgɑɚd, -z
vend, -s, -ing, -ed, -or/s 'vend, -z, -ɪŋ, -ɪd, -ɚ/z
vendetta, -s venˈdeɾə, -z
vendible 'vendɪbl̩
veneer, -s, -ing, -ed vɪˈnɪɚ, -z, -ɹɪŋ, -d
venerab|le, -ly, -leness 'venəɹəb|l̩, -lɪ, -l̩nɪs
venerat|e, -es, -ing, -ed, -or/s 'venəˌɹeĭt, -s, -ɪŋ, -ɪd, -ɚ/z
veneration ˌvenəˈɹeĭʃn
venereal vɪˈnɪɚˌɹəl [-ˈnɹɹəl]
venery 'venəɹɪ
Venetia, Venetia, Chi non ti vede non ti pretia (*It.*) (LLL, IV.ii.93,94) veˈneˑtia veˈneˑtia ki non ti 'veˑdɛ non ti 'prɛˑtia
Venetian (MWW, MV), **-s** vɪˈniʃn̩, -z
veney (*var. of* **veny***; a bout of fencing*), **-s** 'venɪ, -z
veng|e, -es, -ing, -ed 'vendʒ, -ɪz, -ɪŋ, -d
vengeance (V.), **-s** 'vendʒəns, -ɪz

venial, -ly, -ness 'vinɪəl, -ɪ, -nɪs
Venice (ADO, MV, OTH, TS) 'venɪs
Venice, The Duke of (*MV, OTH*) ðə ˌdjuk əv 'venɪs
venison 'venɪsən [-ɪzən]
veni, vidi, vici (*L.*) (LLL, IV.i.68) 'venɪ 'vidɪ 'vitʃɪ
venom, -s, -ed 'venəm, -z, -d
venom-mouthed 'venəmˌmaŏ̆ð [-ˌmaŏ̆θt]
venomous, -ly, -ness 'venəməs, -lɪ, -nɪs
vent, -s, -ing, -ed 'vent, -s, -ɪŋ, -ɪd
ventage, -s 'ventɪdʒ, -ɪz
Ventidius (*AC, TIM*) ven'tɪdɪəs, -'tɪdʒəs [-djəs]
ventilat|e, -es, -ing, -ed 'ventɪleĭt, -s, -ɪŋ, -ɪd
ventilation ˌventɪ'leĭʃn
ventricle, -s 'ventɹɪkl̩, -z
ventur|e, -es, -ing, -ed, -er/s 'ventʃɚ, -z, -ɹɪŋ, -d, -ɹɚ/z
venturous, -ly, -ness 'ventʃəɹəs, -lɪ, -nɪs
venue, -s 'venju, -z
Venus (AC, ADO, AYLI, CYM, 2HIV, 1HVI, LLL, LUC, MSND, MV, RJ, TC, TEM, TIT, VA), **-es** 'vinəs, -ɪz
Ver (*L.*) (LLL, V.ii.883; TNK, I.i.7) 'vɜ ['vɛɚ̆]
Note.—It should be noted that 'Ver' in TNK *rhymes with 'harbinger'*
ver (*from 'for'*) 'vɚ (*see* **vere**)
verb, -s 'vɜb, -z
verb|al, -ally 'vɜb|l̩, -əlɪ
verbatim vɜ'beĭɾɪm
verbiage 'vɜbɪɪdʒ
verbose, -ly, -ness vɜ'boŏs, -lɪ, -nɪs
verbosity vɜ'bɒsɪtɪ
verdict, -s 'vɜdɪkt, -s
verdigris 'vɜdɪgɹɪs [-gɹi]
verdour *or* **verdor** (*var. of* **verdure**) 'vɜdə
Verdun (1HVI) vɜ'dʌn
verdure 'vɜdʒə [-djə]
vere (*from 'where'*) 'vɛʁ ['vɛɚ̆] (*see Note for* **varld**)

Vere, Lord Aubrey (3HVI) ˌlɔɚ̆d 'ɔbɹɪ 'vɪɚ̆
verg|e, -es, -ing, -ed 'vɜdʒ, -ɪz, -ɪŋ, -d
Verger (HVIII), **-s** 'vɜdʒə, -z
Verges (*ADO*) 'vɜdʒɪs
verier (*from* **very**) 'veɹɪə
veriest (*from* **very**) 'veɹɪɪst
verification, -s ˌveɹɪfɪ'keĭʃn, -z
verif|y, -ies, -ying, -ied, -ier/s 'veɹɪf|aĭ, -aĭz, -aĭɪŋ, -aĭd, -aĭɚ/z
verily 'veɹɪlɪ
veritab|le, -ly, -ness 'veɹɪtəb|l̩, -lɪ, -l̩nɪs
verit|y (**V.**), **-ies** 'veɹɪt|ɪ, -ɪz
verjuice 'vɜdʒus
vermil(l)ion, -s, -ing, -ed və'mɪljən, -z, -ɪŋ, -d
vermin 'vɜmɪn
vermouth, -s və'muθ, -s
vernacular, -s, -ly və'nækjʊlə, -z, -lɪ
Vernon (*1HIV, 1HVI*) 'vɜnən
Vernon, Sir Richard (*1HIV*) ˌsɜ ˌɹɪtʃəd 'vɜnən
Verolles, Monsieur (PER) mə'sjə və'ɹɒləs
Verona (RJ, TGV, TS) və'ɹoŏnə
Note.—In TS, II.i.47, *this name is arguably pronounced as a disyllable, i.e.,* ['vɹoŏnə], *depending on how one chooses to scan the line*
Verone(s)sa (OTH) ˌveɹo'nesə
versal (*from* **universal**) 'vɜsl̩
versatility ˌvɜsə'tɪlɪtɪ
vers|e, -es, -ing, -ed 'vɜs, -ɪz, -ɪŋ, -t
versification ˌvɜsɪfɪ'keĭʃn
version, -s 'vɜʒn̩, -z
versus 'vɜsəs
vertebr|a, -ae, -as 'vɜtɪbɹ|ə, -i, -əz
vertebrate, -s 'vɜtɪbɹɪt [-bɹeĭt], -s
vertigo, -(e)s 'vɜɾɪgoŏ ['vɜtɪ-], -z
verve 'vɜv
ver|y, -ier, -iest 'veɹ|ɪ, -ɪə, -ɪɪst
vesper, -s 'vespə, -z
vessel, -s 'vesl̩, -z
vest, -s, -ing, -ed 'vest, -s, -ɪŋ, -ɪd

---

vestal, -s 'vɛstəl -z

vestibul|e, -es, -ing, -ed 'vɛstɪbjul, -z, -ɪŋ, -d

vestige, -s 'vɛstɪdʒ, -ɪz

vestment, -s 'vɛstmənt, -s

vestr|y, -ies 'vɛstɹ|ɨ, -ɨz

vestur|e, -es, -ing, -ed 'vɛstʃɚ, -z, -ɹɪŋ, -d

vet, -s, -ting, -ted 'vɛt, -s, -ɪŋ, -ɪd

vetch, -es 'vɛtʃ, -ɪz

vetch (*from 'fetch'*) 'vɛtʃ (*see Note for* varld)

veteran, -s 'vɛɾəɹən, -z

veto (*s.*), -(e)s 'vitoŭ, -z

veto (*v.*), -es, -ing, -ed 'vitoŭ, -z, -ɪŋ, -d

vex, -es, -ing, -ed 'vɛks, -ɪz, -ɪŋ, -t

vexation, -s vɛk'seĭʃn̩, -z

vexatious, -ly, -ness vɛk'seĭʃəs, -lɨ, -nɪs

vherefore (*from 'wherefore'*) 'vɛɚfɔʁ [-fɔɚ] (*see Note for* varld)

via (*L.*) (LLL, V.i.139) 'viɑ

via (*prep.*) (*by way of*) 'vaĭə, 'viə (*It.*)

via (*var. of* fia, *meaning 'hurry away'*) 'vaĭə

viability ˌvaĭə'bɪlɪtɨ

viable 'vaĭəbl̩

viaduct, -s 'vaĭədʌkt, -s

vial, -s 'vaĭəl, -z

viand, -s 'vaĭənd, -z

vibration, -s vaĭ'bɹeĭʃn̩, -z

vibrato, -s vɪ'bɹɑtoŭ, -z

vicar, -s 'vɪkɚ, -z

vicarage, -s 'vɪkɚ,ɹɪdʒ, -ɪz

vice (V.), -s 'vaĭs, -ɪz

vicegerent, -s ˌvaĭs'dʒɪɚɹənt [-'dʒeɹ-], -s

viceroy, -s 'vaĭsɹɔĭ, -z

vicinity vɪ'sɪnɪtɨ

vicious, -ly, -ness 'vɪʃəs, -lɨ, -nɪs

victor, -s 'vɪktɚ, -z

victoress, -es 'vɪktɚɹɪs [-ɹɛs], -ɪz

victorious, -ly, -ness vɪk'tɔɹɪəs, -lɨ, -nɪs

victor|y (V.), -ies 'vɪktɚ,ɹ|ɨ, -ɨz

victual, -s, -led, -ler/s 'vɪtl̩, -z, -d, -ɚ/z

videlicet vɪ'dɛlɪset [vaĭ-, -'di-, -'deĭ-], (*L.*) (LLL, IV.i.70; MWW, I.i.130) vi'dɛlɪsɛt
Note.—In the MWW *instance of this word, it is spoken by the Welshman, Evans, and the text actually says 'fidelicet,' indicating his Welsh accent (see Note for* prief)

Videsne quis venit? Video et gaudeo (*L.*) (LLL, V.i.29–30) vi'dɛsne kwis 'vɛnɨt 'video ɛt 'gaŭdeo

vie, -s, vying, vied 'vaĭ, -z, 'vaĭɪŋ, 'vaĭd

Vienna (HAM, MEAS) vɪ'enə

view, -s, -ing, -ed, -er/s; -able 'vju, -z, -ɪŋ, -d, -ɚ/z; -əbl̩

viewless 'vjulɪs

vigil, -s 'vɪdʒəl, -z

vigilan|ce, -t/ly 'vɪdʒɪlən|s, -t/lɨ

vigitant (*most likely Dogberry's [rather than a compositor's] corruption of 'vigilant' in* ADO, III.iii.92) 'vɪdʒɪtənt

vigor 'vɪgɚ

vigorous, -ly, -ness 'vɪgɚɹəs, -lɨ, -nɪs

vild (*archaic var. of* vile), -er, -est, -ly, -ness 'vaĭld, -ɚ, -ɪst, -lɨ, -nɪs

vile, -r, -st, -ly, -ness 'vaĭl, -ɚ, -ɪst, -lɨ, -nɪs

vile-concluded 'vaĭlkən,kludɪd

vile-drawing 'vaĭl,dɹɔɪŋ

Vilia miretur vulgus; mihi flavus Apollo Pocula Castalia plena ministret aqua (*L.*) (VA) 'vilɨɑ 'miɾetʊɚ 'vʊlgʊs 'mihi 'flavʊs ɑ'polo 'pokulɑ kɑ'stalɨɑ 'plɛnɑ 'minɪstɹet 'ɑkwɑ
Note.—This is from the Epigraph to Venus and Adonis and technically not spoken

vill (*from 'will'*) 'vɪl (*see Note for* varld)

village, -s, -ry 'vɪlɪdʒ, -ɪz, -ɹɨ

villager, -s 'vɪlɪdʒɚ, -z

villain, -s 'vɪlən [-lɪn, -leĭn], -z

villain-like 'vɪlən,laĭk [-lɪn]

villainous, -ly, -ness 'vɪlənəs, -lɨ, -nɪs

villain-slave 'vɪlən'sleĭv

villain|y, -ies 'vɪlən|ɨ, -ɨz

villein, -s; -age 'vɪlɪn, -z; -ɪdʒ

villiago (*var. of 'viliaco'; meaning 'scoundrel,' 'contemptible person'*) vɪl'jagoŭ [-lɪ'agoŭ]

Vincentio (*MEAS, TS*) vɪn'senʃɪo, -ʃjoŭ [vin'tʃensɪo, -sjoŭ]

vindicat|e, -es, -ing, -ed, -or/s 'vɪndɪkeĭt, -s, -ɪŋ, -ɪd, -ɚ/z

vindication ˌvɪndɪ'keĭʃn̩

vindicative vɪn'dɪkətɪv ['----']
Note.—Stressed on the second syllable, i.e., [vɪn'dɪkətɪv] *in* TC, IV.v.107

vine, -s 'vaɪn, -z
vinegar, -s 'vɪnɪgə·, -z
vinegary 'vɪnɪgə·ɹɪ
vinewed'st (*moldy*) 'vɪnjudst
　　Note.—*In* TC, II.i.14, *the First Folio*
　　gives whinid'st *(q.v.) instead*
vineyard, -s 'vɪnjə·d, -z
vintage, -s 'vɪntɪdʒ, -ɪz
Vintner (1HIV) 'vɪntnə·
vintner, -s 'vɪntnə·, -z
viol, -s 'vaɪəl, -z
Viola (*TN*) 'vaɪələ
　　Note.—*In* TN, V.i.242, *this name is*
　　disyllabic, i.e., ['vaɪ(ə)lə] *in order to*
　　better suit the meter and rhythm of the
　　verse line
violat|e, -es, -ing, -ed, -or/s 'vaɪəleɪt, -s,
　　-ɪŋ, -ɪd, -ə·/z
violation, -s ˌvaɪə'leɪʃn̩, -z
viol-de-gamboys (*var. of* '*viol da gamba*')
　　ˌvaɪəldə'gæmbɔɪz [-'gɑm-, -bəz]
violen|ce, -t/ly 'vaɪələn|s, -t/lɪ
Violenta (*ALL'S*) ˌvaɪə'lentə
violet, -s 'vaɪəlɪt, -s
violin, -s ˌvaɪə'lɪn, -z
viper, -s 'vaɪpə·, -z
viperous, -ly 'vaɪpə·ɹəs, -lɪ
virago vɪ'ɹeɪgo [-'ɹɑgo]
Virgilia (*COR*) və·'dʒɪlɪə
virgin, -s, -ed 'vɜ·dʒɪn, -z, -d
virginal, -s 'vɜ·dʒɪnəl, -z
virginalling 'vɜ·dʒɪnəlɪŋ
virginit|y, -ies və·'dʒɪnɪt|ɪ [vɜ·'dʒ-], -ɪz
Virginius (TIT) vɜ·'dʒɪnɪəs, -njəs
virgin-knot, -s 'vɜ·dʒɪn'nɒt, -s
virgin-like 'vɜ·dʒɪnˌlaɪk
virgin-violator ˌvɜ·dʒɪn'vaɪəleɪtə·
Virgo (TIT) 'vɜ·goʊ
Vir sapit qui pauca loquitur (*L.*) (LLL,
　　IV.ii.77) 'vɪɹ· 'sɑpɪt kwi 'paʊkə 'lokwɪ-
　　tʊɹ·
virtue (**V.**) (3HVI), **-s** 'vɜ·tʃu [-tju], -z
virtuous, -ly, -ness 'vɜ·tʃʊəs [-tjʊəs], -lɪ,
　　-nɪs

virus, -es 'vaɪɹəs ['vaɪɹ·ɹəs], -ɪz
visage, -s, -d 'vɪzɪdʒ, -ɪz, -d
viscount (**V.**), **-s; -ess/es** 'vaɪkaʊnt, -s;
　　-ɪs/ɪz
vision, -s 'vɪʒn̩, -z
visionar|y, -ies 'vɪʒn̩ə·ɹ|ɪ, -ɪz
visit, -s, -ing, -ed, -or/s 'vɪzɪt, -s, -ɪŋ, -ɪd,
　　-ə·/z
visitating 'vɪzɪteɪtɪŋ
visitation, -s ˌvɪzɪ'teɪʃn̩, -z
visor, -s, -ed 'vaɪzə·, -z, -d
Visor, William (2HIV) 'wɪljəm 'vaɪzə·
vista, -s 'vɪstə, -z
visual, -ly 'vɪʒʊəl, -lɪ
visualization, -s ˌvɪʒʊəlɪ'zeɪʃn̩, -z
visualiz|e, -es, -ing, -ed 'vɪʒʊəlaɪz, -ɪz,
　　-ɪŋ, -d
vi|tal, -tally 'vaɪ|ɟl ['vaɪ|təl], -ɟlɪ [-təlɪ]
vitality vaɪ'tælɪtɪ
vitlars (*pronunciation spelling of*
　　'*victuallers*') 'vɪtlə·z
viva voce (*L.*) (HVIII, II.i.18) 'viva 'votʃe
vive le roi (*Fr.*) (KJ, V.ii.104) viv lʊ 'ʁwɑ
vixen, -s 'vɪksn̩, -z
vizaments (*alt. form of* '*advisements*' *or*
　　'*visements,*' *its aphetic*) 'vaɪzəmənts
vizard, -s, -ed; -like 'vɪzə·d [-ˌzaɹ·d], -z,
　　-ɪd; -ˌlaɪk
vizier (**V.**), **-s** vɪ'zɪɹ·, -z
vlouting-stocks (*from* '*flouting-stock*')
　　'vlaʊtɪŋˌstɒks (*see* **prings**)
vlouting-stog (*from* '*flouting-stock*')
　　'vlaʊtɪŋˌstɒg (*see* **prings**)
voc|al, -ally 'voʊk|l̩, -əlɪ
vocalic vo'kælɪk
vocalist, -s 'voʊkl̩ɪst, -s
vocative, -s 'vɒkətɪv, -z
vocativo (*L.*) (MWW, IV.i.45) ˌvoka'tivo
vocatur (*L.*) (LLL, V.i.22) 'vokɑtʊɹ·
vodka, -s 'vɒdkə, -z
vogue 'voʊg
voic|e, -es, -ing, -ed 'vɔɪs, -ɪz, -ɪŋ, -t
voiceless, -ly, -ness 'vɔɪslɪs, -lɪ, -nɪs
void, -s, -ing, -ed 'vɔɪd, -z, -ɪŋ, -ɪd

---

i w**e** ɪ c**i**ty ɪ h**i**t e l**e**t ɛ d**e**but æ c**a**n a p**a**ss ɜ· b**i**rd ʌ h**u**t ə **a**gain ə· supp**er** u y**ou**
ʊ sh**ou**ld o **o**bey ɔ **a**wl ɒ c**o**p ɑ f**a**ther eɪ p**ai**d aɪ h**igh** oʊ g**o** ɔɪ v**oi**ce aʊ f**ou**nd ɪɹ· **ear**
ɛɹ· **air** ʊɹ· p**oor** ɔɹ· f**or**k ɑɹ· p**ar**k aɪɹ· f**ire** aʊɹ· h**our** b **b**oy p **p**it d **d**og t **t**op g g**o**t
k **k**id h **h**ow fi be**h**ave dʒ **j**ot tʃ **ch**ew z **z**any s **s**oft v **v**at f **f**at ʒ trea**s**ure ʃ **sh**ip ð **th**e
θ **th**in m **m**an n **n**o ŋ ha**ng** l **l**ip j **y**es w **w**on ʍ **wh**ew ɹ **r**igger, ai**r**y ɟ ma**tt**er

'voided (*from* avoided) 'vɔɪ́dɪd

volcano, -(e)s vɒl'keɪnoŭ, -z

volk 'voŏk (*from* 'folk')
Note.—This is from LEAR, IV.vi.233, an example of S.'s direction to the actor (via semiphonetic spellings) to adopt the rustic dialect common to the southwestern counties of Devonshire and western Worcestershire, more or less, for the purpose of giving Edgar a "vocal disguise" (cf. Kökeritz's Shakespeare's Pronunciation, pp. 37–39)

voll|ey, -eys, -eying, -eyed 'vɒl|ɪ, -ɪz, -ɪɪŋ, -ɪd

Volquessen (KJ) vɔl'kesən

Volsce (COR) 'vɒls

Volsces (COR) 'vɒlsɪz

Volscian (COR) 'vɒlʃən

Voltemand *or* Voltimand (*HAM*) 'vɔltɪmænd, -mɑnd

volubility 'vɒljʊbɪlɪtɪ

volub|le, -ly, -leness 'vɒljʊb|l̩, -lɪ, -l̩nɪs
Note.—Sometimes, to reconcile the metrical requirements of a verse line, a word's regular syllabic stress may shift (see chapter 'Shakespeare's Verse' § 1.7 of this dictionary, and cf. **revenue**). In her annotation for TNK, I.ii.67, Lois Potter (editor, The Arden Shakespeare, 1997) asserts that 'voluble' is stressed on the second syllable; however, rules of scansion do not demand it in this case

volume, -s 'vɒljum [-jəm], -z

Volumnia (*COR*) və'lʌmnɪə [vo'l-]

Volumnius (*JUL*) və'lʌmnɪəs [vo'l-], -njəs

voluntaries 'vɒləntəɹɪz

voluntarily ˌvɒlən'tɛə̆ɹɪlɪ [-'teɹ-]

voluntary 'vɒləntəɹɪ

voluptuous, -ly, -ness və'lʌptʃʊəs [-tjʊəs], -lɪ, -nɪs

vomit, -s, -ing, -ed 'vɒmɪt, -s, -ɪŋ, -ɪd

vor 'vɔə̆ (*from* 'for')
Note.—This, from LEAR, IV.vi.240, is an example of S.'s direction to the actor (via semiphonetic spellings) to adopt the rustic dialect common to the southwestern counties of Devonshire and western Worcestershire, more or less, for the purpose of giving Edgar a "vocal disguise" (cf. Kökeritz's Shakespeare's Pronunciation, pp. 37–39). This particular word is also from MWW, II.iii.82; for more about the condition of its use in this play, see **vorld**

vorld (*from* 'world') 'vɜ·ld (*see Note for* **varld**)

vortnight 'vɔə̆·tnaɪt (*from* 'fortnight')
Note.—This is from LEAR, IV.vi.235, an example of S.'s direction to the actor (via semiphonetic spellings) to adopt the rustic dialect common to the southwestern counties of Devonshire and western Worcestershire, more or less, for the purpose of giving Edgar a "vocal disguise" (cf. Kökeritz's Shakespeare's Pronunciation, pp. 37–39)

votaress, -es 'voŏtəɹɪs ['voŏʃə-, -ɹes], -ɪz

votarist, -s 'voŏtəɹɪst ['voŏʃə-], -s

votar|y, -ies 'voŏtəɹ|ɪ ['voŏʃə-], -ɪz

votress, -es 'voŏtɹɪs, -ɪz

vouch, -es, -ing, -ed, -er/s 'vaŏtʃ, -ɪz, -ɪŋ, -t, -ə·/z

vouchsaf|e, -es, -ing, -ed vaŏtʃ 'seɪf, -s, -ɪŋ, -t

vow, -s, -ing, -ed 'vaŏ, -z, -ɪŋ, -d

vow-fellow, -s 'vaŏˌfeloŏ, -z

vox (*L.*) (TN, V.i.295) 'vɒks ['voks]

vox humana (*L.*), -s ˌvɒks hju'manə [-'mɑnɑ], -z

Vulcan (ADO, HAM, TC, TIT, TN) 'vʌlkən

vulgar, -s; -er, -est, -ly, -ness 'vʌlgə·, -z; -ɹə·, -ɹɪst, -lɪ, -nɪs

vulture, -s 'vʌltʃə·, -z

vurther 'vɜ·ðə· (*from* 'further')
Note.—This is from LEAR, IV.vi.231, an example of S.'s direction to the actor (via semiphonetic spellings) to adopt the rustic dialect common to the southwestern counties of Devonshire and western Worcestershire, more or less, for the purpose of giving Edgar a "vocal disguise" (cf. Kökeritz's Shakespeare's Pronunciation, pp. 37–39)

vying (*from* vie, q.v.) 'vaɪɪŋ

Ww

W (*the letter*), **-'s** 'dʌblˌju, -z
wad, -s, -ding, -ded 'wɒd, -z, -ɪŋ, -ɪd
wad|e, -es, -ing, -ed, -er/s 'weɪd, -z, -ɪŋ,
   -ɪd, -ɚ/z
wafer, -s 'weɪfɚ, -z
wafer-cake, -s 'weɪfɚˌkeɪk, -s
waffle, -s 'wɒfl̩, -z
waft, -s, -ing, -ed; -age 'waft, -s, -ɪŋ, -ɪd;
   -ɪdʒ
wafture, -s 'waftʃɚ, -z
wag, -s, -ging, -ged 'wæg, -z, -ɪŋ, -d
wag|e, -es, -ing, -ed 'weɪdʒ, -ɪz, -ɪŋ, -d
wager, -s, -ing, -ed, -er/s 'weɪdʒɚ, -z,
   -ɹɪŋ, -d, -ɹɚ/z
waggish, -ly, -ness 'wægɪʃ, -lɪ, -nɪs
wagg|le, -les, -ling, -led 'wægl̩, -l̩z, -l̩ɪŋ,
   -l̩d
wagon, -s 'wægən, -z
wag(g)oner, -s 'wægənɚ, -z
wag(g)on-spoke, -s 'wægənspoʊk, -s
wagtail, -s 'wægteɪl, -z
waif, -s 'weɪf, -s
wail, -s, -ing/ly, -ed, -er/s 'weɪl, -z, -ɪŋ/lɪ,
   -d, -ɚ/z
wail|ful, -ly 'weɪl|fʊl, -fəlɪ
wain, -s 'weɪn, -z
wain(-)rope, -s 'weɪnɹoʊp, -s
wainscot, -s, -(t)ing, -(t)ed 'weɪnskət
   [-skɒt], -s, -ɪŋ, -ɪd
waist, -s 'weɪst, -s
wait, -s, -ing, -ed 'weɪt, -s, -ɪŋ, -ɪd
waiter, -s 'weɪʃɚ, -z
waiting-|woman, -women
   'weɪtɪŋ|ˌwʊmən, -ˌwɪmɪn
waiting-gentle|woman, -women
   ˌweɪtɪŋ'dʒentl̩|ˌwʊmən, -ˌwɪmɪn
wak|e, -es, -ing, -ed, woke, woken 'weɪk,
   -s, -ɪŋ, -t, 'woʊk, 'woʊkən
Wakefield (3HVI) 'weɪkfild
waken, -s, -ing, -ed 'weɪkən, -z, -ɪŋ, -d

Wales (CYM, 1HIV, 2HIV, HV, RIII)
   'weɪlz
Wales, Prince of (1HIV, RII, RIII) 'pɹɪns
   əv 'weɪlz
walk, -s, -ing, -ed, -er/s 'wɔk, -s, -ɪŋ, -t,
   -ɚ/z
wall (**W.**), **-s, -ing, -ed** 'wɔl, -z, -ɪŋ, -d
wallet, -s 'wɒlɪt, -s
wall-eye, -s, -d 'wɔlaɪ, -z, -d
wall-newt, -s 'wɔlˌnjut, -s
Walloon (1HVI) wɒ'lun
wallow, -s, -ing, -ed, -er/s 'wɒloʊ, -z, -ɪŋ,
   -d, -ɚ/z
walnut, -s 'wɔlnʌt, -s
walnut-shell, -s 'wɔlnʌtˌʃel, -z
walrus, -es 'wɔlɹəs ['wɒl-], -ɪz
Walter (1HIV, 2HVI, RIII, TS) 'wɔltɚ
   Note.—In 2HVI, IV.i.35, *there is a*
   homophonic pun set up that depends on
   how closely one pronounces the name
   'Walter' to sound like 'water' (cf. Note
   for **'Fitzwater** *or* **Fitzwalter***')
waltz, -es, -ing, -ed, -er/s 'wɔlts, -ɪz, -ɪŋ,
   -t, -ɚ/z
wan, -s, -ning, -ned, -ner, -nest, -ly, -ness
   'wɒn, -z, -ɪŋ, -d, -ɚ, -ɪst, -lɪ, -nɪs
wand, -s 'wɒnd, -z
wander, -s, -ing, -ed, -er/s 'wɒndɚ, -z,
   -ɹɪŋ ['wɑndɹɪŋ], -d, -ɹɚ/z
wand-like 'wɒndˌlaɪk
wan|e, -es, -ing, -ed 'weɪn, -z, -ɪŋ, -d
wanny 'wɒnɪ
want, -s, -ing, -ed 'wɒnt, -s, -ɪŋ, -ɪd
wanton, -s, -ly, -ness 'wɒntən, -z, -lɪ, -nɪs
want-wit, -s 'wɒntwɪt, -s
wappened 'wapənd
war (**W.**), **-s, -ring, -red** 'wɔɚ, -z, -ɹɪŋ, -d
warb|le, -les, -ling, -led 'wɔɚbl̩, -l̩z, -l̩ɪŋ,
   -l̩d
warbler, -s 'wɔɚblɚ, -z

---

i wɛ ɪ city ɪ hɪt e lɛt ɛ dɛbut æ cæn a pass ɚ bɪrd ʌ hʌt ə again ɚ supper u you
ʊ should o obey ɔ awl ɒ cop ɑ father eɪ paid aɪ high oʊ go ɔɪ voice aʊ found ɪɚ ear
ɛɚ air ʊɚ poor ɔɚ fork ɑɚ park aɪɚ fire aʊɚ hour b boy p pit d dog t top g got
k kid h how fi behave dʒ jot tʃ chew z zany s soft v vat f fat ʒ treasure ʃ ship ð the
θ thin m man n no ŋ hang l lip j yes w won ʍ whew ɹ rigger, aiɾy ɾ matter

ward, -s, -ing, -ed 'wɔɚˑd, -z, -ɪŋ, -ɪd
warden, -s 'wɔɚˑdn̩, -z
warder, -s 'wɔɚˑdɚ, -z
Ware (TN) 'wɛɚˑ
w'are (*contr. of* **we are**) 'wɪɚˑ
war|e (*archaic; watchful of*), **-es, -ing, -ed** 'wɛɚˑ, -z, -ɹɪŋ, -d
ware (*items that are alike*), **-s** 'wɛɚˑ, -z
ware-a 'wɛɚˑɹə

Note.—*This word, along with its counterparts, 'dear-a' and 'wear-a,' appears in a ditty in WT, IV.iv.316–324; the extra syllable there merely to provide for another musical beat in the line of song. An attempt to retain a strict rhyme with 'dear-a'—as once the two presumably could rhyme (cf. Kökeritz's* Shakespeare's Pronunciation, *p. 208)— is unprofitable*

warlike 'wɔɚˑlaɪ̆k
warm, -s, -ing, -ed; -er, -est, -ly, -ness 'wɔɚˑm, -z, -ɪŋ, -d; -ɚ, -ɪst, -lɪ, -nɪs
war-man 'wɔɚˑˌmæn
war-marked 'wɔɚˑˌmɑɚˑkt
warmth 'wɔɚˑmθ [-mpθ]
warn, -s, -ing, -ed 'wɔɚˑn, -z, -ɪŋ, -d
warning (*s.*), **-s** 'wɔɚˑnɪŋ, -z
warp, -s, -ing, -ed 'wɔɚˑp, -s, -ɪŋ, -t
war-proof 'wɔɚˑpɹuf
warrant, -s, -ing, -ed, -er/s 'wɒɹənt, -s, -ɪŋ, -ɪd, -ɚ/z
warrantee, -s ˌwɒɹənˈtɪ, -z
warrantize 'wɒɹənˌtaɪ̆z
warrantor, -s 'wɒɹəntɔɚˑ [-tɚ], -z
warrant|y, -ies 'wɒɹənt|ɪ, -ɪz
warren, -s 'wɒɹɪn, -z
warrener, -s 'wɒɹɪnɚ, -z
warr'nt 'wɒɹ(ə)nt

Note.—*This syncopated version of 'warrant' is what some editors prefer over some of S.'s usual spellings in the First Folio, such as 'warne,' 'warnt,' and 'warnd' (cf.* **spirit***)*

wart, -s 'wɔɚˑt, -s
Wart, Thomas (*2HIV*) 'tɒməs 'wɔɚˑt
war-thoughts 'wɑɚˑˌθɔts
Warwick (*2HIV, HV, 1HVI, 2HVI, 3HVI, RIII*) 'wɒɹɪk ['wɔɹɪk]

Warwickshire (1HIV, 2HVI, 3HVI) 'wɒɹɪkʃɚ [-ʃɪɚˑ]
war|y, -ier, -iest, -ily, -iness 'wɛɚˑɹ|ɪ, -ɪɚˑ, -ɪɪst, -ɪlɪ, -ɪnɪs
was 'wɒz (*strong form*), 'wəz (*weak form*)
wash, -es, -ing, -ed, -er/s; -able 'wɒʃ, -ɪz, -ɪŋ, -t, -ɚ/z; -əbl̩
Washes (KJ) 'wɒʃɪz
Washford (1HVI) 'wɒʃfɚd
wasp, -s 'wɒsp, -s
waspish, -ly, -ness 'wɒspɪʃ, -lɪ, -nɪs
waspish-headed 'wɒspɪʃˌhedɪd
wasplike 'wɒsplaɪ̆k
wasp-stung 'wɒspˌstʌŋ
wassail, -s 'wɒseɪ̆l [-sl̩], -z
wast 'wɒst (*strong form*), 'wəst (*weak form*)
was't (*contr. of* **was it**) 'wɒzt
wast|e, -es, -ing, -ed, -er/s 'weɪ̆st, -s, -ɪŋ, -ɪd, -ɚ/z
waste|ful, -fully, -fulness 'weɪ̆st|fʊl, -fəlɪ, -fʊlnɪs
Wat (VA) 'wɒt
watch (W.), **-es, -ing/s, -ed, -er/s** 'wɒtʃ, -ɪz, -ɪŋ/z, -t, -ɚ/z
watch-case, -s 'wɒtʃˌkeɪ̆s, -ɪz
watch-'ords 'wɒtʃˌɝˑdz (*see* **prings**)
watch-word, -s 'wɒtʃˌwɝˑd, -z
water, -s, -ing, -ed 'wɔɾɚ, -z, -ɹɪŋ, -d
water-flower, -s 'wɔɾɚˌflaʊ̆ɚ, -z
water-flowing 'wɔɾɚˌfloʊ̆ɪŋ
water-fl|y, -ies 'wɔɾɚˌfl|aɪ̆, -aɪ̆z
Waterford (1HVI) 'wɔɾɚˌfɚd
water-gall, -s 'wɔɾɚˌɡɔl, -z
waterish 'wɔɾɚˑɹɪʃ
water-pot, -s 'wɔɾɚˌpɒt, -s
water-rug, -s 'wɔɾɚˌɹʌɡ, -z
water-side 'wɔɾɚˌsaɪ̆d
water-spaniel, -s 'wɔɾɚˌspænjəl, -z
water-standing 'wɔɾɚˌstændɪŋ
Waterton, Sir Robert (RII) ˌsɝˑ 'ɹɒbɚt 'wɔɾɚˑtən
water-walled 'wɔɾɚˌwɔld
waterwork, -s 'wɔɾɚˌwɝˑk, -s
watery 'wɔɾɚˑɹɪ
wav|e, -es, -ing, -ed; -eless 'weɪ̆v, -z, -ɪŋ, -d; -lɪs

wawl or **waul** (*cry of the newborn babe or animal*) 'wɔl

wax, -es, -ing, -ed; -en 'wæks, -ɪz, -ɪŋ, -t; -ən

wax-red 'wæks‚ɹed

wax|y, -ier, -iest, -iness 'wæks|ɪ, -ɪɚ, -ɪɪst, -ɪnɪs

way, -s 'weɪ, -z

way|lay, -lays, -laying, -laid, -layer/s 'weɪ|leɪ, -leɪz, -leɪɪŋ, -leɪd, -leɪɚ/z

wayside 'weɪsaɪd

wayward, -ly, -ness 'weɪwɚd, -lɪ, -nɪs

waywarder 'weɪwɚdɚ

weak, -er, -est, -ly, -ness 'wik, -ɚ, -ɪst, -lɪ, -nɪs

weak-built 'wik‚bɪlt

weak|en, -ens, -ening, -ened 'wik|ən, -ənz, -ənɪŋ [-n̩ɪŋ], -ənd

weak-hearted 'wikfiɑɚˑtɪd

weak-hinged 'wikfiɪndʒd

weak-kneed 'wik‚nid [‚-'-]

weakling, -s 'wiklɪŋ, -z

weal, -s 'wil, -z

wealsmen 'wilzmən

wealth, -s 'welθ, -s

wealth|y, -ier, -iest, -ily, -iness 'welθ|ɪ, -ɪɚ, -ɪɪst, -ɪlɪ, -ɪnɪs

wean, -s, -ing, -ed 'win, -z, -ɪŋ, -d

weanling, -s 'winlɪŋ, -z

weapon, -s, -ing, -ed; -less 'wepən, -z, -ɪŋ, -d; -lɪs

weaponry 'wepənɹɪ

wear, -s, -ing, wore, worn, wearer/s 'wɛɚ, -z, -ɪŋ, 'wɔɚ, 'wɔɚn, wɛɚɪɚ/z
Note.—Like so many other words in S. that no longer match their would-be rhyming counterparts, 'wear' in LC, 291 wants to rhyme with 'tear' (lachrymal) and 'here.' In such cases, the rhyme is typically forsaken in favor of meaning to the modern ear (cf. 'Shakespeare's Verse' § 1.9 of this dictionary)

wear-a 'wɛɚɹə

Note.—This word, along with its counterparts, 'dear-a' and 'ware-a,' appears in a ditty in WT, IV.iv.316–324; the extra syllable there merely to provide for another musical beat in the line of song. An attempt to retain a strict rhyme with 'dear-a'—as once the two presumably could rhyme (cf. Kökeritz's Shakespeare's Pronunciation, *p. 208)— is unprofitable*

wear|y, -ies, -ying, -ied; -ier, -iest, -ily, -iness 'wɪɚ‚ɹ|ɪ, -ɪz, -ɪɪŋ, -ɪd; -ɪɚ, -ɪɪst, -ɪlɪ, -ɪnɪs

weasand or **wezand** 'wizənd [-zand]

weasel, -s 'wizl̩, -z

weather, -s, -ing, -ed 'weðɚ, -z, -ɹɪŋ, -d

weather(-)beaten 'weðɚ‚bitn̩

weather(-)bitten 'weðɚ‚bitn̩

weathercock, -s 'weðɚkɒk, -s

weather-fend, -s, -ing, -ed 'weðɚ'fend, -z, -ɪŋ, -ɪd

weav|e, -es, -ing, wove, woven 'wiv, -z, -ɪŋ, 'woŭv, 'woŭvən

weaved-up 'wivdʌp

weaver, -s 'wivɚ, -z

web, -s, -bing, -bed 'web, -z, -ɪŋ, -d

wed, -s, -ding/s, -ded 'wed, -z, -ɪŋ/z, -ɪd

wedding-day, -s 'wedɪŋdeɪ, -z

wedding-dower 'wedɪŋdaŭɚ

wedding-garment, -s 'wedɪŋgɑɚ‚mənt, -s

wedg|e, -es, -ing, -ed 'wedʒ, -ɪz, -ɪŋ, -d

wedlock 'wedlɒk

Wednesday (COM, COR, 1HIV, 2HIV, MV, OTH, RII, RJ, WT), **-s** 'wenzdɪ [-deɪ], -z

wee 'wi

weed, -s, -ing, -ed 'wid, -z, -ɪŋ, -ɪd

weeder-out ‚widɚ'ɹaŭt

weed|y, -ier, -iest, -iness 'wid|ɪ, -ɪɚ, -ɪɪst, -ɪnɪs

week, -s 'wik, -s

weekday, -s 'wikdeɪ, -z

ween, -s, -ing, -ed 'win, -z, -ɪŋ, -d

---

i w**e**e ɪ cit**y** ɪ h**i**t e l**e**t ɛ d**e**but æ c**a**n a p**a**ss ɝ b**ir**d ʌ h**u**t ə **a**gain ɚ supp**er** u y**ou** ʊ sh**ou**ld o **o**bey ɔ **aw**l ɒ c**o**p ɑ f**a**ther eɪ p**ai**d aɪ h**igh** oŭ g**o** ɔɪ v**oi**ce aŭ f**ou**nd ɪɚ **ear** ɛɚ **air** ʊɚ **poor** ɔɚ **fork** ɑɚ **park** aɪɚ **fire** aŭɚ **hour** b **b**oy p **p**it d **d**og t **t**op g **g**ot k **k**id h **h**ow fi be**h**ave dʒ **j**ot tʃ **ch**ew z **z**any s **s**oft v **v**at f **f**at ʒ trea**s**ure ʃ **sh**ip ð **th**e θ **th**in m **m**an n **n**o ŋ ha**ng** l **l**ip j **y**es w **w**on ʍ **wh**ew ɹ **r**igger, ai**r**y f **m**a**tt**er

weep, -s, -ing/ly, wept 'wip, -s, -ɪŋ/lɪ, 'wept

weeping-ripe 'wipɪŋ'raɪp

weet, -s, -ing, -ed 'wit, -s, -ɪŋ, -ɪd

weigh, -s, -ing, -ed; -able 'weɪ, -z, -ɪŋ, -d; -əbļ

weight, -s, -ing, -ed 'weɪt, -s, -ɪŋ, -ɪd

weightless, -ly, -ness 'weɪtlɪs, -lɪ, -nɪs

weight|y, -ier, -iest, -ily, -iness 'weɪt|ɪ, -ɪə·, -ɪst, -ɪlɪ, -ɪnɪs

weir, -s 'wɪə·, -z

weird, -er, -est, -ly, -ness 'wɪə·d, -ə·, -ɪst, -lɪ, -nɪs

Weïrd Sister (*MAC*), **-s** 'weɪə·d 'sɪstə·, -z
Note.—The Folio version of MAC *gives the spellings 'wayward' and 'weyard,' coming from the Middle English word for 'fate' (cf. Kenneth Muir's note for* MAC, *I.iii.32, The Arden Shakespeare, 1951). It is always disyllabic (cf. 'dieresis,' Introduction § 3.14 of this dictionary)*

Weïrd Women (*MAC*) 'weɪə·d 'wɪmɪn
(*see Note for* **Weïrd Sister**)

welady *or* **weladay** 'welədɪ

welcom|e, -es, -ing, -ed, -er/s 'welkəm, -z, -ɪŋ, -d, -ə·/z

welcomest 'welkəmɪst

welfare 'welfɛə·

welkin (**W.**) (LLL, MWW) 'welkɪn

well, -s, -ing, -ed 'wel, -z, -ɪŋ, -d

well(-)a(-)day ‚welə'deɪ ['---]

well-advised ‚weləd'vaɪzd

well-a-near ‚welə'nɪə·

well-apparelled ‚welə'pæɹəld

well-appointed ‚welə'pɔɪntɪd

well-balanced ‚wel'bælənst (*when att.,* ['-,--])

well-behaved ‚welbɪ'ɦeɪvd

well-beloved ‚welbɪ'lʌvd [-bɪ'lʌvɪd]

well-beseeming ‚welbɪ'simɪŋ (*when att.,* ['--,--])

well-born ‚wel'bɔə·n (*when att.,* ['-,-])

well-breathed ‚wel'bɹeθt (*when att.,* ['-,-]) (*see Note for* **breathed** [*adj.*])

well-deserving ‚weldɪ'zɜ·vɪŋ

well-famed ‚wel'feɪmd (*when att.,* ['-,-])

well-favored ‚wel'feɪvə·d (['---] *in* TGV, II.i.48)

well-foughten 'wel‚fɔtņ

well-found ‚wel'faʊnd (*when att.,* ['-,-])

well-graced ‚wel'gɹeɪst (*when att.,* ['-,-])

well-hallowed ‚wel'hæloʊd

well-laboring ‚wel'leɪbə·ɪŋ

well-minded ‚wel'maɪndɪd (*when att.,* ['-,--])

well-learned ‚wel'lɜ·nɪd

well-nigh 'welnaɪ

well-noted ‚wel'noʊtɪd

well-painted ‚wel'peɪntɪd (*when att.,* ['-,--])

well-reputed ‚welɹɪ'pjutɪd (*when att.,* ['--,--])

well-seeming 'welsimɪŋ

well-spoken ‚wel'spoʊkən

well-steeled ‚wel'stild (*when att.,* ['-,-])

well-tuned ‚wel'tjund (*when att.,* ['-,-])

well-warranted ‚wel'wɒɹəntɪd

well-willer, -s 'wel‚wɪlə·, -z

well-wish, -ed, -er/s 'wel‚wɪʃ, -t, -ə·/z

Welsh (1HIV, HV, MWW) 'welʃ

Welsh|man (1HIV, HV, 3HVI), **-men** 'welʃ|mən, -mən

Welshwomen (1HIV) 'welʃwɪmɪn

wen, -s 'wen, -z

wench, -es, -ing 'wentʃ, -ɪz, -ɪŋ

wenchless 'wentʃlɪs

wench-like 'wentʃ‚laɪk

wend, -s, -ing, -ed 'wend, -z, -ɪŋ, -ɪd

went (*p.t. of* **go,** *q.v.*) 'went

weraday 'weɹədeɪ [-dɪ]

were (*from* be) 'wɜ·

wert 'wɜ·t

west (**W.**) (COM, CYM, 2HIV, 2HVI, KJ, MAC, MSND, RII, RIII, Sonn. 132) 'west

westerly 'westə·lɪ

western (**W.**) 'westə·n

West Indies (MWW) 'west 'ɪndɪz

Westminster (2HIV, 1HVI, 2HVI, RII, RIII) 'westmɪnstə·

Westminster, Abbot of (*RII*) 'æbət əv 'westmɪnstə·

Westmoreland (*1HIV, 2HIV, HV, 3HVI*) 'westmə·lənd
Note.—This name is so subordinated and spoken so colloquially in HV, *IV.iii.34, that it becomes almost a disyllable, i.e.,* ['wesmələnd]

westward, -s, -ly 'westwɚd, -z, -lɪ
wet, -ter, -test, -ness 'wet, -ɚ ['wefɚ], -ɪst ['wefɪst], -tnɪs
wether, -s 'weðɚ, -z
wet-nurse, -s 'wet,nɚs, -ɪz
wezand (*obscure form of* **weasand**) 'wizənd [-zand]
whal|e, -es, -ing, -ed, -er/s 'ʍeɪl, -z, -ɪŋ, -d, -ɚ/z

Note.—In LLL, V.ii.332, the Quarto and the First Folio give the words '. . . whales bone.' It is often emended to '. . . whale's bone' or '. . . whales' bone.' In any case, the word 'whales' must be disyllabic to meet the metrical demands of the verse line and may be pronounced either ['ʍeɪl'ɪz] *or* ['ʍeɪəlz]. *I prefer the former because it suggests the loose contr. of the possessive 'whale's.' Editors who opt to stay with the Second through Fourth Folios' version of the text give '. . . whale his bone' (cf. TC, IV.v.254, TN, III.iii.26, 3HVI, V.vi.89, and Sonn. 55.7), in which case 'whale' remains monosyllabic (see Abbott's* A Shake-spearian Grammar, *§ 217, and* The Oxford Companion to the English Language, *§ 'Apostrophe—Posses-sion'). The same case could be made for 'moon's' in MSND, II.i.7, and 'night's' in MSND, IV.i.95, etc. for the same reasons (see Note for* **month***)*

whar|f, -ves, -fs 'ʍɔɚ|f, -vz, -fs
what 'ʍɒt (*strong form*), 'ʍət (*weak form*)
whate'er ˌʍɒ'fɛɚ
whatsoe'er ˌʍɒtsoŭ'ɛɚ
whatsome'er ˌʍɒtsʌm'ɛɚ
whatsomever ˌʍɒtsʌm'evɚ
What-ye-call't, Master (AYLI) 'mastɚ 'ʍɒtʃə,kɔlt ['ʍɒtjə-, -tjɪ,k-]
w'have (*contr. of* **we have**) 'wiv ['wæv]
wheak 'ʍiːk

Note.—This word, given twice in TIT, IV.ii148, is meant to stand for the sound

imitative of a pig's squeal, and therefore any egressive or ingressive high-pitched cry carrying the basic feel and shape of the phonetics given above will serve

wheat, -en 'ʍit, -n̩
wheel, -s, -ing, -ed 'ʍil, -z, -ɪŋ, -d
whe'er (*contr. of* **whether**) ʍɛɚ
Wheeson (2HIV) 'ʍisn̩
whelk, -s, -ed 'ʍelk ['welk], -s, -t
whelm, -s, -ing, -ed 'ʍelm, -z, -ɪŋ, -d
whelp, -s, -ing, -ed 'ʍelp, -s, -ɪŋ, -t
when 'ʍen
whenas 'ʍenæz
whence 'ʍens
whencesoever ˌʍenssoŭ'evɚ
whene'er ʍen'ɛɚ [ʍe'n-]
whenever ʍen'evɚ [ʍe'n-]
whensoever ˌʍensoŭ'evɚ
whe'r (*from* **whether**) 'ʍɛɚ
where 'ʍɛɚ
whereabout, -s 'ʍɛɚɹəbaŭt [ˌ-'-], -s
whereat 'ʍɛɚɹæt [-'-]
whereby ʍɛɚ'baɪ (['--] *in* OTH, III.i.9)
where'er ʍɛɚ'ɹɛɚ
wherefor(e) 'ʍɛɚfɔɚ ([ˌ-'-] *in* MSND, III.ii.272)
wherefore 'ʍɛɚfɔɚ
wherein ʍɛɚ'ɹɪn
whereinto 'ʍɛɚ ɹɪn,tu
whereof ʍɛɚ'ɹɒv (*arguably* ['--] *in* Sonn. 63.6)
whereon ʍɛɚ'ɹɒn
whereout ʍɛɚ'ɹaŭt
wheresoe'er ˌʍɛɚso'ɛɚ
wheresoever ˌʍɛɚso'evɚ
where't (*contr. of* **where it**) 'ʍɛɚt
wherethrough ʍɛɚ'θɹu
whereto ʍɛɚ'tu (['--] *in* JUL, III.i.250)
whereuntil ˌʍɛɚ ɹʌn'tɪl
whereupon ˌʍɛɚ ɹə'pɒn
wherewith ʍɛɚ'wɪð
wherewithal 'ʍɛɚwɪðɔl
whet, -s, -ting, -ted 'ʍet, -s, -ɪŋ, -ɪd
whether 'ʍeðɚ

i we ɪ city ɪ hit e let ɛ debut æ can a pass ɚ bird ʌ hut ə again ɚ supper u you ʊ should o obey ɔ awl ɒ cop ɑ father eɪ paid aɪ high oŭ go ɔɪ voice aŭ found ɪɚ ear ɛɚ air ʊɚ poor ɔɚ fork ɑɚ park aɪɚ fire aŭɚ hour b boy p pit d dog t top g got k kid h how fi behave dʒ jot tʃ chew z zany s soft v vat f fat ʒ treasure ʃ ship ð the θ thin m man n no ŋ hang l lip j yes w won ʍ whew ɹ rigger, airy f matter

whetstone, -s 'ʍetstoʊn, -z
whey 'ʍeɪ
whey-face 'ʍeɪˌfeɪs
whew (interj.) 'ʍju
which 'ʍɪtʃ
whichever ʍɪtʃ'evɚ
whiff, -s, -ing, -ed 'ʍɪf, -s, -ɪŋ, -t
whiffler 'ʍɪflɚ
whil|e, -es, -ing, -ed 'ʍaɪl, -z, -ɪŋ, -d
while-ere ˌʍaɪl'ɛɚ
whilst 'ʍaɪlst
whim, -s 'ʍɪm, -z
whimper, -s, -ing, -ed, -er/s 'ʍɪmpɚ, -z,
  -ɹɪŋ, -d, -ɹɚ/z
whims|y, -ies 'ʍɪmz|ɪ, -ɪz
whin|e, -es, -ing/ly, -ed, -er/s 'ʍaɪn, -z,
  -ɪŋ/lɪ, -d, -ɚ/z
whinid'st 'ʍɪnɪdst
  Note.—The OED cites 'whinid' as a var.
  spelling of 'finewed,' an obsolete word
  meaning moldy. In TC, II.i.14, the First
  Folio's 'whinid'st' is often emended to
  'vinewed'st.' The OED does not assert a
  pronunciation for 'whinid,' 'finewed,' or
  'vinewed,' but orthoepic evidence points
  to the pronunciations ['ʍɪnɪd], ['fɪnɪd,
  'fɪnjud], and ['vɪnjud], respectively
whin|y, -iness 'ʍaɪnɪ, -ɪnɪs
whip, -s, -ping/s, -ped, whipt 'ʍɪp, -s,
  -ɪŋ/z, -t, 'ʍɪpt
whipper, -s 'ʍɪpɚ, -z
whipping-cheer 'ʍɪpɪŋˌtʃɪɚ
whipster 'ʍɪpstɚ
whipstock 'ʍɪpstɒk
whipt (p.t. and p.p. of whip, q.v.) 'ʍɪpt
whir, -s, -ring/s, -red 'ʍɝ, -z, -ɹɪŋ/z, -d
whirl, -s, -ing, -ed 'ʍɝl, -z, -ɪŋ, -d
whirlpool, -s 'ʍɝlpul, -z
whirlwind, -s 'ʍɝlwɪnd, -z
whisk, -s, -ing, -ed 'ʍɪsk, -s, -ɪŋ, -t
whisker, -s, -ed 'ʍɪskɚ, -z, -d
whiskey, -s 'ʍɪskɪ, -z
whisper, -s, -ing/s, -ed, -er/s 'ʍɪspɚ, -z,
  -ɹɪŋ/z, -d, -ɹɚ/z
whissing 'ʍɪsɪŋ
whist 'ʍɪst
whist|le, -les, -ling, -led, -ler/s 'ʍɪs|l̩, -l̩z,
  -lɪŋ [-l̩ɪŋ], -l̩d, -lɚ/z
whit 'ʍɪt

whit|e, -es; -er, -est, -ely, -eness; -ing, -ed
  'ʍaɪt, -s; -ɚ, -ɪst, -lɪ, -nɪs; -ɪŋ, -ɪd
white-bearded 'ʍaɪtbɪɚdɪd
whitecap, -s 'ʍaɪtkæp, -s
white-faced 'ʍaɪtˌfeɪst
Whitefriars (RIII) 'ʍaɪtˌfɹaɪɚz
white-haired 'ʍaɪtˌfiɛɚd
Whitehall (HVIII) 'ʍaɪtfiɔl
White Hart (2HVI) 'ʍaɪt 'hɑɚt
white-limed 'ʍaɪtˌlaɪmd
white-livered 'ʍaɪtlɪvɚd
whither 'ʍɪðɚ
Whitmore, Walter (2HVI) 'ʍɔltɚ
  ʍɪtmɔɚ
  Note.—In 2HVI, IV.i.35, there is a
  homophonic pun set up that depends on
  how closely one pronounces the name
  'Walter' to sound like 'water' (cf.
  Fitzwater)
whitster (one who bleaches clothes), -s
  'ʍɪtstɚ, -z
Whitsun (HV, WT) 'ʍɪtsn̩
whitt|le, -les, -ling, -led 'ʍɪt|l̩, -l̩z, -lɪŋ
  [-l̩ɪŋ], -l̩d
whiz(z), -es, -ing, -ed 'ʍɪz, -ɪz, -ɪŋ, -d
whoa 'ʍoʊ ['woʊ]
whoa-ho-hoa ˌʍoʊfioʊ'fioʊ [ˌwoʊfi-]
whoe'er hʊ'ɛɚ
whoever hʊ'evɚ [hu'e-]
whole, -ness 'hoʊl, -nɪs
wholesome, -st, -ly, -ness 'hoʊlsəm, -ɪst,
  -lɪ, -nɪs
wholly 'hoʊllɪ ['hoʊlɪ]
whom 'hum
whomsoever ˌhumsoʊ'evɚ
whoo-bub (var. of hubbub) 'ʍubʌb
whoop (call or cry; paroxysmal gasp or
  cough), -s, -ing, -ed 'ʍup ['hup], -s, -ɪŋ,
  -t
whoops (sudden surprise; mild apology)
  'ʍʊps ['wʊps], 'ʍups ['wups]
whor|e, -es, -ing, -ed; -edom/s 'hɔɚ, -z,
  -ɹɪŋ, -d; -dəm/z
whoremaster, -s; -ly 'hɔɚˌmastɚ, -z; -lɪ
whoremonger, -s 'hɔɚˌmʌŋgɚ, -z
Whore of Babylon (HV) 'hɔɚ (ɹ)əv
  'bæbɪlɒn
whoreson, -s 'hɔɚsn̩, -z
whorish, -ly, -ness 'hɔɚɹɪʃ, -lɪ, -nɪs

whose 'huz
whoso 'husoŏ
whosoever ˌhusoŏ'evɚ ['--ˌ--]
whosomever ˌhusə'mevɚ [-sʌ'm-]
why 'ʍaɪ
wi' (*short for* **with**) 'wɪ
wick, -s 'wɪk, -s
wicked, -est, -ly, -ness 'wɪkɪd, -ɪst, -lɨ, -nɪs
wicker 'wɪkɚ
wide, -r, -st, -ly, -ness 'waɪd, -ɚ, -ɪst, -lɨ, -nɪs
wide-chapped 'waɪdˌtʃæpt
wide-chopped 'waɪdˌtʃɒpt
wide-enlarged 'waɪdɪn'lɑɚ̆dʒd
wid|en, -ens, -ening, -ened 'waɪd|n̩, n̩z, -n̩ɪŋ [-nɪŋ], -n̩d
wide-skirted 'waɪdˌskɚtɪd
wide-stretched 'waɪdˌstɹetʃt
widow, -s, -ing, -ed 'wɪdoŏ, -z, -ɪŋ, -d
widow-comfort 'wɪdoŏˌkʌmfɚt
widow-dolor 'wɪdoŏˌdoŏlɚ [-ˌdɒlɚ]
widowhood 'wɪdoŏɦʊd
widow-maker, -s 'wɪdoŏˌmeɪkɚ, -z
width, -s 'wɪd̪θ ['wɪt̪θ], -s
wield, -s, -ing, -ed 'wild, -z, -ɪŋ, -ɪd
wi|fe, -ves 'waɪ|f, -vz
wife-like 'waɪfˌlaɪk
wig, -s, -ging, -ged 'wɪg, -z, -ɪŋ, -d
wight (W.), -s 'waɪt, -s
wild, -s, -er, -est, -ly, -ness 'waɪld, -z, -ɚ, -ɪst, -lɨ, -nɪs
wild-boar, -s 'waɪldˌboɚ, -z
wild(-)cat, -s 'waɪldˌkæt, -s
wilderness, -es 'wɪldɚnɪs, -ɪz
wildfire, -s 'waɪldˌfaɪɚ, -z
wildfowl 'waɪldˌfaŏl
wild-goose 'waɪldˌgus
wil|e, -es, -ing, -ed 'waɪl, -z, -ɪŋ, -d
wilful, -lest, -ly, -ness 'wɪlfʊl, -ɪst, -lɨ, -nɪs
wilful-blame 'wɪlfʊl'bleɪm [ˌ--'-]
wilful-negligent 'wɪlfʊl'neglɪdʒənt
wilful-opposite 'wɪlfʊl'ɒpəzɪt
will (W.) (2HIV, 2HVI, Sonn. 135, 136), **-s, -ing, -ed** 'wɪl, -z, -ɪŋ, -d

William (*AYLI*, 2HIV) 'wɪljəm
William of Hatfield (2HVI) 'wɪljəm əv 'hætfild
William of Windsor (2HVI) 'wɪljəm əv 'wɪndzɚ
Williams, Michael (*HV*) 'maɪkl̩ 'wɪljəmz
willing, -ly, -ness 'wɪlɪŋ, -lɨ, -nɪs
Willoughby (*RII*) 'wɪləbɨ
willow, -s, -ing, -ed; -y 'wɪloŏ, -z, -ɪŋ, -d; -ɨ
will't (*contr. of* **will it**) 'wɪlt
wilt (*archaic auxiliary v.; second person singular p.t. of* **will**) 'wɪlt
wilt (*v.*), **-s, -ing, -ed** 'wɪlt, -s, -ɪŋ, -ɪd
Wiltshire, Earl of (3HVI, RII) 'ɚl əv 'wɪlt.ʃɚ ['wɪlt.ʃɪɚ]
wimple, -s 'wɪmpl̩, -z
win, -s, -ning/s, won, winner/s 'wɪn, -z, -ɪŋ/z, 'wʌn, 'wɪnɚ/z
winc|e, -es, -ing, -ed 'wɪns, -ɪz, -ɪŋ, -t
winch (*s.*), **-es** 'wɪntʃ, -ɪz
winch (*v.*) (*archaic var. of* **wince**), **-es, -ing, -ed** 'wɪntʃ, -ɪz, -ɪŋ, -t
Winchester (1HVI, 2HVI, HVIII, TC) 'wɪntʃestɚ [-tʃɪstɚ]
Wincot (TS) 'wɪŋkət
wind (*adj., s.*) (*moving air; type of instrument*), **-s** 'wɪnd, -z
Note.—There is probably little to be gained by making this word adjust to the rhyme scheme in AYLI, III.ii.86–93, 99–110 (which practically demands the pronunciation ['waɪnd]*), and little harm in retaining its traditional modern pronunciation*
wind (*v.*) (*coil*), **-s, -ing, wound** 'waɪnd, -z, -ɪŋ, 'waŏnd
wind (*v.*) (*out of breath*), **-s, -ing, -ed** 'wɪnd, -z, -ɪŋ, -ɪd
windfall, -s 'wɪndfɔl, -z
wind-fanned 'wɪndˌfænd
windgalls (*tumor on a horse's leg*) 'wɪndgɔlz
wind-instrument, -s 'wɪndˌɪnstɹəmənt, -s

---

i wɛ ɨ cɪty ɪ hɪt e lɛt ɛ dɛbut æ cæn a pæss ɚ bɚd ʌ hʌt ə agaɪn ɚ suppɚr u yọu
ŏ shọuld o ọbey ɔ awl ɒ cɒp ɑ fɑther eɪ paɪd aɪ hɪgh oŏ gọ ɔɪ vɔɪce aŏ fọund ɪɚ ẹar
ɛɚ aɪr ŏɚ pọor ɔɚ fọrk ɑɚ pɑrk aɪɚ fɪre aŏɚ họur b bɔy p pɪt d dɒg t tɒp g gɒt
k kɪd h họw ɦ behave dʒ jɒt tʃ chew z zany s sɒft v vat f fæt ʒ treạsure ʃ shɪp ð thẹ
θ thɪn m mæn n nọ ŋ hang l lɪp j yẹs w wọn ʍ whew ɹ rɪgger, aiɹy ɾ matɹer

windlass, -es 'wɪndləs, -ɪz
Windmill (2HIV) 'wɪndmɪl
windmill, -s 'wɪndmɪl, -z
window, -s, -ed 'wɪndoŭ, -z, -d
windpipe, -s 'wɪnd‚paɪp, -s
windring (probably a portmanteau-
word of wandering and winding)
'waɪndɹɪŋ
wind-shaked 'wɪndʃeĭkt
wind-shaken 'wɪndʃeĭkən
Windsor (1HIV, 2HIV, 1HVI, MWW)
'wɪnzɚ ['wɪndzɚ]
Windsor Forest 'wɪnzɚ ['wɪndzɚ]
'fɒɹɪst
Windsor, William of (2HVI) 'wɪljəm əv
'wɪnzɚ [-'wɪndzɚ]
wind-swift 'wɪnd‚swɪft
wind|y, -ier, -iest, -ily, -iness 'wɪnd|ɪ, -ɪɚ,
-ɪɪst, -ɪlɪ, -ɪnɪs
win|e, -es, -ing, -ed 'waĭn, -z, -ɪŋ, -d
winer|y, -ies 'waĭnəɹ|ɪ, -ɪz
wing (s., v.), -s, -ing, -ed 'wɪŋ, -z, -ɪŋ, -d
winged (adj.) 'wɪŋd ['wɪŋɪd]
Wingfield (1HVI) 'wɪŋfild
Wingham (2HVI) 'wɪŋəm
wing-led 'wɪŋ‚led
wink, -s, -ing, -ed, -er/s 'wɪŋk, -s, -ɪŋ, -t,
-ɚ/z
winner, -s 'wɪnɚ, -z
winn|ow, -ows, -owing, -owed, -ower/s
'wɪn|oŭ, -oŭz, -oŭɪŋ, -oŭd, -oŭɚ/z
winsome, -ly, -ness 'wɪnsəm, -lɪ, -nɪs
winter (W.) (CYM, 2HIV, KJ, RJ), -s,
-ing, -ed 'wɪntɚ, -z, -ɹɪŋ, -d
winter-cricket, -s 'wɪntɚ‚kɹɪkɪt, -s
winter-ground 'wɪntɚ‚gɹaŭnd
winterly 'wɪntɚlɪ
wintr|y, -iness 'wɪntɹɪ|ɪ, -ɪnɪs
wip|e, -es, -ing, -ed, -er/s 'waĭp, -s, -ɪŋ,
-t, -ɚ/z
wir|e, -es, -ing, -ed 'waĭɚ, -z, -ɹɪŋ, -d
wireless, -es 'waĭɚˑlɪs, -ɪz
wir|y, -ier, -iest, -iness 'waĭɚˑɹ|ɪ, -ɪɚ, -ɪɪst,
-ɪnɪs
wisdom, -s 'wɪzdəm, -z
Wisdom, Lady (RJ) 'leĭdɪ 'wɪzdəm
wise, -r, -st, -ly, -ness 'waĭz, -ɚ, -ɪst, -lɪ,
-nɪs
wise|man, -men 'waĭz|mən, -mən

wish, -es, -ing, -ed, -er/s 'wɪʃ, -ɪz, -ɪŋ, -t,
-ɚ/z
wished-for 'wɪʃt‚fɔɚ
wishtly (perhaps a portmanteau-word of
wishly and wistly; perhaps an error)
'wɪʃtlɪ
Note.—This word in RII, V.iv.7, is given
as 'wishtly' in the First and Second
Quartos only. In the Third through Fifth
Quartos and in the First Folio, 'wistly'
is given. The OED asserts that 'wishtly'
is an obsolete form of the adv. 'wishly'
and cites no instance of its usage. The
OED's stance on 'wishly' however (now
obsolete except dialectally) is that it is
probably an alteration of 'wistly'
influenced by 'wish'
wist, -ly 'wɪst, -lɪ
wit (W.), -s 'wɪt, -s
witch, -es, -ing, -ed 'wɪtʃ, -ɪz, -ɪŋ, -t
witchcraft (W.) 'wɪtʃkɹaft
wit-cracker, -s 'wɪtkɹækɚ, -z
with 'wɪð
withal(l) wɪ'ðɔl
with|draw, -draws, -drawing, -drew,
-drawn wɪð|'dɹɔ, -'dɹɔz, -'dɹɔɪŋ, -'dɹu,
-'dɹɔn
wither, -s, -ing, -ed 'wɪðɚ, -z, -ɹɪŋ, -d
without wɪ'ðaŭt (['--] in 1HIV, IV.iii.96;
JUL, III.ii.104; KJ, III.ii.58; LEAR,
I.i.223; TIM, I.ii.189; TN, III.iii.24)
with|hold, -holds, -holding, -held
wɪð|'hoŭld, -'hoŭldz, -'hoŭldɪŋ, -'held
within wɪ'ðɪn
without wɪ'ðaŭt (['--] in PER, I.i.38)
without-book wɪ'ðaŭt‚bʊk
without-door wɪ'ðaŭt‚dɔɚ
with|stand, -stands, -standing, -stood
wɪð|'stænd, -'stændz, -'stændɪŋ, -'stʊd
witless, -ly, -ness 'wɪtlɪs, -lɪ, -nɪs
witness, -es, -ing, -ed 'wɪtnɪs, -ɪz, -ɪŋ, -t
wit-snapper, -s 'wɪtsnæpɚ, -z
Wittenberg (HAM) 'wɪtn̩bɚg
wittol (archaic term for an abetting
cuckold), -s; -ly 'wɪtl̩, -z; -ɫ
witt|y, -ier, -iest, -ily, -iness 'wɪt|ɪ ['wɪʂ|ɪ],
-ɪɚ, -ɪɪst, -ɪlɪ, -ɪnɪs
wiv|e, -es, -ing, -ed 'waĭv, -z, -ɪŋ, -d
wizard, -s, -ry 'wɪzɚd, -z, -ɹɪ

woe, -s 'woŭ, -z
woe-begone 'woŭbɪˌgɒn
woeful, -ly, -ness, -lest 'woŭfʊl, -ɨ, -nɪs, -ɪst
woe-wearied 'woŭ'wɪɚ̆ɹɨd
woke (*p.t. of* **wake**, *q.v.*) 'woŭk
woken (*p.p. of* **wake**, *q.v.*) 'woŭkən
wold, -s 'woŭld, -z
Wolsey, Cardinal (*HVIII*) 'kɑɚ̆·dn̩l̩ 'wʊlzɨ
wolt 'woŭlt ['wʊt]
Note.—This word appears in the First Quarto version of PER, IV.i.61, and is the subject of some debate. It probably stands merely for the colloquial form of the auxiliary v. 'wilt' from 'will,' in which case the pronunciation is ['wʊt] *(cf.* **woo't**)*. This form is used in HAM, V.i.270 and AC, IV.ii.7; IV.xv.59. If, however, it stands for the obsolete p.t. of 'wieId,' then the pronunciation is* ['woŭlt]*. Commentators interpret the phrase in which it appears in PER differently. The Fourth Quarto gives 'wilt' instead of 'wolt'*
wolvish 'wʊlvɪʃ
wolvish-ravening 'wʊlvɪʃˌɹævn̩ɪŋ
woman, women 'wʊmən, 'wɪmɪn
womaned 'wʊmənd
womanhood 'wʊmənfiʊd
womanish, -ly, -ness 'wʊmənɪʃ, -lɨ, -nɪs
womaniz|e, -es, -ing, -ed, -er/s 'wʊmənaɪz, -ɪz, -ɪŋ, -d, -ɚ/z
woman|kind, women- ˌwʊmən-, ˌwɪmɪn-|'kaɪnd ['---]
womanl|y, -iness 'wʊmənl|ɨ, -ɨnɪs
woman-post 'wʊmənˌpoŭst
woman-queller 'wʊmənˌkwelɚ
woman-tired 'wʊmənˌtaɪɚ̆·d
womb, -s; -y 'wum, -z; -ɨ
Woncot (2HIV) 'wʊŋkət
wonder, -s, -ing/ly, -ed, -er/s, -ment 'wʌndɚ, -z, -ɹɪŋ/lɨ, -d, -ɹɚ/z, -mənt
wonder-wounded 'wʌndɚˌwundɪd
wondrous, -ly, -ness 'wʌndɹəs, -lɨ, -nɪs

won (*p.t. of* **win**, *q.v.*) 'wʌn
wont, -ed 'woŭnt, -ɪd
woo, -s, -ing/ly, -ed, -er/s 'wu, -z, -ɪŋ/lɨ, -d, -ɚ/z
wood, -s, -ed 'wʊd, -z, -ɪd
woodbine, -s 'wʊdbaɪn, -z
wood-bird, -s 'wʊdbɝd, -z
woodcock, -s 'wʊdkɒk, -s
wooden, -ly, -ness 'wʊdn̩, -lɨ, -nɪs
woodland, -s 'wʊdlənd, -z
wood|man, -men 'wʊd|mən, -mən
woodmonger, -s 'wʊdˌmʌŋgɚ, -z
woodpecker, -s 'wʊdpekɚ, -z
Woodeville, Anthony (RIII) 'æn̩θənɨ 'wʊdvɪl
Note.—In RIII, I.i.67, this surname is meant to be, in order to fit rightly into the verse line, trisyllabic, i.e., ['wʊdəvɪl]*. Editors often supply this accepted spelling of the name—with the middle 'e'—to help lead one to this conclusion*
Woodstock, Thomas of (2HVI) 'tɒməs əv 'wʊdstɒk
Woodvil(l)e *or* **Woodvill, Richard** (*1HVI*) 'ɹɪtʃəd 'wʊdvɪl
wood-wind, -s 'wʊdˌwɪnd, -z
Wooer (*TNK*) 'wuɚ
woof (*s.*) (*threads, web*) 'wuf
woof (*s., v.*) (*dog's bark*), **-s, -ing, -ed** 'wʊf, -s, -ɪŋ, -t
wool, -s 'wʊl, -z
wool(l)en, -s 'wʊlɪn, -z
wool-sack 'wʊlˌsæk
woolward 'wʊlwɚd
woosel (*obsolete form of* **ousel**, *q.v.*), **-s** 'wuzl̩, -z
woo't (*colloquial for auxiliary v.* **wilt** *from* **will**) 'wut ['wʊt]
Worcester (1HIV, KJ) 'wʊstɚ
Note.—In order for both 1HIV, I.iii.14 and 1HIV, III.i.4 to be considered regular pentametrical lines of verse, either the caesura after 'Worcester' must absorb the value of one beat, or

---

i we ɨ city ɪ hit e let ɛ debut æ can a pass ɝ bird ʌ hut ə again ɚ supper u you
ʊ should o obey ɔ awl ɒ cop ɑ father eɪ paid aɪ high oŭ go ɔɪ voice aŭ found ɪɚ̆ ear
ɛɚ̆ air ʊɚ̆ poor ɔɚ̆ fork ɑɚ̆ park aɪɚ̆ fire aŭɚ̆ hour b boy p pit d dog t top g got
k kid h how fi behave dʒ jot tʃ chew z zany s soft v vat f fat ʒ treasure ʃ ship ð the
θ thin m man n no ŋ hang l lip j yes w won ʍ whew ɹ rigger, airy ɾ matter

'Worcester' itself must be trisyllabic, i.e.,
['wʊsɪstə]
Worcester, Earl of (RII) 'ɜ·l əv 'wʊstə
word, -s, -ing/s, -ed; -less 'wɜ·d, -z, -ɪŋ/z,
-ɪd; -lɪs
work, -s, -ing/s, -ed, -er/s 'wɜ·k, -s, -ɪŋ/z,
-t, -ə·/z
working-day, -s 'wɜ·kɪŋˌdeǐ, -z
working-house 'wɜ·kɪŋˌhaǔs
work|man, -men 'wɜ·k|mən, -mən
workmanly 'wɜ·kmənlɪ
workmanship 'wɜ·kmənʃɪp
workshop, -s 'wɜ·kʃɒp, -s
worky-day 'wɜ·kɪˌdeǐ
world, -s 'wɜ·ld, -z
worldling, -s 'wɜ·ldlɪŋ, -z
worldl|y, -ier, -iest, -iness 'wɜ·ldl|ɪ, -ɪə·,
-ɪɪst, -ɪnɪs
world-sharer, -s 'wɜ·ldʃɛ·ə·ɹə· [-'---]
world-wearied 'wɜ·ldwɪə·ɹɪd (*when att.*,
[ˌ-'--])
worm, -s, -ing, -ed 'wɜ·m, -z, -ɪŋ, -d
Worm, Don (ADO) 'dɒn 'wɜ·m
worm-eaten 'wɜ·mˌitn̩
worm-hole, -s 'wɜ·mˌhoǔl, -z
Worm, Lady (HAM) 'leǐdɪ 'wɜ·m
worms-meat 'wɜ·mzˌmit
wormwood (**W.**) 'wɜ·mwʊd
worm|y, -iness 'wɜ·m|ɪ, -ɪnɪs
worn (*p.p. of* **wear**, *q.v.*) 'wɔə·n
worn-out 'wɔə·ˌnaǔt
worse, -r 'wɜ·s, -ə·
worsen, -s, -ing, -ed 'wɜ·sn̩, -z, -ɪŋ, -d
worship, -s, -ping, -ped, -per/s 'wɜ·ʃɪp,
-s, -ɪŋ, -t, -ə·/z
worshipful, -ly, -ness 'wɜ·ʃɪpfʊl, -ɪ, -nɪs
worst, -s, -ing, -ed 'wɜ·st, -s, -ɪŋ, -ɪd
worsted (*s.*) 'wʊstɪd
worsted-stocking 'wʊstɪdˌstɒkɪŋ
wort (*plant; type of beer*), **-s** 'wɜ·t
['wɔə·t], -s
wort (*from '*word*'*), **-s** 'wɜ·t ['wɔə·t], -s
Note.—*Evans (in* MWW*) is a Welsh-*
man, and speaks in a Welsh accent, if
somewhat inconsistently. This is an
example of S.'s direction to the actor (by
way of semiphonetic spellings) to adopt
such an accent, more or less, for the
sake of wringing the most satire out of

plays on words stemming from confu-
sions with, and corruptions of, English
pronunciation via the Welsh tongue; thus
the humor of MWW, I.i.113,114, *when*
Evans means 'words'
worth, -s 'wɜ·θ, -s
worthless, -ly, -ness 'wɜ·θlɪs, -lɪ, -nɪs
worthwhile ˌwɜ·θ'ʍaǐl
Worthies, The Nine (LLL) ˌðə 'naǐn
'wɜ·ðɪz
worth|y, -ies, -ier, -iest, -ily, -iness
'wɜ·ð|ɪ, -ɪz, -ɪə·, -ɪɪst, -ɪlɪ, -ɪnɪs
wot, -s, -ting 'wɒt, -s, -ɪŋ
wouldn't 'wʊdnt̩
wound (*p.t. of* **wind** *[coil], q.v.*) 'waǔnd
wound (*injure*), **-s, -ing/s, -ed; -less**
'wund, -z, -ɪŋ/z, -ɪd; -lɪs
woundingly 'wundɪŋlɪ
wove(n) (*p.t. and p.p. of* **weave**, *q.v.*)
'woǔv(ən)
wrack, -s, -ed 'ɹæk, -s, -t
wrackful 'ɹækfʊl
wrack-threatening 'ɹækˌθɹetnɪŋ
wrang|le, -les, -ling, -led, -ler/s 'ɹæŋg|l̩,
-l̩z, -lɪŋ [-l̩ɪŋ], -l̩d, -lə·/z [-l̩ə·/z]
wrap, -s, -ping/s, -ped *or* **-t** 'ɹæp, -s,
-ɪŋ/z, -t
wrast|le, -les, -ling, -led, -ler/s 'ɹasl̩, -l̩z,
-l̩ŋ [-lɪŋ], -l̩d, -lə·/z [-l̩ə·/z]
wrath 'ɹaθ
wrath|ful, -fully, -fulness 'ɹaθ|fʊl, -fʊlɪ,
-fʊlnɪs
wrath-kindled 'ɹaθkɪndl̩d
wreak, -s, -ing, -ed 'ɹik, -s, -ɪŋ, -t
wreakful 'ɹikfʊl
wrea|th, -ths 'ɹi|θ, -ðz [-θs]
wreath|e, -es, -ing, -ed 'ɹið, -z, -ɪŋ, -d
wreck, -s, -ing, -ed, -er/s 'ɹek, -s, -ɪŋ, -t,
-ə·/z
wren, -s 'ɹen, -z
wrench, -es, -ing, -ed 'ɹentʃ, -ɪz, -ɪŋ, -t
wrest, -s, -ing, -ed 'ɹest, -s, -ɪŋ, -ɪd
wrest|le, -les, -ling, -led, -ler/s 'ɹesl̩, -l̩z,
-l̩ŋ [-lɪŋ], -l̩d, -lə·/z [-lə·/z]
wretch, -es 'ɹetʃ, -ɪz
wretched, -ly, -ness 'ɹetʃɪd, -lɪ, -nɪs
wring, -s, -ing, wrung 'ɹɪŋ, -z, -ɪŋ, 'ɹʌŋ
wrink|le, -les, -ling, -led 'ɹɪŋk|l̩, -l̩z, -l̩ŋ
[-lɪŋ], -l̩d

wrinkly 'ɪɪŋklɨ

wrist, -s 'ɹɪst, -s

writ (s., and archaic p.p. and p.t. of
  write), -s 'ɹɪt, -s

writ|e, -es, -ing/s, wrote, written 'ɹaɪt, -s,
  -ɪŋ/z, 'ɹoŭt, 'ɹɪtn̩

writer, -s 'ɹaɪɾ ɚ, -z

writh|e, -es, -ing, -ed 'ɹaɪð, -z, -ɪŋ, -d

writhled 'ɹɪðl̩d

wro(a)th (sufferance) 'ɹoŭθ

wrong, -s, -ing, -ed; -ly, -ness 'ɹɒŋ, -z, -ɪŋ,
  -d; -lɨ, -nɪs
  Note.—In ADO, V.i.52, 'wrongs' must
  be disyllabic, i.e., ['ɹɒŋɪz], in order to
  fulfill the meter of the verse line (cf.
  whales)

wronger (one who wrongs another), -s
  'ɹɒŋ ɚ, -z

wroth (anger) 'ɹɒθ ['ɹoŭθ]

wrought 'ɹɔt

wrung (p.t. and p.p. of wring, q.v.) 'ɹʌŋ

wr|y (adj.), -ier (-yer), -iest (-yest), -yly,
  -yness 'ɹ|aɪ, -aɪ ɚ, -aɪɪst, -aɪlɨ, -aɪnɪs

wry (v.) (deviate from properness), -s,
  -ing 'ɹaɪ, -z, -ɪŋ

wry-necked 'ɹaɪ.nekt

Wye (1HIV, HV) 'waɪ

Xx

X (the letter), -'s 'eks, -ɪz

Xanadu 'zænədu

Xanthippe (TS) zæn'tɪpɨ

xanthous 'zænθəs

xebec, -s 'zibek, -s

xenia 'zɪnɪə [-njə]

xenocurrenc|y, -ies ˌzeno'kʌɹəns|ɨ, -ɨz

xenogam|y, -ous zɪ'nɒgəm|ɨ, -əs

xenogenesis ˌzenə'dʒenəsɪs

xenophobe, -s ˌzenə'foŭb, -z

xenophobia ˌzenə'foŭbɪə

xenophobic ˌzenə'foŭbɪk

xeric 'zɪɚ.ɹɪk

xerography zɪɚ'ɹɒgɹəfɨ

Xerxes 'zɝ ksiz

xi (Greek letter) 'saɪ

xiphoid 'zaɪfɔɪd

Xmas, -es 'kɹɪsməs [-stm-], -ɪz

X-ray, -s, -ing, -ed 'eksɹeɪ, -z, -ɪŋ, -d

Xuthus 'zuθəs

xylem 'zaɪləm

xylograph, -s, -ing, -ed 'zaɪlə gɹaf, -s,
  -ɪŋ, -t

xylograph|er/s, -y zaɪ'lɒgɹəf|ɚ/z, -ɨ

xyloid 'zaɪlɔɪd

xylophone, -s 'zaɪləfoŭn, -z

xylophonist, -s 'zaɪləˌfoŭnɪst, -s

Yy

Y (the letter), -'s 'waɪ, -z

yacht, -s, -ing, -ed 'jɒt, -s, -ɪŋ, -ɪd

yachts|man, -men 'jɒts|mən, -mən

yahoo, -s 'jɑfiu ['jeɪ-], -z

Yahweh or Yahveh 'jɑweɪ [-veɪ]

yak (s.), -s 'jæk, -s

ya(c)k (v.), -s, -(k)ing, -(k)ed, -(k)er/s
  'jæk, -s, -ɪŋ, -t, -ɚ/z

Yale 'jeɪl

yam, -s 'jæm, -z

yammer, -s, -ing, -ed, -er/s 'jæmɚ, -z,
  -ɹɪŋ, -d, -ɹɚ/z

yank (Y.), -s, -ing, -ed 'jæŋk, -s, -ɪŋ, -t

Yankee, -s 'jæŋkɨ, -z

yap, -s, -ping, -ped, -per/s 'jæp, -s, -ɪŋ,
  -t, -ɚ/z

yard, -s 'jɑɚd, -z

yardarm, -s 'jɑɚdɑɚm, -z

yardstick, -s 'jɑɚdstɪk, -s

yare, -ly 'jɑɚ, -lɨ

y'are (contr. of you are) 'jɑɚ

yarmulke (-mel-) 'jɑməlkə ['jɑɚ-]

yarn, -s, -ing, -ed 'jɑɚn, -z, -ɪŋ, -d

yarrow 'jæɹoŭ

i we ɨ city ɪ hit e let ɛ debut æ can a pass ɝ bird ʌ hut ə again ɚ supper u you
ʊ should o obey ɔ awl ɒ cop ɑ father eɪ paid aɪ high oŭ go ɔɪ voice aŭ found ɪɚ ear
ɛɚ air ʊɚ poor ɔɚ fork ɑɚ park aɪɚ fire aŭɚ hour b boy p pit d dog t top g got
k kid h how fi behave dʒ jot tʃ chew z zany s soft v vat f fat ʒ treasure ʃ ship ð the
θ thin m man n no ŋ hang l lip j yes w won ʍ whew ɹ rigger, airy ɟ matter

yashma(c)k, -s jaʃ 'mɑk ['jæʃmæk], -s
Yaughan (HAM) 'jɔn, 'jɔən
y'have (contr. of ye have) 'jæv
yaw, -s, -ing, -ed 'jɔ, -z, -ɪŋ, -d
yawl, -s 'jɔl, -z
yawn, -s, -ing, -ed 'jɔn, -z, -ɪŋ, -d
yaws 'jɔz
y-clad ɪ̆'klæd
ycleped (p.p. of clepe, cf. yclept) ɪ̆'klipt
   Note.—For the pun on 'clipt' to work in
   LLL, V.ii.593, 594, some slight variance
   in pronunciation is perhaps called for
yclept (p.p. of clepe, cf. ycleped) ɪ̆'klept
ye (archaic nom. pl. of 2nd pers. pron.
   you) 'ji
ye (archaic spelling of the, q.v.) 'ði, 'ðɪ,
   'ðə
yea, -s 'jeɪ̆, -z
yea-forsooth 'jeɪ̆fɚˌsuθ
yeah 'jeə
yean, -s, -ing, -ed 'jin, -z, -ɪŋ, -d
yeanling, -s 'jinlɪŋ, -z
year, -s, -ly 'jɪɚ, -z, -lɪ
   Note.—In Frank Kermode's (editor, The
   Arden Shakespeare, 1958) annotation
   for TEM, I.ii.53, there is a brief but
   valuable discussion about monosyllabic
   words that sometimes receive the value
   of two metric beats in S. lines of verse
   "whether or no it is [they are] pronounced disyllabically . . ." In TEM,
   I.ii.53, 'year' is arguably pronounced
   disyllabically or given, as Kermode puts
   it, "a heavy emphasis." Cf. Abbott's
   A Shakespearian Grammar, §§ 475, 479,
   484
yearbook, -s 'jɪɚˌbʊk, -s
yearling, -s 'jɪɚˌlɪŋ, -z
yearn, -s, -ing/s, -ed 'jɝn, -z, -ɪŋ/z, -d
yeast, -s, -ing, -ed, 'jist, -s, -ɪŋ, -ɪd
yeast|y, -ier, -iest, -iness 'jist|ɪ, -ɪɚ, -ɪɪst,
   -ɪnɪs
Yedward (1HIV) 'jedwɚd
ye'll (contr. of ye will) 'jiəl
yell, -s, -ing, -ed 'jel, -z, -ɪŋ, -d
yellow, -s, -ing, -ed 'jeloʊ, -z, -ɪŋ, -d
yellowhammer, -s 'jeloʊˌhæmɚ, -z
yellowish, -ness 'jeloʊɪʃ, -nɪs
yellowness 'jeloʊnɪs

yellowy 'jeloʊɪ
yelp, -s, -ing, -ed 'jelp, -s, -ɪŋ, -t
yen, -s, -ning, -ned 'jen, -z, -ɪŋ, -d
yenta 'jentə
yeo|man, -men 'joʊ|mən, -mən
yeoman|ly, -ry 'joʊmən|lɪ, -ɹɪ
ye're (contr. of ye are) 'jɪɚ
yerk (s., v.) (reaction to a smarting blow,
   or to give one), -s, -ing, -ed 'jɝk, -s, -ɪŋ,
   -t
yes 'jes
yes|man, -men 'jes|mæn, -men
yesterday, -s 'jestɚˌdeɪ̆ [-dɪ], -z
yesternight 'jestɚˌnaɪ̆t
yesteryear 'jestɚˌjɪɚ
yest|y (frothy; var. of yeasty), -ily, -iness
   'jist|ɪ, -ɪlɪ, -ɪnɪs
yet 'jet
yet-appearing 'jetəˌpɪɚˌɹɪŋ ['jeɹə-]
ye've (contr. of ye have) 'jiv ['jɪv]
yew, -s 'ju, -z
yew-tree, -s 'juˌtɹi, -z
y'have 'jæv
yield, -s, -ing/ly, -ed, -er/s 'jild, -z, -ɪŋ/lɪ,
   -ɪd, -ɚ/z
yielder-up 'jildəˌɹʌp
yieldings 'jildɪŋz
yok|e, -es, -ing, -ed 'joʊk, -s, -ɪŋ, -t
yoke-devil, -s 'joʊkˌdevl̩, -z
yoke-fellow, -s 'joʊkˌfeloʊ, -z
yokel, -s 'joʊkl̩, -z
yolk, -s 'joʊk, -s
yon(d) 'jɒn(d)
yonder 'jɒndɚ
yore 'jɔɚ
Yorick (HAM) 'jɒɹɪk
York (1HIV, 2HIV, HV, 1HVI, 2HVI,
   3HVI, HVIII, RII, RIII), -s 'jɔɚk, -s
York, Duchess of (RII, RIII) 'dʌtʃɪs əv
   'jɔɚk
York, Edmund (RII) 'edmənd 'jɔɚk
Yorkist, -s 'jɔɚkɪst, -s
York-place (HVIII) 'jɔɚkˌpleɪ̆s
Yorkshire (RIII) 'jɔɚkʃɚ [-ʃɪɚ]
you 'ju (strong form) 'ju (weak form)
you'd (contr. of you would) 'jud
you'ld (contr. of you would) 'jud
you'll (contr. of you will) 'juəl
young, -er, -est 'jʌŋ, -gɚ, -gɪst

young-eyed 'jʌŋˌaɪ̆d
youngling, -s 'jʌŋlɪŋ, -z
youngly 'jʌŋlɨ
youngster, -s 'jʌŋstɚ, -z
younker, -s 'jʌŋkɚ, -z
your 'jɔɚ (*strong form*), 'jɚ (*weak form*)
you're (*contr. of* **you are**) 'jʊɚ
yours 'jɔɚz
yoursel|f, -ves jɔɚ'sel|f, -vz (*strong form*), jɚ'sel|f -vz (*weak form*)
you|th, -ths 'ju|θ, -ðz
youth|ful, -fully, -fulness 'juθ|fʊl, -fəlɨ, -fʊlnɪs
you've (*contr. of* **you have**) 'juəv ['juv]
y-ravished ɹ'ɹævɪʃɪd
y-slacked ɹ'slækɹd
Yule, -tide 'jul, -taɪ̆d
ywis *or* **iwis** ɹ'wɪs

Zz

Z (*the letter*), **-'s** 'ziː, -z
zamindar (**zem-**), **-s** 'zæmɪndɑɚ ['zem-], -z
zan|y, -ies 'zeɪ̆n|ɨ, -ɨz
zap, -s, -ping, -ped 'zæp, -s, -ɪŋ, -t
zapper, -s 'zæpɚ, -z
zeal, -s 'zil, -z
zealot, -s, -ry 'zelət, -s, -ɹɨ
zealous, -ly, -ness 'zeləs, -lɨ, -nɪs
zebra, -s 'zibɹə, -z
zebrawood 'zibɹəwʊd
zebu, -s 'zibu [-bju], -z
zed 'zed
zemstvo, -s 'zjemstvə ['zemstvoŭ], -ʐ
Zen 'zen
Zenelophon (LLL) zɹ'nelʊfɒn [-fən]
zenith, -s 'zinɨθ, -s
zephyr, -s 'zefɚ, -z
zeppelin (**Z.**), **-s** 'zepḷɪn ['zepəl-], -z
zero, -s 'zɪˌɹoŭ ['zɪɚˌɹoŭ], -z
zest, -y 'zest, -ɨ

Zeus 'zus ['zjus]
ziggurat, -s 'zɪgʊɹɑt [-gə-], -s
zigzag, -s, -ging, -ged 'zɪgzæg, -z, -ɪŋ, -d
zinc, -s, -(k)ing, -(k)ed 'zɪŋk, -s, -ɪŋ, -t
zinfandel (**Z.**) 'zɪnfənˌdel
zing, -s, -ing, -ed, -er/s 'zɪŋ, -z, -ɪŋ, -d, -ɚ/z
zinnia, -s 'zɪnɪə, -z
zip, -s, -ping, -ped 'zɪp, -s, -ɪŋ, -t
zipper, -s 'zɪpɚ, -z
zipp|y, -ier, -iest 'zɪp|ɨ, -ɪɚ, -ɨɪst
zir 'zɚ (*for* '*sir*')
    Note.—This is from LEAR, IV.vi.231, *an example of S.'s direction to the actor (via semiphonetic spellings) to adopt the rustic dialect common to the southwestern counties of Devonshire and western Worcestershire, more or less, for the purpose of giving Edgar a "vocal disguise" (cf. Kökeritz's* Shakespeare's Pronunciation, *pp. 37–39)*
zirconium zɚ'koŭnɪəm
zither, -s 'zɪθɚ ['zɪðɚ], -z
zloty 'zlɔtɨ ['zlɒtɨ]
zo 'zoŭ (*from* '*so*')
    Note.—This is from LEAR, IV.vi.235, *an example of S.'s direction to the actor (via semiphonetic spellings) to adopt the rustic dialect common to the southwestern counties of Devonshire and western Worcestershire, more or less, for the purpose of giving Edgar a "vocal disguise" (cf. Kökeritz's* Shakespeare's Pronunciation, *pp. 37–39)*
zoa (*var. pl. of* **zoon**) 'zoŭə
zodiac, -s 'zoŭdɪæk, -s (['zoŭdjæk] in TIT, I.i.506)
zodiacal zoŭ'daɪ̆əkḷ [zo'd-]
zombie, -s 'zɒmbɨ, -z
zon|al, -ally 'zoŭn|ḷ [-əl], -əlɨ
zon|e, -s, -ing, -ed 'zoŭn, -z, -ɪŋ, -d
zonk, -s, -ing, -ed 'zɒŋk, -s, -ɪŋ, -t
zoo, -s 'zu, -z
zoographic|al, -ally zoŭə'gɹafɪk|ḷ, -əlɨ

---

i we ɨ city ɪ hit e let ɛ debut æ can a pass ɚ bird ʌ hut ə again ɚ supper u you
ʊ should o obey ɔ awl ɒ cop ɑ father eɪ̆ paid aɪ̆ high oŭ go ɔɪ̆ voice aŭ found ɪɚ ear
ɛɚ air ʊɚ poor ɔɚ fork ɑɚ park aɪ̆ɚ fire aŭɚ hour b boy p pit d dog t top g got
k kid h how ɦ behave dʒ jot tʃ chew z zany s soft v vat f fat ʒ treasure ʃ ship ð the
θ thin m man n no ŋ hang l lip j yes w won ʍ whew ɹ rigger, airy ɾ matter

zoographer, -s zoŏ'ɒɡɹəfə·, -z
zoography zoŏ'ɒɡɹəfɨ
zoology zoŏ'ɒlədʒɨ
zoologic|al, -ally zoŏə'lɒdʒɪk|l̩, -əlɨ
zoologist, -s zoŏ'ɒlədʒɪst, -s
zoom, -s, -ing, -ed 'zum, -z, -ɪŋ, -d
zoon (*see* **zoa**), **-s** 'zoŏɒn, -z
zouave (**Z.**), **-s** zu'ɑv, -z
zounds 'zundz ['zaŏndz]

Note.—In Frank Kermode's (editor, The
Arden Shakespeare, 1958) annotation
for TEM, I.ii.53, there is a brief but
valuable discussion about monosyllabic
words that sometimes receive the value
of two metric beats in S. lines of verse
"whether or no it is [they are] pronounced disyllabically . . ." In TIT,
IV.ii.73, 'zounds' is arguably pronounced disyllabically or given, as

Kermode puts it, "a heavy emphasis."
Cf. Abbott's A Shakespearian Grammar,
§§ 475, 479, 484

zoysia 'zɔĭʃɪə ['zɔĭzɪə]
zucchini zu'kinɨ
zwaggered 'zwægə·d (*from
'swaggered'*)

Note.—This is from LEAR, IV.vi.234, an
example of S.'s direction to the actor
(via semiphonetic spellings) to adopt the
rustic dialect common to the southwestern counties of Devonshire and western
Worcestershire, more or less, for the
purpose of giving Edgar a "vocal
disguise" (cf. Kökeritz's Shakespeare's
Pronunciation, pp. 37–39)

zwieback 'zwibæk [-bɑk, 'tsvibɑk]
zydeco 'zaĭdɪkoŏ
zygote, -s 'zaĭgoŏt, -s

Made in United States
North Haven, CT
03 February 2022

15588387R00219